USS INDEPENDENCE CVL-22

A War Diary of the Nation's
First Dedicated Night Carrier

Author:

John Gordon Lambert

Contributing Writers:

Donald Edward Labudde

& the

Officers, Crew and Air Groups of CVL-22

Enhanced 2021 Edition

USS INDEPENDENCE   CVL-22

A War Diary of the Nation's First Dedicated Night Carrier

Author: John G. Lambert
Contributing Writers: Donald E. Labudde
& the Officers, Crew and Air Groups of CVL-22

The author is grateful (as is further acknowledged within the text of the book) for permission to utilize major portions of: "The Sea Time, A Bluejacket's Memoir" by Donald E. Labudde, with the copyright held, and permission kindly granted, by Dorothy E. Labudde,
The author is also grateful for permission to utilize minor excerpts from the following copyrighted book: "Fading Victory, The Diary of Admiral Matome Ugaki, 1941-1945" published in 2008 by the Naval institute Press, (granted by Rick Russell, Director).

First **published & edited** in 2011, and amended in 2012, 2013, 2015, 2021 and 2022 by: John G. Lambert
        EMAIL: **CVL22history@conwaycorp.net**

12th hard cover edition revision, printing by: **Lightning Source** in 2022

ISBN: 978-0-9838869-1-4

Library of Congress Control Number: 2011914899

This is the culmination of a 14 year research effort to document the non-fiction history of the USS INDEPENDENCE CV/ CVL-22.
Due in part to the enormity of the project, there have been numerous updates to the print file to add (what I have viewed as author / historian) important material.
Additionally, unforeseen events (the 2015 & 2016 NOAA) missions have enhanced the knowledge extending the historical timeline.
This revision is my FINAL review, edit and inclusion of material. I consider my work complete!
This finished work now features roughly 560 photos, maps, charts & graphs within 896 pages.

ENHANCED 2021 EDITION

Revised Feb 2022 file update - FINAL Edits

SHE was long, low, and lean. Sired by Necessity, her mother was Hurry—attended, it was said, by midwife Panic. Into her obstinate iron soul was built just enough crank to let you know unmistakably that in a made-up quartering sea she always felt a trifle unsure of herself. Atop the thin rectangular box that was her island sat the monarch commanding her. Forward of the island was mounted a large boat crane whose naked beams resembled the skeletonized neck of a stork. Four low, squat stacks jutted just above her flightdeck abaft the island. Narrow catwalks lined the deck. Halfmoon buckets of thin armorplate that overhung her sides like cantilevered warts contained her inadequate guns; in a heavy rolling sea the great green walls of the water loomed close enough to touch, as if reminding her how uncertain was existence, how indifferent fate. As dumpy and dowdy a sea-going scow as ever outraged a shellback's critical eye, she had speed aplenty, power to spare, and a will and a way of her own. She thrust her high and haughty clipper bow forward with an air of pugnacious vanity that had in it not a trace of humility or shame.

To the Navy she was the *U.S.S. Independence CVL-22,* and her men were young then at sea and strong.

DONALD E. LABUDDE

(The above photo taken 20 October 1945 in Portland, Oregon on the Columbia River)

USS INDEPENDENCE CV / CVL-22
A War Diary of the Nation's First Dedicated Night Carrier

Contents

Preface

With her hull breached once again, unwelcome salt water rushed within. As she succumbed to her fate the Mighty-I rolled on her side. Gravity pulled her toward the bottom, her island structure, having been decorated with eight battle stars and 124 Japanese flags, slipped beneath the surface. Stern first, she submerged on a one way descent into the cold dark depths. Permanently obscured from view, settled on the bottom in her unmarked watery grave, her headstone was to be the vast Pacific.

Her remaining crew members, having survived the war, ravages of disease, and the undefeated hunter Father Time, will one day also slip away as surely as the ship with which they once proudly served their nation in a time of dire need.

Rust is consuming the Mighty-I's hull, and the passage of time eroding memories of the ship and her crew.

History of the USS INDEPENDENCE and her fine crew is becoming relegated to the dark confines of various file cabinets and boxes of documents in places such as the National Archives, or other historical centers, that few eyes will ever see.

I was asked by the historian of the ships reunion group, Al Hiegel, to write a book detailing the time when her decks were dry, and aircraft were launching. Attending a reunion in 2007, the surviving crew members felt historically underrepresented. In researching this book, it occurred to me that this was true of most of our vessels serving the nation during WWII. Reading thru the documents, it is a fine story, deserving to be told, of how the crew earned those eight Battle Stars boldly delivering the war back to the enemy.

As a casual observation, ships do not build ships ... People build ships. Ships do not fight conflicts. People fight conflicts manning the instruments of war upon which they serve. Ships are simply those instruments / weapons created and served upon by man for the purpose of carrying out the will of their nation when diplomatic means fail. We tend to have a lasting affection for those connections with our past that influenced our lives, be it a girl friend, an automobile, motorcycle, airplane, and / or ... The vessel upon which we served. For the Reunion Group, the ship, their ship, was USS INDEPENDENCE.

This book was written in honor of the wide array of shipyard craftsmen who toiled to rapidly build the USS INDEPENDENCE , the crew and aviators that served on her, the workers in the Naval Yards who repaired and serviced her, along with the ship's companies manning the numerous support vessels (that often slip thru history silently in the background without due recognition) that made her contribution to the Pacific war and final victory possible.

It is written to document the birth of the ship, her death, and the days between. It is inclusive of the Air Wings that served aboard, as the aviators and their aircraft were the carrier's offensive weapons of war. As our nation's first dedicated night aircraft carrier, the USS INDEPENDENCE had an impact on US Naval doctrine.

World War II was a time when the fires of hatred were fanned and fueled on both opposing sides and countless millions of lives were directly affected. A time when our nation sent our young men to sea, launching and recovering bold fliers from the rolling decks of mighty ships.

Life is an individual adventure, a collection of day to day, second to second experiences that differs for each and every one of us, even from within the small confines of a ship at war. Visualize the sights, sounds and knowledge of the threat level experienced by the crew on the flight deck during a Kamikaze attack, versus a sailor fighting the war in more obscure confines, in the relative dark, far below decks. Or a Hellcat pilot aloft in his cockpit facing a solitary encounter with the enemy. A gunner in an Avenger trusting his pilot to bring him back aboard alive, and in one piece. Each individual had his own window to the war, different from his fellow shipmate. As much as I feel it deserved, it is not practical to tell a detailed story of each and every individual within the covers of this book.

I desire to present an accurate portrayal of the history of the INDEPENDENCE thru the eyes of those that took the time to document their perspective. I hope I have served the entire crew well. I also give an overview of the war as it relates to the INDEPENDENCE, trying to hold a compass heading true to a course that delivers a sailors view to the life and time aboard the USS INDEPENDENCE, when she and her crew steamed on vast conflicted seas.

John G. Lambert

This document made possible with grateful recognition the following people and organizations;

Don Labudde was born in Oshkosh Wisconsin in 1922. He served on the INDEPENDENCE as an Aviation Ordnanceman. He was both slave and task master extraordinaire to a fine accounting of his time walking her decks. His prolific, detailed and colorful writing paint a story that captures the essence of the life, thoughts and attitudes in the navy during the great Pacific war. The talented writing of Don Labudde above all else, gave me the hope that I might be able to take the reader on a historical journey back to WWII, into Harms Way aboard an aircraft carrier thru the eyes of her crew. Youngsters called to serve their nation during a time when the music of the day was played on vacuum tube radios, before the cell phone, the PC, the Apple or the IPod. No internet. There was the telephone back then, and the telegraph. A ship crewed with young men melding together from the great expanse of farms and cities sprawled across our nation cradled in its protective isolation of two vast oceans. A time of innocence shattered by the call to war across unfathomable expanse of both the Atlantic and the Pacific. Don gives us insight of what it was like when a typical eager youth first goes aboard ship, matures with the experience taught by life at sea on a new vessel, hastily redesigned, purposefully built, manned and ordered to take battle to the enemy.

Don kept a detailed diary. In later years, he wrote an unpublished book on his experiences titled; **"The Sea Time, A Bluejacket's Memoir"**. Don's account of the events had the hindsight of history to assist with his work.

I had served on an aircraft carrier during the mid 60's, the USS BON HOMME RICHARD. She was like the INDEPENDENCE in that she was born and launched during WWII. But unlike the Mighty-I, her hull was originally designed as an aircraft carrier. Also an "Airdale" like Don Labudde, his writing restored to my faded memory the feelings and emotions I experienced as I first went on board, as she carried me to strange lands, far away places and grew crusty with the salt from the sea. The sea … she builds barnacles on ships hulls, and builds character into the hearts and souls of the men that ride her. If you've been to sea, may you once again recall those days thru Don's writing!

Mrs. Dorothy E. Labudde who kindly gave permission to utilize her late husbands work. Dorothy encouraged Don to continue his writing to completion, accompanied him on his research trips, and as an English teacher, was a kind critic and good proof reader.

Don Edward Labudde in San Francisco, 1944   **Dorothy & Donald E. Labudde**

Carol Peterson Don suffered a stroke prior to completion of his writing and Carol provided assistance to Don and Dorothy in the final completion of Don's work. Don expressed his gratitude to Carol for her "great help" and stated without her help and encouragement the task would never have been completed.

Al Hiegel was born in Conway, Arkansas in 1926. As historian for the ship's reunion group, through years of dedication and devotion, Al gathered much of the initial written material that made this book possible. Al went aboard the Mighty-I in early 1945. He was a radar operator on the INDEPENDENCE in C.I.C. during the war. This book was compiled and written at Al's request. He is "The Chief Instigator", expressing his desire that the story of the INDEPENDENCE and her crew not be consigned to the dark forgotten recesses of storage boxes, or pullout drawers, buried and lost in countless walls of filing cabinets, in a large overwhelming archive. History out of sight and out of mind like the Indy herself, so many fathoms down in the vast hidden archives of King Neptune's Realm.

Al Hiegel

Herman Bell, Frank R. Capka, Harvey Carlisle, Russell J. Carothers, Anthony M. D'Aiuto, Karl O. Drexel, Jean Richard Goemmer, Donald E. Labudde, George J. Leedecke, Charles Edward McKie, George Newbauer and Milton F. Popp. These men were crewmates on the INDEPENDENCE who also kept dairies, stories, and written records contributing additional color, depth, detail and background material to the history of the ship. Diary entries capture the human element to a tale of steel hulls and aluminum airframes. The insight they provide is without the benefit of after war historical correction. There are thoughts, hopes and fears expressed as pen was put to paper on the day they made the diary entry. Those entries, from the point of view of the war they were immersed in, with the limited (and sometimes inaccurate) knowledge of what was going on.

Crewmembers who provided photos and documents over the years to the historian, and more recently, to myself.

The National Archives and Research Administration (NARA - College Park, MD & San Bruno, CA). The ship's original Deck Logs, Standing Orders Logs, ship's War Diaries, Combat Action Reports, Aviation Action Reports and numerous other official documents provide the backbone of the historical content. This book is largely made possible by the officers and crewmembers that drafted and typed or made hand entries, creating the volumes of documents that today provide an accounting and hindsight into the inner workings of the gigantic and complex clock works of the Pacific war machine. A war machine sometimes well oiled, often missing cogs, gears and teeth, a point of view much depending on who was reading the clock face, and, the time it was being read. Credit must be given to massive contribution to the Captains and Executive Officers, Navigators, officers that stood watch, making the countless deck log entries, Naval aviators and officers that debriefed and crafted the Aviation Action Reports, and to the yeomen that typed them. The files I accessed were transferred to the NARA by the Navy after the Navy had declassified them.

Photographs are mainly from the **National Archives and Research Administration (NARA)** and the US Navy. Many were provided by USS INDEPENDENCE historian, **Al Hiegel.** The original source the US Navy.

The crew's diaries and Don's book are first hand observations that, when compared and combined with official naval documents and records, present a good accounting of the history of the USS INDEPENDENCE and her crew.   (Additionally, see the contributors to this publication pages in the back of the book.)

Reading this book   (John Lambert)

This document is a chronology narrated in a day by day, hour by hour, ordered structure.
We use the 24 hour clock, each new day starting off at the stroke of midnight, 0000. Time is in local time. The US Navy adjusted the clocks aboard ship to the local time zone the ship was in.
(The Imperial Japanese Navy utilized Tokyo time, where ever their vessel may be.)

The book is written with detail enough to help visualize what the crew saw and experienced in selected cases throughout. If you paint a mental picture as you read, you will learn from; *"course 000° T, speed 22 knots, USS NEW JERSEY, guide, bearing 280° T, distance 2,500 yards"*, that a pilot sitting in his cockpit waiting to launch, or gunners in a gun tub overhanging the water, could look out toward the port (left) side of the INDEPENDENCE to see Halsey's flagship, battleship NEW JERSEY. It was only 2,500 yards away. It also tells that the formation was being lead by the NEW JERSEY, as she was listed as guide. You will know they were steaming due north (course 000° T) and the bows of their hulls were knifing thru the ocean at a speed of 22 knots.
There are numerous entries from the Deck Log as written, many more altered for brevity or to provide better flow, or to integrate other data or information.

If you fly an airplane, or sail on the open ocean, you will feel at home with the 360 degrees of the compass. Some perhaps will feel the need to catch up.

Many calls to general quarters or torpedo defense are detailed to give the reader a feel for the hours of the day, and number of times the crew was called to their battle stations to let the reader better know what granddad really had to endure (the loss of sleep, exposure to the weather, etc. as they ran to and manned battle stations) and give detail of the condition the Air Department was set to for the very same reason. As you read thru, if and as you desire, you should find it easy to skip over those details. This is a true story of the crew and it is my intent to give the reader a feel for what a crew experienced on a fast light aircraft carrier in WWII.

Course and speed changes are given in parts of the book to orient the reader for direction or better paint the picture. General headings are given most days to keep historic perspective as to where she was heading.

This is an effort to bring together detail from thousands of documents, condensing it to form a reasonably complete well ordered story and history, and give the reader easy access.

There are Charts, Track Charts and Maps in the back of the book, with others throughout. See the Index under Maps.

Where there is great temptation to rewrite sections of the book in my own hand, I give preference to use of the crewmembers version, giving the reader a story as portrayed by those that were there, from a point of view of those living the experience, with no knowledge of tomorrow, and groping their way thru the "Fog of War"! This is their story.

Welcome aboard!

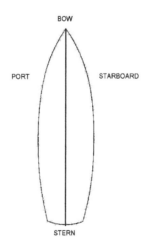

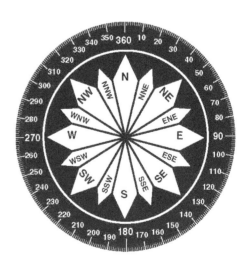

Reading this book - Don's notes   (For the entries in this document attributed to Don Labudde)

THIS is an ex-sailor's recollection of his World War II service on an aircraft carrier, one ship among a magnificent fleet of many ships. She was built just for that war and spent most of her life fighting it. I would never have known her but for the war, which was a long chapter in my life. We were made for each other.

I was an obscure Naval Reserve petty officer whose name, like those of my immediate shipmates, was not meant to appear in any history book. We did what our country asked of us. Most survived the war. So did our ship, falling victim only to the peace.

*Surnames, except for historical personages, have been deleted. ***

Probing into a remembered time, when time seemed to stand still for weeks only to burst into sudden action so violent it stunned a young man's sensibilities, is an old man's only advantage.

When a former sailor seeks a long-ago battlefield on a pilgrimage of remembrance, his goal often turns out to be a mere crossgrid of latitude and longitude on a limitless sea. No stone marks the place, no monument can be erected. His lodestone is…memory.

Don Labudde

(* Note: Surnames were only deleted in Don's accounting.)

Key to sources of Diary Entries & Memoirs.

Throughout this book, the initials will appear before and after their diary or memoir entry.

RA	Robert G. Anderson
HB	Herman Lee Bell
FC	Frank Richard Capka
HC	Harvey Carlisle
RC	Russell Jamison Carothers
AD	Anthony Mario D'Aiuto
KOD	Karl Oscar Walter Drexel
JG	Jean Richard Goemmer
DL	Donald Edward Labudde (Photos page 2)
GL	George J.ohn Leedecke
CEM	Charles Edward McKie
GN	George Edward Newbauer
DrP	Milton F. Popp (Flight Surgeon)

Herman L. Bell   Russell J. Carothers

Anthony M. D'Aiuto   Jean R. Goemmer   George J. Leedecke   Charles E. McKie George E. Newbauer

Additionally: **Guam**   A document that was a partial compilation of news cleared through the Advance Headquarters located on Guam Island, <u>and from other sources</u>. News from this was broadcast throughout the ship during the evenings, typically at 1900 on the public address system by the ship's padre, **Lt. L.A. Failing**. Father Failing's program was known as **"The Road to Tokyo".** The ship's Chaplin included news of the Third Fleet, the INDEPENDENCE, events at home and in Europe. Some of Lt. Failing's own observations appear to be included.

Definitions

AA   Anti-Aircraft fire

AAR   Aircraft Action Report or After Action Report

ACI   Air Combat Intelligence (The ACI officer debriefed pilots & aircrews after the action, creating AARs)

AE   Ammunition Replenishment Ship   (named for volcanoes)

AIA   Aircraft Radar - **A**irborne **I**ntercept "Model **A**" Radar

Aircraft (Air Group) Conditions of Readiness:

>   **Condition 10**   Pilots and aircrew ready and in planes or standing by on deck near their planes. Engines warmed up and planes ready to launch, except engines not running.
>
>   **Condition 11**   Pilots, aircrew and aircraft ready to launch on ten minutes notice.
>
>   **Condition 12**   Pilots, aircrew and aircraft ready to launch on twenty minutes notice.
>
>   **Condition 13**   Pilots, aircrew and aircraft ready to launch on thirty minutes notice.
>
>   **Condition 14**   Pilots, aircrew and aircraft ready to launch on one hours notice, with fuel and armament at discretion.

AK   Cargo Ship   (named for stars, or counties in the United States)

Angels   Aircraft altitude in thousands of feet. "Angels twelve" would be 12,000'.

AO   Oiler   (named for rivers)

ASD   Aircraft search & homing Radar, used by the Navy in Avengers (and PV-1Venturas) - also referred to as "Dog" gear or "Dog" radar.   See Author's note at the bottom of page 437.

ASP   Anti-Submarine Patrol

BatDiv   Battleship Division

BatRon   Battleship Squadron

BB   Battleship (named for states)

Bogey or **Bogie**   Unidentified aircraft (assumed to be a threat unless proven otherwise)

Buster   A request / order for the pilot (s) to fly at maximum continuous speed.

B.W. I.   British West Indies

C&R Department Construction & Repair Department

CA   Heavy Cruiser (named for cities or towns)

CAG   Commander Air Group or Carrier Air Group

CAP   Combat Air Patrol

CASCU Commander Aircraft Support Control Unit

CAVU   Clear Air Visibility Unlimited

CIC   Combat Information Center

CO   Commanding Officer

ComBatDiv   Commander Battleship Division

CL   Light Cruiser   (named for cities or towns)

CruDiv   Cruiser Division

CruRon   Cruiser Squadron

CTF   Commander, Task Force or Carrier Task Force

CTG   Commander, Task Group or Carrier Task Group

CTU   Commander, Task Unit or Carrier Task Unit

CV   Fleet Aircraft Carrier   (named for famous Navy ships or famous battles)

CVE   Escort Aircraft Carrier (named for bays, sounds, or WWII battles)

CVL   Light Aircraft Carrier   (named for famous Navy ships, or famous battles)

DCAP   Day Combat Air Patrol

DD   Destroyer   (named for distinguished Naval / Marine Corp officers or enlisted men)

DE   Destroyer Escort (named for distinguished Naval / Marine Corp officers or enlisted men)

Degaussing   Removing the magnetic field (or magnetic signature) of the ship. Also called Deperm or Deperming.

DesDiv   Destroyer Division

DesRon   Destroyer Squadron

Disposition   The way ships are arranged in a formation / group. See pages 840-842 for disposition diagrams.

>   **Disposition Easy Modified**   A special formation for gunnery exercises.
>
>   **Disposition 3L**   A night or low visibility formation suitable for the defense of carriers.
>
>   **Disposition 3R**   A formation for low visibility or night READY cruising with close screens on heavy units.
>
>   **Disposition 3V**   A day high visibility cruising formation suitable for defense against both aircraft and subs.
>
>   **Disposition 4V**   A day high visibility cruising formation for the defense of a small carrier force used against probable or actual enemy air attack. Guide is normally in the carrier at fleet center.
>
>   **Disposition 5F**   A carrier force day fueling formation for defense against subs
>
>   **Disposition 5LS**   A combination low visibility and antisubmarine cruising formation for night or low visibility day conditions when heavy ship protection against subs is a paramount factor.
>
>   **Disposition 5V**   A cruising formation for air defense, suitable for use for a carrier force under enemy air attack. Guide is normally at the center, and /or the flagship of the OTC.
>
>   **Disposition 5VB** A cruising formation for air defense. A tighter disposition where heavy support ships are in closer to the carriers for better AA defensive coverage.

Disposition 5VC	A cruising formation for air defense. Gives all ships, including destroyers, a 180° clear arc for AA firing.
Disposition 5R	A normal carrier force day or night high visibility formation suitable for defense against enemy aircraft or subs. Guide is normally at the center.
Disposition 6R	A normal carrier force day or night high visibility formation suitable for defense against enemy aircraft or subs. Guide is normally at the center.
Disposition 6VC	Used in gunnery exercises, this formation places all ships in a circle to give each ship a greater clear arc in which to fire.

"Dud" aircraft   Aircraft that were no longer up to par for combat due to damage or need for maintenance.

"Dumbo"   Flying boat, frequently utilized for air-sea rescue. A PBY was commonly referred to as a Dumbo.

F4F / F6F   Aircraft - Grumman "Wildcat" (F4F) and "Hellcat" (F6F) Fighters.

Fathom   Unit of measurement - Depth measurement of the water - 1 fathom = 6 feet

FDO   Fighter Direction Officer - stationed in CIC, the FDO uses radar to vector the fighters to the bogey.

Flight Quarters The Air Department and other necessary ships personnel are at their stations for air operations.

Fox Tare Charlie   Freighter-transport with the deckhouse and smokestack (engines) aft of amidships.

Fox Tare Dog   Freighter-transport with the deckhouse and smokestack (engines) aft of amidships 150-300 G.T.

"Gee-Dunk"   A compartment or ship's store that dispensed fountain sodas, candy, cigarettes, etc.

General Quarters (GQ)   A condition of the ships combat readiness where all hands man their battle stations, and the vessel is closed down for maximum watertight integrity.

GP Bombs   General Purpose Bombs

Guide   The vessel in a formation that other vessels reference to maintain proper station (position).

Gunnery Department Conditions of Readiness: (for aircraft carriers like the CVLs without larger guns)

Condition 1	All Battle Stations fully manned and alert. Ammunition read for instant loading. It is assumed action may be imminent. May be set during the dawn-alert period, (normally 1 hr. before sunrise to sunrise) and from sunset until dark. Cond. 2 set only when surface, submarine or aircraft attack is improbable.
Condition 2	Section watches. 1/4 to 1/3 personnel available. Fire Control, CIC & Communications sufficiently manned for immediate use.
Condition 3	Like Cond. 2. Ammunition at guns manned ready for instant loading. For conditions 2 &3, batteries having sufficient ready ammunition to sustain max. rate of fire until higher cond. of readiness is set need not man lower handling rooms & magazines.

HEI   High Explosive Incendiary

HVAR   High Velocity Aircraft Rocket

Hull down   A vessel at distance low on the horizon with the hull not showing (due to the curvature of the earth). giving view to the upper superstructure, stacks and / or masts. (Hull up - the hull is visible).

IDL   International Date Line

IFF   Identification Friend or Foe

IJA   Imperial Japanese Army

IJN   Imperial Japanese Navy

Jack Patrol   Low altitude anti "Snooper" (enemy scout) Combat Air Patrol.

Lifeguard   An assignment to pick up downed aviators usually tasked to submarines or destroyers.

LSO   Landing Signal Officer

Lugger   Small freighter-transport with the deckhouse and smokestack (engines) aft of amidships 50 - 100 G.T.

NAS , NAAS   Naval Air Station, Naval Auxiliary Air Station

NCAP   Night Combat Air Patrol

NOB   Naval Operating Base

OS2U Kingfisher   Vought observation floatplane. See photo on page 439.

OTC   Officer in Tactical Command

Pelorus   A stand with a compass repeater and typically a sighting apparatus for navigation and relative direction or bearing.

PBY   Consolidated Aircraft *"Catalina"* Navy patrol seaplane. See photo on page 434.

PB4Y-2   Consolidated Aircraft *"Privateer"* Navy long range patrol bomber modified / derived from the B-24 *"Liberator"*.

Point Option   The projected place the carrier will be when the pilots are ready to return for recovery.

"Popeye"   Instrument Meteorological Conditions (reduced visibility) requiring flight relying on instruments.

Port   To the left side of the ship or aircraft center line.

RAPCAP   Radar Picket Combat Air Patrol to provide airborne support for the line of picket destroyers.

RPPI   Radar Plan Position Indicator (or **PPI**) Basically the radar Cathode Ray Tube - Radar visual display. The image on the "Scope" or PPI gives a plan view of the overall area extending out from the ship.

SB2C   Curtis Aircraft *"Helldiver"* Scout Dive Bomber

SBD   Douglas Aircraft *"Dauntless"* Scout Dive Bomber   (replaced by the SB2C)

Sea Truck   Small transport with the deckhouse and smokestack (engines) aft .

SC-2 Radar   Air Search Radar (SC, SC-1 & SC-2 Radars are Air Search).

SG Radar   Surface Search Radar. Basically utilized to see other vessels (and land masses).

SK Radar   Air Search Radar.

SM Radar   Ship borne Microwave Radar with aircraft altitude determining capabilities.

SNASP   Search Navigational Anti-Submarine Patrol.

Snooper   Enemy scout / observation plane.

SOC   Scout Observation Aircraft - Commonly, the Curtis Seagull floatplane. (See photo on bottom of this page).

SOL   Standing Orders Log - A log of the Captain's orders / notations left (for the next watches) when he retired from the bridge at night.

SOPA   Senior Officer Present Afloat

Starboard   To the right side of the ship or aircraft center line

SubCAP   Combat Air Patrol over (for the protection of) our lifeguard submarines.

Sugar Able   Large oiler with the deckhouse and smokestack (engines) aft

Sugar Baker   Freighter-tanker with the deckhouse and smokestack (engines) aft   over 1,000 G. T.

Sugar Charles   Freighter-tanker with the deckhouse and smokestack (engines) aft   300 -1,000 G. T.

Sugar Dog   Freighter-tanker with the deckhouse and smokestack (engines) aft   150 - 300 G. T.

Sugar Fox   Freighter with the deckhouse and smokestack (engines) aft

T   True - coarse or bearing

TAD   Temporary Active Duty (a temporary duty assignment).

TAQ   Main Radio Transmitter (Medium Frequency, high power).

TBD   Douglas *"Devastator"* Torpedo Bomber. (Replaced by the TBM / TBF)

TBF   General Motors built (Grumman Aircraft designed - TBM) *"Avenger"* Torpedo Bomber

TBK   Radio Transmitter (High Frequency)

TBM   Grumman Aircraft *"Avenger"* Torpedo Bomber

TBM   Main radio for communication between the Fighter Director Command and fighter planes. This was replaced by TDQ (HF transmitter) and RCK (HF receiver).

TBS   Talk Between Ships - Short Range ship to ship radio intended to be limited to the horizon for communication within a task force, task group or convoy (though longer range contacts are recorded).

TBY   A portable Talk Between Ships - (VHF) low power ship to ship radio

TCAP   Top CAP, high altitude or upper layer Combat Air Patrol

TCE   Auxiliary radio for communication between the Fighter Director Command and fighter aircraft.

TF   Task Force   Example T**F** 38

TG   Task Group   (subset of a Task Force)   Example T**G** 38.**1**   (38.**1**, 38.**2**, 38.**3**, etc.)

TU   Task Unit   (subset of a Task Group)   Example T**U** 38.1.**1**

Torpecker   Navy slang reference to a torpedo plane

Torpedo Defense   A condition of combat readiness, downgraded from general quarters, where all gunnery positions were manned and the vessel in a watertight condition, however other personal not necessary to that threat level condition were at their normal work / duty stations. Torpedo defense was most frequently utilized with the threat of aircraft attack.

Two-block   Hoisting the flag or signal flag to the full upward extent.

Two-block Fox   Signals air operations

VF   Fighter plane   (V = Heaver than air   F = Fighter)

VF(N)   Fighter plane (night)

VT   Torpedo Plane

VT(N)   Torpedo Plane (night)

WEP   War Emergency Power

Window   A foil like material (like Christmas tree tinsel) used to fool enemy radar. It was thrown or ejected from the aircraft reflecting a false radar return.

XO   Executive Officer

YE / YG   A homing signal (in 30° sectors or segments) sent out from the aircraft carrier as a navigation aid for the pilots returning to the carrier. The pilot would tune into the alpha code signal from the ship which gave him the sector he was in, and fly the reciprocal course to the carrier (See below). The Morris code was changed daily. See photos of the ships (rotating) transmitting antenna on pages 32 & 33. The YG was a portable lower power version of the YE system. Also see ZB (below).

ZB   The aircraft receiver for the ships YE homing system.

YE Homing Code   **SOC - Curtis Seagull floatplane**

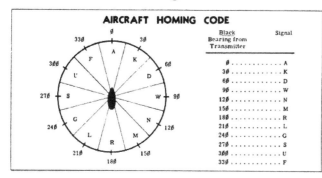

USS INDEPENDENCE CVL-22

Chapter 1

"I wish to have no connection with any ship that does not sail fast;
For I intend to go in harm's way."

John Paul Jones

1
A <u>Brief</u> Pacific War Overview

Japan was not dormant prior to Pearl Harbor. In 1910, Japan annexed Korea. Hirohito became the Japanese emperor in 1926. Japan invaded Manchuria in 1931 and established a "Puppet State" they named Manchukuo. In 1937 Japan invaded China. A Tripartite Pact was signed with Germany and Italy in 1940. Invited to join Germany in its war on Russia, Japan declined, with its Imperial eye focused on expansion south, further assisted by the Vichy French government ceding their Indochina holdings to Japan, for "protection" against the British. In mid 1941 the US and its allies established a trade embargo and froze Japan's assets. Tensions rose. Severely crippled by loss of trade, Japan felt the need to act.

1941

Should hostilities begin in the Pacific involving the United States, we would need to fight a multi-ocean war. We had seven aircraft carriers in 1941, a number grossly insufficient. Consider also the wartime probability of the loss of one or more of those carriers, or damage taking it out of action for weeks or months. A massive fleet expansion program had begun the previous year in 1940. Within the planned Navy buildup were orders for 17 carriers of the new ESSEX Class. These carriers were large and complicated, with the assumption they would consume a lot of precious time to build. Time however was a luxury the nation would most likely not have.

President Franklin D. Roosevelt had both a keen interest and special knowledge in Naval history. In the administration of President Wilson, FDR had served as Assistant Secretary of the Navy. Foreseeing the need to project airpower from the sea, Roosevelt set to work with the task of convincing the "Battleship Navy" (AKA the "Gun Club") they would need a stopgap measure to fill the carrier shortage if war, that appeared to be looming beyond the horizon, became a reality.

The Navy would place orders for thirty six CLEVELAND Class Cruisers, with some keels already laid down at the New York Shipbuilding Company (**NYSB**) yards in Camden, New Jersey. The first to be launched (CL-55, USS CLEVELAND) was on 1 November 1941, and commissioned in June of 1942. President Roosevelt, in August 1941, asked Naval planners to look at the possibility of converting some of the cruisers into aircraft carriers, as a way to rapidly respond to the projected need, until the ESSEX Class carriers were floated, outfitted and fully operational for war.

He knew he had an uphill fight with the Navy and enlisted the help of his friend, Secretary of the Navy, Frank Knox. Together, Roosevelt and Knox successfully persuaded the Navy to proceed with the conversion. As a result, a new class of aircraft carrier, the fast INDEPENDENCE Class light carrier emerged.

First in her class, USS INDEPENDENCE would be followed in amazingly rapid succession by her eight siblings;

CRUISER NAME	CV NAME	KEEL LAID	COMISSIONED
AMSTERDAM (CL-59)	**INDEPENDENCE CV-22**	1 May 1941	14 Jan 1943
TALLAHSSEE (CL-61)	**PRINCETON CV-23**	2 Jun 1941	25 Feb 1943
NEW HAVEN (CL-76)	**BELLEAU WOOD CV-24**	11 Aug 1941	31 Mar 1943
HUNTINGTON (CL-77)	**COWPENS CV-25**	17 Nov 1941	28 May 1943
DAYTON (CL-78)	**MONTEREY CV-26**	29 Dec 1941	17 Jun 1943
FARGO (CL-85)	**LANGLEY CV-27**	11 Apr 1942	31 Aug 1943
WILMINGTON (CL-79)	**CABOT CV-28**	16 Mar 1942	24 Jul 1943
BUFFALO (CL-99)	**BATAAN CV-29**	31 Aug 1942	17 Nov 1943
NEWARK (CL-100)	**SAN JACINTO CV-30**	26 Oct 1942	15 Dec 1943

(The designation for the new class of fast light carriers would later change from **CV** to **CVL**.)

The Japanese attack on Pearl Harbor three months later expedited plans for the conversion. An all out effort was set into motion to have the first of the new carriers, USS INDEPENDENCE, launched in just one year, prior to the end of 1942.

Global events during 1940 and 1941 made the possibility of the United States being drawn into armed conflict an unfortunate reality. Europe and Asia were aflame, and with the tragic attack on December 7th, 1941, like it or not, we were at war. Japanese aircraft sent the pride of our Navy to comingle with the silt at the bottom of Pearl Harbor.

In the early months of the war against the United States (and our allies) Japan was building an impressive list of victories. Islands were occupied and vast stretches of ocean territory fell victim to the Japanese battle flag. These captured territories would become enveloped in the growing circle of "*The Greater East Asia Co-Prosperity Sphere*". The onrushing tide of war at first looked overwhelming as Japan racked up one victory after another in its drive to secure land, oil, natural resources and its destiny as a global power. Additionally, on December 11th, Germany and Italy declared war on the US.

December 1941 is remembered in the United States most for the Japanese attack on Pearl Harbor. Hawaii was not their only success**. They would shell Midway Island, attack and make numerous landings in the Philippines, Thailand, capture Guam, and Wake Island. While Pearl Harbor was under attack, the Japanese Army landed in Malaya. Thailand surrendered. The British surrendered Hong Kong. British warships PRINCE OF WALES and REPULSE were lost in action against Japanese land based aircraft. In the Gilberts, they occupied Makin Island and Tarawa. And, if not enough for the month of December 1941, the Japanese army also landed in British Borneo near Miri. December 9th China declared war on Japan, Germany, & Italy, and on the 11th war was mutually declared between the US and Germany & Italy. At the end of December Admiral Ernest J. King would become the Commander in Chief of the US Fleet and Admiral Chester W. Nimitz would assume duties under Admiral King in command of the Pacific Fleet.   (** Limited success. Two US aircraft carriers were at sea , and the fuel, port and fleet repair infrastructure at Hawaii was relatively untouched. This major Japanese error in planning (or implementation) would allow the US to begin to change the tragic course of war at a more rapid pace, to Japans great disadvantage)

January 1942 started off with the surrender of British Borneo to Japan. A declaration of war against the Netherlands East Indies, occupation of Celebes, the capture of Tarakan & Balikpapan, Dutch Borneo, then capping the busy month of January off with a landing on Ambon Island. Further north, Japanese would occupy Kavieng in New Ireland and Rabaul in New Britain. Rabaul would become one of Japan's premier naval bases. USS SARATOGA and USS NECHES (AO-5) were damaged by torpedoes.

In **February 1942** Japan fought battles in Makassar Straits, occupied Timor, Bali-Lombok, Bangka Island, Palembang, Sumatra and Gasmata, New Britain. England staggered under a sledge hammer blow as Singapore was surrendered by Lt. Gen Percival, and the IJN (Imperial Japanese Navy) raided Port Darwin, Australia, where DD USS PEARY was sunk. At the end of February, into the beginning of March saw the British loss of HMS ENCOUNTER and HMS EXETER, and the US loss of USS POPE and USS LANGLEY (CV1 converted to AV-3, former aircraft carrier - now seaplane tender), the Battle of the Java Sea, and the Battle of Sundra Strait. General Douglas MacArthur was ordered out of the Philippines by President Roosevelt. IJN sub I-17 shelled the Ellwood oil fields near Santa Barbara, California causing only minor damage, but created invasion jitters that rattled the west coast like an earthquake.

As February rolled into **March 1942**, the British evacuated Rangoon, Java surrendered, and the busy Japanese forces occupied large parts of New Guinea (Lae and Salamaua). Next came the Admiralty Islands, Halmahera, and other islands in the Bismarck Sea. The Andaman Islands were occupied (Bay of Bengal).

As one tragedy followed another, US Navy "Gun Club" members were forced to scrap their entrenched traditional strategic thinking in developing a response to the sudden and seemingly ever-growing trail of the crisis in the Pacific. The Navy's spear was broken. The aged leviathans at its tip were sunk, capsized or damaged in Hawaii. The shock induced handwringing after the Japanese attacks had long since past, and make do solutions were needed.

The Navy would just simply have to proceed to fight the war with the assets that floated until shipyards cranked out new hulls and repair yards refloated and repaired the wounded. Fast creative holding actions would become the resolve driven order of the day.

The broken lance of the navy would now be crowned by the few aircraft carriers, the submarines, cruisers, destroyers, destroyer escorts, patrol boats --- anything available to hold the Japanese at bay, and begin to nibble at their tough exposed and rapidly over-expanding hide.

Creativity forced by necessity to deal with the Pacific problem forged new tactics and reshaped the strategic approach. Aircraft Carriers would become the newly crafted tip of the fast hard hitting lance, punctuated by aggressive sub skippers (with undependable torpedoes) silently striking to deplete the enemies capability to freely move their shipping, so vital to the Japanese war machine.

Combat against the Japanese Empire was reshaping the US Navy. It would never be the same. Gold wings worn by Naval Aviators were emerging from the red hot crucible, hammered into form as the cutting edge of the spear as it was re-crafted in the forge of war. The "Gun Club" still vital, drifted aft toward the handle, in a reordered and more supporting roll. Battleships would still see plenty of action, and would carry Halsey into Tokyo Bay. Meanwhile …. April approached.

April 1942 marked the Japanese occupation of the Admiralty Islands and raids against Ceylon, where the British would lose their carrier HMS HERMES, DD HMAS VAMPIRE and corvette HMS HOLLYHOCK. Then Japan struck near Calcutta, India. The British would lose CAs HMS CORNWALL & HMS DORSETSHIRE. At the end of April, Japan planted its flag in the Solomon Islands. As the Japanese battle flag surged in, on an onrushing tidal wave of success, capturing countless allied vessels and assets in the process, its ocean bound area of control and influence swelled. In the background was Japan's massive military commitment to the long, brutal and ongoing war in China.

But April was not entirely one way. For on 18 April, 1942 Jimmy Doolittle led a B-25 air raid on Japan, launched from the carrier HORNET (Task force 16 under Admiral Halsey). This stunned many who felt the Japanese mainland to be safe and secure. Rear admiral (and Chief of staff of the IJN* Combined Fleet) Matome Ugaki would observe in his diary with regard to the Japanese lack of readiness for the raid, "This is extremely regrettable"! (*Imperial Japanese Navy)

Meanwhile, back in Camden, New Jersey, USS INDEPENDENCE was taking shape as workers crafted steel. Once she floated, and entered the Pacific, INDEPENDENCE would be one of the many players that would cause Ugaki to find events "Regrettable" thru to the end of the conflict. But INDEPENDENCE was still high and dry, out of water and not yet a completed war ready vessel.

In **May of 1942,** General Wainwright surrendered at Corregidor (Philippines), leading to the infamous "Death March". The Japanese continued to expand their gains, landing on Florida Island (Solomons), and attempt to isolate sea lanes to Australia in an effort to cut off shipping from the United States. The capture of Port Moresby in southwestern New Guinea was deemed to be vital in that effort. A naval carrier sea battle would ensue as the IJN invasion fleet steamed toward Port Moresby to become known as the Battle of the Coral Sea. Japan would lose light carrier SHOHO. Heavy carrier SHOKAKU would sustain moderate damage, sending it back to Japan for extensive repair. The United States would lose USS LEXINGTON, fleet oiler USS NEOSHO and DD USS SIMS. USS YORKTOWN was damaged. Our loss of LEXINGTON (CV-2) was serious at a time when we were still critically short of aircraft carriers, however this engagement prevented Japan from continuing on to Port Moresby. This setback for Japan prevented the isolation of Australia. Equally important, this action would cost Japan the loss of precious aircraft, and experienced aviators.

Understandably overconfident from rapid successive and expansive victories in the first four months since opening the war against the Allies, planners in Japan craved a "Decisive Battle" against the US fleet. It was felt that invasion and occupation of Midway Island by Japan would cause the US fleet to come out to engage the IJN, with the US assumed to be at a very severe disadvantage.

June 1942 - EBB TIDE.   Unknown by Japan, the US and Brittan had been making inroads at breaking into their numerous codes. Though much was uncertain, gathered intelligence pointed to a planned surprise attack on Midway. With the limited information and resources we had available, and at overwhelming odds in Japan's favor, an ambush was set up. Japan lost heavily in their campaign at Midway. Sunk were Japanese aircraft carriers AKAGI, KAGA, SORYU and HIRYU. We lost YORKTOWN (CV-5) (after her quick repairs and turnaround at Pearl Harbor).

The loss of 5 IJN flight decks in May & June (SHOHO at Coral Sea), with heavy loss of aircraft, skilled aviators and maintenance personnel, on top of other operational and combat losses since the beginning of hostilities, crippled the ability of Japan to continue to prosecute its fast paced offensive ocean war.

Japan's sudden inability to project massed Naval Airpower would mark a point in the conduct of the war where Japan, previously jubilant with *"Victory Disease"*, off balance from the unforeseen rout, would transition from being on the offense, to a defensive posture, in an effort to solidify and hold its expansive gains. History tells us this today, and there were a growing number recognizing the reality of the futility of further conflict. However, the perspective of many in the Japanese military held that, the real " Decisive Battle" was yet to be fought and the final outcome then to be written.

The **I**mperial **J**apanese **N**avy was crippled. The Army seemed blind to this fact or simply ignored it. The Imperial Japanese Army succeeded in their territorial gains, in large part with cooperation and reliance of the Navy for transportation of troops, supplies, and for the critical air support. The very success of these gains were largely due to the ability of the **IJN** and **IJA** to work in concert, (but not necessarily in agreement) always under a highly protective umbrella of ample Japanese air cover. The Army would continue to demand the expansion toward Australia. The Imperial Japanese Army would need the full support of the Navy.

To secure Japan's gains, and serve as a spring board for future operations, construction of a Japanese airfield on Guadalcanal began in June. Still important to planners was the capture of Port Moresby. The Navy however, spread thin, short on fuel, and suffering from losses, was finding itself, more-and-more, in a position where it could provide this critical support, less-and-less.

The US, with its own plans for the area, viewed the Japanese airfield on Guadalcanal to be a future strategic threat to open sea lanes and lines of communication with Australia. With foothold bases (to the south) at Espiritu Santo (New Hebrides) and Nouméa (New Caledonia), US forces moved to capture the island.

In August, their sudden loss of Guadalcanal peaked Japanese concern, who decided it not in their own strategic interest for the US to remain. In response, Japanese cruisers and destroyers would sink the USS ASTORIA, USS QUINCY, USS VINCENNES and severely damage HMAS CANBERRA** in a quick, startling, bold and decisive night action off Savo Island. (** sunk by our own destroyers the following morning.)

The stage was now set for a series of violent and costly surface, air and land battles over ownership of the island that would continue on thru the end of November. Savo Island would be front row center as torpedoes were launched, shells pierced the air, and bloodied battle-torn steel hulls of the Japanese and American Navies were sent to the bottom, or limping off seeking relief and repair. So many ships holed, blown apart, sunk, the battle littered sea floor between Savo and Guadalcanal would become referred to as "Iron Bottom Sound". The futile investment in Guadalcanal further crippled the Japanese Navy. In the Battle of the Eastern Solomons USS ENTERPRISE was damaged however IJNs carrier RYUJO was sunk by aircraft from USS SARATOGA, making RYUJO the sixth Japanese carrier lost in 1942.

The Japanese military steadily experienced inconceivable setbacks. The last half of 1942 would see the emerging trend continue as Japan continued to reel from losses, after its easily won gains. It would see the Imperial Japanese Army lose confidence in its Navy. The Imperial Japanese Navy in turn pointed fingers at its Army, with an erosion in the cooperation that was so critical to the early mercurial expanse of its vast empire. Fixed assets spread out over great expanse that would prove to be a liability to resupply and defend against the highly mobile and growing US Fleet.

Toward the end of 1942 the United States, initially stunned and on the defensive, was seeing glimmers of light at the end of the initially dark tunnel. Isolated by two large oceans, with a homeland basically safe ** from attack, wartime production and training was rapidly ramped up. And, the war in the Pacific was unfolding within the realm of years of prediction. Prediction placed on paper. Paper called "War Plan Orange". (** German U-Boats initially enjoyed an almost free reign off the Atlantic coast.)

"War Plan Orange" and its "Rainbow" follow-on plans had been secretly developed by our military in the event war broke out between the United States and Japan. It slowly evolved over a long period of years as war colleges and strategic military planners played out "what if" war games in response to geopolitical events forming across the vast reaches of the Pacific. The war with Japan would unfold somewhat as predicted by the array of strategic thinkers that contributed to the War Plan. However an unplanned two prong offensive (headed by General Douglas MacArthur and Admiral Ernest King) would drive up the Pacific to capture or bypass Japanese bases.

Plan Orange (though as events emerged was not used) predicted early heavy losses to Japan, with a defensive holding action until we could build up our war machine. Then swift bold counter strikes against Japan, moving from a starting point in the South Pacific, aggressively north to the very door steps of Tokyo.

Orange (and Rainbow plans) could be thought of turning the mighty vast Pacific into a gigantic high stakes game board. The Japanese game pieces, Orange, the Unites States game pieces Blue.

When she was floated, the USS INDEPENDENCE and her crew would become a Blue game piece about to be thrust into the gigantic conflict by the Admirals forced to play the high stakes life & death reality of Pacific War. The Admirals under Ernest J. King (Nimitz, Halsey, McCain, Radford, Bogan, Mitscher, etc.) would be moving game piece INDEPENDENCE with a strong determination to emerge victorious.

As a small mountainous nation of islands, smaller in land mass than California, Japan lacked natural resources such as oil, and the ores needed to make aluminum and steel. Japan relied on shipping. The nations survival depended on it.

We would deprive Japan of her shipping and cut off the supply of oil and the raw materials she would need for the prosecution of war.

As we moved closer, we would build support bases to get within striking distance of industrial and military targets on her homeland.

We would bypass many Japanese bases, first destroying their airpower and shipping, then leaving the Japanese garrisons stranded in desolation to fight tropical disease, cutoff from a fresh supply of food medicines and materials needed to fight a war. Bypassed islands would often continue to suffer bombing by aircraft as a drop site of opportunity for unused ordnance after a mission, and shelling by ships, as well as occasional raids to assure that the beleaguered garrisons withered and remained a non-threat.

The enormous US industrial engine would massively outpace Japan in the necessary food, fuel, supplies and machines of war. The USS INDEPENDENCE was a part of that production ramp up as vast array of shipyard workers toiled on her hull, and the hulls of her sisters. But for now, 1943 is still in the future and, the war is still in the early stages.

Aggressive raids against Japanese held islands were well under way as INDEPENDENCE was floated and put into play, to eventually become a part of Halsey's "Big Blue Blanket".

2
From Concept to Launching

The Shipyard

New York Shipbuilding Corporation (**NYSB**) designed and built the USS INDEPENDENCE and her siblings. The company laid its first keel on 29 November, 1900. Located on the Delaware River in Camden New Jersey, the company grew building tankers, cargo ships, passenger ships, military ships and other vessels. The facilities expanded, helped with orders placed during WW1.

Above is a photo of the shipyard taken in 1921. The NYSB Corporation by then had 5 miles of roads and 15 miles of standard gauge railroad track within its facility, with 115 cranes of various capacities up to 200 tons.

When WWII began the shipyard devoted its entire facility to the production of vessels for the Navy. The facility geared up for the production of cruisers and aircraft carriers. NYSB has considered the building of the INDEPENDENCE class carriers one of that companies "most significant contributions to the war effort."

The work force at NYSB grew to roughly 34,000 during WWII. Trades included Boilermakers, Coppersmiths, Draftsmen, Drop Forgers, Electricians, Engineers, Joiners, Loftsmen, Machinists, Pattern Makers, Painters, Pipe Fitters, Plumbers, Press Men, Punchers, Riveters, Ship fitters, and Welders, to name a few. To run the Company were the typical office positions shuffling the paperwork necessary to run the organization, hire, manage and pay the employees and interface with the government. Metal, once procured, needed to be designed, machined, bent, formed, cut, drilled, assembled, welded, riveted and painted. Miles of pipes cut, threaded, fitted. Wire and cables run.

Congress authorized construction of three CLEVELAND class 10,000 ton light cruisers in June 1940, and on 1 July 1940 the NYSB was issued a contract. The fixed price contract (adjusted for labor & materials) called for the construction of the CL59, CL60 and CL61. These would carry the names USS AMSTERDAM, USS SANTA FE, and USS TALLAHASSEE.

Purchase orders were placed with subcontractors for key components for CL59 in August 1940. The Keel for the CL59, USS AMSTERDAM, was laid on 1 May 1941 in Ways "T" ** of the NYSB yard. Work was well along on the AMSTERDAM at the beginning of 1942, with much of the hull constructed to the main deck level. (** Ways T is located within the middle yard complex, just to the left of the white arrow.)

"Replacement of Naval Vessels"

AUTHORIZING ACT—APPROVED JUNE 14, 1940, AND JUNE 28, 1940

APPROPRIATION ACT—APPROVED JUNE 26, 1940

CONTRACT

FOR THE

CONSTRUCTION OF THREE LIGHT CRUISERS
Nos. CL 59, CL 60, AND CL 61

This contract, entered into this first day of July 1940, by the United States of America, hereinafter called the Department, represented by the contracting officer executing this contract, and the New York Shipbuilding Corporation, a corporation organized and existing under the laws of the State of New York and doing business at Camden in the State of New Jersey, hereinafter called the contractor, witnesseth that the parties hereto do mutually agree as follows:

ARTICLE 1. (a) The contractor, subject to the provisions hereinafter set forth, including the **General Provisions**, will construct at its plant at Camden, New Jersey (hereinafter called the plant of the contractor) three (3) light cruisers Nos. CL 59, CL 60, and CL 61 each of about ten thousand (10,000) tons standard displacement (hereinafter called the vessel/vessels), complete in all respects, both hull and machinery, including the installation of ordnance and ordnance outfit, and of other articles to be furnished by the Department, in conformity with the approved plans and specifications, including changes therein which shall be authorized as hereinafter provided. The said plans and specifications and afore-

AMSTERDAM (CL59)

PURCHASE ORDERS PLACED WITH SUBCONTRACTORS, AUGUST 1940

Boilers, superheaters, economizers, oil burners,
    soot blowers, etc.
Air compressors, low, medium & high
Centrifugal pumps
Forgings for shafting
Turbine driven fuel oil service pumps; turbine
    driven fuel oil booster & trans. pumps; turbine
    driven main lub. oil pumps; motor driven main
    lub. oil pumps; motor driven Diesel oil service
    pumps
Port fuel oil service pumps & fuel oil tank drain
    pumps
Reciprocating pumps - emergency feed & fire & bilge
Main turbines & reduction gears
Hendy lathes
Floor type grinder, Hisey Wolf type 5-USN
25 ton hydraulic press, Manley No. 29A-49
Power hack saw, Marvel No. 4B
No. 2 Cincinnati Universal MH type milling machine
Wade screw cutting lathe
16" sensitive drill, floor type
36" x 9" round column radial drill
Buffer, bench type
16" Universal crank shaper
Refrigerating plant
Deaerating feed tanks
Auxiliary turbo generator sets, 600 KW
36" high intensity arc type searchlight
Motor-generator sets, AC/DC - for searchlight
    & battery charging supply & for interior
    communication
Electric cable
Underwater log system

(CONFIDENTIAL)
U. S. S. AMSTERDAM - CL 59
MAIN DECK LOOKING AFT FROM FRAME 126
NEW YORK SHIPBUILDING CORP., CAMDEN, N. J.
JANUARY 13TH, 1942

Note the photos (taken days after the contract was issued for the conversion) show the work is well along toward the main deck, with the vessel still designated as the USS AMSTERDAM.

(CONFIDENTIAL)
U. S. S. AMSTERDAM - CL 59
MAIN DECK LOOKING FORWARD FROM BULKHEAD 27
NEW YORK SHIPBUILDING CORP., CAMDEN, N. J.
JANUARY 13TH, 1942

U.S.S. ANTIETAM CV 59

BOW VIEW - STARBOARD SIDE

NEW YORK SHIPBUILDING CORP., CAMDEN, N. J.

JANUARY 13TH, 1942

(CONFIDENTIAL)
U. S. S. AMSTERDAM (CL 59)
STARBOARD SIDE LOOKING AFT FROM FRAME 14
NEW YORK SHIPBUILDING CORP., CAMDEN, N. J.
JANUARY 13TH, 1942

Chapter 2

25

(CONFIDENTIAL)
U.S.S. AMSTERDAM - CL 59
STARBOARD SIDE LOOKING AFT FROM BULKHEAD 106
NEW YORK SHIPBUILDING CORP. CAMDEN, N.J.

(CONFIDENTIAL)
U.S.S. AMSTERDAM - CL 59
STERN VIEW — STARBOARD SIDE
NEW YORK SHIPBUILDING CORP. CAMDEN
JANUARY 13TH, 1942

The NYSB Corporation had designed the Cleveland class cruisers and were called upon to carry out the engineering for the conversion of the cruiser into a new class of aircraft carrier. Design change for the conversion was carried out by marine architects at the NYSB Corp., instead of the Bureau of Ships, to speed the process. She was needed quickly. On 9 January the contract was officially issued by the USN Bureau of Ships. The US war with Japan (and her Axis allies) was now 1 month old.

On 10 January 1942, construction on the light cruiser **USS AMSTERDAM** (CL-59) stopped as the orders to convert the emerging cruiser into an aircraft carrier were received. The converted vessel was destined to become the first of her class. She would be identified within NYSB as Contract Number 427 (within Contract Number 1437, for 3 ships). She would carry a proud name of major historical significance to our nation to commemorate the signing of the Declaration of Independence, by action of congress on 4 July, 1776. She would become the **USS INDEPENDENCE, CV-22** .

With the keel for the light cruiser USS AMSTERDAM laid, the hull well underway, and a new contract in hand, the workers at the New York Shipbuilding Corporation yard began the conversion process in January, 1942. The war in the Pacific was slightly more than a month old, and our losses to Japan were mounting. NYSB workers set about in earnest to deliver the lead ship, in a new class of warship to the US Navy.

Work progressed rapidly during 1942 and by mid August the new fast light aircraft carrier was nearing its time for launch.

USS INDEPENDENCE Evolves

Built on a narrow light cruiser hull, 600 feet long at her waterline, the USS INDEPENDENCE would be fast, a necessity for how she would be utilized. She would run in, deliver the war back on the enemies' doorstep. Then she could move quickly out of harm's way after her aircraft had carried out their assigned mission. A rapid raider to put the US on the offensive as we licked our wounds, recovered from our losses across the Pacific, and converted US industry into massive full scale war time production.

Her redesign would need to be expedited to push her out into the war as soon as possible, but careful consideration needed to be given to the conversion details to assure her success.

DON LABUDDE describes the design evolution of Mighty-I this way:

> *"Independence and her eight sisters began life conceived as beauties. In the very act of birth they were caught in circumstances beyond their control. Designers were forced to change plans, forced to create something new and untried out of a desperate need as ineffable as the brevity of man's time on earth.*
>
> *Each was laid down as a sleek new light cruiser. She would boast a long narrow hull for speed and strength. Into it would be placed powerful steam turbines. Coupled to them would be machinery necessary to turn the four great bronzed screws. Magazines holding the projectiles for main and secondary batteries would be buried deep within her hull. Their superstructures, cragged mansions of steel amidships, would be split in two by tall stacks leaning gently aft. Jutting from the main deck would grow the armored mounds of four turrets, proudly pointing *8-inch rifles forward or aft.*
>
> *As designed, as dreamed, they would be everything a dedicated cruiser sailor could wish them to be: fast, handsome, and useful; a pleasure to command, fight, and live on.*
> *** But before a plate could be forged or a seam welded, the inscrutable gods of war stepped in and tossed these best-laid plans of architects and strategists into the nearest wastebasket. The sly old mind of the East, appropriating the sea-borne winged invention of the West, turned it upon them with a reckless determination of purpose that soon studded the floor of the Pacific Ocean with the torn hulks of proud warships and fertilized it with the blood and bones of two thousand men.*
>
> *Yorktown and Wasp, the lady named Lexington, and Hornet all were sunk. Saratoga's ill luck made her queen of the drydocks. Ranger's small size and lack of speed tied her to the Atlantic. And Enterprise, her niche in the halls of immortality already reserved, was doing the work of a Division, her scarred deck mute evidence of the agony through which she had passed, her seared and battered hull pitiable proof of the gossamer thread on which had hung for a time the fate of her nation. Essex, name-ship of a new breed, was still shaking down, while the rest of her handsome progeny were months from their first taste of the sea. Hence Mighty I and her eight sisters.*
> *The powerful turbines, four great screws, and beautiful sleek hulls were theirs to keep. But the super-structures were not to be, nor the turrets or twin tall stacks. Into the basin of their hulls were crammed instead additional tanks to hold a hundred-thousand gallons of aviation gasoline. Magazines were rebuilt to berth fat, ugly aerial bombs and torpedoes and to house ammunition for the winged chariots they would nest, both on the slab mounted high over the hulls and within the cavern that now occupied the greater length of the main deck. Galley, mess deck, and living quarters had to remain as they were; they would only be more crowded, called upon to feed and bed the many more hands required to service radically different main batteries. There was only so much space available. By the time they were ready to grease down the ways alongside river Delaware, even their designers had trouble remembering their original conception. "* ***DON LABUDDE***

Author's notes: Don is a truly wonderful writer, but has a couple of technical errors. Had he not had his heart attack, he may well have caught these had he the opportunity to finish and review his work; * Note: the Cleveland Class light cruisers had 6" guns. ** Note: Don would be correct if he had written "Before the Independence was launched" as the events of this and the next paragraph happened after the keel was laid down, and work commenced on the USS AMSTERDAM.

Flight deck length of the USS INDEPENDENCE was 552 feet, and did not extend to the bow. Width of the flight deck was 73 feet. To aid with aircraft deck movement and placement, an 8 foot wide by 60 foot long side structure was added to widen the flight deck on the port side of the ship across from the island. The photo below shows how this additional width helps the utility of the flight deck as a Dauntless taxies around the forward elevator while it is down. (Photo: May 1943)
A single H2-1 pneumatic hydraulic catapult was installed flush with the flight deck on the port side, to shorten the precious flight deck space needed to launch aircraft.

Located between the flight deck, and the original cruiser hull main deck, the hangar bay (or hangar deck) was utilized for both aircraft storage and maintenance. It was 285 feet long and 55 feet wide. Two hydraulic elevators conveyed aircraft between the flight deck and hangar deck. The hangar deck needed to be flat so the deck was elevated above the cruiser hull's main deck which was concave from bow to stern. The original cruiser main deck was retained of necessity for structural integrity, without undergoing major redesign.

The additional mass above the main deck would make the hull more top heavy (a higher metacentric center in naval parlance). To compensate, tapered side blisters were added to both sides of the hull, increasing the beam roughly 5 feet. The blisters were also functional as they were utilized to hold additional aviation gas and fuel oil. There would be a small speed penalty from the blisters but the added hull stability and range would make the modification worthwhile. Some of the port side blister capacity was taken by Portland cement concrete ballast, poured in to compensate for the added weight of the offset island, exhaust uptakes and antennas on the starboard side of the ship.

The top heaviness, though helped by the blisters, would require extra attention by the helm in foul weather.

The INDEPENDENCE Class carrier's smaller size would limit the number of aircraft she could carry, with smaller flight decks and cramped hangar bays. Not only would the number of aircraft be limited, but consideration would have to be given to aircraft type and size. Best utilization of the carrier and its aircraft compliment would be resolved only after the ship floated and went on her shakedown cruise. Then the mix would still not be idealized, this only happening thru war time experience. The proper mix was also influenced by the evolution in new aircraft designs and their entry into the war.

Having a short and narrow flight deck would make the INDEPENDENCE class carriers slightly "sporty" for pilots to land on compared to the larger carriers. When weather made flight operations less than ideal, the ships rolling could transition the flight deck into a fright deck.

Initial conceptual drawings for the conversion had the island and stacks located on top of the flight deck. It was realized that was untenable due to the crowding of precious flight deck space.

To conserve flight deck space, the island structure was mounted outboard of the flight deck, as you can see in the photo below. The very small island structure contained the bridge, a sea cabin for the captain and one for the navigator, plus a chart room. In addition there were small observation platforms to monitor air operations, and for spotters and signalmen.
 Atop the island was a mast structure supporting the ships yardarm, searchlights, radar, IFF and beacon antennas.   (See photos on next two pages)

This photo most likely shot in 1944, as evidenced by modifications with the addition of a second yardarm and a new antenna mast (both added during the torpedo damage repair and modification period at Hunters Point, to be discussed later).

Arresting Gear Cables

Barricade cables

Additional radar antenna mounting was provided on an offset antenna mast structure between the two pairs of offset stacks. This photo also shows four (of the nine) arresting gear cables, held slightly elevated off the flight deck to making it easier for the aircraft tail hooks to snag, on landing.

Also in plain view, are the support stanchions with their barricade or barrier cables, shown in the up or erected position. They are hydraulically raised and lowered, used to attempt to stop aircraft from striking other aircraft forward of the barricades, should the landing turn into an undesirable adventure.

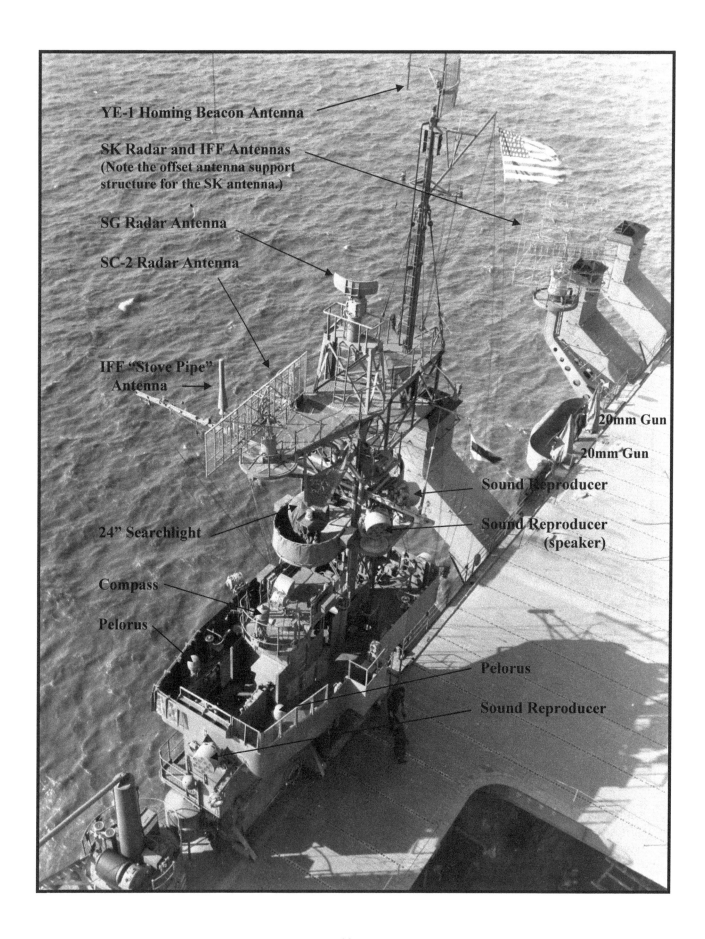

YE-1 Homing Beacon Antenna

SK Radar and IFF Antennas
(Note the offset antenna support
structure for the SK antenna.)

SG Radar Antenna

SC-2 Radar Antenna

IFF "Stove Pipe"
Antenna

24" Searchlight

Compass

Pelorus

20mm Gun

20mm Gun

Sound Reproducer

Sound Reproducer
(speaker)

Pelorus

Sound Reproducer

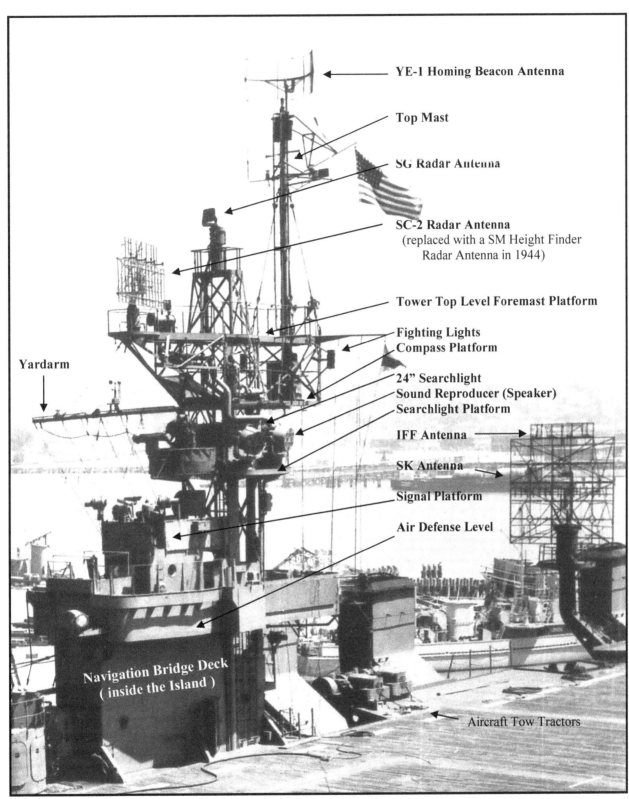

YE-1 Homing Beacon Antenna

Top Mast

SG Radar Antenna

SC-2 Radar Antenna
(replaced with a SM Height Finder
Radar Antenna in 1944)

Tower Top Level Foremast Platform

Fighting Lights
Compass Platform

24" Searchlight
Sound Reproducer (Speaker)
Searchlight Platform

IFF Antenna

SK Antenna

Signal Platform

Air Defense Level

Yardarm

Navigation Bridge Deck
(inside the Island)

Aircraft Tow Tractors

The photo on this page (and on the previous pages) identifies some of the of the decks, platforms, antennas and components on the island structure. After her trip to the navy yard for repair in the first half of 1944, the ship will
gain a second yardarm, a new large vertical antenna mast structure (aft of the offset SK antenna mast, between the 3rd
& 4th stack) and many electronic upgrades. The SC-2 Radar Antenna on the Foremast Platform will be replaced
by a new SM Air Search Radar. These modifications are noticeable in later photos in the book shot after mid
1944.

Not having the cruisers big guns, the ammo storage magazines were converted to aviation ordnance storage to accommodate bombs and other aircraft ordnance. A space was created aft of the hangar bay to store torpedoes. Workshops were also there, slightly cramped with their limited space.

Much of the CLEVELAND cruiser design remained below the main deck.

Four Babcock & Wilcox "Express" boilers burned fuel oil, in turn providing high pressure steam to drive the four General Electric 25,000 shaft horsepower geared (cross compound, double reduced) steam turbine assemblies. The four turbines generated a combined total of 100,000 shaft horsepower to propel the ship with its four massive screws. Separate watertight compartments were utilized for the turbines and boilers, with fore & aft engine rooms and fore & aft boiler rooms. The structural as well as watertight integrity was fairly robust.

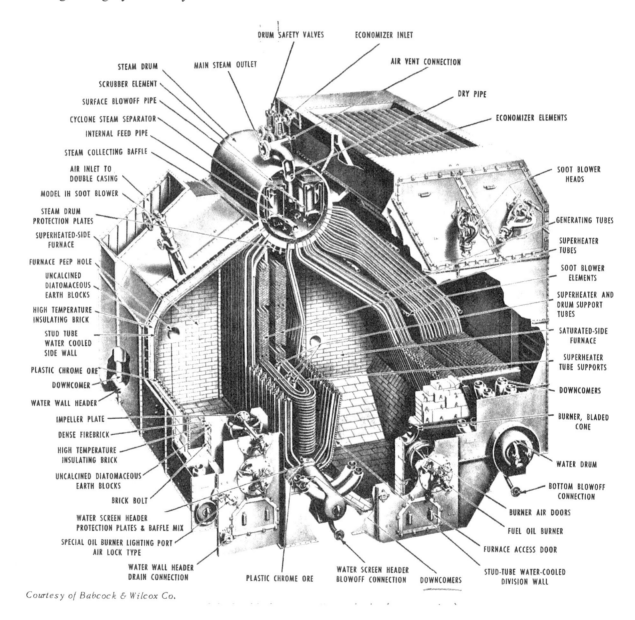

Courtesy of Babcock & Wilcox Co.

Two boilers, much like this, were in each of the forward & aft fire (boiler) rooms, below decks.
(See drawing on next page for boiler & turbine layout)

Hold Deck

Bow

Stern

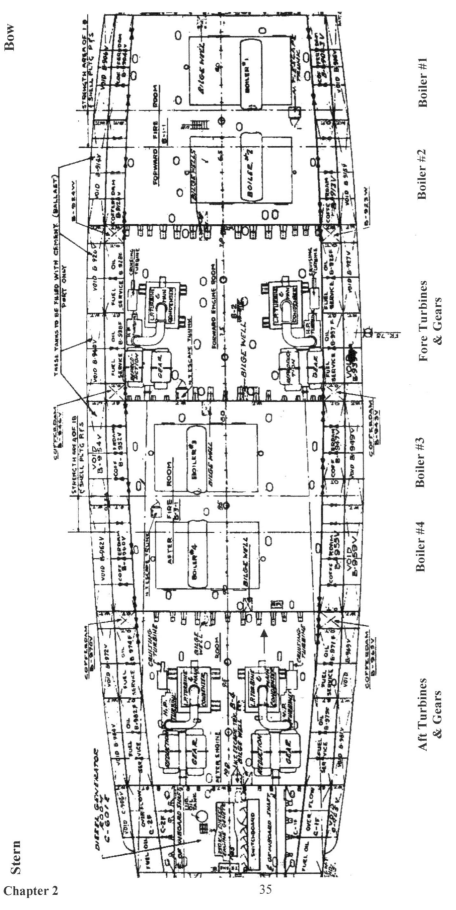

Boiler #1

Boiler #2

Fore Turbines
& Gears

Boiler #3

Boiler #4

Aft Turbines
& Gears

This is from a Hold Deck drawing of the CL55. The CV/ CVL–22 would have been much the same with regard to major machinery layout. Note the inboard prop shafts were driven by the aft turbines. Not shown on the outside of the hull are the added blisters.

Electrical power was provided by four GE geared turbine generators, providing 600 KW each (450 Volt, 60 cycle, 3 phase A.C.). Two diesel 250 KW auxiliary generators provided back-up / stand-by power.

The original design called for an added armor belt around the waterline, however, due to a shortage of the steel amour plate needed, and for expediency, this additional armor was left off the USS INDEPENDENCE.

There also was no additional armor protection provided between the wood flight deck and the hangar deck. The main deck armor (beneath the hangar deck) was only 2 inches thick, from the CLEVELAND cruiser design. With the thin hide, she had better be nimble and fast.

Living quarters became challenged for space. Originally designed for a complement of 114 officers, 65 Chief Petty Officers and 1,236 enlisted men, the numbers would swell to roughly 1460 officers, C.P.O.'s and enlisted men. Actual in-service needs called for crowding the living quarters even more to accommodate roughly 1570 crew members. Additionally, pilots ready room spaces would need to be provided for the Air Group.

Messing Accommodations were designed to seat a total of 745 men, broken down as follows:

Captain's Cabin	(Seats at dining table)	10
Officers Wardroom Messroom	(Seats at dining table)	100
Warrant Officer's Messroom	(Seats at dining table)	14
C.P.O. Messroom		62
Crew Messroom		559

The crew was seated, 488 at tables (8 per table), 44 at parachute packing tables, and 27 at counters.

The Captain, Officers and Warrant Officers dined in separate eating areas (as listed above) and also had separate galleys where food was prepared. They were served by stewards.

> The galley was on the Second Deck, one deck below the Officer's Wardroom. The prepared food was hoisted up on a hand operated dumb waiter.

> The US Navy during WWII was segregated, and the INDEPENDENCE was no exception. The stewards were black. Blacks and whites were berthed in segregated compartments. Battle station assignments were also largely segregated.

The ship's organizational structure aboard USS INDEPENDENCE included the following Departments:

> Air Department   (Divisions - V1, V2, V3, V4, V5 and the squadrons)
> Chaplain
> Communications Department   (Divisions - K1, K2)
> Construction and Repair Department   (Divisions - R, R2)
> Engineering Department   (Divisions - A, B, E, M)
> Gunnery Department   (Divisions - First, Second, Third, Fourth, Fifth, Sixth)
> Medical Department   (Division - H)
> Navigation Department
> Supply Department   (Division - S)
> US Marine Corps

Enlisted Mess - May 1943 - Bench seating and trays.

Above: Aft. Squadron Ready Room

Below: Officer's Wardroom (Capt. Ewen beneath the poster). Table cloths, chairs and plates.

NEW YORK SHIPBUILDING CORPORATION
CAMDEN, NEW JERSEY

SCHEDULE SHOWING OVERTIME AND SHIFT WORK,
AND ATLANTIC COAST ZONE STANDARD LABOR INCREASES
UNDER NOd CONTRACT 1437
(CONTRACT COVERING MORE THAN ONE VESSEL)
FROM SEPTEMBER 28,1942 TO NOVEMBER 1,1942,INCL.

Contract No.			Direct and Indirect Labor	Social Security Tax	Total
NOd 1437					
427	CV22	USS INDEPENDENCE	$324,439.67	$ 7,480.39	$ 331,920.06
428	CL60	" SANTA FE'	478,544.34	11,033.50	489,577.84
429	CV23	" PRINCETON	191,910.17	4,424.75	196,334.92
TOTAL NOd 1437			$994,894.18	$22,938.64	$1,017,832.82

Office of Cost Inspector, USN
18 November 1942.

Left - **18 November 1942**

**Detail of overtime, shift work
and labor increases.**

Below - **1 June 1942**

Voucher
16th payment for $663, 818.00
with
$7,408,117.00 outstanding

(Gen. Acct No. 6. Supp. No. 7)

GENERAL ACCOUNTING OFFICE PREAUDIT

Certified for payment in the sum of $............

Comptroller General of the United States

By ....

U. S.   NAVY DEPARTMENT
(Department, bureau, or establishment)

Voucher prepared at Camden, New Jersey June 1, 1942.

THE UNITED STATES, Dr.,

To NEW YORK SHIPBUILDING CORPORATION,
(Payee)

Address Camden, New Jersey.

Payee's Account No.

PAID BY

(For use of Paying Office)

No. and Date of Order	Date of Delivery or Service	Articles or Services (Enter description, item number of contract or general supply schedule, and other information deemed necessary) Terms ....% Discount Cash .... days	Quantity	UNIT PRICE		AMOUNT	
				Cost	Per	Dollars	Cts.
		Brought forward from continuation sheet(s)					
NOd-1437 7/1/40	11/15/43	Sixteenth (16th) Payment U.S.S. INDEPENDENCE(CV22) EX-CL59, building at New York Shipbuilding Corp. Camden, New Jersey.				$663,818.00	
		Outstanding........ $7,408,117.00					

Shipped from .... to .... Weight .... Government B/L No. ....   Total $663,818.00
(Payee must NOT use this space)

I certify that the above bill is correct and just; that payment therefor has not been received; and that except as otherwise noted all of the articles, materials, and supplies furnished under purchase order No. ....; if unmanufactured articles, materials, and supplies, have been mined or produced in the United States; if manufactured articles, materials, and supplies, they have been manufactured in the case may be, in the United States from articles, materials, or supplies mined, produced, or manufactured, as the case may be, in the United States; and that State or local sales taxes are not included in the amounts billed.

(Memorandum—Do not sign)

Payee NEW YORK SHIPBUILDING CORPN.

Per ....   Title ....

Differences ....

Account verified; correct for ....

(Signature or initials)

Date ....   Date ....   Invoice Rec'd ....

Contract No........   Date ....   Reg. No........

Pursuant to authority created in me, I certify that the above articles were received in good condition, after due inspection, acceptance, and delivery prior to payment is required by law, or the services were performed as stated; that they were procured under the contract numbered above or the unnumbered contract attached hereto, or that they were procured without written contract, in open market, and with or without advertising, under the circumstances stated in No. .... of "Method of or Absence of Advertising" shown on reverse hereof, and were necessary for the public service; and that the prices charged are just and reasonable and in accordance with the agreement.

(Memorandum—Do not sign)

/Approved for $ 663,818.00

NOTE: "THE INSURANCE TERMS OF THE CONTRACT HAVE BEEN MET".

R. W. HYDEN, Rear-Admiral, U.
Title Supervisor of Shipbuilding

ACCOUNTING CLASSIFICATION (for completion by Administrative Office)

Appropriation, limitation, or project symbol	Appropriation title		Limit'n or Proj't Amount	Appropriation Amount

NOTE: "Ultimate delivery to The Commandant, Navy Yard, Phila., Pa.

17X0603   Increase and Replacement of Naval Vessels-
          Construction and Machinery.

		COST ACCOUNT		OBJECT OF EXPENDITURE	
Allotment	Amount	Encumbrance Liquidated	Symbol	Amount	Symbol	Amount

Account 10
Title 1-A

.... dated .... 19.... for $........   on Treasurer of the United States in favor of payee named above.

Check No. ....   Paid by .... on ....   Per ....

Launching the USS INDEPENDENCE

Saturday 22 August 1942   *Launched at New York Shipbuilding Corp. Camden, N.J.*

Secretary of the Navy, Frank Knox was present on this notable day, along with other dignitaries such as **Assistant Secretary of the Navy - Ralph A. Bard**, Mrs. Bard, **Admiral Ernest Joseph King - Commander in Chief, US Fleet / Chief of Naval Operations** (Nimitz's superior), Mrs. King , Rear Admiral A.E. Watson, (Commandant, Forth Naval District), Mrs. Watson, and Rear Admiral R.W. Ryden (Supervisor of Shipbuilding, Camden, N.J.). The Sponsor was Mrs. Rawleigh Warner (wife of the Pure Oil Co. President). Her daughter, Suzanne Warner, was maid of honor. (see photo on next page)

Those attending from New York Shipbuilding Corporation included; Henry Lockhart (Chairman), J.F. Metten (Vice Chairman), R.S. Campbell (President), N.R. Parker (V.P. & Treasurer) and T.H. Bossert (V.P.).

It was Knox who had teamed with President Roosevelt to arrange for the conversion of the INDEPENDENCE and her 8 sisters. She was the first of her breed. The military leaders present urgently needed her in the Pacific.

USS INDEPENDENCE sat with her centerline on the slot of Ways "T". The temperature was 86°F, wind was at 13 mph and the current in the Delaware was running at .28 knots upstream. The tide gauge at 5'9". To help her slide into the Delaware, the ways were greased with a 7/16" base coat of Keystone Grease, followed up with Paragon and Neptune lubricants for slip coats. 16,700 pounds of lubricant total. The prizefighter INDEPENDENCE weighed in at an estimated 7,565 tons. She was lean on those ways, but not yet ready for war. She would have to bulk up to take on the enemy.

CONFIDENTIAL
U.S.S. INDEPENDENCE CV 22
LEFT TO RIGHT
ASSISTANT SECRETARY - RALPH A. BARD
SECRETARY OF THE NAVY - FRANK KNOX
MRS. RAWLEIGH WARNER - S[...]
MISS SUZANNE WARNER - MAID OF HONOR
ADMIRAL ERNEST J. KING U.S.N.
NEW YORK SHIPBUILDING CORP., CAMDEN, N. J.

In accordance with tradition, Mrs. Rawleigh Warner broke a bottle of Renault's Champagne (a New Jersey wine) on her bow for the christening.

Declivity of the keel was 9/16" per foot. A 1,960 ton hydraulic nudge would start her on her 683' trip down the inclined way into the waiting river. Her first foot of travel (to begin her long dangerous journey toward the shores of Japan) would take 300 seconds. It began at 1124 AM. She slowly accelerated her slide into the Delaware, and then began moving briskly down the greased ways.
She breezed by the tall yard crane on her port beam, and past erected scaffolds. Stern first she plunged in as her rudder and keel submerged, quickly moving, momentum from thousands of tons of freshly unharnessed energy plowed her almost directly across the river to the Philadelphia side.
Waiting tugs made fast. They eased the Mighty-I to the south side of pier #1 where she was tied up at 1535. Her newly wetted surface, 49,500 Sq. Ft.

Her launching had gone well, no damage to her hull. She was proudly afloat, new, fresh and ready for outfitting. Outfitting work would be carried out at the Philadelphia Naval Yard.

2 December 1942

NYSB Vice President T.H. Bossert sent a letter to the Chief, Bureau of Ships (confirming a telephone conference they had) stating that due to the status of the ship, it was reasonable to request official dock trials for the INDEPENDENCE to begin 15 December 1942. He then stated on completion of the dock trials and machinery inspection, it was deemed possible to complete the majority of the post trial items required by the inspection, and conduct a second inspection on 28 December 1942.

At the completion of the Hull and Ordnance inspection, the earliest possible date could then be set for the delivery of the INDEPENDENCE to the Navy.

4 December 1942

A conference to determine the completion of USS INDEPENDENCE in the NYSB board room was arranged by letter from Rear Admiral R.W. Ryden (Supervisor of Shipbuilding, Camden, N.J.) to the Bureau of Ships, set for 1100, Friday 11 December 1942. The meeting goal was to set tentative dates for "delivery, commissioning, and readiness for sea". Additionally the meeting was to determine whether NYSB or the Navy Yard would finish the uncompleted work.

5 December 1942

Another letter from Rear Admiral R.W. Ryden (Supervisor of Shipbuilding, Camden, N.J.) was sent to the Bureau of Ships. It proposed a date of 15 December 1942 for official dock trials and inspection of machinery. It further proposed a date of 28 December 1942 for inspection of hull equipment, auxiliaries and ordnance installations.
The Bureau of Ships was requested to issue authorized changes covering the omission of dry docking, hull bottom painting and 15 other items of work listed to be accomplished by the Philadelphia Navy Yard, at which time the INDEPENDENCE would be dry docked.

11 December 1942

A conference was held in the NYSB board room. Attendees were from the Office of Vice Chief of Naval Operations, Bureau of ships, Philadelphia Navy Yard, Office of Supervisor of Shipbuilding - Camden, and the NYSB Corp. Additionally the prospective Executive Officer of USS INDEPENDENCE, Comdr. R.L. Johnson and the prospective Captain of sister carrier USS PRINCETON, Captain G.R. Henderson were present.
The meeting opened with Rear Admiral Ryden reviewing instructions from the Secretary of the Navy to accelerate in every way possible the ultimate delivery of USS INDEPENDENCE to the fleet. The 15 items of uncompleted work, the list to be completed by the Philadelphia Navy Yard were discussed with a determination that it was important to complete the work by 31 January 1943. To facilitate this, a division of work was agreed to by NYSB and the Philadelphia Navy Yard.
Rear Admiral Farber pointed out that a key factor remaining that would influence the commissioning was the availability of officers and crew. Comdr. R.L. Johnson, speaking on behalf of the prospective Commanding Officer of USS INDEPENDENCE, stated that every effort had been made to accelerate the ordering of officer and enlisted personnel, in belief that sufficient necessary ratings would be available for commissioning as early as 30 December 1942. He further specified the need of 5 weeks from the date of commissioning to the date of the "river run trials". Captain G.R. Henderson, USS PRINCETON, agreed with the 5 week requirement. During that period of time the ship needed provisioning, and the initial organization and drilling of the crew needed to be accomplished.
Captain Seiller of the Philadelphia Navy Yard stated that the USS INDEPENDENCE would have Number 1 priority over all other work in the yard with the men available to deliver the vessel at the earliest possible date.
NYSB committed to (at the request of the Secretary of the Navy) make every effort to deliver the ship on time. NYSB was also asked to assure all present that the USS INDEPENDENCE would be fully habitable for the crew on whatever date the ship was delivered.
It was the consensus of the group that:
 1. A tentative delivery date of 30 December 1942 would remain unchanged unless it became apparent to NYSB or the Supervisor of Shipbuilding the date could not be met.
2. The Trial Board should be asked to inspect the vessel on 28 December as previously planned.

3. NYSB would make all preparations to assist in the completion of Government-responsible work concurrently in order to assist the Navy Yard in carrying out its outfitting work.

4. The Supervisor (as directed by the Secretary of the Navy and Vice Chief of Naval Operations with the advice of the Navy Yard) would decide which items of authorized or requested work should be carried out, or deferred, keeping the Secretary of the Navy and Vice Chief of Naval Operations advised.

19 December 1942

A letter from R.A. Dyer (President, Board of Inspection and Survey) to Rear Admiral R.W. Ryden, listed members (and their assistants) of the Board of Survey and representatives of the Navy Department that would witness the dock trials and conduct the inspection of the INDEPENDENCE. They were scheduled to arrive in Camden N.J. on the evening of 27 December, to stay at the Walt Whitman Hotel. Transportation to be available at the hotel at 0800 the morning of the 28th to proceed to the ship.

21 December 1942

A letter was conveyed to NYSB from the Department of Navy, Office of the Judge Advocate General, Washington, D.C., stating:

"*Gentlemen: You are hereby authorized to deliver the U.S.S. INDEPENDENCE (CV22) to the Commandant, Navy Yard, Philadelphia, Pennsylvania. The Commandant has been authorized to preliminarily accept the vessel on or about December 30, 1942, when the status of the work and the condition of the vessel are satisfactory in all respects to the Commandant and the Supervisor of Shipbuilding, and preliminary acceptance is recommended by the Trial Board. By direction of the Secretary of the Navy.*"

The letter was signed by Rear Admiral Woodson, Judge Advocate General of the Navy.

4 January 1942   *Dock Trials and Material Inspection*

Dock trials and material inspection basically was a process of checking that all machinery, plumbing, elevators, electronics and systems throughout the ship were functioning as they were designed and specified to function, dockside. River trials and sea trials would follow as the new vessel went thru its "shake down".

As prearranged in the letter of 19 December, a team of inspectors and observers departed the Walt Whitman Hotel and proceeded to USS INDEPENDENCE.

Testing proceeded on the boilers, the turbines and the generators. A 15% overspeed test of the turbines and reduction gears for dynamic balance and rigidity of all parts had been conducted by GE at their plant on individual uncoupled major components, and was bypassed. Pressure testing, and soapsuds testing for pressure leaks, hydrostatic tests, pressure valve and overspeed trips, vibration, leaks, lubrication, drainage, boiler pressures, operation of soot blowers with steam at full boiler pressure, etc.

A battery of tests of transmitters and receivers in the radio rooms, radar equipment and other electronic and electrical gear in C.I.C. were typical of inspections conducted throughout the vessel.

In a letter from the Supervisor of Shipbuilding, Camden, N.J. addressed to the President, Board of Inspection and Survey, Navy Department, Washington D.C., a **Certificate of Completion of Hull** was provided stating that the USS INDEPENDENCE has been built in accordance with the contract, plans, specifications, is of good quality and satisfactorily completed except as noted on a list provided. A "**Report of Inspection of Bottom of Vessel**" noted that the vessel had not been dry docked to date, so an inspection of the bottom of the hull could not be carried out. Likewise for the "**Certificate of Draft Figures**" as checking and installation of outside draft could not be accomplished until the ship was high and dry.

NOT TO BE RELEASED FOR PUBLICATION.

Note the 5" Gun Mount is installed on the bow (and on the stern)

CONFIDENTIAL

U.S.S. INDEPENDENCE CV - 22

STARBOARD & TOPSIDE ARRANGEMENT AT TIME OF INCLINING EXPERIMENT

NEW YORK SHIPBUILDING CORP., CAMDEN, N. J.

JANUARY 2, 1943

OFFICIAL PHOTOGRAPH
NOT TO BE RELEASED FOR
PUBLICATION

No. 7 Gun Tub

The ship's radar antennas are yet to be installed
Note the offset radar antenna mount between the
two pairs of stacks.

CONFIDENTIAL
U. S. S. INDEPENDENCE CV - 22
STARBOARD & TOPSIDE ARRANGEMENT AT TIME OF INCLINING EXPERIMENT
NEW YORK SHIPBUILDING CORP., CAMDEN, N. J.
JANUARY 2, 1943

CONFIDENTIAL
U. S. S. INDEPENDENCE CV - 22
STARBOARD & TOPSIDE ARRANGEMENT AT TIME OF INCLINING EXPERIMENT
NEW YORK SHIPBUILDING CORP., CAMDEN, N. J.
JANUARY 2, 1943

CONFIDENTIAL
U. S. S. INDEPENDENCE CV - 22
STARBOARD & TOPSIDE ARRANGEMENT AT TIME OF INCLINING EXPERIMENT
NEW YORK SHIPBUILDING CORP., CAMDEN, N. J.
JANUARY 2, 1943

Note the sister CVL behind the INDEPENDENCE.

CONFIDENTIAL
U.S.S. INDEPENDENCE CV - 22
PORT & TOPSIDE ARRANGEMENT AT TIME OF INCLINING EXPERIMENT
NEW YORK SHIP BUILDING CORP., CAMDEN, N.J.
JANUARY 2nd 1943

OFFICIAL PHOTOGRAPH
NOT TO BE RELEASED FOR
PUBLICATION.

CONFIDENTIAL
U.S.S. INDEPENDENCE CV - 22
STARBOARD & TOPSIDE ARRANGEMENT AT TIME OF INCLINING EXPERIMENT
NEW YORK SHIPBUILDING CORP., CAMDEN, N.J.
JANUARY 2, 1943

Note the stacks of the sister CVL forward of the island & the ships crane.
Stacks aft of the island are those of the INDEPENDENCE.

Note the antenna mast supporting 3 antenna wires, 2 pairs of these on the port side. ➜
Also note the tracks and weight sled for the "Inclining Experiment".

No. 7 Gun Tub

USS INDEPENDENCE riding high in the water, and not yet commissioned.
Note the covered 5"/38 gun on the bow and the 20mm gun (also covered) in the gun tub to the left side of
the ladder, under the flight deck. The ship would be commissioned with 16 single 20mm guns. You can
see barrels of a twin 40mm gun elevated beneath the ships crane. Fresh paint, pristine.
Note in the photos on the previous page, the 20mm guns. Covered and pointed skyward, they almost
give the appearance of unopened umbrellas for outdoor seating. Note the pairs of exposed shields with
each gun. Further aft (bottom photo), in the last gun tub, a covered twin 40.

The Crew

It was the early years of the 20th century. Their mothers and fathers were witness to the invention of the flying machine, the transition of the horse & buggy to the automobile, the telephone. The "Great War" had left vast quantities of blood spilled in fields and trenches in Europe. "The war to end all wars" had at last ended. Soldiers, sailors and airmen came home and a new generation of "whoopee" babies were born. Many had electricity and indoor plumbing in their homes. Some not. They lived in cities, they lived near timber, and they toiled on the farm, their own, or someone else's. Youngsters in the roaring twenties, they grew into their teens thru the stock market crash and great depression era of the thirties. It was a time when communication was slower. News spread by newspaper and the radio, or by word of mouth via the milk man, the paper boy, friends on the street, and neighbors over the fence. Their dads worked, their moms housewives, cleaning, cooking, raising the kids. They were safe, doors unlocked, isolated by two great oceans. These things had shaped the now young adults, from across the broad expanse of the United States. On December 7th, 1941, a new war descended on the unready nation.

Emmett Russell Edwards, "Eddy", was born in 1921. Eddy worked at JC Penney's while attending the University of South Carolina. His dad was a sailor in WWI who became a steam fitter in Fort Jackson. Eddy enlisted in 1942, earned his wings as an aviator in Texas in November 1943. Eddy married Margaret Eargle and days later drove his 1938 Chevrolet to Jacksonville, Fl. He would see his young wife again briefly on a short leave before departing for the war with Night Fighter Squadron 41 on USS INDEPENDENCE. Eddy, embraced by the sea, would not return from the Pacific.

Leo Ghaston Jr. was 17 when he enlisted. Leo went thru boot camp in Great Lakes, IL and was sent to Memphis, TN for training as a Radioman. His dad had been too young for WWI, and drove a milk truck, was a baker, and while Leo was aboard USS INDEPENDENCE, worked for GM during WWII. Leo would serve aboard as an ARM3c in Torpedo Squadron 27, flying as aircrew in Avengers.

Ed Seace's dad, born in 1898, was a foreman of a garage performing maintenance of power company vehicles in Harrisburg, PA. Ed Seace was born in 1922. Ed had a number of jobs; cabinet making, driving a truck for Coca-Cola, and working at a hardware store. He was 19 as he listened to the news of Pearl Harbor on the radio. He went first to his grandmother's house to tell her he was enlisting. She tried to talk him out of it. His older brother in the Air Force, Ed was sworn into the Navy on 7 September 1942. Like so many crewmen that were plank owners on the Mighty-I, Ed had been ordered to report to the Philadelphia Navy Yard. Most were from the tri-state area around Philly. There, in temporary barracks, he drilled under the tutelage of warrant officers and petty officers. Not the normal "boot camp", it was a hasty solution to convert young civilians to men of the sea, in the hectic hurried effort to fill the needs of ships newly floated by the massive industrial military expansion. Half of Ed's group would be assigned to the not-yet-ready-for-war USS INDEPENDENCE. Most of the others sent to the USS NEW JERSEY (commissioned 4 months after the INDEPENDENCE). Ed would board as a S2c (Seaman 2nd class), with brief training in fire fighting, and aircraft & ship recognition.

Joe Rodgers was born in 1919. 19 months later his mom died. In 1932 his dad died, struck by a police car. Joe was raised by his older brother Jim, and his sister-in-law, Ruth. Joe graduated high school, and worked at a local grocery store / butcher shop, waiting on customers and making deliveries. In 1940, at 21 years of age, he enlisted in the Navy. He served on the DD, USS MAYO in Atlantic convoy duty, with radio schooling in 1941. He was on watch when war broke out. He became a Plank Owner as he reported for duty aboard the Mighty-I, before she was commissioned. Still young. Already an old salt!

Onboard they would come, reporting for duty. Roughly fifteen hundred young men. Each with his own tale of their past. Each with his own individual story in the future, as yet to be written. A huge blank slate for them to write it on. As large as the vast outstretched sea.

3
Commissioning to Sea Trials

Thursday 14 Jan 1943   *Commissioned at the Philadelphia Navy Yard*

The USS INDEPENDENCE was commissioned at the Philadelphia Navy Yard. Her new master was Captain George R. Fairlamb, Jr., USN of Richmond Va.

Deck Log entry: *Having been accepted by the Commandant Fourth Naval District upon delivery at pier #2 Navy Yard, Philadelphia, Pa. by the contractor, New York Shipbuilding Corp. of Camden N.J., the U.S.S. Independence became a ship of the United States Navy at 1532 on this date.*
1532 Rear Admiral Milo F. Draemel, Commandant, Fourth Naval District, after a stirring speech to the officers and men of the crew already assembled, ordered the USS INDEPENDENCE placed in full commission. Captain G.R. Fairlamb Jr. read his orders and assumed command.
There were many distinguished guests present consisting of high ranking officers of the US Navy with their families. The senior officer present amongst the guests was Secretary of the Navy for Air, Artemus Lamb Gates.

Moored port side to pier #2 with 6 manila lines and 2 wire hawsers with No. 4 boiler on line for auxiliary purposes. Receiving fresh & flushing water, telephone and electrical services from the dock.
1555 "Set the watch and manned four 20mm guns for anti-aircraft defense.   H.B. Lyon, Lieut. Comdr. USN."
The Commandant, Fourth Naval District hauled down his personal flag, hoisted the commission pennant and left the ship.

Friday 15 Jan 1943   *Moored - Philadelphia Navy Yard*

War Diary entry: *Moored port side to pier #2 at Navy Yard, Philadelphia, Pa. for unrestricted availability for Navy Yard work in conjunction with completion of the vessel and making approved alterations, for fitting out and equipping and for preliminary organization and training of the crew.*

0805 Held quarters for muster. During the morning, received fresh provisions. Throughout the day an additional 435 men reported aboard for duty.

Saturday 16 Jan 1943   *Moored - Philadelphia Navy Yard*

0810 Mustered crew on stations. Today they continued taking on fresh provisions.
Forty crewmen temporarily left the ship to receive 20mm & 40mm gunnery instruction.
2305 Commenced taking steam from the dock, then secured No. 4 boiler.

Sunday 31 January 1943   *Drydock # 2, Philadelphia Navy Yard*

0805 Moored as before to the east side of pier #2, Philadelphia Navy Yard. Mustered crew at quarters.
0850 Received 7 tugs alongside for assistance with power and steerage.
0915 Made all preparations for getting underway.
0929 Underway with the assistance of tugs, to move from Pier # 2 to the drydock.
1025 Passing over the drydock sill.
1100 Drydock gate closed. Water was pumped from the drydock and she settled on keel blocks at 1250 in drydock # 2, Philadelphia Navy Yard. The vessel began receiving fresh & flush water, steam, electricity and telephone service from the drydock. Crew would bring aboard fresh stores, go on liberty, leave, attend navy schools, and work at their daily assigned tasks. New crewmembers were reporting aboard.

14 January 1943 - USS INDEPENDENCE is commissioned as a ship of the US Navy

The Mighty-I would set on keel blocks, hull out of water, until February 8th, as she was made ready with final outfitting for her maiden voyage to prove her seaworthy, beginning the task of preparing a newly constructed Naval vessel to go to war.

Saturday 6 February 1943   *Resting on keel blocks - Drydock # 2*

Resting on keel blocks as before.
2025   Held practice air raid.
2032   Sounded general quarters. Manned guns, repair stations and battle dressing stations.
2042   Secured from general quarters. Set regular port watch on ready guns.

8 February 1943   **Moved from *Drydock # 2 to Pier #2, Philadelphia Navy Yard***

1528 Commenced making preparations for leaving the drydock.

At 1535 on 8 February 1943, USS INDEPENDENCE floated off her keel blocks. Assisted once again by yard tugs, at 1614 the stern floated over the drydock sill. 16 minutes later the bow cleared and the USS INDEPENDENCE was moved to be moored port side, to the east side of pier #2 in five and a quarter fathoms of water at the Philadelphia Navy Yard. There, secured with 8 manila lines and 2 wire hawsers, and receiving service from the pier, she would remain moored, waiting her celebratory appearance six days later. Then she would begin her river trials. Work continued in a focused effort to make ready for that day.

Original Marine Detachment assigned to the USS INDEPENDENCE
for the commissioning. Photo taken at the Philadelphia Navy Yard in 1943

Tuesday 9 February 1943   *Pier #2, Philadelphia Navy Yard*

Moored as before. Received stores for the general mess;
900 dozen eggs, 505 lbs. of scallops, 1200 lbs of fresh headless shrimp, 50 gallons of oysters (grade B), 4143 lbs. of pork loins (whole frozen), 200 lbs. of pig liver, 1000 lbs. of white trimmed cabbage, 570 lbs of fresh white topped turnips, 20,000 lbs. of potatoes, 920 sweet potatoes, 975 lbs of celery, 1350 lbs. of lettuce, 800 lbs. of tomatoes, and 495 lbs. of corn flakes cereal.

2009 Sounded fire quarters. Two alarm fire along outboard bulkhead of air conditioning machinery space, gallery deck, frame 42, port side. Fire caused by burning of steel (torch) by yard workers, causing insulation and rags to ignite on the opposite side, resulting in only slight damage. Fire extinguished.
2022 Secured from fire quarters.

Above: Stern shot. Sitting on keel blocks in the drydock. Notice the 5" gun mount.

Still on Keel blocks in Drydock #2, tomorrow she will once again float as the drydock is flooded.

Thursday 11 February 1943   *Pier #2, Philadelphia Navy Yard*

Moored as before in 5 1/4 fathoms of water.
1006 Commenced Dock Trials. Navigator on the bridge.
1129 Completed Dock Trials. Test satisfactory.

Sunday 14 February 1943   *Pier #2, Philadelphia Navy Yard - River Trials begin*

This would be a big day in the history of the USS INDEPENDENCE. She would take to the Delaware River channel under her own power and begin feeling her way with the early steps, as a new ship, of a new design, in preparation for the sea. The Captain and crew would experience a first taste of the challenges that would lay ahead, aboard the vessel they had received orders to man and make ready for war.
0400 Moored as before. Lighted fires under boilers No. 1, 2 & 3.
0402 Lighted fires under boiler No. 4.
0520 Tested main engines by electricity.
0530 Set condition 13.
0610 Tested main engines by steam.
0612 Received river pilot on board.
0630 Set the special sea detail.
We will let the ship's War Diary take over from here, picking up again where it leaves off.

War Diary;
UNITED STATES SHIP INDEPENDENCE

ZONE DESCRIPTION +4

<u>+ 4</u>

REMARKS

February 14, 1943.

0-4 Moored as before.   F. S. Robertson, Lieut., (JG) USN.

4-8 Moored as before. 0630 Made all preparations for getting un-
    der way. 0700 Navy Yard Pilots A. R. Duriss and J. Vitts and
    river pilot J.R.Ingram came aboard. 0720 underway with aid
    of tugs. # 2 and #3 boilers cut in on main steam line. The
    following passengers were aboard.

LIST OF PASSENGERS - RIVER RUN

    Captain Henderson - Commanding Officer, U.S.S. PRINCETON
    Commander J. B. Moss - Executive Officer, U.S.S. PRINCETON
    Lt. Comdr. D. L. Roscoe - U.S.S. PRINCETON
    Lt. Comdr. A. C. Aichel - U.S.S. PRINCETON
    Lieut. V. A. Mortoret - U.S.S. PRINCETON
    Lieut. A. C. Smith - U.S.S. PRINCETON
    Lieut. Long- U.S.S. PRINCETON
    Ens. Trehanow - U.S.S. PRINCETON
    Commander H. G. Simms - BuShips
    Lt. Comdr. W.B. Armstrong - BuShips
    Lt. Comdr. H. M. Thorpe - BuShips
    Lieut. J. A. Milburn - BuShips
    Mr. E. Pallange - BuShips
    Mr. J. R. Cole - BuShips
    Mr. J. J. Davey - Gen. Elect. Co.
    Mr. H. J. Chase - Gen. Elect. Co.
    Mr. R. B. Barton - Gen. Elect. Co.
    Mr. O. H. Scott - New York Ship.
    Mr. C. S. Nicks - Worthington Pump Co.
    Mr. L. M. Sibole - Gen Elect. Co.
    Mr. S. W. Robinson - New York Ship
    Mr. Wilsey - Arma Co.
    Lieut. A. St. C. Walden - Navy Yard Phila. Pa.
    Lieut. R. V. D. Ford - Navy Yard Phila., Pa.
    Lt. (JG) W. J. Otto - Navy Yard Phila., Pa.
    Lieut. J. G. Houpis - Raytheon
    Mr. A. A. Farrar - Raytheon
    Mr. C. Ray - Navy Yard Phila., Pa.
    Mr. D. Heist - New York Ship
    Lieut. J. F. Bronson

    0735 steering various courses at various speeds conforming
    to the channel. 0746 Navy Yard pilots left the ship all tugs
    clear. Passed bell buoy #44 abeam to port. Captain and Navi-
    gator on the bridge
    Pilot J. R. Ingram at the conn.

                                 W. Floyd Cole, Lieut., USNR.

8-12 steaming as before. 0805 passed buoy #1 F Abeam to star-
    board. 0815 passed buoy #5 T abeam to starboard 0834
    passed Chester Range Forward Light abeam to starboard 0838
    passed Buoy #6 C abeam to port
    0851 passed buoy #2 C abeam to port 0911 passed
    Buoy 1/2 M abeam to port   0910 cut in #1 boiler on
    main steam line. 0925 passed buoy #2 B abeam to port 0930
    passed Christiana River light abeam to starboard
    0941 passed buoy #1 C abeam to starboard 0955 passed buoy #1 D abeam
    to starboard 0957 passed buoy #8 N abeam to port 1012 passed buoy # 2 N
    abeam to port 1026 passed buoy #2R abeam to port 1032 passed buoy #2 B
    abeam to port 1124 arrived at Ship John Shoal Lighthouse and turned to
    right to reverse course 1136 completed the turn 1142 passed buoy #42 abeam
    to starboard.
                                H. B. Seim, Lieut., USN.

Approved: Examined:

Radio Direction Finder Loop Antenna

USS INDEPENDENCE island structure, fresh paint, clean, pristine, a wartime virgin.
Yet to have the first squadron number, or Japanese flag painted under the credited squadron number
(as seen in later photos, each enemy flag designating a squadron or ship's gunner's kill).

1420 Steaming as before. Let fires die out under No. 4 Boiler.
1645 Moored port side, bow facing the river, to the west side of pier #2, Philadelphia Navy Yard.
1725 Secured the special sea detail. Secured main engines and No.1 boiler.
1754-2026 Secured No.3 and No.2 boilers. Began receiving steam from dock.

Monday 15 February 1943

1737 Completed the dead load testing of the catapult.

Tuesday 16 February 1943

1530 Received on board, 9 torpedoes and 12 boxes of miscellaneous torpedo parts.
During the 1600-2000 watch they received more fresh provisions for the mess.

Wednesday 17 February 1943

2045 Received on board 18 torpedoes.

Friday 19 February 1943

0730 Commenced taking on fuel from trucks alongside on pier #2.
1850 Received on board 5,460 gallons of aviation lubricating oil.

On the flight deck looking forward, elevator down, 20s covered, ship's bell silent.

REPORT ON MACHINERY OF ... NEW YORK SHIPBUILDING CORPORATION, CAMDEN, N. J.

427

Aircraft Carrier INDEPENDENCE (CV22) 25 February, 43

Group No.	N. Y. S. Structure No.	ITEM	WEIGHT (pounds)	ALLOTMENT Total	ALLOTMENT Material	ALLOTMENT Labor	VALUE MATERIAL RECEIVED	LABOR COMPLETED
S-3		General superintendence, office expense, bond, etc.		$431,698	$213,767	$217,931	$213,767	$217,931
S-1		Drawings		84,610	19,600	65,010	19,600	65,010
S-8		Trials and delivery	23,946	138,887	42,630	96,257	42,630	96,257
S-38	481	Heating system	32,157	123,209	29,836	93,373	29,836	93,373
S-59	483	Refrigerating system	9,520	49,619	39,358	10,261	39,358	10,261
S-48	485	Fire system	14,167	15,919	6,073	9,846	6,073	9,846
S-48	486	Bilge and ballast system	603,462	27,448	9,355	18,093	9,355	18,093
S-41	539	Main turbines and reduction gears	188,190	1,508,383	1,472,039	36,344	1,472,039	36,344
S-46	516	Condensers		174,416	96,831	77,585	36,831	77,585
S-41	534	Turbine maneuvering and operating gear	4,650	21,702	4,468	17,234	4,468	17,234
S-45	536	Oil and water service	91,603	161,806	80,766	81,040	80,766	81,040
S-43	541	Shafting and bearings and spares	481,557	265,343	190,902	74,441	190,902	74,441
S-44	546	Propellers, including spares	159,676	75,377	35,964	39,413	35,964	39,413
S-91	551	Hoisting and hand gear	13,000	12,323	2,112	10,211	2,112	10,211
S-16	552	Floor plates, ladders	92,095	62,600	17,360	45,240	17,360	45,240
S-47	553	Independent machinery	232,461	450,662	330,513	120,149	330,513	120,149
S-56	554	Fresh water drain collecting tank	1,123	605	106	499	106	499
S-87	555	Instruments and gages	6,000	70,086	35,369	34,717	35,369	34,717
S-91	556	Engine outfit and workshop machinery	66,868	132,940	99,885	33,055	99,885	33,055
S-51	561-2	Main boilers and spares						
S-51	563	Furnace fittings	651,392	454,130	410,335	43,795	410,335	43,795
S-51	564	Boiler fittings						
S-55	565	Fuel-oil system including fuel-oil burners	172,251	324,341	127,452	196,889	127,452	196,889
S-51	570	Fireroom fittings, including soot blowers	16,532	20,734	13,312	7,422	13,312	7,422
S-52	571	Uptakes and smoke pipes	66,137	154,564	131,620	22,944	131,620	22,944
S-39	573	Covering and lagging boilers	26,708	25,965	6,417	19,548	6,417	19,548
S-53	574	Forced-draft system	60,727	171,726	151,023	20,703	151,023	20,703
S-48	581	Copper and brass piping	67,144	153,676	20,870	132,806	20,870	132,806
S-48	582	Iron and steel piping	165,432	175,117	49,330	125,787	49,330	125,787
S-48	583	Stop valves and cocks	157,534	213,421	126,291	87,130	126,291	87,130
S-48	584	Sea chests, strainers, and castings	7,925	64,938	8,989	55,949	8,989	55,949
S-39	585	Covering and lagging	78,877	86,190	21,832	64,358	21,832	64,358
S-41	592	Installing main engine and shafting		78,550	182	78,368	182	78,368
S-51	594	Installing main boilers		8,798	31	8,767	31	8,767
S-41	595	Foundation, bolts, and packing	8,196	2,918	1,065	1,853	1,065	1,853
		Machinery spares	22,946	51,278	39,454	11,824	39,454	11,824
S-49	813	Compressed-air system	27,277	60,760	55,579	5,181	55,579	5,181
S-61	621	Generating outfit	218,538	429,282	361,972	67,310	361,972	67,310
S-62	622	Switchboards (radio, sound, power, I. C., testing, and lighting)	44,151	346,366	332,879	13,487	332,879	13,487
S-66	623	Searchlights	10,150	84,665	80,312	4,353	80,312	4,353
S-62	624	Power system	146,922	419,118	224,050	195,068	224,050	195,068
S-64	625	Miscellaneous electric spares	2,500	29,825	29,253	572	29,253	572
S-64	626	Lighting system	123,217	410,693	194,698	215,995	194,698	215,995
S-64	627	Signaling apparatus (underwater sound and running and signal lights)	4,699	19,483	11,503	7,980	11,503	7,980
S-67	628	Radio	5,220	31,589	7,236	24,353	7,236	24,353
S-65	631	Call-bell and alarm system	21,340	109,720	54,930	54,790	54,930	54,790
S-65	632	Signal and indicator system	23,945	130,073	76,190	53,883	76,190	53,883
S-65	633	Telephone system	56,688	328,777	197,638	131,139	197,638	131,139
S-71	634	Telegraph system	13,519	53,843	32,851	20,992	32,851	20,992
S-24	635	Fire-control system	60,535	245,746	115,786	129,960	115,786	129,960
S-65	636	Gyrocompass and dead reckoning tracer system						
S-62	637	Mechanical system	5,892	24,421	10,384	14,037	10,384	14,037
	638	Motor generator sets and storage batteries	294	1,834	569	1,265	569	1,265
S-65	639	Sound motion picture	33,347	48,439	40,446	7,993	40,446	7,993
			2,232	13,975	10,750	3,225	10,750	3,225
		TOTALS	4,323,142	8,582,588	5,672,163	2,910,425	5,672,163	2,910,425

NOTE: Vessel was delivered 1/14/43.

Total allotment for machinery 8,582,588

Credit for material at subcontractor's works

Earned on material (sum of col. 5) 5,672,163

Earned on labor (sum of col. 6) 2,910,425

Total earned, labor and material 8,582,588

Amount paid contractors on previous installments on account of machinery 8,325,110

Estimated amount due contractors to date on machinery 257,478

Percentage of completion of machinery (See note No. 2) 100%

CHIEF OF BUREAU OF SHIPS,
NAVY DEPARTMENT, Washington, D. C.
Copy to Bureau of Supplies and Accounts.

R. W. RYDEN,
REAR ADMIRAL, USN
Supervisor of Shipbuilding.

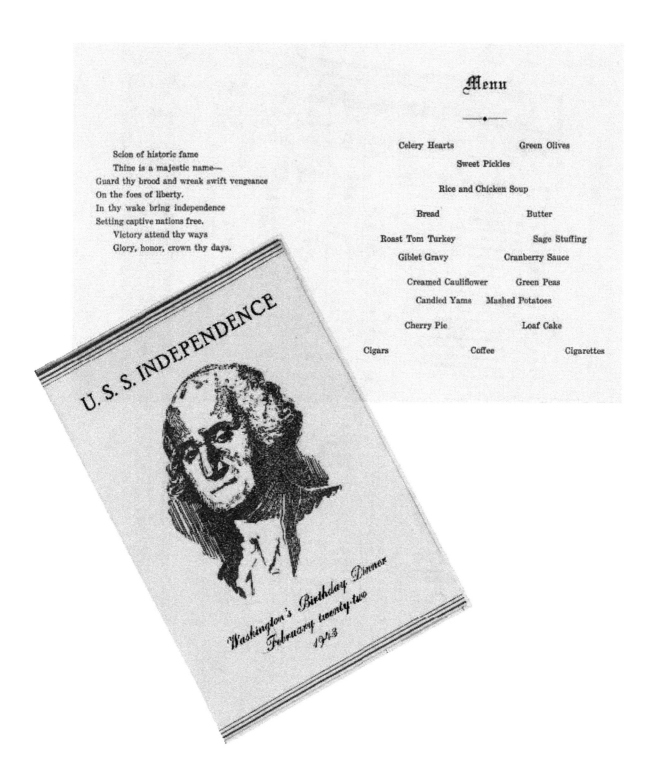

Menu

Celery Hearts   Green Olives

Sweet Pickles

Rice and Chicken Soup

Bread   Butter

Roast Tom Turkey   Sage Stuffing

Giblet Gravy   Cranberry Sauce

Creamed Cauliflower   Green Peas

Candied Yams   Mashed Potatoes

Cherry Pie   Loaf Cake

Cigars   Coffee   Cigarettes

Scion of historic fame
Thine is a majestic name—
Guard thy brood and wreak swift vengeance
On the foes of liberty.
In thy wake bring independence
Setting captive nations free.
Victory attend thy ways
Glory, honor, crown thy days.

U. S. S. INDEPENDENCE

Washington's Birthday Dinner
February twenty-two
1943

Monday 22 February 1943   *Fighting Squadron 22 begins to board*

Enlisted men from Fighting Squadron 22 began to report onboard for duty.
1735   Commenced loading ammunition from the dock.
At 2400 ammunition was still being transferred from the hangar deck to the magazines.

Note the aft pair of antenna masts with the three radio antenna wires strung between them. These masts were lowered during flight operations.

Note the 20mm gun mounts.
The guns elevated skyward with canvas covers.

Snow on the flight deck (looking aft) in Philadelphia

Tuesday 23 February 1943   *Loading ammunition*

1015 Commenced loading ammunition from freight cars.
1320 A fuel oil barge came alongside and commenced fueling the ship.
1716 Completed unloading ammunition from box cars.
2107 Completed stowing ammunition in the magazines.
2235 Completed fueling the ship having received 394,017 gallons of fuel oil.

Wednesday 24 February 1943   *Shifting berths*

1630 Disconnected services from the pier and made preparations for shifting berths.
1745 Underway to shift berths steaming to the quay pier.
1826 Moored portside to the quay wall between drydock No.4 and Shipbuilding Ways No.3 in 5 fathoms of water, Philadelphia Navy Yard. CV-22 began receiving services from the pier.

Monday 8 March 1943

1550 Commenced loading ammunition from the Dock.

In each of these photos, both pair of radio antenna masts are visible.

U.S.S. CV22.
AIR VIEW, DECK FROM OVERHEAD.
NAVY YARD, PHILA, MAR 12-1943.
546-43.

USS INDEPENDENCE on the Delaware River.
Note the SK Radar Antenna between the fore and aft pairs of stacks.
Also note the absence of any antenna mast between the aft pair of stacks. It will be added in 1944.

Tuesday 9 March 1943   *Underway - River trials & deperming*

Moored as before, portside to the quay wall.
0815 Gasoline lighter came along the starboard side.
0820 Disconnected services from the pier.
1320 Ceased taking gasoline from lighter, having received 93,900 gallons of aviation gasoline.
1350 Received onboard two NE-1 aircraft. (The NE-1 was a dual control 65 hp version of the Piper Cub.)
1400 Commenced making preparations for getting underway.
1532 Singled up all lines.
1556 Received tugs alongside.
1613 Got underway for pier 46, Philadelphia, Pa., Captain at the conn.; Executive Officer and Navigator on the bridge, speed 15 knots, steaming up the Delaware River, maneuvering to conform to the channel.
1751 Moored starboard side to the south side of pier 46, Philadelphia, Pa. in 5 fathoms of water, for the purpose of deperming* the vessel. (* Deperming - Removing or decreasing the ship's magnetic field.)

Wednesday 10 March 1943   *Underway - River trials*

0145 Moored as before. Commenced receiving current from the pier for deperming.
0610 Secured from deperming and commenced unrigging deperming gear.
0800 Mustered crew on stations. At 0900 they sounded general quarters.
0931 Completed deperming.
0940 Secured from general quarters.
1100 Commenced making preparations for getting underway.
1130 Set the special sea detail. Made the daily inspection of the magazines.
1251 Got underway, backing out of the slip. Captain at the conn.; Executive Officer and Navigator on the bridge, speed 15 knots, steaming up the Delaware River, maneuvering to conform to the channel.
1401 Moored to the quay wharf, Philadelphia Navy Yard.
1430 Secured main engines.

Friday 12 March 1943   *Sea Trials - Underway from Philadelphia on a shakedown trip*

1436 Moored as before. A river pilot reported aboard ship.
1500 Got underway, maneuvering to conform to the Delaware River channel, standard speed, 15 knots.
2014 Anchored in berth A, Delaware Bay in 6 fathoms of water with 45 fathoms of chain on the starboard anchor, off of Brandywine Shoal and Fourteen Foot Bank.

Saturday 13 March 1943   *Sea Trials - Delaware Bay*

0325 Anchored as before in berth A, Delaware Bay. Commenced swinging at anchor to flood tide.
0445 Completed swinging at anchor.
0726 Got underway at 15 knots with the river pilot at the conn.; Captain, Executive Officer and the Navigator on the bridge.
1219 Anchored in Delaware Bay, in 10 fathoms of water with 60 fathoms of chain to the port anchor, off of Brandywine Shoal Light.
1225 Secured main engines and No. 1 & 2 boilers.

Sunday 14 March 1943

0700 Anchored as before. Lighted fires under No. 1 & 2 boilers.
0800 Mustered crew at quarters.
0845 Got underway.

0900 Began compensating the magnetic compass.
1317 Anchored in the Delaware Bay off of Brandywine Shoal and Brown Shoal Light Buoy.
2210 USS YP49 came alongside to pick up 11 boxes of transmitters, casting off at 2240.

RC Arrived in Chesapeake Bay. Trained squadron in the bay until 4 April 1943. RC

Monday 15 March 1943   *Anchored in Chesapeake Bay*

0815 Anchored as before. Made all preparations for getting underway.
0830 Got underway, steaming in the Delaware Bay.
1730 Anchored in the Delaware Bay.
1800 Commenced making preparations for getting underway for the purpose of shifting anchorage.
1900 Underway with the Captain at the conn.; Executive Officer and Navigator on the bridge.
1906 Darkened the ship.
1936 Anchored, 10 fathoms of water, in the Delaware Bay off of Brandywine Shoal (near Cape May).
2030 Commenced swinging to the flood tide, stern to starboard.

Tuesday 16 March 1943

Anchored as before in 10 fathoms of water, with 60 fathoms of chain to the port anchor.
0805 Commenced sounding the fog signal due to reduced visibility, continuing thru 1025.
1300 Commenced swinging to the flood tide, stern to port.

Wednesday 17 March 1943   *Anchored in Hampton Roads, Va.*

0005 Anchored. Commenced swinging to the flood tide, stern to port, completing swinging at 0305.
0531 Commenced getting under way, speed 15 knots, maneuvering to conform with the channel. They
were steaming toward the Delaware Bay entrance (to exit the bay to enter the Atlantic Ocean).
0600 Entered the swept channel. At 0658 INDEPENDENCE commenced sounding the fog signal.
0800 Mustered the crew.
0920 On base course 171°T, began zigzagging to Plan 6.
1338 Passed the entrance buoy to Chesapeake Bay. Commenced structural firing.
1637 Sighted land on the starboard bow, 5 miles.
1846 Anchored, berth 22, in 14 fathoms of water with 75 fathoms of chain to the port anchor, Hampton
Roads Virginia.
2122 Sounded general quarters. Antiaircraft drill was conducted by orders of SOPA.
2140 Secured from general quarters.

Thursday 18 March 1943   *Anchored in Hampton Roads, Va. - VC-22 reports aboard*

0225 Anchored as before. Commenced swinging to the flood tide, stern to starboard.
0810 Mustered the crew at quarters. (Sometime during the day, **no entry in Deck Log**, it was overlooked, YO-140
came along side. Its departure is noted below at 2325. See photos on next two pages. It appears they offloaded fuel to perhaps
perform repairs or modifications, possibly the fuel was contaminated, then reloaded aviation gasoline on March 20th.)
0815 Enlisted men (131 of them) of Composite Squadron VC-22 reported on board for duty.
1040 Commenced swinging stern to port with the ebb tide. Completed swinging at 1130.
1510 Commenced swinging stern to starboard with the flood tide.
2325 Completed discharging 83,263 gallons of aviation gasoline to barge. The barge cast off.

Friday 19 March 1943   *Anchored in Hampton Roads, Va.*

1934 Anchored. The Blue Troupe of the United Service Organization boarded the ship to perform.

18 March 1943

18 March 1943

Saturday 20 March 1943   *Anchored in Hampton Roads, Va.*

Anchored as before, in berth 22, 16 fathoms of water with a mud bottom. The ship would continue to swing at anchor with the ebb and flow of the tide while they remained at anchor in Hampton Roads.
0250 BYMS#37 scraped the starboard bow putting a small dent in the plating.
0740 Received a lighter along our starboard side.
0758 Received gasoline barge YO-140 along our starboard side. Received gasoline from the YO-140 from 0833 thru 1100. The barge cast off at 1113.
1412 Secured from fire quarters.
1530 Lighter removed from starboard side.

Monday 22 March 1943   *Hampton Roads, Va. to the Chesapeake Bay*

1600 Anchored in berth 22, in Hampton Roads Va. Got underway, steaming to the Chesapeake Bay.
1903 Anchored in 8 fathoms of water in the Chesapeake Bay 5,000 yards off Old Plantation Light.

4
The Air Group 22 Comes Aboard

AIR GROUP - The Squadrons

Fighting Squadron 22 (VF-22) and Composite Squadron 22 (VC-22) - the first CVL squadrons.

VF-22 was formed at NAS Norfolk, Virginia on 30 September 1942. This was roughly one month after the INDEPENDENCE was launched, and four months before she began her dock trials. As VF-22 coalesced, Lt. Philip H. Torrey, Jr. commanded (30 September 1942 thru 13 August 1943).
Lt. Leland L. Johnson (Executive Officer under Torrey) assumed command from 13 August 1943 thru 29 December 1944.

VF-22 was at this period of time flying the Grumman F4F-4 "Wildcat".

On 2 December 1942 fighter squadron (VF-22) transferred from NAS Norfolk to NAAS Manteo, on north end of Roanoke Island. The island is south of Albemarle Sound, located within the outer banks. It lies across a narrow sound west of Nags Head, just south of Kill Devil Hills where the Wright Brothers made their first flights. Manteo was a public airport as war broke out, and transitioned into a NAAS (to be commissioned by the Navy at the beginning of March, four months after VF-22 first arrived). Conditions at Manteo were somewhat primitive during the hasty transition, as described by VF-22:
"Facilities at Manteo were extremely limited, and physical hardships abound for all hands. Especially uncomfortable were the barracks-type living quarters, which were inadequately heated. At first there was no hangar, but later a nose hangar was constructed. Lacking recreational facilities, the squadron operated a canteen in one of the unused buildings. Operational training at Manteo included the usual shakedown activities of any new squadron, plus operations with the U.S.S INDEPENDENCE on its trial run."

VF-22 pilots made their first catapult assisted takeoffs from a land based catapult in Philadelphia. They were qualified for carrier landings on the USS CHARGER, CVE-30.

VC-22 first started as VS-22 (Scouting 22). It had been commissioned at NAS Norfolk on 1 October 1942. VS-22 was equipped with a mix of 9 each of the Douglas SBD-4 "Dauntless" and the new Grumman TBF-1 "Avenger". They were among the first squadrons to be equipped with the TBF-1s. During the eventual "shakedown" aboard the INDEPENDENCE, Lt. Comdr. Peters suggested (in an informal letter to Captain Fairlamb) that the SBDs were unsuitable for use on the CVL due to the lack of wing folding capability.

While the fighter pilots trained at Manteo, the combined torpedo and dive bombing squadron of Scouting 22 departed on 10 December 1942 for training at NAAS Creed's Field, an auxiliary of NAS Norfolk. Creeds Field was south of Oceana NAS (Virginia Beach) near Back Bay, and was finally commissioned at the beginning of April, 1943. Officers and enlisted men lived in Quonset huts. Conditions in December of 42 were described as cold with mud, slush and snow. *"On very quiet evenings, local pilots jokingly tell of hearing a sucking sound emanating from the swamplands near where Air Group 22 trained, as the Great Dismal Swamp tries to inhale unwary airplanes flying overhead."* Like Manteo, Creeds Field had no hangars, with aircraft maintenance performed in the open exposed to the elements.

Lt. Comdr. James McClelland Peters, VC-22 Commanding Officer was also the Carrier Air Group 22 Commander (CAG). Lt. Comdr. Thomas H. Jenkins was VC-22 Executive Officer.

Scouting 22 lost pilot Ensign S.F. Summers and his radioman, ARM3c R.L. Newman in an accident on 29 December 1942. Their aircraft had failed to pull out of a dive (thought to have been caused by the pilot being temporarily incapacitated by a blackout with the resultant momentary loss of control).

Prior to boarding the INDEPENDENCE, while still at Manteo, VF-22 also lost its first pilot.

The date was 15 January 1943. Ensign Roy L. Lee was flying his F4F Wildcat roughly 20 miles east of Oregon Inlet, N.C. (just southeast of Manteo) when his life raft fouled the tail assembly. It was never established if it was blown out of the cockpit, or tossed from it. The parachute opened when Roy Lee bailed out, however he was not recovered from the water due to "a high sea running at this time". If he threw the life raft out of the Wildcat, it indicates the probability of some mechanical or fuel related problem with the aircraft, and due to the state of the sea, he likely felt a bailout a better option than a rough sea water landing.

VS 22 pilots were present for the commissioning of the INDEPENDENCE in Philadelphia. The TBF pilots trained at Quanset Point, R.I. for torpedo drops, and were checked out on catapult takeoffs at Mustin Field, Philadelphia. They carrier qualified onboard the USS CHARGER in the Chesapeake Bay.

In mid-March 1943, VF-22 returned to NAS Norfolk, to be transferred to the INDEPENDENCE and Scouting Squadron 22 (VS-22) was renamed Composite Squadron 22 (VC-22).

On 23 March 1943, Carrier Air Group 22 (VF-22 and VC-22) flew aboard USS INDEPENDENCE.

25 March, 1943 - On landing a SBD (Bu. No. 6903) **drops into the port catwalk. No injuries.**

Fighting Squadron 22 photos and squadron logo (dated <u>September</u> 1943). Missing are photos of the CO, Lt. Comdr. Philip H. Torrey, Jr. and Ens. Edward J. Rohner

Air Group - The Aircraft

The USS INDEPENDENCE would go to war against Japan with her aircraft and aircrew as her primary offensive weapons. The aircraft are very briefly introduced here as the Mighty-I receives her first fliers, Air Group 22. It would take time and some experimentation for the Navy to decide the proper mix of aircraft for this new class of carrier.

F4F-4 Wildcat (fighter)
The F4F-4 entered service in 1942. It was designed by Grumman Aircraft, and featured hand cranked retractable landing gear. The dash 4 introduced folding wings. In April 1942 production of the fighter transitioned to Eastern Aircraft so Grumman Aircraft could concentrate on the production of its new F6F design. The Eastern Aircraft units would be designated FM-1 & FM-2.
The F4F-4 had self-sealing fuel tanks, bullet resistant glass and fore & aft armor plate for pilot protection. USS INDEPENDENCE would first operate with the F4F-4s, later switching over to the new F6Fs.

General characteristics
Crew: 1
Length: 28 ft 9 in.   Wingspan: 38 ft   Wing area: 260 ft²
Empty weight: 5,760 lb   Max takeoff weight: 7,950 lb
Powerplant: Pratt & Whitney R-1830-86 double-row radial engine, 1,200 hp with an electric c. s. prop.
Performance
Maximum speed: Approx. 320 mph *(at 18,800 feet)*
Fuel capacity: 144 gallons *(plus 1 or 2 drop tanks @ 58 gals each)*
Combat radius (sm): 120 *(Main tank)* / 282 *(1 drop tank)* / 374 *(2 drop tanks)*
Range max: 830 *(Main tank)* / 1050 *(1 drop tank)* / 1275 *(2 drop tanks)*
Service ceiling: 39,500 ft   Rate of climb: 1,950 ft/min

Guns: Wing mounted 6× 0.50 in M2 Browning machine guns, 1440 rounds (240 rounds/gun)

F6F Hellcat (fighter)
The F6F entered service in 1942. It was designed by Grumman Aircraft, and featured hydraulic actuation for the retractable landing gear, slotted flaps, gun charging and oil cooler doors. The F6F had self-sealing fuel tanks, bullet resistant glass and fore & aft armor plate for pilot protection. The USS INDEPENDENCE would enter combat in the Pacific with F6F-3s later receiving dash 5s. As a night carrier, it would have F6F-5Ns with ASH / APS-4 search / attack radar, or later with AN/APS-6.

General characteristics (F6F-5)
Crew: 1
Length: 33 ft 7 in.   Wingspan: 42 ft 10 in   Wing area: 334 ft²
Empty weight: 9,238 lb   Max takeoff weight: 15,300 lb
Powerplant: Pratt & Whitney R-2800-10W double row radial engine, 2 stage 2 speed Supercharger, water injection, 2,000 hp max. with a constant speed prop.
Performance
Maximum speed: Approx. 379 mph *(at 23,400 feet)*
Fuel capacity: 250 gallons total internal in 3 tanks *(plus 1 external drop tank @ 150 gals each)*
Combat radius (sm): 391 *(internal tanks)* / 590 *(1 drop tank)*
Range max: 1,130 *(internal tanks)* / 1,650 *(1 drop tank)*
Service ceiling: 35,100 ft   Rate of climb: 2,980 ft/min

Guns: Wing mounted 6× 0.50 in M2 Browning machine guns, 1,600 rounds

**F4F
WILDCAT**

**F6F
HELLCAT**

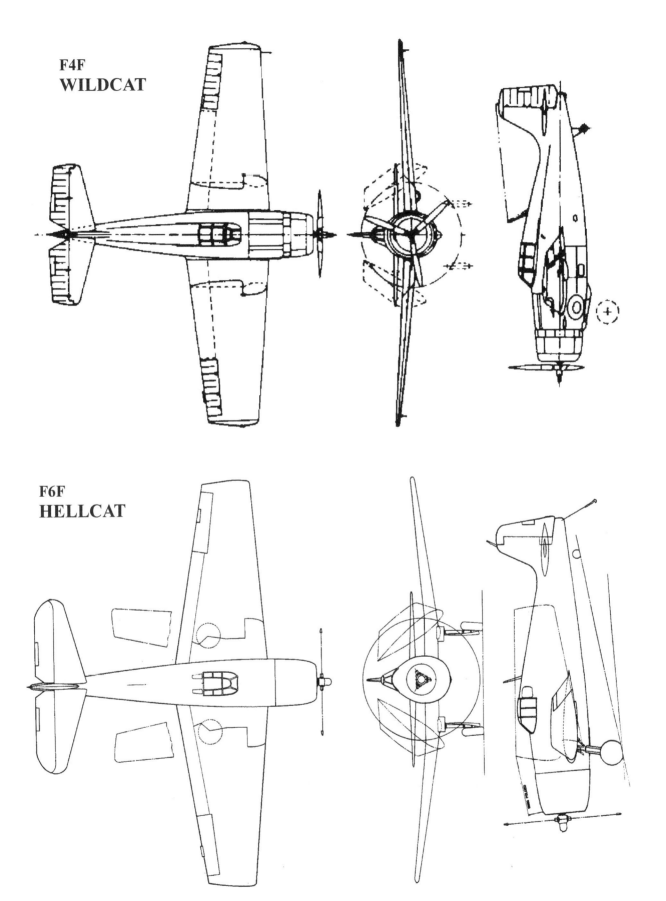

SBD DAUNTLESS (Dive Bomber)

The SBD, manufactured by Douglas Aircraft, entered service as a naval dive bomber in 1940 and would be produced thru early 1944. In 1943 the SBD would begin to be replaced by the SB2C Helldiver. The wings would not fold and required a lot of deck space. When the USS INDEPENDENCE completed trials and entered combat operations, Avengers would be utilized.

General characteristics (SBD-5)
Crew: Two
Length: 33 ft   Wingspan: 41 ft 6 in   Wing area: 325 ft²
Empty weight: 6,404 lb   Max takeoff weight: 10,700 lb
Powerplant: 1× Wright R-1820-60, 9 cylinder radial engine, 1,200 hp
Performance
Maximum speed: 255 mph
Range: 1,565 mi max.
Service ceiling: 25,530 ft

Guns: 2 × 0.50 in - forward-firing fixed Browning M2 machine guns in the engine cowling.
         1 or 2 × 0.30in - flexible-mounted Browning machine gun in the rear cockpit.
Bomb load: 2,250 lb

TBM / TBF AVENGER (Torpedo Bomber)

The **TBF Avenger** was designed and manufactured by **Grumman Aircraft**. Like Grumman's new fighter designs, it had folding wings and retractable landing gear. When produced by the **Eastern Aircraft division** of **General Motors**, it is called the **TBM**. It entered the service in 1942 as a replacement for the TBD Devastator. It was a rugged aircraft with self sealing gas tanks. A night (N) version was built with radar. The pilot was isolated with the only set of flight controls. Avenger squadrons would fly off USS INDEPENDENCE throughout the war.

General characteristics (TBF / TBM-3)
Crew: Three - Pilot, turret gunner, and a radar operator, ventral gunner,
Length: 40 ft 11 in   Wingspan: 54 ft 2 in   Wing area: 490 ft²
Empty weight: 10,555 lb   Max takeoff weight: 17,893 lb
Powerplant: 1× R-2600-20, 14 cylinder air cooled radial engine, 1,900 hp
Performance
Maximum speed: 276 mph
Range: 1,105 mi max.   Fuel capacity: 335 gallons
Range / fuel capacity extended with droppable internal or external tanks. Note: Bombs or torpedoes not carried if internal droppable tank is installed.
Service ceiling: 23,400 ft

Guns: 2 × 0.50 in - Forward-firing fixed Browning M2 machine guns in the wings.
         1 × 0.50in - Turret mounted Browning machine gun in the rear cockpit.
         1 × 0.30in - Browning machine gun in the dorsal.

Bomb load: 2,000 lb of bombs or depth charges, or 1 Mk 13 torpedo.

SBD
DAUNTLESS

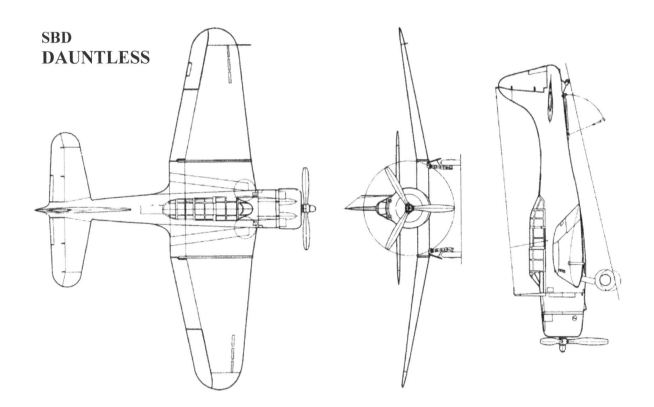

TBF /TBM
AVENGER

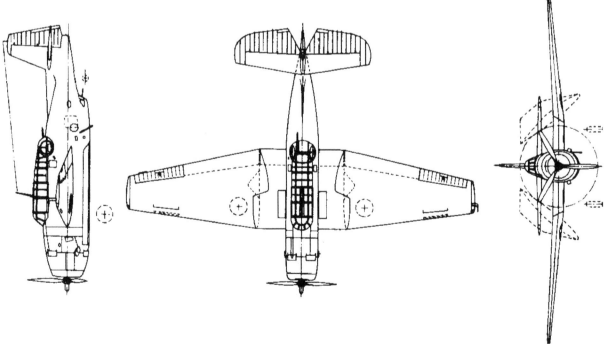

23 March 1943 *The first aircraft lands on the flight deck of USS INDEPENDENCE*
VF-22 and VC-22 fly onboard

0800 Anchored as before. Set special sea detail. Commenced making preparations for getting underway.
0836 Underway at 15 knots at various courses at various speeds while conducting flight operations.
Commenced operations in Chesapeake Bay and received on board Air Group 22, commanded by Lt.Cdr.
James M. Peters, USN, and consisting of VF-22, (12 F4Fs), and VC-22, (8 SBD-4s and 9 TBF-1s).
0926 Commenced landing aircraft. Received the first plane onboard.
1051 Launched first aircraft. Completed launching aircraft at 1156. They carried out routine flight
operations thru the afternoon.
1815 Anchored in 7.5 fathoms of water off New Point Comfort, and York Spit.
2215 Thirty two enlisted men returned onboard, having attended 20mm & 40mm gunnery school, and
forty four enlisted men returned onboard, having attended fire fighting school.

Wednesday 24 March 1943 *Chesapeake Bay - First operational accident*

Anchored as before. Made all preparations for getting underway.
0745 Underway in the lower Chesapeake Bay. Today, they carried out routine flight operations.
0949 Lt. John R. Behr approached to land. He missed the arresting gear wires and his F4F-4 (Bu. No.
12105) paid the price, crashing into the barrier cables. Lt. Behr was uninjured. Unfortunately, flight deck
mishaps were a part of routine flight operations while learning the art and honing the skill of landing on
an aircraft carrier, especially a carrier with a snooker table sized flight deck. Lt Behr just became the
first of a long list of the Mighty-I's operational accidents, and barrier cable incidents.
1224 Anchored in 10 fathoms of water, starboard anchor, lower Chesapeake Bay off Wolf Trap, New
Point Comfort and York Spit.
1347 Underway, steaming at various courses at various speeds to conduct routine flight operations.
1635 A SBD (Bu. No. 6833) failed to snag an arresting gear cable, and crashed into the barrier. No injuries
to the pilot, or his flight crew.
1915 Anchored in 6.75 fathoms of water with 45 fathoms of chain, port anchor, lower Chesapeake Bay
off New Point Comfort.

Thursday 25 March 1943 *Chesapeake Bay*

0600 Anchored as before. Underway in the lower Chesapeake Bay conducting routine flight operations.
1200 Anchored as before, lower Chesapeake Bay off Wolf Trap and New Point Comfort.
1458 Got underway again to conduct routine flight operations.
1543 SBD (Bu. No. 6903) flown by Ensign James F. Prinz hooked an arresting gear cable on landing and
crashed into the port catwalk. He and his gunner, ARM3c W.J. Mahoney exited the bent warplane
uninjured.
1602 Anchored in 6 fathoms of water with 30 fathoms of chain, port anchor off Wolf Trap, New Point
Comfort and York Spit.

Friday 26 March 1943 *Chesapeake Bay - Routine flight operations*

1325 Anchored as before. Set the special sea detail.
1355 INDEPENDENCE got underway. At 1408 they secured the special sea detail.
1418 Sounded flight quarters.
1730-1901 Conducted routine flight operations.
1903 Anchored in 13 fathoms of water with 60 fathoms of chain, starboard anchor off Wolf Trap, New
Point Comfort and York Spit.

Saturday 27 March 1943   *At anchor in Chesapeake Bay*

2050-2128 Anchored as before. Coast Guard Cutter 83302 was alongside to deliver 23 crewmembers. They returned aboard having attended an aircraft training school.

Sunday 28 March 1943   *Our first aviation fatality*

Anchored as before.
0815 Mustered the crew at quarters, followed by a Captains inspection of the crew and living spaces.
1254 Got underway to conduct flight operations. Today would not be exactly routine.

1659 VF-22 pilot Ensign Edward Jilberto Rohner was landing, caught a wire, and his F4F-4 (Bu. No. 3481) broke apart on the flight deck. In what had to have been an unfolding nightmare, the pilot was helpless to further control the outcome as the remaining momentum carried Ensign Edward Rohner and the forward section of his Wildcat into a gun bucket, continuing over the side into the sea. He sadly was not recovered. His younger brother, John R. Rohner, a US Marine, received the tragic news of "Eddie's" death while he was undergoing boot camp in San Diego.

2044 Anchored in 9 fathoms of water, lower Chesapeake Bay off Wolf Trap, New Point Comfort and York Spit.

JG We lose our first pilot and plane, tail is pulled off as the plane hits gun bucket, plane sinks immediately. JG

Monday 29 March 1943   *Chesapeake Bay*

0730 Anchored as before. Got underway to conduct routine flight operations.
1417 Commenced 20mm gunnery practice, hypothetical runs to port and starboard.
1046 Secured from torpedo defense.
1632 Conducted structural firing tests of the 40mm gun mounts.
1815 Anchored in 13 fathoms of water, lower Chesapeake Bay off York Spit, Wolf Trap, New Point Comfort and Old Plantation Light.

Tuesday 30 March 1943   *Underway - Collision avoidance during flight operations*

0800 Anchored as before. Mustered crew on station. Made preparations for getting underway.
0840 Underway to conduct routine flight operations. The ship also trained for "Anti-aircraft runs", securing at 1629.
1000 A column of Sub-Chasers crossing ahead from port to starboard placed SC #692 (third in column) on a collision course. Sounded "Danger Signal". Repeated the "Danger Signal" two more times without any reaction from the Sub-Chasers.
1010 All engines stopped, then all engines back full to avoid collision with SC#692.
1011 All engines ahead standard.
1746 Dropped anchor, 9 fathoms of water in lower Chesapeake Bay off Wolf Trap, New Point Comfort and Old Plantation Light.

Wednesday 31 March 1943   *Underway for routine flight operations*

0800 Anchored as before. Commenced making preparations for getting underway.
0840 Underway to conduct routine flight operations.
1635 Dropped anchor in 8.5 fathoms of water, mud bottom in lower Chesapeake Bay off Cape Charles Beacon and Old Plantation Light.

Thursday 1 April 1943   *Underway for fueling at sea drills and flight operations*

0606 Anchored as before. Generator #1 dropped its load due to low vacuum.
0620 Generator #2 was cut in.
0623 Regained power to all stations.
0750 Commenced making all preparations for getting underway.
0841 Underway steaming up Chesapeake Bay for the operating area.
0923 Sounded torpedo defense.
1018 Made daily inspection of the magazines.
1255-1506 Alongside tanker USS NIOBRARA to conduct fueling at sea drills. In the afternoon they conducted routine flight operations.
1942 Anchored in 10 fathoms of water, lower Chesapeake Bay off Old Plantation Light and York Spit.

Friday 2 April 1943   *Underway for flight operations, fueling at sea and drills*

0830 Anchored as before. Made all preparations for getting underway.
0858 Got underway at 15 knots maneuvering to clear the anchorage.
During the day the ship went to flight quarters to conduct routine flight operations, and torpedo defense. They also conducted fueling at sea exercises from 1350 to 1442 with the DD (destroyer) USS MAYO.
1509 Commenced steering and engine controls casualty drills, shifting control to various stations.
1538 Returned control of engines to the pilot house.
1707 Anchored in 6.75 fathoms of water, lower Chesapeake Bay off York Spit, Wolf Trap and New Point Comfort.
1930 Completed dead load testing of the catapult.

VC 22 & VT 22 squadron insignia

Saturday 3 April 1943   *Underway for flight operations*

0853 Anchored as before. CV-22 got underway for flight operations.
1000 Sounded flight quarters.
1128 Secured from flight quarters.
1223 Anchored in 8.5 fathoms of water, lower Chesapeake Bay off Stingray Point and Wolf Trap

Sunday 4 April 1943   *Underway for battle practice*

0555 Anchored as before. Commenced jacking over main engines by steam.
0730 Manned all stations for getting underway.
0800 Underway for rehearsal for short range battle practice (0830-1130).
1135 Dropped anchor off Windmill Point.
1337 Got underway at standard speed (15 knots) maneuvering to clear the anchorage for short range battle practice.
1617 Anchored in lower Chesapeake Bay off York Spit, Wolf Trap and New Point Comfort.

Monday 5 April 1943   *Underway for drills*

0800 Anchored as before. Mustered the crew on stations.
0905 Sounded general quarters for damage control problem.
1357 Having made all necessary preparations, USS INDEPENDENCE got underway.

1503 Conducted collision drill. Minutes later they conducted an abandon ship drill.
1526 Secured from collision and abandon ship drills.
CV-22 returned to moor, starboard side to pier #7, NOB, Norfolk, Virginia with the aid of tugs.

Tuesday 6 thru Thursday 8 April 1943   *Moored NOB, Norfolk, VA.*

Moored as before, receiving fresh water and telephone service from the dock. Today CV-22 received fuel oil, stores and supplies. With trials in the Chesapeake Bay completed, the ship would be made ready for sea and a shakedown cruise to Trinidad. Men would temporarily leave and re-board the ship for training on shore. New crewmembers would also continue to report aboard. On the 8th they took onboard munitions delivered from the U.S. Ammunition Depot in Portsmouth, Va.

Friday 9 April 1943 *Underway from Hampton Roads Va. en route Gulf of Paria Venezuela.*

0745 Moored as before. Held quarters for muster.
0826 Pilot came aboard and reported to the bridge in preparation for getting underway.
0846 Got underway, steaming on boilers #2 & 4 at various speeds on various courses, with the pilot conning and navigator & Executive Officer on the bridge. CV-22 proceeded out to sea en route to Gulf of Paria, Venezuela under orders (COMAIRLANT 091837) . They were accompanied by DDs (destroyers) USS SIGSBEE and USS GUEST as their screen.
0857 The pilot (H.T. Treakle) left the ship.
1053 Lighted fires under boiler #3.
1133 Connected boiler #3 to the main steam line.
Commenced flight operations from 1649 to 1851.

Saturday 10 & Sunday 11 April 1943   *At sea*

Steaming as before, zigzagging south with the destroyer screen, conducting routine flight operations.

Monday 12 April 1943   *At sea*

0541 Aircraft were warming up on the flight deck for the days flight operations and Edward A. Erickson (ships clerk) made contact with a spinning prop. He was taken to sick bay with his left arm mangled. It later had to be amputated 2" below the shoulder.
0800 Mustered crew on stations.
1143-1152 Held steering casualty drill.

Tuesday 13 April 1943   *At sea*

Steaming as before. CV-22 had routine flight operations from 0700 thru 1015.

Wednesday 14 April 1943 *Anchored at NOB, Trinidad, in the Gulf of Paria.*

0003 Steaming as before. Ship is darkened and boilers No.1 & 4 are in use. Changed speed to 2/3rds.
0004 Changed speed to full.
0330 Completed blowing tubes on all steaming boilers.
0422 Shifted steering to port unit.
0549 Commenced flight operations.
0455 Sounded general quarters, securing at 0555.
0800 Mustered the crew on stations.
0832 Ensign E.L. Alstott was taking off for a routine flight and crashed into the water. He and his radioman ARM3c C.F. Prince were saved. The SBD Dauntless (Bu. No. 10426) sank.

April 1943 Norfolk, Va.

Aircraft taxing and being towed up the dock to be hoisted aboard by the ships crane.
Note the 40mm gun sight on the right, and vehicles of the era on the dock.
(F4Fs taxiing with engines running, TBF being towed)

Flight operations were completed at 1541.
1755 Anchored 8 fathoms of water, port anchor, off Nelson Island, Gulf of Paria.
1803 Secured main engines.
1833 Stationed picket boat.
2104 Green alert signal. Turned out anchor lights.
2125 All clear signal. Turned on anchor lights.

RC Arrived in Trinidad. Operated in the bay training squadron. Liberty in Port of Spain. RC

A Grumman F4F-4 Wildcat on the dock being readied to hoist aboard.

The ship's crane is lowering a F4F-4 to the flight deck, hoisted from the pier at Norfolk, Va.

15 April, 1943. Flight deck crew man-handling Lt. McConnell's F4F-4, the right main landing gear collapsed on landing. Prop is bent. (Bu. No. 11852)

Thursday 15 April 1943   *Anchored at NOB, Trinidad, in the Gulf of Paria.*

0830 Anchored as before. Edward A. Erickson* was taken from the ship to the Naval Air Station dispensary.   (* Erickson was struck by the prop on April 12th.)
1030 Made routine tests prior to getting underway.
1108 Underway, maneuvering to clear the anchorage. Captain at the conn.
1127 Secured the special sea detail.
1321 Commenced flight operations.
1621 Lt. James H. McConnell landed his F4F-4 (Bu. No. 11852) . His landing gear collapsed. He was uninjured.   Flight operations were completed for the day at 1820.
1824 Set the special sea detail.
1949 Anchored in 8 fathoms of water, mud bottom, 50 fathoms of chain to starboard anchor.
1957 Secured the special sea details, and hoisted out the No.2 motor whale boat.

Friday 16 April 1943   *Gulf of Paria*

0702 Anchored as before. Got underway to conduct flight operations.
0750 Commenced flight operations.
1605 ACMM Charles W. Leet was thrown into the elevator pit by the tail of an aircraft and its prop wash. He suffered multiple injuries.
1746 Dropped anchor in Gulf of Paria off Nelson Island, Diego Island and Cronstadt Island.

Saturday 17 April 1943   *Gulf of Paria*

Anchored as before. At 0631 CV-22 got underway for flight operations.
0944 Flying in a Wildcat, Lt. Philip H. Torrey crashed into the water off NAS Trinidad. The F4F-4 sank. Lt. Torrey was uninjured. (Bu. No. 11856)

Routine flight operations would continue and at 1013 Lt. Clement M. Craig crashed his F4F-4 on the aft end of the flight deck, with collapsed landing gear. Lt. Craig was uninjured.
1825 Dropped anchor, Gulf of Paria.

Sunday 18 April 1943   *Gulf of Paria - Flight operations*

0622 Anchored as before. Got underway.
0743 USS SIGSBEE came along port side to take on fuel.
0852 Completed fueling at sea operations.
1354 Commenced flight operations.
1517 Sunday would not be a day of rest from aircraft accidents. Ens. Billy Burk Laughren "crashed on flight deck and hit barrier". His TBF suffered only minor damage and he had no injuries.
That afternoon, the Mighty-I served as a target. In *"formation battle practice"* exercises, the INDEPENDENCE maneuvered to avoid practice torpedoes fired at it. While hoisting the torpedoes aboard after the exercise, one torpedo was not recovered.
1846 Dropped anchor in the Gulf of Paria.

14-28 April 1943   *Gulf of Paria, Trinidad (Venezuela) - Conducting training exercises*

During this period of time, the crew of the USS INDEPENDENCE would continue to shake down the ship and sharpen their knowledge and skills at sea. The days would pass with variations of a routine that would begin at anchor. Crew mustered generally at around 0800, inspected the magazines, and prepared to leave the anchorage.
VC-22 would train, learning to launch and recover off the new class of aircraft carrier.
They would also operate from Edinburgh Field, Trinidad (with the now familiar inadequate meager shore facilities) as they honed their skills at gunnery, bombing, search exercises and radar* training.
In the late afternoon / early evening, INDEPENDENCE would once again drop anchor, settling in for the night.   (* Not defined, the radar training was either ship or land based radar, as the aircraft were not radar equipped as yet)

Monday 19 April 1943   *Gulf of Paria - Gunnery practice*

0637 Anchored as before. Got underway, commencing flight operations at 0736.
Today in the early afternoon they conducted 20mm gunnery practice, returning to anchor at 1353.

20-21 April 1943   *Gulf of Paria*

Tuesday and Wednesday would go much as before with normal flight operations. Tuesday CV-22 took on 320,514 gallons of bunker fuel oil.
The Mighty-I dropped anchor inside the net off Five Islands at 1604 on the 21st.

Thursday 22 April 1943   *Gulf of Paria - Flight operations*

1130 Got underway to conduct flight operations, completing those daytime flight operations at 1612.
1626 Commenced swinging the ship to compensate the magnetic compass. They completed the compass compensation at 1815.
2050 **Commenced night flight operations.** Pilots, the LSO and deck crews would be given the opportunity to explore a new facet of the learning curve.
2118 Lt. Commander Philip Torrey was uninjured when his F4F-4 Wildcat (Bu. No. 11663) crashed into the barrier on landing.
2142 Likewise, Ens. John C. Maxey was uninjured with his crash when the number 5 arresting gear cable carried away (broke) as he landed in his F4F-4 (Bu. No. 11851), hitting the barrier.
2333 Anchored in the Gulf of Paria.

Refueling at sea exercises with the USS MAYO (DD-422) on 2 April 1943

Refueling the USS SIGSBEE (DD-502) on 18 April 1943

Muster on the flight deck, 1943. **"Attention to Colors!".** Flag is being hoisted aloft. Note the bugler.

Lower Photo to the right: Fire Room Number 2 crew - 1943

Muster on the flight deck - Gulf of Praia in late April 1943

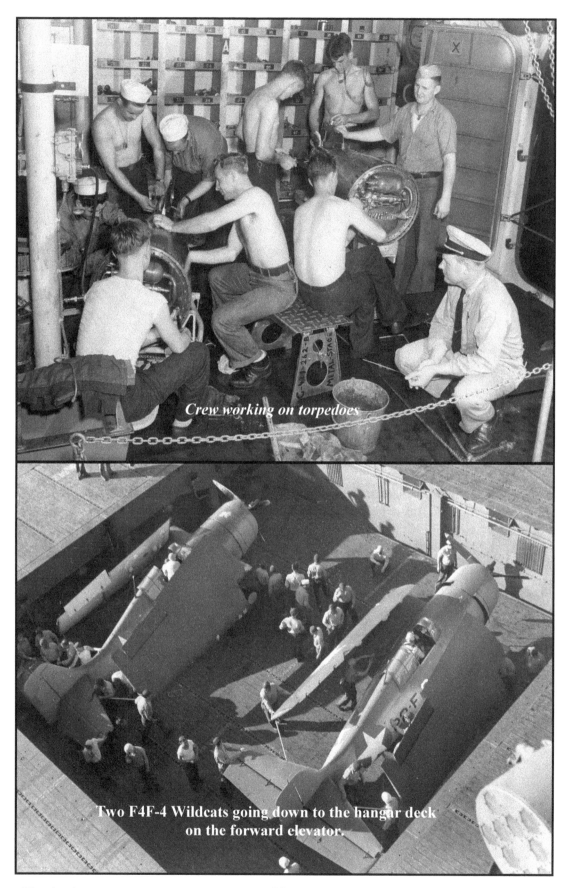

Crew working on torpedoes

Two F4F-4 Wildcats going down to the hangar deck
on the forward elevator.

Air Group 22 relaxing in the Forward Squadron Ready Room

Briefing in the Forward Squadron Ready Room - Air Group 22

Deck crew prepares to pull wheel chalks as a TBF readies to taxi

Assist. Air Officer Lt. Comdr. R. B. Moore and V-1 Div. Officer Lt. Richard Ashley Teel work out flight deck spotting.

Catapult launching. The Avenger pilot has completed his pre-launch checks and with takeoff power applied, brakes released, he has signaled he is ready, and waits for the catapult officer to drop / arc his raised right arm forward to signal for catapult crew to start the launch. The aircraft is restrained from movement against the thrust of the engine by an assembly holding the tail (not visible behind the catapult officer's left leg). A calibrated aluminum hold back ring will break in the restraint allowing the aircraft to move forward when the applied force from the catapult finally launches the Avenger.

Chapter 4   92

Deck launching. Unassisted by the catapult, much further aft on the flight deck, an Avenger pilot runs
up his 14 cylinder 1,700hp Wright Cyclone and performs last minute (more correctly - last second) cockpit
checks as the launch officer has signaled for run-up. When the pilot is ready, he will signal the launch
officer, and when he sees launch ready conditions, the launch officer will swing the flag in a fast forward
and downward arc, signaling the pilot to release his brakes and begin his takeoff run.

Just launched, a pilot climbs out as other aircraft move forward to the catapult.
A plane guard destroyer steams astern.

TBF-1 Avengers in these two photos;
Above a low level fly-by.

Below deck launching - note the tail wheel.

Also note; the ship's radio antenna mast is
shown, lowered for air operations.

Crew members relax by the rail, looking out at the fleet oiler USS NIOBRARA (AO-72)

TBF-1 Avenger - Landing gear, flaps & tail hook down, engine cowl flaps open,
with an ample coating of oil and exhaust residue on the belly.

24 March 1943 - A Dauntless in motion., after missing the wires and hitting the barricade. Not what his flight instructor envisioned, but, any landing you can walk away .from .....

Navy Blimp on patrol overhead above this Douglas SBD "Dauntless"

Coffee & sandwiches being served during general quarters

Photos of the "Mighty-I" from the USS SIGSBEE (DD-502)

Looking out on a schooner as the USS INDEPENDENCE approaches Dragons Mouth, the north entrance to the Gulf of Paria, Trinidad. TBF-1 Avengers on the bow.

USS INDEPENDENCE approaches Dragons Mouth, the north entrance to the Gulf of Paria, Trinidad, with her destroyer screen USS Sigsbee (DD-502) & USS Guest (DD-472) off the bow.

Early model TBF-1 Avengers are seen on the flight deck as crew members look out at the scenic view.

During this time period, the INDEPENDENCE had on board 9 TBF-1 Avengers, 12 F4F-4 Wildcats and 9 SBD-4 Dauntless'.

Ensign Alsotott's SBD stalling into the sea after launch. (See: 14 April 1943)

Friday 23 April 1943　　　　　　*Gulf of Paria - Flight operations*

1259 Anchored as before. Got underway to conduct flight operations.
1930 Commenced night flight operations.
1953 Ens. W.C. Cummings was picked up by a crash boat, uninjured after his F4F-4 plummeted into the water off the starboard side of the Mighty-I. The plane sank. The number one 40mm gun mount caught an unexpected and unwanted piece of the action as the Wildcat (Bu. No. 2114) meandered thru, injuring S2c C.E. Temple. He reported to sick bay with a fractured right arm and a lacerated scalp.
2053 The anchor chain played out once again in the Gulf, off Quarantine Station and Alice Point. Due to the number of night landing accidents on board, the decision was made for VF-22 to hold night bounce landing practice at an army airfield.

Saturday 24 April 1943　　　　　*Gulf of Paria - Flight operations*

1130 Anchored as before. Got underway to conduct flight operations.
1420 Ens. Billy B. Laughren skidded into the starboard catwalk in his TBF (Bu. No. 5880) upon landing. There were no injuries. However, pilots were finding new ways to crash their airplanes aboard the Mighty-I and the starboard side of the vessel was just put on notice it was not immune. The crews manning the catwalks and gun mounts were by now becoming well aware that they would have more to watch out for than the Japanese when the ship went to war, as the environment surrounding the flight deck was indeed a dangerous place during air operations. They would need to keep alert.

Sunday 25 April 1943　　　　　　*Anchored, Gulf of Paria*

CV-22 received onboard from a Naval Air Station lighter, one F4F-4 Wildcat (Bu. No. 11052).

Monday 26 April 1943　　*Gulf of Paria - Flight operations*

0603 Anchored as before. Got underway to conduct flight operations.
0922 A F4F-4 Wildcat had landed and an explosion occurred in the aircrafts tail section. Machinist Harold L. Stalker needed to be treated for nose injuries when a flying piece of the assembly struck his face. There were no other injuries.
1702 Completed flight operations.

Chapter 4

1753 Anchored in the gulf off Pelican Island and Cronstadt.

Tuesday 27 April 1943   *Gulf of Paria - Flight operations*

0630 Anchored as before. Got underway to conduct flight operations. They began flight operations at 0740, and were back at anchor at 1653 as before.
This was a shakedown cruise for all hands as they learned their craft, and the idiosyncrasies of the good ship INDEPENDENCE. As well the aviators. Slightly bent airplanes were building up. They transferred 3 damaged F4F Wildcats to the Naval Air Station via a lighter.

Wednesday 28 April 1943   Anchored - *Gulf of Paria*

Anchored as before. CV-22 took on board military passengers for transportation to the United States.

Thursday 29 April 1943   *Underway from NOB, Trinidad, en route to Philadelphia, Pa.*

0700 Weighed anchor and got underway. CV-22 conducted flight operations from 0920 thru 1120.
1618 Changed course to 000°T, leaving the Gulf of Paria. CV-22 headed back to Philadelphia.
1640 Accompanied by the USS BUCK, USS SIGSBEE and USS SWANSON, INDEPENDENCE commenced zigzagging on base course 034°T in accordance with zigzag Plan #7.
On the return voyage to Philadelphia, Jean Goemmer noted;
"We weigh anchor and head for Philadelphia. We make sub contact outside the harbor. Destroyers with us drop depth charges. We run into bad storms off Cape Hatteras. Most of the crew gets sea sick. **JG**

Friday 30 April 1943   *Underway from NOB, Trinidad, en route Philadelphia, Pa*

Steaming as before, accompanied by the DD screen, USS BUCK, USS SIGSBEE and USS SWANSON. They were operating as an independent unit of the Atlantic Fleet.
0542 Sighted land (Martinique), distance 20 miles bearing 340°T.
0645 USS SIGSBEE dropped one depth charge on a sound contact (proved to be false).
During the day CV-22 conducted brief flight operations.

Saturday 1 May 1943   *Underway from NOB, Trinidad, en route Philadelphia, Pa.*

0537-0544 Steaming as before. Exercised crew in an abandon ship drill.
0543 Conducted steering casualty drill.
CV-22 conducted flight operations from 0842-1030, 1151-1249 and 1537-1644.
1453 USS SWANSON reported a steering casualty, which was repaired within 22 minutes.
At 1856 during routine general quarters, the 5" gun mounts were fired at an improvised target balloon.
1902-1919 Exercised crew in a fire drill.

Sunday 2 May 1943   *Underway to Philadelphia, Pa.*

Steaming as before. CV-22 was en route zigzagging on base course 330°T, speed 20 knots. They conducted flight operations three times today; 0845 until 1122, 1440 until 1609, and 1714 until 1725.

Monday 3 May 1943   *Underway to Philadelphia, Pa.*

Steaming as before. At 0330 CV-22 ceased zigzagging to commence a full power run, recording 31.5 knots (345 rpm), on course 286°T. The DD screen stayed with her, except the USS BUCK, which lagged behind. At 0800 they changed course to 006°T as they proceeded north.
1000 Completed full power run and commenced smoke prevention run. Sighted a ship on the horizon, ten miles ahead port, identified as a merchant ship.
1258 USS BUCK was sighted and took her station.

Chapter 4

2030 USS INDEPENDENCE ran afoul a storm off cape Hatteras and tried various courses and speeds to reduce the ships roll and protect the aircraft on the flight deck.
2215 Radar contact was made on a convoy 18,000 yards off the port quarter.
2324 Reduced speed to 15 knots.

Tuesday 4 May 1943   *Moored Navy Yard, Philadelphia, Pa.*

1048 Made landfall on channel buoy "Point XM", marking the entrance to Delaware Bay. Changed course to 315°T, speed 25 knots. Off Cape May, VC-22 flew ashore bound for NAAS Willow Grove, Hatborough, PA. where most men were granted leave prior to departure for overseas combat.
1327 Received a pilot onboard and steamed up the Delaware River.
1910 Arrived off the Philadelphia Navy Yard and dropped anchor at 1935.
2200 Aided by yard tugs, CV-22 got underway to moor, portside to the east side of pier 2, at the Philadelphia Navy Yard, and began receiving water, steam, electrical and telephone services from the dock. The USS NEW JERSEY (to be commissioned in 19 days), USS BROOKLYN, sister carriers USS BELLEAU WOOD, USS PRINCETON and various other ships were present.

Tuesday 4 May 1943 thru 11 June 1943

Underwent post-shakedown repairs and alterations at the Philadelphia Navy Yard. The 5" gun mounts on the forecastle and the fantail were to be replaced with 40mm quad gun mounts.

On May 5th, numerous crew members left the ship for 6 days of leave. Some transferred for training or other duty. During the days that followed many new crew members reported aboard. These new sailors would become acclimated to the ship and their new assigned duties. Ship's company would continue to go ashore for various training classes such as; anti-aircraft gunnery, fire fighting, etc.

On 7 May 1943, the USS INDEPENDENCE was still moored at pier 2. Don Labudde had received his orders and came aboard. He described it as follows:

DL *"Our actual arrival in Philadelphia, the transfer to the Navy Yard, the stay of a few days (or maybe a week, surely less than a month) in a receiving barracks, was and is a blur.*

What will always stick in mind, though, was the day I crossed the quarterdeck for the first time and became a bluejacket assigned to U.S.S. Independence, CVL-22.

Late afternoon. Scattered remnants of morning fog. Puddles everywhere from recent squalls. Distant echoing thunder.

She emerged like a benign ghost from behind a gossamer shroud. At her truck flew the red flag Baker, denoting the significant presence of the small Yard oiler hugging her starboard side. A long line of sailors in dungarees trudged up and down the after gangway, lugging final stores aboard. She was almost ready for sea.

The good earth that had provided the warp and woof of her being still restrained her. Hovering over the flightdeck was the long boom of a giant gantry crane, dipping, grabbing, lifting, depositing, its elevated cab partly obscured in the mist. From within her came the sound of chipping hammers, the stutter of rivet guns. Now and then a welding torch sparkled brightly in the cavern of her hangar deck, lighting it with cold blue fire. Yard workers in steel hats and leather work clothing scurried to and fro, paying scant attention to the draft of new men reporting for duty. Everybody appeared oblivious to the long-hulled warships in various stages of construction that lined both sides of the dock.

I also ignored those ships, having eyes only for this vessel, my ship. I looked her over up and down, admiring the great flukes of her anchors and the up-curving sweep of her clipper bow. She was not beautiful; perfection had eluded her. She was a long crate some imbecile had topped with an over-sized slab. All that crappy water pouring out of her sides made her a floating sewer dumping its fecal wastes into a polluted stream. Hard straight lines belayed her gentler curves. Mundane items of ship gear cluttered her sides, breaking her smooth symmetry: half-round gun sponsons, great baskets of floater nets. A long-hulled whaleboat was secured near the port quarter. I saw all this, and didn't see it.

Chapter 4

Aware that I'd be wise not to make a show of my eagerness to go aboard, I said in my most worldly manner to Phil alongside me, "Man alive, isn't she ugly though?"

"That she is," said a genial Phil. "Welcome aboard, sailor."

My heart sang. I was sure I would remember that salutation all the days of my life. Welcome aboard!

A young coxswain sauntered down the gangway, looked us over with enthusiastic contempt, and blew a blast on his whistle. We stirred, tugging at our jumpers and squaring our hats sea-going style, not wishing to appear more lubberly than we could help. Everyone herded toward the gangway.

I held back, struck by the thought that the next step would be one of the most important of my life. Looking up once more at this ponderous structure confronting me, I searched for some small indication that she knew who I was and was glad to see me, that she recognized a mutual need for one another. But all I saw was an impervious wall of cold gray steel looming in front of me with stoic indifference. She didn't care if I came or went, loved or hated her. I was young that day and immortal.

It took a while for Phil and me to settle in, to find our way around. A ship's innards are a maze. There were vital locations to discover: sleeping racks stacked closely one-on-one between aisles so narrow they made our quarters at 87th and Anthony seem like suites at the Waldorf. It was lucky we were so skinny. Messing compartments, the gedunk stand, the barbershop. Sick Bay, the unprivate crews' heads and shower rooms.

Roaming willy-nilly was frowned upon, especially for airdales. Every ship abides by ancient rules of the sea. Mighty I was a carrier of aircraft, meaning that aviation ratings existed by sufferance of the true seamen, as if we were along for the ride. Her reason for being was almost irrelevant. We didn't conn her, tie her to a dock, fire her guns in self-defense. We were on the ship, not of her.

My initial search for the aviation armory, our sanctum sanctorum, enlightened me on this point. I was stumbling about aft of the hangar deck. Coming blindly around a bulkhead, stepping clumsily over a coaming into a narrow passageway leading farther aft, I collided belly-to-belly with a tall, slender officer who looked as startled as I. This wasn't supposed to happen. Enlisted men were required to watch for approaching officers and immediately give way. "Hit the rail!" was the traditional command.

But I had not seen this man in time to avoid him. His cap was speckled with goldleaf scrambled eggs. I had already learned that the only three-stripe commander aboard was the Exec, so this must be he. It was. He was as tall as I'd read Abe Lincoln had been. No beard, though. No genial smile of welcome, either. I saluted, he returned it. His voice was stern. He demanded my name and rate, how long I had been aboard, and what I thought I was doing here. I recited the requested stats (including my service number 305 30 04 although he hadn't asked for it) and then said that I was looking for the aviation armory. The look on his face revealed that he wasn't quite sure himself where it was. Then his memory clicked in and he gave gruff but reasonably polite directions. We exchanged another battery of salutes and he continued on his way without cracking a smile. I left the scene with relief.

Within a few months this officer, Rudy L. Johnson, became Captain of the good ship Independence. A fine one. I'm sure our accidental meeting faded quickly from his memory. Not from mine. The armory was a small rectangular steel-walled room large enough to hold about a dozen men, just forward of the fantail, where the after 40-mm quad gun was mounted. It was a supply bin, not a hangout for cracker-barrel philosophizing. A long, uncluttered workbench lined one bulkhead. Atop it were bins crammed with spare parts, each part in place. A vertical row of Browning .50-caliber aircraft machine guns at the far end was secured to the bulkhead with strong metal straps. The deck was unpainted, rubbed almost to a shine with steel wool. Various manuals were stacked in a small metal bookcase. The room contained everything a dedicated ordnanceman could want--except pinups.

Before we went to sea, I learned how CVL-22's construction would impact our jobs. She was a jury-rigged compromise. Every officer and man aboard had to make her work. All airdales envied the classy, long-planned facilities for living and fighting rumored to be enjoyed by the big new Essex-Class carriers, some being built right here in Philly. We were orphans of the storm. Needed orphans. President Roosevelt himself had overruled high Navy brass, which didn't want any part of us. It was the bomb elevator and its long dark shaft, the hatch to cover the shaft, and the method of raising and lowering the hatch that brought me up short. I detested it from that day forward.

A long time later, while discussing the problem, I said to a grinning, ever-patient Bob, "I guess to get certain things you gotta give up certain others. I see that. What gets me is why they couldn't come up with a better hatch arrangement. Something electric maybe, or hydraulic. But this...."

The rectangular hatch sealing the elevator and its long deep shaft was located amidships, just ahead of the forward aircraft elevator and the island structure to the right. Because the hatch weighed nearly half a ton, it had to be lifted by a block-and-tackle hoist, which needed to be hooked to a tall portable stanchion curved at its upper end. After the hatch had been undogged with a special tool, the hook of the hoist was inserted in a cleat on the hatch; the man at the hoist then raised the hatch with a rapid-fire series of pulls on a chain. When the hatch had been lifted to a right angle to the deck, the curved end of the stanchion was swung around and the hatch folded back and lowered. Only then could the bomb elevator, concealed and protected by the hatch, be put to work. It was a jury-rigged setup tolerable only on a jury-built ship. I never got used to it. On this day of initiation to the ship's mysteries, this device shocked me.

"You mean," I moaned to Whitey, "we've got to go through this nonsense every time we open this thing?"

"No way else to open it. Or close it."

The elevator platform was a grooved steel plate slightly smaller than the hatch opening. Phil suggested that we take a ride on the elevator down to the magazine. I shot him a disgusted look, wishing he'd kept his mouth shut. I wanted no part of this thing. Whitey, perhaps, sensed my attitude.

"Okay," he said looking carefully at the two of us. "When we start down, fellas, don't touch the bulkheads."

"I don't intend to," I flipped.

"That's good. You'd lose your arm."

Whitey stood between Phil and me. I was more puzzled than upset by the smirks of the strikers looking on. What the hell, I thought, it's just a damn ride on an elevator, isn't it?

It was more than that. Down we went. The fast rate of descent scared me. The bulkheads erected themselves like tall narrow barriers, closing in like movable panels in a chamber of horrors. My apprehension amazed and shamed me at how quickly it turned into fear; I froze, not daring to move a muscle. The strikers' smirks topside made sense. They had done this before, I hadn't. I forced myself to relax as my knees bent slightly with the platform's approach to its pit stop. A gust of relief came from Phil. The clumsy hatch cover arrangement had earned my immediate detestation. Loathing was what I felt for the bomb elevator and the shaft it resided in. I'm glad I had no idea on that day how many times I'd have to use these accoutrements.

A heavy, vault-like armored door swung slowly open with a few creaks of resistance. Whitey led us into the dim, oppressive gloom of the bomb magazine. The strong paint odor which permeated the entire vessel was a stench here in her subterranean depths.

The magazine's cargo had not yet come aboard. The space was large, dimly lighted, with a low overhead. Sections were divided by vertical aluminum stanchions mounted deck to overhead. Claustrophobia had never been a problem for me, but this place gave me the willies.

Whitey dashed whatever hopes I might have entertained about staying clear of it.

"You two," he said blandly, "will probably spend a fair amount of time down here."

Whitey led us back onto the elevator and the three of us pulled the door shut. He secured the dogs.

"Small arms mag next," he ordered.

"Who takes care of that one?" Phil asked.

"We do. No ordnanceman gets out of any of this. We take the daily mag temps, too."

This compartment was on the same deck level but forward and was reached by a circuitous route through a maze of passageways and up and down several ladders, the final one a seemingly endless affair.

We descended into a sweat box, our shirts pasted to our backs. My nostrils narrowed; the air stank. The smell of creosote came from stacks of wooden ammo boxes containing unbelted rounds for aircraft machine guns.

We returned topside. I was dead tired. Whitey kept us at it. I began to understand how big the damn ship really was.

We explored both topside rearming rooms. Starboard was a narrow steel chamber just forward of the island, with an opening off the catwalk near a twin-barreled 40mm gun mount manned by the ship's Marine contingent, commanded by a stocky young captain. Its long bulkheads were lined with bins for ammo cans supplying the wing guns. It was meant as a storeroom only, but was a good place to cork off between strike missions--or to ease a hangover between the end of liberty and 0800 quarters.

Real work was done in the portside ready magazine. Athwart the island, just below flightdeck level, it was located beneath the by-pass ramp designed to give squeezing room for taxiing airplanes or those being spotted forward of the three barrier cables by plane pushers.

A steel workbench that lined one bulkhead was equipped with a portable belting device, used mainly whenever individual air group commanders decided to change the ratio of AP bullets to tracers in a belt. Their frequent revisions were a pain in the tail. Of course we complied; orders is orders. There was no outside forced ventilation. Filled ammo cans were stacked in bins on the outboard bulkhead. There was a narrow passage between bins and workbench; two rearming crewmen, wearing essential tool belts, couldn't get past one another without pulling in your gut. This led to some annoyance and the passing of enough gas to drain the room of occupants for minutes at a time. We called it the fart factory.

We had our own comfort station. A small crews' head lay just forward of the magazine, lighted by a single weak bulb and equipped with a toilet and urinal. A steel watertight door supposed to be dogged at all times guarded the place, a stricture universally ignored because the smoking light was always OUT in the magazine. The Chiefs looked the other way; no officer was ever known to enter.

Four or five men crammed into this place at one time, smoking. We all had the habit. It was the thing to do; never gave it a second thought. At 50 cents a carton, it was the cheapest and best approved vice we could sustain. The room stank with a sour smell composed of human waste flushed as an afterthought, clothing reeking of sweat from overworked human bodies, and a haze of cigarette smoke that never dissipated. Long minutes after exiting that head, a man emanated a foolproof odor as a clue to where he'd just been.

A man faced a hazard emerging from that magazine or head because he had to bend almost double to fit through the hatch. Reaching the flightdeck from the catwalk could be done, by an agile person, with a single leap; most used a four-rung ladder. A simple jump into the catwalk was the way we came down. You did this with care, however; a misjudgment would land you in the drink or on a dock forty-five feet below.

Practicing this technique not long after I came aboard was how I finally met Ensign Porky. His reputation, as the saying goes, preceded him. Bob, Tom, Dan, Sully, among others, had described him to Phil and me unfavorably before we had set eyes on him. Wait 'til he crosses your path, was the attitude.

But it was quiet, sober-sides Dan whose advice I took to heart: "Better stay clear of that one. He was a piece of work. Stupid he was not. While still ACOM, his antennae smoked out opportunities for ambitious sailors lurking just beyond the 1940 horizon. One night, so the story went, he had caught himself up in a Pearl City bar, drained his glass in one gulp, and trotted back to his ship where he knew he could stay out of trouble. Promotion came in due course. Navy needed him now more than ever.

Porky would become a principal subject years later among us ex-AOM's at our reunions, the memory of his rough edges lubricated by time. We had served under a lot of officers and Chiefs, most of them competent leaders of a Navy with a huge job on its hands and millions of kids to break in. But Porky was the one we remembered.

Since the day Phil and I had reported, the atmosphere about the entire ship had changed. It was quieter, for one thing. No Yard workers were aboard wielding their chipping hammers or rivet guns. The last Yard worker had gone ashore without a backward glance. Yet the shipyard hummed along. We were only one vessel among many about to become another unit in a great fleet building here and across the Delaware River in Camden, New Jersey, the place where Independence had felt her first cold embrace of the sea.

107

Chapter 4

Independence by now was beyond all that. It was exciting just to look around and savor my surroundings. I recall the scene vividly:

A shallow pool of white glare separated the quarterdeck from the gloomy far ends of the hangar. The last dull glow of the early spring twilight had settled over the shipyard, until the gathering darkness of the earth had wed the descending darkness of the sky. Word had gone out that it wouldn't be long now.

Our flightdeck and hangar were clear, awaiting the aircraft to be lifted aboard by cranes from a barge any day now. I knew that supplies from beans to bullets were on hand because I'd been breaking my back helping load and stow them. In my mind's eye I could see the black gang far below in the engine rooms, checking their gauges as they monitored the slow rise of steam in her boilers.

All this time a sort of unofficial melding of working groups took place. Officers and men, as essential to the ship's well being as the skipper who bossed the entire show, disappeared into her bowels and seemed never to show their faces topside again. Aviation mechs, metalsmiths, electricians, instrument technicians, each handicraft in its room similar to our ordnance armory near the fantail, prepared for the approaching time when their skills would be put to the test.

Colored T-shirts and tight cloth helmets were issued to all flightdeck personnel. Officers who would wave the final signal GO to the pilots at takeoff wore bright yellow helmets and shirts.

Everybody was issued waist lifebelts, inflated by an attached small canister of oxygen. For those of us who had to wear belts cluttered with tools needed to accomplish the rearming bit, they were a burdensome joke; nor did they breed confidence.

Seamen stood watches over 20-mm gun mounts along both catwalks, though none of the mounts had a single round on hand.

A work day starting before sunrise usually ended by 1700. Port or starboard liberty was granted daily, ending at the eight strokes of the bell signifying 2400.

Philadelphia, the city, had no intellectual interest for me just then. I regret that. Too many elemental juices were rushing over the dam. It was simply a great liberty town. I made no attempt to visit Independence Hall, and the Liberty Bell was stashed away for the duration. Museums and libraries were by-passed in a taxi loaded with sailors hungrily looking forward to whatever they could discover to assuage their appetites.

The ship was far more crowded now than when Phil and I had reported aboard in early May. Weeks had sped by; only the plankowners seemed to have been aboard longer than we. **DL**

29 May 1943   *Ashore, VF-22 transitions to the new Hellcat*

VF22 became one of the first squadrons to change from F4F Wildcats to the new F6F Hellcats.

Sunday 6 June 1943 thru Wednesday 9 June 1943

On Sunday, 6 June the ship completed fueling, receiving diesel oil, fuel oil and aviation gasoline. Monday, 7 June thru Wednesday 9 June they received a large mix of munitions.

Wednesday 9 June 1943   *Harvard University comes to C.I.C.*

On this day a meeting had been arranged by the office of the 'Navy Department Coordinator of Research and Development' onboard the INDEPENDENCE with Harvard University.

On 8 February 1943, a directive had been issued by the Commander in Chief, U.S. Fleet that all combatant vessels of cruiser type or larger have a Combat Information Center.

The INDEPENDENCE was selected for the participants to receive preliminary education on C.I.C., and to study problems and shortcomings uncovered during the recent shake down cruise. Some of these problems are noted on the next page. The study would help to resolve some of the issues to the benefit of not only USS INDEPENDENCE, but her sisters and other vessels in the growing fleet.

Participants from the Cruft Laboratory and the Psycho-Acoustic Laboratory (Harvard University), the Psychological Corp. (N.Y.), the office of the Navy Department Coordinator of Research and Development, and the Bureau of Aeronautics met with C.I.C. officers from the USS INDEPENDENCE and USS NEW JERSEY. Three conferences were held; 0930 to 1200, 1200 to 1530, and 1530 to 1700.

Combat Information Center, C.I.C. was vital to the wartime operation of the ship. It was the heart of crucial information interpretation, coordination, flow and routing. Radar data, radio communications with ships and aircraft, as well as communication with lookouts, the bridge (and other vital parts of the ship) were all part of the C.I.C tools that would be utilized to evaluate, and correlate the information to provide situation awareness at sea and in combat. This would include dissemination of information to the "Flag", other ships, fire control and aircraft to improve combat effectiveness.

During routine watches, C.I.C. had 4 officers, with 2 additional squadron night controller officers when the ship was operating with a night air group. During G.Q., the number was upped to 12. There were 45 enlisted men (plus technicians) in C.I.C. split into 3 watches (15 men each), to man C.I.C. 24 hours a day. The 3 watches were split up into 5 shifts to try to maximize the time off between watches so the men could get unbroken periods of rest to maintain high efficiency and alertness on watch.
C.I.C. was located on the Gallery Deck beneath the Flight Deck, just forward of the elevator well near the Island. It could be a very busy, noisy and cramped space. Ventilation was not good, and a hatch was frequently left open for fresh air, opening outboard on the starboard side near an AA gun mount. The noise from the guns when firing, aircraft on the flight deck, and from the speakers could make it difficult to discern necessary communication, with concentration a challenge. Piled on top of the noise and poor ventilation was the heat and humidity in the tropics (later in the Pacific).

USS INDEPENDENCE Combat Information Center, C.I.C.

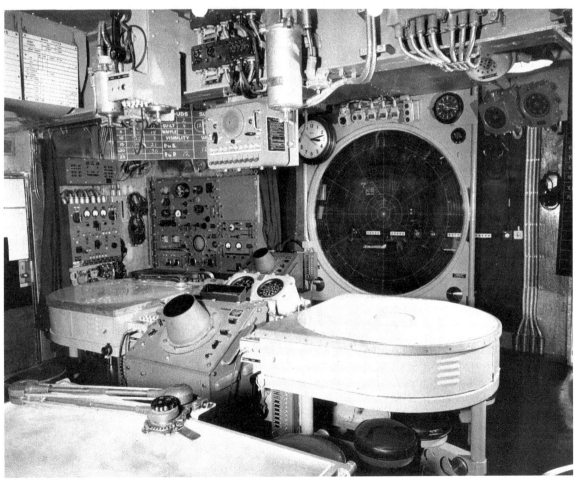

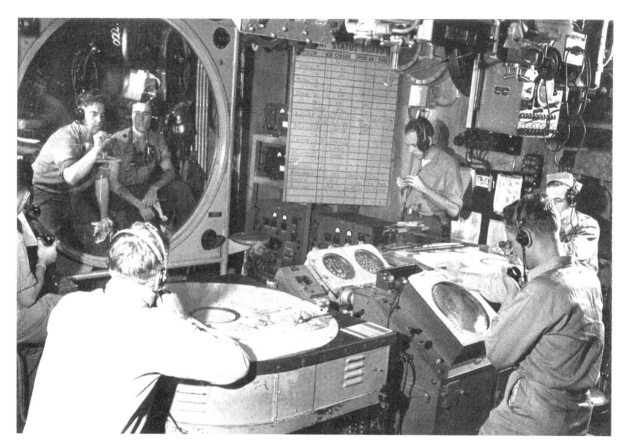

The center table with a Remote Plan Position Indicator is utilized by the Fighter Director Officer. The curved intercept plotting tables on either side are backlit, typically manned by two Interceptor Officers. Plotters stand behind the vertical Master Plot. A radar control room (not shown) is off to the right.
The radar operators aboard the USS INDEPENDENCE had 3 types of radar: SG for surface search, SK for aircraft search and SC-2 - later in 1944, changed out to SM for fighter direction.

Thursday 10 June 1943

In Philadelphia, VF-22 became the first squadron to be catapulted in the new F6F Hellcat.

Friday 11 June 1943

At 0838, CV-22 began receiving aircraft onboard. VC22 was assigned 9 new TBF-1s and 9 SBD-5s.

DON LABUDDE
Our airplanes arrived unceremoniously by barge. They looked clumsy and helpless as one by one the F4F fighters, the fixed-wing SBD dive bombers, and the big new TBF torpedo planes came swinging slowly through the air, props motionless and landing gear down and locked. Each plunked gently to a spot on the flightdeck, where handlers were directed to push them to designated places.
    Pilots, gunners, and technicians assigned to CVG-22 (the reason all the rest of us were here) came up the gangway lugging seabags and suitcases like traveling salesmen and dispersed to their special quarters: officers country for the pilots, crew quarters just below flightdeck level for the gunners and radiomen who manned the TBFs and SBDs.
We airdales were excited to have real airplanes on hand at last. Men from each group of specialists swarmed over them. Ensign Porky had us ordnancemen opening the Dzus buttons on the fighter wings to see if the guns were mounted properly, that the new gun chargers worked, and if sticky tape had been pasted over the muzzles of each barrel. Elementary, but he insisted. ***DON LABUDDE***

5
From the Atlantic Fleet to Hawaii

Saturday 12 June 1943 *Underway from Philadelphia en route Colon, C.Z., Panama.*

Moored as before, portside to the east side of pier 2, at the Philadelphia Navy Yard.

0800 Held quarters for muster.

0835 Tested main engines.

0919 Aided by tugs to pull away from the mooring, CV-22 proceeded to get underway down the Delaware River. They were steaming under CINCLANT orders (281942, May 1943) toward the Delaware Bay. At 1446 all engines were stopped.

1450 The degaussing officer came aboard.

1455 CV-22 got underway steaming at standard speed (144 rpm) on various courses while conducting degaussing runs at Brandywine Shoal Light.

1640-1833 Compensated the magnetic compass.

1944 Dropped anchor in the lower Delaware Bay in eleven fathoms of water off of Harbor of Refuge.

DL   *"SHE'S broke loose!" a Southern voice cried. "Ah think we're underway. She's movin'!"*
No, I thought as my heart lifted. It's the shoreline, the dock, the shipyard that is moving. The sky itself seemed in motion. Clouds scudded by at an odd angle. The sun's bright ball swung through a long arc, casting dark shadows that crawled the flightdeck beneath the airplanes. Dockside sailors who had singled-up our lines and cast the heavy hawsers from the bollards shriveled to tiny figures. Toy-like gantries towered over suddenly miniaturized warships. Multi-stored workshops shrank to a background panorama befitting a model railroad pike.

Independence had come to life. There was a sharp sense of exhilaration as this inanimate steel space I had been occupying trembled under my feet with the stirring of a life all her own.

We paused in mid-channel while the puffing tugs cast off with sharp pooping blasts of their whistles. On either side of us spread a vast industrial complex. Camden on the left, naval shipyard on the right stretching for miles. An awesome sight. Might & Main on display. Both the commercial shipyards and the U.S. Navy shared a long history here:

In this Delaware stream, huge carrier Saratoga had first wet her bottom. Battleships Idaho, Arkansas, and Colorado began life here. Likewise, newer battlewagons Washington, New Jersey, and South Dakota drew their first breath of life in these Yards. And, as my own ship slid past this scene, I wondered how many among the crowds exactly thirty years earlier witnessing BB Oklahoma's journey down these greased ways had been prescient enough to foretell that in 1941 she would be lying at the muddy bottom of a distant harbor called Pearl, her sun-baked topside trussed-up with a long line of bents, their taut cables pulling her slowly back to an even keel, to a semblance of tortured dignity, her ruptured hull contaminated with lethal gas and with garbage heaps of bones that the sea's mindless creatures had long since picked clean of the flesh they had once supported.

My gaze wandered, trying to drink it all in. A lump formed in my throat as I spotted my home state's majestic new representative, huge battleship Wisconsin, BB-64, squatting high and dry in her mother's gigantic womb. Still months from her first taste of the old briny, her one hundred million dollar cost was a bargain.

But it was the sight of Independence's own eight sisters that riveted my attention.

(I now know more of the story than I did then).

The logistics of materiel supply, of available skilled manpower, had forced the decision to build all nine in one location: Camden, New Jersey. Of the six already afloat, only Mighty I had been shaken down. Which meant, on this day of days, that we led the van. From my vantage point in midstream, their appearance briefly dampened my enthusiasm.

All looked skinny, top-heavy, ugly. Seaworthy? How could a landlubber like me judge fairly?

No distant factory whistles or town sirens saluted as we steamed slowly by. No brass bands were heard piping us down the road to glory. Our departure was just another wartime workaday event. Shorelines slid by slowly, receding as the river widened and became an inland sea. **DL**

Sunday 13 June 1943   *Farewell Delaware Bay*

0730 Anchored as before in the Delaware Bay. CV-22 sighted and exchanged signals with Destroyer Squadron 24 (ComDesRon 24 consisting of destroyers USS BROWNSON and USS THATCHER), instructing them to anchor at their discretion.

1258 Got underway to depart the lower Delaware Bay, accompanied by escorts USS BROWNSON and USS THATCHER, maneuvering to clear the anchorage.

1305 Commenced steaming on course 155°T, speed 15 knots.

1319 Sounded general quarters. 1322 Changed course to 135°T.

1530 Departed Delaware Bay passing Buoy XM off port beam, distance 300 yards.

1539 Secured from general quarters. Commenced zigzagging (Plan 17) on base course 135°T.

1640- 1802 Conducted flight operations.

2120 Commenced zigzagging per Plan 3.

DL   *We left the Delaware behind at Cape May and entered the Atlantic before sundown. A destroyer escort tagged along. I remember the gentle swell, the deck rising and falling beneath my feet. Sunset was still, windless. A Wisconsin prairie would have cast dull shadows; here there was room for none. A few shorebirds, not an albatross among them, creaked lonesome cries as they winged past, waiting wisely for the ship's wet trash to be scattered in our wake after dark. I remember the sea smell, the hushed atmosphere. Phil was silent. No one else seemed to want to talk. My first evening at sea.* **DL**

Monday 14 June 1943   *Steaming toward the Canal Zone*

Steaming as before accompanied by USS BROWNSON and USS THATCHER.

0623 Commenced flight operations, with recovery of aircraft for the day completed by 0852.

2000 Sounded general quarters. At 2020 the crew worked out a battle problem, completing it at 2035. The Task Unit steamed thru the night zigzagging on a 180°T base course at 20 knots.

DL   *Witnessing these first landings gave me a problem. My eyeballs acted like movie cameras recording everything they saw. I was mesmerized by the hectic activity. But while the scene etched indelible images, it brought a loud, plain-spoken reminder of where I was and that no unthinking day-dreaming was permitted.*

"Labudde! Get your finger outa your ass or you'll be a dead hunka cheese! Snap outa it!"

I snapped. I was standing behind a fighter spotted forward of the island, watching aft as another plane came around in the groove. This one was a big TBF, the Navy's new torpecker. Before I could blink it had settled to the deck. Once freed of the arresting gear cable, it loomed huge and unwieldy, taxiing quickly forward as its wings folded jerkily to the fuselage under hydraulic pressure. But its great prop was a spinning scythe that would have sliced me to ribbons if I hadn't moved out of the way.

When I looked around, nobody was paying attention to me. I was alone, isolated. They were busy. Whichever ordnanceman had shouted the warning and, perhaps, saved my life, has remained forever anonymous. The whole thing was a much busier scene than I had imagined. Everything happened at once. Between the spinning props, there seemed barely squeezing room for a man to get through. Our long narrow flightdeck had suddenly become woefully short--and a whole lot narrower. Ensign Porky must not have witnessed my attention lapse, because he never mentioned it.

BS47360

U.S.S. CV 22.
SURFACE VIEW. "OFF THE BOW."
NAVY YARD. PHILA. JUNE.19-1943
8-13-43

The Navy caption on the photo is incorrect. On the morning of June 19, 1943 the ship was anchored in Limon Bay, preparing to transit the Panama Canal. This photo was most likely shot on 12 or 13 June, as noted on the photo on the following page. Here calm water. Next photo she is underway.

INDEPENDENCE is underway, note the tug or small boat off her starboard bow.

I did recall the words of Bob, Tom, Sully, and Dan in a casual armory bull session when they had warned Phil and me and other new hands curtly: Keep your eyes open and your brain alert or you'll die on that deck up there.

The lesson I learned that first day didn't scare me. It was similar to the adage about the mere threat of the hangman's noose having a wondrous way of concentrating the mind.

Word had been passed via the grapevine that the small F4F's were to be replaced shortly with a new, war-designed model called the F6F*. Every ordnanceman looked forward to its arrival.

The trip down to and through the Canal Zone was not exactly a springtime cruise.

Flight operations was the principal activity for us airdales, but the whole ship's company was in makee-learn status. Drills, drills, drills. Bugle calls of all sorts. Shrill bosun whistle signals over the P.A. system from the anonymous quartermaster on the bridge: Man Overboard. Abandon Ship. Fire & Rescue. Breakfast, Noon, and Evening Chow. Captain's Mast. Liberty Call. Reveille. Flight Quarters. Most important of all, general quarters: first the bugle call, then the clanging gong, followed immediately by the broadcast command: All hands man your battle stations! (* VF-22 had begun receiving F6Fs on the 10th in Philadelphia)

For me, the multiplicity of bugle calls blended into a rapid blare of toots running up and down the scale. In time I learned them all, of course, because they structured my life. Only GQ, most important of all, refused to dig a groove.

One of the biggest life-changes was getting used to Darken Ship. As the day's light died, bulbs came on below decks. But they came on red, so that every object took on a hellish glow meant to keep us from "night blindness" if we had to rush topside into a suddenly blackened seascape. Men's skin tones took on a ghastly cast; youngsters who hadn't needed to shave suddenly found their chins almost black with a budding beard. Book print was harder to read; color pictures lost their lure. Arguments erupted among poker and cribbage players over the true cast of cards supposed to be red.   ***DL***

Tuesday 15 June 1943　　*Steaming toward the Canal Zone*

0558 Steaming as before. Commenced flight operations, recovering aircraft at 0815.
0907 Sounded flight quarters, securing at 0943. From 1300 to 1340 they held quarters for muster.
1426-1455 Structural firing of all gun mounts.
1930 Sighted patrol plane on port bow.
1935 Sighted four to six vessels on port quarter, identified as friendly.
2040 Commenced zigzagging on base course 210°T.
2315 Sighted Dixon Light, San Salvador, bearing 239°T.

JG 10 miles off San Salvador, on the southern tip of Cuba. JG

Wednesday 16 June 1943　*Steaming toward the Canal Zone*

0021 Steaming as before. Passed the Dixon Light, San Salvador abeam to starboard.
0129 Sighted USS ROCKAWAY on starboard bow bearing 210°T.
0330 Sighted Verde Gras Light on Crooked Island bearing 156°T.
0444 Sighted South Point Light bearing 282°T, 11 miles.
0515-0618 General quarters.
0635 Commenced flight operations.
0643 Sighted South Gay Island, bearing 140°T, 8 miles.
0652 Completed flight operations.
0828 VF-22 pilot Lt. James H. McConnell in a F6F-3 was having engine trouble, and made a forced water landing 3,000 yards off our port beam. McConnell climbed into a rubber raft, was sighted and picked up uninjured by the USS THATCHER. The F6F (Bu. No. 8995) sank.
0835-0920 Conducted flight operations.
0931 USS THATCHER rejoined the formation.
1040 Sighted friendly blimp 8 miles off the starboard beam.
1056 Commenced exercises with the air group.
1152 Completed flight operations.
1605 Commenced air operations, catapulting aircraft. The second aircraft experienced a broken catapult cable, ceasing further launches.
1710-1725 Recovered aircraft.
2131 USS BROWNSON made a sound and radar contact. CV-22 maneuvered to take evasive action.
2134 Contact lost.
2200 Sighted Navassa Island, passing Navassa Light 6 miles abeam to starboard at 2305.

JG We pass through Windward Passage, between Haiti and Cuba. F6F was lost in water, pilot saved. JG
GL Started thru the Caribbean Sea. GL

The Catapult

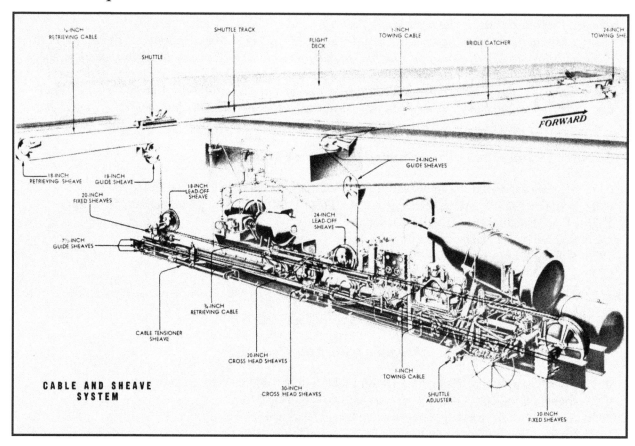

CABLE AND SHEAVE SYSTEM

The USS INDEPENDENCE was originally built with one H2-1 pneumatic hydraulic catapult system.

Aircraft carriers do not have the luxury of long runways like their geographically fixed land based counterparts. Flight deck space is precious. Catapult systems help aircraft being launched to rapidly obtain the forward speed necessary for the wings to generate enough lift to allow the plane to fly. This, while taking up no more of the limited flight deck space than necessary. The H2-1 Catapult system could bring a 16,000 pound aircraft to 60 knots.

A flush track roughly 85 feet long was installed in the port side of the INDEPENDENCE flight deck. Along the length of track ran a "Shuttle". The shuttle would pull the aircraft being launched. The shuttle was in turn pulled by a cable system, located under the flight deck, attached to a pneumatically operated hydraulic "Engine". Stored highly compressed air is released to force hydraulic fluid to drive a ram which pulls the cable attached to the shuttle. There is roughly a ten-to-one ratio of the run of the shuttle vs. the ram travel due to the design of the cable system. So for example, 8 feet of ram travel could provide 80 feet of shuttle travel.

The shuttle features a heavy hook just above the flight deck that pulls a cable bridle attached to the launching aircraft.

Catapult operators would properly adjust the pressure, operate and maintain the machinery to assure the planes got a good launch, keeping both aircraft and aircrew from a saltwater bath. Occasionally, all things mechanical, as well as human, do not work as advertised. In error, a winged Navy aluminum asset is sent plummeting to the ever-waiting and coldly indifferent ocean bottom.

Catapult Machinery room for the H2-1 pneumatic hydraulic catapult.

The bridle is installed around the catapult shuttle hook, and attached to hooks on the aircraft.

In practice, the aircraft would taxi or be pushed up into the launch position. At the tail of the aircraft, a holdback device that utilized a small aluminum ring, would prevent the aircraft from moving forward from where it was "spotted" on the catapult. The bridle would be looped around the catapult shuttle hook and the ends of the bridle attached over the two aircraft hooks under the wing. The shuttle would be tensioned. The pilot would run up his engine to full power. When the pilot was ready, and the timing right on the flight deck, the catapult operator would receive a signal to fire the catapult. When the pneumatic force of the catapult engine was released, the sudden shuttle force pulling the aircraft (combined with the thrust of the planes propeller) would break the calibrated aluminum ring holding back the tail. The aircraft was now off on its fast ride down the rapidly disappearing flight deck. For the aviator in the cockpit, it was fly, or get wet!

During flight operations, the USS INDEPENDENCE would turn into the wind. There might be a 10 knot wind at sea. If the "Mighty-I" was knifing thru the water at 20 knots, directly into that 10 knot headwind, the aircraft wings were getting 30 knots of wind speed across them. When the catapult fired, it would add an additional 60 knots of airspeed. Adding to that was the thrust provided by the aircrafts propeller. The aircraft should be nice and solidly in the air.

Note the bridle falling away as this Dauntless is catapulted.

It sounds somewhat simple but there were many factors for a launch to work well. The mechanics had to do their job right, so that the aircraft engine continued to produce reliable takeoff thrust. The flight deck and catapult crews had to have their act together to hook up the bridal (stay away from the prop), set the shuttle to move with the proper speed at the proper time. The pilot was the last link in the system. The guy in the cockpit had best be alert and really up to the task of keeping his ride in the air, once his fate was cast to the wind. The system all had to work together as a well oiled cohesive machine at the time of the launch.

Photo of the stern port side, Mare Island, 11 July 1943

A TBM-1 Avenger being catapulted from the "Mighty-I"

5085-43
PLAN VIEW, AMIDSHIPS LOOKING AFT.
MARE ISLAND, CAL.   JULY 11

Mare Island, 11 July 1943 . The sled is for testing the catapult. Note only one track in the flight deck. This was while the USS INDEPENDENCE had only a port side catapult.

Thursday 17 June 1943   *Steaming toward the Canal Zone*

0532 Steaming as before with escorts. Sounded general quarters.
0545 Commenced battle problem, completing it at 0605. At 0624 they secured from general quarters.
0740 Commenced launching fighters.
0803 Sounded torpedo defense against air attack (for drill) securing from torpedo defense at 0907.
0955 Completed flight operations. A F6F-3 (Bu. No. 8984) suffered a damaged right main wheel strut during landing.
2013 Steaming on base course 210°T, zigzagging at 19 knots.

GL In the middle of the Caribbean Sea. GL

DL   Long before we left Philly we knew we were headed for the Pacific. The never-ending activity was stimulating and instructive. But day after day? No set hours? No after-chow snoozes? Duty before dawn, concluding long after sunset?
            In spite of this, I began to love the sea. This affair would suffer its share of setbacks. At a distant time the sea would show me an ugly face that brought to mind Shakespeare's line from Richard III: No beast so fierce but knows some touch of pity. On that occasion it showed no pity. Afterwards my love bubbled at a low ebb.
But on this first leg of the trip it was calm. I don't recall any thunderstorms or even overcast skies as we steamed southwest toward Colon. But neither do I remember any "great opalescent and tremulous cloud," as Conrad described it. There was no fog.
            Flight Quarters were held daily. The nights were still, the air gradually warming as we dipped deeper into the Caribbean. After sundown GQ each evening I left my battle station and wandered up and down the flightdeck with Phil or Bob and Sully or with Tom or Dan. I can't remember the phase of the moon then, but it was never totally dark. The shadowed planes became silhouettes outlined against a deep gray seascape.   Then came the Canal.   DL

Friday 18 June 1943   *Steaming toward the Canal Zone   -   Mid-air collision*

Steaming as before en route to the Panama Canal with ComDesRon 24.
0617 Commenced maneuvering for the purpose of conducting a battle problem.

Radioman "Woody" Baughman took his seat in the Douglas SBD "Dauntless", and strapped in behind his pilot Warren Callahan. Born on 1 August 1925, young Woodrow attended grade school and high school in Geronimo Oklahoma. He cut short his high school education and enlisted in the Navy June 6th 1942. "Woody" took his basic training at Great Lakes NTS. He was sent to Radio School at Jacksonville Florida, and was assigned to Air Group 22. Baughman would not celebrate his 18th birthday.

0831 Commenced launching aircraft.

At approximately 0910, 9 TBFs and 9 SBDs had launched to deliver a simulated attack on the Gatun Locks at the Panama Canal. The center attack group reached the target at approximately 0931 and commenced the simulated air raid on Gatun Locks, using evasive tactics, flying at roughly 200 knots at mast heights, about 50' off the water right down the channel. They exited from their run on the initial target, turning left and returned at treetop level strafing strategic targets of opportunity toward the Limon Bay breakwater. The east attack group joined the channel to strike the locks just after the first raid, and also turned left to make low level runs down Limon Bay. On the return flight, two SBDs turned right and flew back along the canal.

Army Air Force fighters were tasked to intercept and make a simulated attack on the INDEPENDENCE raid. They flew out from France Field, C.Z., taking to the air at almost the same time Air Group 22 pilots launched (one hour time zone difference - note 2000 entry).

Warren Ellis Callahan
(pictured here as a midshipman)

Reuben Woodrow Baughman
(1942 photo)

Thomas J. Orzada

Two P-39s appeared dead ahead of Lt(jg) Warren Elias Callahan (and his radioman ARM3c Reuben Woodrow Baughman) to make a frontal run on the SBD. Callahan and Baughman's SBD was almost due west of a coaling plant very low above Limon Bay. Lt(jg) James F. Prinz, flying about 200' above and behind Callahan, witnessed the merge head on, as both the P-39 and the SBD abruptly pulled up, presumably each expecting the other pilot to dive under. Seeing a collision imminent, they both converted to a steep climbing turn and collided. One wing appeared to have been torn from each aircraft.

The SBD (Bu#10881) continued its upward travel, rolled three times and plummeted into the bay. It sank immediately leaving an oil slick on the surface of the bay. Crash boats and other small boats from the surrounding area attempted a rescue. Occupants of both aircraft perished in the accident.

The P-39N (S/N 42-18444) pilot was 2nd Lt. Thomas J. Orzada (52nd AAF fighter squadron). His wingman, 2nd. Lt. Christopher A. Squire, flying off his left wing roughly 250' behind, witnessed the collision, seeing a section of the P-39s right wing come off. It rolled inverted and hit the water, disappearing immediately, leaving an oil slick, a piece of wing (or fuselage) and belly tank floating on the surface.
        (The wreckage of both A/C were later recovered.)

1025 Sounded torpedo defense, securing at 1031. At 1140 they again sounded torpedo defense.
1403 Commenced flight operations.
1415 Army Air Force P-39s commenced a simulated attack, ceasing the simulated attack at 1438.
1525 Completed flight operations.
1635 Sounded general quarters in preparation to entering port.
1636 Commenced maneuvering on various courses toward the channel entrance.
1713 Passed the channel entrance buoy abeam to port into the swept channel.
1738 Passed light ship to starboard. At 1744 the crew secured from general quarters.
1746 Passed through the gates to Limon Bay. At 1747 all engines stopped. At 1807, resumed steaming toward an anchorage, having received on board a pilot and Mr. Boomer, Assistant Port Captain.
1819 Anchored in 7 fathoms of water off Toro Point, and the break waters in Limon Bay.
2000 Turned back all clocks 1 hour to plus 5 zone time.

JG During practice canal attack, defended by US Army planes, one of our planes crashes with an Army plane killing all hands. JG

SBD Dauntless being refueled

Saturday 19 June 1943   *Transited Panama Canal, and moored NOB, Balboa, C.Z.*

0507 Anchored in Limon Bay, Colon Harbor, CZ. Weighed anchor and got underway to transit the canal. At 0517 INDEPENDENCE suffered a steering casualty, regaining steering control at 0519.
0809 Entered lock #3.   0840 Opened the last lock and entered into Gatun Lake. CV-22 began steaming on various courses at various speeds transiting through Gatun Lake and the canal.
1438 Completed transiting the Panama Canal and arrived at Balboa Reach.
1530 Moored port side to the east side of Pier 18, Balboa, CZ in 40 feet of water.
1553 Secured main engines and boilers, except boiler #3, using it for auxiliary purposes.
1637 Commenced receiving fresh water from the shore.

JG Started to transit canal entering Gunter Lock at 0830. Man killed by towing train at Pacific Locks. Growth on both sides of this canal very thick and jungle like. See the hill Balboa was supposed to have stood as he viewed the new ocean, and because of its calm, called it Pacific. Docked at 1530. JG

DL   Millions of people have passed through the Panama Canal since those days and enjoyed the experience. But we seemed to shoot through without a stop. The enclosing green foliage was an armed camp. Cannon and small gun emplacements were everywhere. The U.S. Army surrounded us, watching our every move. Like all vessels, we went up with the rise and down with the flow through the various locks until we began to question if we'd ever find sea level again.

Aircraft crowded on deck kept us from having to undergo formal inspections. A blessing. Being a native mid-westerner, I had a notion I knew all about heat and humidity. The Canal Zone shattered it. And if topside was awful, below decks was unbearable. DL

Repositioning a F4F Wildcat

Sunday 20 June 1943   *Moored NOB, Balboa, C.Z.*

0707-1000 Moored as before. Received onboard, aviation gasoline.
0855-1145 Received onboard, 30 cal and 40mm munitions.

DL   *We anchored in Limon Bay off Colon on 18 June and went through the Canal next day. Very limited shore leave was granted. That limitation was one of the skipper's wiser decisions. None of the ordnancemen were included in a small liberty party. When the party of about fifty returned before midnight, we thanked our lucky stars for having been forced to stay aboard. Guys like myself, ever curious, peered over the flightdeck's edge down at the gangway leading to the quarterdeck. The memorable scene in Tom Heggen's novel Mister Roberts was a mild imitation of what our own Officer of the Deck and his aides had to contend with. Three of our men, each a bloody mess, needed medical attention beyond the scope of our sick bay. A Navy ambulance appeared out of nowhere and hauled them off. Other walking wounded were wrestled below by the ship's shore patrolmen. Torn and rumpled white undress uniforms looked as if the wearer had been used as a broom to sweep an unpaved street. Hats and neckerchiefs were missing. All but the unconscious ones were boisterous, happily belligerent, and exuberant enough to need three days to sober up. How many won brig time I don't remember; the ship had other business ahead of us and we kept moving on. Besides, the Captain was probably thankful to get them back alive.*

But the stories they told! How girls who'd been waiting at the foot of the gangway had squired them from bar to bar, leading to cheap little movie houses where the bill of fare consisted of black-and-white films minus intellectually redeeming attributes. SP's and MP's lined the outboard aisles but didn't interfere unless the entertainment got too raucous.
When it did, the usual cause was one girl taking umbrage at the way another girl blatantly tried to abscond with her man. The military cops broke up the disputes and everybody made their way outside. All this led to excessive drinking, fighting, a rough good time, an escorted trip back shipside, and a memorable hangover.

A few men who spent the night in jail missed the ship--just about the biggest sin a sailor could commit. But these were not ordinary times. A ship needed every hand. The tardy ones were hustled from a Colon military lockup to Balboa. A couple of days on P & P in our own brig was a cheap penalty. *DL*

Monday 21 June 1943   *Underway from Balboa, C,Z. en route San Diego, Calif.*
USS INDEPENDENCE enters the vast outstretched Pacific

0703 Moored as before. Got underway as Task Unit 52.1.5 in company with Task Group 52.1 (of Task Force 52) at various courses at various speeds to clear the harbor. With us are the USS MOBILE (CTG), USS BROWNSON, USS FULLAM, USS SCHROEDER and USS SPENCE. This vessel guide.
0730 Passed through the western entrance of the Panama Canal into the Pacific.
0846 Commenced gunnery practice, firing port gun batteries at a towed sleeve.
0925 Commenced firing starboard gun mounts at a towed sleeve, shooting the sleeve down.
0943 Secured from torpedo defense.
1210 Sounded flight quarters and commenced launching aircraft.
1540 The Task Group came under simulated air attack. Sounded torpedo defense quarters.
1545 Repelled the simulated air attack.
1553 Secured from torpedo defense.
1658 Completed flight operations.
1841-1926   Manned general quarters stations.
2015 Sighted Isla Jicairta Light on starboard bow.
2235 Commenced zigzagging on base course 295°T, speed 18 knots.

JG Left Balboa at 0600. Simulated attack by PT boats. Very much interested as it was the first time I saw them in action. JG

Tuesday 22 June 1943   *Underway, en route to San Diego, Calif.*

0623 Steaming as before. Commenced air operations.

0920 F6F-3 (Bu. No. 8952) piloted by Ensign Edward C. Dale had an accident on landing, hitting the barrier damaging the prop and engine cowling. No injuries.

1437 The ship commenced maneuvering, exercising at defensive maneuvers, ceasing exercises at 1555.

1925 Commenced maneuvering while conducting simulated casualties during battle problem.

DL *We got underway 21 June and were joined soon by light cruiser Mobile, CL-63, and five tin cans for escort. Mobile boasted Independence's original hull design and we found it interesting contrasting her sleek looks against ours. She was much prettier, as were all cruisers of that Cleveland-class. But no faster. She was our shepherd, with AA guns sticking out of her like quills bristling from the back of an outraged porcupine. In fact, it was not long after this that we imperious aircraft carrier sailors became convinced that every ship in the U.S. Navy carried guns mainly as protection for us. The flattops were going to do most of the fighting in this damn war and if they didn't shield us all the cans, cruisers, and battleships might just as well hunker down in their bases for the duration. So, there.*

How long did this insolent stupidity last? For the blink of an eye. We learned quickly to love them all. Next day we sighted the mountains of Costa Rica in the hazy distance. We made good time considering flight quarters and lots of gunnery practice.

The benign Atlantic had barely lifted our hull to meet a large swell, but our first taste of the Pacific was rough, windy, and cool, with overcasts low enough to cancel flight quarters for a few hours each day. *DL*

Wednesday 23 June 1943   *Underway, en route to San Diego, Calif.*

0508 Steaming as before. Sounded general quarters.

0929 Sighted Army B-24 bomber bearing 280°T, 3 miles.

1502 Commenced flight operations.

1653-1721 Manned torpedo defense stations.

1705 Commenced maneuvering while conducting simulated air attacks.

1840 Sounded general quarters.

1855-1916 Exercised a battle problem. At 1939 the crew secured from general quarters.

2133 Steaming as before. Changed speed to 20 knots.

Thursday 24 June 1943   *Underway, en route to San Diego, Calif.*

0419 Zigzagging on base course 300°T at 20 knots. Report of submarine contact by the destroyer screen. Turned left to 195°T.

0422 Changed course to 125°T.

0426 Resumed base course 300°T, and soon resumed zigzagging.

0538 Sighted two ships, 220°T, estimated at 15,000 yards.

0553 Commenced flight operations.

0714 Secured from flight quarters, having launched aircraft.

0742 Sounded torpedo defense, exercising with a simulated air attack.

0756 Secured from torpedo defense. Sounded flight quarters to recover aircraft.

0837 Secured from flight quarters, having recovered the last aircraft.

1013 Commenced gunnery exercises.

1306 Land sighted on the starboard bow.

1332 Commenced air operations. Steered various courses at various speeds maneuvering to avoid simulated air attack by their own air group.

1601 Secured from torpedo defense. Began maneuvering to recover aircraft.

1802 Maneuvered to take up station 1,000 yards behind USS MOBILE.

1910 Sounded sunset general quarters, securing at 2002.

They ended the evening zigzagging on base course 280°T.

The Quad 40mm gun tub on the forecastle deck (on the bow). Note the shell clip storage around the tub.

Twin 40 mm guns in action, in tubs on the gallery deck off the starboard bow.

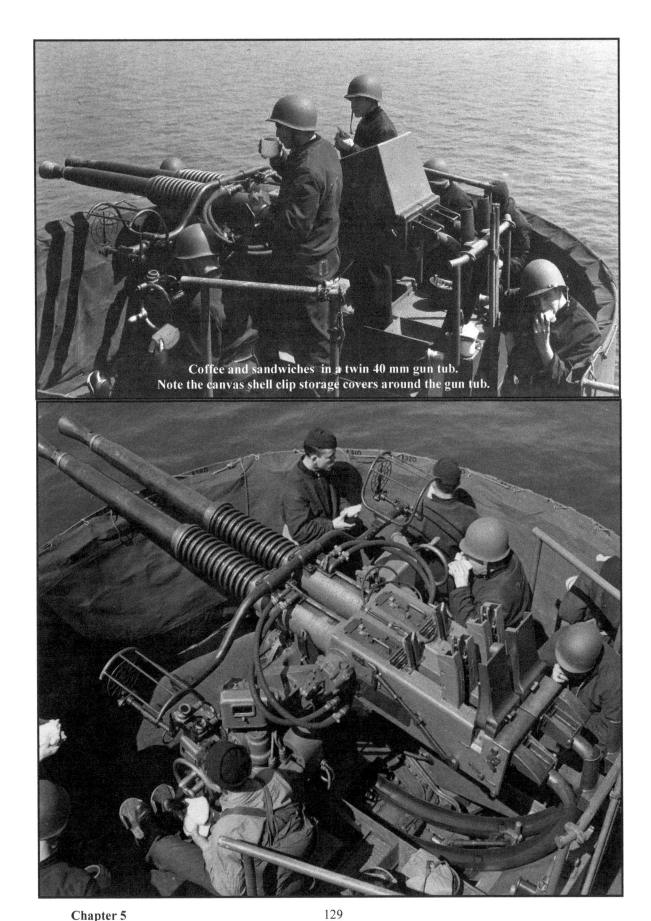

Coffee and sandwiches in a twin 40 mm gun tub.
Note the canvas shell clip storage covers around the gun tub.

Refueling the USS SPENCE on 25 June 1943. This Fletcher class destroyer was destined to fall prey to Typhoon Cobra. On December 18th 1944 she would capsize after a deep roll to port, leaving only 24 survivors. (Photo courtesy of John Doherty)

Friday 25 June 1943   *Underway, en route to San Diego, Calif*

0603 Steaming as before. USS MOBILE commenced gunnery firing practice.

0623 Ceased zigzagging, steadying on course 300°T. Began preparations for refueling destroyers.

0800 Reduced speed to 8 knots as USS SPENCE commenced its approach to port for taking on fuel oil. During the fueling operation they slowly increased speed to 12 knots.

1042 Completed fueling operation, having pumped 72,262 gallons of fuel oil to the SPENCE. As SPENCE moved away, USS THATCHER began her approach to port to take on fuel.

1315 Completed the transfer of 71,092 gallons of fuel oil to the THATCHER.

1518-1538 Launched aircraft for air operations.

1615 Commenced maneuvering to avoid simulated air attack by their own air group.

1807-1847 Recovered aircraft.

1927 Sounded general quarters, securing at 2030.

2200 The ship's Pit Log was discovered to be broken. The Sword Arm needed to be replaced.
          (The Pit Log supplies the ship's speed through the water.)

JG More gunnery practice and flight quarters. Preparing for fueling destroyers at sea. Sight Mexico off starboard beam. JG

Saturday 26 June 1943   *Underway, en route to San Diego, Calif*

0639 Steaming as before. Commenced maneuvering for flight operations.
0742 Completed launching aircraft.
0815 One F6F landed with engine problems.
0854 Commenced maneuvering to thwart simulated air attack.
0940 Commenced recovering aircraft.
1016 A F6F (Bu. No. 8998) landed long catching the last arresting gear cable, striking the barrier. Damage was minor.
1032 Sounded torpedo defense to conduct gunnery burst firing exercises, securing at 1135.
1200 Set clocks back 1 hour to conform to plus 7 time zone.
1300 Commenced gunnery practice, firing on a sleeve towed by the USS MOBILE.
1330 Sighted land bearing 340°T, 72 miles.
1415 Secured from torpedo defense.
1445 Sounded flight quarters to launch aircraft, completing recovery by 1632.
1710 Sounded torpedo defense, securing at 1740.
1915 Commenced zigzagging on base course 304°T, speed 20 knots. At 2000 we were 50 miles west of the tip of Baja California.

Sunday 27 June 1943   *Underway, en route to San Diego, Calif*

0545 Steaming as before. Commenced flight operations.
0915 Completed flight operations.
They steamed north conducting planned exercises, commenced zigzagging on a base course of 330°T from 1138 until 2000, when they changed base course to 339°T.

Monday 28 June 1943   **Moored, NAS North Island, San Diego, Calif.**

Steaming as before. During the morning they commenced flight operations at 1012, and at 1127 underwent a simulated air attack. Afterward, VC-22 flew to NAS North Island. The squadron would utilize their time ashore performing night field carrier landings, night searches and day radar work.
1220 One of the TBFs was damaged when its landing gear collapsed while sitting on the flight deck. AM1c Willard R Brooks was struck by the Avenger as it dropped, suffering a contusion to the right leg.
1306 Completed flight operations.
1523 Commenced zigzagging on base course 068°T.
1532 Sighted Los Coronados Islands, off the starboard quarter bearing 105°T, 17 miles.
1600 Passed the channel entrance buoy to San Diego abeam to port, maneuvering to conform to the channel. At 1732 CV-22 moored starboard side to pier K, North Island, San Diego, California.

DL   On 28 June we entered San Diego Bay and docked alongside North Island. Passing Point Loma lighthouse to port, with the mass of North Island looming ahead to starboard, was a slow, careful process of threading between unmarked buoys separating large menacing anti-submarines nets which were pulled slowly away by special tugs as we made our way north through the channel. No doubt there were artillery emplacements nearby but we couldn't spot them. It was a nervous time.

Soon after we had tied up to North Island and liberty parties had been selected (which this time did include ordnancemen) we scampered down the gangway and, in deference to the great land we had just invaded, many of us knelt down and actually kissed this holy ground. We laughed nervously about this unprecedented action; it was embarrassing, silly, childish. But unforgettable.

Liberty of a few hours in wartime San Diego was no prize. SP's and MP's had the town locked down. The harbor was blacked out. No wide storefront window was bright enough to display its wares.

We wandered aimlessly about like the fools we were. My concern was the whereabouts of my brothers. Ed had already gone through Marine boot camp here. I had no idea where he was; my parents had written that they didn't know. Russ, they wrote, had enlisted in the Corps to follow his brother, but I'd had no word as to whether he was still in Dago (the term we used for the fair city, hated by the natives even more than Frisco was detested by true San Franciscans). I had no way to find out. I did try a Red Cross location, but drew an incredulous look that questioned my sanity at even daring to ask such an unanswerable question. (In truth, Ed was already with Marine Air Group 24 in the South Pacific and Russ was enduring the rigors of a stinking overcrowded troopship on his way to the same area.). **DL**

Tuesday 29 June 1943   Relocated to Destroyer Base, San Diego, Calif.

1605 Moored as before. Got underway to relocate to the Destroyer Base, San Diego, across the bay.
1705 Moored to pier 3, Destroyer Base, San Diego, California.

Friday 2 July 1943   *Underway from San Diego, to San Francisco, Calif.*

1801 Moored as before. Aided by tugs, got underway to clear the berth.
1915 Entered the channel transiting from San Diego Bay into the Pacific.
1941 Departed the channel and turned to 277°T, accompanied by USS SPENCE and USS THATCHER.
1950 Gunnery Department fired 40mm burst practice.
2310 Changed course to 308°T.

JG   *Leave port for speed run to Mare Island, San Francisco California at 1800.* *JG*

DL   *The second day of July saw us underway up the coast for Mare Island, giving us a hint of how rough the sea can be off that coast. Our air group practiced firing at target sleds, expending lots of .50-caliber ammo and creating an impressive popcorn show for sailors watching from the fantail or from the after edge of the flightdeck. For the ordnancemen it was a repetitious, rigorous exercise cleaning and recleaning the guns, reloading emptied ammo wing cans, and occasionally replacing gun barrels because some inattentive pilot had kept his finger too long on the trigger, thus burning away the rifling grooves.*
Yet I didn't realize how valuable the workout would turn out to be. It was all "don't think about it just do it." Again we learned never to let our attention stray from what was going on aft while the planes landed. *DL*

Saturday 3 July 1943   *Moored Navy Yard, Mare Island, Calif.*

0840 Steaming as before. Sighted land bearing 080°T, 20 miles.
1147 Sighted the Farallon Islands bearing 357°T, 17 miles.
1228 Passed within the entrance to the San Francisco Bay channel.
1335 Passed under the Golden Gate Bridge.
1514 Entered Mare Island Strait.
1549 Moored port side to pier 21M, Mare Island Navy Yard.

DL   *Before we entered the Golden Gate our air group flew off to an air station somewhere in central California. We rounded the Farallons to the tinkling sound of a buoy and headed for the fabled bridge thirty miles to the east. The sky was not only overcast but the clouds were a low gray blanket, not unusual, we learned, for this water in the month of July. We slid past the tower of Mile Rock lighthouse to starboard as the channel gradually narrowed and there, dead ahead, was the International Orange spider web of the great bridge, scarcely six years old, looming ever larger as we approached, hanging overhead for a moment as we steamed beneath it. Lime Rock light passed to port as we entered the Bay.*

As with San Diego there were thick anti-sub nets to be pulled away. Heavily armed men on all sorts of small craft watched our arrival like hawks.

Perhaps because Independence was the first CVL to enter San Francisco Bay, the Captain had us assembled in long ranks port and starboard along the flightdeck. Happily, uniform of the day was dress blues. Pea coats would have been appropriate. While July in Wisconsin meant heat and humidity, this wasn't the Fox River leading into Lake Winnebago. This was windy and cool.

No doubt the city paid scant attention to our arrival. Another flattop couldn't have attracted any special notice, even one as ungainly and boxy as the Mighty I.

I couldn't have cared how we looked. I saw only the city piled on the hillsides to the right, the thin sleek skyscrapers lifted upward by the height of the land they were perched upon, slender streets winding their way to unknown but seductive destinations.

And then the city slid silently by until it was on our starboard quarter and fading away--as, I found out, it had a habit of doing. Then another great bridge, under and past, and the Bay narrowed as we steamed east and north, as if the war wouldn't release its firm grip on us just for sight-seeing. And so to our appointment at Mare Island Navy Yard across from Vallejo. Lessons we had learned on our voyage from Cape May demanded that certain modifications to the Class, Carrier Aircraft-Light, had better be made before any of us steamed off for Pearl and beyond. Like everything else so far in her life, Independence was the first to get the treatment.

San Francisco, on my initial visit, proved to be a disappointment. Part of the reason was economic. I was almost broke and most of the rest of my compatriots were at least badly bent. Another part was the effects of the war itself. The city was observing a mandatory brownout. As soon as the sun went down, whatever glitter had given the buildings along Market Street and the narrow canyons of lesser streets leading to the hills beyond a patina of glory and a sheen of majesty, faded quickly into dark shadows unrelieved by sparkling lights. The famed Ferry Building tower was all but blacked out; the bay end of Market Street ended abruptly with a sharp descent into nothingness. Few automobiles moved anywhere, and streetcar headlights didn't deserve the name: they resembled lamps illuminated by glowing candle wicks.
A big part of my discontent was the unexpected weather. It was cold. Dress blues were no match for what our skinny bodies had to endure. I thought I'd freeze.

The long gray Navy buses from Vallejo ("Valley Joe" to sailors) deposited us at the city's transit station south of Market along Mission Street. We wandered up to Market and headed west. Some walked, most hitched a ride on the jammed zero-fare streetcars. Jammed means jammed. Servicemen clung to whatever handholds they could find on either side of the cars, mounted themselves on the lowered steel basket cowcatchers, or somehow retained their precarious perches on the after ends.

At the corner of Market and Ellis or Stockton we struggled our way out of the car and headed for a Maxwell House doughnut shop because its wide interior, while dim, was brighter than any other storefront on the street. And at the counter we found half of the ordnance gang.
We finished our coffee and doughnuts, left a nickel or a dime as a tip, and shoved off. We drifted glumly back to the bus station. By the time we pulled through the gate at Mare Island it was raining lightly. We scattered rapidly and were glad to greet the warmth below decks.

Ensign Porky returned from a three-day leave. He comes back tired and sour-looking and we all wonder if he got enough on the beach to satisfy him. Probably not, for now he's an even greater pain in the ass than before. His ability to dredge up more work for us is boundless. **DL**

8 July 1943   *Moored Navy Yard, Mare Island, Calif.*

Moored port side to pier 21M, Mare Island Navy Yard.

George Leedecke   *I arrived aboard the Independence, my first ship. She sure did look good.* **GL**

These two photos shot off Mare Island California in early July 1943

135

Monday 12 July 1943   *Underway from Mare Island to* **Carquinez Strait**

Moored port side to pier 21M, Mare Island Navy Yard.
2055 Aided by tugs, CV-22 got underway, moving to an anchorage in Carquinez Strait.
2124 Dropped anchor in Carquinez Strait, off Carquinez Light and the breakwater.

DL   *For whatever reason, we departed at night. Three miles, maybe, into Carquinez Strait and then into San Pablo Bay where we dropped anchor for the night. Darken ship was the rule, so every light below decks was red.*   *DL*

Tuesday 13 July 1943   *Underway from* **Carquinez Strait** *to NAS Alameda, Calif.*

Anchored as before in Carquinez Strait.
0800 Weighed anchor and steamed to Naval Air Station Alameda, California.
1034 Moored starboard side to dock, NAS Alameda, California.

DL   *Tuesday the 13th, and with it confirmed rumors that the ship was ready for sea at last. I don't know if my shipmates were ready, but I certainly was. This had been an interlude. So much lay ahead.*
       Reveille was before 0500 and when the sky lightened with the sun obscured there was land piled close aboard on either side and we were standing still. Felt strange. Chilly and gray. The hull strained against the tug of unseen currents. Uniform of the Day was dungarees. Most of us wore black sweaters over our shirts, some had donned black watch caps due to the cold; not for many months would we put them on again. general quarters didn't break off until we got underway slowly down San Pablo Strait about 0800, passing The Brothers to port and then into San Francisco Bay heading for Alameda.
       As we slowly closed the pier and tied portside-to, our planes were waiting in rows, wings folded (except those of the sturdy but deck-clumsy SBD's), propellers shining and motionless, each airplane's crew chief standing proudly alongside its cockpit waiting for the ship's crane to lift it aboard. Big TBF torpeckers and, the spanking new Grumman F6F fighters the tax-payers would soon get to know as Hellcats and every airdale already knew was going to win the war. What a thrill!*
       Next stop, Pearl. *DL*   (* Air Group 22 operated out of NAS, North Island (CASU-5) from 28 June thru 11 July when they were ordered to NAS, Alameda. On the 14th Air Group 22 was ordered again to INDEPENDENCE where they were loaded aboard from the dock.)

Wednesday 14 July 1943   *Underway from NAS, Alameda, Calif. to Pearl Harbor T.H.*

Moored as before. Made all preparations for getting underway.
1128 Underway to Pearl Harbor, T.H.. CV-22 was accompanied by USS BOYD, in accordance with CINCPAC secret dispatch 112357, dated July 1943.
1424 Departed seaward from the channel entrance of San Francisco Bay, course 320°T.
1526 Changed course to 270°T.
1557 Commenced gunnery practice, firing 20mm and 40mm guns, completing the firing at 1705.

Thursday 15 July 1943   **At Sea - *USS INDEPENDENCE Reclassified***

Steaming as before. Today would be a day of air operations.
0604-0625 Launched 7 SBDs and 8 TBFs.
0659-0707 Launched 11 F6Fs.
0723 Launched 1 F6F, 1 SBD and 1 TBF.
0900-0952 Recovered all aircraft.
1557-1608 Resumed air operations catapulting aircraft.
1620-1623 Launched 11 F6Fs.
1753-1845 Recovered all aircraft.
2245 Changed base course to 248°T.

Prior to this date, the INDEPENDENCE class carriers carried a Navy classification of **CV**.
USS INDEPENDENCE was the **CV-22**.
On July 15th, all nine fast light INDEPENDENCE class carriers were reclassified as **CVL's**.
USS INDEPENDENCE became **CVL-22**.

Friday 16 July 1943   *At Sea - En Route to Pearl Harbor*

Steaming as before. Today would be another day of air operations.
0602-0634 Catapulted 7 SBDs and 8 TBFs.
0642-0649 Launched 11 F6Fs.
0846 Commenced recovering aircraft. Upon landing, a F6F (Bu. No. 8989) piloted by Lt. Robert K. Ashford failed to engage an arresting gear cable and struck the barriers. Lt. Ashford was unhurt. All aircraft were back aboard by 0953.
1534 The afternoon flight operations commenced, catapulting 10 F6Fs, 2 SBDs, and 7 TBFs.
1744 Landing back aboard commenced with all aircraft on deck by 1835. At 1746 Lt(jg) Marsh paid his respects to the barrier. The arresting gear cable his F6F Hellcat (Bu. No. 8985) hooked failed to hold. He was unhurt.
2106-2120 The USS BOYD fired star shells during gunnery practice.

DON LABUDDE writes;   *FROM my dad to my brothers, from my dear wife to complete strangers, even from my admired uncle who survived nearly as much sea time as I did as the Exec's yeoman aboard light cruiser Columbia, CL 56, the question has been the same: "Did you ever get seasick?"*

The quick answer has always been, No. But like Daniel Boone's response when asked if he'd ever been lost, he is reputed to have replied, "Not lost. Bewildered."

My first and worst touch of queasiness hit me on the second day out of San Francisco. The sea was rougher than a cob. The ship rolled more than she ever had before. Chow that went down my gullet didn't want to stay down and my whole body ached something awful.

I was with Whitey's rearming crew on the flightdeck when I decided to give up and turn myself into sick bay. I asked his permission to leave. He nodded. I ignored the smirks of the other guys. I had no more than reached the level of the hangar deck when I saw Whitey following me. I stopped. He stopped. He looked real concerned.

"You gonna be all right?"

"I need something," I wheezed. "Maybe an aspirin."

He looked straight into my eyes. (I would have forgotten the incident except for that piercing examination.) "Hold it in," he said.

"Ugh," I moaned.

"Hold it in," he snapped. "We're only two days out. It's gonna get calm and warm tomorrow. We're going southwest. Hold it in."

"Jeez, I dunno."

"We need you topside," he said in his quietly firm voice and left me standing there on my wobbly legs. When he left, he never looked back.

Maybe it was a test. At least I took it that way. I remember swallowing a few times (learning what bile tasted like), forced my legs straight while flexing my knees to ride with the rolling motion of the deck. After a couple of moments I followed Whitey up the outside port ladder back to the flightdeck. My record stood. No seasickness. But it was close.

Our four-day cruise to Pearl Harbor turned into five days and probably taught everyone aboard a few things. It surely made some of the ordnancemen wonder if we had picked the right specialty back in boot. It all was very entertaining. With the sea calm and the air warmed, I caught myself unexpectedly wondering what my mother would think if she could see me now, holding on with a death grip to a shaking airfoil suspended over a most unfriendly sea below. How many of my shipmates, faced with the same challenge, called out "Momma!" in fear and protest, I don't know. I never did, but I suppose I considered it.

At the end of that first full day of learning what this new aircraft would mean for us from now on out, we laid down to the aviation armory and collapsed in exhaustion on the steel deck, dogged the door, and bitched about our fate. Suddenly the door, undogged from outside, opened, and there stood Ensign Porky looking puffed-up and official and announced that tomorrow, July 17, we'd be having our first real rearming drill.

"I want you to do it right," he said trying to look each of us down. "And I ma-mean right! Got that?"

Oh, we got it all right. And away he went.

Saturday 17 July 1943   *At Sea - En Route to Pearl Harbor*

0600-0647 Steaming as before. Catapulted 4 F6Fs and launched 6 SBDs.
0801 Underwent simulated air attack by our air group. All aircraft were back onboard by 0908.
2000 Changed course to 238°T.

DL   *Everything began remarkably well the next morning (the 17th). Welcome sun replaced the two-day overcast after leaving the Golden Gate. The state of the sea was calm. The speed of the soft wind down the deck was muted. The sound of the sea was muffled. The turns into the groove of each plane as it approached were precise. The confident snapping of the landing signal officer's paddles as he waved each chicken aboard were neat. The ship swung about with our single escort destroyer on the starboard quarter with a handsome twenty-five-knot bone in her teeth.*

Well, Ensign Porky's and Lieutenant Harry's ordnancemen failed them from the word Go. We let down V2 Division, the Air Department, ourselves, and, most important, Independence.

I don't know why. Each ordnanceman carried the lovely pride that without us the roaring airplane engines and fine communication gear and skilled pilots and mechanics and metalsmiths were as nothing if the airplane's guns didn't work when called upon, if the bombs and torpedoes didn't exit the bomb bays properly because we hadn't hung them correctly or explode on the target because they'd not been fuzed and armed skillfully. Without our special talents, in fact, the whole aircraft carrier concept as a major weapon of naval warfare was a windy farce.

So, what happened? We thought we knew our jobs. We even knew what not to do. We had done all of this a dozen times. What had been lacking, what stunned us, was the sudden pressure, the close-to-the-war-zone awareness. Those drills had almost been games; this was deadly serious and we knew it and blew it. No one was more surprised than we. Or more embarrassed.

We fumbled the drill into a fiasco that sent Porky into such convulsions of anger and frustration that some of us thought (or hoped) he'd bust a gasket. He didn't, but probably only because Lieutenant Harry saw enough early-on and drew him aside so we could mend our ways without the Ensign's menacing presence.

It was amazing to me how this mustang could allow his professional wisdom and judgment to leach his need to lead, guide, and teach into pure harassment of his troops. We needed a boost, not a blast.

But even with Porky temporarily off to the sidelines (not very far off) we continued our clumsy ways. Rebel's crew down in the bomb magazine did its job so well that we in the rearming crews couldn't get the skid-mounted bombs off the elevator platform and aft to the waiting planes fast enough to clear the skids and send them below again for new loads.

We hung a thousand-pounder GP under each squatting SBD and another in the yawning bay of each TBF in what I naively thought was damn good time but was actually molasses. The length of the flightdeck from bomb elevator aft to where the planes were spotted had never seemed so long. The pipe handles on the bomb skids (carts) had never weighed so much, the little hard-rubber wheels had never turned so reluctantly, my arms had never supported a greater strain and my chest had never come so close to bursting.

I wasn't alone. Tom and Dan and Bob and Sully, First or Second Class men boasting lots of experience, were as clumsy as guys like Phil and me or any of the strikers. Not one of the Chiefs

USS Independence (CVL-22) in San Francisco Bay, Calif., on 15 July 1943, the day her hull number was changed from CV-22 to CVL-22. She has nine SBD scout bombers parked amidships and aft, and nine TBM torpedo planes parked amidships and forward. Official U.S. Navy photo, now in the collection of the National Archives. [80-G-74433]

managed to square things away enough to prove that he deserved his khaki uniform. I'm sure all of us felt the gimlet eyes of the Air Officer (if not the Captain) staring grim-faced down from the bridge as we fumbled like blind and crippled gnomes in some demented factory at the hottest end of Hades.

By noon it was all over. We had done everything the drill called for. We just hadn't done it very well. We averted eyes from each other. The individual plane captains smirked.

The bombs and their arming wires were removed from the shackles and sent back below to Rebel with good riddance. When the elevator hatch cover door had been closed and dogged, a handful of us retreated to the sanctuary of the portside ready rearming room below the flightdeck while a few more jammed into the adjacent head for a pee and a smoke. We felt pretty low. We knew we were better than what we had just displayed. We knew we couldn't be that bad. But it did make you wonder.

Ten minutes or so went by. Suddenly the dogs securing the door flipped to the open position, the door swung wide, and Mister Harry and Ensign Porky squeezed their way in. We sucked in our guts trying to stand at attention. Everybody pulled off his blue-dyed hat. The room stunk with perspiration. Oh-oh., I thought., here it comes: the ass-chewing trip to the woodshed.

Both officers removed their caps. The lieutenant looked into each man's face without blinking. Porky's face displayed molten emotions he had temporarily capped.

"We had a good drill," Mister Harry said with soft determination, a statement we had not expected to hear. "We did make mistakes," he continued. "The timing was a little off. We'll all do better next time. We'll have to. We shall, gentlemen."

Porky wagged his head in instant agreement.

"We ga-gotta drill," he stuttered and to our surprise added, "you fellahs can do it."

Whitey spoke up, nodding to Porky but turning to Mister Harry: "We know we can, sir. Thank you, sir."

"We'd like some coffee," said the lieutenant. "Can we get a cup in the armory?"

"You bet," Phil piped up.

"Yes, sir," Tom exclaimed with a glare at Phil's temerity.

The two officers replaced their caps, spun on their heels, and departed without redogging the door-- thank heavens. It was stifling and the sweat stink was awful.

That was all. I don't remember that we said anything. We learned later that the lieutenant and the ensign had laid down to the armory, spoke to a few more downcast guys, and left just as quickly after giving a lift to their spirits.

But not many hours had gone by before we heard that their performance before the Chiefs in a separate, private meeting had been anything but cordial. More than one asshole had been reamed, in language no one had suspected this stock broker Reserve Lieutenant knew. The ensign hadn't opened his mouth. And within a day or two after docking at Pearl we watched a couple of the more inept Chiefs leave the ship for the beach: the ultimate downer for a true seaman.

Well, that was that. But it was instructive. A drill is both practice and training, a seeking for perfection. We really didn't know everything. How many of our lives it may even have saved in the long run is impossible to say. Soft-spoken Lieutenant Harry showed us smarts we hadn't suspected; he earned our respect and never lost it. Even Ensign Porky seemed subdued. It wasn't in his make-up to stay down very long, of course, and he didn't; but perhaps he too had learned something he wasn't apt to forget. In fact, we all did.   ***DL***

Sunday 18 July 1943   *At Sea - En Route to Pearl Harbor*

0534-0548 Steaming as before. Launched 7 SBDs and 6 TBFs.

0548 Observed flashing light off the starboard beam. USS BOYD investigated, reporting back the light was from a flare dropped by one of CVL-22's aircraft.

0627-0636 Launched 2 TBFs and 9 F6Fs.

0715 Air group simulated an air attack.

0735-0833 Recovered all our aircraft.

1404-1406 Catapulted 3 TBFs.
1425 USS BOYD commenced fueling from CVL-22, completing taking on fuel at 1633.
1645-1648 Recovered all aircraft.

Monday 19 July 1943   *At Sea - En Route to Pearl Harbor*

0915 Steaming as before. Gunnery Department commenced burst firing 20mm and 40mm guns.
1005 Gunnery Department completed its exercise.
1459-1503 Catapulted 2 TBFs.
1749-1753 Recovered our 2 TBFs. At 2103 they changed base course to 233°T.

Tuesday 20 July 1943   *USS HALFORD joins up*

0304-0315 Steaming as before. Catapulted 6 TBFs.
0320-0330 Launched 3 TBFs and 9 SBDs.
0356-0420 Launched 9 F6Fs.
0800 USS HALFORD joined the formation.
1034 Sighted Molokai bearing 205°T, distance 30 miles.
1342 Commenced gunnery practice, completing firing at 1520.
1538 USS HALFORD catapulted 1 aircraft. (The HALFORD, DD-480, is one of 3 FLETCHER Class destroyers modified with a catapult / tracks and crane to launch a plane, as a trial to ascertain the feasibility of putting a scout plane on destroyers. The float plane would land in the water and be hoisted back onboard. The catapult & crane were removed when she entered the yards in October of 1943 and she was reconverted to the FLETCHER Class Configuration. The perceived need disappeared as more carriers became available.)
1540 Escorts commenced firing 5" guns for surface firing practice.
1626-1634 Launched 9 F6Fs.
1710 The air group commenced a simulated air attack on Pearl Harbor, then proceeded to Luke Field on Ford Island.
1727 Commenced maneuvering to approach the channel entrance to Pearl Harbor.
1807 Entered the swept channel to Pearl Harbor.
1912 CVL-22 moored with her starboard side to pier F-10, Ford Island, Pearl Harbor, T.H

GL 7/20-24/43 Arrived in Pearl Harbor. Ship made some gunnery runs outside the harbor. We have some good shooting gun crews. Did better than the other ships. GL

JG Sighted Hawaiian Islands at 0830. Diamond Head a pretty sight. Moored to dock at Island of Oahu at 1900 Pearl Harbor. Tied up near sunken wreckage of Battleship Utah, sunk December 7th. JG

RC Arrived in Pearl Harbor. We were in & out of Pearl Harbor training squadron till August 22nd. RC

DL   Landfall on Oahu came late Tuesday morning, 20 July. Reveille had been at 0145, Flight Quarters an hour and a half later. We launched the whole deckload for a mock attack on Pearl, after which the planes were to fly to ground stations on Maui at sunup. The morning darkness was warm and soft. Pale cold blue bursts of exhaust flame spurting from the nacelles as the engines roared into life and the planes swept down the deck were like gemstones fading rapidly with height and distance. A beautiful sight.

*   We secured from Quarters shortly after the launch, went below to the third deck for breakfast, responded to morning GQ, stood around twiddling our thumbs until dismissed, and did routine chores. I recall a suppressed air of excitement at the thought of finally getting to see Pearl Harbor with our own eyes, to find out what this storied anchorage really looked like.*

*   It took half the day before we found out. Whether we circled the entire island chain is an open*

Maintenance crews work hard to keep the planes airworthy, on the flight deck - July 1943

question. It just seemed that way. After sunrise, for hour after hour, there were mounded shadows of land on the horizon, but they remained teasingly far-off. Every one that came into view vanished but was soon replaced by another as we kept steaming relentlessly along. The naked flightdeck became a platform for off-duty swabbies strolling forward to peer ahead. At last the shadows became darker, we could see hints of green foliage. All these islands were mountains, of course, but some stuck taller out of the sea than others. Most of us knew Oahu was not one of the larger mounds, so it became a guessing game as to which one it would be. We envied the navigator, the quartermasters, all those intellectual guys who had to know where we were exactly. Of course they didn't tell us. It was well after we had chowed down at noon that we noticed one mound getting darker and assuming a more solid shape as we approached. Suddenly the bugle call and clanging gong of general quarters confirmed that this was it. Everybody hopped to his duty station with unusual alacrity.

Unfamiliar planes buzzed down out of nowhere, looking us over carefully. (Surely they knew we were coming, didn't they? That we are friends?) Some Army P-40 fighters even dived at us, clearing the deck at great speed but not by many feet of altitude. Our gunnery officer had his men tracking them as they approached, following through till they disappeared. A big PBY patrol plane examined us from a near distance, wagged its long wings at last in a friendly fashion (as if it had consulted with someone in authority to make sure we were OK) and flew away. Small patrol boats, scattered higgledy-piggledy, popped up all over the place, officers and lookouts scanning us with glasses bow to stern.

Ahead were two mighty mountain ranges. I knew them to be Waianae to the northwest, and Koolau in the distance dead ahead.

The ship slowly approached the channel, everybody marveling at the myriad colors of the water, and then the channel narrowed, the antisubmarine nets were pulled apart, and at long last we were there!

(Twenty-three years after the war I reentered Pearl for the first time as a civilian, with Dorothy, aboard a sight-seeing tour boat. This was at a time when Navy still demanded that all cameras be stowed in a locked storage box while within the confines of the harbor, a requirement silly and annoying. As the crowded boat putt-putted up the channel past Hospital Point, the navy yard, and the submarine base, there was scarcely a ship or a man to be seen. The boat paused for a long moment close aboard the long white structure recently erected above and athwart what was left of Arizona.

Our tour did not allow us to climb the steps to the monument, and for that I was grateful. We continued north and west around Ford Island to the left past sunken and abandoned Utah, slid by Fox 10, which was the mooring immediately aft of Utah where Independence had first docked in 1943, past the old Pan AM Airways base at Pearl City on the right where the big Boeing 314 flying boats had begun the weekly 21-hour flight east to San Francisco, and then continued back out to sea the way we had entered. Within minutes we were headed back to Honolulu, a city which had transformed itself in response to the invasion of postwar tourists.

I anxiously retrieved my camera from a smiling Hawaiian who insisted on calling me "Sir", no doubt in recognition of my age, and sat down again without saying anything. The slippage of time had hit me hard. Dorothy took my hand, letting me stew, I suppose, in whatever juice she may have thought was souring my memory. But there was no sourness and the memory, if bittersweet, was mainly good. What haunted me had been the harbor's unexpected emptiness. Where, oh where had all the virile young sailors and the mighty warships gone...?)

Ancient target ship Utah, which had turned turtle when she'd taken a Long Lance fish during the raid on Pearl, was still squatting at her mooring nineteen months later, her naked brown bottom upended for every curious sailor to gaze upon. Independence slowly approached Fox 10 and was tied to the short new aircraft carrier dock that had since been erected. A small brass band on the dock greeted us with the evocative strains of "Aloha". What really caught our attention, though, was a number of grass-skirted girls in sandals swaying to the music, their arms waving seductively, small flowers in their hair, their necks and chests embroidered with garlands we later learned were called leis. We were enchanted. All this just for us? No other port had offered such a welcome.

A few ordnancemen hung around on the flightdeck long past sunset. Without airplanes aboard most airdales had a vacation. We knew it wouldn't last, but that first evening in Pearl was a delight. Magnificent scenery, darkening quickly as the sun lost its glow, a threatening line of clouds from the Koolau Range seeming to hesitate as if on a signal before blanketing the harbor and then backing-off: a diurnal manifestation.

(I knew that fact from friend Judd's and my avid reading of Alec Hudson's short stories about prewar Pearl and Hawaii in the Saturday Evening Post. I had no way to know that "Hudson" was a pen name and that at this very moment the author was in naval intelligence just across the way.)

The breeze was warm and soft. Airplane engine noise from neighboring Ford Island split the silence, disturbing the wondrous scene; yet the noise was so much a part of our lives we hardly noticed it. There were few lights anywhere. The ship was darkened below decks same as if at sea. We were excited to be here. Now to get ashore and see it all!

Our liberty trips to the beach, which commenced the next day, soon told me I'd never be able to see everything. Maybe I expected too much. I wasn't disappointed, just sort of let down because the whole of it was unattainable and I had to acknowledge the fact. It was all so exciting, such a splendid dream for this country boy from Wisconsin.

Phil and I and Rebel and Charlie were included in the first group from V2 Division. Uniform of the Day was white undress uniforms, spit-shined shoes and carefully tied neckerchief. White caps were squared sea-going style. Phil had doused himself so generously with cologne that nobody wanted to sit beside him.

Our trip to the beach began by stepping into a bobbing yard boat tied to the dock. The ride took about fifty of us out into the loch and around the north end of Ford Island. As the boat came abreast the rusting wreckage of battleship Arizona, our coxwain surprised us by uncovering and slowing the boat to give us a moment to tune into the solemnity of the scene. All of us had seen the newsreel shots of her magazine exploding in a horrendous flash of flame and fire on that Sunday morning--which still seemed as if it had happened yesterday. Now, as we passed slowly by, I wondered what would come of her, if she would ever be salvaged or her remains put to other work. How long, in fact, would she even be remembered?

As we resumed our trip to the boat landing at the navy yard, we saw two other grim items of 7 December interest: the black oil scum still coating the rocks and boulders that lined Ford Island, and the great long hull of overturned battleship Oklahoma, like Utah holed by torpedoes and stuck in the mud. But she was so huge she couldn't be ignored like Utah; her hulk had to be removed just to clear passage to the channel. Two days after the attack, work had begun. We saw it in its final stages. Naval and civilian salvors were even then slowly bringing her back to an even keel, a myriad array of tall headframes supporting 3-inch cables anchored to embedded concrete forms on the island. So, even a year and a half since that Day of Infamy, the harbor, the navy yard, Ford Island, all still showed deep scars. We were suitably impressed and awed. But already as our craft continued toward the boat landing, we were treated to a sign of hope and restored strength: U.S.S. Essex **, name-ship of her class of new fleet aircraft carriers, was docked at Ten-Ten pier, opposite from Independence (name-ship of her class) on the other side of Ford. The two of us would begin to make the bastards pay for all this!

Liberty expired at 1800. We'd been warned that that meant the quarterdeck, not the boat landing. There were three ways to get into Honolulu (or four, if you wanted to walk): jitney bus, taxi, or a rattling little narrow-gauge railroad with a spur running between base and city. We just took it for granted that it belonged to one of the plantations supplying pineapple juice to the outdoor fountains (which we never found) that were reputed to be all over Honolulu. We happened to be in time for the departure schedule, so we ordnancemen chose it. The cars were uncomfortably small, hot, with sticky seats. Smoke from the tiny engine came through the open windows and it was so noisy no one tried to talk. The whole shebang moved at such a leisurely pace it made the elderly R F & P that Phil and I rode between Washington and Richmond seem up-to-date and luxurious. I thought it was wonderful.

** Author's note: The USS ESSEX was commissioned less than eight months ago … on 31 December 1942.

Chapter 5   144

Come to think of it, we never did get into downtown on this first visit, although we came close. After leaving the train and slapping the dust and dirt out of our clothing, we wandered willy-nilly not too far from the harbor, up one street and down another, gawking like the malihinis we were. The buildings looked different from any in Oshkosh. Phil's comment said it all: "Hey, this is an old town." Stores, shops, what might have been staircase openings to living quarters were two-storied, small, usually white or painted a dull pastel color. Big broad awnings, some of them spanning an entire block. Most had corrugated tin sheets shielding the stucco siding. The street names we first came across were ordinary: Hotel Street, River Street next to a canal of some sort with a splendid view of distant mountains. One street boasted a longer name, Beretania, that crossed the other two. All were narrow. Auto traffic was light; cars had blackout shields mounted over their headlights. Civilian pedestrians were few. Yet every street, every block, swarmed and hummed and jostled with human activity. The whole scene was tropical, exotic, like no other place we were familiar with. **DL**

Photos of Waikiki Beach. Below Diamond Head (Courtesy of John Doherty)

Wednesday 21 July 1943   *Moored Ford Island, Pearl Harbor, T.H.*

0800 Moored as before. Mustered crew at quarters.
1100 Made daily inspection of the magazines. Opened doors and scuttles to reduce temperatures on magazines above 90°. (They would have to also do this on Friday the 23rd.)
2000 **Arthur W. Radford** this day assumed duties as COMCARDIV 11 in USS INDEPENDENCE.

On this date, VF-22 was transferred to a shore based status at NAS Ford Island, Oahu, T.H. On 4 August VF-22 will be transferred to NAS Puunene, Maui, T.H. VF-22 would be reassigned to sister CVL, USS BELLEAU WOOD on 22 August for the Baker Island raid. VF-22 transferred back to the USS INDEPENDENCE on 29 September 1943 on time for the Wake Island raid.

Saturday 24 July 1943   *Moored Ford Island, Pearl Harbor, T.H.*

0832 Moored as before. Inspection party boarded to conduct an annual military inspection of the ship.
0848-1022 Conducted personnel inspection.

While focus remains on the USS INDEPENDENCE as she about to be immersed in the massive Pacific War, the action has been hot and deadly elsewhere. To touch on the events ever so lightly:

From 7 August 1942 when U.S. troops first landed, through February 1943 when the Japanese finally succumbed to the weight and determination of the U.S. invasion (evacuating the remainder of their withering forces), **Guadalcanal was finally secured in Solomon Island chain.**
Japan was deprived of their southern seaward drive to capture Port Moresby.

Guadalcanal was viewed as a holding action, to contain the further movement south by Japan, but also served as a solid starting point with its airfield (Henderson Field) to begin the U.S. offensive north.

The US goal was to move north and take Rabaul. The two pronged plan to capture Rabaul, initially starting out as **"Elkton III"**, evolved into **"Operation Cartwheel"**.
On the pathway to Rabaul, McArthur's forces would make landings near Lae (New Guinea) and on Rendova, Kiriwina and Woodlark Islands as they progressed north along New Guinea, then on to New Georgia to capture Munda Airfield.
Halsey (under general directives from McArthur) was tasked to move up the Solomon's.

But war plans usually have unexpected occurrences to muddle the neat, tidy ink & paper. A series of naval surface battles ensued as Halsey's forces advanced north: (see map on following page)

5 - 6 July 1943 The Battle of Kula Gulf   Action was already hot when destroyer USS STRONG was lost after a torpedo attack by Japanese destroyers led by IJN's NIIZUKI. The death toll rose aboard the STRONG as Japanese shore battery shells hit, and while settling, her depth charges went off. Roughly 46 men were lost. STRONG was supporting US landings off Vila.
A night surface action erupted (off Kolombangara) in Kula Gulf between U.S. Task Group 36.1 with 3 light cruisers and 4 destroyers intercepting a Japanese "Tokyo Express" run of 10 destroyers bringing combat troops down "The Slot". USS HELENA (CL-50) was sunk with 168 killed. Japan lost 2 destroyers (NIIZUKI sunk & NAGATSUKI ran aground), with 324 killed.

12 - 13 July   The Battle of Kolombangara   In another night surface action; destroyer USS GWIN was scuttled and light cruisers USS HONOLULU, USS ST. LOUIS and HMNZS LEANDER (Royal New Zealand Navy) were severely damaged with Allied losses of 89 killed as the Japanese torpedoes found their targets. The Japanese lost light cruiser JINTSU and suffered 482 killed. Their "Tokyo Express" run succeeded in landing roughly 1,200 men at Vila.

6 - 7 August   The Battle of Vella Gulf   The Imperial Japanese Navy sent another "Tokyo Express" run, still trying to reinforce the contested airfield at Munda by dropping troops and supplies at the port of Vila under cover of night (the U.S. claimed the air by day). The IJN lost destroyers ARASHI, HAGIKAZE and KAWAKAZE.
US destroyer Task Group 31.2 consisting of six DDs utilized night eyes (radar) to pounce. The fourth Japanese DD (SHIGURE) escaped in the dark. Japanese losses were heavy with roughly 1,210 listed as killed. US losses - None.

These naval surface actions represent a distinct reversal of the rolls between Japan and the U.S. with the beginnings of both the U.S. Naval offensive, and Japan's unrecoverable defensive collapse toward its very shores.

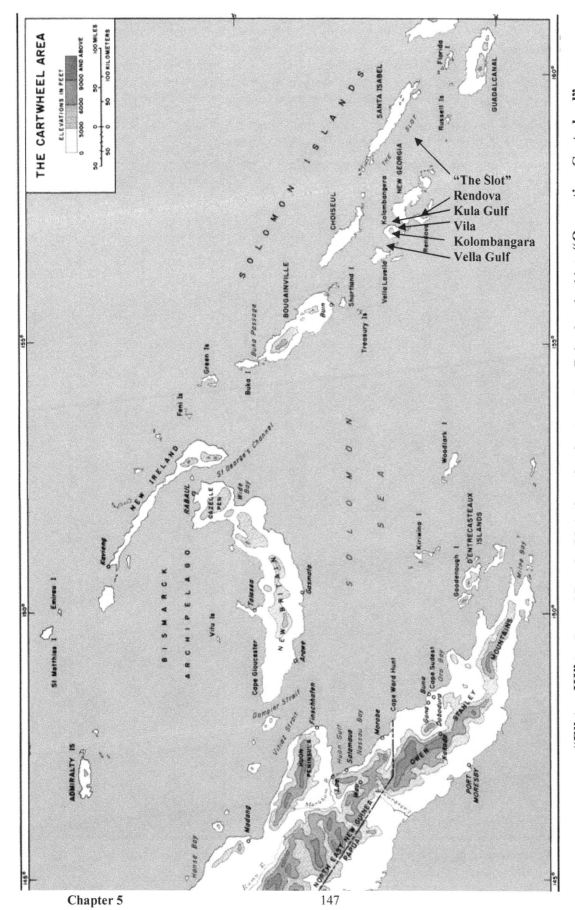

THE CARTWHEEL AREA

"The Slot"
Rendova
Kula Gulf
Vila
Kolombangara
Vella Gulf

Originally conceived as "Elkton III" by General Douglas McArthur, the plan to capture Rabaul evolved into "Operation Cartwheel".
In a two pronged effort, McArthur's forces would move north, up along the east coastal area of New Guinea, and Halsey's forces would move from
Guadalcanal north thru the Solomon Island chain.   Plans in wartime are just that - "Plans"!   Rabaul would later be isolated and bypassed.

Chapter 5   147

Still **"feeling out the waters"**, the U.S. Navy was also about to strengthen the offensive with its rapidly expanding carrier fleet. To practice for tough well hardened targets of the newly forming Fast Carrier Task Groups (as INDEPENDENCE Class and the new ESSEX Class carriers were joining the fleet), the Admirals would first utilize rapid hard hitting surprise raids to gain real exposure and experience in the development of doctrine and procedures for the tougher operations that would lay ahead.

The early Fast Carrier "learning" raids would also to serve to keep IJN planners off balance, attempting to guess where in the vast Pacific, Nimitz's Admirals would strike next.

Weighing anchor to go to war.   Anchor chain being hosed off with fresh water as it is hoisted by the capstan to then descend into the chain locker.

6
Training for War - Enter VF-6

26 July to 21 August   *Overview*

The INDEPENDENCE Class of carrier was new to the Pacific Fleet, and would begin conducting training exercises out of Pearl Harbor (in accordance with ComCarDiv 11 Op Order 1-43). During this time, the best mix of aircraft was evolving. The 9 Douglas SBD Dauntless' of VC-22 were eventually removed from the ship, and pilots of VF-6 reported aboard flying F6Fs, with Lt. Comdr. Edward Henry (Butch) O'Hare, commanding.

Larger issues were also in a state of evolution. The Navy was strategizing on the best use and mix of its available compliment of carriers for the upcoming offensive operations against Japan.

Monday 26 July 1943   *Out to Sea - Training Exercises*

0818 Moored as before. Underway, taking departure of the channel at 0925.
0936 Formed cruising disposition 5-LS accompanied by USS DASHIELL, USS MCKEE and USS TERRY. Conducted gunnery exercises from 1043 thru 1133, and again from 1242 thru 1455.
1100 Made daily inspection of the magazines. Opened doors and scuttles to reduce temperatures on magazines above 90°.
1626 Underwent simulated air attack.
1717-1735 Recovered 7 TBFs.
1926-1928 Recovered 2 TBFs.

DL   At 0800 the ship went out for a couple of days' gunnery practice and flight operations. Planes came aboard at 1630 after their guns had shot up all the available towed targets, and we ordnancemen were busy from then on.

Now came the Word, and we spent the night burdened with the knowledge that the next day we would undergo another rearming drill. The previous disaster still stuck in our craws. This one commenced differently. Orders were passed quietly, sternly, decisively. No Chief's face cracked a smile. Ensign Porky was grim. Lieutenant Harry was said to have personally inspected every space from the bomb mag to the flightdeck rearming rooms to the armory's steel-wool polished deck. No one heard him mouth a complaint or a word of encouragement. We were on our own. If we hadn't grown up since the last fiasco, we wouldn't get another chance.

This time, we did it like clockwork. The leaders--Tom, Sully, Bill, Dan, Bob, Whitey, a new guy whose initials B.C. were the only name we were to know him by and was already striking for Chief-- worked like slaves and drew every lesser man after them. Everything meshed no matter how tight the flight schedule. When a striker wasn't available to haul ammo cans, Dan showed up lugging four and sometimes six full ones. Down below, Rebel was said to have driven his crew so hard his men slipped and slopped in their own sweat. Bombs appeared on the elevator at a steady clip. We flopped to the deck as the planes moved over us to their take-off position, straining against the stiff relative wind that made flight possible and our leg muscles into hard lumps. We jumped with relief and exhaustion into the port catwalk, watching with critical eyes as each plane struggled into the air for another gunnery run. When they returned an hour later, we reversed the whole drill.
We settled down finally with a sigh of relief when two-blocked Fox whistled into its slot in flagbags and flight quarters came to an end. We had done it!

This time, however, even as we rejoiced, I noticed a change that was less than subtle. It was deliberate. Neither Porky nor Harry offered pats on the back. Nor was there, so I heard, no repeat visit to the aviation armory for coffee; nor did any CPO get his ass chewed or lose his khaki uniform. We were big boys who'd come of age and were going to be commanded that way from now on. Do it or lose your stripes! **DL**

Tuesday 27 July 1943

0600-0621 Steaming as before. Catapulted 2 TBFs and launched 6 TBFs and 8 SBDs.
0731-0735 Launched 8 F6Fs. At 0748 the ship underwent simulated air attacks.
0800-0854 Recovered all aircraft.
1015-1156 & 1300-1403 Gunnery Department conducted firing exercises.
1501-1624 Launched 8 SBDs and catapulted 9 TBFs and 9 F6Fs.
1731-1926 Recovered all aircraft.
2155-2201 Escort vessels conducted night gunnery firing practice.

Wednesday 28 July 1943

0601-0700 Steaming as before. Launched 9 TBFs, 4 SBDs and 9 F6Fs.
0740 Underwent simulated air attack.
0842-0921 Recovered all aircraft.
1014-1130 Gunnery Department conducted firing exercises.
1159-1248 Catapulted 9 F6Fs and 9 TBMs. Launched 8 SBDs. VC-22 flew out to operate out of Puunene Air Field on the island of Maui. Living conditions were described as very poor as they worked on tactics with VF-22 and practiced torpedo and glide bombing. VC-22 rejoined CVL-22 on 22 August.
1248 Entered the swept channel to enter Pearl Harbor.
1447 The Mighty-I moored starboard side to pier F-10, Ford Island, Pearl Harbor.

Wednesday 4 August 1943   *Fighting Squadron Six comes onboard*

0800 Moored as before, starboard side to pier F-10, Ford Island, Pearl Harbor. Held quarters for muster.
0915 **Officers from Fighting Squadron Six** commenced reporting aboard for temporary duty aboard USS INDEPENDENCE.
0930 Daily inspection of the magazines. Finding temperatures above 90°, opened all doors and scuttles.
0943 An aviation tractor plunged over the bow of the flight deck, down to the forecastle, continuing on into the water. During the accident, AMM3c William J. Zoeller was knocked from the flight deck to the forecastle deck, receiving "extreme multiple injuries". AMM1c John D. Ivey was driving the tractor as it took its plunge from the flight deck and he too went into the water. Watching the action, AMM1c Charles P. Boyer and S2c James Strange dove from the flight deck into the bay and assisted in the rescue of Ivey. At 0950 Ivey was pulled from the water with a fractured right arm.
1030 **Enlisted men from Fighting Squadron Six** commenced reporting aboard for temporary duty aboard USS INDEPENDENCE.
1115 Both John Ivey and William Zoeller were transferred off the ship for further medical treatment.

Fighting Squadron Six on this day began reporting aboard the ship. The squadron evolved out of VF-3, which had been reformed at NAS San Diego, California, with 36 new F6F-3 Hellcats, and 54 pilots. The squadrons Commanding Officer (and first Navy Ace) was Lt. Comdr. Edward *("Butch")* H. O'Hare and the Executive Officer was Lt. George *("Bull")* C. Bullard.
On 15 June 1943, VF-3 had departed stateside for Hawaii on CVE USS PRINCE WILLIAM with 48 pilots and 36 Hellcats. On 23 June 1943, VF-3 arrived at NAS Puunene, Maui, Hawaii (off Maalaea Bay, to later become Maui Airport, then a drag strip) and began training operations. The navy would utilize VF-3 as a talent pool, striping off numbers of its original aviators to join or form other squadrons. VF-3 was officially re-designated VF-6 on 15 July 1943.
(Divisions of Fighting Six would operate off USS INDEPENDENCE and her sister CVLs, USS BELLEAU WOOD, USS COWPENS, and USS PRINCETON thru the end of November, 1943).

Thursday 5 August 1943   *Put out to Sea - Training Exercises*

Moored as before. Made all preparations for getting underway.

0758 Got underway for training exercises.

0915 Forming Task Group 59.15.2 with USS INDEPENDENCE as guide and OTC, she steamed in cruising disposition 5-LS with the DD screen, USS FULLAM and USS TERRY.

1005-1058 Gunnery Department conducted firing practice exercises.

1116-1149 Recovered 12 VF-6 F6F Hellcats.

1205-1221 Recovered 11 F6F Hellcats.

1401-1412 Launched 15 planes.

1422-1439 Recovered 15 Aircraft.

1506 Underwent simulated air attack.

1515-1529 Launched 15 planes.

1536 Commenced recovering aircraft.

1552 F6F (Bu. No. 4877) broke a landing gear upon landing, no injuries.

1607 "Completed landing 26 F6Fs". (CVL-22 War Diary)

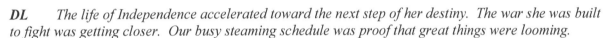

Fighting Squadron Six Insignia

1658-1711 Launched 19 aircraft.

1716-1739 Recovered 19 aircraft.

1815-1824 Recovered 6 aircraft.

1856 Joined up with Task Group 59.15.1 (USS ESSEX, USS DASHIELL, USS MCKEE and USS SCHROEDER), forming cruising disposition 5-LS. COMCARDIV 2 in ESSEX assumed OTC and guide.

DL   The life of Independence accelerated toward the next step of her destiny. The war she was built to fight was getting closer. Our busy steaming schedule was proof that great things were looming.

We had gone to sea to pick up an air group new to us that had been sitting unemployed on a Navy field on Maui. Its ground support personnel had already come aboard.

Thirty-six brand new F6F fighters came in booming that morning, sweeping past to starboard, making a swing to the left and left again downwind, turning finally into the groove for landing--led by the almost legendary LCDR Edward Henry "Butch" O'Hare of Lady Lex and Enterprise fame.

O'Hare's was first plane down. The grapevine had carried rumors of his arrival the day before; our Air Officer confirmed them. Every sailor aboard without duties elsewhere probably was lurking in unauthorized places in the catwalks to watch him come aboard. No other fighter pilot in the Navy bore a name recognized by more flattop seamen than he did. Scarcely twelve months ago most had been undergoing the rigors of boot camp. Many who panted with hope to serve aboard an aircraft carrier, as I did, had got the idea from reading about his exploits in early 1942 while flying off doomed CV-2 Lexington as well as war-battered CV-6 Enterprise.

As closed-mouthed as Navy had to be in those desperate days, he helped give it, and the nation, something to cheer about. His award of the Medal of Honor by President Roosevelt for defending Lady Lex by single-handedly shooting down five Japanese planes and damaging another was front page news for days. Later, when my friend Judd and I pored over the black headlines in the Oshkosh Daily Northwestern of Lexington's sinking at Coral Sea in May that year, our resolve to become carrier sailors was a patriotic urge for revenge we took into the recruiting office thirteen months later. Most critical of all the men watching O'Hare's plane approach were the airdales. We knew this wasn't just another pilot coming aboard, but we wanted to see him prove it. He did.

Landing gear seemed to just touch the deck, tailhook caught and held the correct cable, and the plane quickly taxied forward past the lowered barriers and screeched to an abrupt stop. The way he simply jumped from cockpit to deck delighted his wiseacre audience and won its regard. Here was a man who clearly knew his business. He was big; his cockpit must have been a closet. He waved a casual half-salute with his gloved right hand; the left hand and arm clutched the plotting board. Bareheaded, he strode quickly into the island and half a minute later appeared on the bridge with the

Captain and the Air Officer to observe the rest of his group come in. Arthur Radford, our resident rear admiral, also, looked on. It was an honor for Independence to have Butch and his people aboard.

His pilots were experienced and skilled. But like all such, some made occasional eggs-on-the-face mistakes. **DL**

Friday 6 August 1943   *At Sea - Training Exercises*

During this day the INDEPENDENCE Air Group would be tasked to try to intercept simulated raids flown against the Task Group to determine if a CVL could handle defensive CAP requirements, while the larger ESSEX Class carriers operating with her could be freed for purely offensive strike missions. It would be determined that CVL-22 could not fend off all the incoming raids unaided. Lesions learned during this period of time helped to mold naval doctrine on the utilization of light fast carrier operations as her sister CVLs were entering the fleet.

0611-0620 Steaming as before. Launched 8 aircraft.
0837-0850 Recovered 8 aircraft.
0952-1002 Launched 16 aircraft.
1015 Recovered 1 aircraft.
1016 Underwent simulated air attack.
1039-1041 Launched 4 aircraft.
1046-1112 Recovered 23 aircraft.
1301-1303 Launched 4 aircraft.
1313-1316 Recovered 4 aircraft.
1456-1502 Launched 9 aircraft.
1527 Underwent simulated air attack.
1543-1544 Launched 4 aircraft.
1547-1605 Recovered 21 aircraft.
1728-1733 Launched 8 aircraft.
1737-1741 Recovered 4 aircraft.
1939-1948 Recovered 5 aircraft.

Photo: Courtesy of Philip H. Torrey III

**Lt. Comdr. Philip H. Torrey, Jr.
CO of VF 22**

3 aircraft were still aloft. The ship was operating in less than ideal conditions with scattered rain squalls and nightfall upon them. The pilots had not yet fully trained for night carrier landings. The decision was made to land one aircraft on the larger USS ESSEX and send the other two to the beach.
2016 One of the aircraft, still aloft, landed onboard the USS ESSEX. The remaining two VF-6 pilots were directed to return to land on the islands. Ensign Robert B. (*Bob*) Locker landed his F6F safely at Hilo. They had become separated and Ensign Henry (*Hank*) T. Landry, low on fuel was forced to land off airport. He received injuries when his Hellcat flipped inverted on landing on Hilo.

Saturday 7 August 1943   *At Sea - Training Exercises*

0703-0709 Steaming as before. Catapulted 4 aircraft.
0759-0807 Catapulted 8 aircraft.
0815-0818 Launched 5 aircraft.
0837-0841 Launched 8 aircraft.
0947 Underwent simulated air attack.
1011-1021 Recovered 8 aircraft.
1123-1124 Catapulted 2 aircraft.
1200-1205 Launched 9 aircraft.
1248-1351 Gunnery Department conducted firing exercises.
1505 Steamed into the swept channel entrance to Pearl Harbor.
1549 Moored with our starboard side to pier F-10, Ford Island, Pearl Harbor, T.H.

Monday 9 August 1943

Today sister carrier, CVL-23, the USS PRINCETON arrived in Pearl Harbor.

DL   CLANG! CLANG! CLANG! went the General Alarm, followed immediately by the quick-step notes of the bugle sounding general quarters over the PA system.

On this morning it jarred me into instant reaction, cementing itself into my memory so that I never forgot it again. Blaring earlier than regular morning reveille in port, it was unexpected. The notes seemed to warble with anxiety. Nobody could forget that this was Pearl Harbor. We moved, leaping out of our sacks, scrambling into dungaree pants, shirt and shoes, and rushed out of the compartment up or down ladders topside or below decks to our battle stations. Mine had been changed to the flightdeck; I'd been assigned to Sully's rearming crew, which to me meant only one thing--I'd be able to see whatever happened! What I saw was sudden death.

We knew that new carriers were coming into Pearl this morning. Their air groups were to make mock attacks on the base. What we didn't know was when these would begin.

Traditional 0800 quarters had been delayed. Tension triggered by that early GQ. even though it was false, remained. All gun mounts were manned and ready. The Captain was visible on the bridge chatting with his staff; a few officers scanned the geography through large field glasses.

Essex was across Ford Island from us. Yorktown had just steamed slowly past her on her way to the channel for a day of gunnery practice at sea.

Suddenly the sky was full of diving planes. They seemed to come from nowhere. Of course we knew they were ours, but even so we received an indelible hint of what it must have been like to the thunderstruck sailors manning those violated ships on that Sunday morning nineteen months ago. The demonstration was stunning. Dive bombers, fighters, torpeckers diving, swooping, climbing--a growling, swarming ballet sparked with flashes of sunlight glancing off wing and fuselage.

Someone stood beside me on the starboard side forward of the island structure.

"Hey!" he yelled and pointed across the harbor at a single plane just above the navy yard.

A TBF with open bomb bay doors was making a rather sharp glide-bombing run at Essex. As we watched, the airplane's angle of attack increased and before I could gulp the plane pitched over onto its back and flew straight into the ground. A flash of bright orange flame burst upward followed instantly by a long plume of oily black smoke.

We stood open-mouthed. Aircraft noise continued to buzz above the harbor. Planes which had been participating in the mock attack broke off and disappeared. Whatever activity was taking place in the navy yard where the plane had crashed couldn't be seen from my vantage point. Within moments the sky was clear of smoke. Silence commandeered the scene, a hush that masked what had happened minutes ago.

Scuttlebutt, particularly among the airdales, circulated throughout the ship after GQ was secured. All sorts of explanations and reasons for the accident were offered. Two pragmatic items everybody agreed with were that the three men in the TBF had at least died instantly, and Essex herself was damn lucky she hadn't been hit.

That afternoon Phil and I made liberty in Honolulu. Going through the navy yard, we learned that the plane had struck a tall derrick next to a drydock before plunging into a yard personnel tram. It was reported to have been carrying twenty-seven people, including a half-dozen sailors. The collision had destroyed the tram and killed its occupants.

Yesterday, our joint plan had been to go ashore as early as possible after GQ, but Ensign Porky for reasons unknown had seen fit to delay permission. Only hours later did we realize that he had possibly saved our lives.

Day by day new warships entered the harbor. Pearl was filling fast. Every pier, dock and anchorage in all the lochs seemed to be occupied. Essex, Yorktown and Independence were joined by cruiser Mobile, the Limy carrier Victorious (which never was in a task group that included us), as well as battleship Indiana, which I jealously thought got a special welcome. Navy brass had a love for those behemoths that carrier sailors felt was misplaced. Flattops and submarines were going to win the war out here.

On 9 August the carriers that had supplied planes for the mock attack, Essex-class Lexington, Independence-class Belleau Wood and Princeton, and CVE Long Island, came aboard. Heavy cruiser Pensacola had arrived a few days earlier. On this date, then, there were seven carriers, a battlewagon, a heavy and a light cruiser, and so many destroyers and auxiliaries I could not count them all. An untold number of submarines were based north of the navy yard in their separate enclave.

Every sailor had plenty to do. Between reveille and Taps the workday was long. Liberty was stingy, granted only by sections. Some of us, including me, had never done so much manual labor in his life. Labor-saving devices seemed to have been designed for every gang of airdales but the AOM's.

Friends who had visited Essex came back envious, but strangely satisfied at their lot; no one wanted to serve in such a big ship. But we continued to feel sorry for ourselves. **DL**

Wednesday 11 August 1943   *The Air Group undergoes changes*

Moored as before, with the starboard side to pier F-10, Ford Island, Pearl Harbor, T.H.
0749 Got underway, steaming toward the channel to exit the harbor.
0900 Took departure of the channel seaward to form cruising disposition 5-LS with USS STEVENS and USS HARRISON.
1018-1200 Gunnery Department conducted AA practice.
1158 A single 40mm gun in mount number 11 exploded injuring several members of the gun crew. Seaman second class James J.M. Clevenstine along with Seaman second class Malcolm M. Allen immediately put a stream of water on the gun to cool both the gun and exposed ammunition, even though Allen was struck in the throat by a shell casing fragment and was bleeding profusely. (Sadly, J.J.M. Clevenstine would die later in the war aboard the USS INDEPENDENCE as a direct result of friendly fire).
The following men were admitted to sick bay with injuries; S2c Malcolm M. Allen, S2c Harold E. Addington, S1c Edward L. Arthur, S2c Maurice C. Heath, and S2c Francis D. Spack.
1247-1337 Recovered 32 Fighting Squadron Six F6F Hellcats, and 2 Hellcats from VF-22. **
1503-1514 Catapulted 8 aircraft.
1541-1548 Launched 12 aircraft.
1625 Underwent simulated air attack.
1635-1636 Catapulted 2 aircraft.
1701-1728 Recovered 22 aircraft.
1830 Joined Task Group 59.16.2 with USS YORKTOWN, USS MCKEE, USS SCHROEDER and USS THATCHER.
1910-1924 USS YORKTOWN recovered aircraft.

** VF-22 would be replaced onboard USS INDEPENDENCE by Fighting Six (VF-6). Additional transition was in process for Air Group 22. On 13 August Lt. Leland L. Johnson became VF-22s new Commanding Officer. VC- 22 became "streamlined" and Bombing 22 (VB-22) was detached, remaining on Maui. Torpedo 22 (VT-22) with their TBF-1s stayed onboard the INDEPENDENCE. The Mighty-I would go to sea with VF-6 and VT-22. VF-22 would return for assignment aboard the INDEPENDENCE on 29 September, once again reuniting with VT-22.

Thursday 12 August 1943   *At sea - Air Group training*

0549-0610 Steaming as before. Launched 8 aircraft.
0727 Underwent simulated air attack.
0740-0757 Launched 14 aircraft.
0810-0830 Recovered 2 TBFs and 9 F6Fs.

TOP ROW - John Staniszewski, John Johnston, Robert Hobbs, Ashton Roberts, George Rodgers, Harvey Odenbrett, James Nichols, Robert Locker, Charles Palmer, Edward Philippe, Sy Mendenhall, Charles McCord

3RD ROW - Bayard Webster, Tom Hall, Robert Merritt, Bascomb Gates, Cliff Seaver, William Davis, Don Kent, John Benton, Herschel Pahl, Robert Klinger, Lindley Godson

2ND ROW - John Ogg, Tom Willman, Wilton Hutt, Thaddeus Coleman, Allie Callan, Alexander Vraciu, Richard Trimble, Al Niquist, Malcoomb Loesch, William Rose, Sandy Crews

BOTTOM ROW - Richard Loesch, John Altemus, Foster Blair, Henry Fairbanks, George Bullard, Edward O'Hare, Paul Rooney, Joe Robbins, Alfred Kerr, Robert Neel, Cyrum Chambers

VF-6 on Maui in July, 1943

VF-6 Enlisted

Top Row, standing: James E. Alexander, H.A. Barrett, Chief Lunsford
Third Row: Willis S. Dawson, Lead Chief J.C. Williams, Chief Frank Shamro, Chief Wilton K. Decker, Chief Yoeman Hansen
Second Row: Roger W. Gunn, Harold F. Peeler, N. A. Aiello, A.A. Anestasio, Frederick J. Ahern
First Row, sitting: Steven L. Piwetz, Clyde E. Baur, Steel, J.S. McNight, G.R. Budd

0831 Underwent simulated air attack.
0908 Launched 2 TBFs.
0942-0949 Launched 14 aircraft.
1043 Underwent simulated air attack.
1053 Underwent simulated air attack.
1155-1200 Launched 14 aircraft.
1207-1223 Recovered 15 aircraft.
1304 Underwent simulated air attack.
1413-1415 Launched 8 aircraft.
1422-1436 Recovered 13 aircraft.
1648-1652 Launched 8 aircraft.
1700-1707 Recovered 8 aircraft.
1914-1920 Recovered 8 aircraft.

Friday 13 August 1943

0547 Steaming as before. Catapulted 1 aircraft.
0613-0619 Launched 11 aircraft.
0702-0710 Launched 14 aircraft.
0718 Recovered 1 aircraft.

Chief Cyrus R. Berkheimer was a "Plank Owner"
His son would later fly aboard in VF(N)-41

0839 Approaching to land his F6F (Bu. No. 4877) aboard
the INDEPENDENCE, VF-6s Ensign John Ogg
touched down and ended up in the port catwalk, damaging both the Hellcat and the 40mm gun director.
John Ogg was not injured.
1044-1105 USS YORKTOWN launched aircraft.
1058-1102 Launched 5 Aircraft (none could land onboard until they extricated John's wayward F6F).
1305-1340 Gunnery Department conducted antiaircraft practice.
1508 Steamed into the swept channel entrance to Pearl Harbor.
1601 Moored port side to pier F-1, Ford Island, Pearl Harbor, Oahu, T.H..

DL   Rather heavy seas, low overcast, gusty winds. Flight quarters, scheduled for all day, were
abruptly terminated shortly before noon because one of the landing fighters skidded to the right and slid
into a gun director aft of the stacks, giving men in the adjacent gunbucket a scare. No one, including the
pilot, was hurt.
*   Asbestos Joe came lumbering over in his big white protective suit lugging his fire-fighting gear,*
but it wasn't needed. The flight surgeon and two pharmacist mates checked the pilot as soon as he had
extricated himself from the cockpit, then walked him to the island structure. A quick look at his face as
he went by startled me: he was as young as I!
*   Airdales like myself, suddenly idle, examined the aircraft; how clumsy and odd that sleek*
machine looked, hung up with its starboard wing dangling over the sea, the snout of its engine nacelle
an open maw appearing to weep with embarrassment. But that was just my heated imagination working
overtime. From a practical point of view its frozen position with one wing protruding over the
flightdeck made further flight ops impossible. Move it, deep-six it, or go back into Pearl.
*   Because it made sense, most of us correctly decided what that decision would be. Wise sailors,*
of course, knew that what made sense didn't always win a blue ribbon. This time it did.
*   So back into Pearl Harbor we went. Word of our arrival had preceded us. As we slid past Hos-*
pital Point we encountered the first of several Bronx-cheer galleries. Wheelchair patients with white-
uniformed nurses in attendance waved us through the channel from the wide lawn fronting the water.
Moving past the drydocks, navy yard workmen and sailors paused and stared at our helpless passenger-
pigeon with its propeller motionless and one leg of its gear stuck in the catwalk. Everyone seemed to be
waiting to watch as we came by, heading for our berth alongside Ford Island. A whistle blew some-
where in the yard; others followed. We could only listen to these sarcastic poops and toots and grit our

teeth. Pondering this incident long afterward, Big Dan's opinion fit my own: not a thing would have been made of the affair except that this particular pilot happened to be a member of the famous Butch O'Hare's hotshot fighter group. He certainly wasn't the first kid to botch a carrier landing in bad weather and he wouldn't be the last. **DL**

Replaced by Lt. Leland L. Johnson (as previously noted), Lieutenant Commander Philip Huston Torrey, Jr. * was transferred from VF-22 to assume command of VF-9 aboard the USS ESSEX.
The Navy was shifting qualified and experienced personnel to fill its needs due to rapid expansion, as industry produced new hulls, and new air groups formed. Experienced aviators were also rotated to training assignments to pass their knowledge to new aviators. Scouting 22 had also lost its Executive Officer as Lt. Cdr. Richard L. Fowler had been selected to form a new Squadron.
 (* Shot down in combat with a Ki-44 "Tojo" over Habu, Japan on 16 February 1945, Philip H. Torrey, Jr. would not survive the war. He was flying off the USS LEXINGTON.)

Monday 16 August 1943   *Moored, Ford Island, Pearl Harbor*

0800 Moored as before. Mustered the crew at quarters.

0820 CVL-22 held **meritorious mast to award commendations for action above the call of duty** to:

AMM1c Charles Paul Boyer and **S2c James Strange** for diving from the flight deck to rescue their fellow shipmate on August 4th (when the aviation tractor went into the bay).

S2c Malcolm M. Allen and **S2c James Jefferson M. Clevenstine** for their action of 11 August when the 40mm gun mount barrel blew up, thought to have prevented further causalities.

DL   *Decisions made by that anonymous, all-knowing entity which ruled our lives and controlled our destinies called "higher authority" played one of its mysterious games three days after our humble return to Pearl.*
Orders were given to Lieutenant Harry and passed through Porky and the chiefs to us coolies who did the work (the Chain of command) to remove all .30-caliber ammo and all parachute flares from the magazines and send this materiel ashore.
Okay. Hard, hot labor in the respective mags. All pitched in. Flightdeck rearming crews joined Rebel's men below decks. They were glad to see us prove that we, too, had muscles. In the fetid air, we all stunk together. Topside went the stuff, stacked in layers on the bomb elevator. Good riddance. We thought we'd seen the last of it.
That afternoon, one thousand thirty-six wooden cases of unbelted .50-caliber ammunition came aboard, hoisted from dockside trucks onto the flightdeck and sent below to the small arms magazine. Rebel's crew couldn't handle all this by itself, so we rearming guys didn't make it back topside as soon as we'd expected to.
This was on a Monday. That night, before hitting the sack, word was passed that we'd begin working 12-hour shifts until belting was complete. All liberty was cancelled for ordnancemen till the job was done. **DL**

Tuesday 17 August 1943   *Moored, Ford Island, Pearl Harbor*

DL   *Tuesday was a long day, broken only by chow at noon and late chow after 1800, when the night shift took over. Belting the rounds on the hangar deck was easy. Removing them from their wood cases needed labor, and I became a laborer.*
In the magazine the stink of creosote emanating from each box fouled the air, stuck to our dungarees, clung to our hair. Claw hammers needed to pry off the box covers made the wood slats screech with pain as each was torn open to reveal shiny, mean-looking cartridges by the many hundreds. **DL**

Wednesday 18 August 1943   *Moored, Ford Island, Pearl Harbor*

DL   On Wednesday the ship's Gunnery Department was ordered to give a hand with the belting machine. It was a simple device; eight or ten rounds at a time were forced into a cartridge belt fed to it by a bored sailor. Hard work remained in the magazines, where we toiled. The 12-hour shifts wore everyone down. When I turned in that night only half the job had been done. *DL*

Friday 20 August 1943   *Moored, Ford Island, Pearl Harbor*

DL   That Friday afternoon, another blow fell. The TBF stuff we had sent to the beach five days ago would be returning. Today. Pronto. Higher Authority had decreed that Independence would, after all, carry a complement of torpeckers as well as fighters next time she went to sea. Which meant the .30-caliber ammo would come back aboard and, as it was a new consignment, would also have to be belted. *DL*

Saturday 21 August 1943   *Moored, Ford Island, Pearl Harbor*

DL   Saturday saw us adding this new assignment to our workload. We stowed the boxes, opened them, and sent the contents to the hangar for belting. That was an easier job and I envied those guys, but even they were bushed. Yet no one gave up or tried to. Probably each man suffered a little from the disheartening knowledge that what he was doing was no more than a back-breaking, soul-stifling bout of hard labor. In it there was no glory, certainly no pleasure, and little likelihood of any thanks. Its miniscule effect on the war would be lost to history. If recorded at all, it would rate no more than half a line in the ship's log. But when, in years to come, we would recall this time of travail and perhaps question if it had really been as bad as we now knew it was, we'd have one indisputable fact to remember: we hadn't quit.   *DL*

Sunday 22 August 1943   *Got Underway with Task Group 59.16*

Moored as before, port side to pier F-1, Ford Island, Pearl Harbor, Oahu, T.H.
0837 Got underway, aided by tugs, in accordance with ComCarDiv 11 OpOrder 3-43, with Task Group 59.16.
0945 Departed the swept channel at Pearl Harbor seaward toward the designated operating area.
0953 Joined up with USS YORKTOWN (OTC), USS HARRISON, USS JOHN RODGERS, USS LA VALLETTE, and USS SIGSBEE, forming cruising disposition 5-LS.
1057 USS YORKTOWN commenced gunnery exercises firing its 5" guns.
1232-1332 The Mighty-I Gunnery Department conducted AA practice firing at a towed sleeve.
1602-1658 USS YORKTOWN recovered aircraft.
1607-1725 CVL-22 recovered onboard 24 F6Fs of VF-6 and 9 TBF-1s of VC-22.

DL   On Sunday we went to sea. I almost joined the crowd going to church services on the hangar forward of where the belting continued, but I was afraid I'd go to sleep and fall off my chair.
     VF-6's fighters and VC-22's torpedo planes came aboard maybe a hundred miles at sea. Sunset GQ came, and any sluggard among us came-to with a jolt.
     "Now hear this!" barked the loudspeaker. The Captain had something to say, a message we wanted to hear. For some reason, after GQ was secured, I wrote down his exact words:
     "This is not a training cruise. Just a year after our ship's launching we are going to make a strike. I want every man and officer to put his heart in his job."
     All the strain and pain of our recent labor vanished. In our compartment there was happy noise I hadn't heard before. On the mess deck, it was said, sailors actually toasted each other by clinking coffee mugs together. At last! was our mood.   *DL*

7

Into Harms Way
Marcus Island and Wake Island Raids

Monday 23 August 1943   *Steaming with Task Force 15*

Became a unit of Task Force 15, and commenced operating in accordance with ComTaskForce 15 Op Order 50-43 dated 20 August, 1943.

0701 Steaming as before. Sighted USS INDIANA with 3 escorts, bearing 004°T at 16,000 yards.

0800 Sighted USS ESSEX. Proceeded to join up to form Task Force 15 consisting of:

TG 15.5   USS INDEPENDENCE, USS ESSEX (CTG 15.5) and USS YORKTOWN (OTC).

TG 15.1   USS INDIANA, USS MOBILE and USS NASHVILLE.

TG 15.4   DESRON 24 (minus USS MURRAY) plus USS LA VELLETTE & USS THATCHER.

TG 15.6   USS GUADELOUPE (Fleet Oiler) and USS HALFORD (See page 141).

1012 Commenced steaming on base course 320°T, fleet speed 18 knots.

0951-0954 Launched 4 TBFs.

1210 Changed course to 300°T.

1318-1324 Recovered 4 TBFs.

DL   When I got to the flightdeck next morning we were surrounded. Carriers Yorktown and Essex, each boasting about three times our number of planes, looked handsome and formidable. Battleship Indiana had been joined by light cruisers Nashville and Mobile, our friend from Canal days. A long-hulled oiler plugged along on the fringe. Tin cans scurried here and there like watchdog busybodies.

An hour before noon chow the Captain's voice told us where we were headed. Marcus Island. A hit-and-run raid.

The skipper had barely ended his announcement before maps and charts appeared from the lockers of guys I'd never have given credit for even being interested. Shows how much I knew of human nature! All were aware that Marcus was pretty close to Tokyo, but not until the maps were unfurled did we find out how close. Less than a thousand miles. Did Rear Admiral Radford, our skipper's boss, know what he was doing'? (Good question, one we'd be asking of other higher ups in the future.)

The task group kept to a steady 15-knot pace west and then northwesterly to give Japanese-held Wake Island a wide berth. Flight operations were minimal, which made us happy. Scuttlebutt about all sorts of things buzzed throughout the ship. The atmosphere was decidedly different from what it had ever been. The rumor grapevine continued to spew tales that might have been true but were disturbing regardless of their validity. Yorktown was supposed to have lost three SBDs last night and two men. One plane had tried to land aboard our ship but its engine had conked out before it could reach us; pilot and gunner got out okay (which made me happy; my Marine brother was an SBD gunner himself.) One plane was supposed to have hit the water in our wake and blew up. The third SBD had gone over Yorktown's side upon landing.

*What to believe? No official account of such an episode was made; unofficial accounts were figments of dreams and nightmares. **DL***

JG   Joined the carrier Essex and the battleship Indiana and their escorts. We are told by Captain Fairlamb that we are out to hit Jap held Marcus Island, 950 miles from Japan proper.

*RC Leave Pearl harbor to make our first strike against Japs. We had 3 carriers in task group, Yorktown, Essex and Independence escorted by 3 cruisers and eleven destroyers.   **RC***

Allie Callan (VF-6) would note: *" Our communication equipment was quite old and outdated, but was the only type available at the time. Shortly after our initial operation aboard the Independence, we received our new radio equipment. It was the first VHF in the fleet. The VHF (Very High Frequency) was static free and very reliable."* **A. W. Callan** (Sea Eagle By: A.W. Callan)

Tuesday 24 August 1943   *Steaming with Task Force 15*

0611-0617 Steaming as before. Catapulted 4 TBFs.
0944-0946 Recovered 4 TBFs.
1641-1645 Catapulted 4 TBFs.
1931-1938 Recovered 4 TBFs.
The three carriers took turns putting aircraft up during the day (a practice that would continue) to scout for submarine and surface threats.

JG We are 400 miles from Midway. JG (Note: In the morning of the 24th the INDEPENDENCE was roughly 400 miles east of Midway, passing to within 225 miles NE at 2000 that evening).

Wednesday 25 August 1943   *Steaming to attack Marcus Island*

0300 Steaming as before. Changed base course to 290°T.
1042 Recovered 1 TBF from USS YORKTOWN, in a deferred forced landing.
1307-1311 Catapulted 4 TBFs.
1625 Underwent simulated air attack.
1631-1637 Recovered 4 TBFs.
1655 Changed base course to 260°T.
1800 Changed base course to 288°T (speed 19 knots).

JG An officer goes out of his mind, runs about the ship with loaded revolver. Caught and locked up in isolation ward. JG

Thursday 26 August 1943 *Steaming to attack Marcus Island - Cross the IDL*

0715 Steaming as before. Crossed the International Date Line, local date not changed.
0928-0932 Catapulted 4 TBFs.
1238 Recovered 1 TBF, emergency landing.
1323-1325 Recovered 3 TBFs.
1711 Recovered 1 TBF belonging to the USS YORKTOWN.

DL All fighters were lined up on either sides of the flightdeck, noses pointing outward, as every pilot fired his guns into the sea. Not a gun malfunctioned. I guess that made Butch O'Hare happy. Of course, no one wearing our dungarees called him Butch. He was an officer and we were sailors who knew their place. With the AOM's, he made a hit even though it caused lots of extra work. Down the line from Mister Harry to Ensign Porky to the Chiefs came the order: Do what he wants. (Or words to that effect.)
   What he wanted was his ammunition to be belted in a different ratio from the usual three black-tipped armor piercing bullets to one red-tipped incendiary, to a potent ratio of seven AP-to-one incendiary. All his section's guns had already been boresighted to impact a single point not too far ahead of the airplane. This augmented ratio would be a real killer; nothing could have withstood it. DL

Friday 27 August 1943   *Steaming to attack Marcus Island*

0622-0620 Steaming as before. Catapulted 4 TBFs and launched 4 F6Fs.
0730 Commenced steering various courses at various speeds during fleet fueling operations.
0928-0945 Recovered all CVL-22 aircraft.
1852 Catapulted 1 TBF belonging to the USS YORKTOWN.
1935 Resumed fleet course of 285°T.

Saturday 28 August 1943   *Steaming to attack Marcus Island*

0649 CVL-22 commenced operations to take on fuel from USS GUADELOUPE. Roughly 3 hours later fueling was completed, and the YORKTOWN launched planes. At 1300 CVL-22 launched 4 TBF's as YORKTOWN was recovering her morning launch. Two hours later at 1505 the fleet changed course to the east. At 1633 the 4 TBF's were brought back on board at 1 minute intervals.
The ESSEX took over air operations launching and recovering her chicks from 1700 thru 1916.

DL All ships refueled, some from the oiler and the destroyers from the big carriers or the battlewagon. We were working hard. I came to the conclusion that the guys who did the work on aircraft carriers were the AOM's and the AMM's.
Had an ordnance hangar deck 4-hour watch last night. Wore a sound-powered phone headset, tied into a lot of circuits. Interesting chatter. Hard to stay awake, but I did. Hangar kind of ghostly at night, all doors closed, lights dim, shielded flashlights used with care by guys working on engines and guns. DL

JG Fueled from tanker, officer* is passed over to tanker or provision ship. Made sub contact. JG
          (* Lt.Jg. W. H. Wright was transferred to the USS GUADLOUPE)

Sunday 29 August 1943   *Steaming to attack Marcus Island*

At 0605 ESSEX began the day launched planes as preparations were made for INDEPENDENCE air operations with 8 TBF's catapulted near 0930. At 1112 base course changed to 270°T. At 1300 air operations again began with launches of 21 F6F's. The TBF's were recovered after the fighter launch, and at 1400 YORKTOWN underwent a simulated air attack. 50 minutes later it was the Mighty-I's turn for the simulated air pasting. From 1604 for the next 35 minutes CVL-22 would recover all her aircraft. Clocks were set back 1/2 hour at 1830.
The base course changed to 290°T between our simulated air attacks that day, remaining somewhat on westerly headings. Then, at 2100, a large swing toward the southwest commenced, steaming on a new base course of 233°T .

Monday 30 August 1943   *Steaming to attack Marcus Island*

On this day the INDEPENDENCE conducted no flight operations. YORKTOWN and ESSEX launched and recovered aircraft throughout the day.

DL 0930. A voice from the loudspeaker pronounced: "We are now five hundred miles from Marcus Island. We will increase our speed tonight and make a long run in. Commander Task Force 15 has sent the following message to all ships, 'Inform all hands what we are up to. All TBF's flying with fighter escort, have orders to destroy any Jap picket boats sighted. Tomorrow morning is the time. Good Luck. Hit 'em hard and let's go!'" DL

For the non-aviators, a little lesson as we enter the war:

This is the "clock" face from an aviator's perspective.

A Japanese Zero at 9 o'clock would be off his left (port) **wing.**

If he is on the Zero's 6 o'clock, then he is on the Zero's tail. If the inverse is true .....

Well, one way or the other, it's deadly serious.
          Pull the trigger and smoke happens!

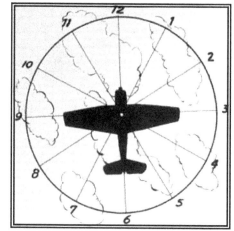

Tuesday 31 August / Wednesday 1 September 1943 (International Date Line crossed)

Marcus Island Raid

PLAN OF THE DAY

TUESDAY 31 August 1943.

0245 Reveille. Breakfast.

0410 General Quarters.

0615 Launch Aircraft.
Thereafter operate as directed by Commander Task Force.

0645 Sunrise - Light ship.

0700 (about) Commence serving hot meals in B-322-L port and Starboard sides.*

0800 Muster on Stations.

1824 Darken ship.

1854 Sunset. General Quarters.

R. L. Johnson

R. L. JOHNSON,
Commander, U. S. Navy,
Executive Officer.

*See Addenda.
Word will be passed when men can go below to eat.
RETURN PROMPTLY TO STATIONS

HIT HARD! HIT FAST!

The "Plan Of The Day" was published daily and posted in a conspicuous location to inform the crew of the days "planned" events and additionally a "Watch List" of the officers and enlisted men assigned to the various watches. Additionally it disseminated other information deemed necessary to communicate to the crew. The ship also published a "Breakfast Bulletin" to give news from home, and news of the war. Much of the news within the Breakfast Bulletin was the "Radio Press News" delivered thru the Advanced Communication Center on Guam Island.

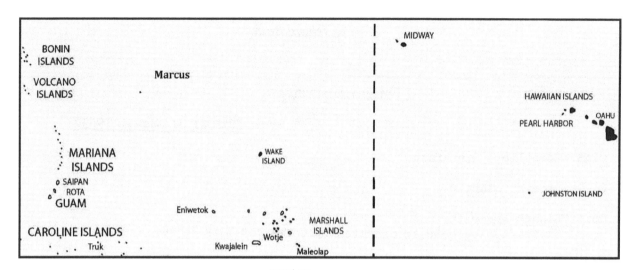

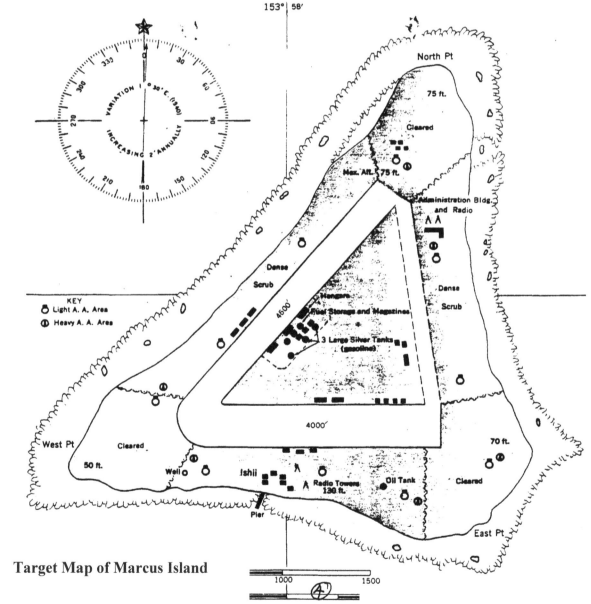

Target Map of Marcus Island

**Photo of Marcus Island shot by a plane from the USS YORKTOWN,
fires burning and Japanese aircraft visible.**

Frank Capka notes: *"The Mighty I's first squadron was "Fighting 22" and Lieutenant Commander Peters was Air Group Commander. When Cdr. Peters led his fighters over the island of Marcus on 1 September 1943, it marked the beginning of the carriers battle career. Together, this carrier force attacked the enemy from dawn until dusk, and when the force retired 70% of the buildings and emplacements on Marcus were reduced to shambles."*

GUAM 1 September 1943, the first action for the carrier. Lt. Cmdr. James Peters, commanding Fighting 22, had wheels painted on the bottom-side of the Hellcats wings to give them the appearance while in flight of Wildcats. This was done to trick the Japs into believing that the Hellcats, considered to be the best carrier fighters, were not yet in use. GUAM

Note: Errors are in both above observations. Lt. Cmdr. J..M. Peters led VC-22 (TBM Avenger squadron), not VF-22. VF-22 would not participate in the Marcus raid off the CVL-22 as VF-22 was temporally reassigned to the BELLEAU WOOD (**see page 154** - Wed 11 Aug.). **VF-6** hellcats were aboard (under Lt. Cmdr. O'Hare), along with **Lt. Cmdr. Peters' VC-22 TBMs**.

The captain noted after the raid:
"Aircraft ordnance stowage is too inaccessible for efficiency under battle conditions. The location of the bomb elevator in the center of the flight deck forward conflicts with respotting and landing operations, and makes rearming planes a slow cumbersome maneuver. Doubling the number of bomb skids will alleviate this handicap and permit a greater degree of pre-spotting of bombs."

Marcus Island   (Minami Tori Shima)

The Mighty-I was part of a fast hard hitting raid against the Japanese perimeter. They were in Task Force 15 led by Rear Admiral Charles A. Pownall. In addition to the USS INDEPENDENCE, Task Force 15 was composed of carriers USS ESSEX and USS YORKTOWN, battleship USS INDIANA, light cruisers USS MOBILE and USS NASHVILLE and a screen of 10 destroyers (BOYD, DASHIELL, HALFORD, HARRISON, JOHN RODGERS, LA VALLETTE, MCKEE, RINGOLD, SIGSBEE and STEVENS) as it steamed toward Marcus Island. Submarine USS SNOOK was with them for lifeguard duty, and the Cimarron class fleet oiler USS GUADELOUPE was assigned to refuel the group.

This was a mission of new beginnings:

> It would be the start of Admiral Chester W. Nimitz's drive across the Pacific.

> Marcus Island would catapult the Mighty-I off on her zigzag path toward Tokyo with her first combat against the Imperial Japanese Empire.

> This raid would be the first use of the Grumman F6F Hellcats in combat against the enemy. The Hellcat would become one of the premier fighters of WWII carrier aviation.

> Utilization of the submarine USS SNOOK was to lead to the use of subs for rescuing downed aviators, serving "Lifeguard" duty along the airmen's proposed flight paths throughout the war against Japan, not only for Navy fliers, but AAF as well.

This would also serve as a training raid for future fast carriers operating in Task Groups at slash and dash missions targeting Japanese bases. They would make a fast run in, attempting to make the approach undetected, catch the Japanese off-guard, maximize the damage, and withdraw to strike again. It was like a shell game they would learn to play. A deadly game of making the Japanese guess which of their islands Blue pieces would strike next, obscured by a vast mighty expanse of ocean. At this stage of the war Japan was thinly spread over a large domain. We could overwhelm their stationary islands with brutal attacks from flexible non-stationary elements tailored and focused for the task. This was a stage of the war Japan was ill prepared for. It would be high stakes for both sides, paid for with blood markers on the table.

Marcus Island was a base for long range "Betty" bombers. US forces were to destroy the aircraft, radar and the infrastructure.

On this raid, the Task Group would not take a direct route, but sweep in with a powerful right hook as it came steaming up from the southeast, passing wide and well to the east, then curving west to hit them from the north. While this was happening, US forces were also securing Baker and Holland Islands.

On the day of the raid the INDEPENDENCE was directed to provide; a Combat Air Patrol for the task Force, a search in assigned sectors 200 miles out toward Japan's mainland to intercept and report incoming forces or aircraft, ASPs, and to join ESSEX aircraft on an attack on the 4th run on the island.

The sea was calm and the visibility excellent. The winds were light and variable, necessitating high carrier speeds for the launches.

More than 90 aircraft participated in the pre-dawn attack. Catching the island defenders by complete surprise, aided by taking advantage of area thunderstorms to evade the enemy radar, numerous Mitsubishi "Betty" bombers were destroyed on the ground. The destruction at Marcus (with 275 sorties flown) was at a cost of 1 TBM and 3 F6Fs lost in action.

Tuesday 31 August / Wednesday 1 September 1943 (International Date Line crossed)
Marcus Island Raid

Steaming in Task Force 15, formation 5LL. Base course is 228°T, axis 270°T, speed 25 knots.
0350 Changed speed to 28 knots, course 204°T. The morning presented no wind or clouds. Ships produced a green phosphorescence glow, as if magically ignited, within the churned bow wave and stern wake as they steamed thru the darkness.
0410 Sounded general quarters. The crew had been called early and sent to breakfast.
0422 USS YORKTOWN began launching aircraft, completing its first launch at 0505, and they were over target, commencing their attack at 0605.
0545 USS ESSEX commenced launching its aircraft for the second attack wave to hit Marcus, completing its launch at 0611.
0612-0640 Catapulted 12 F6Fs and 8 TBFs for Combat Air Patrol.
0858-0910 Catapulted 12 F6Fs for second Combat Air Patrol. At 0910 the YORKTOWN launched its second attack.
0929-0941 Recovered 12 F6Fs launched at 0640 (first CAP).
1014 USS MCKEE picked up an ESSEX Hellcat pilot forced down in the water astern of the TF.
1041 USS NASHVILLE catapulted 2 aircraft.
1042-1052 Recovered 1 F6F and 9 TBFs (one TBF from the USS YORKTOWN).
1235-1243 Catapulted 5 F6Fs and 3 TBFs for the eighth wave of attacks on Marcus along with ESSEX planes. Due to a catapult problem, the deck had to be respotted for deck launching.
1256-1306 Launched 6 TBFs and 4 F6Fs.
1336-1337 Launched 2 F6Fs. The flight of 8 Avengers were led by Lt. Cdr. James M. Peters (VC-22) was escorted by a division ** of 4 Hellcats led by Lt. Comdr. E.H. O'Hare of VF-6, reaching Marcus at 1435. They bombed buildings and hit the radio mast on the island. The ninth Avenger was from the YORKTOWN (that had made a forced landing at 1052). O'Hare's Hellcats strafed the runway area leaving twin engine bombers burning. On the return trip they attacked a ship looking like a tanker which was seen to violently explode, break in two, then sink. The nature of the explosion led them to believe the vessel may have been an ammunition ship rather than a tanker. (** See photo page 171 for O'Hare's Div.)
1340-1400 Recovered 12 F6Fs (the second CAP).
1543-1550 Launched 9 F6Fs (for CAP). Six minutes later 1 F6F was recovered.
1558 Commenced maneuvering close in to heavy vessels for better mutual anti-aircraft defense.
1612 Launched 2 F6Fs to reinforce the CAP.
1615-1650 Recovered 13 F6Fs and 7 TBFs. One TBF had a hung bomb, that dropped on the flight deck after the Avenger landed, with a partially armed nose fuse. Ensign Reece (in charge of aircraft ordnance) bent up the arming impellers, removed the nose and tail fuses, and threw them overboard. The bomb was returned to bomb storage.
1833-1850 Recovered 7 F6Fs from our third CAP. One F6F landed aboard the USS ESSEX due to a landing gear problem.
2015 Sounded general quarters. USS SIGSBEE dropped depth charges on a submarine contact. The Task Force maneuvered to clear the area.
2047 Secured from general quarters. The SIGSBEE lost contact with its prey.
2100 Set Fleet speed to 18 knots.
2136 Set Fleet course to 050°T.

JG   General quarters at 0410. Water smooth as glass, not enough wind to launch loaded planes. Forced to use catapult. Planes look great flying in formation with running lights lit. One of our planes made a forced landing on the island. Crew must have been given up for lost.   JG

Note: While CVL-22 was attacking Marcus Island, sister CVLs BELLEAU WOOD* & PRINCETON were supporting the Army 804th Aviation Battalion occupation of Baker Island. (* With VF-22 aboard for the Baker Island raid - see entry bottom of page 145)

1 September 1943   *Marcus Island Raid*

The USS INDEPENDENCE Executive Officer, **Karl O. Drexel**, lays out the first day of the Marcus operation;

DOG DAY   MARCUS   1 SEPTEMBER 1943

The Nipponese call it Minami Tori Shima, we call it Marcus, but tonight its name is mud.
The first taste of combat was experienced by the Mighty Eye when, she, in operation with the ESSEX and YORKTOWN (plus the INDIANA, Cruisers and Cans), moved within 900 miles of the Japanese Mainland to blast this little triangular rock until it seemed that it most surely sunk.
Marcus outwardly appears insignificant. It rises some 75 feet above the sea, protected by a coral reef, surrounded by a shingle beach, covered with palms and brush, and is only about four miles in circumference, consisting of 740 acres. Actually, its significance is predicated on the fact that the Nips are using it as a land based "Carrier" to ferry their planes to Marshall and Gilberts. To stop this ferrying business for awhile and to gain experience for future engagements is the purpose for this task force.
Everyone up at 0230 for breakfast-steak and eggs-general quarters at 0330.
The first wave's being launched at 0400. A beautiful sight to see the hundreds of planes taking off in the darkness, rendezvousing at a couple thousand feet altitude and starting out for Marcus. Everyone was tense and a little nervous but ready for whatever these Yellow Bastards might throw at us. Our gunners have been practicing all the way out and they are good. We didn't know whether we had been spotted or not-it hardly seemed possible that we hadn't been picked by snoopers, subs or both in the long trip out here.
As the sun rose on Marcus it was the sunset for the Garrison that was maintained there for it was at this moment that the first wave hit them. From this time until late this afternoon wave after wave struck at the Island. No other piece of land per sq. mile in the world, including German targets, has been the recipient of such a terrific beating. One hundred pound incendiaries, 500 and 1000 lb. daisy cutters, demolition bombs of all sizes, 12 hour and 24 hour delayed action bombs--all spelled hell for those on the rock.
Went to ready room to greet pilots as they came back from their first taste of the real McCoy. It was their first "non-dry run" and their first time under fire and did they show it when they returned! Excited as a gang of kids who got away with the stealing of the farmer's favorite apples. Everyone talking at once. French La Fleur strafed and bombed a re-fueling vessel of some sort and was so elated over it that to understand his New Orleans drawling stutter was impossible until after a cup "O joe" and cigarette was shoved at him. Too much bedlam in ready room, so left happy that everyone returned from this encounter.
Late this afternoon all waves had returned and the combat patrols were taken aboard and we ran like hell-on the way home. All of us happy that we had gotten away with it but just a shade disappointed that no slant eyes showed up for us to take a pot shot at. The pilots had had all the fun! There was still a remote possibility of a night attack from the receding mainland but most of us had re-laxed. It had been a long and successful day. The OTC sent all hands a "well done."
Now, as this is written, the war seems remote. Everything is quiet about the decks. Very little card playing tonight. Too much tension developed over the last 24 hours of waiting for action. We are now out of range of any possibility of attack.
Although this was a comparatively small attack, it was significant in that it had blasted an island almost in the shadow of the enemies stronghold. It was an attack preliminary to the day when the Pacific War would be enlarged and in-tensified and would soon be forgotten. It had served a dimly-understood end: The ultimate big scale Aerial Bombardment of Japan itself. The Japanese now realize that, knowing that we can collect enough air and sea power to smash at them anywhere in this biggest of all oceans, henceforth they will never know when to relax.   ***Karl O. Drexel***

DON LABUDDE gives his perspective of the Marcus events as they unfold on the Mighty-I; *Tuesday, 31 August (actually Wednesday, September 1). Reveille at 0300, general quarters forty-five minutes later. (Time for hurried breakfast and a too-short stop in the head; no wonder most of us were constipated.) Dark topside, sea very calm. Ship's wake quite phosphorescent, like rippled satin. Brilliant. Tell-tale markers on the sea. From an airplane they must have resembled four-lane highways. In any other location, Lake Winnebago for instance, they would have delighted me.*

Essex and Yorktown launched first, their aircraft making a single circle of the task force before disappearing. Our own planes took off about 0545. We installed nose fuses on those anti-submarine missiles in addition to the normal hydrostatic, so they could be used either way. Early reports, buttressed by the grapevine, reported first attacks successful.

Our second deckload went off about 1000, less than an hour after the first one had returned. What that really meant, in the plain English historians seldom use, was that everybody topside worked their asses off; or to put it more politely, like the coolies we were. From the TBF's we replaced the depth charges with four 500-lb GP bombs. The fuelers finished their job while we secured the bomb elevator hatch cover, clearing the deck for the next launch. Some guys were so tired they didn't bother to jump into the catwalk, just slumped to the deck and let the planes roar past on their way into the Wild Gray Wonder of the overcast.

The third deckload repeated the second's quick turnaround. The fighters had shot up most of their ammo and the torpeckers had dropped most of the bombs. By now we didn't care what they'd shot at or where the bombs had been dropped. None of our rearming drills from Philly and San Francisco had prepared us for this.

"What the hell," Sully grumbled, "it's war. Enjoy."

Commander Task Force 15, so the story went, had intended still another strike, but it started to rain buckets and he cancelled it. We'd begun reloading the TBF's as the rain and the word of the cancellation came down together. We were pissed; a lot of labor had gone for naught. But relieved, too. We'd had enough for one day. (If anyone had told us we'd soon be doing this as a daily routine and thinking nothing of it, we'd have tossed him overboard).

So we finished our hitch by singing, at the top of our lungs, naughty songs for the benefit of the skipper and his staff staring down from the bridge. Porky came over, hopping up and down with embarrassed rage. Mister Harry, concerned, looked like a discarded dishrag, his tailored officer's cap slopping over his ears, his expensive shoes as soaked as our boondockers.

We had a great time: wheeled the last unused bombs and depth charges to the elevator, sent them dripping below, secured the hatch, and jumped into the catwalk, crowding the portside rearming room where landlord Bill groaned in futile protest as we dripped on his pristine deck. Nobody entered the adjacent head to smoke; the slashing rain had ruined all cigarette packs. How many shivering guys came down with colds and aching bodies afterward is lost to memory.

The task force turned tail immediately and didn't spare the horsepower on our way out of the vicinity and back to Pearl. Losses among the air groups of all the carriers were reported to have been small, but they were still losses. Our padre, a likable Irish priest some of the crew loved, others liked, still others tolerated because he was the only preacher-man around and would have to do, held a memorial service in the shelter of the hangar. I didn't attend. No disrespect for either the dead aviators or the good Father. I was doomed to suffer anonymous loss privately. If that attitude sometimes felt like a curse, the anguish was just as deep. **DL**

GL *Sent our planes over just before dawn, repeated attacks all day. Met no opposition. "Butch" O'Hare and his squadron VF-6 are on our ship. Burned planes on the ground, shot and bombed the airstrip, barracks, radio shack, A.A. guns and positions. Our planes sunk a Jap tanker.* **GL**

VF-6 Pilots – 6 September 1943

<u>Rear Row:</u> L-R John Staniszewski, Willie Callan, Sy Mendenhall, Henry Fairbanks, John Johnston, George Rogers, John Ogg, Robert Neel, Cyrum Chambers, Tom Kerr, George Bullard.

<u>Center Row:</u> L-R J.D. Butler, William Searl, Robert Locker, Clifford Seaver, Herschal Pahl, Alex Vraciu, Paul Rooney, Edward "Butch" O'Hare, Foster Blair, Tom Hall, Charles McCord, Wilton Hutt.

<u>Front Row:</u> L-R James Nichols, Bayard Webster, Robert Hobbs, Malcomb Loesch, Robert Merritt, Robert Klinger, Bascom Gates.

O'Hare's Division

VF-6 pilots L-R: Alex Vraciu, Edward "Butch" O'Hare, Sy Mendenhall, Willie Callan

Third Division

VF-6 pilots L-R: Robert A. Hobbs, Robert S. Merritt, Bascomb Gates, Tom A. Hall, Wilton H. Hutt

Sixth Division

VF-6 pilots L-R : Bud Loesch, Foster Blair, James Nichols, Hershal Pahl, Cliff Seaver

Fifth Division

VF-6 pilots L-R : George Rogers, John Johnston, Al Fairbanks, Robert Locker, John Ogg

Thursday 2 September 1943   *Returning to Pearl Harbor*

0559-0621 Steaming as before. Launched 8 TBFs and 4 F6Fs to search for submarine and surface threats.
0800 USS ESSEX, INDIANIA and YORKTOWN commenced fueling destroyers.
0931-0944 Recovered all aircraft launched at 0621. YORKTOWN aircraft took over CAP duties.
1257-1313 Launched 8 TBFs and 4 F6Fs for CAP and ASP (Anti-Submarine Patrol).
1628-1638 Recovered all aircraft launched at 1313. The ESSEX launched aircraft to fly CAP, recovering them 1844-1854.
2130 Changed base course to 089°T.

Friday 3 September 1943   *Returning to Pearl Harbor*

1301-1311 Launched 8 TBFs and 4 F6Fs for CAP and ASP.
1630-1642 Recovered all aircraft launched at 1311.
The ESSEX and YORKTOWN also flew CAPs and ASPs throughout the day.
2130 Changed base course to 105°T.

Saturday 4 September 1943   *Returning to Pearl Harbor*

0549 Steaming as before. Crossed the 180th meridian. The date was not changed.
0702-0909 Fueled the USS RINGGOLD.
1215 Changed base course to 110°T.
1258-1308 Launched 8 TBFs. The ESSEX and YORKTOWN also flew CAPs and ASPs throughout the day.
1630-1649 Recovered all aircraft launched at 1308. One TBF (Bu. No. 23879) crashed into the barrier on landing. No injuries.
2130 Changed base course to 114°T.

Sunday 5 September 1943   *Returning to Pearl Harbor*

0904 Steaming as before. Launched 1 TBF.
0911 Launched 1 TBF.
1004 Launched 1 TBF.
1044-1045 Recovered 3 TBFs.
1305-1325 Launched 4 TBFs and 11 F6Fs.
1451 Launched 8 F6Fs.
1502 Recovered 1 F6F.
1504 Recovered 1 F6F from USS YORKTOWN.
1520 Underwent simulated air attack.
1600-1641 Recovered all aircraft.
2100 Changed base course to 117°T.

Monday 6 September 1943 *Fires onboard - Returning to Pearl Harbor*

1904 Steaming as before. Fire reported in the forward fireroom.
1943 Fire reported extinguished in the forward fireroom.
1959 Fire reported to have broken out again in the forward fireroom.
2129 Fire reported extinguished again in the forward fireroom. Fire party secured.

Tuesday 7 September 1943   *Moored Navy Yard, Pearl Harbor, T.H.*

0644 Steaming as before. Sighted land bearing 180°T, 36 miles.
0902-0944 Launched 8 TBF Avengers and 21 F6Fs. They flew out to Hawaii. VT-22 flew to Puunene, Maui, and rejoined with the VC-22 SBD-5s.
1324 Changed base course to 140°T.
1342 Formed Task Group 15.2 accompanied by USS INDIANA, USS DASHIELL, USS RINGGOLD, USS SCHROEDER and USS SIGSBEE.
1456 Changed base course to 050°T.
1647 Commenced maneuvering approaching the channel entering Pearl Harbor.
1716 Entered the channel to Pearl Harbor.
1850 Moored starboard side to pier B-22, Pearl Harbor Navy Yard.

DL We reentered Pearl Harbor. Independence docked at the navy yard for repairs to the catapult. A truckload of mail was waiting on the dock. Manna from heaven! Ten of the letters were mine. Mother and Dad, sister Dona, a cousin or two, even a Get Well card from someone (I must have mentioned my sunburn; now I wanted to forget it forever.) None from Ed or Russ. Things were getting tough at home. Not much gasoline, tires pretty scarce, people cheating on the black market (in Oshkosh?), not much good meat or butter to be had. Rationing taking hold of everybody's life. (Not mine, was an empty thought I suppressed.) Come home soon, some letters pleaded. Right.   The Honolulu newspapers were full of stories about the Marcus Island raid. Made us feel good. Still, we snickered at the skill of the writers or editors who wrote lots of words telling little of what we had experienced. I admired their skill in filling columns with verbiage that dressed to a fare-thee-well what Navy had permitted them to say. The civilian navy yard contract workers had no such reluctance to tell us what we had done. They knew everything.

Tuesday we swabbed down the magazine and repainted it top to bottom. God, no wonder I detest the odor of paint to this day!

Wednesday, a single day of liberty. Ooh for Philly or Chicago. Had to settle for Honolulu. Phil, Rebel, Charlie and I searched for another restaurant. Found a different slop-chute off Beretania. Once again ignored the cat houses on River Street. Duplicated our first trek ashore but this time placed two sunnyside-up eggs between each pancake in an even taller layer. Had gut aches all night long. Phil and I haven't yet revealed the secret of our gourmet horsemeat palace on Kalakaua.

By Sunday, the bomb mag's paint had dried sufficiently, and its resident load was brought aboard. Below, where I worked under Rebel's direction, the task seemed endless but hardly boring. The heavy armored door would creak open to the elevator shaft, bombs would be trundled in by ones or twos depending on size, door secured behind the cart, and the block-and-tackle hoist would lift each piece high enough so that we could trundle it back to its assigned location. This went on hour after hour, until the magazine was burdened deck to overhead with these round green oversized slugs whose purpose in life was to smash things and kill people. Grinning hand-tightened nose plugs guarded the holes where a fuse to set off their lethal load would be inserted when the time came.

What, I wondered, would my gentle Ma think of her eldest child now, dealing in such a commodity? Working like a slave in a dungeon many feet below the waterline late into the night?   DL

RC Arrived back in Pearl Harbor, were in and out of here till 29 September for gunnery practice. RC

Wednesday 8 September 1943   *Moored Navy Yard, Pearl Harbor, T.H.*

DL Our rest period came to an end. Bombs out of the magazine. Every single one. Hell of a job. Big empty compartment when they had all gone. Dim, shadowy, ominous; vertical stanchions standing alone like stripped trees in a dead forest. Chiefs gave the word: Get out the chipping tools and rust scrapers. Paint buckets and brushes not far behind. DL

Thursday 9 September 1943 *Moored Navy Yard, Pearl Harbor, T.H.*

DL *On Thursday the scraping began. Dirty job, tiresome, endless. Hot, smelly. Dungarees ruined in half a day's labor. Bad dusty air, hacking cough. Headache. Breath of fresh air topside to clear the lungs. Seamen ordnancemen, strikers, Third, Second, even First Class guys worked together on hands and knees till the job was done.* **DL**

Saturday 11 September 1943 *Moored Navy Yard, Pearl Harbor, T.H.*

0907 Fire reported frame 101, second deck, port side. Galley panel leads overboard.
0909 Secured from fire quarters.

Monday 13 September 1943 *Captain G.R. Fairlamb transfers off USS INDEPENDENCE*

0903 Deck Log entry: *"In accordance with medical form G, Captain G.R. Fairlamb, Jr., USN, was transferred to USNH* for treatment."* (* US Naval Hospital)

Tuesday 14 September 1943 *Herschel Pahl and Robert Locker collide mid-air*

Mighty-I's squadrons were operating from shore bases during her stay in the Navy Yard. During squadron exercises, Ensign Herschel Pahl (VF-6 - F6F-3 Bu. No. 25983) flying from Puunene Maui, had a sudden violent mid-air collision with Lt.(jg) Robert Bratcher Locker (VF-6). Herschel Pahl was rescued by a boat, and taken to a hospital. Robert Locker's F6F was observed to plummet straight in. Robert Locker was not recovered.

Saturday 18 September 1943 *Moored Navy Yard, Pearl Harbor, T.H.*

1555 Moored as before. Got underway to shift berths.
1624 Moored to starboard side of pier B-7, Pearl Harbor Navy Yard.

Monday 20 September 1943 *Captain G.R. Fairlamb returns onboard USS INDEPENDENCE*

1116 Deck Log entry: "Captain G.R. Fairlamb., USN, returned aboard ship having completed treatment at U.S. Naval Hospital."
1320 Moored as before. Got underway with the aid of tugs to shift berths.
1358 Moored starboard side to pier B-22, Pearl Harbor Navy Yard.

Monday 27 September 1943 *Captain G.R. Fairlamb Relieved of Command*
       Commander Rudolf Lincoln Johnson Assumes Command

1357 Deck Log entry: ***"Pursuant to orders of the Commanding Officer, dated 27 September, 1943, letter # CVL22/P16-4/00 serial # 565, George R. Fairlamb, Captain, USN was properly relieved * and ordered to report to Comfair West Coast as C.O. for duty via first available aircraft."***
(* See two page letter on next two pages)

Captain George Remington Fairlamb, USN, relieved as Commanding Officer by Comdr. Rudolph Lincoln Johnson, USN of Glendale California. Rudolf L. Johnson was the ships Executive Officer. Commander Walter Fred Rodee replaced Johnson as the new Executive Officer.
Rear Admiral Arthur W. Radford, USN, ComCarDiv 11 and his staff were transferred from the ship.

Wednesday 29 September 1943 *Underway to form Task Force 14*

1100 Moored as before. Made all preparations for getting underway.
1219 Got underway, maneuvering to conform to the channel leaving Pearl Harbor.

UNITED STATES PACIFIC FLEET
AIR FORCE, PACIFIC FLEET

Serial

21 September 1943

PERSONAL AND CONFIDENTIAL

Dear John:

I must ask your help on a very important and rather delicate matter. I have done my best to solve it here, but cannot manage it.

Immediately upon arrival of INDEPENDENCE, it was noted that something was wrong and it did not take long to find out that it was Fairlamb. I directed the Division Commander (Radford) to make a surprise military inspection, but the results were not conclusive. Very shortly the word got around that the morale of the ship was very low. I made a personal inspection and later went to sea in the ship. It was quite obvious all the time that Fairlamb was in bad shape, either mentally, physically, or both. We all knew his medical record included several months hospitalization for stomach ulcers while he was down at Jacksonville. It was noted that he lived on a special diet and was subject to vomiting when under stress. In fact, this happened on the occasion of his official call on me immediately after his arrival here. The medical officer of INDEPENDENCE insisted to Fairlamb that he be hospitalized, but he refused.

As a result of my observations over a period of 24 hours at sea in the ship, I became extremely concerned. Unfortunately, Radford went off on a special mission with PRINCETON and BELLEAU WOOD and therefore was not aboard during the operations against Marcus. Prior to the departure of the ship for those operations, I had the Executive Officer, Commander R.L. Johnson, in and told him I was cognizant of the situation and reminded him of his responsibility under the regulations to relieve the captain if it became necessary. I informed Pownall, the Task Force Commander, of these instructions.

Upon return to port after Marcus, Johnson came to me and detailed certain happenings which were convincing to his mind and to mine that Fairlamb had to be taken out of the ship. I then got hold of the ship's medical officer and he reported to me that he was convinced Fairlamb should be hospitalized. He was instructed to strongly recommend to Fairlamb that he be hospitalized and report results to me. He reported that Fairlamb refused. I then got Fairlamb up and told him I was going to send him to the hospital. He demurred at first, but I showed him the transfer papers prepared by the Force Surgeon and signed by me and he finally accepted without further demur.

-1-

Letter from Rear Admiral John Towers to Vice Admiral John S. McCain regarding the relief of Captain Fairlamb. Page 1 of 2   Document from: David F. Anderson

UNITED STATES PACIFIC FLEET
AIR FORCE, PACIFIC FLEET

Serial

As a result of one week's hospitalization and complete examination, Captain Ceres, MC, in charge of the hospital, who knew all the background, reported that no "pathology" had been discovered and that it was believed to be a combination of a weak stomach and a highly nervous condition.

I would like to say at this point that I am informed that both squadron commanders of the squadrons who were aboard during the Marcus operations, Peters and O'Hare, who are very sound, expressed a fervid hope they would never have to go to sea again in that ship with that Captain.

The long and short of it is that we all know—and by "we" I mean the Ship and Force Medical Officer, Sherman, Radford, and me—that Fairlamb has no business in command. Yet we have little tangible upon which to relieve him. I know that he is not on the list of those selected for flag rank and am sure he never will be. Therefore, it seems to me the best interests would be served by ordering him to shore duty at once, and I am asking you if this can be arranged.

In view of immediate, prospective and prolonged operations, it is highly desirable that his relief be an officer experienced in carrier operations. I consider that the best man in sight within the rank brackets is Doyle, with the second best choice Logan Ramsey. Doyle is a splendid CO and had lots of good experience in command of NASSAU. I am sure he would be the first to admit that he is not suited for the type of duty to which he has just been ordered.

If you agree with me about this matter and can convince the Bureau of Naval Personnel, I consider a despatch detachment warranted in view of extended operations to start very shortly. Johnson is perfectly capable of handling the ship if there is a delay in getting the relief here.

Sincerely,

Vice Admiral J.S. McCain
Deputy Chief of Naval Operations
(Air)
Navy Department
Washington, D.C.

1337 Steamed clear of the swept channel seaward to form up in company with sister ship USS BELLEAU WOOD, USS BRAINE, USS BULLARD, USS HAZELWOOD, USS KIDD and USS TRATHEN. CVL-22 is OTC and guide operating as Task Group 15.16 in accordance with dispatch 290830 of ComTaskGroup 15.16. Fleet course 180°T, speed 18 knots, both carriers in column with destroyers forming the screen.
1441 Changed course to 215°T.
1502-1553 Gunnery Department conducted gunnery firing exercises.
1615-1701 CVL-22's squadrons returned on board as she recovered 24 F6Fs (VF6 & VF22) and 9 TBFs (VT22). The SBD half of VC-22 was transferred to Ford Island to join VB-98.
1755 USS INDEPENDENCE joined Task Unit 14.5.1 consisting of USS YORKTOWN, USS ESSEX (OTC and guide), USS BOYD, USS BRADFORD, USS BURNS, USS CHAUNCEY and USS CONNER, forming disposition 5LS, course 180°T, speed 18 knots.
CVL-22 became part of Task Force 14, and commenced operations in accordance with ComTaskForce 14 OpOrder 52-43. At 2020 they changed course to 250°T.

DL   Off we go again. Lexington left this morning with a flock of destroyers and several cruisers. We got underway at 1300, followed through the channel by sister CVL Belleau Wood. Yorktown and Essex soon joined us. Our planes landed aboard commencing about 1600, consisting of twenty-four fighters from VF-6 and VF-22, and nine VT-22 TBF's.

At quarters this morning over the PA System, the Skipper gave us the word that we were headed for something "mighty big". Almost blocking the significance of his announcement, however, was the different sound of his voice. No wonder. It came from another man.

The day after we finished restowing bombs in the magazine, our section had been granted liberty. No matter how bushed from all that work, I couldn't pass up the opportunity: never could tell what you'd find on the beach.

What took place on the ship in our absence was the relieving of our Skipper and the advancement of CDR Rudy L. Johnson, the exec, to Captain. No formal flightdeck change-of-command ceremony, no ship's company lined up in ranks, no speeches. The grapevine buzzed for days, in a subdued mood, reporting that something had apparently disturbed some officers about a certain individual's conduct on the bridge the day of our Marcus strike. The skipper's relief was handled discreetly. Only the change in the Captain's voice alerted all hands to a new chapter in our ship's life, right at the onset of this new war cruise.   DL

RC   Leave Pearl Harbor to hit Wake Island. We have 6 carriers Essex, Yorktown, Lexington, Belleau Wood and Cowpens escorted by 7 cruisers and 24 destroyers. RC

Thursday 30 September 1943   *At sea, forming Task Force 14*

0601-0608 Steaming as before. USS ESSEX launched 8 planes for a Combat Air Patrol.
0606 Sighted **Task Unit 14.5.2** composed of the USS LEXINGTON, USS COWPENS, USS DASHIELL, USS HARRISON, USS JOHN RODGERS, USS MCKEE, and USS MURRAY.
0608 Sighted **Task Group 14.6** with USS CIMARRON, USS KASKASKIA, USS DALE and USS HALFORD.
0658 Sighted **Task Unit 14.2.1** and Task Unit 14.2.2 consisting of USS BIRMINGHAM, USS MINNEAPOLIS, USS MOBILE, USS NASHVILLE, USS NEW ORLEANS, USS SAN FRANCISCO and USS SANTA FE with destroyers USS BANCROFT, USS CALDWELL, USS COGHLAN, USS HULL, USS RINGGOLD, USS SIGSBEE and USS SCHROEDER.
0800 Formed disposition 3L with Commander, Task Force 14 (OTC), in USS ESSEX. Guide in USS CIMARRON. Fleet course 270°T, speed 18 knots.
0936-0941 Launched a 6 plane CAP. Sister carriers BELLEAU WOOD and COWPENS would share CAP duties with the Mighty-I during the day.

1308-1314 Recovered the CAP launched at 0941. COWPENS would recover their planes, the last CAP of the day, by 1817.

DL   *CVL Cowpens joined up, to bring carrier strength to six. Advertised as largest aircraft carrier strike force in history. Also four light cruisers, Nashville, Santa Fe, Birmingham and Mobile, as well as three heavies, New Orleans, Minneapolis, San Francisco, were scattered throughout the task force. Oilers Kaskaskia and Cimarron were along to provide fuel for everybody, including the twenty-four greyhound tin cans galloping about. Somewhat to our surprise, there were no battleships traipsing along this time.* **DL**

JG   Captain Johnson tells us "We are with the most powerful carrier force ever put to sea" (6 carriers, 7 cruisers and 24 cans, 2 tankers.). **JG**

Friday 1 October 1943   *At sea, steaming to raid Wake Island*

Steaming as before. Today was a day of rest for the INDEPENDENCE air group, with BELLEAU WOOD putting up the first CAP at 0559, followed by LEXINGTON, then ESSEX, with YORKTOWN closing the day recovering the last CAP at 1806.
1930 Changed fleet course to 275°T.

Saturday 2 October 1943   *At sea, steaming to raid Wake Island*

Steaming as before. LEXINGTON put up the first CAP of the day, beginning launching at 0559.
1330 Commenced Phase III of the operational plan reforming into separate Task Groups, the Second Cruising Group, 14.13 in cruising disposition 8L with OTC in LEXINGTON, guide USS CIMARRON. USS INDEPENDENCE formed up in the First Cruising Group, 14.12 in cruising disposition 7L with carriers BELLEAU WOOD, ESSEX (OTC and guide), and YORKTOWN, cruisers BIRMINGHAM, MOBILE, NASHVILLE and SANTA FE, destroyers BANCROFT, BRAINE, BURNS, CALDWELL, CHAUNCEY, COGHLAN, CONNOR, HAZELWOOD, KIDD and TRATHEN, along with fleet oiler USS KASKASKIA.
2212 Crossed the 180th meridian at 20° N latitude, fleet course 270°T.

Sunday 3 October 1943   *At sea, refueling*

0559-0622 Steaming as before. Launched inner and intermediate CAPs for the fleet.
0615 Formed cruising disposition 7F coming to course 070° T, reducing speed to 9 knots.
0635 Commenced fueling operations steering on various courses at various speeds as signaled by OTC.
0931-0937 Recovered the aircraft launched at 0622 (replaced by aircraft from BELLEAU WOOD).
1152 USS SANTA FE assumed guide.
1242-1254 Launched inner and intermediate CAPs for the fleet.
1603-1620 Recovered our aircraft launched at 1254 (replaced by aircraft from BELLEAU WOOD).
1838 Completed Task Group fueling operations. Reformed cruising disposition 7L on course 270° T, speed 18 knots with OTC and guide in USS ESSEX. USS KASKASKIA, accompanied by USS DALE, departed the formation.
2100 Changed fleet course to 263° T.

JG   Destroyers are fueling from the tanker 600 miles from Wake. Band plays on the flight deck for the boys. **JG**

DL   3 October saw the task force refueling destroyers. We finished the calibration job, but meanwhile there was no slacking any other ordnance job. Captain told us we'd be furnishing fighter protection for the cruisers bombarding the island. Warned us to be ready for anything. **DL**

WAKE ISLAND

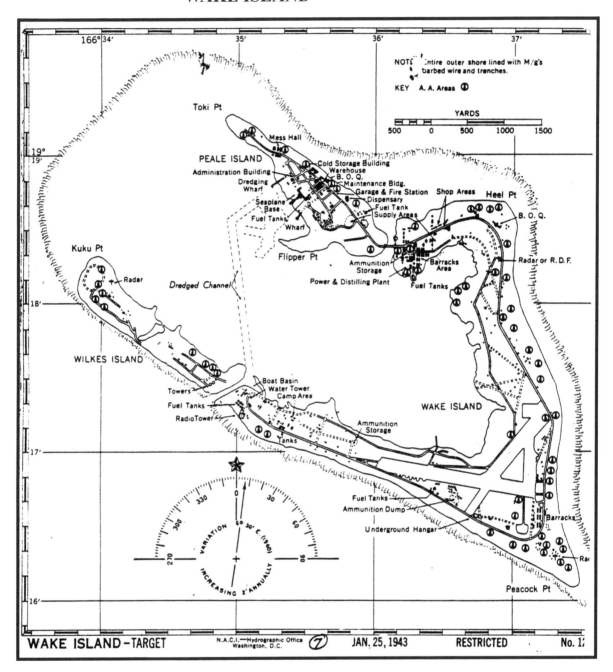

Wake Island Overview

Wake Island is a coral atoll that consist of three islands with a fringing coral reef. The islands are Peale island, Wake island and Wilkes island. Wake, the largest island, is "V" shaped with Peale and Wilkes close in at the top of the "V". A US possession, it was a base for the Pan American Airways. The US military constructed a base in January of 1941. Wake was taken from American defenders by the Japanese at the beginning of the war. The Wake Island raid, following closely on the heels of the Marcus Island raid, would keep the Japanese on the defensive, serve as a training vehicle for multi-carrier Task Groups, and help shape future carrier operations.

Breakdown of Wake Raid Task Force 14 *Groups/Units*

Task Force 14 - (Commander Task Force 14, Rear Admiral Alfred E. Montgomery, in USS ESSEX)

Task Group 14.2 -

  Task Unit 14.2.1 - USS MINNEAPOLIS (Commander Task Group 14.2 & Commander Task Unit 14.2.1), USS NEW ORLEANS, USS SAN FRANCISCO and USS RINGGOLD (ComDesDiv 50), USS SIGSBEE and USS SCHROEDER.

  Task Unit 14.2.2 - USS SANTA FE (Commander Task Unit 14.2.2), USS BIRMINGHAM, USS MOBILE, USS NASHVILLE, USS BANCROFT (ComDesDiv 28), USS CALDWELL, USS COGHLAN and USS HULL.

Task Group 14.5 -

  Task Unit 14.5.1 - USS ESSEX (Commander Task Force 14, Commander Task Group 14.5 & Commander Task Unit 14.5.1, Rear Admiral Alfred E. Montgomery,), USS YORKTOWN, USS BOYD, USS BRADFORD, USS BURNS, USS CHAUNCEY and USS CONNER.

  Task Unit 14.5.2 - USS LEXINGTON (Commander Task Unit 14.5.2, Rear Admiral Arthur W. Radford), USS COWPENS, USS DASHIELL, USS HARRISON, USS JOHN RODGERS (Commander Screening Group), USS MCKEE, and USS MURRAY.

  Task Unit 14.5.3 - USS INDEPENDENCE (COMCARDIV 22, Admiral Van H. Ragsdale, Commander Task Unit 14.5.3), USS BELLEAU WOOD, USS BRAINE, USS BULLARD, USS HAZELWOOD and USS KIDD.

Task Group 14.6 - USS CIMARRON (Commander Task Group 14.6 & Commander Task Unit 14.6.2), USS KASKASKIA (Commander Task Unit 14.6.1), USS DALE and USS HALFORD

First Cruising Group 14.12 - USS ESSEX, USS INDEPENDENCE, USS BELLEAU WOOD, USS YORKTOWN, USS SANTA FE, USS BIRMINGHAM, USS MOBILE, USS NASHVILLE, USS KASKASKIA, USS BANCROFT, USS BOYD, USS BRADFORD, USS BRAINE, USS BULLARD, USS BURNS, USS CALDWELL, USS CHAUNCEY, USS COGHLAN, USS CONNER, USS DALE, USS HAZELWOOD, USS KIDD and USS TRATHEN.

Second Cruising Group 14.13 - USS LEXINGTON (Commander Task Group 14.13), USS ESSEX, USS INDEPENDENCE, USS BELLEAU WOOD, USS SANTA FE, USS BIRMINGHAM, USS MOBILE, USS NASHVILLE, USS KASKASKIA, USS BANCROFT, USS BOYD, USS BRADFORD, USS BRAINE, USS BULLARD, USS BURNS, USS CALDWELL, USS CHAUNCEY, USS COGHLAN, USS CONNER, USS DALE, USS HAZELWOOD, USS KIDD and USS TRATHEN.

Screen Group - USS JOHN RODGERS (Commander Screening Group), USS BANCROFT (ComDesDiv 28), USS BOYD, USS BRADFORD, USS BRAINE, USS BULLARD, USS BURNS, USS CALDWELL, USS CHAUNCEY, USS COGHLAN, USS CONNER, USS DALE, USS DASHIELL, USS HALFORD, USS HARRISON, USS HAZELWOOD, USS HULL, USS KIDD, USS MCKEE, USS MURRAY, USS RINGGOLD, (ComDesDiv 50) with USS SIGSBEE, USS SCHROEDER and USS TRATHEN.

Monday 4 October 1943   *At sea, steaming to raid Wake Island*

1203-1206 Steaming as before. Launched inner and intermediate CAPs.

1330 Radar contact bearing 335°T, 58 miles. Radar contact was then lost.

1414 USS SANTA FE assumed guide.

1430 Formed cruising disposition 7R on base course 275°T, speed 18 knots.

1601 Changed speed to 25 knots.

2052 Radar contact reported by USS KIDD, bearing 238°T, 32,700 yards. The contact proved to be friendly.

JG   We are split into three formations, keeping sharp lookout for Jap patrol planes. Ship adds knots so as to be in position for the raid. We are to provide fighter protection for the cruisers that are going in to shell the island. JG

Wednesday 5 October 1943   *Wake Island raid*

The INDEPENDENCE proceeded from roughly 100 miles north of Wake with sister carrier BELLEAU WOOD. They accompanied cruisers (formed as a bombardment group) to an area 30 to 50 miles out, 060°T from Wake. The two carriers were tasked with CAP duties protecting both the cruisers and themselves. Weather for the attack was 2'000' overcast with 6 tenths sky coverage, 15 miles visibility, surface winds at 10-14 knots with light swells. CVL-22 would have two fighters from the YORKTOWN and two fighters and one Avenger from the BELLEAU WOOD make emergency landings onboard during the course of the day.

0415 Sounded general quarters. Thirty minutes later, ESSEX and YORKTOWN commenced launching the first strike on Wake, then an hour later, their second strikes.

0614 Commenced catapulting 4 F6Fs for CAP, 2 TBFs for ASP and 6 TBFs for Air Search Patrol #1. The main objective of the 6 Avengers on the Air Search Patrol was also to look for Japanese submarines in assigned sectors 200 miles out from the INDEPENDENCE.   BELLEAU WOOD would do the same commencing 0615.

0636 A destroyer recovers 3 pilots from the sea that crashed on takeoff (from other carriers).

0644 Formed cruising disposition 7RR with the 2nd Bombardment Group, as the Bombardment Support Unit (14.5.3).

0715 Secured from general quarters.

0825 Cleared the flight deck for emergency landings. Two YORKTOWN fighters, low on fuel, landed at 0830, reporting the first strike a success with 6 or 7 Zeros shot down, many fighters and bombers destroyed on the ground and large fires burning on Wake. CVL-22 refueled and rearmed her YORKTOWN guests.

0916 The Mighty-I commenced launching 8 F6Fs for CAP #2 and 1 TBF for ASP #2. (BELLEAU WOOD does the same).

0930-0935 Recovered 5 TBMs. Air search reported no contacts in their assigned sectors.

0947 2nd Bombardment group (SANTA FE Group) proceeded on scheduled assignment. CVL-22 commenced operating independently with BELLEAU WOOD and screen (DES DIV 92) BRAINE, BULLARD, HAZELWOOD, KIDD and TRATHEN forming cruising disposition 5L, INDEPENDENCE guide and OTC.

1017-1019 Launched 4 TBMs for ASP.

1023-1028 Recovered 3 F6Fs and 3 TBFs.

1100 Flying CAP in their Hellcats; Lt.(jg) Sy E. Mendenhall, wingman Lt.(jg) Bayard Webster, with Lt. (jg) Robert L. Klinger and wingman Ens. John P. Staniszewski dropped in to strafe Wake, when relieved from their patrol. Attacking from the NE, they machine gunned Japanese antiaircraft positions, barracks and an administration building, exiting toward the south.

1145-1152 Launched 10 F6Fs for CAP.

Between 1145 & 1230, VF-6 pilots Lt. Comdr. Edward H. "Butch" O'Hare, Ens. Henry T. "Hank" Landry, Lt.(jg) Alex Vraciu and Ens. Allie W. "Willie" Callan, Jr. were on CAP, assigned to cover the cruisers with the possibility of strafing runs against Wake afterwards. They were at 8,500' when given vectors for a southbound intercept, which turned out to be three Zekes in a "V" formation northbound at between 4,000' to 5,000'. The Hellcats descended to attack. Butch dropped the first Zeke, making a high side head-on firing pass, then pulling around to pick up the attack from the stern, scattering the other two Zekes. Vraciu selected the trailing Zeke on the right, opened fire and noted his tracers making hits, then smoke immediately pouring from the engine cowl, followed by it bursting into flames. Alex had to abruptly pull up, passing over the burning Zeke to avoid colliding with it. Hank scissored with the third Zeke, in an ensuing dog fight, and shot it down firing head-on. The pilot did not get out as it went down. A short time later, 20 miles south of Wake, O'Hare and Landry shot down a Betty bomber using the same type of attack as they had made on the Zeke. Firing head on (Hank hit the engine) they then attacked from the stern, shooting at the gunners, the Betty then went down. O'Hare and Landry claimed one Zeke each, and shared the Betty.

Vraciu and Callan had dropped in on Wake and made three strafing runs on ground targets. Vraciu left a Betty in an "exploded" condition, and a Zeke burning as he took departure with violent "S" turns to evade the heavy fire of all caliber (7.7mm, 20mm, 3" & 5") rising up from Japanese AA positions. Alex had used a total of 1800 rounds (a mix of incendiary, armor-piercing and tracer) from his six .50 caliber guns. "Willie" Callan departed leaving one Zeke and two barracks buildings in flames.

1200 After his CAP over the cruisers, Lt.(jg) M.E. Frelisen (VF-22) strafed barracks near Peacock Point on Wake, then picked out a Japanese ship roughly 200' long (much like one of our destroyer escorts) at anchor outside the reef east of the entrance to the lagoon, and strafed it.

He encountered a lot of AA fire, expending 1,800 rounds with no damage to his Hellcat.

1246-1300 Completed recovering 12 F6Fs.

1320 Lt. Harold McMillan and Lt.(jg) Leo Meacher were flying VC-22 TBF-1 Avengers on an ASP at about 500' over the cruisers about 10 miles south of Wake. They had been within clear view of the 3 cruisers and 3 destroyers for roughly two hours, when 2 Haps appeared. One Hap made a firing run on the underside of Meacher's TBF, then broke off in a rapid climb. McMillan's top turret gunner opened fire on the Hap. Seconds later they observed a SOC spinning down in flames from close to where the Hap had climbed. Two parachutes were seen to have open. At that time, the cruisers and destroyers began to open fire on McMillan and Meacher.

1330 The FDO (Fighter Director Officer) in USS MINNEAPOLIS vectored two VF-22 Hellcats (flying CAP over the cruisers) to a bogey. Both pilots, Lt. Clement M. Craig and Lt. Robert K. Ashford, made firing runs on a Dave biplane, which burst into flames and crashed.

1345 INDEPENDENCE Hellcats flying a CAP over the CVLs were given a vector to intercept a bogey by the BELLEAU WOOD FDO. LT. John R. Behr, Lt.(jg) James A. Bryce, Lt.(jg) Donald C. Stanley and Lt. James H. McConnell found a Betty bomber at 5,000'. The VF-22 division proceeded to make runs on the Betty, a total of 12 passes firing their six 50's. The Betty tried to seek cloud cover to evade the high side and beam runs, firing back with guns from its tail, top turret and side turrets. Descending, the Betty burst into flames at 2,500', exploded and crashed.

1348-1358 Launched 8 F6Fs for CAP and 1 TBF.

1406 Sounded general quarters. Enemy bombers approaching from the south, distance 30 miles. Changed course to 270°T.

1423 Radar contact bearing 225°T, 15 miles.

1430 CVL-22 turned into the wind (085°T) to recover aircraft.

1434-1437 Recovered 6 F6Fs.

1448 One F6F damaged his landing gear upon landing.

1453 Large group of bogies (30-40) was sighted on radar, bearing 205°T, 85 miles and closing.

1511-1530 Launched a CAP of 5 F6Fs. (BELLEAU WOOD launched 11 F6Fs).

1534 Formed cruising disposition 5V, course 290°T, speed 25 knots. Bogies soon closed to 22 miles.

1553 BELLEAU WOOD recovered 1 F6F , emergency landing.

1600 Lt.(jg) John C. Maxey (VF-22) finished his assigned CAP over the cruisers and he then strafed the old U.S. Marine barracks and adjacent buildings on Wake.

1601 Enemy aircraft opened to 60 miles. Four VF-6 Hellcats flying CAP were vectored, making visual contact on three Zekes, but they could not close on the enemy due to the Japanese altitude advantage. Launched 3 F6Fs for CAP.

1606-1610 Recovered 4 F6Fs.

1621 Enemy aircraft closed to 22 miles, bearing 240°T. Changed course to 055°T.

1638 Sighted T.U. 14.2.1 bearing 270°T, 9 miles.

1655 Enemy aircraft closed to 8 miles. Sounded general quarters. Changed course to 085°T.

1715 T.U. 14.2.1 and T.U. 14.2.2 of T.G. 14.2 formed up in cruising disposition 5LSS.

1738 Sighted T.U. 14.2.2 bearing 030°T, 8 miles.

1743 CVL-22's T.U. 14.5.3 commenced taking station in formation 5LSS.

1808 Sighted T.U. 14.5.1, bearing 330°T, 8 miles.

1818 Secured from general quarters.

1819 USS BELLEAU WOOD departed this T.U.14.5.3 to join up with T.U. 14.5.1.

1820 CVL-22's T.U. 14.5.3 commenced operating independently while recovering aircraft.

1831- 1844 Recovered 6 F6Fs and additionally (emergency landings) 2 F6Fs and 1 TBF from BELLEAU WOOD.

1902 CVL-22's T.U. 14.5.3 (less BELLEAU WOOD) joined with T.U. 14.5.2 and T.U. 14.2.1 forming up in cruising disposition 8R under T.G. 14.13 (CTG in LEXINGTON, guide in USS MINNEAPOLIS).

Karl O. Drexel   *DOG DAY ONE*   **5 October 1943**

Today the greatest Carrier Task Force (6 Carriers, 8 Cruisers and 17 Destroyers) ever assembled lambasted Wake Island. My one thought has been that this is my first real chance to help make the Japs pay for Chuck Hahn, Dave Lilly and the many other Americans that were on Wake on Dec. 23, 1941. This mornings routine was similar to the Marcus raid. Up at 0230 for the steak and eggs breakfast~ general quarters at 0330 with the first strike taking off at 0430. It was a beautiful sight to see the Hellcats, Dauntless and Avengers with their blue and red exhausts blazing in the pre-dawn darkness. We have been within easy striking distance of the Jap-held Marshall Islands for two days. Naturally during these past two days we've been expecting the works to be thrown at us. We never saw a bogie on the screen yesterday and no dawn attack today so secure from general quarters went at 0700.

Talked with the pilots as they came back. The first wave met very little anti-aircraft fire and no planes. Once again the Japanese man was caught with Honorable "pants down". The second strike, however, met with all kinds of ack-ack and some Zeros. All our planes returned to base safely although a little shot up.

This afternoon we were assigned the "hot corner." We provided air coverage (CAP) for the cruisers and cans who went in to shell the Islands (Wake, Peale and Wilkes). For two hours they pumped 454 tons of high explosive bombardment into the quaking atoll. During this bombing we were in the "front line trenches" - the only carrier close enough to the Island to intercept any attacks from the Marshalls. We figured this would be some show since it was evident that we were expendable so to speak. However, nothing developed and at the end of the bombardment period we rejoined our force.

We were told yesterday by our Skipper that this force was not going to leave Wake with an 85% completed job (as on Marcus). It was to be a 100% devastation. So with this view in mind, this evening Navy Liberators from Midway rubbed salt into the already gaping wounds by adding more bombs and bullets to ours. They reported to the task force commander, Admiral Montgomery, that there was still some anti-aircraft still being thrown up, so we are going in again tomorrow. **Karl O. Drexel**

DL *On Tuesday 5 October (6th, west of the IDL) reveille was at 0250, first launch at 0615. All day long planes left and returned. Most had fired their guns or dropped their bombs and we recleaned and reloaded until about 1000 when GQ sounded and we had to don our steel helmets. Bogeys reported within thirty miles. A nuisance, never showed up. Our work continued without much a break until 2330. A few planes had flak nicks, one TBF came back with a bay door damaged after its bombs had exited.* ***DL***

GN *We hit Wake Island for the first time since it was taken by the Japs.* ***GN***

JG *Reveille at 0240. general quarters at 0415.. Some other carriers lose planes taking off. Planes go over in waves bombing the hell out of them. Some of the planes come back with holes in them from Jap AA fire on the island. Butch O'Hares boys attached to our ship keep Jap planes away from ship. We hang around all day and night just looking for trouble.* ***JG***

GL *Hit Wake Island. Planes took off just before dawn. Sent in repeated attacks all day long. Planes destroyed 30 Jap planes in the air and 31 on the ground. "Butch" O'Hare still flying from the Evil I.* ***GL***

Captain Johnson addresses the crew during the Wake Raid. The opening in the flight deck, called the "Glory Hole" by the Aviation Ordnance Men, was the bomb elevator. Not a good location, it was a make-do design necessitated by the conversion.

Chapter 7   185

With bakers standing by, and the ships band playing in the background on the flight deck, VF-6 fighter pilot Lt.(jg) Alex Vraciu gives a piece of cake to Captain Rudy Johnson. The cake (in the shape of the carrier) was in celebration of the carrier's 2,000th landing on USS INDEPENDENCE flight deck. The date of the landing was 5 October 1943. Alex was the pilot. Alex survived the war, an ace credited with 19 victories, awarded the Navy Cross, the D.F.C. and Air Medal.

Thursday 6 October 1943   *Wake Island raid*

Steaming as before in T.U. 14.5.3 (less BELLEAU WOOD) with T.U. 14.5.2 and T.U. 14.2.1 in cruising disposition 8R.

0430 Sounded general quarters.

1515 USS ESSEX and USS YORKTOWN launched their first strikes of the day.

0530 USS LEXINGTON launched its first strikes of the day.

0615-0633 Launching a strike of 8 Avengers and 8 Hellcats (escorts) against Wake Island. During this period of time, USS COWPENS began launching.

0651 Secured from general quarters.

0702 Lt.(jg) Sy E. Mendenhall had climbed into his F6F-3 (Bu. No. 8849) and strapped in. Wings were unfolded and locked, a plane director helped position him on the catapult, and the deck crew readied him for launch. With the R-2800 Pratt & Whitney turned up, prop tips biting at the air, he was ready for his mission. "Fly-One" swung his arm forward in an overhead arc and off Sy ambled into the wild blue. The wrong wild blue. Something had gone amiss mechanically with the catapult and Sy Mendenhall and his Hellcat settled into the wild blue sea. Sy exited the sinking aircraft.

0714 Completed launching 10 F6Fs.

0718 Lt.(jg) Sy E. Mendenhall was rescued, uninjured, by the USS SCHROEDER.

0732 Recovered two fighters making emergency landings.

0800 Sighted 1st Cruising Group (plus BELLEAU WOOD), bearing 150°T, 6 miles.

0815 Behind a rain squall moving in over the target area, Comdr. James M. Peters led the VT-22 bombing strike in on Wake Island targets, having flown 95 miles from launch on heading 202°T, dropping bombs as follows;

Comdr. James M. Peters - twelve 100# bombs on a fuel storage facility, starting fires.

Lt. Comdr. Thomas H. Jenkins - four 500# bombs on a mess hall and barracks on Peale Island.

Lt. Harold W. McMillan - one 2,000# daisy-cutter on central Peacock Point.

Lt.(jg) Silas R. Johnson - twelve 100# incendiary clusters on a barracks area starting a large fire.

Lt.(jg) Robert M. Soule - four 500# bombs on a mess hall and barracks on Peale Island.

Lt.(jg) Billy B Laughren - four 500# bombs, 1 on a building, one near miss near a bridge, 2 on a runway.

Lt.(jg) Robert W. Scholk dropped four 500# bombs on large buildings in central Peale.

Due to the rain storm, pilots were forced to attack at low altitudes, making AA more of a problem, and damage assessment difficult. (AA was described as light but numerous, from all over the island.)

The 4 VF-6 Hellcats (flown by Lt.(jg) R.S. Merritt, Lt.(jg) R.A. Hobbs, Ens. T.A. Hall and Ens. B.E. Gates) were escorts for the avengers. They now proceeded to strafe targets of opportunity on the island.

VF-22 fighter pilots (Lt. Leland L. Johnson, Lt. R.K. Ashford, Lt. C.M. Craig and Lt. J.H. McConnell) strafed targets on Peale Island leaving ammunition dumps exploding, and fuel trucks & fuel storage areas exploding & burning.

0852-0940 Recovered 6 Avengers and 8 Hellcats.

0941 A F6F-3 from USS COWPENS could not lower its tail hook and was forced to make a water landing 180°T from this vessel. (The VF-23 pilot Ens. C.N. Seaver was recovered by USS DASHIELL)

0941 Radar surface contact, 25 miles, bearing 030°T.

0956 COWPENS reported its pilot (Ens. Orson H. Thomas - VF-25) was sighted in the water, uninjured, 2-3 miles off Peacock Point. Unable to give assistance.

1043-1046 Completed launching 7 Hellcats for CAP, and 4 Avengers for ASP.

1050-1055 Recovered 8 F6F Hellcats.

1313-1321 Recovered 8 F6F Hellcats.

1436-1437 Recovered 3 Avengers (ASP).

1515 Launched 2 Hellcats to escort 2 SOCs launched by the USS SAN FRANCISCO to attempt the rescue of two aviators reported in a raft.

1550 A F6F-3 from the COWPENS struck the ramp and crashed over the port side into the water. (VF-25 25 pilot Ens. Eldin Robert Arms was not recovered.)

1629 A destroyer was unable to recover the COWPENS pilot.

1642 Radar contact 25 miles, bearing 325°T.

1650 The SOCs and CVL-22 escorts were unable to locate the downed aviators in the raft.

1828 Sighted T.G. 14.12. Minutes later, at 1833, general quarters was sounded on order of the OTC.

1838 Recovered the (two) CVL-22 Hellcat escorts (and USS SAN FRANCISCO recovered its SOCs).

1930 Secured from general quarters.

1938 Rendezvoused with T.G. 14.12 (OCT in ESSEX and guide USS MINNEAPOLIS).

2013 Departed from T.G. 14.12. Formed cruising disposition 8R, with T.U. 14.5.2 & 14.5.3 on base course 080°T, speed 18 knots, zigzagging per plan 6.

USS INDEPENDENCE aircraft damage during the two day raid included:

1 F6F lost - Lt.(jg) Sy E. Mendenhall - Defective catapult launch.

1 F6F - Damaged longeron broken due to plane handling.

1 TBF - After bulkhead shorn due to successive hard landings.

1 TBF - Lt.(jg) B.B. Laughren - 6 holes in wings, and severed ruder cable - 7.7mm enemy AA.

1 TBF - Lt.(jg) R.W. Scholk - Hole in wing - 7.7mm enemy AA.

1 TBF - Lt.(jg) R.M. Soule - Hole in wing - 7.7mm enemy AA.

1 TBF - Lt..(jg) L. Meacher - Holes in wing & damaged hydraulic system - 7.7mm & 20mm enemy AA.

Also, Lt. Meacher and Lt. McMillan received friendly fire from the cruisers while flying ASP for them.

During the action on 5 October, Willie Callan caught sight of fresh game sporting meatballs on the wing. He turned in toward his target and began firing. In startled disbelief, Sy Mendenhall evaded as his wing-man tried to shoot holes in his tail. Willie recalls the event over a half century later: *"I soon realized the recognition error and after the mission we both told Butch about the incident."* Butch essentially replied: *"Willie, I've been telling you, you haven't been using enough lead on your targets"."*

The problem had been with the Navy insignias on the aircraft. During a transition to new insignias, in certain lighting conditions, the over-painted insignia would appear to be a solid meatball. The problem was of enough concern to have been noted in the **USS INDEPENDENCE Action Report - Recommendations Based on this Action:** (the Wake Action). Some exerts from the report follow;

(C) Several fighter pilots almost made runs on aircraft of their own force due to poorly executed painting-out of former insignia. The over-painting shows up as a darker-toned, round blotch on the gray-blue background. The result at long range greatly resembles the dark circle of the Jap insignia. It is strongly recommended that this defect be remedied immediately. (The round insignia was replaced in late June. Locations on the on the planes had also changed, with some over-painted - see flight deck photos)

Additionally: **Old Insignia**   **New Insignia**

3. The conduct, performance and skill displayed by ALL hands on board during this action were excellent and in accordance with the traditions of the service. The measure of success contributed to the operation by this command is largely due to the outstanding work and spirit of the Aircraft Crews, the Fighter Director - Radar team and the Landing Signal Officers. That other ship's departments (than Air) were less conspicuous is due entirely to the splendid performance of the Air Department components which denied the enemy access to our forces.

4. During this operation two Fighters landed against wave-offs and "got away with it". While this is not recommended as a standard procedure, it demonstrates what can be done under stress even on a small flight deck.

5. The Catapult can be a tremendous asset to a CVL when forced to jockey for a launching position within a disposition confined by a screen; conversely the lack of a catapult may be of great handicap to the entire disposition, It is urged that effective steps be taken to provide spare parts and ample servicing facilities for catapults at Pearl Harbor.

Up again this morning at same time for same routine as yesterday. We expected the Nips to come up in droves today. At 1500 general quarters was sounded. We all thought this was it and we were thanking the Good Lord we were not in the same position as we were yesterday afternoon. The attacking groups were picked up on the screen about 90 miles away. The "blip" on the screen showed the groups to be a 50 or 60 plane formation. But as it turned out our fighters intercepted two groups of 15 planes each about 20 miles out. Soon afterward we secured from general quarters with a sigh of relief.
Now we are on our way out. We saw no action. Being in enemy water for this length of time with an at-tack expected any moment has left everyone kind of limp. It's surprising how the tension mounts under such conditions. You don't realize that you are keyed up until you begin to leave the danger area. Even then the danger of a sub is imminent, especially when recovering or launching aircraft and we are out of the destroyer screen. During these two days of attacking more than 800 sorties were carried out. More than 400 tons of projectiles deposited on the Island by bombardment and over 300 tons by aircraft. Barracks, administration buildings, power plants, water distillation plants, gun emplacements, runways, etc. were destroyed or severely damaged. At least 60 aircraft, 30 of which were in the air, were destroyed.   ***Karl O. Drexel***

DL   *On Wednesday 6 October (7, west of the IDL) when reveille again rousted us, everyone was so tired it was difficult to shake the remnants of whatever sleep we'd received out of our heads. Work today actually not as intense as yesterday; maybe we're getting used to it.*
    "God," said a bleary-eyed Whitey, "I hope this gets over with soon."
    Last deckload landed before dusk and we began to haul ass back to Pearl.
    Friday morning Independence lost a fighter over the side on take-off. Catapult malfunctioned and dumped plane and pilot* into the drink. I remember jumping to the deck to see whatever I could see, which was only a brief glimpse of the plane's tail just before it disappeared. A sharp-eyed OD on the bridge snapped quick orders to the helmsman to avoid the pilot by swerving the ship just enough to miss him, though he must have got a bellyful of salt water as the hull rushed by fast enough to thrust him out of the way. Picked up later by a destroyer named Schroeder, maiden name of my Mother.
    (Fifty-six years after this incident I received a letter from the dunked pilot, an ex-member of VF-6, a retired commander. Wrote that he knew immediately the catapult hadn't given his plane sufficient boost. He struggled to exit the cockpit as soon as he hit water, apprehensive that the looming hull would run him down, and endured a long wait for a boat from the can to pluck him to safety. Still a vivid memory. This letter to me only because I mentioned to our reunion group's historian that I'd recorded such an incident in my little note book, and he happened to know the pilot.)   ***DL***

(*Sy E. Mendenhall was the pilot of the F6F-3 that was lost to the sea due to the bad cat shot)

JG *10/7/43 Headed back for Pearl. Rig for fueling at sea. Boilers leaking, no showers. Only enough water for drinking.* ***JG***

CINCPAC Communiqué No. 15, dated 10 October indicated that 320 tons of bombs were dropped on Wake, 30 or more Japanese aircraft were destroyed in the air and 31 on the ground. Two small vessels were destroyed. The Task Force lost 13 planes in combat. Additionally, (not in the Communiqué) the Task Force lost approximately 14 planes operationally due to deck crashes, or other causes.

Note: The US would later learn the Japanese executed 98 civilian contractors they had captured in December 1943, as a direct result of this raid. Presuming a US landing would be attempted, the execution was ordered by Rear Admiral Sakaibara Shigematsu and was carried out on 5* October to eliminate the civilian contractors as a possible problem or threat.
(* The 5th per R. J. Cressman's Chronology with other sources indicating the 7th.)

Captain Rudy L. Johnson with Admiral Alfred E. Montgomery

"Butch" O'Hare in a VF-3 Grumman F4F Wildcat (most likely shot at a Naval Air station).
O'Hare, with VF-6, flew F6F Hellcats off the "Mighty-I".

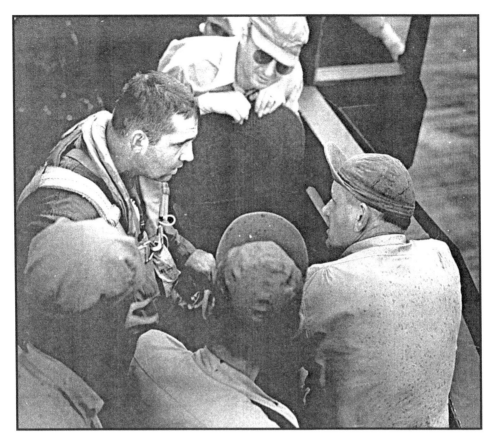

"Butch" O'Hare with Rear Admiral Alfred E. Montgomery - 5 October 1943

Alex Vraciu with Rear Admiral Alfred E. Montgomery

On the flight deck during refueling operations. The tanker USS KASKASKIA is alongside to starboard (note the wake in the water on the starboard side). The destroyer aft is possibly USS BOYD.

Note the "poorly executed" over-painted National Aircraft Insignia on the folded F6F wing in the foreground, that presented a problem of being mistaken for a Japanese "Meatball" (see 6 October 1943, 4 pages back). Insignias had been removed from the upper right and lower left wings. Also note the F6F behind it (wings extended) still in transition with the new insignias painted on, but the old insignia not yet over-painted on the upper right wing.

Thursday 7 October 1943   *Withdrawing from Wake Island*

Steaming as before with T.U. 14.5.2 & 14.5.3 on base course 080°T, speed 18 knots, zigzagging per plan 6. Commander T.G. 14.13 in USS LEXINGTON (guide), Commander T.U. 14.5.3 in this vessel.
0622 USS MINNEAPOLIS assumed guide.
0705 Sighted T.G. 14.12, 8 miles.
0740 Rendezvoused with T.G. 14.12., and they joined the formation.
0816 USS CIMARRON assumed guide.
1159-1226 Launched 4 TBFs for ASP and 10 F6Fs for CAP.
1527-1602 Recovered all aircraft launched at 1226.
1840 USS LEXINGTON assumed guide.
2000 Changed course to 095°T.

Friday 8 October 1943   *Refueling*

0540 USS INDEPENDENCE left Task Group 14.13 to conduct fueling operations with Task Group 14.12. INDEPENDENCE, ESSEX, LEXINGTON, YORKTOWN and BELLEAU WOOD would provide air patrols during the day.
0640 Assumed station with fueling group, disposition 8F, course 070°T, 12 knots.
0730 USS KASKASKIA came along the CVL-22 starboard side and USS BOYD fueled off the tankers starboard side.
1059 Cast off from USS KASKASKIA having completed fueling.
1127-1335 USS HAZELWOOD was along our port side to take on fuel.
1419 Having completed fueling operations with T.G. 14.12, commenced maneuvering to take station in T.G. 14.13, Commander and guide of T.G. 14.13 in USS LEXINGTON.
1458-1500 Launched 4 TBFs for ASP.
1459 Crossed 180th meridian at 21 N Latitude.
1732 Formed cruising disposition 8R, course 090°T, 20 knots.
1810 T.U. 14.6.2 departed the disposition.
1831-1836 Recovered the ASP launched at 1500.

Saturday 9 October 1943   *Steaming toward Pearl Harbor*

0800 Joined T.G. 14.12. (Commander and guide in ESSEX). Formed cruising disposition 3L, course 090°T, 18 knots.
0942-1011 Launched 7 TBFs for ASP.
1301-1306 Recovered the ASP launched at 1011. COWPENS, ESSEX and YORKTOWN provided patrols throughout the day as well.

Sunday 10 October 1943   *Steaming toward Pearl Harbor*

0652-0703 Steaming as before. Launched 6 TBFs for ASP.
1012-1022 Recovered the ASP launched at 0703.
1530 Commenced operating independently by Task Units. This vessel OTC and guide of T.U. 14.5.3 operating in company with USS BELLEAU WOOD, USS BRAINE, USS BULLARD, USS HAZELWOOD and USS KIDD.
1712 Formed cruising disposition 5LS.

Monday 11 October 1943   *Moored Pearl City, Oahu, T.H.*

0509 Radar picked up landfall on the Island of Kauai (bearing 040°T, distance 73 miles).

0653-0723 Launched 23 F6Fs and 3 TBFs, headed for Hawaii.

0751-0752 Launched 2 TBFs. The TBFs of VT22 flew to NAS Hilo (moving to Luke on the 19th).

0829-0903 Conducted target practice on 3 balloons.

1102 Sighted Barbers Point (082° T, 22 miles).

1149-1151 Launched 4 TBFs. Number 22-C-7, a TBF-1 was lost over the side as it failed to take off, and splashed into the water. USS KIDD picked up the pilot (Lieut. Harold W. McMillan) and his crew, with no injuries.

1257 Destroyers deployed to screen the entrance into Pearl Harbor.

1330 Passed channel buoy #1 to port entering the swept channel.

1440 Mooring starboard side to berth V-2 at in Pearl City, Oahu, T.H. in 40 feet of water.

DL *Entered Pearl Harbor this afternoon, docked near Pearl City.* *DL*

Thursday 14 October 1943 *Moored Pearl City, Oahu, T.H.*

1915-2230 Moored as before. Received munitions from NAD, Oahu.

DL *On the 14th took six hundred cases of AP ammo from the magazine. All bad, will have to be exchanged. Went into Honolulu. Must have been half the U.S. Navy in port all at once. Streets never so jammed. Almost no civilians anywhere, except behind store counters peddling cheap goods to rich swabbies.* *DL*

Friday 15 October 1943   *Underway for Training Exercises near Hawaii*

0907 Moored as before. Cast off lines and got underway.

1002 Departed the swept channel.

1008 Formed up with TG 19.17 with USS LEXINGTON, USS YORKTOWN (guide and OTC) and a destroyer screen consisting of USS BOYD, USS BRADFORD, USS BROWN, USS CHARRETTE, USS IZARD, USS MCKEE, USS SCHROEDER and USS SIGSBEE, cruising disposition 5LS modified.

1115 Changed course to 235°T.

1205 Reformed in a column formation for firing practice runs with INDEPENDENCE in trail behind the YORKTOWN and LEXINGTON.

1250-1535 Gunnery Department conducted firing exercises.

1601 Formed cruising disposition 5LS modified on course 230°T, 18 knots.

1644-1729 Conducted qualification landings with TBF's. The other two carriers also conducted flight operations, with the YORKTOWN conducting operations at night.

1850 USS LEXINGTON departed the formation to conduct night flight operations.

1908 Changed course to 250°T.

Saturday 16 October 1943 *At Sea - Training Exercises near Hawaii*

0625 Radar contact with USS LEXINGTON and her escorts, bearing 075°T, 33,000 yards.

0730 Formed disposition 5LS modified, USS YORKTOWN guide and OTC.

0833-0834 Launched 2 TBFs.

0841 INDEPENDENCE assumed guide. During the day she conducted gunnery exercises.

1835 USS LEXINGTON departed the formation to conduct night flight qualifications.

Sunday 17 October 1943 *At Sea - Training Exercises near Hawaii*

0809 Steaming as before. USS LEXINGTON rejoined the formation. Formed cruising disposition 5LS.

0905 The three carriers formed up in a column disposition, USS INDEPENDENCE guide.

1015-1127 Gunnery Department conducted firing exercises.

1110 Sighted Oahu, bearing 035°T, 29 miles.

1130 Formed cruising disposition 5LS modified.

1231 Task Group under simulated attack by the USS BUNKER HILL Air Group.

1504 Passed through entrance channel to Pearl Harbor.

1549 Moored with the starboard side to berth V-1, Pearl City, T.H. in 40' of water. (The V-1 berth was near the tip of the Pearl City Peninsula near where the Pan Am Clippers landed daily)

2105 Completed fueling the ship.

Monday 18 October 1943   *Moored Pearl City, Oahu, T.H.*

JG Spent most of the day loading ammunition. Some fun. JG

Wednesday 20 October 1943   *Moored Pearl City, Oahu, T.H.*

DL Wednesday 20 October was a long day that didn't end until after midnight. Phil and I tagged along with Rebel into Honolulu. Saw a movie I have no memory of, ate too much indifferent food (Rebel found a place serving ham, grits, and gravy; was beside himself with delight), bought more books and a lot of magazines.
Upon crossing the quarterdeck just before 1800 the JOD informed us the new belted ammo would be arriving at midnight and all ordnancemen were assigned to unload it from the trucks and stow it in the small arms mag. If any of us could have got his hands on the stateside machinists who'd screwed up that original supply of ammo, he (assuming it was a he) would have ended up ground to bits by his own lathe. DL

Thursday 21 October 1943   *Underway from Pearl Harbor, T.H.*

0210 Moored as before. Completed receiving munitions from NAD Oahu.

0830 Made all preparations for getting underway.

1002 Underway, maneuvering to clear the berth, in accordance with ComCarDiv 4 OpOrder 1-43.

1104 Departed the channel from Pearl Harbor seaward.

1138 Formed up on USS ESSEX (OTC) in T.U. 53.3.1 in company with USS BUNKER HILL (guide), and the DD screen; USS BULLARD, USS CHAUNCEY, USS KIDD, USS HAZELWOOD and USS HEERMANN.

1309 Formed cruising disposition 5LS.

1312-1346 Landed onboard 24 F6Fs and 1 TBF.

1525 Sighted Task Unit 53.3.2.

1530 Sighted Task Unit 53.3.7.

1613-1621 Landed onboard 8 TBFs.

1717 Task Group 53.3 formed cruising disposition 3LS on course 180°T, 15 knots. OTC in USS TENNESSEE, guide is USS GUADALUPE.

DL Underway at 1000, which meant a lot of grumpy ordnancemen going to quarters half asleep. A good many ships went through the channel to the open sea before we did, and another long string followed. The grapevine says we're headed southwest this time, maybe to New Caledonia. DL

Friday 22 October 1943   At sea - *Underway from Pearl Harbor, T.H.*

0820 Steaming as before. Changed course to 210°T.

0906-0917 Launched an inner and intermediate Air Patrol of 6 Avengers.

1317-1322 Recovered our patrols launched at 0917.

1400-1447 Exercised crew on abandon ship stations.

1853-1913 Exercised crew at fire quarters.

8
The Rabaul Raid

Breakdown of the Task Group 53.3 *Units*

Task Group 53.3 - (Commander Task Force 53.3 in USS TENNESSEE)

> **Task Unit 53.3.1** - USS ESSEX (Commander Task Unit 53.3.1), USS BUNKER HILL, and USS INDEPENDENCE.

> **Task Unit 53.3.2** - USS GUADALUPE (Commander Task Unit 53.3.2), and USS PLATTE.

> **Task Unit 53.3.4** - USS SANTA FE (Commander Task Unit 53.3.4), USS BIRMINGHAM, and USS PORTLAND.

> **Task Unit 53.3.7** - USS TENNESSEE (Commander Task Force 53.3, Commander Task Force 53.3.7), USS COLORADO, USS INDIANA and USS MARYLAND.

Screen Group - USS JOHN RODGERS (Commander Screening Group), USS BULLARD, USS CHAUNCEY, USS DASHIELL, USS HARRISON, USS HAZELWOOD, USS HEERMANN, USS HULL, USS KIDD, USS MCKEE, USS MURRAY, USS RINGGOLD, USS SIGSBEE and USS SCHROEDER.

DL *Although the Wake Island task force had been powerful and impressive to look at, the number of ships going to sea with us this time bore a touch of majesty, a command presence beyond compare. With no flight quarters planned for a couple of days, and an occasional break between bouts of replacing good AP ammo for bad, I had a chance to enjoy the sight of all those vessels spread out on all sides. Four battlewagons and four cruisers had accompanied the three carriers out of the channel, as well as a pair of oilers and a whole division of tin cans. Our next operation was pretty sure not to be another pinprick hit-and-run raid as Marcus and Wake had been. We were on our way for the kill.*

Confirmation of a long voyage ahead came that evening through the dependable grapevine. All shellbacks, officers and men, were to report to Chief's quarters for proper identification. Meaning that a crossing of the Equator lay dead ahead. We pollywogs (at least three-quarters of the personnel aboard) began to shiver in our boots. No mercy could be given or expected....

When USS Independence, CVL-22, slid through the Pearl Harbor channel on that October day in 1943 to join up as a member of the task force, not an officer or man aboard had the ghost of an idea how glad he would be to enter that jeweled harbor again.

Too many young men were fated never again to see it. *DL*

JG *Sunrise at 0700, sunset at 1930. Sailing in deep blue today. Awake this morning to find that we had joined quite a large sized Task Force. GQ at 1935 tonight.* *JG*

Saturday 23 October 1943

0649 Launched one Avenger for air patrol, when further launching was stopped by the OTC.
0723 Recovered the Avenger, launched at 0649.
1026 Radar contact reported bearing 075°T, 63 miles. The contact was then lost.
1440 Gunnery Department test fired all 20mm and 40mm guns.
1551-1557 Launched an inner and intermediate Air Patrol of 6 Avengers.
1759-1808 Recovered the patrols launched at 1557.

Sunday 24 October 1943   *Splash 1 TBF Avenger*

1000 Steaming as before. Changed course to 190°T.
1605-1631 Launched 6 TBFs for an inner and intermediate Air Patrol. A catapult bridal broke during the launch of TBF-1 (Bu. No. 23963) and the aircraft splashed down in the failed attempt to get airborne. The VC-22 pilot (Lt..jg William M. Comegys) and his two aircrew members were rescued by the USS KIDD uninjured.
1834-1838 Recovered the air patrol launched at 1631.

Monday 25 October 1943

0138 Steaming as before. USS TENNESSEE reported surface radar contact, bearing 349°T, 18,000 yards. The contact was lost.
0636-0720 Air activity started the morning with the BUNKER HILL losing a SB2C as it crashed into the water during a launch.
0719 Commenced fueling operations as directed by OTC. Formed fueling disposition F1, guide USS GUADALUPE. Course 150°T, speed 11 knots. AOs began to fuel the destroyers.
1016 USS ESSEX assumed guide.
1042 A TBF from the ESSEX made an emergency landing aboard our vessel.
1215 Fueling operations completed. Reformed cruising disposition 3VS.
1257-1302 Launched an inner and intermediate Air Patrol of 6 Avengers.
During the afternoon destroyers lined up to begin transfers.
1335 USS BULLARD came alongside to transfer the SB2C pilot recovered from the BUNKER HILL crash.
1416 USS SIGSBEE came alongside to transfer secret guard mail.
1428 USS KIDD transferred the aircrew from the failed VC-22 launch on 24 October.
1646-1654 Recovered the air patrol launched at 1302.

JG Sunrise 0558. Sunset 1830. The day today nearly perfect, the water was smooth with sunshine all day. JG

Tuesday 26 October 1943   *King Neptune's Royal Court*

0417 Steaming as before. **Crossed the equator** at Longitude 170-56.2W.
0623-0645 Launched an inner and intermediate Air Patrol of 6 Avengers.
1009-1014 Recovered the air patrol launched at 0645.
1837 Launched 1 TBF for return to USS ESSEX.

The Mighty-I had crossed the equator. Only two types of sailors were in the Task Force that day as they sailed across the invisible line in King Neptune's domain.

You were a Shellback or a Pollywog !

Certificate of initiation into the *" Solemn Mysteries of The Ancient Order of The Deep"*

Signed by Davey Jones *"His Majesty's Scribe"*
&
Captain R.L Johnson acting *"Servant"* of
Neptunus Rex
"Ruler of the Raging Main"

DL   *That evening every pollywog, officer and man, received an elaborate copy of his personal Subpoena and Summons Extraordinary, printed over an idealized sketch of the ship:*

To All Who Shall See These Presents
Greetings

WHEREAS, the good ship INDEPENDENCE, bound southward, is about to enter our domain and whereas the aforesaid ship carries a large and loathsome cargo of land lubbers, beach-combers, guardo-rats, sea-lawyers, lounge-lizards, parlor-dunngans, plow-deserters, chicken-chasers, four-flushers, dance-hall sheiks, drugstore cowboys, asphalt arabs, and other living creatures of the land, masquerading as seamen of which low scum you are a member, having never appeared before us; and
WHEREAS, The Royal High Court Of The Raging Main
will convene on board the good ship INDEPENDENCE on the (26th) day of October 1943, in Latitude Zero degrees Zero minutes Zero seconds Longitude [Censored] and whereas an inspection of the Royal Roster shows that it is high time your sad and wandering nautical soul appear before Our August Presence:
BE IT KNOWN, That we hereby summon and command you Donald E. LaBudde (sic) AOM3c U.S. Navy to appear before the Royal High Court to be examined into your fitness to be taken into the citizenship of the deep and to hear your defense on the following charges:
CHARGE I: In that you have hitherto willfully and maliciously failed to show reverence and allegiance to our ROYAL PERSON, and are therein and thereby a vile landlubber and pollywog.
CHARGE II: In that You   (Blank; maybe they'd run out of suitable insults)....

Given under our hand and seal.

Davey Jones, *scribe*   **Neptunus Rex**, *Supreme Ruler*

There were signatures affixed to this document, but I didn't recognize the names or else they were figments of someone's imagination. B.C., being the only shellback in the ordnance gang, almost got deep-sixed that night in self-defense by us pollywogs. All in good fun, of course.

All through the ship there was an ominous atmosphere of dark thoughts and dark doings running rampant. Shellback sailors with long-held grudges against pollywog shipmates finally had a quasi-legal opportunity to square things in almost any way they could devise. In a few rare cases, pollywog officers would have to watch their backs when confronted by deputized shellback sailors they'd had to discipline formally in the past.

Fact was, nobody could be sure what would happen. Anticipation swung between trepidation and downright fear.

Independence wasn't alone in this hectic scene. The task force was big, covering hundreds of square miles. Every vessel from tin can to battlewagon was setting up for the same ancient ritual. Pollywog admirals vied with shellback seamen. Every man for himself--sort of. Rank did have its privileges.

It turned out to be a great day, a mixture of anxiety and relief. The weather was good. A Combat Air Patrol (CAP) from another carrier was the only flight of planes aloft.

On Independence the huge pollywog contingent from Captain to seaman striker had his dignity and body saved from insult or injury, thanks to a timely intervention by an obscure but deadly unit of the Imperial Japanese Navy.

Just before noon the GQ alarm began clanging away. Sailors had never reversed their planned roles faster than we did that day. general quarters, every man knew, was never part of any playtime drill. Skirted, big-bosomed swabbies of all ranks and ratings rushed to their battle stations topside or below decks. All guns were manned and ready within minutes. All flightdeck eyes were fastened on the big bedspring radar antenna aft of the island structure, a habit we'd started on the way to and from milkrun Marcus. This cruise, we knew, was taking us deep into an active war area. Our concentration never faltered, nor did the antenna halt its circular traverse of the sea.

There was nothing out there. This time.

An hour later Captain Johnson announced that a Jap sub had been detected at the fringe of the task force. Tin can sound gear having indicated a genuine target, the admiral in charge called off all ceremonies connected with inducting all pollywogs into The Ancient Order of the Deep.

For half an hour after the All Clear everyone held his breath. The Japanese Long Tom [1.] *torpedo had earned a dread reputation among American sailors. The mere threat of a submarine in the vicinity alerted not only an admiral but raised the hackles on every man's chest.*

GQ was secured. As our costumed crew went its various ways, the Captain's voice broke into the barely suppressed sighs of relief to announce that, despite the interruption, all pollywogs had dutifully crossed into Neptune Rex's Domain and therefore were now and forevermore authorized Shellbacks.

Fun and frolic turned to tragedy early the next morning. Independence was assigned the dawn anti-submarine patrol, which meant it was only half-light when we began launching eight torpedo bombers. We had armed each with a pair of 250-lb depth charges, the usual load.

Four planes swept down the deck into the gray sky without incident. I was in the port catwalk, blue cloth helmet tied at my chin, dungaree shirt a thin sheet in the brisk wind. Lieutenant Harry and Ensign Porky were alone together off to one side. Bill and Tom and, I think, Big Dan, were in the catwalk beside me. Our phone talker, little Frank, stood with his special gear mounted on his chest. Every eye was on each airplane as it roared by.

The sixth plane swept by and began a climb that almost immediately went awry. Two of us very stupidly leaped to the deck for a better look. The plane just seemed to hang in the air. Then the nose dipped slightly and the wings leveled out. A half-second later the port wing dipped sharply and into the drink the big plane went with a huge splash.
"CLEAR THE DECK!" boomed the bull horn from the bridge.
We never got a chance to. The depth charges exploded and the plane vanished. Just like that.
A brief flash of flame, a great splash of water mixed with solid chunks of debris. I felt the ship swerve slightly to starboard. We must have been doing thirty knots. Other guys by then had joined us on the flightdeck.
I staggered back to the catwalk and jumped down, trying to ignore Ensign Porky's angry shaking head.

Nobody spoke. Airplane numbers Seven and Eight were instructed to kill their engines. A windy silence followed.

That afternoon an informal hearing was held by the Air Officer in the wardroom. Harry and Porky attended, as did the rearming crew leader and a couple of other ordnancemen, one of whom was B.C. Not yet having been assigned to a specific job, he had wandered under this TBF as it was being loaded. His testimony that nothing he'd observed had been incorrect or unauthorized had significant influence with the examiners--and cemented his relationship with all of us. An honest man. If he had seen something wrong, he'd have said so.

The brief investigation was inconclusive. Aircraft maintenance personnel were the most thoroughly grilled; ordnance was almost a sideshow. Not even a rumor of a problem with the engine or the aircraft structure came to light. Three men were dead.

I was sickened almost to nausea. Once again I'd seen violent death. This time it was closer than before. Big Dan, who had comforted me weeks before in Pearl Harbor after that mock attack accident, said nothing. His warning that something like this could happen again rang in my ears. This time, though, it was worse. These were our men; the plane had been assigned to Independence.

Next day, as the good Padre held a memorial service on the hangar, I was busy in the rebelting room helping Bill square it away. Later we listened to a shipwide broadcast of the Notre Dame-Navy football game. Most everybody bet on Notre Dame.
Few men were as nationally famous as Butch O'Hare; it was an honor to have him aboard. But the other members of his section of Fighting Six were as anonymous to the public as we were. It had to be that way, really. A large percentage of ships company seldom got to the flightdeck.

[1.] Don Labudde referred to the **Japanese "Long Lance"** (Type 93) **Torpedo** as the Long Tom.

But even to us airdales who were topside everyday, most pilots were strangers. They became as faceless to us as we surely were to them. That's why some dubbed us "deck apes." A form of humanity beneath them, necessary to have around but mostly avoidable.

I felt no resentment at this, though it galled some of my shipmates. These men did most of the dying connected with aircraft carriers, they were the ones taking the war to our enemy. But when a pilot and his crew died violently before the eyes of some, all the men felt it in the gut of his heart. No broadcast of a football game thousands of miles away could drown our silent grief.

Besides, our time to begin dying was fast approaching. **DL**

(The fatal accident Don witnessed was that of Ensign James Samuel Behrens, in a stall /spin accident on takeoff. The date was 27 October . The aircraft a TBF-1C Bu No 23881) (Note: the date was listed as the 27th in the CVL22 War Diary and the 29th in the VT22 Squadron History)

JG 10/26/43 Sunrise 0600 Sunset 1758. A nice day today, a few clouds in the sky but everything cleared up making it another warm day. Ship crossed the equator this morning at 0445. Initiation of the Pollywogs this morning was canceled because enemy submarines had been contacted. General quarters at 1808, Condition III watch set on the battery. **JG**

Wednesday 27 October 1943 *We lose three men in an accident*

0641-0653 Launched an inner and intermediate Air Patrol of 7 Avengers and 1 Hellcat. A TBF-1 (Bu. No. 23881) crashed after take off in a probable stall/spin accident, with depth charges appearing to detonate on impact. USS SCHROEDER recovered only minor items from the wreckage. Lost were pilot Ensign James Samuel Behrens and his aircrew members William Marvin Martin ARM3c & Roy Alfred Utter AMM3c.
1007-1015 Recovered our air patrol.
1117 USS BULLARD came alongside to deliver guard mail.

JG 10/27/43 Sunrise 0708 Sunset 1934. Weather today cloudy with showers this afternoon. This afternoon the ship lost a TBF over the side taking off. All three men lost. The plane exploded as soon as it hit the water. Information was given to us tonight that the plane captain had taken the regular radioman's place in the plane in order to get in time for flight pay. The band played on the flight deck this afternoon, because of Navy Day, playing tunes that brought back many fine memories. General quarters at 2005, Condition III set on the battery. All clocks were set back 1/2 hour at 1900 tonight. **JG**

RGA   Had a piece of blueberry pie with dinner. The war seemed so far away with all the entertainment on board today. **RGA**

Thursday 28 October 1943

0800 Steaming as before. Changed course to 000°T.
0932-0944 Launched an inner and intermediate air patrol of 7 TBFs and 1 F6F, with 4 additional F6Fs for an exercise.
1200 Changed course to 130°T.
1302-1314 Recovered the aircraft launched at 0944.

JG   Sunrise 0708 Sunset 1921. Water smooth and clean. Set all clocks back one half hour at 1900 again tonight. GQ at 1954. **JG**

Friday 29 October 1943 (& Saturday 30 October 1943)   *We cross the IDL*

0607 Steaming as before. USS PLATTE lost power and stopped dead in the water.
0639 USS PLATTE Resumed station under her own power. Battleships launched aircraft.

0852 Battleships commenced recovering their aircraft.

1158 Crossed the 180th meridian (International Date Line) at 12° South Latitude.

1209 Changed to East Longitude date, 30 October, 1943, zone minus 13.

1235-1242 Launched an inner and intermediate air patrol of 6 TBFs and 1 F6F.

1456-1506 Recovered the air patrol launched at 1242.

The group steamed south, course 180°T, speed 15 knots.

JG 10/29 & 10/30 Sunrise 0708. Crossed the 180 degree meridian at 1000 today, therefore shifting the time ahead twenty four hours. So today is now Saturday the 30th instead of Friday. Sunset Saturday night 1845. JG   ***RGA***   *Thundershowers in the afternoon*   ***RGA***

Sunday 31 October 1943   *Steaming to Espiritu Santo*

0156 Steaming as before. USS DASHIELL reported a sound contact, and investigated. Unable to locate the contact, she resumed her station at 0250.

0442 USS MARYLAND reported a sound contact, bearing 037°T, 7 miles. USS HEERMANN was sent to investigate, with negative results.

0631 Formed fueling disposition F2. Fleet course 310°T, 11 knots.

1130 USS RINGGOLD came alongside with guard mail.

1304 Landed 1 TBF from USS BUNKER HILL, flown over as a replacement aircraft.

1620 The Independence took aboard a second replacement TBF from the USS BUNKER HILL.

1734 Fueling operations were completed. Formed cruising disposition 3VS, on course 320°T, 15 knots, with USS TENNESSEE (OTC), and USS GUADALUPE (guide).

1900 USS SCHROEDER came alongside with guard mail.

JG GQ at 0543. The water today was smooth and clean, hardly a ripple except the ships wake. GQ at 1900. JG

Monday 1 November 1943   *Steaming to Espiritu Santo*

0000 Steaming as before, changed course to 230°T. At 0600, began north easterly course changes to form fueling disposition F1 with a fleet course and axis 070°T, at a speed of 11 knots.

0724   With water as smooth as glass, the USS PLATTE came up along the starboard side to deliver fuel oil. Over the next hour and 1/2, five small 5° course changes would slowly bring the course and axis to 95°T while fueling was in progress. The Gunnery Department set condition IV instead of condition III while the tanker was along side. With fueling completed and hoses recovered, at 1003 all lines were cast off from the USS PLATTE. Just under an hour later air operations began with the launching of 7 TBMs and 3 F6Fs for inner and intermediate air patrols. At 1149 one TBF was recovered from the air patrol for an emergency landing. Twenty minutes later 1 F6F was launched as a replacement.

The USS ESSEX took up the watch launching air patrols (1422-1429), losing one aircraft on takeoff at 1424 with the sea claiming the airframe, a TBF Bu.No. 05892. The USS JOHN RODGERS successfully rescued the air crew, its second "Plane Guard" rescue of the day.

1448–1459 CVL-22 recovered the air patrol launched 3 hours before. Course changes made throughout the afternoon would point the Task Group to southeasterly headings.

1554 Fueling operations were completed and the Task Group formed cruising disposition 3VS with the guide in USS TENNESSEE course 248°T, axis 215°T, speed 12 knots.

1726 USS KIDD briefly came along side to deliver Guard Mail.

USS ESSEX recovered her chicks and the USS BUNKER HILL stood watch for the fleet.

At 1800 & 1845 BUNKER HILL aircraft reported surface contacts that disappeared as the plane closed on the contact. USS SIGSBEE investigated, reporting the contact to be a whale.

1900 All clocks were set back 1 hour (zone minus 12).

2000 Changed course to 217°T, and the crew settled in for the evening.

Tuesday 2 November 1943   *Task Groups join up*

0500 Steaming as before. With fueling operations completed, USS PLATTE & USS GUADALUPE accompanied by USS HAZELWOOD & USS HEERMANN detached from the Task Group and proceeded to NANDI. As the tanker group pulled away the USS BUNKER HILL launched the days first air patrols.

0550 The Task Group formed cruising disposition 3LC, course and axis 217°T, speed 15 knots, Guide USS TENNESSEE. Shortly after 0700 BUNKER HILL recovered her air patrol, and at 0720 with her aircraft recovered, the course and axis changed to 245°T. Fifteen minutes later USS KIDD reported possible sound contact.

0745 Task Group 53.2 was sighted hull down on the horizon, bearing 250°T, distance 13 miles.

0805 USS KIDD again picked up another sound contact and began dropping depth charges. Negative results.

0818 Our Task Group (53.3) was joined by Task Group 53.2 forming disposition 3L with a course and axis 215°T, speed 15 knots, guide is USS ESSEX, OTC in USS WASHINGTON. In addition to the WASHINGTON, 53.2 ships included USS SOUTH DAKOTA, USS ALABAMA, USS MASSACHUETTS. Their screen is; USS FLETCHER, USS RADFORD, USS JENKINS, USS LA VALLETTE, USS NICHOLAS, and USS TAYLOR.

0925-0933 Launched 8 TBFs for inner and intermediate air patrols as eyes for the Task Group. One TBF was recovered ten minutes later and launched again at 0954.

1016 Radar contact was made on an unidentified plane, bearing 85°T distance 60 miles. Contact closed to 40 miles and then faded.

The USS ESSEX then took over inner and intermediate air patrol duties as the carrier launched her birds at 1235-1239. A few minutes later INDEPENDENCE recovered her TBF Avengers. ESSEX recovered her air patrols from 1612-1618 with a course change to 195°T.

1700 Changed axis to 270°T and the USS ESSEX assumed guide. Courses for the afternoon basically westerly with a speed of 15 knots. BUNKER HILL stood watch from 1519-1823.

JG *"Water all around couldn't be better except for the heat. GQ at 1830 tonight."* *JG*

Wednesday 3 November 1943   *Steaming to Espiritu Santo*

0523 Steaming as before. USS ESSEX kicked the morning air operations off launching inner and inter-mediate patrols.

0810 Formation axis changed to 215°T. Within 15 minutes USS BUNKER HILL was launching the next group of air patrols and the ESSEX began recovery of her early birds (0859-0905).

0925 The Task Group formed disposition 0L, with course & axis 215°T, speed 13 knots. OTC and guide USS WASHINGTON. Course and disposition changes were made over the next 2 hours, settling in with disposition 3V.

1200-1210 Launched air patrols for the Task Group.

The afternoon would get busy, with the ESSEX also launching aircraft (1231-1303) for a simulated air attack on the Task Group.

1449-1511 Course and axis changes commenced and the ships crew went to torpedo defense to repel the simulated air attack.

1520 USS ESSEX began recovery of her Air Group. One minute later a TBF from BUNKER HILL made an emergency landing on our flight deck.

1538-1546 We recovered our flyers (launched at noon).

1603 The Task Group formed cruising disposition 3L on a course of 130°T, axis 090°t, speed 15 knots, OTC USS WASHINGTON, guide USS TENNESSEE.

1730 Changed axis to 050°T. 1831-1837 BUNKER HILL recovered her air patrol.

2000 Changed course to 085°T.

JG "Water calm today. Joined forces with three more cruisers, Portland, Salt Lake City & Birmingham. Today the force passed within sight of Berwice Island." (Vanua Levu) *JG*

GL "Stayed off Fiji Island and picked up rest of task force." *GL*

Thursday 4 November 1943   *Steaming to Espiritu Santo*

JG "Sunrise 0630. Sunset 1800. Cool last night. Air quiet and sky clean. All of the light cruisers left the formation today early, leaving us only heavy cruiser Portland." *JG*

0000 Steaming as before. Changed course to 050°T.
0540-0545 The USS BUNKER HILL kicked off the morning air operations with the dawn patrol during the early morning hours. The course was changed to the north and at 0730 changed to 320°T.
0831-0839 Launched 2 F6Fs and 8 TBMs, relieving the BUNKER HILL aircraft.
0915 Formed contact disposition 0L, USS WASHINGTON OTC, USS ESSEX guide, with a course and axis 320°T, speed 15 knots.
1141 BUNKER HILL began launching their air group to replace INDEPENDENCE aircraft on inner and intermediate combat air patrols.
1207-1214 Recovered all aircraft launched at 0839.
1436 The Task Group formed cruising disposition 3L. USS MASSACHUSETTS assumed guide.
Essex launched the last air patrols of the day, allowing the BUNKER HILL to recover her air crews.
1635 ESSEX assumed the Guide, recovering her patrols just after sunset.
1930 Changed course to 245°T.
2330 Changed course to 300°T.

Friday 5 November 1943   *Steaming to Espiritu Santo*

JG "Sunrise 0635 Sunset 1748. All of the battleships left the force at 0600 this morning to go into port. We will follow them in this afternoon. Pulled into Espiritu Santo, northern most island in the New Hebrides group. Dropped the anchor at 1605. The harbor lies closely between two islands in the group, in what is called the Diamond Passage." *JG*

0525-0535 Steaming as before. USS ESSEX launched her air patrols.
0554 In accordance with operational schedules, battleships departed from the formation. Task Group 50.3 formed in cruising disposition 5LS, axis 120°T course 300°T, speed 25 knots. CVL-22 was in the company of USS ESSEX (guide & Commander Task Group), USS BUNKER HILL, USS KIDD, USS CHAUNCEY and USS BULLARD.
0614 Changed course to 305°T. Nine minutes later clocks were set back 1 hour (Time Zone minus 11).
0750-0753 BUNKER Hill launched the next air patrol, and ESSEX recovered her air patrol.
1047 Lopevi Island was sighted bearing 230°T at 25 miles. Seven minutes later Pauuma Island came into view bearing 260°T at 23 miles.
Were it not for the war, today could shape up into a nice scenic cruise. Certainly a geography lesson with remote islands the crew had never heard of appearing at different compass points on the horizon. Those less fortunate, with duties in the bowels of the ship were visually deprived.
1106-1110 While BUNKER HILL was recovering her air patrol, 5 TBF's were launched from the INDEPENDENCE flight deck for intermediate air patrol duty.
1138 Lookouts sighted Ambrym Island, bearing 305°T at a distance of 27 miles along with Pentecost Island, bearing 296°T, 28 miles distant. Changed course to 300° T.
1230 The T.G. passed thru the Selwyn Strait. An hour later the Mighty-I steamed past the USS MATSONIA abeam on the port side, followed shortly with the sighting of Malekula Island at 230°T, 23 miles and Aoba bearing 008°T at 22 miles distance.

1401 CVL-22 passed the abeam of the USS ARCTIC, SS FRANK C. DRUM and YP 419 off the port side. Minutes later the BUNKER HILL launched her patrols, ESSEX recovered her anti-submarine air patrols, and we began to recover our 5 TBF's.

Over the next hour 3 more course changes would occur, and on a new heading of 246°T, CVL-22 would pass within 8 miles of Tutuba and Malo islands. At 1513 they sighted Espiritu Santo, bearing 345°T, 10 miles out. A half hour later, with speed dropping to 20 knots, CVL-22 formed up on ESSEX, minutes later slowing again to 15 knots.

1607 Passed Point XRAY abeam entering a swept channel into Pallikulo Bay, Espiritu Santo, New Hebrides, dropping anchor in 45 fathoms of water between berths 32 & 34.

Don Labudde *wrote:*

"Even though we were anchored off shore, the jungle could be seen growing right to water's edge. Warships and auxiliaries cluttered the harbor. In the distance no Sea Bee construction battalions could be seen tearing up the real estate. They'd long ago finished their task here. We had cruised past a number of hazy islands as we approached. One of them reached quite a way into the sky, decorated with a garland of white clouds.

For the first time, I felt a long way from home. It was not only hot but sultry. Clothing stuck to the body. Nothing ashore looked inviting. The Plan of the Day stated that liberty would be sharply restricted. Wandering off into the jungle was not a wise idea. No drinking water and no food of any sort would be available. Manpower was too short to make up rescue parties. Above all, the ship would be leaving soon with little notice.

Which she did. But not until we all had worked our tails off in that stifling air. One morning's chores began with reveille at 0430. Never saw so many cases of Spam in my life!

Next day we replaced all the ammo in twelve fighters and I didn't get to Sunday services again. I always seemed able to find an excuse. Did receive several welcome letters and cards; too many cards that spoke good wishes in sophomoric verse with nothing but a signature scribbled below. What a waste! What vapid salutations!

An hour's unexpected notice was all it took to get the ship underway at 1630. Big hurry. Rumors shot through the ship that a Japanese task force was heading our way from Truk, the so-called Pearl Harbor of the southwest Pacific, an area the Japs had been taking over until their conquest had been halted at Guadalcanal.

Everybody topside got a thrill when, just before sundown, the task group was joined by a squadron of four new battleships charging toward us from the starboard quarter. Of course the occupants of the bridge knew they were coming, but we coolies didn't. They were beautiful but looked mean. Neat bow waves gleamed pink in the lowering sun; long 16-inch rifles jutted from their turrets like rounded steel toothpicks: U.S.S. Washington, Alabama, South Dakota, and Massachusetts. Handsome. Fast. Mighty fighting machines. Next morning battlewagons and the threat from Truk had vanished. Most airdales were sorry the big ships were gone. Loaded with ample anti-aircraft batteries, they'd be great to have along for protecting the carriers.

Dusk was still hours off when we got underway about 1730 and made passage through the same channel between small islands. No flight quarters were scheduled, but our officers and Chiefs couldn't bear to let us alone for a few hours. I almost fell asleep watching a mandatory training film about loading TBFs with torpedoes. Not much different from the lessons we were supposed to have learned in Chicago. Here in the after ready room where the film was shown, even rolled-up shirt sleeves would have been a blessing. Porky and the Chiefs frowned at those who tried it (including me). Harry removed his cap and wiped his brow but left his sleeves buttoned; Navy had learned by sad experience that shirt sleeves worn properly helped protect bared skin from being scorched by fire.

So we endured the stink of each other's sweat and smoked till the air turned into a blue haze.

The film flicked away, a voice droned on through the projector's tiny speaker. Cigarette followed cigarette. Air in the room became opaque. Hacking coughs, burning eyes.

The film ended and we stumbled into the passageway, which felt almost cool. And heard a new rumor from someone hurrying by: "Ship's headed for Rabaul."

As Independence headed roughly north and westerly with carriers Bunker Hill and Essex and our nine escorting destroyers, Rear Admiral A. E. Montgomery in charge of Task Group 50.3 (SOUTHERN CARRIER GROUP), we left LCDR Butch O'Hare behind. Combat-battered Enterprise had returned from yard repair at Bremerton and he would assume command of a new air group. No shipwide announcement of this transfer was made, so the first we airdales suspected something like this was when he failed to show up at flight quarters. Fate decreed that we were never to set eyes on him again.
Everybody was too busy to dwell on his absence. The whole atmosphere had changed. The Marcus and Wake Island raids had been exciting. What was approaching excited us in a different way. This was for real. They'd been training exercises--except for the airmen who were lost. Up to now no one on the ship had even been shot at." **DL**

Saturday 6 November 1943   *Anchored in Pallikulo Bay, Espiritu Santo, New Hebrides*

Anchored as before. 1602– 1806, received fuel oil and Aviation fuel from USS ATASCOSA.

Sunday 7 November 1943   *Anchored in Pallikulo Bay, Espiritu Santo, New Hebrides*

Anchored as before.   *Frank Capka would note:*

FC *"The Mighty I was temporarily detached from the large task force being assembled by Vice Admiral Raymond A. Spruance, USN, and issued orders to report to Rear Admiral Frederick Sherman, USN, who was at that time in command of a carrier force pointing for a strike at Rabaul.*
"Something was Up" there and all hands on the Mighty I knew it, particularly when it was disclosed that the USS ESSEX and the USS BUNKER HILL were also picked for the mission. Nevertheless, the three flat-tops were given only two days to prepare for the unexpected "detour" in the planned operations, and Rear Admiral Alfred E. Montgomery, USN, was elected to command the triumvirate." **FC**

(Halsey organized a fast hit & run raid on Rabaul just prior to the upcoming Gilbert's operation. With very tight timing, he sent the SARATOGA - PRINCETON carrier group led by Sherman. Sherman would attack from waters north of Bougainville. The ESSEX - INDEPENDENCE - BUNKER HILL carrier group, under Admiral Alfred E. Montgomery, would join the attack from the Solomon Sea off the south side of Bogainville. Halsey also ordered air support from the Solomon Island air bases.)

At 1629 the crew began making preparations for getting underway. 105 fathoms of wet anchor chain began cascading down into the port anchor chain locker. COMSOPAC dispatch 070050 set the wheels in motion for steaming out of the berth into the channel. At 1725 the USS INDEPENDENCE once again passed Point XRAY forming up on USS ESSEX. CVL-22 was joined by USS BUNKER HILL, USS BULLARD, USS KIDD and USS CHAUNCEY becoming Task Group 50.3.
The destroyers steamed up ahead to form a screen. USS ESSEX OTC & Guide, axis 000°T on a course of 120°T at 20 knots.
2150 Passed Cape Cumberland abeam at 10 miles off to port finishing the day off on a course of 278°T, speed 22 knots.

JG *"We were told early today that the ship is on 1 hour notice for getting underway. The sun shone all day and the water was very smooth. The ship got underway at 1600 for parts unknown."* **JG**

GL *"Had a full moon and place was under possible air attack so we had to pull out at night and return in the morning."* **GL**

Monday 8 November 1943   *Coral Sea - Underway to attack Rabaul*

0137 Changed course to 125°T.

0147 Sighted Cape Cumberland, 10 miles, bearing 180°T.

0551 Changed speed to 22 knots, course 190°T.

0656 Passed Pallikulo Point abeam to port, and began maneuvering to conform to the channel.

0708 Anchored in 45 fathoms of water between berths 32 & 34 in Pallikulo Bay, Espiritu Santo, New Hebrides.

1532 The crew once again began preparations to get underway.

1556 Underway in accordance with Commander Task Group 50.3 dispatch 080358. Steered various courses at various speeds to clear the channel and passed point XRAY at 1620. In addition to carriers ESSEX & BUNKER HILL, CVL-22 was accompanied by destroyers USS BULLARD, USS CHAUNCEY, USS EDWARDS, USS KIDD, USS STACK, USS STERETT, and USS WILSON. As before, Mighty-I took up position off USS ESSEX (OTC, guide and Commander Task Group*[1]). Course & axis 350°T, speed 25 knots.   *[1] Rear Admiral Montgomery Commanding.

2035 Sighted Cape Cumberland, bearing 265°T, 18 miles

2211 Changed course & axis to 278°T.

GL   *"Pulled out of New Hebrides to attack Rabaul Harbor in New Brittan Island, also Bougainville Island. We went through the Coral Sea. Had routine G.Q. this morning and night."*   *GL*

Tuesday 9 November 1943   *Coral Sea - Underway to attack Rabaul*

0500 The Task Group maneuvered into the wind by signals from USS ESSEX (OTC & Guide). USS BUNKER HILL launched the dawn air patrols and 1 hour later the fleet formed into disposition 5LS on a course of 278°T, axis 270°T at 18 knots.

0817-0839 Deck crews on INDEPENDENCE catapulted 8 TBF's for inner & intermediate air patrols. One hour later USS STERETT came along side to deliver guard mail.

1129-1147 Launched 12 F6F fighters for exercises and then recovered 8 TBF Avengers. At the same time ESSEX & BUNKER HILL put aircraft into the air for exercises, and the Task Group turned to 088°T.

1231-1240 Launched 9 more F6F's.

1256-1319 Sounded torpedo defense to repel a simulated air attack. Torpedo defense was again re-peated 1401-1439. Minutes after torpedo defense concluded, CVL-22 recovered 11 fighters and 30 minutes later recovered the balance.

1547 The Task Group changed course to 278°T and eleven minutes later the ships Gunnery Department began test firing our automatic weapons, expending 98 rounds of 20mm and 100 rounds of 40mm. The crew ended the busy day, once again, ready to go into combat against the enemy.

DL   *"All fighters flew today. Most pilots fired their guns at something. We cleaned and oiled them and pasted tape over their muzzles.*

Later in the day skipper Johnson finally gave ship's company the word: We are to hit the major Japanese base at Rabaul on New Britain Island, a place so tender the Japs are sure to rise up in righteous wrath in defense. Old Saratoga and CVL Princeton, which had been beating up on the area for a few days, are to support us. Captain Johnson said we'd be going up the western side of the Solomon Islands and should be passing legendary (he didn't use that word) Guadalcanal this afternoon. We'll be in Empress Augusta Bay tomorrow.

Everybody listened to his voice. From the by-pass ramp we could look up at the bridge and see him speaking into the mike. I don't remember anyone in the ordnance gang making a snide or comical comment. All that concerned us was what the TBFs would carry. It was a sleepless night."   *DL*

JG *"Reveille at 0355, GQ at 1427 at sea. We have been under the command of Admiral Halsey for the past two days. The weather is perfect and the sea is smooth. The ship had nearly all her planes in the air today. GQ tonight at 1930."* **JG**

Wednesday 10 November 1943   *Underway to attack Rabaul*

0520 Steaming as before. The USS ESSEX turned the Task Group into the wind and launched the intermediate and combat air patrols.
0805 USS MCKEE and USS MURRAY joined up with the Task Group (50.3) to assist with screening. ESSEX recovered & BUNKER HILL launched. CVL-22 would take up the call for air patrol duty launching 4 Hellcats and 4 Avengers from 1203-1211. They were recovered 1518-1527. One hour later, USS MURRAY came along side with guard mail.
1741 The T.G. began the high speed run toward its launching point for the attack on Rabaul at 30 knots.
1755 Changed fleet course to 325°T.

JG *"GQ at 0428 this morning. The Captain informed us this afternoon that we would enter Augusta Bay tomorrow, and will attack shipping around Rabaul. At 1800 tonight the ship starts doing 30 knots, course 345° continuing this speed and course throughout the night. The main Jap submarine base is near here, accounting for the fact that there are so many submarines in these waters. No GQ Tonight. Rain pounds down through the night."* **JG**

DL *"No flight quarters this morning. The sea looked the same to me, except that it might have been a shade more gray. Choppy water. Plenty of wind. From time to time a hazy shadow of an island slid by. We must have been doing twenty knots.*

    Word came down from on high early this afternoon: all torpeckers to carry fish. Up they came from their storage in a special magazine not manned by ordnancemen but by torpedomen, whom we seldom dealt with except when they needed us. Like now.

    Loading went smoothly without a hitch. Even Porky was surprised. But any sweet-talking AOM who ever struggled while handling those long, heavy sausage-shaped mechanical denizens of the deep came away from the loading task spouting language he hadn't realized he knew.

    "Practice makes perfect," a sweating Sully mumbled at Porky half under his breath. "Sir."
    Porky made as if he didn't hear, never cracked a smile.
    This is what we were being paid for. Less than a hundred bucks, most of us, once a month."
DL

Thursday November 11, 1943   *Solomon Sea - Rabaul*
Rabaul Overview

The USS INDEPENDENCE, as an element of TF 50.3, was about to raid one of the most important and heavily defended Japanese Army and Naval bases in the South Pacific. Rabaul was a key hub and a major threat that needed to be removed as we advanced toward Japan.   (See maps on pages 147 & 215)

Rabaul is located on the north eastern side of New Britain, which lays off the eastern side of Papua New Guinea. It is 500 miles northeast of Port Moresby. It is at the northern end of the Solomon Islands, northwest of Bougainville. To the south is the Solomon Sea, to the north, the Bismarck Sea. To the east New Ireland, the Pacific Ocean is on New Ireland's eastern shore.

A volcanically active area, the harbors were formed in a large sunken caldera nestled between two volcanoes, Tavurvur and Vulcan. Rabaul was deemed too heavily occupied and defended to invade (for the blood price we would pay), made additionally difficult with its large complex of volcanic tunnels, it was wisely decided to bypass and isolate Rabaul. Shipping and its aviation infrastructure would be attacked to defang "Fortress Rabaul" and remove it as a threat to allied forces. This was part of a larger plan to cut off shipping of raw materials going to Japan, and contain military assets from spreading out to hit us in secured areas.

Other more lightly defended islands in the area would be taken and air bases quickly established to keep Rabaul isolated and neutralized, and reduced as a threat, with constant raids.

While the INDEPENDENCE was steaming towards Pallikulo Bay in Espiritu Santo, a few days earlier on November 5th, Rear Admiral Sherman led the first raid of carrier air strikes against Rabaul, inflicting damage to several ships of the Japanese Fleet. He was returning to decimate vessels in the bay. It was now CVL-22s turn to join in. Unknown to Rear Admiral Sherman, the Japanese had moved many of its ships out of the bay to safer waters.

November 11th would be the second carrier air assault against this bristling military bastion. Defended with over 350 antiaircraft guns, and over 40 coastal guns and numerous airbases, it held promise of a target rich environment.

Rabaul however would be target rich for both opposing forces. Who would best swing that sharp double edged sword?

This would be a fast hit and run follow-up raid to sink shipping targets and further deplete the Japanese aviation assets.

From the INDEPENDENCE "Action with the Enemy Report":
" Aircraft operating from the USS INDEPENDENCE throughout the action of November 11th, were:
VC-22 9 TBF-1's under Comdr. James H. Peters, U.S.N., Air Group Commander.
VF-6   12 F6F-3's under Lt. Comdr. Harry W. Harrison, U.S.N.R., Squadron Commander.
VF-22 12 F6F-3's under Lieut. Leland L. Johnson, U.S.N.R., Squadron Commander.
VF-33 11 F6F-3's under Lieut. John Coney Kelley, U.S.N. "

Thursday November 11, 1943   *Solomon Sea - Rabaul*

Reveille at 0330. general quarters sounded at 0512 (secured at 0624).
0517 Sighted shore based CAP on an early morning with clear skies and calm water. Pilots feasted on their usual Steak & egg breakfast. Afterword in the ready room they would obtain their briefings, fidget with plotters to work out navigation problems and prepare for the mission.

KOD "Pilots man your planes," comes over the squawk box. All file out, some grim faced, some laughing, most of them scared a little (as who wasn't). **KOD**

0545-0553 Sighted 8 other friendly vessels, hull down, on the horizon (3 CL's and 5 DD's).
0611 Sighted Bougainville Island, bearing 070°T, distance 40 miles.
0640 The INDEPENDENCE was off Bougainville near Empress Augusta Bay when she commenced launching the first strike consisting of 9 Avengers of VC-22, each armed with one MK.13 torpedo using Torpex warheads. The 9 Avengers were escorted by a total of 16 F6F-3 Hellcats, 8 each from VF-6 and VF-22. The mission targets were enemy shipping in and around Simpson Harbor. 8 Hellcats from these two squadrons (4 each) remained on board in event they were needed to launch as additional CAP.
Land-based VF-33 fighter pilots flew 11 Hellcats in from Segi Point, New Georgia to serve as CAP over the Task Group. At 0700 CVL-22 received word to be prepared to land them aboard at 0745. They began landing aboard the INDEPENDENCE at 0836. She refueled and rearmed the aircraft, fed the pilots, and began launching them at 1022. One pilot would remain onboard due to nausea. They would use INDEPENDENCE as a support base to refuel and rearm. VF-17 pilots flying F4U-1s operating out of Ondongo, New Georgia were also tasked with top cover for TF 50.3. They would refuel and rearm off other carriers. Avengers would be catapulted. Hellcats would deck launch, using an average of 390'.

Aircraft from the USS BUNKER HILL (VF-18) and USS ESSEX (VF-9), would make strikes on shipping in the same general area. Sherman's PRINCETON and SARATOGA aircraft (on the Pacific side of Bougainville Island) would find their operations hampered by weather.

The Avengers flew toward Simpson Harbor at 11,000 feet. Flying conditions were average throughout the day with Cumulus clouds present in a layer from twenty five hundred to three thousand feet presenting 3 tenths cover. Winds became light and variable after 0800. Higher Cirrus, Alto-Cumulus and Alto-Stratus clouds would give 6 tenths sky cover supplying scattered showers throughout the area all day. Weather was a factor. It could help or hinder, providing cover for both attacker and target.

Two divisions of 4 fighters each, flew out in front on either side roughly 1,200' above the Avengers. Another two divisions flew 3,000' higher ahead of the group. One of the higher divisions of Hellcats would remain at altitude as top cover when the Avengers and fighter escorts dropped in for the torpedo attack.

The flight spotted a Japanese Cruiser* and two Destroyers steaming south roughly 8 to 10 miles NW of Duke of York Islands outside of Simpson Harbor. All the aircraft, except the top cover, pushed over to drop in for the attack. Aircraft from other carriers had also spotted the Japanese warships. They were finishing their strikes while the Avengers were setting up to make their torpedo runs on the cruiser. As the Avengers began their approach to the target the Hellcats commenced strafing runs on the cruiser and one destroyer. The Japanese took exception to the affront with a stiff barrage of AA fire described as a "virtual blanket" from both the cruiser and the destroyer. Two divisions strafed the cruiser and one division strafed both ships.

The Avengers released their torpedoes at an altitude of 275' to 300' off the water, roughly 1,000 to 1,600 yards from its starboard side, airspeed 190—200 knots. Eight torpedoes dropped thru open bomb bay doors at angles of 45° to 90° off the cruisers bow. One hit was observed at or near the stern on the starboard side, with no apparent change in the cruisers speed. The ninth TBF-1 Avenger (flown by Walter L. LaFleur) was unable to drop his torpedo, its bay doors jammed shut due to damage to the aircraft during catapulting from the INDEPENDENCE. One torpedo was seen to veer off at a right angle to the direction of launch. One "or possibly two" torpedoes were reported to have failed to run.

Following the attack, the Avengers turned back toward the fleet. Most of the fighters after their strafing runs made an attempt to rejoin with the Torpedo Planes but mistakenly hooked up with nine Avengers from another carrier. The only fighter to successfully rejoin to protect the returning Avengers was flown by Lt. Earl Willis Marsh (VF-22). Flying back to the INDEPENDENCE, Marsh, as sole escort, saw two Zeros appearing to commence a run on the flight. Marsh immediately turned into them to counter their attack. Two other Zeros dropped in from a higher altitude to join the fray. Marsh shot down one Zero, but from all appearances, sustained vital damage to his fighter. Rolling over on his back and bailing out of the crippled Hellcat (F6F-3 Bu. No. 8834) at 800', the chute was seen to open only 100' above the sea in St. Georges Channel, off Cape Palliser. His doomed fighter crashing into the water some distance away. Seconds after March had parachuted into the water, the remaining 3 Zeros each made a strafing run on Marsh. Marsh, an expert swimmer, was hoped to have had a good chance to make it to the shore of New Britain or New Ireland on either side of the channel, if he had survived the strafing. "His action in defense of the TBF's is considered to have saved VC22 from probable losses of planes and men."

The group of 4 Hellcats that remained top cover during the low level attack on the Japanese ships, lost sight of the Avengers due to the low cumulus layer. Looking for their Avengers, they were jumped by an estimated 12 to 18 Zekes near Gazelle Point. In the ensuing fur ball, Ens. R.A. Hobbs (VF-6) became a Zero magnet, finding two on his tail, and taking hits. Lt. R. S. Merritt (Division Leader) gave Hobbs a hand with his problem shooting down both Zekes, hitting one in the engine from above at 9 o'clock, stitching the other in the Fuselage, firing his six 50's level at 12 o'clock. The action continued as Ens. T.A. Hall pulled the trigger and took out a Zeke from 12 o'clock level, then went after another only to find himself scrapping for pieces of it with Lt. J. R. Behr & Ens. B.E. Gates. The three eager Hellcat pilots would have to share credit for the Zeke morsel. As this action continued Hall found a Zeke attached to his tail, which in turn was jumped by Behr. Behr hot on the tail of the Zeke was in turn jumped by two others from above. A quick split "S" shook off the two Zeros, only to be jumped by two more. A dive for speed and gradual full power climb at 160 knots allowed him to outrun the Zeros making good his escape. A Zeke was observed on the tail of Ens. Bascom Eugene Gates, Jr. (VF-6) during the melee. Hall dove on the Zeke causing the pilot to break off the attack. This was the last time Gates was seen.

Hobbs was not without problems after Merritt relieved him of his Zekes. With his hydraulics shot up, he could not extend his landing gear and had to make a water landing. He was picked up by the USS STACK.

Aircraft returned to the INDEPENDENCE to refuel and rearm for the next strike. The first hellcat returned at 1043. The 9 Avengers recovered by 1112. A total of 19 Hellcats completed recovering by 1115.

The Japanese cruiser the INDEPENDENCE aircrews attacked was not identified by the pilots, as it was not in a known class. Its features were forwarded to intelligence. The unidentified cruiser would turn out to be the light cruiser AGANO. She was floated in Sasebo near the time the INDEPENDENCE was launched and like the INDEPENDENCE, AGANO was namesake ship in her class.

Her crew would make emergency repairs to the stern and proceed to Truk. Nor was it known by returning INDEPENDENCE pilots that Rear Admiral Osugi Morikazu was injured in the raid and taken off the following day by the Japanese destroyer URAKAZE, which also sustained minor damage from strafing on November 11th. Three months later AGANO would be sunk off Truck by submarine USS SKATE on 16 February 1944.

A second light cruiser, YUBARI, was also damaged in the raid. YUBARI would be sunk by submarine USS BLUEGILL in April, 1944.

Aircraft from other carriers sank a Japanese destroyer and damaged two others.

IJN destroyer SUZUNAMI was sunk with the loss of her Captain (Commander Kamiyama) and 147 of her crew.

In addition to URAKAZE, IJN destroyers damaged were NAGANAMI (heavy damage to stern, dead in water, she was towed into Rabaul by MAKINAMI), and WAKATSUKI.

NAGANAMI and WAKATSUKI would be sunk 11 November 1944 in Ormoc Bay by TF38 aircraft. URAKAZE would sink with a loss of all hands by a torpedo shot from submarine USS SEALION off Formosa on 21 November 1944.

1030 Two divisions of VF-33 pilots (under Lt. John C. Kelley and Lt. Tom Purcell) were launched to fly CAP for the Task Group. They would see plenty of action as the Japanese hornets nest finally began to buzz over the Task Group (at approximately 1400).

F C The first strike--an outstandingly successful one--was comparatively easy, with relative little opposition from either Nip planes or antiaircraft batteries. But just as the second strike was getting under way 'the tables' were suddenly reversed and the carriers were subjected to the heaviest air attack ever unleashed upon a United States carrier force.
The attack, which began at 1:30 P.M., lasted for more than an hour, with the Japs attacking in three waves and their number conservatively estimated at 120. F C

1305 Received notice to prepare to launch the second strike at 1330, along with a CAP of 8 aircraft.
1315 Radar reported many bogies bearing 000°.
1328 The afternoon launching of the second strike commenced, with the same objective as the morning strike. 12 Hellcat fighters and 2 Avengers had been launched when the Task Group was hit by an enemy air strike. The afternoon strike against Rabaul was then abandoned.

Eight Avengers were readied for the mission. The second Avenger had just been launched when an estimated (as noted by Harrison) 24 Japanese dive bombers pushed over to commence their attack. Later, during a lull in the action between the dive bombing attack, and the torpedo attack, 6 additional Hellcats were launched.

SK radar first picked up the Japanese aircraft 115 miles out. The raiders were sighted with binoculars 25 miles out and finally by naked eye at 20 miles. BM2c Walter Scott McGill made the binocular contact.

1355 Increased speed to 30 knots and began maneuvering to avoid enemy dive bombing attack. Evasive action was taken for 45 minutes during the attack.

1356 Commenced firing on five dive bombers attacking this vessel.

1357 One bomb exploded mid-air 30' from the island. The flight deck was strafed and a near miss (bomb) hit the water 75' astern sending shrapnel at the after gun buckets. Four other bombs hit the water close to the ship. Two bombs were duds.

1358 Three torpedo planes commenced runs on the port bow. One plane was shot down by a 40mm mount. One plane dropped its torpedo, which ran down the port side on a parallel opposite course.

At approx. 1400, VF-33 (in the air for roughly 3.5 hours) was vectored by Royal Base into the fray. Lt. Kelley and Lt. Purcell leading the VF-33 Hellcats were joined in the CAP by 24 VF-17 "Jolly Roger's" pilots flying F4U Corsairs. Lt. John Coney Kelley did not return. He was missing in action.

1411 Three torpedo planes commenced a run on the port quarter. One was shot down by CVL-22 guns.

1432 Enemy plane commenced run on starboard quarter, and was shot down by a fighter.

1434 Two Enemy torpedo planes commenced a run on the starboard quarter. The run was broken up when ship's guns opened fire. The aircraft turned astern, with one brought down by the ship's guns.

ESSEX (Royal Base) and INDEPENDENCE (Red Base) served as fighter director for four divisions each. Montgomery's TG caught the action. AAR's (Aircraft Action Reports) indicate the Japanese sent up 100 - 110 aircraft. Other sources estimated 120. The mix was identified as Zekes, Tonys, Hemps, Vals, Kates and a Betty. Three INDEPENDENCE F6Fs were lost in the days action. VF-33 lost two. The toll on the Japanese aviators and aircraft was heavy. VF-17 listed 18 destroyed, and 7 damaged. VF-33 claimed 5 1/2 kills with 1 Kate shared with a F4U (AAR #5). USS INDEPENDENCE squadrons bagged 5 Zekes and 2 Vals.

The attacking Japanese aircraft that made it by the CAP then faced a terrible barrage of anti-aircraft fire from the Task Group they were hunting. The ships were not going to take it laying down.

INDEPENDENCE gun crews blasted down 6 Japanese aircraft. The Japanese did no damage to the fleet however they succeeded in stopping the second strike of the day.

DL Armistice Day. Nobody mentioned the date until we went below for noon chow (served at 0930) and were greeted at the steam tables by a special menu in its honor.

We had launched a deckload of fighters and bombers, and they started to return just as we finished dinner. Three fighters didn't make it back at all. We reloaded the F6's and waited for orders whether to rearm the TBFs with bombs or fish. Torpedoes it was. We had almost finished with the last plane when general quarters clanged and bugled. Word came that enemy bombers were coming in on the port quarter. No torpedo bomber ever had its load secured and armed so quickly than the one I was working on.

A hush settled down. The "port quarter" story had been false. We waited. My tin hat, with loose strap about the chin, made my scalp itch. I remember how utterly silent it had become. The wind had died to a faint whisper.

Then I glanced up at the bridge. The gunnery officer was training his binoculars forward and upward. In an instant everybody on the bridge was at his side. Probably Captain Johnson too, but I didn't see him.

I stared straight up and saw a formation of airplanes very high. They could have been ours, I suppose, but when they started peeling off I changed my mind and started shouting at anyone who'd listen. No one would, until a tin can just off our starboard bow started firing its 5-inchers. Bang-bang-bang.

"TAKE COVER!" roared the bull horn.

We all scrambled. Essex was portside of us and the diving airplanes seemed headed right for her. Two huge white-and-black explosions burst just aft of her flightdeck, sending mountainous gobs of the sea down upon her fantail.

Independence's own guns came to life. I'd heard them before, in practice, but the sound was different, rapid, frantic, as if they really meant it this time. Every ship was firing. The sky was covered with black shell bursts. The noise was the loudest pounding, pounding sound I had ever heard. As the ship turned I saw a Jap torpedo bomber (known as a Kate) hit the water off the port bow and flash into a wall of orange-red flame.

For a minute or two there was silence once again. The guns had stopped shooting. We airdales (some of us) jumped to the deck to look around. The sea had been transformed into a flat prairie with bonfires blazing in every direction. All ships were turning up flank speed, but it seemed as if motion had stopped for a moment, permitting the wild scene to etch itself forever in memory.

"TORPEDO BOMBERS COMING IN ON PORT QUARTER!" roared the bull horn, interrupting my bemused reverie.

We dropped again into the catwalk but could see, with a stretch of the neck, everything to starboard. One plane flew parallel with the ship. Out of nowhere came an F4U with a very brave pilot who dived at the attacker in the midst of all that ack-ack shooting at friend as well as foe. Foe went down, bouncing twice before staying put.

Which guns killed him no one could say. The F4U screamed over us and away and I lost sight of it as the pilot fought desperately for altitude and freedom from friendly fire.

Another Kate gave up trying to hit us and picked on a destroyer close by on our starboard side, heading for its fantail. The little can fought fiercely for its life. Just before the Jap must have been about to release his Long Tom fish the plane was hit in its nose by 5-inch and 40-mm shells and smashed into the sea, flames engulfing it while the sea took its time smothering them.

It was a terribly thrilling sight. Of course I'd never seen anything like it. Or imagined what it would feel like. Whitey in the catwalk beside me stared wide-eyed when my language apparently got too much for him.

"I never heard you scream that way!" he screamed.

"What way?" I screamed back.

"You think this is a football game? Men are dying out there!"

"But they're Japs!" I yelled back.

(Yes, I actually said that. And they were.) And this was war. Nobody but these guys had ever tried to kill me. I was resenting it.

(Whitey and I remained friends till the day he died in the 1990's, a retired California school principal.)

The history books are filled with stories of this day's fight. Not until the Marianas Turkey shoot in 1944, for which Independence was unable to be present, did so many attacking enemy planes splash in their abortive attempt to sink our ships.

Long before the books were written (and many of the authors were born) we celebrated our day's victory by congratulating and making fast friends with the guys who'd manned the 20- and 40-mm guns in the catwalks and on the bow and fantail. They had watched us work every day in sunshine and rain, we had watched them practice firing at sleds and sleeves until the ammo ran out. This time their targets were real airplanes with flesh and blood pilots and gunners trying to slaughter all of us. These guys, most of them as young as we, who stood in the catwalk buckets while airplanes thumped to the deck at great speed and sometimes didn't stay put but ended atop the guns mounted in those buckets, these anonymous happy mess mates were suddenly our buddies for life. Merely clicking coffee mugs together would have to do until something better came along, although some of the guys we were toasting wouldn't be there to enjoy another swig. **DL**

JG At 1345 the ship was attacked by Jap dive bombers and torpedo planes. The main attack lasted 55 minutes, consisting of four waves. The first dive bombers were the first to attack the ship. The next were torpedo planes coming in from port and starboard bow. The forth raid was shot down by our own fighters before they reached the force. The Ship was credited with shooting down 3 planes and our planes 14. Gun Mount 3 was credited with one of the planes, hitting a bomb released by the plane mid air, shrapnel from the resulting explosion downing the plane. After this we put on full steam and got into a little safer waters. JG

Twenty four Vals on the left, and 6 Vals on the right came in high and fast to hit the Task Group, diving to release their 100 lb bombs at roughly 2,200'. The second group of aircraft were 3 Kates followed by the last group of 4 Kates (1 may have been a Betty). The Kates approached low and fast, releasing their torpedoes at approximately 2,000 - 2,300 yards.

The 12 Hellcats launched as escorts for the Avengers remained on station at high altitude under direction from the FDO aboard the ESSEX.

Ens. J.B. Thomas, pilot of the first TBF catapulted, turned left 180 degrees flying up the port side of the INDEPENDENCE. He had just reached a point roughly 75' high off the water, 200 yards out abeam, when a Val that had just completed its diving attack on the ship, was pulling up and exposed its underbelly to Thomas's top turret gunner (V.C. Thomas, AOM3c) who fired 275 .50 cal rounds into the length of the Val's fuselage and engine from 9 o'clock low. The Val burst into flames and crashed into sea.

KOD At one time four enemy torpedo planes headed for a carrier when a can moved in and shot down three of the four with one volley of her guns. The fourth was picked off by fighters. KOD

Flying his Hellcat at 3,000', Lt. Craig jumped a Val in a power dive attacking one of our DD's. Making a high side run from 4 o'clock (with his six .50 cal machine guns), the Val burst into flames and crashed into the sea.

Today, bombs had hit the water close to the ship 20, 30 and 50 yards distant, but the INDEPENDENCE escaped any real damage other than taking 7.7MM rounds during a strafing run in the wood flight deck. Two bombs that were near misses were duds. One released bomb was hit by the ships 40mm AA round and exploded mid air. Ships guns accounted for the destruction of 2 Vals and 4 Kates.

KOD Went back to Ready Room to visit with pilots and wait for our second strike.
But here the Japs proved the old axiom that "a strong offense is a good defense." general quarters sounded "All hands man your battle stations." Bogies reported at 45 miles.

Central station passes word to don flash proof clothing and hit the deck--Dive Bombers approaching. "Here they come-everyone on deck." The ship fairly leaps out of water as we zig zag at 34 knots with every gun blazing away. As we lay on deck, we hear a roaring rumble that sounds as though our fantail took a beating from a near miss. We hear it really was a miss but near-50 yards. No damage done to rudder however. "Dive bombers hit!" Shouts of hooray from all hands below decks.

"Torpedo Planes coming in from starboard." Ship turns into them and to right to give port guns a chance. They don't even get off their fish when our guns and fighter planes get them. More shouts of joy-Repair II gang singing "Praise the Lord and Pass the Ammunition."

"More Torpedo Planes coming in from Port Quarter." I lay there in all my gear sweating profusely in this compartment with no ventilation. Temp. about 100^0, hot and smelly. Doing plenty of powerful praying. Not as scared as I thought I'd be but hoping that the skipper doesn't zig when he should have zagged. Funny I think of the Armistice Day two years ago when my ball carriers were zigging down football field to win for us.
Am wondering if the Mighty Eye will repeat? She does! Again Torpedo planes knocked down like flies before they get their fish off.

Comes a lull in battle (which turns into the end) and you go up to hangar deck wringing wet. To hell with your chances of catching cold--you feel like you have to have air or you'll pass out from heat

x

x

exhaustion. Everyone who saw the "show" are like kids. Remarks like "No matter where you look you could see smoke from Jap planes burning in water. " "Boy those yellow son's of bitches really burn when they're hit." A bright orange flame. "You should have seen that Torpedo plane coming straight for us--all of a sudden mount 10 hit him right on the button. Christ, did he burn!"

You wander around talking to pilots, gun crews, flight deck officers and men. Everyone says never did they see such a sight. Jap planes going down on all sides. At least 30-35 enemy planes shot down and no hits scored on any of the task force!

One mount, firing at a Dive Bomber, hit its bomb as it was released from plane! Bomb exploded and blew up the plane. Wouldn't happen again in thousands of tries.

Men on the Bridge tell about the skipper moving from one side to the other calling out course changes and mixing his changes with "There's one-get the bastard! Wow! Did you see that son of a bitch go up in flames!"

The Exec. moving along from mount to mount after it was over asking "How many did you get? Nice going!" Slaps them on the back like quarterback giving his team the old go spirit.

The catapult Officer Lt. (jg) Bachman was turning up a TBF on the catapult when Dive Bombers came in on first wave. "I looked up and stood there for a minute dumb-founded; I didn't know they were in so close. I gave Si Johnson (Silas Robert Johnson) a cut gun while on the run."

Si said, "When Jack gave me cut gun looking like a rabbit in search of a hole, I looked up and jumped out of cockpit at same time. Climbed under bomb bay, realized where I was with Torpedo two feet overhead and moved to hell out of there in a hurry."

Little Bill Comegys, sitting in his TBF waiting for Si to be catapulted, said, "Christ, I looked up and that bomb looked like it was headed straight for me so I ducked my head, closed my eyes and waited." *KOD*

KOD Ensign Thomas, a new TBF pilot-first time in action-was catapulted for the strike when Dive Bombers were overhead. He didn't know they were around until he heard his tail gunner firing away. He looked back just in time to see Jap bomber go into a smoking, flaming spin. "Boy was Ah scared!" he exploded in his southern accent. Instead of hi-tailing out of the Task Force, he circled carriers until he realized they were firing at him, so from then on he dipped from one side to the other to show all and sundry that he was a friendly. Finally located two cans who wouldn't fire on him and circled them for an hour or so.

Captain Johnson's report, in part, to O.T.C.: "One torpedo plane came in so close we were prepared for a hit but our automatic weapons (Mount 10 - McElwee) knocked him down before he could release his fish. What a pretty sight to watch that yellow bastard burn."

In the evening routine G.Q. extended an hour because of Bogies from Bouganville. Again at 2000 general quarters sounded but despite full moon not an attack ensued.

Skipper called Father Kelly up to bridge and asked him if he could pray.
Padre replied, "Yes, a little bit, Captain."
"Well, pray for clouds like you've never prayed before." "I'll try," responded Kelly.
Clouds arrive tonight and the Padre blamed the delay on Navy Red Tape. *KOD*

JG GQ was secured at 1600 and Condition II was set on the battery (4 hours on & 4 hours off). Radar continued to make contacts of the enemy. 1830 sunset. Full moon making us very vulnerable to attack by the enemy.The Princeton and Saratoga were in on the attack of Rabaul from the northern side of the island, we came in from the south, and the Army made their attack from the east with P40's. *JG*

GN Noticed for the first time how nice the Jap planes burn. *GN*

Tactical Comments: (From VF-17 AAR # 21)

"The most obvious tactical comment must concern the failure of the Fighter Director aboard the ESSEX to put the covering fighters in a position where they could intercept the enemy attack. Had the Fighter Director aboard the INDEPENDENCE had all divisions under his control instead of only one division, he could have had 32 fighters over the enemy before their attack could have been launched. As it was the ESSEX Fighter Director vectored 16 fighters out 30 miles from the Task Force to intercept 12 friendly planes, and when the enemy was sighted, ordered all fighters to continue still farther out on the same vector. It was only when the Task Force was actually under attack that he summoned them back."

Sickbay was busy today with minor injuries. The plane crew unfolded a wing, wedging Bernard W. Kutz between a wing and the fuselage. He received multiple contusions. Washington L Shelton sprained his right ankle working with a plane, J.W. Miller fell from the hangar deck into the elevator pit, dislocating his thumb and in another fall down the elevator shaft, John C. Foster received a contusion on his head. Head contusions common aboard ship, most from not ducking low enough going thru hatchways dashing to battle stations.

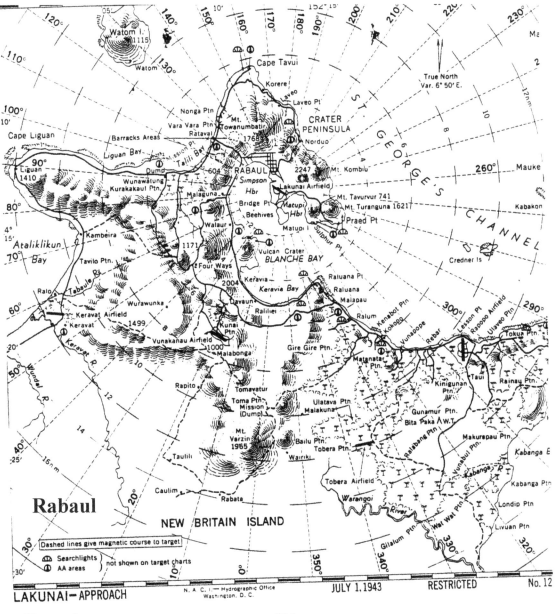

RABAUL RAID

UNDATED PACIFIC WAR:- Navy planes from aircraft carriers and land based bombers making a raiding force of more than 200 sank three Japanese war-ships and damaged twelve others at Rabaul, New Britain last Thursday, Allied Southwest Pacific Headquarters announced today. The enemy lost sixty-four planes in four unsuccessful attempts to sink the carriers. One cruiser and two destroyers were sunk at Rabaul *[1] and eleven destroyers were damaged and twenty-four enemy interceptors were shot out of the sky in the massive assault which opened Wednesday night and extended into Thursday's daylight hours. As the Naval Task Force was withdrawing, the Japanese made a supreme attempt to sink our carriers. Their dive bombers and torpedo planes were so consistently cut down by anti-aircraft fire' of the ships and covering planes that none of the Japanese first three waves scored a single direct hit on the vessels, headquarters said. The fourth wave never even reached its targets. General MacArthur's spokesman said light damage was sustained by some warships but the seaworthiness of none was impaired. There were minor casualties among the personnel. The heavy smash at the key enemy stronghold was the work of Admiral William F. Halsey's Air Arm. In all the actions seventeen Allied planes were lost against the Japanese plane toll of eighty-eight. Some of the Allied pilots were saved. There was no change in the situation on Bougainville where Marines and Army Troops have secured a firm beachhead at Empress Augusta Bay. Japanese positions near the beachhead took an aerial pounding.

JAP CLAIMS ON RABAUL RAID

DOMEI NEWS AGENCY:- The following Japanese propaganda broadcast received stated that the Imperial Naval Air Force spotted and attacked an American Naval Force off Bougainville Island during the day and night of Nov. 11th, in face of inclement weather and obtained following results: sunk instantaneously - one cruiser or large destroyer; damaged - one battleship; severely damaged - two large aircraft carriers, 1 heavy cruiser; heavily damaged and set ablaze - three cruisers or large destroyers, one destroyer; and shot down two planes. Thirty of our planes lost, which deliberately crash-dived into enemy objectives, as yet have not returned to base, the report said. This air battle was designated as the third off Bougainville Island. Imperial Naval Air Force and surface craft units attacked and shot down seventy-one enemy planes out of approximately 200 which raided Rabaul on November II. In this engagement one of our cruisers was damaged slightly and one destroyer was sunk while ten of our planes as yet have not returned to base.

*[1] Japanese losses were: DD SUZUNAMI was sunk; CLs AGANO & YUBARI and DDs NAGANAMI, URAKAZE & WAKATSUKI were damaged. (See page 210 - Sources include: R.J. Cressman -Chronology / Parshall - Combined Fleet / Wiki)

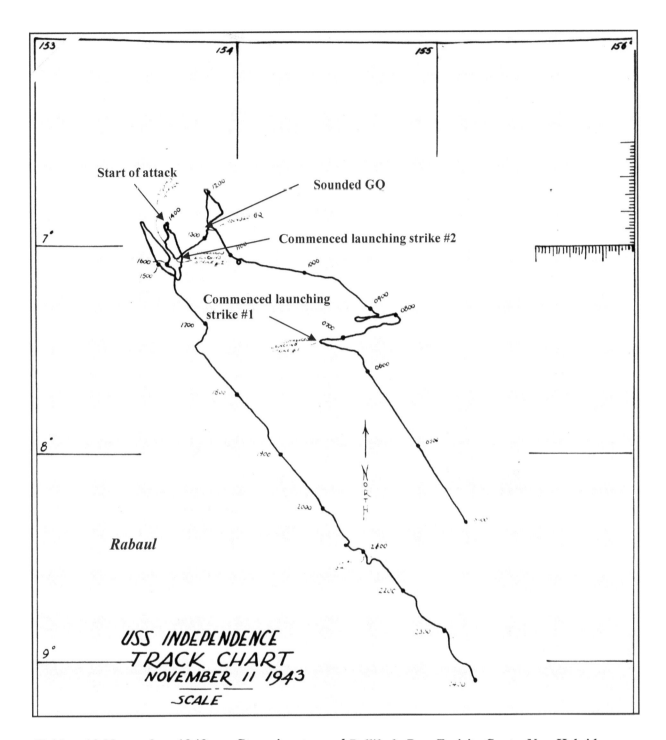

Start of attack

Sounded GQ

Commenced launching strike #2

Commenced launching strike #1

Rabaul

USS INDEPENDENCE
TRACK CHART
NOVEMBER 11 1943
SCALE

Friday 12 November 1943   *Steaming toward Pallikulo Bay, Espiritu Santo, New Hebrides*

Steaming in company with (Task Group 50.3) USS ESSEX, USS BUNKER HILL, USS BULLARD, USS CHAUNCEY, USS EDWARDS, USS KIDD, USS MCKEE, USS MURRAY, USS STERETT, and USS WILSON. Fleet course 140°T, disposition 5LS.

0400 USS MCKEE & USS MURRAY detached from the group. Ninety minutes later, ESSEX launched air patrols for the group.

0550 Formed fueling disposition F1 with guide in BUNKER HILL and destroyers screening ahead. Speed decreased to 12 knots.

0610-0756 USS EDWARDS pulled up along Mighty-I's starboard side to take on fuel oil.

0812 As EDWARDS pulled away, she was replaced by the USS CHAUNCEY. At 0956 CVL-22 completed fueling the CHAUNCEY.

1029 USS STACK positioned herself in close on the starboard side and transferred on board a pilot and his aircrew of a TBF from Torpedo Squadron 9, and Lieut.(jg) Robert A. Hobbs with VF6, who had put his crippled Hellcat down in the sea yesterday. USS STACK had rescued them after crash landings, and now also began to take on fuel oil.

1246 The fleet completed fueling operations, formed up disposition 5LS on a course of 100°T at 20 knots. OTC & guide USS ESSEX.

1252 INDEPENDENCE launched a Hellcat for return to its shore base. Minutes later, fleet speed increased to 25 knots.

JG Ship in much safer waters today having headed on a course of mainly due south all night. Main job undertaken today, refueling of destroyers. Number of destroyers refueled, 406, 619, 667. Condition IV set all day for fueling, and left on through out the night. No routine GQ tonight. JG

Saturday 13 November 1943 *Anchored in Pallikulo Bay, Espiritu Santo, New Hebrides*

Steaming ESE, it was Mighty-I's turn to provide air patrols for the Task Group. CVL-22 launched 6 Hellcats at 0540 over a 5 minute period. They were recovered at 1106.

1226 Fleet course changed to 120°T and nine minutes later they passed Cape Cumberland abeam starboard at 8.5 miles.

1400 CVL-22 launched 1 TBF manned by the Torpedo 9 flight crew (rescued by the USS STACK) for their return to the USS ESSEX.

1443 The carriers formed up on ESSEX (disposition 18), Fleet course & axis 175°T at 25 knots.

1608 Passed Pallikulo Point, Espiritu Santo abeam on the port side. The INDEPENDENCE was dropping anchor in Pallikulo Bay eleven minutes later, between berths 32 & 34.

That evening the USS CACHE pulled along side and CVL-22 commenced taking on fuel oil and gasoline from her at 1928. NAB* Espiritu Santo delivered 9 Mk 13 Mod. 1 torpedoes to replace what had been used at Rabaul.   (* Naval Air Base)

2220 INDEPENDENCE completed receiving fuel oil from the CACHE.

JG Dropped the hook and immediately started taking fuel and stores aboard. Doesn't look like we'll be here long. JG

DL   Back at Espiritu Santo, the Padre had a service of deliverance in the rain after the anchor had been let go. Even I attended. All joined in the Lord's Prayer. The scene was solemn and impressive. Light rain felt good.
Captain Johnson gave us the score. The Mighty I had shot down planes herself. No warship in the task group had been touched. Air group numbers were untallied as yet. The grapevine was already broadcasting: Get ready fellahs. We ain't hardly got started!   DL

RGA Movies on the hangar deck tonight. RGA

Sunday 14 November 1943 *Underway from Pallikulo Bay, Espiritu Santo, New Hebrides*

1545 Anchored as before. Started making all preparations for getting underway in accordance with ComTaskGroup Op. Order 1-43.

1608 Underway, steering various courses at various speeds to clear berthing and conform to the channel. Exiting the channel at 1630, they steamed east at 15 knots.

1705 Formed up 135° relative to the USS ESSEX at 2,000 yards, new course 045°T stepping the speed up to 20 knots. Thirty minutes later INDEPENDENCE recovered three Avengers and one Hellcat.

1744 Forming disposition 18 on USS ESSEX (OTC & guide), new course of 035°T, with USS BUNKER HILL, USS BULLARD, USS CHAUNCEY and USS KIDD (as Task Group 50.3).
1900 Steaming as before, they set the clocks back 1/2 hour.
2030 Sighted Moralav Island bearing 20°T at 23 miles. Passed Aurora Island to our starboard, abeam.
2204 Last fleet course change closed the day turning to 050°T.

JG Still taking on stores. At 1200 we were put on 1 hours notice for getting underway. At 1630 we got underway. JG

HB On the 14th, we got underway to cover the invasion of Tarawa in the Gilbert Islands, arriving on the 18th. HB

Monday 15 November 1943   *Underway for the Gilbert Islands*

0506-0511 Steaming as before, they launched six Hellcats for Task Group inner and intermediate air patrols. Three and one half hours later Mighty-I recovered her fighters as the USS BUNKER HILL took up the watch. They were still formed up on USS ESSEX.
1820 Changed fleet course to 068°T and steamed east.

Monday 15 November 1943 — *Again (The Second Monday 15 November 1943)*

0200 Steaming in **Task Unit 50.3.3**, they crossed into time zone +12, changing clocks ahead 1/2 hour. This also put them across the dateline, so today is yesterday, Monday 15 November 1943, all over again.
0830 They began launching inner, intermediate and the combat air patrols. They put six Avengers and 4 Hellcats into the morning air in eleven minutes time.
0833 Sighted a PBY on a bearing of 51°T, 11 miles out.
0850 Admitted AMM2c B.W. Steadman to sickbay. He was struck by a propeller when a starting charge went off, spinning the prop.
1142 Sighted the oiler USS NESHANIC (AO-71) & USS WINTLE (DE-25) bearing 120°T, 16 miles out. Five minutes later INDEPENDENCE recovered the aircraft from the morning launch.
1240 Sighted Task Unit 50.3.2 bearing 081°T, distance 14 miles.
1249 Formed fueling disposition Fox 1, fleet course & axis 025°T at a reduced speed of 9 knots as the NESHANIC took position on CVL-22's starboard side to begin to deliver fuel oil.
Those on deck during the fueling operation could watch as ESSEX launched her air patrols. They might have observed as two aircraft crashed into the sea during their launching.
1733 Sighted Nuku Island, bearing 023°T, 20 miles.
1838 Formed cruising disposition 5L, fleet course 315°T, axis 070°T, speed 14 knots with USS ESSEX OTC & guide. Ships with CVL-22 were: **Task Unit 50.3.1** composed of ESSEX, BUNKER HILL, INDEPENDENCE, OAKLAND, BULLARD, KIDD AND CHAUNCEY. **Task Unit 50.3.2** CHESTER, SALT LAKE CITY, PENSACOLA, ERBEN, HALE, NESHANIC & WINTLE.
2131 Changed fleet course to 135°T.

*JG Water smooth as glass all day. The Captain announced we are to raid Tarawa air base, the southern most island in the *[1]*Marshal Group. (*[1] Note: Tarawa is in the Gilbert Island Group)
        This is the second Nov 15th as we again crossed the Date Line, all clocks are set back 24 hours. We take fuel from a tanker today, also pick up more ships. During fueling 2 planes*[2] off another carrier break into flames and drop into the water. No one knows the reason. We pass Funafuti at night, there are still fires burning on it where the Japs had bombed it the day before. JG*
[2] The two planes lost were off the ESSEX. At 1501 a TBF (Bu#47599) crashed into the sea on take-off and exploded. No trace of the pilot and his crew were found. At 1506 a F6F (Bu#04883) crashed into the sea on take-off. The pilot survived, rescued by USS ERBIN.

GL We are on our way to hit the Gilbert Islands. Other half of the task force headed for the Marshal Islands. GL

9
Operation Galvanic - Tarawa

Tarawa is in the Gilbert Island group, on the eastern line of the Japanese outer ring of island holdings. Japan captured Tarawa and Makin Islands two days after the raid on Pearl Harbor. The coral atoll is roughly 2,400 miles southwest of Oahu. Rear Admiral C.A. Powell was tasked with the occupation of the Gilberts. Centerpiece of the operation were Marine Corp and Army landings on Tarawa and Makin Island scheduled for November 20th, and Apamama ** on the 21st.

Makin Atoll is north of Tarawa, and Apamama ** lies south. All three possessed airfields. The Independence Air Group would hit targets in support of invasion.

* *Note: Apamama Atoll - also known as Abemama, Apemama and Hopper Atoll.

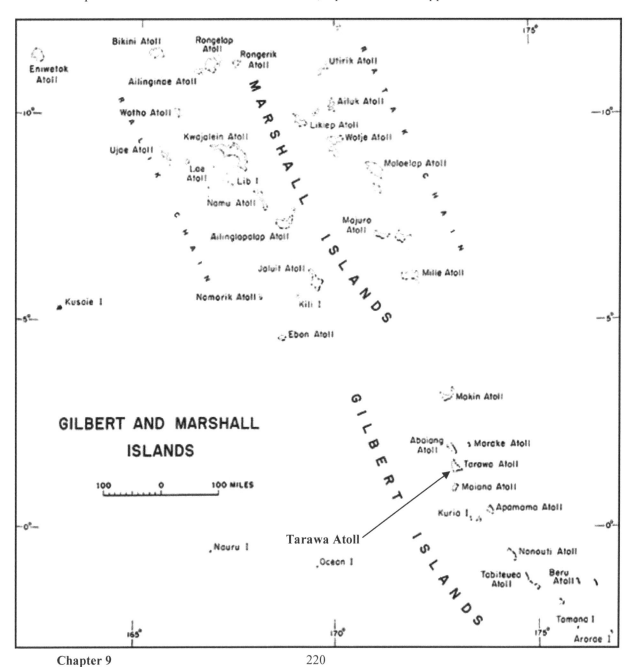

Tarawa Atoll & Betio Island

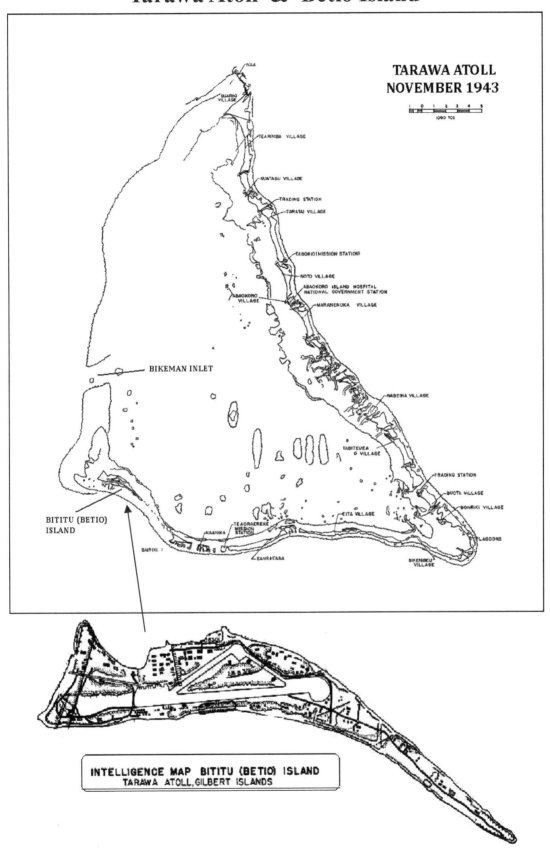

TARAWA ATOLL
NOVEMBER 1943

NAA

BUARIKI
VILLAGE

TEARINIBA VILLAGE

NUATABU VILLAGE

TRADING STATION

TARATAI VILLAGE

TABORIO (MISSION STATION)

NOTO VILLAGE

ABAOKORO ISLAND HOSPITAL
NATIONAL GOVERNMENT STATION

ABAOKORO
VILLAGE

MARANENUKA VILLAGE

BIKEMAN INLET

NABEINA VILLAGE

TABITEUEA
O VILLAGE

TRADING STATION

BUOTA VILLAGE

BONRIKI VILLAGE

EITA VILLAGE

BITITU (BETIO)
ISLAND

NAANIKA

TEAORAEREKE
MISSION
STATION

LAGOONS

BAIRIKI I

BANRAEARA

BIKENIBEU
VILLAGE

INTELLIGENCE MAP BITITU (BETIO) ISLAND
TARAWA ATOLL, GILBERT ISLANDS

Tuesday 16 November 1943   *Underway for the Gilbert Islands*

0019 Steaming as before, changed fleet course to 225°T. At 0430 course changed to 180°T.
0438 Began launching 6 Avengers and 5 Hellcats for Intermediate and Combat Air Patrols.
0530 Formed fueling disposition Fox 1 on a fleet course & axis 080°T, speed reduced to 9 knots with the USS NESHANIC. Twenty six minutes later CVL-22 recovered one of her Hellcats.
0834-0838 Mighty-I recovered her patrols as the BUNKER HILL launched its aircraft as replacements.
1525 Changed fleet fueling course to 315°T. A little over an hour later, having completed fueling operations, the fleet formed cruising disposition 5L settling in on a course & axis of 310°T at 20 knots, guide USS ESSEX.
1657 Oiler USS NESHANIC & USS WINTLE detached from the Task Group to proceed as they were directed. Three minutes later as NESHANIC & WINTLE were departing, sighted 14 LST's and 2 escort vessels hull down on the horizon, bearing 292°T.
1820 Changed fleet course to 305°T. At 1844 they sighted lights on Funafuti Atoll, bearing 335°T on the horizon. They would change fleet course at 1935 to 300°T, and again at 2346 to 310°T.

JG *The Captain tells us that we are part of the largest Task Force that was ever assembled in the Pacific. He says we are going to take the Marshal & Gilbert Islands, bombing them for two days and landing troops on them on the 20th. At night enemy planes again attack Funafuti. We pick up the attacking planes on radar, but make no move to intercept them. We will catch them tomorrow when we attack their base. One group will hit Makin and the other Abemama. We are hitting all parts of the islands at once.* **JG**

Wednesday 17 November 1943   *Underway for the Gilbert Islands*

JG *A sub is sighted 50 miles away, we are on alert. We pass a group of troop transports that are going to land on Tarawa after we bomb the hell out of it. We leave the transports behind.* **JG**

Thursday 18 November 1943   *DOG DAY (MINUS TWO)   TARAWA*

Steaming with the Southern Carrier Group (Task Group 50.3) which included Task Units 50.3.1, 50.3.2 and 50.3.3. As part of 50.3.3, they steamed in cruising disposition 5L, guide and OTC in USS ESSEX at 22 knots with a base course of 337°T, axis 310°T and zigzagging in accordance with Plan 6. They were proceeding to the point of launching to once again deliver the war back to the Japanese. Mighty-I was in good company. In addition to ESSEX, with them were BUNKER HILL, OAKLAND, CHESTER, SALT LAKE CITY, PENSACOLA, and the Screen Group; BULLARD, CHAUNCEY, ERBEN, HALE and KIDD.
Reveille (0200 per JG / 0230 per KOD).
0314 They crossed the to the north side of the Equator at 172°E Longitude.
0315 Flight quarters sounded. Preparations were made to launch aircraft for attacks on Tarawa. The Attack Plan for the INDEPENDENCE Air Group was to carry out the following schedule on both the 18th & 19th of November:

TIME	TYPE	NUMBER	MISSION
0415	F6F-3	8	Strike #1
0415	F6F-3	8	C.A.P. #1
0430	F6F-3	8	Strike #2
0430	TBF-1	9	Strike #2
0945	F6F-3	12	Strike #4
0945	TBF-1	9	Strike #4
1120	F6F-3	8	C.A.P. #3
1330	F6F-3	8	C.A.P. #5

All Hellcats were loaded with 2,400 rounds of .50 caliber ammunition. Those assigned C.A.P. would carry belly tanks with extra fuel. Those Hellcats assigned with strikes would launch with only 250 Gallons of fuel.
Avengers would launch with 300 gallons of fuel. They would be armed with twelve 100lb. GP bombs or 12 incendiary clusters.

Weather for the day presented a moderate sea with 15 knot winds out of the east, visibility 8-10 miles, ceiling unlimited with scattered clouds at 2,500'.
0330 General quarters.
0415 The INDEPENDENCE on a new course of 100°T, her bow knifing thru the water at 20 knots, commenced the first launch into the dark predawn sky. 32 to 35 knots of wind was over the bow for the morning launches. Strike One flew off the deck to carry out attacks against assigned targets on Bititu (Betio), 120 miles distant. Strike Two launched at 0440. Fighter aircraft and torpedo planes from ESSEX and USS BUNKER HILL would be also attacking their own targets. The Avengers would hit their targets with General Purpose Bombs and Incendiaries. 10 Hellcats from VF6, 12 Hellcats from VF22 and 8 Avengers from VC22 participated, with 7 of the Hellcats remaining on CAP over the target area until relieved.

The large number of aircraft launching from three carriers into still dark skies would cause problems during join up, one pilot accidently merging with a squadron from BUNKER HILL. Over Bititu as the hunters strafed their targets, brilliance of the flash from tracer rounds proved blinding to their sensitive night time vision.

The first strike began at 0559 with strafing aircraft making runs from 4,000' down to 200'. Avengers with bombing assignments approached at 6,000' releasing their ordnance from 1,500 to 1,000'. Targets included aircraft, buildings, AA weapons, munitions, fuel storage and supplies.

Hellcats assigned as CAP would proceed to make strafing runs against AA positions once they had been relieved, prior to returning to the ship. 4 Avengers and 4 Hellcats received battle damage, repaired aboard the ship by busy mechanics. Damage to 3 of the Avengers was caused by the incendiaries being blown back by the slipstream into the bomb bay windows upon release. An Avenger took a nasty 20mm AA hit to one wing. AA guns were silenced but considerable machine gun and rifle fire was encountered by pilots coming from areas around the runways and taxiway. 18,760 rounds of 50 Cal were expended by the twenty two INDEPENDENCE VC22 and VF6 Hellcats.

The ship would then make a series of course changes settling in to a zigzagging base coarse of 280°T. They would continue to make numerous course changes throughout the day.
0620 Secured from general quarters, *set Condition III*
0702 Commenced recovering of 15 Hellcats and 8 Avengers from Strike One on a new course of 110°T, speed 18 knots.

JG Our planes start coming back from the raid. Some with pretty bad holes in them from AA fire, but they do come back. JG

0743 USS ERBEN made a submarine contact and dropped 8 depth charges.

JG At 0745 a can on our starboard bow starts dropping depth charges on what is believed to be a sub. Explosions shake the ship, it is only 300 yards away. JG

0835 CVL-22 resumed recovery of the remaining 7 Hellcats from Strike One.
0945 Commenced launching Strike Four consisting of 12 Hellcats and 8 Avengers. Strike Four would also be joined with aircraft from ESSEX and BUNKER HILL for additional attacks on Bititu. The eight

VC22 Avengers would each carry four 500 pound AN–MK43 GP bombs. They were to hit buildings, machine gun emplacements and covered artillery positions. Fighters would strafe AA positions near the runway, along the south shore and the pier area. Fighters from another carrier bagged a Pete (5 to 10 miles west of Tarawa).

1116 Commenced launching 8 additional Hellcats for CAP.

1136 CVL-22 recovered 1 Hellcat making an emergency landing with a fuel leak.

Aircraft returning from the attack once again had battle damage that was repairable aboard ship. One TBF with port wing damage from 20mm AA fire, another with the tail wheel shattered and holes in the fuselage from 7.7MM AA, another with 20mm AA damage to hydraulics and electrical wiring in the bomb bay. Three F6F's drew AA fire. One with 12.7mm damage to a right main fuel tank, the two others with 7.7 mm holes in the fuselage & port horizontal stabilizer.

1204 CVL-22 was on a course of 100°T when radar picked up a contact bearing 302°T, 83 miles out and closing. general quarters sounded.

1211 CVL-22 scrambled 4 additional Hellcats for CAP.

1258 Changed course to 180°T.

1301 Secured from general quarters.

1323 Sighted 16 B24's on a bearing 220°T at 8 miles.

1432 On a new course of 110°T they recovered 7 of the Hellcats from the CAP.

1500 Crossed the Equator once again, southbound at Longitude 172°-12'E.

1533 A bogy was picked up 63 miles from INDEPENDENCE on a bearing of 328°T. Four Hellcats were directed to intercept them by the ESSEX FDO. One Dave was shot down.

1632 With continued fleet course changes during the day, now on a basic course of 180°, USS PENSACOLA assumed guide while USS CHAUNCEY slid into position alongside ESSEX. She cast off from ESSEX at 1710 and minutes later ESSEX resumed as guide.

1809 General quarters sounded with a radar contact closing to 13 miles, bearing 210°T.

1843 Various radar contacts were picked up closing to 12 miles.

1855 Cruisers and destroyers commenced firing on various targets using radar control.

1904 USS PENSACOLA reported loss of steering control warning all ships to steer clear. Five minutes later she regained control of her steering.

1930 Raiders designated raids one & two and split up into single planes.

JG Just at dusk we have another GQ. A Jap Betty can be seen on the horizon coming toward us. Three others spread out around us. All of our planes are aboard, too dark for them to be of much help anyway. When the bombers come within range the cruisers open fire. Carriers do not fire their guns after dark, it only helps the enemy to find them. The orange bursts from the muzzles with the green and red tracers reflecting against the clouds make a nice sight but I can't appreciate it much. About 50 more bombers are reported near. We out maneuver them by putting on more knots and making sharp turns. We can see them dropping flares off our stern about 30 miles trying to pick up our wake. They drop further behind us and we can begin to breath again. JG

1946 No planes observed within 30 miles. Four minutes later flares were reported off the port quarter.

2000 Position Lat 01°- 07.5'S Long 172°- 20.5'E

2055 All radar screens clear. Secured from general quarters.

2135 Course 040°T at 18 knots.

2214 2 radar contacts identified as friendly.

Karl O. Drexel *Would describe the events of the 18 November 1943:*

It looks as though this is becoming a weekly habit of the Mighty Eye's. Yesterday marked the beginning of the largest Naval Offensive in the Pacific Theater of the war. The ESSEX, BUNKER HILL and I NDEPENDENCE (plus escorting cruisers and destroyers) concentrated their full offensive power on

Tarawa, the Jap stronghold in the Gilberts. A Carrier group hit Naru at the same time. Today Carrier groups, Battleships, Cruisers and Destroyers move in on Millie and Makin in the North. Tomorrow the landing forces take over Tarawa, Makin and Apamama. By this time next month the Gilberts will be Allied property-Marshall Island Truk watch out!

Yesterday morning at 0230, reveille sounded the Death Knell of Tarawa. The "Shuttle Service Bombing, Inc." that devastated first Marcus, Wake, and last week attacked Rabaul, again began its service creating a groove in the air between the task force and the Island of Bititu on Tarawa. Five strikes of bombing, TBFs, SBDs, SB2Cs and strafing F6Fs begun a two day assault on assigned targets. The Japs promised us a warm reception if we came down here so we fully expect the fireworks. We are operating between Truk and Tarawa-the hot corner again. From time to time Bogies appeared on our Radar Screen but all eventually proved to be "friendlies." It looked as though our only general quarters call would be the routine thing from reveille until sunrise.

Our pilots encountered much anti-aircraft opposition but no planes were visible either in the air or on the ground. This should have given us some inclination as to what was to come but it didn't. By evening we began to feel quite secure-another Marcus and Wake raid. (Ho hum!)

A group of us were gathered on foc'sle smoking and talking about the attack.
Pilots were talking about the mad scramble above the ships at the rendezvous point. The same pilots who were so elated after their first attack on Marcus were now talking like the veterans that they are. (All had returned to "base" safely with but a few holes to show that they had been out on nothing more than routine patrol.) All hands were visibly happy that our day was not what had been anticipated. An interruption in our chatting came from the forward gun mounts lookout. He had laconically commented, "Bogie-bearing 300." The tenseness that had been dissipated over a period of 12 hours returned in a period of 12 seconds. "All hands man your battle stations," was sounded almost immediately. This was the beginning of one of the most fantastic night raids on record in the Pacific.

A group of 30-40 bombers-torpedo planes-closed from 50 miles to 16 miles, and coming in high, fast and in three groups from the stern. Again we were in our flash proof clothing, helmets and flat on the deck hoping and praying. This was like going into a dark alley knowing there are thugs waiting to kick hell out of you and your chances of slipping by them are 1 in a 1000. It was pitch black out-no moon and scattered clouds. How could we stop them with our effective A.A. when we couldn't see them? True, Radar could give us their bearing, but the effectiveness of this kind of shooting is questionable. We didn't launch our fighters because of this reason. We would have shot down as many of our own as we would have Japs. If we thought Rabaul attack was rough, this stab in the dark was rough and tough! The task force made a 90° turn to starboard and running like hell-making 30 knots. We could feel the ship shudder from the abrupt turn. We thought such evasive action could be of little value-how the hell could they miss? But as we lay on our stomachs sweating and panting from the heat and excitement, we began to wonder what was going on. They should be launching torpedoes and bombs by now but no word came to us. After a period of time that actually seemed like hours, Commander Fowler announced that the same enemy planes that were 16 miles dead astern, were now 25 miles away and paralleling our course! How could they miss? But they did for the moment.
Again word came that snoopers were within 10 miles. This meant that it'll simply be a matter of moments before these same snoopers would radio our positions to their gang. It was inevitable or so we thought. As it turned out the snoopers didn't spot us-the attack opened to 60, 70, 100 miles and finally disappeared!!
Our prayers were answered. For three and one half hours we were in Condition I, waiting for that attack.
Secure from general quarters at 2130 was the sweetest sound ever played by a ship's bugler. We went into Condition II, Watch I, and I remained on Patrol until 2400. Two hours later we were up again for

today's operation. Who knows what the night will bring? Let's pray that by now every Jap plane has been destroyed!
As an indication of what it's like to go through something like last night's nightmare, I quote Commander Peters, the Air Group Commander and pilot of a TBF:
"I would rather fly through all the Ack-Ack they can throw at me than go through last night again."
Karl O. Drexel

JG At around 2400 we turn and head back so we will be in position to attack again in the morning. JG

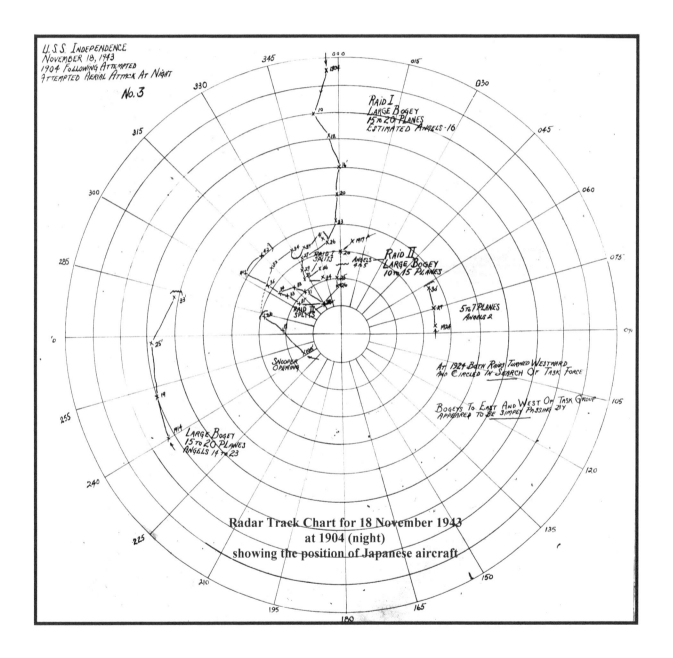

Radar Track Chart for 18 November 1943
at 1904 (night)
showing the position of Japanese aircraft

Friday 19 November 1943   *DOG DAY (MINUS ONE)   TARAWA*

Steaming with the Southern Carrier Group (Task Group 50.3) which included Task Units 50.3.1, 50.3.2 and 50.3.3. INDEPENDENCE in 50.3.3, was cruising in disposition 5L, guide and OTC in USS ESSEX at 18 knots with a base course of 040°T, axis 270°T and zigzagging in accordance with Plan 6.

0315 Sounded flight quarters.

0330 Sounded general quarters.

0335 Changed course to 270°T.

0402 Task Unit 50.3.2 began departing the formation under orders. Ships include CHESTER, HALE, PENSACOLA, and SALT LAKE CITY.

0415 Increased speed to 22 knots.

0435 Coming around to 090°T, 23 knots they commenced launching Strike One, VF22 flying 6 Hellcats, 95 miles from Tarawa. The sea was moderate with winds from 105°T, visibility 10 miles, ceiling unlimited with 2 tenths sky cover.

Five minutes later, Strike Two launching commenced. VC22 launched 6 Avengers, and VF6 launched 6 Hellcats. The targets once again were on Bititu. As on the previous day, aircraft launched from ESSEX and BUNKER HILL would strike their targets at almost the same time. Today, the weather was the same as on the 18th.

Lt. M.E. Kirkpatrick (ACI) - *As the TBFs commenced their bombing run, Lt. J. Pincetich, leading his flight, observed one Betty taking off eastward from the field at Bititu and another Betty taxiing westward for takeoff. Pincetich altered his course, dropped his bombs near the buildings just south of the NW end of the NE-SW runway, overtook the Betty which had just taken off, and made two high side runs, firing both 50 cal wing guns (TBF-1C). His top turret gunner had a no deflection shot during these runs, but his gun jammed. As the Betty gained speed, it turned North, closely following the N.E. leg of Tarawa Is. shore line and pulled away from Pincetich. The Betty taxing for takeoff was not observed to leave the field. A fire observed by several pilots near the Eastern end of the landing field was thought to be from this Betty.* **MEK**   (Chart on page 221)

Pilots again strafed buildings and the pier area. Two Avengers returned with AA damage that was repaired aboard the ship.

0543 Turned to 270°T.

0616 Radar contact, bogy bearing 191°T, 29 miles from INDEPENDENCE. 4 ESSEX fighters were vectored to intercept.

0624 Secured from general quarters, set condition II.

0629 ESSEX planes shot down 1 Betty Bomber, 235°T, 35 miles from INDEPENDENCE.

0720 Commenced recovering Strike One on new course 000°T.

0746 Changed course to 280°T.

0800 Position Lat 00°- 27.9'S Long 173°- 30.4'E with zigzagging and course changes throughout the morning.

0805 Word came to cancel Strike #4 and maintain deck spot for A.S.P. and C.A.P.. Belly tanks were installed on all Hellcats.

0815 Four F6F Hellcats from VF 22 were scrambled. A bogey was picked up, bearing 163°T, 36 miles. The pilots of all four Hellcats almost immediately dropped their belly tanks after launch and joined up. Vectored by the FDO, they sighted the Betty 25 miles south of INDEPENDENCE. The dark olive drab Betty was boring in on the INDEPENDENCE to deliver a torpedo attack, flying at roughly 200 knots and 1,000'. The two sections of Hellcats maneuvered in from 4,000' to bracket the twin engine Betty. Lt. Clement M. Craig made the first high side run knocking out the tail gunner. Ens. Edward C. Dale made a similar run from the opposite side of the Betty, which made a diving 90° turn for the water. Dropping quickly to 50 feet above the surface it released its torpedo, gaining speed as it shed the weight. Ens. Dale, breaking off his run at the last second, barely avoided the water.

Lt.(jg) Robert A. Richardson and Lt.(jg) James H. Roberts made flat runs on either side of the Betty. Lt. Craig and Ens. Dale then made similar firing passes. Fire was observed from the engines as Lt. Craig was completing his attack, followed by an explosion in the engine area. The doomed Betty crashed into the sea and burned. The victors circled the burning wreckage for 30 seconds, received another vector and departed, as two late arriving ESSEX F6F's strafed the slick where the Betty had submerged.

1334 On a course of 105°T at 20 knots, CVL-22 launched a CAP of 8 Hellcats. They began recovering them at 1750.
1819 Sounded general quarters.
1842 On a course of 342°T, radar contact was made bearing 301°T, 26 miles. The radar contact was Task Unit 50.3.2 rejoining.
1911 Changed course to 220°T. Secured from general quarters at 1932.
2000 Position Lat 00°- 21'S Long 172°— 49.7'E.
2030 New course, 320°T. Sighted Task Unit 50.3.2, bearing 250°T, distance 4 miles. They did not rejoin due to poor visibility, but took station on a parallel course, bearing 290°T at 4,400 yards.

JG Dog Day minus 1. This morning we again pick up a bogey. Our fighters take off. One bomber reported downed 5 miles off our starboard beam. Later in the morning, one of our fighters downed another Betty. We sleep by our guns tonight, just in case. JG

KOD Not much happened on this day. We spent a good deal of time running to our battle stations to find out a B-24 didn't have his IFF on.
When I say not much happened, it is meant as far as we were concerned. As far as the Japs are concerned, plenty happened throughout the Gilberts and particularly in our "little" spot-Tarawa. Not only did we send as many strikes at them as we did yesterday but also shelled the hell out of them with two Cruisers. We think they are now wishing that Tojo hadn't boasted that Tarawa would not be taken. KOD

18 November 1943 - Bititu Island at the end of a bomb run.
Viewed from the north side of the island looking south.
A sea plane ramp is in the foreground.

Saturday 20 November 1943   *Tarawa (Invasion) - Torpedoed*

Steaming in company with units of Task Group 50.3 zigzagging (Plan 6) on a base course of 320°T, axis 270°T, speed 18 knots in cruising disposition 5L, fleet guide and OTC in USS ESSEX.

T.U. 50.3.2 on station bearing 290°T, 4,400 yards. Ships with INDEPENDENCE include; BUNKER HILL, CHESTER, HALE, PENSACOLA, and SALT LAKE CITY, OAKLAND, and a destroyer screen group; BULLARD, CHAUNCEY, ERBEN, HALE and KIDD.

0415 Sounded general quarters.

0538 Commenced catapulting strike #1 (4 Avengers), base course 110°T, speed 22 knots.

0546-0557 Launched 12 Hellcats.

0715-0721 Launched second wave of 4 Avengers and 8 Hellcats. The F6F-3 Hellcats were tasked with a CAP over T.U 50.3.1. Visibility was estimated to be 6-8 miles under high scattered stratus at 20,000'. A Betty was sighted flying low at 100' off the water by a division led by Lt.Cdr. Harry Harrison. The four Hellcats dropped in from 2,000' and bracketed the Betty which was flying at an estimated 230 knots. Harrison and his wingman Lt.(jg) Robert Klingler were on the starboard side as Lt.(jg) Alex Vraciu and his wingman Ensign Robert Bloomfield crossed over the Betty which had dropped to 50' and began making a slow turn to the left. This set up Vraciu and Bloomfield, to make flat side runs on the twin engine bomber. Low to the water, the Betty dropped its torpedo in an effort to gain speed and maneuverability. It didn't help. Vraciu saw a glow from the wing root just before the Betty hit the water.

1144-1154 Recovered the first wave of Hellcats and Avengers.

1336 Commenced launching a C.A.P. of 8 Hellcats, base course 115°T, speed 22 knots.

1425 Commenced launching 3 Avengers for A.S.P.

1452-458 Recovered 4 Avengers.

1625 On a course of 330°T, all engines were signaled ahead flank speed. A submarine periscope was reported in the Mighty-I's wake, distance 2,000 yards, bearing 170°T by the Landing Signal Officer. USS KIDD was dispatched for hunter killer operations against the sub.

1637 Base course 060°T.

1732 Commenced zigzagging 5° left and 5° right of base course, 100°T at 20 knots.

1750 Darkened ship.

1754 Ceased zigzag, on a new course 115°T. Minutes later we recovered our C.A.P. of 8 Hellcats.

1758 Course 100°T. A radio warning received by C.I.C. from Lt. Harold McMillan (VC22) flying on A.S.P. in his Avenger, informed the ship of a large group of low-flying Bettys approaching very low to the water from the west, avoiding radar detection. Sighted 15 Betty Bombers approaching disposition on the starboard beam bearing approximately 250°T, distance 7 miles, altitude 200' flying at high speed. The USS BUNKER HILL had a C.A.P. in the air at 10,000'. They attacked the Bettys at 9 miles out claiming 2 shot down and 3 probable.

1800 Sounded general quarters, set material condition Afirm and broadcasted the visual contact over T.B.S.. All Damage Control Personnel were moved up to at least above the second deck due the threat coming from a torpedo attack. They donned helmets, flash proof clothing & gloves and were ordered to lie prone on the deck.

INDEPENDENCE went to flank speed, commenced maneuvering various courses to avoid torpedo attack. The ship made a turn with 20° left standard rudder, to present a stern attack to the oncoming enemy. Steadied up at approximately 50°. Commenced turning to the right with standard rudder to avoid enemy planes working around ahead. Steadied up to approximately 100°T, commenced turning left.

The Bettys were deployed in a line when they appeared over the horizon, heading for the Task Group, then made a big circular sweeping turn in toward INDEPENDENCE.

Three of the Bettys had broke off from the group to attempt to get ahead of the ship. One of the Bettys in this group of three was shot down and the attack broken up by guns from the USS HALE.

Twelve of the Bettys had turned in and began to close on the INDEPENDENCE. The Bettys flew into a hale of AA. INDEPENDENCE gunners opened up with 9 twin 40mm, 2 quad 40mm, and 16 single 20mm guns. Six Bombers were shot down by ships guns. Two on the port side, four on the starboard side. Three of the attacking Bettys got to within 100 yards or less. Three other Bettys were shot down by other ships, and one was shot down by a fighter. A number of the Bettys absorbed a lot of damage before being splashed. Four burst into flames as they hit the water.

1806 Sighted a torpedo wake approaching from the starboard quarter on a 140° track angle, the ship on a course of approximately 060°T. Commenced turn to port. The ship, at high power, with all boilers in line, was making approximately 30 knots.

1807 A Japanese torpedo struck the INDEPENDENCE at frame 103 on the starboard side, roughly 8-12 feet below the water line, flooding after engine room and vicinity. Radio Central lost all receiver power. It shifted to emergency power. Radio II also lost power and lighting. It filled with suffocating smoke. TBS became unreliable. Radio IIA lost power and lighting, flooded with oil and water and had to be abandoned. The TAQ, TBK and the TBM transmitters were rendered inoperative.
All ventilation was secured except for Sickbay, Radar Plot and engineering spaces.
       The INDEPENDENCE began to list and slowly went over to 12 degrees starboard, then quickly righted itself to a 7 degree starboard list. Engineering Department commenced immediate measures to correct the list. The Flight Deck Crew would also began repositioning aircraft to attempt to help, using aircraft on the flight deck as ballast. Eventually the list was corrected to 3 degrees to port.
Many compartments below the third deck were flooded between frames 91 and 113, with the third deck flooding to 5 or 6 feet between those frames.
       The after engine room filled with heavy black smoke, some flame, lighting was lost, and it flooded to the overhead. It was abandoned with both throttles open, without loss of life. No.3 & 4 boilers had to be secured and they flooded with sea water.
       The after fire room began flooding slowly (water coming from the after engine room), but was brought under control by lowering emergency pumps down into the space, and rigging emergency power leads for the pumps. Water settled to below the lower grating level with the additional aid of a fire and bilge pump. Bulkheads were shored up and leaks were plugged. (The compartment was emptied of water within eight hours.)
       A fire had started burning when oil ignited floating on top of the water in compartment C-301-L. As the compartment continued to flood, the fire self-extinguished due to the inrushing sea water. The compartment was completely open to the sea due to the explosion.
The sprinkling system was activated when the explosion occurred to prevent fire in the hangar bay. It was shut off when it became evident that there was no longer a hazard.
The explosion caused the loss of steering control on the bridge, as well as loss of communication with aft steering. Steering was operated from an alternative feed aft. Steering was facilitated using magnetic compass, using telephone communication to Central Station from the bridge, out to the CPO mess room, and from there by word of mouth to the after steering station. She was making 4 to 5 knots at 160 RPM.
       USS INDEPENDENCE limped on with forward engine room steam provided by No. 1 & 2 boilers. Within minutes of the explosion, the No. 1 shaft began a heavy vibration. It rapidly broke in two and was secured. The INDEPENDENCE now had only No. 4 shaft available.
The after gyro compass room was flooded to the overhead. The forward gyro compass was knocked out.

1810 Radio II, now filled with smoke, was abandoned on orders from Central Station.
1812 A TBY transmitter was setup on the bridge as a standby for the TBS.
1820 Emergency power failed in Radio Central, to be restored 15 minutes later.
1833 Sighted submarine on port bow, distance about 300 yards. INDEPENDENCE gunners opened fire on the sub. Radio communication was not available as radio circuits were inoperative. USS HALE dropped one depth charge on the contact.
1850 INDEPENDENCE steamed on an easterly course (after the explosion) at a speed of 4 to 5 knots.
1935 Speed 13.3 knots (by the pitometer log), making full speed on No.4 propeller shaft, turning 255 RPM. This speed would be maintained for 48 hours. Steering 180°T (still by magnetic compass, using telephone communications from the bridge, to central station, to the CPO mess room, and from there by word of mouth to the after steering station).
2015 Forward gyro back in commission.
2047 Ship on even keel.

2235 Regained steering control from the Pilot House. Heavy cruiser PENSACOLA, with destroyers KIDD and HALE stood by INDEPENDENCE and escorted us out of danger.

Post war interrogation of IJN Commander Goro Matsuura indicates that 16 Japanese aircraft participated in the raid. They were said to have flown 600 miles directly from Wotje, with a loss of 8 aircraft in the attack. *(Note: Morrison Vol. VII suggests that half were from Roi, half from Maloelap.)*
** The Betty raid was part of the IJN 775th Air Group that was night trained: Lieut. Nobuki Miyamae led the First Squadron; Lieut. Yoshiaki Akiyama led the Second Squadron. Neither survived.
          (** Source: "Titians of the Seas" - Belote & Belote)

Independence crewmembers would describe the events of the day;

GL   *D-day – sent planes in and softened it up for the "gyreenes" going in. In the evening we were attacked by 15 twin engine torpedo planes (Bettys). Torpedoes were flying everywhere. We were missed by quite a few. The new A.A. cruiser (Oakland) was firing with every 5 inch she had and she couldn't hit a bull in the ass with a base fiddle. We were hit under the island structure and forward island by two fish but they were both duds. The Independence shot down 6 Bettys and probably 3 more. Then the torpedo hit us, what a flash, a moment I'll never forget. It hit aft between the mess deck and the fire room and curled our 3" armor deck like tissue paper. It blew off our 40M.M. mount *[1] on the starboard side aft. It blew it clear over the flight deck. It was an 8 ton mount so you can imagine the force behind that fish. The dead were lying all over. The blood was ankle deep. It knocked out three of our screws, so we only had one to go on. The ship was dead in the water and a submarine started to surface on the port side about 400 yards away. Port side guns opened fire on it. A destroyer came over fast and dropped depth charges. Sun disappeared. Planes dropped flares but they couldn't find us. Next day we buried our dead at sea. Something a guy will never forget.*   **GL**

(*[1] **The 40mm gun mount was in gun tub number seven. See photo on page 45**)

HB   *On the 20th, the Marines landed at Tarawa and were slaughtered due to the fact the tide was not such as to allow the landing boats to deploy the Marines on the beach. Our ship was hit by a Japanese torpedo on the starboard side. I was lucky to have escaped any harm, since seconds before, I had been closing all water-tight doors and ventilation in the main mess hall in the compartment where the torpedo hit. I had just finished my duties and was closing a water-tight door between compartments, heading back to my battle station. About this time I heard Father Kelly our Chaplain on the loud-speaker, saying to hit the deck, as we were about to be hit by a torpedo.*

*   I dove to the deck, and all Hell broke loose. We did get hit by a very powerful aerial torpedo from a twin-engine Betty. Then word came over the speaker to abandon ship. I surely hated to hear such a command. Luckily, almost immediately, the order was canceled. This was good news, since I really was not looking forward to going into the water with all the sharks, and possibly the Japanese coming back to finish us off. After being dead in the water for 7 minutes, what a relief it was to get our power back on.*

*   We heard a man was trapped in the shaft alley, and help was needed to get him out. I was in the work party that cut a hole in the deck over the shaft alley where this man was trapped. We got him out just in time. When we got to him, the water was up to his chin. He climbed out of the hole we had cut, made it to the second deck, and passed out. I knew this man since I slept near his sack. He was a really nice fellow, from Colorado, I believe. He was sent back to the states, the lucky stiff.*
There we were, with a hole in our side large enough to put a good size house in. We were taking on an awful lot of water, which caused our ship to list to starboard. We pumped water over to the port side to level the ship so we could get underway and head to a small island named Funafuti.

*   We lost 17 people on November 20, and had to bury most of them at sea; some were lost overboard when the torpedo hit. It was an extremely sad experience to see our buddies pushed over the side in burial bags that were weighted down with sand. I will never forget that day.* **HB**

DON LABUDDE *(Don was on a catwalk beside the flight deck)*

"A gigantic sledgehammer slammed into Independence's side, clawed its way into her bowels, and with an ear-splitting explosive roar ripped her open to the sea. She jumped almost vertically into motion, dancing a clumsy jig, trying to lift herself out of the water as if the sea had rejected the weight of her hull. An instant later it grabbed her back. Two thousand tons of seawater gushed through a hole in her side we learned later was big enough for a locomotive.

The catwalk had come up and collapsed my legs. Someone fell on me. We fought each other furiously trying to untangle arms and legs. I got loose, jumped up, and looked aft.

A black geyser was shooting skyward with immense force. At its apex gravity quickly pushed it back down in a strong descending wave. Concealed within it was a chunk of Independence--and a team of her men.

The torpedo had exploded directly beneath a starboard 40mm gun bucket. It broke the bucket loose and hurtled it up and over the width of the flightdeck, bucket, guns and all the sailors in it, from starboard to port and into the water below--right before my eyes and those of others. Several gunners tumbled from the bucket and fell away to the deck. One thudded to a gory death in a portside gunbucket opposite the point of torpedo impact. The rest, arms flailing wildly, rode their broken mount into the sea.

Dumbfounded, I opened my mouth to shout, to make sure someone else saw what I saw. But before I could make a sound the flying gunbucket and its passengers had vanished in a cloud of spray without leaving a trace.

Aft along the deck two fighter planes had snapped their manila lines and slid over the side. Another pair skipped precariously to the edge of the deck, their fate hanging on the ship's next move.

Independence had all she could do to control her own fate. The force of the sea and the laws of motion tossed her back and forth. Like a gutshot animal cut down in flight, she staggered on, oscillating ponderously from side to side. Every frame and beam, every rivet and seam had absorbed the shock and pain of her hurt. With a mighty effort, she threw the strength of her ruptured hull into a battle against the unwelcome weight of the water trapped inside her. Clouds danced across the sky as she wobbled and wavered. Water alongside her burbled in confusion as she lost forward momentum. Fuel oil gushed from her gaping wound; a telltale black spoor dyed what remained of her wake. She began to settle as if an enormous boulder had dropped into her belly and was dragging her to a reluctant halt.

Finally she stopped. Three of her four engines had quit. The last of her four great screws revolved slowly, keeping us barely moving.

Independence refused to die."   **DL**

VF-6 Pilot Allie Willis "Willie" Callan standing on the starboard side at an open hatch forward of the ready room watching the action would note* [1.] : *"One Betty approached from the starboard quarter and turned to parallel the ship's course. He was so close that we could see the pilot and co-pilot in the cockpit. All guns on the starboard side opened up on him point blank and he blew up in a sheet of flame."* Willie continued: *"At the same time we heard and felt a tremendous explosion that shook the whole ship. It almost knocked us to our knees."* **A.W. Callan** (* [1.] Sea Eagle By: A.W. Callan)

KOD   At 1800 general quarters was sounded and the lookout on the No.1 gun mount said, "Enemy planes bearing 170° (relative) range 20 miles. Before going to my station, I glanced out along the 170° bearing and was stopped in my tracks by surprise. The nearest destroyer almost dead astern and about a mile or so back was firing her guns at the setting sun! But upon more searching of the horizon for the can's objectives, I sighted Torpedo Planes (Bettys) coming in for us about 40 feet off the water and moving in fast as hell!

I'll let my "official" action report take over from here:

ACTION REPORT FROM GENERAL QUARTERS 20 NOVEMBER 1943 TO 0800, 21 NOVEMBER 1943.

TIME 1759 - GENERAL QUARTERS SOUNDED

(A) At approximately 1800 GENERAL QUARTERS was sounded. The writer stayed on forecastle long enough to get range and bearing of enemy planes from lookout on No. I gun mount. What seemed to be but a minute or two later, torpedo planes were seen coming in from our starboard quarter bearing 170 degrees (relative.) Knowing that the Repair Parties had had little time to set Material Condition Afirm throughout the Ship, it was this Roving Patrols intentions to expedite the setting of Condition Afirm. The writer did not get any further than Repair IV when our guns started firing and word from Central Station was to "Don all flash proof clothing and hit the deck".

(B) We in Repair IV area felt impact of the torpedo hit about one minute after Central had passed the above word. nearly all men were on the deck when the hit was felt. Immediately Repair IV men moved into the 'smoke filled compartments B-204-2L and C-201-L with hoses and fog applicators to extinguish any resultant fires. Hangar deck crew brought hoses down from hangar deck into compartment C-201-L. All power aft was gone. Approximately one minute after hit we met the Engineers force from after Engine room as they were moving forward along second deck. Ass't Engineer Lieut. Sloan, asked to have steam shut off. This request was relayed to Central Station.
" Screams for help were coming from the after messing compartment C-301-L. Carrigan, C.F., SF1c went down port ladder into this compartment to assist men in getting out. At the same time, the writer accompanied by Lt. Aylsworth, Ass't Supply Officer, went down starboard side into C-301-L to get men out. We found no men on our side.
Writer reported to Central Station that this compartment was flooded. The First Lieutenant requested that we make certain: that all doors and hatches in and leading into 2-101, 2-112 and 2-107 be dogged down tightly. This action was taken and it is felt that were it not taken, it would have been virtually impossible to rescue man trapped in S.A. C-604-E. Water was pouring into trunk 2-112 until door leading from C-301-L into trunk was properly dogged; The hatch on " third deck in this trunk was also improperly secured ".
It was at this time that men were reported to be trapped in the compartment C-601-E. A bucket brigade was started and continued until power was obtained to start submersible pump. When power was available, two submersible pumps were dropped into trunk. Headway against the oil and water was made for a short time only. Pumps were secured when it was found that no rising was evident.
At approximately the same time a crew of men under the direction of Carp, Higgins and Roberts, J.C., CSF worked for some four or five hours getting trapped man out of S.A. C-604-E.
During this time Commander Fowler and Carrigan, C.F., SF1c made a thorough inspection of after part of ship. Commander Fowler, Ensign Wyckoff accompanied by Carrigan, C.F., SF1c and Rodis, E.J., SF3c again went into compartment C - 301-L to look for men and attempt to determine extent of damage in that compartment.
Ensign Knox and Rodis, E.J., SF3c went into the flooded compartment B-322-L to close watertight door at frame 101. Two submersible pumps then dropped into this compartment. No damage noted at this time.
Shored bulkhead 113 on first platform deck between flooded compartment C407L and dry compartment C-408-L. Very little water in latter compartment. Sometime later six submersible pumps dropped down into after fire room.
(C) No comments on Material and Design.
(D) No deficiencies noted. Lack of 440 power on 2nd deck.
(E) No recommendations as to improvements of Material and Training.
(F) Commendations. None. All of the men of the Repair Parties were excellent in performance of their duties, a few of them were outstanding.

(*KOD* Contd.) *This report doesn't of course include how miserable we all were that night. Our wardroom was seemingly littered with the dead and wounded. It smelled to high heaven as if in query to God - Why? Doctors, corpsmen, negro mess attendants, repair party men, a couple aviators, all working as fast as they could to save lives and stop pain. Officers' beds were being used for the near dead-giving them as much plasma as was necessary.* **KOD**

The oil made the deck so slippery that at times it was almost impossible for the doctors to stand up. The dead were lying on the deck in a corner with blankets over them. None of the wounded groaned or moaned much-they were still too shocked by the suddenness and the fury of the torpedo. It seemed odd to me as I moved through the wardroom that so many of the wounded were suffering from leg, arm and skull fractures but still were not burned. I had been down in the damaged area and knew that no one could have been in the forward or amidships stbd messing compartment at the time of the hit and not be burned. Went into my room to take the oily clothes off and found two more of the wounded being cared for in there. It was at this time that I learned that the upward explosion of this one damned torpedo had shot up along the side of the ship and blown No. 7 gun mount off of the ship! Thousands of pounds of men and metal blown completely from their position by a torpedo hit many feet below. It seemed incredible but the twisted legs and unseeing eyes were mute testimony.

The rest of the early morning was a nightmare. We made burial sacks for the dead, moved the wounded to sick bay, tried to clean up wardroom so that men could be fed "bread line" style. The food was oil smelly sandwiches and coffee. Despite the gruesomeness of it all we were still able to eat almost heartily. After eating, all men except Engineers gang and C&R people dropped to the deck for an hours sleep before the expected dawn attack. The Engineers gang under Chief Machinist Snow, a survivor of the Wasp, were affecting miracles with the one engine room and one screw- 13 knots! Although this was twice as much as we had hoped for it still wouldn't be fast enough to zig and zag when we should. However, the dawn came with its usual So. Pacific beauty without the accompaniment of Jap planes. One cruiser, and two cans were escorting the limping INDEPENDENCE to Funafuti. We felt safer at 13 knots, with those three ships, than we had in the previous days with the task force.

It was learned during the day that we were lucky that only one torpedo hit home. Fifteen Torpedo Planes attacked us, seven were shot down by our ship, four by the destroyer and two by Fighters. It was believed two got away. At one time, according to those on the Bridge, five torpedoes were in the water at one time. As if this wasn't enough, the periscope of an enemy sub was seen almost in the middle of our task force-about 200 yards off the port beam! It is believed by the Captain and the Navigator, a former sub captain, that the sub heard the explosion and stuck its periscope up to see what damage had been done not realizing he was so close to the damaged ship. Finding himself in such a position made it impossible to fire a torpedo, it would never have armed itself if it had, and the explosion concussion would have damaged himself. Thank the good Lord for that!

After two and a half days of slow travel and lots of hard work with little sleep, we arrived in Funafuti - a British held island but protected by Navy, Army and Marines. **KOD**

JG *Dog Day. Reveille at 0230. Word is passed over the PA "Enemy planes picked up at 17 miles coming this way being attacked by our planes" - Later, A/C our planes shot down identified as a Betty. I go up topside for routine GQ, sit around talking to the fellows and watch our planes come in, when GQ sounded without the usual 5 minute warning. When I get to my GQ station, the crew on watch says something about 15 twin engine bombers off the starboard quarter coming in fast. Just about that time I saw them just over the horizon. All guns on the starboard side open up, the planes come in so close that if you had known the pilot, you could have recognized him on sight, too close. The main thing bothering me was his little guns firing at us, due to the bank of the plane he doesn't seem to be making any hits. Planes seem to be going down right and left. Just then there is a terrific blast shaking the whole ship like nothing I have never felt before. It shakes a TBF ** off the flight deck forward. There is no doubt we have caught a fish. I look back aft where it hit and see bodies strewn across the deck. The 40 mm mount that weighs 5 tons had been thrown across the deck and into the water on the other side. Another attack is expected so we keep a sharp look out as two planes go over the horizon we find ourselves dead in the water. When it looks like we are dead ducks, we start to move again at 3 knots, then as it started to get dark the word came over the speaker "We are doing 13 knots" with one carrier and two cans as escorts. We eat down in the ward room sandwiches taste of fuel oil. Not hungry anyway. Cloudy for the whole trip to Funafuti. JG* (**Note: It was a F6F-3, Bu.No. 8990)

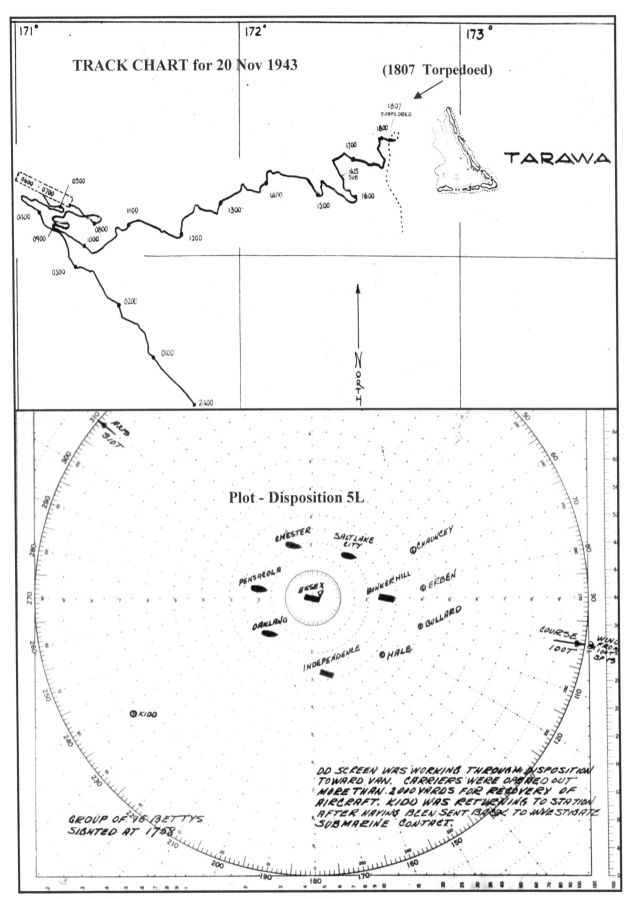

TRACK CHART for 20 Nov 1943

(1807 Torpedoed)

1807
TORPEDOED

1800

1700

1625
SUB

1600

1500

1400

1300

1200

1100

1000

0900

0800

0700

0600

0500

0400

0300

0200

0100

2400

TARAWA

NORTH

Plot - Disposition 5L

CHESTER

SALT LAKE CITY

CHAUNCEY

PENSACOLA

ESSEX

BUNKER HILL

ERBEN

BULLARD

OAKLAND

INDEPENDENCE

HALE

COURSE 100T

WIND FROM 100T 3KTS

KIDD

DD SCREEN WAS WORKING THROUGH DISPOSITION TOWARD VAN. CARRIERS WERE OPENED OUT MORE THAN 2000 YARDS FOR RECOVERY OF AIRCRAFT. KIDD WAS RETURNING TO STATION AFTER HAVING BEEN SENT BACK TO INVESTIGATE SUBMARINE CONTACT.

GROUP OF 16 BETTYS SIGHTED AT 1758

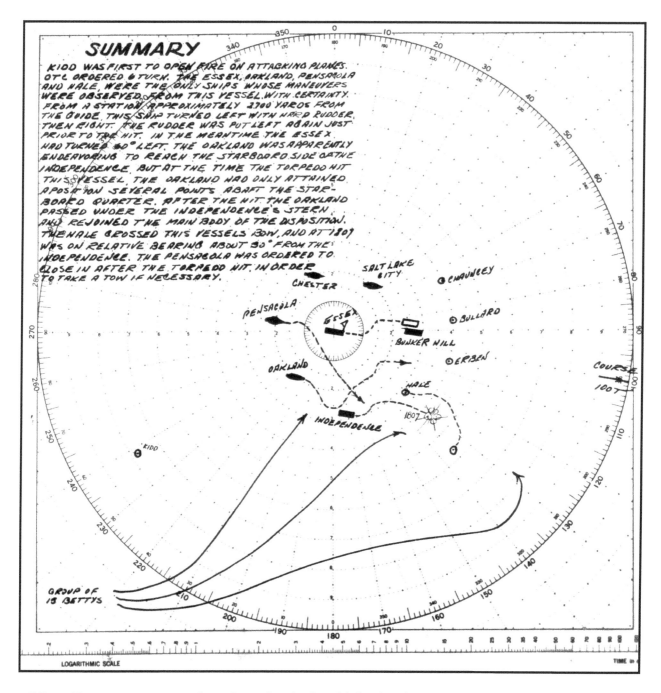

SUMMARY

KIDD WAS FIRST TO OPEN FIRE ON ATTACKING PLANES. OTC ORDERED 6 TURN. THE ESSEX, OAKLAND, PENSACOLA AND HALE, WERE THE ONLY SHIPS WHOSE MANEUVERS WERE OBSERVED FROM THIS VESSEL WITH CERTAINTY. FROM A STATION APPROXIMATELY 2700 YARDS FROM THE GUIDE THIS SHIP TURNED LEFT WITH HARD RUDDER, THEN RIGHT. THE RUDDER WAS PUT LEFT AGAIN JUST PRIOR TO THE HIT. IN THE MEANTIME THE ESSEX HAD TURNED 60° LEFT. THE OAKLAND WAS APPARENTLY ENDEAVORING TO REACH THE STARBOARD SIDE OF THE INDEPENDENCE, BUT AT THE TIME THE TORPEDO HIT THIS VESSEL, THE OAKLAND HAD ONLY ATTAINED A POSITION SEVERAL POINTS ABAFT THE STARBOARD QUARTER. AFTER THE HIT THE OAKLAND PASSED UNDER THE INDEPENDENCE'S STERN AND REJOINED THE MAIN BODY OF THE DISPOSITION. THE HALE CROSSED THIS VESSELS BOW, AND AT 1807 WAS ON RELATIVE BEARING ABOUT 30° FROM THE INDEPENDENCE. THE PENSACOLA WAS ORDERED TO CLOSE IN AFTER THE TORPEDO HIT, IN ORDER TO TAKE A TOW IF NECESSARY.

DL   *AS primitive man must have done when he first felt his fragile mortality, huddling deep within his caverns at Lascaux and Altamira, so too did Independence's airdales gather in clusters on the flightdeck that first night. No one would have admitted it, but we all needed shelter from the threat of the dark and succor for the wounds to our spirits.*

Merciful clouds remained overhead. Occasional warm gusts of wind were a welcome balm. Gentle vibrations from the solitary working screw spinning slowly in its shaft were those of a kitten's purr.

There was long silence at first, scant talk later. Somebody would boldly make a joke, a jarring note of sacrilege followed by a moment's hush. Then a ripple of redeeming laughter. There was a studied, casual note in the half-heard chatter. Yet, to a man we were scared, lonely, and a long way from home. *DL*

An attacking Betty bomber absorbs fire from INDEPENDENCE gunners
with tail surface partially shot away
seconds before exploding and impacting the sea.

Looking aft just after the torpedo hit.

This was gun tub number seven.
See photo on page 45)

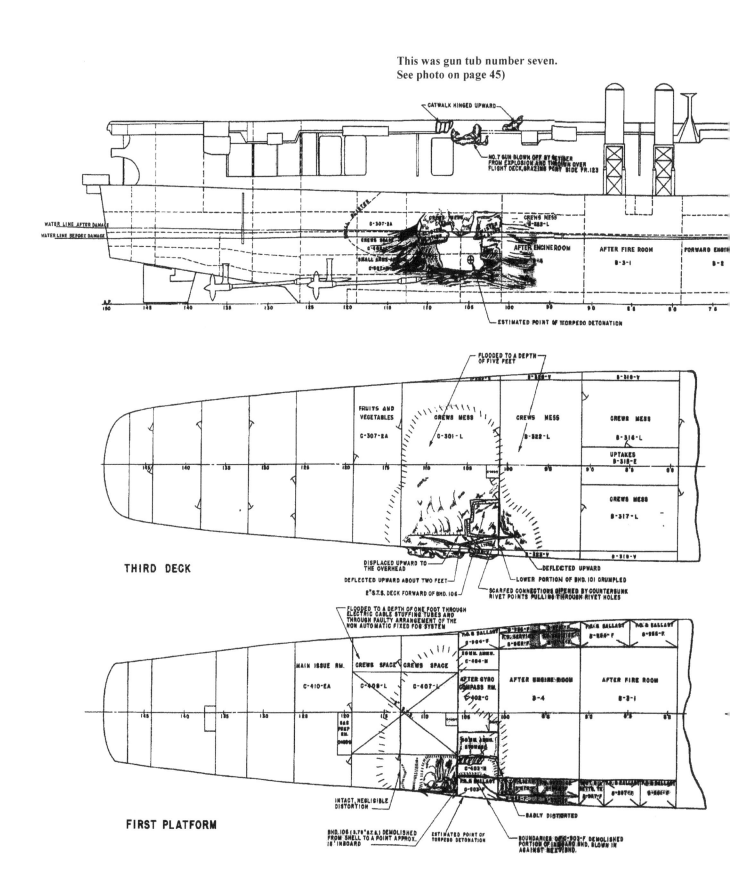

THIRD DECK

FIRST PLATFORM

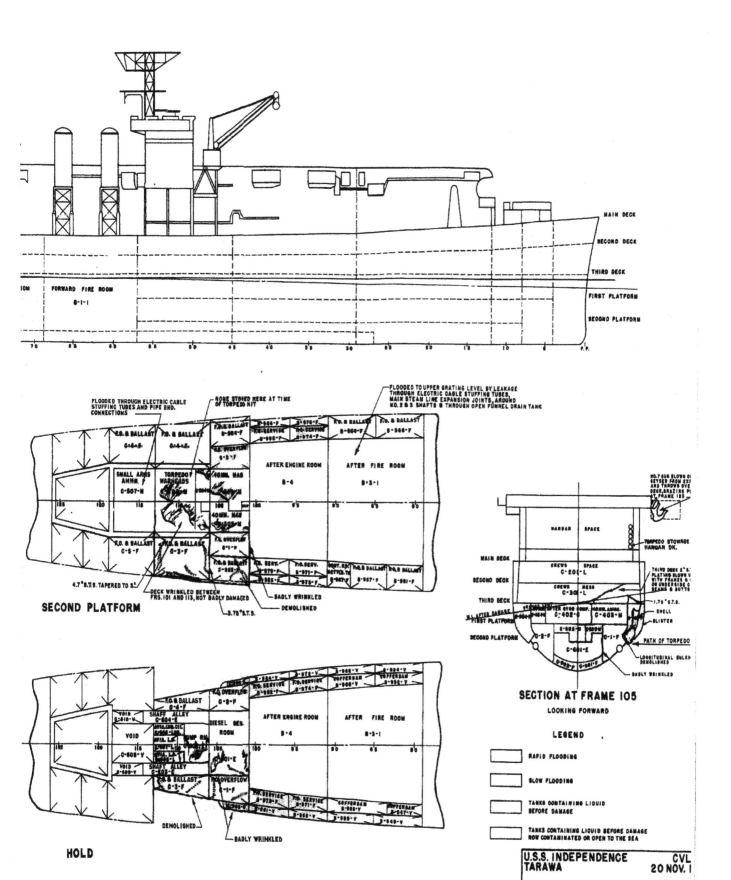

SECOND PLATFORM

HOLD

SECTION AT FRAME 105
LOOKING FORWARD

LEGEND

RAPID FLOODING

SLOW FLOODING

TANKS CONTAINING LIQUID
BEFORE DAMAGE

TANKS CONTAINING LIQUID BEFORE DAMAGE
NOW CONTAMINATED OR OPEN TO THE SEA

U.S.S. INDEPENDENCE   CVL
TARAWA   20 NOV. I

TORPEDO DAMAGE

Enclosure (H) Part 3
#3
Catwalk, starboard side, looking forward. This portion of
the catwalk together with 40 MM gun mount No. 7 were blown
over the flight deck.

Enclosure (H) Part 3
#2
Catwalk, starboard side, looking aft. This portion of the
catwalk together with 40 MM gun mount No. 7 were blown over
the flight deck.

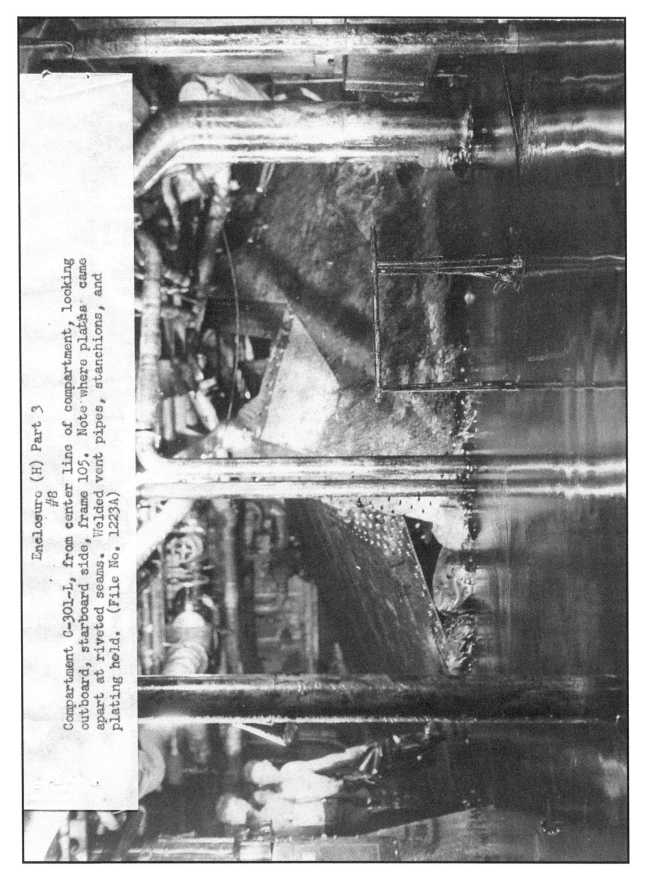

Enclosure (H) Part 3
#8

Compartment C-301-L, from center line of compartment, looking outboard, starboard side, frame 105. Note where plates came apart at riveted seams. Welded vent pipes, stanchions, and plating held. (File No. 1223A)

Enclosure (H) Part 3
#5
Compartment C-301-L looking starboard and forward from frame
109. Note buckled deck. (File No. 1228)

Enclosure (H) Part 3
#15
Compartment B-316-L, showing method of shoring door 3-91-4.
Note seepage at base of door and oily deck. (File No. 1073)

Enclosure (H) Part 3
#1

Hole in the side looking aft from catwalk. Ship underway.
(File No. 1108)

Shortly after the torpedo impact & explosion. Smoke and / or steam coming up over the flight deck from the hole in the aft starboard side of the ship.

10
The Torpedo's Aftermath

Sunday 21 November 1943   *Retiring from Tarawa, they bury their dead*

DL   *Sunrise revealed an unfamiliar scene. The ship's forward progress was a crawl compared to what we were used to. The deck aft of the stacks was a shambles. Jumbled airplanes, their manila lines loosened by the immense jolt as the deck had responded to the torpedo's impact, were pointed every which way. Folded wings, vulnerable tail surfaces, tender bellies had been abused by kinetic forces they hadn't been designed to absorb without damage.*

One F6F sat teetering at the edge of the deck just aft of the gap in the starboard catwalk. The oval snout of its nacelle stared like the gaping maw of an animal pleading to be put out of its misery. At the air officer's order, we helped the plane pushers and plane captains to do just that. Its ignominious journey into the deep was accompanied by a jeering chorus celebrating the expenditure of another bundle of War Bonds. Seventy-five thousand dollars worth, I heard. A fortune.

Aft of the stacks the pool of oil hadn't yet congealed. Walking was treacherous. Oil-soaked detritus cluttered the deck: a single shoe, its laces still knotted neatly; a black sopping rag torn from somebody's dungaree shirt; tarred chunks of steel separated from the dislodged gunbucket as it blew skyward. The long portside HF radio antennas, like telephone poles, were limp and sagging; only the ships's starboard list suspended their wires above water. Our wake was no more than a lazy disturbance clutching the stern.

Never had I imagined I would ever see my ship in such a muddled state. Over it hung a feeling of exhaustion after a wild evening during which the players had squandered reserves of mind and spirit in unthinking debauchery.

All of us, officers and bluejackets, were as disheveled as Mighty I. Water was available only for drinking (not much of that) and for cooking and medical use. Sailors bathed last night in fuel oil rubbed it off their faces, out of their eyes, off their hands and arms as best they could. Nobody could get to his locker below decks to change reeking dungarees. Bodies stunk. Each guy maneuvered to keep upwind of the other guy.

Breakfast, piped down soon after quarters, consisted of sausage between hunks of unbuttered bread, washed down with gallons of coffee. From the flightdeck just forward of our portside catwalk station, long lines of hungry men snaked down a ladder and along a short passageway into the officer's wardroom. Temporary cafeteria along the port bulkhead. Temporary hospital starboard side. Aft along that bulkhead, temporary morgue.

There lay the dead. Shipmates now in the absolute sense, uniformed in shrouds of canvas. Delivered from pain and fear. Bright hopes gone.

Oh, come off it, I thought, cursing myself for being so sentimental and literary. This was war. These mummies were part of the cost. I was angry, confused, unable to escape this abattoir. Many mummies breathed--the living dead, the burned wounded bound tightly in head-to-toe bandages, parked on tables against the starboard bulkhead behind jittery messmen doling out food for the living and able. Scurrying surgeons and corpsmen binding, patching, sewing, all oblivious to the hungry customers waiting to be served at the nearby lunch counter.
Now and then muffled sobs escaped from clean white wrappings that stank of roasted flesh and sour medicine. Eyes that showed traces of torture stared at me with a glazed look of envy or recognition. Envy it must have been, for I knew no one here.

Who were they, anyway? A martinet officer hated by his men? A buddy who had stood as Best Man at his shipmate's wedding just before we left Philly? A seaman second from whom I had gladly accepted a trayful of chow last evening while brooding about his life on the mess deck?

We healthy coolies gawked, sympathized, thanked our lucky stars, accepted our rations, and got outside to let the wind blow our minds clear.

This simple-minded son of Maude and Ed examined the broad face of the sea that morning, curious to see if it had changed. The cataclysm I had witnessed yesterday couldn't have happened before. I was sure it had shaken the earth, changed history, interrupted the flow of time.

Father Sea had not changed. It bore no scar, boasted no wound or blemish. The flaming man-wreckage that had rained into it had vanished. Immense, impassive, inviolate, it merely waited in silence for the next act in Man's mad drama.

Still, I could not help but look at it with different eyes. Gray and chill, it was minus the travel-poster blue of the day before. The sky was an opaque, back-lighted screen that reminded me of the November landscape back home, waiting breathless for winter coming.

War's iron fist had at last bludgeoned me where it hurt. The wearing of the uniform, the look and smell and sounds of a dozen strange and wonderful places, the restless spirit of youth that commanded see, see, see. All had conspired to lead me straight to this--fear, sorrow, destruction and death, permitting me to glimpse a narrow sliver of truth and reality. I had awakened this morning a survivor, but no longer the same person. Only the sea was the same. It would endure. I would not.

Rumors concerning our next destination had begun swooshing along the grapevine almost from the moment we were sure Independence wasn't going to sink. A strange name, Funafuti, began kicking around. Captain Johnson cleansed the speculation when he broadcast that we were heading for the Ellice Islands group, some seven hundred miles south of Tarawa. An anchorage at a place called Funafuti already had a repair vessel awaiting our arrival, U.S.S. Vestal, a survivor of the Pearl Harbor attack.

Shortly after securing from sunrise GQ on the day after our wounding, interment services were held at the after end of the flightdeck. Men retrieved from below decks and a few who'd fallen off the gun bucket were confined to the deep. **DL**

DL   *Attendance at this ritualized ceremony was not mandatory; too much vital work occupied too many officers and men. But seamen and others showed up who saw in the services a chance to escape fifteen minutes' labor—such as airdales like me. The air group commander was there together with a handful of his pilots. Captain Jim had a Marine honor guard on hand to fire the customary salute. A brace of enlisted men, guard-belted and wearing leggings, stood by as pall bearers, ready to give the final push overboard.*

The remains, each one shrouded with an airplane engine tarpaulin weighted with defused 40mm shells, were lined head-end forward on plywood planks at the edge of the deck. Each shroud was overlaid with a Stars and Stripes.

At precisely one minute before the ceremony was set to begin, Captain Johnson descended from the bridge, took his place front and center, and nodded curtly to the chaplain.

That good man acknowledged the gesture and opened his little black book and began to read. Only once did he interrupt his monologue, pausing to look upward at the sky.

Independence steamed slowly on, heading for Funafuti and an emergency repair job.

By now the good padre was bareheaded and down on his knee, facing aft, tilted slightly to the right. Far below I could hear the water burbling at our stern. The sea was liquid glass. Not a cloud spotted the sky. I recall only two details of the ceremony.

First was the small size of the audience. It troubled me. Of some fifteen hundred officers and men, less than a tenth saw fit to attend—a poor showing for such a solemn occasion. What I didn't understand was that the crew had had enough of death. They thought they were through with it.

The second detail is a single quote from the padre's brief talk at the end of his prayers. He got off his knees, faced us, and took from his black book a slip of paper, which the breeze tried to rip from his fingers.

"I'd like to conclude with a quotation from a great writer who knew the sea like few men," he said in a wavering voice. "It's a question, really. From Joseph Conrad. 'Who would be a sailor if he could be a farmer?'"

Independence hissed quietly through the water. A quartering breeze tugged at us as we stood. The padre nodded. A phone talker in the catwalk spoke an instruction and on the bridge a bugler three times sounded Attention on Deck over the PA system. All nonessential work throughout the ship came to a halt.

From the bullhorn sounded the Exec's voice:

"All hands, bury the dead."

The Marine corporal of the guard barked a command. Rifles slanted skyward. Three loud volleys shattered the silence.

Immediately at the edge of the deck began a flurry of activity, as if those charged with the duty couldn't wait to be done with it. Alongside each corpse a pair of sailors lifted each wooden slab to a sharp angle and turned its burden loose one by one in succession. A slip, a slide, a soft scraping sound of fabric on wood. Each flag, suddenly bereft of its inflating support, collapsed about the board.

The bugler sounded Taps. It was complete.

A few voices mumbled quietly. My angered shipmate had disappeared. I was compelled to stare aft at the sea but saw nothing but water. The door to the great tomb had already been sealed.

Silence prevailed. Long thoughts plagued me, such as Fate apparently having decided that we would all have to wander a little longer on a trail that led nowhere. ***DL***

0735 The Latitude 01° 20' S, Longitude 172° 52' E. USS INDEPENDENCE held burial at sea services for enlisted men killed in action.

0745 Solemnly, they had committed the following shipmates to the deep:

Joseph Edmond Byrne	S2c	Philadelphia, Pa.
Lawrence Lewis Swartz	S1c	Philadelphia, Pa.
Edward Newman Jones	S1c	Redding, Pa.
Joseph Thermon McGowan	S2c	Philadelphia, Pa.
Bela Sobek	S2c	Wilkensburg, Pa.
Wallace Gardner Lee	S1c	Pitman, N.J.
Walter Robert Hunt	S2c	Worcester, Ma.
Joseph Christy Sedgwick	S2c	Bristol, Pa.
James Boydell MacKenzie, Jr.	GM3c	Narberth, Pa.

PERSONNEL KILLED IN ACTION

Joseph Christy Sedgwick	S2c	Bristol, Pa.
Wallace Gardner Lee	S1c	Pitman, N.J.
Edward Newman Jones	S1c	Redding, Pa.
Bela Sobek	S2c	Wilkensburg, Pa.
Joseph Edmond Byrne	S2c	Philadelphia, Pa.
Edward McLean	Cox	Topton, N.C.

DIED FROM INJURIES RECEIVED

Lawrence Lewis Swartz	S1c	Philadelphia, Pa.
Joseph Thermon McGowan	S2c	Philadelphia, Pa.
James Boydell MacKenzie, Jr.	GM3c	Narberth, Pa.
Walter Robert Hunt	S2c	Worcester, Ma.
Fredrick Paul Lockwenz	S2c	Schenectady, N.Y. Died 11/23/1943

PERSONNEL MISSING IN ACTION

Clarence Thornton Roberts	Cox	Philadelphia, Pa.
Thomas Eugene Streeter	Cox	Lilbourn, Mo.
George Edward Castro	S2c	Richmond, Ca.
Oliver Ashton	F1c	Northbridge, Ma.
John Floyd Grant, Jr.	F1c	Dayton, Oh.
Joe Ervin Fretwell	S1c	Macon, Ga.

PERSONNEL WOUNDED IN ACTION, and or listed as transferred for further treatment

Joseph Vincent Abramovitch	F1c	1	David Lehman	S2c	2
John Baptiste Ashton	F2c	2	George LeRoy	S1c	1
Ray Bragg	S2c	3	Walter Richard Lucas	S2c	2
Charles Kilborn Brown	S2c	2	John Robert Newman	S2c	1
Harold Cecil Bryant	S2c	1	Fredrick Charles Schroeder	S2c	2
Eugene Edward Bull	S2c	1	Charles Eugene Struckhoff	Pfc	Ukn.
John Randolph Bullard	S1c	1	Washington Lee Shelton	AMM3c	1
James Lawrence Burns	S2c	1	Edward Paul Sikora	SK3c	3
James John Cuff	S2c	3	Francis William Sminchak	F1c	3
Carl Joseph Gorman	S2c	2	Joseph Swider	S2c	2
Albert Henry Huelsman	S1c	2	Robert Thomas Utter	S2c	2
Oswald Lewis Johnson	MoMM1c	2			

(Transferred To: **1** USS CASCADE   **2** USS CURTISS   **3** USS RELIEF   Unknown)

Additionally, the following men were injured: Joseph James Bianco, Raymond Chester Bronikowski, Edward William Buckley, Ralph Theodore Coppola, John Edward Crowther, James Edward Davies, Raymond Leland Feltey, Leo Joseph Fitzgerald, Carl Kenneth Harsh, Joseph Hollock, Anthony Joseph Janiak, Lewis Wilmer Jones, Dwight Palmer Kilbourn, Philip Francis Leonard, James Vincent Lucchino, Robert John Mac Quaid, James Edger Murphy Jr., Virgil Pace, Melvin Theodore Pechman, Benjamin Henry Roe Jr., Edward Norman Ruest, Walter Charles Ryan, Edward Robert Seace, James Howard Severt, John William Shultz and Jesse Charles Swift. Injuries included; Burns, fractures, contusions, lacerations.

Steaming on course 180°T, speed 13.2 knots, en route to Funafuti Atoll, Ellice Islands for preliminary repairs. Boilers No1 & 2 in use. During the day a PBY flew overhead providing ASP.

GN We are headed for Funafuti and turning on one screw. So far the weather has been very favorable to us with a low ceiling and rain squalls every once in a while. GN

Monday 22 November 1943   *Steaming to Funafuti Atoll*

Steaming as before in company with USS PENSACOLA, USS HALE and USS KIDD.
0456 Sounded general quarters.
0617 USS PENSACOLA launched 2 SOCs for ASP.
0650-0730 USS HALE took on fuel from USS PENSACOLA, resuming fueling from 0843-1002.
0741 Two fighters reported on station for CAP.
0830 Sighted Nanumea Island (Nanumea Island), bearing 135°T, 22 miles.
0831 A SBD reported on station for ASP.
1042 Transferred official mail to USS HALE.
1050 USS PENSACOLA and USS HALE departed the formation to proceed as assigned.
1055 Made daily inspection of the magazines. Magazines C-403, C-502, C-503, C-504 and C-506-M are flooded. Magazines C-404-M and C-507-M have been pumped out.
1352 Sighted USS RINGOLD.
1424 Catapulted 2 F6Fs, course 080°T. Changed course to 115°T.
1507 Sighted Niutao Island, bearing 130°T, 10 miles.
1520 USS RINGOLD took station as a screen.
1532 USS KIDD came alongside to take on fuel.
1628 Passed Niutao Island abeam 15 miles to our starboard.
1738 USS KIDD cast off and departed for assigned duty.
1746-1916 Routine evening general quarters. At 1900 they changed course to 125°T.
2040 Sighted search light beams in the distance, bearing 169°T thought to be on Nukafetau Island (Nukufetau Island) 90 miles away, and bearing 150°T, assumed to be on Vaitopo Island (Vaitupu Island), distance 75 miles.

From the diary of **Lt.Cdr. H.W. Harrison**;

"Still plugging along! The ship has been getting more organized as the time passes. A few of our planes that were on the hangar deck that were flooded with salt water when the sprinkler was turned on after the torpedo hit, were only slightly salted, and we got them a fresh water bath today. The officers and crew likewise got a bath, as we were beginning to get a little ripe. The ready room after GQ smells like a monkey pit.
The CA and one DD left us this A.M. to return to the fight. We fueled the other one in the P.M. and it did the same. We got a DD from Funafuti for the rest of the trip, plus a VF and 2 VB and a PBY as air cover all day." **HWH**

JG Planes sent out from one of our bases to cover us. The cruiser and one of the cans leave us to go back to Tarawa. The captain as they are leaving shouts to them "Get as many of those bastards as you can while we are laid up, Good hunting!". We sight a couple of small islands and begin to feel a little better. JG

Tuesday 23 November 1943   *Anchored at Funafuti Atoll, Ellice Islands*

Steaming as before in company with USS RINGOLD.
0043 Sighted a glow on the horizon off the starboard stern quarter, believed to be a passing hospital ship.

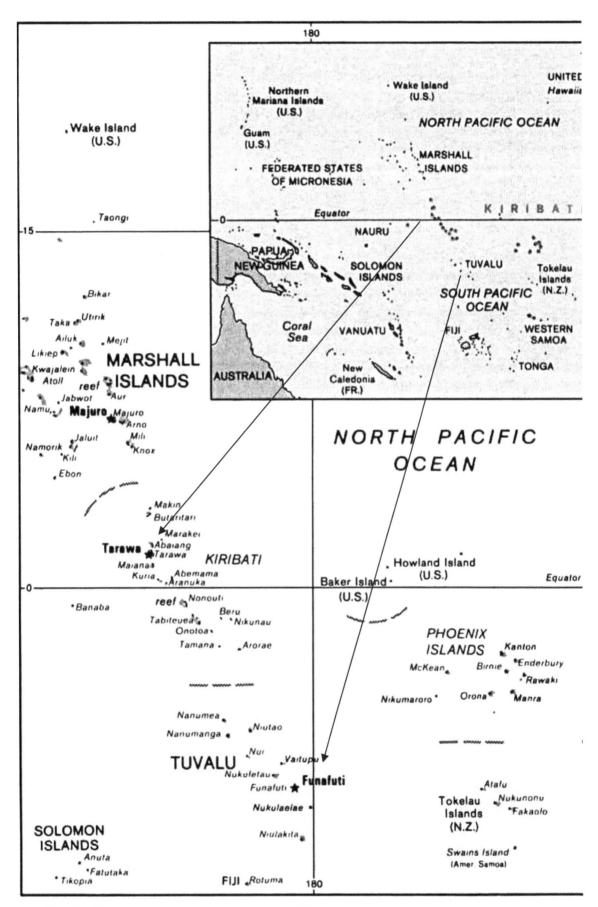

0430 Changed course to 180°T.

0713 Sighted Funafuti Atoll, bearing 167°T, 20 miles. At 0802 they changed course to 200°T.

0900 Commenced reducing speed to 8.8 knots, by reducing shaft speed 5 RPM every 2 minutes.

0940 Changed course to 078°T.

1002 Passed through the entrance to Te Ava Fuagea Channel, maneuvering to conform to the channel.

1037 Received a Pilot aboard to guide the Mighty-I to her berth.

1139 Dropped port anchor in 25 fathoms of water, coral bottom, 90 fathoms of chain, berth Baker 13, Funafuti Atoll, Ellice Islands.

GL *Got 13.1 knots out of one screw. Ate sandwiches and drank coffee for three days. Everybody ate in the ward room. Everything tasted of oil. It was a horrible sight below decks, no lights, fuel oil everywhere. Made port in the Ellice Islands (Funafuti). Seabees and the repair ship Vestal fixed us up a little. Managed to get on the beach a few times. We laid in port for about two weeks. We transferred our wounded men to the hospital ship.* **GL**

JG *We anchor at Funafuti, the northern most island of the Ellice Group of islands. This island has been bombed only a few days ago.* **JG**

From the diary of **Lt.Cdr. H.W. Harrison**;

"Entered Te Bua Bua Passage into Funafuti Atoll this A.M. at 0945 and came to anchor at 1100. Our speed this morning and the later part of the night has been reduced to 8 knots due to salt in the boilers. It seems we got here on our last gasp, and will remain for one month. I hope that's an extravagant estimate.

All VFs are being turned in to the Supply Officer on the island as replacements for losses on the other CV's in the battle, so it looks as we'll just sit on our duffs for a month.

Got a laugh at Whitey Moore's expense this morning. He came in and took a shower with his clothes on, explaining he'd worn them for about a week. The ship's laundry is out of commission among other things. Spent the P.M. washing my clothes and stringing them around the room. I wish I had a picture of the place, as it looks like One Hung Low's laundry." **HWH**

DL *LANDFALL came mid-morning 23 November, third day of our retreat. I had joined a few idlers leaning against the safety chain at the foremost end of the flightdeck. Nobody had binoculars, so we just stared. Phil was there but we didn't speak.*

Land emerged as a speck far ahead, an indistinct smudge where water met the edge of a sky more pale than the ocean it roofed. Soon the speck took on size and shape, gradually revealing itself as a tiny oasis surrounded by the sea, marooned at the center of a watery world of silent light. Its appearance made us blink with surprise.

But it was real enough and we were glad to see it. In spite of its exotic name, though, we soon discovered that distance alone lent Funafuti enchantment. As the Mighty I closed its lush shoreline, a slight off-shore breeze wafted from its jungle a fetid stench of ageless decay that sent us reeling in disgust. No legendary Moorea, this! A brilliant bauble of nature, it was a clump of primitive beauty, its hot air spiced with the pungent odor of putrefaction.

But, who cared? We were glad to be alive, glad to be greeted by sailors waving from repair ship Vestal. We were the wounded patient its skilled mechanic surgeons awaited. Navy had stationed her here as a precautionary measure in case of damage at the Gilberts to a major ship.

*It was over now, that invasion, and a success. Victory hard-won at great cost. Lessons learned, techniques perfected, Tarawa now another paragraph in history's bloody epic. The Marines and the Army had paid most of the cost. But Navy had suffered more than the loss of Independence. Elderly battleship U.S.S. Mississippi ***[1]** had lost forty-three men in an explosion in a 14- inch main battery gun. And the day after we arrived at Funafuti, CVE U.S.S. Liscome Bay ***[2]** was hit by a Long Lance and sent to the bottom with almost all hands: six hundred forty-four men and officers including a rising young rear admiral.*

Which meant that Independence and her men, her dead and those yet to die, were already a half-forgotten sideshow. Even as we bound our wounded and began the task of repairing the rents and fissures disfiguring our ship, the war and the wide world moved on without us, casting vessel and sailormen aside as poor relations.

Dirty poor relations. We found ourselves living in a shabby hovel that insulted our sense of the fitness of things nautical. Work toward restoring our ship's habitability in this tropic heat began ten minutes after the anchor had dropped. It continued for days. Airdales, out of a job (or so we thought) were ordered by Ensign Porky and other aviation officers to join deck crews in what turned out to be a monumental Field Operation. Aviation petty officer ratings counted for next to nothing. All were conscripted to swab decks, scour bulkheads, sweep up and shovel debris, chip rust, man paint brushes, and shine every inch of brass brightwork till the ship gleamed more than she had the day we left Philadelphia.

Cooks resurrected beans from a cornucopia that seemed to contain nothing but beans. Breakfast and noontime and evening chow was navy beans and lima beans and green beans and yellow beans—all spooned onto our trays as a special treat. Lima beans were over-abundant and became favorite delicacies that were transformed into soup and succotash, fried into cakes, baked into loaves of bean bread soaked in powdered milk to soften the resulting granite to a palatable form of hardtack. A genius C & R artisan repaired a broken ice cream machine one day and the next day lima bean sundaes became a source of delight at the gedunk stand. (Years later it took my bride a long time to convince me to accept lima beans as a normal vegetable.)

Showers had to be endured under a cold spray of salty sea water and a special bar of soap that failed to produce suds no matter how hard it was rubbed. Such water and soap left the showeree feeling neither clean nor refreshed.

One day, a big Mariner twin-engine patrol plane flew in with a ton of mail. Our skipper won unofficial promotion to an admiral's star from the crew for allowing an interruption in our cleaning chores while letters from home were devoured. I suspect our officers enjoyed the hiatus as much as we did. **DL**

(Note: *[1] The turret explosion on the USS MISSISSIPPI occurred on 20 November.)

(Note: *[2] The USS LISCOME BAY was sunk on 24 November by IJN submarine I-175, commanded by Cdr. Tabata Naoshi. I-175 will be sunk with the entire crew by DD USS CHARRETTE and DE USS FAIR on 4 February 1944 off Kwajalein. Rear Admiral Henry M. Mullinnix (ComCarDiv 24), aboard USS LISCOME BAY, injured on the carrier's bridge, did not survive. LISCOME BAY lost 54 officers and 648 enlisted men.)

Also anchored in the lagoon at Funafuti Atoll was USS VESTAL. It was fortuitous that she had steamed in yesterday.

VESTAL had been moored outboard, next to USS ARIZONA on December 7th, 1941 when the Japanese struck Pearl Harbor. Damaged from the horrific blast when ARIZONA's magazines blew up, and additionally, also being hit by two Japanese bombs, her CO - Commander Cassin Young beached her to save the VESTAL. VESTAL was repaired and returned to duty. With Cmdr. W.T. Singer at the helm, good ship VESTAL was now about to help obtain partial payback for her wounds at Pearl by helping the Mighty-I stay off the bottom, with her hard working crew, doing what they could to patch up the INDEPENDENCE. Temporary repairs in the initial effort to return the CVL-22 back into the war.

Wednesday 24 November 1943   *Anchored - Funafuti Atoll, for temporary repairs*

DL *Captain Johnson gave us a rundown on the battle we had survived. Our ship shot down six Jap planes, small recompense for our casualties. Said he didn't know where we'd be going next. Food, he said, is still scarce but who's starving?*

Took the planes off the ship by crane and barge today. Really sorry to see them leave. Phil and I agreed that it was impossible to imagine when we'd be able to house them again.

USS VESTAL

Repair ship Vestal had a real job of work to do on Independence. Torpedo damage we could see from topside was minimal except where the gunbucket had been blasted away. We all heard plenty of tales describing what had happened. The detonation had opened a yawning hole in the side ranging from bilge keel to second deck. The blast had demolished the after engine room, smashed a fueling station, continued its thrust upward where it made of the crew messing compartment and the galley a mass of warped and tangled junk. Welds cementing the armored deck had torn loose and the overhead had collapsed. Bulkheads had bent. Hinges on watertight doors had been strained to the breaking point. Into this cavity had flooded the sea, contaminated not only with black oil but fouled with bodies of men unable to escape the carnage.

A large wooden raft had been moored immediately to our starboard side just forward of the torpedo hole. From this raft Vestal's deep divers attempted to cut away the jagged edges of steel surrounding the opening. The idea was to lessen the immense drag our single functioning engine would have to push against once we resumed our journey to Pearl Harbor. With the bent edges cut loose, a temporary patch plate would be welded over the opening and the hull pumped as dry as possible.

The skipper wanted this job done quickly. A berth awaited him at Pearl and he wanted to get there before some other wounded ship swiped it.

It was, really, a simple engineering plan—burdened with one hitch. Funafuti's lovely lagoon was infested with sharks. The voracious hunger of these local denizens had responded to a new food supply within minutes after we had dropped anchor.

The divers would barely submerge before they had to be hastily retrieved. They stood-by patiently until our Marines had driven off the marauders with rifle or BAR fire.

All day long the silvergray fins could be seen slicing through the lagoon a few hundred yards out. Whatever their motivation—instinct, bloodlust, plain meanness—the sharks would get up their courage and come streaking for the ship's side like a raiding war party. The Marines would permit them to approach within a hundred yards and then open a barrage of fire, aiming always at a single fin. As the bullets struck home, the selected target crashed into an invisible wall. Instantly a cold-blooded, mad thrashing scramble followed as its distracted fellow raiders turned to gorge themselves on its punctured flesh--a maelstrom of primordial fury.

From our gallery on the flightdeck, forty-five feet above, we coolies watched the pellucid blue water turn ghastly pink and then brilliant red, the glare of the sun magically transforming the roiling froth into a million tiny jewels. The scene upset tender stomachs (including mine) and raised hairs on the backs of sensitive necks. Yet for all its entertainment value, it slowed the work and something had to be done.

Remove the attraction, obviously. Volunteers were selected—I mean, encouraged. No one picked later talked about the job—not for half a century, and even then not much. It had been gruesome, I was told in a private conversation by an elderly man who'd been a hardnosed youngster at the time but now was a gentle great-grandparent. He had a partner in his youthful adventure, but that one was no longer alive. They had gone below to the second deck, opened a scuttle to the third deck, and descended slowly into a dark steaming charnel house reeking with the combined stenches of all the rivers of hell.

Bodies immersed since the torpedo hit were balloons. They floated clumsily before the men pushing them and were perfectly tractable until a hatch was encountered that was too small for their watery bulk. So the live men squeezed the dead men through one hatch after another until relieved of their burden by hands reluctantly grabbing from above.

A subsequent burial-at-sea ritual was held as before, but I don't know of anyone not ordered to go that attended. I didn't. But the job had to be done on the Mighty I, and was. A forgotten, unheralded incident by anonymous men. When medals were handed out a few days later, nobody heard their names. To me, they've always been heroes. **DL**

Thursday 25 November 1943   *Thanksgiving Day*

JG *Thanksgiving Day. We got our first hot meal since we were hit. Beef, potatoes & gravy, bread, butter and coffee. It made us feel that we were eating like kings. It really tasted good. A repair ship comes along side and starts repairing the hole in our side. It is about 30' long and 20' wide with ragged steel plates hanging from it.* **JG**

DL *Thanksgiving Day! Didn't have much of a feast but who cares? We're alive and even the beans taste good. Cooks and bakers and messmen doing a stand-up job.* **DL**

Friday 26 November 1943   *Anchored - Funafuti Atoll, for temporary repairs*

VF-6 was detached and ordered to duty with ComTaskGroup 50.3 in accordance with a ComCenPacForce dispatch. Pilots flew to Nanumea, then to Tarawa, for a difficult and unpleasant overnight stay on the newly captured island. A PB4Y-2 was assigned as pathfinder for the long overwater flight (with its onboard navigator). The following day they flew aboard the USS ESSEX.

Saturday 27 November 1943   *Anchored - Funafuti Atoll, for temporary repairs*

VF-22 was also detached and ordered to duty with ComTaskGroup 50.3 in accordance with a ComCenPacForce dispatch.

Sunday 28 November 1943   *Anchored - Funafuti Atoll, for temporary repairs*

Anchored in berth 13 Funafuti Atoll, Ellice Islands in 25 fathoms of water, coral bottom. USS VESTAL along starboard side.
During the stay for temporary repairs, he crew of USS VESTAL would secure the No. 1 shaft and her divers removed the No. 1 propeller and secured No. 2 and 3 propellers together with a cable to prevent rotation while the INDEPENDENCE was under way. Munitions and gasoline would first be removed as well the transfer off of aircraft and spare parts. The flooded third deck was made water tight, dewatered, and damaged blister plating protruding from the hull was removed. A ruptured fire main was temporally repaired to restore fire main water pressure to the ship.

DL *Vestal found extra food in its locker and sent over enough fresh chow for our belly-robbers to provide the crew with a real Thanksgiving Dinner.* **DL**

JG *Today we had another Thanksgiving dinner, a few days late. Well worth waiting for. Turkey and all the trimmings. We ate it on portable tables in the hangar deck, it was good. We still haven't received any mail. After dark while the movie was on, Admiral Nimitz comes aboard. We don't see him.* **JG**

Wednesday 1 December 1943   *Anchored - Funafuti Atoll, for temporary repairs*

Anchored in berth 13 Funafuti Atoll, Ellice Islands in 25 fathoms of water, coral bottom. USS VESTAL along starboard side. Boiler No.2 in use for auxiliary purposes.

Thursday 2 December 1943   *Anchored - Funafuti Atoll, for temporary repairs*

0845 Anchored as before. Conducted diving operations in the after gyro room.

Sunday 5 December 1943   *Anchored - Funafuti Atoll, for temporary repairs*

0758 Anchored as before. With temporary repairs completed, USS VESTAL cast off from the starboard side and shifted to an assigned anchorage.
1108 Made daily inspection of the magazines. C-403, C-502, C-503, C-504 and C-506 are flooded.
1620 A damaged TBF was hoisted to the flight deck.
1650 Miscellaneous aviation gear was taken onboard.
1845 A lighter on the starboard beam was removed by tug USS ONTARIO.
         (USS ONTARIO was also built by NYSB, commissioned in 1912)

JG Work on the ship by repair ship Vestal completed, and as repair ship pulls away from us the ship is put on 1 hour notice for getting underway. Crew resumed eating down in the old mess hall today, having eaten chow on the hangar deck since being torpedoed. The ship is pretty well cleaned up with the exception of the after engine room, which is still flooded and C407L, a crew living compartment, also still flooded. Then, nearly all compartments need a coat of paint. JG

Monday 6 December 1943   *Anchored - Funafuti Atoll, for temporary repairs*

1515 Anchored as before. Received aboard 2 TBFs*.
1615 Commenced transferring 80 depth charges to a boat for delivery to Funafuti Atoll.
1820 Tanker USS SEPULGA moored alongside the port quarter to deliver fuel oil.
1825 Received onboard 2 TBFs*.   (*These were aircraft in need of repair.)

DL Removed depth charges from the magazine today and began to transfer them to the beach via barge. When we quit for the day there were still about eighty under a tarp topside. About 2330 all AOMs were roughly awakened and ordered to strike the loose depth charges below. Jap bombers reported to be in the vicinity. Ship went to GQ. An anchored vessel with a hole in its side is in a helluva situation to beat off an assault!

Nothing happened. Rode the bomb elevator down and up and down so many times I almost got used to it. Must really be getting Asiatic! DL

Tuesday 7 December 1943   *Underway from Funafuti Atoll, Ellice Islands en route Pearl Harbor*

0045 Anchored as before. Completed receiving 410,000 gallons of fuel oil from USS SEPULGA. Ship commenced swinging stern to port.
0800 USS SEPULGA cast off all lines and proceeded to its assigned anchorage.
1542 Made all preparations for getting underway.
1605 A pilot came onboard to guide us out of the Atoll.
1612 Got underway for Pearl Harbor in accordance with Movement Order No. 10-43 of 6 Dec 1944 from Commander Service Squadron 4. Commenced maneuvering at 5 knots to clear the channel.
1650 Steamed pass buoy #1 taking departure of Funafuti Atoll thru Bua Bua Channel.
1705 Formed up Task Unit 16.19.1, course 090°T, speed 12 knots (230 rpm) on No. 4 screw, in company with USS DEWEY, USS MONAGHAN and USS ARAPAHO (ATF-68). INDEPENDENCE is guide, OTC and Commander Task Unit. At 1800 they turned to base course 000°T.

A lengthy report titled *"ACTION WITH THE ENEMY REPORT of the U.S.S. INDEPENDENCE November 18, 19, and 20, 1943"* contained within a letter from the captain titled *"Action Report - Galvanic"*, dated 4 December 1943. Within the letter were observations / recommendations from Captain R.L. Johnson. Some (not all of the letter) of the most noteworthy items follow:

---

4. As preparations were being made on Dog Day to recover the Anti-Submarine Patrol, warning was received (from one of our own patrolling TBFs) that a large group of strange aircraft had been sighted. This was followed almost immediately by the sighting from the bridge, of approximately 15 Bettys on the starboard beam on the horizon. From then on things happened very fast as described in Appendix (1). The wakes of four torpedoes, excluding the one which struck the ship, were observed; one passed close aboard on the starboard side on a parallel course, and three torpedoes were seen to pass astern across the ship's wake.

5. References (e) and (f) have been reviewed in light of experiences and observations gained during the Rabaul Attack and Galvanic. It is interesting to note the paralleling if incidents and the applicability of conclusions drawn therein a year ago. There is very little to distinguish this attack from those discussed in references (e) and (f) except:

    (a) Low altitude of approach which appears to have defeated timely Radar Detection.

    (b) Sparse destroyer screen; five destroyers to three (3) carriers and four (4) cruisers. At the time of the attack the effective screen was reduced to four, one destroyer having been ordered to investigate a submarine contact.   (Author's note: These deficiencies would be helped later in the war with not only more destroyers, but with the stationing of Radar Picket Destroyers further out from the main body of the task groups, to give early warning of incoming enemy raids. These pickets would take a horrible beating from the kamikazes.)

7. The expeditious and orderly withdrawal from the scene without outside assistance, once the damage had occurred, was not due exclusively to fortune. Months and months of drill and instruction paid dividends during the 29 minutes required to work up to 13.5 knots. Actually the ship was never completely dead in the water and the quartermaster on watch in the steering engine room undertook to steer a zig-zag course when he found himself out of communication with the bridge. The effective handling of Damage Control facilities and the quick manipulation of remaining power by the Engineer's Force were responsible for the saving of this ship in highly dangerous waters. It is hoped that higher authority will see fit to recognize those who are so richly deserving for this outstanding piece of work.

8. It is a moot point just how much stack gases interfered with the fighting of the ship. By coincidence or design the main attack came from the direction in which the stack gases were being swept by the ship's motion. The attacking planes on the starboard quarter could not be seen distinctly from the bridge and the lookouts were unable to follow torpedo wakes accurately. As a result, the exact bearing of the hitting torpedo was lost as it neared the ship.

    At one time or another, stack gases have hampered lookouts, guns' crews, flight deck crews on the starboard side, and the receiving and transmission of signals by flag hoist and flashing light.

    It is understood, unofficially, that alterations to stack arrangements on CVLs is contemplated. It is further understood that these alterations envision the amalgamation of all four smoke pipes into one stack. In view of this possibility, it is recommended that the alterations incorporate the wet exhaust principle so that gases will be led down and clear of guns, directors, lookouts, etc. It is further recommended that such an installation be given high priority on an experimental basis.   (Author's note: The USS INDEPENDENCE would never have the stacks changed or have these design related problems resolved)

9. After the explosion many electrical circuits had to wait for casualty power before they could be re-energized. This was true of both the incinerator and the garbage grinder. Consequently piles of burnable trash and tare accumulated which could not be disposed of because the ship did not dare leave a trail.

When casualty power restored the incinerator circuit it was necessary to fire the incinerator day and night which, in turn, heated adjacent spaces excessively due to ventilation difficulties.

This is not to be taken as a condemnation of the incinerator. Actually the incinerator is doing a whale of a job during normal conditions. The real difficulty is the excessive tare and packing material in which practically all items are received.

It is recommended that serious and productive effort be given to the elimination of tare. There is not much point in ships eliminating fire hazards through the disposal of essential items only to have all supplies (including small arms ammunition) delivered in inflammable containers.

11. This ship joins the ranks of those who consider the 20mm gun an ineffective ship's weapon - at least for the CVL class. The argument is frequently advanced "stick on all the guns you can" which may be appropriate for larger ships with ample top side weight tolerances. However, even the 20mm installation weighs something and once the weight has been added something should be realized in return. That no such "dividends" have been paid by the 20mm guns has been demonstrated in recent actions in which this ship has participated.

The 20mm rate of fire is approximately four times that of the 40mm. The weight of 40mm projectile is roughly four times that of the 20mm whereas the ranges compare as two to one. Since the purpose of the CVL armament is to destroy the enemy before he can drive his attack home, it follows that the "revenge" weapon is not only of dubious value but may be a source of false hope and security.

This ship has made a study of substituting 40mm barrels for 20mm barrels and firmly believes that 6 40mm twin mounts plus 8 MK 51 directors can be substituted without unacceptable top side weight increases. (20mm guns to come off include those six now scheduled to be added forward as an alteration.) It is recommended that this change in armament be accomplished during the current availability for battle damage repairs. (Note: The substitution of the 40mm gun mounts on the scale Captain Johnson requested would not occur, perhaps due to the impact of additional weight on the vessels stability. Not only the weight of the weapons, but the larger gun tubs and munitions storage. The listing in later typhoons may have been worse with these modifications. Changes in weapons would occur in an early 1944 repair / refit.)

12. Damage Control measures and steps taken to restore power are described briefly in Appendices (2) and (3) for those who are interested in these phases. While the full extent of damage to the hull and machinery cannot be ascertained until the ship is docked and freed of water, the ship was by no means completely crippled. Two planes were launched before entering port, an escorting destroyer was fueled at sea. Had there been more wind, routine air operations could have been conducted especially with the aid of catapult (for launching) in spite of the fact that the airplanes were utilized for counter-listing and trimming purposes.

DL Lifted the depth charges topside again and swung them to a lighter without incident.

Underway at 1615. Now I know what a sailor feels like when his ship is alive again. Slow, though. One engine, one screw. Rumor says thirteen knots top speed to Hawaii, but that turns out to be wrong. Seldom on our 2300 mile trip to Pearl did we top five or six knots. Navy either must think we are safe enough. So far our luck has been good. Our single escort is no more than a big sea-going tug.

Second anniversary of attack on Pearl. A year ago Phil and I were striving to earn a third class aviation ordnance badge at school in Chicago. Boy, what they didn't tell us about duty out here! DL

GL Left Funafuti to go to Pearl Harbor. Could only use one screw. Made 13.1 knots. GL

Wednesday 8 December 1943   *Steaming to Pearl Harbor*

0910 Steaming as before. Crossed the 180th meridian at 05° - 56' Latitude.
1803 USS ARAPAHO reported a sound contact. Changed course to 290T.
1830 Commenced zigzagging on base course 038°T.
1858-1956 Routine evening general quarters.

Thursday 9 December 1943   *Steaming to Pearl Harbor*

0533-0635 Steaming as before. Routine morning general quarters.
0800 Mustered crew on stations
0900 Exercised abandon ship drill.
1430-1437 Exercised crew at fire quarters.

Friday 10 December 1943   *Steaming to Pearl Harbor*

0213 Crossed the equator at 175° - 36.5' West Longitude.

DL   Crossed Equator for sixth time since departing Pearl in October. Rumor started that because we'd had an abbreviated initiation first time, the "old" shellbacks would get another crack at the "new" shellbacks who'd gotten off so easy. Who starts such tales?

All AOMs started classes in the AA version of the 20mm anti-aircraft gun. Much different from the aircraft type. None of our present aircraft complement is equipped to use the weapon; only the SB2C dive bomber has it, and that plane is too big for our deck. Thank heavens.   DL

Saturday 11 December 1943   *Steaming to Pearl Harbor*

0800 Steaming as before. Mustered crew on stations.
0941 Gunnery Department commenced burst firing with automatic weapons.
1325 Sighted USS NASSAU and her escort vessel, hull down on the horizon, bearing 314°T.

Monday 13 December 1943   *Steaming to Pearl Harbor*

0800 Steaming as before. Mustered crew on stations.
1030 Exercised abandon ship drill.
1430-1437 Exercised crew at fire quarters.
1842 Sounded routine evening general quarters.
1923 Sighted star shell and tracer firing bearing 045°T. Changed course to 020°T and commenced zigzagging per plan No.6.
1940 Ceased zigzagging and resumed on base course 040°T.
1951 Changed course to 010°T.
1955 Sighted star shell and tracer firing bearing 060°T, 27 miles. Radar contact 070°T, 27 miles.
2000 Radar contact 082°T, 25 miles.
2007 Sighted star shell and tracers from automatic weapons, bearing 075°T.
2008 Changed course to 040°T.
2017 Secured from general quarters.

Tuesday 14 December 1943   *Steaming to Pearl Harbor*

DL   Believe it or not, doing little or nothing. Must be driving Porky crazy with frustration. Sea is getting rougher as we go north and ship's speed has dropped. Taking green water now and then over the bow. Love to stand at the forward end of the flightdeck with the wind in my face. Now and then I get a pussful of an angry Pacific Ocean.   DL

INDEPENDENCE steamed along on one (No.4) screw. Divers had removed No.1 propeller at Funafuti, and used cable to secure No. 2 & 3 propellers together, preventing rotation with the ship underway.

Wednesday 15 December 1943   *Steaming to Pearl Harbor*

0505 Steaming as before. Intercepted a TBS transmission of destroyer escort USS EMORY to oiler USS TALLULAH, reporting radar contact on this Task Unit, bearing 049°T, distance 18 miles.
0609 Sounded general quarters.
0616 Surface radar contact bearing 238°T, 31,000 yards.
0700 Sighted 2 ships bearing 237°T and 239°T, 15 miles.
0709 Secured from general quarters
0800 Mustered crew on stations.
0815 Sighted 2 ships bearing 258°T, distance 12 miles, on an approximate parallel course.
1935 Radar contact, friendly aircraft bearing 105°T, 78 miles.
2200 Commenced zigzagging on base course 090°T.

Thursday 16 December 1943   *Steaming to Pearl Harbor*

0629-0729 Steaming as before. Routine general quarters.
0843 Sighted ship hull down on the horizon bearing 198°T, 28,000 yards.
1205 Flooded voids A507B, A508B, A903B, A904B, A905B and A 906B to trim the ship.
1254 Sounded fire quarters. A mattress on the catwalk on the starboard side at frame 50 caught fire and was extinguished with CO_2 extinguishers.
1257 Secured from fire quarters.
1300 Changed course to 002°T.
2020 Gun fire and star shells sighted bearing 015°T, 75,000 yards.
2030 Radar contact on land: Mauna Kea peak on Hawaii bearing 082°T, 132 miles, Mauna Loa peak bearing 091°T, 132 miles.
2245 Surface radar contact bearing 045°T, 14 miles.
2252 Sighted signal light on port bow and exchanged calls with the USS JET, a coastal yacht.
2300 Sighted carrier force bearing 048°T, 4 miles.

Friday 17 December 1943   *Moored starboard side of Fox 1, Ford Island, Pearl Harbor*

Steaming as before as Task Unit 16.19.1 on No. 4 screw (boilers No. 1 & 2 are in use) in company with USS DEWEY, USS MONAGHAN and USS ARAPAHO. The ship is darkened.
0633 Sounded routine general quarters.
0720 Changed course to 290°T. Commenced maneuvering in preparation to entering the swept channel.
0733 Sunrise.
0746 Passed channel entrance buoys No.1 & 2, followed by the harbor entrance gate net.
0757 The harbor pilot came onboard. Commenced steering various courses to conform to the channel.
0800 Mustered the crew on stations. At 0908 the firemen secured the No.2 boiler.
0918 Moored starboard side to Fox 1, Ford Island, Pearl Harbor, T.H. in 38 feet of water.
1005 Commenced receiving services from the dock.
1018 Rear Admiral Dunn (ComSerForPac) came aboard, leaving the ship at 1110.

DL   Entered Pearl this morning. The chain of islands looked like emeralds as we approached. I never dreamed I'd be so glad to see them again.
We received quite a reception when we tied up to a dock at Ford Island across from the navy yard, not too far from wrecked Arizona. A large Navy band played "Anchors Aweigh". I think every sailor responded to the traditional marching tune the same way: with unexpected pride. Out of the corner of my eye I noticed guys pull in their belly and puff up their chests. I admit to letting air out of my own lungs. A chorus line of grass-skirted girls wearing leis sang "Aloha" and performed a sweet swaying dance routine.

*Dat ole dabil rumor had claimed we'd be ordered to wear undress whites for entering port, but the order never came. Story is that Captain Johnson considered it but because we had gone to war in dungarees it was fitting that we wear them coming back alive. Nice story. Would like to believe it, but—Doubting Donald. **DL***

JG *Reveille this morning at 0300 due to pulling into Pearl Harbor. At about 0700 we started to enter the mouth of the harbor and at 0900 we pulled along side dock at Ford Island across from Oahu.* ***JG***

Saturday 18 December 1943　　*Moored starboard side of Fox 1, Ford Island, Pearl Harbor*

1401　Moored as before. Commenced diving operations off the starboard side and stern.
1410　A yard tug removed a barge from the port side.
1413　YO-30 moored along the port side.
1449　Secured from diving operations.
1617　Completed fueling from YO-30.
1700　Began transferring torpedoes, warheads and detonators off the ship.

Sunday 19 December 1943　　　　*Moved to a drydock for repairs*

0810　Moored as before. Turned over main engines by steam.
0816　Commenced testing the steering engines, finding them satisfactory. The protective net was then removed from the port side.
0835　Singled up all mooring lines.
0908　All departments ordered to report readiness for getting underway.
0947　A pilot came aboard to guide the movement of the ship.
0950　Tugs 142 and 146 secured to the port bow and port quarter.

1007 Underway with the assistance of tugs 142, 146 and Mikioi from Fox 1, Ford Island to shift to a drydock for repairs.
1100 Passed over the sill into Drydock No. 2, Navy Yard, Pearl Harbor.
1101 First line passed to dock. Began securing main engines and boilers.
1155 Caisson was closed. At 1215 they commenced pumping water from the drydock.
1315 Main generators secured.
1320 USS INDEPENDENCE is resting on keel blocks.
1405 Began receiving services (telephone, steam, water, electricity, etc.) from the drydock.

JG   At 0900 this morning the ship shoved away from the dock at Ford Island and went into the dry dock No. 2 at the Pearl Harbor Yard. Movie on board again tonight. JG

DL   Stood at rail watching Independence maneuver into Drydock #2 this morning. Fascinating. More fascinating was the water draining away. Soon we were left high and dry with only thick poles stabbing at us on both sides to keep the ship level. Strange sight to see walls of concrete close aboard to port and starboard with a great thick movable gate aft to keep out channel water. Gangway lifted by crane to quarterdeck. Liberty for some sections was granted. River Street whorehouses, stand by!
When we were allowed on the dock we couldn't wait for a looksee at the hole in her side. My reaction surprised me. Tears formed at the sight of my ship's gaping wound, so rudely patched by Vestal's workers. I couldn't let anybody see me in this state, so I blew my nose hard and damn near drew blood. Phil was nearby, but he was as moved as I and stayed by himself. No one looked at anyone else. After months of enforced intimacy where no secret could be concealed, the sight of our injured ship clapped shut every man's mouth and shuttered his face. This was personal.
It was exactly here that a story got started (possibly by a yard worker) that we had been hit by three torpedoes but only one had detonated. If that is true, we truly are lucky. What one did to the ship was horrendous; three would have had us sharing the sea with the creatures born to it. Most would not have lived that long.
(The apocryphal story of three fish but one explosion lost its legendary character when it turned out to be true officially. Some former shipmates enjoy bragging about a trio of torpedoes, not appreciating how close we came to never having a reunion anywhere at all.)
A big shock to every man aboard Independence and especially to the airdales, officers and men, was the word (delayed by mandatory radio silence) that LCDR "Butch" O'Hare had been lost 27 November in a mysterious night flying incident no one seemed to know anything about.
I can't say that we ordnancemen felt his loss more than any other group of airdales, but because he had gone out of his way to make himself known personally to each of us made him more of an individual than any other pilot. I would conjecture that AMMs and AOMs enjoyed especially close relationships with pilots even though none knew our names—the mechs because they kept the planes flyable and the ordnancemen because we kept the guns they needed to fight with shooting when they needed them. Most everybody took O'Hare's loss hard. Years later, a seaman friend who had nothing to do with flight was compelled to research the facts of this officer's life and Navy career and published a fine short book about it. He was also the driving force behind the official City of Chicago finally honoring its famous son—letting its citizens know the man who O'Hare International Airport was named after. DL

Monday 20 December 1943   *Resting on keel Blocks in Navy Yard Dry Dock No. 2.*

Resting on keel blocks as before.

JG   The water still in the Dry Dock at reveille this morning but at 0900 it started to drain out and by 0930 it was completely empty of water. At about 1030 I looked down the pier and noticed quite a fleet of cars headed for the ship with motorcycle escorts. It turned out to be a number of high ranking officers of the Pacific Fleet, including Admiral Nimitz, Admiral King, General Marshal and others. Our Captain Johnson and Executive Officer Roddl met them on the dock, and a tour of inspection of the damage to the ship was made. Some decision seems to have been made, after which they all got into the cars and drove off again. **JG**

Tuesday 21 December 1943   ***Resting on keel Blocks in Navy Yard Dry Dock No. 2.***

Resting on keel blocks as before.
With access gained to the damaged magazines, munitions were removed and transferred by box car to the Naval Ammunition Depot, Lua Lua Lai, Ohau.

DL   *A line of gray Navy trucks brought over five hundred bags of mail and a work party deposited them on the dock. How it all got sorted I can't imagine. We gorged on cakes that somehow had survived the trip from Anywhere U.S.A.*   **DL**

Friday 24 December 1943

DL *Christmas Eve! My diary says a bunch of us went to a "good" movie in town, but I don't remember it. Doesn't seem very seasonable; too warm and sunny for a Wisconsin Xmas. Spent lots of time thinking of my family and how far away I am. Strange how we've all been separated by this war.*   **DL**

6799-4

LBL AT DAMAGED AREA AFTER SOME WATER HAD BEEN PUMPED FROM DOCK

Bottom of ship starboard side looking forward. note wrinkles in hull of ship. note broken no 1 shaft.

Saturday 25 December 1943   ***Christmas Day***

DL *Amazed myself by attending church services on the hangar deck. Several guys went, so I weakly joined the crowd. Padre surprised me with a fine sermon I determined to remember, but I'm sure that's a lost cause. Before his sermon, he announced that we had lost seventeen shipmates at Tarawa. Not a great number, really, but to the families it must have been devastating. I know how the news would have been received by my family.*

What a feast we had today! Our belly-robbing cooks and bakers and messmen did themselves proud. If this goes on, we'll need a new nickname for the galley guys. (Hold on! We ain't through this war yet. They can't keep this up!)

The print shop outdid itself by coming up with a fancy, folded menu on good deckle-edged paper. A copy was placed at each diner's plate. (Yes, plate.) For some reason I sent mine home the next day, never dreaming anyone would save it. But Ma and Pa did. On the backside of the last flap was printed a short verse I've never been able to find in any reference book:

> *And the night shall be filled with music,*
> *And the cares that infest the day,*
> *Shall fold their tents like the Arabs*
> *And as silently steal away.*

If we stole away from the tables it was because we were stuffed and unable to move very fast. I had consumed more than a little of everything the menu had offered . **DL**

JG *Christmas Day. The Plan of The Day reads "Holiday Routine". Christmas carols being played over the speakers all morning. Christmas dinner, turkey and all the trimmings. After dinner a Christmas Program for the military was broadcast over the ships speakers. Jack Benny, Bob Hope, Red Skelton, Bing Crosby, Bob Burns and others put on a program enjoyable by all.*
The afternoon was spent in R&R. The movie tonight was "Dixie" with Bing Crosby and Dorothy Lamour, a new movie all hands seemed to enjoy very much. In all, a very complete Christmas Day. **JG**

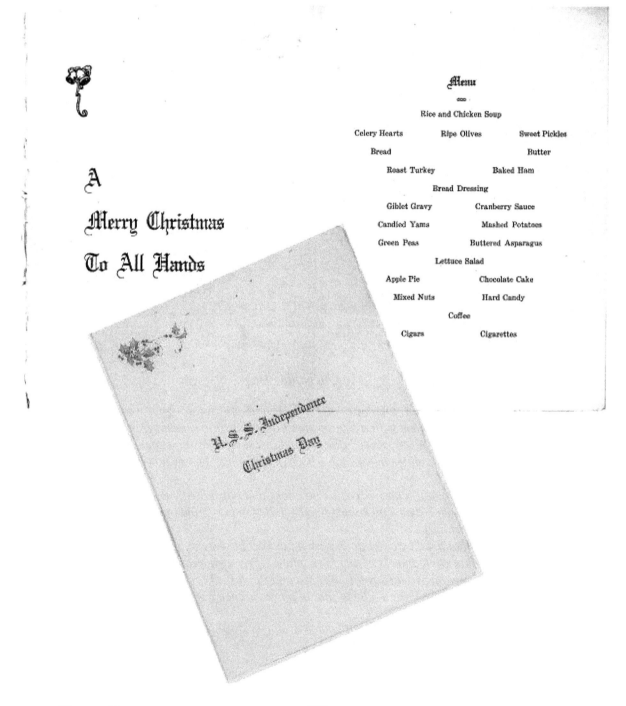

Sunday 26 December 1943　　　*Resting on keel Blocks in Navy Yard Dry Dock No. 2.*

0614 Resting on keel blocks as before. Lighted fires under No.1 boiler.
0953 Commenced flooding the drydock.
1005 Disconnected water hose to the dock.
1011 Water seepage reported in after engine room. Stopped pumping water into drydock.
1035 Commenced pumping water from the drydock. Repairs began on water leak in after engine room.
1135 Commenced receiving fresh water from the pier.
1335 Completed pumping water from the drydock.
1740 Commenced flooding the drydock.

DL Channel water came flooding into the drydock early today but had hardly got a good start when a serious leak was discovered in the after engine room. Seemed to take a long time to drain. Everybody twiddled their fingers. Porky used the time to have us move ammo boxes from one side of the small arms magazine to the other. Gad, in his day he must have served under some sons of bitches Chiefs! DL

Monday 27 December 1943　　　*Underway for San Francisco, California*

0635 Resting on keel blocks as before. Tested the steering engines.
0700 Cut in generators No.1 & 2.
0710 Shifted the steam and electricity loads from the pier to the ship.
0730 Lighted fires under No.2 boiler. At 0800 they mustered the crew on stations.
0816 Made all preparations for shifting berths.
0846 The INDEPENDENCE became waterborne and damaged areas once again flooded: C407L, After Gyro Room, Radio 2A, C602E, C603E, C604E, C504M, C601E, C-1F,C-3F, C901F, C902F and C903F. Leaks again developed in the after engine room, but was managed with the use of submersible pumps.
1107 Underway to shift berths, aided by tugs. Captain at the Conn, Executive Officer, Navigator and Pilot on the bridge.
1203 Moored, port side to fueling pier H4, Navy Yard Pearl, Harbor, in 40 feet of water.
1255 Commenced fueling from the dock.
1330 Made preparations for getting underway.
1448 Completed receiving fuel oil from dock.
USS INDEPENDENCE had been taking on passengers for transportation to the states.
1517 Got underway for San Francisco, California as Task Unit 15.19.2 with our escort USS YOUNG. CVL-22 began making 230 RPM on No.4 propeller, maneuvering on various courses to clear the harbor.
1545 Sounded general quarters for sortie from Pearl Harbor.
1550 Lost power on gyro repeaters. Commenced steering by the ship's magnetic compass.
1558 Power restored to gyro repeaters.
1620 Departed the swept channel and steered on course 153°T.
1645 Lost power on the gyro repeaters. Commenced steering by the ship's magnetic compass.
1710 Changed course to 080°T. At 1830 the helm changed course to 011°T.
2235 Changed course to 020°T. With power restored, commenced steering by the gyro compass.

DL Yard workers toiled all night but when the water flowed back into the dock everything held this time and we backed out and took on fuel. Underway at 1500. The bow dove into a rough trough right outside the channel. Wind blowing a near gale. Have a single destroyer as escort. Should be able to make thirteen or fourteen knots. Home for New Years Eve! Watched dusk gray Diamond Head fade into the dark distance and wondered when we'd see it again. DL

GL Left Pearl harbor for the good ole USA. All hoping to get a nice leave. Johnson says we will be out again in 6 or 8 weeks. Everyone is happy as hell. GL

Tuesday 28 December 1943   *Underway for San Francisco, California*

0000 Steaming as before. Changed course to 044°T.
0605 Radar surface contact on bearing 132°T at 37,000 yards.
0630-0731 Routine morning general quarters.
0930 Mustered crew at quarters.
1804-1905 Routine evening general quarters.

Wednesday 29 December 1943   *Underway for San Francisco, California*

0630 Steaming as before on boilers No.1 & 2, on No.4 propeller, 14.1 knots average speed. USS YOUNG screening at 3,000 yards. INDEPENDENCE is OTC and guide. Commenced zigzagging on base course 044°T. They would zigzag during the daylight hours and cease zigzagging during the night. Clocks were set ahead as they steamed through the time zones.
0810 Changed base course to 060°T.

Thursday 30 December 1943   *Underway for San Francisco, California*

1500 Steaming as before. Sounded general quarters and exercised crew at abandon ship drill.
1507 Gunnery Department test fired automatic weapons.
1535 Secured from general quarters.
1645 Changed speed to 16.2 knots.

Saturday 1 January 1944   *New Years Day*

Steaming on course 064°T, making 17 knots (270 rpm) on #4 screw. Boilers 1&2 are in use.
CVL-22 was in company with USS YOUNG in Task Unit 19.15.2, this ship OTC, CTU and guide.
0702-0803 Routine morning general quarters.
0910 Commenced zigzagging on base course 080°T.
0930 Held quarters for muster, followed by captain's inspection of crew and meritorious mast.
1115 Secured from captain's inspection and meritorious mast. Made daily inspection of the magazines. Conditions normal except in the damaged areas.
1802-1902 Routine evening general quarters..

***DL** Blowing a gale outside the hangar bay where Captain Johnson had us lined up for a full dress inspection. Which was okay, but most of us would have enjoyed being in town for the holiday. Everybody suspected our arrival had been delayed just so our fifteen hundred guys weren't added to the pack of sailors already on Frisco's streets.*

*Had meritorious mast. Solemn occasion. Lots of medals and commendations. Johnson's Silver Star was partially for his conduct during our trial by fire. He deserved it, as did every other sailor no matter how humble or honored. **DL***

Sunday 2 January 1944   *San Francisco Bay - Hunters Point*

Steaming as before on No. 4 screw averaging 16 knots through the water.
0650 Radar contact, distance 20,500 yards. IFF was showing the contact as friendly.
0703 Sounded routine general quarters.
0731 Commenced zigzagging on base course 080°T.
0732 USS LAWRENCE joined the formation screen.
0821 Set all clocks ahead 1/2 hour to zone plus 7.
1013 Radar contact of land bearing 072°T, 90 miles.
1243 Sighted Farallon Islands bearing 038°T distance 35,000 yards.

1254 Ceased zigzagging and changed base course 060°T.

1256 Changed base course to 052°T.

1302 Commenced zigzagging on base course 052°T.

1334 Ceased zigzagging and changed base course to 050°T.

1341 Passed Farallon Islands abeam to port.

1344 Sounded general quarters for entering channel.

1345 Changed course to 068°T.

1348 Commenced decreasing speed gradually to 200 r.p.m.

1449 Passed swept channel #1 buoy abeam to port, entrance to San Francisco Bay. Steering various courses at various speeds to conform with the channel.

1516 Passed Bonita Point light and Mile Rock light abeam passing from International waters to Inland waters.

1516 Secured from general quarters. The pilot A. Oakley came aboard.

1659 Moored port side to pier, Berth 1, Hunters Point Navy Yard, San Francisco, California, in 7 ½ fathoms of water with 10 wire hawsers and one 8" manila line. Draft 23'5" forward, 25'0" aft.

1717 Secured main engines and let fires die out under boiler No. 1. Boiler No. 2 and generators No. 1 and No. 2 in use for auxiliary purposes.

1718 Shifted watch to quarterdeck, set regular in-port routine.

1743 Receiving fresh water from the dock.

1850 Receiving telephone service from the dock.

1851 United States Customs Inspector came aboard.

1942 Let fires die out under Boiler No. 2."

GL Arrived at San Francisco, Golden Gate Bridge sure looked good. Got a 14 day leave.
*Note: Our score for six months; 39 Jap planes, one heavy cruiser, one tanker, raided 4 islands. **GL***

*GN Hit Frisco and tied up at Hunter's Point and will I ever forget that place. Went on Liberty that night through the Int'l Settlement and celebrated all the holidays that had passed so inconspicuously while at the business of making war. Called up Edna that night and although she got a big kick out of it I think I got a bigger one. While here had two weeks leave and spent seven days and six nights of the latter part of January at home. **GN***

*DL Ended the first cruise of the Independence today after six months, two weeks and two days of hard, strenuous sailing that covered over 30,000 miles. The Golden Gate looked swell to us and it was a big thrill to glide beneath that huge red bridge. We docked at Hunters Point which is near San Francisco, so we won't have so far to go. Going ashore tonight with the gang and get what has been denied to us for a long time. I think we deserve it. San Francisco as I viewed it from the deck of my proud ship that day whispered to me and I listened: Here, boy, here. I've been waiting for you. Come to me and I'll show you life and give you love and you won't be sorry. But hurry, lad. Nothing like this moment will ever again be the same. I was home. **DL***

Monday 3 January 1944   *Moored - Hunters Point*

0800 Moored as before to port side of berth # 1 Hunters Point Navy Yard, San Francisco, California. The ship was in 45 feet of water, receiving all services from the dock including fresh & salt water, steam, electricity and telephone services. Mustered crew at quarters.

DL   At precisely 1700 on the third day of the year 1944, Independence unleashed her men and the invasion of San Francisco was on.
        First, though, we had to line up in ranks extending the length of the flightdeck and endure a speech by our skipper. Bless the man, he kept it short....

"All right," he concluded. "Liberty for the starboard watch 1700 to 0730, port watch tomorrow same time. You will find San Francisco a friendly city with a warm and generous heart. It can also get you in trouble. I'm telling you now, stay out of trouble. And take a few precautions. I don't want anybody turning up in sick bay in a few days with a leaky faucet. Have a good night. Dismissed!"

Thus duly warned, we hurried below to prepare for our first bout with the city's night.

Much of the preparation had been accomplished weeks before. At Funafuti, a couple of days after Independence hauled in her anchors to begin the first leg of the trip to the States, moldy dress blues had magically appeared from beneath stacks of dungarees. Evenings saw the fantail as well as the catwalk railings—clear of the gun mounts—draped with freshly laundered blue uniforms. Off-duty sailors used old toothbrushes to scrub white jumper striping. Lost buttons were replaced, patches made where needed. I observed guys struggling to ease bellies into trousers that had fit perfectly last time worn. Shoes gleamed under successive polishing. White hats withheld from the mandatory blue-dyeing process endured washing and bleaching and rinsing before being set aside to dry, each man's name inked black on the inside rim so no mistakes in identification would be made when retrieved. Neckerchiefs were ironed by whatever means could be devised, folded into thin strips, and stowed lengthwise beneath clean mattress covers for permanent pressing. Ships Store was cleaned out of new skivvies and socks and every other article that could be expected to be of use when the time came.

Such as, Right Now. Tonight.

Since Tarawa, all ordnancemen had been confined to a compartment on the Poop just below the flightdeck. It was quieter because with only one screw operating there was much less vibration. Besides, no landing airplanes thumped to the deck overhead. Sleep came easier.

The price we paid for this luxury was space. The place was jammed. And this particular afternoon not only jammed but perfumed, aromatic, smelling with all the paste and powder the stiff-legged male animal on the make could possibly smear or spray upon his muscular frame in this most unprivate of boudoirs. In short, the joint stunk.

The San Francisco that greeted us looked the same as it had in July during our brief forays into town from Mare Island. Her fabled night-lighted glory was hidden by wartime; the neon flash of commerce was almost nowhere to be seen—as if someone in a position of responsibility had neglected to pay the light bill. For most of us, this first night of freedom in a real American city (Honolulu had been real enough but with a distinctly Oriental feel to it) began at the corner of Third and Market Streets. Jitney cabs disgorged their loads, spun about in tight U-turns, and went roaring back to Hunters Point for more of the same.

INDEPENDENCE under repair suffered mightily. Her crew endured every agony, mainly because no one in authority permitted us to escape it.

No more than a few days after mooring at Hunter's Point Navy Yard—and after all ordnance and unneeded fuel had been removed to barges and small yard oilers—she moved ponderously under her own power into the yard's newest drydock. It was almost as if she was putting up a final show of defiance.

From the flightdeck we watched the slow rigamarole as she entered her new berth. There had been plenty of speculation about how long we would be here, but I don't recall any rumor that had predicted she would be on the blocks the better part of four months.

Encouraging rumors that claimed we would be placed ashore in naval barracks were quashed quickly, and buried forever on the fourth day of our arrival.

A full dress, all-hands awards formation was held on the flightdeck. Commendations and medals from Purple Hearts to Navy Crosses were awarded to men and officers who had earned them the hard way. Our good skipper received the Silver Star from some Stateside admiral for having brought his ship home. During his blessedly short acceptance address, he claimed that while it was an honor to receive it, the medal really was to Independence and her crew. "She and you," he said, "have got us here to San Francisco."

We took Captain Johnson at his word. Although we couldn't show our respect for the man visibly or audibly (no Three Cheers and a Hear-Hear on an American man-o-war!) I remember seeing a few heads nod in agreement with the admiral's words of commendation.

But then Johnson dropped the other shoe.

"Because of impossibly crowed conditions ashore," he said, "all of us, officers and men, will live aboard ship while repairs are being made. Married men with wives hereabouts will be permitted overnight and weekend liberty depending on workload. All unmarried men will be granted liberty between 1730 and 0730 on alternating port and starboard nights and occasional seventy-two hour leaves, again depending on the needs of the ship. All crewmen, married and unmarried, will be granted fourteen-day leave commencing the second week in January." Then his voice switched to gravel: "Any man AWOL from liberty or leave will be dealt with per Navy Regulations. Dismissed!"

Grumble-grumble. Piss and moan. The formation did not break up as usual. It collapsed.

Doesn't the Old Man know how noisy it's going to be?

Not in his quarters!

He'll be living on Nob Hill with his wife, why should he care?

The Yard's gonna tear us up bit by bit.

First welder scorches my tail's gonna get a torch shoved up his well-paid fanny!

Okay, so we hated it, lived with it, and survived. No one liked the daily confinement, the unlimited upset to ordinary living standards, the mounds of dirt, the unholy noise. Skipper was good as his word, though: liberty was so plentiful that pretty soon we all were singing a current, supposedly patriot ditty about Twenty-one Dollars a Day Once a Month.

And then the entire ship began to ring with an endless, dissonant passage from a madman's Anvil Chorus. It was made up of enormous chipping hammers, stupendous rivet guns, and other demonical steel machinery designed to uproot from their foundations other hard steel machinery. And our personal Simon Legree named Ensign Porky came back from an extended leave. He put us to work like chain gang coolies in the magazines located a single deck above the metallic core of all this uproar. Ratings from striker to ordnanceman first class got the same treatment.

This gentleman seemed to glory in upholding his reputation as a slave driver. While we stumbled around groggily, suffering from the excess of the night before, he squeezed every ounce of whiskey or rum or gin from our pores with a satanic expression. Gleefully he assigned work he had to know strained almost to the breaking point leg and thigh muscles which had not yet recovered from their vigorous exertions of a few hours earlier. And while we coolies sweated in the cool San Francisco air (even in the magazines the air was chill), he perspired so profusely watching us work that his khaki shirt darkened at the armpits as if he were standing atop the Equator. I suspected, hopefully, that his fellow officers considered him a jerk. Even if they did, we who had to endure him knew him as a stupid jerk.

(In the month of July in a year so distant from that time neither of us could have dreamt we'd live to see it, I received a letter from my shipmate Bill which expressed surprise at a mention I had made of Ensign Porky in a letter of my own:

"Your memories of ---- ----- ---- seem less harsh than mine. I thought he was the most stupid, ignorant, uneducated person I ever met, and a poor leader. I hope I am not being offensive, I'm just being honest.")

We felt that it would be nice if mother Navy would send him somewhere else. It was impossible to know that this devil would still be around for our next cruise—the longest one of all.

Our small group was not the only one suffering under this draconian type of supervision. Wounded Independence was our home too, but our artisan jobs had departed with the guns and shackles mounted in the airplanes we had been trained to service. So we were assigned to various menial jobs we had scarcely known existed on the ship. It startled me how quickly we all settled into this routine. Within two weeks of the ship's keel grounding on the blocks of the drydock and the water which was her element was pumped out, we accepted our new existence as if it were all part of the game. The denizens of the mess deck and galley still fed us three squares a day. It wasn't easy for them.

Their quarters had been smashed when the fish hit at Tarawa and it would be months before yard workers could rebuild them. Only the forward mess deck could be utilized. The lack of refrigeration was replaced by large crates placed dockside. Each held mountains of food from fresh eggs to pork chops and steaks.

There had to be an explanation from somebody for this virtual imprisonment. Sure enough, our faithful rumor factory came up with a beauty that went a long way toward relieving our anxieties. Rudy Johnson's political tendrils (so the story went) had detected a danger in his original desire to find shelter for his crew on the beach while his Mighty I got the full roughhouse treatment. New construction was producing new aircraft carriers monthly. Each new bottom required new hands. Each new skipper dreamed of taking an experienced crew to sea on his own first cruise as Captain of the Pinafore, pip-pip. If Johnson beached his crew he'd lose it man by man. So he made a deal with high brass—which may have won him an admiral's star later because it got them off the hook. He would save mother Navy lots of trouble finding room for us refugees by keeping his crew intact aboard his ship while she endured evisceration at the hands of skilled men whose ministrations would be long, hard, rough, and loud beyond imagining. And his men, so he bragged, would enjoy every day of it.

Now, that is one version of why we stayed aboard and it may have been true. Whether he really claimed that we would enjoy it is questionable. If he did, Captain Jim's Marine contingent should have been ordered to rinse out his mouth with water from a scupper whose ball check valves had gone bad.

Our confinement had its good points. A solid roof, comforting warmth, chow three times a day the like of which bluejackets didn't get west of Pearl. If that wasn't enough, fifty yards from the drydock was a large soup-and-sandwich emporium where sailors could buy a real New York Kosher pastrami on rye for half a buck or a Chicago-style hot dog with sauerkraut and trimmings for 35 cents, potato chips included. A mug of joe for a dime, a thick malt two-bits, soft drinks a nickel. And if your butt supply was low, a carton of smokes went for half a dollar.

Our fllightdeck was cluttered with mounds of gear protected by huge tarps. Construction had begun on a second catapult, for Mighty I would return to sea with the first double cat of any of the nine CVLs. But I was looking at the inviting downtown buildings in the distance. They gleamed pink at sunrise whenever fog didn't blot them out. The Mark Hopkins hotel, perched fat and sassy on its hill, displaying the broad windows of its topdeck bar, beckoning from five miles away. Life aboard was tolerable if noisy, laborious, and untidy.

As the skipper had promised, liberty was generous. Large leave parties departed weekly. LEAVE parties were met at the Oakland Mole by a Chief or a yeoman PO with a sheaf of papers on which we were checked off as having arrived promptly on the designated day.
A seaman driver commanding a gray, flat-nosed GM diesel bus with U.S. Navy painted in small black letters high on its side transported us across the Bay Bridge straight to Hunters Point.

Looking down at San Francisco from the elevated vantage point of the bus window, the city seemed to be welcoming me home. The Ferry Building tower, the Hills Brothers sign with a bearded man in a yellow caftan draining a huge mug of coffee, the buildings piled high on the hills, Twin Peaks in the distance, the busy waterfront: all had become part of my life.

I was due to report back to the ship "on or before 1500 Thursday 24 February 1944." My train had been almost on time. With little traffic to contend with anywhere along the route, the driver got us to the Point with half an hour to spare. First concern was the appearance of my ship. I plunked my bag down at the foot of the gangway and made a walking tour along Mighty I's starboard side.

God, what had they done to her? Gutted by the torpedo, in my absence these workers had completed her evisceration. Repair ship Vestal's hardy artisans at Funafuti had done the best they could under the emergency situation, but their patch-up ministrations had been gentle compared to the way she looked on this day. Half her hull from flightdeck to keel had been stripped of the steel sheeting that covered her nakedness from the eyes of man and the power of the sea. So much machinery had been extracted that she had become a defenseless, empty maw. Strakes and stiffeners held decks and bulkheads together. Welding torches sparkled in the half-darkness of her innards.

An unholy racket, only partly muffled by distance, emanated from inside her as if buzzing insects were enjoying a grand old time.

I turned away in distress. Oh man, I moaned. This is going to take half a year!.

But as I swung about, on the dock behind me towered great new Babcock & Wilcox boilers and turbines covered with tarps large enough for circus tents, as well as other machinery to replace what had been removed days ago. She was on the mend. These guys were taking care of her. **DL**

During the time the ship was in drydock Robert Anderson would note:

RA *The crew was given 14 days leave. Mine started around Feb. 2nd. Took a United Airlines plane from Richmond Field Calif. to East Boston Airport. Made it in 23 hours. Only a few stops were made. I remember stopping at Elko Nevada, Iowa, Chicago, Cleveland, N.Y.C. and Hartford. Made return trip by plane as far west as Cheyenne Wyoming. Took a train for remainder of trip.* **RA**

Saturday 1 April 1944   *Off the keel blocks and out of drydock*

Resting on keel blocks in 16 feet of water, Drydock No.3, Hunters Point, San Francisco.
0545 Commenced additional flooding of the drydock.
0610 USS INDEPENDENCE lifted off the keel blocks with a 3/4° starboard list.
0612 Disconnected from shore services supplied by the dock.
0635 A harbor pilot reported on board to aid undocking the ship.
0658 Underway, with the assistance from yard tugs YT 189, YT 462 and YT 477, from Drydock No.3 to shift berths.
0714 The bow of the INDEPENDENCE crossed the drydock sill.
0749 Moored in 8 fathoms of water with the starboard side to berths No.1 & 2, Naval Drydocks, Hunters Point.
0800 Mustered crew on stations.
0825 All yard tugs cast off and the harbor pilot departed the ship.
The INDEPENDENCE began receiving services from the dock.

Friday 28 April 1944   Secretary of the Navy, Frank Knox dies

Secretary of the Navy, Frank Knox died at age 70. On Sunday, flags of the nation are flown at half mast. The USS INDEPENDENCE and her eight sister ships would have been the Cleveland class cruisers had it not been for Franklin D. Roosevelt and Frank Knox. He will be replaced by James Vincent Forrestal.

William Franklin Knox
Secretary of the Navy

Frank Knox was in the photo at the launching on 22 August 1942 (page 41)

Above: **Moored with the port side to berths No. 1 & 2, Naval Drydocks, Hunters Point looking aft** (toward the south) **from the island. These photos possibly taken in April to June 1944 timeframe.**

The photo below shot at the same location as photos on pages 278 & 282

Above: **Moored with the port side to berths No. 1 & 2, Naval Drydocks, Hunters Point looking across the flight deck from the island toward the north.**

In the background in the fog / haze is the Oakland Bay bridge and the city of San Francisco. Note the open bomb elevator Don Labudde so detested. Beyond the dockside crane is a barge floating in front of Drydock #2, and behind the building complex is the entrance to Drydock #3.

Photo below: **Date** (possibly 15-17 June 1944) **and Location in San Francisco Bay unknown. Note the new antenna mast between #3 & #4 stacks** (not the radar antenna).

Monday 21 May 1944   *Repairs and modifications continuing*

Moored starboard side to berths No.1 & 2, U.S. Naval Drydocks, Hunters Point. With the aid of tugs, INDEPENDENCE was "wound" (rotated) and pushed port side to the berth.

Monday 29 May 1944   *Repairs and modifications continuing*

Moored as before, port side to berths No.1 & 2, U.S. Naval Drydocks, Hunters Point.
1600 Conducted tests on the port catapult by firing catapult shots of 9,900 lbs of dead load.
2000 Completed catapult testing.
2100 Tested all night landing lights (except three marker lights, not yet installed at the forward end of the flight deck). Completed testing at 2125.

These photos were (possibly) **shot at Hunters Point, Berths Nos. 1 & 2 between 21 May and 15 June 1944** (or at Pier 31, Magnetic Proving Grounds for deperming on 15 June)**.**

Originally painted in standard "Measure 21" camouflage (Navy Blue) paint, USS INDEPENDENCE is wearing a fresh coat of paint in camouflage scheme Measure 3x* Design 8A utilizing Light Gray, Ocean Gray, Navy Blue and White. (*See next page)

During the time in the Navy Repair Yard at Hunters Point, in addition to the torpedo damage repair, the ship had received many upgrades. To name a few major upgrades:

USS INDEPENDENCE received the addition of a second catapult. After fretting over the proposed location of the catapult track (to be located starboard, or, in tandem with the port catapult), the installation (starboard location) was approved on March 31st as an experimental installation. She was the first CVL to receive an additional catapult and proper flight deck spotting was a necessity. See pages 886-893 for a selection of photos depicting the study of aircraft spotting with two catapults on a CVL.

She (the vessels of the US Navy are said to be referred to in the female vernacular, due to the cost to keep them in powder and paint *) would steam out of Hunters Point with a fresh new coat of Measure 3x - Design 8A Camouflage paint and countershading, per a *"request"* dated 5 January 1944.
(Note: The letter calls out Measure 33, the Bu. Ships drawings BU AER 170023 & 170024 call out Measure 3_, with a reference 32 / 8A at the lower left corner of the drawings. The letter requesting Measure 33 contains no indication as to the actual implementation.) (John W. Snyder - Naval Historian - with a background in naval paint chips, indicates 3x referring to measure 31, 32 or 33 and that the CVL-22 "was, in fact, wearing Measure 32". The three measures said to be the same design, the difference between 31, 32, & 33 being the colors of the paints used within the design.) (*A close rendition - attributed to Nimitz)

As for the powder, changes were made to the INDEPENDENCE gun count. One additional 40mm twin gun mount had been approved.

To compensate for the added weight of the new starboard catapult, its machinery, and the new twin 40mm gun mounts, 18 of the 20mm guns were removed and a reduction in torpedo stowage was made to correspond to the new allowance of 18 torpedoes (these were torpedoes for the Avengers).

The **new "Authorized Battery"** was:
       2 - 40mm Quadruple Gun Mounts
      10 - 40mm Twin Gun Mounts
       4 - 20mm Guns

All guns (other than the Quad 40^s on the bow and stern) were to be located on the Gallery Deck Level.

The loss of most of her 20mm guns was most likely not much of a real loss. Called "Revenge Weapons", the 20mm gun was a short range weapon that made noise, but lacked real punch. It most likely could distract and perhaps somewhat deter a pilot resolved to live after delivering an attack on the ship, but would only knock him down after he had ample opportunity to deliver his ordinance to the ship - hence - "Revenge Weapon".

She also had her **SC-2 radar replaced with SM search radar**. When originally fitted out to first enter the war, <u>S</u>hipborne <u>M</u>icrowave Radar was both desired and targeted to be installed on the INDEPENDENCE. SM Radar was under development and the INDEPENDENCE was inspected by engineers from both the Massachusetts Institute of Technology and the General Electric Company. The problem that made it untenable was SM Radar at that time was still too big (many times the originally allocated space, weight and power requirements) and the antenna too heavy for the island structure. Radar was undergoing extensive research with rapid development by MIT and GE, but SM Radar was still not far enough along in its ongoing refinement. It was said to be *"in a very nebulous state of design"* as stated in a 4 November 1942 memo to Bu. Ships from the Supervisor of Shipbuilding. So in its place, the then lighter SC-2 radar had been fitted. INDEPENDENCE didn't have the luxury of time to wait for the R&D in 1942.

Obviously, the R&D had been both fast and productive, as the CVL-22 was now (little more than a year and a half after that memo) reentering the war with SM Radar. Close inspection of the later photos will show the new SM Radar Antenna dish in place of the earlier 4.5' x 15' rectangular "bedspring" antenna on the front of the Foremast Platform on the island structure.

Additionally, a second yardarm was added to the island, and a new antenna mast was installed between the last two aft stacks. (A photo of the new antenna mast is on page 397)

The photos on these two pages show some island detail of the CVL-22 after the 1944 repairs at Hunters Point.   Note the ability to open up or close off the bridge area.

(The photo on the top right was 2-hole punched, and has slight storage damage)

This photo is looking down on the ("flagbag") signal flag stowage.

Note in this photo the 20mm gun tubs have been removed from under the flight deck overhang that were above the Quad 40 mount on each side.

First Division in June 1944 (San Francisco area location not known in this partially damaged photo)

While INDEPENDENCE had been on the mend at the hands of diligent yard workers, the U.S. forces were progressing from their foothold at Guadalcanal steadily north up through the Pacific. The Gilberts were behind us (along with the torpedo damage) and Nimitz had zeroed in on the Marshal Islands. VADM Marc Mitscher would replace Pownall. Under Mitscher the islands of Kwajalein, Roi and Namur (on Kwajalein Atoll) fell prey to landings by the Army and Marines, with the islands declared secured from the 2nd thru the 5th of February. **(Also see Map on next page)**

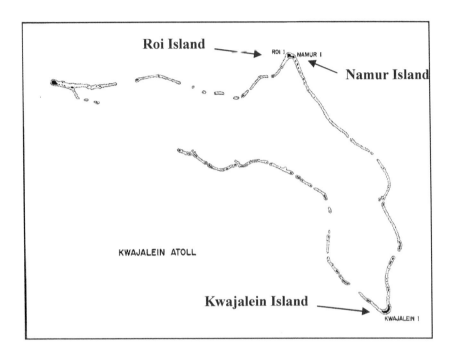

Mitscher then jumped to the Carolines and struck at the massive Japanese presence at Truk atoll. Eniwetok was at first bypassed, as untouched, Truk would have posed an overbearing and highly dangerous threat to the Eniwetok invasion, which occurred on February 19th. With Eniwetok captured and Truk effectively defanged and isolated, Japanese airbases and installations at Jaluit, Maloelop, Mili and Wotje were also isolated and bypassed.

With the Gilberts, Marshals and now the Carolines cutoff from Japan, isolated and contained, further Marine and Army invasions of those islands had become needless, saving many U.S. lives.

Admirals eyes now focused on the Marianas.

The Emperor's bathtub was being drained at an alarming rate as the ocean empire Japan so rapidly had seized was now quickly evaporating. Gallant submarine crews were also hard at work sending Japan's transport vessels to the ocean bottom along with their cargos of troops, food, oil, supplies and other vital materials of war.

During these campaigns Japan also suffered a continuing toll on its aviation assets. Newly trained Japanese aviators were manning their aircraft with far less flight experience than American aviators, and the wide disparity in training and flight time was starting to show as with a much higher rate of Japanese combat losses.

On **4 June 1944** U.S. troops captured Rome and, two days later, on **6 June 1944** blood spilled on and around the beaches of Normandy as the massive Allied Invasion of Europe commenced.

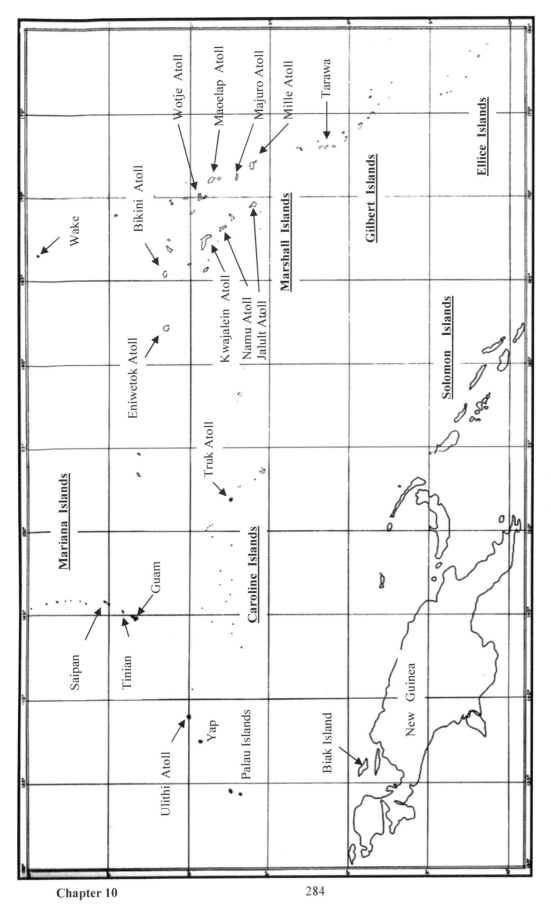

Map of the Central Pacific

Thursday 15 June 1944   *Readying to get underway*

Moored in 8 fathoms of water, port side to berths No.1 & 2, U.S. Naval Drydocks, Hunters Point. Receiving services from the dock. At 0035 they commenced jacking over No.2 & 3 main engines.
0230 Commenced testing after diesel engine. Yard Tug 478 placed YN-74 along the starboard side to pump fresh water to the main feed tanks.
0315 Secured from jacking over No.2 & 3 main engines.
0405 Secured aft diesel engine, testing having proven unsatisfactory due to failure of governor control.
0730 Yard Tug 478 removed barge YN-74 from our starboard side, having pumped 51,480 gallons of fresh water on board.
0750 Services had been disconnected from the dock, a Bar (harbor) Pilot had come aboard, and all preparations were completed for getting underway.
A number of officers and over 50 civilians reported aboard for post repair sea trials.
0800 Mustered crew at quarters.
0818 Set the special sea details and lookouts.
0831 Aided by tugs, INDEPENDENCE got underway for post repair trials in San Francisco Bay.
0839-0841 Yard tugs 462 and 478 cast off from our starboard side.
Stopped all engines due to "guard over the counter gear rubbing on all shafts".
0855 Underway on all shafts. Commenced post repair trials at various speeds on various courses.
0927 Anchored in 8 1/2 fathoms of water, mud bottom.
0932 Pilot A. Oakley left the ship.
0943 Made preparations for getting underway.
0951 Underway, continuing sea trials with a Bar Pilot on the bridge.
1029 Anchored in San Francisco Harbor in 7 1/2 fathoms of water, starboard anchor.
1200 Made preparations for getting underway.
1211 Underway, continuing post repair trials in San Francisco Bay at various speeds on various courses.
1229 Forced to reduce speed due to unusual noise coming from the No.4 main engine reduction gear.
1239 Stopped No.1 & 4 screws and proceeded ahead on No.2 & 3 screws at 10 knots.
1248 Restarted No.1 & 4 screws, proceeding on all 4 screws at 15 knots.
1312 Made a westerly run through the magnetic survey range, and then reversed course and made an easterly pass through the magnetic survey range.
1402 Commenced maneuvering to position the ship for mooring at Pier 31 to deperm the ship.
1439 Moored to Pier 31, San Francisco with the aid of yard tugs HENRY J. BIDDLE and YT-181 in 5 1/2 fathoms of water.
1510 Commenced rigging deperming cables. Tested after diesel engine, testing having proven unsatisfactory due to failure of governor control.
1521 Secured No.3 generator.
1740 Completed rigging deperming gear. At 1910 the ship commenced deperming.

Friday 16 June 1944   *Post repair sea trials*

Moored at Pier 31, Magnetic Proving Grounds, San Francisco, California.
0045 First Officer reported a cable fouled in No.2 screw. The Engineering Officer was notified not to turn over the screws. A diver was tasked to free the cable.
0235 Diving operations commenced to free the screw and by 0330 the cable was removed.
0600 Commenced making all preparations for getting underway.
0722 Underway from Pier 31, Magnetic Proving Grounds, San Francisco with the assistance of the yard tug HENRY J. BIDDLE, to continue post repair sea trials.
0725 HENRY J. BIDDLE cast off and CVL-22 commenced maneuvering to conform to the channel as they proceeded to sea. They were under orders from the Commander, Western Sea Frontier.

0755 Passed through the anti-submarine nets proceeding seaward.

0758 USS KING and U.S. Navy Blimp K-121 reported for escort duty.

0800 Sounded general quarters for sortie.

0814 Passed Point Bonita light abeam to starboard, then passing from inland to international waters. Numerous course and speed changes were made during the day.

0934 Secured from general quarters.

1033-1109 Conducted torpedo defense for structural firing tests.

1120 Sounded torpedo defense to exercise A.A. practice on towed sleeves.

1200 Sounded flight quarters.

1201 Commenced two 360° turns to calibrate the new SM Radar.

1220 Secured from torpedo defense.

1223 Commenced another 360° turn to calibrate the SM Radar.

1239 Completed recovering 4 F6Fs and 4 TBMs (based at Watsonville, California).

1443 Exercised crew at torpedo defense, and resuming A.A. firing practice.

1540 Catapulted 4 F6Fs and 2 TBMs to proceed to Watsonville and 2 TBMs to fly to NAS Alameda.

1636 Secured from flight quarters.

1658 Testing of the turbines, reduction gears and shafts progressed through the day with small increases in speed with the maximum speed obtained reaching 34.4 knots (341 RPM).

1704 Reduced speed due to a failure of a feed pump in the after fire room.

1705 Secured from torpedo defense.

1800 Commenced full power run, with engine room putting out 345 RPM.

1905 Lost sight of destroyer USS KING as it gradually fell astern.

1945 Darkened ship.

2029 Sounded routine evening general quarters.

2050 Full power runs were suspended early due to failure of three forced draft blowers (Blowers Nos. 2, 9 and 12). Commenced slowing the ships speed to 20 knots with 10 RPM decreases every 5 minutes.

2100 The U.S. Navy Blimp K-121 departed to return to its base.

2131 Secured from evening general quarters.

Saturday 17 June 1944   *Sea Trials*

Steaming as before, zigzagging on base course 009°T.

0239 Sighted USS KING, bearing 155°T, 2,780 yards.

0350 USS KING assumed screening position ahead, 2,000 yards off the starboard bow.

0435 Report of radar contact with an unidentified aircraft bearing 110°T, 30 miles.

0455 Sounded general quarters.

0525 Rendezvoused with escort, U.S. Navy Blimp K-105.

0552 Secured from general quarters.

0850 Made landfall (Farallon Islands) on radar, bearing 013°T, 45 miles.

0925 Commenced testing of the aft diesel engine. Commenced transfer of 10,000 gallons of gasoline and conducted test of the gasoline system.

0930 Sighted the Farallon Islands, bearing 006°T, 27 miles.

1005 Made daily inspection of the magazines, and weekly test of the magazine sprinkler system.

1035 Commenced maneuvering approaching to enter swept channel entrance to San Francisco Bay.

1042 Sounded general quarters. At 1043 the ship passed buoy Able abeam to port.

1114 Stopped all engines.

1116 All engines ahead standard, speed 15 knots.

1159 Passed Point Bonita lights abeam to port.

1210 Secured from general quarters.

1216 Passed through the anti-submarine nets of San Francisco Bay.

1234 Anchored in 13 fathoms of water, 60 fathoms of chain, mud bottom, in San Francisco Bay.

1254 Yard tug 136 tied up along the port side aft, breaking her mast in the process, as the tug's mast struck the overhanging gun bucket for mount 8. No hull damage to INDEPENDENCE occurred, but the signal light bar on gun bucket 8 was damaged beyond repair and some damage was sustained to support brackets for the propeller guard.

1258 Yard tug 136 cast off from our port quarter, undesired modifications too both vessels completed.

1325 Most of Navy and civilian personnel that had come aboard to assist with the post repair sea trial testing now departed the ship. INDEPENDENCE took aboard 6 people for degaussing and compensating the ships magnetic compasses.

1402 Got underway to proceed through the channel east of Red Rock, to the San Rafael Magnetic Survey Range.

1454 Proceeded to make runs north & south at the San Rafael Magnetic Survey Range to calibrate degaussing coils, completing the calibration at 1606.

1513-1524 Exercised the crew at fire quarters.

1627 Began steering various courses to compensate the magnetic compass, completing the task at 2014.

2023 Anchored in 13 fathoms of water in San Francisco Bay off Hunters Point.

2055 The team that compensated the compass departed the ship.

Sunday 18 June 1944   *Sea Trials continue*

0555 Anchored as before. Jacked over the main engines.

0630 Made preparations for getting underway.

0700 Stationed the special sea detail.

0717 Stationed the anchor and windlass details.

0720 Yard tug brought a pilot aboard.

0730 Got underway on various courses at various speeds, remaining off Hunters Point while calibrating the radio direction finder.

0800 Mustered crew on stations.

1037 Completed calibration of radio direction finder. Proceeded to Hunters Point.

1053 A second pilot reported aboard to assist with mooring.

1055 Commenced maneuvering to moor with the assistance of yard tugs 136, 181 and 462 on the starboard side of the ship.

1135 Moored with the port side to berths No.1 & 2, U.S. Naval Drydock, Hunters Point, San Francisco.

1203 Yard tugs cast off from starboard side. Secured the special sea details.

1233 Commenced receiving services from the dock.

1755-2030 A yard diver commenced diving operations to inspect the rudder, propellers, struts and shafts to ascertain if damage occurred when the deperming cable fouled the propeller. None found.

Monday 19 June 1944

0930 Moored as before. Received rocket components from Naval Ammunition Depot, Fallbrook, Ca.

1030-1140 Conducted testing of the aft emergency diesel engine, finding it was unable to carry a load.

Tuesday 20 June 1944   *Sea Trials continue*

0350 Moored as before. Lighted fires under No.1 boiler.

0650 The INDEPENDENCE crew began making preparations for getting underway, first securing steam from the dock, then other services.

0800 Mustered crew on stations.

0850 Leak reported in the No.2 lube oil pump.

0919 Got underway with assistance of yard tugs YT-136 and YT-462 and two pilots on the bridge. The CVL-22 maneuvered to conform to the channel as it steamed seaward at 15 knots.
0926 A pilot left the ship.
0955 USS KING reported for escort duty.
1017 Passed the anti-submarine nets guarding the entrance to San Francisco Bay.
1025 Sounded general quarters.
1035 Passed Point Bonita light abeam to starboard and Mile Rock light abeam to port.
1040 U.S. Navy Blimp K-155 reported for escort duty.
1043 The INDEPENDENCE began the process of slowly increasing the speed. They passed buoy A abeam to port at 1150 and continued to increase speed in one knot increments. They performed vibration testing and slowly brought speed up for full power runs.
1304 Sounded torpedo defense for tracking drill. The INDEPENDENCE conducted evasive maneuvering during practice torpedo runs on the ship by two B-26s.
1425 While slowly stepping the speed down, the crew secured from torpedo defense.
1437 Stopped all engines.
1438 Backed all engines full.
1442 Ship dead in the water.
1447 Starboard engine ahead full, port engine backing full.
1448 Port engine ahead full.
1518 Passed buoy A abeam on approach to San Francisco Bay.
1621 Passed Point Bonita light abeam to port and Mile Rock light abeam to starboard.
1640 Passed the anti-submarine nets at the entrance to San Francisco Bay.
1645 Commenced maneuvering to conform to the channel, steaming toward Hunters Point.
1739-1750 A pilot came aboard and yard tugs tied up to our starboard side to facilitate mooring.
1807 Moored with our port side to berths 1 & 2, U.S. Naval Drydock, Hunters Point, San Francisco.
1831 Tugs YT-136, YT-351 and YT-462 have cast off, and the pilots have departed the ship.
1845 Commenced connecting services from the dock (water, power, telephone).

Wednesday 21 June 1944

Moored. Work continued on the ship to address last minute problems, in preparation to return to service.
1100 Lt. M.H. Planck returned onboard from the Bank of America with $237.00 in silver (paper exchanged for coinage) and $40,000 from the Federal Reserve Bank, of San Francisco.
1300 Received onboard 250 gallons of milk from Dairy Bell Farms for the general mess.
1405 Secured the aft distribution board for cleaning, with electric power provided to the aft portion of the ship by the aft emergency diesel.

Thursday 22 June 1944

Moored as before. Received onboard 157,962 gallons of fuel oil, 5,236 gallons of diesel oil and 70,619 gallons of aviation gasoline.

Saturday 24 June 1944   *Sea Trials continue*

0230 Moored as before. Lighted fires under No.1 boiler. At 0240, lighted fires under No.3 & 4 boilers.
0330 Cut in No.3 boiler to main steam line.
0430 Made all preparations for getting underway. Nine yard workers came aboard to assist with post repair sea trials. A pilot then reported aboard to assist with undocking.
0440 Singled up all lines.
0445 Cut No.1 boiler into main steam line and at 0455 cut No.4 boiler into main steam line.

0500 Got underway from berths No.1 & 2, U.S. Naval Drydock, Hunters Point, maneuvering to stand out from San Francisco Bay.

0517 Yard tug 136 secured to the fantail to remove the pilot, casting off at 0519.

0555 USS KING reported for escort duty.

0559 Passed the anti-submarine nets at the entrance to San Francisco Bay.

0610 Passed Point Bonita light abeam to starboard as they steamed seaward.

0709 Passed the Farallon Islands light abeam to starboard.

0735 Commenced sounding fog signals as visibility decreased to 1.5 miles.

0745 Changed speed to 30 knots.

0815 Discontinued use of fog signal.

0840 Increased speed to 31.5 knots, commencing full power trials.

0910 Sighted U.S. Navy Blimp K-75.

0928 Steadied up on course 190°T.

0933 Blimp K-75 commenced patrol 30° off each side of the bow to a distance of 10 miles.

1024 Changed course to 085°T using 2° left rudder.

1230 Made radar contact with land, off our bow, course 080°T, 39 miles.

1300 Completed full power run.

1310 Sounded flight quarters.

1321 Commenced maneuvering to land aircraft.

1410 Completed recovery of 8 TBMs and 2 F6Fs from NAS Alameda.

1441 USS KING approached the starboard side to take on fuel.

1540 Secured from flight quarters.

1547 USS KING cast off having received 5,000 gallons each from the forward and aft fueling stations.

1552 Sounded flight quarters. Commenced maneuvering to launch aircraft.

1615-1617 Catapulted 2 F6Fs to return to NAS Alameda.

1626 Sounded fire quarters.

1628 Passed abeam the Farallon Islands light, distance 1.9 miles and entered the channel to San Francisco Bay.

1634 Secured from fire quarters.

1635 Sounded general quarters.

1702 USS KING was directed to return to base.

1728 Passed Point Bonita light abeam to port.

1734 Secured from general quarters. Then changed speed to 10 knots.

1742 Passed through the anti-submarine nets of San Francisco Bay. Blimp K-75 was directed to return to base. Maneuvered to proceed to an anchorage.

1830 All engines stopped.

1830 Anchored in San Francisco Bay, 9.25 fathoms of water, with 90 fathoms of chain, mud bottom.

1846 Yard tug YTB-136 came alongside to port to remove the pilot, yard workers that assisted with the post repair trials, and Naval Officers that had observed. YTB-136 cast off at 1850.

2140 Commenced swinging stern to port.

Sunday 25 June 1944   *Underway to NAS Alameda*

0800 Anchored as before. Mustered crew on stations.

0806 All departments were manned and ready for getting underway.

0815 Set the special sea and anchor details, and at 0826 they heaved short on the starboard anchor.

0902 Underway to NAS Alameda from an anchorage off Hunters Point, San Francisco, steering various courses at various speeds.

1019 Moored port side to berth 9, NAS Alameda, California. Mooring was assisted by commercial Crowley tug No. 23.

1350 Yard Oiler YO-91 moored along the starboard side to deliver fuel oil.
1425 YOL-2 moored outside YO-91.
1605 YOL-2 cast off having delivered 13,800 gallons of diesel oil.
1909 Sounded fire quarters due to a fire in the Bake Shop.
1919 Secured from fire quarters. Damage was described as "negligible" and was due to a failed exhaust blower over a hot oven.

RC Left Hunters Point for Alameda to pick up planes and squadron. RC

Monday 26 June 1944   *Moored at NAS Alameda*

Monday saw the INDEPENDENCE continue to prepare for the next step on the long and broken sea journey to the shores of Japan. Next stop, the return to Pearl Harbor. Now docked at Naval Air Station Alameda, the ship continued in its preparations for going back to war. She now was taking aboard aircraft for delivery to the islands. 12 PV-1 Lockheed Venturas of VB-133 were stowed onboard.

In early June, Biak Island, at the northwestern end of New Guinea had been targeted for U.S. invasion. Japan reluctantly and belatedly set into motion "Operation Kon" to back up the island defenders with reinforcements as they decided the island's airfields would be too vital to lose. They tasked RADM Matome Ugaki with the "Kon Operation" utilizing battleships, heavy cruisers and destroyers to deliver the landing force and their supplies to Biak, with the U.S. invasion already well in process. However, "Kon" was canceled due to far higher pressing priorities.

The trigger was pulled on "A-Go" as USS INDEPENDENCE was being made ready for Sea Trials.

"A-Go" or "Operation A" was a required Japanese Combined Fleet response if the U.S forces threatened the perimeter defensive island holdings surrounding Japan. The plan was to draw the U.S. fleet into a trap west of Palau for a "Decisive Battle". A-Go was set in motion by **"Operation Forager"**, the U.S. invasion of the Marianas. "Kon" was dropped as Ugaki received orders to *Stand by for Operation A"*. The U.S. forces were invading the beaches of Saipan.

Ugaki's force of 2 BBs, 2 CAs and 9 DDs departed Batchian Anchorage at Halmahera. Refueling at sea got off to a bad start when the First Tanker Force was misplaced, and DD SHIRATSUYU turned her minor collision with tanker SEIYO MARU into a full blown calamity as the DD's own depth charges went off with the resultant self sinking. A bad omen for things to come as the force proceeded north.

VADM Jisaburo Ozawa had steamed out of Tawi Tawi through the Sulu Sea joining with other elements converging at the Guimaras Anchorage. Ozawa's force would emerge into the **Philippine Sea** via San Bernardino Strait to join up with Ugaki's group (east of Leyte and northwest of the Palau Islands). They would form three groups: **"Vanguard Force"** (RADM Takeo Kurita), **"A Force"** (VADM Ozawa) and the **"B Force"** (RADM Takaji Joshima) with 3 carriers in each.

On **19 June 1944** Japanese carriers sent off 4 large air strikes during the day to attack the U.S. fleet. VADM Marc Mitscher's Task Force 58 was waiting and the resulting aerial carnage that would ensue would become known as **"The Marianas Turkey Shoot'** as American pilots overwhelmed and decimated the attacking Japanese aviators. Those Japanese planes that got through flew onward, only to face waiting shipboard AA gunners. Damage to the U.S. fleet was minimal.

U.S. Submarines scored big as USS ALBACORE and USS CAVALLA made torpedo attacks hitting Japanese carriers TAIHO and SHOKAKU. TAIHO, after taking a torpedo to the port side, succumbed to internal explosions from fuel vapors due to errors by damage control, losing roughly 1,650 men. SHOKAKU plunged to the bottom after a series of explosions with a loss of over 1,200 men.

Task Force 58 pursued west that evening. Carrier pilots from INDEPENDENCE Class sister ship USS BELLEAU WOOD attacked the carrier HIYO the next day. Hit by bombs and torpedoes, HIYO eventually slipped under, upending as it sank, with a loss of roughly 250 lives. Japanese battleship HARUNA, cruiser MAYA and carriers CHIYODA, JUNYO and ZUIKAKU were also damaged as the remainder of the Combined Fleet was retiring, most to the Japanese homeland. Tankers GENYO MARU and SEIYO MARU were severely damaged, then scuttled.

Japan lost roughly 200 land based aircraft, over 430 carrier based aircraft and float planes, 3 aircraft carriers, with a number of ships damaged and sunk, and a large loss of life. Japan could ill afford the massive and crippling setback to its already lean carrier aviation assets.

The Combined Fleet got the "Decisive Battle" they sought. The disastrous aftermath however, was not the outcome the planners had so hopefully envisioned.

The combined action would be written into history as the **"Battle Of The Philippine Sea"**.

Marine landings on the island of Saipan had begun on June 15th. After the Naval actions on June 19th & 20th, the Imperial Japanese Army on Saipan, Tinian and Guam (fighting against unrelenting superiority) will fall to the U.S. invasion forces. Marines will invade Guam on July 19th, and Tinian on July 24th, as the crew of USS INDEPENDENCE and her air group makes ready to reenter the war.

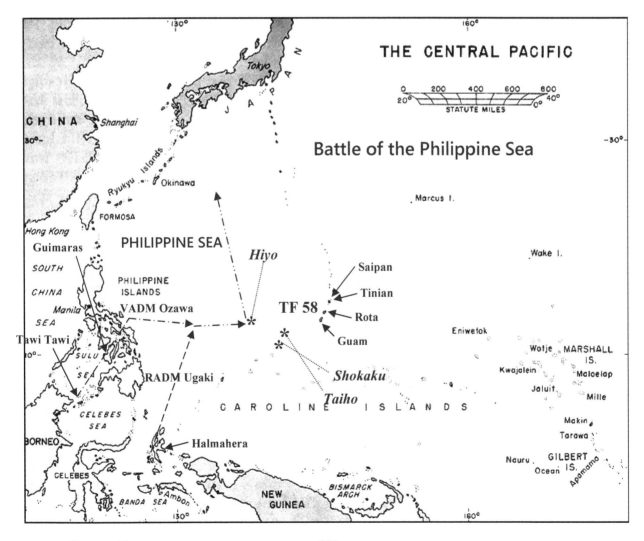

11
Steaming to Pearl Harbor

Tuesday 27 June 1944   *Underway to Pearl Harbor - Air Group 22 is back onboard*

Moored port side to berth 9, NAS Alameda, California. Supplies continued to come aboard.

Officers and enlisted men of VB-133 came aboard for transportation to Hawaii.

3 additional PV-1 Ventura airplanes of VB-133 were stowed onboard.

Hoisted aboard 22 F6F-5 Hellcats and 1 TBM avenger of Air Group 22, and 1 NE-1.

INDEPENDENCE took aboard 393 additional enlisted personnel for transportation to Hawaii.

Received on board in pouches, $35,000,000 in currency for delivery to the Bishop National Bank, Honolulu.

Received onboard secret cargo escorted by Ensign R.Y. Sims.

The crew of the USS INDEPENDENCE made all preparations for getting underway.

1340 Two commercial tugs secured to the starboard side of INDEPENDENCE. U.S. Coast Guard Reserve pilot Lt.Cdr. J.G. Diggs came aboard and proceeded to the bridge 20 minutes later.

1415 With assistance from the Red Stack tug RELIANCE, and Crowley tug No.23, got underway. Began steaming on various courses at various speeds to clear the berth and move to conform to the channel.

1430 Both commercial tugs cast off.

1432 All engines ahead two thirds.

1437 Proud ship USS INDEPENDENCE ground to a halt as she ran aground on a mud-silt bar, becoming stuck fast in the channel between the carrier pier at NAS Alameda and the San Francisco Bay. INDEPENDENCE was mired in the grasp of mud from frame 50 to the vessels stern. Backed all engines. The engines were backed both together, and alternately in a frustratingly futile effort to free the ship. The stern swung starboard.

1500 Tugs No.23 and RELIANCE once again came to the aid of INDEPENDENCE and pushed, and pulled to try to free the ship.

1515 Engineering Department commenced pumping voids.

1620-1715 Flooded void C-18-V. Cut in No.1 boiler to the main steam line.

1625 Made inspection of magazines and forward spaces for damage as the result of the grounding.

1737 Yard tug YTB-181 came alongside port to carry out the anchor and chain.

1750 Yard tug YTB-477 and Army tug boats ST-149, LT-3 and RICHMOND joined the effort to push and pull free the forlorn carrier, along with tugs YTB-261, YTB-169, YTM 478, KRAUTHAUF and FEARLESS.

1759 Tug boat YTB-181 dropped the INDEPENDENCE's port anchor and the INDEPENDENCE commenced heaving on the port anchor chain.

1828 With all engines backing full, heaving in on the anchor chain, and all tugs assisting, the tenacious bay bottom finally let go its hold and the USS INDEPENDENCE was free to proceed.

1833 Cast off from all tugs.

1842 Underway, conforming to the channel.

1855 Anchored in San Francisco Bay in 8 fathoms of water with 45 fathoms of chain. Inspection was once again made of all accessible spaces, voids, and the hull bottom. No damage to the hull, propellers or machinery was noted.

1940 Completed re-flooding the previously pumped voids and pumped out void C-18-V.

1952 Hove short on the port anchor chain.

1958 Got underway conforming to the channel as INDEPENDENCE proceeded seaward.

2007 Darkened ship.

2034 Passed through the anti-submarine nets that were shielding the entrance to San Francisco Bay.

2044 Sounded general quarters for sortie.

2058 Passed abeam Mile Rock 2,400 yards to port, and Bonita Point light 1,600 yards to starboard.

2138 The USCGR pilot left the ship.

2244 Passed channel buoy "A" abeam 500 yards to port. At 2250 they secured from general quarters.

2350 Commenced zigzagging on base course 254°T.

DL On the jacket cover of an outsized book published in 1983 by the U.S. Naval Institute titled U.S. Aircraft Carriers, An Illustrated History, there is a fine blueprint drawing of the port side of Independence. Below it is reproduced a port quarter photo taken that very day as we were getting underway. This view shows "the unusual tumble-home form of her class." Her new camouflage paint scheme almost gleams. Our deckload of Hudson** twin-engine bombers "en route to the combat area" take up the entire flightdeck. A swarm of sailors in dungarees or undress whites are scattered among the aircraft. A sizable group is clustered on the fantail near the quad-40mm gun. Somewhere in that mass, I am standing too.

What neither the photograph shows nor the text has a line of explanation about, is that shortly after we backed from the Alameda dock with the aid of Navy tugs, we scraped our bottom on an unmapped sand bar. We came to a sudden, crunching halt that almost knocked us off our pins. Shocked silence. Burbling water about the hull. Confusion galore and questions: What happened? Hey, we gonna go back in? Back to Hunters Point and the drydock?

On the bridge brief pandemonium surely set in. I saw more officers running about than I had the day we were torpedoed. Captain Johnson must have suffered visions of his career gone down the tubes with this one act of—What? Carelessness? Ineptitude? Lack of proper charting of the harbor? And even if any of his officers had led the ship astray, it was his back that bore the monkey clinging to it. Action, however, came fast. Tugs scurried around getting better fixes on our hull. Bigger tugs were ordered from Mare Island. Rumor and speculation was rife. Were we too heavy? Did that bullion in the vaults weigh too much? Do those damn bombers topside weigh too much?

What saved us from having to go back in, what saved Captain Johnson (a man we admired) from disgrace, what killed the dreams of some that they'd have one more night on the beach, was a large and powerful tug from, of all places, the United States Army. It took a couple of hours to get to us, but when it came an efficient crew tied lines to somewhere on our stern. Together with embarrassed U.S. Navy tugboat crews, off we slid from the mud and sand.

The rest of the story was anticlimax. Until a Navy deep diver went below to make a quick inspection to ascertain how much damage had been inflicted on the hull (there was none), we sat where we were. The view of my beloved San Francisco was magnificent. It was the home of my loved one. I only hoped that she had not joined the crowd of women on the Golden Gate Bridge waiting for Mighty I to pass below at the commencement of our grand journey. DL
** Note: The PV-1s were the Lockheed (Vega) Ventura, not the Hudson (Thank you Doug Siegfried at Tailhook)

GL We are on our way to Pearl Harbor and the blue Pacific. We carried planes for the islands and the payroll for the islands. It sure was tough to say good bye to Frisco as we passed once more under the Golden Gate. Every man had a lump in his throat. GL

Wednesday 28 June 1944 *Underway to Pearl Harbor*

0355 Steaming as before. Radar contact was made of friendly aircraft, 20 and 45 miles distant.

2145 Froward gyro compass failed due to blown out fuse. The fuse was replaced.

AD Choppy Sea, Passengers were sea sick. What fun. AD

Thursday 29 June 1944   *Underway to Pearl Harbor*

1237 Steaming as before. Secured No.3 main engine due to a steam leak.
1346 With repairs completed, placed No.3 main engine back on the main steam line.
1504 Commenced increasing speed for additional vibration testing.
1620 Having completed the vibration testing, reaching a speed of 30 knots, tests were considered satisfactory, reduced speed to 16 knots, all ahead standard. At 1800 they set all clocks back 1 hour.
2019-2119 Manned general quarters stations.

On this date, Carrier Air Groups were classified under the following designations:

CVBG   **Large carrier air group**
CVG   **Medium carrier air group**
CVLG   **Light carrier air group**
CVEG   **Escort carrier air group**

AD Still at sea, all by our self, no escort vessels. AD

Friday 30 June 1944 *Underway to Pearl Harbor*

Steaming as before, zigzagging on base course 246°T, speed 16 knots.
0415 Exercising steering control drill, shifting control to aft steering.
0510 Secured steering control drill, shifting control back to the pilot house.
2100 Changed base course to 240°T.

Monday 3 July 1944 *Underway to Pearl Harbor*

Zigzagging on base course 233°T, speed 16 knots, steaming singly en route to Pearl Harbor.
0157 Commenced steering casualty drill, simulating steering casualty and shifting steering control aft.
0218 Completed steering casualty drill, returning steering control back to the pilot house.
0412 Sounded general quarters for practice bombing attacks by land based aircraft.
0755 Sounded torpedo defense for practice firing runs.
0815 Gunnery Department commenced firing on sleeves towed by land based aircraft.
0830 Secured No.3 boiler, placed out of commission due to a steam leak.
0943 Completed gunnery exercises. Secured from torpedo defense.
0945 PC 486 and PC 578 reported for duty to serve as escort screens.
1037 Sighted Molokai Island bearing 159°T, 22 miles, and Oahu Island bearing 225°T, 22 miles.

USS INDEPENDENCE in her new camouflage paint scheme with F6Fs, TBMs and PV-1s on board for transportation to Hawaii

The ship's band plays on the trip over to Pearl Harbor.
Note the PV-1 Lockheed Venturas of VB-133 being transported to Hawaii.

1045 The trip to Hawaii from San Francisco was to see more danger from food and beverage, than the Japanese, for the crew of USS INDEPENDENCE. William Shiver was admitted to sickbay for treatment of first and second degree burns to his abdomen and left arm when a wayward coffee pot fell over as the ship rolled. Days earlier, W. Sedor visited sickbay for a contusion to a finger working in the spud locker.
1240 Zigzagging on base course 270°T, passed Makapuu Point abeam to starboard, 7 miles.
1314 Commenced zigzagging on base course 295°T.
1346 Changed course to 338°T.
1349 Sounded general quarters for entering port and commenced maneuvering to enter the channel.
1408 Passed buoy No.2 abeam to starboard approaching Pearl Harbor. Continued steering various courses at various speeds to conform to the channel and steaming toward our berth.
1417 A pilot came aboard and made way to the bridge.
1418 Passed through the anti-submarine nets at the entrance to Pearl Harbor, T.H.
1430 Secured from general quarters.
1438 Yard tugs made fast to our port side to assist us in mooring.
1451 Moored, starboard side to berth F-13, in 40 feet of water at Ford Island, NAS Pearl Harbor.
1510 The pilot departed the ship and yard tugs YT-142 and YT-146 cast off. our port side.
1530 Officers and enlisted men of VB-133 departed the ship. The 393 enlisted men transported as passengers from NAS Alameda also left the ship.
1605 Commenced receiving telephone service from shore.
1630 Secured the main engines.
1645 650 bags of U.S. Mail, carried as cargo was delivered off the ship to Fleet Post Office authorities.
1810 A submarine net was placed around the ship.

DL INDEPENDENCE returned to a new war. Pearl Harbor presented a display of naval might making my memories of what the place had looked like when we left for the States in December spare and scattered. There were many new ships big and little. Some were so new their hulls still bore fresh paint. So did ours, of course, but under our new coating were battle scars they could not boast.

As our bow poked its way through the channel into the harbor, a few flags broke out from the signal tower on Ford Island. Were they welcoming us back? A nice thought.
Today was 3 July 1944. On the same date one year ago we had tied up at Mare Island with a faulty

aircraft elevator on our way west. So much had happened since. Today we moored at Fox 10-10 where barges and cranes were already in place to accept our deckload of Hudson** bombers. Unloading began immediately. Everything seemed to be in a hurry.

Although we were not a virgin arrival, things were not in such a hurry as to deprive us of another traditional Hawaiian welcome: pretty girls in shimmering grass skirts, leis of plumeria blooms and red hibiscus about their necks as they danced their hip-swaying routines. A small band's rendition of Aloha, with female voices as background, made toughened sailors turn their faces away so shipmates wouldn't notice their reaction. I had the same trouble.

The Koolau Mountains still wore their tiara of sun-wreathed cumulus. Aft of our location, battleship Arizona was now no more than a rusting skeleton, neglected while the war that had begun with her destruction was being fought. She had contributed her big guns and a few little ones. The bones of her men had long ago been interred. But she would have to wait a while before mother Navy—and the nation itself—would decide what to do with her sunken remains.

If any of our crewmen had believed we would be docked long enough at Pearl to renew the delights he had enjoyed during previous Honolulu liberties, he was rudely brought back to reality four days later.
DL   (** As previously noted: Lockheed Venturas, not Lockheed Hudsons.)

Tuesday 4 July 1944   *Moored at Ford Island, Pearl Harbor, T.H.*

0745 Moored as before. Mustered crew on stations.
0810 CVL-22 commenced unloading the 15 PV-1 Venturas, 24 F6F-5 Hellcats, and 9 TBF-1c Avengers she transported from NAS Alameda.
0955 Removed from the INDEPENDENCE and delivered to a representative of Bishop National Bank, Honolulu, 50 pouches said to contain 35 million dollars in currency, delivered aboard by the Federal Reserve Bank of San Francisco. Unloaded a secret cargo of an undisclosed nature.

Wednesday 5 July 1944   *Moored at Ford Island, Pearl Harbor. Change berths*

0800 Moored as before. Got underway to exchange berths.
0839 Moored, starboard side to berth F-2, NAS Ford Island, Pearl Harbor.
0927 Received onboard 6,972 gallons of diesel oil.
1412 Received onboard 185,462 gallons of fuel oil.
CEM *Tonight, the crew's movie - "Hitler's Gang"* **CEM**

Thursday 6 July 1944   *Moored at Ford Island. Exchange Air Groups*

Moored, starboard side to berth F-2, NAS Ford Island, Pearl Harbor. Today, 6 Officers and 40 enlisted men reported aboard with VFN-78 and VFN-79. Air Group 22 officers and enlisted men left the ship to proceed to NAS Barbers Point, as a temporary assignment, prior to reporting to USS COWPENS. INDEPENDENCE crew also transferred munitions off the ship to the Navy Ammunition Depot.

Friday 7 July 1944   *Underway for Air Group training*

0410 Moored as before. Commenced removing the torpedo net.
0605-0613 Tested the steering engine.
0719 All preparations made for getting underway.
0723 With a harbor pilot on the bridge, singled up all lines.
0739-0740 Yard tugs YT-142, YT-223 and YT-306 moored to the port side.
0743 Got underway from pier F-2.
0747 Yard tugs cast off and CVL-22 commenced steaming toward the channel entrance to the open sea. At 0813 the harbor pilot departed the ship.

0817 Passed the anti-submarine nets, with vessels abeam on the port and starboard sides.
0830 Joined up with USS FLUSSER and USS SMITH (anti-submarine screen) to form Task Group 19.4.
0845-0903 USS SMITH came along the starboard quarter to deliver guard mail.
0912 Sounded torpedo defense.
0953 Gunnery Department conducted anti-aircraft gunnery practice against towed sleeve targets, expending 2,877 rounds of 40mm and 1,146 rounds of 20mm ammunition.
1227 Sounded flight quarters.
1318 Conducted flight operations for refresher and familiarization flights with aircraft of **VF(N)78** and **VF(N)79**.
2147 Sounded flight quarters.
2217 Conducted night flight operations for **night** refresher and familiarization flights with aircraft of VF(N)78 and VF(N)79.

GL Arrived back at Pearl Harbor again. We made our usual gunnery runs. Started training night fighter pilots. Was in and out of Pearl for about a month. GL

DL   Our lines were singled-up and we pulled away from 10-10 dock, presumably to move over to the new carrier dock Fox 10 behind sunken Utah on the other side of Ford Island. Instead, we made a complete circle of Ford and within minutes were heading once again through the channel outbound into the open sea.

We AOM's were not the only airdales who guessed what we'd be doing—recovering our air group. I looked forward to it. At least we would once again be doing work we had been trained for. No more of these chicken-shit nit-picking tasks Ensign Porky was able to dream up to keep us busy.

Oh, I almost forgot: Lieutenant Junior Grade Porky, an important promotion. And his boss, Mister Harry, had picked up a half-stripe for his uniform sleeves, lofting him to Lieutenant Commander. I heard of nobody begrudging the latter's boost upward, but more than one man wasted energy shaking his head (and maybe his fists) at the unknown hand which had lifted his assistant to a higher level of command. Gad, some thought, now Porky'd be really impossible to live with.

On that day, it didn't matter. Suddenly, twenty or thirty miles from Oahu, Air Group airplanes returned in a swarm from their land base at Maui. We became so busy dodging them as they landed and taxied forward that we forgot Ensign (whoops—Lieutenant j.g.) Porky. Immediately we jumped to it, checking each F6F's six wing guns and other mechanisms, inspecting the open bomb bays of the big new TBF's (mostly TBM's now, made by General Motors.) DL

Saturday 8 July 1944   *At sea for Air Group training*

Steaming as before. Ship is darkened with the exception of flight deck landing lights.
0015 Completed night flight operations.
0539-0639 Manned routine morning general quarters stations.
0800 Mustered crew on stations.
0930 Sounded flight quarters.
1430 Secured from flight quarters.
1953-2053 Routine evening general quarters.
2147 Sounded flight quarters.
2313 Commenced night carrier flight operations.

Sunday 9 July 1944   *At sea for Air Group training*

Steaming as before with USS FLUSSER and USS SMITH as Task Group 19.4. Ship is darkened with the exception of flight deck landing lights.

0238 Completed night flight operations.
0536-0636 Routine morning general quarters.
0800 Mustered crew on stations.
1145 Sounded torpedo defense for scheduled gunnery exercises.
1201 Commenced anti-aircraft gunnery firing runs.
1338 Commenced maneuvering while launching target drones.
1540 Having completed gunnery exercises, secured from torpedo defense.
1953-2049 Routine evening general quarters.
2245 AMM3c Marion Clifton Tipton was admitted into sickbay for treatment of a lacerated scalp, received from a fall into the elevator pit during general quarters.
2302 Sounded flight quarters to conduct night refresher air operations.

Monday 10 July 1944   *At sea for Air Group training*

Steaming as before at 15 knots on boilers No.2 & 4.
Conducting air operations. Ship is darkened with the exception of flight deck landing lights.
The destroyer screen was re-tasked with plane guard duty.
0129 Completed night flight operations. Escort destroyers resumed screening operations off the bow.
0352 Exercised crew at flight quarters.
0400 Exercised crew at general quarters for night fighter intercept problem.
0424-0430 Launched aircraft to conduct flight operations.
0635 Secured from general quarters.
0716 USS SMITH took departure from the Task Group.
0901 Sounded torpedo defense for gunnery exercises.
0918 Commenced gunnery practice, firing at towed sleeves towed by a B-26.
1028 Secured from torpedo defense.
1137 Sighted land, bearing 031°T, 30 miles.
1140 Commenced pumping ballast overboard.
1228 Sounded flight quarters to launch aircraft.
1430 Completed flight operations.
1437 Commenced steering various courses at various speeds to enter the channel to Pearl Harbor.
1502 Passed channel buoys No.1 & 2 abeam to port and starboard.
1510 Passed through the anti-submarine net. At 1512, a harbor pilot came aboard.
1515 Maneuvering to conform to channel, proceeding to berth F-9, NAS Ford Island, Pearl Harbor.
1534-1536 Yard tugs YT-142 and YT-308 made fast to our port side to aid our docking.
1544 Moored starboard side to berth F-9, NAS Ford Island, Pearl Harbor.
1550 The yard tugs cast off our port side.
1605 The harbor pilot departed the ship.

Tuesday 11 July 1944   *Moored at NAS Ford Island, Pearl Harbor, T.H.*

Moored as before, starboard side to berth F-9, NAS Ford Island, Pearl Harbor. Receiving services from the dock.
0700 The INDEPENDENCE held quarters for personnel inspection and presentation of awards.

Captain Rudy L. Johnson presented the **Distinguished Flying Cross** to **Lt. Leland Lamas Johnson**, and the **Air Medal** to **AOM3c V.C. Thomas***. (*Thomas shot down Val - see page 213)

Received onboard 206,094 gallons of fuel oil.
Received onboard 20mm and 40mm ammunition from the Navy Ammunition Depot, Oahu, and transferred to the depot boxes of 20 and 40 mm empty brass shell casings.

Captain Rudy L. Johnson presents the Distinguished Flying Cross to Lt. Leland Lamas Johnson

Wednesday 12 July 1944   *Moored at NAS Ford Island, Pearl Harbor, T.H.*

Moored as before, starboard side to berth F-9, NAS Ford Island, Pearl Harbor.
0643 Made all preparations for getting underway. At 0645 a harbor pilot came aboard.
0704 Got underway to go out to sea.
0805 The harbor pilot departed the ship.
0816 Passed channel entrance buoys No.1 & 2.
0824 USS SMALLEY joined up as an escort, forming Task Group 19.4.
0903 Sounded torpedo defense.
0921 Commenced anti-aircraft gunnery practice at a towed sleeve.
1035 Completed gunnery exercise. Secured from torpedo defense.
1039 Sounded flight quarters.
1050-1111 Recovered VF(N)78 aircraft consisting of 12 F6F Hellcats and 1 TBM Avenger.
1415 Commander Ernest Cain Hillyer was admitted to sickbay for treatment to multiple injuries of his left arm, legs and back when he was blown off balance by the prop wash of an aircraft on the starboard catapult and fell from the flight deck to the signal station on the starboard catwalk.
1645 Completed flight operations.
1712 Secured from flight quarters.
1942-2038 Routine evening general quarters.

Thursday 13 July 1944   *Underway for Air Group training*

0145-0440 Steaming as before. Conducted night flight operations.
0532-0632 Routine morning general quarters.
1135 USS HALLIGAN joined the Task Group as an additional escort.
1324 Sounded flight quarters.
1336 Commenced flight operations, VF(N)78 launching and recovering for refresher training.
1432 While landing, Ensign E.J. Baudinot crashed into the port catwalk and gun mount No.8. His F6F (Bu.No. 41112) suffered a damaged prop, engine and left wing. The 40mm gun received damage to its automatic loader, a guard rail was damaged, a landing light, high pressure air line, a loud speaker, and 180 rounds of 40mm ammunition.
1556 Completed recovery of VF(N)78 aircraft.
1707-1728 Recovered 8 F6Fs of VF(N)79, flown onboard from Barbers Point, Oahu.
1806 Sounded flight quarters.
1810-1819 Launched the 8 F6Fs of VF(N)79 that landed at 1728, for return to Barbers Point.
1823 Secured from flight quarters.
1941-2038 Exercised general quarters.

INDEPENDENCE Bakers
(Photo courtesy of Pat Caffee)

Friday 14 July 1944   *Underway for Air Group training*

Steaming as before with destroyers USS HALLIGAN and USS SMALLEY, forming Task group 19.4.
0800 Mustered crew on stations, sounded flight quarters.
0829-0839 Catapulted 10 VF(N)78 F6Fs to return to their shore base.
0841 Secured from flight quarters.
0849 Sounded torpedo defense.
0909 Gunnery Department commenced firing at target drones launched from this vessel.
INDEPENDENCE steered various courses at various speeds while firing at (then recovering) the drones.
1041 Secured from anti-aircraft gunnery exercises.
1300 Sounded flight quarters.
1310 Secured from flight quarters.
1402 Sounded torpedo defense for an aircraft tracking drill.
1418 CVL-22 reeled out a target sled astern for strafing runs by planes of VF(N)79.
1509 Secured from torpedo defense.
1518-1550 Recovered aircraft of VF(N)79.
1943-2040 Routine evening general quarters.
2045 Sounded flight quarters.
2124 Secured from flight quarters.
2241 Sounded flight quarters.
2250 The destroyer escort shifted tasks to assume the roll of plane guard 1,000 and 3,000 yards astern.
2313 Commenced launching aircraft.

Saturday 15 July 1944   *At sea for Air Group training*
                                     VF(N)-78 Departs

Steaming as before. Ship is darkened except necessary flight deck landing lights.
0111 Commenced recovering aircraft.
0113 Increased speed to 31.2 knots.
0131 Completed recovery of 1 F6F and 1 TBM.
0147 With a wind velocity "too low and too uncertain to safely attempt further landing operations", 3
TBMs and 5 F6Fs of VF(N)79 were ordered to return to Barbers Point.
0218 Secured from flight quarters. Our speed now 18 knots.
0530-0630 Routine morning general quarters.
1030 Sounded flight quarters.
1107-1133 Launched 7 VF(N)79 aircraft to return to Barbers Point.
1137 Secured from flight quarters.
1226 Sounded torpedo defense for gunnery exercises.
1257 Commenced firing on a towed sleeve.
1337 Secured from torpedo defense.
1345 Sighted Oahu, bearing 346°T, 30 miles.
1458 Sounded general quarters for purposes of entering port.
1505 Passed swept channel buoys No.1 & 2 abeam to port and starboard.
1513 Passed through the submarine net entering Pearl Harbor. At 1515 a harbor pilot came aboard.
1522 Secured from general quarters.
1543 Moored starboard side to berth F-10, NAS Ford Island.
1645 Officers of Night Fighting Squadron Seventy Eight - VF(N)78, departed the INDEPENDENCE.

12
A Night Carrier Emerges

Sunday 16 July 1944   *Moored at NAS Ford Island, Pearl Harbor, T.H.*

Moored as before, starboard side to berth F-10, NAS Ford Island.
Received onboard 159,054 gallons of fuel oil, aircraft starter cartridges, and 20mm & 40mm ammunition from the Navy Ammunition Depot, Oahu.

Monday 17 July 1944   *At sea conducting Air Group training*

Moored as before. Made all preparations for getting underway.
1016 With a harbor pilot on the bridge, CVL-22 got underway for refresher training.
1059 The harbor pilot left the ship.
1112 Passed channel entrance buoys No.1 & 2. USS BUSH and USS MAHAN joined up as escorts.
1247 Sounded torpedo defense to exercise Gunnery Department in anti-aircraft practice.
1314 Gunnery Department commenced firing at towed sleeves.
1425 Secured from torpedo defense.
1430 Sounded flight quarters.
1458-1539 Landed onboard 16 F6Fs and 12 TBMs of VF(N)79.
1542 Secured from flight quarters.
2155 Commenced launching 6 F6F Hellcats for night operations.
2247 INDEPENDENCE turned into the wind in preparation to recover aircraft. Ensign "Joe Sam" Allen crashed into the safety barrier on landing. He was uninjured, but the F6F (Bu.No. 43022) sustained damage to the prop, engine, both wings and the radar equipment on the wing.
2318 The remaining 5 Hellcats were ordered to return to NAS Barbers Point, Oahu.

Tuesday 18 July 1944   *At sea for Air Group training*

0005 Steaming as before. Secured from flight quarters.
0915 Sounded flight quarters.
1013 Commenced catapulting aircraft.
1034 Sighted the island of Oahu bearing 060°T, 30 miles.
1051 Completed catapulting 10 F6Fs and 12 TBMs of VF(N)79, for return to NAS Barbers Point.
1105 Sounded torpedo defense for anti-aircraft gunnery practice.
1110 Secured from flight quarters.
1125 Gunnery Department commenced firing at a towed sleeve.
1128 USS MAHAN departed under orders to return to Pearl Harbor.
1213 Secured from torpedo defense.
1356 USS BUSH departed (USS BUSH would be sunk by a Kamikaze off Okinawa 6 April 1945).
1404 Passed channel entrance buoys No.1 & 2 approaching Pearl Harbor.
1414 A harbor pilot came aboard and CVL-22 proceeded toward its berth.
1441 Moored starboard side to berth F-10, NAS Ford Island, Pearl Harbor.

19-20 July 1944   *Moored at NAS Ford Island, Pearl Harbor, T.H.*

Moored starboard side to berth F-10, NAS Ford Island, Pearl Harbor.
During these two days the ship took on fuel oil, aviation gasoline and ammunition.

Friday 21 July 1944   *Underway conducting Air Group training*

Moored starboard side to berth F-10, NAS Ford Island, Pearl Harbor.

0545 Making preparations for getting underway.

0715 Got underway and proceeded counterclockwise around Ford Island seaward with a harbor pilot onboard. At 0808 the harbor pilot departed the ship.

0819 Passed channel entrance buoys No.1 & 2 leaving Pearl Harbor.

0820 Escort DDs USS LEUTZE and USS SMALLEY formed up on CVL-22 as Task Group 19.4.

0844 Sounded torpedo defense for anti-aircraft gunnery practice.

1059 Secured from torpedo defense. At 1240 they sounded flight quarters.

1314-1401 Manned torpedo defense and maneuvered to repel a simulated torpedo attack by VF(N)79 aircraft.

1410 Commenced landing aircraft.

1420 Ensign "Joe Sam" Allen was landing his F6F (Bu.No. 40992) and once again encountered difficulty. He broke the No.5 deck pennant, skidded and went over the starboard side between the No.2 & 3 stacks. Destroyer USS LEUTZE recovered him and reported "Joe Sam" to have only minor injuries..

1428 The paravane chain was reported parted.

1445-1505 Recovered 15 F6Fs and 6 TBMs of VF(N)79.

1517 Hauled in the paravane chain using the anchor windlass and secured it to the deck.

1830 Sounded flight quarters.

1855 Commenced launching 6 F6Fs.

2025 Recovered the 6 F6Fs, completing flight operations.

Saturday 22 July 1944   *At sea conducting Air Group training*
                               Lose a TBM and ARM3c Edward John Glaser

0400 Steaming as before as Task Group 19.4. Sounded flight quarters.

0450-0456 Launched 4 TBMs.

0500 TBM No. 25 reported down, in the water bearing 010°T, 16,000 yards. A flare light was then reported in that position.

0508 Completed launching 6 F6Fs.

0538 Sounded general quarters.

0544 Commenced steering on courses to take the ship back to the position of the downed TBM.

0636 Secured from general quarters.

0650 Sighted smoke from a smoke bomb at the accident site.

0658 Commenced steering various courses around the location of the accident.

0706 USS LEUTZE picked up two survivors of the downed TBM. The pilot, Ensign J.D. Haigler and gunner AOM2c Alvin R. Huss were rescued, however ARM3c Edward John Glaser is presumed to have gone down with the TBM (Bu.No. 25588). Haigler received a gash on his head. Huss fractured his ankle.

0728-0747   Recovered 3 TBMs and 6 F6Fs.

0836 Sounded flight quarters.

0848-0901 Launched 2 TBMs to search for E.J. Glaser, then secured from flight quarters.

1130 Sounded flight quarters.

1141-1149 Recovered the 2 TBMs launched at 0901, with negative results during the air search.

1155 Secured from flight quarters.

1300 Sounded flight quarters.

1319 Launched aircraft for strafing runs on a target sled towed astern.

1400 Secured from flight quarters.

1516 Sounded flight quarters.

1647 Completed recovery of aircraft launched at 1319.

1724 Secured from flight quarters.

Sunday 23 July 1944   *At sea conducting Air Group training*

0010 Steaming as before. Radar picked up 4 large ships and their screen, bearing 232°T, 24,000 yards.
0031 Passed the group of ships 7,900 yards abeam to port.
0210 Conducted simulated steering casualty, shifting control of steering aft.
0218 Transferred steering control to central station.
0223 Completed the exercise and shifted steering back to the bridge.
0331 Sounded general quarters on receipt of a secret dispatch from Commander, Hawaiian Sea Frontier.
0600-0603 Launched a 3 plane Combat Air Patrol.
0630 Launched 1 additional plane for CAP.
0852-0909 Recovered 4 F6Fs.
1013 Steering control lost during shift from the starboard to the port steering unit.
1015 Shifted steering to the starboard unit.
1018 After steering station recovered control.
1022 Steering shifted to the central station.
1116 Sounded torpedo defense for gunnery exercises.
1153 The steering casualty problem was reported to be a ball check valve not seating properly in the port steering unit, and repaired.
1157 Shifted steering control from starboard to port unit.
1224 Gunnery Department completed firing on towed sleeves. Secured from torpedo defense.
1915 Sounded flight quarters.
1947-1950 Launched 6 F6Fs to conduct night flying operations.
2019-2105 Recovered the 6 F6Fs launched at 1950.
2340 Simulated steering casualty, shifted steering to the central control station.
2345 Completed steering casualty exercise and shifted control back to the pilot house.

Monday 24 July 1944   *At sea conducting Air Group training*

0437-0445 Steaming as before with escorts USS LEUTZE and USS SMALLEY. Launched 6 TBMs.
0509 Sounded flight quarters.
0619 Completed recovery of the 6 TBMs launched at 0445.
0900-0915 Catapulted 14 F6Fs and 6 TBMs of VF(N)79 to return to Barbers Point.
0923 Secured from flight quarters.
1004 Sighted Island of Oahu bearing 030°T, 31 miles.
1232 Passed channel entrance buoys No.1 & 2 approaching Pearl Harbor.
1240 Passed through the submarine net entering Pearl Harbor.
1243 A harbor pilot came aboard and INDEPENDENCE proceeded toward her berth.
1350 Moored starboard side to berth F-1, NAS Ford Island, Pearl Harbor.
1418 The harbor pilot departed the ship.

Tuesday 25 July 1944   *Moored at NAS Ford Island, Pearl Harbor, T.H.*

Moored starboard side to berth F-1, NAS Ford Island, Pearl Harbor. The ship took on aviation gasoline.
        CEM   The V-2 Division had a picnic at the Navy qualifying pool & field. CEM

**Wednesday 26 July 1944   *Captain R.L. Johnson detached, relieved by Captain E.C. Ewen
F.D.R. arrives in Hawaii***

The day was notable in the history of the ship, starting with a change of command. Ceremonies were held on the flight deck with **Captain Rudy Lincoln Johnson** reading orders of the Commander-in-Chief, U.S. Pacific Fleet dated 9 July 1944, relieving him of command of the USS INDEPENDENCE.

He was detached with orders to report to the Vice Chief of Naval Operations in Washington D.C. Then, **Captain Edward Coyle Ewen** read orders dated 11 July 1944, giving him command of the vessel. Captain Ewen would lead the crew on their return to the Pacific War.

At 1438, the cruiser USS BALTIMORE *, flying the flag of the President of the United States, passed to port. USS INDEPENDENCE rendered full passing honors, short of the gun salute. President Franklin Roosevelt made a trip to Hawaii to meet with General Douglas MacArthur (who flew in) and Admiral Chester Nimitz to discuss strategy for the coming campaigns. MacArthur with his agenda to retake Luzon and Nimitz with his own, favoring first, invasion of Formosa. (* Photo page 526)

Roosevelt's decision would not shape the general direction the new captain (Ewen) was to steam, for the nations compass was pointed steadfast at Japan by all parties present. But it would determine the path the Mighty-I would steam to deliver the war directly on the emperors doorstep, the invasion stops on the way, and the places where soldiers, sailors and flyers would spill their blood.

After the ceremonies, after the President passed in the BALTIMORE, work aboard INDEPENDENCE went on as usual. Crew members now in dungarees flushed fuel oil and lube oil tanks into a sludge barge that came alongside to port at 1600, and took on additional ammunition from the Naval Ammunition Depot at 1700. (See photo of the BALTIMORE passing by INDEPENDENCE on page 526)

DL   Pearl Harbor. Change of Command ritual. The flightdeck was lined end to end with ranked sailors in undress whites, squared hats, and spit-polished shoes. We were about to say good-bye to Rudy L. Johnson.

Although our skipper was a harsh disciplinarian, nobody had ever condemned him for being an unfair man. The only other grudge against him some men would always remember was the decision to keep us locked aboard ship during her repair job at Hunters Point. Six months of hell! Still, as sorry as we were to see him go, he deserved bigger and better commands.

The officer who took the podium was a smaller man than Johnson. His skin was darker. He had a pug nose that looked as if it had got that way in a slugging match. (We were never to find out. But later we learned that he'd been a champion boxer at the Academy.)

I remember nothing of the speech Captain Johnson made. He did pay the ship a compliment by calling her the Mighty I. Then he was gone.

Edward C. Ewen of Portsmouth, N.H., assumed command and stood silently looking us over. We would wait and see what he would do with the ship—and with us.

Liberty was granted by port and starboard watches till 1700 for a few days. As before, Honolulu looked as beautiful, as lush, and as beaten up and rundown as it had a year ago. There must have been another hundred thousand sailors in town. The crib houses on River Street and around Beretania fronted even longer lines of men, mostly sailors. Most of them stood with legs crossed, trying to hide the sausages in their pants. How the kamaainas put up with the onslaught, I have no idea. Wartime prosperity no doubt helped.

Rebel, Charlie, Bobbie, Chuck, Dan and now and then Tom made forays into the Black Cat, a downtown bar. The rotgut imitation whiskey it served seemed to begin an ulcerating process as it descended down your gullet. I couldn't imagine anyone getting drunk on such a mixture.

Without much notice, these unsatisfactory liberties ended abruptly and we went to sea again. This time we headed south and west. We had no way to know it, but Pearl Harbor and Honolulu would become something of a dreamy memory. We would not see either again until January 1945.

The grapevine said our destination was Eniwetok. It was one of the Marshall Islands that had been captured while we were at Hunters Point. More importantly, other rumors said we were about to get another assignment. This one was said to be the result of long planning by high ranking officers— including the unforgotten LCDR Butch O'Hare, one of its triggers. We took the news in stride. The almost universal reaction aboard the ship was: Of course, who could do it better?

Whatever "it" might turn out to be.   DL

27 July 1944 - 30 July 1944

Moored as before, starboard side to berth F-1, NAS Ford Island, Pearl Harbor.
The "Mighty-I" transferred the air groups rocket parts, rocket bodies, motors and fuses to her sister ship, the "Mighty Moo" - USS COWPENS. On the 29th CVL-22 received 155,160 gallons of fuel oil.

Monday 31 July 1944   *Underway in Task Group 19.4*

1210 Moored as before. A yard tug removed the torpedo net from around the port side of the ship.
1212 Commenced turning over our main turbines by steam, made all preparations for getting underway.
1255-1257 Yard tugs YT-307 and YNT-12 secured to our port side.
1301 Got underway with a harbor pilot on the bridge.
1306-1308 The yard tugs cast off as INDEPENDENCE proceeded on various courses at various speeds to conform to the channel.
1323 Sounded general quarters for leaving port.
1330 The harbor pilot departed the ship.
1332 Passed through the submarine net as INDEPENDENCE took departure of Pearl Harbor.
1342 Passed channel entrance buoys No.1 & 2 steaming seaward.
1351 Secured from general quarters.
1409 Maneuvered to assume station and formed up into Task Group 19.4, accompanied by USS COWPENS and screening destroyers USS CUSHING, USS HALLIGAN and USS ROWE.
(Note: USS HALLIGAN would strike a mine on 26 March 1945 and sink after grounding on a reef off Okinawa.)
1456 Formed cruising disposition 5-R, course 180°T, 20 knots, COWPENS (OTC and guide) bearing 150° T, 2,000 yards.
1502 Sounded torpedo defense.
1514 Formed special disposition "George" with the COWPENS for conducting anti-aircraft gunnery practice, with COWPENS 1,000 yards ahead of us, bearing 230°T, course 230°T.
1516 Commenced firing at towed sleeves.
1638 Sounded flight quarters.
1641 Secured from anti-aircraft gunnery exercises and from torpedo defense.
1701 Commenced maneuvering to reform cruising disposition 5-R.
1715-1808 Landed onboard 13 F6Fs and 9 TBMs of VF(N)79.
2010 Reformed special disposition "George" to conduct night anti-aircraft gunnery exercises.
2035 Gunnery Department commenced night firing exercises.
2200 Secured from night anti-aircraft gunnery exercises and from torpedo defense.
2202 Resumed disposition 5-R.
2215 Sounded flight quarters.
2230 USS INDEPENDENCE assumed tactical command and became guide. INDEPENDENCE would serve as OTC and guide during night operations. COWPENS resumed OTC and Guide at all other times.
2249-2258 Launched 3 F6Fs and 4 TBMs.

Tuesday 1 August 1944   *At sea conducting training exercises in Task Group 19.4*

Steaming as before with USS COWPENS, USS CUSHING, USS HALLIGAN and USS ROWE.
0057-0104 Catapulted 3 F6Fs and 2 TBMs.
0113-0133 Recovered 3 F6Fs and 4 TBMs that were launched at 2249.
0319-0324 Catapulted 3 F6Fs and 2 TBMs.
0324 Increased speed to 22 knots.
0332 Lighted fires under boilers No. 2 & 4 to boost steam pressure.
0336-0349 Recovered 3 F6Fs and 2 TBMs that were launched at 0057.
0350 Reduced speed to 17 knots.

0540 Recovered 3 F6Fs and 2 TBMs launched at 0319.

0550-0656 General quarters.

0800 Mustered crew on stations.

1147 USS HOWORTH joined the formation.

1227 USS ROWE departed the formation to return to base.

1405 Catapulted 2 TBMs to return to base.

1409 Completed flight operations.

1459 Formed special disposition "George" for conducting gun mount testing.

1502 Sounded torpedo defense to conduct firing exercises and testing of 40mm gun mount No.4.

1605 Secured from torpedo defense due to reduced visibility, gun mount No.4 had test fired 2 rounds.

1607 Resumed disposition 5-R.

1645 Sounded flight quarters.

1652-1706 Steered on various courses at various speeds while COWPENS conducted flight operations.

1730-1733 Recovered 2 TBMS launched at 1405.

1827 Secured from flight quarters.

2030-2038 Catapulted 3 F6Fs and 4 TBMs.

2243-2245 Catapulted 3 F6Fs.

2255-2308 Recovered 3 F6Fs and 4 TBMs (that were launched at 2030).

Wednesday 2 August 1944 *At sea conducting training exercises in Task Group 19.4*

Steaming as before. INDEPENDENCE continued refresher night training for the Air Group.

0136 Completed launching 3 F6Fs and 2 TBMs and the recovery of 3 F6Fs (launched at 2245).

0356 Completed launching 3 F6Fs and 2 TBMs. Recovered 3 F6Fs and 2 TBMs (launched at 0136).

0540 Sounded general quarters.

0551 Completed recovery of 3 F6Fs and 2 TBMs (launched at 0356).

0636 Gunnery Department test fired 40mm gun mount No.4.

0641 Secured from general quarters.

0735 USS COWPENS assumed guide and tactical command.

0800 Mustered crew on stations.

1346 Sounded torpedo defense for the purpose of tracking exercises on USS COWPENS aircraft.

1416 Secured from torpedo defense.

2033 Completed launching 3 F6Fs.

2255 Launched 3 F6Fs and recovered the 3 F6Fs (launched at 2033).

Thursday 3 August 1944   *At sea conducting training exercises in Task Group 19.4*

Steaming as before in cruising disposition 5-R.

0055-0115 Catapulted 3 F6Fs, then recovered 3 F6Fs (launched at 2255).

0224-0235 Catapulted 4 TBMs and 2 F6Fs.

0257 Completed recovering 3 F6Fs (launched at 0115).

0317 Completed catapulting 4 F6Fs.

0501 Commenced recovering aircraft.

0514 Ensign R.H. Klock's landing did not go as planned (as often happens with carrier landings) and his F6F crashed into the port catwalk, continuing in a harrowing journey over the side of the ship. In its path, the Hellcat bent the ships No.2 antenna boom. The No.3 antenna boom, 15 feet of hand railing, and a life raft were carried away and not recovered. The F6F-3N (Bu.No. 40844) was claimed by the sea.
 "Bob" Klock was retrieved uninjured by the USS HOWORTH.

0555 Completed recovering 4 TBMs and 1 F6F launched at 0235 (1 F6F lost over the side) and 4 F6Fs launched at 0317.

0600 USS COWPENS became OTC and guide.

0636 Launched 2 F6Fs and 1 TBM which proceeded to NAS Barbers Point, and 1 F6F departing for NAS Ford Island.

1019 Sounded torpedo defense for the purpose of tracking exercises on USS COWPENS aircraft.

1040 Formed special disposition "George" for conducting gunnery exercises.

1053 Steadied on course 055°T. Gunnery Department commenced firing on towed sleeves.

1202 Sighted Oahu, bearing 020°T, 23 miles.

1229 Completed firing on towed sleeves. Secured from torpedo defense.

1333 Departed the formation to proceed into Pearl Harbor.

1354 Passed channel entrance buoys No.1 & 2 approaching Pearl Harbor.

1406 Passed through the submarine net entering Pearl Harbor.

1407 A harbor pilot came aboard and proceeded to the bridge.

1417 Sounded fire quarters due to a fire near the incinerator.

1422 Secured from fire quarters, the fire having been extinguished, with no reported damage.

1447-1448 Harbor tugs YTB-142 and YTB-371 secured to the port side to assist with mooring.

1455 Moored starboard side to berth F-1, NAS Ford Island, Pearl Harbor.

1512-1514 The yard tugs cast off.

1519 The harbor pilot departed the ship.

1950 YD-82 was being moored alongside to port by yard tug YT-152 when it struck the ship. Damage was minor (repaired by the Navy Yard, Pearl Harbor) and mooring to the port side so that the two damaged radio booms (Ensign Klock's accident) could be repaired was complete at 1955.

Friday 4 August 1944   *Moored at NAS Ford Island - S2c J.E. Hogan drowns*

Moored as before. Today the duty section of the crew took onboard aviation gasoline and fuel oil. The liberty section went ashore. At 1300 while on liberty, S2c James Edward Hogan drowned at Waikiki Beach, his death reported by the Honolulu Coroner's office.

Saturday 5 August 1944   *Moored at NAS Ford Island, Pearl Harbor, T.H.*

Moored as before. Transferred munitions both from and too the Naval Ammunition Depot, Oahu.

Sunday 6 August 1944   *Out to sea, conducting training exercises*

Moored as before, starboard side to berth F-1, NAS Ford Island, Pearl Harbor.

0030 Completed taking ammunition aboard.

0500 Commenced jacking over main engines by motor (electric).

0545 Disconnected fresh water from the dock.

0630 Commenced turning main engines by steam.

0733-0735 Yard tugs YT-146 and YT-152 secured to the port side.

0736 Got underway with the assistance of tugs, and with a harbor pilot on board.

0741-0741 Both yard tugs cast off.

0756 Sounded routine general quarters. At 0806 the harbor pilot departed the ship.

0810 Passed through the submarine net departing Pearl Harbor.

0821 Passed channel entrance buoys No.1 & 2 steaming seaward.

0833 Secured from general quarters.

0841 Commenced maneuvering to take station off USS COWPENS (OTC and guide) in company with USS BLUE, USS DE HAVEN and USS MAHAN as our screen, in Task Group 19.4, disposition 5-R.

0943 Began maneuvering to form special disposition George (in column 1,000 yards astern the COWPENS) for gunnery exercises.

0948 Sounded torpedo defense and at 0952 Gunnery Department commenced firing at towed sleeves.

1124 Having completed firing practice, secured from torpedo defense.

1158 Reformed in disposition 5-R, course 180°T, COWPENS bearing 170°T, 2,000 yards.

2015 Sounded torpedo defense for gunnery exercises, firing at towed sleeves.

2210 Sounded flight quarters.

2217 Secured from torpedo defense. Planned anti-aircraft firing practice was canceled due to a failure of the lighting in the towed sleeve targets.

2258-2322 Catapulted 7 F6F Hellcats and 6 TBM Avengers of VF(N)79.

2329 A F6F returned to land due to engine trouble.

Monday 7 August 1944   *At sea, conducting training exercises*

Steaming as before. The ship is darkened. 6 F6Fs and 6 TBMs are in the air, 3 F6Fs assigned CAP, the remaining planes simulating an attack group.

0052-0058 Launched 2 F6Fs for CAP.

0109-0141 Recovered the 6 F6Fs and 6 TBMs launched at 2322.

0305-0317 Launched 3 F6Fs and 4 TBMs.

0325 Recovered 2 F6Fs launched at 0058.

0530-0550 Recovered 3 F6Fs and 4 TBMs launched at 0317.

0624 USS COWPENS commenced launching aircraft.

1325 Commenced steering various courses in a signal drill exercised by OTC.

1518 Sounded torpedo defense.

1527 Commenced maneuvering to form special disposition George for gunnery exercises.

1545 Gunnery Department commenced anti-aircraft exercises, firing at a drone.

1605 Maneuvered to recover the drone. Then reformed in disposition George.

1622 Resumed anti-aircraft exercises, firing at a drone.

1629 Commenced maneuvering to launch an additional drone.

1648 Reformed in disposition George.

1724-1730 Resumed anti-aircraft exercises, firing at a drone.

1740 Secured from torpedo defense.

2000 USS INDEPENDENCE assumed tactical command and guide to conduct night air operations.

2002 Sounded flight quarters.

2028 Launched 4 F6Fs.

2240 Launched 3 F6Fs for a CAP, and 3 F6Fs and 6 TBMs for a simulated attack group.

2304 Recovered 4 F6Fs launched as 2028.

Tuesday 8 August 1944   *At sea conducting training exercises in Task Group 19.4*

Steaming with USS COWPENS in company with USS BLUE, USS DE HAVEN and USS MAHAN.

0038-0108 Recovered 6 F6Fs and 6 TBMs.

0154 Secured from flight quarters.

0430 USS COWPENS assumed tactical command and guide.

0606 USS INDEPENDENCE departed the formation accompanied by USS MAHAN to proceed independently to return to Pearl Harbor.

0700-0749 Launched 10 F6Fs and 5 TBMs, then secured from flight quarters.

0752 Commenced swinging the ship to calibrate the radar, completing the task at 0812.

As was done previously, CVL-22 entered Pearl Harbor, and at 1009 was moored starboard side to berth B-2, U.S. Navy Yard.

9-12 August 1944   *Moored at the U.S. Navy Yard, Pearl Harbor, T.H.*

The night air group traded out (swapped) all its F6F-3(N)s for new F6F-5(N)s from VF(N)-102. It was noted that *"the 102 boys just <u>loved</u> the deal"*.

Sunday 13 August 1944   *Out to sea conducting training exercises in Task Group 19.3*

Moored as before at berth B-2, U.S. Navy Yard, Pearl Harbor.

0955-1030 Commenced jacking over main engines by motor (electric).

1430 Made preparations for getting underway.

1607 Got underway for training exercises with the assistance of a harbor pilot, and two yard tugs (YT-142 and YT-195) secured to the port side. CVL-22 maneuvered to conform to the channel, steaming counterclockwise around Ford Island.

1654 Passed through the submarine net and took departure of Pearl Harbor.

1706 Passed channel entrance buoys No.1 & 2 steaming seaward in company with USS CUSHING and USS HALLIGAN as escorts, forming Task Group 19.3, with INDEPENDENCE (OTC and guide).

1830 Sounded flight quarters.

1857-1930 Steering various courses at various speeds into the wind, they landed onboard 15 F6F Hellcats and 5 TBM Avengers of VF(N)79.

2010-2133 Pumped out all bilges and engineering spaces.

2022 Zigzagging on base course 160°T, speed 15 knots, INDEPENDENCE made visual and radar contact on friendly forces off the port quarter, 7,850 yards.

2147-2151 Catapulted 4 F6Fs.

2241-2245 Blew tubes on boilers No. 2 & 4.

2320-2348 Lighted fires under boilers No. 1 & 3 and cut them into the main steam line.

Monday 14 August 1944   *At sea, conducting training exercises as Task Group 19.3*

Steaming as before. Air Department is at flight quarters.

0013-0050 Launched 5 F6Fs and recovered 4 F6Fs launched at 2245.

0103 Commenced reeling out the target sled for strafing runs by the 5 F6Fs.

0154 Air Group strafing runs were completed and the target sled was retrieved.

0223-0247 Recovered the 5 F6Fs launched at 0050.

0955 Sounded torpedo defense to conduct anti-aircraft gunnery practice on towed sleeves.

1000 Maneuvered into a column for gunnery exercises.

1012-1133 Conducted anti-aircraft gunnery firing practice. Then secured from torpedo defense.

1133 Reformed the cruising disposition.

1420-1442 Launched 6 TBMs and 16 F6Fs, completing flight operations.

1448 Secured from flight quarters.

1515 Streamed out the target sled astern of the ship.

1530 The Air Group commenced strafing and bombing runs against the towed target sled.

1613 Commenced recovery of the target sled.

2232-2305 Launched 6 F6Fs.

2334 Streamed out the target sled astern of the ship for strafing runs by the 6 F6Fs.

Tuesday 15 August 1944   *Moored at NAS Ford Island, Pearl Harbor, T.H.*

0052-0126 Steaming as before. Recovered 6 F6Fs launched at 2305.

0126 USS CUSHING departed to return to Pearl Harbor.

0133 Secured from flight quarters.

0440 Changed course to 320°T.

0648 Sighted land off the starboard bow, bearing 350°T, 31 miles.

0825 Commenced maneuvering toward the channel entrance to Pearl Harbor.

0856 USS HALLIGAN departed to proceed independently.

0900 Passed channel entrance buoys No.1 & 2 approaching Pearl Harbor.

0919 Passed through the submarine net entering Pearl Harbor.

1020 With the assistance from a harbor pilot, and yard tugs YT-142 and YT-306, CVL-22 moored starboard side to berth F-1, NAS Ford Island, Pearl Harbor. The ship then connected to dockside utilities, took on fuel oil, diesel oil, aviation gasoline and munitions.

Wednesday 16 August 1944   *Underway to return to the Pacific War*

Moored as before starboard side to berth F-1, NAS Ford Island, Pearl Harbor in 6 3/4 fathoms of water.
0430 Lighted fires under No.4 boiler.
0445 Commenced jacking over main units by hand.
0557 Cut No.4 boiler into main steam line.
0635 Harbor pilot, Chief boatswain G.L. Carter came aboard.
0717-0720 Yard tugs YT-195 and YT-371 made fast alongside to port.
0731 Got underway from berth F-1, pilot on the bridge, in compliance with secret Movement Order 1-44 from Commander, Task Group 12.3.2, Rear Admiral Fredrick C. Sherman in USS ENTERPRISE.
0735 Both tugs cast off from the port side.
0748 Pilot, Chief boatswain G.L. Carter left the ship.
0751 Sounded routine general quarters for sortie out of the harbor.
0809 Passed by channel buoys No.1 & 2, taking departure of Pearl Harbor. Commenced maneuvering to gain position in formation with USS ENTERPRISE (guide & OTC), USS INTREPID, USS BLUE, USS CUSHING, USS DE HAVEN, and USS MAHAN forming Task Group 12.3.2.
0826 Secured from general quarters.
0949 Gained position in disposition 5-R.
1156 Commenced maneuvering to form a column behind USS ENTERPRISE for gunnery practice.
1212 Sounded torpedo defense.
1426 Commenced anti-aircraft firing practice against towed sleeve targets.
1526 Having completed gunnery practice, secured from general quarters. Commenced maneuvering to reform disposition 5R, 3,000 yards from USS ENTERPRISE.

GN We head from Pearl toward Eniwetok and we have drawn the squadron which to our mind was the best of the two. Captain Ewen takes over command making the third skipper we have had since she slipped down the ways. GN

GL Left Pearl Harbor for Eniwetok Island, in the Marshals. Ready to rejoin the fleet again. The only night carrier in the fleet. GL

Thursday 17 August 1944   *Out to sea, en route to Eniwetok, in Task Group 12.3.2*

0100 Steaming as before, course 266°T, 19 knots. Sounded flight quarters.
0130-0145 Catapulted 4 F6Fs and 3 TBMs. (4 TBM's were downed on the deck with squawks.)
0400 F2c W.F. Garvey was admitted to sickbay with first and second degree burns received when a coffee pot fell over in a roll of the ship.
0450-0512 On a vary dark and rainy night, recovered 4 F6Fs and 3 TBMs catapulted at 0145.
1055-1100 Conducted an emergency drill simulating an air attack, steering various courses at various speeds. USS ENTERPRISE and USS INTREPID conducted flight operations during the day.
2100 Changed course to 265°T.

Saturday 19 August 1944   *At Sea en route to Eniwetok*

Steaming at 19 knots (192 rpm), course 160°T. INDEPENDENCE would cruise a base course of 160°T throughout the day with course changes for zigzagging (Plan No.6), air operations, etc.
0030 Sounded flight quarters.

0206 Completed launching 4 F6Fs.

0400 Sighted friendly ships opposite course.

0422 Completed recovery of 4 F6Fs launched at 0206, and launching 4 F6Fs and 5 TBMs.

0428 Changed course to 000°T to avoid crossing track of friendly ships.

0512 Sounded routine general quarters, securing at 0612.

0633 Changed Fleet axis to 120°T, ENTERPRISE guide 090°T at 3,000 yards.

0800 Mustered crew on stations.

0839 Landed SB2C #64 from USS INTREPID for emergency landing.

0859 Commenced steering various courses and speeds while ENTERPRISE and INTREPID completed flight operations.

1005 On a base course of 260°T Fleet disposition changed to V-5, commenced streaming target sled.

1022 Began steering various courses and speeds during simulated dive bombing and torpedo attacks.

1100 Made daily inspection of magazines.

1134 Began steering various courses and speeds during simulated dive bombing and torpedo attacks.

1144 Reformed cruising disposition 5-R.

1200 Launched SB2C #64 (from USS INTREPID). Took target sled aboard.

1857 Commenced steering various courses and speeds during ENTERPRISE and INTREPID flight operations.

Sunday 20 August 1944   *At Sea en route to Eniwetok, in Task Group 12.3.2*

Steaming at 19 knots - 192 rpm, course 160°T. INDEPENDENCE would cruise a base course of 160°T throughout the day with changes for zigzagging, air operations, etc.

Cruising in Task Unit 12.3.2 with USS ENTERPRISE, USS INTREPID, USS BLUE, USS MAHAN, USS CUSHING, USS DE HAVEN in cruising disposition 5-R, axis 120°T, spacing 1,000 yards. Rear Admiral Fredrick C. Sherman (OTC) in ENTERPRISE (guide).

0230 Sounded flight quarters.

0325 - 0335 Launched 4 VF(N)79 TBMs for antisubmarine patrol.

0537 Sounded routine general quarters.

0616 Completed recovery of the 4 TBMs launched at 0335.

0637 Secured from general quarters.

0800 Mustered crew on stations.

0914-0926 Catapulted 13 F6Fs and 9 TBMs.

1019 Recovered 1 F6F, emergency landing.

1025 Formed disposition 5-V.

1053 Maneuvering on various courses to avoid simulated attack from air group.

1138 Formed cruising disposition 5-R.

1145 Sounded flight quarters.

1240 Completed recovery of 12 F6Fs and 9 TBMs launched at 0926.

1245 AOM1c Bernard C. Lewis was checking guns on an aircraft when he was struck on the side of his neck by the tail of a TBM being spotted. He was admitted to sickbay with a fractured cervical vertebra.

1500 Commenced gunnery exercises.

1604 Completed launching 4 TBMs for antisubmarine patrol.

1908 Completed recovery of the 4 TBMs launched 3 hours before.

1937 Radar surface contact, reported friendly.

2110 Changed course to 260°T.

Monday 21 August 1944   *At Sea en route to Eniwetok, in Task Group 12.3.2*

Steaming at 19 knots, course 260°T. INDEPENDENCE would cruise a base course of 260°T throughout the morning with changes for zigzagging, air operations, etc.

Cruising in Task Unit 12.3.2 with USS ENTERPRISE, USS INTREPID, USS BLUE, USS MAHAN, USS CUSHING, USS DE HAVEN in cruising disposition 5-R, axis 090°T. Rear Admiral Fredrick C. Sherman in ENTERPRISE (OTC and guide).

Ship is darkened, material condition Baker is set, Gunnery Department in condition 2, Air Department in condition 14, all other departments condition 3.

0230 Sounded flight quarters.

0329 Catapulted 6 TBM(N)s for ASP.

0405 Secured from flight quarters.

0532 Sounded general quarters.

0607 Commenced steering various courses and speeds during flight operations being conducted by INDEPENDENCE, ENTERPRISE and INTREPID.

0615 Completed recovery of 6 TBMs launched at 0330.

0800 Mustered crew to stations.

0926 Changed course into the wind while ENTERPRISE and INTREPID conducted flight operations.

1023 Base course 255°T, commenced zigzagging per plan No.6.

1042 Maneuvered to avoid simulated air attack.

1227 Commenced steering various courses and speeds during ENTERPRISE and INTREPID flight operations.

1315 ENTERPRISE and INTREPID completed flight operations. Steadied course 255°T, and changed to disposition 5-R.

1435 Sounded torpedo defense.

1516 Sounded flight quarters, secured from torpedo defense.

1614 Steering into the wind in preparation for launching aircraft by BAKER method.

1619 Launched 4 TBMs for Anti-submarine Patrol.

1622 Mustered crew at quarters for physical drill.

1632 Secured from flight quarters.

1745 USS INTREPID became formation guide (by order of OTC), bearing 360°T, at 3,000 yards.

1846 Sounded flight quarters.

1848-1852 Recovered the 4 TBMs that were on Anti-submarine Patrol.

1930 Changed course to 285°T.

1934 Made radar contact, surface craft, bearing 185°T, distance 16.5 miles.

2138 Surface radar contact bearing 255°T, 22 miles on converging course.

2154 Changed course to 215°T to avoid course of surface contact.

2203 Passed surface contact abeam, starboard, distance 10.5 miles.

2223 Changed course to 260°T.

Wednesday 23 August 1944   *At Sea en route to Eniwetok*
                                     AOM2c Daniel Lee Rinick lost at sea

0000 Changed to minus 12 zone time, making this date 23 August 1944.

Steaming in Task Unit 12.3.2 with USS ENTERPRISE, USS INTREPID, USS BLUE, USS MAHAN, USS CUSHING, USS DE HAVEN in cruising disposition 5-R, axis 090°T. Rear Admiral Fredrick C. Sherman in ENTERPRISE (OTC), USS INTERPID guide, bearing 180°T, 3,000 yards.

Ship is darkened, material condition Baker is set, Gunnery Department in condition 2, Air Department in condition 14, all other departments condition 3.

0428-0628 Manned general quarters.

0815 Mustered crew to stations.

0830 Sounded flight quarters.

0941 Completed launching 12 F6Fs and 9 TBMs.

0946 Secured from flight quarters. Air Department set condition 13.

0957 Commenced streaming target sled. At 1009 the target sled was secured at 1,500 feet.

1200 Sounded flight quarters.

Chapter 12

1215 Air group completed gunnery exercises, recovered target sled.

1232 Commenced recovering aircraft.

1238 F6F-5N piloted by Ensign William A. Shipman, in his third attempt to land, ignored a wave-off and crashed into aircraft parked on the forward end of the flight deck after clearing the barrier, then went over the port side. In addition to the plane lost, three others were damaged. One crewman was knocked over the side and six others injured. AOM2c Daniel Lee Rinick was lost to the sea.

Don Labudde describes the event:

DL   *Reveille was early enough to promise a long day for all hands. Breakfast began with the usual sloe-eyed looks at one another as we gradually came awake. Coffee and cigarettes helped. Talk was sparse, low keyed, and mostly on one subject--all airdales were trying to get used to the demands being made on them by the presence of the ship's new air group.*

Air Group 22's pilots and planes had been replaced by CVLG(N)-41. It consisted of sixteen spanking new F6F-5(N) fighters and nine new TBM(N) torpeckers. The airplanes looked the same except for a large bulbous bulge near the right end of the starboard wing. Inside the bulge was concealed a movable round radar antenna with a small orange scope in the cockpit. Really neat.

These devices were the mechanical and electronic manifestations of the beginning of Independence's new role in life. The pilots had been specially trained for night flying. We took their quality for granted. Any Navy pilot qualified for aircraft carrier duty was certifiably good.

What did concern the ordnancemen that morning was a flight detail included in the Plan of the Day: target practice on a sled pulled by the ship itself. We had gone through this exercise before with previous air groups, but this would be our first chance with Group 41. It was a given that the pilots would enjoy shooting at the sled (it wouldn't shoot back!). But how long each man kept his finger frozen on the trigger was the question. Its answer, we had learned, was the clue to how much extra work we'd have to do.

"Rat-tat-tittie-tat-tat," one guy groaned sourly.

"Yeah," said someone else. "Start shootin', can't stop, ziiiip goes the rifling."

"What're you gonna do about it?" asked Dan. "Come on, if we were sitting in those cockpits taking a bead on a target we'd do the same thing. It's only a coupla extra seconds. Hard to ease off."

We listened. Dan was the calming influence among us. He looked at each man in turn.

"Right," Sully said. "And all that ammo available."

"Shootin' ducks at two hundred and fifty knots," Tom added. "And Uncle Tax Payer footin' the tab. What more could you want?"

Then somebody else said, possibly me because I hated extra work, "Bet they'd be more careful if they had to change those damn barrels!"

Fox two-blocked just before sunrise and the planes roared off. The new starboard catapult installed at Hunters Point had cut our launch time in half. I never tired of watching the drama unfold as each plane moved forward in the semi-darkness. Their props spun like half-seen discs, slicing the natural moisture in the air into willowy wisps torn to bits before they reached the nacelle. At each wheel a goggled, helmeted plane pusher knelt, holding his wooden chock at the ready to jam it against the wheel if so signaled by the deck officer guiding the planes forward. And off they went.

Our morning was pretty much routine while the planes went through their gunnery exercises. The TBMs flew off on scouting missions. A normal gallery from below decks gathered to watch aft as the fighters peeled off and screamed downward toward the big sled that rode about a mile behind the ship. Thousands of bright tiny water spouts blossomed as bullets speckled the sea all around the sled. We AOM's paid close attention.

As each fighter's six guns fired simultaneously, rapid puffs of smoke burst from each barrel. Distance made the ripping sound resemble the violent shredding of stiff cloth. Empty cartridge cases spewed in a steady stream from under the wings. Sixty rounds per second per airplane.

The gallery, composed mainly of guys who were rarely allowed topside during flight quarters, dissipated reluctantly at the orders of their officers. The sled exercise came to a close and preparations were made to recover.

Over the bullhorn an unfamiliar voice spoke up, maybe to remind everyone that he was watching, too.

"Keep alert," boomed Captain Ewen. "Think smart!"

(Now, for a moment, permit Independence's official Log to have its say. This is what I copied as Dorothy and I researched it in August 1960.)

"1215 Air Group completed gunnery exercise; recovered target sled.

"1226 Ceased zigzagging; changed course to 115 deg T.

"1232 Commenced recovering aircraft.

"1238 F6F-5N piloted by Ensign _____ AV(N), USNR File Nr-----------, in attempting to land, picked up No. 9 arresting wire, cleared the barriers, and crashed into another F6F parked on the flight deck forward, port side, and then went over the side. The rudder was put over hard left; all engines were stopped and rudder was put hard right. Stern of the ship swung well clear of personnel in the water...."

Three fighters had already been recovered and spotted well forward per the deck plan. One had found its roost on the forward starboard bow. Another had ended up in the middle of the deck with its engine nacelle peering over the fo'c'sle. The third perched on the extreme port bow, its folded port wing suspended forty-five feet above the water—which was rushing by below at nearly thirty knots.

Coffin Corner. Little Frank the talker, sound-powered headphones affixed to his ears, was standing next to me in the catwalk athwart the island structure. Others were present, I don't remember who. Porky and LCDR Harry were off to one side aft of the entrance to Bill's rearming magazine.

I was awaiting the airplane already assigned to me by my crew leader. When it hit the deck, I'd be up and after it even while the hydraulic mechanism activated by the pilot was folding its wings and before the plane pushers could squeeze it into place. The ordnancemen who had met the first three planes were busy-busy. Already they had signaled proof that our concern at breakfast had been on the mark: the rifling in many barrels had been stripped smooth as a baby's bottom. Replacements would be necessary.

Not a one of us questioned that the ordnanceman already perched on the outboard port wing of the plane at Coffin Corner was Dan. He had a habit of getting there before anyone else—mostly because he seldom had competition for the honor. His working partner, Joe T____, was handling the starboard guns.

I glanced aft at the next approaching airplane. It was coming up the Groove. I saw the LSO wave him aboard. Its starboard wing guns belonged to me. I nerved myself to react quickly, oil can and barrel brush in hand, the instant he touched down and began to taxi forward.

Time skipped a beat.

The landing fighter bounced as it thumped hard to the deck. Its tail hook hopped and skipped over the first available arresting gear cable, across the second cable, over the third and fourth cables and then across them all but Number 9—which was too late. Forward up the deck the airplane came rushing at over seventy knots.

On the bridge the air officer immediately recognized what was about to happen. From the throats of the bullhorn screeched a mind-piercing electronic BeeeeEEEeeeEEEP!

Every soul forward of the barrier cables was galvanized into action. Scattering every which way, they rolled and tumbled toward the outer reaches of the deck, ducking into the catwalk. Time and action froze. My eyes became slow-motion cameras.

By now only three chest-level strands of the barrier cables stood between this unleashed fighter and the helpless aircraft parked forward—with airdales already concentrating on their jobs. Nothing could have stopped that airplane but a wall of steel or the hand of God. Neither was present.

It chopped its way through the barriers as if they were made of butter and unleashed it to freedom, chaos, and death.

The port wing swept over my head as I ducked beside Frank. We both instantly popped up again to gawk as we watched what happened happen. No one had time to scream a warning to Dan.

If the hurtling fighter had veered left a little, it would have fallen into the port catwalk and possibly wiped out the gunners manning the 40-mm mounts there. Instead, it crashed with a cracker-box roar into Dan's plane and cut it in two. The shock sent the forward end into the sea. Dan, his arms flailing, was already in the water when the broken airplane crashed down upon him.

To return to the Log, it tells the official tale in cold, Officer-of-the-Deck-style statistics:

"Damage to the ship, a) Three holes made by propeller in flight deck, Frames 58, 59, and 60 centerline. b) Base for landing signal light bent, Frame 22 port. c) Rack for bridle-catcher bent, Frame 26 port. d) Safety rail slightly bent, Frame 26 port. e) Splinter shield braces, Gun No. 4, badly bent.

"Damage to aircraft. a) Plane F6F No. 3: port elevator smashed (no repair). Rudder sheered (no repair). Fin sheared. Fuselage bent at tail, rivets sheared. Starboard elevator dented. b) Plane F6F No. 9: Port wing cut through. c) F6F plane No. 10: Went into gun bucket. Engine and propeller assembly appear to be all right. Remainder of plane total loss. d) Plane F6F No.6: Lost over the side.

"Injuries to personnel: a) Ensign W.A. Shipman missing. b) Rinick, D. L., AOM2/c, USN, missing Rinick was working on the flight deck and knocked over the side by F6F No. 6.

"The U.S.S. DeHaven was ordered to attempt rescue of Ensign W.A. Shipman and D.L. Rinick, but reported being unable to find them, although debris of the plane was found floating in the water astern of the disposition.

"1240. Changed speed to 19 knots 192 r.p.m. Steadied up on course 115T; continued recovering aircraft.

"1302. TBM No. 26, serial No. 25582, crashed into the barrier, snapping barrier cable and damaging propeller of plane.

"1317. Completed recovering aircraft, having landed aboard 12 VF, and 9 VT including plane lost over the side. Changed course and commenced zigzagging in accordance with Plan No. 6 on base course 260T.

"1323. Ceased zigzagging and resumed base course 260T.

"1333. Changed course to 252T.

"1433-1508. Exercised crew at torpedo defense."

And what did I do after this dreadful incident, this removal from my life of a shipmate who had welcomed me to Independence at Philadelphia and had become a friend and a sympathetic and wise counselor? I went back to work, just the way every other rearming crew member did.

After the doctors and corpsmen had taken the injured below and the C & R guys had cleared the deck of debris and had restrung the barrier cables, another landing F6F was recovered and spotted in Coffin Corner.

We took Dan's loss hard. If we were looking for sympathy, though, the adage about finding it most easily in the dictionary applied. I was so naïve I thought perhaps Mister Porky would show up in the armory to say a few words, but he never did. LCDR Harry, I suppose, was swamped with paper-work. This concerned Dan's demise and Slim's injuries. He was the other AOM injured by debris that flew like shrapnel when the two planes came together. Fact is, we didn't discuss the accident very much at all. That's what it was—an accident. Professionals had to accept it that way. Like the way the dead Ensign pilot's friends did, I presume. Tomorrow would be another day. The business toughened you.

Besides, any one of us could have been the victim. Dan's death amounted to an intersection of several factors, all involving time, circumstance, and personality. First plane spotted at Coffin Corner, that port wing hanging over the water. Both constituted an irresistible attraction that met the demands of Dan's belief in his indestructibility. When young, we all suffer from it.

Of course there was a religious service for the pilot and petty officer second class Dan a couple of days later on the hangar deck. I believe they were the first men lost at sea for which no bodies survived to deep-six. Other AOM's attended and perhaps Porky and Harry did. I did not. Nobody asked me why, and I was grateful. **DL**

The following men were injured in the accident and admitted to sickbay:
S1c Andrew D. Leaskey, AOM2c Tray L. Haynes, AMM2c Albert W. Krajewski, SK2c Ignatius R. Musech, AMM2c William F. Lust, and S2c Ivan E. Thompson.

1600 Commenced steering various courses during ENTERPRISE and INTREPID flight operations.

Thursday 24 August 1944   *Anchored at Eniwetok Atoll, Marshall Islands*

0500 Steaming as before. Sounded flight quarters

0524 Sounded routine general quarters.

0555 Changed course to 120°T. Steered various courses into the wind while catapulting antisubmarine patrol.

0558-0600 Catapulted 4 Avengers. Changed course to 0228°T, and commenced zigzagging in accordance with Plan No. 6 on a base course of 248°T.

0655 Secured from general quarters.

0715 USS ENTERPRISE assumed guide.

0730 Set clocks back one-half hour to zone minus 11.

0825 Changed course to 270°T.

0843 Sounded flight quarters.

0855 Sighted land bearing 230°T, distance 15 miles.

0915 Commenced steering various courses into the wind during flight operations.

0921 Completed recovery of 4 Avengers launched at 0600, changed course to 270°T, speed 17 knots.

0949 Commenced steaming various speeds and courses while maneuvering into special disposition for entering the harbor of Eniwetok.

1012 Steadied up on course 285°T, speed 15 knots, and commenced zigzagging independently.

1018 Commenced maneuvering to conform with harbor channel.

1026 Passed buoy No.2 abeam to starboard.

1028 Secured from flight quarters.

1134 Anchored in "A" anchorage No. I-9 in 25 fathoms of water with 110 fathoms of chain to port anchor, on a sand and coral bottom, in Eniwetok Harbor, Eniwetok Atoll, Marshall Islands.

RC Arrived at Eniwetok, the island had just been taken from the Japs and there is hardly a tree left standing. RC

AD Arrived at Eniwetok at 1030. Hundreds of ships are anchored here. Island is a wreck due to the bombing and shelling our forces did while taking it away from the Japs. AD

Friday 25 August 1944   *Eniwetok Atoll - CVLG(N)41 forms*
     Conducted training exercises out of Eniwetok as part of Task Group 58.2

0417 Anchored as before. Lighted fires under No.3 boiler.

0435 Commenced jacking main engines.

0618 Commenced spinning main engines by steam every 4 minutes until underway.

0638 Commenced walking in port anchor.

0728 Got underway in obedience to secret orders Commander Task Group 58.2, dated 22 August 1944. Steaming on various courses and speeds while standing out of Eniwetok Harbor.

0733 Sounded routine general quarters.

0802 Passed through the channel entrance to Eniwetok Atoll, departing as part of Task Unit 58.2.1, consisting of USS BUNKER HILL (OTC), INTREPID, CABOT, SAN DIEGO, OAKLAND, OWEN, MILLER, THE SULLIVANS, and TINGEY. Rear Admiral G.F. Bogan is Commander Task Unit 58.2.1 in BUNKER HILL. Base Course 070°T, speed 16 knots.

0809 Secured from general quarters. Assumed position in column 3,000 yards astern BUNKER HILL.

0825 Mustered crew to stations.

0845 Sounded torpedo defense.

0851 Changed course to 020°T.

0917 Commenced firing anti-aircraft practice on various types of towed sleeve runs.

1111 Assumed position in disposition 5-R, base course 345°T, speed 16 knots, axis 100°T. Guide USS CABOT bears 100°T, distance 2,000 yards.

1158 Changed course to 100°T.

1200 USS INDEPENDENCE assumed Task Unit guide.

1230 Task Unit changed course to 345°T.

1241 Commenced zigzagging (Plan No. 6), USS CABOT assumed guide from USS INDEPENDENCE.

1320 Ceased zigzagging, steadied up on a new course of 015°T.

1331 Began maneuvering in a special column with guide in USS OAKLAND, bearing 120°T, distance 6,000 yards, 16 knots, axis 120°T.

1524 Began maneuvering to take position in disposition 5-R.

1529 USS CABOT assumed formation guide bearing 280°T, 2,000 yards.

1559-1612 Launched 11 Hellcats and 9 Avengers.

1724 Changed course to 090°T to come into the wind, commenced steaming various courses and speed into the wind for flight operations for INDEPENDENCE and USS INTREPID.

1751 Completed recovery of Hellcats and Avengers launched at 1612.

1755 Secured from flight quarters.

1806 Changed course to 270°T, speed 25 knots.

1815 Formed cruising disposition 5-R, axis 090°T with guide in USS BUNKER HILL.

2300 Sounded flight quarters

2355 Changed course to 065°T, speed 18 knots.

On this day a dispatch was received dissolving VF(N)79.

VF(N)-79 was decommissioned, and became CVLG(N)-41.

CVLG(N)-41 led by Commander Turner F. Caldwell, was to be comprised of :

VF(N)-41   Night Fighter Squadron Forty One.
Commander Turner Foster Caldwell ("Stinky") leading the night fighter squadron.
17 pilots and 16 F6F-5Ns

VT(N)-41   Night Torpedo Squadron Forty One.
Lieutenant William R. Taylor ("Reb") leading night torpedo / bombing squadron.
9 pilots and 9 TBM-1Ds.

CVLG(N)-41   History

The Navy had programs at Naval Air Station Quonset Point, Rhode Island that evolved into Project "Affirm" to develop night fighter squadrons, utilizing aircraft with British developed (and US refined and produced) Airborne Intercept "Model A" radar (AIA).

Commander Harvey B. Seim USN would write: *"Here, through the combined efforts of the Navy, the Sperry Company, and the Massachusetts Institute of Technology, the equipment and pilots necessary to gain command of the night sky were developed".* As the Pacific war progressed an early effort was established in the Solomon Islands referred to as "GCI Moon". The shore based group, VF(N)-75, of six specially equipped F4U Corsairs (with AIA) and six Lockheed Vega Venturas were set up in October 1943 on Vella Lavella, aided by mobile Ground Controlled Intercept. Harvey Seim points out Navy fighter director officers needed time to gain experience in the art of providing a continuous flow of "Bogey" information required for successful night fighter intercepts.

Carrier based experimental night intercepts were carried out off the USS ENTERPRISE, under Admiral Radford, in the Gilberts by Lt. Cmdr. Edward H. O'Hare (after he transferred off the CVL-22) and Lt. Cdr. John L. Phillips. They were given permission to attempt night intercepts with a "Team" using the Hellcat and Avenger aircraft. On 24 November1943 a unsuccessful attempt to break up a Japanese night raid on Tarawa was attempted using two Avengers. Two nights later on the 26th two Hellcats operating with a radar equipped Avenger (Phillips) broke up a Japanese attack shooting down the "Tail-End-Charlie" and Butch O'Hare piloting one of the two Hellcats was lost in the "melee". This was believed to be the first carrier based night intercept.

The Naval leaders went through a slow difficult learning curve on the proper use and implementation of the night intercept program. Early on VF(N)-76 flying F6F-3(N)s with AIA, and later APS-6, helped to pave the way. In addition to the development of new equipment, procedures and techniques for its effective use needed to jell. Near the end of 1943 they relocated to NAAF Charleston, RI.

VF(N)-79 had formed on 20 January 1944 at NAS Quonset Point, Rhode Island. The skipper, Commander Turner Foster Caldwell, Jr., had three Navy Crosses since his graduation from Annapolis in 1935. He had just enough rank and respect to have a slight edge on getting things done. And equally important, he had vision of how a night fighting group should be utilized. He would have to work around Admirals that had no such vision. Around his core group of Lieutenants with combat experience flying in the Solomon's, they turned a fresh batch of Ensigns into a dedicated well trained cohesive night fighting squadron, flying F6F-3(N) Hellcats and TBM Avengers prepared for night action.

Training included night intercept (to find the enemy), combat tactics (to outfight the enemy) and cross country navigation (to find their way to target, and equally important, successfully recover back onboard the carrier).

In February 1944 they continued their training at NAAS Charleston, Rhode Island. Carrier qualifications were off the CV-4, USS RANGER in the Atlantic Ocean. Night carrier qualifications were to take place on the CVE-30, USS CHARGER in the Chesapeake Bay. In June, 1944 the mixed squadron (fighter pilots, torpedo pilots and aircrews) proceeded to San Diego where they boarded the USS BARNES for transportation to Pearl Harbor. There, they began flying off the USS INDEPENDENCE continuing to hone their skills and effectiveness. On 25 August, VF(N)-79 dissolved and reformed as CVLG(N)-41. With the assignment of CVLG(N)-41 to the CVL-22, the Mighty-I was in the early stages, on the way to becoming our nations first dedicated Night Carrier. She was not the first carrier to conduct night operations. In early 1944 night fighters were tried (typically in *"four plane sections"* with very limited success by small numbers of pilots on other carriers without adequately implementing a night fighter program that worked well. A major source of the dilemma was the vary nature of aircraft carrier design. The modern carriers of the day were straight deck carriers.

Irvin H. ("Hebe") Lee, VFN-41 Hellcat pilot explains the problem:

"Planes on the deck of WWII vintage carriers, when not carrying out flight operations were parked on the aft end of the flight deck. As flight operations began, the aircraft were moved forward to the launching position for takeoff. The planes not taking off were then moved all the way forward, ahead of the protective barriers, which left the aft end of the flight deck clear for landing aircraft. After all the aircraft landed, this ballet started all over again. The aircraft were serviced and parked on the aft end of the deck. During combat conditions, keeping up to eighty planes properly spotted on the deck throughout the day is like a dog chasing its tail. If a couple of night aircraft are launched, after they become airborne, every damn plane on the deck is moved forward again to clear the landing area of the deck. Rotating the night patrols until daybreak and then going back to full-blown day operations was more work then a ship's Captain wanted to ask of his deck crew." **I.H. Lee**

A carrier trying to conduct both day and night operations would, simply stated, wear its crew to a frazzle. And sleep would be difficult at best, with the round-the-clock noise and beehive of activity. It would evolve that the solution for the problem was to operate a dedicated carrier within a task group to conduct night operations exclusively, while the other carriers, assigned daylight operations slept snugly at night. The nocturnal creatures would catch their rest during the day.

The USS INDEPENDENCE would become the nations first dedicated nocturnal carrier, and the airmen of CVLG(N)-41 would become the night hunters for the Task Group, working diligently to refine and improve the skill of night attack. But it would take time for the concept to evolve. And evolve it would, with a resounding success. USS ENTERPRISE *[1] would take up the night carrier duties later in the war, to become the nations next dedicated night carrier, joined later still by USS BON HOMME RICHARD.

(*[1] USS SARATOGA very briefly filled the roll before ENTERPRISE, however she was damaged (her first operation in that assignment) at Iwo Jima by kamikaze attacks, and out of action the remainder of the war.)

CVLGN-41 aboard the INDEPENDENCE would set the course and lead the way. Operating under shade and concealment of night, they would name themselves the **"SHADEMAIDS"**.

CVLG(N)-41 insignia

Note: The squadron insignia was drawn by Milton Caniff (Terry and the Pirates).

MIGHTY I RETURNS TO PACIFIC ... AND NEW ASSIGNMENT

Frank Capka *It was in June, 1944, that the damage sustained by the Mighty I at Tarawa was completely corrected at Hunter's Point, California, and that certain improvements over the ship's original fighting strength were made one of which was the installation of an additional catapult thus making her the first ship of her class to be equipped with two catapults.*

Back at Pearl Harbor in July, 1944, the Mighty I set out immediately to prepare herself for her new assignment-namely; the developing of operational procedures and combat tactics for night carrier operations.

As stated earlier, the assignment established a precedent in carrier operations. On the Atlantic Coast, a CVE (Escort Carrier) was reported to have used night fighters for night anti-submarine patrol duty, and in the Pacific ESSEX-class carriers were known to have had night fighter pilots of "Black Chickens" in their complements.

But the Mighty I was the first carrier to boast an entire air group especially trained for night operations, and was the first carrier to function exclusively as a Night Operating Carrier.

"Why was the Mighty I selected for this all-important role in Naval Aviation?" The answers obtained from the ship's crew members vary only with respect to their phrasing, and the opinion, although not official **, is that the choice was based on the Mighty I's excellent operational record and the experience of its personnel, the greatest portion of which served with the carrier since its commissioning.

In any event, the switch from day to night operations required considerable revamping of the ship's organization, and not a small amount of modification in the living habits of the crew.

And in each case, the metamorphosis was successfully accomplished. Under Captain E. C. Ewen, USN, who relieved Captain Johnson as the Commanding Officer in July, 1944, the job of planning the new ship's organization fell into the lap of Commander Edwin J. S. Young, USN, who, until he relieved Commander W. F. Rodee as the Executive Officer was the Mighty I's Air Officer.

These changes formed the nucleus for others. Commander Richard A. Teel, USN, who was Assistant Air Officer, was elevated to the Air Officer's post, while Lieutenant Commander J. H. Arnold, USN, came aboard in July, 1944, to act as his assistant. Meanwhile, succeeding Commander Goldman, USN, as Engineering Officer, was Lieutenant Commander E. VJ. Sloan, USN, formerly Commander Goldman's assistant.

At this time, also, the Mighty I welcomed aboard Commander Turner F. Caldwell, Jr., USN, a veteran of Guadalcanal and the Solomons, and regarded by many as the "ring leader" of night fighting tactics-the popular belief persisting that he conceived the idea of the night fighter during his tour of duty in the Solomons. .

At any rate, Comdr. Caldwell was to be the leader of the Mighty I's nocturnal airmen, all of whom were especially trained in night operations and night interception prior to reporting aboard that they were ready for their new role was borne out in the months to come when they amassed a record of 46 planes destroyed and four damaged.

Designated as a Night Operating Carrier when it returned to the Pacific in July, the Mighty I did not function solely as such until after the early raids on Palau in September, 1944, which were launched on 6-7 of the month. She did, however, conduct routine night patrols throughout this period.

It was in the coming Philippine operations that she was to gain prominence as a night carrier. And what busy days those were to be for the Mighty I and her crew.   ***Frank Capka***

** Another possible explanation of tasking the USS INDEPENDENCE as a dedicated night carrier is that it was said that Admiral John McCain shared the vision Lt. Commander Turner F. Caldwell, Jr. had of the need for the Navy to own the night.

In addition, **Lcdr. C.B. "Cy" Heinrich** (after the war) offered up his insight:

"The following narrative I feel should be part of the history of air group CVLG(N)41 and the USS INDEPENDENCE CVL22.

Following the torpedoing of the ship in the campaign for Tarawa and the return to Pearl Harbor and on to San Francisco for repair, I received orders to report to COMPFAIR WEST COAST at San Diego, reporting in there, I was assigned to the staff of Captain Cromlain, chief of training.

(An interesting side note I discovered later: Capt. Cromlain, his chief of staff Jim Daniels, Turner Caldwell and Bill Henry all were part of the same Dive Bomber group flying out of Guadalcanal.)

The six to seven months the ship was in the yard at Hunter's Point Navy Yard were most productive in creating training procedures for new air groups being readied for assignment to new carriers about to join the Pacific Fleet.

The Independence, following trial runs to the satisfaction of crew and yard personnel, was docked at Alameda Naval Air to load cargo for Pearl Harbor.

With every square inch of hangar and flight deck filled with aircraft and spare parts plus almost a thousand passengers, the Independence was to get under way a 0500 the next morning. Not 400 yards from the dock she ran aground. It was determined that tugboats would not be able float the ship and that the best was to hope for a exceptional high tide at noontime. The expected tide floated the Independence again; thus, Captain Johnson became the de facto commander, as NavRegs say any commander who grounds his ship shall be relieved of his command. Even though a harbor pilot was on board, the commanding officer was responsible.

After discharging cargo and passengers in Pearl Harbor the Independence spent several weeks at sea doing night operations with VFN79 air group, which was stationed at Barbers Point Naval Air Station.

While the ship was docked at Ford Island one day, I had finished a leisurely breakfast, as I was not on the day's "Duty Section," when I heard on the ship's PA system, "Lt. Heinrich, report to the duty officer on the double. "Expecting trouble, I found Capt. Johnson, Cdr. Young and Cdr. Teel waiting, and I was wondering why I had to be called as we were to attend a conference at fleet headquarters. (I still think I was a late addition to the party.) The Captain's shore boat was along the port side and proceeded to take us to fleet headquarters.

The purpose of the meeting was to determine which ship was to be designated as the Night Operating Carrier with the fleet.

At that time there were two carriers in Pearl Harbor without assigned air groups, the Independence and one of the escort carriers. The escort carriers were so called because their primary duty was to escort convoys in the Atlantic and Pacific war zones. They were built on "Liberty Ship" hulls in the Kaiser Ship Yards in Seattle.

Attending the conference was more gold braid then I had ever seen in one place before, with a senior admiral as the moderator. As the meeting continued, the pros and cons of the ships were advanced.

The escort carrier had a broader beam* and thus less roll in a cross sea, larger elevators that could take a F6F or a TBF without folding the wings**, a larger hangar deck and more storage space, and an eight-foot-wider flight deck. As the discussions went on it seemed as though the escort carrier was being promoted. Presently the moderating admiral said he understood the young man sitting in the far corner was the Landing Signal Officer on the Independence and he felt that everyone present would be interested in any comments that officer had to offer.

I addressed the group with my knees shaking and almost unable to vocalize. The Independence had a flank speed of 32 knots, *** versus approximately 14 knots for the escort carrier. Thus, under a no-wind condition at sea the Independence could always provide a 30 knot-wind down the flight deck. In my estimation this more that offset all the advantages mentioned previously for the escort carrier, I said.

The mediator's next statement was, "Can anyone disagree that the Independence shall join the fleet as the designated Night Operating Carrier?" Designation of the Independence became CVLGN and Air group VFN79 was assigned to the Independence and became CLVGN41.
For those who do not understand, when an aircraft carrier conducts flight operations it is always headed into the prevailing wind. Approach speed equals the air speed of an aircraft preparing to land on the carrier (90 knots) minus deck wind speed (30 knots) equals landing speed (60 knots).

Respectfully submitted, C. B. "Cy" Heinrich, LCDR USNR RET"

*   Note: Most specs seem to indicate no advantage in the CVE Beam, the CVE flight deck is wider.

**   Note: The elevators may have been too small for these A/C with unfolded wings.

*** Note: As a casual observation, the 32 knot flank speed of the CVLs also meant that a CVL night carrier could run in a pack with the big dogs where the CVEs due to their slower speeds were not ideal for fast raids directly into harms way, as the day carriers would typically be tasked. Higher speed also gave better stand-off capabilities should highly undesirable direct contact with major enemy surface threats suddenly transpire (as would happen with the CVEs off Leyte). With no disrespect to the CVEs, a CVE dedicated to night warfare might better be suited for operations with tankers, transports, supply and service vessels, and or utilization within close proximity to a fixed geographic area, such as a landing support mode, where CVEs offered very high value in providing air cover, ASP and search operations.

The CVL could only handle a limited number of aircraft, which combined with her speed made it ideally sized and suited for early night carrier operations. She also now, after the repairs and refit, had two catapults, which gave redundancy in event of a catapult failure, and could effectively double the night launch rate. The main drawback was the narrow and relatively short flight deck, which would call for pilots to be on top of their craft!

Commander Harvey B. Seim USN would write: *" Experience was another factor which led to the choice of the INDEPENDENCE. It was the first of its type to be commissioned, and had pioneered in the development of an effective CVL shipboard organization. It was the first of the class to see action against the Japanese*[1], and had participated in several hotly-contested engagements. It had been bloodied in action, and its crew was experienced, resolute and eager to accept the challenge of the new task."*   (*[1] The USS BELLEAU WOOD was on the Baker & Howland Island raids at roughly the same time.)

Saturday 26 August 1944   *Eniwetok Atoll*
Conducted training exercises out of Eniwetok as part of Task Group 58.2

0007-0015 Steaming as before. Launched 3 TBMs and 4 F6Fs.
0337 Turned into the wind for flight operations. Launched 4 F6Fs and 3 TBMs and recovered 3 TBMs launched at 0015.
0414 Completed recovery of 4 F6Fs launched at 0015. Changed speed to 16 knots.
0502-0603 Manned general quarters stations.
0532 Commenced various course and speed changes to conduct flight operations.
0534 Completed launching 3 TBMs for ASP.
0549 Completed recovery of 4 F6Fs and 3 TBMs launched at 0337.
0616 Changed course to 060°T, speed 16 knots.
0645 Task Unit 58.2.2 consisting of the USS HOUSTON, MIAMI, VINCENNES, MARSHALL, STEPHEN POTTER, BENHAM, and WEDDERBURN joined the disposition.

Chapter 12

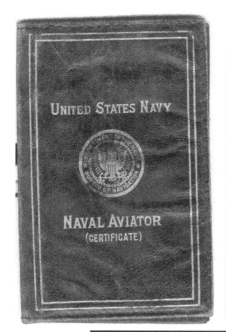

LSO (Landing Signal Officer) Lt. Cyrus B. Heinrich was highly praised by the aviators for his skilled, devoted and focused work helping to guide the pilots back onboard. If a landing aircraft became too threatening, he could dive for cover in the net near his foot on the left side of the photo, to escape beneath his platform.

A "black light" would light up the florescent material of his paddles, leg stripes and arms at night. Cy developed the first florescent suit, and his wife sewed it up. He got the idea as he and his wife Patsy, attending the Ice Follies, had observed the use of a black light to illuminate costumes of the ice skaters.

This was a typical business office of a lethal night hunter, the VF(N)-41 pilot.
The photo shows the cockpit of a Grumman F6F-3 Night Fighter equipped with AN/APS-6 radar.

(The Bu No. - 65960 on the S/N plate riveted to the lower right side of the instrument panel identifies the F6F as a dash 3. The radar display ("Indicator Unit") is in the center of the instrument panel. The control unit for the display was located near the pilots seat pan (out of sight on the left) and an Auxiliary Control Unit is visible above the throttle quadrant (small panel with the single toggle switch and a circular black knob).   (Photo courtesy of Patrick Clancey - Hyperwar)

The further refined AN/APS-6 Radar (MIT Radiation Laboratory led development with Westinghouse Electric selected as the prime contractor) **replaced the earlier AIA Radar** (MIT Rad. Lab. & Sperry Gyroscope Co.) **in the Hellcats.**

VFN-79 in April 1944, taken at N.A.A.F. Charlestown, Rhode Island

Top Row (standing) L-R:
Jesse T. Barker, Meredith

Middle Row (standing) L-R:
Gale V. Williams, Irvin H. Lee, Robert W. Klock, Emmett R. Edwards, Harrold E. Johnson, James A. Barnett, Roland K. Thies, William R. Taylor, William P. Phelps, Joseph J. O'Shaughnessey, Walter J. Seekamp, Robert R. Deuel, John S. Gaines III

Bottom Row L-R:
William A. Shipman, Reuben F. Peterson, John E. Dewis, George W. Obenour, Robert R. Fegraeus, William E. Henry, Turner F. Caldwell, John E. Williams, Forrest M. Archer, Joseph F. Moore, Jack S. Berkheimer, Elmer M.Towers, Floyd A. Fisher

CLVG(N)-41 Torpedo Squadron Pilots - VT(N)-41

Top Row (standing) L-R: **Colburn C.** *"Coly"* **Hardy, Robert R.** *"Bob"* **Campaigne, Frank H. McNair, William R.** *"Reb"* **Taylor, William P.** *"Bill"* **Phelps, Donald M.** *"Don"* **Linton, Milton F.** *"Doc"* **Popp**

Bottom Row L-R: **John E.** *"Jug"* **Williams, Forrest M.** *"Polly"* **Archer, James** *"Jim"* **Taylor, John E.** *"Jack"* **Dewis, Robert N.** *"Hobby"* **Hobson**

0706 Secured from flight quarters, set condition 13.

0800 Mustered crew to stations.

0804 Sounded flight quarters.

0853 Commenced various course and speed changes to conduct flight operations.

0900 Having recovered 3 TBMs launched at 0534, completed flight operations and commenced maneuvering to regain position in formation.

1240 Air Department secured from flight quarters.

1304 Task Unit 58.2.2 departed from the formation.

1335 Commenced zigzagging on base course 245°T in accordance with Plan No. 7, speed 16 knots.

1349 Sighted land bearing 230°T, 9 miles.

1404 Let fires die out and secured No.1 and 3 boilers.

1423 Changed speed to 23 knots.

1427 Ceased zigzagging, changed course to 220°T.

1438 Changed cruising disposition to column astern of USS BUNKER HILL, distance 2,000 yards.

1439 Commenced steaming at various courses and speeds to conform to the Deep Entrance channel and harbor of Eniwetok Atoll.

CLVG(N)-41 Torpedo Squadron Aircrew - VT(N)-41

Top Row (standing) L-R: **Joseph J. Krejci, Harvey M. Nye, Robert Mahaffey, Peter T. Julsen Jr., John P. Conroy, John L. Flanagan, Alvin R. Huss, Foster V. Cooper**

Middle Row L-R: **Howard Parry, Howard F. Murphy, Robert J. Doane, R.J. Metelko, Richard G. Larson, John M. Foster Jr., Ralph C. Milliron, George L. Franke Jr.**

Bottom Row L-R: **William D. Hetman, Stafford E. Hardwick**, Robert S. Barnes, **W.T. Heagney, Robert E. Chadwell, James F. Mitchell, William Lumpkin**

1503 Sounded routine general quarters.
1535 Secured from general quarters.
1659 Anchored in "A" anchorage, Berth Item 9, in 25 fathoms of water, sand and coral bottom, with
110 fathoms of anchor chain to the port anchor.
1715 Let fires die out and secured No. 4 boiler.
1909 Secured main engines.
> *CEM*   *The movie tonight was- "A Guy Named Joe".*   *CEM*

AD *Back at Eniwetok. Went swimming over the side in the afternoon. Water was warm.* **AD**

Monday 28 August 1944   *Eniwetok Atoll*

0645 Anchored as before. YT-470 moored two spacer barges port side amidships.

CLVG(N)-41 Fighter Squadron Pilots - VF(N)-41

Top Row (on wing) L-R: **Emmett R.** *"Eddy"* **Edwards, Warren G. Light, James A.** *"Barney"* **Barnett,
Lester H.** *"Les"* **Diskosky, Robert W.** *"Bob"* **Klock, Reuben F.** *"Pete"* **Peterson**

Middle Row (standing) L-R: **Charles H.** *"Chuck"* **Kesler, Gayle V.** *"GeeVee"* **Williams, Benjamin R.**
"Spike" **Houden, Arthur H.** *"Art"* **Hansen, Floyd A.** *"Fish"* **Fisher, Baker A.** *"Brady"* **Bradenbaugh,
Russell D.** *"Otis"* **Otis, Irvin H.** *"Hebe"* **Lee**

Bottom Row L-R: **Glen R. Earl, Kyle H.** *"Mo"* **Morris, Fred Allen** *"Honey"* **Hunziker, Robert R.** *"Fergie"*
Fegraeus, Turner F. *"Stinky"* **Caldwell, Wallace E.** *"Wally"* **Miller, William E.** *"Bill"* **Henry**

0745 USS NIOBRARA came alongside to port.
0815 Mustered crew at quarters. Captain E.C. Ewen presented letters of commendation for meritorious
action to crew members for the events of 20 November 1943, the day the Mighty I was torpedoed;

- **Kenneth J. Smith**, WT3c from the Secretary of the Navy.
- **Frank R. Samson**, QM1c from the Secretary of the Navy.
- **James H. Cook**,   MM2c from the Secretary of the Navy.
- **Neil L. Rennie**,   S1c from Rear Admiral A.E. Montgomery.

0820 Commenced receiving fuel oil and aviation gasoline.
0930 Completed receiving aviation gasoline.
1000 Made daily inspection of the magazines.
1040 Barge with dry stores moored alongside port quarter.

1115 Received aboard 3 F6F-5(N)s from C.A.S.U. No. 35 plane pool, Eniwetok Atoll.
1405 Completed receiving fuel oil from the USS NIOBRARA. At 1445 she cast off from port side.
1455 YT-470 removed two spacer lighters from port side.
2110 Yard Oiler No. 76 came alongside port side.
2200 Commenced receiving fuel oil.

Tuesday 29 August 1944   *Underway for Operation Stalemate II**
(*A part of "Operation Forager" - the Mariana and Palau Islands campaign)

The Mighty I on this day got underway in accordance with orders of ComTaskGroup 38.2.
Task Group 38.2 is part of Task Force 38 with Vice Admiral Marc Andrew Mitscher commanding.
Task Unit 38.2.1 consist of four aircraft carriers; BUNKER HILL, CABOT, INDEPENDENCE and
INTREPID and cruisers OAKLAND and SAN DIEGO along with a screen of 8 destroyers. Flagship for
38.2 is USS BUNKER HILL with Rear Admiral G.F. Bogan commanding (CTG).
They will join up with Task Group 38.1 and 38.3 to take part in Operation Stalemate II. The primary
purpose of this operation is to secure the Palau Islands to protect MacArthur's flank from Japanese air or
naval attacks while he takes back the Philippines. A Marine Corp landing is scheduled for September
15th, and the Navy is tasked to soften the area up, including air strikes on targets, attacks on shipping
and Japanese aviation assets. Task Force 38 will strike at targets in the Palau Islands and the central
Philippines.

The original intention as they steam toward Eniwetok Harbor channel is to have INDEPENDENCE
operate as a Night Carrier, except for routine daytime patrol missions. The group will steam south (past
Kusaie Island in Micronesia) prior to turning west in an attempt to avoid detection.

Anchored as before. Yard Oiler 76 and Buffalo Camel tied alongside to port.
0036 Completed receiving fuel oil from Yard Oiler 76.
0130 LCI-392 came alongside starboard side to unload bomb fuses.
0230 Small boat M-1 came along starboard side to unload 40mm ammunition, bombs and bomb tails.
Additional munitions were received from USS PIEDMONT (AD-17).
0429 LCI-392 Cast off and stood out in the harbor.
0555 Commenced jacking over main engines.
0559 Small boats M-1 and SP-58 cast off starboard side.
0712 YO-76 cast off the port side.
0715 Commenced spinning main engines by steam.
0720 Buffalo Camel cast off the port side.
0754 Cut in degaussing. At 0800 the crew was mustered on stations.
0829 Underway steering various courses and speeds conforming to the channel while standing out from
the harbor.
0830 Sounded routine general quarters.
0847 Passed buoy No.2 abeam port and took departure from Eniwetok Harbor. Steadied on course 105°
T, 25 knots in company of Task Group 38.2 with carriers USS BUNKER HILL, INTREPID, CABOT,
cruisers OAKLAND and SAN DIEGO, destroyers CUSHING, COLAHAN, STOCKHAM, BENHAM
and YARNALL. Formation 5-R1, axis 090°T, at 16 knots. Guide and OTC in BUNKER HILL, bearing
090°T, distance 2,500 yards. CTG 38.2 in BUNKER HILL is Rear Admiral G.F. Bogan.
0859 Secured from general quarters.
0916 Changed course to 225°T.
1720 On a course of 165°T, 18 knots, sighted ships bearing 105°T, 20 miles out, on a converging
course.
1820 Merging with Task Groups 38.1 and 38.3. Joined up to form cruising disposition 5-X.
2000 Changed course to 150°T, and at 2010 began zigzagging (per Plan No.8) on base course 150°T.

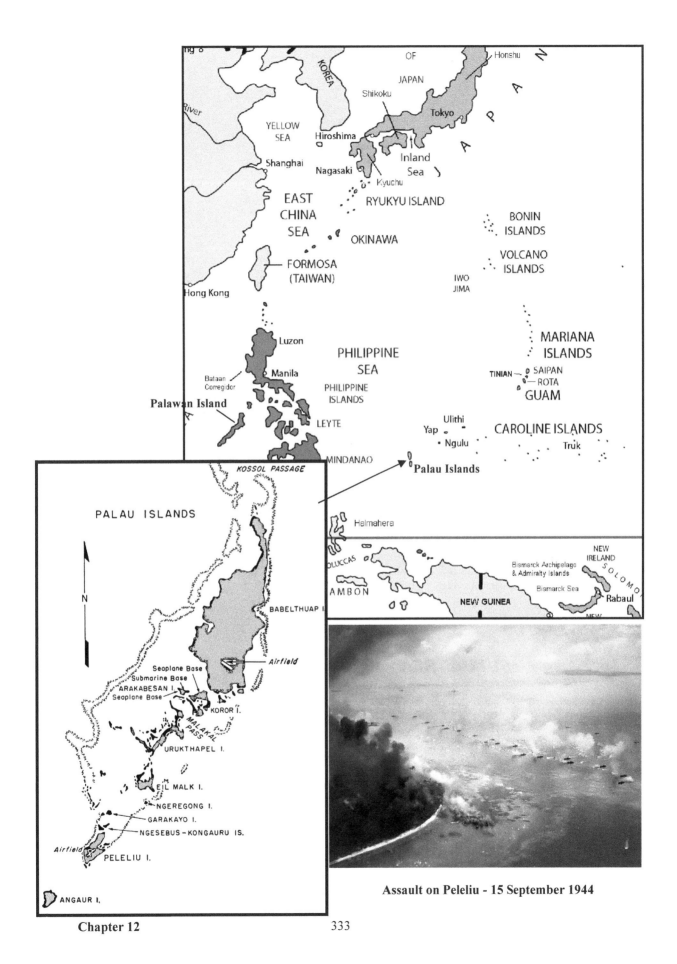

Assault on Peleliu - 15 September 1944

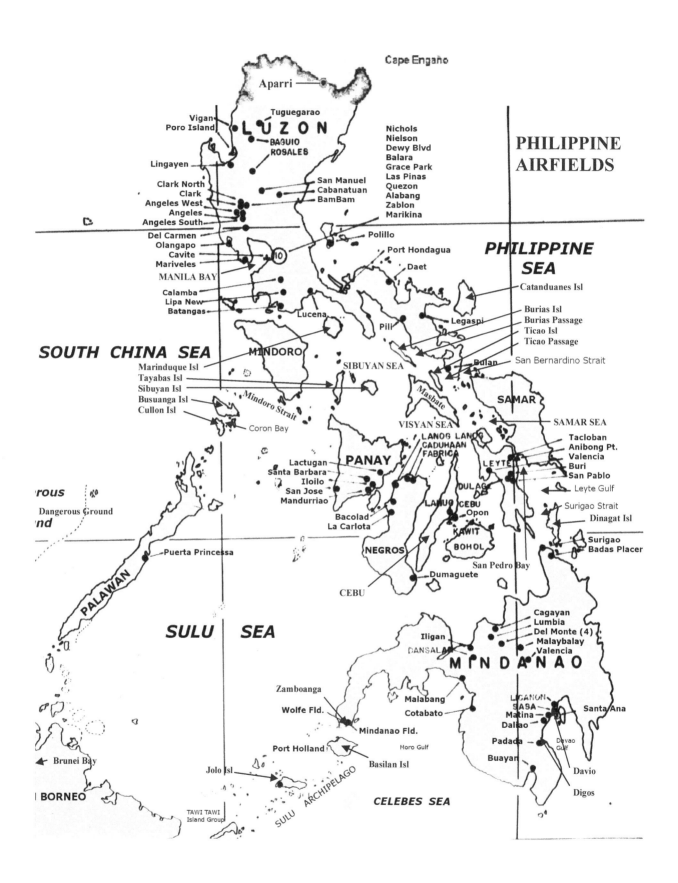

PHILIPPINE AIRFIELDS

Cape Engaño

Aparri

Vigan
Poro Island

Tuguegarao

LUZON

BAGUIO
ROSALES

Nichols
Nielson
Dewy Blvd
Balara
Grace Park
Las Pinas
Quezon
Alabang
Zablon
Marikina

Lingayen

Clark North
Clark
Angeles West
Angeles
Angeles South

San Manuel
Cabanatuan
BamBam

Del Carmen
Olangapo
Cavite
Mariveles

10

MANILA BAY

Polillo

Port Hondagua

Daet

PHILIPPINE
SEA

Calamba
Lipa New
Batangas

Lucena

Pili

Catanduanes Isl

Burias Isl
Burias Passage
Ticao Isl
Ticao Passage

SOUTH CHINA SEA

MINDORO

SIBUYAN SEA

Legaspi

Bulan

San Bernardino Strait

Marinduque Isl
Tayabas Isl
Sibuyan Isl
Busuanga Isl
Cullon Isl

Mindoro Strait

Coron Bay

Masbate

SAMAR

Lactugan
Santa Barbara
Iloilo
San Jose
Mandurriao

VISYAN SEA

PANAY

LANOG LANOG
CADUHAAN
FABRICA

LEYTE

SAMAR SEA

Tacloban
Anibong Pt.
Valencia
Buri
San Pablo

Leyte Gulf

rous

Dangerous Ground
nd

Bacolad
La Carlota

NEGROS

Puerta Princessa

SULU   SEA

CEBU

PALAWAN

Dumaguete

DULAG

LANUO CEBU
Opon

KAWIT
BOHOL

San Pedro Bay

Surigao Strait

Dinagat Isl

Surigao
Badas Placer

Cagayan
Lumbia
Del Monte (4)
Malaybalay
Valencia

Iligan

DANSALAN

MINDANAO

LIGANON
SASA
Matina
Daliao

Santa Ana

Zamboanga

Wolfe Fld.

Malabang

Cotabato

Mindanao Fld.

Port Holland

Moro Gulf

Padada

Davao
Gulf

Buayan

Brunei Bay

Basilan Isl

Jolo Isl

Davio

Digos

BORNEO

TAWI TAWI
Island Group

SULU ARCHIPELAGO

CELEBES SEA

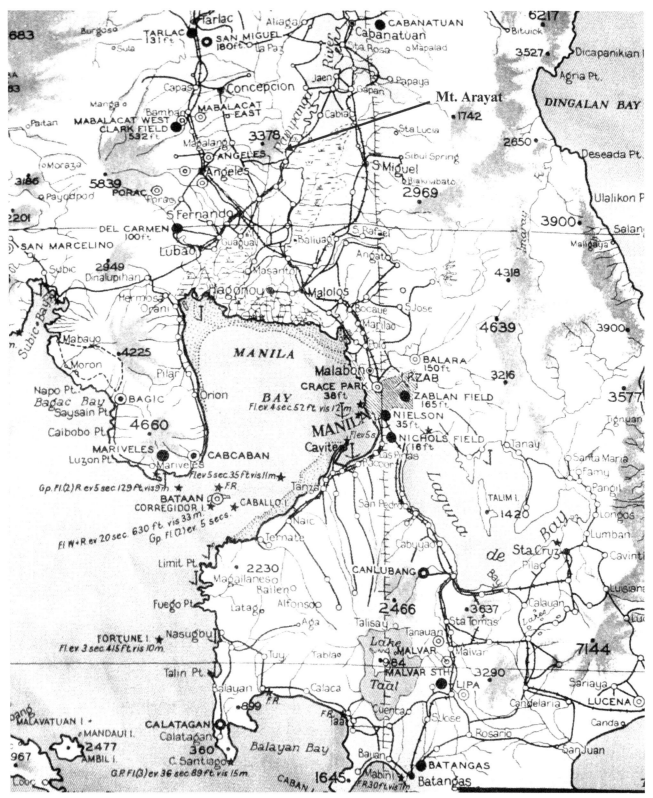

Manila Bay Area - Partial section of silk Luzon chart issued to aviators during WWII.
This shows the area that Night Air Group 41 covered in their assigned missions over Luzon .

13
Return to War - Operation Stalemate II

Wednesday 30 August 1944   *Underway for Operation Stalemate II*

0458 Steaming as before. Sounded general quarters.

0749 Sounded flight quarters.

0840 Changed course to 090°T, speed 28 knots as INDEPENDENCE, BUNKER HILL, CABOT and INTREPID prepared for flight operations.

0843 Completed launching 4 F6Fs.

1009 Commenced steering various courses, maneuvering to avoid simulated air attack.

1010 Task Group formed cruising disposition 5-V1.

1103 On a course of 225°T, the Task Unit formed cruising disposition 5-R1.

1155 Changed course to 060°T for flight operations.

1201 Commenced various courses and speeds into the wind for flight operations by all four carriers.

1210-1213 Recovered the 4 F6Fs launched at 0843.

1227 Secured from flight quarters, Air Department set condition 14.

1247 Commenced zigzagging (per Plan 6) on base course 210°T.

1325 USS CUSHING reported a sound contact.

1330 Changed course to 330°T in an emergency turn signal from Commander Task Group 38.2.

1351 Resumed zigzagging on base course 210°T.

With various course changes thru the afternoon and evening, INDEPENDENCE closed the day at 1916 on a course of 250°T, speed 18 knots.

Thursday 31 August 1944   *Underway for Operation Stalemate II*

Steaming as part of Task Group 38.2 with USS BUNKER HILL (OTC and guide, at 270°T, 2,500 yards, Disposition 5-R, axis 090°T.), INTREPID, CABOT, OAKLAND, SAN DIEGO, CUSHING, COLAHAN, BLUE, STOCKHAM, BENHAM, HALSEY POWELL and WEDDERBURN.

0200 Sounded flight quarters.

0257-0302 Launched 4 F6Fs.

0606 On a new course of 045°T, speed 24 knots, completed recovery of 4 F6Fs launched at 0302.

0611 Commenced maneuvering to regain station in disposition 5-R1.

0932 Formed in column for firing as follows: USS INTREPID, BUNKER HILL, CABOT, INDEPENDENCE, spacing 1,000 yards.

0937 Commenced zigzagging (Plan No.6) and sounded torpedo defense for purpose of anti-aircraft firing practice on a towed sleeve.

1031 Secured from torpedo defense.

1052 Completed forming disposition 5-R, zigzagging on base course 250°T, speed 16 knots.

1155 Ceased zigzagging, steadied up on course 270°T.

1156 USS INDEPENDENCE designated as guide. USS BUNKER HILL, INTREPID and CABOT left the formation to proceed to flying stations.

1300 BUNKER HILL assumed disposition guide

1325 Sounded routine general quarters. At 1330 the crew held an abandon ship drill.

1400 Secured from abandon ship drill.

1415 Secured from general quarters.

1437 OTC designated this vessel as disposition guide.

1642 BUNKER HILL assumed disposition guide.

1900 Set clocks back 1 hour to zone description minus 10.

The day ended zigzagging on a base course of 250°T, speed 18 knots.

Friday 1 September 1944   *Underway for Operation Stalemate II*

Steaming as before with Task Group 38.2. Ship is darkened, in material condition Baker. Gunnery Department is in condition 2; Air Department in condition 12; Engineering Department in condition 31, all other departments in condition 3. Zigzagging in accordance with Plan No.6 on base course 250°T.

0430-0537 Manned routine general quarters stations.

0708 Disposition axis changed to 280°T, course to 250°T. Commenced maneuvering to new position.

0732 Arrived at new position in the disposition. BUNKER HILL (guide) bears 100°T at 2,500 yards.

0800 Mustered crew on stations.

0809 Commenced steering various courses at various speeds while USS BUNKER HILL, CABOT and INTREPID conducted flight operations.

0846 Changed course to 300°T as the formation took evasive action while undergoing simulated dive-bombing and torpedo attack. At 0910 they changed course to 270°T.

1042 Sounded torpedo defense.

1134 Commenced steering various courses and speeds while USS BUNKER HILL, CABOT and INTREPID landed aircraft.

1355 USS HALSEY POWELL came alongside starboard quarter to receive mail.

1649 Changed course to 210°T.

1702 USS HALSEY POWELL returned alongside to deliver guard mail.

1744 Changed speed to 24 knots, began catapulting 4 F6Fs as CAP, and 4 TBMs as ASP, for this Task Group. Then reduced speed to 21 knots.

1751 Commenced Zigzagging (Plan No.6) on base course 270°T.

2019 Steering various courses at various speeds into the wind to recover aircraft.

2044 Completed recovering 4 F6Fs and 4 TBMs launched at 1748. TBM # 27 (Bu No. 46267) crashed into barrier No.2 upon landing, with only slight damage to the ship, and the TBM.

2102 Regained position in disposition 5R-1. Began zigzagging on base course 275°T.

2349 Made emergency turn to 335°T to avoid sound contact, which later proved false.

Saturday 2 September 1944   *Underway for Operation Stalemate II*

Steaming as part of Task Group 38.2 with USS BUNKER HILL, INTREPID, CABOT, OAKLAND, SAN DIEGO, CUSHING, COLAHAN, BLUE, STOCKHAM, BENHAM, HALSEY POWELL and WEDDERBURN. CTG Rear Admiral G.F. Bogan in BUNKER HILL, which is OTC and guide at 120° T, 2,500 yards. Disposition 5-R1, axis 120°T, base course 275°T, speed 18 knots. Ship is darkened.

0456 Sounded general quarters, set material condition Able.

0535 Sighted group of tankers and escorts bearing 270°T, 15 miles, on a converging course.

0556-0557 Secured from general quarters. Let fires die out under and secured boilers Nos. 1 and 3.

0605 Tankers joined the formation to refuel the Task Group.

0630 Changed course to 110°T, speed 10 knots (98 rpm).

0632 Commenced various courses at various speeds while proceeding alongside tanker to receive fuel.

0637 USS CABOT became formation guide.

0640 USS CACHE in the center of the fueling group became formation guide.

0650 Formation axis shifted to 110°T.

0737 USS CACHE came along starboard side.

0802 After fueling hose connected. 0803 Commenced pumping from USS CACHE.

0808 Commenced pumping from forward pumping station from USS CACHE.

0925 All lines cast off, having received 184,245 gallons fuel oil.

0930 Changed speed to 15 knots. Draft after fueling; fwd 24'1", aft 26'2".

0938 Began maneuvering various courses and speeds to regain proper station.

1000 Sounded flight quarters.

1040 Lighted fires under boiler No.1.

1054 Changed speed to 12 knots, steadied on course 115°T.

1100 Lighted fires under boiler No.3.

1107-1115 USS YARNALL was along starboard quarter for transfer of guard mail.

1117 Increased speed to 20 knots; proceeding to flying station, steering various courses into the wind preparatory to launching aircraft.

1137-1142 Catapulted 4 F6Fs as a CAP and 4 TBMs for ASP. Boilers 1 & 3 were put on line. With the launch completed, changed course to 110°T, speed reduced to 15 knots.

1444 Completed launching a second CAP and ASP of 4 F6Fs and 4 TBMs, changed course to 080°T, speed 28 knots.

1451 Changed course to 285°T and commenced steaming on various courses and speeds while recovering 4 TBM's and 4 F6F's launched at 1142.

1510 Changed course to 125°T, commenced on various courses and speeds to regain position within the disposition.

1550 Main Control reported main feed pump placed out of commission due to frozen rotor.

1615 Changed course to 310°T.

1625 Changed to disposition 5R-4, maneuvering to new position from guide USS SAUGATUCK, bearing 270°T, 10,000 yards. USS COLAHAN and USS STOCKHAM are plane guards.

1738 Commenced steaming on various courses and speeds proceeding to flying station.

1745-1749 Commenced catapulting 4 F6Fs for CAP and 3 TBMs for ASP.

1759 Turned into the wind to begin recovery of aircraft.

1802-1811 Landed on board 4 F6Fs and 4 TBMs launched at 1444.

2004 Commenced steaming on various courses and speeds to regain position in disposition 5R-4.

2035 Changed course into the wind for flight operations.

2056 Recovered 4 F6Fs and 3 TBMs launched at 1749.

2240 Assumed position in disposition 5R-4.

2324 Resumed zigzagging on base course 310°T.

Sunday 3 September 1944   *Underway for Operation Stalemate II*

0100 Steaming as before. Changed course to 355°T.

0200 Sounded flight quarters.

0232-0302 Catapulted 4 F6Fs and 4 TBMs.

0454 Sounded routine general quarters.

0537 Changed course to 348°T, speed 25 knots and began recovering aircraft launched at 0300, then changed course to 080°T (and speed - 20 knots) while maneuvering to regain position in disposition.

0557 Secured from general quarters.

0800 Mustered crew on stations. Cleveland Class light cruisers USS HOUSTON, MIAMI, VINCENNES and screen joined the formation.

0830 Commenced maneuvering to form disposition 5R-3 with USS SAUGATUCK, guide bearing 120°T at 4,500 yards, base course 120°T.

1112 USS BUNKER HILL designated as formation guide. Began maneuvering into position on new guide, bearing 120°T at 2,500 yards.

1132 USS VINCENNES was designated the new formation guide, bearing 120°T at 6,500 yards. Numerous course changes were made throughout the afternoon and evening.

1900 Set all clocks back one hour to zone minus 9 time.

The evening of September 3rd ended zigzagging on a base course of 260°T.

Monday 4 September 1944   *Underway for Operation Stalemate II*

Today passed much the same as yesterday. No flights were logged from the INDEPENDENCE. The Task Group continued to steam toward the west.

0640 A plane was sighted "landing in the water", bearing 002°T, 10 miles distant.

0937 USS HALSEY POWELL made a sound contact bearing 225°T at 10,000 yards, later classified as a non-submarine.

1713 USS COLAHAN came alongside starboard quarter to deliver guard mail.

2330 USS TINGEY made a sound contact. Seven minutes later the contact was also classified a non-submarine.

2352 Resumed zigzagging on base course 290°T.

Tuesday 5 September 1944   *Underway for Operation Stalemate II*

0422 Steaming as before with Task Group 38.2, disposition 5R-3, base course 290°T, speed 17 knots. USS BUNKER HILL is guide, 110°T, 2500 yards. Sounded general quarters.

0435 USS VINCENNES assumed guide, 110°T, 6,500 yards.

0542 Let fires die out under boilers Nos. 1 and 3.

0800 Mustered crew on stations.

1017 Steadied on course 310°T. USS YARNELL came alongside to starboard to transfer guard mail.

1023 Mail transfer completed, YARNELL cast off.

1045 Commenced zigzagging on base course 290°T.

1545 BUNKER HILL assumed guide.

1600 Mustered crew at quarters for battle gear inspection.

1650 Lighted fires under boilers Nos. 1 and 3.

1738 Cut in boilers Nos. 1 and 3 on main steam line.

1741 Darkened ship.

2015-2105 Pumped bilges. At 2140 the fleet speed changed to 18 knots.

Wednesday 6 September 1944   *Operation Stalemate II - Palau (Palau, Angaur & Peleliu)*
(see map - page 333)

0444 Steaming as before. Sounded general quarters.

0548 Secured from general quarters, Air Department set condition 14. Changed fleet speed to 12 knots.

0600 Mustered crew on stations. Commenced zigzagging independently (per Plan No. 19) on base course 290°T.

1120 Ceased zigzagging.

1121 VINCENNES assumed guide, formed disposition 5R-5 on axis 290°T, guide bearing 290°T at 7,500 yards.

1127 Changed speed to 20 knots.

1157 USS OAKLAND designated as guide, bearing 290°T, 2,500 yards.

Today at noon Task Group 38.2 began air operations against Palau Islands (held by the Japanese).

1257 Sounded general quarters. Four unidentified aircraft reported at 355°T, distance 35 miles.

1301 Changed speed to 22 knots.

1305 Aircraft identified as friendly.

1307 Changed course to 300°T.

1335 Secured from general quarters.

1530 Sounded flight quarters and prepared flight deck for landing aircraft of other carriers, if necessary, upon returning from sweep.

1553 Secured from flight quarters, Air Department set to condition 13.

1752 Changed speed to 15 knots, steadied up on 320°T while USS STOCKHAM came alongside to deliver mail.

1805 Sounded torpedo defense, set Air Department set to condition 11.

1806 USS STOCKHAM cast off.

Chapter 13   339

1810 Changed speed and course to regain station.
1830 Changed course to 065°T, speed 18 knots.   This vessel launched no aircraft today.

Beginning today, USS INDEPENDENCE will conduct torpedo defense daily at sunset. Air Department will be set condition 11 and C&R Department set to condition 2, unless otherwise noted.

Thursday 7 September 1944   *Operation Stalemate II - Palau*

0430 Sounded flight quarters.
0458 Sounded general quarters.
0518 On a base course of 275°T, increased speed to 25 knots.
0525-0534 Launched 4 F6Fs for CAP and 4 TBMs for ASP.
0558 Launched 4 F6Fs for CAP, then changed speed to 29 knots.
The Hellcats had full fuel with belly tanks and weighed 13,500 lbs. The avengers carried two 325 lb bombs with a full load of fuel and launched weighing 15,600 lbs. The flight had smooth seas with a wind of 4 knots from the NW. Wind over the deck averaged 27 knots.
0605 Secured from general quarters. Air Department remained at flight quarters.
0624 Changed speed of disposition to 18 knots.
0635 HOUSTON, MIAMI and VINCENNES left the disposition to form a new column inside the destroyer screen on the right flank.
0715 CruDiv 14 consisting of light cruisers HOUSTON, MIAMI and VINCENNES left the formation to shell the Palau Islands. The three cruisers were of the Cleveland Class, sharing the basic original hull design of the INDEPENDENCE.
0804 Changed fleet speed to 25 knots.
0813 Changed course to 255°T. The sea was calm with the wind over the deck registering 30 knots.
0819-0827 Catapulted 8 F6Fs for CAP and 4 TBMs for ASP.
0844-0859 Steering various courses at various speeds to recover 8 Hellcats and 4 Avengers launched this morning prior to 0600.
The Independence assumed various courses and speeds until 1154 when, pointed into the wind, she catapulted 8 Hellcats for CAP and 4 Avengers for ASP.
1206 BUNKER HILL pilot Lt.(jg) H.T. Brownscome landed aboard the INDEPENDENCE. Brownscome's Hellcat was hit in the cockpit by anti-aircraft fire over target on Palau Island. He was admitted to sickbay for treatment of superficial shrapnel wounds to his face and chest.
1228 Changed course to 310°T, speed 30 knots.
1243 Completed recovery of aircraft launched at 0819. They then steered on various courses at various speeds to regain station.
1320 Changed course to 280°T, speed 25 knots.
1355 Reduced speed to 18 knots.
1440 USS MILLER reported sound contact bearing 290°T from that vessel. Changed course on signal to 205°T. Minutes later the contact report was classified as non-submarine.
1510 After various course and speed changes, INDEPENDENCE once again was turned into the wind for launching the next CAP of 8 Hellcats and ASP of 4 Avengers. By 1538 they also had recovered the patrols launched at noon. INDEPENDENCE returned to station within the disposition only to again pull out of position at 1800. Meanwhile CruDiv 14 slipped back into the formation at 1550, having shelled its target assignments.
1813 Completed recovery of the 8 Hellcats and 4 TBMs launched at 1520. The ship then returned to station on a fleet course of 100°T.
2030 INDEPENDENCE ended the day zigzagging on a base course of 090°T at 18 knots.
2106 The Air Department set condition 12. It was a very busy and exhausting day for all aboard the Mighty I. Engineering received a deserved "well done" for maintaining the 16 Hellcats in an "up" status at all times.

RADIO PRESS NEWS   SEPTEMBER 7, 1944   **PAGE ONE**

THE EXTREMELY DIFFICULT WE DO IMMEDIATELY
THE IMPOSSIBLE TAKES A LITTLE WHILE LONGER

REPORTS FROM 38.1, 38.2, 38.3 OVER PALAU

Our planes arrived over the target at 1405 and commenced attack.
Little or no opposition was encountered, except that at one time it was mentioned that two rescue planes
South of Peleliu were under attack and several planes sent to their aid. All planes returned and landed
aboard safely.

REPORTS FROM 38.4 AT YAP.

Attacks on Yap were going on at the same time. From conversations heard, opposition was a little
heavier, with zeros in the air. Two to three planes were missing when the groups rendezvoused to return
to base, and it was reported that two had crashed, one while making a dive on the town.

Reports intercepted by planes from 38.1, 38.2 and 38.3 over Palau were highly favorable all day. There was
no air opposition whatsoever, and A.A. fire of all types was meager. No surface ships were encountered,
but one small boat was reported burning between Angaur and Peleliu. A couple of badly shot up planes
were the only things visible on the runways. In the afternoon, our planes were picking their targets
leisurely and carefully. Judging from conversations, a camouflaged radio station and radar installations
were coming in for a good deal of attention. The cruisers bombarded the islands throughout the day, but
no results have been stated. No tally could be kept of our own casualties, but they appeared to be
extremely light.

Reports from 38.4 from Yap were very fragmentary, the only reports intercepted being from planes
bombing warehouses and radio installations.

GUAM   <u>**7 September 1944**</u>
*Well, that night passed without incident. Seems almost too good to be true. Today, a five deck load strike
(approximately 1300 sorties including a fighter sweep) hit Palau and Angaur. At the same time 38.4 hit
Yap and Ulithi Islands in the north. The little yellow men are probably wondering what the hell and
where are they coming from?*
*For 48 hours this task group has been roaming the ocean between the Palau Islands and the Philippines
with out a sign of the Jap air arm or their fleet. Their silence has provoked many discussions—some say
they are waiting for us to hit in the Philippines proper.*
*Others claim their air fleet has been moved back to Formosa and to Japan itself. Our submarines,
scouting and screening north of us, report a few cruisers and DD's in Manila Bay.*
*So far it has been so quiet that there are some aboard who are giving odds that our gun's won't fire in
Angaur. However, I'm not one to tempt fate in this manner.*
*In addition to our strike this morning, this afternoon we fueled the entire fleet within 500 miles of Davao
in Mindanao. This surely should stir up something because we are now on our way to hit Mindanao.*
GUAM

***DL** PRECISELY what it meant for Independence to become a full-fledged night operating carrier was
made clear within days of its announcement. Almost everything was turned upside down. No single
person, officer or enlisted man, escaped. Ordinary seatime activities had to be adjusted to the new
reality.*

A small, vital revision to the ship's structure had to be made before she assumed her new role. The jury-rigged method the electricians of the 4th Division devised to illuminate an extremely narrow path along the port side of the flightdeck won the prize. Approaching pilots would use it to line up with as they sought their way home in darkness. The ship's original design had called for the installation of electric conduits fore and aft on either side. That wasn't the problem. The problem was how to shield the glow of the lights from any lurking enemy submarine or snooping aircraft.

Simple solution: soup cans! Campbell Soup? Tomato? Chicken and Rice? The galley was told to preserve a score or more such containers. The paint shop dulled the interiors with a coat of bland reflecting paint while the exteriors received a flat black treatment. These were then secured along the port edge of the deck, with a hole drilled in each to accept the wiring the electricians hooked up to complete the job. A primitive setup, but it worked.

My personal belief, however, has always been that a major reason the whole shooting match came together and held was the quiet, insistent drive of our new Captain Ewen. He had help, of course. But deck officers need a driving force to push them as well as coolies do. He must have laid down a strict demand that they do the job he wanted or take a walk on the plank back to Pearl and beyond. This in turn triggered incentives causing every sailor aboard to turn-to with an eagerness that probably surprised every hand.

*It surprised me. Dan's recent loss[*1.] was not forgotten, of course, but the fact of it receded into the rush of things that had to be done today. His life was over, ours were subject to daily change.*

What the new Captain did for his ship, the fresh skipper of Air Group 41 did for his new breed of night flying pilots and aircrewmen. His name was Turner Caldwell, a full Commander. Because our normal life had been disrupted by the arrival of this group, we wisenheimer airdales looked carefully at the man in charge of this band of winged warriors. He must possess something extra, something that made him stand out above his peers. He did, indeed. ([*1.] Daniel Lee Rinick on 23 August)

To most of us (and certainly to me) every flattop pilot was a hero to begin with. But these particular kids were going to be launched well after dark, in almost any weather, to search black skies to see what they could see. If they met enemy planes and pilots, an immediate kill-or-be-killed bout of combat would ensue. If they survived such an encounter, they would return to our pencil-thin deck in the dead of night and do their best to come back aboard in one piece without smashing any hardware or killing anyone including themselves. And do it night after night, not as a matter of routine but because they were trained and ready and probably would not have wanted any other assignment. That they were young and sharp was taken for granted. A few AOM's thought they must be nuts.
Their skipper didn't think so. Commander Caldwell held their lives in his heart.

While AOM's were not the only airdales affected by Mighty I's night carrier designation, we lived and worked pretty much in a closed, self-protective world all our own. What problems any other craft had to adjust to were their problems.
But there had been holes in our training. At the Chicago school Phil and I had graduated from almost eighteen months ago, not once had we received instruction in field stripping or otherwise tearing down an aircraft machine gun in the dark. We had learned to do it under a hood—like changing film in a camera. Now it became clear that was an inadequate technique. Nor had we loaded or unloaded mock bombs and depth charges or—heaven forbid—aerial torpedoes in our backyard TBF. Nor had performed the simplest mechanics of servicing F6F guns. Or replaced ammo cans or changed rifling-stripped barrels. Or tried bore sighting while wearing very dark glasses.

Independence had missed the great sea/air fight known to history as the Battle of the Philippine Sea. But from the day she rejoined the fleet in July at Pearl and sortied south and west to Eniwetok under a new skipper and carrying a new air group as well as a new assignment, she was in the thick of everything involving the Third Fleet's mighty Task Force 38. And when it became the Fifth Fleet and Task Force 58 under a new command structure, she was still there. There was not much of anything in the subsequent Pacific War that did not involve either TF 38 or TF 58. Both were powerful beasts, but only the designations and a few top officers changed. The ships stayed the same.

For the Philippine Campaign that was shaping the force was divided into four carrier Task Groups made up eight new, big Essex-class CV's, mighty Enterprise—the only Pacific survivor[1.] *of the prewar flattops—and eight of the nine CVL's. Together, these carriers were able to loft one thousand combat aircraft. Nothing so daunting had ever split the planet's ocean seas.*

Of the CVL's, CTG 38.1 under VADM McCain had Monterey and Cowpens. 38.2 under RADM Gerry Bogan were graced with Cabot and Independence. Carrier Task Group 38.3 under RADM Freddie Sherman boasted Princeton and Langley, while CTG 38.4 under RADM Ralph Davison possessed Belleau Wood and San Jacinto. ([1.] Correcting Don: The USS SARATOGA CV-3 also survived)

Bossing TF 38 was VADM Mark Mitscher, but his boss was the redoubtable Admiral Bill Halsey, Commander of the Third Fleet in battleship New Jersey. Halsey's reputation as a bulldog had preceded him. Some high-ranking younger men had their doubts, but the job was his and he seemed ready for the slashing carrier war that lay ahead. Many lives were at the mercy of his personality.

Independence was sort of an odd-man-out member of TG 38.2. With our night Air Group 41 under Turner Caldwell, we would be part of the Task Group all day long, enjoying the protection of its massive strength as well as adding ours. After dark, however, our fate was dumped pretty much into our own hands. We would break away, with a destroyer as escort, steaming most of the time at flank speed to put as much distance between us and the task force somewhere beyond the horizon. We all knew it was there, but Jeezus—those first few nights alone on the enemy's sea were scary.

And yet there was light in the dark. An anonymous philosophic jerk somewhere was of the opinion that you can get used to anything—and maybe it's true. It was true in the speed with which we became accustomed to the darkness as we moved about the flightdeck, as we hastily opened and closed our notorious bomb elevator magazine hatch cover, or when we trundled those clumsy skids to and from the aircraft.

On most nights there was light on the water and a dim and dull silvery glow from the sky between layers of clouds. No wonder Halsey wanted us clear of the task force! No wonder our engineering officers worried that sooner or later some crucial gear would break, some indispensable valve would fail to close, that the constant demands from the bridge for speed and more speed would prove to be the camel's backbreaking straw. And no wonder that no single destroyer accompanied us night after night. It was always a different one. Duty with Independence was demanding.

The worst moments came when the planes taxied forward up the deck in single file to the catapults. Hot, bluish fire spouted from engine exhaust and lighted ever-so-slightly the whole show. We'd follow it as the airplane shot into the air, struggling for altitude, while we hoped no lurking Jap submarine was watching.
While the planes were away, we would often go below to partake of Frenchie's galley crew's horsecock [2.] *sandwiches and sugar sweet black coffee. Almost nobody talked. Everyone's eyes were bleary. Every airdale's shoulders slouched with weariness. No one's task was harder than the next guy's. We would march to the nearest head and piss the coffee away before climbing the nearest ladder back to the flightdeck. There we awaited the return of our chickens.*

In the morning Independence would resume her place in formation. Our friendly destroyer faded into the swarm of small ships. Her men, too, were bushed.

Tomorrow night and the next one and all the nights between now and January would be the same. We were lucky we didn't know what the forces of wind and weather and the savage, suicidal hatred of men at war would reveal. **DL** ([2.] slang for bologna sandwiches)

GUAM

On this date the 3rd fleet under Admiral Halsey, started the ball rolling in Tojo's front yard by striking the Palau Islands in the Caroline Islands. 516 Miles from Mindanao of the Philippines.
The Independence, a part of the fleet (38.2) {being one of four carrier task forces) is on its way for the first time since it was torpedoed at Tarawa. This time we are planning a new and very difficult role. We are the first combat carrier to carry a complete night air group. It is Air Group N 41, and is under the

command of Commander Turner F. Caldwell holder of 3 navy crosses.

Since we are within striking range of the Jap's land bombers and torpedo planes, our group does not strike Palau today but is held in readiness to intercept the night attacks that may emanate from the Philippines.

Much speculation has been ventured as to how much of an air attack we will be subject to during the forth coming operations, we know that MacArthur's Liberators are pounding the three major airfields (Digos, Davao and Davao 11) on the island of Mindanao nightly but it's a cinch for the Japs to stage an attack from the north.

Question number 2 is, will the Jap fleet come out, we are ready if they do and of course we are hoping they will. We have the largest group of combat ships ever assembled for one under-taking. All told we have approximately 6BB's including Halsey's Flagship the New Jersey, and 8 CV's and 8 CVL'S, 20 cruisers and 60 DD's, these ships are divided into five task groups 38.1,38.2, 38.3, 38.4, 38.5. The first four groups are carrier task groups while the latter is the BB group. It is obvious that we have plenty with which to meet the Japs.

Getting back to our strike of today, it went off with a great deal of ease. A 100 fighter plane sweep went in. No air opposition was encountered and not too much AA fire. We had bogies on the screen but nothing to worry about yet. Perhaps tonight will be the time for all good Betty's to prowl. ***GUAM***

Friday 8 September 1944   ***Operation Stalemate II - Palau***
                                        Palau, Angaur & Peleliu

0430 Steaming on course 285°T, 18 knots. Sounded flight quarters.

0440 USS VINCENNES assumed formation guide from USS OAKLAND. INDEPENDENCE bears 090°T, 7,500 yards from guide.

0458 Sounded general quarters.

0530-0538 With a calm sea, wind over the deck at 31 knots, INDEPENDENCE launched 8 Hellcats for CAP and 4 Avengers for ASP. ASP searches had become dull and routine, but a necessity, hunting for enemy subs. Aircraft availability was described as "remarkable", due to diligent maintenance crews.

0600 Secured from general quarters. USS MIAMI, YARNALL, CUSHING, COLAHAN, HALSEY POWELL, BENHAM, and TINGEY departed the Task Group to proceed to the fueling area.

0610 Mustered crew on stations.

0613 Changed course to 240°T, speed 22 knots for BUNKER HILL flight operations.

0715 Changed course to 090°T, speed 18 knots.

0815 USS BUNKER HILL became guide. INDEPENDENCE bears 135°T, 3,500 yards from guide.

0823 Changed fleet course to 240°T, speed 20 knots.

0854-0905 Recovered aircraft launched at 0530.

0920 Secured from flight quarters.

1108 Changed fleet course to 260°T, speed 20 knots.

1126 USS YARNELL came alongside to transfer a passenger to this vessel.

1143 With the transfer of Capt. Edward W. McClure, USMCR, aboard for special temporary additional duty, YARNELL cast off and pulled away.

1200 In company of USS CABOT and SAN DIEGO, changed course to 160°T, and speed to 24 knots, then commenced various courses and speeds while proceeding to the fueling area.

1220 Arrived at fueling area and commenced approach to fleet tanker USS KASKASKIA steaming on course 285°T, speed 10 knots.

1306 Passed first line to USS KASKASKIA, on starboard side. 1330 Commenced receiving fuel oil.

1509 Completed fueling having received 282,961 gallons of fuel oil and cast off all lines.

1514 Commenced various courses and speeds while CABOT completed fueling.

1535 In company with USS SAN DIEGO and CABOT, INDEPENDENCE is guide steaming on course 292°T, speed 27 knots to rejoin Task Group 38.2.

1619 Sighted Task Group 38.2 bearing 270°T, 18.5 miles.

1707 Changed speed to 28 knots. Commenced maneuvering to regain position in formation with guide USS VINCENNES, disposition 5R5, axis 270°T, fleet speed 25 knots.

1755 Resumed position, guide bears 270°T, 7,500 yards.

1823 USS OAKLAND became guide.

1826 Sounded torpedo defense.

1900 Changed course to 295°T.

2116 Air Department set condition 12.

GL *Still at Palau. Have had no opposition. This evening headed for the Philippines. They say the Japs have 1500 planes in the Philippines.* *GL*

RC *Our planes hit the islands of Palau, Angaur & Peleliu. We hit these islands for three days and refueled in the late afternoon of the 8th.* *RC*

HB *On September 8, we left to go on to the Philippines. This was the first time the Americans had been back near the Philippines since the Japanese took them early in the war.*

We continued raids on the Philippine islands of Mindanao and Cebu for several days until pulling back to refuel at sea. One of my jobs, when we refueled, was to operate the huge drum holding the lines securing the ships at a safe distance apart. The lines were necessary because of the rough seas. Eight to ten seamen manned these lines. Quite a few hands were required since the lines were four or five inches in diameter. These lines were wrapped several times around the drum I operated; then they went over to the oil tanker. My job was to keep any slack out and to hold the bows of the two ships together.

Many times, as we got the oil lines all connected, the Japanese would send planes out, and we would have to break loose the lines and separate our ships a safe distance apart. Our planes were launched and shot the Japanese down so we could get the tanker back alongside to take on our fuel. Sometime it would take 2 or 3 days to get fueled up and ready for another raid. *HB*

Saturday 9 September 1944   *Philippines, Mindanao*

The days operations were off Mindanao.

Steaming with Task Unit 38.2.1 in company with USS BUNKER HILL (OTC), CABOT and INTREPID, disposition 5R5, base course 295°T, speed 25 knots. INDEPENDENCE bears 090°T, 2,500 yards from USS OAKLAND, guide.

0345 THE SULLIVANS, stationed as a picket, reported a surface contact bearing 250°T, 15,000 yards from that vessel.

0521-0754 Manned general quarters stations.

1252 Made daily inspection of the magazines. Conditions normal except for fuel oil leak in overflow vent lines in A516-M and 517-M. (The "M" suffix indicating an Ammunition storage compartment.)

1303 The oil is being removed and these magazines cleaned.

1611 Changed course to 150°T, speed 25 knots.

1630 Sounded flight quarters.

1726 Commenced launching 4 Hellcats for a night fighter picket. The time to launch these 4 fighters was 1 minute and 16 seconds.

1853 Changed course to 250°T, speed 20 knots.

1856 BUNKER HILL again became guide. INDEPENDENCE bears 135°T, 3,500 yards from guide.

1909-1913 On a course of 250°T, speed 30 knots, recovered the 4 Hellcats launched at 1726.

2120 Changed course to 090°T, speed 18 knots.

UNITED STATES PACIFIC FLEET
CVLG-(N)-41   **NIGHT INTRUDER MISSION**   **8 September 1944.**

1. Launch three and one half to four hours before dawn, a total of two planes for each airfield to be heckled. If the total number of planes exceeds six, two groups should be formed and they should proceed to the target independently.

2. The rendezvous should be executed with lights on and the last plane to join up should blink turtle back light until all planes have rendezvoused. At this time the planes will depart for target with all lights out.

3. All radios should be checked on the deck by listening to planes in the air if possible. A good fast procedure for checking would be as follows: Check with another ship rather than own. "Hello Tiger" this is "Cupid ll" checking, over. All planes (in order if possible) do the same. "Hello Tiger" this is "Cupid 12", checking etc.

4. Good interplane communication is necessary over the target area. and *no* plane should be launched without it.

5. Pilots may open out to check their gear, but should not lose the leader as a delay in a second rendezvous may mean failure of the mission. While opened out test all guns.

6. Pilots should check ZBX to determine how far out they can expect to receive the Y.E. when they return.

7. The ideal load for the F6F would be a belly tank incendiary and one 500 pound fragmentation bomb or incendiary cluster. The F6F can carry one flare, but the TBM can carry twelve. Neither plane can carry both bombs and flares.

8. The use of flares is more helpful in blinding the ground personnel than aiding the pilot, while the belly tank bomb would light the area for other attacks. A flare striking the ground before it goes out will set a good fire for target illumination.

9. A TBM could lay a stick of four (4) 500' pound bombs along the main runway and thereby prevent aircraft from taking off.

10. Conserve your ammunition! Use two guns at a time when feasible. Such as destroying a search light or strafing a fire party trying to put out fires around the field. Don't use the out board guns until daylight as they are loaded with tracer.

11. If AA gets too hot, retire and come back when things quiet down. You need not go very far and remember that every burst looks like it is right on top of you at night, but you are OK unless you feel the explosion.

12. Night evasive action for anti-aircraft fire should be primarily keeping "plenty of speed" and change altitude as you notice the burst. Remember they cannot see you and they are most likely firing at a set altitude.

13. Destroy any and all search lights as soon as they come on. Don't get so steep as to tumble your gyros, as you'll probably have to make an instrument pull out.

14. Watch carefully for aircraft taking off, and try to get them before they get their wheels up. Don't go too close before shooting; remember bore-sight pattern.

15. If conditions are as good as they are ever going to be, start your attacks. Each plane announcing his attack and direction such as: "SMITH ATTACKING FROM SOUTH" - then "SMITH COMPLETED ATTACK".

16. If a plane notices a good target on a run he should tell the other plane about it if it can be easily described or hit it himself on the next run. Prime TARGETS would be: 1. Aircraft, 2. Ships, 3. Gas facilities, 4. Hangars, and 5. Buildings.

17. (a) A good method of rendezvous is all planes take a magnetic heading away from the target and most likely it will be light by the time you get to far from the target. Planes should return in at least two plane sections with identification on.
    (b) For full dark rendezvous, choose some prominent landmark such as a point, or small island which can be seen under any light conditions. Also have an alternate rendezvous in case a rain squall covers the primary one.

18. When nearing the formation do not go below 2000 feet if ceiling permits. If forced very low, come in, in a series if course changes; to indicate you are not boring in for an attack. If you do not get instructions, orbit outside ten miles distance, flash emergency lights. This will wake them up.

Japanese Aircraft

All aircraft designs are compromises. The Japanese entered the war with advanced designs for the period, however they too had their share compromises. For speed, rate of climb, maneuverability, and range, many of their designs lacked features that offered pilot and aircrew protection, such as self sealing fuel tanks and armor plating in critical areas (to save weight). This strategy depends on the aircrafts agility, and the pilots ability, to stay out of the adversaries gun sights. Japanese pilot ability degraded as the war progressed (and, as US aircraft designs advanced) . The following pages give a very brief look at some of Japan's aircraft that are noted within this book.

"**Frank**" Nakajima Ki-84 fighter

"**George**"   Kawanishi N1K fighter

"**Oscar**" Nakajima Ki-43 Type *1 Hayabusa* fighter

"**Tojo**"   Nakajima Ki-44 *Shoki* fighter

"**Tony**" Kawasaki Ki-61 *Hien* fighter

"**Tony**" Kawasaki Ki-100 Type 5 fighter

"**Zero** or **Zeke**" Mitsubishi A6M Type 0 *Reisen* fighter (**HAP** Type 2)

Japanese Aircraft

"**Nick**" Kawasaki Ki-45 *Toryu* heavy fighter

"**Frances**" Yokosuka P1Y *Ginga* bomber

"**Dinah**" Mitsubishi Ki-46 reconnaissance aircraft

"**Jill**" Nakajima B6N *Tenzan* torpedo bomber

"**Betty**" Mitsubishi G4M medium bomber

"**Sally**" Mitsubishi Ki-21 Type 97 bomber

"**Grace**" Aichi B7A *Ryusei* torpedo dive bomber

"**Judy**" Yokosuka D4Y *Suisei* dive bomber

"**Val**" Aichi D3A dive bomber

"**Topsy**" Mitsubishi Ki-57 transport

Japanese Aircraft

"**Emily**" Kawanishi H8K Type 2 flying boat

"**Mavis**" Kawanishi H6K patrol flying boat

"**Jake**" Aichi E13A Type Zero
reconnaissance seaplane

"**Rufe**" Nakajima A6M2-N *Suisen 2*
float seaplane, fighter bomber
(Zero on floats)

Japan was not able to keep pace with the U.S. in the supply of desperately needed aircraft. Another issue that would hamper them operationally was the problem of having correct spare repair parts on hand, for the changing mix of widely dispersed aircraft currently at the specific individual airfields, when the parts were needed.

Equally critical was the failure to keep pace with a steady stream of well trained replacement pilots ready for combat. This was a major flaw in Japan's planning, especially within the aviation ranks. A worsening shortfall of skilled aviators and technicians would prove fatal to the Empire's increasingly futile efforts. After late 1943, due to fuel shortages and the ever pressing need for replacement pilots, the intermediate phase of the pilot training program was scraped in favor of operational training in combat aircraft with tactical units. "This would result in heavy losses"*. Additionally, Japanese planners would underestimate the attrition rate.   (* post war interrogation of Rear ADM Seizo Katsumata, IJN)

GUAM   **9 September 1944**
This morning we again sent in the fighter sweep to prepare the way for our TBFs and SB2Cs. No shipping has been found as yet so many operational air fields and the city of Davao will be the targets. While we, 38.1 and 2 and 3 are wanging away at Mindanao. 38.4 is hitting the Palau islands again. This bombing and shelling has been done with remarkable smoothness and precision. Our planes have encountered no air opposition and only a moderate degree of AA fire. They were scheduled to go in and heckle the target tonight. But the trip was cancelled much to our pilot's disgust. ***GUAM***

Sunday 10 September 1944   *Philippines, Mindanao*

Steaming as before. The Task Group is continuing strikes against Mindanao today.
0521 Sounded routine morning general quarters.
0621 Secured from general quarters. Air Department set condition 14.
0710 USS OAKLAND designated group guide. Changed axis to 225°T.
1113 Commenced zigzagging (Plan No. 6) on base course 215°T.

Chapter 13   349

1130 Sighted land, Mindanao, bearing 270°T, distance 60 miles.

1256 Changed fleet course to 225°T, fleet speed 20 knots.

The sea was moderate and wind over the deck averaged 26 knots as crews made ready for launching aircraft. Pilots would have 6 miles visibility, with an overcast ceiling at 7,000'.

1307-1314 Catapulted 8 Hellcats for CAP and 4 Avengers for ASP. Changed speed to 23 knots.

1327 Catapulted 1 F6F Hellcat as a replacement for one returning with a mechanical problem. At 1329 INDEPENDENCE then recovered a Hellcat from the group launched twenty minutes earlier, returning back to the flight deck due to an oil leak. At 1330, fleet course changed to 090°T.

1522 Changed speed to 24 knots and ceased zigzagging.

1541-1546 Catapulted 8 Hellcats for CAP and 4 Avengers for ASP.

1550 Changed speed to 30 knots.

1603 Changed course to 240°T and commenced maneuvering preparatory to recovering aircraft.

1630 Completed recovery of 7 F6Fs and 4 TBMs (launched at 1307) and 1 F6F launched at 1327.

1755 At a speed of 25 knots, we changed course to 069°T, proceeding to station to recover aircraft.

1827 Changed course left to 240°T, then began maneuvering into the wind to recover aircraft.

1832 Sounded torpedo defense.   1837 Darkened ship.

1841 Completed recovery of 8 F6Fs and 4 TBMs launched at 1541. Steering various courses at various speeds to regain position in Task Group.

1920 Arrived in position, USS OAKLAND guide, bearing 225°T at 2,500 yards, zigzagging on a base course of 090°T, speed 18 knots.

1932 Secured from torpedo defense.   2131 Air Department set condition 12.

GL *Attacked Mindanao again today. Still no opposition. They say the Japs took all their planes to Luzon.* *GL*

GUAM   10 September 1944

Today was a repeat of yesterdays attack. Fact of the matter is, so little was left of the targets the 4th and 5th strikes were called off. It looks like we are wasting our time around here. 38.4. is still alternately bombing and fueling at Peleliu and Angaur. They are having a field day with no air opposition and almost no AA fire.

*We arm chair strategists feel that we should forget about our bombing attacks scheduled for Mindanao on the 12th and 13th and 14th and go after bigger game, namely the Island of Luzon. There perhaps we will find enough aircraft and shipping to make this trip a grand slam. Knowing Admiral Halsey's reputation for fighting, we expect such a move. Flash---at 1800 we received word that the Island of Luzon has been picked to come in for a share of 3rd fleet might. Further word concerning where, when and how is forthcoming, maybe now we will see some action. This new move is a welcome one for the past five days have been boring. Our only excitement came from the sighting of the Island of Davao from the Ship. The entire fleet had moved within two miles off the island and the mountain range east of Davao was plainly visible from the forecastle. *GUAM**

Monday 11 September 1944   *Philippines, Mindanao - Fueling*

Steaming with Task Unit 38.2.1 (of Task Group 38.2) in cruising disposition 5R5, course 090°T, speed 19 knots, axis 225°T. INDEPENDENCE bears 045°T, 2,500 yards relative to USS OAKLAND (guide).

0501 Sounded general quarters. Air Department set condition 14.

The INDEPENDENCE would make numerous course changes throughout the day as the fleet retired to an area to refuel.

0601 Secured from general quarters.

0705 On a fleet course and new fleet axis of 315°T, speed 12 knots, guide shifted to tanker USS PATUXENT. INDEPENDENCE bears 135°T from the guide at 6,500 yards.

0719 Changed fleet speed to 10 knots.

0824 Commenced zigzagging independently and changed speed to 12 knots.

1025 Steadied on course 315°T.

1104 USS EVANS came alongside starboard quarter, delivered & received mail, and conveyed over Lt. (jg) W.E. Lamoreaux for the purpose of returning the F6F to USS BUNKER HILL that Lt.(jg) Brownscombe had landed aboard on September 7th.

1123 Cast off from USS EVANS. Commenced maneuvering on various courses and at various speeds to approach the tanker USS PATUXENT, on a course of 315°T, speed 12 knots.

1210 Arrived in position with USS PATUXENT for refueling.   1250 Receiving fuel oil.

1407 USS NEW JERSEY and IOWA, with two cruisers and four destroyers sighted hull down on horizon, bearing 180°T.

1430 Cast off all lines from USS PATUXENT having taken on 195,918 gallons of fuel oil and 25,000 gallons of aviation gasoline. Maneuvering to assume position off guide, USS PATUXENT.

1450 In position, bearing 135°T, 6,500 yards from guide.

1500 USS NEW JERSEY and IOWA joined the disposition.

1536 Began emergency maneuvers to avoid carrier conducting flight operations into the wind.

1548 Resumed position in the disposition after emergency maneuvering.

1646 Formed cruising disposition 5R5.

1657 USS NEW JERSEY became guide, axis 225°T, course 315°T, speed 20 knots.

1709 Catapulted 1 Hellcat of Air Group 17 for return to USS BUNKER HILL (see 1104 - above).

1732 Changed course to 315°T.

1748 USS STEPHEN POTTER steamed up alongside the starboard side to deliver guard mail.

1749 Maneuvered to regain position in the formation, course 315°T.

1818-1918 Exercised routine sunset torpedo defense.

2120 Air Department set condition 12.

Tuesday 12 September 1944   *Philippines - Cebu, Bohol, Leyte, Negros*

Steaming with Task Unit 38.2.1 in cruising disposition 5R5 of Task Group 38.2., course 315°T, speed 20 knots, axis 225T. INDEPENDENCE bears 180°T, 2,500 yards relative to (guide) USS NEW JERSEY. Course 315°T, speed 20 knots.

0450 Sounded flight quarters.

0519 Sounded general quarters.

0609 Commenced various courses at various speeds into the wind to launch aircraft.

0610-0612 The sea was moderate, visibility 5 to 6 miles with 8/10 cloud cover, ceiling 7,000' when 8 F6F-5Ns were catapulted for a four quadrant sector search to extend out 200 miles ahead of the Task Force for Japanese presence.

0620 Secured from general quarters.

0632 Secured from flight quarters. Air Department set condition 13.

0707 Changed course to 310°T, speed 19 knots. USS THE SULLIVANS pulled alongside the starboard quarter to deliver mail.   0721 USS THE SULLIVANS cast off.

0725 Fleet axis changed to 300°T. Maneuvered to new position on guide USS NEW JERSEY, bearing 300°T, 2,500 yards.

0755 Flying in pairs in their search sector, Ens. R.W. Klock and his wingman G.W. Obenour were at 500' when they sighted a Model 11 Betty bomber flying at 700-1000' altitude 4 miles ahead and closing. The squadron was eager for action and *"The two kids jumped it like hungry wolves"*. The brown Betty, sporting red meatballs, did not see the two Hellcats at first as it passed over Klock and Obenour. They were roughly 200 miles from the INDEPENDENCE. The Hellcats climbed to an altitude of 800-1000' above the Betty and executed a highside run approaching from the rear at 5 to 7 o'clock. They caught the Betty crew napping. Short bursts from all six guns fired from 250 yards put tracers into the starboard engine, which flamed immediately. Both Hellcats repeated their runs concentrating on the port engine and wing roots. Flames erupted from the engine and fuselage. *"One Jap was seen to jump from the plane; another was seen to attempt to do so, but failed."* The Betty exploded upon impact with the water. A considerable amount of flaming debris was strewn on the water for several hundred feet. The two Ensigns drew first blood for VF(N)-41, with a shared kill, half for each Ensign.

0904 Changed course to 120°T.

0928 Commenced various courses at various speeds into the wind to recover aircraft launched at 0612.

0930 Klock and Obenour entered the traffic circle and landed back aboard *"Cupid"*.

0942 Completed recovering the 8 F6Fs. Sounded torpedo defense.

0943 Secured from torpedo defense.

INDEPENDENCE steamed at various courses and various speeds throughout the afternoon.

1613 Ceased zigzagging, steadied on course 010°T.

1617 Changed fleet course to 270°T. Proceeded to station to launch aircraft.

1633 Completed catapulting 4 TBMs for ASP, and 12 F6Fs for CAP covering the Task Group under FDO (Fighter Direction Officer) direction. The patrol split into divisions of 4 each, one division took station at 5,000', the other at 10,000'. (1 division = 4 planes, 1 Section = 2 planes)

1634 Steered on various courses at various speeds to resume station in the formation.

1803 Changed course to 265°T. Steamed on various courses at various speeds for recovery of aircraft.

1824 Lt. W.E. Henry, and Ens. J.S Berkheimer, J.A. Barnett and F.A. Fisher where in their Hellcats on CAP at 10,000', flying 340°T, when they were informed by the FDO of a bogy crossing to port 30 miles ahead. At 1824 they were given new vectors with the updated report of two bogeys reported high almost above the fleet. Applying W.E.P. (Wartime Emergency Power) Henry and Berkheimer climbed to 24,000'. Barnett and Fishers W.E.P. malfunctioned and lagged behind in the climb.

Late evening twilight, dull skies, freezing rain, sleet at 20,000', rain squalls lower. Flying thru a sleet—like rain squall, Henry spotted a twin engine plane 1,000' below at 2 miles. The silhouette was that of a Dinah, which ducked into a large cloud and disappeared. Then Henry spotted another Dinah 1,000' below him, 2 miles away. The second Dinah flashed a red join up light several times, indicating the Dinah pilot thought that Henry was his wingman (the other Dinah). Henry obliged, and closed for a high run from the rear firing from 7 o'clock at 750'. Tracers hit the starboard engine, which started to smoke. The Dinah nosed over sharply leveling again at 16,000'. Berkheimer at first, had a difficult time seeing Henrys target. He watched as Henry made a second pass, opening fire from 8 o'clock high at a distance of 500 feet. Henry's tracers sprayed the Dinah from engine to engine. Both engines began to flame, and pieces of wing flew off. Then flames died down. Berkheimer made his run from 5'oclock high, closed to 1,500', opened up and hit the starboard wing root and engine. He pulled off his target at 500' after 3 short burst, taking away additional pieces of wing and tail section. Henry made a third pass level from the stern pulling the trigger briefly at 200', and the Dinah started to burn again. The sand colored Dinah pulled up slowly, rolled over and exploded *"like a magnesium flare"*.

At 1846 Henry announced on VHF *"Splash one Dinah"*.

1830 Sounded torpedo defense.

1841 Completed recovering 8 of the 12 F6Fs, and 4 TBMs launched at 1633.

1846 Commenced maneuvering to resume station in formation.

1930 Secured from torpedo defense.

1945 Changed course to 250°T and began maneuvering on various courses at various speeds for recovery of aircraft.

2000-2007 Recovered the 4 F6Fs launched at 1633 flown by Henry, Berkheimer, Barnett and Fisher. *"Bill"* Henry and *"Berky"* Berkheimer each shared the Dinah. Both pilots complimented Lt. W.J. Sullivan for his efficient vectors as FDO aboard the INDEPENDENCE.

2037 Course 130°T, speed 21 knots.

2125 Enemy aircraft detected on radar bearing 250°T at 45 miles.

2127-2128 Sounded flight quarters. Then sounded torpedo defense. Changed fleet course to 220°T.
2140 Changed course to 130°T.
2145 Changed course to 100°T.
2148 Enemy aircraft closed to 18 miles, bearing 300°T. Flares reported, bearing 300°T.
2156 Changed course to 130°T.
2200 Enemy aircraft departed and faded from radar screen.   2209 Secured from torpedo defense.
2301 Changed course to 123°T.

GUAM   THE CENTRAL PHILIPPINES

Targets selected for this days working over the central Philippines, Leyte, Samar, Cebu, Negros, Panay, etc. Also the southern tip of Luzon. The usual five deck load strike proceeded by the fighter sweep are to be launched.

CVL(N)41 out of the strike scored first when Ensign Obenour and Ensign Klock knocked down a Betty, it was their first time in combat and they did all right.

The usual bogies appeared on the screen. Torpedo defense and condition 2 watches were set but all bogies were friendly.

During the evening CAP Lt. Bill Henry and Ensign Berkheimer got themselves a Dinah (reconnaissance plane). Both were vectored to the bogie until visual contact was made. Admiral Halsey called, personally over the TBS with a "GOD DAMN GOOD, CUPID (our call name) GOD DAMN GOOD". Admiral Bogan gave our pilots and CIC a well done.

During the day a 50' motor launch with 44 survivors was picked up by a destroyer**. The flagship New Jersey asked the Can to ascertain the most intelligent Japs and be prepared to transfer them to that ship.
GUAM   (** Note: The 44 survivors captured by USS MARSHALL were from the Japanese light cruiser NATORI, sunk by submarine USS HARDHEAD on 18 August 1944 off Samar.)

On this day, seeming small events transpired that will change the prosecution of the war. A Hellcat piloted by Ensign Thomas C. Tillar from USS HORNET ditched his F6F and was rescued by Filipinos. He learned from his rescuers that the Japanese forces were weak on Leyte. He was transferred to a SOC (Scout Observation Plane from the USS WICHITA) for return to the fleet. Admiral Halsey combined this aviator's report with other intelligence, drawing the conclusion that the Japanese forces on Leyte had been overestimated, and pushed for the date of the planned Leyte Campaign to be accelerated by two months.

Wednesday 13 September 1944   *Philippines - Cebu, Bohol, Leyte, Negros*

0430 Sounded flight quarters.
0522 Sounded general quarters.
0530 On a course of 290°T, 24 knots, completed launching 4 F6Fs (scrambled on orders of OTC).
0559 On a course of 260°T, 22 knots, completed catapulting 8 F6F-5Ns for a 200 mile sector search utilizing four 2 plane sections.
0645 Commenced various courses at various speeds into the wind for flight operations.
0654 As INDEPENDENCE was recovering the 4 Hellcats launched at 0530, 12 miles off on the port quarter Task Group 38.1 was observed firing on unidentified aircraft. (INDEPENDENCE is in TG 38.2)
0658 Changed course to 130°T, speed 20 knots.
0717 Secured from general quarters.
0724 Ens. J.A. Barnett and F.A. Fisher sighted a small submarine, which crash-dived as they approached. At 0800 they sighted another small sub, which took the same evasive action.
0810 Ens. R.W. Klock and E.R. Edwards sighted a third sub 80 miles east of Batag Island. It also crash-dived.
All three subs were on bearings that would have put them heading toward San Bernardino Strait. One of the subs was later identified as friendly.

0812 Ens. W.E. Miller and R.F. Peterson were in their Hellcats 135 miles north from "Cupid"* flying at 400'-500' when they sighted a Model 12 Betty 10 miles out flying at roughly 180 knots, only 50' above the water. The Hellcats closed at 260 knots indicated. The Betty crew sighted them and pushed the throttles forward to give a speed of 240 knots and descended to roughly 15' above the sea. The chase was on. Miller and Peterson closed and commenced a series of flat side runs back and forth on the bracketed Betty, hosing the engines and fuselage. The Betty flew through two rain squalls trying to lose the Hellcats. Barnett and Fisher searching in an adjoining sector observed the chase from about 1 mile away and joined the action. The Betty had lost speed due to damage inflicted by Miller and Peterson. Barnett made a highside run from the starboard forward side sweeping his tracers across the nose. The Betty pilot hit the water, bounced back into the air, then smacked into the water a second time. The Betty broke in two and floated on the surface without burning. Three survivors were observed on the wreckage. Miller, Peterson and Barnett each were given 1/3 credit for the Betty.   (* Cupid was the radio code name for INDEPENDENCE)

0926 Completed recovering the 8 Hellcats launched at 0559.
1330 Sighted Dinagat Island, bearing 242°T, distance 41 miles. (Dinagat Isl. is near Leyte Gulf - map page 334)
1336 Changed course to 100°T.
1356 USS MARSHALL came alongside starboard quarter to deliver and receive mail. MARSHALL cast off 1408.
1457 Changed course to 260°T and commenced steering various courses at various speeds to keep clear of USS BUNKER HILL while she recovered aircraft.
1622-1626 On a course of 180°T, launched 12 Hellcats for CAP and 4 Avengers for ASP.
1816-1830 Recovered 10 (of the 12) F6Fs and 4 TBMs launched at 1626.
1843-1844 Recovered the two remaining F6Fs launched at 1626.
1946 Changed course to 040°T, 18 knots
2100 On signal from OTC, changed course from 040°T to 120°T to avoid a possible submarine contact bearing 300°T, distance 8 miles, as reported by USS YARNALL. Contact was lost. The original course of 040°T was then resumed.

GUAM   13 September 1944   Philippines Mindanao
We launched the usual striking forces this day. Our air group picked off another Betty this morning during their CAP. Ensign Peterson and Ensign Miller made the first couple of passes and called Ensign Barnett to finish the Betty off when their guns jammed.
A sizable hornets nest was stirred up by our first fighter sweep.
*35 Zeros jumped 16 F6Fs - result, 20 Zekes shot down and 8 damaged. No information today on our own casualties. We are expecting them to be heavier than in the past few days since the Japs evidently staged in planes during the night. So far, the unofficial score is as follows: 38.2 – 63 planes shot down, damaged or destroyed. 38.3 -73 planes shot down and 118 damaged or destroyed.   **GUAM***

***GL**   Attacked Mindanao again. Task force got 63 planes, sunk a sub chaser *¹·, two 2500 ton ships. Our C.A.P. got another Betty.   **GL**   (*¹·* Three Subchasers; MOGAMI MARU, CH-12 KYO MARU & CH-55 were sunk. Numerous transports and cargo ships were sunk: NICHIEI MARU and RAKUTO MARU are a close match.)

Thursday 14 September 1944   *Philippines - Cebu, Leyte, Negros, Panay*

Steaming with Task Unit 38.2.1 (in cruising disposition 5R5) of Task Group 38.2, course 040°T, speed 18 knots, axis 300°T. INDEPENDENCE bears 120°T, 2,500 yards relative to guide. Rear Admiral G.F. Bogan is CTU in BUNKER HILL.
0430 Sounded flight quarters.
0522 Sounded general quarters.
0557 Began maneuvering on various courses at various speeds while launching aircraft.
0606 Completed launching 8 F6Fs for a search. The sea was moderate, wind 31 knots over the flight deck, launching the sector search into a sky with a 6 mile visibility, and a ceiling of 3,000'.

Six Hellcats were recovered at 0926. The remaining two were safely back on the flight deck at 1004.

1103 Secured from flight quarters.

1155 On a course of 255°T, speed 20 knots, sighted Dinagat Island bearing 242°T, distance 60 miles.

1545 Sounded flight quarters.

1632 Commenced steaming on various courses at various speeds while proceeding to flying station.

1706 Completed launching 12 F6Fs as a CAP, and 4 TBMs for ASP. These patrols were recovered from 1822 thru 1833.

1833-1935 Manned torpedo defense stations. Air Department was then set to condition 11.

GUAM   14 September 1944

Repeat of the 13th and 14th. Still hitting central Philippines. Air opposition was nil and AA fire less than yesterday and day before. Maybe they figure enough is enough. **GUAM**

GL *Was standing by to provide the air protection if needed for the invasion of the Palau Islands.* **GL**

AD *Still bombing Japs at Cebu.* **AD**

Friday 15 September 1944   *Palau Invasion (Marines begin landing on Palau)*

Cruising in disposition 5R5, base course 110°T, axis 300°T, speed 18 knots. USS NEW JERSEY (guide) bears 120°T at 2,500 yards. The ship is darkened. At 0150 they sounded flight quarters.

0257 Commenced steering various courses at various speeds while conducting flight operations.

0300-0309 Launched 4 F6Fs and 4 TBMs on a search mission, then changed course to 110°T.

0400 Secured from flight quarters.

0613-0620 Recovered all aircraft launched at 0309.

0630 Mustered crew on stations, then secured from general quarters.

0702 Changed fleet course to 110°T.

0945 USS BUNKER HILL assumed duties as guide. This vessel 165°T, 3,600 yards.

0949 Bat Div 7, Cru Div 14, and Des Ron 52 left the Task Group to form with Task Force 34. They were tasked to shell the Palau Islands.

1006 Changed station to circle 2, bearing 165°T, 2,800 yards from guide.

1015 USS OAKLAND became formation guide. INDEPENDENCE bears 120°T, 2,000 yards.

1450 Changed fleet axis to the left to 245°T, speed 12 knots.

1508 Changed fleet course to 200°T, speed 18 knots.

1615 Changed fleet course to 110°T, speed 15 knots.

1633 Opened distance to 2,500 yards to guide.

1705 Bat Div 7, Cru Div 14, and Des Ron 52 rejoined the Task Group.

1736 Changed fleet course to 220°T.   1737 INDEPENDENCE was designated guide.

1810 Changed course to 110°T. Sounded torpedo defense.

1820 USS IOWA and NEW JERSEY took positions in formation.

1824 NEW JERSEY designated guide, bearing 245°T, distance 2,500 yards.

1911 Secured from torpedo defense.

2100 Changed fleet course to 180°T.

2130 Air Department set at condition 12.

GUAM   15 September 1944

Left central Philippines area to be ready for anything the Japs might send to harass landings on Peleliu and Angaur. Also on our way to fueling position, about 100 miles from Peleliu.   **GUAM**

GL *Bombed Manila Bay on the 15th & 16th.* **GL**

RC *Marines landed on Palau, opposition pretty heavy. Our planes covered landings.* **RC**

Saturday 16 September 1944   *Refueling*

Today they retired, steaming to a designated fueling area.

0458 Sounded general quarters. One hour later, secured from general quarters. Air Department set to condition 14, all other departments set condition 3.

0610 Mustered crew to stations. Commenced maneuvering to approach the fueling area.

0755 Changed fleet speed to 10 knots.   0800 Changed fleet course to 245°T.

0820-0827 USS STOCKHAM was along starboard side to receive Lt. A.R. Allen and Comdr. Turner F. Caldwell for transfer from INDEPENDENCE to USS LEXINGTON for a conference.

1100 Steadied on course 254°T, speed 10 knots.

1107-1116 USS STEPHEN POTTER was alongside starboard side, delivering and receiving mail.

1123 Commenced steering various courses at various speeds to come alongside fleet tanker USS CACHE, on course 245°T, 10 knots.

1216 Draft forward 23'; draft aft: 25'4". Commenced receiving gasoline from USS CACHE.

1230 Commenced receiving fuel oil.

1401 Castoff all lines from USS CACHE having received 24,500 gallons of gasoline and 212,952 gallons of fuel oil. Draft forward 24'4"; draft aft: 24'11".

1404 Sounded flight quarters.

1409 Commenced maneuvering to assume position on (guide) USS CACHE.

1426 Took up position on USS CACHE, bearing 232°T, 6,500 yards.

1524 Secured from flight quarters. Air Department set condition 14. Then steadied on course 245°T, speed 10 knots as USS STOCKHAM came along starboard side to deliver Lt. Allen and Comdr. Caldwell back aboard INDEPENDENCE from their conference on the LEXINGTON.

1539 STOCKHAM cast off.

1622 Sounded flight quarters, then proceeded to flying station, steering at various courses, and speeds.

1653-1702 Landed on board 4 F6Fs (Bu. Nos. 58817, 58865, 58853 and 58881). These Hellcats were transferred from USS BARNES to the USS INDEPENDENCE as an additional combat team, piloted by; Ensigns D.A. Naughton, B.W. Piper, E.H. Nygaard, and W.E. Stephans.

1702 Steamed steering at various courses and speeds to regain position in the formation.

1745 Regained position in the formation, began zigzagging independently.

1806 Sounded torpedo defense.

1820 Task Group 38.2 formed cruising disposition 5R5 on base course 340°T, axis 245°T, speed 15 knots. USS NEW JERSEY assumed guide, INDEPENDENCE bearing 065°T, 2,500 yards from guide.

1830 Secured from flight quarters. Air Department set condition 14.

1903 Secured from torpedo defense.

2057 Changed fleet course to 340°T, speed 16 knots.

GB We pulled back on September 16 to refuel near Palau. GB

AD Still at sea refueling, received mail. AD

GUAM   16 September 1944

Nothing happened yesterday as far as we are concerned. Our BB's and CA's went in to cover landings which incidentally, are reported to be pretty tough sledding, Marines ran into about 10,000 Japs with tanks, mortars and the works. Again they, like their bereaved brethren at Tarawa, went under ground while we bomb and blasted. The little yellow rats finally came out of their holes but ran into such a mess of trouble they probably wished they could crawl back into them and crawl back to Japan.   GUAM

Sunday 17 September 1944   *Palau Islands*

Steaming as before. Air Department is in condition 11.

0455-0557 Manned general quarters stations.

0717 Changed course to 330°T, speed 18 knots.

0802 USS BUNKER HILL assumed guide, bearing 165°T, 2,500 yards. USS NEW JERSEY, HANCOCK, HUNT and MARSHALL left the formation.

0824 Began steering various courses at various speeds to proceed to flying station.

1039 USS VINCENNES assumed fleet guide, bearing 300°T, 2,500 yards.

1048 Sounded flight quarters.

1116 Changed fleet course to 180°T.

1119 1123 Launched 4 F6F-N5s and 2 TBMs for transfer to USS BUNKER HILL to make room for 4 day fighters. Additionally pilots Lt. W.P. Phelps and Lt.(jg) F.M. Archer were transferred to BUNKER HILL for temporary additional duty.

1144 Secured from flight quarters.

1247 Sounded flight quarters.

1315 Changed fleet course to 180°T, speed 26 knots.

1318 Commenced steering various courses at various speeds into the wind while landing aircraft.

1334 Landed 3 F6F-5s (day fighters) from USS BUNKER HILL, assigned to INDEPENDENCE.

1521-1523 Launched 4 F6F-5Ns for CAP over Kossol Passage (Palau Islands) and an anti-shipping sweep in the Babelthuap - Koror area.

Attacking under low ceilings they strafed a heavily camouflaged vessel of a type they were not able to identify, and an AK.

1611 Landed aboard one F6F-5 from USS BUNKER HILL, assigned to USS INDEPENDENCE.

Day fighter pilots were being brought aboard. The mission of the INDEPENDENCE as a dedicated night carrier had not yet fully evolved. The new pilots would pick up missions during daylight hours. The lengthy hours (involved operating both day and night schedules) would make it difficult for the crew.

1615 Secured from flight quarters.

1710 Changed fleet course to 035°T.

1744 USS BUNKER HILL assumed formation guide. INDEPENDENCE bears 345°T, 3,500 yards from guide.

1802 Sounded flight quarters, then sounded torpedo defense.

1807 Changed fleet course to 065°T. Commenced steering various courses at various speeds while recovering aircraft.

1822 Completed recovery of 4 F6Fs launched at 1520, and steadied on course 065°T, speed 20 knots.

1836 Secured from flight quarters. Set condition 14 in the Air Department.

1843 USS NEW JERSEY assumed guide. INDEPENDENCE bears 300°T from the guide, 2,500 yards, on a new fleet course of 270°T.

1903 Secured from torpedo defense.

2326 Changed course to 260°T.

Monday 18 September 1944   *Palau Islands*

0100 Changed fleet course to 090°T.

0421 Sounded flight quarters.

0458 Sounded general quarters.

0520 Changed speed to 27 knots for flight operations.

0535 On a calm sea with 12 mile visibility, completed launching 9 F6Fs and 5 TBMs. Four Hellcats were assigned CAP and the remainder of the launch were tasked with ASP and anti-snooper patrols.

0815-0836 INDEPENDENCE gunners test fired the ships automatic weapons. Then commenced steering various courses at various speeds proceeding to flying station.

0842-0854 Recovered all aircraft launched at 0535.

0907 Secured from flight quarters. Set condition 14 in the Air Department.

1239 Sounded flight quarters for purpose of re-spotting the flight deck.

1308 Secured from flight quarters.

1411 Sounded flight quarters. On a base course of 020°T commenced steaming various courses at various speeds while landing aircraft.

1426 Completed landing four F6Fs transferred to INDEPENDENCE from USS SAN JACINTO, along with the following pilots; Lieut. Robert A. Alexander, Lt.(jg) Rufus R. Henderson, & Ensigns John G. Hansen and William T. Howard.

1440 Secured from flight quarters.

1537 USS YARNALL came alongside starboard quarter to deliver guard mail, then cast off at 1544.

1625 Fleet axis changed to 240°T. Returned to base course 000°T.

1638 USS BENHAM came alongside starboard quarter to deliver guard mail, casting off at 1640. Commenced maneuvering to arrive at new station.

1658 On station with guide, NEW JERSEY, bearing 240°T at 2,500 yards, speed 16 knots on base course 000°T.

GUAM   <u>18 September 1944</u>

We are leisurely heading north today. Are still in vicinity of Peleliu and Anguar in case help is needed but it is quite obvious we will not be called on. The Army has all of Anguar while the Marines have the air field at Peleliu and are working their way to the northern part of the island.   ***GUAM***

Tuesday 19 September 1944   *Philippines Underway for Manila*

0455 Steaming as before in company with Task Unit 38.2.1 in cruising disposition 5R5. Ship is darkened, Air Department in condition 14. Sounded general quarters.

0613 Changed fleet course to 130°T, speed 15 knots.

0614 USS INTREPID assumed guide, bearing 195°T, 3,500 yards.

0629 USS NEW JERSEY assumed guide, bearing 240°T, 2,500 yards.

0642 Changed fleet course to 240°T, speed 10 knots.

0644 USS ENOREE assumed guide bearing 295°T, distance 6,500 yards from INDEPENDENCE.

0811 On a new course of 318°T, speed 18 knots prepared for launching aircraft.

0817 Launched one F6F piloted by Commander Turner F. Caldwell to proceed to the USS BUNKER HILL for a conference.

0946 Steadied on a new course of 250°T, speed 13 knots as USS MILLER steamed up along the starboard side amidships to receive Lieut. A.R. Allen and Lieut. W.R. Henry aboard, to be delivered to the USS LEXINGTON for conference. At 1010 USS MILLER cast off.

1027 Zigzagging independently while maneuvering to gain position 3,000 yards astern USS ENOREE.

1115 Commenced approach to port side of USS ENOREE.

1148 Steadied on course 240°T, maneuvering to bring USS ENOREE along the starboard side, speed 10 knots. 1221 Connected fueling hose to aft fueling station and commenced pumping fuel.

1305 USS TWINING came alongside port quarter to deliver guard mail.

1310 Connected forward fueling hose and commenced pumping fuel oil at forward pumping station.

1330 Having received 137,811 gallons of fuel oil, cast off all lines from USS ENOREE.

1355 Changed speed to 17 knots and maneuvered to regain station in the formation.

1422 Resumed station, changed speed to 12 knots.

1609 Sounded flight quarters. Proceeded to flying station.

1635 Recovered one F6F piloted by Comdr. Turner F. Caldwell, returning from BUNKER HILL.

1638 Secured from flight quarters, Air Department set condition 14.

1646 Commenced zigzagging on base course 240°T, 18 knots.

1730 Task Group 38.2 formed cruising disposition 5R5, axis 240°T. USS NEW JERSEY assumed guide. INDEPENDENCE bearing 060°T, 2,500 yards from guide.

1811 Sounded torpedo defense, then changed fleet course to 235°T. USS MILLER came alongside to return Lieut. A.R. Allen and Lieut. W.R. Henry aboard from their conference on the LEXINGTON.

Also coming aboard from the MILLER were the following pilots reporting for duty from the USS WASP to the INDEPENDENCE; Lieut. E.J. Becker, Ens. H.S. Meacham and Ens. W.K. Jackson.
1908 Cast off all lines from USS MILLER.
1914 Secured from torpedo defense.
1945 Changed fleet course to 340°T.

Wednesday 20 September 1944   *Philippines Underway for Manila*

0506-0606 Manned general quarters stations.
0916 Steadied on a new course of 290°T, speed 15 knots, USS MILLER came alongside port quarter to deliver baggage of pilots recently transferred aboard.
0929 USS MILLER cast off.
0943-0945 USS BENHAM was alongside port quarter to deliver guard mail.
1015 Regained station in disposition.
1110 Sounded flight quarters.
1131 Proceeded to flying station.
1206-1211 On a "slight sea", visibility 6 miles under a 3,000' ceiling, catapulted 8 F6Fs for CAP. Independence regained station, then once again at 1433 proceeded to flying station.
1525-1529 Launched 8 F6Fs for a second CAP of the day. INDEPENDENCE then proceeded to land the aircraft of the noon CAP, completing the recovery at 1605.
1715 USS INDEPENDENCE regained station in the disposition zigzagging on a base course of 310°T.
1726 Steadied on course of 300°T, speed 18 knots while the USS YARNELL came along the starboard side, delivered and received mail, then cast off at 1727.
1742 Resumed position in the formation returning to a course of 300°T, speed 22 knots.
1747 Changed fleet speed to 23 knots, course 305°T. INDEPENDENCE was proceeding to flight station on various courses at various speeds into the wind while recovering aircraft from the 1529 CAP.
1824-1825 Recovered all eight F6Fs.
1834 Sounded torpedo defense, began maneuvering to regain position in the formation.
1840 Secured from flight quarters. Air Department set condition 14.
1905 Regained position in the formation.
2100 Ended the day steaming on fleet course 325°T, fleet speed 23 knots.

GL Headed this day for Luzon the biggest island in the Philippines. We were told that's where all the Jap planes were. We are hoping they come in after us. Its like shooting ducks only these ducks burn. GL

USS INDEPENDENCE now had received onboard 8 day Hellcat fighters and 12 new pilots. The ships aircraft complement now consisted of 16 F6F-5s, 8 F6F-5Ns, and 7 TBM-1C(N)s.

The fleet was steaming in to conduct strikes on Luzon.

GUAM   20 September 1944
Today we start for Manila. At noon we began our high speed run, and pour it on all the way. By 0600 we should be 80 miles from the island of Luzon and in a direct line (about 130 miles) from Manila. Comdr. Caldwell is going to lead the first fighter sweep into Clark field, one of the principal targets. GUAM

Thursday 21 September 1944   *Philippines, Luzon - Manila*

0000 Steaming as before, changed course to 270°T. Air Department in condition 14.
0540 Sounded general quarters.
0756 On a new fleet course of 010°T, commenced launching aircraft.
0819 Completed launching 20 Hellcats and 4 Avengers for ASP. The Hellcats carried one 500lb GP

bomb each, and also had belly tanks attached. 16 Hellcats were tasked with a fighter sweep over the Clark Field area on Luzon, 4 utilized for CAP. The strikes were in conjunction with sweeps and strikes by other carrier groups from Task Group 38. Aircraft were sent aloft into weather described as really foul with rain and heavy seas. Wind over the deck as much as 42 knots.

Weather was overcast and "very squally" near the carrier. It improved over Luzon, with a high overcast at 20,000 feet, a broken cumulus layer at 3,000', and a light haze layer over the ground.

The Hellcats flew west at 10,000' to target via Dingalan Bay, then southwest to Mt. Arayat. Arayat is an inactive volcano rising over 3,100' above surrounding terrain, making it an easy to see landmark for targeting Japanese held primary airfields. Led by Comdr. Caldwell, they proceeded to Clark Field where they bombed and strafed targets. Climbing out through 5,000' flying back toward Arayat for rendezvous after the strike, they ran into two Tonys, which appeared to have flown into the Hellcats unexpectedly from the north. Caldwell, Berkheimer, Henderson, Allen, Obenour, Barker, Miller, Williams and Lee engaged. One Tony escaped the uneven fray smoking, with a split-S followed with a quick dive through clouds, after Caldwell, Berkheimer, Henderson and two other fighters from the CABOT each got a piece of him.

The other Tony pilot ended his mission shot up in the engine and cockpit area, exiting in an evasive tight turn into a half spin, violently smoking as it plunged through broken clouds crashing into the ground NW of Arayat. The kill, logged at 0930, was shared by Barker, Miller, Lee and Williams with a 1/4 claim each. Barker also was credited with damage on the other Tony from a 12 o'clock level attack. This was the first action for many of Caldwell's new VF(N)-41 pilots and the day was still young.

In the meantime, back at the Task Group;
Ens. R.F. Peterson had fuel problems and landed aboard the USS COWPENS (T.G. 38.1).
0823 Changed course to 230°T.   0853 Changed course to 010°T.
0858 Launched 1 Hellcat to replace a Hellcat with engine trouble, then recovered the returning Hellcat.
0915 Formation shifted to 5V5, axis 000°T.

The Hellcats reformed over Arayat heading west. They ran into 2 Oscars and 2 Zekes (Zeros) flying east at high speed. In the ensuing fray that started off with Caldwell's head on firing pass. Fegraeus was credited with a probable on a Zeke with high runs from 3 & 5 o'clock scoring on the engine and wing roots. In a separate action Johnson and Henry were jumped by two Oscars and one Zeke from 8 o'clock low. Johnson and Henry both received hits, Johnson's Hellcat taking 20mm rounds to the underside damaging his hydraulic system. Henry after receiving Zeke bullets thru his starboard wing tangled with two Oscars, was credited with a probable Oscar scoring hits from 6 o'clock into the Oscars wing roots. Fisher and Barnett found 3 Topsys below them at 5,000' in a V formation. Berkheimer and Henderson, also sighted the enemy transports. They were at a lower altitude, in better position for the attack, and beat them to the Topsys.

Berkheimer's runs on one of the Topsys brought it down with hits from astern into the port engine and wing root. It crashed and exploded N.E. of Dau East Field.
0951 Proceeded to flying station, steadying on course 030°T.
0959 Commenced launching 4 F6Fs for CAP, into rain, with heavy seas.
1055 Commenced recovering aircraft from the 0756 launch.
1123 Lieut. Bill Henry floated down the deck on landing, crashing into the barricade and overturned, flipping the Hellcat over on its back. A fire broke out from within the engine cowling, and was immediately extinguished with a fog spray by quick reacting deck crew members. Bill was uninjured. F6F-5 (Bu.No.70147) was written off as a total loss and jettisoned over the side of the ship. On its way over the side, the bent Hellcat struck and dislodged a life raft, and it too was lost to the sea. At 1155 Ens. Harry Johnson set his crippled F6F-5 (Bu.No.58502) down for a water landing, due to shot up hydraulics. Harry was uninjured and was fished out of the sea by the USS BENHAM. Ens. Henderson landed aboard the HORNET, ENS Klock landed aboard PRINCETON, Ens. Berkheimer landed aboard the WASP. By 1205, all other pilots in the 0800 launch were recovered back aboard.

1254 With the deck cleared of the wrecked F6F and re-spotted, 4 F6Fs and 4 TBMs were then launched with the carrier turned into the wind on a course of 355°T. The Hellcats assigned CAP, the Avengers ASP. Wind over the deck averaged 36-40 knots.

1304-1316 Recovered 4 F6Fs.

1344-1350 Launched 10 F6Fs. The mission was a fighter sweep over Clark Field and Lingayen Field areas. Last minute changes in plans for this launch instead provided high cover over Luzon at 17,000-20,000'. No enemy aircraft were observed.

1410 Landed 1 F6F flown by Comdr. Caldwell from the 1350 launch, returning with engine trouble. His generator had failed and, as he was flight leader, the remaining 3 Hellcats in his unit were not launched.

1454 Launched 3 F6Fs and 3 TBMs for CAP and ASP.

1505 Sounded torpedo defense due to a reported unidentified aircraft in the area.

1513 Secured from torpedo defense.

1514 Recovered 1 F6F flown by "Berky" Berkheimer (who was returning from the USS WASP).

1520 Recovered 3 F6Fs, launched at 1254 and 1 F6F launched at 1350.

1642 Landed on board 2 F6F Hellcats flown by Henderson and Peterson, returning from the USS HORNET and USS COWPENS, and recovered 1 Hellcat launched at 1454.

1703-1706 Launched 4 F6Fs for a dusk CAP.

1708-1715 Recovered 8 F6Fs.

1732 Recovered 1 TBM.

1800 Sighted Luzon, bearing 270°T, distance 40 miles.

1812 Changed course to 000°T.

1819 Recovered aboard 2 F6Fs and 2 TBMs.

1823 Changed course to 345°T.

1845 Sounded torpedo defense.

1859 Landed 4 F6Fs launched at 1706.

1912 Changed course to 120°T, speed 20 knots.

1925 Secured from flight quarters. Air Department set condition 14.

1945 Secured from torpedo defense.

2100 Changed fleet course to 110°T.

2230 Commenced zigzagging (Plan no.6), base course 110°T, fleet speed 18 knots.

All aircraft were back aboard except the Hellcat piloted by Ens. Klock (landed aboard USS PRINCETON).

GN   Hit Manila. Things have turned out fairly well so far and we are getting by nicely as a night carrier. The boys haven't really started smacking the Japs down in the dark as yet but we are not molested in the period when they are flying. Food supply is getting very low with the exception of salmon and we are good and sick of that. GN

DL   Historic hindsight considers the invasion of the Palau Islands to have been unnecessary. Halsey had suggested that the islands be bypassed. Nimitz, the Grey Eminence, disagreed. "It was useful," wrote naval historian Morison, "but hardly worth the expenditure of 1950 American lives."
As carrier sailors far from the gruesome scenes on the beach, we had the inestimable good fortune of not having to undergo what our Marine brethren did. I hoped brothers Ed and Russ were a thousand miles from the place. The very name, Umurbrogol Ridges, still has a connotation of dark caves bristling with weapons and enemies. The fighting was a dirty slugging match in tropical humidity combined with a terrible lack of drinkable water. Weapons and iron determination dug them out. The last five defenders did not surrender until the first day of February 1945.
We stuck around only until other urgent tasks demanded our attention. There were many. Strategic decisions were being made that would inevitably put our own heads at greater risk.
One such decision was the familiar story of the fortuitous way the date for the planned invasion of Leyte was advanced two months, from 20 December to 20 October. A Naval Reserve ensign pilot

from CV Hornet was forced to ditch his F6F close to an island near the southwestern coast of Leyte. While awaiting rescue, he learned from his Filipino saviors of the paucity of the Japanese garrison. His information, along with other clues, prompted Halsey to recommend to the Joint Chiefs of Staff, then meeting at Quebec [*1.], *to advance the dates. It was done. Our enemies thus got an earlier fight for the Philippines than expected. So did we. It was a beast.* **DL** ([*1.] The "Octagon" Quebec Conference, occurred on 11-16 September 1944 to discuss the war in Europe and the Pacific with Roosevelt, Churchill and the Joint Chiefs of Staff present. In the Pacific, it pushed forward the Philippine invasion. Essentially, the Army oriented toward an eventual land invasion of Japan. Admiral Leahy [*2.] was convinced Japan would be defeated by the Navy with Army air assistance.) ([*2.] Hoyt)

GUAM   21 September 1944

Up at 0330 this morning for breakfast and early general quarters. Our fighter sweep was expected to be launched at 0615 but due to the extremely foul weather all operations were cancelled. At 0710 the schedule was again put on the active list and the skipper Com. Caldwell, took off with 12 fighters, loaded with a 500 AP and plenty of ammunition.

Due to many snoopers in the area (none of which would come very close) we remained at our general quarters stations from 0530 to 1500. A small matter 10 hours. However, since we were not attacked at any time we have no reason to bitch. This is especially so when one of the pilots who was flying in weather that would normally ground ducks.

All in all, our fighters, dive bombers, and torpedo bombers from 38.1, 2,3 did ok by themselves and here is the score;

110 enemy planes destroyed in the air. 95 enemy planes destroyed on the ground. Ships Sunk; 1 DD, 2 Large AOs, 1 Large AP, 10 Large AK, 12 Medium AK, 1 Floating Dry Dock, and 2 Luggers. This is not bad considering we lost only 15 planes.

This evening we were 27 miles from the island of Luzon. The weather had cleared sufficiently to enable all hands to see the Sierra Madres Range on the east coast. It is unbelievable to all that the Japs have allowed a task force of this size to go hit the their strongest points in the Philippines without offering resistance, and yet, that is exactly what has been happening for the past two weeks. What the hell are they doing with their air force is a mystery. Our photo planes got shots of many single and twin engine planes dispersed amongst the trees surrounding Clark and Nichols Field. Why aren't they flying them at us today is a question no one can answer. Tomorrow it will be too late for them to fly. We'll get them the first thing in the morning, weather permitting.   *GUAM*

Friday 22 September 1944   *Philippines, Luzon - Manila*

0453 Sounded flight quarters.   At 0529, sounded general quarters on report of approaching aircraft.
0613-0631 Launched 12 Hellcats for a combat sweep over Clark and Lingayen Fields in central Luzon, and 4 Avengers for ASP. The aircraft were launched in heavy seas, wind over the deck 36-37 knots with 2 mile visibility under a 1,500' ceiling. By the time the Avengers were launched, green water was coming over the deck, rain and thick clouds prevailed.

If the thought of launching in heavy seas from a rising, falling, and rolling flight deck, into rotten weather from the bow of the INDEPENDENCE is of concern to a pilot ready to launch, then also consider fact that those pilots and aircrews would have to find the ship and land on the stern in that same foul weather and moving deck, after combat with the enemy. Having survived the enemy, they would now need to survive the landing. Over central Luzon the fighter sweep would have better conditions over target with very thin scattered cumulus at 3,000' and high overcast at 17,000'.
0652 Sighted Luzon on starboard bow at approximately 35 miles.
0658 Landed a Hellcat from USS CABOT for an emergency landing. Formation axis changed to 270°T.

INDEPENDENCE Hellcats had launched with belly tanks and a single 500lb bomb each. They would attack Clark Field, Angeles West Field, and O'Donnell Field. Join up was made with fighters from USS CABOT inbound, approaching central Luzon at 12,000'. CABOT fighters then climbed to 18,000' to give VF(N)-41 pilots high cover when fighters from T.G. 38.1 failed to show (which had been tasked with high CAP). AA fire from the Japanese over target was moderate and rated as inaccurate - to - accurate.   ([*2.] Hoyt - How They Won The War In The Pacific)

It had improved over yesterdays raids, the Hellcats having provided the enemy with opportunity to practice and hone their skills on actual live moving targets.

Typical bomb release was made following a 30° to 70° glide at from 2,500' altitude down to as low as 1,500'. Numerous parked aircraft and AA positions were hit with reports of damage or destruction.

The INDEPENDENCE sweep had bombed and strafed Clark and O'Donnell Fields.

Regrouping with CABOT fighters, they proceeded toward Lingayen. Caldwell & Allen, not effecting a rejoin with the group, flew S.S.W. to discover Angeles West Field with many single engine and twin engine aircraft targets sitting on the ground. They proceeded to make strafing runs, "burning out" a cluster of 3 Bettys, a mix of a Judy, a Zeke and a Betty, and direct hits on 5 Zekes parked in front of a hanger. The strafing run completely destroyed all 5 Zekes, with "flames spreading mushroom-like from one to the other, and into the hangar".

The main group, back together at 12,000', was 10 miles South of the Lingayen Gulf when they spotted 6 Vals escorted by 1 Zeke, which were below at 8,000'.

The entire group of INDEPENDENCE and CABOT pilots dropped in on the enemy.

Moore, with multiple bursts on a Val finally laid in a burst from level at 6 o'clock astern. The Val flamed and exploded, entered a slow spiral crashing into the ground N.E. of the Agno River.

Berkheimer made a pass at a Zeke from 4 o'clock high, in clouds, which had just been hit by 2 or 3 CABOT pilots. The Zeke, right wing burning, lost altitude rapidly and crashed into the side of a mountain in a small ravine.

Bill Henry made multiple passes on 1 Val, finally seeing it explode during a 1 o'clock level run with hits into the engine and fuselage. His next Val was killed with bursts into the engine and wing roots, level from 6 o'clock. The Val caught fire in the port wing, rolled, then entered a smoking descending circle crashing into the ground, " splattering flame on both sides of the Agno River".

Lingayen Field was obscured by low cloud. Moore and Peterson managed a diving pass on a Pete floatplane. Moore, overshooting his run, observed pieces flying off the Pete's starboard wing as Peterson made his firing pass. The Pete disappeared into clouds and poor visibility.

0904 Launched a CAP of 4 Hellcats and the CABOT Hellcat that had landed two hours ago. They recovered 10 of the 12 Hellcats and the 4 Avengers launched and 0631, and recovered the Hellcat piloted by Ens. Klock, who had landed yesterday aboard USS PRINCETON.

0959 Recovered the remaining 2 Hellcats from the 0631 launch.

1137 Weather had continued to deteriorate and all other flights were called off with the exception of the launching of 8 F5FN Hellcats for CAP and 5 Avengers for ASP. 1151 Recovered 4 Hellcats launched at 0904 and 1 Avenger (most likely just launched, and returning with a mechanical problem).

"Weather conditions at this time were next to impossible; ships 500 yards away were almost obliterated by the downpour: winds of 35-40 knots over the deck were the rule. Such conditions caused one pilot to call in after about an hour and with a sigh and a certain amount of nonchalance state, "Well, I'm still airborne."

1321 Commenced emergency turn to avoid USS WEDDERBURN, out of control due to loss of steering.

1415 WEDDERBURN reported she regained normal steering.

1440 Recovered 8 Hellcats and 4 Avengers launched at 1137.

1500 Secured from flight quarters, Air Department set condition 14.

1831 Resumed disposition 5R5, axis 270°T, guide NEW JERSEY. INDEPENDENCE is 330°T, 2,500 yards from guide, course 120°T, 15 knots.   1916 Changed fleet speed to 24 knots.

GUAM   22 September 1944

Today's routine was just a little rigorous for the ships company as general quarters only lasted 6 hours. As was scheduled again, regardless of the stinking weather (a 50 knot wind with high seas and rain) our fighter sweep was launched at 0615, and as scheduled, the Japs have fewer aircraft to hide than yesterday. Our group of 12 planes accounted for 4 in the air and 14 on the ground, the reports from the rest of the force have not come in yet.

At 1100, all strikes against Manila and Manila Bay and the air fields were cancelled because of the weather. A typhoon is on its way and we'll have to run like hell to get out of its path.
Later reports still incomplete tell us that another medium AK, 1 medium AO, 3 small AOs were sunk.[1.]
Also 6 floatplanes. The weather is really bad but the aerologist tell us we are going to be out of it in another 12 hours.   **GUAM**   (*[1.] AK DAKAR MARU, and oilers NO.7 TAKASAGO MARU, NO.9 HAMMEI MARU, & NO.24 NANSHIN MARU and other vessels were sunk - Robert J..Cressman)

Saturday 23 September 1944   *Philippines, Luzon - Refueling*

0515 Sounded general quarters, securing from general quarters at 0615.
1130 At a new fleet speed of 10 knots, fleet course 280°T, USS HUNT came alongside starboard to receive Ensigns F.A. Fisher and J.F. Moore to proceed to USS NASSAU to pick up replacement aircraft.
1139 USS HUNT cast off.
1149 Changed fleet speed to 12 knots followed by a fleet course to 160°T at 1153.
1237 Steaming at various courses and various speeds to come alongside tanker USS MASCOMA on course 280°T, speed 12 knots.
1302 Secured boilers 1 & 3, first line secured to MASCOMA.
1317 Commenced receiving fuel oil.
1329 Commenced receiving aviation gasoline. Exchanged mail with the tanker.
1420 Sounded flight quarters.
1431 Lighted fires under No.1 boiler, followed by No.3 boiler at 1444.
1453-1456 No.1 & 3 boilers cut into main steam line.
1459 Cast off from tanker USS MASCOMA having received 208,000 gallons of fuel oil and 32,000 gallons of gasoline.
1500 Commenced steaming on various courses at various speeds while launching aircraft.
1514 Completed launching 12 F6Fs and 4 TBMs. Commenced maneuvering to take position 6,500 yards astern tanker USS CHIKASKIA (AO-54), fleet guide, on course 280°T, speed 12 knots.
1535 Secured from flight quarters, Air Department set condition 14.
1600 USS BENHAM came alongside to transfer Ens. H.R. Johnson back aboard ship. (Johnson was rescued by the BENHAM after he set his crippled Hellcat down alongside her two days ago in his forced water landing.)
1625 USS BENHAM cast off and INDEPENDENCE commenced to proceed to the night flying station.
1644 Maneuvering into the wind, they landed on board two replacement F6Fs flown over from USS NASSAU. Then commenced maneuvering to regain station.
1725-1726 USS LEWIS HANCOCK (DD-675) came alongside to transfer mail.
1805 Maneuvering at various speeds on various courses into the wind while recovering aircraft.
1818 Completed recovering 12 Hellcats and 4 Avengers launched at 1514.
1819 Sounded torpedo defense.
1830 Secured from flight quarters, Air Department set condition 14. Darkened ship.
1845 Regained position in the disposition.
1920 Secured from torpedo defense.
2100 Changed course to 305°T, speed 22 knots.

GUAM   23 September 1944
Today the sea is calm as the word Pacific implies. We are on our way southeast to fuel ship. Much speculation as to where we are going afterward. Latest reports have it that Ulithi, a group of atolls that will make a good fleet anchorage, is being invaded today. Also Yap, a former cable and weather station that we had polite words over with the Japs over 25 years ago. Both of these islands in the North Caroline's Group are rather important for future and all our operations against the Philippines. It is scuttlebutt that after fueling, we will again go back to the Philippines for a few more strikes. By that time Ulithi will have been taken and we can use it for a rearming and reprovisioning base. Inserted on this page are 3 messages that we received today;

NO. 1
FROM:SECNV ACTION CIMCPOA
INFO READRESSED FR0M RADIO HONLULU TO ALL US NAVY SHIPS
FOR DELIVERY TO ADMIRAL F. HALSEY X YOU ARE LIVING UP TO YOUR REPUTATION FOR
SINKING THE JAPS X THE NAVY DEPARTMNT IS PROUD OF THE LATEST EXPLOIT OF THE THIRD
FLEET X I SEND CONGRADULATIONS TO YOU AND VICE ADMIRAL MITSCHER AND HIS CARRIER
FORCE AND TO ALL SHIPS AND MEN WHO PARTICAPATED IN THESE SUCCESSFUL OPERATIONS.
JAMES FORRESTAL.

No.2
FROM CTF 38 ACTION TF38
ANOTHER COMMENDATION TO THE OFFICERS AND MEN OF THIS TASK
GROUP FOR A JOB WELL DONE. IN THE ATTACKS ON LUZON OUR PILOTS
AND AIR CREW MEN HIT THE ENEMY ANOTHER DIASTEROUS BLOW IN SPITE OF HAZARDOUS
WEATHER. THE UNCOMPLETED SCORE SHOWS 144 PLANES SHOT DOWN AND
140 DESTROYED ON THE GROUND. 35 SHIPS SUNK AND 27 DAMAGED AND PROBABLY SUNK.
MANY DESTRUCTIVE HITS ON AIR-FIELDS AND HARBOR INSTALLATIONS.

NO.3
FROM COM THRID FLT. ACTION 38.2
INFO. THIRD FLEET CINCPAC
ALTHOUGH THE CAPACITY AUDIENCE HISSED THE MAGNIFICENT LUZON PERFORMANCE THE
GATE RECEIPTS WERE GRATIFYING AND VERY LITTLE WAS THROWN AT THE ACTORS.
THE SHOW GOES ON THE ROAD AGAIN SOON AND KEEPS ON GOING SO LONG AS THE AUDIENCE
HAS A SPOT TO HISS IN.   X HALSEY   *GUAM*

Sunday 24 September 1944   *Philippines, Coron Bay Raid*

The Task Group is steaming as before in the Philippine Sea roughly 170 miles east of San Bernardino
Strait, approaching in cruising disposition 5R5 on a 305°T base course at 22 knots. Air Department is in
condition 14. Throughout the day they would turn generally southeast taking them roughly 50 miles off
the shore line of the Island of Samar.
0430 Sounded flight quarters.
0520 Sounded general quarters.
0610 Catapulted 16 Hellcats (for a fighter sweep, and fighter-bomber shipping strike), and 4 Hellcats &
4 Avengers for SNASP. Aircraft headed toward Coron Bay, Busuanga, Culion and Coron Islands
(located off the northern tip of Palawan, between Palawan and Mindoro). They joined up with squadrons
from the BUNKER HILL, CABOT, INTREPID and LEXINGTON as part of a large strike (with "Tiger
99" from USS BUNKER HILL designated as strike leader). This was to be a large anti-shipping strike.
INDEPENDENCE pilots would have to fly a total in excess of 600 miles to and from the target areas.
Eight VF(N)-41 Hellcats carried 500# GP bombs with 4-5 sec. delay tail fuses. Eight Hellcats were
assigned to fly as cover.
0718 Secured from general quarters.
0727 Ens. Barnett, catapulted at 0610, immediately had an in-flight problem with his aileron controls
freezing. The trim tab torque tube had corroded badly and froze in place. He dropped his bomb outside
the screen and landed his F6F5 back onboard INDEPENDENCE, while the remaining 15 Hellcats flew
west. Due to low cloud cover, Ens. R.F. Peterson and Lt.(jg) R.R. Henderson became separated and
joined up with strikes from other carriers.
On the way in to the target area, Japanese vessels were sighted and pilots from other carriers were
assigned to attack. As the INDEPENDENCE Hellcats approached Coron Bay, it was noted that most of
the shipping lay outside the bay in surrounding waters (see chart on page 367).

Over Coron Bay, the group was dispersed by the strike leader for low level attacks. Lt. W.E. Henry and Ens. J.S. Berkheimer flew down the east coast of Coron Island crossing the bay to the NW. They bombed and strafed a 260' long unidentified ship north of Chindonan Island. They thought Henry got a hit but no results were reported.

Peterson dropped in on a DE (Target 4) along with some SB2Cs from the CABOT near Cabulauan Island. He was unable to observe his results. He rejoined CABOT fighters, looking around noted an AK in North Busuanga Harbor was smoking, and an AO in Lusong Bay was heavily smoking. Returning to the ship he noted a small trawler burning fiercely.

Henderson had joined a flight from the Lexington attacking targets at North Busuanga. He strafed an AK with no visible results. LEX fighters got near misses with most of their bombs, but later someone got a direct hit on the most northern vessel in the group.

From the AAR II-8:

"Barker's division, less Peterson, had swung Westward over Culion Island, and Barker picked out one of the 2 large AOs, which together with one large AK, were lying in the Bay entrance, West of Lamud-Marily Bay. The 2 AOs were not underway, but headed towards the Southeast. The AK was steaming slowly Northwest, between them. Barker's target was the AO to the Southwest (target #1). His division swung up from Culion, crossed the bay and up the Western Busuanga Island coast a short distance. A turn to port brought them around to a position for a broad side attack on the AOs starboard beam.

Barker, the first one down, pushed over from 5000', heading East. He made a diving turn to water level, released from 50' and Lee (in his division), saw Barker's bomb strike the AO squarely amidships, just under the amidships superstructure, from 3 o'clock; just above the water line. Since the fusing was 4-5 sec. delay, Klock who was now well into his own approach, was severely buffeted by the explosion. Barker had also strafed before and during release. He pulled up in a climbing turn to 3,500', looked back and saw a great eruption of gray smoke and water. Klock made his run, but at the last minute, found he had no bomb. It had detached, same as Johnson's, somewhere on route to the target area. Lee then came down, strafing, from 7000' leveled out at 75' and released from 3 o'clock for a potential broadside. His aiming point was just forward of the stern bridge superstructure. The bomb was thought by Lee and Barker to have struck slightly high, but with damaging effect. Lee then went over and strafed the AO to the Northeast (target #2) getting hits in the superstructure on the stern.

Barker in the meantime began a strafing run up the stern of his AO, firing from 4000' down to 1000'. Using the ship's stern gun as his aiming point, he put a full 5 sec. burst into his target. When he was down to 1000', his tracers hit what was apparently ammunition on the deck, or a magazine, as the whole superstructure on the stern blew out like a mushroom shaped ball of flame. Barker immediately pulled out. Lee, who had come around to strafe this AO again, saw the explosion. Klock who had, just after his "DUD" run, strafed a DE lying in Lamud-Marily Bay (target #9), had also pulled around and had strafed Barker's target. The three of them then restrafed the DE, and another one near by. The first one was burning when they retired to the East for more targets.

Barker's AO was seen by many pilots, including AGC Caldwell, to be burning fiercely, listing 15-20° and settling by the stern, in a sinking condition. It is claimed as definitely sunk.

These three then swung South over Coron Bay to rendezvous, but saw 4 VF making runs on three motor launches in the bay, off South central Coron Island. One was smoking when they arrived. Barker took the one closest to the island, strafing from port quarter to starboard bow, and saw it burn.

Klock and Lee worked over the other two, and saw one of them burning when they retired. The three joined up on 10-12 SB2Cs and 16-20 VF, and returned to base.

Having determined by now that there was to be no air opposition, Comdr. Caldwell led his and Alexander's divisions down for strafing attacks. Alexander was, as mentioned, minus Henderson. All seven VF made runs over the AK (target #5) lying just west of the North tip of Tangat Island.

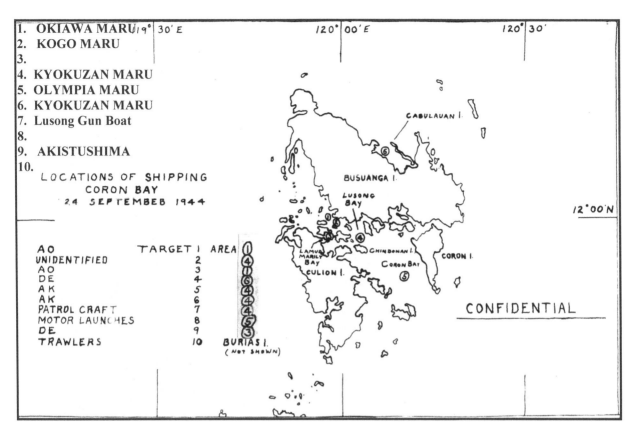

1. OKIAWA MARU
2. KOGO MARU
3.
4. KYOKUZAN MARU
5. OLYMPIA MARU
6. KYOKUZAN MARU
7. Lusong Gun Boat
8.
9. AKISTUSHIMA
10.

LOCATIONS OF SHIPPING
CORON BAY
24 SEPTEMBEB 1944

	TARGET	AREA
AO	1	
UNIDENTIFIED	2	
AO	3	
DE	4	
AK	5	
AK	6	
PATROL CRAFT	7	
MOTOR LAUNCHES	8	
DE	9	
TRAWLERS	10	BURIAS I. (NOT SHOWN)

CONFIDENTIAL

Coron Bay Strike map enclosure from the CVL-22 Action Report - 1to 30 September

It was given a very severe going over, and was seen to be burning when they retired.

Moore then swung over and strafed another AK (target #6) three times, seeing a column of steam spout up as he pulled away. The others, Fegraeus, (with a special camera rig), Hansen and Alexander, were joined by Moore and all of them strafed what was recognized by photos (attached to the ship's action report) to be an ex-killer whale boat. This target (#7) lay roughly between targets #5 and #6, and was strafed once by all four, and twice by Moore and Fegraeus. It was smoking when they left it.

Howard, after the attack on target #5, saw below what he thought was a speedy small vessel skimming across the water North of Chindonan Island, heading southeast. Suddenly its violent wake stopped, and Howard saw the "boat" continue on. Realizing it must have been a seaplane he tallyhoed it, peeled off and dived down. He made a modified highside run and wound up on the tail of the plane, which turned out to be a Jake. The Jap had by now gotten up to 2500', and instead of wrapping it up, straightened out. Howard gave him a burst at 6 o'clock, level, into the starboard wing stub, and the Jake started to burn. Then the tracers went into the floats below, and they started to burn. The rear seatman started to fire with no effect. Howard gave the Jake another burst "for pictures" and the Jap crashed into the water South of Tambon Island (0845 I). Several pilots saw the action; it was the only one involving enemy planes. The CABOT's flash reports confirmed the shooting down of an enemy plane by some VF of another group.

Caldwell's and Alexander's divisions then joined up and returned to base. Upon returning, Comdr. Caldewell gave his impression of the attack:
"During the action in Lusong Bay bomb hits were seen on every vessel present except one small AK (target #5). There were many misses also. A very large AO on the southeast side of Lusong Bay had

three dive bomber hits, the last causing a violent flame. The AO continued to burn with ever increasing intensity, and the entire ship was ablaze when the strike left the scene. Just Northwest of this AO was a probable oil barge, which was listing 40° and down by the stern. All of the ships were smoking or burning. Bomb hits were likewise seen on two AKs in the harbor West. In the area West of Lamud-Marily Bay, the Southern most ship (target #1) blew up and burned with great intensity. The other two in this vicinity were hit by bombs.

Anti-aircraft came from the ships under attack as well as from seemly well camouflaged positions in the surrounding hills.
As Caldwell's and Alexander's divisions passed over the Southern portion of Burias Island, they saw three trawlers (target #10) trailed by 6-7 small craft, proceeding Southeast along the Eastern coast. These three trawlers were strafed by all three VF of Alexander's division, and all of Comdr. Caldwell's division. One was left burning. (Klock also made a strafing pass at one of these on his way home.)"

The problem Ens. Barnett had with his frozen aileron controls was caused by severe corrosion in the F5F-5s trim-tab torque tube. The steps were taken to correct the problem in other INDEPENDENCE aircraft, with the engineering officers suggesting the problem to be of faulty design and inadequate inspection.

0730 Mustered crew on stations. No absentees.
0754 Rotated fleet axis to the left to 180°T.
0848 Changed disposition to 5V5. INDEPENDENCE took station 000°T, 2,000 yards from guide, USS NEW JERSEY.
0851 Sounded flight quarters.
0933 Recovered 4 Hellcats & 4 Avengers launched at 0610.
1000 Sounded fire quarters, 2 alarm fire in hangar deck amidships. An electrical fire erupted in TBM No.24 and was extinguished within 2 minutes.
1006 Secured from fire quarters.
1047 Launched 8 Hellcats as CAP.
1113 Launched 4 Avengers as ASP, carrying two 350 lb depth bombs each.
1149 Recovered 15 Hellcats launched at 0610.
1435 Recovered 8 Hellcats launched at 1047 and 4 Avengers launched at 1113.
1602 Shifted axis to 080°T.
1629 Assumed disposition 5R5. INDEPENDENCE bears 260°T, 2,500 yards from guide.
1635 Launched 4 Hellcats and 4 Avengers for SNASP.
1832 Recovered 4 Hellcats and 4 Avengers launched at 1635.
1942 Changed fleet course to 077°T, and fleet speed to 20 knots.

GUAM   **24 September 1944**   *Philippines Visayan Island & Colon Harbor*
As was suspected we did go back to the Philippines for another crack before heading for re-arming and reprovisioning area.
*Today we sent a strike of F6Fs some with 500lb AP bombs. And SB2Cs ** with wing tanks. A mere distance of 340 miles (one way) to Coron Bay. Evidently the hot dope indicates shipping in there, maybe part of the fleet that scurried out of Manila Bay. (** The SB2Cs were off other carriers)*
Later as it turned out there were no combatant ships (except a couple of DE's) but plenty of AO's and AK's. Terry Barker, flight officer of the air group flying ace fighter scored a direct hit on an AO with his bomb, then strafed it. Between the two they sank same. All told 16 of which 8 carried bombs from the Independence sunk an AO, scored direct hits on two more and strafed 8 others. Plus shooting down one lone Jake (float plane) who tried like hell to get out but didn't make it. This strike was followed by more aimed at the air fields on the Visayan group again. The complete score for the entire task force of the third fleet had not come out yet. As a result of the past two weeks bombing and strafing of the

Philippines from the southern tip of Mindanao to Manila Bay, Subic Bay, Clark and Nichols Field in Luzon, the Puppet Government at Manila declared war on the U.S.A., Ironic .. no'? **GUAM**

DL First proof that we were hurting them came when Japanese shipping began to shift south from Luzon. Task Force 38 followed like a hungry wolf. Our planes hit targets all the way from the Calamian group between Mindoro and Palawan to the Visayas. **DL**

DrP *Sunday, Raid Coron Bay (38.2) - Bag 1 Jake, 1 ship—Oiler, 3 boats.* **DrP**

Monday 25 September 1944

0515-0617 Sounded general quarters. Course 077°T, speed 20 knots.
0810 USS CABOT assumed guide.
0820 Changed disposition to 5R3, INDEPENDENCE bears 260°, 2,500 yards from CABOT.
0950 Formed a column, course 080°, bearing 260° at 3,000 yards from USS INTREPID (guide) .
1000-1122 Manned torpedo defense stations for anti-aircraft gunnery practice, firing on a towed sleeve.
1123 CABOT reassumed guide; reformed cruising disposition 5R3.
1413 Commenced zigzagging (Plan 6) on fleet base course 089°T.
1802-1902 Manned torpedo defense stations.
1959 Changed speed to 14 knots.
2000 Ceased zigzagging in accordance with Plan No.6, commenced zigzagging in accordance with Plan No.7, base course 089°T.

GL *On our way to Saipan to get bombs and ammo.* **GL**

Tuesday 26 September 1944   *Join up with Task Group 34*

Steaming as before in company with Task Unit 38.2.1 consisting of USS INDEPENDENCE, INTREPID, CABOT (guide) and BUNKER HILL (OTC). Rear Admiral G.F. Bogan in BUNKER HILL is also CTU 38.2.1 operating in accordance with secret orders dated 27 August, 1944 modified and supplemented 11 September, 1944 to Commander First Carrier Task Force, Vice Admiral M. A. Mitscher, Operation Order 10-44. Ship is darkened. Air Department is in condition 14.
0350 Sounded flight quarters.
0500 Ceased zigzagging, steered on various courses at various speeds proceeding to flight station.
0513-0518 Launched 4 F6Fs and 4 TBMs.
0813 Changed fleet course to 275°T, 14 knots. Commenced steaming on various courses at various speeds while recovering aircraft.
0824 Completed recovery of 4 F6Fs and 4 TBMs launched at 0513.
0835 Secured from general quarters on a course of 068°T, speed 25 knots.
0843 Changed course to 086°T. Pursuant to orders from CTG 38.2, left Task Unit 38.2.1 in company with USS BENHAM and USS COLAHAN to join and report to CTF 34 for duty as Task Group 34.9.
1030 Sighted picket destroyer of Task Force 34 bearing 103°T, distance 19 miles.

AD *We left the task force and joined up with a battleship division, cruisers and destroyers, heading for Saipan.* **AD**

1130 INDEPENDENCE, BENHAM and COLAHAN reported for duty to CTF 34, Vice Admiral Willis A. "Ching" Lee Jr., in USS WASHINGTON (Lee's flagship), in accordance with Battle Plan 1-44 dated 9 September, of CTF 34.
1201 Changed course to 070°T, speed 18 knots.
1206-1215 USS HUNT was alongside starboard quarter to deliver mail. Sounded flight quarters.
1217 Commenced zigzagging on base course 070°T to Plan No.23 while gaining position on guide,

USS VINCENNES, bearing 070°T at 11,500 yards, disposition 4N.

1227 Ceased zigzagging and turned into the wind for flight operations.

1237 Launched 2 TBMs (Reb Taylor & Jack Dewis) ordered to proceed to Guam with highly secret dispatches.

1302 Commenced maneuvering with Task force 34 to remain on the disengaged side while the Task Force conducted battle exercises.

1319-1519 Conducted simulated flight operations.

1532 Completed simulated battle exercises.

1552 Gained position in Task Force, disposition 4S, 070°T, speed 15 knots, USS VINCENNES bearing 070°T at 11,500 yards.

1627 Commenced zigzagging independently on station. INDEPENDENCE bears 270°T at 11,500 yards from VINCENNES.

1739 Sounded torpedo defense, Air Department condition 14.

Wednesday 27 September 1944   *Refueling and exercises while steaming to Saipan*

Task Force 34 steaming in disposition 4S, axis 090°T with C.T.F. Vice Admiral Willis A. Lee Jr. in USS WASHINGTON. INDEPENDENCE (T.G. 34.9) maintaining position 6,000 yards from guide, USS MASSACHUSETTS, bearing 090°T, zigzagging (Plan No.25) on base course 090°T, speed 15 knots. Ship is darkened, Air Department is in condition 14.

0354 On signal, ceased zigzagging, changed fleet course to 200°T to turn away from sound contact reported by USS STEPHEN POTTER.

0417 Sounded general quarters and changed course to 130°T.

0520 Left formation, maneuvering to fueling station. Secured from general quarters.

0525 Commenced maneuvering into the wind for air operations.

0534 Launched 3 TBMs for ASP. Changed course to 270°T and speed to 15 knots maneuvering into position along port side of tanker USS NANTAHALA. Changed course to 090°T, speed to 12 knots.

0903 Cast off USS NANTAHALA having received 19,000 gallons of aviation gasoline and 251,000 gallons of fuel oil, and proceeded to flying station.

0918-0920 Catapulted 1 F6F and 2 TBMs for ASP, course 290°T, speed 28 knots.

0935-0937 On a course of 280°T, recovered 3 TBM's launched at 0534.

0940 Began maneuvering to regain station in fueling formation.

1007 Assumed position 4,000 yards astern fuel line, zigzagging independently.

1031 Ceased zigzagging for maneuvering to form column 1,500 yards astern of USS NEW JERSEY, course 125°T, speed 20 knots.

1226 Commenced maneuvering various courses at various speeds to form a column astern the USS ALABAMA and USS NEW JERSEY respectively, spacing 1,000 yards.

1254 Commenced maneuvering into the wind for flight operations.

1301 Launched 4 Hellcats for CAP and 3 Avengers for ASP.

1318 Recovered 1 Hellcat and 2 Avengers launched at 0918. Commenced maneuvering to regain position in the formation.

1330 Resumed station 2,000 yards astern USS ALABAMA.

1353 Commenced gunnery practice on towed sleeve.

1607-1615 Recovered 4 Hellcats and 3 Avengers launched at 1301, and the 2 Avengers from Guam, sent there yesterday from this vessel. Formed disposition 4S, bearing 270°T, 6,000 yards from guide, USS MASSACHUSETTS.

1712 Commenced zigzagging (Plan No. 25) on base course 030°T.

1720-1820 Manned torpedo defense stations.

2300 Changed base course to 100°T.

Destroyer USS COLAHAN, DD-658, transferring a patient on board.
9/28/1944

Thursday 28 September 1944   **Anchored Garapan Harbor, Saipan, Mariana Islands**

Steaming as before, as Task Group 34.9 with USS BENHAM and USS COLAHAN, this vessel OTC and guide. In company with Task Force 34 (USS MASSACHUSETTS guide for TF34). We bear 270°T, 6'000 yards from MASSACHUSETTS. Ship is darkened. Air Department is in condition 14.

0410-0510 Ship at general quarters.

0420 Sighted Saipan Island bearing 130°T, 31 miles.

0433 Changed axis to 130°T.

0455 Formation changed disposition to 4N.

0525 CTF 34 released Task Group 34.9 to proceed to anchorage.

0546 USS COLAHAN came alongside starboard side to transfer a patient (Lt.Jg. R. B. Patch) with an acute appendicitis to this vessel for admission to sick bay. (photo on previous page)

0557 USS COLAHAN cast off, then USS BENHAM and USS COLAHAN were released to proceed independently.

0613 Changed course to 110°T.

0627 Sounded general quarters. Commenced steering various courses at various speeds conforming to channel.

0633 Let fires die out and secured boilers No. 2 & 4.

0637 Lieut. W.W. Hodgkins (harbor pilot) came aboard and proceeded to bridge.

0646 Passed through anti-submarine net at entrance to Garapan Anchorage, Saipan.

0654 Secured from general quarters.

0712 Anchored in berth H-31, in 13 fathoms of clear blue water, rocky bottom, with 80 fathoms of chain to port anchor. Various units of the 3rd fleet and assorted small craft and auxiliaries present.

0720 Harbor pilot Lieut. W.W. Hodgkins left the ship.

0730 Mustered crew on stations.

0740 LCV 997 came alongside starboard to deliver bombs and depth charges.

0803 Let fires die out and secured No. 3 boiler.

0916 LCV 997 cast off. At 0930 INDEPENDENCE secured all 4 main engines.

0942-0955 LCV 258 was alongside to starboard to deliver bomb tail vanes.

1255 LCT 357 moored alongside port and delivered 120 GP 100 lb bombs, .50 cal ammo and .50 cal belt links.

GN   Pull in at Saipan but don't take on any chow.   GN

RC   Went ashore in the afternoon for two hours. Still several hundred Japs on the island causing plenty of trouble.   RC

GL   The island was a mess, they were still fighting up in the hills. Jap ammo, tank and bodies lying around. Land mines were everywhere. But on the whole the climate was swell and the island was green with trees grass and so on. It sure made a beautiful sight after being at sea so long.   GL

HB   On the 28th we were treated to a 30 minute beer party on Saipan. We could not stay too long due to the risk of so many unexploded shells and hand grenades. Bodies were still in fox holes. This is unforgettable.   HB

DrP   Go ashore at Saipan. Get Jap money, bayonet, Marine knife. Hot, rain, mud & terrible destruction.   DrP

1355-1415 Jacked over No. 4 main engine by electricity.   At 1420 LCT 357 cast off.

1430-1520 LCT 349 was moored alongside to port to receive from this ship 120 fragmentation bomb clusters to deliver to Service Squadron 10.

1525-1540 LCMS 29 was moored alongside to port quarter to deliver fuses and detonators.
2330 LCMS 29 came alongside port quarter to deliver 3600 Type D Starter Cartridges (for starting the aircraft engines), 3360 rounds of 40mm HEI (High Explosive Incendiary), and 1080 rounds of 20mm HEI.

Friday 29 September 1944   *Saipan - Underway*

0015 Anchored as before. LCMS 29 cast off.
0130-0445 LCMS 22 moored to port quarter to deliver 40mm ammunition.
1416-1518 Lighted fires under boilers.
1622 Commenced heaving short on port anchor.
1639 Got underway from Saipan Harbor, Mariana Islands per secret orders of CTG 38.2, dispatch No.
29054 dated 29 September 1944. Steaming on various courses at various speeds standing out of harbor.
1658 Sounded routine general quarters.
1713 Passed through anti-submarine nets taking departure from harbor.
1717 Steaming on various courses at various speeds taking proper station in formation.
1738 USS BENHAM and USS COLAHAN took anti-submarine stations, forming Task Unit 34.9 with
INDEPENDENCE (OTC), operating with Task Force 34, Vice Admiral Willis A. Lee Jr. (OTC in USS
WASHINGTON). Course 270°T, 15 knots. TF 34 is in disposition 4S axis 270°T. INDEPENDENCE bears
090°T, 6,000 yards from (guide) USS MASSACHUSETTS.
2136-2140 Rotated fleet axis and course to 225°T.
2150 Commenced zigzagging (Plan No.25) on base course 225°T.
*HB On September 29, we set sail to an island named Ulithi, arriving on October 1. We were to visit
this island on many occasions to refuel and take on supplies. HB*

*GL Pulled out of Saipan for the Ulithi Islands to get supplies. Island is within bombing range of Jap
held island of Yap. GL*

Saturday 30 September 1944   *Underway to Ulithi Atoll*

Steaming as before. Ship is darkened, Air Department in condition 14. No planes are in the air.
At 0235 USS MILLER reported sound contact, bearing 040°, distance 1500 yards. Ceased zigzagging,
emergency turn to 115°T.
0252 Changed fleet course to 205°T and resumed zigzagging (Plan No.25), base course 225°T.
0335 Sounded flight quarters.
0420 Sounded general quarters.
0445 Ceased zigzagging, changed course to 125°T, speed 22 knots while launching aircraft.
0459 Completed launching 4 Hellcats for Combat Air Patrol.
0524 On a course of 245°T, speed 25 knots, sounded torpedo defense for the Gunnery Department to
repel a simulated air attack by planes from TG 38.2.
0530 Task Force 34 assumed disposition 4V. INDEPENDENCE bearing 225°T, 6,000 yards from
guide, USS MASSACHUSETTS.
0552 From a base course of 225°T, speed 17 knots, commenced maneuvering to avoid simulated air
attack, making a number of emergency turns until 0639, when we secured from the maneuvering
exercise. TF 34 assumed disposition 4V back on base course 225°T, speed 17 knots.
0640 Secured from torpedo defense. Proceeded to flying station.
0656 Changed course to 086°T, commenced steaming on various courses at various speeds for while
recovering aircraft.
0708 Recovered 4 Hellcats launched at 0455. Changed course to 256°T, speed 25 knots, commenced
maneuvering to regain position in the formation.
0744-0746 Changed course to 150°T, 22 knots while launching 4 Hellcats, then commenced
maneuvering to regain station.

0843 Changed course to 245°T, speed 25 knots, commenced maneuvering to disengaged side of formation for battle exercises.

0853 Sounded torpedo defense.

0910 Gained position 10,000 yards on bearing of 315°T from Task Group 34.1 and commenced maneuvering to follow movements of TF 34 while maintaining position on disengaged side.

1029 Completed exercises and secured from torpedo defense. Steered various courses at various speeds while proceeding to flying station.

1037 OTC ordered CAP to remain aloft.

1102 Steamed at various courses and various speeds into the wind to recover aircraft.

1106-1108 Recovered 4 Hellcats launched at 0746.

1110 Maneuvered to regain position with guide, USS MASSACHUSETTS, bearing 225°T, 6,000 yards.

1203 Formed disposition 4V, base course 225°T.

1215 OTC ordered course change to 300°T, maneuvered to avoid simulated air attack.

1301 Proceeded to flying station.

1302-1304 Catapulted 4 Hellcats.

1344 Formed cruising disposition 4S.

1349 Proceeded to flying station.

1400-1407 Recovered 4 Hellcats launched at 1134 and 4 Hellcats launched at 1302. Maneuvered to regain position in the formation.

2308 Changed fleet course to 180°T.

Sunday 1 October 1944   *Underway - Ulithi Atoll*

Steaming as before. Part of the Forth Carrier Division, in company with USS BENHAM and USS COLAHAN. INDEPENDENCE is OTC & guide of TG 34.9, operating with Task Force 34 in cruising disposition 4S, axis 210°T, base course 180°T, speed 17 knots. Ship is darkened, Air Department is in condition 14.

0409 Changed course to 210°T.   0419 Formed disposition 4N.

0430 Sounded routine general quarters.

0444 Took station in disposition 4N with guide in USS IOWA.

0445 Sighted Ulithi Atoll, bearing 245°T, 15 miles.

0457 TG 34.9 detached from TF 34 and ordered to rejoin Task Group 38.2 (Rear Admiral G.F. Bogan).

0531 Secured from general quarters. Air Department set condition 14, all other departments condition 3.

0540 Commenced maneuvering to take station with TG 38.2 for entrance into Ulithi Atoll.

0606 USS SAN DIEGO assumed guide of TG 38.2.

0635 Changed course to 295°T.

0700 Entered Mugai Channel, steering various courses at various speeds to conform to channel.

0741 Anchored in berth No. 8, Ulithi Atoll, Caroline Islands, in 23 fathoms of water, coral bottom, with 125 fathoms of chain to the port anchor.

0800 Mustered crew on stations.

0805 LCI 1292 came alongside with provisions, ramming into our starboard side. The LCI struck INDEPENDENCE at frame 10 1/2, strake H-1 causing a hole thru the plating roughly 5 inches in diameter leading into compartment A303A. The damage, above the water line, was repaired by ships crew later this day.

DL   Independence had entered Ulithi Atoll for the first time near the end of September 1944. This was shortly after it had been occupied without Japanese opposition by an Army Regimental Combat Team from the 81st Division. We came in with the fleet formed at Eniwetok after steaming from Pearl. Eniwetok anchorage, captured only after fierce and bloody opposition, was too far east of where the war was obviously headed.

Ulithi's lagoon was enormous: nineteen miles long, five to ten miles wide. Over seven hundred big ships could be anchored safely at a time. Guam was four hundred miles to the northeast—a mere stepping stone in such a vast ocean.

A fond (?) memory for tens of thousands of sailors was a small, "helmet-shaped" island (Sam Morison's description) called Mogmog. On one occasion, some twenty thousand men were said to have spent a day there. Any individual who had secret dreams of a lubricious afternoon on a vaunted South Sea Island paradise, with an abundant supply of native girls running about half-naked, quickly learned that he'd been snookered. Just over ten degrees north of the Equator, Mogmog's heat was stifling. The straggling palm trees growing all over the place proved the delusion: they looked like tall, desiccated weeds.

The entertainment began with a bumpy ride of three or four miles in a landing craft. We were swabbies boasting lots of sea duty, but the contrast between life on a big ship and an hour in a bouncing boat was a divine comeuppance. So many of my shipmates became seasick during the trip landward and so many more did the same returning to Mighty I that I never made a repeat trip. It was a wrenching, retching, stinking experience. The coxwain manning our boat had apparently been splashed with vomit before, for he had sheathed himself head to toe with foul weather gear before we shoved off. Despite this, Mother Navy did her best to provide a wholesome American-style picnic grounds. Mogmog was a godsend. What else to do with a stadium-full bevy of young sailors a long way west of River Street and Beretania? Every eager recreation officer and every grinning Padre sweated puddles trying to keep us amused and happy. We had a grand time dashing about in sun and sand, wearing short-cut old dungarees, hats inside out, smoking too many cigarettes, trading our allotted four cans of weak beer (except when we got caught) for twice as many soft drinks. We played raucous games of softball in scratch teams made of would-be Babe Ruths or spindly-legged Joe Dimaggios. We got into hot-tempered discussions with sailors from other ships about the blessings of serving on our particular bucket versus some other—which meant harsh words and belly-to-belly confrontations. Not much blood was shed; nobody lost teeth or an eyeball. What few fights developed were broken up by determined SP's who, I sensed, were a trifle scared as they surveyed the overwhelming multitude they were duty-bound to control.

When 1700 finally came and this glorious day of recreation eight thousand miles from home ended, each man faced a long, sickening, exhausting ride in another pitching rowboat. Our ship never looked so good as she did when I staggered wearily up the accommodation ladder (a Jacobs ladder would have dumped us into the lagoon) and fell into my sack. Mister Porky granted us a night's rest. We decided his boss had ordered him to.

This was one of Ulithi's aspects. It was also a place of patriotic glory if you looked at it with eyes that saw. No man could scan the full extent of the atoll's great lagoon without observing the might and majesty of America spread out before him. Neither at Pearl Harbor nor San Francisco Bay nor at Camden along the Delaware could one bask in the sight of all these warships gathered together.

Carriers large and smaller, battleships new and older, heavy cruisers and light ones, destroyers from World War I four-pipers to modern Fletchers and Somner-class—on which the brunt of the kamikaze craze was to fall. There were strange looking craft never seen before: LST's, LSD's, LCM's, many others. Big fleet oilers (one of which, U.S.S. Mississinewa, from which we had refueled a number of times, was torpedoed in this anchorage). Subs, as vital to the Pacific War as the flattops, lurked like menacing tortoise shells half-submerged beside their tenders.

The day finally dawned when the lagoon came alive with the slow turning of great brass ship screws. We formed into our respective task groups of carriers and battleships and cruisers and destroyers. Hour by hour and ship by ship we went to sea. Thus began the long, hard, seemingly endless journey back to the States by way of, as a starter, the Palau Islands to the north, with an initial target named Peleliu. Anything could happen. Everything did.   **DL**

CEM   *"Address Unknown" was the movie we saw tonight beneath a tropical sky and a large full moon.*
   CEM

Ulithi Atoll

. "No man could scan the full extent of the atoll's great lagoon without observing the might and majesty of America spread out before him."
Donald Labudde

These two Navy photos from NARA are of the fleet within Ulithi Atoll. The well known bottom photo titled "Murders Row at Ulithi Atoll" (possibly taken 8 December 1944) **shows carriers WASP** (CV-18)**, YORKTOWN, HORNET, HANCOCK, and TICONDEROGA (front to back).**

14
Typhoon at Ulithi Atoll

Monday 2 October 1944   *Ulithi Atoll*

1048 Anchored as before. Sounded torpedo defense; unidentified aircraft picked up by radar.
Torpedo defense secured at 1053 when the aircraft was indentified as friendly.
This evening the wind increased beyond 25 knots, with the barometer slowly dropping. Many small boats were reported adrift within the anchorage.
Rear Admiral Bogan transferred his flag to the USS INTREPID.

GN Pull in at Ulithi and start to take on chow as fast as we can. Word is passed to be prepared to get under way on one hour's notice as Typhoon is on the way. GN

GL Had to pull out of island because of approaching hurricane. GL

AD At Ulithi taking on provisions. Raining like hell. AD

Tuesday 3 October 1944   *Ulithi Atoll - Typhoon at Sea*

Anchored in berth No. 8, Ulithi Atoll, Caroline Islands, in 25 fathoms of water, with 125 fathoms of chain to the port anchor. Wind continued to pick up.
0100 LCVP No.5 parted lines while tied astern of this ship and drifted away. No.2 motor whaleboat was sent to recover it. Both the LCVP and motor whaleboat were secured alongside USS MIAMI at 0230.
0501 Commenced heaving short on port anchor.
0544 Got underway with TG 38.2 per orders in Com Third Fleet dispatch, dated 3 October 1944.
Steering various courses at various speeds conforming to the channel.
0705 INDEPENDENCE headed south to ride out the storm with TU 38.2.1 forming cruising disposition 5R5, guide and OTC in USS INTREPID bearing 160°T, 2,500 yards, fleet axis 160°T, speed 12 knots.
0829 USS INDEPENDENCE became guide.
0840 USS BUNKER HILL joined the formation.
0850 Assumed station at fleet center.
0930 Entered heavy rain squall with heavy seas.
0950 USS CABOT joined the formation.
1313 Commenced zigzagging (plan No.6) on base course 090°T, fleet speed to 15 knots.
1356 With the storm growing worse, wave troughs deepened and peaks grew. A roll to port reached 27 degrees. Amidships on the flight deck, a portable crane was lost over the side, while on the starboard quarter a F6F (Bu.No.58853) slid into the sea. Green water was battering the ship and the damage list grew as the ship staggered under the relentless action of the storm driven waves. Below the flight deck in the hangar bay, aircraft broke free destroying 1 TBM (Bu.No.46255) and 3 F6F's (Bu.Nos.58431, 58726, 58817), and damaging structure within the hangar bay. The following damage was reported:
    1. Ventilation ducts, intake and uptake, were bent, ruptured and crushed.
    2. Foamite station was wrecked.
    3. Steam pipe to the ventilation heater was bent.
    4. Water supply line to the spark arrester for the incinerator stack was carried away.
    5. Eight feet of pipe safety rail around a flight deck catwalk was carried away.
    6. The splinter shield around the quad 40mm platform mount on No.1 forecastle was bent in and ammunition stowage damaged.
    7. Fixed fog nozzle connection was carried away from the forecastle.
    8. Nine 2 inch pipe life line stations were carried away from the forecastle.

9. Two stowage boxes for helmets and protective clothing for mount No. 1 were carried away.
10. Mount No. 1 power drive sustained mechanical damage.
11. The cooling system for mount No. 7 was damaged.
12. 20 feet of lagging was torn off salt water piping on the forecastle, port side.
13. All sheet metal linkage covers for 40mm mount No. 1 were carried away.
14. Fresh water service line on forecastle was badly distorted, requiring replacement.
15. Emergency salt water 1 1/2" pipe connection (on the forecastle port side) to magazine sprinkling system was carried away.

Damage to the ship was repaired by ships crew over the next 3 days.
2100 Final course for the day, 250°T, speed 15 knots.

DL *It was, truth to tell, Mother Nature driving our departure on that Tuesday, the 3rd day of October 1944. Independence had sent a work party of some sort ashore before 0800 quarters. As we mustered on the flightdeck, a wind that freshened even as we stood in formation began to blow with increasing force. Rigging atop the bridge and in flagbags aft of the island structure jiggled noisily.*
Our work party was left on the beach. We were, I believe, the second major ship to leave for the open sea behind the destroyers. The admirals apparently felt that any lurking submarine would ignore the cans but might readily pick off a CVL, thus giving itself away before the big Essex-class CV's or a battlewagon poked their bows outside. By the time we had crossed the bar, visibility was down to a few hundred yards. The wind was beginning to howl.

What we were steering into was our first typhoon—a mild one dubbed a tropical storm. It taught everyone aboard Mighty I some hard lessons. Wild seas and strong winds and poor visibility made it appear that we were alone on a planet gone mad. It was a new experience, but no one forgot it.

In 1960, while perusing our expurgated Log with Dorothy, I found one page that had not been removed. Forty-three lines long, it revealed the extent of damage inflicted on our ship. I understood why. Our skipper and his minions, probably through their lack of seatime experience, had let us down by not thinking through this new challenge. As the wind screamed and the sea erupted, airplanes tied down but not secured tried their best to fly and, in the process, things broke loose. Landing gears had been tied with ample manila lines, but no one had instructed the mechs to drain the hydraulic oleos and double-up with ¾-inch cables. So the lines gave with the constant up-and-down, in-and-out pressure and, finally, either snapped or stretched too far. This happened to planes lashed to cleats topside and to those parked in two parallel rows on the hangar.

One bobbing F6F on the starboard quarter of the flightdeck loosened its restraints. I saw it tumble over the side because I was stupidly wandering around the deck, in and out of the catwalks and between the palisades erected forward of the elevator. The wind and the boiling green sea, flecked with white foam, fascinated me. Holding on for dear life in the port catwalk, I was staring across the deck when this airplane gave up the ghost. Men were hopping up and down beside it. Some officer gave a prudent order and they left it to its fate.

In the morning the hangar was a shambles. Why the wreckage had not caught fire, no one cared to say. The official Log, written during the 1200-1600 watch, reported the loss of the topside F6F due to a 27-degree roll. "Also damaged beyond repair were the following planes on the hangar deck: 1 TBM, 3 F6F. The following damage was caused by heavy seas, all of which damage can be repaired... within the next three days."

Together with all the other airdales, we AOM's worked like dogs for days. Every spare Browning mounted on the armory bulkheads was used. Those in storage were broken out, cleaned of their cosmoline, and set aside. The guns in the TBM and the three ruined F6F's were salvaged.

Independence survived. An LCT was sunk. The wind died and the sea calmed and nobody said much of anything next day at chow.

On my study wall is a large framed 18x12 enlargement of a portside picture of Mighty I in the throes of this mild October blow. Just which Navy photographer took it, and from which ship, had been unknown to the Archives attendant, where I first saw a much smaller print. A thick gray overcast melds sky and ocean. Her bow is smashing into a quartering sea as a gust of wind tears the bow wave to shreds. The stern seems to be lifting out of the water. Planes, whose moorings have held in spite of the strain, are clustered alongside the stacks and at the after end of the flightdeck. Not a living man can be seen anywhere along the port catwalk—certainly not me. Perhaps by then I had learned my lesson. **DL**

DrP *0530—Departed lagoon Ulithi due to storm. Wind 36+ knots. 1530—Aircraft damaged on hangar deck. Typhoon type storm. No personnel casualties to speak of. What a mess—worse than enemy damage to airplanes.* **DrP**

CEM *"Everything was going O.K. in spite of heavy seas. I was lying in my bunk with my shoes off at about 1400 when the drawers commenced to come out . Although they were replaced as soon as they came out, they began to fall out faster then they could be taken care of.*
Suddenly all hell broke loose. A tool box broke loose, spilled its contents, and started sliding back and forth across the deck. A bin opened letting all the buckets (about a dozen) fall into the stowage; an office chair followed; the rest of the chairs, benches, and personnel were sliding about making a heck of a racket."
" Then a racket broke out on the hangar deck and one of the fellows who was standing at the double hatch said, that the planes had broken loose".
"It looked as though all the planes on the hangar deck had broken loose and since they were filled with gas, there was an immediate danger of fire. No fire call was sounded but the fire hoses were broken out almost at once which goes to show what an excellent fire fighting gang we have." **CEM**

McKee reported F6Fs and TBMs had snapped securing lines striking each other, pushed against bulkheads, smashing into torpedoes, and two spare engines. Aircraft with smashed tails and battered wings slid back and forth across the deck.

CEM *"We'd almost gotten the planes secured when the ship made several large lurches. Boy, you should have seen everybody scram. I climbed on top of the torpedo racks and stayed there until things quieted down. As soon as the ship smoothed out a little, we put more lines on the planes, because they'd smashed about more."* **CEM**

GN *Underway again and we are really hit but by the elements. Think I would rather face the Japs for at least we can fight back. A bad time is had by all and you have all you can do to hang on in the daytime, no less trying to lay in a bunk at night. I tried my best and I just don't think it can be done. Ruined 12 planes on hangar deck and lost one over the side from the flight deck. A lot of gray hair for George here.* **GN**

RC *Got underway, got caught in typhoon and lost one plane over the side and had several damaged.* **RC**

HB *On October 3, we had to leave Ulithi to ride out one of the many typhoons we had to deal with. The Independence was a cruiser to start out with and was converted to a carrier. It was said it could easily turn over. In fact I was told, if we rolled over to 32 degrees it might go belly up. I saw it roll to 28 and 29 degrees several times and it was no fun. When you went to chow, you had to hold onto your tray for dear life, or you could be eating out of someone else's tray. One time I remember the waves being so high, you could look out and see a battleship one minute and the next thing it wasn't there. The waves were hiding the battleship which was a good hundred feet from the water line to the very top, so you know the waves were pretty high.* **HB**

AD *Got underway at 0500. tried to outrun a Typhoon. No luck—we are right in the middle of it. Plenty rough too. We lost some planes over the side and banged up some on the hangar deck. Still plenty rough at night.* **AD**

Wednesday 4 October 1944　　　　　*Ulithi Atoll*

Steaming as before with TU 38.2.1 consisting of this vessel (center of formation & guide), USS CABOT, USS BUNKER HILL, and USS INTREPID.　　0200　fleet course changed to 295°T.
0423-0523　Ship was at general quarters.
0628　Changed fleet course to 270°T.
0845　Changed course to 340°T, speed 10　knots.
0847　Sighted Ulithi Atoll, bearing 310°T, distance 16,000 yards.
0915　Commenced maneuvering to gain column formation with guide in USS SAN DIEGO, 2,000 yards distance, as forth ship in column.
0922　Gained position in column and proceeded on various courses at various speeds proceeding into Ulithi Atoll.
0930　Entered the channel on approach to the anchorage.
1045　Anchored in anchorage No. 8, Ulithi Atoll in 27 fathoms of water, coral bottom, with 110 fathoms of chain to port anchor.
1122　A LCI had broken down forcing the INDEPENDENCE to get underway to a different anchorage.
1232　Anchored in anchorage No. 10, Ulithi Atoll in 18 fathoms of water, coral bottom, with 125 fathoms of chain to port anchor at waters edge.
The Captain has directed the ship stand ready for getting underway on one hour's notice. Provisioning was resumed, however it was hampered due to lack of small boats, which were damaged in the storm. All ships had the same problem.
1800　The ladder of the starboard gangway was damaged, due to heavy seas, by the motor launch returning a working party that had been sent aboard the USS ALDEBARAN.

GN　Back to Ulithi even though the storm is still here. It has let up considerable. GN

GL　Pulled back into Ulithi to get our supplies. Found out the LCI with our supplies sunk during the storm. GL

RC　Weather improved so we go back to Ulithi to repair damage. RC

HB　When the storm was over, we had lost one of our whale boats and had thirteen damaged planes. We dropped anchor at Ulithi again on the 4th. HB

AD　At Ulithi. Air dept. repairing planes. AD

Thursday 5 October 1944　　　　　*Ulithi Atoll*

Anchored in anchorage No. 10, Ulithi Atoll. Continued provisioning the ship.
0730　Mustered crew on stations.
0840　USS SAN DIEGO stood out.
0930　USS OAKLAND underway to refuel.
The ships No.2 whale boat had been dispatched to try to recover LCVP No. 5 on October 3rd. at 0100. The whaleboat crew had tied up alongside the USS MAIMI. They later took shelter from the worsening storm aboard the USS DIXIE. The No. 2 whale boat was reported lost adrift today when the lines were discovered parted from the DIXIE's stern.

Friday 6 October 1944　　　　　*Ulithi Atoll - Underway*

Anchored as before in anchorage No. 10, Ulithi Atoll.
1000　Made daily inspection of magazines. Maximum temperature 93°F.
1015　Commenced jacking over all main engines by electric motor.

Above: **Lashed down on the flight deck.** Below: **Typhoon damaged aircraft on the Hangar Deck.**

Palisades are erected to help break up the wind on the aft side as it blows down the flight deck.

Typhoon damaged aircraft on the Hangar Deck.

1400 Commenced receiving fresh provisions from USS ALDEBARAN.

1420 Ensigns D.M. Pearson and R.M. Nielsen reported aboard to ferry 2 Hellcats to the HANCOCK.

1450 Hoisted aboard No. 1 whaleboat.

1520 Completed receiving fresh provisions.

1600 Got underway from anchorage in Berth No. 10. Commenced steaming on various courses at various speeds conforming to the channel.

1606 Sounded routine general quarters.

1642 Took departure of Ulithi Atoll, Mangejang Island bearing 260°T, distance 1.8 miles. Steaming on course 115°T, 18 knots, maneuvering to form disposition 5R5 with USS INTREPID (OTC), HANCOCK and CABOT constituting Task Unit 38.2.1, Rear Admiral G.F. Bogan (Commander, Carrier Division Four) in USS INTREPID. Cruising with Task Group 38.2 on a course of 225°T, axis 150°T, guide USS NEW JERSEY which is 150°T at 5,000 yards from this vessel. Proceeding to fueling area.

1651 After stripping them of useable parts, jettisoned overboard 1 TBM and 2 F6Fs, damaged beyond repair during the heavy weather on October 3rd.

1702 Secured from general quarters. Air Department set condition 14.

1729 Sounded routine torpedo defense.

1754 Changed course to 205°T, speed 24 knots.

1810 Gained new position on (guide) NEW JERSEY, bearing 060°T, 2,500 yards, pursuant to signal from OTC. Steadied on course 290°T, speed 15 knots.

2340 Commenced zigzagging on base course 350°T, speed 19 knots.

GN Underway for action. This time we hope it's a good bit. The weather is still pretty bad and we continue to take a beating but we are getting used to it this time. GN

GL Pulled out of Ulithi got very few supplies. Last operation was 35 days at sea, don't know how long the next one will be. Scuttlebutt is that we will raid an island just off of Japan then Formosa, and then back to the Philippines again. GL

Overview

1. The U.S.S. INDEPENDENCE departed Ulithi Atoll on October 6th, in company of other units of **Task Group 38.2**, which consisted of : CVs INTREPID (Flag), HANCOCK, and BUNKER HILL; CVLs CABOT and INDEPENDENCE; BBs IOWA and NEW JERSEY; CLs VINCENNES, HOUSTON, and MIAMI; A/A CLs SAN DIEGO and OAKLAND, and 17 DDs. At the time of the departure Ulithi was in the outer perimeter of a rather severe storm which had been blowing since early October 3rd.

PLAN: To join with **Task Groups 38.1**, **38.3** and **38.4** in operations designed to support the invasion and occupation of Leyte and other islands in the Philippines.

2. The INDEPENDENCE had been ordered converted back to a night carrier after the Palau action. It was intended to operate the INDEPENDNCE as a night carrier during the coming operations, except for routine patrols.

3. On board the INDEPENDENCE was Night Air Group 41- **CVLG(N)-41**, Commander Turner Foster Caldwell, Jr., USN, Air Group Commander (CAG).
     This group consisted of:
          VF(N)-41 - 25 pilots - 3 F6F3; 9 F6F5N; 12 F6F5
               Comdr. T. F. Caldwell, Jr., USN, Squadron Commander
          VT(N)- 41 - 7 pilots - 8 TBM-1C; 1 TBM-lD
               Lieut. W. R. Taylor, USNR, Squadron Commander

By October 15th the transfer of day pilots and planes had been completed and the composition of this group was then:
          VF(N)-41 - 16 pilots - 1 F6F3N; 2 F6F5; 12 F6F5N
               Comdr T. F. Caldwell, Jr., USN, Squadron Commander
          VT(N)-41 - 9 pilots - 8 TBM-1C (Most, if not all, were most likely night equipped)
               Lieut. W. R. Taylor, USNR, Squadron Commander

Saturday 7 October 1944   *Underway*

On October 7th Task Group 38.2 made the scheduled rendezvous with Task Groups 38.1, 38.3, and 38.4. The four groups proceeded in the outer perimeter of the storm toward Okinawa Shima in the Nansei Shoto Island chain, against which the first strikes were scheduled to be made on October 10th.
Only routine patrols were flown prior to October 10th.
Steaming as before, ship is darkened, Air Department is in condition 14.
0434 Sounded general quarters.
1700 Changed course to 015°T, speed 17 knots.
1705 Commenced zigzagging (Plan No.6) on base course 015°T.

AD At sea, in another storm, sea is pretty rough. AD

15
Nansei Shoto and Formosa

Sunday 8 October 1944   *Underway - Refueling*

Steaming as before, ship is darkened, Air Department is in condition 14.
0625 Changed course to 260°T, changed speed to 10 knots.
0639 Rotated axis to 260°T. USS NECHES became guide. Maneuvering to gain position on guide.
0723 Gained position on USS NECHES, bearing 223°T, distance 3,200 yards. Commenced zigzagging independently, steering various courses at various speeds, while maintaining position on guide.
0915 Ceased zigzagging, maneuvered into position for approach on tanker USS NECHES (*AO-47) .
    (* Note: USS NECHES AO-5 was lost to torpedoes from Japanese submarine I-72 on 23 January 1942.)
1145 Commenced pumping fuel oil starboard side aft. 1147 Commenced pumping fuel oil starboard side forward. USS BUNKER HILL joined the formation to become a part of TU 38.2.1.
1226-1231 USS MILLER was alongside port quarter to deliver guard mail.
1302 Sounded flight quarters.
1329 Cast off USS NECHES having received 250,000 gallons of fuel oil. Commenced steering various courses at various speeds while proceeding to flying station.
1339-1346 Steering into the wind, launched 4 F6Fs. 2 F6Fs were sent to the USS HANCOCK and 2 to the USS INTREPID, pursuant to orders from CTG 38.2. The INDEPENDENCE was sending off day fighters for use by other carriers, in exchange INDEPENDENCE would receive night fighters.
1405 Steering various courses into the wind for flight operations.
1421 Completed recovering 2 TBMs, (Bill Phelps and "Polly" Archer) launched from the USS BUNKER HILL, that had been on temporary loan. (They had detached on loan on 17 September)
1434 Commenced steering various courses at various speeds while regaining position in the formation.
1443 Regained station, course 260°T, guide USS NECHES, bearing 087°T, distance 7,900 yards, speed 10 knots.
1602 Commenced steering various courses at various speeds proceeding to flying station.
1623-1629 Catapulted 4 F6F day fighters sent to the USS BUNKER HILL, pursuant to orders from CTG 38.2 for use by her air group.
1700 Formed cruising disposition 5R5, guide USS NECHES, bearing 047°T, 1,900 yards. Changed fleet axis to 000°T.
1735-1835 Ship was at torpedo defense. Air Department set to condition 11.
1840 USS INTREPID became guide, bearing 330°T, 5,500 yards.
1920 TG 38.2 completed fueling.
2100 Changed speed to 18 knots, USS NEW JERSEY designated guide bearing 000°T, distance 5,000 yards.
2035 Air Department set to condition 12.
2100 Changed course to 295°T.
2110 Commenced zigzagging (Plan No.6) on base course 295°T.

AD At sea, taking on fuel, prepared for another raid on the Japs. AD

Monday 9 October 1944   *Underway*

Steaming as before in company with TU 38.2.1. At 0400, changed to base course 010°T.
0446 Sounded general quarters.
0550 Secured from general quarters, Air Department set in condition 14.
0802-0803 Launched 2 TBMs, sent to the USS SAN JACINTO.
0819-0853 Received on board 2 F6F3(N)'s transferred from USS INTREPID. Received on board 3 F6F5(N)s transferred from USS BUNKER HILL.

USS MILLER pulls alongside the port quarter for transfer of guard mail.
In the background; USS NEW JERSEY, USS CABOT, USS BUNKER HILL and USS INTRIPID.

1120 Changed course to 110°T.

1220 USS COLAHAN came alongside to starboard to transfer mail and a patient for treatment in sickbay, and received back the patient (now recovered) for the emergency appendectomy performed aboard the INDEPENDENCE.

1232 OTC changed fleet course to 286°T.

1250 USS COLAHAN cast off.

1252 Changed course to 276°T, speed 28 knots while regaining position in the formation.

1423 Regained position in the disposition, changed fleet course to 020°T.

1431 Received onboard 1 F6F5(N) from USS BUNKER HILL.

2100 With numerous course changes throughout the evening, the INDEPENDENCE closed the day on a course of 300°T, speed 25 knots, beginning a high speed run in to strike Nansei Shoto.

GUAM   *9 October 1944*

Again the Third Fleet is on its way to help set the rising sun, after rearming at Saipan and reprovisioning at Ulithi. We are now on our way to Nansei Shoto, the stepping stones of Japan. This crack we are taking is a diversionary one only and just a sample to the 820,000 Japs on these islands, as to what is to come in the very near future.

Tomorrow at 0545, 38.2 will send a search group (for both reconnaissance and bombing) north around the island of Yaky Shima while 38.3 has a similar search to the south near Formosa. All four task units will send four or five deck loads to raise hell with the main island in the Nansei Shoto group. Okinawa Shima. This Island, in addition to having a fine fleet anchorage (where fleeing Jap fleet from the Philippine Sea battle hid out) is the communication center for Japanese forces in Formosa, Philippines and western Pacific.

The population of this one island is 443,000 and that of Naha, the largest city in the Nansei Shoto Group is 66,000, the island has been used extensively for staging aircraft from Japan to Formosa.

After the October 10th strike at Okinawa we fuel and head for Formosa. On the 12th and 13th all task groups will hit their assigned targets on the island of Formosa.

After this operation we again retire for fueling purposes and head for the largest undertaking the Pacific has yet seen. The beginning of the Philippine campaign by the taking of Leyte in the Visayan group.

Four divisions of army will do the invading with the 7th fleet (amphibious) and the Third fleet supporting. It's a MacArthur show. After the landings have been established, the Independence will continue to provide night fighter coverage.

Latest intelligence tells us that part of the Jap fleet is in the Japanese Sea while, the other part is between the Malay Straits and Borneo in the South China Sea.

Flash •••• A sub report tells us that a Jap CV just left Manila and that if it continues on its course and speed, it will probably cross our course sometime tomorrow providing the two subs who are hot on its trail don't bag it first.   *GUAM*

Tuesday 10 October 1944   *Nansei Shoto Archipelago*
Ryukyu Okinawa-Shima & Amami Oshima

Steaming as before in TU 38.2.1 with USS INTREPID, BUNKER HILL, HANCOCK, and CABOT, as a **Task Unit** of **Task Group** 38.2. (Rear Admiral G.F. Bogan is CTG in INTREPID). Cruising in disposition 5R5, axis 000°T, course 300°T, speed 25 knots, bearing 180°T, 5,000 yards from the guide, USS NEW JERSEY. Ship is darkened, Air Department is in condition 14.

0515 Sounded general quarters.

0629 Changed fleet course to 000°T, axis to 045°T, and fleet speed to 15 knots.

0653 Changed disposition to 5V5, axis 045°T, we bear 225°T, 3,500 yards from guide.

0823 Steering various courses into the wind for flight operations.

0830 Landed 2 TBM(N)s as replacements from the USS SAN JACINTO.

0900 Axis rotated to 045°T, INDEPENDENCE assigned to position bearing 000°T, 3,500 yards to guide. Commenced maneuvering into position.

1023 Secured from general quarters, Air Department set to condition 11. It had become apparent no enemy attacks were developing.

1451 Changed course to 190°T.

1519 Changed speed to 22 knots.

1523 Sounded torpedo defense on report of an approaching enemy aircraft.

1524 Sounded flight quarters, then changed course to 045°T.

1530-1550 Launched 16 Hellcats and 4 Avengers. 12 Hellcats were assigned CAP and 4 Hellcats were assigned to the Avengers which were tasked with SNASP.

1606 Changed course to 190°T.

1615 Secured from torpedo defense. The threat from enemy aircraft failed to materialize.

1643 Sounded flight quarters.

1700 Changed course to 050°T, speed 18 knots.

1704–1710 Steering various courses into the wind, recovered 7 F6F Hellcats launched at 1530.

1754 Completed recovery of 4 F6Fs and 4 TBMs launched at 1530. At 1758 sounded general quarters.

1801-1805 Recovered 2 F6Fs.

1825-1827 Recovered 3 F6Fs. All of our aircraft were now safely back onboard.

2208 They started retirement from the area to refuel, changing course to 190°T.

2340 Received report of radar contact of enemy aircraft on bearing 040°T, distance 40 miles.

2341 Sounded flight quarters, then changed fleet course to 080°T.

2345 Commenced launching 2 F6Fs to intercept the unknown aircraft.

2350 Changed speed to 30 knots, then changed fleet course to 220°T.

2350 Changed course to 250°T.

DL Today began the first occasion since the Marianas campaign (which Mighty I had missed) that all four Task Force 38 carrier groups operated together as one unit. What a unit it was! I have no idea how many hundreds of square miles it covered. We could see all the ships except some of the hulldown destroyers guarding our flanks. The other groups were invisible except when course changes brought us briefly within sight of each other. TF 38 planes pounded Japanese shipping and military installations on Okinawa "and other islands" in the Ryukyus.

Each night Independence snoopers flew search missions. We airdales almost got used to working like dogs in the dark. Frenchie in the galley kept the joe hot and fresh, the sandwiches stuffed with horsecock meat, pickles and mustard, and the soup kettles brimming. A slice of papaya would have been nice. DL

GN Strike at Formosa. Jap planes got to within 16 miles of us but were splashed by our CAP. Up practically all night with GQ. GN

GL Attacked Nansei Shoto and Okinawa Shima Islands in the early morning. Okinawa Shima is our principal target. Air opposition was slight. Shot down a few Jap planes in the air and destroyed a few on the ground. Ships were found in the harbor, we eliminated them. Sank 2 subs, a large sub tender, 14 tankers and cargo ships and 14 small craft. Damaged 1 CL, 1 small sub tender, 18 tankers and cargo ships and 14 small craft. Had GQ midnight and 0300 in the morning. Nothing happened. C.A.P. shot down a couple snoopers. Still about 300 miles from Japan.
Note: We listened to Radio Tokyo to amuse ourselves. They claim to have sunk almost all our whole fleet. GL

DrP Strike Okinawa Shima as part of 38.2 Task Group. Score: 2 subs, 1 large sub tender, 1 tanker, 2 cargo ships, 1 sampan, 2 small craft, 1 landing craft, 2 ammo lighter, 8 small ships, 2 Frances, one twin engine bomber, 1 Tony. All we did was wreck 7 aircraft on deck on a scramble at 2400.**
Obenour, pilot, uninjured. DrP   (** See 0137 - 11 October 1944)

There were 1396 sorties flown over Okinawa hitting 4 airfields (three on the main island, one located the smaller island Ie Shima) close in off the western shore. Warehouses were hit in the city Naha destroying food and munitions. Ships sunk would further harm the ability of the Japanese to supply the island.

GUAM   <u>10 October 1944</u>   **Ryukyu Okinawa-Shima & Amami Oshima**

As scheduled, the third fleet hits all parts of Okinawa Shima in the Nansei Shoto Archipelago. If early returns are any indication, the operation was a success in more ways than one. Not only did we give the Nips something to think about by coming within 200 miles off the empire itself, but our pilots did right well by themselves.

During our five hour GQ this morning our anti snooper patrols knocked down at least 2 Frances and 1 Betty. They came out to snoop but not for long.

Our first wave of bombers spotted some shipping in one of the anchorages and it wasn't long before an 8,000 ton Sub Tender plus assorted Cargo ships and small craft were sunk. And a cruiser and a destroyer and a badly damaged destroyer.

As the planes left this area, they spotted another Sub Tender, four submarines afloat, 2 subs in dry dock and other craft lying in anchorage. Now devoid of their bombs and rockets, it was necessary for them to leave this choice morsel to wave no. 2. By the time the 2nd striking force hit, the shipping, the four subs were gone but those that were left, well, they're gone too •••••

All told the two striking forces from 5 carriers of 38.2 sunk 17 ships and small craft and damaged 38 ships and small craft. These are the first returns only. We know that all other objectives, air fields all AA positions buildings etc, took a beating.

This evening three large formations of enemy planes were reported on their way to get us but somewhere along the line the switch was pulled and they didn't come.

At midnight, more bogies on the screen sent us scurrying to our battle stations. We launched two night fighters to intercept, but before any contact was made, the snooper bogey headed for greener pastures (good thing to if our night chicks ever got to him goodby Jap)

Again at 0230 we were roused from our sacks to man our GQ stations because of bogies. After our night fighters chased him or them around the sky for an hour or more he too headed home and we went to our sacks.

Today we fuel and tomorrow we hit Formosa, everybody, especially those who have not been in the Pacific before are getting pretty cocky. Here's hoping they will have more reason to be after the next operation or two.   **GUAM**

F6F5Ns being spotted and made ready to catapult

Avengers being catapulted (note the radar).

An Avenger just catapulted as a Hellcat prepares to launch.
(note the difference in the cowl flaps)

0100 Steaming as before in TU 38.2.1. USS CUSHING and USS YARNALL were detached from TG 38.2 to act as plane guards for the INDEPENDENCE when operating outside the screen.

0110 Commenced steering various courses at various speeds into the wind for flight operations, operating independently in company with YARNALL and CUSHING from TG 38.2.

0137 The two F6Fs that were scrambled to intercept the bogey at 2345 were returning to land. Ensign G.W. Obenour (Bu.No.58392) floated down the deck in the rain and dark of night, crashing through the barrier damaging his Hellcat, two other Hellcats, and three Avengers beyond repair. Luck prevailed (if the loss of 6 aircraft can be used with the word luck in the same paragraph) as "Obie" was uninjured, and there were no personnel injuries.

0147 Landed the second F6F.

0200 INDEPENDENCE, YARNALL and CUSHING maneuvered to overtake TG 38.2.

0234 Sounded general quarters due to radar contact bearing 050°T, distance 25 miles.

0243 Jettisoned 1 F6F-3N (Bu.No.58392) overboard, damaged beyond repair in crash at 0137.

0342 Secured from general quarters.

0345 Radar contact faded from the screen.

0521 Sounded routine general quarters. Air Department set condition 14.

0557 Changed course to 210°T. 0601 Formed cruising disposition 5R5.

0704 Rotated formation axis to the right to 080°T.

0729 Commenced maneuvering to approach USS MISSISSINEWA for fueling operations.

0730 Mustered crew on stations.

0807 USS MANATEE designated as guide of fueling disposition.

0819 Maneuvered alongside USS MISSISSINEWA to starboard.

0852 Commenced taking on fuel oil.

0915-0936 USS MARSHALL was along side port quarter to receive pilots of replacement aircraft to be flown from USS NASSAU.

1026 USS MISSISSINEWA cast off having delivered 204,000 gallons of fuel oil and 795 gallons of lubricating oil. Commenced maneuvering to regain station.

1129 Regained station, INDEPENDENCE bearing 215°T, 2,500 yards from the guide. Commenced zigzagging independently on base course 260°T, speed 12 knots.

1254 Jettisoned 1 F6F-5N (Bu.No.58796) overboard, damaged beyond repair in the storm on October 3rd.

1337 Jettisoned 1 F6F-5N (Bu.No.58970) and 3 TBM(N)s (Bu.Nos.25582, 45619, 46247) overboard, damaged beyond repair in crash at 0137.

1412-1420 USS HICKOX was alongside starboard quarter to transfer mail. (Note: Deck log has USS Hickock)

1427 Sounded flight quarters.

1441 Commenced steering various courses at various speeds proceeding to flying station.

1448 Guide shifted position in the formation, INDEPENDENCE to bear 249°T, distance 8,900 yards from guide.

1448-1452 Landed on board three replacement F6F5Ns and three replacement TBM-1Cs, received from the USS NASSAU.

1456 Secured from flight quarters, Air Department set condition 14. Commenced steering various courses at various speeds to regain position in formation.

1603 Commenced zigzagging independently on course 260°T, speed 12 knots.

1750 USS WEDDERBURN came along the starboard side to deliver mail, casting off at 1754.

1821 Changed course to 080°T.

1833 Changed course to 320°T, speed 24 knots.

2333 INDEPENDENCE turned into the wind and catapulted 2 F6F(N) Hellcats piloted by Ens. W.E. Miller and Ens. R.W. Klock, upon orders to scramble from OTC. Enemy aircraft were tracked on radar to a distance of 28 miles, bearing 025°T. Sounded general quarters. Miller and Klock had been launched into a night that was black, squally, six tenths cumulonimbus cloud cover with bases at 2,000 feet. Moonrise would occur at 0227. Klock's IFF was out and he was instructed to orbit.

Refueling alongside USS MISSISSINEWA (AO-59) on 11 October 1944

Miller discovered hydraulic problems immediately after being launched.

He was also having transmitter problems. The hydraulic problems translated to having to pump up his gear, flaps, and charge his guns manually.

He was given vectors toward the bogey and intercepted a Mavis. During the ensuing night chase he made numerous approaches on the slower Mavis, getting off a few shots, with problems of overshooting his target ("at least six times"), loosing it in clouds, and loosing it off his onboard radar screen, without being able to bring it down. When the night pursuit reached 50 miles out, Klock was instructed to give up the chase on the elusive Mavis. Another factor making the intercept difficult was lack of night interception practice with radar intercept gear due the squadron being used as a day carrier since returning to combat.

2355 Secured from general quarters. Air Department remained in condition 11.

GN   We refueled and kept a good C.A.P. for we are way in enemy waters. Up again early with bogies and a Jap sub that was picked up at midnight.   GN

GUAM On 11 October we fueled our task force within easy range of Jap bombers (and they found that range easy enough). All during the day Bettys, Francis's, and Nells paid us visits. Such visits were occasional, only came in singles or at the most pairs. No concentrated attacks were made and our fighters took care of them all. Our fueling operations were never interrupted. GUAM

Refueling alongside USS MISSISSINEWA (AO-59) on 11 October 1944

DL   *The tempo kept heating up. TF 38 pounded shipping, airfields, and industrial targets on Formosa. The island was regarded as "the strongest and best-developed base south of the homeland proper..."*

Planes from CVs Lexington, Essex, and CVL Langley sank a host of ships off the Pescadores **. The strikes drew heavy Japanese counterattacks, which was the purpose of our strikes. Forty-two enemy planes were splashed. A Combat Air Patrol was maintained by planes from Cabot and Independence.

By now the Third Fleet (Halsey in New Jersey) and Task Force 38 (Mitscher in Lexington) was a typhoon in itself. This is what it consisted of (according to historian Morison). Mark it well, for such a naval powerhouse is not likely to ever again sail the Seven Seas:

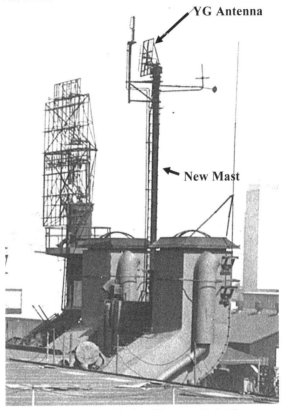

YG Antenna

New Mast

TG 38.1 (McCain)
CV Wasp & Hornet
CVL Monterey, Cowpens, Cabot
CA Wichita, Boston, Canberra
15 DD

TG 38.2 (Bogan)
CV Intrepid, Hancock, Bunker Hill
CVL Independence
BB Iowa, New Jersey
CL Houston, Vincennes, Miami, San Diego, Oakland
17 DD

TG 38.3 (Sherman)
CV Essex, Lexington
CVL Princeton, Langley
BB Washington, Massachusetts, South Dakota, Alabama
CL Santa Fe, Birmingham, Mobile, Reno
14 DD

TG 38.4 (Davison)
CV Franklin, Enterprise
CVL San Jacinto, Belleau Wood
CA New Orleans
CL Biloxi
12 DD   **DL**

New Antenna Mast added at Hunters Point between the No.3 & No.4 stacks. Photo courtesy of: Steve Wiper

(** *Author's note:* The Pescadores are an archipelago [AKA Penghu Islands - in the Taiwan Strait] located between the western shores of Formosa [today Taiwan] and the mainland of China.)

GN *Make strike on Formosa. Japs are really out in force. Our pilots had a sort of a field day and the Nips kept us going all night. Dropped flares all around us and that at night is a bit scary. Loading 100 lb bombs for a night strike when a Jap came over the starboard quarter. Dropped a flare that was a bit aft. Bunker Hill was on our port side and he dropped seven directly over her. Looked like broad day light out and our two ships stood out like a sore thumb. Waited for bombs to drop but thank God they never came. Finished loading bombs and went to starboard belting room. Was on the deck topside a short time when two five-inch shells from another outfit burst close aboard. Could hear the shrapnel hit the water. About half an hour later a dive bomber made a run on us. For the third time that night I tried to dig myself a foxhole in the flight deck. He didn't release his bomb but from the way it sounded to me he came within 100 feet. A few more gray hairs.* **GN**

GUAM
The 12th was the big day, or should I say the big night. The day went as expected. All four task groups split the island into four sections and attacked their respective areas with the usual fighter and bombing raids, for the first time since we've been operating out here the Japs really put their fighters into the air. Estimated figure not authenticated yet, were something like 150 planes shot down. No enemy planes attacked our groups during the day. Usual snoopers were picked off intermittently all day.

Those sporadic snoopers attacks, were discontinued when at 1845 they started their first real torpedo attacks.

At that time we went to general quarters and remained there until 0230 this morning, those eight hours in torpedo junction were the longest eight hours I've ever put in. The screen was covered with bogies.

We had six night fighters in the air earlier in the evening but two had landed when the attack began. The four fighters left intercepted with Bill Henry establishing himself an ace (five planes) by bagging two Bettys in quick secession. This was enough to break up the initial attack, but not for long.

The entire eight hours was a nightmare of bogies at 010° 10 miles, bogey 190° 8 miles, and so on all around the screen.

Night landings in the rain and so on. Windows being dropped, flares dropped and lighting up the entire task group and Bettys being splashed, a myriad of events. That let us pretty well bushed.

We were relieved when secure was sounded, a few interesting moments were experienced in the early stages of the attack when we were hit by a dud torpedo aft, about frame 95.

Only one other thing could have jarred the ship in this fashion. A bomb (or depth charge).

Of the four fighters we had in the air only two were pancaked.

Obenour and Moore disappeared. Obie was heard over one of the task groups begging for some light to make his landing, but the dangers involved was obvious and he was told to make a water landing, he was never seen or heard from after that. Moore must have been shot down. He was never heard from either. It's tough to lose two good kids! Obie didn't go in much for night fighting but Moore ate it up. He was always eager to get into the air day or night, to get himself some red flags on his plane. Our only hope is that he got it quick or makes his way to Formosa.

We searched all day but found no trace of either. **GUAM**

DrP *Formosa. TG good bag. Swell weather. 1800—Attempt to land 8 VF. Edwards in second plane to land goes into stbd catwalk & holds up landing of 6 VF airborne. Bogies reported and Henry gets 2 Betties, Barnett 1 Betty. Joe Moore lost, probably shot down. Obenour lost in pancake into sea. Concerted bogie attacks by waves using flares hit us strafing or torpedo attacks lasted from 1930 to 0100. Saw 4 bogies splash into the sea burning & exploding. Beautiful AA fire. We had 2 chances but missed with AA. Big night.* ***DrP***

Thursday 12 October 1944   *High Speed Run to Attack Formosa*

0209 Steaming as before in TU 38.2.1. Left formation with USS TINGEY and USS MILLER as screens.

0234 Commenced steering various courses at various speeds into the wind for flight operations.

0246 Landed 1 F6F.

0330 Landed 1 F6F, changed course to 302°T to rejoin formation. Changed speed to 28 knots at 0340.

0535 Sounded flight quarters. At 0537 general quarters was sounded.

0705 Regained position in Task Group 38.1 in disposition 5V5, axis 080T, bearing 240°T, 3,500 yards from guide.

0730 Secured from general quarters. Air Department set to condition 13.

0900 Changed fleet course to 055°T.

0944 Enemy aircraft reported by OTC, bearing 355°T, 100 miles, on course 160°T. Sounded flight quarters. At 0950 the bogey was reported to be friendly.

1558 Sounded flight quarters.

The INDEPENDENCE was now transitioning into a dedicated night carrier. TG 38.2 was in the air making strikes against enemy targets against Formosa, while Air Group 41 pilots rested during the daylight hours. Like fabled vampires, or bats, they would now eagerly come out to stalk prey at night. The **"Shademaids"** would mount their aircraft to hunt the enemy, under cover of darkness. They would defend the fleet from Japanese night hunters and snoopers, while the day shift carriers slept.

1615-1619 Catapulted 8 Hellcats for CAP. The two divisions of 4 Hellcats were led by T.F. "Stinky" Caldwell and W.E. "Bill" Henry.

1629 Secured from flight quarters. Air Department set to condition 14.

1715 Sounded torpedo defense.

1730 Comdr. Caldwell's division was vectored to intercept bogies which turned out to be friendly.

1830 Four of the eight Hellcats (Caldwell's division) were instructed to return to land.

1831 On a course of 065°T, 15 knots, began recovering aircraft.

1835 With one Hellcat recovered (Comdr. Caldwell), Ens. Emmett R. Edwards landing gear dropped into a gun director bucket, planting his F6F3N (Bu.No.58052) into the starboard catwalk amidships near the forth stack, fouling the flight deck for the next half hour. The Hellcat prop and flap were damaged. There was a need to clear the deck quickly, in the haste, the Hellcat was further damaged beyond repair. No injuries to pilot or deck crew. In addition to the loss of the Hellcat, the ship lost one 25 man life raft over the side and sustained other minor damage. Obenour and Allen were delayed landing, then further delayed when enemy planes appeared, Obenour and Allen continued to orbit.

At 1840 Bill Henry's division were vectored to a group of bogeys roughly 25 miles out flying at 1,000' altitude crossing in front of the Task Group. Henry after following vectors, spotted a Betty one mile ahead. Closing in rain, he opened fire at 700' astern (not using his outboard guns for fear of being blinded by tracers). After a couple of bursts, both engines began to burn brightly. The Betty turned slightly to port in a flaming glide, hit the water and exploded. No survivors were seen.

The flight was then given a new vector for two more bogeys. Bill Henry and James Arden Barnett spotted the two Bettys off their port beam flying at 500' altitude in a single column. Bill Henry fired from 6 o'clock level with all six guns.

As with the previous Betty, this one went the same way, as a flamer with both engines burning, exploding as it hit the water from a port turning dive. It was Bills second Betty that evening.

"Barny" Barnett closed on the remaining Betty which had dropped down to 200' off the water. Barny closed to 600' level astern putting rounds in to the bomber. He placed three 2 second burst into the Betty observing the entire plane become engulfed in flame, burning fiercely before it crashed into the water. As Bill and Barny departed the area, flames from both downed Bettys burned on the oceans surface.

1855 Sounded general quarters. Enemy aircraft (mostly Bettys) attacked the Task Force. CAP pilots had been instructed to remain outside of the 15 mile circle of the formation during the attack to avoid friendly fire from the fleet guns. The Task Group opened fire. AA fire from the ships "shot down several that burned spectacularly within the group". The first plane shot down was roughly 7,000 yds. off the port bow.

1913 The second A/C (Type 2 Betty) was shot down (by USS CABOT ?) roughly 1,200 yds. off the port quarter. The third plane 6,000 yds. on the port bow by a BB.

1916 The forth A/C crashed on the horizon off the port beam.

1925 INDEPENDENCE opened fire, with its stern quad 40mm mount, on two Bettys crossing astern, the first at 1,600 yds., the second at 3,000 yds. No hits observed. By 1945, all attacking enemy planes not shot down had withdrawn. No damage was inflicted on the Task Group.

2008 Commenced dropping astern of screen to recover night fighters. OTC directed INDEPENDENCE to remain inside screen during recovery of aircraft.

2037 Commenced steering various courses at various speeds during aircraft recovery.

2045-2052 Bill Henry, Barny Barnett, F.A. Fisher and J.S. Allen landed their Hellcats from the CAP launched at 1615. Two pilots failed to return aboard. Ensign Joseph F. "Joe" Moore was last seen during the action with the first Betty. His fate unknown. He was never seen again. (F6F-3N Bu.No. 41209)

Ensign George W. "Obie" Obenour ran low on fuel circling the TG trying to find a carrier to land on, in the dark of night with low visibility. His receiver seemed to be bad, but his transmissions were heard asking for a carrier to show a light. With fear of showing their position to a possible enemy sub or aircraft, the vast dark lonely ocean remained dark. Obie had been instructed to make a water landing. He, like Joe Moore, was never seen again. (F6F-5N Bu.No. 58728)

Obie's friend and fellow VF(N)-41 aviator Irvin H. "Hebe" Lee would write in his book *"Shademaid"*; *"The admiral was responsible for weighing the loss of an aviator who he didn't know personally, to the possibility of allowing a light to be shown that could guide an enemy torpedo bomber to its target. My feelings still are if they put us in harm's way to protect the fleet, there is some responsibility to one in dire need. 'One for all and all for one'. Fifty years later I can still hear Obie's radio plea, a haunting memory that fails to go away."*
I.H. Lee

2125 INDEPENDENCE opened fire with two 40mm twins and two 20mm guns on enemy aircraft crossing overhead at 3,000'. No hits observed.
2225 A fifth A/C was shot down astern on the horizon by a DD.

2335 Enemy aircraft flying at roughly 4,000' dropped 2 magnesium parachute flares* on the port side, eight on the starboard side, illuminating Task Force 38.2 very brightly. No attack followed the flare plane.

* This attempt to locate the fleet was recalled later in an article (Saturday Evening Post - 11 August 1945) by Cdr. Turner Caldwell, Jr. who wrote: *"Tojo the Lamplighter came out to make his rounds".*
He noted: *"A string of these million-candlepower chandeliers lit up our own group brilliantly."*

2341 A sixth A/C crashed on the port quarter roughly 20 miles out, and a seventh at 0200 on the port quarter horizon. All seven appeared to be in flames before crashing.

Importantly, it was noted (in a Revised Report "AA Action by Surface Ships") the need for radar control of the gun batteries of CVL type ships armed only with 20mm & 40mm gun batteries during this night action. Additionally the need for Mark 15 sights ASAP as the Mark 14 sights provided no magnification. Targets seen with 7x50 binoculars could not be tracked by the Mark 14 gun sights.

GL Attacked. Will be about 100 miles off of the China coast all the time hoping the Japs will come out and play. Raid was very successful. Force shot down 124 planes and destroyed on the ground 96. We lost 22 planes. What a night!! Just what we have been waiting for, the Japs to come after us. They attacked the force at 5:15 and kept it up until 2:20 in the morning. There was A.A fire everywhere you looked. Our C.A.P. got 3 Bettys as they were coming in, the rest got into the task force. The Japs claim to have sunk 9 carriers, 5BB's, numerous light and heavy cruisers, everyone got a big kick out of it. The Japs sure used a lot of flares and it was as bright as day. The burning planes came so close you could almost touch them.

HB On October 12, we attacked Formosa which is the big island between Japan and the Philippines. The Japanese attacked, and we were under attack until 0230. Things I remember about this day are eating pork chops and, also being hit by two dead fish, which simply means torpedoes that malfunctioned. Thank the Lord! One torpedo was enough! HB

Friday 13 October 1944   *Formosa*

Steaming as before in TU 38.2.1 with Task Group 38.2 in cruising disposition 5V5, axis 080°T, course 100°T. New Jersey guide bearing 060°T, 3,500 yards. Ship is darkened, at general quarters. Throughout the evening a number of enemy aircraft have been reported over the Task Group, have dropped flares illuminating up the area about the INDEPENDENCE, and have been fired upon by vessels in this group.
0052 Sounded general quarters for purpose of repelling imminent air attack.
0148 Sounded general quarters for purpose of repelling imminent air attack.
Nothing developed from either anticipated air strike. It kept the crew awake.
0222 Secured from general quarters, Air Department remaining at flight quarters. Gunnery Department set in condition 3.
0346-0348 Set fleet course to 055°T, 15 knots and catapulted 4 F6F5N Hellcats (Berkheimer, Caldwell, Klock and Miller) and 4 TBM-1C Avengers (Linton, McNair, Phelps and Taylor) to make night heckling attacks on targets over Southern Formosa. Targets were the Tainan, Takao and Toko areas.

Chapter 15

Hellcats were carrying one 500 lb GP bomb each, the Avengers twelve 100 lb GP bombs each. 15 miles off Garambi Point they encountered extremely heavy weather.

0359 Changed fleet course to 359°T.

0500 Ensign Jack S. "Berky" Berkheimer on the way to target, flying at 3'000'over Toko S/P base, roughly 1 mile off the shoreline saw three 4 engine flying boats anchored in the Toko lagoon.
He dropped down to 700' turning in to make a strafing pass when aircraft wing lights passed to his port. Berky executed a wingover, pulling up on the tail of an Emily, and fired a burst from 5 o'clock level, hitting both inboard engines, which started burning. The next burst into the hull also produced flames. The Emily made a descending glide, crashing into the sea just outside the seaplane base. Berky dropped his Bomb on Toko Seaplane base hangar aprons and made two strafing runs. Climbing out, Berky noticed the wing lights of another Emily. Maneuvering to the Emily's 6'oclock level position, he placed a burst between its port engines. A fire started. Another burst into the hull once again produced a fire and soon the entire flying boat was enveloped in flames. It exploded midair, and crashed 1 mile from Berkheimer's first Emily.

0600 Ensign Robert W. "Bob" Klock was separated from his wingman inbound to target having encountered a heavy frontal area and rough air, on a very dark night. After Klock had dropped his bomb on a large military storehouse, there appeared to be a number of Japanese flying boats orbiting over Ryukyu Island that were thought to have been returning from reconnaissance on the Task Force. Klock picked up an Emily, aided by his AIA, closed on its 6 o'clock, level, 1,500' altitude, and fired two short bursts into the engine areas. The Emily started to burn, spiraled into the ocean and exploded. This was S.S.W. of Ryukyu Sho.

Bombs were dropped on the Toko seaplane base hangars and shops, aircraft parking areas at Okayama and Reigaryu airfields and the shipyard area at Kigo. Due to the darkness, strafing and bomb damage assessment was not possible unless immediate fire or explosions occurred. Pilots reported they "were highly pleased with the radar mapping ability of their ASD and AIA, being easily enabled to orient themselves with terrain with little trouble".

0635 Commenced steering various courses into the wind, at various speeds for recovery of aircraft.

0645 Recovered 1 Hellcat and 1 Avenger.

0718 Commenced steering various courses into the wind while recovering aircraft.

0725 Recovered 3 Hellcats and 3 Avengers

0730 Mustered crew on stations.

After their recovery onboard from their missions, pilots reported seeing a series of float lights (believed to be electric) in the sea roughly 10 miles apart, 65 miles west of the Task Force in a line toward Garambi Point. These were most likely to aid Japanese planes on patrol to find our fleet. Also 4 or 5 trench fires or lights were sighted lit on shore between the Toko Seaplane Base and Garambi Point thought to serve as navigation aids for their pilots on patrol near our Task Force.

0802 Jettisoned overboard 1 F6F-3N, damaged beyond repair while landing on 12 October 1944. This was the Hellcat (Bu.No.58052) flown by Ensign Emmett Edwards.

0901-0902 Catapulted two Avengers to search for the fighter pilots that failed to return (Joe Moore and George Obenour) from CAP last night. Changed course to 045°T, speed 17 knots.

1150 Sounded flight quarters.

1234 Recovered the two Avengers launched for the search, returning with negative results. Secured from flight quarters, Air Department set to condition 13.

1835 Sounded general quarters for purpose of repelling imminent air attack.

1854-1950 Nine course changes were made. Considerable antiaircraft fire was put up by ships of this Task Group. INDEPENDENCE did not open fire. CVL-22 intercepted a report the USS CANBERRA in TG38.1 had been hit by two aerial torpedoes, and was taken in tow.

2037 Secured from general quarters. At 2345 they changed course to 270°T, and steamed west.

GUAM Well, the night finally ran into day without any more trouble from the nips. We launched a heckler mission at 0330 to start off this mornings activities. When the skipper came back from this mission he told us that the Japs had a string of floating beacons (flares light's or drums) in a direct line from their northern groups of islands, and thus the attacking planes had only to follow the lights to come within range of the groups. This seems to indicate one or all three things. One the Japs are poor navigators. Two, the attacking planes were originally from Luzon and didn't know the area or three, their radar is none to accurate.

An hour ago we secured from another intensive attack on our two outer most groups. This time it started 18 minutes earlier than last night. But only lasted until 0230. It is sincerely hoped that the bastards stay at home for the rest of the night but you never can tell ..... rotten flying weather has developed and that may keep them away.
On the night of Friday 13, we are no longer attacking the island of Formosa, but moving away in the most leisurely manner imaginable. One would think there wasn't an enemy plane within miles (fact is there isn't one within 20 miles at present writing).

Word has been received for the reason of our leisurely withdrawal. Plans were changed and we will again hit Formosa in the morning. So far we have not received any word on the score from the last two days. We may have to wait for Admiral Nimitz's communiqué from Pearl Harbor.
The following message was sent from CTG 38.2 and 33 this morning: Will launch hecklers mission as planned. Ships guns took care of guest and night fighters 3 during the party.
Halsey sent back ••• X ••• Very good. As I am glad I came to the party. NOTE •••• Beside bombing and strafing 4 important air fields, our hecklers came back with three more planes to their credit. Berkheimer got two Emilies and Klock got one. GUAM

AD The morning of the 13th we were hit by a torpedo but it was a dud. Our planes again made an attack on Formosa, In the late afternoon until 2200 we were under constant attack by Jap planes. The heavy cruiser USS Canberra was torpedoed. AD

DL Friday 13 October. Payback day. We had stung them so badly they had to react. Death came at all hours day and night on both sides. CV Franklin was hit a glancing blow by the survivor of four Betty bombers. Three were shot into the drink. The final one died sliding "horribly" straight across Franklin's flightdeck, spewing its wreckage into the sea alongside.
*   The Japanese boasted to the homefolks and to the world that the American navy had suffered grievous losses in this hectic three-day battle. They exaggerated, prompting a famous cartoon that showed Halsey (with John Paul Jones, James Lawrence, Oliver Hazard Perry, David Glasgow Farragut, and George Dewey sketched in shadow) holding up a large sign announcing:*
*   WE ARE RETIRING AT HIGH SPEED TOWARD THE JAPANESE FLEET.*

*   Still, that night the first major USN surface ship in this episode, heavy cruiser USS Canberra, was struck by a Long Lance torpedo ninety miles off Formosa and "badly crippled." She had been hit between her two firerooms below the armor belt, "blowing a huge, jagged hole and killing twenty-three men instantly." She came to a dead stop. About four and a half thousand tons of water rushed in before a damage control party could isolate compartments.*
*   Cruiser Wichita was assigned to take her under tow. DL*

Admiral Matome Ugaki noted in his diary: *" Since early this morning the above enemies* raided with ease and grace"! (*4CVs & 4 CVLS)* The diary gives no historical insight as to his thoughts as he emoted the reality ... A mixture of what? Consternation, contempt, anger, helplessness, envy, solemn desperation? Ugaki further recorded the Japanese had struck back in response to the Formosa strike by sending out roughly 100 planes in seven assaults. 70 had been equipped with torpedoes.

GN Another strike on Formosa. Ships are firing all around us but I'm too tired to watch the fireworks. Went to sleep in the starboard belting room with all battle gear handy. 38.4 got a bit of a beating this time.

GL   Our planes went over at night, no sleep for the Japs. Nothing happened during the day but we expected trouble during the night. They did, but hit one of the other task units. They got a hit on a new cruiser Canberra. Named after the one sank in the battle of Savo Sea. She shot down 8 planes before being hit. The cruiser Wichita is towing her and the Cabot left to supply her with air cover. The carrier Wasp was also hit by a burning plane, little damage resulted. GL

DrP   0330 - 4VF & 4 VT to shore at strip Formosa on specific targets. Berkheimer -2 Emlies, Klock -1 Emily. Targets hit satisfactorily. All return safely @ 0630.
0900 - 2VT (Taylor & Dewis) on search for Moore & Obenour. Approx 22Nx123E, unsuccessful. Storm coming with strong winds & rain.
Eve - Wild bogie attacks for approx. 1 1/2 hrs. Rain wind & overcast. 9512 mi (Naut) since P.H.**
Canberra takes 2 fish and is under tow with difficulty. DrP   (** Pearl Harbor)

Saturday 14 October 1944   *Formosa*

Today, the plan was for the Task Group to retire to refuel, then to proceed to the Philippines to commence strikes. In war, plans change. Further fighter sweeps against Formosa were ordered to provide cover for the crippled CANBERRA, delaying the planned departure.

0542   Steaming as before. Sounded general quarters.

0714   Commenced steering various courses at various speeds to assume new station in formation.

0732   Changed course to 250°T, 15 knots, having gained position, INDEPENDENCE bearing 270°T, 3,000 yards from guide, USS NEW JERSEY.

0740   Secured from general quarters on a new course of 070°T, speed 10 knots.

0745   Mustered crew on stations.

1753   Changed fleet course to 065°T.

1107   USS CABOT, HOUSTON, THE SULLIVANS and STEPHEN POTTER left the task group to protect the crippled CANBERRA, which was taken in tow by cruiser USS WITCHITA to make the 1,300 mile trip to Ulithi.

1120   Changed position in the formation, bearing 225°T, 2,000 yards from the guide.

1143   Changed Fleet course to 135°T, fleet speed 16 knots. The Fleet began to retire to the southeast.

1329   Changed Fleet course to 140°T, fleet speed 24 knots.

1510   Radar contact, large groups of enemy aircraft low on the water were reported by CIC, bearing 230° T, 25 miles. These were first sighted by a SNASP. Ships radars did not pick them up until they were close in. 42 aircraft (Nicks, Bettys, Judys, and Tonys) were shot down, many by the Task Group CAP between 1500 and 1800 (hours).

1513   Sounded general quarters for purpose of repelling imminent air attack.

1517   Task Group opened fire on enemy aircraft. Several enemy planes were shot down.

1526   INDEPENDENCE opened fire on enemy aircraft.

1552   Commenced maneuvering on signal to avoid air attack, making emergency turns and speed changes.

1655   Secured from general quarters.

1700   Commenced maneuvering to new flying station bearing 050°T, 15 miles to the windward side, from the center of the TG. 38.2 formation. This unit will maintain flying station outside the screen through the night in company with USS WEDDERBURN, STOCKHAM and YARNALL.

(Note: This procedure would be consistently followed to give INDEPENDENCE greater freedom to launch and recover aircraft, especially during air attack, while at the night flying station). Axis for this unit 050°T, with destroyers in a 1,500 yard circle. INDEPENDENCE guide and OTC with WEDDERBURN bearing 110°T, YARNALL bearing 230°T and STOCKHAM bearing 350°T.

1708   Task Group 38.2 was attacked by enemy aircraft, sounded general quarters. CVL-22 had not yet cleared the screen and remained inside the screen of TG 38.2, following the evasive turns of the TG as directed by TG 38.2 OTC in USS INTREPID.

1716 TG 38.2 opened fire on a lone enemy aircraft that got past the CAP.

1743 Enemy attack ended. CTG TG 38.2 ordered INDEPENDENCE to proceed to night flying station. Changed speed to 27 knots to proceed in company with USS WEDDERBURN and STOCKHAM.

1835 Sounded general quarters. Several bogies appeared between 1800 and 1945, but the decision was made not to launch night fighters due to rotten weather, and poor flying conditions.

1843 USS YARNALL joined this unit and took up station.

1845 Enemy aircraft again attacked TG 38.2.

1933 Sighted light off port beam, dispatched STOCKHAM to investigate. Light appeared to be a float light dropped by the Japanese as a marker.

By 2000 weather had cleared up enough for flight operations.

2147 Sounded general quarters upon approach of unidentified aircraft bearing 230°T, 25 miles. CVL-22 prepared to launch fighters for the intercept. At 2152 changed course to 090°T.

2153 Launched one F6F.

2158 Launched one F6F.

The INDEPENDENCE would keep two night fighters aloft as CAP for the TG the remainder of the night, launching relief CAP's at 0100 and 0300 the morning of the 15th.

2159 Observed heavy AA barrage from TG38.2, bearing 230°T, distance 12 miles.

2245 Secured from general quarters.

2305 Rotated axis of this Task Unit to 070°T.

2314 Sounded torpedo defense on approach of unidentified aircraft.

2341 Secured from torpedo defense, as contact with the bogy was lost. INDEPENDENCE CAP ran it off.

Near dusk on this day the USS HOUSTON was hit by an aerial torpedo. She was taken in tow by the USS BOSTON. Less than 100 miles from Formosa, the "Cripples" were to be used as bait for the Japanese, using the COWPENS, and CABOT along with escorting destroyers for protection.

DL   *Light cruiser Houston was torpedoed only eighty miles from land at 1845, and damaged more heavily than Canberra. Houston's skipper refused to abandon ship, thus adding another vessel to Halsey's problems. Either ship probably would have been lost if these attacks had happened two years before in the grim early days of the naval war. How they survived is a great story of luck, pluck, courage, and sacrifice. It has become a legend in the Navy. We became part of the legend merely by being near at hand.*

Halsey decided to use the plight of these two cripples as bait to bring out the enemy's main fleet. U.S. ships of all sorts were ordered into the act. In the end, the bait failed but the torpedoed ships were saved to fight again. They became known, unofficially, as Crip. Div. 1. The names of sailors who had to be deep-sixed at the scene have joined the eighteen thousand chiseled into big stone markers at Punchbowl National Cemetery, located in the verdant bed of an ancient volcano overlooking Honolulu.

Meanwhile, we and other ships on the sidelines of this battle of Formosa had a struggle surviving an air attack that hit us just before a certain midnight.

This wild fight occurred shortly after Houston had taken her fish. She and Canberra were miles from us, but the Japs must have been desperate to find any American ships to strike. They found us and our escorts. Radar for once had failed to detect anything lurking in the sky.

All of a sudden, as we worked in pitch darkness preparing our night snoopers for launching, the black sky burst into the brightest incandescent light I had ever imagined possible.

We had already loaded torpeckers with 100-pound frag bombs and were in the process of bombing-up a section of F6Fs with two 500-pounders each when Whitey, B. C., and other Chiefs came around with orders from Porky to remove the bombs from the fighters and stow them below. Unusual. Neither the air officer nor the skipper liked having the bomb elevator hatch uncovered once it had been secured—and especially at night. A half-dozen skids with two frags each, fuses and arming wires installed, were sitting along the starboard side of the flightdeck. They would be used on TBM's waiting in the hangar. No time now to stow them.

A fighter sat on either catapult ready to go, its pilot waiting word from the bridge. The night itself didn't seem right. Something was hovering overhead, a shadow clouding the back of my mind. The darkness was pitch black, although visibility was clear. Working near the after end of the deck, we could see a long tail of phosphorescence following Mighty I's stern. Other ships barely a thousand yards on either side trailed similar, faintly visible spoors.

We unloaded the bombs off the fighters, the hatch was raised with the usual strains, grunts and farts, the bomb elevator went up and down the necessary number of times, and then we buttoned everything up. Frank, listening on his headset, reported to Porky that the magazine door had been shut and dogged.

And so we strolled forward toward the port catwalk for a smoke in the tiny head adjacent to the ready magazine. We never made it.

POOF! and the night's blackness vanished as bright lights snapped on overhead.

POOF! and the flightdeck end to end, port to starboard, as well as the sea hundreds of yards on either side, burst into a glaring, painful noontime daylight that must have been brighter than a massive array of synchronized floodlamps turned on all at once. I shielded my eyes with my hands. How I or anyone kept from ramming into the razor edge of an airplane prop or the edge of a wing or tail surface is a mystery. Each man ducked instinctively into the starkly outlined shadows beneath the planes for shelter. BOOM! BANG! CRASH! Our guns sent bright red incendiary shells streaking into the brightened night sky. Two, and then a third, parachute flares slowly descended--messengers from heaven meant to aid whoever it was up there determined to kill us. Guns from all the other ships joined in. It was such a frightening display of blood red anger that it killed forever my delight in Fourth of July fireworks.

In the distance to port, a flash of wild flame came from a shot-up airplane diving into the drink. One of ours? Men were running all over the deck. I saw faces peering upward, a direction that must have caused instant if temporary blindness. A torpedoman friend named Nelson (nicknamed Bob) piled into the port catwalk and almost fell upon Mister Porky, who was already there.

Bombs began erupting within the sea. Everybody looked up to see where they came from. It was an unthinking, helpless mass gesture. Geysers shot skyward, as if propelled by some great subterranean eruption.

But that massed light! It was so blinding, so intense, that the impulse to escape it was compelling. Talk about being caught naked in front of Henderson Hoyt's Department Store on Main Street, Oshkosh at high noon!

But then came the real kicker: the still-bright flares dropping into the water continued to burn for many fathoms as they descended, lighting the sea below its surface with a ghastly green glow as if it were an enormous aquarium.

And that raised the greatest fear of all. If one of those devil devices happened to drop onto the flightdeck its heat would instantly burn a hole clean through the deck into the hangar, parked full with fueled and bomb-laden airplanes. It would have been an inferno.

No ships were hit during that pyrotechnic display. Our snoopers were launched without bombs two hours after midnight.

Rumors were that the pilots sitting in the cockpits when the first flares dropped out of the black night sky needed a change of skivvies. If true, they were not alone. **DL**

DrP *Cond. II all day. Others in 38.2 have field day on C.A.P. & fighter sweeps shooting down over 40 planes.*
Eve. - Wild bogie attack - I see a SB2C shot down & Jap dive bomber make get away after near miss on Hancock. - no damage.
Night - Interception of Emily & splash by Bill Henry in all night fighter action. **DrP**

GL *Hit Formosa again and met no opposition. I guess we play to rough. Food on board is running low. We are going to invade the Philippines on the 20th and we are leaving Formosa. The Japs attacked us again at 3:30 pm & kept it up all night. Another plane fell very close to our ship. The force shot down 36 planes in the dark & brother that is really some shooting. A dive bomber got a very near miss on the Hancock. A Jap plane crashed on the fantail of the Reno. Our fighters shot down two more bombers.* **GL**

Sunday 15 October 1944   *Formosa*

Steaming as before, as Task Unit 38.2.1, on course 135°T, speed 24 knots, bearing 020°T, 10 miles from TG38.2 guide, on a parallel course. Ship is darkened, Air Department is at flight quarters, Gunnery and C&R departments in condition 3, Engineering Department in condition 31. INDEPENDENCE has 2 night fighters in the air.

0021 Sounded torpedo defense. The Japanese sent aircraft out, but no attack developed.

0052-0053 Launched 2 F6FNs, piloted by Bill Henry and Ensign Reuben F. "Pete" Peterson for night CAP. It was a black night with no moon. The ship then secured from torpedo defense.
Peterson was instructed to orbit by USS HANCOCK's CIC. Henry was given a "Buster" vector to a bogey, reported at 25 miles, angels 3, crossing NE-SW. Henry flew out 22 miles ... the bogey was lost. First instructed to orbit, he was then given a fresh bogey at angels 2.5 (2,500'). He got a radar contact, closing, and loosing altitude, until he started feeling the buffeting from slipstream of the bogey at only 200' altitude. He found two targets 700'-1,000' ahead. He put bursts into the inboard port engine, then the inboard starboard engine. The two engines on the four engine Emily glowed, and he saw 2.7 cal. tracer fire coming from the top turret. Bill pulled out to the port side, then dropped back in behind the tail for another shot when the Emily's port fuel tanks or engine finally started to burn brightly. The Emily banked in an uncontrolled turn to the right and crashed into the water at a 50° angle. Splattered all over the water, it burned for 15 minutes. It had gone down at 0305, 45 miles from INDEPENDENCE. Henry was given a bearing to the second bogey, flying in soup with visibility that had dropped to zero, he broke off the chase twice feeling he would likely ram into the enemy, then returned to base.

Bill Henry had encountered problems with the targeting of the Emily due to the brightness of his gunsight. It may have prevented him from bagging the second Emily. He would report:
"The Mark III gunsight is not satisfactory for night fighting. The illumination it provides, no matter how much it can be dimmed down, is essentially wrong, since light between the pilot and his target impairs night vision and also materially reduces the contrast between the object and the background.
It is suggested that a telescopic sight would be more suitable than the present illuminated reflecting sight. It should have a small magnification, high light-gathering power, and an exit pupil to take advantage of the wide aperture of the dark adapted eye."

0113-0127 Recovered two Hellcats launched at 2153.
0235-0243 Manned torpedo defense stations.
0330-0331 Launched 2 F6FNs.
0333 Sounded flight quarters.
0351 Commenced recovering Hellcats (Peterson & Henry) launched at 0053.
0523 Sounded general quarters.
0624 Recovered 2 hellcats launched at 0330. Secured from general quarters.
0626 Changed course to 150°T, speed 28 knots. Left night flying station and commenced maneuvering to regain position with TG 38.2.
0643 Secured from flight quarters.
0745 Regained position with TG 38.2, guide NEW JERSEY, bearing 045°T, 2,000 yards, on course 135°T, speed 24 knots.
1012 Changed course to 160°T.
1025 Sighted fleet tankers 5 degrees to starboard, bearing 165°T at 15 miles.
1105 Commenced maneuvering to approach port side of tanker, USS ESCAMBIA. Speed 10 knots.
1130 Came alongside USS ESCAMBIA and at 1200 commenced taking on fuel oil. Transferred 5 officers* to USS ESCAMBIA for transfer to the USS INTREPID. (* Ensigns D.A. Naughton, E.H. Nygaard, W.E. Stephens, W.R. Jackson and H.S. Meacham)
1325 Completed transfer of fuel oil having received 244,624 gallons.

1342 Cast off from USS ESCAMBIA. Maneuvering to clear fueling group and steadied on course 060°T, 12 knots.

1408-1424 USS UHLMANN was alongside starboard amidships. Lieut. R.R. Fegraeus and Ens. J.A. Barnett were transferred to the UHLMANN to bring replacement planes back to the INDEPENDENCE.

1434-1439 USS COLAHAN was alongside to starboard to receive an officer (Lt.Cdr . G.S. Heston) previously transferred to INDEPENDENCE (on 9 October) for medical treatment.

1521 Took station in formation and commenced zigzagging independently on station.

1610 Formation changed disposition to 5R5, axis 045°T, course 060°T, speed 10 knots.

1714 Sounded flight quarters.

1734 Commenced maneuvering to proceed to flying station.

1750 Landed 2 F6F3N replacement aircraft launched from the USS BARNES. (Bu.No. 58308 & 58977)

1751 Secured from flight quarters, then proceeded to regain station.

1759-1859 Ship was at torpedo defense.

2000 Changed fleet course to 330°T, speed 23 knots. Proceeding toward Formosa again.

GUAM Today we fueled the force and for the first time in four days, I got myself some real honest to goodness sack time. I have had 4 hours sleep in the previous 42 hours. Between the tenseness of the situation, lack of sleep and improper eating most of us were pretty well done in. After today and tonight we'll be ready for whatever awaits us at Luzon our target for the next two days.   GUAM

GL We left the Formosa area, don't know how many ships were sunk. They delayed our next attack as we made contact with a section of the Jap fleet.   GL

RC Refueled, "Tokyo Rose" reports 11 carriers, 2 battlewagons, 4 cruisers and several destroyers have been sunk in the three days battle off Formosa.   RC

DrP Sunday - Slept all day, no action. Quiet night with a few bogies on screen. None attack.   DrP

Monday 16 October 1944   *Formosa*

0526 Sounded routine general quarters.

0626 Secured from general quarters, Air Department set to condition 14.

0750 Sounded flight quarters.

0817 Commenced zigzagging (Plan No.6) on base course 140°T.

0837 USS CUSHING steamed alongside our port quarter to deliver onboard Lieut. C.C. Hardy from VF105 for duty in connection with air combat intelligence.

0844 Sounded torpedo defense, reported unidentified aircraft bearing 300°T, 12 miles.

0846 Secured from torpedo defense, received a report the aircraft was shot down. One minute later USS CUSHING cast off. Commenced steering various courses at various speeds to regain station.

0856 Regained station.

0929 Changed course to 140°T. 0937 Changed course to 065°T.

0938-0950 Half-masted colors, following movement of USS BUNKER HILL.

1004 Changed course to 320°T.

1014 Observed firing at an unidentified aircraft, 240°T, on the horizon, flying low over the water. The aircraft got away.

1016-1029 Manned torpedo defense stations.

1600 Sounded flight quarters.

1607 Changed fleet course to 200°T.

1700 Sounded flight quarters.

1755 Changed fleet course to 070°T.

1757-1802 Launched 8 F6Fs for CAP over TG 38.2. Task Group formed disposition 5V5.

Commenced maneuvering to close on guide to 2,000 yards. Sounded torpedo defense.
The CAP was sent out to orbit in assigned stations 25 miles from fleet center. Four were under control of the INDEPENDENCE FDO, and four directed by the HANCOCK FDO. There were no enemy contacts during this patrol.
1815 Gained station and changed course to 070°T, speed 19 knots. Then proceeded to night flying station, bearing 070°T, 12 miles from center of TG 38.2.
1826 Changed speed to 27 knots, course to 025°T.
1828 USS HICKOX took station on the INDEPENDENCE, bearing 070°T, 1,500 yards.
1840 Changed course to 020°T, speed 25 knots.
1903 Secured from torpedo defense.
1930 USS YARNALL took station on the INDEPENDENCE, bearing 250°T, 1,500 yards.
1945 Having gained night flying station, changed course to 070°T, speed 22 knots.
1951 Recovered 1 F6F launched at 1800.
2147 Launched 7 TBMs and 2 F6Fs for search. The two Hellcats were launched to replace the eighth Avenger scheduled for the search that was a "dud' (had mechanical problems). The mission was to search for the Japanese fleet, which had sortied to "annihilate" the remains of the "crippled US fleet".
2211 Recovered the second F6F launched at 1800.
2212 The third F6F launched at 1800 crashed into the barrier upon landing, causing minor damage to the F6F.
2228 Changed course to 180°T.
2244 Recovered the remaining 5 F6Fs launched at 1800.
2330 Changed course to 235°T.

AD   At sea. Part of the Jap fleet some 300 miles away. We are waiting for our chance to get them. No luck today, maybe tomorrow. At this point the Japs have reported that they sank practically all of our carriers and escort vessels. If they did sink us I sure must be riding on air and all those carriers, battlewagons, cruisers and destroyers I see all around us is just an illusion.   AD

GN   Supposed to make a strike on Luzon but search planes spot Jap fleet and "Bull" Halsey decides to have it out with them during the night we lost contact with their fleet.   GN

GUAM   Today we are out searching for a Jap task group. They, believing that "Bulls" third fleet has been all but annihilated, are thought to be steaming toward the "remnants" of our fleet with the idea of sending what little is left to the bottom of the Taiwan Ocean (as they call the body of water off Formosa).
Our search planes located the nip force some 300 miles to the north of us late this afternoon. But due to the lateness in the day, no strike could be launched. The force was said to consist of 1 CV, 2BB 4 CA, and 8 DD. This indicates that they really believe most of our fleet has been sunk or severely damaged. They wouldn't send such a puny force out to do battle with what we've got ready and rarin for them. Tonight "Rebel Taylor" and his night flying VT squadron went on a 350 mile search, but had no luck in relocating the Jap forces. Since the Japs spotted our reconnaissance planes in the afternoon, they have evidently high-tailed it for home.   GUAM

Damage inflicted on the US fleet was vastly overstated by Japanese pilots returning from combat. With wildly exaggerated reports of over 50 US ships said to be sunk or damaged, Vice Admiral Shima boldly steamed out to "clean up" the "cripples".
Time to sortie, arrive on scene (two days), and lack of fuel oil added to decisions preventing additional elements of IJN's main fleet from steaming out of the Japanese homeland. IJN was suffering severe fuel shortages which hindered major fleet action, and needed to preserve precious fuel oil for the all important defense of the Philippines, and the Japanese mainland. The IJN fleet was to be preserved for "The Decisive Battle" predicted to come. Vice Admiral Shima's force would have to handle it.

Halsey's Third Fleet waited, smacking their lips, trying to find the Japanese morsel that took the bait. Shima however wisely turned back when the true nature of what he would be up against became apparent. With his small force of three cruisers and four destroyers, annihilation was guaranteed.

An important factor that would influence events to happen shortly, was the loss of Japanese pilots and aircraft off Formosa. Admiral Matome Ugaki would record in his diary three days later (October 19th) that Imperial Headquarters announced 312 Japanese planes had failed to return from their missions against the US fleet. That does not include aircraft and pilot losses on the ground incurred during our strikes upon their airbases.

On the 19th Ugaki would also still be of the impression that US Fleet losses were severe, as Imperial Headquarters also (inaccurately) reported that eleven carriers, two battleships, and three or four cruisers had been sunk, with an almost equally large number of Halsey's fleet damaged.

DrP 16 Oct 1944 Monday - Plans changed when Jap fleet reported steaming out. High excitement & *expectancy. We search all night (16 planes VF & VT) but fail to locate any Jap fleet. Reports have it* *Houston is in tow by Washington, crippled by 2nd fish. Canberra reported still afloat & under tow.* ***DrP***

Tuesday 17 October 1944   *Formosa Area*

Steaming as before. This vessel is (OTC and guide) in company with USS HICKOX and USS YARNALL, as a detached Task Unit in a night flying station 10 miles windward of TG 38.2, bearing 060°T from TG 38.2. Base course 235°T, speed 27 knots.

0050 Changed course to 050°T, speed 22 knots for flight operations and recovered 1 F6F.

0104 Recovered 2 TBM's.

0203 On a course of 060°T, speed 22 knots, recovered 4 TBMs.

0219 Seaman R.C. Myers was admitted to sick bay for multiple shrapnel wounds. While sitting in a crew's shelter leading to the forward ready room, he was struck by shrapnel caused by a projectile that passed through the flight deck after a wing gun of a folded port wing of a TBM fired one round.

0221 Recovered 1 F6F and 1 TBM. All aircraft launched at 2147 for the search were now recovered. The search reported sighting 1 submarine, appraised to be friendly. The Japanese fleet was not found.

0230 Changed course to 215°T, speed 29 knots to close distance on TG 38.2.

0528 Sounded general quarters.

0632 Secured from general quarters, Air Department set to condition 13.

0840 Changed fleet course to 060°T, speed 18 knots.

0900 Changed fleet disposition to 5R5, INDEPENDENCE bearing 225°T, 2,500 yards from guide, USS NEW JERSEY.

0907 CIC reported radar contact, bogey bearing 320°T, 20 miles.

0909-0918 Manned torpedo defense stations to repel air attack.

1131-1156 USS WEDDERBURN was alongside on port quarter to deliver mail.

1451 USS HALSEY POWELL came alongside and transferred guard mail.

1455 USS HALSEY POWELL cast off. Changed speed to 26 knots to regain position.

1501 Reduced speed to 20 knots preparatory to the HALSEY POWELL returning alongside.

1512-1515 HALSEY POWELL was alongside to receive guard mail improperly delivered to this vessel.

1640 Changed fleet course to 203°T, speed 21 knots.

1654 Rotated fleet axis to 110°T. Maneuvered to assume new position 2.5180 * from guide.

1736 Sounded flight quarters.   (*Note: 2.5180 = 2,500 yards, 180°)

1754 Launched 2 F6Fs.   (**Note: 1.5000 = 1,500 yards, 000°)

1807 Sounded torpedo defense.

1817 Changed course to 165°T. Left the formation and maneuvered to proceed to night flying station, 10 miles windward side of guide, to operate with the USS YARNALL (stationed at 1.5180) and USS STOCKHAM (stationed at 1.5000 **) as a detached unit. Changed speed to 22 knots.

1837 Changed course to 125°T for flight operations, then Launched 1 F6F.

1915 Secured from torpedo defense.

1920 Landed 1 F6F. Changed course to 190°T, speed 24 knots to regain station.

2057-2100 Changed course to 115°T and launched 2 F6Fs. Changed course to 205°T.

2113-2136 Changed course to 080°T and recovered 4 F6Fs.

2138 Changed course to 215°T, increasing speed to 28 knots 4 minutes later.

GL   Due to a stroke of bad luck we lost the Jap fleet. Everyone is cussing mad. They must have seen the strength of our fleet and ran like hell.   GL

GN   Halsey is desperate in trying to find their fleet. Must be hiding around Formosa somewhere.   GN

GUAM   17 October 1944
Spent a fair part of this day searching for the lost fleet but no luck. Late this evening, we began to steam for Luzon again. This time to hit the North Aparri airfield to isolate another air group from taking any part in the defense of Leyte when General MacArthur lands there, No opposition of any kind was encountered. Evidently 38.1 had done a pretty good job of lambasting this place two days ago.   GUAM

DrP   Tuesday - Quiet day. Night C.A.P.   No bogies   DrP

Wednesday 18 October 1944   *Steaming toward Luzon, Philippines*

0000 Steaming as before. Changed fleet course and detached unit course to 260°T.
0159 Sounded flight quarters.
0206 Changed course to 010°T to launch aircraft.
0206-0212 Changed course to 010°T to launch aircraft. Completed launching 2 F6Fs. Then changed course to 260°T, speed 25 knots while regaining night flying station.
0450 Changed speed to fleet speed, 22 knots. 38.2 bears 260°T at 6 miles.
0529 Sounded general quarters.
0613-0616 Commenced maneuvering into the wind and recovered 2 F6Fs.
0632 Changed course to 260°T, speed 28 knots, maneuvering to regain position in Task Group 38.2.
0634 Secured from general quarters. Air Department set condition 14.
0720 USS YARNALL and USS STOCKHAM were detached to rejoin their TG screening stations.
0751 Changed speed to 18 knots, course 240°T. Regained disposition 5R5, axis 110°T, guide bears 110°T at 2,500 yards.
0756 Turning to port, changed fleet course to 090°T.
1004 Sounded flight quarters. All fighters were placed in condition 11.
The Task Group steamed toward the southeast. Task Group 38.2 carried out air strikes against air installations and shipping over and around northern Luzon. INDEPENDENCE pilots did not participate, however remained in condition 11 from the return of the first strike, remaining throughout the night.
1825 Sounded flight quarters.
2000 Base course changed to 129°T.

Thursday 19 October 1944   *Luzon, Philippines - Fueling*

Steaming in company with Task Unit 38.2.1 consisting of this vessel, USS INTREPID (OTC), USS BUNKER HILL, and USS HANCOCK. TU 38.2.1 is in company with TG 38.2 in cruising disposition 5R5, axis 110°T, course 129°T, speed 16 knots.
0523-0623 Ship was at general quarters. Air Department set in condition 14.
0818 USS CUSHING came alongside to deliver mail.
0829 Steered various courses, stopped all engines. USS CUSHING cast off to allow maneuvering.
0921 Changed Fleet course to 110°T.
0927 Changed fleet speed to 10 knots. Shifted guide to forward center tanker USS CALIENTE. INDEPENDENCE bears 290°T, 3,000 yards from guide.
0938-0940 USS CUSHING was alongside to starboard to transfer mail.
1101-1118 USS COLAHAN was along the starboard side to transfer 3 pilots* onboard to fly aircraft to the USS HANCOCK. (* Ensigns E. Falkowski, R.E. Tedford and T.L. Herring)
1204 Changed speed to 15 knots and commenced approaching fleet tanker USS PATUXENT.
1231 Passed first line to tanker.

1306 Commenced receiving fuel oil and aviation gasoline. Transferred Lieut. William Perry to the tanker for further transfer to Washington, DC.

1440 Having received 228,245 gallons of fuel oil and 23,000 gallons of aviation gasoline, cast off from USS PATUXENT.

1451 Changed course to 105°T, speed 20 knots.   1504 Changed fleet course to 020°T.

1506 Changed fleet course to 295°T and commenced launching 3 F6Fs for delivery to USS HANCOCK by pilots transferred to this ship by the USS COLAHAN.

1510 Commenced maneuvering to regain position in disposition.

1523 Changed fleet course to 310°T, speed to 18 knots. USS NEW JERSEY designated guide.

1550 Regained position in disposition 5R5, guide on bearing 290°T, distance 2,500 yards.

1803-1905 INDEPENDENCE was at torpedo defense. At 1904 they changed fleet course to 009°T.

2300 Changed course to 273°T. At 2310, commenced zigzagging (Plan No.6) on base course 273°T. The INDEPENDENCE was assigned no flight operations this evening.

GUAM   We refueled today--250 miles from Luzon. A month ago we wouldn't have dared. Two months from now we'll be fueling that close to Taiwan.   GUAM

This flight deck photo shot in August 1945 (ten months forward from the time period of this page in the book). Note the new antenna mast and new yardarm from the Hunters Point repairs and refit as future Air Group Twenty Seven readies to launch. F6F hellcats, props turning, external belly fuel tanks mounted, and HVAR rockets beneath the wings for strikes on Japan.

16
Leyte
Leyte Invasion - Overview - Japan reacts

General Douglas MacArthur was fulfilling his promise, at last. Supported by a vast invasion fleet, troops would go ashore on the beaches of Leyte, with landings at Tacloban and Dulag. MacArthur would go ashore on the afternoon of the 20th. **(See map on page 334 for this chapter)**

The US invasion of the Philippines at Leyte Gulf pulled the trigger for "Sho 1", which was one of four Japanese options covered under an umbrella military strategy of the "Sho-Go" plan. The Philippines, if reoccupied by the US, would cut off sea routes to the island nation of Japan. It would isolate Japan from oil, food and raw materials vital for the war. It would further cut off and isolate Japan from its rapidly shrinking territorial gains. The Philippines could not fall with the Imperial fleet left sitting at anchor. The Leyte invasion would pry the IJN fleet out from its protected waters for a hoped for "Decisive Victory". "Sho 1" was, as played out, a desperate plan against overwhelming odds. Odds made worse by the accelerated schedule of the US invasion.

Japanese military planners opted for complex plans, often dividing their forces. The "Decisive Battle" would send the powerful Imperial Fleet in a pincers movement to decimate the Leyte invasion force. IJN would advance on Leyte with four separate naval forces. The IJN was to receive air support from Imperial Japanese Army air bases in the Philippines.

Japans military aviation however, was in shambles, with a shortage of trained Naval Aviators. IJN needed time to retrain and replenish. It had carriers, with insufficient pilots, aircrew and mechanics. Experienced battle hardened aviators had been consumed in a large string of IJN losses. Vital aircraft and aviators were also diverted for the defense of Formosa. With time, the IJN could rearm and retrain, just a few precious months were thought to be necessary. However, Sho No.1 sprung early. The carriers were not ready. Japans remaining aircraft carriers (unknown to US battle planners) were basically empty shells (with skeleton air wings) that would steam out (**Northern Force**) to be used as decoys to bait Bull Halsey away from the beaches at Leyte. Wave the cape (the IJN battle flag) and pull the Bull's vast naval air armada away in pursuit, so the mighty Japanese BB's, CA's and DD's of the **Center** and **Southern Forces**, unhindered, could bring their large guns and Long Lance torpedoes to bear, causing havoc and the destruction of the US invasion forces.

At 0830 on 17 October, the Japanese Combined Fleet was issued an Operational Telegram Order to "Stand by for Sho No.1". At 0928, another Order was issued to start the "First Attack Force" to sortie, advancing forward to Brunei for refueling.

The stage was now set for the horrific collision of mighty opposing naval forces in what would turn into separate major actions; Battle of the Sibuyan Sea, Battle of the Surigao Strait, Battle off Samar, Battle off Cape Engaño, when lumped together to be called the "Battle of Leyte Gulf".

Vice Admiral Takeo Kurita (**Center Force**) sortied from Lingga Roads, proceeded to Brunei Bay, Borneo to take on fuel oil, and would attempt to steam to the invasion beaches at Leyte thru San Bernardino Strait. He departed Brunei at 08:00 on 22 October. On a most convluted route, Center Force would plot its course thru the Palawan Passage, the Sulu Sea (via the Mindoro Strait) entering the Sibuyan Sea thru Tablas Strait, and proceed north of Burias and Ticao Islands to San Bernardino Strait.

Vice Admiral Shoji Nishimura (**Southern Force**) steamed from Brunei Bay to attack Leyte thru the Surigao Strait. He would traverse the Sulu Sea.

Vice Admiral Kiyohide Shima sortied from Bako to attack Leyte thru the Surigao Strait. He received his orders on 21 October, to support Nishimura's Southern Force.

Vice Admiral Jisaburo Ozawa (**Northern Carrier Force**) had the critical (and sacrificial) task to decoy and pull off Halsey's Third Fleet. He would form his battle group and depart on 22 October from the Inland Sea, to steam down across the Philippine Sea from the north.

The events of these few days would be some of the most notable in naval history. Decisions and actions of the admirals in both navies would be shaped and marred by the notorious "Fog of War", unimaginably poor communications, and flawed command structures. Decisions and actions would be the subject of many questions and much debate by future historians. I choose not to second guess, but will put forth comments by those that were there aboard USS INDEPENDENCE, on those violent days nearing the end of October, 1944.

The composition of the IJN forces were as follows: (Vessels in <u>underlined</u> type would be sunk)

Northern Force: Vice Admiral Jisaburo Ozawa

>
> Carriers (CV): <u>ZUIKAKU</u>
> Carriers (CVL): <u>CHITOSE</u>, <u>CHIYODA</u>, <u>ZUIHO</u>
> Battleships/Carriers: (hybrids): HYUGA, ISE
> Light Cruisers: ISUZU, <u>TAMA</u>, OYODO
> Destroyers: <u>AKIZUKI</u>, FUYUZSUKI, <u>HATSUTSUKI</u>, KIRI, KUWA, MAKI,
>   SHIMOTSUKI, SUGI, SUZUTSUKI, WAKATSUKI

Center Force: Vice Admiral Takeo Kurita

>
> Battleships: HARUNA, KONGO, <u>MUSASHI</u>, NAGATO, YAMATO
> Heavy Cruisers: <u>ATAGO</u>, <u>CHIKUMA</u>, <u>CHOKAI</u>, HAGURO, KUMANO, <u>MAYA</u>, MYOKO,
>   SUZUYA, TAKAO, TONE
> Light Cruisers: <u>NOSHIRO</u>, YAHAGI
> Destroyers: AKISHIMO, ASASHIMO, FUJINAMI, HAMAKAZE, HAMANAMI,
>   <u>HAYASHIMO</u>, ISOKAZE, KISHINAMI, KIYOSHIMO, NAGANAMI,
>   <u>NOWAKI</u>, OKINAMI, SHIMAKAZE, URAKAZE, YUKIKAZE

Southern Forces: Vice Admiral Shoji Nishimura followed by Vice Admiral Kiyohide Shima (operating independently)

Vice Admiral Shoji Nishimura
>   Battleships: <u>FUSO</u>, <u>YAMASHIRO</u>
>   Heavy Cruisers: <u>MOGAMI</u>
>   Destroyers: <u>ASAGUMO</u>, MICHISHIO, SHIGURE, <u>YAMAGUMO</u>

Vice Admiral Kiyohide Shima
>   Heavy Cruisers: ASHIGARA, NACHI
>   Light Cruisers: <u>ABUKUMA</u>
>   Destroyers: AKEBONO, KASUMI, SHIRANUHI, USHIO

Ship against ship action would start first with submarines USS DARTER and USS DACE sighting Admiral Kurita's Center Force off the western side of Palawan, near the southern tip. Contact reports alerted Halsey something was up. An ambush was set up further up the Palawan Passage, while Kurita's Center Force steamed with Palawan to their starboard and "Dangerous Grounds" off to port. Early morning on 23 October DARTER and DACE drew first blood. Kurita had his flag ship (heavy cruiser ATAGO) blown out from under him by DARTER's torpedoes. Kurita, dripping wet, transferred his flag to battleship YAMATO. DARTER also crippled the IJN heavy cruiser TAKAO, retiring it from the operation. Heavy cruiser MAYA was rapidly sent to the bottom by torpedoes from DACE.
Admiral Ugaki was viewing the action commanding YAMATO would observe in his diary:
"Nothing was left (of MAYA) *after the smoke and spray subsided.."*

Naval action had now started, that would display courage and sacrifice by both opposing forces.

(Note: The **bold** type used on **24 thru 26 October** are to assist the reader reference to the action related to the above IJN forces.)   We return to 20 October.

Friday 20 October 1944   *Philippines - "A" Day - Leyte Invasion*

0524-0617 Steaming as before. INDEPENDENCE was at routine torpedo defense.
0650 Changed course to 160°T while USS UHLMANN came alongside to starboard, delivered mail and cast off at 0710. Maneuvered to regain position in the disposition.
0713 Regained position and commenced zigzagging on base course 179°T.
0745 Ceased zigzagging, resumed base course 179°T.
0749 Commenced maneuvering to rotate axis to 045°T and assume position on new axis.
0910 USS CABOT rejoined TG38.2.1 from her temporary duty escorting the cripples away from Formosa. She was assigned to a position bearing 225°T, 2,500 yards from (guide) NEW JERSEY. INDEPENDENCE was positioned bearing 090°T, 4,000 yards from guide on a new course of 025°T.
0932 Fleet changed course to 255°T, speed 16 knots.

A massive gathering of naval vessels would be involved in support of the invasion to retake the Philippines by the **Sixth Army**. The combined vessel count of **Seventh Fleet** and the **Third Fleet** was approximately:   9 fleet carriers, 8 light carriers, 18 escort carriers, 12 battleships, 9 heavy cruisers, 11 light cruisers, 3 anti-aircraft cruisers, 92 destroyers, 17 escort destroyers, 280+ amphibious & support vessels, and 110+ auxiliaries. As a side note: Sister carrier USS COWPENS now has on board the Air Group INDEPENDENCE had aboard in 1943 from shake down to Tarawa; VT-22 and VF-22.

0943 Waves of landing craft were beginning their advance toward the beaches on Leyte, with landings scheduled for 10:00 to take advantage of high tides.
1217 Changed fleet course to 030°T.
1230 USS MILLER came along starboard side amidships to transfer US Mail.
1243 Changed fleet course to 260°T.
1415 Sounded flight quarters.
1529 Changed fleet course to 035°T.
1532-1539 Launched 8 Hellcats for CAP and 4 Avengers for SNASP.
1605 Changed course to 000°T, speed 17 knots.
1634 USS HUNT came along starboard quarter to deliver guard mail, casting off at 1638.
1749 Changed course to 030°T to proceed as a detached unit to our night flying station with USS UHLMANN and THE SULLIVANS, 10 miles windward of the formation, bearing 045°T from guide.
1750 Launched 2 Hellcats for night CAP.
1805 Commenced recovering aircraft.
1809 Sounded torpedo defense.
1814 Upon landing, Lt.(jg) Forrest M."Polly" Archer crashed into the island structure when the tail hook broke, and he opted for the island structure, rather than hitting the aircraft in front of him. The TBM-1C Avenger (Bu.No. 25539) was damaged beyond repair. A fire ensued. Polly had scalp wounds and second degree burns. His radioman & gunner, ARM2c P.T. Julsen Jr. also sustained a lacerated scalp. The INDEPENDENCE lost some of its communication capability in the accident and logged the following damage: Forward flag bag badly bent & torn, all signal halyards destroyed, after end of the island structure bent in, flight deck scuttlebutt badly damaged, four steam lines were broken including lines to the whistle and siren, lines to the antenna cut knocking out the primary and secondary TBS, ships bell was lost over the side, voice tube to the bridge from the signal station bent in, two portable 15 pound CO_2 bottles lost over the side, damaged barrier piston and no. 3 barrier pennant broken.
A small portable TBY was quickly broken out to reestablish communication with the Task Group. (The TBY was a portable version of the TBS - Talk Between Ships.)
1815 Aircraft recovery was completed, having recovered 7 Hellcats and 4 Avengers.
1816 Sounded fire quarters.
1822 Changed course to 220°T.

1823 Shifted repeaters to after gyro due to overload on forward gyro.

1830 Fire brought under control and extinguished.

1909 Secured from torpedo defense.

2104-2108 Changed course into the wind and completed recovery of 2 Hellcats for night CAP.

2142 Completed recovering 2 Hellcats launched at 1800 and 1 Hellcat launched at 2108. Then changed course to 210°T, speed 28 knots.

2202 Changed course to 000°T and launched 1 Hellcat. Changed course to 220°T.

2400 Changed course to 040°T into the wind, speed 17 knots.

GUAM *Most of our force is orbiting about 200 miles off Luzon--maintaining a strategic supporting position. If the Japs send any part of a fleet down to oppose MacArthur's landings today, they will be in the " bite" to be intercepted. If they have staged many aircraft in (which is unlikely) and air attacks become too severe, we will be in close enough to give 38.1 a hand in supporting the landings from the air. The Independence was originally scheduled to provide night fighter coverage to the landings but since there is a remote possibility of a run in with the Jap force, that was out this way four days ago, We are still with the " Bull" and that means we will be where every major action is expected.* *GUAM*

DL *With massive help from the U.S. Navy, General MacArthur and the United States Army returned today to the Philippines at Leyte. It would be a long, brutal, hard-fought campaign that the general considered a strategic necessity and a political and moral imperative. He was right in my opinion. Among other regional bloody fights in World War II, this one could not be avoided.*

But my purpose is to relate how USS Independence CVL-22 fit into the big picture. She was only one of nearly two dozen fast carriers*—the shock troops, as it were, of the sea forces. Her role was singular and vital. *DL* (* Roughly 17 fast carriers)

GN *D-Day on Leyte. We patrol around the Philippines.* *GN*
(Note: It was actually "A-Day" on Leyte, D-Day was already taken by Eisenhower for the Normandy Invasion)

RC *Army invades Leyte. Were standing by to intercept any of the Jap fleet who might try to aid their armies.*

DrP *Off Samar & Leyte. Night C.A.P. for MacArthur landings.* *DrP*

Saturday 21 October 1944   *Philippines - Leyte Invasion*

0004 Launched 2 F6FNs for night CAP off Samar (McArthur landings). Changed course to 210°T.

0020 Catapulted 1 F6FN.

0045-0106 Recovered 3 F6FNs.

0317 Catapulted 2 F6FNs for night CAP.

0343-0348 Recovered 2 F6FNs.

0530 Sounded torpedo defense.

0532 Jettisoned overboard "Polly" Archer's TBM, damaged from the crash into the island structure yesterday at 1814.

0600 Recovered 2 F6FNs launched at 0317.

0635 Assumed position with TG 38.2 in disposition 5R5, bearing 090°T, 4,000 yards from (guide) USS NEW JERSEY on course 090°T, speed 22 knots. Secured from torpedo defense.

During the day the TBS was repaired, the signal halyards were replaced, and other damage from the TBM accident were repaired as possible.

Task Groups 38.2 and 38.3 attacked the Visayas, southern Luzon and Coron Bay. INDEPENDENCE pilots did not participate in the attacks due to assignment to provide Combat Air Patrols scheduled to cover the disposition all night.

1803 Sounded flight quarters.

1816 Sounded torpedo defense.

1830 Proceeded to night flying station, bearing 050°T, 10 miles from TG 38.2, accompanied by destroyers USS TWINING and USS THE SULLIVANS.

1843 Launched 3 F6Fs.
1847 Recovered 1 F6F.
1917 Secured from torpedo defense.
1919 Launched 1 F6F.
1923 Gained night flying station.
1955-2000 Recovered 2 F6Fs launched at 1843, and 1 F6F launched at 1919. This night CAP was recalled early, and no further CAPs were launched this evening due to weather that was progressively worsening, causing remaining scheduled patrols to be canceled.

GUAM   *21 October 1944*
Part of our carrier force struck Coron Bay again. This Bay is directly west of Leyte and on our last attack there, much shipping was sunk. It was hoped that the Japs had brought in more ammunition ships, AO's, AK's to aid their forces on Mindanao and on the Visayan Islands but not much was found. This afternoon we heard radio Tokyo analyze the Battle of Taiwan (October 12, 13, 14). It seems they considered it necessary to explain to their listening public why such discrepancies appear between the Jap communiqués and those of Admiral Nimitz. They attempt to lend more credit to their claims of 25 warships sunk by asking if Admiral Nimitz's statement of "no aircraft carriers damaged and only two in the entire fleet damaged and none sunk, what was Admiral Halsey's fleet doing on 15 and 16 October in dangerous water under range of our land based bombers?" They weren't striking against Taiwan nor were they striking Luzon (all of which is true on the 15th we were fueling and on the 16th we were searching and chasing alternately the Jap task force).
This announcer went on to say that the American Third Fleet's back was broken "and were not striking Taiwan or Luzon because most of their fleet was at the bottom of the Taiwan Ocean or being towed home".
It is evidently their belief that our activities against Taiwan were brought to an abrupt close by their devastating air attacks, (they were terrific in a sense, but far from devastating), they believed we were attempting to sever the life line of the Philippines by rendering Taiwan completely helpless. Obviously no one single striking force could accomplish such a purpose on so large and formidable an island. Especially since it lies so close to the empire itself and to Jap held China coast. *GUAM*

Sunday 22 October 1944   *Philippines - Leyte Invasion*

Operating with Task Groups 38.1 and 38.4, Task group 38.2 was in bad weather with low visibility. No flight operations were conducted by INDEPENDENCE as the fleet was conducting long range searches.
1422 USS HANCOCK detached from TG 38.2 to join TG 38.1.
1552-1608 Steadied on a course of 120°T, speed 15 knots. The USS BENHAM came alongside amidships, starboard, to deliver mail.

They steamed the remainder of the day toward a fueling rendezvous on numerous headings toward the north east finishing the 22nd of October off zigzagging on base course 077°T, speed 16 knots with the Air Department in condition 11.

Monday 23 October 1944   *Philippines - Leyte Invasion*

0526 TU 38.2.1 is steaming as before. Sounded torpedo defense.
0536 Ceased zigzagging, changed course to 200°T.
0540 Sighted fueling ships, 200°T at 15 miles.
0544 Changed course to 240°T.
0614 Changed course to 270°T, secured from torpedo defense, Air Department set to condition 14.
Left our position in the disposition and commenced maneuvering to come astern of tanker USS CACHE.
0635 Gained position 3,000 yards astern USS CACHE, fueling course 270°T, speed 10 knots.

Commenced approach on USS CACHE.

0655 Changed axis to 090°T. Guide shifted to tanker USS TOMAHAWK, bearing 270°T at 3,000 yards from fleet center. Gained position alongside USS CACHE to starboard. Guide now bears 270°T at 2,000 yards. Commenced pumping fuel oil at 0731.

0901 Cast off from USS CACHE having received 170,830 gallons of fuel oil, 15 drums of lubricating oil, 17 CO_2 bottles, and 8 acetylene bottles. Commenced maneuvering to regain station.

0945 Regained station 500 yards, bearing 270°T from guide, USS CACHE. Commenced zigzagging independently on base course 270°T.

1108 USS NEW JERSEY designated guide. USS BUNKER HILL had been reassigned and departed from Task Group 38.2 during the 0800-1200 watch.

1146 Changed fleet course to 240°T, speed 16 knots.

1200 Gained station 2,500 yards, bearing 090°T from guide. The Task Group had completed its refueling and once again, reformed disposition 5R5. We proceeded toward an area just north of central Samar, where the Task Group would launch a "Reinforced search" extending west to include Coron Bay.

1340-1356 USS YARNALL was alongside to starboard amidships to deliver mail.

1400 Sounded flight quarters.

1452 Changed speed to 25 knots for flight operations.

1504 Completed launching 8 F6Fs for CAP and 4 TBMs for ASP. Changed speed to 16 knots.

1722 Changed fleet speed to 24 knots proceeding to flying station.

1803 Change course to 060°T into the wind, changed speed to 28 knots to recover aircraft.

1817 Completed recovery of 8 F6Fs and 4 TBMs launched at 1504. This had turned out to have been a routine patrol, with negative sightings. Changed course to 275°T and commenced maneuvering to regain position in the disposition.

1852 Regained position in the disposition and commenced zigzagging on base course 240°T.

They ended the day at 2010 zigzagging on base course 249°T.

Task Group 38.2 now had 3 carriers, INTREPID, CABOT and INDEPENDENCE.

GUAM Fueled Ship today. Late in the afternoon our orders were changed. We aren't going to Ulithi but are heading full steam for a new position north of Samar Island. 38.4 will be north of us and 38.3 south. 38.1 is going to Ulithi as originally planned.

Later today we received word that a Jap task force is entering a passage in the Visayan group evidently on its way to "clean up" on our landing groups off of Leyte Island. We'll go after them the first thing in the morning. GUAM

October 22-25, 1944 — Philippine Sea Battle

DL

The Battle of Leyte Gulf was, according to military historians, the greatest naval clash of all time. The Official Chronicle calls it a succession of fleet engagements. In one way or another, Mighty I and her snoopers took part in most of them.

In spite of doubts among some high-ranking Navy officers about the IJN's willingness to give battle, when it did come out it meant to win, to annihilate. Unable to ignore this great American intrusion into the Philippines, it was loaded for bear. Although the bear it chose to fight was bigger and more powerful, the fight turned into a mighty struggle between titans.

Independence bared her fangs at 1935 when one of our night fliers spotted the IJN Center Force (ADM Kurita) headed 120 degrees, the course for San Bernardino Strait. Report was radioed to the ship at 1958 and retransmitted so that Halsey received it at 2004.

Around 2030 another of our night chickens reported Kurita's force twenty-five miles nearer the strait than it had been at 1935. Fate, and what some have called the bullheadedness (or the fighting spirit) of one man, Bill Halsey, had altered the battle in ways no one could have foreseen. Wrote naval historian Morison: "Halsey's thoughts as well as his forces were streaking northward and the night fliers from Independence, which had lost track of Kurita after 2320, had been pulled off to search for Ozawa's Northern Force."

The battle had indeed changed. The fiercest fighting went on in our vicinity, including the loss of sister ship CVL Princeton, hit by an enemy bomb. Light cruiser Birmingham had been ordered to assist fighting her fires and to rescue as many men as possible. She was close alongside when Princeton's aft torpedo magazine exploded in a cataclysmic blast that doomed the vessel as well as many of her sailors. Birmingham was showered with so much shrapnel that streams of blood ran in her scuppers from dead, dying, mutilated men. Decapitations, arms and legs torn off, butchered torsos disfigured her topside. Two hundred twenty-nine died, two hundred-eleven were seriously wounded, two hundred-fifteen received minor wounds. Destroyers Morrison, Gatling, and Irwin were also damaged and suffered casualties of their own. Eventually that evening Princeton had to be scuttled. A torpedo from cruiser Reno did the trick.

Many American seamen rued the day they had first heard Princeton's name. We knew her well. She had been the first CVL to follow us down the Delaware to the open sea at Cape May, and would be the only Independence-class carrier to be lost in the war. She was the first fast carrier to be sunk since prewar Hornet was torpedoed 27 October 1942 near Guadalcanal.

Meantime, Halsey in New Jersey was racing north and we were in his train. He would not be dissuaded despite evidence that he might be wrong. Reports from Mighty I search pilots that they had spotted the Japanese Center Force resuming an easterly course were forwarded to his staff. RADM Bogan, our Captain Ewen's boss, discussed the reports via TBS with the skipper. After confirming them, Ewen mentioned that our snoopers had noticed "the ominous fact" that all navigation lights in San Bernardino Strait were "brightly lighted", a sure sign that ships were intending to come through. Bogan, disturbed, drafted a message to Halsey, then called him personally to make sure it got through. He was rebuffed, apparently by a staff person, and made no further attempt at direct communication. What had been lost? Only the weary gods of War know. The battle went on to its destined end. Many books offer different sides of the story. A stateside magazine called it The Battle of Bull's Run. Halsey was impervious to any real or implied insult. He was certain he knew what had to be done—sink the rest of the Jap carriers in open battle while the rest of his fleet took care of itself.
What about our story—the Independence crewmen who were along for the ride? We went temporarily from a night operating carrier to a day operating carrier. How easily our snooper pilots adjusted, I don't know. The biggest change for us ordnancemen while we raced north was a heavier armament load on all the planes. Aviation mechs and metalsmiths worked like mad keeping the airplanes flyable. The snipes in the black gang sweated blood keeping critical engine equipment functioning beyond the normal call of duty. At times the annunciator on the bridge rang up flank speed. Halsey was in a hurry. Get those Jap flattops!

The great battle south of us, meanwhile, raged throughout the day. The Japanese fought well, but the Americans were the tigers in this fight. Ships earned their places of honor in USN annals, their sailors dying in the effort. DD's Hoel, Johnston, and DE Samuel B. Roberts were sunk in determined torpedo attacks against the enemy; Johnston's skipper, badly wounded, never lived to see his Medal of Honor. DD Heermann as well as DE Dennis were damaged while trying to divert gunfire away from escort carriers not designed or intended to fight Japanese battlewagons and cruisers. If there is any glory in such vicious action, this was one area where it took place. Many sailors must have thought the day would never end—yet were astonished when the Japs turned tail. **DL**

Tuesday 24 October 1944   *Philippines - Leyte Invasion*

Steaming as before. Ship is darkened zigzagging on base course 249°T at 15 knots.
0124 Radar reported two bogeys bearing 310°T, distance 65 miles.
0128 Changed course to 070°T, speed 25 knots, leaving the formation to launch aircraft.
INDEPENDENCE (guide) is accompanied by USS YARNALL (station 1.5000) and USS STOCKHAM (station 1.5180), axis 060°T.

0132 Completed launching 2 F6F's scrambled for the interception of the unidentified radar contacts. Sounded flight quarters. Changed course to 060°T, speed 15 knots.

Ens. J.S. "Berky" Berkheimer and Ens. Harry E. Johnson were launched into a dark, no moon night sky, 5/10 cloud cover with bases at 1500' and squalls. Berky was given vectors that led him in a sweeping circular path as he closed on the bogey. At one point he drew friendly fire from a destroyer in the fleets screen. With vectors and his AIA scope in his cockpit, he would pick up the bogey on his scope, have it fade, then maneuver to reacquire it. He finally was able to pick it up on his radar 2.5 miles ahead at angels 10.5, and closed to within 1/4 mile by radar until he finally had visual contact with 4 exhaust stack flames. The large four engine Emily flying boat did not appear to know it was being stalked. Berky put bursts into the inboard starboard engine, the inboard port engine, then a third burst into the sand brown colored hull, from level 6 o'clock astern. It immediately started to burn in a gliding turn to port. Pieces of hull were flying off after the third burst and, as the flaming flying boat descended thru 7,000' it blew up mid air, and then "it went down to crash in a mass of flames".

During this time Harry Johnson hunted another bogey for a considerable distance, but broke off the pursuit when his radar and communications gave out. Berky was vectored to Harry's prey. But this tail chase was more difficult as the Japanese crew appeared to know they were being hunted. There were violent turns with changes in altitude, repeated several times as Berkheimer hung on with radar and vectors, continuing to close. At one time he caught a visual glance of the exhaust flames and saw a Mavis in a hard starboard turn. Berky lost him both visually and on his scope, but new vectors brought Berky back in hot pursuit. The Mavis pilot was now making check turns to port and starboard flying over the cumulus layer of cloud with tops at 4,500 feet. For some reason the Japanese pilot did not think to duck into the clouds. Berky was finally able to get him on his AIA scope and flew up to within 100' underneath the black painted Mavis for positive identification. He dropped back to 200' astern, climbed to level at 6 o'clock behind it and fired into the wing, and inboard engines, then the starboard outboard engine which started to burn. The Mavis ended up in the water burning. Berky made a strafing run on it for gun camera photos.

0138 Assumed flying station bearing 056°T, 7 miles from TG 38.2.

0142 Commenced zigzagging (Plan No.6) on base course 250°T.

0153 Sounded torpedo defense, Bogey reported bearing 260°T, distance 25 miles.

0214 Secured from torpedo defense.

0403 Changed course to 060°T, speed 20 knots for flight operations.

0409 Launched 2 F6Fs to relieve our night CAP. Changed course to 250°T, speed 25 knots.

0434 Completed recovery of 2 F6Fs launched at 0132 (Berkheimer and Johnson). During his recovery Berkheimer made an uneven hard night landing, and the fuselage buckled, leaving it badly wrinkled. The F6F5N (Bu.No. 58724) was written off as totaled for salvage.

0522 Regained night flying station.

0530 Sounded torpedo defense.

0552 Changed course to 065°T, speed 25 knots for flight operations fleet disposition to 5V5. INDEPENDENCE now bears 090°T, 2,000 yards from guide.

0557 Completed recovery of 2 F6Fs launched at 0409.

0620 Commenced maneuvering reentering the formation to regained station.

0640 Secured from torpedo defense, Air Department set condition 14.

0651 Gained station in the disposition (course 030°T, speed 15 knots, bearing 090°T, 2,500 yards from guide).

The other carriers of the TG launched strikes against the Japanese Fleet reported moving through the Visayan Sea.

0810 A Japanese surface force of 4 BBs, 8 CAs and 13 DDs (Kurita's Center Force) was reported south of Mindoro Island on a course of 050°T steaming at a speed of 10-12 knots, by one of TG 38.2's search planes. (This was possibly a report from INTREPID aircraft.)

0813 Changed fleet course to 230°T.

0829 Sounded flight quarters.

0845 Changed fleet course to 070°T.

0905-0918 Launched 11 F6Fs for CAP over TG 38.2 and 4 TBMs for SNASP. Maneuvered to regain position in the formation.

The launch would put up 10 F6F5Ns and 1 F6F5, for a total of 11 Hellcats out of 12 scheduled for the mission. Ens. Berkheimer was not launched due to problems with the Hellcats carburetor.

The CAP consisted of 2 divisions. The Hellcats were launched into a bright day with scattered clouds and visibility estimated at 15-20 miles.

Division 1 led by Turner F. "Stinky" Caldwell made no contacts, however they were witness to the destroyer USS CUSHING shooting down a Betty Bomber with its AA fire.

Division 2 led by Lt. J.T. "Terry" Barker reported no activity.

Division 3, led by Lt. Erwin J. "Jack" Becker had Ensigns Wallace E. "Wally" Miller and Reuben F. "Pete" Peterson as wingmen. They were vectored toward 2 Vals at angels 8 over the fleet but had to give a wide berth due to friendly AA fire put up by Task Group DD's. They never made contact with the Vals, continued in the general direction of the bogeys and were instructed to orbit. Fanning out in a large orbit, Miller tallyhoed a very low flying bogey. Miller saw twin floats and recognized it to be a Jake as he peeled off in pursuit. He closed descending at 260 knots on the Jakes tail, put multiple burst into the Jakes tail from level at 6 o'clock until the Jake blew up scattering debris in all directions. The debris hit the water at 1006, 60 miles out on a bearing of 330° from the Task Group.

Becker and Peterson witnessed the action and rejoined with Miller. In less than 5 miles from the first kill, Peterson tallyhoed a Francis at 2 o'clock and 4-5 miles flying at 1,200', just below the base of 5/10 cumulus cloud cover. Peterson pursued, Miller and Becker on his tail. Instead of using the clouds for cover, the Francis pilot dove for the water. Miller released his belly tank and began to pull closer. Becker dropped his tank and went to W.E.P (War Emergency Power). The Francis was fast and Miller and Peterson were firing out-of-range bursts to try to force a turn. Becker pulled past Miller and started putting bursts into the Francis. After a long burst down its fuselage, the dark-mottled green-brown Francis dropped its right wing and slid off in a glide, "hit the water and splattered".

0939 Sounded torpedo defense. An enemy torpedo attack was expected.

0948 Sounded general quarters.

0959 Changed fleet course to 240°T to refuel returning aircraft from other carriers.

1009 Landed one F6F, low on fuel, from USS CABOT.

1010 Commander THIRD Fleet directed Task Groups 38.3 and 38.4 to concentrate on Task Group 38.2.

1032 Landed one SB2C, low on fuel, from INTREPID. Maneuvered to regain position in the formation.

1047 Regained station, secured from general quarters.

1053 Launched the refueled USS INTREPID SB2C.

1055 Changed fleet course to 115°T. Sounded general quarters.

1124 Secured from general quarters.

1136 Sounded torpedo defense, an enemy air attack was expected.

Task group 38.2 was off San Bernardino Strait.

1225 Changed fleet course to 090°T, speed 23 knots.

1229 Launched one F6F for return to the USS CABOT.

1233-1244 Recovered 11 F6Fs and 4 TBMs launched at 0918. Changed speed to 15 knots.

1255 Sounded general quarters, changed fleet course to 250°T, speed 20 knots.

1306 Secured from general quarters (The expected air attack had not developed).

1445 Air Department set to condition 12.

1712-1717 Launched 4 F6FNs for CAP and 2 TBMs. The mission of the TBMs was to shadow the enemy BBs and CAs (Kurita's Center Force) in the Sibuyan Sea.

1740 Launched 1 F6FN.

1745 Recovered 1 F6FN.

1800 Increased speed to 25 knots and commenced maneuvering to gain flying station, bearing 090°T, 10 miles from TG 38.2 as a detached Unit, accompanied by USS YARNALL and USS STOCKHAM.

1920 Changed course to 120°T.

1925-1928 Launched 2 TBMs (Jim Taylor and John "Jack" E. Dewis) **to relieve on station the 2 TBM's launched at 1717 to shadow the Japanese.** Changed course to 290°T.

1948 Changed course to 180°T.

2005 A report from an INDEPENDENCE night search TBM (possibly John E.Dewis) **placed the main battleship-cruiser force at 12° 45' N., 122° 40' E., course 120°, speed 12 knots, time of sighting 1935. (This sighting was Admiral Kurita's Center force, in the Sibuyan Sea, advancing toward San Bernardino Strait under cover of night. The sighting information was given to Admiral Bogan, aboard INTREPID by Captain Ewen via TBS — Talk Between Ships.)**

2019 Changed course to 000°T.

2032 The main battleship-cruiser force was again sighted passing between BURIAS and MASBATE Islands by VT(N)-41. The INDEPENDENCE Avengers would continue to track Kurita's force.

2039 Unidentified aircraft bearing 010°T, 12 miles. Sounded torpedo defense.

2047 Changed course to 180°T. Observed firing on port bow, 10 miles.

2050 Sounded general quarters. Changed course to 310°T.

2109 Changed course to 000°T.

2122 Secured from general quarters.

2141 Changed course to 080°T, speed 18 knots for flight operations.

2148 Completed recovering the 4 F6Fs launched at 1717, and at 1740 (for the Combat Air Patrol). They reported no contact with the enemy.

2302 A TBM's report (from the INDEPENDENCE night Air Group) gave the enemy position as 12° 45' N., 123° 22' E., 12 knots.

2243 Recovered 2 TBMs launched at 1717.

2340 Changed course to 075°T for flight operations.

2343 Recovered 2 TBMs launched at 1928. These TBMs were recalled after showing the enemy force reached the southern tip of Burias Island and started steaming northeastward between Burias and Ticao Islands. Periodic contact reports were made to the OTC.
Kurita had turned toward San Bernardino Strait.

2345 Changed course to 355°T, speed 27 knots.

DrP Tuesday 0200 - Berkheimer splashes Emily. 0320 - Berkheimer splashes a Mavis. 1000 (about) Miller splashes a Jake. 1030 (about) Becker splashes a Francis. Total airborne splashes - 21, 1 ship sunk. 1200 - Jap fleet located SW of Mindoro & tracked steaming S.E. 1500 - one BB (Jap) dead in water. **DrP** *(IJNs BB MUSASHI was sunk. BBs YAMATO & NAGATO; CAs MYOKO, MOGAMI & TONE and DDs KIYOSHIMO, FUJINAMI & URANAMI were damaged.)*

GUAM   24 October 1944
WE launched two small strikes--all that one group could afford at present at 4BB's, 8CA's, 13DD's. Results not know yet. Scuttlebutt has it that the first strike didn't go so well--scoring only two hits, second strike supposed to have sunk 2 cruisers and 4 cans. Two BB's seemed out of control -- going around in circles. We have gone to GQ four times, none of the attacks were coordinated as usual. One or two bogies at a time. (this was not true of the attacking Japs on 38.3 who claim 150 planes in a 4 hour raid). One Jake sneaked in unobserved and dropped a bomb which missed the Cabot by about 50 yards. The last GQ sounded today at about 2045. When torpedo defense was sounded, some of us went out to the forecastle to watch the cans and cruisers open up on the bogey, For most of us, it was our first chance to see night firing, It was awe inspiring – in fact it was more than that- It was scary as hell! Just after we left the forecastle for our battle stations, two five inch shells from our task force burst over

our flight deck. No damage done or injury sustained so it was O.K. - Close though. All night our TBM's shadowed the force. They had high tailed it for the China Sea[1] on the first strike against them and were pretty well out of range by evening. Sometime during the night, however, they came back and seemed to be heading toward. Leyte again. We kept them well shadowed all this time. The search planes of 38.4 also discovered a Jap carrier force north of us about 300 miles. Looks like tomorrow is going to be a busy day for everybody.* **GUAM**

[1] Misleading Halsey, the Japanese Center Force was not going to the South China Sea. Plagued by harrowing attacks pressed home by five waves of attacks from US aviators, the IJN's "First day of the decisive battle" left MYOKO (CA) damaged and withdrawing to Brunei, and MISASHI (BB) sinking. This had followed the loss (the previous day on the 23rd) of ATAGO (CA - Kurita's flagship), MAYA (CA) and damage to TAKAO (CA) causing its withdraw to Brunei by the action of US subs DARTER & DACE. Center Force briefly withdrew to feint retreat, and distance them from US aviators, until they could resume pressing through the San Bernardino Straits utilizing the cover of nightfall. Both sides would be hampered by fatigue and plagued with poor communications. IJN gained the advantage of surprise, though INDEPENDENCE would send alerts to Halsey in vain. Halsey was left to sleep, and when alerted, he by then, wanted the Japanese carriers .. Not knowing the Japanese Northern Carrier Force were essentially empty shells lacking aircraft strength, and those available flown mainly by lower time aviators. IJN pilots with insufficient training for carrier landings were instructed to land on the Philippines.

GN *Again spot Jap fleet. One heluva big outfit of planes go in for the kill. We get word that the Princeton, our sister ship has been hit and sunk.* **GN**

HB *On October 24, our pilots shot down one Emily, one Mavis, one Francis, and one Jake. The Japanese fleet, consisting of four BBs, eight CLs, and thirteen destroyers, was sighted 200 miles away. We sent an attack group, and damaged two battleships on the first wave. A second enemy force, consisting of three CVs, two CLs, and five destroyers, was sighted 300 miles to the north. Our ship and the rest of our task force was under attack all night. We had two near hits by 500 lb. bombs dropped by Vals.* **HB**

The 24th had been a busy day for both our fleet and the opposing Japanese. To the north, Sherman's TG 38.3 sent raids against targets on Luzon. The Japanese reciprocated sending out three raids (of 50-60 aircraft each) against the fleet. USS PRINCETON was hit with a bomb, and due to the resulting collateral damage (beginning with a gasoline fed fire in the hangar bay), had to be scuttled. Light cruiser USS BIRMINGHAM, attempting to assist close in, was damaged by a massive secondary explosion from within PRINCETON (thought to have originated in the torpedo storage area) with heavy casualties. The Japanese surface forces were also moving in earnest. IJN's Southern force of Vice Admiral Shoji Nishimura was closing on Surigao Strait. Not far behind him was the force of Vice Admiral Kiyohide Shima. Nishimura and Shima were steaming steadfastly into a trap set by the eagerly waiting Rear Admiral Jesse B. Olendorf. BBs, CAs, CLs, DDs and PT boats were ready for action. The historic lethal nighttime ship-to-ship naval engagement would begin at just before 2300 and extend into the 25th of October.

INDEPENDENCE had just recovered the Avengers that had been shadowing Vice Admiral Takeo Kurita's Center Force.

Over the horizon, out of sight and sound of the crew of the INDEPENDENCE, roughly 250 miles south, Olendorf's battle ships and cruisers held fire as PT boats (to be followed by destroyers) at the leading edge, were just springing Olendorf's massive deadly trap that would decimate the Southern Force thru the early morning hours of the 25th. The bloody "Gun Club" action would go down as "The Battle of Surigao Strait" as the Japanese steamed up the narrow strait into the horrific effective shelling from US battleships and cruisers at the top of a "T". Vice Admiral Shoji Nishimura would not survive.

Kurita was less than 200 miles SW making steady progress on his approach toward San Bernardino Strait. He was also steaming into naval history books, toward the "Battle off Samar". These historically important actions have been detailed in other books. They are lengthy tales that divert focus from the CVL-22. The brief overview is intended only to better clarify overall perspective.*[2]

([2] I suggest the following books: "Battle of Surigao Strait" by Anthony P. Tully; "Sea of Thunder" by Evan Thomas; "The Battle For Leyte Gulf" by C. Vann Woodward; "Last Stand of the Tin Can Sailors" by James Hornfischer)

Chapter 16

We pick up aboard the INDEPENDENCE ending the 24th of October with the ship's clocks ticking over to the 25th. At 0800 she will be roughly 240 miles north of her 2000 position (on the 24th) when her aircrews had sighted Kurita in the Sibuyan Sea. INDEPENDENCE (Captain Ewen, steaming in TG 38.2 under Admiral Gerald Bogan), will be with Halsey taking the bait and chasing after Vice Admiral Jisaburo Ozawa's Northern Carrier Force, at Ozawa's pre-planned invitation.

Wednesday 25 October 1944   *Philippines - Leyte Invasion*

Steaming as before in company with USS YARNALL and STOCKHAM as a detached Unit of TG 38.2. on the weather side of the fleet. **They are heading north to intercept a Japanese carrier group with Task Force 38 in Task Group 38.2.**

0039 Changed course to 340°T.

0049 Forward gyro temporally out of commission due to a "burnt out" rectifier tube. Repeaters shifted to after gyro.

0050 Changed course to 040°T, speed 16 knots.

0054-0058 Launched 5 TBMs tasked to carry out a 350 mile sector search ahead of TG 38.2's track. The INDEPENDENCE made numerous course and speed changes throughout the night.

0126 Launched 1 TBM. This was a replacement for a returning TBM with "material problems".

0140 Recovered 1 TBM launched at 0058.

0144 Sounded torpedo defense upon report of a radar contact showing unidentified aircraft bearing 290°T, 23 miles.

0153 Forward gyro back in commission.

0209 **A northern Japanese carrier force was reported by an INDEPENDENCE TBM** (flown by Jim Taylor) **which made contact at 0205 in position 16° 43' N., 125° 37' E. and gave the composition of the group as 5 ships -- 2 large, 2 small and one undetermined.**

0212 **An amplifying report corrected the 0209 report to 3 large ships and 3 small ships on course 110°, speed 15 knots.**

0218 **The same INDEPENDENCE TBM reported another force 40 miles astern of the 6-ship group on the same course and speed.** (These two sightings were Admiral Ozawa's carrier groups, sacrificially tasked to draw Halsey away from Leyte.)

0228 Recovered 1 TBM launched at 0058.

0232 Secured from torpedo defense. The aircraft threat had disappeared.

0315 Commander Task Force THIRTY-EIGHT ordered all radars silent except SM search radars.

0328-0331 Launched 3 F6Fs and 1 TBM.

0333 **Commander Task Force 38 designated Task Group 38.2 "Battle Line Carrier Group".**

0353 Recovered 1 TBM launched at 0058.

0405 Recovered 1 TBM launched at 0331.

0531 Sounded routine general quarters.

0548 Regained our station within Task Group 38.2, course 050°T, speed 25 knots, disposition 5V5, axis 090°T, guide USS INTREPID bearing 210°T, 2,500 yards. **Battleships, cruisers and several destroyers began to split off to reform as Task Force 34, along with battleships from other Task Groups.**

0655 Maneuvered into the wind to 060°T for air operations.

0706 Completed recovery of 3 F6Fs launched at 0331, 2 TBMs launched at 0058 and 1 TBM launched at 0126.

0745 Regained position in the formation, course 000°T, speed 18 knots.

0841 Sounded general quarters due to unidentified aircraft.

0853 Secured from general quarters. Aircraft identified as friendly.

1110 **Task Group 38.2 along with Task Force 34 changed course to 180°T, speed 20 knots in response to requests for help from CVE's of the Seventh Fleet being attacked off Samar. The "Battle off Samar" had been in progress since just before INDEPENDENCE turned into the wind at 0655. Escort carrier group - "Taffy 3" was in severe trouble, slow, short on defensive options, and never imagined to be within range for ship-to-ship combat, was fighting for its life, dodging shells raining down from Admiral Kurita's massive guns as the Japanese continued to close.**

Historically bold action by destroyers, destroyer escorts & aviators would save "Taffy 3"!
Japanese pursuers, unsupported by IJA aviation, with poor communication, fatigued from 3 days
of continuous action, surprised, harassed, battered, restrained by low fuel ...... Turned back!

1201 Changed fleet course to 100°T.

1205 Unidentified aircraft reported on radar bearing 238°T, 15 miles.

1210 Changed fleet course to 315°T. From 1212 thru 1218 the crew manned torpedo defense stations.

1221 Maneuvered to gain new station bearing 090°T, 2,500 yards from guide.

1323 Changed fleet course to 240°T.

1329 **The ships of Task Force 34 were consolidated into Task Group 38.2.**

1333 Maneuvered to gain new station bearing 090°T, 2,500 yards from (guide) USS NEW JERSEY, in disposition 5R5.

1626 Maneuvered to gain station in new disposition 5V5, USS SOUTH DAKOTA having assumed guide. **BatDiv 7, CruDiv 14, and several destroyers left the formation to form TG 34.5. This was to be an advanced striking force proceeding ahead of Task Group 38.2, in an attempt to intercept the enemy (Kurita). IJN's "Center Force" would attempt retiring back thru San Bernardino Strait.**

1645 USS INTREPID became guide. Changed course to 180°T, speed 2 knots.

1800 Changed course to 137°T, speed 26 knots proceeding to night flying station as a detached unit outside of TG screen. Accompanied by USS CUSHING and USS TWINING, INTREPID bears 070°T, 8 miles.

2000 On a course of 120°T, speed 23 knots, commenced launching 2 F6Fs and 6 TBMs, then changed course to 180°T. **The night Avengers were assigned a sector search 250 miles ahead to cover the entrance to San Bernardino Strait to find Kurita's retiring fleet.**

2058–2102 Changed course to 070°T. Launched 2 F6Fs, and recovered 1 TBM launched at 2000.

2145 One of CVL-22's TBMs made visual contact with 15 Japanese ships off the NE tip of Samar steaming west at 18 knots. The Avenger shadowed the enemy, making periodic position reports.

2324 Launched 1 TBM to replace our snooper shadowing Kurita.

2330 Recovered 2 F6Fs launched at 2000.

2353 Changed course into the wind to 070°T for flight operations

DL 25 October 1944 was one of the U.S. Navy's longest days ever. Off Cape Engaño to the north, our night-day planes stood by as CAP, as aircraft from CV's and other CVL's wreaked havoc on what was left of the Imperial Japanese Navy's carriers. But due to mixed signals that led to crucial misunderstanding among his own admirals as well as between Halsey and Nimitz and the Navy boss of bosses in Washington, Admiral King, he relented and we began to head south. (History records that he ranted and raved in New Jersey's flag quarters as he made his decision.)

I remember how it looked and what it felt like when all attacks were suspended while everybody waited to see what the Big Guy was deciding. Word came down that we were about to reverse course. We couldn't figure out why; we hadn't yet had time to sink every Jap ship confronting us.
Picture a gray, almost table-flat sea lumped with the sleek shapes of dozens of warships big and small. A wan sun shone through a high overcast. Forward speed was urgent, all bows pointed in a northerly direction. Every flattop had planes in the air. All, suddenly, were ordered back.

Not long before our own chickens came home to roost, Rebel and I walked aft down the flight-deck looking at the grand panorama on all sides. Mighty I, in union with the other ships, had already swung around into the prevailing wind. The stiff wind at our backs pushed us along easily. What

impressed me was the sudden way the whole task group had seemed to hesitate, slow its forward motion, and come nearly to a halt, as if someone had slammed on the brakes.

Changing direction was not a simple maneuver for the three task groups (TG 38.1 had previously been detached and sent to Ulithi for refueling and rest; it was immediately recalled.) We, with all the carriers as well as the battleships and cruisers, could have done it by a simple twist of the wheel once a new course was set. The destroyers could not. Even the latest models could only steam at flank speed for a very limited time. The faithful tin cans badly needed a drink. They sucked up every drop they got, but it took valuable time. DL

Thursday 26 October 1944   *Philippines - Leyte Invasion*

Steaming as TU 38.2.1 in company with USS CUSHING and USS TWINING as a detached Unit of TG 38.2, guide USS INTREPID, bears 090°T, 8 miles. Course 070°T, speed 18 knots. Ship is darkened, at flight quarters, with 6 Avengers and 2 Hellcats in the air. **INDEPENDENCE is steaming towards San Bernardino Strait. Her TBM's had tracked the enemy steaming, in single column, back thru the Strait. (These were the surviving ships of Admiral Kurita's retreating Center Force. They were picked up in the Strait and tracked thru Ticao Pass to the southern tip of Burias Island)**
(See map on page 334 for this chapter)

0000-0006 Recovered 3 Avengers launched at 2000 and 1 Hellcat launched at 2058.
0120-0124 Recovered 2 Avengers launched at 2000.
0131 Recovered 1 Hellcat launched at 2058.
0227-0229 Launched 2 Hellcats, course 090°T, speed 18 knots to serve as communications relay planes for the upcoming airstrike launch.
0311-0321 Launched 5 Hellcats armed with 500 lb bombs, and 4 Avengers loaded with torpedoes to strike the fleeing Japanese ships. The strike would run into severe weather. Due to the weather and limitations of the night search radar, the Japanese escaped detection. The returning Avengers would have to jettison the three torpedoes, with a fourth brought back on board fouled in the bomb bay.
0507 Recovered 1 Avenger launched at 2324. The VT(N)-41 pilot and his aircrew tracked the retiring enemy fleet until roughly 0230 when contact was lost in severe widespread thunderstorms.
0527 Sounded general quarters.
0630-0633 Recovered 4 Avengers launched at 0321 and 2 Hellcats launched at 0229.
0639 Secured from general quarters.
0646 Course 330°T, commenced maneuvering to regain position in TG 38.2.
0721 Changed course to 065°T, speed 20 knots for flight operations.
0732 Completed recovery of 5 Hellcats launched at 0321.
0750 Regained station within the screen of TG 38.2, bearing 030°T, 2,500 yards from guide, axis 090°T, disposition 5V5. Changed course to 072°T, speed 20 knots.
0800 Mustered crew on stations. At 0807 the ship secured from flight quarters.
1023 Changed course to 180°T.
1050 Formation changed to cruising disposition 5R5, then changed course to 070°T.
1150 Changed course to 240°T, speed 20 knots.
1154 USS ALABAMA became guide. INDEPENDENCE bears 303°T, 3,100 yards from guide.
1200 Changed speed to 26 knots, course to 220°T.
1201-1204 Manned torpedo defense stations.
1233 Changed course to 240°T after resuming position in formation.
1339 Sounded torpedo defense.
1347 USS INTREPID designated fleet guide, bearing 210°T, 2,500 yards.
1404 Secured from torpedo defense.
1415 Sounded flight quarters.
1505 On a new fleet course of 080°T, commenced launching aircraft.
1523 Completed launching 12 F6F Hellcats for CAP and 4 TBM Avengers for SNASP. Changed fleet course to 240°T, speed 20 knots.
1718-1733 Maneuvered to assume a new disposition station, 270°T, distance 2,500 yards from guide.
1759 Launched 2 F6Fs for CAP.
1806 Commenced recovering aircraft.
1821 Changed speed to 22 knots and proceeded to the night flying station with USS COLAHAN and USS WEDDERBURN, as a detached unit.
1825 USS HANCOCK rejoined TG 38.2.
1849 Completed recovering 12 F6Fs and 4 TBMs launched at 1523, and 1 F6F launched at 1759.

1916 Launched 1 F6F for CAP.
1918 Assumed night flying station bearing 120°T, 8 miles from TG38.2 guide, USS INTREPID.
2100 Launched 2 F6Fs for CAP.
2131 Recovered 1 F6F launched at 1916, and 1 F6F launched at 1759.
2359 Completed recovery of 2 F6Fs launched at 2100. Changed course to 085°T, speed 15 knots.

GUAM   *26 October 1944*
Our night torpedo planes took off after Japs, escorted by night fighter last night but had to come back. 1,000 foot ceiling wouldn't permit them to get over the mountains on the east coast of Samar and Luzon. Our planes (TG 38.2) were able, however, to make a couple more strikes on the force before they were completely out of range. Following is the total score to date. Since early on the 24th, 3 Jap task groups were sighted.

        The northern group east of Luzon was composed of 4 BB, 2 CV, 1 CVL, 2 CA, and 4 DD.
        The northern Visayan group was composed of 4 BB, 8 CA, and 10 DD.
        The southern Visayan group composed of 2 BB, 2 CA, and 2 DD.
With the exception of some carriers, this is practically the entire Jap fleet.
Damage Done.
        Ships Sunk. 1 CV, 2 CVL. 2 BB. 4 or 5 CA and 10 DD.
        Ships Damaged. 5 or 6 BB, 2 0V, 1 OCA and 5 DD.
Note; Under ships sunk there are 10 DD's listed. An early morning battle between our BB's and the Jap task group ended up with the remnants of 10 ships floating around off the Leyte coast. These 10 are considered and conservatively listed as DD'S. There may have been a few cruisers in the group.   *GUAM*
(Note: This was as known at the time. Refer back to page 417 for a correct breakdown of Japanese vessels)

DL   *Mighty I reverted to night carrier status as we made our way south. By now, the battle for Leyte Gulf (of which Engaño had been a major offshoot) was over. The fight for the Philippines was not. Wreckage from ships and boats of all sorts became navigational hazards. Torpedoed cruisers Canberra and Houston completed the first leg of their long journey to the States when they reached the haven of Ulithi on 27 October. Our planes spotted targets that would be hit by the day planes later. For the airdales, our working lives once again became day-night shift work, any hour of which could turn into a general quarters alert.* *DL*

GL We are still in a running battle with the Jap ships. Our TBM sighted astern of us another Jap task group consisting of 3 battleships, 3 carriers, 3 cruisers, 10 destroyers. They say the Japs have brought out their whole fleet. We are getting rid of them one by one.
We have been running to GQ for about 2 days now. We just received a report that our sister ship the Princeton was sunk. A bomb hit her gas line then a magazine blew up. The cruiser Birmingham stood by and took off the crew. They saved 133 officers and 1227 men. Our destroyers had to sink her. *GL*

Friday 27 October 1944   *Philippines - Leyte Invasion*

Steaming as before in company with USS COLAHAN and USS WEDDERBURN. They are at their night flying station to the windward side of TG 38.2, approximately 7 miles, bearing 100°T from guide USS INTREPID. Ship is darkened, Air Department is at flight quarters. They are retiring to take on fuel.

0106 Changed course to 100°T.
0107 Scrambled 2 Hellcats to intercept unidentified aircraft, bearing 230°T, distance 90 miles. Ensigns I.H. "Hebe" Lee and E.R. "Eddy" Edwards were launched into a no moon night, visibility 2 miles.
0123 Ens. Jack S. "Berky" Berkheimer was launched in his Hellcat and instructed to orbit.
0147 Recovered 1 Hellcat launched at 0107. Edwards had a bad radio, necessitating a return to the ship.

Lee (Cupid 2) proceeded toward the bogey, which seemed to be a snooper, thought to have radar as it closed to within 80 miles and withdrew numerous times. Lee had a 60 mile restriction on his intercept. The restriction was lifted and Lee was vectored for the intercept to a point 80 miles out at angels 12. 0229 Tally Ho, Lee made radar contact, 3.5 miles from the bogey on his 4 mile scale, dead ahead at 12,000'. The bogey made a 180° turn, Lee following. He picked up the flames from four exhaust stacks. Lee closed to 150' back, low behind the bogey to verify it wasn't a friendly. Lee identified it as a Mavis flying boat, nosed up and fired with his inboard guns (outboard had tracers). The 3 second burst from Lee's four 50's (from 5:30 low) hit the Mavis inboard engine and wing area between the two starboard engines. The Mavis burst into flames and exploded. Lee pulled off to port to avoid the flaming debris, the burning Mavis turning with him. Reflections from the flaming mass, just under him, caused Lee to think he was on fire. He radioed Cupid base he was preparing to bail out. Then, after unbuckling, pulling back the canopy, Lee recognized his Hellcat was OK, that it was the burning Mavis beneath him. Lee followed the Mavis as it circled down to the water. He could see the large red meatballs from the glow of the flames. Lee made a strafing run on it (to get gun camera footage, he had forgotten to turn the camera on), and remained near his prey for 5 minutes as the still floating Mavis burned fiercely. It was Lee's first kill.

0315 Ensigns Lee and Berkheimer landed their F6F5(N) Hellcats safely back onboard. USS Wasp reported the Mavis was using radar on 147 m.c. using its frequency searching gear, that ceased at the time of the shoot down. Ens. Charles Knuckle, assisted by Ens. J.O. Coates in CIC, computed the bogey speed & bearings for Hebe Lee, the team producing a near perfect night fighting intercept, despite the fact that INDEPENDENCE SM radar was not functioning properly during the intercept. Bogey altitude information was provided by USS INTREPID only once to Lee during the mission. It was stated in the Aircraft Action Report; *"it is emphasized here that seldom in the experiences of a night fighting squadron will the degree of perfection attained in this action be approached again"*.

0520-0620 Ship was at torpedo defense.

0624 Air Department secured from flight quarters, regained station in the formation, USS INTREPID bears 300°T, 2,500 yards.

0624 Changed fleet course to 090°T. Guide shifted to USS NEOSHO. Commenced steering various courses at various speeds to gain fueling station.

0648 Commenced approach on (fleet oiler) USS NEOSHO.

0710 Came alongside USS NEOSHO to starboard side.

0735 Commenced receiving fuel oil aft, and gasoline forward.

0822 Lost power to fore and aft gyro compass repeaters, commenced steering by magnetic compass.

0826 Gyro repeaters back in operation, resumed course 120°T.

0922 Cast off all lines from USS NEOSHO, having received 224,000 gallons of fuel oil and 30,000 gallons of aviation gasoline.

0951 Lost power to fore and aft gyro compass repeaters, commenced steering by magnetic compass.

0952 Gyro repeaters back in operation, resumed course 120°T.

1238 Changed speed to 8 knots, course to 134°T, to take station 2,500 yards astern USS NEOSHO.

1256 Changed course to 120°T, speed to 12 knots, having gained station.

1403 Came right to avoid USS VINCENNES which maneuvered dead ahead of INDEPENDENCE to keep clear of tankers departing this task group.

1410 Task Group 34.5 rejoined the formation. BatDiv 8, BatDiv 9, and USS WASHINGTON departed to rejoin TG 38.3, as originally assigned. USS NEW JERSEY assumed formation guide, disposition 5R5, axis 120°T. INDEPENDENCE taking station 120°T, 2,500 yards from guide, steaming westward.

1430 Sounded flight quarters.

1507 Changed course to 180°T, speed 15 knots.

1532-1538 USS WEDDERBURN was alongside to deliver a Radio Electrician onboard for temporary duty from USS CABOT, then changed speed to 22 knots, course to 095°T.

1544-1547 Launched 8 Hellcats for CAP, and 4 Avengers for ASP.

1610 Changed fleet course to 300°T, fleet speed 16 knots.

1759-1808 Recovered all 12 aircraft launched at 1547. Proceeded on course 000°T, speed 25 knots toward night flying station in company with USS LEWIS HANCOCK and USS TWINING, operating as a detached Unit with INDEPENDENCE (guide & OTC).

1925 Changed course to 280°T, speed 16 knots, having arrived on station 8 miles, bearing 060°T from TG 38.2 guide.

1932 Commenced zigzagging (plan 6) on base course 300°T.

GL The battle with the Japs was over for present. We beat the hell out of them and they are still running. GL

GN Nips have scattered so we refueled and kept searching. Jap sub got in close to outfit but was sunk by can. GN (IJN submarine I-26 was presumed sunk off Leyte on the night / morning of 25-26 October by DEs USS COOLBAUGH or USS RICHARD M. ROWELL after launching torpedoes at USS PETROF BAY - CVE-80)

Saturday 28 October 1944   *Philippines - Leyte Area, East of Samar*

Steaming in company with USS LEWIS HANCOCK and USS TWINING off Samar Island, at the night flying station, 8 miles, bearing 060°T from TG 38.2 guide, USS NEW JERSEY. Base course 300°T, speed 15 knots. The CVL-22 was prepared to render support to forces in the vicinity if necessary.

0529 Sounded routine general quarters.

0610 Commenced maneuvering to regain position within the TG 38.2 formation.

0636 Secured from general quarters, Air Department set to condition 13.

0650 Gained position within the disposition, 5R5, axis 120°T, bearing 120°T, 2,500 yards from USS NEW JERSEY. Steadied on fleet course 120°T, speed 20 knots.

0954 Changed fleet course to 240°T.

1114 Changed fleet course to 223°T.

1348 Sounded torpedo defense, unidentified aircraft bearing 050°T, 15 miles.

1350 Secured from torpedo defense on reports the aircraft was shot down.

1405-1407 Changed course to 095°T for flight operations. Launched 1 Hellcat and 1 Avenger for SNASP, then commenced steaming at various speeds and on various courses to regain position in the formation.

1715 Sounded flight quarters.

1758-1759 Course 070°T, speed 25 knots, launched 2 F6F Hellcats for CAP.

1805 Recovered the Hellcat & Avenger launched at 1407. The aircraft had assisted in the rescue of 14 men from a downed Mariner of VPB-21. Sighting a life raft, the 2 INDEPENDENCE aircraft orbited until USS CUSHING arrived to pick up the crew.

1813 Left the formation to proceed to the night flying station in company with DDs USS LEWIS HANCOCK and USS TWINING.

1839 Arrived at the night flying station, bearing 070°T, distance 8 miles from NEW JERSEY, course 315°T, speed 25 knots.

2157 Changed course to 025°T. Launched 2 Hellcats for CAP as replacements for our returning CAP.

2207 On a new course of 060°T, speed 18 knots, recovered 2 Hellcats launched at 1759. Then changed course to 310°T.

2238 Changed course to 315°T, speed 25 knots.

GUAM   October 28 1944
Back off the east coast of Visayan again prowling for the Japs ships. Chances are we'll not find anything after the last few days battling. Me thinks it will be a long time before they are able to muster enough first line ships to give anyone a bad time, This afternoon the following words were passed over the loud speaker system:

At 1405 Now knock off all sun bathing.

At 1405 Now man all torpedo defense stations.

At 1406 Now secure from torpedo defense.

At 1406 A Helen was just splashed 15 miles astern of us.

At 1407 Now sunbathing is permitted.

(no sense in letting the war interfere with our pleasure for too long a period.)

GUAM

Sunday 29 October 1944   *Philippines*

Steaming in company with DDs USS LEWIS HANCOCK and USS TWINING, off Samar Island, at the night flying station 8 miles, bearing 060°T from TG 38.2 guide, USS NEW JERSEY. Base course 315°T, speed 25 knots. We are proceeding to a position east of Polillo Island, off the east coast of central Luzon. TG 38.2 will strike at targets near Manila and Manila Bay during the day.
INDEPENDENCE pilots will provide night CAP.

0157 Changed course to 015°T, and launched 2 Hellcats for CAP.

0205 Commenced recovering aircraft.

0210 The F6F-5N Hellcat (Bu.No. 58722) returning from the 2158 launch piloted by Cdr. Turner F. Caldwell Jr. landed hard, broke the tail hook and hit the barrier. Cdr. Caldwell was uninjured.
Four pieces of flight deck planking were damaged by the prop cutting into the deck.

0236 Recovered the second Hellcat from the 2158 launch.

0323 Launched 2 Hellcats for CAP.

0525 Sounded general quarters.

0557 Changed course to 080°T, speed 20 knots for flight operations.

0603 Recovered 2 Hellcats launched at 0323.

0622 Secured from general quarters, Air Department set condition 13.

0627 Commenced steering various courses at various speeds to rejoin TG 38.2.
Released USS LEWIS HANCOCK and USS TWINING from this detached Unit.

0720 Gained position in formation bearing 120°T, 2,500 yards from guide USS NEW JERSEY, OTC in USS INTREPID, in cruising disposition 5R5, axis 120°T, course 270°T.

0800 Mustered crew on stations.

0906 Changed fleet course to 085°T, speed 25 knots.

1037 Changed fleet course to 270°T, fleet speed 20 knots.
During the day, the Task Group flew strikes against Japanese installations on Luzon.

1047 Shifted fleet axis left to 090°T. INDEPENDENCE bears 090°T, 2,500 yards from NEW JESEY.

1121 Changed fleet course to 080°T, fleet speed 25 knots.

1143 Sounded general quarters, expecting an air attack.

1200 Changed course to 020°T.

1202 Observed other vessels of this TG firing guns off our starboard quarter. The Task Group came under attack by Japanese dive bombers that got thru the CAP screen. A Zero was seen to dive on the INTREPID, the plane hitting her gun tub, and another aircraft dove at the HANCOCK with an apparent near miss. None of the attacking aircraft came close enough for INDEPENDENCE to open fire. Another bomber observed overhead retired. One group of dive bombers was reported to have jettisoned their bombs after approaching to within 20 miles of the Task group, and turned back toward base.

1205 Changed fleet course to 090°T, fleet speed 20 knots.

1301 Secured from general quarters, Air Department remained at flight quarters.

1306 Changed fleet course to 240°T.

1330 Sounded torpedo defense on report of approaching enemy aircraft.

1508 Changed fleet course to 080°T.

1645 Sounded torpedo defense on report of approaching enemy aircraft.

1727-1730 Launched 7 Hellcats for CAP.

1733-1737 Half-masted colors following movements of OTC in USS INTREPID.

I.H. Lee would note; *"After the launch, some genius running the store had our task force steam to the east where we penetrated a violent weather front."* Lee was referring to earlier launches by the Task Group. CVL-22 pilots (launched above) were now clear of the weather on the carrier's side of the front. The last strikes sent out by the Task Group were returning late, low on fuel, several with bad radios, in bad weather, attempting to locate their flattops. The day pilots needed to penetrate a severe weather front to return to their carriers. CVL-22 night fighters were directed to try to locate cripples and guide them back thru the weather to their carriers. Many of the returning aircraft, out of fuel, or nearly so, and not desiring to attempt a dangerous ditching at night, made water landings while there was still enough remaining daylight. Destroyers would be busy all night plucking downed airmen from the water.

1836 Recovered 1 F6F from USS HANCOCK.

1855 Changed speed to 28 knots and proceeded to night flying station accompanied by USS LEWIS HANCOCK and USS TWINING as a detached Unit, INDEPENDENCE OTC and guide.

1916 Changed course to 130°T, speed 24 knots.

2011 Gained night flying station, changed course to 315°T. INDEPENDENCE now bears 120°T at 8 miles from NEW JERSEY.

2025 Commenced steering various courses at 20 knots into the wind for flight operations.

2041 Recovered 2 F6Fs launched at 1730. One Hellcat flown by Ens. Lee, crashed into the barrier, with no injuries, slight damage to aircraft, and first barrier wires destroyed. Lee credited the event to a broken arresting gear cable. The belly tank parted from the aircraft, went thru the prop, causing a small fire that was quickly extinguished. Lee was one of the pilots sheepherding the lost flock thru the weather. Exciting ending to a tiring flight. INDEPENDENCE pilots assisted in the rescue of at least 1 downed aviator, having sighted and reported his float light.

2106 Recovered 2 F6Fs launched at 1730, and at 2119 recovered 1 F6F, also launched at 1730.

2208 Recovered 2 F6Fs launched at 1730. All our planes were back aboard. Changed course to 295°T.

2233 Launched 2 F6F's for CAP.

2309 Commenced zigzagging on base course 293°T, speed 18 knots.

RC Hitting Manila Bay. Land based Jap planes attacks fleet but did no damage. RC

HB Eleven Japanese planes were shot down over our task force group on October 29. We had 26 pilots down in the water, in heavy rains, and our night pilots helped locate them so the destroyers could pick them up. HB

GL Received word that Canberra & Houston reached port safely. GL

GN Strike northern Luzon. During noon chow we are called to a fast GQ. Just about got topside when I got word that 11 Nips were splashed. Good for our side. Received word that a good storm is approaching and from the way it looks now it will get dark very early. Looks bad for a lot of the day pilots for at least half of them are still in the air milling around or else on their way back with our pilots leading the way. All carriers are lit up like Xmas trees but some planes are starting to hit the water. Very low on fuel and having a hard job getting aboard their carriers. Hope the Nips don't come snooping around now but got word that one got too close. Can see a beautiful fire on the Cabot where a plane *[1.] *made a bad landing. Storm getting worse. GN* (*[1.] That was the fatal crash killing Ens. E.B. Cook and the fighter's pilot Lt.(jg) H.M. Wagstaff, Jr. aboard the CABOT. They were committed to the sea at 1315 on October 30th.)

DL Sunday 29 October. TG 38.2 attacked targets including airfields near Manila and shipping in Manila Bay. CV 11, Intrepid, was crashed by a kamikaze; light damage, ten sailors killed. DL

Note: The Japanese attack on the INTREPID was filmed by INDEPENDENCE photographer Ed Schultz. The film shows a battleship (possibly USS NEW JERSEY) on the port side of the INDEPENDENCE. The Japanese plane (estimated at 250' to 300' altitude) proceeded forward in a long low-level shallow high speed dive, along the port side of the BB, proceeding forward toward INTREPID. Slowly trading altitude for speed, the fast moving aircraft was hit by AA fire, and suddenly at about 800' astern (about the length of the CV-11) it flamed like a bright burning comet, as it continued for the carrier. The flaming aircraft broke up midair, just before the burning wreckage hit the #10 gun tub. (Ed Schultz's footage was used in the movies "Midway" & "Task Force")

Monday 30 October 1944   *Philippines*

Steaming in company with USS LEWIS HANCOCK and USS TWINING, 8 miles from USS NEW JERSEY bearing 120°T. They were off SE Luzon, generally north and east of Catanduanes Island, retracing the previous day's track, hoping to locate surviving downed aviators from the last strike.

0153 Ceased zigzagging.

0157–0205 Launched 3 F6Fs.

0214-0216 Recovered 2 F6Fs launched at 2233, and 1 F6F launched at 0157. Then changed course to 300°T, speed 21 knots. INDEPENDENCE now bears 210°T, 10 miles from guide.

0316 Commenced zigzagging (Plan No. 6) on base course 293°T.

0537 Sounded routine general quarters.

0611 Maneuvered into the wind to 065°T for flight operations.

0621 Completed recovering 1 F6F launched at 0157, and 1 F6F launched at 0205. (Fegraeus and Klock)

0630 Secured from general quarters.

0636 Changed course to 240°T and commenced maneuvering to regain position within TG 38.2.

0713 Regained station in the formation, USS NEW JERSEY bears 270°T, distance 2,500 yards, commenced zigzagging on base course 135°T.

0749 Air Department set to condition 14.

0800 Mustered crew to stations. Half-masted colors following movements of USS HANCOCK.

0835 Two-blocked colors.

1250 Changed fleet course to 300°T.

1251 Unidentified aircraft reported by ships radar. Sounded torpedo defense.

1254 Aircraft identified as friendly.

1256 Secured from torpedo defense.

1300-1315 Half-masted colors following movements of USS CABOT. (Burial service on previous page)

1547 Changed fleet course to 103°T.

1705 Sounded flight quarters.

1738 Launched 1 F6F from the USS HANCOCK's air group (which landed onboard at 1836 on the 29th) for return to the HANCOCK.

1748 Changed course to 110°T, speed 24 knots, leaving the formation to proceed to the night flying station, in company with USS LEWIS HANCOCK and USS TWINING, as a detached Unit.

1908 Gained night flying station bearing 135°T, 8 miles from USS NEW JERSEY.

2009 Changed course to 100°T, speed 18 knots to conform to TG 38.2 changes.

2149 Launched 2 F6Fs for CAP.

2204 Changed course into the wind to 140°T, speed 24 knots.

2208 Recovered 2 F6Fs launched at 1757, then changed course to 100°T, speed 18 knots. INDEPENDENCE would maintain a two Hellcat CAP thru the night.

GN Our skipper gets a " Hearty Well Done " from " Bull " Halsey. Our pilots did do good work in bringing back some of the-day planes and one pilot brought in about eleven by himself. Reminds me of a hen with her brood of chicks. GN

AD Patrolling, very quiet day. Jap fleet has definitely been beaten. AD

Tuesday 31 October 1944   *Fueling*

Steaming as before in company with USS LEWIS HANCOCK and USS TWINING, 8 miles from USS NEW JERSEY, bearing 135°T. Course 100°T, speed 18 knots. Air Department is at flight quarters.

0155 Launched 2 Hellcats for CAP.

0202 Changed speed to 25 knots, on a new course of 130°T.

0206 Recovered 2 Hellcats launched at 2149, then changed course to 100°T and speed to 16 knots.

0518 Sighted tankers bearing 108°T, 16 miles.

0524 Sounded torpedo defense.

0607 Speed, 25 knots, recovered 2 Hellcats launched at 0155.

0613 Secured from torpedo defense. Air Department set to condition 14.

0616 Commenced maneuvering to rejoin TG 38.2 in the fueling disposition. USS SABINE is guide. INDEPENDENCE was ordered to receive fuel from USS SABINE.

0704 With boilers 1 & 3 secured, came alongside to starboard of the SABINE, steadied on course 100°T, speed reduced to 11 knots.

0910 Cast off from SABINE having received 209,000 gallons fuel oil, 16 drums of lube oil, 4 cylinders of helium, and 22 cylinders of aviation breathing oxygen. Then commenced maneuvering to take up station 1,500 yards, bearing 100°T from guide.

0930-0937 USS WEDDERBURN was alongside amidships starboard to transfer R.A.A.F. Flying Officer A.R. Talbot for temporary duty involving briefing of pilots.

1040-1047 Half-masted colors following movements of USS HANCOCK.

1300 Guide USS SABINE shifted position, now bears 280°T, 2,500 yards.

1430 The Task Group completed fueling operations. Base course 100°T, guide shifted to the USS NEW JERSEY, bearing 100°T, 2,500 yards.

1630 Rotated fleet axis to 090°T. INDEPENDENCE now bears 090°T, 2,500 yards from guide.

1700 Cut in boilers 1 & 3 on main steam line.

1750-1850 Routine torpedo defense.

CVL-22 remained with the Task Group this evening. The TG would remain in the general fueling area.

2000 Changed fleet course to 150°T.

2010 Commenced zigzagging (Plan No.6) on base course 150°T.

2047 Air Department set condition 12.

GL Our food is scarce. We sure get enough salmon. GL

Photo of a US Navy Consolidated PBY "Catalina" flying boat (taken off NAS Jacksonville Florida)

On the following pages are excerpts follow from:

- The Action Report Captain E.C. Ewen sent off to The Commander-in-Chief, U.S Fleet at the end of October, 1944 - Action Report for U.S.S. INDEPENDENCE for period 1- 31 October 1944

- Letter from Rear Admiral Gerald Francis Bogan (CTG 38.2)

- Letter from Vice Admiral John Sidney McCain (CTF 38)

U.S.S. INDEPENDENCE

CVL22/ A16-3
Serial No. 0017
S-E-C-R-E-T
From: The Commanding Officer
To: The Commander-in-Chief, U.S. Fleet.
Via: (1) The Commander, Task Group 38.2.
      (2) The Commander, Task Force 38.
      (3) The Commander, Western Pacific task Forces and Commander, THIRD Fleet.
      (4) The Commander-in-Chief, U.S. Pacific Fleet and Pacific Ocean Areas.
Subject: Action Report for October, 1944.
Action Report for U.S.S. INDEPENDENCE for period 1- 31 October 1944

1. During the period covered by this report, it has been the usual procedure for the INDEPENDENCE, with two destroyers as escort, to operate as a detached unit of Task Group 38.2 at a distance of approximately 8 miles from the center of the Task Group in the direction of the wind. This position has been taken in order to permit freedom of maneuver for air operations and yet if possible to prevent a separation from the Task Group beyond TBS contact as a result of these air operations. Only once during this period had the wind direction been in the same semi-circle as the fleet course and on many occasions it has been the exact opposite, or practically so.
The usual speed of the ship during recovery has been between 25 and 30 knots, resulting in a speed separation which has reached as high as 48 knots. Upon completion of air operations, with the INDEPENDENCE Group traveling at 28 knots, the overtaking speed has been reduced to 3 knots, when, upon one occasion the fleet speed was 25. If, however, a station closer than 8 miles is taken, which is actually but 9,000 yards from the outer screen circle, and the Task Group turns into the wind, the TBS circuit can become clogged up to the point where it becomes extremely difficult to get change in course signal through to the escorting DD's until such time as the Task Group and its detached unit close to an uncomfortably short distance.

2. If, however, the wind direction is in the same semi-circle as the next fleet course, a station of 10 miles is recommended, and this should be fairly easy to maintain.

3. Above everything else, care must be taken to so station the detached unit that regardless of the tactical maneuvers of the Task Group, it can never get on the windward side of the detached unit.

4. Due to the limited number of available DDs, it has only been possible to assign two as the INDEPENDENCE screen. Inasmuch as protection against air attack has been considered paramount, these DDs have been assigned stations 1.5000 and 1.5180**. With the direction of the axis into the wind, the DD stationed at 1.5180 changes to 1.5170 during actual operations. The rotation of the axis with an appreciable change of wind direction is all that is required in the way of TBS transmission, except for the usual changes of course and speed required for conducting the launchings and recovery. However, at times this results in an inefficient anti-submarine screen when the course and axis are such as to place both DDs nearly abeam. This condition, however, must be accepted unless the TBS is to be jammed with continual transmissions directing the DDs to new stations. With a third DD available, an adequate anti-submarine screen as well as a good anti-aircraft screen would always be available. In this case the three DDs would be stationed 1200 yards apart around the 1.5 circle with one at 1.5180 to perform the duties of plane guard during operations.

5. The recovery of aircraft at night will always be a slower process than the similar operation during the day. Not until the carrier has actually turned into the wind and settled down on its course are the planes able to commence to form their landing circle. It is necessary for the planes to wait until this time before flying the initial leg, which is parallel to the landing course and along the starboard side of the carrier. Maintaining the semblance of a landing circle during the period in which the carrier is turning, so as to be able to land on board as soon as the carrier is into the wind, as is the case in daytime procedure, is not feasible for night recovery. With the exception of the two planes already spotted on the catapults, launching intervals at night may be expected to be appreciably longer than those requlted during daytime operations. Re-spotting of the deck for last-minute change of plans also will result in what may appear to be unreasonably long delays.

        (Authors Note**: 1.5 circle is 1500 yards from center, 1.5180 is 1500 yards, at 180 degrees.**)**

6. Maintenance difficulties for night operations, particularly in radio and radar equipment, far exceed those which confront the day carrier group. Radio, radar, IFF, gyro horizon and instrument lighting, as well as ZB must be 100% reliable or the plane becomes a "dud" as soon as it is airborne. Where an aircraft operating in the daytime can perform its mission reasonably well by simply staying with the rest of the group, during night operations the failure of any of the above renders the plane not only useless, but it becomes a liability. Every effort has been made to develop maintenance methods to meet the required standards with resultant check-off lists unbelievably long, and yet to date, while improvement has undoubtedly been achieved, we still have a long way to go. The obvious reasons for the altogether too frequent failure of this equipment are:

(1) The equipment is too fragile. It is not rugged enough to withstand the rough treatment to which it must be exposed.

(2) Every launching is a catapult launching, with the consequent high rate of acceleration that undoubtedly
(3) affects the operation of both the radio set and the radar, as well as instrument lights and gyro horizon. Plane radios are always checked out on deck to the pilot's satisfaction, either with other planes in the air or with the ship, only to suffer complete failure as soon as the plane is airborne. Radar failures, instrument lights and occasionally a gyro horizon are rendered useless in the same manner.

(3) The high percentage of hard landings inherent in night operations as compared to those made during day
(4) recoveries are a matter of fact, normal landing at night would be considered hard landings in the daytime.

7. It is felt that the night carrier should have on board a carefully selected radio and radar maintenance section in the Air Department. Later models of airborne radio and radar, which have built into them a far higher degree of reliability, may be available, in which case they should be installed in night operating aircraft first. It may even be desirable to back up the radio set with a complete second set as a stand-by. Additional experience, however, is necessary before making this a definite recommendation. In this connection, auxiliary lighting for instruments has apparently eliminated the instrument lighting failures.

8. Pilots flying at night are also prone to demand more nearly perfect operation of the power plant and accessories than the same pilot making a flight in daylight. This is perfectly natural, but again emphasizes the higher standard of maintenance required for the successful continuous operation of aircraft from carriers after sunset.

9. While the VF(N) and VT(N) pilots are undoubtedly more expert in instrument flying than are the average day pilots, nevertheless weather limitations must be recognized for the night fliers the same as it is for the average day pilot. The effect of thunderstorms upon lights, instruments, radio and radar is unpredictable and certain of these conditions nullify the usefulness of the night fighter by filling his radar scope with storm blips, through which he is unable to see his target. Other conditions which would render his radio useless is likely to result in the loss of the pilot and the plane.

10. Night operations appear to place an unusually heavy mental strain upon the Landing Signal Officer. As long as planes are in the air, he is ever on the alert. This is particularly noticeable during the nights that we have maintained an all-night Combat Air Patrol. It doesn't seem possible for him to relax between landing periods in the same manner that Landing Signal Officers controlling daylight operations have always been able to do. In this connection, it is recommended that, if possible, two fully- qualified signal officers for night operations be assigned to night operating carriers. If two Landing Signal Officers for night operations are not available, then an additional signal officer fully qualified for day operations should be assigned.

11. The work of the Air Group on board this ship during the past month has definitely been commendatory. From every angle improvements have been noted. The added experience has resulted in a general feeling of confidence among the pilots in their ability that is most gratifying. There is every reason to believe that this improvement will continue.

E.C. Ewen

AIR OPPERATIONS SUMMARY
CVL-22, CVLG(N) 41

During the period of operation from October 6 to October 31, 1944, INDEPENDENCE, with night fighter group 41 participated in the' attack on enemy forces at Okinawa, Formosa, and the Philippine areas. A balance sheet drawn for these operations would show on the credit side of the ledger that the group shot down 10 planes at night, 2 planes in the day; flew 153 Combat Air Patrols; 8 strikes at night on Formosa, 24 Anti-Submarine Patrols and 27 searches. These searches, flown at night by TBM-1Cs with "Dog" gear, were successful in locating enemy forces on two occasions. A large number of pilots, forced down at sea, can thank the pilots of the group for early rescue on several occasions. The debit side of the ledger would show the loss of 11 planes as the result of operational casualties, and the failure to break up the one real night attack which this Task Group underwent off Formosa. That this attack was not broken up by night fighters may be attributed to the fact that the INDEPENDENCE was operating inside the screen and could not launch and recover aircraft without jeopardizing the Task Group. Doctrine now calls for INDEPENDENCE to move outside the screen to flying station about ten miles up wind at 1800 and remain there for the night. INDEPENDENCE is accompanied by two destroyers. One almost impossible situation arose from this condition when the base course was near the reciprocal of the wind. Under these conditions the INDEPENDENCE would open the range at a rate of 40-45 knots while landing or launching aircraft and close at a rate at 4-5 knots. However, this method of operation permits the Task Group to keep batteries released at all times and permits INDEPENDENCE to launch and recover aircraft at will. Practically split-second decision to launch aircraft is necessary and vital when a bogey appears on the screen at night and the time used to obtain permission to launch and to navigate through the Task Group might well prove fatal to successful interception.

One great element of successful operation came to light and it is of paramount importance; that is that equipment, for planes operating at night, must be the best obtainable. At the head of this list must come communication. When a fighter loses communications with base he is not only helpless, he is a liability rather than an asset and may jeopardize the entire Task Group. The desirability, in fact necessity, of providing units operating in the combat areas with the latest, and best equipment, while those groups in training in the rear areas use the older equipment cannot be stressed too much. Out of three pilots lost by this group, two were the direct result of failure of communication. It might be stated here that it is standard practice to make radio checks either with planes in the air or a nearby carrier before launching.

TBMs with "Dog" gear twice proved their value as night search planes for locating enemy units. On October 24 at 1715 four TBMs were launched to search for enemy units in the Sibuyan Sea area. Wing tanks were loaded with gasoline giving the planes 408 gallons and no bombs were put on. A few hours later, contact was made with enemy forces off the southwest tip of Burias Island. These forces were reported and their course and speed. Planes were recovered at 2200.

Part IV – Page 1

Author's note: ASD or "Dog" gear was airborne radar used in the night Avengers. AN/APS-3 (ASD) was first provided [produced by Philco] in 1943. A later and much lighter version (300 lbs vs. 150 lbs installed weights) AN/APS-4 (ASH)[produced by Western Electric] became available in 1944.

AIR OPPERATIONS SUMMARY CVL-22, CVLG(N) 41 (Continued)

At 2000 on October 25 five TBMs were launched to search an area from Catanduanes Island through San Bernadino strait south to a point 100 miles east of the Southeast tip of Samar. Contact was made with the enemy as they were in San Bernadino strait and they were shadowed, up through Ticao Pass to the southern tip of Burias Island. This intelligence aided in locating this force on strikes later in the day. One comment concerning pilot morale might be mentioned here. Pilots had been told to contact Commander, Support Air when off the southern coast of Samar, upon making this contact, one of the TBM pilots was asked if he was a night fighter whereupon he replied, "No, but I'll chase any bogies if you've got 'em! Again the YM or "Granny", as she is affectionately known, proved her worth. Granny has been picked up at 80 miles and given the pilots a vector to base when a Point Option course would have led them astray.

The one night intruder mission upon which 4 TBMs and 4 F6Fs were sent proved to be, a distinct success. At 0350 on October 19, 4 TBMs loaded with 12-100lb GPs and 4 F6Fs each, armed with 1-500lb GP were launched to "heckle" installations on the southwest Formosa coast. One fighter and one TBM teamed up and divided the various fields in that area. Bombs were dropped without incident in the parking and operation areas and Ensign Berkheimer shot down two Emilys while Ensign Klock shot down another. All planes returned to base safely.

Landing and take-off data will not be repeated here since times remain essentially the same as previously reported. Suffice it to say that an average interval of 30 seconds for groups (8-12VF - 4VT) launchings in the daytime is readily attained while night launchings of more than two planes will average 55 seconds interval. All launchings are by catapult.

It is believed that it is not necessary actually to maintain a Combat Air Patrol during the entire night but that 2 pilots in Condition ELEVEN backed up by two more in Condition TWELVE is adequate. However, in keeping pilots aloft at night, an opportunity is provided for running intercept problems and allows the pilots to "keep their hand in." Reliance can be put on the search radar and the fact that with the night carrier operating outside the Task Group, planes can be launched instantly the bogey appears on the screen. That this is true was demonstrated on the night of October 26 or rather at 0100 October 27 when a bogey was picked up at 105 miles on a closing course. Two fighters were launched immediately and Ensign Lee chased the bogey to 12,000 feet distance 75 miles and shot him down.

One further comment should be made that 4 night fighters in the air at one time is all that can be handled by C.I.C. Any more planes in the air prevent an accurate track being kept, someone gets lost and then the troubles really begin. Two planes on patrol is best, but not more than four should ever be launched for intercept purposes at night.

Pilot morale in this group is extremely high and this in spite of the fact that they see pilots of other ships being sent on strikes and engaging the enemy with the usual results. It is generally hoped on this ship that greater use of both fighters and torpedo planes will be made in night attacks on both land installations and shipping. That the pilots and the ships crew are "rarin to go" in such an operation cannot be doubted.

Part IV – Page 2

AIR OPPERATIONS SUMMARY CVL-22, CVLG(N) 41 (Continued)

COMMUNICATIONS

1. Fox Schedule - The Primary Fox still provides reliable communication at least 95% of the time although interfered with by rain static and subject to periodic fading and even occasional echo, timely reruns have enabled us to keep our files complete. The Jump Fox has not as yet proven as reliable. Its weaker signal fades completely out at times, whole messages being sometimes missed. Also the Jump Fox shifts from 4125 kcs to 16500 kcs at 1930 GCT and it has been our experience that signals on 12375 kcs and 16500 kcs are not readable before about 2000 GCT.

2 . VHF Communication - Frequent failures were experienced in the fighters AN/ARC-5 equipment. Much of this is ascribed to the constant shock at catapulting, which this set seems less able to stand than the AN/ARC-4. New and more rugged equipment, understood to be forthcoming in the near future, may provide an answer to this problem.

3. Search Plane Communications - Contact reports made on the nights of 24-25 and 25-26 October were made on the search frequency, 6420 kcs, and paralleled by VHF relayed by a communication plane over the force. Serious interference was experienced on 6420 kcs from powerful signals, apparently from nearby land stations. There was no indication of deliberate interference, the frequency appeared to be one used by the Japanese as well as ourselves. A change in our primary search frequency is recommended. All but one of the ungarbled reports were received by VHF. In spite of this fact it is not recommended that much faith be placed in this method of transmitting contact reports. There are inevitable delays caused by atmospheric vagaries, especially at night, which are intolerable from the point of view of speed of reception. This method of making contact reports is recommended only as a back-up of HF CW reports.

Contact reports were relayed to the OTC on the night of 24-25 October via the primary TBS and on the night of 25-26 October by the relay plane via the U. S. S. IOWA.

The importance of the contribution of the USS INDEPENDENCE to the development of the US Navy's carrier based night fighting doctrine is further evidenced here within the endorsement letters of the Action Report by Rear Admiral G.F. Bogan and Rear Admiral J.S. McCain. Their endorsement copies are on the following two pages:

**Vought OS2U "Kingfisher"
scout observation float plane**
(photo shot in 1942)

UNITED STATES PACIFIC FLEET
COMMANDER CARRIER DIVISION FOUR

FB2-4/A16-3

SECRET

1 Nov 1944

FIRST ENDORSEMENT to:
USS INDEPENDENCE Secret
ltr. CVL22/A16-3 Serial
0015 dated 1 October 1944.

From: Commander Task Group THIRTY EIGHT POINT TWO.
To :   Commander in Chief, U. S. Pacific Fleet.
Via :   (1) Commander Task Force THIRTY EIGHT.
            (2) Commander Western Pacific Task Forces and
                Commander THIRD Fleet.

Subject: Action Report on Stalemate II.

    1.   Forwarded.

    2.   Subsequent to the completion of this report the
complement of the INDEPENDENCE has reverted to that of a night
operating CVL. It is felt that the most advantageous method of
operating such a unit is to detach it at dusk with suitable
escort in order that night operations may be conducted without
hindering the tactical movements of the Carrier Task Group.

    3.   Maintenance of a patrol of two VF(N) during all
hours of darkness is considered an effective way of combating enemy
attacks and snoopers. In the case of night attacks, interception at
a distance of 50-80 miles with subsequent destruction of one or more
enemy planes (preferably the leader) may successfully break up an
incoming attack. Japanese apparently employ a "homing" plane for
night attacks. Early destruction of
this plane may avert attack completely.

                                G. F. BOGAN.

Copy to:
    USS INDEPENDENCE.

UNITED STATES PACIFIC FLEET
**SECOND CARRIER TASK FORCE,
PACIFIC FLEET**

23 DEC 1944

SECOND ENDORSEMENT to
CO, USS INDEPENDENCE,
Secret ltr., CVL22/A16-3,
Serial 0015 , dated 1 October 1944.

From: Commander SECOND Carrier Task Force, Pacific.
             (Commander Task Force THIRTY-EIGHT).
To: Commander-in-Chief, United States Fleet.

Via: Commander Western Pacific Task Forces and
             Commander THIRD Fleet.

Subject: Action Report on Stalemate II.

1.   1.   The comments of Commanding Officer U.S.S. INDEPENJENCE and
of Commander Task Group THIRTY-EIGHT POINT TWO are generally concurred in. The
Task Force Commander now envisions a task group of night trained CV's and CVL's for
use in night heckling and attack missions as well as for night Combat Air Patrol and anti-
submarine patrol.

          2.   As the operations of the Task Force penetrate deeper into
the inner defenses of the enemy, night attacks upon the force can be expected with greater
frequency and determination. These cannot be defeated unless proper training and
experience have prepared the night groups for such operations.

          3.   In order to fully exploit the obvious value of a night task
group it must be placed under the command of an officer not only with experience in
training and in developing new tactics but one who has an active interest in the subject.

                              J. S. McCAIN.

Copy to:
     CO, USS INDEPENENCE
     CTG 38.2

Note item No. 3 in the above letter.
**Obviously, the full value and proper application of a dedicated night carrier was not appreciated
(understood or both) by some members of the command structure.** However, in an attempt to not be overly
critical with hindsight, I suggest that the art of war is a learned experience, a costly evolving moving target, the
price of learning to be paid with markers of blood. It should also be realized that dedicated carrier functions were
made possible only as the numbers of hulls grew, and the navy had to rethink the utilization of their expanding
inventories of assets.

The Mighty-I made its contribution to the advancement of night carrier combat in the Pacific.

GL Note: Here I will enter the official report on our action against the Jap Fleet from CINPAC.

```
Communiqué #168

1. The Japanese fleet has been defeated and routed by the 3rd and
7th fleets. The second battle of the Philippines ranks as one of
the major sea battles of World War II in the Pacific. Others were
Coral Sea 5/4 to 8/42, Midway 6/3-6/42, Guadalcanal 11/12 to
15/42, Philippines 1/19/44.

2. Movement of the Jap fleet northward from Singapore area were
detected 10/21/44. Sub scouts sighted enemy forces and sank 2
Atago class cruisers and hit a third. Ships of the 3rd fleet
moved eastward of the Philippines off Surigao Straits, San Ber-
nardino Straits and Polillo Islands on 10/23/44. Carrier search
planes discovered 2 strong enemy forces moving eastward through
the Sibuyan Sea and the other through the Sulu Sea.

3. Photos by carrier planes showed the force moving eastward
through the Sibuyan Sea consisted of 5BB's thought to be Yamato -
Musashi - Nagato - Kongo - Haruna, 8 CA's & CL's, 2 Mogami - 2
Tone - 2 Nachi, 1 Atago, 1 Noshiro and 13 destroyers. The force
moving through the Sulu Sea consisted of 2 BB's Yamashiro class,
2 CA's, 2 CL's and 8 DD's.

4. As soon as the Japs were discovered on 10/23/44 fighters,
torpedo planes & dive bombers from the 3rd fleet were launched to
attack both forces. In the Sibuyan Sea 1BB & 1 CA were damaged,
set afire and maybe sunk. 3 BB's received bombs and torpedo's
capsized and sunk. In the Sulu Sea both BB's were bombed and hit.
CA's & DD's were strafed with rockets and machine guns.

5. Meanwhile into the east of the Philippines enemy shore based
planes were attacking our carriers. In the aerial battle which
ensued, more than 150 enemy planes were shot down. Our losses
were light. The carrier CVL23 Princeton was hit & badly damaged
so our destroyers sunk her.

6. Also on 10/23/44 a land based search plane discovered an enemy
carrier force about 200 miles off Cape Engano; on North Luzon
heading south. There were 17 warships in the force, 1 large CV
believed to be of the Zuikaku class, 3 CVL's of the Chitose &
Zuiho classes, 2 BB's of the Ise class with flight decks aft, 1
CA of the Noshiro class, 3 cruisers of the Kisko class and 6
DD's.

7. To meet this serious threat Halsey concentrated several of his
carrier groups and started north at high speed for a dawn attack.

8. The 3rd fleet caught the enemy completely by surprise on dawn
of 10/24/44, that there was no effective air opposition. Later in
the afternoon planes which had refueled ashore in the Philippines
flew out to join the ships which already met disaster. The planes
arrived late and our C.A.P. shot down 21 of them. In this action
the enemy lost 1 CV Zuikaku class and 1 CVL Zuiho class and 1 CVL
Chitose class, 1 CL or CA sunk by gun fire, 1 DD sunk, 1 cruiser
damaged later sunk by one of our subs.
```

442

9. Damaged- 1 BB hit by 2-4 torpedoes and many bombs. 1 BB hit by many bombs, 3 cruisers damaged by bombs & gunfire, 4 destroyers bombed and strafed. None of our ships were damaged. Before the bombed ships could be tracked down we had to go to the assistance of the 7th fleet off Samar Islands.

10. The enemy force of BB's CA's & DD's which had been attacked in Sibuyan Sea had started through the San Bernardino Straits. In spite of the damage done they attacked units of the 7th fleet off Samar Island during the morning of 10/24/44. In the battle most of the enemy ships were badly damaged by units of the 7th fleet assisted by our planes. 1 CA Mogami class was sunk, 1 destroyer was dead in the water. The enemy fleet fled from the battle and during the darkness through the San Bernardino Straits. About 0200 a straggling cruiser was sunk by gunfire of the 3rd fleet.

11. Meanwhile the southern enemy force had crossed the Sulu Sea into the Mindanao Sea attempting to pass through the Surigao Strait and met the 7th fleet in a night action 10/24&25/44. All units of the enemy fleet were sunk or routed.

12. On 10/25/44 carrier planes of the 3rd fleet were launched against the crippled enemy force fleeing through the Sibuyan Sea. Damage done by the 3rd fleet, 7th fleet & shore based planes sunk 1 CA Mogami class off Mindoro Island, 1 CL Noshiro, 1 BB also 3 BB's damaged and 3 more cruisers.

13. The total damage done to the Jap fleet during 10/22 to 27/44 included sunk
2 Battleships
5 Heavy Cruisers
4 Large Cruisers
3 Light Cruisers or Large Destroyers
6 Destroyers
Damaged & probably sunk
1 BB, 3 CA, 2 CL, 7DD
Damaged 6 BB's, 4 CA's 1 CL, 10 DD's.

14. During the same action our losses were 1 CVL-23 (Princeton) 2 CE's *, 2 destroyers (the Johnson – Hale **), 1 DE (the Roberts ***) & a few small craft.

15. The following BB's damaged at Pearl harbor took part in the action; West Virginia, Maryland, Tennessee, California & the Pennsylvania. Also the carriers Wasp, Hornet, Lexington.

The End *GL*

(Authors Notes: To clarify, the above two pages were within *G*eorge *L*edecke's diary. This was a copy of Naval Communiqué #168 he had included, as he noted at the beginning.
Additional corrections & clarifications:
Correct spelling and accounting for the Japanese losses are noted at the beginning of this chapter.
 * The CVEs lost were the ST. LO and the GAMBIER BAY.
 ** This was incorrect. The destroyers lost were the JOHNSTON and the HOEL.
 ***The DE lost was the SAMUEL B ROBERTS. The few small craft referred to were most likely PT boats in the opening action in Surigao Strait.)

Wednesday 1 November 1944   *Training Exercises*

Steaming as before in Task Unit 38.2.1 consisting of USS INDEPENDENCE, USS HANCOCK, USS CABOT and USS INTREPID. INTREPID is flagship with Rear Admiral G.F. Bogan, Commander, Carrier Division FOUR, as part of the THIRD Fleet, Admiral W.F. Halsey, Commander in Flagship USS NEW JERSEY. Formation 5R5, axis 090°T. Conducting various training exercises operating in the fueling area.

0115 Commenced zigzagging on base course 225°T.
0501-0610 Manned torpedo defense stations. Air Department set to condition 14.
0631 Commenced zigzagging on base course 133°T.
0800 Mustered crew on stations.
0930 Commenced zigzagging on base course 265°T.
1242 Ceased zigzagging, changed course to 285°T, speed increased to 21 knots to gain position for AA gunnery practice.
1248 Sounded torpedo defense for AA gunnery practice.
1300 Changed course to 265°T, speed 16 knots having gained position 1,000 yards astern USS INTREPID, guide. The heavy ships in the Task group maneuvered to form two columns at intervals of 1,000 yards, distance 5,000 yards. Cruisers and destroyers formed a bent line screen, and the formation commenced steering a series of 20° turns to the left & right of base course.
1318-1351 INDEPENDENCE gunners fired on towed sleeves, expending 618 rounds of 40mm, and 90 rounds of 20mm ammunition.
1440 Steadied on course of 265°T having regained disposition 5R5.
1529 Changed course to 090°T, speed changed to 20 knots.
1535-1543 USS LEWIS HANCOCK steamed alongside amidships to starboard to receive R.A.A.F. Flying Officer A.R. Talbot from INDEPENDENCE, having briefed CVLG(N)-41 personnel.
1613 Commenced zigzagging (Plan No.6) on base course 265°T.
1945 USS INTREPID became guide, bearing 135°T, 3,500 yards from INTREPID.
1955 BatDiv 7 and CruDiv 14 and several destroyers left the formation to form Task Group 34.5.
2100 Commenced zigzagging (Plan No.6) on base course 250°T.

GN Started back for supplies but that has been cancelled so we head back for battle. GN

HB Four Japanese BBs, two CLs, and several Tin Cans were sighted November 1, but got away. HB

Thursday 2 November 1944

Steaming as before in the same general area.
0514-0615 Ship was at routine general quarters.
0557 Air Department set to condition 14.
0647 Ceased zigzagging, made emergency turn to 140°T on report of sound contact by USS YARNELL. Numerous course changes were made throughout the day.
At 0832 we gained a new position in the disposition, having shifted to 5V5.
1530 Sounded flight quarters.
1619 Changed fleet course to 070°T.
1650-1656 Launched 8 F6Fs as CAP.
1703 Launched 1 F6F.
1706 Recovered 1 F6F. Maneuvered to regain station within the formation.
1921-1930 Recovered 4 F6Fs launched at 1656.
2013-2017 Recovered 3 F6Fs launched at 1656 and 1 F6F launched at 1703, then changed course to 070°T, speed 18 knots.
2030 Commenced zigzagging on base course 078°T.

2130 Air Department set to condition 12.

GN We heard that remnants of Jap fleet is around and " Bull " really wants to polish it off. GN

Friday 3 November 1944   *Refuel & Replenish*

0502 Steaming as before in our fueling area roughly 450 miles NE of Leyte. Sounded torpedo defense.
0553 Secured from torpedo defense.
0604 Commenced zigzagging on base course 110°T.
1056 Changed fleet course to 295°T.
1100 Changed speed to 15 knots, course to 110°T while proceeding to flying station.
1105 Launched 1 TBM ferrying a pilot to the USS HORNET to pick up a replacement F6F. Changed course to 295°T, returning to formation.
1120-1122 USS YARNALL came alongside to transfer mail, then cast off.
1132 Resumed station in the formation. Then commenced maneuvering on various courses at various speeds proceeding to the fueling station.
1238 Came alongside port side of fleet tanker USS TAPPAHANNOCK.
1301 Commenced taking on provisions.   1305 Commenced receiving fuel oil.
1330 Completed receiving the following dry provisions, sufficient for 3 days;

Bacon, Canned	168 lb.	Salt	200 lb.
Luncheon Meat	252 lb.	Corn Beef Hash	231 lb.
Tongue Beef, Canned	108 lb.	Yeast	48 lb.
Beans, Kidney	100 lb.	Butter, Canned	159 lb.
Beans, Lima	100 lb.	Beef, Corned Canned	144 lb.
Beans, Navy	200 lb.	Jam	144 lb.
Peaches	486 lb.	Baking Soda	36 lb.
Tea	40 lb.	Baking Powder	30 lb.

1343 Completed receiving fuel oil, taking on 129,000 gallons.
1400 Cast off all lines from USS TAPPAHANNOCK. Then changed course to 290°T, speed 20 knots.
1420 Assumed station bearing 110°T, 2,500 yards from fleet center, speed 12 knots, course 293°T.
1435 Changed speed to 15 knots, course to 075°T into the wind for air operations.
1442 Sounded flight quarters.
1449-1452 Speed 18 Knots, recovered 1 TBM launched at 1105, and 1 F6F delivered to INDEPENDENCE, transferred from USS HORNET.
1547 Regained position in the formation, speed 12 knots, course 293°T.
1615-1645 USS WEDDERBURN was alongside amidships to starboard to transfer provisions.
1649 Commenced maneuvering to take position in cruising disposition 5R5.
1710 Changed speed to 18 knots, course to 265°T.
Today, battleships, cruisers and destroyers, that had formed TG 34.5 2 days ago, rejoined the formation.
1722 USS NEW JERSEY assumed formation guide. INDEPENDENCE began taking position, bearing 110°T, 2,500 yards from guide.
1741 Changed course to 215°T.
1744 Changed speed to 10 knots "to avoid embarrassing USS HANCOCK who was conducting flight operations".
1759 Changed speed to 20 knots.
2149 Commenced zigzagging on base course 330°T (Plan No.6), speed 15 knots.
2334 Ceased zigzagging, changed course to 250°T to clear TG 38.3 after collision involving the USS RENO. (**HB** *On November 3, cruiser Reno and CVL Langley collided.* **HB**)
2337 Changed speed to 25 knots.

2357 Changed course to 240°T.

GN   Lost their fleet again so we again start back to take on supplies. No dice though we refuel and take aboard some chow from tanker. Food has gotten very low again and we are back on the good old standby of salmon and rice. I think they are preparing our stomachs for the invasion of China.   GN

Saturday 4 November 1944

Steaming in company with USS INTREPID, USS HANCOCK and USS CABOT in cruising disposition 5R5 on base course 240°T, axis 110°T, speed 25 knots, guide USS NEW JERSEY bearing 315°T, 2,500 yards. We have no planes in the air. At 0012 fleet course changed to 330°T.
0021 Commenced Zigzagging on base course 330°T, speed 18 knots.
0200 Changed course to 000°T.
0400 Changed fleet course to 300°T.
0515-0619 INDEPENDENCE was at routine torpedo defense.
0828 Commenced maneuvering to gain station in disposition with axis rotated to 060°T.
0856 Maneuvered for air operations.
0857 Launched 1 F6F Hellcat to proceed for transfer to USS CABOT for her air group.
1200 Changed course to 265°T, speed 25 knots.
1245 USS OWEN was ordered to come alongside to receive aviation parts.
1315 Commenced maneuvering into position astern the formation to receive the OWEN.
1322 USS OWEN came alongside to starboard, both vessels commenced steaming at 15 knots.
1341 USS OWEN cast off having received 1 F6F propeller and 1 F6F carburetor.
Proceeded to maneuver to regain station in Task Group 38.2.
1418 Sounded flight quarters.
1442 Regained station in the TG.
1453-1456 Changed speed to 28 knots to launch aircraft, launched 2 F6F(N)s for CAP, then reduced speed to 18 knots.
1612 Changed course to 265°T.
1746 Changed course to 015°T for flight operations.
1755 Completed recovery of 2 F6Fs launched at 1456.
1800 The Task force started a high speed approach toward Luzon on a course of 265°T, speed 22 knots for scheduled arrival near dawn.

Sunday 5 November 1944   *Luzon, Philippines*

Zigzagging on base course 265°T, bearing 060°T, 2,500 yards from guide, USS NEW JERSEY.
0539-0638 Routine general quarters.
0800 Mustered crew on stations.
0810 Changed course to 140°T.
0813 Sounded torpedo defense after the report of an unidentified aircraft bearing 160°T, 30 miles out.
0814 Secured from torpedo defense upon report that a Betty bomber was shot down.
0840 Sounded flight quarters.
0927 Changed course to 040°T for flight operations.
0941 Completed launching 12 F6Fs for CAP. The 12 Hellcats split off into three 4 plane divisions. INDEPENDENCE would maintain a CAP while pilots from other carriers of TG 38.2 flew sweeps and attacked targets in southern Luzon, Lubang Island and the Bicol area throughout the day, while the other Task Groups struck central Luzon. Targets were air fields and aircraft to further sap the Japanese air strength in the Philippines.
0948 Secured from flight quarters. Air Department set to condition 13.
1051 Changed course to 200°T.

1059 Sounded flight quarters.

1102 Sounded torpedo defense - unidentified aircraft reported bearing 140°T, distance 20 miles.

Comdr. T.F. Caldwell's division was given a vector by C.I.C. to a bogey. Caldwell was out of the action, forced to orbit due to an engine problem. His 3 wingmen pursued the bogey. They descended gaining speed and ducked under a 2,500' cloud base. Lt. R.R. Fegraeus tallyhoed the bogey 4 miles ahead at 2 o'clock at 1,500 feet. Fegraeus, with Ensigns E.R. Edwards and J.S. Allen also in hot pursuit, pulled up on the tail of a Judy 800-1,000' astern, described as being drab with red meatballs. Fegraeus fired off a 2-3 second burst from 7 o'clock level as the Judy began a gentle turn to port. It began to burn fiercely in the port wing and engine. Allen almost simultaneously pulled up over the top of Fegraeus and squeezed off a burst that sprayed the fuselage. The burning Judy glided down striking the water, slipping under the surface 4-5 seconds after impact, "leaving an oil slick where it went under". The time, 1105.

1115 Secured from torpedo defense upon report that a Judy was shot down, bearing 140°T, 9 miles.

1117 Secured from flight quarters.

1121 Changed course to 045°T.

1122 Sounded flight quarters.

1126 Launched 1 F6F (Ens. R.A. Fisher) to replace a F6F with an engine problem.

1128 Recovered 1 F6F (Comdr. Caldwell) with a bad engine, launched at 0941.

1132 Secured from flight quarters. Air Department set to condition 13.

1209 Changed fleet course to 180°T, fleet speed 17 knots.

1223 Sounded flight quarters.

1307 Changed fleet course to 055°T.

1315 Sounded torpedo defense, upon the report of an unidentified aircraft.

1316 Commenced recovering 11 F6Fs launched at 0941 and 1 F6F launched at 1126.

1319 Secured from torpedo defense. Aircraft was identified as a friendly.

1336 Changed fleet course to 210°T.

1355 Fleet speed 20 knots, sounded torpedo defense.

1404 Secured from torpedo defense.

1436 Air Department set condition 12.

1601 Sounded flight quarters.

1658 Changed course to 055°T.

1659-1706 Launched 8 F6Fs for CAP, then changed course to 210°T. TG 38.1 controlled 2 Hellcats, TG 38.3 controlled two, and the remaining four were retained by 38.2.

1748 In a new type of mission, a TBM-1(N) night Avenger, flown by Lt. William R. "Reb" Taylor, was launched to assist destroyers USS BROWN and USS BOYD in hunter killer tactics against Japanese submarines in the vicinity of the Task Groups.

Making matters slightly more complicated, the DD's were also subjected to enemy air attack throughout the evening, and the Avenger was vectored off out of range to orbit during these attacks so as not to become a target of friendly fire from the DD's guns.

1754 Changed course to 050°T.

1806 Launched 1 F6F(N).

1812 Launched 1 F6F(N). These two Hellcats were tasked with CAP duties were added to the eight others already on station. It was observed that 10 night fighters aloft simultaneously were becoming difficult for effective control.

1814 Sounded torpedo defense.

1820 Sounded general quarters. *RA All night we were in condition 1 easy. Reason: Bright moon all night. RA*

1825 Changed speed to 23 knots. Proceeded to night flying station, bearing 040°T, 8 miles from guide, in company with DDs USS MARSHALL and USS TWINING as plane guards.

1851 Commenced maneuvering for flight operations.

1907-1942 Recovered 6 F6Fs.
1951 Recovered 1 F6F.
2011 Changed course to 335°T.
2019 Changed course to 050°T for flight operations.
2022 Recovered 1 F6F(N) Launched at 1706.
2054 Recovered 1 F6F(N) Launched at 1706.
2155 Steadied on course 355°T for flight operations.
2202-2207 Launched 2 F6F(N)s and 1 TBM(N).
2219 Recovered 1 F6F(N) launched at 1812.
2255 Recovered 1 TBM(N) launched at 1748.
2259 Changed course to 355°T, speed 19 knots.
2301 Commenced zigzagging (Plan No.6)
on base course 355°T.
At 2350 The INDEPENDENCE night CAP picked up
unidentified surface radar contacts.

MK 51 Gun Director

AD What a day. GQ from 1815 to 0700. Our squadron of night fighters have been heckling the Japs all night. Our ship and fighters have been making history and we have received many "well dones" from Admirals Nimitz and Halsey, also Mitscher. Note: Striking Luzon. Food situation is getting worse, may receive supplies soon. AD

Monday 6 November 1944   *Luzon, Philippines*

Zigzagging on base course 335°T, in company with USS MARSHALL and USS TWINING, bearing 040°T at 8 miles from the guide, at their night flying station. Ship is darkened and has 2 F6Fs and 1 TBM in the air.
0159 Changed course to 075°T.
0205 Completed launching 1 F6F(N) and 1 TBM(N).
0230-0240 Hellcats flown by Lt. W.E. "Bill" Henry, Ens. Gale V. "GV" Williams, Ens. J.A. "Barney" Barnett and Lt. J.T. "Terry" Barker were catapulted into the night. They were tasked with a predawn heckling mission over Clark field in Manila. This mission was intended to interfere with any predawn efforts the Japanese might make to attack Task Force 38. The hecklers each had two 350 lb bombs.

After launch, Gale Williams jettisoned his bombs returned with a bad radio. Trouble with the AN/ARC-5 radio "had been chronic" with the VF(N)-41 Hellcats, thought to be aggravated by catapulting and hard landings. Then, 35 miles out, Terry Barker returned with a rough engine, as he observed dropping and fluctuating oil pressure.

Bill Henry and Barney Barnett continued on climbing, crossing the east coast of Luzon at 8,000' near Baler Bay. Visibility was 10 miles on a cloud free night with a bright 6/10s moon. Better still, lights were showing, the island was not blacked out.
Proceeding via Mt. Arayat, Henry buzzed Clark Field looking for target aircraft. Over Clark at 5,000', Barnett reported 2 Topsys (Japanese transports) with lights on preparing to land. Henry made a tight turn, pulling up behind one in the landing pattern at 800' and fired 2 bursts from 6 o'clock level, hitting the port engine and wing root. The Topsy went into a steep glide, crashing within 100' west of the runway, exploding and burning on impact. As Henry was targeting the first Topsy, Barnett S-turned down behind the second Topsy pulling in 300' astern. Barnett fired off a long burst from 6 o'clock level. The port engine caught fire and the Topsy dropped down heading quickly for the runway to land. Barnett put another burst into the burning transport, now at 200'. It dove into the ground just east of the runway and exploded. The time, 0445.
After bombing targets on the ground, heading north toward Lingayen Gulf looking for more Japanese transports, they spotted a third bogey 20 miles north of Clark at 3,000'. Henry pursued, but the Topsy pilot became aware of it, dove for the deck, doused his lights and vanished. Bill tried to find it on his AIA radar, without results.

They spotted two other F6Fs, made contact over VHF and explained the two fires at Clark. The WASP pilots bagged the third Topsy just north of Clark a short time later. Henry and Barnett headed back to the ship, never encountering any searchlights or anti-aircraft fire.

0250-0307 Recovered 1 TBM(N) launched at 2207, and 3 F6F(N)s; one had been launched at 2205, and the other 2 had been launched at 0240 (Williams & Barker).

0330 Completed recovery of 1 F6F(N) launched at 2203.

0408 Recovered 1 F6F(N) launched at 0205.

0634 Recovered 1 TBM(N).

0655 Recovered 1 F6F(N).

0657 Secured from general quarters, Air Department remained at flight quarters.

0718 Recovered 2 F6F(N)s (Henry & Barnett).

0800 Mustered crew on stations.

0810 Received report of radar contact, bogey bearing 290°T, 85 miles.

0813 Sounded torpedo defense due to radar contact.

0928 Secured from torpedo defense, Air Department set to condition 13.

1354 Changed course to 190°T, speed 12 knots to avoid USS HANCOCK, conducting flight operations.

1355 Changed course to 175°T, speed 17 knots.

This afternoon they began their retirement from the area to the northeast.

1525 Sounded torpedo defense on signal from OTC, securing at 1537.

1600 Sounded flight quarters.

1655-1700 Changed speed to 22 knots, launched 4 F6Fs for a dusk CAP.

1704 Changed course to 035°T.

1726 Launched 1 F6F, changed speed to 24 knots.

1753 Maneuvered to night flying station in company with USS MARSHALL and USS TWINING, 8 miles from the center of TG 38.2.

1809 Changed course to 060°T. Then sounded general quarters.

1836 Recovered 1 F6F launched at 1700, which crashed into the barrier. Changed speed to 22 knots.

1905 Released 5 radar decoy balloons to help cover our retirement from the area.

1912 Secured from general quarters.

1928 Recovered 3 F6Fs. 2 were launched for the dusk CAP at 1700, 1 at 1756.

2000 Changed course to 100°T, then changed fleet speed to 18 knots.

2107 Changed course to 060°T to recover aircraft.

2118 Recovered 2 F6Fs.

2142 Launched 2 F6Fs for night CAP, then changed course to 100°T.

2153 Launched 1 F6F.

2211 Recovered 1 F6F.

2242 Commenced zigzagging on base course 100°T.

Tuesday 7 November 1944   *Retiring to refuel*

Zigzagging on base course 100°T (at their night flying station), in company with USS MARSHALL and USS TWINING, bearing 240°T at 8 miles from the USS NEW JERSEY, at the center of Task group 38.2 . The ship is darkened. 2 F6Fs are in the air.

0155 Maneuvered into the wind, 045°T, for flight operations.

0206-0207 Recovered 2 F6Fs launched at 2142. Then commenced maneuvering to regain night flying station.

0259 Gained night flying station, commenced zigzagging on course 135°T, speed 18 knots.

0531-0641 Manned routine torpedo defense stations.

0605 Commenced maneuvering to rejoin TG 38.2.

0623 Detached USS MARSHALL and USS TWINING to rejoin TG 38.2.

0640 Regained position in the disposition, 5R5. NEW JERSEY (guide) bears 240°T, 2,500 yards. Air Department set to condition 14.

0727 Ceased zigzagging and resumed base course 135°T.

0735 USS BILOXI, HUNT and YARNALL took departure of TG 38.2 to join TG 38.3.

0800 Mustered crew on stations.

0900 Half-masted the Colors following USS CABOT. Changed course to 125°T, speed to 22 knots.

0910 Changed course to 135°T.

0911 Sighted tankers bearing 110°T, 11 miles. Various course and speed changes were made as the Task Group and Tanker refueling group maneuvered to join up.

1100 Tankers joined TG 38.2. Fueling disposition was set, USS TAPPAHANNOCK as guide. INDEPENDENCE was ordered to receive fuel from port side of USS TAPPAHANNOCK. Commenced maneuvering to gain position alongside the tanker.

1124 Came alongside the TAPPAHANNOCK.

1148 Commenced pumping fuel oil fore & aft.

1312 Cast off from the tanker having received 199,000 gallons fuel oil, 15 drums of lubricating oil, and 8 drums of aviation lubricating oil. Commenced maneuvering to regain station.

1340 Arrived on station bearing 254°T, 5,300 yards from USS TAPPAHANNOCK (guide). Commenced zigzagging independently on base course 060°T, speed 10 knots.

1400 USS WASP, USS LOUISVILLE, USS BROWN and USS BOYD joined the formation.

1655 Guide shifted positions. INDEPENDENCE bears 250°T, 7,500 yards from guide.

1805 Ceased zigzagging, steadied on course 060°T.

1822 USS NEW JERSEY assumed guide, bearing 090°T, 2,500 yards, axis 060°T. They were leaving the tankers proceeding toward Ulithi.

2347 Changed course to 100°T, speed is 18 knots.

RA Tonight the wind is blowing quite hard. Sea is moderately rough. RA
GN We got word that a good storm is on the way and word is passed to lash down everything. GN
AD Sure would appreciate some good chow. AD

Wednesday 8 November 1944   *Proceeding to Ulithi - Typhoon*

Underway as before in Task Unit 38.2.1 consisting of USS INDEPENDENCE, USS HANCOCK, USS CABOT, USS WASP and USS INTREPID (OTC). The ship is darkened.

0040 Changed speed to 14 knots. The Task Unit is in a storm area, with rough weather and heavy seas.

0506-0606 Manned routine torpedo defense stations. During the day heavy seas periodically submerged the forecastle. The forward quad 40mm mount was damaged and forecastle gear was carried away by the heavy seas. The forward bulkhead of the forward catapult room was pushed in.

0816 Changed fleet course to 122°T.

1442 Changed fleet course to 082°T, speed reduced to 11 knots.

1522 Changed fleet course to 122°T, speed increased to 17 knots.

1604 USS WASP, USS BROWN and USS BOYD left the formation to proceed to Guam.

1730-1815 Manned routine torpedo defense stations.

HB We left for Ulithi and got into another typhoon which lasted 2 days. The waves were so high we got water in our gun buckets. These guns are 30 or 40 feet above the water line, so you know the waves were pretty high. We had been at sea so long, our food supply was almost depleted, except for salmon, rice, and beans, which we had plenty of, and which we ate three times a day. I could not eat salmon for several years after that. (We had run out of soap during the battle of the Philippines.) HB

GN We are really in it. I thought the last storm was bad but I'm just patiently waiting now for the ship to start breaking up. Got word that three of our sister ships are having trouble. All have fires on hangar decks where planes broke loose. I'm surprised myself that the flight deck continues to stay put. GN

RC Had a bad storm, bow of ship caved in. RC
GL Another Hurricane, bow under water all the time. Waves are smashing our catapult room.
Note: This in the second hurricane we hit in this area in the space of a month. GL

Thursday 9 November 1944   *Ulithi Atoll*

Steaming as before. Ship is darkened. Air Department is in condition 14, Engineering Department condition 33, all other departments condition 3.
0439-0539 Sounded torpedo defense.
0800 Mustered crew to quarters.
0812 Changed course to 135°T.
0829 Sighted Ulithi Atoll, Caroline Islands, bearing 160°T, 19 miles.
0840 Changed course to 060°T and launched 1 F6F, ordered to the USS HANCOCK.
0844 Changed course to 090°T.
0858 Changed course to 131°T.
0907 Commenced maneuvering, taking our place in column to a position 4,500 yards behind USS INTREPID, for entrance into Ulithi Atoll.
0930 USS VINCENNES assumed guide.
1001 Commenced maneuvering while approaching and conforming to the Mugai channel.
1010 Sounded general quarters for entrance into the anchorage.
1027 Received report of unidentified aircraft, 28 miles on bearing 055°T. Set condition RED. This aircraft was proved friendly.
1037 Secured from condition RED.
1130 Passed through anti-torpedo nets at entrance to the anchorage.
1135 Secured from general quarters. Made all preparations for anchoring.
1209 Stopped all engines.
1213 Anchored in Berth No.23, Ulithi Anchorage in 25 fathoms of water, coral bottom with 120 fathoms of chain, port anchor, having been underway continuously for 33 days and 20 hours.
1233 Set the in port watch. Ens. J.S. Berkheimer reported back aboard.

We began to take on supplies from ComServRon TEN, "which did an excellent job".
With aid supplied from a tender, the ships crew started repairs of typhoon damage to the forecastle, including replacement of the quad 40mm gun mount.

1315 LCT 87 moored along port side aft to transfer ammunition.
1340 Main radio issued RED Alert.
1342-1355 Manned torpedo defense stations.
1430 LCT 87 cast off port side.
1840-2321 Two 35-foot motor launches from USS CASTOR were alongside to deliver supplies.

RC Anchored at Ulithi repairing ship. RC
HB We were back at Ulithi, taking on some much needed supplies. HB
AD Arrived at Ulithi for supplies. Storm beat the bow of our ship. Will need repairs. Plenty of ships at this anchorage. AD

Friday 10 November 1944   *Ulithi Atoll*

0800 Anchored as before. SOPA is in USS NEW JERSEY. Mustered crew on stations. During the day
   we received dry and fresh provisions from various supply ships at anchorage.
1155 Received on board 1 F6F from a barge from USS SITKOH BAY.
1555 Received on board 1 F6F.

GN   Took on stores and supplies. Hope to get a fried egg or two out of the deal.   GN
AD   Anchored—receiving ammo and supplies. Ham & eggs for breakfast. Oh boy, good chow again. AD

Saturday 11 November 1944   *Ulithi Atoll*

Anchored as before. The ship was under 24 hours notice for getting underway.
0800 Mustered crew on stations.

During this stop at Ulithi, crew that could be spared from watches and work details were taken on recreation parties to "a nicely developed fleet recreation center" on Mog-Mog Island. Junior officers would unwind and soak up booze at "Crowley's Tavern". Night fighter pilot I.H. Lee would note; *" It lacked "Mothers" touch, but no one cared"*.

GL   We continued loading stores – saw a few movies. GL

Sunday 12 November 1944   *Ulithi Atoll*

Anchored as before. The ship was under 24 hours notice for getting underway.
0157 LCT 179 moored to port side to deliver lubricating oil.
0230 Received an aircraft engine from a small craft on the starboard side.
0500 Removed the No.1 40mm quad mount from the forecastle (storm damaged on 8 November) to the
        salvage tug USS MARION.
0620 LCT No. 179 cast off from port quarter.
0800 Mustered crew on stations.
0915 YT 80 placed YO 104 alongside port.
1000 USS KANKAKEE came alongside to port.
1036 Commenced taking on fuel.
1159 Having received 108,000 gallons of fuel oil and 23,100 gallons of aviation gasoline, USS
KANKAKEE cast off.
1209 LCT 173 moored alongside to starboard.
1356 Received aboard one F6F-5N.
1408 LCT 173 cast off.
1603 Floating crane moored alongside, starboard bow.
        (This was possibly to replace the new No.1 gun mount)
1916 Floating crane cast off from starboard bow.

GN   Eddie Peabody came aboard. He was a bit late and as it was about the first show I've been to aboard ship in about a year I feel as though he is not coming. He arrived with his band though and put on a very good show. This crew really needed something like that. About this time we were trying to figure out what the word liberty means. Asked all the fellows but they don't know. GN

Father Kelly

AD   Anchored - Today Father Kelly is getting transferred. He is the finest person I ever knew and every fellow on the ship hates to see him go. AD   (Note: Chaplin Kelly was replaced by Rev. Failing.)

RA   Got a new quad 40mm gun in place of the one that got smashed by the tropical storm. RA

Monday 13 November 1944   *Ulithi Atoll*

Anchored as before. The ship was under 24 hours notice for getting underway.

0015 Having delivered aviation stores, LCM cast off.

0100 LCM came alongside starboard gangway to deliver small stores, then cast off.

0800 Mustered crew on stations. Assumed SM and SK radar guard.

0830 Admitted crewmember* to sickbay with two crushed toes from accident embarking motor whale boat alongside.   (* S1C Frank Wesley Dickerson)

0835-0850 Proceeded with jacking over main propulsion units.

1410 LCI No. 865 came alongside starboard quarter to load empty oil drums, casting off at 1500.

GN Painting throughout the ship. Looks like a long time before the next liberty. GN

AD Anchored. Carriers Franklin and Belleau Wood are returning home due to damage occurred in battle with Jap fleet. AD

Tuesday 14 November 1944   *Ulithi Atoll - Getting Underway*

Anchored as before. No.1 boiler in use for auxiliary purposes.

0130 Transferred bomb fuses to LCT 916.

0300 Received Bomb fuses from LCT 996.

0714 LCM 85 came alongside starboard with ammunition.

0800 Mustered crew on stations.

0900 Jacked over main engine by hand.

0903 LCM 85 cast off.

1152 Lighted fires under No.3 boiler.

1251 No.3 boiler cut into main steam line.

1300 Lighted fires under No.2 & 4 boilers.

1455 Commenced heaving short on port anchor.

1517-1522 Boilers No. 2 & 4 cut in on main steam line.

PHOM2C Edward Schultz

1534 With anchor chain on short stay, 30 fathoms, commenced heaving in on port anchor.

1536 INDEPENDENCE got underway prior to dark with Task Unit 38.2.1, carrier unit of Task Group 38.2, in accordance with secret orders dated 12 November, 1944 of Commander Task Unit, rear Admiral G.F. Bogan, who is also C.T.G 38.2 in USS INTREPID. They were to operate east of the Philippines in support of the Philippine Islands Campaign with the forces on Leyte and Samar.

Commenced maneuvering to conform to channel while leaving the harbor.

1610 Sounded general quarters.

1620 Passed between buoys No. 1 & 2 at the entrance of Mugai Channel, Ulithi Atoll.

1625 Changed course to 071°T, speed 20 knots for flight operations.

1626 Launched 1 F6F. Then reduced speed to 18 knots.

1634 Landed 3 F6Fs; 1 launched at 1626, and 2 replacement F6Fs from Ulithi Air Base.

1636 Took departure from Ulithi Atoll with right tangent of Falalop Island bearing 035°T, 4.5 miles. Then commenced maneuvering to take station in the formation.

1658 USS NEW JERSEY became guide.

1715 Formed cruising disposition 5R, axis 060°T.

1845 Proceeding westward on course, 270°T, speed 17 knots.

Wednesday 15 November 1944   *At Sea*   *Proceeding Toward Luzon*

Steaming in company with TG 38.2.1 consisting of USS INDEPENDENCE, USS CABOT, USS HANCOCK and USS INTREPID (OTC). Zigzagging on base course 270°T, 17 knots, Disposition 5R, axis 060°T. INDEPENDENCE bears 060°T, 2,500 yards from USS NEW JERSEY (guide).

0443 Sounded torpedo defense.

0547 Changed course to 065°T.

0547 USS INTREPID designated guide, bearing 285°T, 3,500 yards. Secured from torpedo defense, Air Department set to condition 14.

0600 Commenced maneuvering to gain position 1,200 yards astern USS INTREPID in column formation with USS PASADENA third vessel in column. The heavy ships formed up in two columns for AA practice against towed sleeves.

0610 Gained position, changed course to 270°T, speed 17 knots.

0625 Sounded torpedo defense for gunnery exercises.

0640 Commenced firing exercises on target sleeves.

0725 Secured from torpedo defense and gunnery exercises. Expended 1058 rounds of 40mm and 180 rounds of 20mm during gunnery exercises.

0750 Commenced maneuvering to gain position 5R with guide bearing 285°T, 3,500 yards.

0943 USS NEW JERSEY became guide, INDEPENDENCE bears 060°T, 2,500 yards.

1029 Sounded torpedo defense for a simulated attack by aircraft of TG 38.2 carriers.

1049 All gyro repeaters were cut in on the after gyro due to a casualty in the forward gyro.

1125 Forward gyro back in commission after replacement of an amplifier tube.

1126 Changed course to 280°T.

1127 Secured from torpedo defense.

1415 NEW JERSEY shifted position in the formation (5V) preparatory to 5" AA practice. Guide shifted to USS INTREPID.

1502 Returned to disposition 5R.

1544 USS NEW JERSEY assumed guide bearing 240°T, 2,500 yards.

1629 Sounded flight quarters.

1724 Changed fleet course to 075°T. Commenced launching aircraft.

1733 Sounded routine torpedo defense.

1734 Completed launching 5 F6F(N)s.

1750 INDEPENDENCE left the formation to proceed to their night flying station, accompanied with the USS HUNT and USS HALSEY POWELL as Task Unit 38.2.10.

1805 Assumed night flying station bearing 085°T, 8 miles from USS NEW JERSEY.

1855 Recovered 5 F6F(N)s launched at 1734. Bad weather prevented further flight operations.

2118 Commenced zigzagging on base course 278°T.

GL We had target practice & New Jersey & Iowa fired 16 inch guns. GL

Thursday 16 November 1944   *Refueling - Proceeding Toward "Ready"*

Steaming as before at the night flying station with USS HALSEY POWELL and USS HUNT.

0130 Sounded flight quarters.

0301 Ceased zigzagging, changed course to 070°T for flight operations.

0319 Completed launching 4 F6Fs and 3 TBMs. Then changed course to 280°T.

0326 Changed course into the wind and launched 1 TBM.

0507-0617 INDEPENDENCE was at torpedo defense.

0619 Recovered 4 F6Fs and 4 TBMs. All aircraft were back on board. INDEPENDENCE then started maneuvering to gain position alongside tanker USS MONONGAHELA.

0650 Secured from flight quarters. Air Department set to condition 14.

0759 Alongside tanker to our starboard, commenced passing fueling lines.

0834 Commenced receiving fuel oil.

0928 Cast off from USS MONONGAHELA having received 93,787 gallons of fuel oil and transferring to the tanker 14 empty helium bottles and 5 bags of mail.

0931 Changed course to 060°T and maneuvered to gain position on USS MONONGAHELA, 2,000 yards, bearing 230°T. USS MONONGAHELA is stationed 3,000 yards bearing 075°T from fleet center.

1115 Station of USS MONONGAHELA changed to 4,000 yards, bearing 255°T from fleet center.

1245 Gained new position on USS MONONGAHELA, 6,500 yards, bearing 255°T.

1345 Task Group 38.2 completed fueling and formed cruising disposition 5R, fleet axis changed to 090°T. INDEPENDENCE assumed station bearing 090°T, 2,500 yards from USS NEW JERSEY. USS PASADENA left the formation to join TG 38.4.

Task Groups 38.1, 38.2 and 38.4 were steaming toward operating area "Ready", roughly halfway between Ulithi and the Philippines, to conduct various training exercises.

1401 Sounded flight quarters. Changed course to 090°T, speed 12 knots.

1418-1422 USS LEWIS HANCOCK came alongside to transfer 3 sacks of US Mail, then cast off.

1445 Changed speed to 16 knots for flight operations.

1502 Completed launching 6 F6Fs for CAP.

1516 Resumed position in the formation.

1530 USS NEW JERSEY assumed guide.

1704 USS STOCKHAM came alongside to starboard to deliver guard mail.

1715 USS STOCKHAM cast off. Changed speed to 22 knots to regain station.

1740 Sounded torpedo defense.

1745 On a new course of 084°T, speed 20 knots, completed launching 3 TBMs for ASP.

1754 Upon landing, a F6F crashed into the barrier, destroying the barrier. Slight damage to the Hellcat.

1805 Completed recovery of 6 F6Fs launched at 1502. Then changed course to 040°T to proceed to the night flying station in company with USS HUNT and USS HALSEY POWELL, as TU 38.2.10.

1840 Secured from torpedo defense.

1904 Changed course to 010°T having arrived at the night flying station to the windward side of TG 38.2, bearing 090°T, 14,000 yards from NEW JERSEY.

2130 Changed course to 060°T to launch aircraft.

2154 Launched 3 TBMs for ASP.

2216 Changed course to 100°T.

2221 Recovered 3 TBMs launched at 1745 and 1 TBM launched at 2154.

2324 Changed course to 255°T and launched 1 TBM.

Friday 17 November 1944   *Proceeding Toward "Ready"*

0205 Steaming as before in company with USS HUNT and USS HALSEY POWELL. There are 3 TBMs in the air. Changed course to 100°T into the wind for flight operations.

0211 Completed launching 3 TBMs for ASP.

0225-0238 Recovered 2 TBMs launched at 2154, and 1 TBM launched at 2324.

0240 Maneuvered to regain night flying station.

0406 Regained night flying station, changed course to 260°T, speed 18 knots.

0522-0622 Torpedo defense.

0546 Changed course to 055°T, commenced recovery of aircraft.

0550 Completed recovery of 3 TBMs launched at 0211.

0554 Commenced maneuvering to regain position within TG 38.2.

0608 Air Department secured from flight quarters, set condition 14.

0632 Assumed position in TG 38.2, bearing 090°T, 2,500 yards from guide, USS NEW JERSEY. Changed course to 260°T, speed 20 knots.

0810 USS HANCOCK, THE SULLIVANS and STEPHEN POTTER left the formation to effect the transfer of the flag of Vice Admiral J.S. McCain, Commander Task Force 38, from USS WASP to USS HANCOCK.

1345 USS HANCOCK, THE SULLIVANS and STEPHEN POTTER rejoined the formation.

1428 USS TINGEY came along the starboard side. Captain E.C. Ewen and Commander T.F. Caldwell

Jr. left INDEPENDENCE for transport on TINGEY, having been called to a conference aboard USS HANCOCK. Commander Edwin James Steven Young temporarily became Commanding Officer.

1435 USS TINGEY cast off.

1600 Sounded flight quarters.

1721 Received mail from USS UHLMANN.

1726 Changed fleet course to 080°T.

1745 USS INTREPID designated guide, bearing 285°T, 3,500 yards.

1805 Changed fleet course to 245°T.

1809 USS TINGEY came along starboard side to return Captain Edward Coyle Ewen and Commander Turner Foster Caldwell Jr. from the conference aboard USS HANCOCK.

> TG 38.2 was assigned primary targets, Nielson, Nichols, Lipa and Batangas airfields, and shipping in Manila Bay.
>
> TG 38.1 was assigned the Tarlac-Mabalacat area, AA positions to the north, Aparri, Loag and San Fernando Airfields and the shipping in Lingayen Gulf.
>
> TG 38.4 was assigned Clark Field and airstrips to the south to include Manila Airfields, and shipping in Subic Bay.

1823 Cast off all lines from TINGEY.

2100 Changed course to 100°T.

2146 Changed course to 030°T, changed speed to 24 knots. Departed the formation with USS HUNT and USS HALSEY POWELL to the night flying station.

2155-2201 Launched 2 TBMs and 2 F6Fs.

2218 Gained night flying station bearing 260°T, 7 miles from USS NEW JERSEY. Changed course to 000°T.

AD At sea, everything very quiet. AD

Saturday 18 November 1944   *Take Aboard Reporters and Refuel - Approach Luzon*

Steaming as before in company with USS HUNT and USS HALSEY POWELL, as TU 38.2.10. There are 2 F6Fs and 2 TBMs in the air.

0000 Changed course and axis to 270°T. Commenced zigzagging ten minutes later.

0107 Ceased zigzagging, steadied on course 310°T to avoid the USS CUSHING which had dropped behind TG 38.2 due to an engineering casualty.

0120 USS CUSHING was rejoining her formation. Resumed zigzagging on base course 270°T.

0200 Ceased zigzagging, changed course to 080°T for flight operations.

0208 Completed launching 2 F6Fs and 2 TBMs.

0237 Completed recovery of 2 F6Fs and 2 TBMs launched at 2201. Changed course to 270°T, speed 25 knots, to regain station.

0529 Sounded torpedo defense.

0608 On a course of 080°T, speed 20 knots, recovered 2 F6Fs and 2 TBMs launched at 0208. Then returned to course to 270°T.

0631 Secured from torpedo defense.

0640 Regained station within TG 38.2, bearing 060°T, 2,500 yards from NEW JERSEY (guide).

0644 Secured from flight quarters. At 0700 they changed course to 180°T.

0855 Changed Fleet course to 060°T.

0945 USS INTREPID was designated guide. They then formed a firing disposition with heavy ships in two columns for anti-aircraft practice, INTREPID bearing 295°T, 3,000 yards from INDEPENDENCE.

0957 Sounded torpedo defense.

1013 Commenced AA practice firing our port batteries.

1113 Completed gunnery exercises, secured from torpedo defense.

1131 USS UHLMANN transferred two war correspondents to INDEPENDENCE; Charles P. Gorry of the Associated Press, and Phillip S. Heisler of the Baltimore Sun.

1139 USS NEW JERSEY designated guide, formation 5R, bearing 240°T, 2,500 yards from INDEPENDENCE. Changed fleet course to 215°T.

1210 Sighted tankers 260°T, 9 miles. Commenced maneuvering to fueling area.

1245 Maneuvered to approach fleet tanker USS KENNEBAGO, on course 300°T, speed 10 knots.

1336 Commenced receiving fuel oil. We transferred mail to the KENNEBAGO, and completed the fueling at 1421, having received 98,100 gallons of fuel oil.

1439 Cast off all lines and commenced maneuvering to gain position bearing 300°T, 1,500 yards from USS KENNEBAGO.

1615 TF 38.2 formed cruising disposition 5R5, axis 060°T, NEW JERSEY guide. Assumed station 060°T, 2,500 yards from guide.

1739 Changed Fleet course to 050°T. With fueling operations completed, and the fleet reformed, they commenced a high speed approach toward Luzon.

1756 Sounded torpedo defense, changed course to 295°T, speed 25 knots.

"Water over the bow". If any crew members were in the No.1 quad 40mm gun tub, they were taking a chilly saltwater bath. (Photo courtesy of John Doherty. Date and details are unknown)

17
Philippines - Luzon

Sunday 19 November 1944   *Luzon - Philippines*

Steaming as before with Task Group 38.2 with USS CABOT, USS HANCOCK and USS INTREPID. Rear Admiral Bogan is OTC in INTREPID. Air Department is at flight quarters, in condition 11. The Task Group is approaching Luzon at high speed for strikes against Japanese air strength at various air fields on Luzon. The plan is to arrive at dawn. TGs 38.1 and 38.4 are also approaching Luzon. Radar condition 4 was in effect. All air searching was provided with SM. SK was to be turned on only if night fighters were intercepting a bogey.

0035 Scrambled 2 F6F5Ns due to radar contact of unidentified aircraft, 050°T, 32 miles out. Lt. W.E. Henry and Ens. J.A. Barnett were sitting in their Hellcats on the catapults. They were launched into a black moonless night. The bogey disappeared from radar before they could close. Barnett was recalled.
0145 Sounded torpedo defense on reports of an unidentified aircraft. Henry, orbiting, was vectored to a second contact. It proved to be a very difficult intercept, but Henry finally was able to make contact at 1,000 feet astern, closing fast for the identification. It was a four engine Emily. Bill Henry put bursts into the engines and wing roots from 4-6 o'clock level at angels 7. The Emily, in a sweeping starboard turn, descended and began to fiercely burn. At 1,500 feet, the entire starboard wing separated, and the aircraft plummeted into the water. Bill announced the splash at 0205. This was his eighth shoot down.
0159 Secured from torpedo defense when the Emily was driven off (shot down by Bill minutes later).

0302 Launched 2 F6Fs to relieve the two in the air for CAP, and 2 TBMs for ASP and search. INDEPENDENCE then formed Task Unit 38.2.1 in company with USS HUNT and USS HALSEY POWELL and proceeded to a night flying station outside the Task Group screen.

During the intercept of the Emily, Bill Henry had noted a float light on the surface of the water. This was probably dropped as a marker for other Japanese aircraft to aid in finding our fleet.

With our presence discovered, OTC ordered our aircraft to be quickly armed and launched as night heckler missions over Luzon airfields. They were tasked to cover Clark, Tarlac, Mabalacat, Lingayen, Aparri, Nichols, Nielson, Lipa and Batangas airfields (see map page 334).

0413 Changed course to 000°T, speed 22 knots for air operations.
0420 Completed launching 7 F6Fs. Six were armed with 350lb depth bombs. Pilots launched were; Cdr. T.F. Caldwell, Jr., Ensigns F.A. Fisher, J.E. Berkheimer, R.W. Klock, E.R. Edwards, J.S. Allen and Lt. (jg) R.R. Fegraeus. The depth bombs were dropped at Clark Lipa and Nichols Fields with mixed results. A Sally was hit, the runway cratered and a fire started in an AA emplacement at Lipa. Three parked planes were hit at Clark.

Cdr. Caldwell experienced radio and gyro problems after launch, and Ens. Allen was catapulted as a replacement, carrying no bombs. They flew off toward assigned targets. Caldwell had jettisoned his bombs expecting to return, however he was able to overcome his technical problems, and though delayed, continued on.
Ensign Floyd A. "Fish" Fisher, flying alone at 5,000 feet, headed toward Clark, passed Baler Gulf and turned south chasing lights on a bogey. He lost it but sighted 2 Topsys at 3,000 feet. Making a circling descent with flaps to slow his speed, he dropped in on the tail of a Topsy and opened fire level at 6 o'clock 1,000' astern. The starboard engine began to burn. The aircraft burst into flames and fell to the ground ablaze. Fisher then searched for the other Topsy, saw blinking lights 15 miles south.

Fisher closed, climbing back to 5,000' and executed the same basic approach, descending to a position astern. Fisher again fired from 1,000 feet back. He hit the port engine, a fire starting, then snuffed out, the Topsy starting a turn to port. Fisher fired again, hitting the starboard wing root. The aircraft burst into flames, crashed and exploded on impact. Time; 0600.

0505 Bill Henry landed his Hellcat. He and Barnett had been aloft on a 5 hour night patrol and fatigue had set in. Henry, approaching to land, was given a wave off, but took a cut (cut the throttle and followed thru with the landing) *"and only with a last instant correction, prevented a crash"*.

0520 Barnett guided his Hellcat down toward the flight deck, took a cut, but was fast, missed the arresting gear wires, and hit the barrier wires. The aircraft flipped over on its back. Barnett got out with only minor scratches. The demolished F6F-5N (Bu.No.58725) was jettisoned into the sea using the ships crane.

0547 Berkheimer, over Lipa Field, sighted an enemy plane taxing. Dropping down to attack, he caught an Oscar, now just taking off, climbing out thru about 300' AGL*[1]. Berkheimer opened fire 1,000' astern, 6 o'clock level, and kept firing until he saw flames between the cockpit and wing roots. The Oscar nosed over into a steep glide, exploding on impact 4 miles from the runway. (*[1] Above Ground Level)

0547 Sounded routine general quarters.
0636 Changed course to 060°T, speed 20 knots for air operations.
0645 Completed recovery of 2 F6Fs launched at 0302.
0652 Secured from general quarters.
0654 Completed recovering 2 TBMs launched at 0302.
0800 Mustered crew on stations.
0816 Completed recovering 7 F6Fs launched at 0420, and also recovered 1 TBM *"which was in trouble"* from the USS INTREPID.
0826 Commenced zigzagging on base course 240°T. Secured from flight quarters, Air Department set to condition 14.
0841 Sounded general quarters on order from CTF due to unidentified aircraft nearing the formation.
0846 Rejoined the TG38.2 formation, assuming station bearing 060°T, 2,500 yards from guide, USS NEW JERSEY.
0852 USS HANCOCK designated guide.
0900 Secured from general quarters. Air Department set to condition 14.
1005 Changed course to 060°T.
1008 Sounded general quarters due to unidentified aircraft nearing the formation, bearing 080°T, 35 miles. At 1026 the aircraft was identified as friendly so they secured from general quarters.
1030 Launched the TBM from the USS INTREPID.
1035 Air Department set to condition 14.
1054 Changed course to 160°T. USS NEW JERSEY resumed guide.
1219 Changed course to 270°T.
1220 Sounded general quarters. Aircraft was reported by TBS to be diving on the formation.
1231 Secured from general quarters when nothing further developed.
1234 Changed course to 065°T.
1310 INDEPENDENCE became guide while USS NEW JERSEY conducted flight operations*[2].
1340 USS NEW JERSEY resumed as guide. (*[2] most likely launching or recovering her float plane)
1349 Changed base course to 180°T.
1412-1418 USS WEDDERBURN was alongside to the starboard quarter to receive ball bearings for a 40mm gun mount.
1500 Sounded flight quarters.
1502 Sounded torpedo defense on report of bogey bearing 240°T, 28 miles.
1526 Changed course to 085°T for flight operations.

1530 Secured from torpedo defense as two Judys were reported shot down by USS CABOT's guns.
1535 On a new course of 055°T, launched two F6Fs for a rescue mission to stay over a life raft, with several men, until a destroyer arrived.
1558 Sounded torpedo defense upon a TBS report of an unidentified aircraft.
1603 Secured from torpedo defense.

1651 Changed course to 050°T and launched 2 F6F5Ns tasked with a night heckler mission targeting Aparri Airfield. Aparri was the closest airfield on Luzon to Formosa and the Japanese Empire, therefore an important stopover point for Japanese planes flying to the Manila area. Ensigns W.E. Miller and R.F. Peterson climbed to 5,000' and started for Aparri, 230 miles away. Halfway to target, in twilight, the night fighters spotted a formation of 5 sand colored model 12 Betty bombers, 10 miles ahead, low to the water and closing, apparently to attack the fleet. The Bettys passed beneath at 8 o'clock. Miller & Peterson dropped in behind them. Peterson was first to pull the trigger on the trailing Betty. On his second burst, his guns jammed. Miller commenced his attack on the tail end Betty and put a long burst into the engine, wing root and fuselage from 6 o'clock level. The Betty dropped down, flying low with its entire starboard wing aflame for two miles, before it hit the water. Miller received permission to jettison his bombs and pursued another Betty. He made a highside run without effect, then dropped in on its tail and fired off a long burst close in from 6 o'clock into both engines. Miller and the Betty briefly disappeared into cloud, remerging with Miller seeing the Betty splash into the water. Down to 3'500 feet Miller spotted a third Betty off his starboard wing, slightly high, going in and out of cloud. Miller gave chase putting 3-4 short bursts into the engines as they passed from one cloud thru another. The Betty was flaming from both engines as it disappeared into a large cloud. Miller, unable to confirm a kill, was given a probable.
The Bettys were on a flight path that would have most likely taken them to the fleet. Peterson and Miller had broken up the attack.

1711 Sounded general quarters upon report of enemy aircraft bearing 243°T, 30 miles.
1723 Launched 2 F6Fs for CAP.
1755 Departed the formation with USS HUNT and USS HALSEY POWELL to proceed to a night flying station as Task Unit 38.2.10.
1815 Recovered 1 F6F launched at 1535. Then changed course to 055°T.
1819 Enemy aircraft reported bearing 248°T, 12 miles.
1820 Observed firing on the horizon astern by various ships of the Task Group.
1903 Secured from general quarters.
1905 Assumed night flying station 090°T, 7 miles from center of TG 38.2.
1919 Recovered 1 F6F launched at 1535.
1955 Recovered 2 F6Fs (Miller and Peterson) launched at 1651.
2101 Launched 2 F6Fs for CAP.
2134 Recovered 2 F6Fs launched at 1723.

GN Hit Luzon and Manila. Under attack at dusk but our fighters drove off their torpedo bombers. Had a night raid and received another hearty " well done " from " Bull' ' the next day. GN

GL We had torpedo defense at 2 o'clock this morning. Our night fighter shot down a four motor flying boat. Our night fighters went over Luzon before dawn and shot down four more Jap planes. During the day raid, 18 more were shot down out of the air, 34 destroyed on the ground. In the harbor they hit 2 cargo ships,[1] 2 DE's and 16 smaller cargo ships. Our night fighters were commended by commander of task group 38.2 and third fleet for a job well done. We had 3 GQ's and 4 torpedo defenses. Today a large group of 15 to 20 planes tried to get in but we shot most of them down. The Japs are using suicide dive bombers so we have to watch our step. GL*

[1] This was possibly convoy MATA-33 off San Fernando from Manila where freighter ESASHI MARU was possibly set afire & beached and sub chasers CH-19 & CH-26 (convoy escorts) were damaged. (Sources: Cressman & Combined Fleet)

Monday 20 November 1944   *At Sea, Retiring to Refuel*

Steaming with USS HALSEY POWELL and USS HUNT zigzagging on base course 090°T at 22 knots. There are 2 F6Fs in the air. The group is retiring to a fueling area near "Ready".
0025 Reduced speed to 15 knots.
0031-0032 Launched 2 F6Fs for CAP.
0047 Ceased zigzagging, changed course to 050°T and speed to 16 knots for flight operations.
0105 Completed recovery of 2 F6Fs launched at 2101. Then resumed course 090°T and changed speed to 25 knots.
0310 Reduced speed to 18 knots for flight operations.
0321 Completed launching 2 F6Fs for CAP.
0343 Completed recovery of 2 F6Fs launched at 0032.
0532 Sounded torpedo defense.

The fleet oiler USS MISSISSINEWA had fueled INDEPENDENCE last month (photos page 397-398). Today (six days after Mighty-I's departure from Ulithi) a Japanese Kaiten would light the dark pre-dawn Ulithi sky (at 0547) with violent explosions as MISSISSINEWA, with its 400,000 gallons of Av-gas, went up in deadly massive blasts that rocked the Ulithi lagoon. She lost 63 crew members.

0614 Changed course to 060°T for flight operations.
0623 Recovered 2 F6Fs launched at 0321. The Task Unit then proceeded to rejoin TG38.2.
0626 Secured from flight quarters, Air Department set to condition 14.
0632 Secured from torpedo defense.
0708 Regained station 2,500 yards, bearing 060°T from guide, USS NEW JERSEY in cruising disposition 5R, axis 060°T, zigzagging easterly on base course 090°T.
1230 Changed fleet course to 040°T.
1238 USS INTREPID assumed guide. INDEPENDENCE bears 105°T, 3,500 yards from guide.
1304 Formed cruising disposition 5V.
1517 USS STEPHEN POTTER came alongside to receive two war correspondents; Charles P. Gorry of the Associated Press, and Phillip S. Heisler of the Baltimore Sun. (Philip would later become Managing Editor)
1529 Changed fleet course to 075°T and formed cruising disposition 5R. USS NEW JERSEY designated guide.
1550 Sounded flight quarters.
1630-1644 Followed USS HANCOCK in half-masting colors.
1717 Commenced maneuvering to a night flying station accompanied by USS THE SULLIVANS and USS MILLER, 14,000 yards on bearing 060°T from USS NEW JERSEY.
1727 Launched 2 TBMs for ASP.
2138 Launched 2 TBMs for ASP.
2155 Changed course to 070°T, speed 12 knots for flight operations.
2202 Completed landing 2 TBMs launched at 1727. Then changed course to 130°T, speed 22 knots.
2345-2348 Steadied on course 115°T for flight operations. Launched 1 TBM.
2356 Changed course to 065°T, speed 12 knots for flight operations.

*GN   Year ago today we took a fish and were laid up for a while. Today was quiet though and only had routine patrols up. **GN***

Tuesday 21 November 1944   *At Sea, Refueling and Transferring Aircraft*

Operating with USS THE SULLIVANS and USS MILLER at a night flying station 7 miles from USS NEW JERSEY. There are 3 TBMs in the air.
0005 Recovered 1 TBM launched at 2138.

0137 Launched 1 TBM.

0215 Recovered 1 TBM launched at 2138.

0522 Sounded torpedo defense.

0540 Recovered 1 TBM launched at 2348 and 1 launched at 0137.

0555 Secured from flight quarters, Air Department set to condition 14.

0633 Regained position in the disposition.

0724 Changed fleet course to 150°T.

0740 Sighted fueling group 10 degrees to starboard, bearing 160°T, 21 miles.

0803 Changed fleet course to 120°T.

0812 Commenced maneuvering to approach fleet tanker USS KANKAKEE.

0835 Passed first line to USS KANKAKEE (fleet guide).

0900 Changed fleet speed to 8 knots. USS WEDDERBURN came alongside the port quarter. The INDEPENDENCE Air Group was to receive ten new F6F night fighters, and 4 new TBM night torpedo plane replacements. Pilots were transferred to USS WEDDERBURN for transport to the CVE, USS SHIPLEY BAY, to fly the aircraft aboard. CVL-22 will turn over ten older fighters and two TBMs to other carriers in the group. Pilots transferred to the WEDDERBURN were; Wolf, Decker, Allen, Williams, Lee, Berkheimer, Barnett, Matheson, Herpick, and Johnson.

0948 Cast off all lines from USS WEDDERBURN.

1118 Cast off all lines from USS KANKAKEE having received fuel oil, oxygen bottles, and transferring to KANKAKEE the mail. Changed course to 075°T, speed to 20 knots.

1126 Changed course to 085°T, speed to 9 knots.

1137 USS HUNT came alongside starboard quarter to transfer 8 pilots on board to receive planes to fly back to the USS HANCOCK, USS CABOT and USS INTREPID.

1159 Cast off all lines from USS HUNT.

1204 Commenced proceeding to flying station.

1234 Changed course to 080°T, and commenced launching aircraft.

1246 Completed launching 6 F6Fs and 1 TBM for transfer to USS HANCOCK and USS INTREPID.

1333 Sounded flight quarters.

1346 Launched 1 TBM for transfer to USS CABOT.

1416 Completed launching 2 F6Fs for transfer to USS INTREPID.

1423-1439 USS STEPHEN POTTER was alongside to transfer 4 pilots and 1 passenger to USS SHIPLEY BAY for delivery of replacement aircraft to the INDEPENDENCE.

1450 Changed course to 045°T for flight operations. Commenced receiving replacement aircraft.

1512 A F6F (Bu.No. 71253), on landing, crashed into the barrier causing slight damage to the Hellcat.

1530 ARM2C W.M. Layburn was admitted to sick bay for a contusion on his upper leg, caused when the barrier accident occurred. He jumped into No.3 gun bucket from the flight deck to avoid the aircraft.

1531 Completed recovery of 10 F6F-Ns, transferred onboard from USS SHIPLEY BAY. The night fighters had new APS6 gear with greater range. Commenced maneuvering to regain disposition position.

1604 Commenced steering various courses at 12 knots for flight operations.

1615 Completed recovering 4 new TBM-3D replacement aircraft from USS SHIPLEY BAY.

1616 Commenced maneuvering to regain position in the disposition.

1653-1655 Changed course to 070°T at 12 knots for flight operations. Launched 2 F6Fs, to be flown for transfer to the USS HANCOCK. Then maneuvered to regain station.

1700 The Task Force completed fueling. USS NEW JERSEY became guide, bearing 080°T, distance 2,500 yards, course 080°T, speed 8 knots.

1719-1730 USS TINGEY was alongside to starboard to transfer US Mail to INDEPENDENCE.

1739 Sounded torpedo defense, then changed speed to 15 knots.

1839 Secured from torpedo defense.

2038 Air Department set to condition 12.

2347 Changed fleet course to 050°T, speed 15 knots. The group stayed in area "Ready".

Wednesday 22 November 1944   *At Sea, Exercises in Area "Ready"*

0021 Steaming as before in area "Ready". Changed Fleet course to 195°T, speed 18 knots.
0520 Sounded torpedo defense.
0559 Secured from Flight quarters, Air Department set to condition 14.
0614 Changed course to 300°T.
0620 Secured from torpedo defense.
0700 USS INTREPID became guide.
0710 (BatDiv 7) USS NEW JERSEY, and IOWA with (CruDiv 14) USS VINCENNES and MAIMI,
accompanied by DesRon 52, left the formation to form Task Group 34.5.
0711 USS INDEPENDENCE designated guide.
0800 Mustered crew on stations.
1140-1152 USS BROWN was alongside the port quarter to transfer 4 pilots who had flown aircraft to
the USS INTREPID and USS HANCOCK, back on board INDEPENDENCE.
1228 Changed course to 250°T.
1309 Sounded torpedo defense upon orders from OTC. Fired on a large spherical object which passed
abeam to port. It appeared to be a large float from an anti-submarine net. Several hits were made, but the
object remained afloat.
1522 Ships that had left the formation at 0710 today, returned to reenter the formation.
1525 USS NEW JERSEY resumed as fleet guide.
1731 Launched 2 TBMs for ASP, and 2 F6Fs for CAP. Maneuvered to proceed to our night flying
station in company with USS THE SULLIVANS and USS MILLER forming TU 38.2.10.
1744 Sounded torpedo defense.
1756 Gained night flying station bearing 060°T, 6 miles from USS NEW JERSEY.
1834 Secured from torpedo defense.
2127 Changed course to 100°T for flight operations.
2134 Completed launching 2 TBMs for ASP, and 2 F6Fs for CAP, then changed course to 180°T.
2148 Changed course to 055°T for flight operations.
2152 Hellcat (Bu.No. 71293) crashed into the barrier on landing, causing minor damage to the aircraft.
2220 Completed recovery of 2 F6Fs and 2 TBMs launched at 1731. Then changed course to 065°T.
Commenced zigzagging on base course 065°T, speed 15 knots.

*GN Routine patrol. Had 4000th landing. Getting along. By the 6th or 7th thousand, we should be in
Japan somewhere. GN*

Thursday 23 November 1944   *At Sea, Exercises in Area "Ready"*

Steaming as before in area "Ready", at a night flying station, windward of TG 38.2, ten miles
from its guide, bearing 060°T. Ship is darkened and has 2 TBMs and 2 F6Fs in the air.
0028 Launched 2 F6Fs.
0048 Recovered F6Fs launched at 2134.
0137 Launched 2 TBMs.
0154 Recovered 2 TBMs launched at 2134.
0336 Launched 2 F6Fs and 1 TBM.
0355 Recovered 2 F6Fs launched at 0028 and 1 TBM launched at 0137.
0513 Sounded torpedo defense.
0555 Completed recovering 2 F6Fs, 1 TBM launched at 0336 and 1 TBM launched at 0137.
0600 Changed course to 220°T.
0607 Commenced maneuvering to regain station within the TG 38.2.
0617 Secured from torpedo defense, Air Department secured from flight quarters.
0633 Regained position, bearing 045°T, 2,500 yards from USS NEW JERSEY.

0810 USS OWEN came along starboard side to transfer equipment.

0833 USS COLAHAN came alongside to transfer passengers. Received aboard Ensigns Klock and Peterson who ferried planes to the USS HANCOCK on 21 November.

1207 Changed fleet course to 264°T, speed 18 knots.

1758 Changed course to 270°T. This evening, the fleet was proceeding west at 22 knots.

1935 USS STEPHEN POTTER dropped behind the formation with a bad shaft, accompanied by USS THE SULLIVANS.

During the day, near noon, TG 38.1 was detached from duty with Task Force 38 and proceeded to Ulithi Atoll. TG 38.3 steamed in from Ulithi joining company with TG 38.2.

GN Routine patrols. Something is up but we can't get any good dope on it. GN

Friday 24 November 1944   *At Sea, - Refueling*

Steaming as before in cruising disposition 5R on course 270°T, 22 knots, guide USS NEW JERSEY.

0535 Sounded torpedo defense.

0537 Changed course to 330°T.

0540 Sighted tanker group off the starboard bow bearing 340°T, at 10 miles.

0554 Maneuvered to avoid collision with fleet tug crossing in the formation path. Then maneuvered to regain position.

0604 Fleet course changed to 010°T.

0625 TG 38.2 commenced fueling operations. Fueling course 070°T, speed 10 knots.

0635 Secured from torpedo defense. USS KANKAKEE became guide.

0755 Gained position 900 yards astern guide.

0810 Commenced maneuvering to fueling station.

0825 Came alongside USS KANKAKEE to our starboard.

0928 Commenced pumping fuel oil from tanker.

1038 Cast off from tanker having received 130,000 gallons of fuel oil and U.S. Mail.

1106-1112 USS MILLER was alongside for transfer of passengers. War correspondent Phillip Reed of International News Service came aboard to cover pending operations. (Phillip G. Reed would become Managing Editor & Asst. General Manager of the U.P.I. after International News Service merged with U.P.I.)

1136 Assumed position in disposition bearing 250°T, at 1,000 yards from USS KANKAKEE.

1218 Commenced zigzagging independently on base course 070°T.

1314-1325 USS BROWN was alongside starboard quarter to deliver registered mail.

1359 USS NEW JERSEY became guide. INDEPENDENCE is bearing 070°T, 2,500 yards from guide.

1433 Changed course to 285°T, speed 25 knots to begin a high speed run toward Luzon.

Saturday 25 November 1944   *Speed Run Toward Central Luzon*

Steaming as Task Unit 38.2.1 in company with USS INTREPID (OTC), USS CABOT and USS HANCOCK in cruising disposition 5R, course 285°T.

0403 Changed course into the wind and launched 2 F6Fs for a "Jack" Patrol per instructions from OTC at 0355. INDEPENDENCE then maneuvered to regain station.

0442 Sounded torpedo defense, due to sighting of an unidentified aircraft, bearing 170°T at 17 miles.

0447 Changed course to the north (355°T), having observed firing on the port bow.

0500 Completed launching 4 F6Fs for Jack Patrol. At 0504, changed course to the west, 270°T.

0520 Secured from torpedo defense, *"the unidentified aircraft having been chased away"*.

0554 Sounded general quarters.

0622 Changed course to 070°T.

0655 Secured from general quarters.

0658-0706 Recovered 2 F6Fs launched at 0403, and then 4 F6Fs launched at 0500.

0710 Secured from flight quarters, Air Department set to condition 14. All aircraft were now back on board. The INDEPENDENCE night fighting group would rest during the day as other carrier squadrons in the Task Group went out on strikes against targets.

1105 Changed course to 220°T.

1216 Sounded torpedo defense due to enemy aircraft reported at 145°T.

1219 Sounded general quarters, condition Able set.

1225 The Task group CAP reported several Hemps* overhead. (*Note: the "Hamp'" was the code name for the Mitsubishi A6M3 Model 32 "Zero" fighter, an improved version of the A6M2. It was later referred to as the "Zeke 32".)

1230 Increased speed to 24 knots, changed course to 075°T. Then changed course to 060°T.

1232 *"Various ships of the Task Group were observed to open fire on enemy planes. One plane, appearing to be a Val was taken under fire diving for the USS HANCOCK. Although repeatedly hit, the plane came in on the USS HANCOCK but blew up into several fragments shortly before she was over the USS HANCOCK. The plane struck the water nearby but a fire was seen to burst out on the forward end of the HANCOCK'S flight deck. This was later reported to have been caused by a burning wing from the disintegrated plane. The fire was soon brought under control and extinguished."*

1233 Changed course to 355°T. The Task Group temporarily ceased firing, as the attack seemed to be over. At least 7 single engine aircraft thought to be Vals, Jills, or Hemps* had crashed within the formation. Ships made evasive maneuvers as signaled by the OTC.

1236 Changed course to 075°T. Various ships of the Task Group again opened fire on enemy planes. One single engine aircraft dove on USS CABOT from the starboard bow, crashing along her flight deck on the port side, proceeding into the water.

1253 Changed course to 125°T. A Japanese Zero carrying a 550lb. bomb approaching from the starboard quarter *"was seen to dive on and strike the flight deck of the USS INTREPID, and a large fire burst out on the USS CABOT's flight deck forward caused by a diving plane or bomb. A number of enemy planes were shot down by the Task Group at about this time. The plane striking the INTREPID caused a large fire which began to increase in size, while the USS CABOT began getting their fire under control." "A large column of fire and smoke rising nearly 150 feet followed almost immediately"* when INTREPID was hit. (INTREPID would suffer the loss of 69 killed and approximately 150 wounded - Source *"INTREPID" by White & Gandt*)

1257 INDEPENDENCE *"opened fire on an enemy plane diving out of the sun, and it was taken under fire by other ships of the Task Group".*

1258 Changed course to 175°T.

1259 INDEPENDENCE *"fired at another enemy plane overhead which was also under fire by other ships of the group".*

1300 *"Changed course to 245°T. The USS INTREPID was now burning furiously and enveloped in smoke from stern to bow to such an extent that the entire ship was hidden. She was also shaken by internal explosions. When the smoke would clear, intense flames were seen to be raging throughout her hangar deck. On the other hand, fires on the USS HANCOCK and CABOT were out."* One attacking aircraft, shot down, crashed into the sea in flames between the INTREPID and NEW JERSEY.

1352 *"Changed course to 065°T for recovery of planes returning from strike. The USS INTREPID was now bringing her fires under control but the after half of the ship still appeared to be burning Badly."*

1358 Changed course to 085°T.

.1437-1443 Launched 9 F6Fs (8 were for a Jack Patrol).

1453 Recovered 1 F6F with a mechanical problem, launched at 1443. The Hellcat's landing gear would not retract after launching.

1505 Launched 1 F6F as a replacement. *"The fires on the USS INTREPID now appeared to be definitely under control and appeared to be out by 1516."*

1519 Recovered 1 F6F launched at 1443 with guns that were jammed, and recovered I F6F launched from the USS INTREPID. INTREPID's aircraft, unable to land on their own flight deck, were disbursing to other carriers for refueling, then on to Leyte's Tacloban Airfield.

1526 Changed course to 075°T, speed to 18 knots. *" The screen was now clear of unidentified planes".*

1559 Secured from general quarters.

1620 Changed fleet course to 065°T.

1651-1652 Launched 4 F6Fs for dusk CAP.

1719 Catapulted 1 F6F as a replacement for a F6F launched at 1651, which had a defective receiver.

1729 Recovered 1 F6F launched at 1443.

1800 Proceeded upwind to a night flying station accompanied with destroyers USS MILLER and USS THE SULLIVANS as plane guards.

1808 Sounded routine general quarters.   1833 Changed course to 090°T.

1855 Gained night flying station, USS NEW JERSEY is guide, 6 miles bearing 275°T.

1858 Launched 1 F6F replacement for a F6F launched at 1651 with a *"Bent Weapon"* (code for bad radar).

1905 Steering various courses into the wind at 24 knots for flight operations.

1906 Commenced recovering aircraft.

1919 Recovered 6 F6Fs; 4 launched at 1443, 1 F6F launched at 1505, and 1 F6F launched at 1652.

1920 F6F-5N (Bu.No. 58364) had been launched at 1443. Returning to land, Lt. T.E. Wolfe had a tail hook fail and crashed thru the barriers, then into the island structure. Pilot Wolfe was uninjured but AMM3c Edward Ricci was lost overboard during the crash. USS MILLER was detached to search for Edward Ricci. A fire ensued from the wrecked F6F and the INDEPENDENCE changed course to 180°T to put the wind on the port beam in an effort to keep the fire from spreading.

1922 Another course change was made to 140°T, and the fire was under control 3 minutes later. By 1930 the fire was completely out and the INDEPENDENCE increased speed to 26 knots and began maneuvering to regain its night flying station. The F6F had been destroyed, there was minor damage to the ships structure, however critical electronics did not fare as well. SG and SM radar were put out of commission, as was the TBS transmitter. Steam lines had been damaged to the ships siren and whistle.

2009 Decreased speed to 20 knots as USS COLAHAN joined the Task Unit as a replacement for USS MILLER (searching for Ricci). Seamen First Class; Frederick C. Haines, Ruben Beasley and Edward N. Ruest were sent to sick bay suffering serious burns from the crash. They were standing by a foamite station on the starboard side of the flight deck when the crashing F6F burst into flames. Seaman Edward Ricci was never seen again. (There is a recent questionable unconfirmed report that Ed Ricci MAY have survived, perhaps found by a DD. Ed Ricci is still listed as missing by the US Government.)

2040 Completed recovery of 5 F6Fs; 1 launched at 1443, 2 at 1652, 1 at 1719, and 1 at 1858.

2142 Launched 2 F6Fs for night CAP.

2210 Recovered 1 F6F launched at 1652.

2320 On a course of 090°T, changed speed to 26 knots.

It was felt the failures experienced by the F6Fs were due to the ten new F6F replacements not having been thoroughly checked out after delivery.

On this day, the Japanese suicide aircraft had been reported as friendly by four ships in Task Group 38.2. It appeared they had caught on to our IFF and were transmitting it, though weaker in transmission, and a narrower code than our normal codes. Some Japanese aircraft employed window, with poor success.

HB *November 25-Attacked Manila. Our group was under attack all afternoon. From our after elevator, I watched Japanese suicide planes dive onto and crash into the Hancock and the Cabot. Two planes hit the Intrepid, causing one hell of a fire. We were the only carrier in our group not hit by suicide planes. We did have a close call when two 1000 lb. bombs hit near us and shook the hell out of our ship, but no damaged was incurred. Also, on the 25th, one of our planes, a TBM *, crashed into the superstructure (or island) aboard our ship, and one of our guys was lost overboard. His name was Ricci.* **HB**   (* Note: It was the F6F Hellcat at 1920)

GL *Today was a day that I or anyone in 38.2 will never forget, especially the Intrepid. We attacked Luzon and sent fighter sweeps and deck loads over the island. I can say I have seen everything now. The Japs used their secret weapon today. I was writing a letter and torpedo defense sounded & followed by GQ. So I went up topside on the bridge to my lookout station. A group of planes were picked up on our radar screen and showed friendly lights but a fighter reported after tallyhoing them as 3 Vals. They had found out our I.F.F. and were coming in. He shot one down and the other two got away.*

Task group 38.4 (Kodiak) sent in a report that they were being attacked by dive bombers and torpedo planes. About 12:10 the first Jap dive bomber started his run on the Hancock. He came down to about 400 yards and he blew up off our starboard beam. It was a suicide dive and his bomb had a near miss. When the plane blew up a piece of it landed on the Hancock flight deck and started a fire. The pilot was blown out of his plane and came down on a parachute. They were in on us now. They were all over the sky. Some came down out of control, others burst into flame and blew up. Then one came down from about 20,000 feet straight for the Intrepid. He kept coming right on and made a suicide dive right onto the aft flight deck right down into the hangar deck. The Intrepid burst into one mass of flames and smoke. Then one dived on the Cabot, a carrier of our type. They must have thought it was us because they were painted black. He crashed on the Cabot's flight deck forward port side and fell into the sea. They then started their attack on the flaming and smoking Intrepid. Two torpedo planes made a run on her, one burst into flames and crashed into the sea. But the other one came straight up and crashed onto the Intrepid's flight deck. This was number two. The sky was black with A.A. fire.

Another Val started a run on the Cabot. We sighted her first and opened fire with our 40's & 20's on the starboard side. Then the Cabot and a cruiser opened fire and hit him, he crashed into the sea a few feet from the Cabot. Another one was directly over us, we opened fire but the Iowa got him with 5 inch.. I think he was looking us over but he looked too long. There were 4 carriers in our group and we were the only one that was not hit or damaged. The action started about 12:15 and ended 3:30. We sure are worried about tonight. There were 26 planes shot down. The other carriers took the Intrepid's planes. Others went into Leyte & a few crashed into the sea, no gas. These Jap suicide planes are really bad. They are damn hard to stop. It is the first time I have ever seen another ship hit. The Japs only attack the carriers[1], they don't bother the other ships. We were in G.Q. all night as we expected trouble. By now the Intrepid had the fire out, she never once slacked her speed. One of our night fighters crashed into the bridge and all but sacred me to death again. It burst into flames, a 4 alarm fire. You can be sure it was getting kinda warm on the bridge. One fellow was lost over the side and others burned. Found out first Jap suicide plane killed everyone in C.I.C. *[2] on the Intrepid.* **GL** (*[1] In the last year of the war more than 45 ships of various types and sizes would be sunk, and roughly 300 damaged by kamikazes)*
(*[2] The C.I.C. crew killed were 32 men in ready room four on standby at the time waiting to relieve C.I.C. - Source "INTREPID" by White & Gandt)*

GN *Hit Manila. Under heavy suicide attack all afternoon by dive bombers. The Hancock was first to be hit when a dive bomber directly overhead received a direct hit. Parts of plane including a wing struck Hancock well forward and started a minor fire. Was under control in a few minutes. Intrepid took a bomb through flight deck. Three torpedo planes had been making a run on her at the time and a two engine job was splashed not more than 200 feet away. Two single engine planes escaped the fire and went aft of her. One made a short climb and came around in a dive and dove on her flight deck. There was a beaut of a fire raging by that time from the bomb hit and the plane really helped it along. She didn't lose speed though and kept her place in the task force. There was so much smoke flowing aft that her guns were useless. The other bogie disappeared. About this time I spotted two planes about 8000 ft and in the sun. Reported to the Marine Captain who immediately had all forward guns trained on them. They came about halfway down and swung over to the Cabot. One hit her flight deck forward but fortunately made a swing at the last moment and came in from the port side. Slid across the deck and overside on the starboard side. The other one was hit before she got to the target and was splashed about 50 feet off starboard side of Cabot. Today was the day I lost a lot of faith in our escorts. About the only big ship that I seen open up was the Iowa. The Jersey and a cruiser on our starboard side didn't fire a shot that I know of and they do have a lot better anti aircraft guns than we do. I guess its just as well not to rely on them. Incidentally we were the only carrier in our unit that wasn't hit. **GN***

DL *Ten days after my twenty-second birthday Independence was the only fast carrier in our group not struck by a Japanese suicide plane on Saturday, 25 November 1944.*

It was our first major encounter with kamikazes. No one aboard Mighty I could have guessed that this would be our fate from now on—to be witness time and again to some other ship's horror. Seen even from a distance, it was awful.

A book called The Official Chronology of the U.S. Navy in World War II supplies details of the fleet's ordeal:

Task Groups 38.2 and 38.3 of Task Force 38 had had a busy day strafing, bombing, and sinking Japanese shipping off central Luzon in the Philippines. Aircraft from Ticonderoga sank a heavy cruiser in Santa Cruz harbor. Hellcats from Ticonderoga and Essex as well as fighters and TBMs from CVL Langley attacked a convoy about fifteen miles southwest of Santa Cruz, on the west coast of Luzon, also sinking a coast defense ship and several landing ships. Planes from CV Intrepid sank two "fast transports" and damaged another as well as a destroyer escort in Balanacan Harbor, Marinduque Island. Essex and Langley aircraft sank an army cargo ship while damaging another off San Fernando. A Japanese merchant tanker was damaged by planes in Manila Bay.
And then we paid the price.

What remained of the Japanese Imperial Navy reacted with the fury any outraged animal that still has a means of defense would. Of fangs and claws, it had plenty. The "Divine Wind" became a scourge that screamed its way into our lives with such insane, savage ferocity that it would leave thousands of American families grieving, staining all Pacific horizons with smoke and flame billowing from our battered, burning ships.

One of the penalties Independence sailors suffered as the result of our night-flying duty was that while we labored all night, our enemies chose mostly to attack in daylight. Thus we got little rest, less sleep. When GQ sounded, we airdales manned our battle stations together with everybody else, no matter how dopey and drowsy we were.

On this unforgettable day in November, a few of our planes had joined the Combat Air Patrol (CAP) after the ship had returned to station at the conclusion of our nighttime isolation. About mid-morning one of our fighters landed badly, cut its way through the barriers, and crashed into the island structure. But what happened next, just before 1300, has wiped my memory clean of details about that incident.

Suddenly the GQ gong clanged a sharp warning, a bugler blew off a few sharp notes, and then someone on the bridge interrupted to roar over the feedback screech of the bullhorn: ALL HANDS! MAN YOUR BATTLE STATIONS!

On the double I hot-footed from the fighter on which I had been working and ran towards Bill's rearming magazine to get my steel helmet. I couldn't run fast enough. Halfway there, closer to starboard near the island, I hit the deck. Guns big and little had been banging away all around me and I cringed with the noise as if I was their target. Rolling over, I was astonished to see our portside 40mm mounts, elevated slightly, firing across the deck to starboard. I felt the shells whistling by over my head. My ears throbbed with pain. Old shipmate ACOM B.C., of all people, ran up, one hand holding his own helmet down, the other offering me another—which I accepted gratefully.
"Are you stupid or what?" he yelled. "Get off the dingdamn deck! Lookit up there! They're comin' down on us!" And away he ran like the Arkansas jackrabbit he was.

I looked up in the direction he'd been pointing. Sure enough, one high, small dot grew rapidly in size as it headed down toward the centerline of our flightdeck. My skinny ass remained glued to the deck. I was mesmerized by the calamity about to strike my ship and me.
Except that it didn't. The tiny dot (now with the visible wings of an airplane) banked sharply to the left and headed straight for sister ship CVL Cabot, two thousand yards on our starboard bow.

On my feet at last, I ran to where Captain Jim, skipper of our Marine contingent that manned the forward starboard 40mm batteries, was observing the action.

Our guns had stopped firing at this attacker due to the danger of hitting Cabot. The enemy plane swept down and down on an invisible string and crashed with a great billowing burst of red and orange flame on Cabot's port bow. Many men died before my eyes; many others probably wished they had. Debris from the flightdeck spewed into the air. The ship itself shuddered and rocked but didn't lose a knot of speed.

Captain Jim, his head concealed within his large communication helmet, ears covered by a headset, was barking into the phone.

From the corner of my eye I saw a ship's photographer lift his camera and focus on an object to starboard behind burning Cabot. The object was another larger plane diving in a sloping descent toward the after end of CV Intrepid, her stern obscured by boiling white water as her screws tried vainly to push her out of danger. The sky was pockmarked with AA bursts.

Our photographer continued to snap away as if he had the whole world in focus. Captain Jim jumped up and down in frustration; his 40mm guns were useless. Every soul there on the bridge or in the gun tubs forward of us was no more than a witness to the inevitable.

From Intrepid's deck near her large island a great flash of flame and black smoke soared skyward as the attacker found his mark. Many more men died.

The piloted airplane had penetrated her flightdeck and crashed through to the hangar, setting off raging fires. But these had barely flashed into life when a second kamikaze approached at high speed, also from aft. It crashed so violently that it too went through the flightdeck. Its bomb also exploded in the hangar. Another great burst of debris, flame, and smoke shot upward and temporarily knocked the ship out of action. Seventy-five airplanes that Intrepid had aloft were forced to land on other flattops.

Alongside us, fifteen hundred yards to starboard, handsome battle cruiser Alaska's bow hove into view. She must have been turning up her advertised thirty-three knots. All guns except the nine rifles of her 12-inch main battery were firing away in every direction—including ours. The instinct to duck was powerful. We all stood there frozen stupidly, unable to move.

Our photographer, less than ten feet from my side, shot so many frames so quickly I thought his camera would burst. He vanished when he ran out of film.

CV's Hancock and Essex in 38.1 were hit that day by other kamikazes but were able to keep operating. Fifteen men died in fire and wreckage on Hancock. Essex escaped serious damage this time because the Judy attacking her struck only an edge of the deck before plunging into the sea. (Neither she nor Hancock would again be so lucky.)

Four of the seven carriers in the two groups had taken hits. A total of one hundred-seven men died. Hundreds were injured. Even Bill Halsey had had enough. He knew he'd been forced to keep his flattops too close to Luzon too long. We all retreated to Ulithi to lick our wounds, repair damage, and allow time for wise ones to decide how to counter this new menace. 25 November 1944 was a hard day.

Never before had the fast carriers suffered such a beating. **DL**

Note; The CABOT was hit by 2 kamikazes - reported as Zekes. One hit the flight deck, the other a near miss hitting close aboard the port quarter, where the #2 gun tub was carried away. (Thirty six CABOT crewmembers were killed and / or were missing in action, with 16 more seriously injured - Source - "Bull Halsey" by E.B. Potter)

Sunday 26 November 1944   *Steaming to Ulithi Atoll*

Steaming as before at a night flying station. Task Group 38.2 is retiring from Luzon to proceed to Ulithi Atoll. INDEPENDENCE has 2 F6Fs airborne on CAP.

0115 Completed recovery of 2 F6Fs launched at 2142. Then changed course to 108°T and began zigzagging on that base course.

0531 Sounded routine torpedo defense.

0552 Commenced maneuvering to regain station within TG 38.2.

0634 Secured from torpedo defense.

0643 Regained position in TG 38.2, bearing 070°T, 2,300 yards from guide USS NEW JERSEY. Commenced zigzagging on base course 108°T.

0800 Mustered crew on stations. Absentees: AMM3c Edward Ricci, lost overboard at 1920 on 25 November 1944 when Lt. Wolfe's landing F6F collided with the island structure.

0930 Jettisoned overboard 1 F6F-5(N) (Bu.No. 58364) damaged beyond repair during the collision into the island structure.

1055 Commenced maneuvering to gain position bearing 090°T, 2,000 yards from USS INTREPID.

1114 Gained position off INTREPID and commenced sending logistic report by semaphore. Semaphore signaling proved unsatisfactory, used visual means to transmit the message.

1125 Commenced maneuvering to regain position off USS NEW JERSEY.

1310 Changed course to 117°T.

1400-1425 Half masted colors following movements of USS INTREPID (as INTREPID held services committing her dead to the sea, from the action on 25 November).

1530 Sounded flight quarters.

1715 Proceeded to our night flying station with USS MILLER and USS THE SULLIVANS.

1729 Launched 2 TBMs for ASP.

1739 Sounded routine torpedo defense.

1753 Launched 1 TBM.

1811 Gained night flying station bearing 060°T, 12,000 yards from guide, NEW JERSEY.

1834 Secured from torpedo defense.

1828 Recovered 2 TBMs launched at 1729.

2130 Launched 2 TBMs for ASP.

2201 Recovered 2 TBMs launched at 1753 and 1811. Then changed course to 130°T, speed to 26 knots.

GL After being awake two days, we headed for Ulithi Island. GL

Monday 27 November 1944   *Steaming to Ulithi Atoll*

Steaming as before proceeding to Ulithi Atoll, Caroline Islands. CVL-22 is operating at a night flying station accompanied by USS MILLER and USS THE SULLIVANS as a detached Task Unit, 38.2.10, bearing 250°T, 12,000 yards from the guide in TG 38.2. There are 2 TBMs in the air as ASP.

0155 Maneuvering into the wind to conduct flight operations.

0157-0203 Recovered 2 TBMs launched at 2131. Then, began maneuvering to regain station.

0503 Sounded routine torpedo defense.

0518 Completed recovery of 2 TBMs launched at 0131.

0530 Commenced maneuvering to rejoin the Task Group.

0606 Secured from torpedo defense. Air Department is set to condition 14.

0623 Assumed station bearing 070°T, 2,500 yards from guide, USS NEW JERSEY, course 124°T, speed 24 knots.

0912-0920 Passed through heavy rain squall. Visibility reduced to 1,000 yards.

1150 INDEPENDENCE became guide.

1520 Sounded flight quarters.

1524 Sighted Ulithi Atoll, bearing 171°T, distance 16 miles.

1604 Landed 1 F6F transferred to INDEPENDENCE from USS HANCOCK.

1630 Commenced maneuvering into column for entering Ulithi Atoll.

1647 Secured from flight quarters. Air Department set to condition 14.

1701 Sounded general quarters.

1715 Changed course to 299°T, speed 20 knots and entered Mugai Channel.

1718 Passed Mangejang Island abeam to port.

1720 Entered Ulithi Atoll, passing the anti-submarine net abeam to starboard.

1733 Commenced maneuvering toward Berth 36.

1753 Secured from general quarters. Gunnery Department set to special harbor condition 2.

1829 Anchored in 16 fathoms of water with 100 fathoms of chain beyond Berth 36, anchoring within Berth 46 due to another vessel being anchored in the center of the Berth 36.

1850 No.4 boiler in use for auxiliary purposes.

AD At 1600 we arrived at Ulithi. Saw a movie on the hangar deck ("The Invaders") in the evening. AD

Tuesday 28 November 1944   *Ulithi Atoll*

0800 Anchored as before, in 16 fathoms of water, coral bottom with 100 fathoms of chain, in Berth 46, Ulithi Atoll. Mustered crew at quarters.

1400 The following replacement pilots reported on board for duty with CLVG(N)-41:

Lt. K.H. Morris, Lt. Baker A. Bradenbaugh, Ensigns Lester H. Diskosky, Benjamin R. Houden, Fred A. Hunziker, Warren G. Light and Donald R. Powers.

RC Went aboard Intrepid, her hangar deck pretty badly burnt. *RC*

AD Anchored at Ulithi. Intrepid is going back. *AD*

Wednesday 29 November 1944   *Ulithi Atoll*

0230 Anchored as before. LCM 68 cast off after delivering foul weather equipment.
0600 LCM 80 secured along port side to deliver stores.
0640 LCM 81 secured along starboard side to deliver stores.
0730 LCM 80 and LCM 81 cast off
0800 Mustered crew on stations.
1000 Ships No.1 motor whale boat was damaged while being hauled out on skids. The hole stove in the bottom of the hull was repaired by the crew.
1459 Launched 1 F6F-5N for return to USS INTREPID air group on the airfield at Ulithi Atoll. The Hellcat had landed on board on 25 November.
2315 LCT 899 secured to port side aft to deliver 5 drums of oil.

AD Anchored, I went on a beer party on one of the islands called Mog Mog. Beer was good, so was land. *AD*

Thursday 30 November 1944   *Ulithi Atoll* - **Captain Ewen awarded Navy Cross**

Anchored as before. The ship is preparing for sea again, receiving stores and ammunition.
0902 Captain Ewen left the ship to proceed to USS HANCOCK.
1035 Tug 143 placed YO-104 along port side.
1145 Captain Ewen returned to the INDEPENDENCE from USS HANCOCK, where he had been awarded the Navy Cross by Admiral William F. Halsey, Commander, Third Fleet.
1230 USS ENOREE moored to the port side. At 1541 USS ENOREE had cast off having delivered 269,300 gallons of fuel oil and 35,820 gallons of aviation gasoline.
2215 LCT 7336 came alongside to deliver ammunition and fuses.
2315 LCT 7336 cast off.

GN Word is received that the Intrepid * is heading for the States (again). She is going to make sure she holds that title " Queen of the Drydocks." Hancock and Cabot are being repaired here. *GN*
    Note: INTREPID would steam to Hunters Point for repairs, from Ulithi, via Eniwetok and Pearl Harbor.

RC Had big Thanksgiving dinner. *RC*

AD Anchored at Ulithi. We had our Thanksgiving Dinner today. *AD*

Friday 1 December 1944   *Ulithi Atoll*

0520 Anchored as before. Lighted fires under No. 4 boiler. Made preparations for getting underway.
0800 Mustered crew on stations. No absentees.
0806 Got underway in company with TG 38.2.1 (less USS TICONDEROGA) with USS LEXINGTON and USS HANCOCK. They were also accompanied by USS HORNET and USS MONTEREY. LEXINGTON has Rear Admiral G.F. Bogan as OTC and CTU 38.2.1, as well as CTG 38.2.
0807 Commenced maneuvering on various courses at various speeds conforming to the channel.
0822 Sounded general quarters.
0825 Passed anti-submarine nets at Mugai Channel entrance, Ulithi Atoll.
0829 Passed channel entrance buoy No.1 abeam to starboard.
0850 Secured from general quarters.
0854 Maneuvered to take station in cruising disposition 5R, axis 060°T. Admiral Halsey directed the

TG to return to the anchorage at Ulithi the following morning. The remainder of the day, the ship conducted training exercises near Ulithi.

0919 Gained station, changing course to 115°T, speed 15 knots, bearing 210°T, 2,500 yards from guide, USS NEW JERSEY.

1458 USS VINCENNES, MIAMI and PASADENA, with accompanying destroyers, joined the formation, taking their respective positions.

1521 Lighted fires under No. 1 boiler.

1530 Sounded flight quarters.

1634 Cut No.1 boiler into main steam line. USS LEXINGTON, PASADENA and SAN JUAN left the formation to form TG 38.5. Rear Admiral Joseph J. Clark is now OTC of TG 38.2 in USS HORNET.

1720 Sounded routine torpedo defense.

1819 Secured from torpedo defense.

2155 Commenced zigzagging (plan No.6) on base course 110°T.

AD   Underway at 0800, cruising around, may go back to Ulithi tomorrow. AD

GL   Left Ulithi but returned next morning because Typhoon around the Philippines. GL

RC   Left Ulithi for battle zone. Run into storm so at noon we head back for Ulithi. RC

(The reason for the return to Ulithi was the delay of a scheduled invasion by McArthur of Mindoro. The Task Force steamed out on December 1st. to support the invasion. The pushback of the schedule allowed the fleet to turn back for the much needed rest and relaxation.)

Saturday 2 December 1944   *Return to Ulithi Atoll*

Steaming as before as TG 38.2.1 in company with USS HANCOCK and USS MONTEREY. Temporarily in command of TG 38.2 is Rear Admiral J.J. Clark in USS HORNET, as USS LEXINGTON is temporarily detached from TG 38.2. Air Department is in condition 11.

0340 Commenced zigzagging on base course 130°T.

0345 Radar reports land, Ulithi Atoll, 60 degrees to starboard bearing 190°T, at 24 miles.

0445 Sounded torpedo defense.

0513 Commenced maneuvering to gain position in column, INDEPENDENCE 4,000 yards from guide.

0543 Launched 4 F6Fs to proceed to Ulithi Atoll airstrip on Falalop Island. The air group intends to conduct refresher training from the airstrip while the ship is at anchor in the atoll.

0555 Gained position in column and commenced maneuvering to conform to channel.

0622 Sounded general quarters.

0637 Passed buoys No. 1 & 2 at entrance to Mugai Channel, Ulithi Atoll.

0653 Secured from general quarters. Gunnery Department set to special harbor condition 2.

0707 Anchored in berth No. 31, in 9 fathoms of water, coral bottom, with120 fathoms of port chain.

0745 Let fires die out and secured No.1 boiler.

0800 Mustered crew on stations.

0930 Set Air Department to condition 11 with 4 Hellcats ready to catapult.

1115 Air Department set to condition 14.

1615 Grant D. Whippin with the Airborne Coordinating Group reported on board for temporary duty with the VF(N)-41.

GL Went on beach island of Mog-Mog and had 4 cans of warm beer, also went swimming and got a mild sunburn. GL

Sunday 3 December 1944   *Ulithi Atoll - Anchored   Repainting the Hull*

During this stopover at Ulithi, the ship took on supplies, topped off provisions and fuel. Maintenance on the ship was carried out and the side of the hull was repainted.

Monday 4 December 1944   *Ulithi Atoll - Anchored*   *Repainting the Hull*

1630 LCT 385 moored alongside starboard returning a liberty party rammed the INDEPENDENCE causing a large 5'4" long hole in the hull roughly 3' above the waterline at frame 102.

Tuesday 5 December 1944   *Ulithi Atoll - Anchored*   *Repainting the Hull*

Damage to the hull caused by LCT 385 ramming the side was repaired by ships crew members.

Wednesday 6 December 1944   *Ulithi Atoll - Anchored*   *Repainting the Hull*

GL *December 3-10 Anchored at Ulithi spent time bringing on supplies and painting ship.* *GL*

Thursday 7 December 1944   *Ulithi Atoll - Anchored*   *Repainting the Hull*

1545 Anchored as before. LCT 385 Came alongside to starboard returning a liberty party.
1602-1605 LCT 388 was alongside port quarter to deliver drums of lubricating oil.
2015 Motor Whaleboat No.1 returned to INDEPENDENCE having sustained damage at about 1900. The boat ran afoul a 200' line running aft from the USS COWPENS, damaging the gunwales, carrying away the aft railing, and losing overboard the compass and binnacle. No injuries to personnel. In the evening, 2 INDEPENDENCE Hellcats flew a mission from the Falalop Island airbase to raid Japanese installations on Yap Island.

Friday 8 December 1944 *Ulithi Atoll - Anchored as before*

1240 YOGL-6 was towed by US Navy Tug 143 and moored to the port side of INDEPENDENCE.
1256 YO-76 came up along the port side and tied up.
1308-1455 Received 70,630 gallons of fuel oil from YO-76. Fifteen minutes later she cast off.
1620 Tug 143 removed YOGL-6 from the port side and took it in tow.
1818 Enemy air raid probable, set condition 2. The shore station reported an unidentified aircraft.
1820 Enemy air raid imminent. Set condition 1.
1822 Sounded torpedo defense. At 1825 torpedo defense was upgraded to general quarters.
1856 All clear issued by SOPA. Secured from general quarters.

AD *Anchored, Jap scare — all hands to GQ. Japs bypassed us.* *AD*

Monday 11 December 1944   *Underway From Ulithi Atoll, Exercises at Sea*

0348 Anchored as before. Lit fires under No.3 boiler, and commenced jacking over the main engines.
0445 Lit fires under No.2 boiler.
0600 Cut boiler No.3 into main steam line.
0716 Got underway with USS LEXINGTON and USS CABOT in company with TG 38.2.
Rear Admiral G.F. Bogan is CTG 38.2 and CTU 38.2.1 in LEXINGTON (OTC). Steaming in accordance with secret operational orders dated 10 December, 1944.
0721 Commenced maneuvering to conform to the channel.
0726 Sounded general quarters.
0730 Passed the anti-submarine nets at the entrance of Mugai Channel.
0747 Departed off Mas Island, bearing 324°T, 4 miles.
0800 Set clocks back 1 hour.
0718 (Clock set back) Commenced maneuvering to gain station in formation 5R. USS HANCOCK and USS HORNET joined the formation.
0723 Secured from general quarters, Air Department remained at flight quarters.
0730 Attained position in the formation, bearing 270°T, 2,500 yards from guide USS SAN JUAN.

Changed course to 000°T, speed 18 knots.

0800 Mustered crew on stations. No absentees.

0828 Changed fleet course to 080°T.

0838 Recovered 4 F6Fs, operating out of the airstrip on Falalop Island (Ulithi Atoll) since launching from INDEPENDENCE at 1000 on December 2nd.

0841 Secured from flight quarters. Air Department set to condition 14.

1128 Changed fleet course to 295°T. At 1146, commenced maneuvering to form a firing disposition 1,000 yards astern the USS LEXINGTON, in a column.

1222 Sounded torpedo defense for gunnery exercises.

1242-1345 Fired automatic weapons for anti-aircraft practice on a towed sleeve. Expended 2,441 rounds of 40mm, and 706 rounds of 20mm ammunition. Then secured from torpedo defense.

1353 Commenced maneuvering with all engines at full speed to regain position in disposition 5R, bearing 270°T, 2,500 yards from guide in center of the formation.

1443 Changed fleet course to 295°T, speed 23 knots.

1530 Sounded flight quarters as an exercise.

1620 USS LEXINGTON designated as guide.

1654 Ships from TG 34.5 joined the formation.

1710 USS NEW JERSEY assumed guide.

1727 Changed course to 300°T, speed 24 knots.

Task Group 38.2 now had 3 CVs, 2 CVLs, 3 BBs, 4 CLs, 1 CLAA and 20 DDs. TG 32.1 & TG 38.3 were of a somewhat similar composition. They headed toward a fueling rendezvous.

GL *Left Ulithi with Lexington, Hornet, Hancock, Cabot, New Jersey, Iowa, Wisconsin.* *GL*

RC *Leave Ulithi for battle zone to cover invasion of Mindoro.* *RC*

Tuesday 12 December 1944   *Underway at Sea*

0518 Steaming as before. Sounded routine torpedo defense.

0549 Changed fleet course to 030°T, speed 24 knots.

0622 Secured from torpedo defense.

0714 Changed fleet speed to 20 knots, all engines ahead standard.

0726 USS CABOT designated guide.

0734 USS NEW JERSEY reassigned guide.

0800 Mustered crew on stations. During the day, air groups from other carriers conducted training exercises in preparation for upcoming operations against the Japanese on Luzon.

0935 Changed course to 300°T. USS LEXINGTON became fleet guide.

1132 USS NEW JERSEY reassigned as fleet guide.

0935 Changed course to 300°T. USS LEXINGTON became fleet guide.

1132 USS NEW JERSEY reassigned as fleet guide.

1530 Sounded flight quarters.

1715 Commenced steering various courses at various speeds while leaving the formation to form TU 38.3.10. Captain E.C. Ewen is CTU.

1746 Sounded routine torpedo defense.

1756 Proceeded to our night flying station windward of TG 38.2. USS NEW JERSEY is 14,000 yards away, bearing 290°T. We are accompanied by destroyers USS BRUSH, USS BLUE, USS TAUSSIG and USS SAMUEL N. MOORE.

1845 Secured from torpedo defense.

GL *They now give us 4 destroyers instead of 2 when we leave the task group for night operations.* *GL*

Wednesday 13 December 1944   *Refueling and briefing for the run in on Manila*

1845 Secured from torpedo defense.

GL They now give us 4 destroyers instead of 2 when we leave the task group for night operations. GL

Wednesday 13 December 1944   *Refueling and briefing for the run in on Manila*

0543 Rejoined Task Unit 38.2.1 in company with USS LEXINGTON (OTC), USS HORNET, USS CABOT, USS HANCOCK, a part of Task Group 38.2. Course 070°T, speed 15 knots Cruising disposition 5R, axis 060°T.
0548 Sounded torpedo defense.
0615 USS MASCOMA became guide.
0648 Secured from torpedo defense. Air Department set condition 14.
0703 Came along side USS MASCOMA to begin taking on fuel oil, speed 8 knots (78 rpm).

AD *At sea. Receiving fuel. Strike tomorrow at Manila area. We are invading Mindoro. Planes from our ship will bomb Japs all through the night. There will be plenty going on and the Japs will be pretty damn busy.* **AD**

0810 Received 10 bottles of aviators breathing oxygen from MASCOMA.
0847 Cast off from the tanker having received 137,100 gallons of fuel oil.
1037-1047 USS MILLER was along the starboard side to transfer guard mail.
1137-1148 USS THE SULLIVANS was along the starboard side to receive personnel. Two pilots left the INDEPENDENCE for transfer to the USS HORNET.
1300 USS NEW JERSEY assumed fleet guide bearing 100°T, distance 2,500 yards.
With fleet speed and course changes throughout the afternoon, at 1530 flight quarters was sounded on a course of 285°T, speed 22 knots.
1742 The INDEPENDENCE Task Unit proceeded to a night flying station.

As Captain Ewen retired for the evening he would leave the following Standing Orders:

*"Cruising as Task Group 38.2.10 consisting of the INDEPENDENCE guide in center with the following DD's: HUNT, HICOCK **, LEWIS HANCOCK, and SPENCE. Axis of this formation is 085°T.*
Guide of T.G. 38.2 bears 260°T at 14,000 yards.
We are making a night "run in" to strike airfields in Luzon tomorrow.
We have 2 VF(N) in condition eleven on the catapults. If Bogy is picked up direct Fly Control to start engines immediately. Call me at the same time.
Call me immediately if radar makes either surface or air contact.
Keep all hands alert. Read over carefully instructions to DD's operating with Group 2. Course 247°T. Speed 23 knots.
Follow Melrose in changes in course and / or speed which may always be expected over T.B.S.
We expect to launch 2 VF(N) at 0400 if we have not done so before that time.
Call me at 0300." (** Note - the correct spelling is HICKOX)

(NY times photo
provided by Roy Berkheimer)

L to R - William E. *"Bill"* Henry, James Arden *"Barney"* Barnett, Wallace E. *"Wally"* Miller, Jack Stanley *"Berky"* Berkheimer. VF(N)41 Night Stalkers counting their kills.

- Lt. Henry received the Distinguished Flying Cross, the Air Medal, the Navy Cross and Gold Star in lieu of a third Distinguished Flying Cross, and a Gold Star in Lieu of a second Air Medal.
- Lt.(jg) Barnett received the Distinguished Flying Cross and the Air Medal.
- Lt.(jg) Miller received the Distinguished Flying Cross and the Air Medal.
- Ens. Berkheimer received the Navy Cross, the Air Medal and Gold Star in lieu of a second Air Medal.

Aboard USS INDEPENDENCE - Avenger crew in VT(N)-41
L to R - Howard Parry, George L. Franke, Jr., Donald M. Linton (pilot)

18
Operation Obliteration
Mindoro Invasion

Task Force 38 was assigned to attack targets on Mindoro and Luzon (Philippine Islands). This was in support of Army landings during the assault and occupation of Mindoro. Naval airpower was to neutralize Japanese air power, and attack shipping to deny access to Luzon's harbors If successful, air operations would prevent enemy attacks from developing against the fleet. (Map page 334)

Aircraft from the INDEPENDENCE would (from 14 December through 16 December) fly 35 night sorties in 9 separate heckling missions. They would also furnish Combat Air Patrols for the Task Force throughout the nights, and predawn periods. These Combat Air Patrols would prevent the Japanese from gaining knowledge of the approaching fleet's location.

INDEPENDENCE with its Air Group CVLG(N)-41 and her screen of 4 DD's split off from Task Group 38.2 to deploy as a Special Task Organization known as Task Unit 38.2.10, assigned to operate as a Night Carrier Unit. As darkness fell, the INDEPENDENCE Task Unit would steam off from 38.2 as she conducted night operations under command of Captain E.C. Ewen.

Thursday 14 December 1944   *Philippines, Luzon - "OPERATION OBLITERATION"*

0350 Steaming on a course of 120°T at 23 knots.
Radar condition Four was in effect during the approach. Only the ships SM radar was being used for air search. The U.S.S. INDEPENDENCE and its DD screen had been operating at its' night station since sunset, with night fighters in condition 11 on the catapults. Orders were received to launch 2 F6F(N)s at 0400 for CAP to cover the dawn strike launchings. Lt. W.E. Henry and Ens. J. A. Barnett were in their planes preparatory to this planned CAP. (At approximately 0330 orders were received to turn on the INDEPENDENCE SK radar, which did not become effective until almost 0400.)

0353 Bogey bearing 260°T, 42 miles reported by USS HANCOCK. CVL-22 launched 2 F6F-5N's immediately (by orders from OTC) and changing course to 247°T. Night, no moon, visibility 5 miles. Henry and Barnett were catapulted. Barnett was sent on a 020°T course, to orbit at Angels 1, 20 miles from base. Henry was immediately vectored south to intercept the bogey which was on a fairly steady 120°T course at Angels 2, speed 120-125 knots, crossing. Apparently this bogey, flying low, was making no attempt to confuse possible night fighter opposition by resorting to the use of window or such usual evasive tactics as changes in speed and altitude, or 360 degree turns. As Henry continued on his southerly vector, the bogey's southeasterly course brought it from 42 miles distant to approximately 30 miles from the INDEPENDENCE, at which point, it began to open again.
Henry made contact on his APS-6A gear at 0411, *"bogey at 2 miles, twelve o'clock"* when the ship's screen showed the bogey at 185°, 38 miles out. Shortly afterwards, when Henry had closed to half a mile, he made visual contact on the exhaust flames of an Emily four engine flying boat, as he continued to close. The Emily was flying at 125 knots (at 1,000'), so Henry lost altitude and speed to get into position to attack. Bill fired three bursts from four of his 50's into the Emily's engine area from 6 o'clock level. The Emily immediately began to lose altitude in a turning glide, crashing into the water at 0415. Flames enveloped it, and the Emily continued to burn for some time. The action occurred approximately 40 miles south of the base.

During portions of Bill Henry's interception, the INDEPEDENCE radar information was poor, due probably to the low altitude at which the planes were flying. The HANCOCK, nearer to the scene of the action, took over the interception on these occasions and provided valuable aid in retaining contact.

Lt. William E. Henry, in shooting down his ninth victim, received a "Well Done" from both CTG 38.2 and CTF 38 for his intelligent, aggressive action. The entire interception required only 22 minutes from the time Lt. Henry was launched, although the Emily was shot down 40 miles out and opening.

0437 Changed course to 050°T. 0440 launched 1 F6F.
Shortly after, Bill Henry's APS 6A gear was not functioning properly. Lt. Fredrick H. Hankins was catapulted at 0439 to replace him. All three VF(N) remained in the air, but no further bogies were reported.
0437 Changed course to 050°T.
0440 Launched 1 F6F.
0605 Sounded routine general quarters on a course of 247°T, 25 knots.
0658 Steaming on a course of 105°T, speed 22 knots.

0707 Lt. Fredrick H. Hankins had launched at 0440. Returning to land, slow and low in the approach, he received a wave off from the LSO. Lifting the nose of the Hellcat in an attempt to comply, he was not able to gain altitude, and trying to avoid the ships structure (radar & stacks) he stalled and spun in.
Lt. Hankins' F6F-5N Hellcat (Bu.No.71253) dove into the sea at a 35° - 45° angle. INDEPENDENCE crew members observed the Hellcat buckle just aft of the cockpits armor plate and sank rapidly.
USS HICKOX steamed to the crash site to attempt to rescue the pilot, however nothing could be found in the area. His position was 16°-20'N, 124°-16'E.

0718 Recovered 2 Hellcats flown by Henry and Barnett, launched at 0355.
0721 Maneuvered to regain position in the Task Group, secured from general quarters.
0743 Secured from flight quarters, Air Department set condition 14. Throughout the morning, numerous speed and course changes were made, and the crew had been mustered to quarters at 0830. During the day, the Task Force maintained a "Big Blue Blanket" of fighters over Luzon to suppress Japanese air strikes against the fleet.
1415 Sounded flight quarters
1440 On a course of 130°T, speed 24 knots they made radar contact with an unidentified bogy bearing 230°T at 30 miles.
1444 Sounded torpedo defense.
1452 Aircraft identified as friendly. 1457 Secured from torpedo defense.
1601 Steamed at various courses and speeds to take up Night Flying Station in company with destroyer screen; USS BLUE, USS DYSON, USS SAMUEL N. MOORE and USS TAUSSIG.
1640 New course 125°T, speed 24 knots for flight operations.

1648 INDEPENDENCE catapulted six F6F-5N Hellcats, each carrying two 500# GP bombs for twilight and night heckling missions against major airfields, AA positions and facilities around Luzon. Visibility was estimated at 20 miles straight and level for lighted objects, but reduced near the ground due to dense haze. No moonlight. The Hellcats encountered no aerial opposition. AA fire put up by the Japanese was described as moderate to intense.

The Hellcats were flown by Comdr. Turner F. Caldwell, and Ensigns Joe Sam Allen, Gayle V. Williams, Irvin H. Lee, Harold E. Johnson, and Rueben F. Peterson.

From AAR #II-22:
"After effecting rendezvous over the ship, they headed west toward Luzon, flying low. As they approached the coast, they climbed to 7000'. The sun was still up, so Comdr. CALDWELL instructed all planes to orbit until sunset. It was felt, since these six planes were to cover practically all of Luzon, it would be too dangerous to arrive over the target areas while it was still daylight, in such small numbers.

As the sun was setting, Comdr. CALDWELL headed for Lingayen Gulf, ALLEN and WILLIAMS for the Clark area. PETERSON, JOHNSON, and LEE headed southwest together, since they were scheduled to cover the Lake Taal area, southern and northern Manila respectively.

PETERSON, JOHNSON and LEE flew at 150' in a three plane closed V formation, with JOHNSON in the lead. When they were about 10 miles northeast of Manila, AA opened up on them from a point apparently just north of the reported site at Balara. JOHNSON immediately radioed to the others that his cockpit was full of oil and that his oil pressure was dropping. PETERSON continued south, but LEE stayed with JOHNSON, suggesting he head east towards the mountains. JOHNSON, after announcing his intention to do so, zoomed up and jettisoned his bombs, and shortly after, his engine froze altogether. LEE saw him head toward and make a perfect forced landing in a small, shallow lake about two miles east of Novaliches Rizal.

This lake is just above the Balara air field site. LEE in the meantime had also jettisoned his bombs, and, with both wheels and flaps down, circled the lake at deck level, until he saw JOHNSON out of his plane and wading toward shore, waving his arms to indicate he was all right.
LEE then left the scene after complete darkness had set in and, proceeding to Grace Park airfield, made a strafing run at 2000' on the wooded area east of the strip.
LEE then climbed above some marginal clouds and headed north to Mt. Arayat hoping to rendezvous with WILLIAMS for the trip back to base. He was unable to contact WIILIAMS, but did notice a plane crash and burn about 2 miles south of Clark #2 airstrip. The whole Clark area was "a solid sheet of AA" and, shortly after, LEE saw a second plane go down in that area, exploding as it hit the ground. It was thought that ALLEN had possibly shot down a Jap plane and had himself been hit by AA just afterward. Allen's plane was the only friendly otherwise unaccounted for in the Clark area.
LEE proceeded back east alone, dropping window as he did so, and landed aboard without further incident.
PETERSON, who had continued south after JOHNSON'S forced landing, went on to Lake Taal area, dropping his bombs in separate runs on the darkened West Lipa airfield. Some AA was thrown up at him, but he evaded it by diving to 500', weaving in the dive. From there he flew down to the Batangas air-field, but was unable to distinguish it in the darkness. On the way back, he saw a lighted truck, near the SW shore of Laguna del Bay, and, after zooming it once, returned to make one strafing run over it. Its lights were immediately doused, so PETERSON does not know what damage he did. He headed north-east toward the sea and base.

WILLIAMS had gone directly to the Clark area from the break-up point on the east coast . Just west of Mt. Arayat, AA began to come up, so he headed north to Mabalacat #1 field. He saw two fresh bomb craters on that field, probably dropped by ALLEN, whose assignment included the two Mabalacat fields. WILLIAMS then headed toward Clark #2. The AA trained on him again, so he turned north and then west toward Mt. Arayat. Seeing red lights moving northward on the N-S highway east of Dan Junction, WILLIAMS made a short strafing run over them. The truck burst into flames as though it were loaded with gasoline.
As WILLIAMS continued toward Arayat, three searchlights from positions around Arayat played on him and AA started to come up from just east of Dan Junction.
Circling Mt. Arayat at 6000', he saw that the lights had gone out. He went back near the positions, blinking his running lights as he did. The lights flashed on again and WILLIAMS dived down strafing. The lights were doused again and WILLIAMS decided to head home.
Just as he started, he heard ALLEN, on radio, asking him if he was the plane " over Clark with the lights". WILLIAMS said he was not, then continued east to the coast and to base. He heard nothing further from ALLEN, although he tried to raise him several times for the trip back home. Information supplied by LEE and WILLIAMS provides the principal clues to ALLENs disappearance. He possibly reconnoitered his assigned field in the northern Clark area, dropping his bombs on Mabalacat #1. After this he may have seen a strange plane, and, after having checked with WILLIAMS to make sure it wasn't he, attacked and shot the plane down. Then he may have been hit by AA and crashed himself. However, Lt. W. R. TAYLOR, VT(N) 41 Commander, was on his way in on the second heckler mission at

the time WILLIAMS had tried to raise ALLEN. TAYLOR is certain he heard ALLEN call, in an interrogating manner, two or more times after the two planes had crashed, in an attempt to contact WILLIAMS. ALLEN did not return, is regarded as missing.

Comdr. CALDWELL proceeded directly from the east coast break-up point past Rosales field where he saw no planes or activity. He continued on to Lingayen field, which he buzzed at 300 knots, 50' off the deck.
No planes or activity were noted here either. Heading up the west coast, he saw a considerable amount of shipping just off Agoo. A small jetty runs out into the water. Just north of it was a Sugar Baker, lying parallel to the beach.
300-400 yards outboard lay another Sugar Baker at anchor; and a few hundred yards north of those two were 2 Sugar Charlies and 3 Sugar Dogs. It was still not dark, so Comdr. CALDWELL continued his reconnoitering up the coastline. Along the road which paralleled the coast, a convoy of 5 trucks doused its lights, one by one, as the VF(N) plane flew over them. At San Fernando Point, a small 1500 ton freighter evidently hard hit, was beached on the south side. Two Sugar Bakers also at anchor off the south side of the point, about 500 yards out from the beach. Inside San Fernando harbor, on the north side of the point, 20-25 Sugar Dogs and miscellaneous other craft and barges were seen. None seemed to be underway. Continuing north, Comdr. CALDWELL made out the Luna field strip. He saw no activity, but east of the strip a heavy clump of woods indicated an excellent potential hiding place for aircraft. Comdr. CALDWELL went on until he reached Laoag field. No planes, nor apparent activity were seen, but Comdr, CALDWELL dropped a 500 pounder on what appeared to be hangars or service buildings on the east side of the field. Whatever it was, he feels he hit the target, although he was unable to check results.
Heading back south, Comdr. CALDWELL made a steep, east to west, gliding beam attack on the outboard one of the 2 Sugar Bakers off Agoo Point. The ship was, by sheer good luck, silhouetted by the narrow beam of light provided by the evening star. As he pulled up sharply after his drop" Comdr. CALDWELL saw smoke from the detonation, indicating his bomb had landed dead center". He circled, then flew low along the side of the ship after the smoke had cleared. The ship had broken in the middle and was going down. As he circled again, Comdr. CALDWELL saw the ship's after portion awash and still settling. Waves were breaking over the stern. This ship was in position 16 - 22 N, 120 - 18 E, Time 1937. It is being claimed as definitely sunk. Comdr. CALDWELL then returned to base alone.

Pilots from the air group have been over Clark Field area several times before at night, yet this is the first time that either searchlights or AA fire has been encountered. The automatic fire was not only intense but accurate and seemed to be synchronized with the searchlights which seemed to be able to get "on" without much hesitation. Practically every important field, with the exception of those assigned to ALLEN and JOHNSON, was flown over or near, yet no airborne planes were seen and the only ground activity came from the fields indicated in the narrative above."   **AAR #II-22**

1757 On a course of 120°T, speed 20 knots (203 rpm) the ship commenced Flight Operations completing the launch of 3 additional Hellcats at 1803.
1815 Sounded torpedo defense. Secured from torpedo defense 1 hour later.
1838 Completed launching 4 TBM-1D Avengers, tasked to relieve the F6F night hecklers. They were each loaded with wing tanks and 12 100# GP bombs with delayed fuses. They would fly more than 200 miles over unfamiliar territory on a dark no moon night to find their assigned targets.

Lt.(jg) Robert R. Champaigne found assigned Bambam and Mabalacat airfields too dark, so he bombed Clark Field. Ensign John Dewis likewise found Del Carmen dark and dropped a flare to light up Clark where he bombed and strafed runways, revetments and dispersal areas. Ensign John Williams used his radar to navigate to his assigned target near the Lake Taal region, and bombed Batangas Field, then continued on to bomb and strafe barracks and a dispersal area at Lipa West. Circling north, he noticed trucks moving south. Near Calamba town, he bombed and strafed a large truck depot and a rail yards.

Lt. W.R. "Bill" Taylor used a flare to light up Nichols #1 and proceeded to bomb and strafe 6 twin engine planes parked beside the runway, setting fires. He stated he was certain he left them severely damaged. Bill continued on to strafe the runways at Las Pinas and aircraft dispersal areas at Nielson.

2109 Launched 3 Hellcats on a course of 110°T, speed 20 knots.

2136 Recovered 5 Hellcats launched at 1648. A F6F-5N Hellcat (Bu.No.71278) piloted by Ensign Joseph Samuel Allen and F6F-5N Hellcat (Bu.No.71309) piloted by Ensign Harold Eddy Johnson failed to return.

It was later learned that Ensign Johnson was rescued by Philippine guerrillas and returned.

2147 Recovered 2 F6F Hellcats launched at 1803.

2237 On a course of 080°T, speed 25 knots, INDEPENDENCE launched 4 Avengers.

2334 Launched 2 F6F Hellcats, course 060°T.

2355 Completed recovering 3 TBM Avengers launched at 1838, speed 22 knots, course 120°T.

One TBM-1D Avenger (Bu.No.45618) crashed into the port catwalk at frame 93. The pilot, Ens. John E. Dewis took the cut and hit the flight deck just as the ship rolled. Dewis and aircrew (Robert S. Barnes & Stafford E. Hardwick) managed to scramble for safety (the aircraft suspended by bent radio masts and its tail hook) before the totaled Avenger was dropped over the side. Davy Jones devoured another military treasure for his locker floor many fathoms below. (Note: The Deck Log list the TBM accident on 14 December. The AAR places the event ten minutes later at 0005 on 15 December)

GN First day of another series of strikes against Luzon and Manila. Are trying new tactics. Keeping a batch of fighters over target at all times to repel any attempts that may be made to get to the task force. Worked all day and night and lost five planes. Rescued two of the pilots. Not very much air opposition. GN

GL At 4:15 in the morning Bill Henry shot down a Emily – the whole operation took 17 minutes. Hit Mindoro during the day, met little air opposition. We are putting up heckler raids & C.A.P. all night. Destroyed 179 Jap planes. GL

HB We then headed back to hit Manila again on the 14th. Our ace, Henry, shot down one Emily. HB

AD Invasion of Mindoro. During the night we lost two of our pilots over Jap fields at Luzon. No dope yet about the invasion. Also no Jap planes over us. AD

Friday 15 December 1944 *Philippines, Luzon*
"OPERATION OBLITERATION" (Mindoro Invasion)

Steaming as before. There are 5 F6Fs and 5 TBMs in the air. Air Department is at flight quarters and the ship is darkened. The ship is at a night flying station in company with destroyer screen, USS BLUE, USS DYSON, USS SAMUEL N. MOORE and USS TAUSSIG. 0008 Changed course to 130°T. 0015-0025 Recovered 3 F6Fs launched at 2104, and 1 TBM launched at 1840.

From Action report Serial # 25:
"With a confused sea in the operating area, the recovery of aircraft on the night of 14-15 December was a hair-raising operation. The unfavorable characteristics of the CVL as a night carrier under normal conditions have been commented on in previous correspondence, but under the existing conditions on the night of 14-15 December the landings were both miraculous and breath-taking." **Captain E.C. Ewen**

0235-0245 Launched 6 F6F5Ns. Four were assigned a heckling mission, each armed with two 500# General Purpose bombs. Flown by Lt. Baker A. "Brady" Bradenbaugh and Ensigns James A. "Barney" Barnett, Benjamin R. "Spike" Houden and Fred A. "Honey" Hunziker, the Hellcats rendezvoused over the ship and headed west for targets over Luzon on a dark moonless night. Bradenbaugh dropped one of his bombs in a dispersal area between the Bambam airfields, and dropped the other at Clark #5 airstrip. Then he noticed a light in the night sky moving at 1,000' off his starboard wing. Maneuvering to its tail, he identified it as a twin engine Nick, Dinah or Irving (later identified as a Nick by checking silhouettes and exhaust flame patterns). He fired two bursts from 6 o'clock level, igniting the port engine. The Nick slipped into a steep glide, burning brightly, striking the ground and exploding southwest of Angeles West field. Barnett and Houden attacked shipping in the harbor at San Fernando Point, making bombing and strafing runs. Two "Fox Tare Dogs" disappeared. Hunziker dropped 1 bomb on Clark field #2 and the second bomb on a truck convoy, followed up with a strafing run on the same convoy. Due to the darkness of the night, the grass or sod airstrips were all but impossible to discern.

0310-0339 Recovered 4 TBMs launched at 2237 and 2 F6Fs launched at 2334.

1 F6F5N (Bu.No.58073) made a hard landing and broke its back. It ended up in the port catwalk at frame 95, causing further damage (to the damage done by the TBM). The pilot was uninjured. (This appears to be a Hellcat from the 2334 launch on 14 December, however it is incorrectly listed within AAR II-25 for the 0235-0245 launch on this date, or the Deck Log entry is in error.) Repair parties would have to attend to damage from both the TBM & F6F accidents, which included damaged wood flight deck planking and two port side antenna booms (frames 94 & 100) that were bent and damaged (they remained operational). The 40mm No.8 gun director was also damaged.

0600-0705 Manned general quarters stations.

0734-0746 Recovered 5 F6Fs launched at 0245.

0800 Changed course to 150°T, speed 27 knots, for flight operations.

0805 Landed 1 F6F launched at 0245. Then changed course to 300°T, speed 22 knots.

Task Group 38.2 had been returning westward since 0200. Steaming into the wind for flight operations required INDEPENDENCE to steer east, causing a separation from the TG by as far as 31 miles.

0821 Changed course to 325°T to avoid TG 38.1.

0824 Secured from flight quarters. Air Department set to condition 14.

0835 Sighted TG 38.2 bearing 295°T. Changed course to 265°T.

0859 Commenced maneuvering to regain station within TG 38.2.

0949 Gained position in the formation, changed course to 030°T, speed 18 knots, bearing 340°T, 2,500 yards from guide, USS NEW JERSEY. Disposition 5R, axis 130°T.

1005 Changed course to 120°T. TG 38.1 reported a torpedo wake astern of them. Changed course to parallel the torpedo track. The reported wake turned out to be a discoloration in the water.

1445 Sounded flight quarters.

1538 Commenced maneuvering to the edge of the Task Group, proceeding to our night flying station.

1600 Proceeding to our night flying station with USS HICKOX, USS LEWIS HANCOCK, USS HUNT and USS SPENCE. NEW JERSEY now bears 300°T, 14,000 yards.

1704 Catapulted 4 F6F5Ns on a night heckling mission to sweep Luzon airfields. Armed with two 500# bombs each, Lt. W.E. Henry and Ensigns James A. Barnett, Wallace E. Miller and Emmett R. Edwards rendezvoused over the INDEPENDENCE and proceeded across Luzon toward Lingayen Gulf at 5,000'. Looking for targets, all four pilots had difficulty finding aircraft at the various enemy airstrips. Miller dropped his bombs on Nichols #1 and #3 airstrips. Henry dropped his bombs on the barracks area between Clark #2 and Fort Stotsenburg. Barnett dropped his bombs on Clark #2 airfield. Edwards dropped a bomb on Nichols #1 airfield and on a searchlight position near Nichols.

1801 Changed speed to 23 knots and launched 2 F6Fs for night CAP.

1809 Darkened the ship and minutes later sounded torpedo defense.

1829 Launched 3 TBM-1D(N)s and a TBM 3D(N) for a night heckling mission over Luzon airfields, each armed with twelve 100# GP bombs. Pilots were Lt. Donald M. Linton and Lt. William P. Phelps, Lt.(jg) Frank H. McNair and Lt.(jg) Forrest M. Archer. They were ordered to continue the job of making life miserable for the Japanese at airfields across Luzon, to intercept and destroy enemy aircraft, and

A crane is brought over to extract a F6FN from a port side catwalk / gun tub.

Night Action !

generally to disrupt any Japanese plans to strike at the fleet. The night shift would maintain the "Big Blue Blanket" over Luzon until it was time for the day shift to take over. This strike replaced the previous 1704 launch.

1836 Launched 1 TBM-3D(N). This was Lt.(jg) Robert R.Campaigne, immediately launched to replace Phelps, who was forced to return with a hydraulic leak..

1903 Recovered 1 TBM (Lt. W.P. Phelps).

Linton bombed Clark #2. McNair hit Neilson field, bombing and strafing, scoring a probable on a Topsy, then returned with a bad oil leak. Archer split his bomb load between Lipa West, Perez, Batangas and he strafed Lucena. He noted, on his radar, ships leaving the harbor, reporting it for the day fighters. Campaigne dropped bombs at Clark #2, Malacat, Porac, Angeles and Bambam. All planes returned safely aboard. The night had no moon and visibility was poor due to haze and low overcast.

2103 Launched 2 F6Fs for night CAP relieving the 2 launched at 1801.

2139-2147 Recovered 6 F6Fs, 4 launched at 1704, and 2 launched at 1801.

2227-2231 Launched 3 TBM-3D(N)s for the next shift in an all night series of heckling missions. The Avengers each carried twelve 100# GP bombs. Taking off in conditions similar to the 1829 strike, Lt. William P. Phelps, Lt.(jg) James Taylor and Ens. John E. Williams headed out toward targets. Phelps hit Las Pinas near Lake Taal. Williams dropped half his bombs at Nichols #1.

He was hit with intense AA during the flight. Combined with shrapnel damage from his own low level bomb release at Nichols, the damage to the Avenger bomb bay and lower fuselage was enough to jettison the remaining bombs over water and return to the INDEPENDENCE. Taylor dropped his bombs thru haze on Angeles field, returning with his radio and radar inoperative.

2310-2312 Launched 2 F6F5Ns. The INDEPENDENCE night torpedo squadron reported enemy planes were airborne over the Manila area. Permission was obtained to launch two night fighters for the hunt. Ensigns Reuben F. Peterson and Jack S. Berkheimer catapulted off looking for prey. Peterson, near Manila Bay spotted the navigation lights of a plane circling to land over Cavite. Peterson maneuvered into position to put a burst into a float plane from 5 o'clock low. The Jake went down burning into the water. Ten minutes later Peterson found an unidentified aircraft with its navigation lights on and put a burst into it from 7 o'clock low. It also crashed into the bay. Peterson observed that both enemy pilots most likely never knew what hit them.
Berkheimer conversed with Peterson after "Pete" bagged his kills. "Berky" reported he was over Manila. "Pete" saw search lights come on around the Manila area, and heard a transmission "Peter ...". Peterson then saw an explosion on the ground in the center of Manila, "which appeared like that resulting from a crashed plane". Peterson called Berkheimer repeatedly, with no response. The time was 0220 in the morning of the 16th.

2333-2334 Launched 2 F6Fs for night CAP relieving the 2 launched at 2103.

2351-2355 Recovered 1 TBM launched at 1829.

The Aircraft Action Report from the 1704 launch stated:

"The point of note in this report is the number of searchlights experienced in the Manila area and to the southwest. These lights were not being turned on at random, but in a well-define pattern. The ones in Manila proper were all flashed on at one time and were seemingly synchronized with AA, which came up almost at the same time. Radar control of both would seem to be indicated. It might be recommended that, since with few exceptions, Manila proper holds no bombing value, particularly to night planes, it be studiously avoided in passing from the north to the Nichols-Nielson and other fields around the per-imeter of the city. It might also be suggested that if it is felt necessary to fly over areas of known searchlight-anti-air-craft concentration at night, the altitude should be either very high or on the deck. Further the pilots must be prepared to clear out of the area immediately, on instruments.
The Clark area, on the other hand, showed-no signs of lights or anti-aircraft. Although heckler missions which covered the Clark fields the previous night experienced considerable of both, the firing being

particularly intense from automatic guns."

GN D-Day on Mindoro. Our planes accounted for three bogies and returned pretty well shot up. GN

RC Yanks land on Mindoro. We're still hitting airfields. RC

GL We lost 1 plane over Luzon, A.A fire, the pilot *[1] got out of the plane OK. We shot down 1 Nick. We had a bit of hard luck in the landings and lost a plane or two. Our night fighters also sunk or damaged 3 ships. GL*   (*[1] Harold E. Johnson on the 14 th)

Saturday 16 December 1944 *Philippines, Luzon*
"OPERATION OBLITERATION" (Mindoro Invasion)
Loss of Jack Stanley Berkheimer and Donald Richard Powers

Steaming as Task Unit 38.2.10 with USS HICKOX, USS HUNT, USS LEWIS HANCOCK and USS SPENCE, axis & course 035°T, speed 22 knots, at our night flying station, bearing 060°T, 10 miles from guide of T.G. 38.2 (USS NEW JERSEY). Ship is darkened and Material condition ABLE modified is set. Air Department is at flight quarters and has 6 TBMs and 6 F6Fs in the air.
Two F6Fs were assigned as CAP for the Task Group.
0002 Landed 3 TBMs launched at 1829.
0017 Landed 2 F6Fs launched at 2103. Speed and course changes were made and at 0242 on a course of 035°T, 22 knots they launched 6 F6Fs. Increasing speed to 24 knots (244 rpm) they landed 2 F6Fs launched at 2234, and 2 TBMs launched at 2231.
0322 Landed 1 TBM launched at 2231.
0435 Recovered 2 F6Fs. One was piloted by Ensign Peterson.

1 F6F-5N (BU.NO.71293) piloted by Ensign Jack Stanley Berkheimer (launched at 2231) failed to return, reported as having been shot down by AA over Manila. (Ensign Berkheimer's aircraft was found in the jungle after the war, and his remains were recovered. He is interned today at Arlington.)

One F6F (piloted by Lt. E.S. Ogle) landed from the USS HORNET.
0605-0701 Manned routine general quarters stations.
0704-0759 Recovered 9 F6Fs launched at 0242.
0900 Task Unit 38.2.10 rejoined T.G. 38.2. The Task Force returned westward to send continuous air strikes against Japanese airfields on Luzon during the day.
1245 Launched Lt. Ogle in his F6F for return to HORNET.
1518 Maneuvered to avoid a destroyer crossing the bow from port to starboard.
1541 Departed the Task Group to take up position 10 miles upwind of 38.2 as a Night Flying Station. With INDEPENDENCE were destroyers USS BLUE, USS DYSON, USS TAUSSIG and USS SAMUEL N. MOORE. They were once again Task Unit 38.2.10.
1758-1803 Launched 6 F6Fs to provide dusk and evening CAP.
1900 The Force began retiring southeast to refuel. Two radar decoy balloons had been deployed at 1831 to cover the retirement.
1911 Secured from torpedo defense. The dusk CAP returned to land at 1907.

The evening CAP returned to land at 2129. As Ensign Donald Richard Powers was approaching to land, his Hellcat (F6F-5N Bu.No. 71155) lost air speed just off the port quarter of the flight deck, and spun into the sea. USS TAUSSIG picked up unconscious Powers. Approximately 45 minutes later Ensign "Donny" Powers died from his injuries. TAUSSIG, to conserve fuel, rejoined the screen of T.G. 38.2.

2156 Changed course to 125°T, speed 23 knots.
2328 Let fires die out under No.1 boiler and secured it to make necessary repairs on the throttle valve.

GN Hancock's planes intercepted six Nips (probably suicide divers) on the way toward us and splashed all. We lost a plane in drink but the pilot was rescued by can. GN   (Ensign Donald R. Powers died of his injuries shortly after the rescue.)

RC   Left battle zone to refuel. We are running into a typhoon.   RC

19
Cobra Strikes

Sunday 17 December 1944   *COBRA STRIKES*

With the barometer falling, a tropical depression was becoming well formed.
Dark towering cumulonimbus clouds covered the sky. Lightning flashes were punctuated with deep rumbles of thunder. Building winds howled as even higher gusts whipped up the sea. The underestimated storm fed by moisture laden tropical air and warm waters grew into a massive typhoon. A typhoon named "Cobra".

Errors in recognition of the building severity by scouts, piled atop of delayed reporting and deciphering of encrypted cipher delays helped assure Halsey's aerologist would not realize the true severity of the weather system until it was too late.

Terms of engagement would not be set this day by Halsey nor the Japanese. Cobra dealt out terms of her own. Cobra arose, tightening its grip on the fleet with deployed venomous fangs of wind driven frothing mountainous swells. The admirals' weapons of war were offensively useless as this now became a life or death tactical battle for some ships to simply remain afloat. Davy Jones smacked his lips for Cobras victims to ad to his treasure trove of vessels settled fathoms below on the oceans bottom. The looming stately stature of the aircraft carrier as she appeared to the sailors as they first walked up to her, duffle bags on their shoulders, on the pier back at the Navy Yard was now reduced to small, perhaps way too small. And INDEPENDENCE was in the company of ships much smaller.

Rear Admiral G.F. Bogan in USS LEXINGTON was commanding TG 38.2.

INDEPENDENCE split off from Bogan's group to a separate night flying station designated Task Unit 38.2.10. Steaming as her screen were USS BLUE, USS DYSON and USS SAMUAEL N. MOORE, INDEPENDENCE as guide and OTC, Capt E.C. Ewen commanding. They were on a course of 125°T, 23 knots, in cruising disposition 5R, axis 050°T, bearing 050°T from the guide USS NEW JERSEY, 10 miles, in accordance with Secret Orders dated 10 December, 1944 (TG 38.2).

0534 Sounded routine torpedo defense. They steamed changing courses and speed, relaxing from torpedo defense at 0645, and secured from flight quarters. (no aircraft had been in the air).
0705 Regained station with Task Group 38.2, guide NEW JERSEY, bearing 080°T at 2,500 yards, making course, speed and bearing changes.
0807 Rotated Fleet axis to 040°T, guide New Jersey, bearing 070°T at 2,500 yards.

The fleet had depleted its fuel during the previous days of operations. With building seas, fuel oil was needed for both maneuvering and ballast. Ballast was necessary to keep the ships upright in the heavy seas. Crucial decisions would need to be made whether to fill spaces dedicated for fuel oil with sea water or fuel oil depending on predicted scheduled time to join up with a tanker, if weather and sea conditions would safely allow the critical coupling. These voids needed to be filled with either for proper ballast.

As Cobra strengthened, smaller escort "Jeep Carriers" were having difficulty, as were their escort destroyers. Older destroyers of the Farragut class design, had undergone ship yard modifications to be updated with additional structure above the main deck including guns, a Combat Information Center, radio and radar equipment. These modifications had made these vessels top heavy. The antennas mounted high would increase these top heavy tendencies in heavy seas and high winds. Even the newer Fletcher Class designs would not prove immune to Cobra's wrath.

1015 Sighted tanker bearing 070°T at 12 miles.
1046 Commenced various courses and speeds to join up on tanker USS MASCOMA at 8 knots.
1110 Came up along starboard side to prepare to pull over fueling transfer hoses.
1156 Commenced pumping fuel oil, increasing speed to 10 knots.

Seas where rough with increasing winds. During the next hour and a half, swells grew in height as the winds worsened, the core of the storm to the southeast. Officers and sailors in the bridges of the two vessels were challenged with the task of maintaining a parallel course and fixed distance to prevent joining in collision, or diverging causing separation of lines and fueling hose.

1300 INDEPENDENCE had taken on 218,150 gallons of fuel to 90% of her capacity when CTG 38.2 ordered a halt to fueling operations due to heavy seas becoming increasingly worse.
1305 Casting off from the tanker, they steamed westward to a rendezvous where weather was projected to be better for fleet fueling to resume the next morning.
1400 Changed course 040°T, 10 knots, bearing 227°T from guide USS MASCOMA at 5,250 yards.
1412 USS NEW JERSEY became guide, bearing 250°T, 2,500 yards.
1425 Course 290°T, speed 15 knots (149 rpm).
1445-1505 Ships colors were half-masted for a memorial service held for those recently lost.
During the afternoon the ship was secured for typhoon weather.
1756-1855 Manned torpedo defense stations. Zigzagging (plan 6) on a base course of 270°T.
1915 Ceased zigzagging, resumed base course 270°T, fleet speed 14 knots.

When Captain Ewen retired this evening he had left the following entry in the Standing Orders Log for the watches:

"Weather conditions are not expected to improve during the night and at midnight new course will probably result in heavy roll. Require half hourly reports from all departments on conditions.
Caution helmsman to use only the minimum amount of rudder required to steer the course. It is better to wander somewhat out of position than to use a large amount of rudder attempting to steer a steady course.
Keep check on all units in the formation. Take any action necessary to keep clear. Call me if an embarrassing situation is indicated."

Near midnight, Cobra strengthened.

HB   *We refueled at sea. That same day we were hit by yet another typhoon. This one almost collapsed our bulkhead in the catapult room. I was in the work party that was sent in to make the bulkhead secure* *by shoring with timber we used for the flight deck. Using the 4x6 timbers, we braced from the forward bulkhead back to the next bulkhead about 15 to 20 feet away. This was a really tough job due to the rough seas. When we would hit a wave the bow of the ship would sink down into the water, and the whole ship would shake, then all of a sudden, the bow would come out the water at least 15 or 20 feet. It would almost take your breath away. This made our job a lot harder, since it was so hard to keep our feet under us. I remember this job took at least several hours. **HB***

AD Fueling. A typhoon is heading our way. Spent a pretty rough night. AD

Monday 18 December 1944   *COBRA - Calvin Milton Becker is lost overboard*

Steaming as Task Unit 38.2.1. In company of TG 38.2 with carriers USS CABOT, USS HANCOCK, USS HORNET, and USS LEXINGTON (OTC). USS NEW JERSEY, guide, bears 250°T, 2,500 yards on a course of 180°T, 14 knots, cruising disposition 5R.

0430 The bad weather stayed with the USS INDEPENDENCE. A luminous electrical discharge presumed to be St. Elmo's Fire was observed (as the carrier passed under a black cloud) from the masthead, yardarm, and antenna tips. No attempt was made at fueling as the storm had strengthened, the center closer then the previous day. The eye of the typhoon was to the southwest and moving closer at a rate of 12 knots. Heading south to attempt to skirt below the storm, by 0900 the INDEPENDENCE was experiencing rolls of 30° to each side.

At about 0830, a heavy roll caused a section of the bomb stowage to carry away, permitting nearly 25 tons of bombs, including 9 blockbusters, to roll around the bomb magazine like beer kegs. By noon, however, all bombs had been shored to prevent further movement, and a dangerous situation had been corrected with only minor damage to the stowage. The ship's only whale boat was lifted out of its skids by a wave, smashed, and carried over-board.

HB Another man was lost overboard. His name was Becker. We were still riding out the typhoon when, somehow, one of our 2000 lb. bombs broke loose. This bomb started to roll around in the bomb storage and started breaking all of our bombs loose. They were sliding from side to side, literally tearing everything in their path to pieces. It was decided the only way to stop the bombs was to drop some of the 4x6 timbers down into that jumble of smashed up bombs and twisted steel. This we did, and it took about a carload of timber to stop things from sliding around. We were told there was no danger of any of the bombs exploding because there were no detonators in them. After we got every thing stabilized, the Ordnance people started hoisting the bombs out. One officer said he didn't see why the bombs hadn't exploded. HB

Damage done to the ship however was relatively light. The aircraft, securely lashed to the deck, had not budged. They had learned how to properly tie down our aircraft in the last typhoon.

0909 During the deep rolling, S1c Calvin Milton Becker fell off the flight deck, lost over the side to the mountainous seas. Winds gusted to 60 knots. Wind driven heavy rain reduced visibility to 1,000 yards.

1145 At 12 knots, INDEPENDENCE started to change course to 120°T in an attempt to clear the storm. It became necessary to back one engine to complete the course change.

At roughly 1400 they passed the center of the storm estimated to be 17 miles to the northeast, moving in the opposite direction to the ships course. Wind speed gusting to 84 knots. The maximum roll was to port 34 degrees, a new high for the INDEPENDENCE.

GN The storm has caught up with us. Gun buckets on the starboard side actually took water. Also, witnessed water coming over the fantail. Didn't feel very well looking at it so I went below. The other storms we have encountered up to this time were child's play compared to this. Every time she goes over the whole structure of the ship groans and it wouldn't surprise me to see flight deck lift off. Bombs broke loose in magazine and we had a merry time of it. Took until about midnight before all was secure. GN

This photo is taken during the next typhoon - exactly one month later, on 18 January 1945, in the China Sea.   Photo: Courtesy of Fredrick Hobson

RC *Still in typhoon, ships taking a terrific beating.* **RC**

GL *This is the worst storm as yet. I don't think we will make it back as it looks as though we will capsize. I was nearly washed over the side coming down the aft port ladder from the flight deck. The water was at least three feet over my head and I hung on for dear life. I made it inside and am scared as hell. The ship is still rolling. the gun buckets and stacks are in the water almost every roll. The screws are also out of the water at times. I stayed in my bunk all day and sure did a lot of praying. I would rather face the Japs than this. The waves were as high as the flight deck and brother that is plenty high. The storm broke a little about five but I still am shit scared and nervous as all hell.* **GL**

At around 1500 the storm began to abate. By nightfall the wind was down to a normal 15 knots. This night they proceeded to another rendezvous with the tankers.

DL **SEVEN HUNDRED-NINETY** *United States Navy sailors, officers and men, drowned on 18 December 1944, in a tropical storm known as Typhoon Cobra. Three destroyers capsized and sank, taking nearly all hands to the bottom; several more were lucky to survive. Numerous ships had men swept off their decks. Many others suffered major damage. Carriers lost airplanes and other gear overboard. Collisions between ships were narrowly avoided when radar screens went blank as antennas blew away. Loose aircraft on the hangar decks of CVLs Monterey and San Jacinto and escort carriers CVE Altamaha and Cape Esperance caused gasoline fires that threatened the ships and the lives of everyone aboard.*
Wherever they lurk in the heavens, the gods of weather must still be shaking their heads at such a wartime tragedy. Why the mightiest unit of the American Navy should have blundered into this maelstrom of nature in an area east of Luzon notorious for these storms is less a matter of metaphysical speculation than a study in the faulty judgment of men under extreme pressure.

Seawise admirals could not agree as to what exactly was confronting the Fleet or where it was coming from. Their own aerologists guessed wrong. No one had access to a magic switch to beam up pictures revealing what they needed to know. Barometers and thermometers, the state of the sea, the look of the sky, the force and direction of the wind, "the laws of storms"--all were considered but not everybody interpreted what they observed the same way.

By forenoon 17 December, it had become apparent to the most obtuse junior officer and enlisted man that he was approaching a crisis in his life of such magnitude that it just might whisk him off the board. War was the triggering culprit. Commitments had been made to continue Third Fleet's raids by planes from its fast carriers against Japanese installations on Luzon and Leyte. The U.S. Army was fighting ferocious battles to retake the Philippines. It depended on us to provide air cover while new landing strips for its own planes were being bulldozed out of the jungle.

Admiral Halsey had informed General MacArthur that Task Force 38, (VADM John McCain), would have to break off to refuel on the 17th and 18th but would be back on the job Tuesday, 19 December. That date would not be met. A few destroyers had been allowed to become dangerously unstable due to lack of fuel and ballast caused by our constant hurry-scurry activity.
Several fueling rendezvous had been set for the 17th. One after another had to be changed to a different location because the sea had withdrawn its welcome. The hungriest destroyers were now in desperate need, bobbing and corkscrewing like floating toys in a bathtub. As they approached the BBs and large CVs, and even closed the big fat oilers that were part of the support screen, the effort to hook up and gulp the fluid that meant life or death to these workaholics became a frenzied dance in a sailor's nightmare. Thick hoses were impossible to manhandle on the rolling, pitching decks. When attachment was made, the heaving sea forced the small ships to veer away. Hoses would part like writhing pythons from the fueling trunks with a violent shoop-snap sound that not only sprayed men but instantly turned decks and fo'c'sles into treacherous black skating rinks.

Every ship survived that night. Yet the sea never forgets. It exacted its revenge next day. Because Third Fleet covered many hundreds of square miles, some vessels experienced no more than gale force winds and seas no rougher than if they had just passed under a heavy thunderstorm. The big flattops, luckily not caught in the vortex of the storm, rode it out relatively smoothly with only minor damage. Battleships Massachusetts, Iowa, Alabama, New Jersey, Wisconsin, North Carolina, South Dakota, and Washington were barely disturbed.

A pertinent question is, How much did this comparatively smooth ride mislead Halsey in New Jersey? Could he have misjudged the impact the storm was inflicting on his smaller ships? Doesn't seem possible. As a young officer he had spent years in destroyers in all kinds of weather. Still, the war was the urgent priority. Did full awareness of what smaller members of his Fleet were enduring come too late? I refuse to believe it. He had already informed MacArthur that he would not be able to resume his planned strikes on the 19th. This headstrong man knew full well what he had gotten into.

USS Spence, DD-512, was survived by one officer and twenty-four men.
USS Monaghan, DD-354, an active witness to the Pearl Harbor attack, left a total of six men alive. A petty officer second class was ranking survivor.
USS Hull, DD-350, another survivor of Pearl Harbor, left eight officers alive (including her captain) and fifty-five enlisted men.

Destroyers pitched and rolled to such degrees that some were caught "in irons" in deep troughs from which they were lucky to escape. Rolls between 75 or even 85 degrees were not uncommon. Men " walked " the bulkheads of many a vessel. The skipper of destroyer Dewey (DD 349) saved himself by hanging horizontally from a bridge fitting while his ship rolled beneath him; he wasn't sure she would right herself or if he could hold on long enough. **DL**

HB   One thing I failed to mention was, after we almost ran out of food, we took on supplies. We put box after box of potatoes any place we could store them. One place they were stored was in the after elevator pit. This was also where we stored all of the sheetmetal we used for various jobs. When we were in the typhoon, all of our sheetmetal got loose, and broke the angle irons that were welded to the deck to hold it. All that metal sliding around broke up the boxes of potatoes and made mush out of them, and the juice was running down into the compartments below. What a mess this turned out to be! It took quite awhile to clean up.

In this typhoon two of our carriers caught fire, and several destroyers sank.   **HB**

AD I've never been through anything this bad before. Waves are like mountains. Much too rough to work. We rolled 37 degrees and we can only take 40 degrees. I was one scared sailor. At 1700 she calmed down considerably. Glad most of it is over. **AD**

DL   Since the day we had entered the Atlantic off Cape May, I was like the happy, homesick swabbie singing the musical comedy complaint: "And what did I see? I saw the sea." It wore a coat of many colors--mostly blue in the Caribbean and in the vicinity of Hawaii, but took on a gray pall under a chilly low overcast. It was green when disturbed by a rapid cross-current, and flecked with a patina of dirty white whenever a sheet of phosphorescence trailed our stern.

But I had never seen anything like this. It was coal black.

On the 16th we ordnancemen had serviced the guns on the planes recovered from the previous night's search. Word came down from Flight that no chickens would be aloft tonight. The sea was already making up. Launching planes in bad weather and then recovering them on a narrow, rolling and pitching deck in the dark would have been shooting craps with liar's dice. Our pilots did fly CAPs all day long, though, and prepared to do the same next day, the planned fueling day. It didn't happen. Not a plane was catapulted from any carrier.

Mister Porky must have sensed something. In his foul weather gear he resembled a balloon. "Ya-ya put it on," he ordered those of us goofing off in Bill's portside rearming magazine. "No flyin' today. Hangar deck, lots to do. And hang a couple more gun spares on the arm'ry bulkhead. May need 'em. 'Member how many we used up in October?" Off we hustled. I went below to the armory using the portside outboard ladder from the flightdeck. The sea was boiling liquefied anthracite. It swept toward me in great black waves that were being torn to shreds of dirty white foam as they rolled aft. The steps of the ladder dipped into whitecaps washing over the tops of my boondockers, tugging greedily at my underpinnings. I shouldn't have been there. Planned fueling day, the 17th, was worse. My belly was used to good-sized rolls, but pitching disturbed it and gave me a headache. Visibility had diminished to the point where the big, indistinct shadow of an Essex-class carrier on the port bow simply disappeared.

The mess deck had been rife with rumors about a real blow coming. Hell, I thought, it's here! All the gunners topside wore foul weather gear. Some were strapped into the gun tubs. The air was thick and heavy, reminding me of what a gathering line of springtime thunderstorm at home had felt like. But it had never scared me. The scene before me now was gut-wrenching.

Nobody slept that night. The whole ship's company seemed to be awake, on alert. Damage control parties roamed fore and aft. Roving patrols headed by the chief boatswain made their rounds, checking bulkheads, fittings, doors, our overall watertight integrity--the heart and soul of any vessel.

On the flightdeck and hangar deck, mechs and aviation metalsmiths tied down aircraft, remembering lessons learned in October about the need for cables as well as manila lines around fuselages and landing gears, draining oil from the oleo struts, securing tarps about the engine nacelles. We ordnancemen checked the security of gear that might become adrift. All small arms magazines and rocket launcher stowage spaces were checked. Neither Porky nor any of the chiefs ordered anything special done to the bomb magazine. Windy had reported that he and Mitch had it under control. (Perhaps the overriding attitude was that nothing more could be done at this stage. I don't know if anyone prayed down there, but they surely held their breath.)

Normally a warship is silent as she goes about her business. But by dawn of 18 December, Mighty I was howling her distress. Wild winds and an aroused sea awakened demons hidden in the steel plates of her hull and among the rivets holding her together. Enormous forces tried to pull her apart. The screeching, warbling wind by itself was deafening. Added to that was the huffing sound of a heaving mass of steel trying to raise itself out of the water only to fall back down into a trough between swells with the full dead weight of its thousands of tons. She sobbed and groaned in agony as every loose piece of gear broke from its restraints and caromed from bulkhead to bulkhead, deck to overhead. Half-deafened sailors staggered down tilting passageways. Cooks and bakers dodged flying utensils. Large coffee urns and huge copper soup kettles tilted off their mountings and crashed to the deck. Quick-stepping galley workers danced out of harm's way. Clumsy ones were scalded.

Topside, vertical palisades to blunt the wind's force had been inserted before sundown on the 17th into the flightdeck's cleats. Tarps already placed about engine nacelles made them look like huge puppies bundled against a blizzard's onslaught. The long, beanpole portside HF antennas had been raised to the vertical position to lessen the port list and to keep the wires out of the sea. It would have torn them loose early on, sheering our communication with whatever world still existed beyond the tempest. To help reduce our built-in starboard list, both aircraft elevators had been lowered. The wide roll-down hangar doors were raised to let the wind blow through, reducing the sail area of our sides but permitting the hangar to be transformed into a slippery, ankle-deep wading pool.

All attempts at refueling destroyers had been canceled before 0800 the 18th. It was too late, they'd have to wait. The exotic word " typhoon" spit from the rumor mill for the first time.   **DL**

19 December 1944 - USS INDEPENDENCE receives the body of Ensign Donald Richard Powers

Tuesday 19 December 1944   *Ensign Donald R. Powers buried at sea*

GN Best part of storm has passed and everyone breathes a bit easier though it is still blowing a bit out.
GN

0546 Sounded routine torpedo defense. Minutes later they changed course to 150°T, speed 20 knots.
0621 Commenced an emergency turn to 110°T as the USS DYSON reported a sound contact, which was later lost. Minutes later they changed course and reduced speed, securing from torpedo defense.
0728 The axis was rotated to 330°T, prior to joining a fueling group. Guide USS NEW JERSEY bears 000°T at 2,500 yards. Changed fleet course to 050°T.
0800 Mustered crew to stations. Calvin Milton Becker (lost at sea in the typhoon yesterday) was the only man absent. The Task Unit would begin zigzagging, making course and speed changes.

The force refueled in comparatively calm waters. Air searches were sent out to locate destroyers, destroyer escorts, survivors un-reported since yesterday's storm. The searchers did sight some ships with super-structures blown off or damaged.

1050 Ceased zigzagging to allow USS MARSHALL to take station on the starboard side amidships. MARSHALL was delivering four replacement pilots picked up from the USS KWAJALEIN. At 1116 USS MARSHALL cast off and minutes later INDEPENDENCE again resumed her zigzagging independently on a base course of 330°T.
1209-1224 USS TAUSSIG was along the port side. INDEPENDENCE received the body of Ensign Donald Richard Powers. (TAUSSIG had picked him up after he crashed into the sea on 16 December.)

From 1300 until 1312, a burial service was held, committing the body of
Ensign Donald Richard Powers to the sea.

GL My prayers were answered as the storm is over and the sun shinning this morning. I still got a funny feeling every time I think of that narrow squeak I had yesterday. We refueled again today. At 13:00 we buried one of our pilots. Had a sub contact – turned out to be friendly. GL

AD *At sea fueling. One of our pilots who crashed over the side was brought aboard ship this morning. He died after he was picked up by a DD. We held burial services on the flight deck. This is the first one I've seen. It's a shame to have men dying like this.* **AD**

1320 The U.S.S. CABOT left the Task Group to join Task Group 38.1.
1430 The ship jettisoned nine 2,000 lb. and six 1,000 lb. GP bombs due to damage of the bomb stowage locker during the typhoon.
1700-1826 At a speed of 10 knots, INDEPENDENCE was alongside USS MANATEE receiving fuel oil, and two drums of lubricating oil. INDEPENDENCE transferred U.S. mail over to the MANATEE.

1915 The Task Group formed disposition 5-R. The screen was formed in a bent line ahead with a line of destroyers on each flank to the screens of the adjoining task groups, this giving good coverage to the water as they retraced the course through the storm area looking for survivors.

Wednesday 20 December 1944

0200 Steaming as before with Task Unit 38.2.1. In company of USS HORNET, USS LEXINGTON (OTC) and USS NEW JERSEY, guide, bears 330°T, 2,500 yards, zigzagging on a base course of 340°T, 17 knots, cruising disposition 5R, axis 330°T. Ship is darkened, Air Department set to condition 14.
A normal screen was formed and they proceeded northward to get into a position for a run-in on Luzon.
0552-0652 Manned torpedo defense stations.
0730 Changed course to 050°T.
0731 Fleet axis changed to 090°T. Commenced maneuvering to assume new position, bearing 180°T, 2,500 yards from guide.
0800 Changed course to 315°T.
0900 Mustered crew on stations. No absentees.
1700 Task Unit 38.2.10 was formed, consisting of this vessel (OTC), USS STEPHEN POTTER, USS THE SULLIVANS, USS HUNT and USS LEWIS HANCOCK, proceeded to a night flying station approximately ten miles upwind. Axis of the cruising disposition is 145°T.
1708 On station for night operations. NEW JERSEY now bears 320°T, 14,000 yards.
1900 The Task-Force commenced a high speed run on Luzon on a course of 258°T, speed 22 knots.

GN *Still pretty bad out. Enough so to keep our planes on deck. We got word that three cans and a CVE [1] were lost due to the weather. We are in the area and lot of debris is floating around. Saw about ten lifejackets and three life rafts. Making a speed run to strike at Luzon in the wee hours of the morning.* **GN** [1] Note: No CVEs were lost, however numerous vessels including aircraft carriers received damage, some requiring major repair.

RC *On our way back to Luzon.* **RC**

GL *Continued to look for survivors from DE [2] that capsized in the storm. Very few have been picked up. Latest report is we have lost Spence, Monaghan and possibly Hull. There is a lot of scuttlebutt going around other ship losses. We are supposed to hit Luzon tomorrow for one day. So a convoy can bring reinforcements on to Mindoro.* **GL** [2] Note: This was in error. 3 DD's (destroyers) were lost: USS HULL, USS MONAGHAN and USS SPENCE. No DEs were lost.

Thursday 21 December 1944   *Search for Survivors*

Steaming at a night flying station with the USS STEPHEN POTTER, USS THE SULLIVANS, USS HUNT and USS LEWIS HANCOCK, 14,000 yards, bearing 140°T from New Jersey. CVL-22 has no aircraft airborne, Air Department is in condition 11 Easy.
Due to weather and high swells, air operations from this carrier are not possible.
0155 Changed course to 110°T to retire from the area, canceling the scheduled strikes.

0426 Lost fires under boilers No. 3 & 4 due to water in the fuel oil.

0530 Relit fires under boilers No. 3 & 4 and cut into the main steam line.

0556-0701 Manned torpedo defense stations.

0626 Commenced maneuvering to regain station within TG 38.2.

0736 Regained position within the formation, guide bearing 090°T, 2,500 yards.

1033 Commenced zigzagging on base course 130°T.

1157 Changed course to 226°T. Proceeding with the Task Group back to make a wide area search of the area in which the Task Force was steaming throughout the storm for survivors in the water.

1807 Changed base course to 095°T, zigzagging per plan 6.

1808-1906 Ship was at torpedo defense.

GN Strike called off. Weather still not right and planes stay on deck. GN

RC Operations canceled due to more storm, picked up a few survivors from DE's*[1] lost in typhoon on the 18th, and head for Ulithi. RC (*[1] Note: Once again, they were DDs, not DEs. I include these entries as written, even when in error, not being critical, but to lend insight today, as to how the shipmates understood the actual events they were then immersed in. This was their war, in real time. We have today, safely with book in lap, the luxury of decades of historical hindsight without the sudden rush to "General Quarters"!)

GL T.D. instead of G.Q., we are not hitting Luzon today. We turned back last night due to the storm in the area. I guess we go to Ulithi or Guam this time. Still searching storm area. We sighted many life rafts and debris but very few survivors. GL

AD At sea. They picked up a few survivors from the storm. I think there were 13 which isn't many considering how many ships went down. AD (Note: There were approximately 91 survivors rescued; 62 from HULL, 6 from MONAGHAN, and 23 from SPENCE. Approximately 775 men were lost from these 3 DDs.)

Friday 22 December 1944   *Refueled*

Steaming as before in company with USS HANCOCK, USS HORNET, and USS LEXINGTON (OTC). Zigzagging on base course 095°T, INDEPENDENCE bears 270°T, 2,500 yards from guide, USS NEW JERSEY. Ship is darkened, Air Department is in condition 14. Boilers 1,2,3 and 4 are in use.

0633 Changed course to 090°T, changed speed to 17 knots, rotated axis to 060°T. Commenced steering various courses at various speeds to regain station bearing 060°T, 2,500 yards from NEW JERSEY.

0828 Commenced steering various courses at various speeds to come along port side of Fleet Oiler USS CHIKASKIA for fueling operations.

0857 Commence fueling on course 060°T, speed 10 knots. Fleet guide shifted to USS NANTAHALA bearing 330°T, 1,000 yards from center.

1103 Cast off all lines from USS CHIKASKIA, having taken on 20,000 gallons of aviation gasoline and 124,200 gallons of fuel oil, steering various courses at various speeds to regain normal position within the formation.

1142 Regained station, guide USS NANTAHALA bearing 060°T, range 6,500 yards.

1320-1324 USS BLUE was alongside port quarter to transfer one napalm mixer to this vessel.

1326 Commenced steering various courses at various speeds to assume new position on USS NANTAHALA, bearing 240°T, 1,500 yards.

1422 USS MILLER came alongside port quarter to deliver mail.

1430 USS NEW JERSEY departed eastward from the Task Group to proceed independently.

1433 USS MILLER cast off.

1512 USS SAN JUAN became guide in position 0000, bearing 060°T, 2,500 yards. Changed course to 090°T, speed 20 knots. Fueling was completed and they were steaming to Ulithi.

1547 Commenced zigzagging on base course 120°T.

GL Still hunting for survivors and doing pretty good. We are about 100 miles off Leyte. GL

Saturday 23 December 1944   *Steaming toward Ulithi Atoll*

Steaming as before. INDEPENDENCE bears 240°T, 2,500 yards from guide, USS SAN JUAN.
0521-0625 Manned torpedo defense stations.
1152 Changed course to 080°T.
1212 Task Group shifted to disposition 5V, guide USS VINCENNES, bearing 078°T, 7,500 yards.
1220 Commenced maneuvering for gunnery exercises.
1221 Sounded torpedo defense for Anti-Aircraft gunnery exercises.
1248 Maneuvered to station bearing 140°T, 12,000 yards from USS VINCENNES. Steadied on fleet course 120°T, speed 18 knots.
1415 Completed gunnery exercises, having fired 1,416 rounds of 40mm, and 928 rounds of 20mm.
1420 Commenced maneuvering to take station in disposition 5R.
1448 Gained station, USS VINCENNES bearing 078°T, 7,500 yards. Steadied on fleet course 080°T.
1546 Changed fleet course to 135°T. USS SAN JUAN designated guide bearing 060°T, 2,500 yards.
1730 Commenced zigzagging on base course 135°T.
1731-1833 Manned torpedo defense stations.

GL Refueled today and received some mail. We are headed for Ulithi. GL

DL A concentrated search for survivors of Spence, Hull, Monaghan and for men who had been washed into the sea from other ships was brought to a halt on 23 December. Task Force 38 was bereft. Courses were set for Ulithi. (Authors note: Heroic determined effort by the Captain and crew of destroyer escort USS Tabberer, who themselves were in extreme peril, stayed on station against orders and rescued 55 survivors.)
Much damage had to be repaired. One hundred forty-six aircraft had been lost or " damaged beyond economical repair" including ninety-four from the CVEs, thirty-three from the CVLs, the rest from cruisers and battleships. Such losses could not be absorbed without immediate replacement. Extensive radar damage had left Third Fleet vulnerable to air attack. Lexington, Ticonderoga, Essex, Cowpens, Cabot, and Langley among the fast carriers were left with no defensive radar. BB Iowa suffered a similar loss.
The war would have to wait. But war, the ultimate evil, never waits. By an ironic coincidence, the U.S. Army in the sultry heat of the Philippines would suffer along with its European counterpart in the freezing first days of The Battle of the Bulge without much help from aircraft. DL

Sunday 24 December 1944   *Anchored at Ulithi Atoll, Caroline Islands*

Steaming as before in company with USS HANCOCK, USS HORNET, and USS LEXINGTON (OTC). INDEPENDENCE bears 240°T, 2,500 yards from guide, USS SAN JUAN. Ship is darkened, Air Department is in condition 14. Boilers 1 and 3 are in use.
0453 Sounded torpedo defense.
0558 Commenced maneuvering to form column open order for AA gunnery practice.
0628 USS VINCENNES designated guide. INDEPENDENCE is fifth in column order, 4,000 yards from USS VINCENNES at head of column. At 0634 the formation commenced firing on towed sleeves.
0658 Sighted land bearing 160°T, distance 19 miles.
0730 Changed course to 090°T.
0742 Completed AA gunnery exercises.
0756 Secured from torpedo defense.
0824 Commenced steering various courses and speeds conforming to the channel.
0839 Sounded general quarters.
0905 Passed buoys No. 1 and 2 at entrance of Mugai Channel, Ulithi Atoll, Caroline Islands.
0911 Secured from general quarters. Gunnery Department set to special harbor condition 2.
0933 Anchored in berth 21 in 29 fathoms of water, coral bottom (125 fathoms of chain to port anchor).

0935 Set all clocks ahead to time zone (-10) time.
1042 Secured main engines and No.3 boiler.
1210 Task Group 38.3 stood in and anchored, followed by Task Group 38.1 at 1340.

GL Had gunnery run in morning then we pulled in and received lots of mail. GL
(Note: During the afternoon, roughly 150 bags of mail were received aboard.)

*AD Ulithi — Anchored at 0900 **Xmas eve.** AD*

Monday 25 December 1944   XMAS Day - *Anchored at Ulithi Atoll, Caroline Islands*

0830 Anchored as before. Mustered crew on stations.
0915 LCM-74 came alongside to starboard. Commenced unloading GSK freight.
1130 Made daily inspection of the magazines.

GN Had a good Xmas dinner although I thought I would miss it due to a working party. It was called for the same time chow was sounded and luckily we were first in line. Never did get to work and it was called off at 8 P.M. GN

AD Anchored Xmas day. Chow was H.O. We all received Xmas packages and had a feast. AD

CEM At the movie this evening, we saw a short Coast Guard subject "Task Force" and the Andrews Sisters in "Swingtime Johnny". CEM

Tuesday 26 December 1944   *Anchored at Ulithi Atoll, Caroline Islands*

0830 Anchored as before. No.1 boiler in use for auxiliary purposes. Mustered crew on stations.

GL Took on stores and ammunition and am hoping a little Xmas rest (plenty of mail) GL

GN The " Bull" and a lot of other big shots were supposed to be aboard for a broadcast to the States but at the last minute it was changed to the Yorktown, " The Lucky Lady." GN

Wednesday 27 December 1944   *Anchored at Ulithi Atoll, Caroline Islands*

0825 Anchored as before. Prepared the ship for fueling operations.
0917 Tanker USS ATASCOSA came alongside port amidships.
0935 LCM#3 came alongside starboard quarter to deliver aviation supplies.
0950 Commenced fueling from USS ATASCOSA.
0959 LCM#3 cast off.
1055 Completed fueling. Received 103,051 gallons of fuel oil and 689 gallons of lube oil.
1119 USS ATASCOSA cast off.
1122 YF699 came alongside starboard forward with a load of bombs.
1950 LCT 899 moored alongside starboard to deliver lube oil.

GN Move bombs aboard and routine work. GN

AD Anchored. Had a smoker on hangar deck, also a movie. All hands had a good time. AD

Thursday 28 December 1944   *Anchored at Ulithi Atoll, Caroline Islands*

1203 LCT# 829 moored on starboard bow with aviation stores. The LCT hit the side of the hull punching a hole 4 inches in diameter at frame 17 about 10' above the waterline and wrinkling a watertight transverse bulkhead.

1319 LCT# 829 cast off from starboard bow.
AD Anchored. Went on a beer party at Mog Mog. AD

During the period from 25 — 28 December the ship reprovisioned and took on fuel and ammunition. Daily recreation parties of about 250 men went to the fleet recreation center on Mog Mog Island.

Friday 29 December 1944   *Ulithi Atoll - Underway*

0830 Anchored as before. Mustered crew on stations.
0845-0920 Turned over main engines.
1146 Cut in boiler No.4 on main steam line.
1200 Tested all main engines by steam.
1220 Received bomb fuses and boosters from ComServRon TEN.
1255-1315 Draft taken prior to getting underway. Made all preparations for getting underway.
1320 Returned LCVP# 184 and fifty foot motor launch to boat pool, Ulithi harbor.

Underway from Ulithi in accordance with ComTaskGroup 38.2 orders. The Mighty-I is now part of ComCarDiv SEVEN under Rear Admiral Matthias B. Gardner (in the U.S.S. ENTERPRISE). Carrier Division SEVEN consist of USS INDEPENDENCE, USS ENTERPRISE and USS BATAAN. BATAAN and ENTERPRISE are not at this anchorage.
1329 Got underway as TU38.2.10 (in company with USS LEWIS HANCOCK, USS MILLER, USS MARSHALL and USS HUNT) to conduct refresher flight operations and training exercises. Standing out of Ulithi anchorage at various courses and speeds conforming to channel.
1344 Sounded routine general quarters.
1406 Passed thru anti-submarine nets.
1409 Passed buoys No.1 and 2 abeam to port and starboard at 18 knots with buoy No.1 300 yards distant. Changed course to 070°T.
1430 Set all clocks back one hour to time zone (-9).
1330 Boilers No. 1 and 3 cut in on main steam line.
1336 Secured from general quarters. Air Department remained at flight quarters.
1357 Commenced steering various courses and speeds while conducting refresher flight operations.
1358-1403 Launched 7 F6F Hellcats for the purpose of practicing approaches and landings.
1451 Completed recovering 3 Hellcats launched at 1358.
1513 Recovered the remaining 4 Hellcats launched at 1358. Changed course to 065°T, speed 18 knots.
1535 Secured from flight quarters. Air Department set to condition 14.
1545 Sounded torpedo defense for gunnery exercises.
1608 Course 100°T. Formed a column 2,000 yards astern USS LEWIS HANCOCK (guide) for gunnery exercises.
1704 Completed firing on a towed sleeve. USS INDEPENDENCE became guide. Secured from torpedo defense. The destroyer screen then resumed stations in the cruising disposition.
1745-1830 Manned routine torpedo defense stations, sounding flight quarters at 1815.
1908 Completed launching 6 F6Fs for the purpose of practicing approaches and landings.
1930-1943 Recovered 4 F6Fs launched at 1908. The remaining two Hellcats stayed aloft to observe tests conducted by the destroyers.
2015-2100 The destroyer escort made smoke during testing to determine the effectiveness of a smoke screen in obscuring the vessels from enemy planes.
2131 Recovered 2 F6Fs launched at 1908. Comments from these pilots determined that one destroyer would effectively hide the Task Unit in bright moonlight.
2227 Completed launching 3 F6Fs and 3 TBMs for the purpose of practicing approaches.

Hawaii

June 1944   R.N.Hobson   G.V. Williams   Joe-Sam Allen   "Hebe" Lee

27 Dec 1944   **MogMog - Ulithi Atoll , A squadron hot dog roast**

L to R: **Donald Linton** (VT pilot), **Russell Edwards** (VF pilot), **Milton Popp** (Flight Surgeon), **Robert Hobson** (Radar Officer), **Rolly Theis** (Radar Officer), **, Herb Wieland** (CVL-22 Catapult Officer)

Underway after departing Ulithi, USS INDEPENDENCE is leading USS Hornet (CV-12), then USS LEXINGTON (CV-16). Light Cruiser USS SAN JUAN (Atlanta Class CL-54) is shown to the right.

USS INDEPENDENCE underway with TG 38.2 to strike Japanese targets on Formosa.

2312 Completed recovery of 3 F6Fs and 3 TBMs launched at 2227. Speed set to 22 knots.

2357 Commenced zigzagging on base course 310°T. They had operated westerly into the wind for flight operations, but were now on easterly headings toward Ulithi for a morning rendezvous with TG 38.2.

Saturday 30 December 1944   *Underway*

Steaming as before as TU38.2.10 in company with USS LEWIS HANCOCK, USS MILLER, USS MARSHALL and USS HUNT (in accordance with secret orders dated 28 December,1944) in a cruising disposition zigzagging on base course 310°T, speed 18 knots.

0415 Changed base course to 215°T.

0455-0556 Manned routine torpedo defense stations.

0858 Launched 1 F6F-5N to proceed to Falalop Island, Ulithi.

0915 Sighted Ulithi Atoll, bearing 225°T, distance 20 miles. Changed course to 185°T. They cruised off the Atoll until 1004 at which time the TU was dissolved. The destroyers were detached to join the screen of TG 38.2.

1008 Commenced steering various courses at various speeds to gain position in column of nine ships, as last ship. Column guide, at its head, is USS PASADENA, bearing 315°T at 9,000 yards.

1031 Gained position in column joining TG 38.2.

1145 Sounded torpedo defense for gunnery exercises.

1248 Sounded flight quarters. Changed speed to 16 knots.

1253 Completed gunnery exercises. Secured from torpedo defense.

1323 Changed course to 350°T. At 1330 Task Group 38.2 formed disposition 5R on axis 090°T, guide USS NEW JERSEY, bearing 090°T, 2,500 yards.

1332-1351 Recovered 7 F6F-5Ns and 1 TBM(N) as replacements.

1355 Secured from flight quarters.

1605-1608 Launched 2 TBMs for the purpose of testing radar jamming equipment.

1710 Recovered the 2 TBMs launched at 1605, with satisfactory results with the tests.

1712 Changed course to 290°T, speed 22 knots proceeding west toward a fueling area.

GN Landed new aircraft and got to work modifying them. GN

Sunday 31 December 1944   *Underway*

Steaming in company with TG38.2 consisting of USS INDEPENDENCE, USS LEXINGTON, USS HANCOCK and USS HORNET, disposition 5R, course 325°T, guide USS NEW JERSEY, bearing 270° T, 2,500 yards. Air Department is in condition 12.

0520-0627 Manned routine torpedo defense stations. Air Department set to condition 14.

0918 Changed course to 270°T.

1117 USS HORNET was designated fleet guide. Battleships and cruisers of this Task Group left the formation to join up with battleships and cruisers of other groups to form Task Force 34.

1130 Changed course to 120°T.

1210 USS SAN JUAN designated as guide. INDEPENDENCE bears 270°T, 2,500 yards from guide.

1214 Changed course to 325°T.

1530 Sounded flight quarters.

1638 USS LEXINGTON designated guide, bearing 045°T, 3,500 yards.

1718 USS NEW JERSEY returned to TG38.2 and assumed fleet guide at fleet center. Course 150°T.

1735 Left the formation to proceed to our night flying station, bearing 150°T, 14,000 yards from USS NEW JERSEY. We are accompanied by destroyer screen USS LEWIS HANCOCK, USS MILLER, USS MARSHALL and USS HUNT, forming TU38.2.1, this vessel guide and OTC.

1745 Changed course to 308°T.

1932 Launched 3 F6Fs for training exercises.

2129 Launched 2 F6Fs and 2 TBMs for training exercises.
2203 Recovered the 3 F6Fs launched at 1932.
2332 Recovered the 2 F6Fs and 2 TBMs launched at 2129.

GL   More gunnery practice. Met up with 5 cruisers, 15 cans. This sure is a big force. I guess we are going to Formosa and Luzon.   GL

Monday 1 January 1945   **Underway - *New Years Day***

GL   Happy New Year. I had the 12-4 watch.   GL

Steaming as before as a night carrier unit under Task Group 38.2 (Rear Admiral G.F. Bogan, Commander, Carrier Division Four, USS LEXINGTON, flagship) at a night flying station seven miles upwind from the center of TG38.2. The Task Group is proceeding northwest to a fueling area, conducting training exercises, on the way to strike Formosa.
0540 Sounded routine torpedo defense.
0620 Commenced steering various courses at various speeds to regain station within TG 38.2.
0701 Changed course to 280°T. Regained position in the formation, disposition 5R, guide USS NEW JERSEY bearing 090°T, 2,500 yards.
0709 USS LEXINGTON designated guide, bearing 045°T, 3,500 yards.
0725 Battleships and cruisers, with destroyers as a screen, left the formation to form Task Force 34.5.
0823 USS SAN JUAN was designated guide at fleet center. Fleet axis rotated to 050°T. Commenced maneuvering to gain station, bearing 230°T, 2,500 yards from guide.
0955 Commenced maneuvering to gain position in a special column 2,000 yards ahead of SAN JUAN for gunnery exercises.
1006 Gained station, new course 270°T, speed 18 knots. At 1007 INDEPENDENCE became guide.
1043-1145 Manned torpedo defense for gunnery exercises.
1146 Gunnery exercises complete, commenced maneuvering to gain station, bearing 050°T, 2,500 yards from USS SAN JUAN, which had reassumed guide.
1415 Sounded flight quarters.
1516 Launched 4 TBMs.
1649 Changed course to 300°T.
1705 USS LEXINGTON assumed guide, INDEPENDENCE bearing 185°T, 3,500 yards from guide.
1730 Battleships, cruisers and their destroyer screen rejoined the formation.
1731 USS NEW JERSEY assumed guide bearing 050°T, 2,500 yards from INDEPENDENCE.
1735-1738 Recovered the 4 TBMs launched at 1516.

Tuesday 2 January 1945   **Underway - Refueling**

Steaming as before 2,500 yards, bearing 230°T from guide, USS NEW JERSEY, zigzagging on base course 310°T, speed 18 knots. Boilers No.2 & 4 are in use. At 0600 the fueling group was sighted.
0604-0704 Manned torpedo defense stations.
0654 Task group commenced fueling exercises in a rough sea. USS SAUGATUCK assumed guide. Commenced maneuvering making an approach on assigned fleet oiler, USS TALUGA.
0728 Came alongside USS TALUGA to starboard.
0756-0800 Lighted fires under No.3 & then No.1 boilers.
0942 Cast off from USS TALUGA having received 223,116 gallons of fuel oil.
1009 Took position in fueling disposition bearing 040°T, 5,500 yards from USS SAUGATUCK.
1114-1119 USS HAZELWOOD was along the starboard side to deliver a box to this vessel.
1154-1213 USS FRANKS was along the starboard side amidships to deliver officer messenger mail, aircraft spare parts, and one passenger to this vessel.
1309-1315 USS LAWS was alongside to deliver mail and one passenger.

1443-1450 USS MILLER was alongside to receive officer messenger mail.

1530 Sounded flight quarters.

1542 TG 38.2 completed fueling operations and formed disposition 5R.

1550 Gained position in formation bearing 225°T, 2,500 yards from NEW JERSEY.
USS NEW JERSEY assumed fleet guide. Then changed course to 287°T.

1559 Changed speed to 25 knots. Refueled, TG 38.2 was beginning a high speed run to the west, for strikes on Formosa.

1730 Commenced proceeding to a night flying station (accompanied by USS LEWIS HANCOCK, USS MILLER, USS MARSHALL and USS HUNT) as Task Unit 38.2.10, upwind of the Task Group.

Captain Ewen wrote in the Standing Orders Log before he retired from the bridge:
"We have an indication that all is not entirely satisfactory with the steering gear. Be alert to notify Crony 2 in the event of a failure.
Keep the watch alert, especially the lookouts. Jap mines (floating) are to be expected in these waters as well as Jap subs.
We are making a high speed run in on Formosa. All hands must be on their toes"
"All messages that come in are to be sent to me immediately over the voice tube BEFORE THEY ARE WRITTEN UP."

GL *We refueled today about 460 miles from Formosa.* **GL**

AD *At sea. Receiving fuel. Tomorrow we will strike Formosa. Crew is uneasy.* **AD**

20
Formosa

Wednesday 3 January 1945   **Formosa**

Steaming as before at a night flying station, accompanied by USS LEWIS HANCOCK, USS MILLER, USS MARSHALL and USS HUNT. Air Department is in condition 11.

0327-0329 Launched 3 F6Fs as night CAP. Pilots and crew were tired from a lengthy briefing.

0627-0727 Manned general quarters stations. Air Department remained at condition 11.

0741 Completed recovery of 2 F6Fs launched at 0329.

0815 Recovered of 1 F6F launched at 0329.

0829 Secured from flight quarters. Air Department set to condition 14. Mustered crew on stations.

0906 Commenced steering various courses at various speeds to gain position in TG38.2.

0931 On station. Guide, USS NEW JERSEY bearing 100°T, 2,500 yards.

The Task Force launched strikes against Japanese installations on Formosa during the morning. With operations hampered by heavily overcast skies (both over the fleet and ceilings down to 1,000' over some target areas) they retired toward the southeast at around 1600.

1643 Proceeding to a night flying station, course 175°T, accompanied by USS LEWIS HANCOCK, USS MILLER, USS MARSHALL and USS HUNT.

1705 Arrived at the night flying station. NEW JERSEY bears 320°T, 12,000 yards.

1746 Launched 4 F6Fs as a dusk / night CAP.

1820 INDEPENDENCE needed to abruptly maneuver, turning sharply starboard to avoid a large floating object. Directly in the ships path, it appeared to be a mine. USS MARSHALL was detached to investigate it, returning to her station at 2220.

2313 Completed recovering the 4 F6Fs launched at 1746.

2340 Changed course to the northwest to return to Formosa.

GN *Strike at Formosa. Everything going smoothly. A constant air blanket of fighters is being maintained overhead and nothing gets close. Very low ceiling to add to our luck.* **GN**

AD Formosa. Our planes are bombing and strafing Jap fields and shipping. Weather is bad. No attacks on our task force. **AD**

Thursday 4 January 1945   Formosa, Ryukyu's, Okinawa-Shima

Steaming as before (OTC & guide) as TU38.2.10 in company with destroyer screen USS LEWIS HANCOCK, USS MILLER, USS MARSHALL and USS HUNT.
INDEPENDENCE bears 140°T, 14,000 yards from USS NEW JERSEY.
0047 Changed course to 140°T, speed 18 knots.
0050 Completed launching 2 F6Fs upon receipt of a report of 2 bogies, bearing 290°T, distance 95 miles. The night interception broke off when the bogey faded from the radar.
0332 Completed launching 3 F6Fs for a night CAP.
0355 Completed recovery of 2 F6Fs launched at 0050.
0627-0729 Manned general quarters stations.
0735 Recovered 1 F6F launched at 0332.
0747 Completed recovery of 2 F6Fs launched at 0332.
0749 Commenced maneuvering to rejoin TG 38.2.
0757 Secured from flight quarters, Air Department was set to condition 14.
0900 Resumed position in the TG, USS NEW JERSEY bearing 045°T, 2,500 yards.
The Task Force again sent air strikes out against targets on Formosa. Once again, overcast weather and rough seas hampered planned operations. The overcast also obscured the fleet from Japanese attackers.
1134 Sounded torpedo defense, due to an unidentified aircraft.
1155 Secured from torpedo defense, aircraft was identified as friendly.
1228 Sounded torpedo defense, due to an unidentified aircraft.
1303 Secured from torpedo defense. The aircraft was identified as friendly.
1530 Sounded flight quarters.
1605 Changed course to 110°T.
1712 Made radar contact of an unidentified aircraft bearing 287°T, range 30 miles. Sounded torpedo defense.
1715 Bogey identified as friendly. Secured from torpedo defense.
1726 Commenced steering various courses at various speeds to proceed to a night flying station (in company with destroyer screen USS LEWIS HANCOCK, USS MILLER, USS MARSHALL and USS HUNT). No INDEPENDENCE aircraft would be launched tonight due to bad weather.
The Task Force retired to the south on a course of 175°T at 19 knots to a fueling rendezvous.

Friday 5 January 1945   Retiring to refuel

0359 Steaming as before. Completed launching 2 F6Fs.
0612 Sounded routine torpedo defense.
0641 Changed course to 100°T.
0642 Sighted tanker bearing 098°T, distance 10 miles. The Task Group and tanker group converged, closing in and completely surrounding the INDEPENDENCE Task Unit. With no maneuvering room, the destroyer screen was released (retaining one destroyer for plane guard during flight operations).
0716 Secured from torpedo defense.
0723 Having turned into the wind, recovered 2 F6Fs launched at 0359.
0724 Commenced maneuvering to rejoin TG38.2. 0751 Secured from flight quarters.
0759 Rejoined TG38.2 in fueling disposition.
0800 Commenced maneuvering, passing thru the formation to approach the assigned fueling tanker, USS KENNEBAGO.
0832 On a course of 120°T, speed 10 knots, came alongside USS KENNEBAGO.
0915 USS ENTERPRISE joined TG38.2. ENTERPRISE was equipped with her crew trained as a night carrier. USS INDEPENDENCE reported to USS ENTERPRISE for duty. ENTERPRISE was flagship of Commander Carrier Division SEVEN, Rear Admiral Matthias B. Gardner. Mustered crew on stations.

1009 Cast off from tanker USS KENNEBAGO having taken on 195,813 gallons of fuel oil, 10 bottles of CO_2, and 6 bottles of Acetylene gas. Commenced maneuvering to regain position in the formation.

1058 Gained position in the formation, guide USS SAUGATUCK. Changed course to 120°T.

1213-1219 USS HAGGARD came alongside to transfer mail.

1412 Launched 1 TBM.

1434-1447 Half-masted colors following movements of USS HANCOCK.

1505-1508 USS MCCORD was alongside to transfer mail.

1510 Sounded flight quarters.

1522 Recovered 1 TBM launched at 1412.

1535-1539 USS WALLACE L. LIND was alongside to transfer mail. Then, CVL-22 commenced maneuvering to regain formation position, altered due to flight operations and destroyer mail transfers.

1610 USS NEW JERSEY assumed formation guide.

1620 Fleet completed fueling operations.

1638 Axis of formation rotated to 050°T. Guide bears 080°T, 2,500 yards.

1752-1754 Launched 4 F6Fs for night CAP.

1811 Sounded routine torpedo defense.

1830 Commenced maneuvering to proceed to a night flying station, accompanied by USS ENTERPRISE, USS HAGGARD, USS HAZELWOOD, USS MCCORD, USS TRATHEN, USS FRANKS and USS BUCHANAN forming Task Group 38.5. USS ENTERPRISE OTC and guide in disposition 5R. INDEPENDENCE bears 205°T, 3,000 yards from guide.

This night carrier Task Group is formed for night operations in the vicinity of the Task Force, to provide night air cover and for completion of various night flying missions in accordance with CTG 38.5's Operation Order 1-45, dated 4 January, 1945. They formed disposition 5R, INDEPENDENCE position 1.5090 and ENTERPRISE at 1.5270. TG38.5 would remerge with TG 38.2 during daylight hours for added protection, and continue to separate from TG38.2 at dusk for night operations, just as INDEPENDENCE had done in the past.

Now two night carrier air groups would share the workload under cover of the dark.

1900 Released radar decoy balloons.

2057 Changed course to 130°T.

2102 Completed launching 3 F6Fs to relieve the night CAP launched at 1754 .

2133 Commenced recovering aircraft. One F6F crashed into the barrier damaging barriers No.2 & 3, and the F6F's engine.

2154 Completed recovery of the 4 F6Fs launched at 1754.

2354 Changed course to 110°T.

TG38.5 proceeded toward Luzon throughout the night with the rest of the Task Force.

AD   At sea. We now have the Enterprise with us as a night carrier.   AD

Saturday 6 January 1945   *Luzon, Philippines*
USS ENTERPRISE joins USS INDEPENDENCE as a Night Carrier

Steaming as before in TG38.5. At 0035 they changed course to 090°T, speed 25 knots.

0048 Recovered the 3 F6F night CAP launched at 2102. ENTERPRISE will take over the CAP for the remainder of the night.

0316 Air Department set to condition 13.

0429-0435 Launched 8 F6F5Ns for a predawn strike against central Luzon airfields. Pilots were Lt. William E. Henry, Lt. Baker A. Bradenbaugh, Lt.(jg) Robert R. Fegraeus, Lt.(jg) James A. Barnett, Ens. Floyd A. Fisher, Ens. Rueben F. Peterson, Ens. Gayle V. Williams and Ens. Irvin H. Lee.

0446 Changed course to 252°T.

Pilots launched at 0435 made a sweep of the assigned airfields, with no enemy aircraft observed in the air or on the ground.

From the Aircraft Action Report:

"As the sweep headed back toward base, they passed east of Mt. Arayat at 6000'. Lt(jg) Barnett tallyhoed a single plane, 12 miles away at two o'clock, ducking around the foothills of the eastern Luzon mountains. Lt(jg) Barnett led his section down, but the Jap, which was identified as an Oscar, had apparently seen them. He fishtailed into the hills at very low altitude. Lt(jg)Barnett and his wing-man had closed rapidly at 250 kts. I.A.S.. Just as he came into firing range of the Jap, the enemy plane turned to starboard, permitting a full deflection shot at him. By the time the F6F5Ns had pulled around, the Jap had slipped through their entire formation, although Lt. Henry and Ens. Williams put burst into him. En route, Lt(jg) Barnett tailed him and put several 6 and 9 o'clock level bursts into the Oscar as it turned sharply again. By now only 50' from the Oscar's tail, Lt(jg) Barnett could see his incendiaries hit close to the engine. As he pulled up, Lt(jg) Barnett watched the Jap burn, and lose his entire port wing, after which he spun violently to earth. He crashed 15 miles east of Mt. Arayat, at 0800(1). All other VFN pilots witnesses the crash.
With all planes low on gasoline, the flight then returned to base, landing aboard at 0940(1)."

0914 Changed course to 070°T for air operations.
0948 Completed recovery of the 8 F6Fs launched at 0435.
1000 Completed recovery of 3 F6Fs from USS ENTERPRISE, her deck being temporarily fouled.
1004 Commenced maneuvering to rejoin TG38.2., then secured from flight quarters.
1030 Gained position in disposition 5R bearing 260°T, 2,500 yards from USS NEW JERSEY.
1410 Maneuvered to avoid a destroyer conducting rescue operations.
The Task Force would launch continuous air strikes against airfields on Luzon today, in spite of being hampered by overcast skies.
1458 Completed launching 4 F6F5Ns for late afternoon airstrikes. The night Hellcats were flown by Lt. Kyle H. Morris, Ensigns Emmett Russell Edwards, Robert W. Klock and Wallace E. Miller. ENTERPRISE launched a similar strike. They rendezvoused and proceeded toward the target area. After arriving over Aparri, the INDEPENDENCE pilots split up into two sections. Klock and Miller split off as Morris and Edwards continued on with the four ENTERPRISE pilots, proceeding down the Cagayan River strafing ground targets.

From the Aircraft Action Report:

" Proceeding down the west coast of northern Luzon, considerable small shipping was seen and the pilots counted at least seven of them burning presumably from an earlier strike. Ens. Klock and Ens. Miller strafed several additional ones without visible results. Upon reaching Port Currimao they found twelve ships of Sugar-Baker and Sugar-Charlie size lying in the small bay off shore. Both Klock and Miller made several strafing runs on one Sugar-Baker and two Sugar-Charlies, starting fires on the latter two. The extent of the damage was not determined as they left the scene.
Ens. Klock, while at the bottom of a fast low level strafing pass, caught a ship-borne 40mm AA shell from directly ahead and slightly below. The shell entered the leading edge of his starboard horizontal stabilizer and upon exploding, ripped off about a fourth of the stabilizer's upper skin surface, and smashed one of the internal braces. Klock retained full control however, and he and Ens. Miller flew back to base, landing aboard at 1925(1). They had seen no enemy airborne planes during the entire time."

Photos: Top -   Wallace E. Miller VF(N)-41
Bottom - William P. Phelps VT(N)-41

Lt. Morris and Ens. Edwards in the meantime, continued down the Cagayan River.

Morris, on a southerly course, spotted three Oscars at 2 o'clock in a "V" formation at 2,000' 4-5 miles away, flying east. As distance closed (now at 1 o'clock) an Oscar peeled off turning in toward Morris to attack. Morris put a burst into the Oscar from 12 o'clock high before the Oscar could bring his guns to bear. The Oscar's starboard wing came off just as the plane exploded, the spinning wreckage falling near the river. Morris, evading the other two Oscars that initially pursued, spotted some Tojos, He applied W.E.P. and pursued. One Tojo started a shallow turn to starboard. Morris with his speed advantage, closed, leveled out and stitched the Tojo with a long burst from 6 o'clock level into the wing roots.

"After 20 seconds of intermittent bursts, the Jap pilot started a shallow turn to port, and continued it until he flew into the ground and exploded."

While Lt. Morris was busy with his two kills, Ensign Emmett R. "Eddy" Edwards was also busy.

From the Aircraft Action Report:
"Morris climbed back up, and heard Ens. Edwards calling, asking Morris to join up on him on a 060 degree (T) course to base. Edwards sounded as though he was in trouble. Morris had 45" (manifold pressure) *and 2400 R.P.M., and immediately turned onto the 060 degree course. He saw 3 Tojos in formation at 4 o'clock,*
2000', a mile away. One of them following the tactics of the other Jap 3 plane sections, peeled off in Morris 's direction, so Morris turned on his W.E.P., and ran away from the scene on the 060 degree course. He contacted Ens. Edwards, who was considerably higher up. After climbing chase of 20 miles, he joined up on Edwards near the east coast. As he pulled up alongside him, he saw Edwards signal for him not to fly too close. Edwards then called him, saying he'd had part of his starboard wing-shot off, but didn't say how it occurred. Lt. Morris then noticed that about five feet of the starboard wing was missing from Edwards 's plane, including the radar antenna housing. The wing seemed to be severed just outboard of the wing flap, with about a foot of main wing spar protruding beyond that point. Edwards was making 180 knots I.A.S., and told Morris he couldn't control his plane at a slower speed. On the way to base, Morris told Edwards he'd knocked down two Jap fighters, and Edwards replied that he himself had gotten a Betty and another plane (the name of which Morris didn't catch).
They both flew to the force, and contacted base. Then 3-4 miles NE of the LEXINGTON, Edwards found himself in a clearing at 2000' altitude. He told Morris he planned to bailout by rolling the plane over and dropping out. Morris saw him roll back his cockpit cover, and then heard him say, " I'll never make it –" Morris called him right back to cheer him, and said, " Roll over and hit the silk ". Edwards didn't call him again, but Morris saw his plane snap over on its back, and plummet down into the water, (Time 1810).
Morris saw no one leave the plane but thought he saw objects that looked like a Mae West and a white helmet (Edwards wore such a helmet) fly from the plane just as it rolled over, before diving in. Morris immediately called the LEXINGTON, which advised that a lookout had already seen the crash, and that DDs had already been sent to the spot. MORRIS circled the oil slick at 17 - 56 N, 124 - 53 E, and saw " THE SULLIVANS " circle it, then go through it. Morris then asked that the DD be instructed to search the adjacent area. Morris then was informed that no survivors or debris had been found, so he headed for base and landed aboard at 1822(I). Edwards is regarded as missing.
The next day, it was discovered that Ens. G. E. Franklin, one of the ENTERPRISE fighter pilots on the same mission, had actually seen Edwards in a midair collision with a Tojo during the melee over Tuguegarao. The Tojo seemed to deliberately turn into Edwards, shearing off a portion of the latter's wing. Immediately after the collision, Franklin saw the Tojo spin in and crash! (This set of facts was also reported in TG 38.5's complete flash report of 7 January 1945 to TF38).
Lt. Morris's two victims were his first; likewise Ens. Edwards had gotten his first three, the last of these by a mid-air collision. It is deeply regretted that he was apparently unable to make a successful bail-out after flying his damaged plane over 200 miles back to the task force."
Ensign "Eddy" Edwards would be listed by the Navy as missing in action for the next 2 years.

1605 Commenced steering various courses at various speeds while forming TG38.5 and proceeding to our night flying station, ENTERPRISE guide, bearing 320°T, 3,000 yards.

1707 Changed course to 050°T.

1726 Catapulted 3 F6Fs that had landed on board at 1000, for return to ENTERPRISE.

1757 Launched 4 F6F5Ns for a night CAP into foul weather conditions.

1540 Changed course to 255°T, speed 17 knots.

1815 Darkened ship.

1817 Sounded routine torpedo defense. Gunners and deckhands would also endure the weather.

1826 Recovered 1 F6F launched at 1458 (Lt. Morris).

1917 Secured from torpedo defense.

1930 Recovered the remaining 2 F6Fs launched at 1458 (Klock and Miller).

1937 Recovered 1 F6F launched at 1757. The remaining 3 F6Fs from the 1757 launch were ordered to divert to the larger ENTERPRISE flight deck. Landing conditions described as being abnormally hazardous, due to winds and high seas. Changed course to 060°T.

2026 Changed course to 330°T.

Due to the weather conditions, the remainder of the planned CAPs for the evening remained on board, in a ready condition. The Task Force headed north toward Formosa during the night. However, due to increasingly foul weather and heavy seas to the north, the decision was made that Luzon would be more desirable for targeting. The fleet changed course toward the southwest.

Sunday 7 January 1945   Luzon, Philippines

Steaming as before in TG38.5 accompanied by USS ENTERPRISE (OTC and guide), USS HAGGARD, USS HAZELWOOD, USS MCCORD, USS TRATHEN, USS FRANKS and USS BUCHANAN. INDEPENDENCE bears 140°T, 3,000 yards from guide. INDEPENDENCE has no aircraft airborne, with 3 F6Fs on board from the ENTERPRISE. At 0330 the ship sounded flight quarters.

0455 Changed course to 075°T. At 0507 the INDEPENDENCE launched 6 F6Fs for predawn fighter sweep over Angeles Airfields area on Luzon.

From the Aircraft Action Report:
"Planes were flown by A.G.C.* T.F. Caldwell, Jr., Lt. B.A. Bradenbaugh, Lt. R.D. Otis, Ens. F.A. Hun-ziker, Ens. W.C. Light and Ens. L.H. Diskosky. They immediately made rendezvous with Ens. A. Hansen and Ens. C.H. Kesler, of this squadron, who were launched from the U.S.S. ENTERPRISE at 0445(1). (These latter pilots had landed aboard the ENTERPRISE at the end of a routine CAP over the task force the night before). (* Air Group Commander)
Only 7 planes proceeded to the target area. Ens. Diskosky landed back aboard shortly after takeoff, because of radio trouble.
The 7 planes flew through bad weather toward the target area, picking up altitude on the way in. They hoped to find clear weather over the target but upon arriving there at dawn, found it completely closed in by 10/10ths clouds. They were unable to break through, after circling at 14,000' for a period of time. They returned to the force, letting down through the overcast on instruments as they approached one of the outlying picket destroyers. They landed aboard at 0915(1)."

0555 Recovered 1 F6F launched at 0507.

0615-0712 Manned routine general quarters stations.

0923 Completed recovering 8 F6Fs, five launched by INDEPENDENCE at 0507, and three launched yesterday at 1757, having to land on the ENTERPRISE at 2055 the same day. These three F6Fs were launched from ENTERPRISE at 0845 this morning.

0927 Air Department secured from flight quarters, set condition 14.

1108 Maneuvered to rejoin TG38.2

1130 Gained position in disposition 5R, NEW JERSEY bearing 080°T, 2,500 yards, OTC in USS LEXINGTON. The weather was "fairly decent" allowing the Task Force to send out blanketing strikes.

1143 Sounded Torpedo defense on report of unidentified aircraft.

1148 Secured from torpedo defense, aircraft identified as a friendly Army B-24.

1400 Sounded flight quarters.

1505-1515 Launched 6 F6Fs as a Target CAP over the Clark Field area on Luzon.

1712 Completed launching 2 F6Fs assigned a night heckler mission over the Clark Field area. Lt. B.A."Brady" Bradenbaugh and Ens. W.E."Wally" Miller found no Japanese aircraft and were hampered by poor visibility.

1715 Changed course to 265°T. Commenced leaving TG38.2 to form up with TG38.5.

1724 Maneuvering to gain position with ENTERPRISE (guide) bearing 350°T, 3,000 yards. Our screen is USS HAGGARD, USS HAZELWOOD, USS MCCORD, USS TRATHEN, USS FRANKS and USS BUCHANAN.

1752 Changed course to 080°T. 1753 Completed launching 4 F6Fs assigned CAP.

1816 Launched 1 F6F.

1820 Sounded routine torpedo defense. Changed course to 085°T.

1825 Recovered 1 F6F launched at 1753.

1853 Launched 2 TBMs.

1920 Secured from torpedo defense.

1932 Launched 2 TBMs.

2047 Completed recovery 6 F6Fs launched at 1513, 1 F6F launched at 1817 due to mechanical trouble, 2 TBMs launched at 1853, 2 TBMs launched at 1932 and 2 F6Fs launched from the ENTERPRISE, due to a fouled deck on ENTERPRISE caused by a landing crash. The TBMs had mechanical difficulties.

2216 Completed launching 3 F6Fs.

2239 Recovered 1 F6F launched at 2216.

2244 Lt. B.A. 'Brady" Bradenbaugh caught the #5 wire during his night landing. The wire broke and Brady's Hellcat swerved into the port gun bucket adjacent to the barrier cables. No personnel casualties or major damage to the ship. The F6F had a damaged port wing and landing gear. It was repaired and flying again two days later. Brady had launched at 1712. 4 F6Fs were in the landing pattern when the crash occurred.

2322 USS ENTERPRISE recovered 1 F6F launched from INDEPENDENCE at 1712 (Wally Miller), and 3 F6Fs launched at 1753 due to the fouled deck on INDEPENDENCE. (Wally had been aloft for six hours, and had no discernable fuel left when he landed.)

2344 Changed course to 085°T.

The Task Force would proceed toward the north during the night for a fueling rendezvous.

GN Enterprise joins us as a night carrier job and hopes are high that we might get to the States or at least to Pearl for some Liberty. Raid Luzon area again. *GN*

GL Still at Luzon. We are waiting around for the landing on Luzon. Report says the island is already a bloody battlefield. Ships of the 7th fleet have been hit so we are here just in case. We land a few of the E's planes that were low on gas. One of our planes crashed into catwalk, little damage done. E lost 4 planes, 2 crashed in air, one in drink, one was shot up. We had a small fire on board but no damage done. *GL*

Monday 8 January 1945   Fueling — Return to Formosa

0018 Steaming as before. Commenced air operations.

0019 Landing, 1 F6F collided with the barrier, causing minor damage to the Hellcat.

0052 Completed recovering 2 F6Fs, 1 launched at 2216 and 1 F6F from ENTERPRISE, returning from a night heckler flight low on fuel. ENTERPRISE maintained the CAP for the remainder of the night.

0629 Changed course to 170°T. At 0630 the tanker group was sighted, bearing 045°T, 10 miles.

Task Group 38.5 was between the converging Task Group and the tankers, maneuvering south and west of the Force to make her approach from astern of T38.2 as it changed course to 070°T for fueling.

0801 Released from TG38.5.

0924 Arrived on station in TG38.2. Changed course to 070°T, speed 10 knots.

1011 Came alongside of tanker USS ATASCOSA.

1045-1100 USS WEEKS was alongside port quarter to transfer mail.

1104-1118 USS ENGLISH was alongside port quarter to receive two pilots to be delivered to CVE USS KWAJALEIN to pick up replacement aircraft.

1136 Having completed pumping 150,465 gallons of fuel oil, tanker USS ATASCOSA cast off from the starboard side.

1137 Commenced maneuvering to regain station within the formation.

1220 Gained position, course 070°T, bearing 078°T, 5,200 yards from guide, USS ATASCOSA.

1250 USS STEPHEN POTTER came alongside port quarter to transfer official mail.

1309 Sounded flight quarters.

1349 USS WEEKS came alongside starboard to transfer U.S. Mail to INDEPENDENCE.

1400 Commenced maneuvering for flight operations.

1406 Launched 2 F6Fs for return to the ENTERPRISE, having landed onboard 2047 last night. Launched 5 TBMs for flight test to "shake out the bugs" (the aircraft recently experiencing reliability problems).

1435 Recovered 2 F6F replacement aircraft, ferried over from the USS KWAJALEIN. Recovered 3 F6Fs that landed aboard ENTERPRISE at 2315 last night due to the fouled INDEPENDENCE deck.

1518 Recovered the 5 TBMs launched at 1406 for flight testing.

1545 Regained position within the formation.

1546 USS NEW JERSEY assumed guide, course 070°T, bearing 100°T, 2,500 yards.

1612-1620 USS MILLER came alongside to transfer Lt. Erwin N. Becker on board from Fighting Squadron 29 for assignment to VF(N)-41.

1621 Maneuvered to form up as TG38.5 (same vessels as before) to proceed to a night flying station.

1710 INDEPENDENCE gained position in TG38.5 3,000 yards from ENTERPRISE.

1715 The Task Force began an approach to Formosa, on a course of 335°T, speed 21 knots.

1751 Changed course to 130°T for air operations.

1757 Completed launching 4 F6Fs for night CAP, and 1 F6F that had landed aboard at 0052 this morning from USS ENTERPRISE (low on fuel).

1821 Recovered 1 F6F launched from the USS ENTERPRISE (that had landed on ENTERPRISE due to our fouled deck).

1839 Completed recovering 2 F6Fs launched at 1757 for CAP. No relief was launched. Remaining CAP aircraft remained on board in a ready condition

1920 Launched 1 F6F.

2123 Recovered 4 F6Fs, 3 launched at 1757, 1 F6F launched at 1920.

2204 Launched 1 F6F. Bogey picked up on radar, bearing 330°T, distance 80 miles (Radar contact later faded). Changed course to 320°T, speed 26 knots.

AD 1/8/45 At sea. Luzon. 7th fleet bombing shore positions. AD

Tuesday 9 January 1945   *Formosa, Ryukyu's ("S"Day - Luzon Invasion)*

0001 Approaching Formosa in TG38.5 accompanied by USS ENTERPRISE (OTC and guide), USS HAGGARD, USS HAZELWOOD, USS MCCORD, USS TRATHEN, USS FRANKS and USS BUCHANAN. Changed course to 165°T, speed 22 knots.

0005 Recovered 1 F6F launched at 2204.   0008 Changed course to 315°T, speed 26 knots.

0520 Sounded flight quarters.

0530 Two destroyers in TG38.2 reported submarine contact. The destroyers stayed with the contacts, aided by two TBMs from the ENTERPRISE.

0748 Commenced maneuvering to rejoin TG 38.2.

0818 Launched 2 TBMs (Reb Taylor & Frank McNair) for a hunter killer anti-sub mission.

0900 Changed course to 000°T, speed 24 knots. Gained position in formation 5R, axis 150°T, guide USS NEW JERSEY, bearing 180°T, 2,500 yards. Mustered crew on stations. Strikes were launched all day by Task Force aircraft against Formosa targets, made more difficult by overcast skies.

0945 Axis changed to 050°T. Maneuvered to assume new position. Guide now bearing 080°T.

From 1130 on, when operations into the wind were not required, the Task Force steamed southwest to close the distance to the entrance of the South China Sea.

1235 Completed recovery of 2 TBMs launched at 0818.

1241 Air Department secured from flight quarters, set condition 14.

1336 Changed course to 180°T.

1343 Sounded torpedo defense, radar contact, unidentified aircraft.

1348 One enemy aircraft (Dinah) shot down by the YORKTOWN CAP, bearing 250°T, 25 miles.

1354 Secured from torpedo defense.

1426 Sounded torpedo defense, radar contact, unidentified aircraft.

1451 Secured from torpedo defense. Aircraft identified as friendly.

1738 Unidentified aircraft reported bearing 350°T, 20 miles, closing. Sounded torpedo defense.

1743 Aircraft identified as friendly.

1745 Secured from torpedo defense.

1824 Sounded routine torpedo defense.

1855 Changed course to 207°T.

1922 Secured from torpedo defense. At 1935 radio & radar silence Condition Two was ordered. Night Combat Air Patrols were kept on deck, maintained in ready condition.

2205 Changed course to 243°T.

2230 Entered Bashi Channel en route to China Sea. They passed Y'Ami Island, the northern most island of the Batan Island group, 13 miles to port. (Map page 515)

GL G.Q. 6:10 – 100 miles from Formosa. Today is big landing on Luzon. Sent strikes into Formosa damage unknown. Had torpedo defense 3 times today. C.A.P. shot down 1 Dina. I guess we are headed into China Sea. No one exactly likes the idea either. The Jap will be all around us. We had two sub contacts this morning. GL

(S-Day. On Tuesday 9 January 1945 the 6th Army went ashore at Lingayen landing 68,000 troops on the first day. From January 4th thru January 12th, 24 ships were sunk and 67 damaged by Kamikazes.)

21
South China Sea

Wednesday 10 January 1945   *Entered South China Sea*

Steaming thru the Bashi Channel into the South China Sea. In company with Task Unit 38.2.1 consisting of carriers INDEPENDENCE, USS LEXINGTON (OTC), USS HORNET, USS HANCOCK and USS ENTERPRISE, in cruising disposition 5R, course 234°T, speed 23 knots (with USS NEW JERSEY guide).

0003 The group now sufficiently beyond the channel to turn toward the southwest. Cloud coverage was thought to have helped all ships to steam thru the passage without any interference from the enemy. Plans called for striking Japanese shipping in the French Indochina area. Every effort was being made to maintain secrecy.

0453 Radar reports of unidentified aircraft bearing 183°T, 80 miles.

0511 Changed course to 040°T, speed 15 knots.

0515 Radar contact now showing unidentified aircraft 27 miles. Lt(jg) Robert R. Fegraeus and Ens. Arthur H. Hansen were catapulted into a cloudy overcast night, with sunrise to occur at 0740. The bogey they were to intercept in their Hellcats, was thought to probably be a routine flight from Luzon and Formosa.

0516 Changed course to 225°T, speed 15 knots.

0518 Sounded torpedo defense. Unidentified aircraft closed to 11 miles, bearing 075°T.

0535 Secured from torpedo defense.

0551 Received report that Ensign "Art" Hansen shot down a twin engine Sally (bomber) 120 miles from the formation.

0635 Unidentified aircraft bearing 188°T, 60 miles, and a second plane bearing 116°T, 69 miles.

0637 Sounded routine general quarters.

0649 Enemy aircraft was shot down by Lt(jg) Robert Fegraeus on our port beam at distance of 2 miles. " Fergie" Fegraeus made his kill high above the cloud layer over the formation. The burning plane, "a streak of fire, suddenly and sensationally, plunged out of the darkness of the clouds overhead, straight to the water three miles away". In the darkness, it was visible for miles.

0657 Received a report that Ensign Arthur Hansen shot down a Nick 72 miles out.

The text from the Aircraft Action Report is provided here to give you a more detailed description of what night combat was like for the VF(N)41 pilots.

From the Aircraft Action Report:

"At 0453(1) on the morning of the 10th, when the force was approximately equidistant from Luzon and Formosa, a bogey made its appearance on the radar screens. Probably on a routine flight from Luzon to Formosa, the Jap first appeared 98 miles out, bearing 180 degrees, closing on a 000 degrees true course at angels 10.5. The INDEPENDENCE had the condition 11 and was prepared to launch immediately, but permission was not received to do so until 0514(I), when the bogey had closed to 27 miles, still on its 000 degrees true course.

Lt(jg) R.R. Fegraeus and Ens. A. Hansen were catapulted immediately, and Fegraeus was sent to orbit at 175 degrees true, 20 miles. Hansen was given a 180 degrees true vector, angels 8, with instructions to buster. He turned on full R.P.M., climbed to angels 8, and shortly after was given a turning vector to put him on the bogey's tail. As he made his turn, he made radar contact, at 0521(I), but it was weak, as the 4 mile scale of his APS6A gear was not functioning properly. He reported his bogey to be 2 1/2 miles, at 1 o'clock. He lost contact three minutes later, but reported at 0528(I) that he picked it up again. He was now directly over the force and both he and the bogey were continuing on their 000 degree courses. INDEPENDENCE base, with poor information now, turned the interception over to the TICONDEROGA.

Hansen had lost contact again but the TICONDEROGA told him at 0540(I) that the bogey should be 12 o'clock, 1 mile, angels 10.5. Three minutes later Hansen was told that the bogeys speed was 180 knots. At the same time Hansen called contact again.

By now the bogey had opened to 62 miles, bearing 012 degrees true, and still on a northerly course. Because of his weak radar gear, Hansen was unable to close for a visual contact and a kill, and at 0555 (I) when he was 85 miles out, the TICONDEROGA gave him a vector back to base. Hansen did not hear this transmission and since he had radar contact on the bogey, continued the chase with no further assistance from C.I.C. On one occasion he switched to gunsight and lined the bogey up squarely between the goal post. Reluctant to fire blind through the clouds, particularly because he had been briefed to make visual identification, he switched back to the 4 mile scale when he could not actually make visual contact ahead.

He lost the contact he'd had, but picked it up again, and after closing to proper range, switched to gunsight again, and put the blip squarely between the goal posts, and with the wings touching the goal posts. Looking out again, he was able to see, a twin-engine plane ahead of him. (He reported that, had he fired from his gunsight contact only, his 50 cal. would have passed to starboard and slightly below the enemy, possibly close enough to put a few slugs in the starboard wing.)

Hansen was now flying at angels 8.3 and his bogey at 8.4. He flew up within 500' of the bogeys tail, and realized he could see only a silhouette, but no flame pattern, indicative of excellent dampeners. He finally identified the plane as a Sally by flying directly under it and observing the wing plan. It was too dark to see the meatballs even as close as Hansen now was. He then dropped back, but found he would have lost visual contact, because of the clouds and the flame dampeners, had he dropped back to his guns' boresight range of 750'. At 250' therefore, he opened up with all six guns, with his pipper on the

Japs tail. His tracers went into the fuselage and both the wing roots of the Sally. After this long burst the bomber's starboard wing root began to burn, and the wing skin around the fire showed a bright red glow. This glow made a good target, so Hansen put another burst into the Jap's starboard engine, and more flames broke out.The Jap should have had plenty of time for evasive action after the first burst, but failed to take advantage of it.

Finally, after a second burst, the Sally started a spiraling turn to port, with the flames burning brightly by now. The glow of the wing skin was also visible, as the Jap was enveloped in clouds on the way down. Hansen followed the Sally down for several hundred feet through the clouds, the flame and glow showing through nicely and giving him something to follow. The Jap was continuing his crazy death spiral as Hansen put another long "blind" burst into the flames and glow.

As he pulled out of his dive and into a 90 degree turn, his instruments having tumbled, Hansen saw a bright fare-up in the cloud area below him indicating the disintegration of the Sally. By this time, 0610 (I) the chase had extended to 21-25 N, 121-08 E, or just a few miles up from and to the east of Garanbi on the southern tip of Formosa. It was the longest night chase in the history of VF(N)41, and also the first time that any of its pilots had fired "Blind", and successfully, at a cloud-enshrouded night target, as described above.

He then headed 190 degrees true, and a few minutes later established radio contact with Fegraeus, and reported that he'd splashed the bogey. He then made contact with the TICONDEROGA who reported him as still being 93 miles from them, on a 013 degree bearing. The TICONDEROGA told him to speed up on his present course as there would probably be more business for him to the east of the force where another bogey was showing. Hansen had in the meantime received a "Well Done" from CTF 38 for his long chase.

  While Hansen was returning from his long chase, another bogey showed up on the radar screen at 0621(I), bearing 185 degrees true, from the INDEPENDENCE, on a course of 000 degrees, distance 90 miles, speed 180 kts., angel 8.5. Fegraeus, who had been orbiting at 175 degrees bearing, 20 miles distant, at angels 8, was sent out for this second piece of business. He was given a 170 degrees vector, and was told by Ens J.0. Coates who handled the entire intercept from the INDEPENPENCE that the bogey should be at 1 o'clock, 60 miles, closing. As the bogey approached on a direct course, Fegraeus was turned on to his course at approximately 45 miles south of the force. His APS6A gear picked up the bogey contact at 3½ mi. while Fegraeus was turning.

The signals were weak on his APS6A, however, and the contact faded. As he straightened out on the bogey's course, Fegraeus regained contact, which showed the bogey at 3 miles, 12 o'clock, on 020 degrees course, speed 155 kts I.A.S., angels 9.4. Fegraeus at angels 9.2, closed to one mile, switched to his one mile scale, and then made visual contact at 1/3 mile; with the bogey at 1230 o'clock and slightly above. Fegraeus closed to 200' on the bogey which he recognized as a Sally, the same as Hansen's first victim. A burst from Fegraeus four inboard guns (outboard guns were tracer loaded) went into both of the Jap's engines, which immediately flared up. The port engine blew up in a few moments, and the Jap nosed over in a 350-400 glide, burning beautifully. Fegraeus, who lost sight of his victim as the Sally plunged through the low overcast. He pulled over, dived through the clouds, and leveling out at angels 1.5, saw his victim, now a flaming mass, hit the water close aboard the Hancock. (20-12 N.,120-20 E.), time 0647(I). Practically everyone in the force saw this Jap crash, and Fegraeus received "Well Dones" from practically all the fleet commands, while still airborne. He was then sent to angels 8 to orbit as he was popeye between angels 1.5 up to 7.5.

  While Fegraeus's interception was in progress, Hansen was returning from his first, having been told by the TICONDEROGA that there was more business to the east. Meanwhile, the HANCOCK had better dope on this eastern bogey, and took over Hansens control. This bogey was picked up at 0627 (I), bearing 125°, distance 72 miles, on a 000° course, at angels 8. Hansen was vectored south, until at 0651(I) he was turned onto the bogey's tail. The bogey was now 063°, 59 miles, and opening on a 000° course at 145 kts. I.A.S. At 0653(I) Hansen called contact, but lost it at 0656(I). Angels had been reported as 8.5, but Hansen's scope showed indications that the bogey was closer to angels 5. Hansen quickly dived to that level, and lost his contact, as indicated above. He then pulled up to

Chapter 21   514

angels 6, and the HANCOCK told him he was ¼ mile behind his bogey .He cracked his flaps and cowl flaps and slowed down to 120 kts., I.A.S. After two vectors of 340° and 010° he reestablished radar contact with the bogy at 0658(I). When he had closed to ½ mile, Hansen made visual contact on the exhaust pattern of a twin-engined plane flying directly ahead of him.   (Continued on next page)

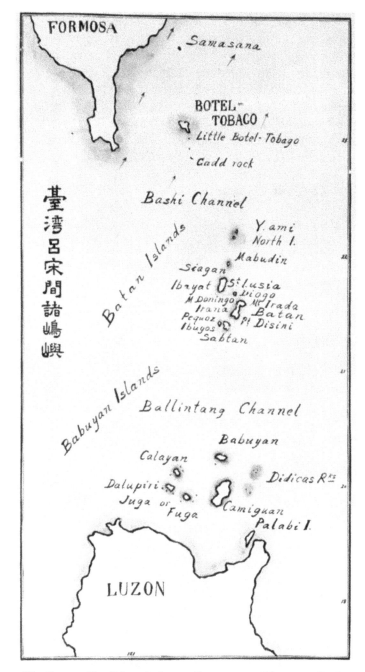

Jack Stanley Berkheimer - VF(N)-41

Alvin R. Huss - VT(N)-41

The Luzon Strait lays between Formosa and Luzon offering passage between the Philippine Sea on the east and the South China Sea to the west. Independence with TG 38.5 steaming west, entered the South China Sea thru the Bashi Channel passing Y'Ami Island, the northern most island of the Batan group, 13 miles to port. The refueling group entered south of the Batan group thru the Balintang Channel.

(Note: Balingtang in modern references, Ballingtang on the map) .
(The letter "B" in the "Bashi Channel" on the map is roughly the location of where Hansen shot down the Sally at approximately 0610.)

Dawn was approaching, so Hansen " sneaked up " on the bogey by ducking in and out of the clouds. When he was only 300' astern, he pulled out to one side and checked the bogey as being either a Dinah or a Nick.(He agreed it was a Nick after returning to base) He then dropped back to 300' to a safe distance astern just in case of an explosion and fired all six guns. Only one starboard gun out of the six actually fired, and it ran dry after a few rounds.

This single gun's fire did the trick however, as the Jap's starboard engine burst into flames for a few seconds. The Jap continued on his course, however, and Hansen tried another 6 gun burst after recharging them all. This time only one port gun out of the six actually fired, and it put out about 20 rounds before it stopped. That was enough, as the Jap burst into flames as Hansen pulled up and directly over him in a sharp port turn. The Nick blew up in the air in a second or two and the debris fell into the sea at 0709(1), 21-22 N., 1.21-04E. Hansen took a 210 steer to base, then 85 miles distant, and received a " very well done " from CTF 38 before he'd landed aboard with Fegraeus at 0735(I).

The above three interceptions were spectacular, and were well handled both by the pilots and the controlling C.I.C's aboard the TICONDEROGA, the INDEPENDENCE and the HANCOCK respectively.

It was Hansen's first night experience in combat, and he was in line as indicated, for numerous congratulatory messages.

Fegraeus, an older hand, did a neat, precise job of interception, and the victim himself added the spectacle effect as he crashed, burning into the water close aboard CTF 38's Flagship, the HANCOCK."

Above AA Report prepared by: Lt. J.J. O'Shaughnessy, VF(N)-41 A.C.I. Officer

0737 Completed recovery of 2 F6Fs launched at 0515 (Hansen and Fegraeus).

The rest of the day was quiet for the crew of the INDEPEPENDENCE as the fleet proceeded southwest past northern Luzon. Small targets, picked up by search planes, were ignored along the way.

0739 Changed course to 225°T, speed 22 knots. Secured from general quarters.
0857 Secured from flight quarters, Air Department set to condition 14.
1530 Sounded flight quarters.
1706 Changed course to 260°T, speed 12 knots and began maneuvering to form TG 38.5.
1726 Gained station in TG 38.5, guide USS ENTERPRISE, bearing 340°T, 3,000 yards.
No patrols were flown this night.

GN Got three Nips who were snooping at dawn. One was splashed in sight of whole outfit by my plane. Pilot only fired about 250 rounds but the Jap sure looked as though he were hit by a couple of 16 inchers. Made a beautiful fire until he hit the drink. GN

GL We are now in China Sea. Had torpedo defense at 5:30. We have two planes in the air. Went into G.Q. at 6:40 had two bogies on the screen. The Bogie which came on the screen was shot down a while later. It was a Sally. We now have two bogies, one at 30, the other at 60 miles. The one at 30 got to within six miles than one of the Cupids pilots splashed him, all eyes turned to the sky to see him come down. He came flaming down at 6:40 right into the middle of task group and looked as though he was going to crash into one of our carriers. He missed and crashed into the sea a mass of flames, what a sight. Our plane followed him all the way down and zoomed up into the sky when he hit. It was a Sally. The other plane at 60 miles had contact with his bogie and splashed him. We got a well done from task group commander and Red Cap (Enterprise), all planes landed safely. One blew out his tire. GL

Thursday 11 January 1945   *South China Sea — Fueling*

Steaming as before in TG 38.5 accompanied by USS ENTERPRISE (OTC and guide), and DESRON 47 consisting of USS HAGGARD, USS HAZELWOOD, USS MCCORD, USS TRATHEN, USS FRANKS and USS BUCHANAN.

A group of tankers had entered the South China Sea through Balintang Channel on the same evening as TG38.5 entered through Bashi Channel. They had accompanied TG38.5 toward the southwest, and today the Task Force will refuel.

0800 Secured from flight quarters.

0809 Changed course to 170°T. Task Group 38.5 commenced maneuvering to rejoin Task Group 38.2.

0910 Commenced maneuvering independently to gain station in TG 38.2.

0922 Commenced maneuvering to take station 1,000 yards astern tanker USS NANTAHALA which is steaming on course of 201°T at 10 knots. The course is downwind allowing progress toward the southwest during the fueling operation. A problem developed on this heading, as they had 25 knots of wind from astern. The bridge was blanketed with stack gas, forcing the bridge watch to wear gas masks for personal comfort. In other words, to keep from being asphyxiated.

The pilots were occasionally faced with the same dilemma with the stack gases, as they sat for lengthy periods strapped into their cockpits, on the catapults, ready to launch at a moments notice.

When wind blew from astern and slightly to port, pilots would become enveloped in the noxious stack fumes, unless the speed of the carrier was enough to blow the gases aft. This while they contend with a mix of weather, and a tired tedium. The effects of tedium, weather and stack fumes suddenly had to be cast astray as a bogy popped up on ships radar. There was an instant need to regain their full wits (and night vision) for a quick engine start and catapult shot, hurling off into a deadly night hunt for the enemy. Then the return to home to a dark bobbing and rolling flight deck.

Also contending with stack gas and weather were the gun mount and flight deck crews.

1014 Commenced approach alongside to our starboard, USS NANTAHALA.

1057 Commenced pumping fuel oil.

1217 Cast off all lines from USS NANTAHALA, having received 192,966 gallons of fuel oil.

1220 Commenced maneuvering to regain station in the formation.

1238 Regained station, guide USS NEW JERSEY, bearing 080°T, 2,500 yards.

1300 USS SAN JUAN designated guide in position 0000. Commenced maneuvering to gain station on USS SAN JUAN.

1400 Gained station on USS SAN JUAN, bearing 080°T, 2,500 yards.

1500 Changed course to 245°T, speed 23 knots.

1634 Sounded torpedo defense. Unidentified aircraft bearing 105°T, 20 miles. TICONDEROGA CAP had shot down 3 Jakes. (COMCARDIV 7 War Diary)

1638 Secured from torpedo defense. Radar contact with unidentified aircraft lost.

1742 Secured from flight quarters, Air Department set to condition 14.

Shortly after 1800 they commenced maneuvering to reform Task Group 38.5 (same vessels as before) and proceeded to a night flying station.

1946 Launched 2 F6Fs for CAP.

2146 Recovered the 2 F6Fs launched at 1946.

GL Fueled ship today. About 1700 Lexington* C.A.P. shot down 3 Jakes. We are still in the China Sea.

GL   (* As noted above COMCARDIV 7 War Diary credits TICONDEROGA CAP. George's source unknown?)

AD At sea. China Sea. Refueling 200 miles off Manila. Crew is a little uneasy about being in the China Sea. Our target for tomorrow will be Jap shipping in Indo China if we can sneak in unnoticed. Halsey says we will throw everything at them including 16" shells. AD

Friday 12 January 1945   *South China Sea   Convoy HI-86*
French Indochina — Camranh Bay, Amoy, Saigon, Quinon Bay

Steaming toward the Camranh Bay region of Indochina, in Task Group 38.5, accompanied by USS ENTERPRISE (OTC and guide), and destroyer screen USS HAGGARD, USS HAZELWOOD, USS MCCORD, USS TRATHEN, USS FRANKS and USS BUCHANAN.

0304 Launched 4 TBMs ("Reb" Taylor, John Dewis, Bill Phelps & John Williams) to participate in pre-dawn searches in the waters off Indochina, in expectation of finding heavy elements of the Japanese Fleet, as well as merchant shipping.

0333 Changed course to 250°T, speed to 26 knots.

0831 Recovered 4 TBMs launched at 0304.

The Task group, steaming 15 miles off the coast, launched strikes against shipping found all along the coast. Against expectations, no heavy Japanese Fleet units were found in the Camranh Bay area.

0900 (approx.) **Japanese Convoy HI-86** had steamed slowly south out of the curved channel of Quinon Bay (Qui Nhon today) to make essentially a sweeping left turning 180° heading change and navigated seaward around the wide tip of the bays protective peninsula to proceed north. The mix of 10 freighters and tankers were shepherded by an escort group of six vessels led by IJN light cruiser KASHII with convoy commander Rear ADM Shiro Shibuya. At about this time the first Navy Hellcats entered the scene.

Convoy HI-86 vessels were:

Tankers & Cargo Ships   (Note all tonnage numbers are approximate tonnage)

BANSHU MARU NO.63	533 ton	Tanker	(crude oil)
EIMAN MARU	6,900 ton	Cargo Ship	(bauxite, natural rubber)
KYOKUUN MARU	10,000 ton	Tanker	(crude oil)
OTSUSAN* MARU	6,800 ton	Cargo Ship	(aviation gasoline, heavy oil, natural rubber)
SAN LUIS MARU	7,628 ton	Tanker	(crude oil)
SHOEI MARU	2,768 ton	Cargo Ship	(heavy oil, natural rubber)
TATEBE MARU	4,519 ton	Cargo Ship	(aviation gasoline, manganese, natural rubber)
TATSUHATO** MARU	6,600 ton	Cargo Ship	(aviation gasoline, heavy oil, natural rubber)
YOSHU MARU	5,711 ton	Cargo Ship	(bauxite, natural rubber)
YUSEI*** MARU	500 ton	Tanker	(crude oil)

Notes: (* AKA OTSUYAMA MARU) (** possibly spelled TATSUBUTO) (*** Possibly spelled USEI)

IJN Escort Vessels

CD-23	745 ton	Type C Escort Ship
CD-27	745 ton	Type C Escort Ship
CD-51	745 ton	Type C Escort Ship
DAITO	940 ton	Hiburi Class Escort Ship
KASHII	61,80 ton	Katori Class Light Cruiser
UKURU	940 ton	Ukuru Class Escort Ship

Back aboard the INDEPENDENCE;

1020 Changed course to 050°T.

1037 Launched 12 F6F Hellcats and 4 TBM Avengers for a day strike against a Japanese shipping convoy. Aircraft were loaded with 500lb GP bombs (1 per F6F, 4 per TBM). This mission would be the largest group attack of CLVG(N)-41 to date, normally operating in smaller numbers for night missions. Briefed and launched to strike a convoy sighted near Cape Sa-Hoi, orders were changed minutes after launching. The new target was to hit another convoy near Cap des Hirondelles (At the tip of the peninsula HI-86 had rounded). Some confusion occurred en route (as might be expected with last minute in-flight mission changes). Clouds covered the convoy (9/10s cover at 3,000') making accurate bombing difficult, but reasonably clear skies to the south otherwise prevailed. The Enemy ships were steaming in parallel columns. (Note: See the table & diagrams on the next 2 pages.) Most of the bombing and strafing runs were made through a crossfire of AA.

During the attack the Japanese escorts were described as being extremely agile in their maneuvering, to avoid bomb hits, and to bring their AA guns to bear. Additional attacks could not be made after the initial strikes due to a follow-on strike by CVG(N)-90 from USS ENTERPRISE.

This was not to be a good day for IJN Convoy HI-86. Ravaged and all but decimated by airborne attacks from the US Carrier strikes during January 12th, only 3 vessels of the original 16 (the more nimble escorts) would escape. The other unlucky 13 either sunk or beached.

Starting first with a description of events as told by IJN Commander Tado Kuwahara in a post war interrogation:

"Three F6F's were sighted at 0855 and the one covering Zero fighter was shot down. At 0955 two more fighters appeared and at 1104 about 16, TBF's and SB2C's appeared. In the attack which lasted 30 minutes the heavily loaded 6,900 ton freighter EIMAN Maru was set afire by a bomb hit and sank. I believe one or two of the attacking planes were shot down by AA fire of the Kashii and other escort vessels. The Ukuru was bracketed by four or five near misses, thirty or forty meters away, which shook up the ship and caused her to stop about 2 minutes; but no damage was sustained. About 1229 a single plane dove on the Ukuru, but only obtained a near miss and did no damage. During the attack the convoy had become scattered due to evasive action and was now reformed. About 20 dive-bombers appeared and circled in the vicinity until 1355 when 50 more of the same type arrived from the north. At 1408 the dive-bombing and torpedo attack by all planes began. The Kashii was sunk almost immediately in an explosion. This was a well executed attack, bombers diving in succession and at the same time a torpedo attack was launched at the Kashii from her starboard side. One torpedo and two bombs hit the Kashii. One of the bombs exploded the after magazine. The ship sank stern first, the bow remained about 10 feet above the water which was shallow. Vice Admiral T. SHIBUYA, Convoy Commander, and his entire staff were killed. At 1416 escort No. 51 on the starboard quarter of the convoy received a hit or a very near miss by bomb, which I believed ignited the depth charges because of the white smoke. She sank very soon. The attack continued practically uninterrupted until dark"

In addition to INDEPENDENCE and ENTERPERSE, other air groups from other carriers were present for the mauling. Lacking their After Action Reports we pick up here from the CVL-22 perspective:

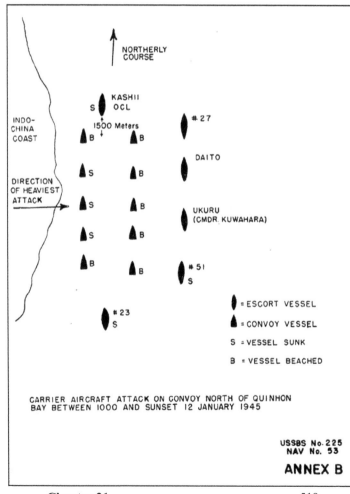

CARRIER AIRCRAFT ATTACK ON CONVOY NORTH OF QUINHON
BAY BETWEEN 1000 AND SUNSET 12 JANUARY 1945

USSBS No. 225
NAV No. 53

ANNEX B

This is the neat tidy disposition of IJN Convoy HI-86 just after rounding the peninsula tip as it proceeded north after leaving Quinon Bay, prior to the beginning of the actual attacks.

At about this time the KASHII was sunk.

The drawing from the INDEPENDENCE AAR on the next page reflects after the attack had begun and was well in progress. IJN Convoy HI-86 had proceeded roughly 21 miles up the coast (plotting reported Lat / Longs on a chart) **to the final resting place of the tankers, freighters, and some of the escorts assigned to protect them. The INDEPENDENCE drawing shows 15 vessels** (the KASHII already consigned to the ocean bottom) **in disarray, and maneuvering for their lives, as the attack was made.**

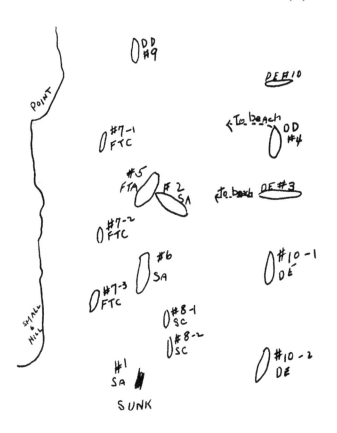

North of Cape des Hirondelles, Indochina :
14°N, 109°-20'E

1. Sugar Able 7000 / 10000 GT
2. Sugar Able 7000 / 10000 GT
3. Destroyer Escort
4. Destroyer, TERUTSUKI Class
5. Fox Tare Able 7000 / 8500 GT
6. Sugar Able 7000 / 10000 GT
7. 3 Fox Tare Charlies 2000 / 4500 GT
8. 2 Sugar Charlies 300 / 700 GT
9. Destroyer, New
10. 3 Destroyer Escorts

(GT = Gross Tonnage)

At the start of the attack, the convoy was in parallel line formation: 2 DE's or 1 DE and 1 DD with 2 FTCs in lead, with rest of the convoy 1 mile behind, DDs and DEs on flanks and rear. Target #1 was sunk early in the attack, so rest of the convoy is shown as having moved northward. The following table only lists the pilots reporting hits, not the misses or runs by pilots without unobserved hits.

PILOT	SHIP	ORD.	HITS	DAMAGE
Caldwell	DE #3	bomb	exploded under stern	trailing oil, headed for the beach
	DE #10	strafing	across deck	fires started, later died out
Henry	DE #4	strafing		burning & smoking
Barnett	SA #6	strafing		burning & smoking
Bradenbaugh	SA #2	bomb	stern of ship	dead in water, decks awash, on fire & in collision with FTA #5
Morris	DE #3	strafing		silenced AA
	SC #8-1	strafing		trailing oil
Kesler	DE #10-3	strafing		silenced AA
Peterson	DE #10	strafing		smoking heavily, trailing oil
Becker	DE #10-2	strafing		silenced AA
Williams	FTA #5	bomb	struck aft	explosion, burning
	DE #10-1	strafing		burning
Linton	SA #1	bomb salvo	2 straddled, 1 amidships	Sunk, blew up, after fire heavy & smoke, broke in two
Archer	SA #6	bomb	aft of mid-ship	heavy smoke, badly damaged

1045 Air Department set condition 14. At 1130 flight quarters was sounded.

1141 Recovered 1 F6F launched at 1037. Ensign Lee returned to land with engine trouble.

1325 Sounded flight quarters.

1345-1416 Recovered 4 TBMs and 11 F6Fs launched at 1037. Then changed course to 240°T.

1418 Secured from flight quarters, Air Department set condition 14.

1600 Sounded flight quarters. At 1704 they changed course to 040°T.

1739-1740 Catapulted 2 F6F5Ns on a mission to heckle the Japanese at Saigon. There had been Japanese aviation activity during the day, and the hellcats would harass the airfields to cover the retirement of the fleet. Ens. W.E. Miller and Ens. F.A. Hunziker flew 235 miles at low altitude to the target area. They scouted the airfields at Tan Son Nhut, Thu Dai Mot and Bien Hoa, as well as the Cat Lai seaplane base and the Saigon wharves. Much of the area had been hit by the days strikes.

1917 Launched 3 F6Fs for a night CAP.

2210 Launched 2 F6Fs for night CAP. Then, first to land from their heckler mission, when Ens. Hunziker hit the flight deck, his Hellcat's port landing gear collapsed, sending the plane into the catwalk. Hunziker was ok, the Hellcat would need to have the wing, port landing gear, engine and prop replaced. With a fouled flight deck, Miller diverted landing aboard the ENTERPRISE minutes later. The 3 F6Fs from the 1917 CAP were also in the landing pattern when the accident occurred, and they also landed aboard ENTERPRISE.   The Task Force retired this evening to refuel tomorrow.

IJN Commander Tado Kuwahara continues:

"The large escort vessels Ukuru and Daito and the small escort vessel No. 27 all were severely damaged, but were able to reach SANGA, HAINAN at 1540 on the 13th. The Ukuru escaped two torpedo attacks by maneuvering. The Ukuru attempted to rescue the crew of the sunken Kashii about 1430, but an attack developed at this time and prevented us from rescuing more than 19. Subsequently we escaped several attacks by maneuvering into nearby rain squalls. The total casualties of the Ukuru were 12 killed and 29 injured. The three remaining escorts arrived at YULIN on 14 January" (Note Japanese loss of life was significant across IJN Convoy HI-86. KASHII alone suffered 621 KIA, her captain and the convoy Rear Admiral.)

GL Independence and Enterprise sent a daylight strike over Camranh Bay. We sent up 4 TBMs & 12 F6Fs. Our planes got bomb hits on four ships (500 pounders). 1 oiler, 1 freighter, 1 DE sunk, 1 DE badly damaged. We sent up a night strike on an airfield and destroyed about 26 planes on the ground. The task group destroyed over a quarter million tons of shipping. We had a few accidents in landing as the sea is running a bit rough. GL

RC Hitting French Indo China, Amoy, Saigon & Camranh Bay. Sank 32 ships, damaged 46 ships, knocked out 100 planes in the air and on the ground. RC

AD South Indo China — Saigon area. The battle wagons weren't able to get in at shipping do to storm, but our planes did a bang up job. Score - 32 ships sunk, 45 damaged, 100 planes destroyed. AD

(Note: Combat action reports from INDEPENDENCE aircraft involve 15 vessels, and somewhat reflect George's observations {ship types don't match}. Richard's & Anthony's diary entries most likely were a combined tally of the numbers of total losses along the coast, including those reported by other carrier air groups, the accuracy not verified by me. Robert Cressman decades after the war would list in his chronology in addition to HI-86, TF-38 aircraft would attack convoys SASI 40, SATA 05 as well as other shipping along the coast. A target rich environment, Japanese shipping losses were indeed very large.)

This book remains focused on INDEPENDENCE. Other carriers involved in the days actions against HI-86 were noted by other sources as the ESSEX CV-9, TICONDEROGA CV-14, LANGLEY CVL-27, and SAN JACINTO CVL-30.

Good hunting! Japanese aircraft targets in this photo marked "USS Independence CVL-22".
(Airfield and date presently unknown)

Saturday 13 January 1945   *South China Sea*

Steaming as before, in Task Group 38.5, accompanied by USS ENTERPRISE (OTC and guide), USS
HAGGARD, USS HAZELWOOD, USS MCCORD, USS TRATHEN, USS FRANKS and USS
BUCHANAN. CTG in ENTERPRISE is Rear Admiral M.B. Gardner. T.G. is in cruising disposition 5R,
course 075°T, speed 21 knots, at a night flying station. INDEPENDENCE bears 140°T, 3,000 yards
from guide. Air Department is at flight quarters, with 2 F6Fs airborne, and 4 F6Fs aboard the

ENTERPRISE.

0022-0026 Recovered 2 F6Fs launched at 2111.

0442 Launched 4 TBMs ("Reb" & Jim Taylor, Bill Phelps & John Williams on sector searches).

0855 Returning to land, Lt. Bill "Reb" Taylor crashed into the barrier. The crew was OK, but the TBM (BuNo 46257) was determined to be damaged beyond repair and jettisoned over the side.

0934 Completed recovery of remaining 3 TBMs launched at 0422. Then secured from flight quarters. Air Department set to condition 14.

0958 Commenced maneuvering to approach a tanker for fueling.

1019 Refueling of the INDEPENDENCE was canceled due to heavy weather. The TG was on the outer fringe of a typhoon. Commenced steering various courses at various speeds to rejoin T.G. 38.2.

1058 Gained position bearing 260°T, 2,500 yards from guide, USS NEW JERSEY, base course 045°T, speed 10 knots. OTC in USS LEXINGTON.

1630 Sounded flight quarters.

1752 Commenced maneuvering to gain position on USS TALUGA, designated guide, bearing 180°T, distance 4,000 yards.

1824 USS NEW JERSEY designated guide in center of formation. Commenced maneuvering to regain formation position on guide bearing 080°T, 2,500 yards.

As Captain Ewen left the bridge to retire for the evening he left orders to *"Keep the look outs alert. We are travelling at very slow speed for these waters and not zigzagging."*

The Task Group steamed toward the northeast with the tankers and their escorts to complete the fueling the following day.

GL We were supposed to fuel today but the weather is rough and only the Cans were fueled. Note: On our January 12th raid the score was much higher than expected. We attacked 4 convoys and sunk 25 ships including a Katori class cruiser, several DDs or DEs. Heavily damaged 133 additional vessels. Shot down 18 aircraft over Saigon, 9 more planes to the north. Also 24 flying boats and seaplanes. GL

Sunday 14 January 1945   *South China Sea*

Steaming in company with Task Unit 38.2.1 consisting of USS HANCOCK, USS HORNET, USS ENTERPRISE, and USS LEXINGTON (OTC). "Wicked weather".

0410 Completed launching 4 TBMs for sector searches, and 2 F6Fs.

0645 Dropped floating smoke marker at the position of a drifting 50 foot fishing boat passing close to port, reporting the boat to the TG commander. The USS AULT was dispatched to pick up the 5 Japanese occupants, sink the vessel, and transfer the prisoners to the USS NEW JERSEY.

0751 Recovered 1 TBM launched at 0410. (Don Linton returned early with a sick gunner.)

0903 Completed recovery of the 4 TBMs attached to this ship, launched from the USS ENTERPRISE, having landed there at 2200 on 12 January. Recovered 3 TBMs and 2 F6Fs launched at 0410.

0912 Secured from flight quarters.

0914-0917 USS THE SULLIVANS came alongside to transfer Officer Messenger Mail to this vessel.

1240 Commenced maneuvering to come alongside the USS NANTAHALA.

1328 Came alongside the tanker and changed speed to 10 knots.

1455 USS LEXINGTON was designated guide and at 1530 directed to take position 5,000 yards ahead of the tankers.

1531 Cast off from USS NANTAHALA, having taken on 16,900 gallons of aviation gasoline, 93,943 gallons of fuel oil, and transferring Officer Mail to the tanker.

1545 Took position on USS LEXINGTON (guide).

1615 USS HORNET designated guide.

1637 Commenced maneuvering to leave TG 38.2, forming TG 38.5. Proceeding to a night flying station.

1728 TG 38.5 formed outside the TG38.2 screen, OTC and guide USS ENTERPRISE.

INDEPENDENCE gained station bearing 140°T, 3,000 yards from guide. ENTERPRISE has the VF(N) ready duty. INDEPENDENCE will take over at midnight.

RC Refueled and headed north to hit Formosa, Amoy, Hong Kong and Swatow. RC

Monday 15 January 1945   *China Formosa — Hong Kong, Swatow, Hainan, Amoy*

Steaming as before, in Task Group 38.5, accompanied by USS ENTERPRISE (OTC and guide), USS HAGGARD, USS HAZELWOOD, USS MCCORD, USS TRATHEN, USS FRANKS and USS BUCHANAN. Air Department is at flight quarters, with no aircraft in the air.
0340 Completed launching 2 F6Fs to investigate unidentified aircraft bearing 045°T, 30 miles.
0356 Aircraft identified as friendly.

0401-0412 Launched 4 TBMs as part of a wide search of sea lanes off the China Coast between Hong Kong and Swatow in preparation of day strikes by TF 38. They launched into weather with bad visibility, 40 knot winds and a near solid low overcast. After launch, Lt.(jg) James Taylor had a defective compass and stayed within 60 miles to serve as a communications relay. Lt.(jg)'s Forrest Archer, John Dewis and John Williams continued on with the search, Dewis dropping his four 500# bombs by radar on shipping, with unobserved results. The other pilots jettisoned their bombs at sea prior to returning. John Williams had new Radar Countermeasures gear installed in his TBM and this would be the first record of combat use of the gear by the squadron. He and his RCM operator would gain valuable data on enemy radar frequencies and pulse rates. The tests indicated the RCM gear could be effective for detecting enemy radar equipped aircraft, giving bearing and range to the bogey for fighter intercept, and allow for jamming the enemy radar so the fighters could make an undetected approach. The TBM test flight with the RCM gear was considered highly successful.

0509 Secured from flight quarters, Air Department set to condition 14.
0746-0752 Recovered the 4 TBMs and 2 F6Fs launched at 0340.
0906 Commenced maneuvering to rejoin TG 38.2.
0930 Gained position in TG38.2, USS NEW JERSEY (guide) bearing 080°T, 2,500 yards.
1026 Sounded torpedo defense. On order of CTG, Gunnery Department set to condition One Easy due to reduced visibility and reported aircraft in the area.
1317 Sounded flight quarters.
1400-1406 Half masted the ensign, for USS HORNET.
1408-1414 Launched 8 F6Fs (to assist ENTERPRISE TBMs) on a fighter sweep over Pratas Island. This was a very small Island in Pratas Reef said to have a radio and weather station. Due to very poor visibility, low ceilings and incorrect bearings to target issued prior to launch, coupled with the small size of the reef, and limited ability of their APS6A radar, the target survived unfound and unmolested. Hellcat pilots Morris, Bradenbaugh, Otis, Fegraeus, Lee, Diskosky, Miller and Houden, receiving no response to their request for a vector to target, jettisoned their bombs and returned to the ship.
1435 Air Department set to condition 13.
1640 Sounded flight quarters.
1720 Completed recovery of 8 F6Fs launched at 1408.
1738 Air Department set to condition 12.
1945 Gunnery Department secured from condition One Easy, set to condition 3.
Due to poor weather conditions, the night CAP remained on the flight deck in a ready condition.
During the night the TG proceeded west for more attacks on the China Coast and Hainan.

GL Had routine G.Q. at 7:00. At 9:30 torpedo defense was sounded and condition one easy was set. We stayed in condition one easy till 20:00. C.A.P. shot down 4 Jap planes. We hit Formosa and Hong Kong and heavy damage was done. The weather is still rough and miserable. GL

Tuesday 16 January 1945   *China Formosa — Hainan & Hong Kong*

Steaming in company with Task Unit 38.2.1 consisting of USS HANCOCK, USS HORNET, USS ENTERPRISE, and USS LEXINGTON (OTC). INDEPENDENCE bears 260°T, 2,500 yards from guide, USS NEW JERSEY. Air Department is in condition 12.

0643 Completed launching 2 F6Fs to serve as communications relays for ENTERPRISE aircraft conducting a pre-dawn search.

0657-0756 Routine general quarters.

0904 Recovered 2 F6Fs launched at 0643.

0910 Air Department set to condition 14.

1104 Admitted Robert L. Hill, S2c, to sick bay for injury sustained when he was struck by the edge of a plane wing while the wing was being unfolded.

1136 Air Department set to condition 12.

During the day, with weather still bad, the Task Force struck at targets ranging from Hainan Island to Swatow, China.

1457 Sounded flight quarters.

1633 Launched 4 F6Fs to assist in a target CAP over Hong Kong. Bill Henry, Russell Otis, Warren Light and Glen Earl joined ENTERPRISE pilots for the mission. Henry and Light chased after an Oscar, shooting long range level 6 o'clock bursts, occasionally scoring hits. Smoking, and spraying oil, the Oscar started for the deck in a long fast glide and pulled into a loop. Henry followed him and caught the Oscar with a burst "stem to stern". The Oscar, at the top of the loop, nosed down crashing into a rice paddy roughly 20 miles from Canton. **The Oscar was William "Bill" E. Henry's tenth kill.**

1756 Commenced maneuvering while leaving TG 38.2 to form TG 38.5 accompanied by (OTC and guide) USS ENTERPRISE , USS HAGGARD, USS HAZELWOOD, USS MCCORD, USS TRATHEN, USS FRANKS and USS BUCHANAN.

1835 Gained position 3,000 yards from USS ENTERPRISE, bearing 140°T.

1849 Catapulted 2 F6Fs to heckle an enemy airfield at Swatow. "Brady" Bradenbaugh and "Mo" Morris headed out toward target, but Bradenbaugh was forced to return due to fuel problems, landing back on board at 2205. Bradenbaugh crashed into the barrier damaging the prop. Morris continued to target (Kilok field), but found no aircraft. He strafed the field, remained over target, finding no aircraft in the air or on the ground, then returned to the ship landing at 2230.

Three aircraft had landed on board at 2100 and another at 2200.

The sea was rough and the INDEPENDENCE was rolling and pitching. "Near typhoon conditions prevailed". The night landings were a test of both pilots and planes. Bill Henry landed, his F6F5N hitting the barrier. A prop and engine change would be needed for his damaged Hellcat.

With the deck cleared, Ens. Glen Earl caught a wire but the entire tail hook section pulled out, then the starboard landing gear collapsed. The broken Hellcat continued skidding across the deck into the barrier. Earl was ok but the F6F5N (Bu.No.71983) was totaled. Carried away on a roll of the ship before it could be secured, the wayward Hellcat struck 2 other F6Fs (Bu.No.71821 & 71782) , damaging them beyond repair. Bradenbaugh's Hellcat was one of them.

All of the INDEPENDENCE aircraft had returned back aboard ship by 2230.

ENTERPRISE was to pick up the CAP duties after midnight, with aircraft in condition 11.

As Captain Ewen retired for the evening he indicated to the watch;

"A heavy swell on the quarter causes a fairly heavy roll, As soon as any change in course is signaled notify the officer in Fly Control. This will be especially important if planes are being re-spotted. A change in course is to be executed with only enough rudder for a relatively slow turn in order to decrease the roll during the turn or at least hold it to a minimum."

During the night they retired toward the south to rendezvous with a fueling group.

Wednesday 17 January 1945   *Retiring to refuel*

0738 Commenced maneuvering to rejoin TG 38.2. Rough seas with "thick weather".

0813 Regained station in TG38.2, USS NEW JERSEY guide, bearing 080°T, 2,500 yards.

0918 Changed course to 170°T. Sighted tankers bearing 160°T, at 20,000 yards.

1000 USS LEXINGTON assumed guide bearing 010°T, 2,500 yards.

1030 Let fires die out under boiler No.3. The second tanker from the left assumed guide, bearing 048°T, 5,300 yards.

1059 Jettisoned over the side a F6F (Bu.No. 71983) damaged beyond repair.

INDEPENDENCE made the first navigation fix in 3 days as the sun broke thru the clouds.

1430 Made periodical inspection of steering gear. Condition satisfactory.

1635 Changed speed to 9 knots.

1645 Five men of the First Division were injured when a heavy sea washed over the forecastle where they were stowing fueling gear.

1652 Reduced speed to 4 knots while securing fueling gear, losing position in the formation. The weather was such that the INDEPENDENCE did not go alongside a tanker today. The tanker group stayed with us this evening.

1654 Let fires die out and secured boiler No.1.

1732 Resumed position in the formation.

1748 USS NEW JERSEY assumed guide.

1915 Launched 2 F6Fs, under "hazardous conditions", to intercept an unidentified aircraft. Per "Hebe" Lee, Captain Ewen had radioed to advise against the launch. CTG ordered it anyway. "Wally" Miller and "Pete" Peterson were catapulted into terrible weather. Pete was told to orbit while Wally made the intercept on what turned out to be a B-24 that forgot to turn on his IFF.

According to Ensign Lee, pilots (in a highly charged squadron ready room) were less than happy with the Admirals decision to launch. Faced with landing in poor visibility and deplorable weather, Miller and Peterson opted to land on the larger ENTERPRISE flight deck, doing so successfully at 2035.

Captain Ewen noted to the evening watch; "Weather conditions are expected to improve as we move to the north. For course changes, use no more rudder than is necessary to bring the ship around slowly. In turns out of the wind it may be necessary to use engines to assist at this slow speed, in which case call me. If you feel uneasy about the way the ship is riding call me. Require half hour reports from all departments on security."

The tanker group stayed with them this evening as they steamed north toward Luzon Straits.

HB We were hit by another typhoon, I was in a work party to repair the flight deck damaged by one of our planes crashing, and we had five men injured by waves over the focsle and the flight deck. The typhoon continues, the forward bulkhead is bent by the waves. **HB**

GL Another typhoon and we are rocking and a-rolling. These storms sure give me an awful feeling. We are supposed to anchor in Leyte Gulf this Sunday. **GL**

26 July 1944 (page 308) - **President Roosevelt arrives at Pearl Harbor aboard USS BALTIMORE to meet with Nimitz & MacArthur**

22
Yet Another Typhoon

Thursday 18 January 1945   *High Water*

Steaming in company with Task Unit 38.2.1 consisting of USS HANCOCK, USS HORNET, USS ENTERPRISE, and USS LEXINGTON. Rear Admiral G.F. Bogan is CTG, CTU and OTC in LEXINGTON. INDEPENDENCE bears 260°T, 2,500 yards from guide, USS NEW JERSEY. Course 000°T, speed 8 knots. Boilers Nos. 2 & 4 are in use. Air Department is in condition 12. Two VF(N)-41 F6Fs are aboard the USS ENTERPRISE ("Pete" Peterson & "Wally" Miller).
0644-0744 Routine general quarters.
0814 Changed course to 105°T. Northeast winds rising to 40 knots increased the size of the seas. As the INDEPENDENCE pitched into the trough of one wave, the bow submerged up to the flight deck. The forward bulkhead above the forecastle dished in from the impact force of the heavy seas. Repair parties promptly shored the bulkhead with temporary wood timbers and made repairs.
0913 Changed course to the 180°T.
1101 Changed course to 200°T.
1115 Changed speed to 12 knots. Due to winds and seas, the ship required engines to maneuver throughout the watch in order to remain on course. These conditions continued throughout the afternoon.
1630 Sounded flight quarters.

"The decision had been made to leave the China Sea via the Sulu Sea and the Surigao Straits. Because the ship tended to stay in the trough of the swell in spite of her rudder, we had to slow and finally back the engines on the inboard side of the turn. Then, to stay on course with the wind and sea on the quarter, the ship requires a difference in turns between port and starboard screws amounting to seven knots. Our maximum roll for the morning was 32 degrees to port. The weather abated slightly during the day."

As Captain Ewen retired for the evening he recorded for the watch; *"We are scheduled to fuel at dawn. If the sea conditions permit we should start pumping ballast around 0430. Watch carefully during the mid-watch to note the state of the sea. Call me at 0400 and discuss your conclusions with me".*

Friday 19 January 1945   *China Sea — Refueling*

0636 Steaming as before. Air Department is in condition 11 with two F6FNs. Sounded routine general quarters. As they steamed south into the lee of Luzon, the wind decreased and the swell leveled off enough to permit normal steering, and fueling. The plan to exit via the Surigao Strait was cancelled.
0724 Commenced maneuvering while approaching the assigned tanker.
0734 Set Air Department to condition 14.
0826 Came alongside of fleet oiler USS MONONGAHELA to the starboard, on course 060°T, speed 10 knots. Guide is USS MANATEE, bearing 330°T, 2,000 yards while refueling.
0918 USS WEEKS came alongside port to transfer guard mail.
1105 Having received 216,127 gallons of fuel oil, cast off from USS MONONGAHELA and commenced maneuvering to regain position in the formation.
The Task Force rounded the Scarborough Shoal and changed course toward the north headed for Balintang Channel. When fueling was completed, the tanker group returned toward the south.
1231 Regained station in the formation, bearing 230°T, 7,000 yards from guide, USS MANATEE, changed course to 040°T, changed speed to 10 knots.
1316-1330 USS TRATHEN was alongside transferring Commander William E. Taylor from USS ENTERPRISE to INDEPENDENCE to observe air operations.
1504 Commenced maneuvering to proceed to our flying station.
1520-1523 Recovered 2 INDEPENDENCE F6Fs flown over from USS ENTERPRISE, having landed there on 17 January during the storm.

1547 Resumed position in the formation.

1630 Sounded flight quarters.

1650 Commenced maneuvering to leave TG 38.2, forming with TG 38.5.

1700 Secured from flight quarters. Set Air Department to condition 14.

1728 Gained position in TG 38.5, USS ENTERPRISE guide, bearing 300°T, 3,000 yards. The USS HAILEY replaced USS BUCHANAN as part of our screen, the BUCHANAN remaining with TG 38.2.

1738 Jettisoned 2 F6Fs (Bu.No. 71821 & 71782) over the side that were previously damaged beyond repair, having all usable parts first salvaged.

2139 Commenced steering various courses into the wind maintaining station on guide while USS ENTERPRISE was conducting flight operations.

2314 Sounded flight quarters.

GL At least the sun is shining and it is a nice day. We are refueling at present. Just heard we are going to stay out longer and not going into Leyte Gulf. GL

Saturday 20 January 1945   *Retired from South China Sea via Balintang Channel*

Steaming in TG 38.5 accompanied by USS ENTERPRISE (OTC and guide), USS HAGGARD, USS HAZELWOOD, USS HAILEY, USS MCCORD, USS TRATHEN, and USS FRANKS. The weather in the area is considerably better than it was two days ago.

0641-0745 Routine general quarters. Air Department set to condition 14.

0900 Commenced maneuvering to proceed to rejoin TG 38.2.

0931 Unidentified aircraft reported on radar bearing 065°T, 45 miles.

0935 Sounded torpedo defense.

0940 Enemy plane reported shot down. (This was a George shot down by the LEXINGTON CAP.)

0950 Secured from torpedo defense.

1020 Sounded flight quarters.

1044 Gained position in TG 38.2, bearing 260°T, 2,500 yards from guide, USS NEW JERSEY.

1114 Secured from flight quarters. Air Department set to condition 12.

1420 Sounded flight quarters.

1530 Lighted fires under Nos.1 & 3 boilers.

1712 Cut in Nos.1 & 3 boilers to the main steam line.

1730 Sounded torpedo defense, unidentified planes reported on radar.

1801 Sounded general quarters. A formation of roughly 12 enemy aircraft are reported 40 miles north. These aircraft appear to be *"in the regular Formosa - Luzon traffic lane"*. The CAP worked these over.

1802 Formation changed disposition to 5V.

1849 Completed launching 4 F6Fs for a heckling mission over lower Formosa airfields.

1905 Completed launching 4 F6Fs for a night CAP.

1913 Observed AA firing from ships in this formation on an enemy plane reported within 5 miles.

1930 Changed course to 090°T, entering approaches to the Balintang Channel * to exit from the South China Sea.   2000 Set condition One Easy. (*Map on page 515)

2120 Sighted Sabtang Island (in the Batan Group) 9 miles off the port side.

2210 Changed formation to disposition 5R.

2230 Recovered 4 F6Fs launched at 1849 and 3 F6Fs launched at 1905.
The fourth F6F from the 1905 launch landed aboard USS YORKTOWN.

2300 Passed by Balintang Island off the starboard beam, officially entering the Philippine Sea, having spent eleven days in the South China Sea.

2333 Maneuvered to form TG 38.5, leaving TG 38.2 this evening to proceed to a night flying station.

2352 Secured from condition One Easy.

The day was a productive one for the Combat Air Patrols all throughout the Task Force, with 22 enemy aircraft credited as shot down.

GN Passing through Straits of Formosa. Five bogies shot down in vicinity of task force. We heard over the radio from Tokyo, quote Tokyo Rose " The Japs have a huge American task force bottled up in the South China Sea and it would be suicide to go through the straits." At 2300 we are informed we are through and in the Pacific. To boot we expect to hit Formosa on the way. GN

(Note: They actually passed thru the Luzon Straits and entered the Philippine Sea on the western side of the Pacific. The Philippine Sea is a marginal sea, separated from the Pacific by the thin line of islands including the Marianas, Guam, Saipan, Tinian, the Bonin Islands and Iwo Jima. The Formosa Strait is today called the Taiwan Strait, located between Formosa and the mainland of China.)

Sunday 21 January 1945   *Formosa—Pacific Ocean*

Steaming in TG 38.5 accompanied by USS ENTERPRISE (OTC and guide), USS HAGGARD, USS HAZELWOOD, USS HAILEY, USS MCCORD, USS TRATHEN, and USS FRANKS, proceeding to the eastern coast of Formosa. Air Department is in condition 11 with no aircraft in the air.

0025 Gained position in TG 38.5, ENTERPRISE bearing 150°T, 3,000 yards.

0119 Completed launching 3 F6Fs to relieve the ENTERPRISE CAP.

0414-0433 Recovered 3 F6Fs launched at 0119.

"The calm water and clear sky were impressive this morning, perhaps because the China Sea had given us such contrary weather. Taking advantage of the good weather, the Task Force sent in strikes all over Formosa. The enemy used the good weather too."

0840 Changed course to 240°T.

0846 Sounded torpedo defense. Unidentified aircraft reported bearing 180°T, 12 miles.

0848 Commenced maneuvering to rejoin TG 38.2.

0857 Secured from torpedo defense.

0918 Regained station within TG 38.2, USS NEW JERSEY is guide, bearing 080°T, 2,500 yards.

0944 Recovered 1 INDEPENDENCE F6F launched from the USS YORKTOWN, that had landed there during the night.

1215 Sounded general quarters. TG38.3 reported they are under air attack, bearing 330°T, 21 miles from this formation. Smoke from damaged ships was plainly visible over the horizon.

1218 Changed speed to 22 knots. Formed cruising disposition 5V.

1315 Changed course to 090°T.

1329 Observed violent explosion on the flight deck of the USS HANCOCK followed by a large fire. The fire covered the aft end of the flight deck to the island structure, apparently due to one of her own torpedo planes crashing as it landed. Within 20 minutes, HANCOCK reported the fire under control, and that within two hours, she should be able to continue flight operations.

1338 Changed speed to 18 knots, changed course to 080°T. Maneuvering to avoid USS HANCOCK. (Note: The HANCOCK explosion killed 62, critically injured 46, and seriously injured 25 of the ships crew, with additional minor injuries. It was caused by the detonation of two 500# bombs adrift aboard a TBM-3 that had just landed. USS HANCOCK left the formation briefly, for freedom to maneuver to fight the fires.)

1516 Changed course to 040°T to avoid USS ENTERPRISE which is returning to station after recovering aircraft. At 1518 changed course back to 090°T.

1523 Secured from general quarters. Air Department set to condition 14.

1605 Unidentified aircraft reported bearing 195°T, 30 miles, at 35,000'. Sounded torpedo defense.

1640 Unidentified aircraft moved off. It was thought the aircraft might be an Army B-29. Secured from torpedo defense.

1650 Launched 4 F6FNs to provide a target CAP "Zipper flight" over Formosa airfields. These were to interfere with dusk attack plans the Japanese might have against the fleet. Lt. Morris, Lt. Otis, Ens. Earl and Ens. Hunziker joined with 8 planes from the ENTERPRISE searching Taito, Alian, Tainan, and Takio airfields, strafing targets of opportunity, then scouting the Takao Harbor area.

1748 Departed TG 38.2 to form with TG 38.5. Maneuvering to gain station on the guide, USS ENTERPRISE, bearing 000°T, distance 3,000 yards.

USS MADDOX (DD-731), serving as a strike picket destroyer was hit by a kamikaze, killing 7 of her crew. USS WISCONSIN left TG38.2 to pick up casualties.

1813 Completed launching 4 F6FNs for a night CAP, and 4 TBMs on a heckler mission to strike airfields on the Sakishima Gunto Islands in the Nansei Shoto group. The purpose of the mission was to suppress night attacks from Japanese airfields. Avengers (with 3 500# bombs each) were piloted by Lieuts. William Phelps, Donald Linton, William Taylor and Lt(jg) Frank McNair. Phelps and Linton hit Ishigaki Airfield and strafed shipping in the harbor. Taylor and McNair were assigned Miyako Shima airfields, with Taylor dropping his bombs on Hirara airfield, then he strafed some shipping. He developed an oil leak after a Japanese AA encounter, and asked McNair to join up for the return trip.

1825 Sounded general quarters.

1931 Observed AA firing from TG 38.2, bearing 290°T, 9 miles.

1935 Commenced maneuvering to form disposition 5V.

1938 Changed course to 075°T, speed 26 knots, gaining station, 180°T, 2,000 yards from guide.

1943 Observed twin engine plane shot down near TG 38.2.

2010 Completed recovering 1 TBM, launched at 1813 (possibly Reb Taylor with an oil tank hit by AA).

2025 All departments set at condition ONE EASY.

2155 Completed recovery of 3 TBMs launched at 1813, 4 F6Fs launched at 1650, and 4 F6Fs launched at 1813. The ENTERPRISE planes relieved the INDEPENDENCE night CAP.

2158 Maneuvered to change from disposition 5V to 5R.

2201 Secured from ONE EASY. Air Department set to condition 11.

2357 Completed launching 3 F6Fs to relieve the ENTERPRISE night CAP.

2359 Changed course to 065°T. The Force steamed toward the northeast for strikes against Okinawa Jima tomorrow.

GL We hit Formosa all day. Had GQ about 12. Bogies all around. 38.3 is under attack. Carrier Langley and Ticonderoga hit by bombs. Langley bomb went down two decks killed one and wounded four. Hangar deck in Ticonderoga was gutted. There are many casualties including Captain & Exec. We are in condition one easy from 12:00 to 3:30. Shot down 48 planes. Hancock had one of its planes crack up on flight deck and explode, there were 127 casualties. GL

(Note: The LANGLEY bomb killed 3 and seriously injured 11. It was released by a Zero that missed the flight deck and crashed into the sea. The TICONDEROGA was hit by 2 Kamikazes, with a loss of over 140 crewmen dead or missing, and over 200 injured.)

Monday 22 January 1945   *Ryukyus - Okinawa-Shima, & Amami Oshima*

Steaming as before. Air Department is in condition 11 with 3 F6FNs in the air as a night CAP.

0006 Launched 1 F6FN.

0026 Recovered 1 F6FN launched at 2355.

0300-0303 Launched 3 F6FNs to relieve our CAP.

0319-0325 Recovered 2 F6FNs launched at 2355 and 1 F6FN launched at 0006.

The sea was almost dead calm with no clouds overhead.

0712 Completed recovery of 3 F6Fs, launched at 0303.

0718 Secured from flight quarters. Air Department set to condition 14.

1012 Commenced maneuvering independently, departing TG 38.5 to regain station in TG 38.2.

1110 Gained station, USS NEW JERSEY guide, bearing 080°T, 2,500 yards, fleet course 050°T, speed 14 knots, OTC in USS LEXINGTON.

1457 Sounded general quarters. Reported visual contact with possible high flying aircraft.

1511 The contact was identified as the planet Venus. *"But as Venus did not dive, we secured"* from general quarters. Air Department set to condition 14.

The day had brought Task Group strikes as scheduled against all of Nansei Shoto. They also swept across to the Island of Kyushu, the southern tip of the Japanese mainland.

1600 Half-masted the ensign following the movements of USS WISCONSIN.

1629 Launched 4 F6Fs as target CAP for a dusk sweep over Okinawa Jima. The pilots ("Bill" Henry, "Barney" Barnett, "Art" Hansen and "Brady" Bradenbaugh) found target airfields well worked over by the daytime sweeps over the islands. They found wrecked and burned out aircraft, described by one pilot "It was like visiting a graveyard, except for the antiaircraft". The Hellcats worked over remaining targets of opportunity, making strafing runs on airfields and shipping. Vessels were hit and many were observed damaged, burning and smoking from the daytime raids.

AD At sea Ryukyu Islands. A beautiful day and they really bombed the hell out of this place. No attack was made on task force. AD

Japanese Admiral Matome Ugaki would note in his diary: *"The enemy task force raided Okinawa area yesterday. They acted as if there was no opponent in front of them."*

1715 Commenced maneuvering to form TG 38.5, departing the screen protecting TG 38.2.

1742 Gained station in TG 38.5 with USS ENTERPRISE (OTC and guide) bearing 300°T, 3,000 yards, with screen USS HAGGARD, USS HAZELWOOD, USS HAILEY, USS MCCORD, USS TRATHEN, and USS FRANKS. Changes in course and speed were given over TBS.

1800 Completed launching 4 F6Fs for CAP.

2052-2106 Recovering 4 F6Fs launched at 1629, and 4 F6Fs launched at 1800. The ENTERPRISE took over the night CAP duties. At 2110 INDEPENDENCE changed speed to 27 knots.

2214 Changed course to 205°T. The Task Force made a high speed retirement toward a fueling area to the south.

GL Striking islands off southern tip of Japan. 3ʳᵈ fleet damaged or shot down 200 enemy planes, sank several small ships. GL

Tuesday 23 January 1945   *Refueling*

0010 Steaming as before. Completed recovery of 2 F6Fs attached to the USS ENTERPRISE.

0302 Air Department set to condition 13.

0707 Commenced maneuvering, leaving TG 38.5, to rejoin TG 38.2.

0734 Gained station within TG 38.2, guide USS NEW JERSEY, bearing 080°T, distance 2,500 yards, fleet speed 25 knots, course 202°T. OTC, Rear Admiral G.F. Bogan in USS LEXINGTON.

0811 USS SAN JUAN warned of a mine 1,500 yards ahead. INDEPENDENCE made a turn using emergency right rudder. The mine drifted by with horns clearly visible, passing 300 yards abeam to port. At 0845 the mine was destroyed astern of the formation by a destroyer.

0900 Sighted tankers on the horizon, bearing 150°T.

0940 Commenced fleet fueling, guide shifting to the USS CACAPON, bearing 104°T, 5,300 yards.

1220 Secured No. 2 & 4 boilers.

1224-1245 USS OWEN was alongside to deliver Officer Messenger Mail, and to receive U.S. Mail. Commander W. Taylor also transferred off this ship for return to the USS ENTERPRISE.

1248 Secured main propulsion unit No.3 for temporary repairs.

1309 Changed speed to 15 knots while approaching fleet oiler USS CACAPON, dropping speed to 10 knots for fueling.

1400 USS NEW JERSEY and USS HANCOCK departed the task group to assist forming TG 38.6. They would proceed the Task Force to Ulithi.

1545 Sounded flight quarters.

1559 Cast off all lines from USS CACAPON, having received 95,313 gallons of fuel oil.

1600 Commenced maneuvering to regain station within the formation.

1608 Completed launching 2 F6Fs from the USS ENTERPRISE which landed aboard at 0010.

1617 USS HICKOX came alongside amidships to starboard to transfer U.S. Mail to INDEPENDENCE.

1748 Air Department set condition 13.

1617 USS HICKOX came alongside amidships to starboard to transfer U.S. Mail to INDEPENDENCE.

1748 Air Department set condition 13.

1753 Lighted fires under No. 2 boiler, then under No. 4 boiler.

When the fleet completed fueling, they parted company with the tankers and began steaming toward Ulithi, zigzagging at 18 knots on base course of 132°T.

GL Refueled and headed for Ulithi. Received some mail. Heard we might go to Pearl as ships screws are fouled up and many numerous things.

Note: When we left, there were four task groups, 38.1,2,3,4. now there are only 1,2,3. No more 4. We have lost Princeton. Those returned for repairs Intrepid, Franklin, Belleua Woods, Bataan, Ticonderoga, Monterey, Hancock, Langley, all carriers. Reno, Houston, Canberra cruisers. Jap suicides always pick on the carriers. We sure have been lucky so far. GL

GN Refueled. Received mail for the first time in three weeks. Headed for Ulithi again. GN

Wednesday 24 January 1945   *At sea—Steaming to Ulithi*

Steaming in company of TU 38.2.1. with USS ENTERPRISE, USS HORNET, and USS LEXINGTON (OTC) in cruising disposition 5R, zigzagging at 18 knots on base course of 132°T. USS WISCONSON is guide bearing 090°T, 2,500 yards. Main propulsion unit No.3 is secured for temporary repairs.

0055 Main propulsion unit No.3 put back in use. All four screws now turning at 181 RPM.

0224 Secured main propulsion unit No.3 again for further repairs.

0700 TG 34.5 departed the formation. USS HORNET assumed guide bearing 090°T, 5,000 yards.

0715 INDEPENDENCE assigned center of the formation, began maneuvering to gain new station.

0731 USS INDEPENDENCE became guide.

0805 Rear Adm. J.J. Clark in HORNET assumed tactical command of TG 38.2..

0824 Main engine No.3 was secured due to a leaking condenser.

0902-0919 USS WEEKS was along the starboard side to transfer mail.

0907 USS LEXINGTON designated guide, bearing 030°T, 2,500 yards. Changed fleet course to 085°T, speed 24 knots.

0928 Commenced maneuvering to regain position (diverted while handling the destroyer).

1000 Regained station in TG 38.2.

1014 USS INDEPENDENCE designated guide.

1226 Changed speed to 16 knots, course 140°T.

1342 USS LEXINGTON became guide, bearing 210°T, 2,500 yards.

1345 Commenced maneuvering to assume a suitable position for gunnery exercises. Sounded torpedo defense for test firing.

1410 Completed test firing 20mm and 40mm guns.

1413 Commenced maneuvering to regain station in the formation.

1442 Regained station, commenced zigzagging on base course 140°T.

1510 Main propulsion unit No.3 was placed back in operation.

1843 USS INDEPENDENCE designated guide.

2000 Commenced zigzagging on base course 133°T.

Thursday 25 January 1945   *At sea - Steaming to Ulithi*

Steaming as before as guide in center of cruising disposition 5R.

0820 Commander of Carrier Division Five, Rear Admiral J.J. Clark in USS HORNET designated OTC.

0910 Sounded torpedo defense for gunnery exercises. USS HORNET was designated guide.

1009 Gained position as fourth vessel in column formed on USS HORNET.

1036 Boiler No. 4 placed out of commission for repairs.

1038 Executed column movement, changing course to 140°T.

1045 Sounded flight quarters.

1103 Completed AA gunnery exercises against a towed sleeve. Secured from torpedo defense having expended 3,905 rounds of 40mm and 771 rounds of 20mm ammunition.

1118 Formed disposition 5R, USS INDEPENDENCE designated guide.

1145 Completed launching 8 F6Fs to fly a CAP until 1430, 7 of which are being transferred to, and will land aboard USS ENTERPRISE.

The following CVLG(N)-41 officers were detached to report to Air Group 90 for flying duty:
Ens. Warren G. Light, Ens. Fred Allen Hunziker, Lt. Russell D. Otis, Ens. Glen R. Earl, Ens. Arthur Hansen, Ens. Charles H. Kesler, Lt. Kyle H. Morris.

1155 Secured from flight quarters. Air Department set to condition 13.

1451 Recovered 1 F6F launched at 1145. At 1456 the Air Department was set to condition 14.

1630 Sounded flight quarters.

1721 Completed launching 3 TBMs for transfer to USS ENTERPRISE.

Friday 26 January 1945   *Anchored in Ulithi Atoll*

0501 Steaming as before as guide in cruising disposition 5R. Zigzagging on base course 133°T, speed 16 knots. Air Department is in condition 14. Sounded routine torpedo defense.

0601 Secured from torpedo defense.

0633 Sighted Ulithi Atoll bearing 160°T, 16 miles.

0637 Changed course to 160°T.

0646 USS LEXINGTON designated formation guide. Commenced maneuvering to take station in column formation.

0703 Gained position as fourth in column, LEXINGTON bears 160°T, 4,500 yards.

0735 Changed course to 227°T, speed 15 knots. Commenced making approach on Ulithi channel.

0800 Mustered crew on stations. 0801 Sounded general quarters for entering port.

0802 Entered Mugai Channel and commenced maneuvering proceeding to the anchorage in Ulithi Atoll.

0842 Secured from general quarters.

0857 Dropped port anchor in 27 fathoms of water with 125 fathoms of chain in Berth 30, Ulithi Atoll, Caroline Islands.

0902 Set all clocks ahead 1 hour to (-) Minus 10 time zone.

1026 Secured No. 3 boiler.

1330 Task Force 34 stood in to anchorage.

1500 LCVP 34-179 arrived for our use. The USS INDEPENDENCE has been without any type of small boat since the typhoon of 18 December washed the last whaleboat out of its skids.

2239 Barge No. 56 came alongside to port to unload GSK stores.

AD Anchored at Ulithi. Movies at night. AD

VT(N)-41
On wing of TBM *"Patty-Mae"*
Left to Right:
Stafford E. Hardwick - Gunner
John E. Dewis - Pilot
Robert S. Barnes - Radar & Radio

Saturday 27 January 1945   *Anchored in Ulithi Atoll*

0930 Anchored as before. Mustered crew at quarters.

1000 The ships company was assembled on the flight deck, the Commanding Officer presented awards and commendations (arranged by seniority of award, followed by seniority of party):

NAVY CROSS; Lt. William E. Henry

LEGION OF MERIT; Ens. Charles W. Kunkle

DISTINGUISHED FLYING CROSS; CDR. Turner F. Caldwell, Lt. William E. Henry, Ens. James A. Barnett, Ens. Irving H. Lee, Ens. Robert W. Klock, Ens. Floyd A. Fisher, Ens. Wallace E. Miller, Ens. Reuben F. Peterson

BRONZE STAR MEDAL; Lt. CDR. Charles E. Thompson, Lt. John W. Sullivan, Ens. James O. Coates, AOM2c Alvin R. Huss (for saving the life of his pilot - Ens. Haigler on 22 July 1944).

AIR MEDAL; Lt. William P. Phelps, Ens. John E. Dewis

COMMANDING OFFICER COMMEMDATION; Lt. Cdr. Harry C. Green, Lt. Cdr. Harvey B. Seim, Lt. John J. Mc Elwee, Lt.(jg) John F. Reece, ChGun Ed D. Arnold, ChGun Thomas M. Harkness, ACOM Norris L. Pratt, CCM Walter A. Rhyne, AOM2c Vite A. Pino, CM2c Herman B. Backlund, TM3c Leopold Martin, TM3c William E. Malong**, TM3c Gerald Maxwell, TM3c Charles C. Nelson, TM3c Walter W. Mc Quatters, AOM3c Donald E. Fry, AOM3c Joseph S. Tinta, S1c Columbus Pezzuti (**Note: Deck log spelling is as above, Muster Rolls list a name Willard Eugene Malone)

1515-1525 Launched 4 F6Fs and 5 TBMs for transfer to CASU 51, Falalop Island.

GL Captain handed out awards and announced we are headed for Pearl. GL

Sunday 28 thru 30 January 1945   *Anchored in Ulithi Atoll*

0000 USS INDEPENDENCE and most of the units of the Third Fleet became part of the Fifth Fleet under Admiral R. A. Spruance, Commander, Fifth Fleet, aboard (Flagship) USS INDIANAPOLIS. Anchored as before.

0645 LCVP #179 was caught under a scupper while moving alongside. Damaged, it was returned to the boat pool.

1937 Commenced receiving fuel oil from oiler YO 76.

2220 YO 76 cast off. INDEPENDENCE had received 186,575 gallons of fuel oil.

GN Routine cleaning up and refuel while at anchor. GN

The INDEPENDENCE was preparing to depart for Pearl Harbor. During the stay in the atoll, radar equipped aircraft were transferred to the USS ENTERPRISE, as well as any gear she might need. Other radar equipped aircraft were transferred to the Falalop Island airstrip. INDEPENDENCE took aboard "dud aircraft" and salvage materials for return to Pearl. Additionally, 410 officer and enlisted passengers reported onboard from various units in the Ulithi Anchorages for transportation to Pearl Harbor.

Tuesday 30 January 1945
        Underway from Ulithi, en route to Pearl Harbor as Task Unit 50.9.7

The crew of The USS INDEPENDENCE made the ship ready for getting under way, bringing boilers on line, pulling up the anchor and at 1537 the ship commenced proceeding toward Mugai Channel.

1549 Sounded general quarters.

1600 Took departure of Mugai Channel passing buoys No.1 and 2 abeam at a speed of 15 knots.

1710 Maneuvered into the wind to conduct flight operations.

1713 Secured from general quarters.

Gunners Mate Crew - Photo (damaged) shot January 1945
Top Row Standing - left to right
Ch. GM John Wimberly, GM2/c William Bradley, GM2/c William Rackawack, GM1/c Woodrow Day
GM1/c Norman Tanner Cramp, GM1/c Walter Radwonski, GM1/c Frank Stasko, Ch. GM Morris Fleming
Middle Row - left to right
GM2/c Leonard Conradt, GM3/c Alfred Henckler, GM3/c Walter Sawdey, GM3/c Theodore Kozil,
GM3/c James Sibbald, GM2/c Thomas Pearson, GM1/c John Rhine
Bottom Row - left to right
GM2/c Earl Carpenter, GM2/c Henry Rushing, GM3/c Paul Deaver, GM2/c Ray Besemer
GM3/c Edwin Seace, GM3/c George Laughlin

1714-1736 Recovered 5 TBMs and 5 F6Fs transferred to INDEPENDENCE from Falalop Airstrip. The Hellcats were "flyable duds".
1740 USS NEHENTA BAY was designated guide. Reduced speed to 10 knots and maneuvered to gain position bearing 005°T, 2,000 yards from guide. Air Department set to condition 14.
With INDEPENDENCE was a screen of 3 destroyers, USS COGSWELL, USS KNAPP and USS MACDONOUGH. They began zigzagging toward Pearl Harbor. Captain Ewen, CTU of TU 50.9.7.

GL Hot Damn Pearl Harbor here we come. GL

Wednesday 31 January 1945   *En route to Pearl Harbor as Task Unit 50.9.7*

0535 Steaming as before. Sounded flight quarters.
0620 Completed launching 1 F6F and 1 TBM.
0720 Sighted 2 YMSs to starboard abeam at 12 miles.
0830 Sounded flight quarters.
0859 Launched 2 TBMs for Anti-Submarine Patrol (ASP). Then mustered crew on stations.
0903 Recovered 1 TBM and 1 F6F.
0907 Secured from flight quarters. Air Department set to condition 13.
1130 Sounded flight quarters.
1201 Completed launching 1 F6F and 1 TBM for ASP.

1203-1204 Recovered 2 F6Fs launched at 0859.

1207 Secured from flight quarters. Air Department set to condition 13.

1323-1328 USS MACDONOUGH was alongside starboard quarter to receive official mail.

1410-1413 USS COGSWELL was alongside starboard quarter to receive official mail.

1429 USS KNAPP came alongside starboard quarter to receive official mail.

1431 Sounded flight quarters.

1432 USS KNAPP cast off.

1452 Completed launching 1 F6F and 1 TBM for ASP.

1458 Recovered 1 TBM and 1 F6F launched at 1201.

1500 Secured from flight quarters. Air Department set to condition 13.

1817 Recovered 1 TBM and 1 F6F launched at 1452.

1820 Secured from flight quarters. Air Department set to condition 14.

1821 USS INDEPENDENCE designated guide.

2000 Set all clocks ahead 1/2 hour.

2040 Commenced zigzagging on base course 067°T.

Thursday 1 February 1945   *En route to Pearl Harbor as Task Unit 50.9.7*

Steaming as before, zigzagging at 15.5 knots. INDEPENDENCE is returning from the forward area (to have needed repairs made in the yard) flying Anti-Submarine Patrols during the daylight hours.

0605 Sounded flight quarters.

0633 Launched 1 F6F and 1 TBM for a dawn ASP.

0635 USS NEHENTA BAY was designated guide, bearing 160°T, 1,500 yards.

0638 Air Department set to condition 13.

0830 Sounded flight quarters.

0900 Launched 1 F6F and 1 TBM for ASP.

0918 Completed recovery of 1 TBM and 1 F6F launched at 0633.

1130 Sounded flight quarters.

1150 Launched 1 F6F and 1 TBM for ASP.

1153 Completed recovery of 1 TBM and 1 F6F launched at 0900.

1218 USS INDEPENDENCE assumed guide.

1430 Sounded flight quarters.

1458 Launched 1 F6F and 1 TBM for ASP.

1501 Completed recovery of 1 TBM and 1 F6F launched at 1150.

1700 Changed course and axis to 098°T.

1741 Sounded flight quarters.

1822 Completed recovery of 1 TBM and 1 F6F launched at 1458.

1824 Secured from flight quarters. Air Department set to condition 14.

2000 Set all clocks ahead 1/2 hour to zone (-) 11 time.

2220 Commenced zigzagging on base course 098°T.

Friday 2 February 1945   *En route to Pearl Harbor as Task Unit 50.9.7*

0612 Steaming as before. Sounded routine torpedo defense. Sounded flight quarters.

0639 Launched 1 F6F and 1 TBM for a dawn ASP. Air Department set to condition 13.

0710 USS NEHENTA BAY assumed guide, bearing 008°T, 1,500 yards. Throughout the day INDEPENDENCE would slip out of position to maneuver during air operations, as necessary, then return to station when air operations were completed.

0712 Secured from torpedo defense.

0830 Sounded flight quarters.

0854-0856 Launched 1 F6F and 1 TBM for ASP.

0901 Completed recovering 1 F6F and 1 TBM launched at 0639.

0902 Secured from flight quarters. Air Department set to condition 14.

1130 Sounded flight quarters.

1151-1154 Launched 1 F6F and 1 TBM for ASP.

1156-1159 Recovered 1 F6F and 1 TBM launched at 0856.

1430 Sounded flight quarters.

1454 Completed launching 1 F6F and 1 TBM for ASP.

1500 Completed recovering 1 F6F and 1 TBM launched at 1159.

1810 Sounded flight quarters.

1826 Completed recovering 1 F6F and 1 TBM launched at 1454.

1828 Secured from flight quarters. Air Department set to condition 14.

2230 Commenced zigzagging on base course 098°T.

Saturday 3 February 1945   *En route to Pearl Harbor as Task Unit 50.9.7*

Steaming as before. Guide, USS NEHENTA BAY, bears 188°T, 1,500 yards, course 098°T, speed 16 knots. Air Department set to condition 14. At 0550 the ship sounded flight quarters.

0618-0621 Launched 1 F6F and 1 TBM for a dawn ASP.

0626 Secured from flight quarters. Air Department set to condition 13.

Today they launched and relieved Anti-Submarine Patrols at 0900, 1150 and 1450.

1206-1349 USS COGSWELL was along the starboard side to take on fuel. INDEPENDENCE pumped 66,318 gallons of fuel oil to her.

2000 Set all clocks ahead 1/2 hour to zone (-) minus 11 1/2.

2118 Radar sighting of 3 small and 3 heavy ships 30 miles ahead on a parallel opposite course. Began a series of course changes to avoid and offset the group 5 miles to the starboard.

2228 Passed Eniwetok Atoll abeam, bearing 000°T, 14 miles to port.

Sunday 4 February 1945   *En route to Pearl Harbor as Task Unit 50.9.7*

Steaming as before. Guide, USS NEHENTA BAY, bears 188°T, 1,500 yards, course 098°T, speed 16 knots. Air Department set to condition 14.

0555 Sounded routine torpedo defense. Sounded flight quarters.

0623 Completed launching 1 F6F and 1 TBM for a dawn ASP.

0631 Completed launching 1 F6F.

0638 Completed recovery of 1 F6F.

0641 Secured from flight quarters. Air Department set to condition 13. Secured from torpedo defense.

0830 Sounded flight quarters.

0853 Completed launching 1 F6F and 1 TBM for ASP. Recovered 1 TBM launched at 0623 and 1 F6F launched at 0631. The F6F Hellcat crashed on the flight deck while landing (causing minor damage to the flight deck) damaging the fighter beyond repair. Pilot, Lt.(jg) James Barnett, was uninjured.

0900 USS INDEPENDENCE left the formation to refuel a destroyer.

0907 Secured from flight quarters. Air Department set to condition 13.

0927 USS MACDONOUGH came alongside starboard to receive fuel.

1010 Jettisoned over the aft end of the flight deck, the Hellcat (Bu.No. 70326) that crashed at 0853.

1030 Completed fueling USS MACDONOUGH, having transferred 42,935 gallons of fuel oil to her.

1147 Regained position within the formation.

1203 Completed recovering 1 F6F and 1 TBM launched at 0853.

1205 Secured from flight quarters. Air Department set to condition 13.

1216 USS KNAPP came alongside starboard to receive fuel.

1312 USS KNAPP cast off having received 30,000 gallons of fuel oil.

1350 Regained station within the formation.

1430 Sounded flight quarters.

1455 Completed launching 1 F6F and 1 TBM for ASP.

1524 Completed recovering 1 F6F and 1 TBM launched at 1150. The Hellcat (BuNo 58825), flown by Lt. Erwin Becker, crashed on landing due to a problem with locking the right main landing gear in the down position. Damage was done to the right wing, engine cowling and the propeller.

1525 Sounded quarters for physical drill.

1526 Secured from flight quarters. Air Department set to condition 13.

1545 Secured from quarters for physical drill.

Photo of a radar equipped Grumman F6F Hellcat

Shown with a belly mounted external fuel tank, two 20mm cannons and four .50 cal machine guns (taken over NAS Jacksonville)

Monday 5 February 1945　　*En route to Pearl Harbor as Task Unit 50.9.7*

0605 Steaming as before. Sounded routine torpedo defense.

0609 Sounded flight quarters.

0634 Completed launching 1 F6F and 1 TBM for a dawn ASP.

0638 Secured from flight quarters. Air Department set to condition 13.

0704 Secured from torpedo defense.

0807 Turned away from reported possible submarine contact, bearing 197°T 3,000 yards from the USS MAC DONOUGH, by changing course to 354°T.

0812 USS MAC DONOUGH lost contact.

0818 Changed course to 074°T. Then commenced zigzagging on base course 074°T.

0900 Mustered crew on stations.

0903 Completed recovering 1 F6F and 1 TBM launched at 0634.

0905 Secured from flight quarters. Air Department set to condition 13.

Maneuvering out of (and returning back into) the formation as necessary, launched relief flights of 1 F6F and 1 TBM for ASPs at 0854, 1154 and 1554. The last relief ASP of the day recovered at 1810.

1814 Secured from flight quarters. Air Department set to condition 14.

Chapter 22　　　538

Tuesday 6 February 1945   *En route to Pearl Harbor as Task Unit 50.9.7*

0556 Steaming as before. Sounded routine torpedo defense. Sounded flight quarters. All anti-submarine patrols would be flown with 2 TBMs today.
0628 Completed launching 2 TBMs for a dawn ASP. Then set Air Department to condition 13.
0650 Conducted firing tests of 20mm and 40mm anti-aircraft guns.
0658 Secured from torpedo defense.
0716 Launched 1 TBM.
0753 Recovered 1 TBM launched at 0628.
0950 Sounded flight quarters.
Maneuvering out of (and returning back into) the formation as necessary, launched relief flights of 2 TBMs for ASPs at 1017 & 1409. Air Department was kept in condition 13 throughout the day. The last relief ASP of the day launched at 1409 and recovered at 1812.
1813 Secured from flight quarters.
1900 Steadied on base course 081°T.

Wednesday 7 and Thursday 8 February 1945   *En route to Pearl Harbor as Task Unit 50.9.7*

Steaming as before. February 7th and 8th would pass much the same as yesterday. Today however they went back to utilizing 1 F6F and 1 TBM on each of the four daytime anti-submarine patrols. INDEPENDENCE proceed on a near easterly heading, closing the distance to Hawaii.

Friday 9 February 1945   *En route to Pearl Harbor as Task Unit 50.9.7*

Steaming as before in accordance with secret orders dated 30 January 1945, of ComServRon Ten (accompanied by the USS NEHENTA BAY (guide), COGSWELL, KNAPP and MACDONOUGH) in cruising disposition, course 085°T, 16 knots, guide bears 175°T, 1,500 yards.
0619 Sounded routine torpedo defense. Sounded flight quarters.
0652 Completed launching 1 F6F and 1 TBM for a dawn ASP.
0655 Secured from flight quarters.
Air Department set to condition 13.
0719 Secured from torpedo defense.
0930 Sounded flight quarters.
0958 Completed launching 1 F6F and 1 TBM for ASP.
1006 Completed recovering 1 F6F and 1 TBM launched at 0652.
 Secured from flight quarters. Air Department set to condition 13.
1044 The TU ceased zigzagging while USS COGSWELL picked up officer messenger mail from ships of the Task Unit.
1103-1107 USS COGSWELL was along starboard side to transfer officer messenger mail.
1115 Resumed zigzagging on base course 082°T.
1156 Completed launching 1 F6F and 1 TBM to proceed to Pearl Harbor (to deliver officer messenger mail prior to the arrival of the TU to that port).
1330 Sounded flight quarters.
1358 Completed launching 2 TBMs.
1400 Completed recovering 1 F6F and 1 TBM launched at 0958.
1804 Sounded flight quarters.
1817-1818 Completed recovering 2 TBMs launched at 1358.
1820 Secured from flight quarters.
Air Department set to condition 14.
1834-1933 Manned routine torpedo defense stations.

PHOM3C Fred E. Owen

Saturday 10 February 1945   *Arrived in Pearl Harbor - CVLG(N)-41 Transfers Off*

Steaming as before. Air Department is in condition 14.

0020 Sighted white flare, bearing 340°T, 12 miles. Made a series of course changes to avoid shipping. This would continue until 0300 as they maneuvered to avoid several successive groups of ships steaming down from the north.

0540 Sighted lights of Honolulu and Pearl Harbor on the horizon bearing 000°T.

0635 Sounded flight quarters.

0637 Changed course to 340°T. At 0642 they changed speed to 10 knots.

0710 Draft of the ship prior to entering port: Forward 22', Aft 24'. Commenced pumping ballast.

0727 Changed course to 328°T.

0734 Completed launching 4 TBMs and 1 F6F for landing at NAS Ford Island.

0737 All engines stopped. Secured from flight quarters. Air Department set to condition 14.

0800 Sounded general quarters for entering the channel.

0803 Commenced maneuvering to conform to channel and making approach to the harbor.

0823 Chief Bos'n G.L. Carter, USN, harbor pilot, reported on board and to the bridge.

0828 Passed anti-submarine net tender abeam to starboard, and secured from general quarters.

0924 Moored the starboard side to berth FOX 1, Ford Island, Pearl Harbor, Oahu, T.H. (assisted by Yard Tug # 146 on the port quarter and Yard Tug # 263 on the port beam). Mooring lines are 9 wire lines and 2 manila lines. At 0934 the harbor pilot (Chief Bos'n G.L. Carter, USN) left the ship.

1005-1020 Let fires die out under boiler No. 3, made the fresh water connection to the dock, and commenced receiving telephone service from shore. They also transferred 4 F6Fs to the pier.

1025 INDEPENDENCE commenced disembarking officers and enlisted passengers.

1110 **CVLG(N)-41 Air Group Officers began transferring off the ship.** Pursuant to orders issued in a confidential despatch from the Commander Air Force, Pacific Fleet dated 8 February 1945, they were to report to NAS Alameda, California for reclassification and decommissioning. However, those orders must have changed. Instead, they boarded the USS GENERAL STURGIS (APA-137) and were transported to Seattle. The actual Squadron celebration and decommissioning of our nation's first night carrier air group occurred at NAS Seattle. **They were decommissioned on 26 February 1945.**

Three CVLG(N)-41 fighter director officers were detached to remain aboard the INDEPENDENCE.

1310 YOG-L-24 moored alongside to port bow.

1410 Commenced receiving fresh water from the dock, taking aboard 30,000 gallons.

1729 Completed discharging gasoline to the YOG.

1820 Commenced offloading bombs onto a freighter.

GN Entered Pearl Harbor and worked all day and night unloading bombs. Received first mail for quite some time. GN

GL Arrived at Pearl Harbor – Girls, girls and more gals. Wow! We spent about 23 days here. They are rushing us like hell to get us out again. They are only doing a half assed job on the ship. No transfers, no nothing. GL

Sunday 11 February 1945   *Pearl Harbor*   *Captain Nolan M. Kindell assumes command*

Moored as before at berth FOX 1, Ford Island. **At 1400, ceremonies were held and Captain E.C. Ewen was ordered detached and relieved by Captain Nolan M. Kindell.**

Monday 12 February 1945   *Pearl Harbor*

1055 Moored as before. Aided by tugs and a harbor pilot, INDEPENDENCE got underway to move to Berth 23, Navy Yard, Pearl Harbor.

1136 Moored our starboard side to Berth 23, in 8 fathoms of water.

The ship was receiving fresh water, salt water, steam, electricity and telephone from the shore.

During the period of 12 February thru 28 February the INDEPENDENCE would undergo a "considerable number of repairs" needed as a result of weather damage, and normal wear and tear.

Friday 16 February 1945 *Pearl Harbor*

0727 Moored as before. Singled up all lines in preparation for moving the ship.
0750 Cut off and secured fresh water, salt water, steam, electricity and telephone from the dock. The ship was moved aft in the berth. During the morning fresh water, salt water, steam, electricity and telephone services from shore were restored.
0945 Mustered crew to quarters. Captain Kindell began a ceremony to present awards as follows:

LEGION OF MERIT;   CDR. Richard Ashley Teel and CDR. Edwin James Stephen Young.
BRONZE STAR MEDAL; Lt. CDR. Earl Ward Sloan and Lt. Cyrus Bernie Heinrich.

1430 INDEPENDENCE received aboard a motor speed boat.

Wednesday 21 February 1945   *Pearl Harbor — Dry Dock No. 1*

0845 Moored as before. Mustered crew on stations.   1035 Secured all services from the dock.
1044-1145 Five Yard Tugs took position in preparation to move the ship.
1150 Got underway being towed by Yard Tugs from Berth 23 to proceed to the assigned dry dock.
1236 Crossed over the sill of Dry Dock No.1.   1240 All tugs cast off.   1248 Caisson in place.
1300 With the ship positioned over keel blocks, water began pumping from the dry dock.
1435 INDEPENDENCE was now connected to fresh water, salt water, steam, electricity and telephone services from the dry dock.
1600 Completed pumping water from the dry dock, resting on keel blocks.

Two days ago, on the 19th (as INDEPENDENCE was being made ready for the drydock), the Marine Corps landed on the volcanic sand beaches of **Iwo Jima**. Later in the grueling fighting over the deadly and hotly contested island, Marine Corp PFC. Charles Curtis Wright (in the 5th Division, 28th regiment, "E" Company) was wounded as a Japanese bullet knocked his steel helmet off his head. A second bullet traversed thru his skull (*"just passing thru"* as Charlie tells it). The first bullet deflected off the helmet, had penetrated his head just below his eye, taking up a more permanent residence in his brain. Surgically too dangerous to remove, he survives with it today. Charles was only one of a massive number of causalities that would occur during intense fighting over the next 34 days.
Over 6,800 killed or missing, and over 19,000 wounded. Japanese losses: over 21,800 killed.
Tonight, on February 21st, as the "Mighty-I" sits dry on keel blocks, the war does not rest. The USS BISMARCK SEA (CVE-95), struck by 2 kamikazes, will sink off Iwo Jima losing 318 men.

Thursday 22 February 1945 *Pearl Harbor — Dry Dock No. 1*

0845 Resting on keel blocks as before. Mustered crew on stations.
1118 Sounded fire call for a one alarm fire in compartment C-201L.
1120 Secured from fire quarters. No damage.

Tuesday 27 February 1945 *Pearl Harbor — Dry Dock No. 1*

0845 Resting on keel blocks as before. Mustered crew on stations.
1600 Received the following engineering report: When the ship was dry docked, inspected all propellers, shafts, strut bearings, engineering sea valves and strainers. All propellers had cracks and nicks. Minor repairs were made to all sea valves by the ships crew. All propellers were repaired and balanced by the yard workers. The Strut and hanger bearings were deemed satisfactory.
1640 Received 1 motor whale boat from the Navy Yard as a replacement for the whale boat lost in the typhoon.

Wednesday 28 February 1945   *Pearl Harbor — Dry Dock No. 1*

Resting on keel blocks as before. During the time in dry dock, along with other necessary repairs completed, the bottom of the hull was scraped and painted. The ship was repainted one color, dark-blue-gray. Also during this period of time, the crew received liberty using port and starboard liberty. Included were 3 days recreational leave at Camp Andrews.

1353 Commenced flooding the dry dock to refloat the ship.

1515 USS INDEPENDENCE was floating and moored in Dry Dock No.1.

Thursday 1 March 1945   *Pearl Harbor — Dry Dock No. 1*

Moored as before in Dry Dock No.1, U.S. Navy Yard, Pearl Harbor, T.H., preparatory to leaving a seven day routine dry dock period with no power.

0909 Harbor pilot Chief Boatswain G.L. Carter came aboard, proceeding to the bridge.

0930 Underway, being backed out of the dock by lines ashore.

0957 With Yard Tugs 119, 146 and 195 assisting, the INDEPENDENCE bow crossed over the sill.

1000 Yard Tugs 152 and 233 joined to assist the tow to Ford Island.

1110 Moored port side to berth Fox 12.

1130 All tugs cast off.. During the day the crew commenced loading ammunition and stores.

GN   Out of drydock and looks like the work is going to be with us thick and fast from here on. GN

1142 Ammunition lighter came along side the starboard bow. Commenced taking on 40mm rounds.

1250 Commenced receiving 18 torpedoes and warheads from the dock.

1315 LCI #1341 came along side the starboard quarter with stores.

1430 Commenced receiving bombs from LCI #1341.

1605 LCI #1341 cast off.

1630 LCI #1273 carrying general stores from the Navy Yard rammed the hull, denting it at frame 111.

1850 Seaplane tender #7 USS SWAN came along the starboard side amidships to furnish feed water.

Friday 2 March 1945 *Pearl Harbor — Berth FOX 12*

Friday would bring an ongoing continuation of resupplying the ship, loading stores and ammunition. Working on a day and night schedule, the entire arming, provisioning, and fueling of the ship was accomplished, disregarding many safety precautions. The USS INDEPENDENCE readied for sea.

The Mighty-I would leave Pearl without an Air Wing they could call her own. Night Fighting Air Group 41 was gone, headed stateside. Today 167 officers and men, comprising Bombing Squadron 86 and Torpedo Squadron 86, came aboard as passengers for transportation. INDEPENDENCE took no planes aboard. Her "Brown Shoes" would board in short order, when they steamed back out to rejoin the war.

The stay in Pearl Harbor would see many crew members being transferred off temporally for additional training (fire fighting, radar, etc.), and shipmates being reassigned. There was also an ongoing supply of new crewmembers making the trip up the gangway for the first time. Noteworthy was S2c Alphonse "Al" M. Hiegel, who would later become historian for the reunion group, and the catalyst for this book.

GN Really turning too, and the gear is starting to come aboard. GN

Saturday 3 March 1945   *Pearl Harbor — Berth FOX 12*

GN Put in 25 hours solid yesterday and looks bad again for today. Did manage to have 4 hours sleep though before we turned too again. GN

Moored port side as before to Berth No.12, NAS Ford Island, Pearl Harbor, T.H., with 8 wire lines and 1 manila line. Receiving fresh water and telephone service from the dock. Boiler No.2 is in use for auxiliary purposes. Fires lighted under boilers No. 3 and 4 for test purposes.

0005 LCI No. 1273 moored alongside starboard bow.

0258 Lighted fires under boiler No. 1 for test purposes.

0523 Cut in Boiler No.1 on the main steam line.   0528 Cut out Boiler No.2.

0720 Received Flash Blue (a drill) from SOP.

0723-0726 Received Flash Red. Manned general quarters stations (a drill).

0745 LCI No.1273 cast off.

0815 YTL 309 came along starboard side to deliver a camel.

0900 Jacked over main engines by hand.

0921 Lighted fires under boiler No 2.

0942 Cut in Boiler No.2 on the main steam line. Secured No.1 Boiler.

1202 Commenced spinning main engines No.1 & 4.

1220 Completed spinning main engines No.1 & 4.

1222 Yard Oiler 47 tied up starboard side amidships. It would cast off at 1847

1300 Yard Oiler 123 was tied up along side YO 47, casting off at 1625.

1543 Yard Oiler 43 tied up to Yard Oiler 123, then at 1943 tied up to the starboard side delivering gasoline and diesel oil.

1730 Commenced spinning main engines No.1 & 3, securing at 1747.

1755 Completed refueling this vessel having received 560,451 gallons of fuel oil.

Work would continue thru the night taking on ordnance, provisions, aviation gasoline and diesel oil.

AD Making preparations to get underway. AD

Sunday 4 March 1945   *Pearl Harbor — Underway to Eniwetok Atoll*

0120 Yard Oiler 43 cast off. INDEPENDENCE received 113,000 gallons of gasoline.

0500 Lighted fires under No.4 Boiler.

0515 Commenced turning over main engine by hand.

0607 Placed Boiler No.4 on main steam line.

0640 Commenced spinning main engine by steam.

0715 Disconnect fresh water supply from the dock. Harbor Pilot came on board.

0738 Cast off stern wire and bow line.

0748 USS YT 263 secured along starboard quarter. (YT - Yard Tug)

0751 Singled up all lines.   0752 Hoisted No.2 motor whale boat on board.

0756 Underway from Berth No. FOX 12.

0801 USS YT 263 cast off.

0802 Commenced maneuvering to leave the channel, Pearl Harbor, Oahu, T.H.

0819 Sounded routine general quarters upon leaving port.

0822 Harbor Pilot departed the ship.

0829 Passed thru nets of the channel.

0840 Took departure of channel between buoys No.1 and 2, changing course to 183°T, speed 15 knots.

0846 Changed speed to 22 knots. At 0847 they secured from general quarters.

0855 U.S.S. CHAUNCEY joined up, forming Task Unit 12.5.3 (Captain N. M. KINDELL, Commanding Officer, U.S.S. INDEPENDENCE, OTC).

1105 Sounded torpedo defense for the purpose of gunnery practice.

1106 Lighted fires under No.1 Boiler.

1125 Commenced firing anti-aircraft practice at a towed sleeve.

1221 Cut No.1 Boiler into the main steam line.

1250 Secured from torpedo defense.

1348 Commenced zigzagging on base course 270°T (zigzagging would cease at sunset).

1900 Changed ships clocks to zone plus 10 1/2.

2100 U.S.S. CHAUNCEY departed, making 25 knots to rendezvous with INDEPENDENCE the next afternoon, after this ships full power run.

AD Underway for battle zone at 0745. We have one DD with us. *AD*

GN Put in another 15 hours solid going. Never have I seen so much gear come aboard this scow. Looks like we are going to fight the Japs by ourselves. We did have five men transferred but not the good workers like we were promised. Haven't had a chance to write Mom in a good while. In fact I need a bath more than anything else but should get it sometime today which incidentally is my birthday. Celebrated in good style too. Fried chicken and ice cream for dinner but with God's help I hope I'll be able to buy my own dinner this time next year. Under way again and it looks like the first stop may be Guam. GN

Monday 5 March 1945   *Underway to Eniwetok Atoll*

0425 Steaming as before. Lost steering control in the pilot house. Shifted control to steering aft.
0426 Shifted steering units from starboard to port due to failure of starboard steering engine.
0432 Shifted steering control back to the pilot house.
0530 Lighted fires under the No. 2 & 3 Boilers.
0549 Sounded routine torpedo defense.
0630-0631 Cut Boilers No. 2 & 3 into the main steam line.
0648 Secured from torpedo defense.
0800 Engineering Department is preparing for a full power run.
During the morning they gradually increased speed to full power, making 31 knots at 1200.
1345 One alarm fire in after uptake. Sounded fire quarters. Paper box in the uptake caught fire and was quickly extinguished. No damage was caused.
1352 Secured from fire quarters.
1430 Antenna wire was carried away from the aft antenna boom due to vibration from the full power run. It was repaired. Maximum speed was maintained until 1600. Slowly the speed was decreased, dropping to 21 knots at 1720.
1817 INDEPENDENCE rendezvoused with the USS CHAUNCEY.
1900 Set all ships clocks to zone plus 11.
2050 Changed speed to 22 knots.
2120-2124 Secured No.2 & 3 Boilers.
2218 Shifted steering control to steering aft to test starboard steering unit.
2240 Completed testing of the starboard steering unit with testing proving satisfactory. Shifted steering control to the pilot house.

Captain Kindell would note in the Standing Orders Log;
"A light, and yellow flare were seen at 17°-55' North 167°—30' West, time 0835 Zebra 5th.
Have destroyers investigate any lights or flares sighted, as we are in area being searched for lost plane survivors.   Call me if anything unusual is sighted or happens."

Tuesday 6 March 1945   *Underway to Eniwetok Atoll*

Steaming as before as TU 12.5.3 in company with USS CHAUNCEY (screen) on course 259°T, speed 22 knots.
0557-0657 Manned routine torpedo defense stations.   0845 Mustered crew on stations.
0852 Put Boiler No.2 out of commission while repairing the control panel.
1650 Crossed the 180th meridian.
1800 Changed course to 240°T. Sighted eight ships consisting of 3 aircraft carriers, 1 cruiser and screening vessels, bearing 330°T, 15 miles.
1838 Sounded torpedo defense.

1858 Darkened ship.

1900 Set ships clocks back 1/2 hour to zone plus 11 1/2.

1903 Changed course to 258°T.

1938 Secured from torpedo defense.

2400 Changed ships time again to minus 12 1/2, thus picking up an East Longitude date.

Captain Kindell would note in the Standing Orders Log;
" At midnight the date changes to 8 March.   No friendly subs will be seen.
Only ships near are those of the GUAM Group to the North of us.
We should draw away from them during the night."

Thursday 8 March 1945   *Underway to Eniwetok Atoll. Poof ... Wednesday 7 March vanishes!*

Steaming as before. **The time zone change at 0000 made this date 8 March 1945.**

0400 Made radar contact with the eight ships sighted before dark, bearing 260°T, 17 miles.

0442 Changed course to 275°T to avoid the group being overtaken by this ship.

0619 Changed course to 255°T.

0845 Mustered crew on stations.

0845 Forced to slow speed of No.3 main engine due to improper functioning of glass sealed valve.

0850 Lost load on after distribution board. After gyro out of commission.

0855 Regained load, after gyro put back in operation.

0900 Regained vacuum on No.3 engine. No.3 main engine back in operation.

1900 Set clocks back 1/2 hour to zone minus 12.

1844 Sounded routine torpedo defense.

2030 Received a report from the "A" Division Engineering officer concerning the condition of the steering engines. Leaving Pearl Harbor both steering units were tested and found to be in good condition. The port steering pump is operating satisfactory. The starboard steering pump is in stand-by status. The servo pump is 140 lbs below its required 400 lbs pressure. The cause is being investigated.

Friday 9 March 1945   *Underway to Eniwetok Atoll*

Steaming with USS CHAUNCEY, course 250°T, speed 22 knots.

0915 Shifted to starboard steering unit.

0930-0935 Conducted rudder test.

1050 Made daily inspection of magazines.

1515 Sighted land bearing 253°T, 17 miles.

1535 Changed course to 285°T, speed is 15 knots.

1600 Changed speed to 10 knots.

1607 Passed buoy, abeam to starboard, at the Deep Entrance to Eniwetok Harbor, Marshall Islands. With the Captain at the conn, the carrier maneuvered to anchor in Berth C-5, anchorage "A", with 125 fathoms of chain to the port anchor, in 30 fathoms of water with a coral and sand bottom.

1900 Set all ships clocks back 1/2 hour to zone minus 11 1/2.

2200 S2c Al Boudreau was admitted to sick bay with a fractured shoulder. He was a member of the motor whale boat crew. A swell caused the boat to heave, and Al lost his balance, getting caught between the boat and the ships hull.

AD Anchored at Eniwetok at 1700. AD

GN Dropped the hook in Eniwetok in the Marshalls. Unfortunately had the duty and spent four hours going here and there on an LCI trying to get stores but to no avail. All we got was good and wet. GN

Saturday 10 March 1945   Eniwetok - *Underway to Ulithi Atoll*

0725 Anchored as before. YOGLs No.18 & 19 were received along the starboard side as camels.
0840 Tanker USS GEMSBOK moored to starboard side.
0840 Mustered crew on stations.
0932 Commenced fueling operation.
1120 Transferred YOGLs No.18 & 19 to the USS GEMSBOK.
1144 Completed receiving 190,021 gallons of fuel oil.
1145 Made preparations for getting underway. Commenced heaving short.
1159 Cast off all lines from USS GEMSBOK.
1207 Got underway to depart the anchorage, maneuvering as required to depart thru the Deep Entrance of Eniwetok Atoll.
1215 Passed channel buoy No.2. USS CHAUNCEY (screen) joined up, reforming TU 12.5.3.
1229 Changed speed to 22 knots, course 211°T. Took departure of Perry Island HECP, bearing 275°T, distance 2 1/2 miles.   (HECP - Harbor Entrance Control Post)
1800 Changed course to 268°T.
1900 Changed all ships clocks back 1/2 hour to zone minus 11.

GN Refueled in the morning and left the Marshalls around noon. Have been headed west ever since and have been hoping to head north. The heat is pretty bad but to be expected I guess around the tropics.
GN

11-12 Mar 1945 GN Routine clean up and squaring away which is a lot. Yard seems to have only half finished their jobs. Off Ulithi and waiting for squadron to come aboard. GN

Sunday 11 March 1945   *Underway to Ulithi Atoll*

Steaming as TU 12.5.3 with USS CHAUNCEY, course 268°T, speed 21 knots.
0638 Commenced zigzagging on base course 268°T. Zigzagging continued during daylight hours, until sunset, when the ship would then proceed on base course during the protection of night.
0840 Mustered crew on stations.
0948-1005 Anti-aircraft gunnery exercises, firing at 5" bursts from USS CHAUNCEY, expending 158 rounds of 40mm ammunition.
1900 Changed all ships clocks back 1/2 hour to zone minus 10 1/2.
1933 Ceased zigzagging, resumed base course 268°T.

Captain Kindell would note in the Standing Orders Log;
"The GUAM Group is about 30 miles ahead."

Monday 12 March 1945   *Underway to Ulithi Atoll*

Steaming as before proceeding west toward Ulithi.
1900 Clocks would once again move back 1/2 hour to zone minus 10.
1930 Decreased speed to 18 knots.
2200 S1c Phillips was admitted to sick bay for multiple contusions when a box of 50 caliber ammunition fell on him from a stack, while he was handling the ammunition.

Captain Kindell would note in the Standing Orders Log; *" No land should be sighted until dawn. Around four an island should be picked up abeam to port by radar. It should not be closer than twelve miles. At least two other formations are arriving at the same time we are. Ships may get close as we approach."*

Tuesday 13 March 1945   *Underway to Ulithi Atoll -* ***CVLG-46 Lands Aboard***

0621 Iar Island sighted bearing 240°, distance 8 miles.

0649 Changed course to 000°T to avoid other ships arriving at Ulithi.

0730 Sounded flight quarters.

0752 Steering various courses into the wind while landing aircraft.

0835 Completed landing 23 F6Fs of the new Air Wing (CVLG-46). Then changed course to 240°T.

0941 Completed landing 9 TBMs and 3 F6Fs of CVLG-46. Changed course to 245°T, speed 24 knots. INDEPENDENCE has 26 Hellcats and 9 Avengers on board, flown in from Falalop Airfield on Ulithi.

1037 Sounded routine general quarters upon approaching port.

1042 Changed course to 298°T, speed 15 knots. Commenced maneuvering while entering channel to Ulithi Atoll, Caroline Islands.

1052 Passed channel buoy No.1 abeam to port, and buoy No.2 abeam to starboard.

1058 Secured from general quarters, manned all mooring stations.

1125 Air Department set to condition 14.

1128 Anchored in Berth 147 using 125 fathoms of chain to the port anchor, in 27 fathoms of water, Ulithi Atoll.

1145 Secured main engines.

INDEPENDENCE reported for duty to Commander Task Force 58 (Vice Admiral Marc A. Mitscher, Commander First Carrier Task Force, USS BUNKER HILL, Flagship).

All of TF 58 was in the anchorage as well other units of the US and British Fleets.

During the afternoon, the rest of Fighting Squadron 46 and Torpedo Squadron 46 reported aboard for duty.

1200 Let fires die out under No.2 Boiler.

1215 Commenced receiving stores and supplies from a barge alongside.

1600 Completed taking supplies from the barge. It cast off.

1755 Damage was reported to our No.1 motor whaleboat at 1630 upon return from a trip to the USS CASCO, AVP-12. While lying off the CASCO to starboard with the motor off, LCM VP34 No. 203 ran down the motor whaleboat, hitting it amidships. Three men were thrown overboard, and severe damage was done to the whaleboat. The men were uninjured.

2105 Sounded torpedo defense due to an unidentified aircraft reported by the shore station.

2120 Secured from torpedo defense as the aircraft was identified as friendly.

GL Received our squadrons. Took on 26 fighters and 9 TBF's. It is the most planes we ever carried. Pulled into Ulithi about 11 and started to take on stores. We missed a little fun as the day before the Japs raided the island, and one of the planes crashed on the island. The Franklin was in, she had her stern pushed in by a Jap suicide. GL

GN Took on squadron 26 F6Fs and 9 TBMs. Will have our hands full this time. Had a slight run in and was chased down to the magazine. Anchored in Ulithi. GN

Wednesday 14 March 1945   *Anchored - Ulithi Atoll - Underway*

Anchored as before in Ulithi Atoll, provisioning.

0040 LCM No.25 cast off from starboard bow.

0045 LCM No.75 cast off with the passengers picked up in Pearl Harbor (officers and enlisted men in VB-86 and VT-86. The squadrons were transferred to proceed to the USS WASP).

0225 LCM No. 125 moored to starboard side to unload provisions, casting off at 0530.

0745 During the morning the task groups of Task Force 58 sortied to stand out from the anchorage. INDEPENDENCE remained at anchor to fuel.

1040 Completed fueling, having received 321,831 gallons of fuel oil.

1155 Turned over main engines by steam.

1202 Tested engine order telegraph and steering engines. The Steering Servo Pump had been repaired during the brief stop.

1241 Underway, pursuant to orders of Commander Task Group 58.4 (Rear Admiral A. W. Radford, USN, Commander, Carrier Division Six, USS YORKTOWN, Flagship) to proceed to a rendezvous with Task Group 58.4. Maneuvering to conform to the channel.

1313 Entered Mugai Channel accompanied by destroyers, USS NORMAN SCOTT and USS HAILEY, as screens, leaving Ulithi Atoll.

1330 Time was changed on ships clocks to zone minus 9. INDEPENDENCE proceeded to the northeast at 22 knots to the rendezvous.

1430 The receiving whip antenna, located on No.4 stack, for the receiver in the auxiliary radio room broke loose. It was replaced by ships company.

1800 Joined up with Task Group 58.4, becoming part of Task Unit 58.4.1 (Rear Admiral A. W. Radford, USN, in YORKTOWN), consisting of the USS YORKTOWN, INTREPID, ENTERPRISE, and LANGLEY, as well as this vessel. INDEPENDENCE will operate in accordance with C. T .G. 58.4 Operation Order 3-45, dated 12 March 1945, as part of the FIFTH Fleet (Admiral R.A. Spruance, USN, Commander, FIFTH Fleet, USS INDIANAPOLIS, Flagship).

1803 Directed USS NORMAN SCOTT and USS HAILEY to join TG 58.4. Commenced maneuvering to take assigned station within the TG 58.4.

1822 Arrived on station in cruising disposition 5-R-l, axis 175°T. Course 350°T, guide is YORKTOWN bearing 075°T, 2,000 yards.   1940 Commenced pumping bilges.

During the night they proceeded toward a fueling rendezvous on a course 335°T, speed 18 knots. The tight schedule and short stay in Ulithi did not give enough time to adequately reprovision.

RC Underway for Japan to hit Honshu, Kobe and Kure. RC

GN Took on some stores and underway at noon. Joined our outfit which is 58.4. Comprises Yorktown, Intrepid, Enterprise, Langley and ourselves for carriers. 'Wisconsin and Missouri for wagons and some cruisers and quite a few cans. GN

Thursday 15 March 1945   *Underway with TG 58.4*

Steaming as before in company with TU 58.4.1 proceeding to the northwest.

0850 The Task Group formed a column astern of the USS YORKTOWN for anti-aircraft gunnery practice against towed sleeves. INDEPENDENCE is 3,000 yards astern.

0919 Sounded torpedo defense for gunnery practice.

1102 Completed firing, after expending 3,886 rounds of 40mm and 1,178 rounds of 20mm ammunition. The Task Group returned to disposition 5-R-1, axis 075°T with USS INDEPENDENCE assigned guide.

1200 Sounded flight quarters.

1312 Launched eight F6Fs and seven TBMs for exercises with the battleship task group. (continued pg 556)

INDEPENDENCE was embarking on a mission tasked to prevent interference by enemy surface and air forces with the invasion, capture and occupation of Okinawa, in the Nansei Shoto Island chain.

From the period covering 14 March thru 11 May, they would be assigned to operate with TG58.4, except from 7 April thru 17 April, when they would be operating in TG 58.2 under Rear Admiral G.F. Bogan. At the beginning of the period, TF 58 was made up as follows:

Task Force 58 - Vice Admiral Mark A. Mitscher - USS BUNKER HILL

Task Group 58.1 — Rear Admiral J.J. Clark — USS HORNET
Task Group 58.2 — Rear Admiral R.E. Davidson — USS FRANKLIN
Task Group 58.3 — Rear Admiral F.C. Sherman — USS ESSEX
Task Group 58.4 — Rear Admiral A.W. Radford — USS YORKTOWN

Task Unit 58.4.1 (Carrier Unit)- Rear Admiral A.W. Radford

USS ENTERPRISE	Hall	Air Group 90
USS INDEPENDENCE	Kindell	Air Group 46
USS INTREPID	Short	Air Group 10
USS LANGLEY	Wegforth	Air Group 23
USS YORKTOWN	Combs	Air Group 9

Task Unit 58.4.2 (Support Unit)- Rear Admiral Low

BatDiv 9	Rear Admiral Hanson
USS MISSOURI	Callaghan
USS WISCONSIN	Stone
CruDiv 16	Rear Admiral Low
USS ALASKA	Noble
USS FLINT	Will
USS GUAM	Lovett
USS SAN DIEGO	Mullan
USS SAINT LOUIS	Roberts

Frigate "Man-O-War" bird
Original artwork for the
VF 46 squadron insignia

(courtesy of the Tailhook Assoc.)

Task Unit 58.4.3 (Screen Unit)- Nunn

DesRon 47	Nunn
DesDiv 93	Nunn
USS HEERMANN	Hathaway
USS HAZELWOOD	Douw
USS MCCORD	Michael
USS TRATHEN	Millett
DesDiv 94	Reynolds
USS FRANKS	Stephen
USS HAILEY	Brady
USS HAGGARD	Soballe
DesRon 54	Mercer
DesDiv 107	Mercer
USS MERTZ	Mattox
USS MONSSEN	Sanderson
USS NORMAN SCOTT	Porter
USS REMEY	Fiala
DesDiv 108	Phillips
USS MC DERMUT	Jennings
USS MCGOWAN	Cox
USS MCNAIR	McCullough
USS MELVIN	Atkins

Original artwork for the
VT 46 squadron insignia

(courtesy of the Tailhook Assoc.)

VT46 Officers

Standing L to R
Frank C. Brooks, Charles Wigham, Jr., James M. Felker, John A. Tschirhart, Robert E. Fitzgerald, unidentified, Burton B. LeTulie, Authur Rosenburgh

Sitting L to R
John Colgate, Harold I. Meyerson, Foster C. Kay, John P. Barron, E.A. Zurlinden, James Street, Daniel R. Harris

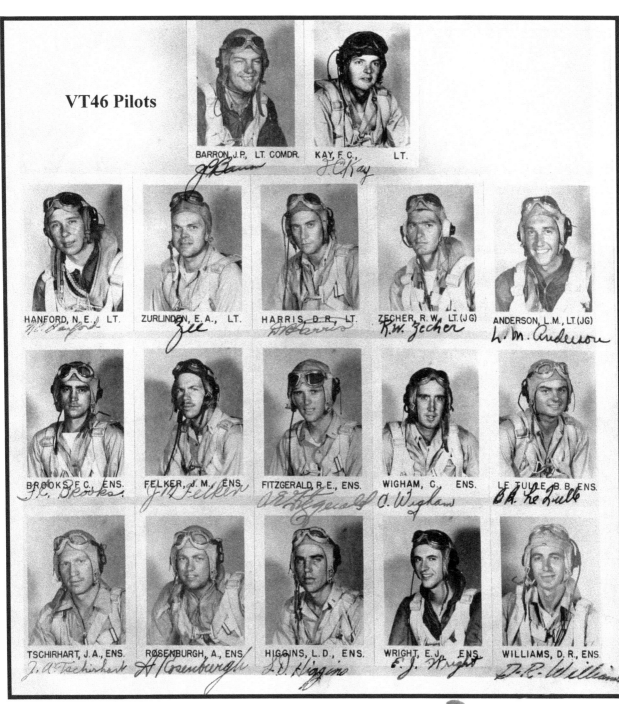

VT46 Pilots

BARRON, J.P., LT. COMDR. KAY, F.C., LT.

HANFORD, N.E., LT. ZURLINDEN, E.A., LT. HARRIS, D.R., LT. ZECHER, R.W., LT. (JG) ANDERSON, L.M., LT. (JG)

BROOKS, F.C., ENS. FELKER, J.M., ENS. FITZGERALD, R.E., ENS. WIGHAM, C., ENS. LE TULLE, B.B., ENS.

TSCHIRHART, J.A., ENS. ROSENBURGH, A., ENS. HIGGINS, L.D., ENS. WRIGHT, E.J., ENS. WILLIAMS, D.R., ENS.

VT46 Pilots & Enlisted Men
(need names)

A flight of seven VT46 TBM-1Cs

• Note the AN/N6 Gun Camera mounted on top of the engine cowls.
• The Yagi Antenna beneath the port wing is for ASB (Air -to-Surface) Radar.
• Atop the port wing tip is the Pitot Tube (positioned to measure airspeed in undisturbed air).

Fighting Forty Six

Training period at Groton, Conn. June 1944

Fighting Forty Six was commissioned at Atlantic City New Jersey on 15 April 1944. They moved to N.A.A.F., Groton Connecticut approximately one month later to complete their training.

The air base at Groton was interesting … Originally a farm (on the Plant estate), the junior officers were quartered in Army barracks, the senior officers in a converted dairy which served as a dormitory and Officer's Club (as well as hospital). The farm silo re-tasked to become the base operations tower. And yes, … Fighting Forty Six was in fact sent to the "Mighty Moo" (USS COWPENS) prior to boarding the USS INDEPENDENCE. Farm raised, what else to expect?

The squadron logo, the Frigate "Man-O-War" bird was selected with the following reasoning presented in the squadron history (describing characteristics common to the bird and the F6F Hellcat) as directly quoted below:
" *(1) In command of wing they are unsurpassed.*
 (2) They are more nearly independent of land than any other birds.
 (3) They are often seen hundreds of miles at sea.
 (4) They delight to soar at astonishing elevations.
 (5) Food is procured by dashing down on wing with unerring aim and by harassing weaker birds until they are
 forced to disgorge or drop their prey.
 (6) They do not leave the nest until they are able to follow their parents on wing.
Let the myopic, buck-teethed, bandy-legged Japs read and beware! We have adopted "Men-O-War" as the nickname of our squadron. " (the closing statement reflecting the attitude, cartoons and rhetoric of the day)

With training completed at Groton, they had proceeded to San Diego, then boarded the USS MAKASSAR STRAIT bound for Pearl Harbor. They would later board the USS BRETON for transportation to Ponam Island Airfield, and eventually end up on the USS COWPENS, (via Manus Island on the USS ALTAMAHA) boarding the "Mighty Moo" at Ulithi Atoll. They would stay aboard COWPENS for one month, from 6 February thru 6 March. Well travelled, the gypsy group was ordered aboard the Mighty-I.

The result of a typical barricade incursion. Air Group 46 aviators would have their landings arrested by the barricade cables a number of times in March and April. Not all were without loss of life.

1437 Launched eleven F6Fs for aerial gunnery exercises.

1611 Completed recovering eight F6Fs and seven TBMs launched at 1312.

1645 Completed recovering eleven F6Fs launched at 1437.

1710 Secured from flight quarters. Air Department set to condition 14.

1756-1856 Manned routine torpedo defense stations.

They continued to the northwest (340°T) at 20 knots during the night.

GL We are headed north to hit Japan is my guess. It is getting colder and colder. GL

GN Quite a bit of sea running and everything is lashed down securely. Still squaring spaces away. Target practice in early forenoon. GN

Friday 16 March 1945   *Underway with TG 58.4*

Steaming as before proceeding to a fueling rendezvous. Air Department is in condition 14.

0430 Changed course to 000°T.

0456 Sounded routine torpedo defense.

0454 Changed course to 320°T.

0540 Two battleships, and two large cruisers, which had been operating in Task Force 59, joined the formation as we formed disposition 5-R, axis 000°T.

0555 Secured from torpedo defense.

0601 Commenced maneuvering while forming a fueling disposition.

0653 Maneuvered alongside the USS CHICOPEE.

0745-0755 USS FRANKS was alongside port quarter to transfer a passenger and mail.

0825 USS CHICOPEE cast off, having pumped 59,774 gallons of fuel oil.

0844 Maneuvered to gain station, bearing 250°T, 4,000 yards from tanker USS CHICKASKIA.

0858 USS FRANKS came alongside to deliver guard mail, then cast off.

1030 Sounded flight quarters.

1125-1132 Launched anti-submarine patrol of 4 TBMs and launched 1 F6F.

1322 USS INDEPENDENCE designated guide.

1345 Formation axis changed to 070°T. The group had completed fueling and parted from the tankers.

1436 Completed launching a CAP of 8 F6Fs.

1456 Completed recovering the 4 TBMs and 1 Hellcat launched at 1132. Secured from flight quarters.

1710 Sounded flight quarters.

1748 Completed recovering the 8 F6Fs launched at 1436. Changed course to 320°T.

1802-1902 Manned routine torpedo defense stations.

The Task Force proceeded northwest towards the Japanese homeland, at a speed of 20 knots.

GN Refueled underway. Routine hops and landings all day. Broke out rockets and readied them for the forthcoming fracas. GN

Saturday 17 March 1945   *Underway with TG 58.4*

0444 Steaming as before towards Japan. Sounded flight quarters.

0535-0542 Launched 3 F6Fs and 3 TBMs for anti-submarine and anti-snooper patrols.

0545 Secured from flight quarters. Air Department set to condition 13.

0805 Sounded flight quarters.

0843-1901 USS HAZELWOOD was alongside to transfer 6 personnel assigned to CLVG-46.

0911 Completed recovery of 3 F6Fs and 3 TBMs launched at 0535.

0915 Secured from flight quarters. Air Department set to condition 14.

1130 Air Department set to condition 11 Easy.

1329-1345 Half-masted the colors following the movement of USS MONSSEN.

1410 Changed course to 000°T. USS YORKTOWN was designated formation guide.

1430-1436 Launched a CAP of 8 F6Fs.

1749 Completed recovery of the 8 F6Fs launched at 1436.

1800 Secured from flight quarters. Air Department set to condition 14. Proceeded north at 19 knots.

GN Routine operations. Made up rockets all day for tomorrow's big smash. GN

AD At sea steaming for Japan. My GQ station is now the bridge. I'll be able to see everything now. Our objective will be shipping and aircraft on the Jap mainland of Kyushu. AD

Captain Kindell would note in the Standing Orders Log;
" Steam darkened. Radio silence. OTC will use TBS only for tactical signals.
Radar silence except for sets above 300 mcs.
Courses set by OTC. Probably zigzagging.
Guide is YORKTOWN at position 2090. Our position 0000.
Enterprise may leave formation during the night if she starts operating.
No friendly contacts are expected. We are in a "Joint Zone" used by our submarines. Our subs are however, not supposed to come within torpedo range of heavy ships."

23
Striking the Japanese Homeland

Sunday 18 March 1945   *TG 58.4 Japan — Honshu, Kobe, Kure*

Steaming as before, approaching Kyushu to launch strikes on the enemy (carrying out Phase "Lucky" of the operation order) accompanied by carriers USS YORKTOWN, USS INTREPID, USS ENTERPRISE and USS LANGLEY. This vessel is 2,000 yards from guide, USS YORKTOWN. Enemy planes were in the vicinity of the Task Force almost continuously after midnight.

0455 Radar reported an enemy plane twelve miles away closing.

0457 Sounded general quarters.

0506 Observed flares and intermittent firing over a neighboring task group, 58.2, twelve miles away, bearing 260°T. The Task Force had been discovered by the enemy.

0557 Other ships in the formation opened fire on a plane reported in the clouds overhead. No results were observed.

0616 Sunrise over the formation, weather clear with scattered clouds at 3,000-4,000 feet.

0630 Changed the formation axis to 345°T, into the wind.

0636 The Task Group went into cruising disposition 5-VB, for better mutual protection in an air attack.

0701 Set condition ONE Easy.

0735 A melee of aircraft were observed ahead of the formation about five miles, apparently fighters of the CAP intercepting some single-engine enemy planes.

0737 One plane (believe to be an Oscar or a Judy) glided down over the center of the formation from ahead and dropped a bomb on the USS ENTERPRISE. This plane escaped the formation low to the water, though the Task Group opened up on him, only to be shot down by fighters astern. The bomb hit the flight deck of the USS ENTERPRISE, bounced against the stack, and fizzled, causing a small fire which was out by 0747. Another enemy plane was shot down by fighters ahead of the formation.

0738 Sounded general quarters. The INDEPENDENCE was strafed by a dive bomber as it passed to starboard. The escaping enemy dive bomber was seen shot down at 0740 by fighters astern. During this attack, a gunner on a forward 20mm mount was wounded in the abdomen by the tracer element of a 5" gun cartridge projectile. S1c James J.M. Clevenstine was taken to sick bay (his "friendly fire" wounds would prove to be fatal). Two unexploded 20mm slugs were later found imbedded in the wood flight deck planks, believed to be from "friendly" 20mm AA guns on other ships.

0759 Two enemy twin-engine planes appeared astern of the group. The first, believed to have been an Irving, came through the formation up the port side, was taken under fire by guns of this as well as other ships. Flames were observed at its wing roots. It crashed in flames 1500 yards ahead of INDEPENDENCE, just short of a destroyer at 0801. The other plane, believed to have been a Frances, came past the starboard side in a long shallow dive, was similarly taken under intense mixed AA fire, and crashed close aboard the USS INTREPID at 0805 (*See note below). The crew immediately observed heavy smoke and fire belching from that ship, subsiding quickly, and appeared to be completely out at 0809.

(*Note on the USS INTREPID: The action as described above reflects data from official Navy documents from the best knowledge of those aboard the INDEPENDENCE, as seen from a distance. INTREPID records indicate the aircraft was a G4M Betty Bomber that exploded close in, as the result of intense AA fire, showering the INTREPID with flaming aircraft parts and gasoline as the aircraft plummeted into the water. Both the Frances and Betty looked similar.)

0822 A friendly night fighter, crossing the formation, was fired upon and crashed outside the screen. The pilot was rescued.

0826 Completed launching 4 F6Fs (of 12 planned) for CAP. Further launching was interrupted due to firing within the formation.

0832-0837 Completed launching the remaining 8 F6Fs for the CAP to relieve planes from other carriers that had been up since dawn.

0843 Changed course to 150°T.

0847 Observed firing ahead.

0941 Set condition ONE Easy.

0957 A friendly plane made a water landing bearing 330°T, distance 2,000 yards.

1105 Changed course to 000°T for flight operations.

1117 Completed launching 12 F6Fs to relieve our CAP.

1148 Completed recovery of 12 F6Fs, 4 launched at 0826 and 8 launched at 0837.

1131 Commenced maneuvering to regain station within the formation.

1310 Sighted a single-engine enemy fighter (thought to be an Oscar) streaking down out of the clouds at 3,000' on the starboard bow. It was aflame, thought to have been hit by the CAP. It was in a shallow dive, dropping a bomb well forward of the USS ALASKA taking AA fire. Heading aft along this ships starboard side intermittently flaming, it crashed out of control in flames roughly 2,000 yards astern.

1315 An enemy single engine plane was sighted high overhead coming out of the clouds, diving on the USS YORKTOWN and taking AA fire. His bomb dropped clear of the YORKTOWN. With its tail shot off, the plane crashed into the water in flames near our screening vessels.

1405 Completed launching 10 F6Fs to participate in a strike against Usa Airfield on the northeastern coast of Kyushu. Usa, a rectangular airfield of about 100 acres, had roughly 60 to 100 planes, reported to consist of Bettys, Helens, Sallys and Vals. Cmdr. Rooney led the strike. Pilots were Lieutenants Badger and McNees, Lt.(jg) Reeder and Stewart, Ensigns Fielding, Pruett and Robinett. They targeted enemy hangars, and aircraft on the ground. Pushing over from 10,000' they fired rockets and strafed with fixed guns. Japanese AA fire over target was described as surprisingly meager and inaccurate. After action reports claimed 6 hangars left burning, 24 A/C destroyed, 6 probable and 10 damaged. They strafed a light house at Mikunoko Shima on the way back.

1500-1530 INDEPENDENCE half-masted colors, following the movements of USS ENTERPRISE.

1502 Sounded general quarters. An enemy dive bomber identified as a Judy, diving suddenly out of clouds on the starboard beam, dropped a bomb exploding close to starboard quarter of USS YORK TOWN. The plane pulled up into a steep climb. It burst into flames at about 2,000' and two parachutes were seen floating down as their burning aircraft crashed and exploded near the screen.

1603 Completed recovering the 12 F6Fs launched at 1117. Additionally, the 2 F6Fs launched at 1405 (Ens. Delehaunty had developed engine trouble en route to target, escorted back by Ens. T.C. Jones) also landed safely back on board.

1620 Set condition ONE Easy.

1659 Observed firing on horizon by Task Group 58.2.

1720-1739 Recovered the 10 F6Fs launched at 1405, returning from the Usa strike.
They had met no airborne opposition and had done considerable damage to parked aircraft and installations. Two of the landing F6Fs hit the battier, with only minor damage to the aircraft and the barrier. They still had rockets hung when they hit the barrier. The rockets were jettisoned.
1815 The formation changed into disposition 5V. Observed firing on horizon to the east at 1844, and again at 1920.
1959 Secured from condition ONE Easy, setting normal conditions.
2345 Changed course to 190°T.
On this day, Lt. John Monsarratt noted * that USS LANGLEY C.I.C. tracked 51 separate Japanese raids from early morning thru nightfall, composed of a single plane, to as many as 8 or 10 aircraft. Diversified attacks with aircraft approaching low level, to above 15,000 feet. (*Angel On The Yardarm)

*RC Sunday, strike day. We expected to surprise Japs today but evidently we didn't for they heckled task group all night long. Went to GQ at 0509. At 0825 Enterprise is hit near island structure by Jap **gasoline tank. 4 men killed, several injured, just minor damage to carrier. 0915 Jap plane dives on Intrepid, five inch guns hit plane before it crashed on flight deck. Yorktown had three near misses. Had 49 attacks today on task group with just minor damage to two carriers. Remained at GQ till 1930. It was longest GQ we have had yet, lasting 14 hours. RC*   (**Note: It was an undetonated bomb, 1 man died.)

GL Had 12-4 watch. That night we had bogies all over our screen. About 3 o'clock I saw gun fire star board beam as on the enterprise night chickens made a contact. I saw him shoot the plane down in flames. Enterprise planes shot down 5 bogies. GQ sounded about 4:56 as the other task group already shot down 2 bogies. About 8 o'clock I heard a shot and turned around in time to see a Oscar drop a bomb or belly tank on the Enterprise on starboard bow. He sneaked right in on us. I could see the pilot, he was so close. He disappeared over the horizon. Damage on the Enterprise was slight. About an hour later I heard gun fire aft. I happened to look up in time to see a Nick come out of the clouds.
All the ships opened up on him. He burst into flames and made a turn for the Yorktown but couldn't make it so he headed for a can up forward, but crashed about 100 yards in front of it. He burned in the water and a few minutes later we saw wreckage float by the port side. Gun fire broke out again back aft as a Diana or Helen made a run the entire length of the task group before it was hit by 5 inch. He burst into flames and headed for the Intrepid. I thought sure he was going to hit hard but he crashed into the sea a few yards from the starboard side, exploded and burst into flame.
There have been causalities on both Intrepid and Enterprise. About noon gun fire broke out on the starboard beam as a Jill made a dive on the Yorktown. His bomb made a near miss. We have had no more attacks. The Japs are still trying to get the Franklin. She is underway and smoking. They are 58.8. We just heard the Enterprise was hit by a 100 pound bomb. Damage is slight. 58.2 is under attack. I can see them firing on the starboard beam. I see one plane go down in flames, they got two more. The CAP has shot down various snoopers. Our planes sighted two bogies on the starboard and attacked them with rockets and 50 cal. Setting them on fire. Smoke is visible on the horizon. We had TD about 9 that night as there was bogies all over the screen. They would come on and go out, dropping window. One closed on starboard quarter and the cans opened fire. He dropped some flares and then burst into flames. The other task group shot down numerous planes. GL

Monday 19 March 1945　　　　*TG 58.4 Japan — Honshu, Kobe, Kure*

Steaming as before. They cruised in the same area to continue the strike against Kyushu and Honshu around the inland Sea. At 0511 they sounded routine general quarters.
0615 Maneuvered to gain proper station as the TG changed to disposition 5VB on an axis of 045°T.
0636 Secured from general quarters, set condition ONE Easy.
0708 Task Group 58.2 was observed under attack and firing, bearing 330°T, twelve miles away. A huge plume of smoke arose from one of the carriers as if she had been hit.
0710 USS FRANKLIN reported that she had been damaged by a suicide plane and was burning badly.
 As the crew watched, the smoke billowed with intensity above the flames that belched out of that ship.

0725 A series of violent explosions, fourteen or more in number, shot fire out engulfing the FRANK-LIN with each. She continued to burn most of the morning, visible to the CVL-22 crew in the distance.

0740 INDEPENDENCE began to launch a CAP of 12 F6Fs, getting only 1 Hellcat launched before they were interrupted by an emergency turn out of the wind, prompted by report of enemy planes bearing 315°T.

0807 Completed launch of 12 F6F s, including the one launched prior to the turn.

Four Hellcats (flown by Lt. John I. Jones and Lt.(jg)s Wesley R. Shaw, Carleton T. Jones and Richard M. Rogg) were vectored by the USS ENTERPRISE FDO toward the bogey. Flying at 3,000' beneath overcast skies, Rogg tally-hoed the bogey flying on an opposite course 1,000' below. The Jill immediately turned left 90 degrees to attempt to avoid contact. With all four Hellcats in pursuit taking shots, the Jill burst into flames. As more hits scored, the Jill began burning violently and started an uncontrolled dive into the water from 1,000'. A single unoccupied parachute was observed floating down to the water. Lt.(jg) Rogg's Hellcat returned with a 12" gash in his port wing, a gift from the Jill's rear gunner. Credit for the 6 o'clock level kill was shared by Carleton Jones and Richard Rogg.

0820 Steaming south, observed firing in Task Group 58.2, bearing 274°T on the horizon, and several bomb explosions near ships of that Task Group.

0920 USS ENTERPRISE, USS FLINT, and Destroyer Division 107*[1.] detached from this Task Group to join Task Group 58.2. These ships were to augment the USS FRANKLIN's Task Group, to provide additional protection during retirement. (*[1.] See page 549 for Des. Div. 107)

1056 Launched 12 F6Fs to relieve the CAP launched at 0807.

1122 Completed recovery of 7 of the 12 F6Fs launched at 0807.

1158 Completed recovery of the remaining 5 F6Fs launched at 0807.

1212 Commenced maneuvering to regain station after recovering aircraft.

1418 Changed course to 160°T.

1420 Observed firing on the horizon bearing 310°T, where enemy planes had been reported.

1437 Launched 10 F6Fs to join a fighter sweep on Oita Jima. Each Hellcat had six 3.5' rockets. INTREPID, LANGLEY and YORKTOWN each launched 12 planes for the raid. Attacks were made on Oita Airfield and Saeki Airfield. 8 A/C were destroyed, with 2 hangars left burning at Oita. At Saeki; 3 A/C were destroyed, and 2 hangars were left burning. The light house, two radio towers and a radar station at Ashikuri Saki Point was strafed on return to base. (Hellcats were flown by Lts. William Schroeder, Jack Rivers, Angus Morrison, and Ensigns Alfred Adair, James R. Butler, Robert J. Byron, Thomas M. Delehaunty, Robert D. Flodquist, James W. Pruett and Samuel A. Sparks.)

1516 Completed recovery of 12 F6Fs launched at 1056.

1531 USS GUAM, USS ALASKA, USS HEERMANN and USS MCNAIR were detached, leaving the formation to join Task Group 58.2.

1747 Completed recovery of the 10 F6Fs launched at 1437 for the Oita Jima strike. The F6F-5 Hellcat (Bu.No.71892) flown by Lt. William Schroeder crashed into the barrier, seriously damaging the aircraft. The entire tail hook assembly had pulled out on landing.

1830 Task Group formed cruising disposition 5-V-2, axis 045°T, course 315°T, speed 18 knots, USS YORKTOWN guide bearing 180°T, 2,100 yards.

1926 Formed cruising disposition 5-VB. At 2140 they commenced zigzagging on base course 270°T.

DL On 19 March we had launched early morning raids when TF 58 was hit badly. I watched three carriers get a display of the enemy's power. CV 18 Wasp was hit with one bomb that put her out of action and caused two hundred casualties. CV 9 Essex was hit with friendly fire from another U.S. ship. But it was CV 13 Franklin which took the brunt of the attack.

Our respective task groups were apart but our cruising radius brought each one momentarily into sight of the others. Standing open-mouthed, I watched hell engulf this huge vessel. My GQ station was on the deck and I had plenty of room, and time, to roam around. But this time I stood still, filled with horror at what I was witnessing. Sheets of bright raw flame burst out and went hurtling skyward. Explosions, each more intense than the preceding one, followed in quick succession. For a moment it appeared that the sea itself was afire. Only now and then could the dim shape of a ship's hull be seen from the distance, like a cast-off derelict fighting for its life in utter silence.

We ordnancemen knew that Franklin was one of the carriers designated to carry the Tiny Tim rocket-propelled missiles. They were new to the fleet with a 1600-lb semi-armor piercing (SAP) bomb for a warhead. Thank God, they were too large for the CVLs. It took less than half a minute to convince us that the flashing, rending explosions we could see so clearly were these things going off. They were enormous oafs. Only SB2C dive bombers and Corsair fighters, too unwieldy for our narrow deck, could lift them. Vicious weapons that were doubly vicious when turned against yourself. A single Jap bomber had swept in out of a clear blue sky and dropped while Franklin was preparing to launch. Its single bomb had penetrated the flightdeck (where it set the first deckload afire) and exploded against the armored deck below and amidst the bombers and fighters already loaded with Tiny Tims. Instantly whooshing forward, the missiles killed dozens of pilots waiting in their ready room immediately forward of the hangar. Mechanics at work and ordnancemen arming the planes, fuelers and gunners, sailors of all ranks and ratings died horribly--until the totals throughout the ship (we learned later) reached eight hundred and two dead and two hundred sixty-five wounded.

The ship did not sink. She was to pave a long patch of the sea with human remains surrendered to it. The last we saw of her was a hull-down smoking remnant sneaking away under her own power--on the first leg of a trip that took her out of the war for good.

Wasp and Essex were out of action also, but only for days. Dead and wounded personnel on both ships were quickly replaced.

It was a silent, thoughtful supper below decks that night. **DL**

AD *At sea Japan — Kyushu. Went to GQ at 0500. Very cold topside. At 0708 Jap planes made an attack on the Franklin and several hits were observed. The ship was burning and exploding very badly. She is dead in the water. In the late afternoon she was taken under tow. Several attacks were made on the task force during the day but all planes were shot out of the sky. Secured from GQ at 1930.* **AD**

RC *Strike Day. Japs had dropped flares all night long but failed to locate us till daylight. At 0745 Franklin was hit by 500 lb bomb. She was all loaded with bombs, rockets & torpedoes in planes to take off for an attack. Many explosions followed bomb hit from her loaded planes burning. The Enterprise, Guam, St. Louis and 4 destroyers fell out of formation and went back to cover her from more attack. She seemed to be on fire all over. At 1045 she lost steam and had to be towed by St. Louis. In the afternoon she got her fires out below decks and got under way on her own at about 1530. Had several attacks during the day but no ships hit but Franklin. She is the worst beat up ship we have had so far in war to still keep afloat.* **RC**

Tuesday 20 March 1945   *Kyushu, Japan — retiring*

Steaming as before. The Task Group retired toward the south remaining near the Franklin. She was making slow but positive progress.

0445 Sounded flight quarters.

0545-0553 Completed launching 12 F6Fs for SNASP.

0700 Flying in a search of their assigned sector, Lt. Richard B. McNees and Ens. Everett R. Robinett tally-hoed a Fox Tare Dog (freighter transport) and engaged it. McNees fired off his rockets and Robinett strafed making 16 runs on the target. 15 minutes later 8 F6F-5s from the USS LANGLEY joined in, leaving the ship dead in the water, aflame, and abandoned by its crew. The ship was later sunk by a destroyer, and its survivors, clinging to debris, were picked up.

0724 Changed speed to 19 knots, course is 115°T.

0737 Observed smoke on the horizon, bearing 144°T. It was believed to be from an enemy Fox Tare Dog, now being attacked by INDEPENDENCE aircraft.

0800 Mustered crew on stations.

0930-0945 Half-masted colors following the movement of USS INTREPID.

0955 USS HEERMANN (DD-532) sank the enemy Fox Tare Dog by gunfire, previously attacked by INDEPENDENCE aircraft. The crew abandoned ship (approx 100' long) as it sunk stern first and USS HEERMANN picked up the survivors clinging to debris. Location 35°35N, 134°57'E.

1014 Sounded torpedo defense. An unidentified aircraft closed to 8 miles, then identified as a F4U.

1017 Secured from torpedo defense.

1051 Sounded torpedo defense due to the expectation of an air attack.

1058 Completed recovery of 12 F6Fs launched at 0553.

1400-1422 Following movements of USS ENTERPRISE half-masted colors.

1431 Sounded torpedo defense, as other Task Groups reported they were under attack.

1441 Launched 12 F6Fs for a CAP and ASP.

1443 Maneuvered to avoid the remains of a spent torpedo which passed about 25 feet to starboard.

1553 Changed course to 090°T, speed 20 knots. Axis rotated right to 140°T. INDEPENDENCE maneuvered regaining station at 1613 in disposition 5VB, guide YORKTOWN, bearing 275°T, 2,800 yards.

1617-1622 USS HAZELWOOD was alongside the starboard quarter, delivering ball bearings and receiving photographs for CTG 58.4.

1645 Sounded general quarters. An attack appeared eminent, however nothing developed, so at 1712 they set condition One Easy.

1826 Completed recovery of 12 F6Fs launched at 1441.

1856 Secured from flight quarters.

2118 Radar contact of unidentified aircraft bearing 108°T, 25 miles.

2121 Sounded torpedo defense.

2127 Observed firing on the horizon, bearing 180°T.

2132 Changed course to 180°T.

2216 Observed firing on the horizon to the northwest, bearing 310°T.

2220 Changed course to 150°T.

2224 Observed firing on the horizon, bearing 350°T.

2320 Observed firing on the horizon to the west, bearing 270°T.

2337 Observed aircraft having dropped flares, burst into flames.

2339 Formation opened gun fire on an enemy plane. It crashed and burned at 2348.

2355 Changed course to 180°T, speed 23 knots.

Wednesday 21 March 1945   *Retiring– Covering USS Franklin*

Steaming as before. Ship is darkened. Gunnery Department is at torpedo defense. Several enemy planes are in the vicinity. Intermittent firing by other Task Groups was observed. They continued retirement toward the south covering crippled USS FRANKLIN. At 0040 the crew secured form torpedo defense.

0440 Sounded flight quarters. At 0504 they sounded routine general quarters.

0541 Completed launching 12 F6Fs as CAP.

0616 Jettisoned 1 F6F-5 (Bu.No.71892) overboard that had hit the barrier on the 19th.

0804 Sounded flight quarters.

0909 Completed recovery of 8 F6Fs launched at 0541.

1022 Completed recovery of 4 F6Fs launched at 0541.

1026 Sounded torpedo defense due to an expected air attack.

1039 Sounded general quarters on direction of CTG 58.4.

1055 Changed to cruising disposition 5V.

1135 At Kanoya Naval Air Base on Kyushu, Japan, Admiral Noritake Toyoda, Admiral Matome Ugaki, and Commander Motohara Okamura attended ceremonies to see off the 1st Cherry Blossom Unit, a part of Japans "Special Attack Forces". A new weapon would be used for the first time against the US Fleet. The Oka (Cherry Blossom) was a one man piloted rocket propelled bomb. It was designed to be carried aloft by a bomber. Powered by 3 rocket motors, it was capable of diving speeds of close to 600 mph. In the nose was a 2,800 pound warhead. 18 Betty bombers (total crew of 137) taxied out to take off.

16 lumbered aloft (with bomb bay doors removed) carrying a 4,700 pound Oka slung underneath. 2 Bettys were navigation and command planes. 30 Zero fighters took off as escorts flying top cover. The Japanese flew out to decimate Task Force 58. Confident, each Oka pilot wore a white headband (hachimaki) given to them by Admiral Toyoda. Each Oka pilot would fly out toward the fleet in the Betty with the bombers crew, then climb down and strap into their Oka as they neared their intended targets. Once released, the pilot would ignite the rocket engines and guide their flying bomb down to destroy a ship.

Japanese Oka (Ohka)
The US Fleet designated the Oka
the "Baka" (Screwball).

1153   Secured from general quarters. Gunnery Department remained at torpedo defense.
1311   Formed cruising disposition 5VB.
1322   Launched 4 F6Fs for CAP.
1417   Launched 4 F6Fs for CAP.
1418   Changed course to 190°T, speed to 22 knots.
1419   Sounded general quarters on direction of OTC due to report of a group of approximately 25 enemy planes approaching this Task Group, bearing 318°T, distance 60 miles.
1419   Formed cruising disposition 5VC.
1430   Launched 4 F6Fs to further augment the CAP.
1455   Information was received that 17 enemy aircraft had been shot down by the CAP and 4 were turned back.

Heavily loaded, the Bettys from Kanoya were extremely slow as they toiled with their under-slung Okas. They were sitting ducks for the fast agile Hellcats that intercepted them. None survived. A few of the Zeros returned shot up, to report they never got within range to utilize the new secret weapons. Okas needed to be released from roughly 15,000 feet, and once dropped, had a range of about 11 miles. They were intercepted 60 miles from the fleet.

According to Matome Ugaki, the Bettys jettisoned their Oka loads when the Hellcats jumped them, but "all were shot down in only a little over ten minutes". All 18 Bettys of the 711 Squadron were decimated that day, along with over half of the escorting Zeros. One Hellcat was lost from VF-17.

1517   Changed speed to 18 knots, formed cruising disposition 5VB.
Gunnery Department set to condition One Easy. Air Department remained at condition 11.
1718   Changed speed to 15 knots.
1727-1728   USS MELVIN was alongside port quarter with medical supplies from USS YORKTOWN.
1731   Changed speed to 18 knots.
1753   Commenced recovering aircraft.
1813   Completed recovering 12 INDEPENDENCE F6Fs and 2 F6FNs from USS ENTERPRISE, for further transfer of planes to the USS INTREPID. The ENTERPRISE, damaged in yesterdays attacks, was proceeding to Ulithi with the USS FRANKLIN and USS WASP. The ENTERPRISE night fighters were to be used by other large carriers with various Task Groups.
1838   Secured from flight quarters.

2000 Changed speed to 24 knots.

2137 Changed course to 225°T. They headed southwest toward a fueling rendezvous.

Thursday 22 March 1945   *Refueling*

0415 Steaming as before. Sounded flight quarters.

0559 Completed launching 8 F6Fs for CAP and 4 TBMs for ASP.

0600-0603 Changed course to 225°T, speed 24 knots.

0640 Formation axis rotated left to 090T. USS LANGLEY designated guide. Commenced maneuvering to gain new position, guide bearing 270°T, 4,000 yards.

0815 Sounded flight quarters.

0927 The Task Group commenced fueling operations from tankers, having maneuvered to merge the groups.

0937 Changed course to 090°T, reduced speed to 10 knots, gaining position in the fueling disposition, guide shifting to oiler USS CACHE (AO-67).

0943 Commenced maneuvering to recover aircraft.

1010 Completed recovery of 4 TBMs and 8 F6Fs launched at 0559.

1014 Secured from flight quarters. Air Department set condition 14.

1024 Regained station in the fueling disposition.

1102-1106 USS HAZELWOOD was alongside port quarter to transfer guard mail for CTG 58.4.

1233-1238 USS TRATHAN came alongside starboard to transfer material.

1326-1330 USS HEERMANN came alongside starboard to transfer mail.

1339-1340 USS MCNAIR came alongside starboard to transfer mail.

1342 Commenced maneuvering to approach assigned oiler, USS TALLULAH.

1430 Came along port side of USS TALLULAH. The guide is oiler USS CACHE, bearing 180°T, 1,500 yards.

1630-1636 USS HAILEY (DD-556) came alongside port to deliver mail.

1730 Launched 2 F6FNs to proceed to (for transfer to) the USS INTREPID.

1752-1806 USS MCNAIR came alongside port to transfer an officer for duty with Air Group 46.

1809 Cast off from USS TALLULAH having received 370 gallons of lube oil, 57,655 gallons of gasoline and 352,230 gallons of fuel oil.

1817 Cruiser Division 16, USS GUAM and USS ALASKA reported to CTG 58.4 for duty.

1818 Sounded routine torpedo defense.

1823 Fueling operations for TG 58.4 were completed. USS YORKYOWN assumed guide, bearing 225° T, 2,800 yards.

1854 USS NEW JERSEY became guide. USS INDEPENDENCE bearing 090°T, 2,000 yards.

1906 USS NORTH CAROLINA, USS UHLMANN and USS COLAHAN reported for duty to CTG 58.4.

1918 Secured from torpedo defense. Changed speed to 18 knots.

2331 Changed speed to 25 knots.

2357 Changed course to 000°T.

GN   Refueled and routine hops all day. Belted .50 cal all day.   GN

DL   Admiral Mitscher reformed TF 58 on 22 March. Independence, now a day carrier, joined Admiral Radford's Yorktown, Intrepid, and Langley. No doubt he was glad to get our Air Group 46 under his command. Among its pilots and aircrewmen were veterans from sunken Princeton.

By now we didn't really care. Such designations were for the high muckety mucks, not for swabbies riding the ships. Books would be written, historians would argue. The faces of the pilots were of strangers and unknowable. All we did was work our tails off and hope we survived, and that the pilots once launched would make it back.

Okinawa was a killer of sailors of all ranks from day one. Even though we never saw the place, our pilots certainly did. It drove the Navy nuts. Land-based Marine air was not strong enough to provide constant support, so the Navy had to stay. Admiral Nimitz would eventually complain that his forces were losing a ship and a half a day and couldn't stand it any longer. DL

24
Operation Iceberg - Invasion of Okinawa

Overview of "OPERATION ICEBERG" - The Invasion of Okinawa

The Ryukyu Islands are a lengthy string running from the tip of Japan south toward Formosa (Taiwan). The Okinawa group of islands is roughly centered in the Ryukyus. On the eastern side of the Ryukyu chain is the Pacific Ocean.

Okinawa has protected anchorages, and ample room for large air bases. On the western shores is the East China Sea. Okinawa (the largest island in the Okinawa group) is approximately 60 miles long and from 2 to 18 miles wide and less then 400 miles from Kyushu Japan. It would give the US a strong foot hold for the final assault on the Japanese homeland. It was an important stepping stone on the Road to Tokyo.

The invasion day was given the designation "L"-Day, and Friday March 23rd would be "Love" Minus Nine. This would be the opening day of the softening up of the island group for the landing.

The 77th Infantry Division would first secure the Kerama Islands which would effectively serve as a staging area for the assault on Okinawa. Slightly over 15 miles west of Naha, the complex of islands are shaped like a ragged torn broken horseshoe that seems to appear that of a sunken volcanic caldera in origin. However, thought to have been connected originally with the mountains of Okinawa, a series of diastrophisms are credited with the islands structures today. Its sheltered bays and inlets would become a valuable anchorage for the fleet, as a refuge to begin repairs of vessels damaged during "Iceberg", as well as for resupply and refueling. It would also serve as a base for seaplanes and their tenders.

The Japanese, of course, had other ideas. Every effort would be made to cripple the attacking US Fleet, as without the fleet, there could be no US invasion of the Japanese homeland.

Friday 23 March 1945   *"Iceberg" - Okinawa — Love Minus Nine*

Steaming as before, as part of TG 58.4.1, accompanying USS YORKTOWN (OTC, Rear Admiral A.W. Radford), USS INTREPID, and USS LANGLEY, in cruising disposition 5VB.
Today, the first strikes against the enemy on Okinawa Jima, Nansei Shoto, will be launched carrying out Phase "Love" of the operational orders. CVL-22 pilots are assigned targets at Naha Airfield, from the Air Target folder "Okinawa Gunto", Revision A, corrected to 22 January, 1945.

0028 The USS HAGGARD rammed an Imperial Japanese Navy submarine amidships aft of the conning tower, sinking it with loss of all hands (IJN submarine I-371). The HAGGARD had first dropped depth charges on the sub, causing it to surface. USS HAGGARD was damaged in the ramming, enough to require it to leave this Task Group to proceed to Ulithi, accompanied by the USS UHLMANN.

0423 Changed course to 270°T. At 0445 the ship sounded flight quarters.
0524 USS GUAM reported sighting a submarine within the formation.
0526 Sounded general quarters.   0535 Changed course to 000°T.
0539 Destroyer dropped depth charges on the sonar contact, bearing 190°T, 10,000 yards.

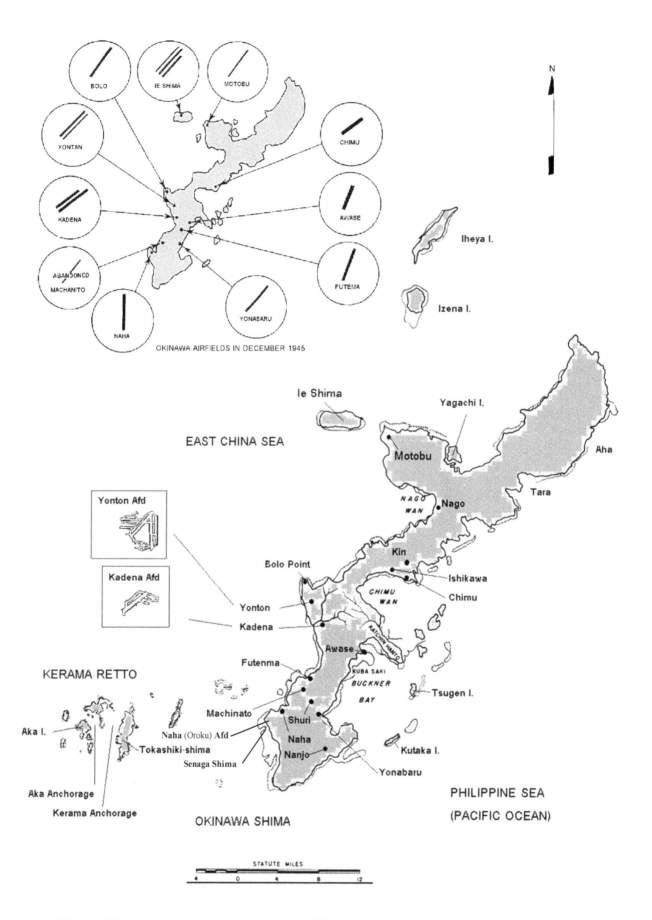

OKINAWA AIRFIELDS IN DECEMBER 1945

N

Iheya I.

Izena I.

Ie Shima

Yagachi I.

EAST CHINA SEA

Motobu

Nago

NAGO WAN

Kin

Ishikawa

Chimu

CHIMU WAN

Aha

Tara

Yonton Afd

Kadena Afd

Bolo Point

Yonton

Kadena

Awase

KATCHIN HANTO

Futenma

KUBA SAKI

BUCKNER BAY

Tsugen I.

KERAMA RETTO

Machinato

Shuri

Aka I.

Naha (Oroku) Afd

Tokashiki-shima

Naha

Senaga Shima

Nanjo

Kutaka I.

Aka Anchorage

Yonabaru

Kerama Anchorage

OKINAWA SHIMA

PHILIPPINE SEA
(PACIFIC OCEAN)

STATUTE MILES

4   0   4   8   12

0554-0612 Launched 8 F6Fs and 9 TBMs for a strike against Okinawa Shima. They were launched 211 miles from the southern tip of Okinawa. Penetrating a cold front, the F6Fs and TBMs encountered low 500'-1,000' ceilings over the target, Naha Airfield. They noted 2 or 3 twin engine planes and 6 to 10 single engine planes (thought to be Tojos) parked on the west side of the runway. Effective normal dive bombing and rocket attacks they had planned could not be made. They instead had to make near level bombing, rocket and strafing runs under difficult conditions. Flying at 50 feet on one of the runs, they noticed Japanese gun emplacements imbedded in caves in the face of a 500' cliff.

Japanese AA fire was described as extremely accurate. Ensign Rosenburgh's Avenger received damage to the wing, a large hole in the starboard side of the fuselage near the turret, many holes aft of the turret in the bilge, the "IFF shot off, part of the radar shot off" and the flaps rendered useless. Two other TBMs also received AA shrapnel damage (flown by Lt. Jg. R.W. Zecher and Lt. Jg. J.M. Felker). The speed of the faster fighters did not provide immunity to the AA. Ensign Everett Robinett, managed to land back aboard the Mighty-I with a shot up tire, flaps not working, with 3' of flap blown away, and holes to the wing root and fuselage. For roughly 15 minutes on the way back, he was accompanied by flames fed by hydraulic fluid near the starboard landing gear well. To add to his list of "All in a day's work" difficulties, he had to shake loose a "hung bomb" before he landed back aboard. His peppered Hellcat (Bu.No.72565) was "stricken from the Navy list" as a result of the damage.

0631 All departments set to condition One Easy.
0908 Passed a drifting mine 300 yards abeam to starboard. Dropped a smoke marker to aid a destroyer to locate the mine, and destroy it.
0948 Changed course to 270°T.
1052 Completed recovery of 8 F6Fs and 6 TBMs launched at 0612.
The remaining 3 TBMs launched at 0612 were recovered by another task group.
1245 Firing within this task group observed at an unidentified aircraft, later found to be friendly.
1246 Sounded general quarters as directed by CTG 58.4.

1315-1317 Recovered 2 TBMs launched at 0612. The group became separated due to bad weather over target. One Avenger had landed on the USS BUNKER HILL and the other two on the USS BENNINGTON. Ensign Arthur Rosenburgh landed his shot up Avenger aboard the BENNINGTON. The TBM-3 (Bu.No.23594) was damaged beyond repair and was jettisoned overboard. Ensign Rosenburgh returned to the INDEPENDENCE. His aircrew men, ARM3c Floyd E. Abbott and ARM2c Elmer V. Rasor both received non-serious AA shrapnel wounds (Abbott also received burns) and remained aboard the BENNINGTON for treatment.

Further strikes against the enemy were canceled due to bad weather.
1330 Commenced zigzagging on base course 000°T. Except for Gunnery Department, secured from One Easy. Air Department set to condition 14.
1554 Sounded flight quarters.
1715 Maneuvered to avoid a floating object in the water, which proved to be a wood box.
1901 Air Department secured from flight quarters, set to condition 14.
2300 Commenced zigzagging on base course 200°T.

Saturday 24 March 1945   *"Iceberg" - Okinawa — Love Minus Eight*

Steaming as before, as part of TG 58.4.1 in the vicinity of Okinawa Shima.
0503 Changed course to 160°T, changed speed to 25 knots.
0507 USS YORKTOWN assumed guide, bearing 225°T, 2,800 yards. USS NEW JERSEY and other battleships are leaving the formation to join a shore bombardment group.
0528 Sounded general quarters.
0556-0603 Launched 8 F6Fs to provide a CAP over US mine sweepers and underwater demolition teams that are working off Okinawa today, in preparation for the landing.

0650-0701 Launched "Strike D1", 8 F6Fs and 7 TBMs*, the first strike by this squadron on Love minus eight day. Led by Lt. Foster C. Kay, 7 Avengers were tasked to bomb, rocket and strafe heavy gun emplacements at Senaga Shima, a small island lying off the southwest coast near Naha, Okinawa. The 8 Hellcats made coordinated attacks giving full support to the Avengers. No Japanese aircraft were encountered. After bombing Naha airfield, Comdr. Carl W. Rooney and Lt.(jg) Marlar E. Stewart strafed and rocketed the villages of Toyama, Gushichan and Kakinohana.

(* VF-46 AAR states 9 TBMs were launched on the "D1" raid, however VT-46 AAR states 7 were launched as does the INDEPENDENCE Deck Log. I give more credence to the VT report as it was their aircraft, and their numbers are supported by the ships Deck Log entries, including returning A/C.)

(Additional Author's notation: I choose to cite both pieces of conflicting official primary documentation throughout this book to help resolve questions future historians may have reviewing pertinent material.)

0831-0834 Launched 8 F6Fs to relieve the CAP over the minesweepers and underwater demolition teams.

0841 Recovered 1 F6F launched at 0834.

0939-0959 Recovered 8 F6Fs and 7 TBMs launched at 0701.

1007 Completed recovery of 8 F6Fs launched at 0603.

1135-1145 Launched "Strike D2", 14 F6Fs and 6 TBMs to strike towns and factories on Okinawa. Also launched to assigned targets were a mix of 63 other aircraft from USS LANGLEY and USS INTREPID. VF & VT-46 pilots headed for the target area. 2 F6Fs returned as one had engine problems. 6 F6Fs and 6 TBMs were turned over to an Airborne Coordinator. They were directed to bomb, rocket and strafe all the Japanese AA positions adjacent to and east of Naha Airfield. This group strafed Okinawa gun positions, towns and a small factory on the way back. In addition, the TBMs dropped propaganda material. 6 F6Fs flew CAP over the minesweeping operations of the DDs and DEs being carried out from the area southeast of Okinawa down to Kerama Retto. After completion of the CAP, Commander Rooney led the F6Fs on strafing runs over Okinawa.

1235 Sounded torpedo defense.

1248-1253 Recovered 7 F6Fs launched at 0834.

1417 Completed launching 8 F6Fs to relieve the CAP over the minesweepers.

1422-1425 Recovered 6 F6Fs launched at 1145.

1520 Upon landing, the tail hook of a Hellcat flown by Lt(jg) Charles K. Purcell missed all 9 arresting gear cables. It shot forward, the propeller snapping thru the barrier cables, hurdling into five Hellcats of the eleven Hellcats and one Avenger spotted forward, having just landed. Lt.(jg) Fredrick Eugene Lieber had just taxied his Hellcat forward of the barriers after landing. He was still sitting in his cockpit when his aircraft was struck. Lieber received multiple mortal injuries from Purcell's propeller during the accident. Four Hellcats (Bu.Nos. 71923, 72287, 72489, 77579) were damaged beyond repair. Two Hellcats needed to have their tails replaced (Bu.Nos. 71013 & 71787). Two barrier cables were in use prior to the accident. Commander Rooney recommended all three barrier cables be utilized from that date forward. A notation on his AAR indicated that all three barrier cables would be used to increase the margin of safety.
        (See accident photo on page 893)
1526 8 F6F's and 6 TBMs launched at 1145 were recovered.

1622 Jettisoned 1 F6F-5 (Lt. Lieber's Hellcat - Bu.No.71923), damaged beyond repair.

1702 Completed recovery of 3 F4U Corsair fighters, two launched from the USS HANCOCK and one from the USS INTREPID. They made emergency landings aboard the Mighty-I because of low fuel levels and having been "somewhat shot up".

1801-1806 Recovered 8 F6Fs launched at 1417.

1832 Secured from flight quarters. Air Department set to condition 14.

2005 Received a report from sickbay that Lt.(jg) Fredrick Eugene Lieber had died of fatal injuries as a result of the accident.

2147 Commenced zigzagging on base course 192°T.

Captain Kindell would note in the S.O.L. as he left the bridge for the evening:
"Other Task Groups are in the vicinity.
No friendly contacts are expected.
Call me if the formation gets tangled up or anything unusual occurs."

RC *Planes bombed while battlewagons shelled Okinawa all day long with no opposition.* **RC**

GN *Another day of rearming and with a capital "R". Really turning too on this business and sending stuff topside. Just got word that a plane went through the barrier. It seems to have got four planes in its path and also the pilot of the plane that landed directly ahead. Heard that he was cut up pretty badly and died before they could remove him from the cockpit. No one else was hurt seriously. Still hitting Nansei Shoto and it should be in bad shape by now.* **GN**

Sunday 25 March 1945   *Okinawa — Love Minus Seven — Refueling*

Today INDEPENDENCE retired to rendezvous with a tanker group to refuel.
0737-0935 INDEPENDENCE was alongside, the tanker USS ASHTABULA to take on fuel.
1025 Maneuvered along the port side of the USS LASSEN to take on munitions. This would be the first time the CVL-22 replenished munitions from an ammunition ship at sea. They used a transfer whip from the ships crane and one of the LASSENs cranes, with the job rapidly completed.
1333 Cast off from USS LASSEN, having received 103 500# bombs, 280 rocket bodies, rocket motors and fuses and .50 caliber ammunition.
1540 Completed launching 12 F6Fs for CAP and 4 TBMs for ASP. In addition, they launched the 3 F4U Corsairs that had landed low on fuel to return to their respective ships.
1600 Mustered crew to quarters.

1619-1626 Burial services were conducted for Lt.(jg) Fredrick Eugene *"Hank"* Lieber who had been killed yesterday in the flight deck accident. The colors were half-masted during the ceremony. Services were conducted in Latitude 22°50.1N / Longitude 128°46.7E. Lieber was remembered as *" an excellent pilot and fine officer"*!

1643 Completed recovery of 6 F6Fs and 1 TBM, supplied as replacement aircraft from a CVE (unnamed). Completed recovery of the 4 TBMs launched at 1540 for ASP.
1706-1715 USS TRATHAN was along side the port quarter to transfer guard mail and cleaning fluid.
1730 USS INTREPID designated guide, bearing 265°T, 2,800 yards. With fueling operations completed they took departure of the tankers and ammunition ships to proceed toward the north.
1758 USS YORKTOWN designated guide, bearing 175°T, 2,800 yards.
1830 Completed recovery of 12 F6Fs launched at 1540 as CAP. Secured from flight quarters.
Air Department set to condition 14.

Captain Kindell noted to the watch as he left the bridge:
"Nearest land is Southern point of Okinawa which at 2000 was 160 miles 335°T.
No landfalls or friendly sightings are expected.
First launch is at 0550 — CAP — 1."

2355 Changed course to 350°T, speed 17 knots.

GL *Fueled the ship today. We also took on bombs & rockets from freighter. This is the first time we received bombs at sea in this manner. Also took on plane replacements.* **GL**

AD *At sea refueling also ammunition. 1545 Burial service for pilot.** **AD**   (* Fredrick Eugene Lieber)

Steaming as before as Task Unit 58.4.1 in company with USS YORKTOWN (OTC and guide), USS INTREPID, and USS LANGLEY, in cruising disposition 5-VB. They are proceeding from replenishment of fuel and munitions back toward an operating area off of Okinawa. Units of the US Army are landing on a small Island west of Okinawa, Kerama Retto, today. The Task Unit will provide air support strikes for the landing.

0445 Sounded flight quarters. At 0547 completed launching 12 F6Fs as a CAP.

0630 USS NEW JERSEY, USS WISCONSIN and USS MISSOURI rejoined the formation.

0642 Changed course to 260°T.

0645 USS NEW JERSEY designated guide, bearing 220°T, 2,000 yards.

0727 Completed launching 8 F6Fs and 9 TBMs for the first mission in support of the landing troops.

VT-46 and VF-46 aircraft joined after launch and then rendezvoused with aircraft from the USS LANGLEY, USS YORKTOWN and USS INTREPID. 87 planes converged to orbit and work with an Airborne Coordinator. The target area was covered with low overcast skies (ceiling 3,000'). In the confusion of the large gaggle circling over cloud obscured targets, and AA from the ground, a F6F piloted by Lt. Fred M. Fox (VFB-9) and a TBM collided midair. Loosing the starboard wing and spinning in, the TBM crashed, exploding on impact killing pilot Lt. Cmdr. Byron Cooke (VT-9 C.O.) and his two crewman; Norman B. Brown and Robert T. Matthews. Lt. Fox Survived his emergency belly landing, and after 3 days on Okinawa was rescued by an OSU2 from USS SAN FRANCISCO.

Due to the mix of weather with the mass of aircraft, normal planned strikes could not be made, and INDEPENDENCE fighters instead diverted for low level attacks on the costal towns of Osunohana, Ise and Ishiza. The Avengers attacked amphibious craft revetments on the coast north of Chatan Mura, and AA gun emplacement positions along the east side of Kadena Airfield, with unobserved results.

As a result of the difficulties encountered with the organization of this strike, it was *"strongly recommended that in adverse weather, strikes or support groups be limited in size to a maximum of 40 A/C"*.

0809 Recovered 1 F6F, launched at 0727.

0845 Recovered 1 F4U Corsair from the USS INTREPID, making an emergency landing. Its engine was "shot up" and deemed damaged beyond repair.

0918-0923 Recovered 8 of the 12 F6Fs launched at 0547.

0933 Completed recovery of the remaining 4 F6Fs launched at 0547.

1019 Jettisoned the shot up USS INTREPID F4U Corsair (Bu.No. 82797) over the fantail.

1055-1111 Recovered the 9 TBMs and 7 F6Fs launched at 0727.

1208-1224 Launched 8 F6Fs as a CAP and 8 TBMs for a strike on Okinawa.

The Avengers (led by Lt. F.C. Kay) targeted a factory and surrounding buildings north of Naha on the west coast. Exploding debris and fires were observed.

1235 Recovered 1 TBM, with engine trouble, launched at 1224.

1525-1529 Launched 12 F6Fs.

1538-1553 Recovered 8 F6Fs and the remaining 7 TBMs launched at 1224.

1815-1828 Recovered 12 F6Fs launched at 1529.

1844 Secured from flight quarters. Air Department secured from condition 14.

2038 Sounded torpedo defense due to an enemy aircraft "snooping the formation".

2045 Secured from torpedo defense. The Bogey was identified as an enemy aircraft and shot down by a night fighter 35 miles from the Task Force.

2113 Changed course to 350°T.

2145 Radar reported an unidentified aircraft bearing 355°T, 10 miles. Sounded torpedo defense.

2204 Changed course to 090°T.

2205 Observed a light on the horizon bearing 085°T, thought to be either a flare or a burning aircraft.

2242 Gunnery Department set to condition One Easy.

2357 Secured from One Easy. Changed course to 270°T.

Opposition from Japan to the invasion of Okinawa until now, had at best, been weak ... tepid. The US Fleet was an onerous thunderous tempest brewing in Japan's very own tea pot. It points to the sorry state of affairs the Japanese military leaders were now in.

Three years ago confident, victorious and massively expanding their ocean bound empire, they were in seemingly solid control of their destiny. Now, they were shaken, withdrawn inward, to the very shores of their homeland. B-29 raids were becoming common and the US Fleet was invading. How to stop the inrushing tide of the allied tsunami?

Japan's precious resources had needed to be rationed. Ships, aircraft, oil and gasoline, food, the materials of war were not available in the numbers needed to meet the overwhelming US threat. Fully trained sailors, airmen, and mechanics at the top of the growing list of critical needs to conduct a war, were now in agonizingly short supply.

Navy carrier pilots flying out on raids were surprised. They had not been seeing robust Japanese aerial opposition (or naval) in volumes they expected. The final defense of the homeland, to keep the enemy from desecrating the soil of their ancestors, had Japan's military leaders withholding those assets in reserve. The decision of when and how best to utilize those men and machines was difficult and debated. At last, the hour glass seems to have emptied.

Today, the Japanese Combined Fleet activated Operation Ten No.1 ordering the Japanese forces to engage the attacking Allied Forces in a "Decisive Battle".

A telling notation from the diary of Admiral Matome Ugaki: *"the Third Air Fleet also came under my command, but they, too, weren't well trained, so I wasn't reassured."* Months prior, in November, he had also noted the ongoing deficit in aircraft production verses Japans urgent needs.

Well trained, or not, a stick was being poked in the Kamikaze nest and they were beginning to buzz with punishing results. US ships around Okinawa took causalities, one was sunk. Damaged: BB NEVADA; CL BILOXI; DDs PORTERFIELD, O'BRIEN & CALLAGHAN, DE FOREMAN; Minesweepers DORSEY & SKIRMISH were damaged by suicide planes, and DD MURRAY was damaged by a dive bomber. DD USS HALLIGAN sunk after hitting a mine.

GN Hit Ryukyu today and this cruise is getting to be more like a madman's dream than anything else. I never heard so many orders issued or countermanded but I guess that is the way of war, though I ask myself why should it fall to the lot of the coolie to do all the work while someone else gets the credit for it. Two strikes today and a few more tomorrow and we should get back out for more fuel and ammo. Bogies around all day but it seems like they are all splashed while still fairly far away. *¹· *Torpedo defense went all day and half the night and the gunnery dept is also taking a beating this time out. Received all kind of mail in the last two days and I hope to get a chance to answer some soon. GN* (*¹· One wonders .... What would have George entered in his diary had he been on one of the vessels struck?)

GL We are still hitting Okinawa. We sent over two strikes. Our TBF's and F6F's are loaded with bombs and rockets. We landed a F4U that was hit with AA. Stripped her and shoved her over the side. We are in condition One Easy all day. About 9:30 that night TD sounded. They had two Bettys on the run. Night chickens of our task group shot them down. We had TD twice more before the night was over. Our Squadron bombed a command post & rocketed installations. (Ryukyu) GL

Tuesday 27 March 1945   Ryukyu Islands, *Okinawa — Love Minus Five*

Steaming as before in the same general area off Okinawa in cruising disposition 5VB, course 270°T, speed 18 knots. INDEPENDENCE bears 070°T, 2,000 yards from guide, USS NEW JERSEY.
0600 Completed launching 12 F6Fs for CAP.
0628 Completed recovery of 1 F6F launched at 0620, and 2 night fighters from USS INTREPID.
0632 Sounded torpedo defense on order from the OTC, who expected an air attack. Set condition One in AA batteries.

0710 Unidentified aircraft, bearing 065°T, 7 miles.

0745 Completed launching a strike of 8 F6Fs, 8 TBMs and the 2 INTREPID night fighters. Air Group 46 rendezvoused with aircraft from the three other carriers. The Hellcats and Avengers were assigned targets for bombing, rocketing and strafing a command post near Kadena Airfield and buildings north of Airfield on Okinawa. They retired east seeking targets of opportunity.

0750 Gunnery Department set One Easy.

0845 A F6F-5 launched at 0600 piloted by Lt.(jg) Alfred W. Thomas made a water landing. The Hellcat (Bu.No.72956) had developed a problem with its engine. USS MERTZ rescued him. Thomas is reported to be in satisfactory condition.

0851-0858 USS MELVIN was alongside the starboard quarter to pick up official photographs.

0928 Recovered 10 F6Fs launched at 0600. Gunnery Department secured from One Easy.

1030 Recovered 8 F6Fs and 8 TBMs launched at 0745.

1158 Commenced launching aircraft.

1159 Sounded torpedo defense.

1207 Gunnery Department secured from One Easy.

1209 Completed launching 6 TBMs for a second strike and 8 F6Fs for CAP. INDEPENDENCE TBMs rendezvoused with aircraft from the YORKTOWN, INTREPID and LANGLEY. VT-46 TBMs then split off with the INTREPID Air Group to attack targets at the eastern tip of a small peninsula. Defensive positions, fortified caves and underground storage areas were hit with bombs and rockets. The AAR states; *"The good weather and complete lack of anti-aircraft fire allowed pilots to definitely identify the target and made accurate bombing possible. The attack was well-coordinated and well-executed and unquestionably caused extensive damage"*.

1415 Gunnery Department set condition 3.

1524-1530 Launched 12 F6Fs to relieve the CAP launched at 1209.

1532-1555 Recovered 8 F6Fs and 6 TBMs launched at 1209.

1806 The Task Group began retiring toward the southeast.

1810-1822 Recovered the CAP of 12 F6Fs launched at 1530.

1831 USS YORKTOWN designated guide. Commenced maneuvering to exchange positions with USS NEW JERSEY.

1903 USS NEW JERSEY designated guide, course 140°T, bearing 115°T, 2,000 yards.

2010 USS GUAM, USS ALASKA and USS FLINT left the formation.

GN Two more strikes today and another island should be leveled fairly well. Condition one easy most of the day and we got a bit of a breather in the afternoon. Expect to refuel and rearm tomorrow but got word that a beautiful storm is in the making so we may get a rest for the next few days. Hope to get some sleep sometime. Had the 8 to 12 this evening and stood watching the cans and cruisers lobbing star shells over some island. Couldn't figure it out for sometime. GN

GL Still ranging through the Ryukyu Islands bombing strafing & rocketing. Our BB's are still shelling Okinawa. Some of our units suffered damage. GL

Captain Kindell noted in the Standing Orders Log this evening as he retired;
"We are heading toward an area for fueling, possibly Glowworm. We also have some operations tomorrow."

Wednesday 28 March 1945 *Ryukyu Islands, Okinawa — Love Minus Four*
Minami-Daito Shima & Kita-Daito Shima

0612 Steaming as before retiring to refuel. Changed course to 240°T.

0614 Commenced maneuvering to make approach on USS TOMAHAWK, the assigned fleet oiler, and designated guide. Changed fleet course to 320°T, speed 11 knots. Guide bears 300°T, 4,000 yards.

0718 Came along port side of USS TOMAHAWK.

0730-0736 USS BULLARD was alongside the INDEPENDENCE port quarter to transfer material.

0915 Having received 31,700 gallons of aviation gasoline, and 128,523 gallons of fuel oil from

USS TOMAHAWK, the fleet oiler cast off.

0917 Commenced maneuvering to take station within the fueling disposition.

0926 Gained station, USS TOMAHAWK guide, bearing 300°T, 4,000 yards.

0958-1014 USS COLAHAN (DD-658) was alongside the port quarter to transfer passengers.

Lt.(jg) Alfred W. Thomas, who ditched his stricken F6F yesterday, was returned to this ship. Ensigns M.B. Albright Jr. and M.L. Bell were transferred to the COLAHAN for delivery back to Air Group 10 aboard USS INTREPID.

1017 Sounded flight quarters.

1039 Recovered 1 F6F attached to the USS LANGLEY, making an emergency landing.

1043 Secured from flight quarters. Air Department set to condition 14.

1109 Changed course to 300°T, speed 11 knots. Commenced maneuvering to exchange stations within the formation with the USS NEW JERSEY.

1120 Gained new position, guide USS TOMAHAWK bearing 300°T, 6,000 yards.

1429 Sounded flight quarters.

1502 Launched 8 F6Fs for a sweep over Minami-Daito Shima & Kita-Daito Shima. The launch was 62 miles out. The fueling course would take the ship to within 10 miles of those islands. *"From the ship we could see our planes working over the land mass of the island, and see the smoke that followed, rise slowly thru the haze."*

Lt. Comdr. Robert A. Weatherup led the Hellcats to make photo and strafing runs across the islands. *"Constant, intense AA, both heavy and light, was encountered during all six runs with the result that on the fifth run the enemy's accuracy improved to the extent of inflicting minor damage to five of eight fighters."* Due to haze, and fogging of the camera lenses, the photos were worthless. Two pilots returned to the ship after 5 passes due to AA damage, the remaining 6 Hellcats made a 6th pass on the targets. The Hellcats attacked an administration building, barracks, warehouses, ammunition storage, and a weather / radio station.

Damage to the Hellcats as listed in the AAR: *"Ensign J.K. Gentry in plane #7, holes in fuselage; Lt.(jg) Samuel A. Sparks in plane #26, holes in elevator; Lt. William Schroeder in plane #16, belly tank shot off; Lt.(jg) Robert J. Byron in plane #15, holes in port wing; Lt. Jack Rivers in plane #2, a 40mm shell passed through his cockpit, blasting away his head rest and cockpit canopy, breaking his rearview mirror and several instruments. Another shell destroyed his hydraulic system leaving several holes in his starboard wing. It was a miracle that Lt. Rivers was not killed instead of suffering minor cuts on his face. He landed aboard without benefit of flaps."*

The USS NEW JERSEY was often between 2,000 to 3,000 yards from the USS INDEPENDENCE.

1510 Secured from flight quarters. Air Department set to condition 13.

1610 Sounded flight quarters.

1628 Launched 1 F6F to return to the USS LANGLEY.

1640 USS NEW JERSEY designated guide.

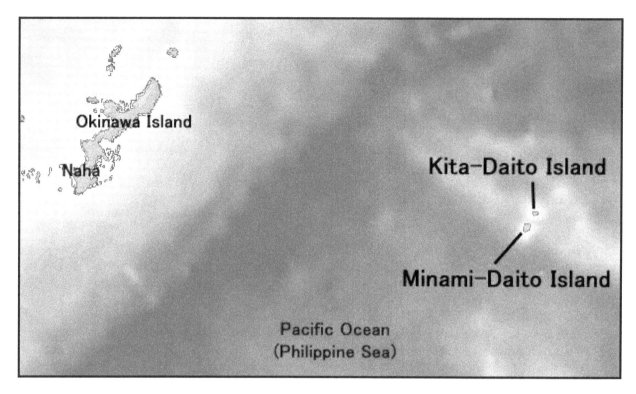

1643 Recovered 2 F6Fs launched at 1502.
1736 Gained station in formation, base course 300°T, 25 knots, guide bearing 300T, 2,000 yards.
1819 Completed recovery of 6 F6Fs launched at 1502.
1827 Secured from flight quarters. Air Department set to condition 14.
1840 Changed course to 350°T.
1935 Put rudder hard left, than hard right to avoid a life raft, and the USS FRANKS standing by investigating the raft, finding it empty.
2002 USS YORKTOWN assumed guide, bearing 255°T, 2,800 yards.
2055 Changed course to 015°T.
2220 USS NEW JERSEY was designated guide, bearing 300°T, 2,000 yards.

The Mighty-I celebrated her 5,000th landing this day.

The group moved north during the night at 21 knots to intercept Japanese naval units, reported to be moving south along the east coast of Kyushu.

GN Refueled and right under the Japs noses. Could hear the wagons and cruisers blasting away practically all day and seen enemy held territory for the first time since the battle for the Philippines. Figured to get some rest today but worked as hard as ever. Looks like we are going right in with the tankers on our tails and at the moment it looks like a good move. Supposedly spotted part of the Jap fleet about 300 miles away so the TBMs were loaded with fish for tomorrows first strike. GN

AD At sea receiving fuel. Spotted land today. Believed part of Okinawa group. Also, received word part of Jap fleet is at Kyushu. We will attack in the morning. AD

HC Raided Okinawa. Could see land, it was only 18 or 20 miles away. HC

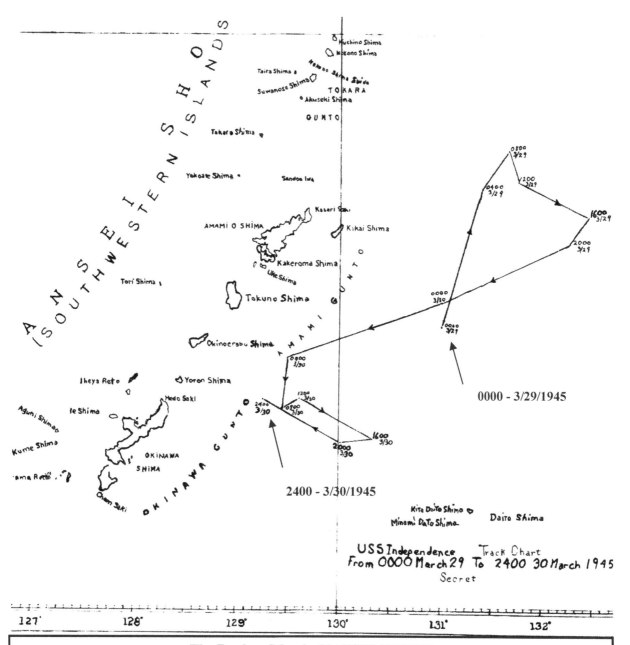

0000 - 3/29/1945

2400 - 3/30/1945

USS Independence   Track Chart
From 0000 March 29 To 2400 30 March 1945
Secret

| 127° | 128° | 129° | 130° | 131° | 132° |

The Ryukyu Islands (NANSEI SHOTO)

INDEPENDENCE Track Chart for 29 and 30 March, 1945. Air strikes on 29 March were launched against the southern tip of Kyushu, just beyond the top edge of this Track Chart. Launch times were shortly after 0600 and 1200 on 3/29. Raids on 30 March were launched and recovered closer to the assigned targets on Okinawa.

Thursday 29 March 1945   *Kyushu*

0445 Steaming as before, headed for Kyushu. Sounded flight quarters.
0505 Sounded routine general quarters.
0605 Completed launching 20 F6F-5s and 8 TBMs. 12 F6Fs were for CAP. 8 F6Fs and 8 TBMS were

sent out on a strike to find heavy elements of the Japanese Fleet seen steaming thru the night around the southern tip of Kyushu. All carriers in Task Group 58.4 launched deck load strikes to find and destroy the Japanese Fleet.

Weather worked in the Japanese favor, for the searching aircraft were faced with hazy skies overcast at 2,000 to 3,000 feet.
During climb out, eager LANGLEY fighters tallyhoed a bogey, firing rounds at a returning SB2C until it was recognized as friendly.

After rendezvous, the group of 132 planes set out for Take Shima, where the YORKTOWN & LANGLEY pilots would proceed up the east coast. INDEPENDENCE & INTREPID aviators would hunt along the west coast, sighting warships ten miles up the coast. Eight friendly destroyers on picket duty. Ten miles further northwest Commander Rooney sighted a sub. The sub fired an incorrect colored recognition flare, then rapidly submerged. The sub captain was served two 500# bombs, most likely without effect. Carl Rooney's division (4 F6Fs) proceeded to investigate Kagoshima Bay for targets. His division bombed hangars and a ramp at Ibusuki Seaplane Station. Lt.(jg) Stewart strafed a twin engine float plane, which burned.

They proceeded at 3,000' toward Kagoshima City when 5 bandits were tally-hoed by Lt.(jg) William J. Schleis at 4 o'clock high. The Enemy fighters started a high stern attack and Rooney's division turned and climbed to meet them. Comdr. Rooney got off a full deflection shot from 1,000 feet, tracers seen to hit the Oscar, which started a shallow glide for the beach (claimed as a probable).

Lt.(jg) Marlar E. Stewart bagged a Frank from 8 o'clock level, which burned and crashed. They were jumped by roughly twelve Franks diving in from 6 o'clock. "A melee ensued in which three Franks were shot down in flames". One by Lt.(jg) Ralph J. *"Rusty"* Reeder from 12 o'clock level, one by Lt. (jg) Schleis from 12 o'clock level, and the third by Comdr. Rooney from 7 o'clock level. The Japanese pilots were *"very aggressive and pressed continuous attacks in pairs. The attack was so hard pressed that our own planes defensive tactics broke down by separation"*. Comdr. Rooney ordered the division to take cloud cover. Rejoining above the cloud layer, they called repeatedly trying unsuccessfully to raise Lt.(jg) Reeder. They retired strafing a barracks, a small village and 4 diesel fishing boats.

INDEPENDENCE TBMs, with 6 F6Fs (Lt. Badger's division plus two from INTREPID) for cover, flew up the west coast and found no Japanese Navy. Seeking other targets they attacked small boats and the dock area in a harbor near Yatsushiro Bay. The covering F6Fs strafed targets of opportunity. A trailing Tojo was spotted by Lt.(jg) Carleton T. Jones, who shot the Tojo down from 2 o'clock level. Jones successfully released a hung bomb causing severe damage to a chemical factory.

The AAR from the VF-46 mission would note:
1. *"Once again the Grumman Hellcat proved its sturdy dependability. With all but one strand of elevator control cable severed, a rudder torque tube holed, and damage from debris in the left wing and aileron Comdr. Rooney continued to dish it out and returned nearly two hundred miles to base for a normal landing."*
2. *Water injection used in combat proved enormously valuable.*
3. *The new type Polaroid goggles afforded a wider field of view and excellent anti-glare properties are a decided improvement over former types.*

0623 Recovered 1 F6F launched at 0605.
0756 Recovered 1 F6F launched at 0605.
0838 Completed recovery of 3 F6Fs with mechanical problems, launched at 0605.
0901 Completed recovery of 10 F6Fs launched at 0605.

1015-1028 Recovered 4 F6Fs and 8 TBMs launched at 0605. One F6F (Bu.No.72455) piloted by Lt.(jg) Ralph Junior Reeder was reported missing over target and failed to return. He was presumed to have been shot down.

1144 Completed launching 12 F6Fs for CAP.

1218 164 miles from Kyushu, CVL-22 completed launching 4 F6Fs to join a special fighter sweep with 8 LANGLEY F6Fs against Kanoya Airfield. One F6F turned back with mechanical problems. Lead by Lt. John I. Jones, the remaining 3 VF-46 planes attacked hangars at Kanoya East and Inujo Airfields.

1305 Air Department secured from flight quarters and set condition 13.

1407 Sounded flight quarters.

1410 Sounded general quarters. Ships of this task group opened fire on enemy aircraft diving at ships in the formation. Two aircraft were seen to hit the water and burn. During this action, two fighters from the USS LANGLEY in hot pursuit were also fired on by the Task Unit and, unfortunately, were also shot down. The pilots were not recovered.

1447 Secured from general quarters.

1451 Commenced maneuvering to avoid hitting a floating mine.

1534 USS YORKTOWN was designated guide by OTC.

1548 Completed recovery of 12 F6Fs launched at 1144 and 4 F6Fs launched at 1218. One F6F crashed into the barrier on landing.

Numerous drifting mines were seen by the task group during the afternoon.

1655 Passed a floating mine 1,500 yards to starboard.

1700 Passed a floating mine 500 yards to starboard. Both mines were marked, reported later as having been destroyed by gunfire.

1810 Secured from flight quarters. Air Department set to condition 14.

2241 Maneuvered to avoid a floating mine, sighted, thanks to the moonlight.

After 1830 they proceeded southwest at 22 knots.

2345 Commenced zigzagging on base course 245°T.

GN Pilots reported that they could not find any Jap warships so they dropped their fish at docks and shore installations. Went all the way up into the sea of Japan looking for some juicy targets and all they found were some fighter planes. Our squadron splashed five of them and we lost one of ours and the pilot in the brawl. About 1400 (hrs) two Jap planes were shot down diving at the Yorktown which is in our outfit. GN

AD At sea Kyushu Japan. GQ 0508. TBM's took off with fish, were over target but elements of Jap fleet disappeared. Dropped fish at docks. Strike on Kyushu going on all day. Secured from GQ 1345. At 1500 Jap planes appeared overhead and dropped bombs off our starboard beam just missing Yorktown. Task force shot down 2 and 1 got away. Our Squadron shot down 4 Japs over Kyushu and one of our pilots was killed. AD

Friday 30 March 1945   *Ryukyu Islands, Okinawa — Love Minus Two*

0025 Steaming toward Okinawa Shima. Unidentified aircraft reported 25 miles toward the west.

0028 Sounded torpedo defense.

0032 USS ALASKA opened fire on the bogey.

0045 Received a report that a night fighter shot down the enemy aircraft.

0048 Secured from torpedo defense.

0556 Completed launching 12 F6Fs for a CAP.

0740 Completed launching 8 F6Fs and 8 TBMs for a strike over Okinawa Shima.

0758 Completed recovery of 1 TBM launched at 0740. This Avenger was the photographic plane for the strike. It developed a propeller governor problem after launch requiring a return to the ship.

The strike group proceeded toward target, encountering near solid overcast at close to 1,000'. The aircraft broke off to look for targets of opportunity. TBMs attacked a bridge, buildings and the village of Ora Wan. Hellcats bombed, rocketed and strafed costal towns of Abe, Arumi, Kawata and Taira.

0945 Completed recovery of 12 F6Fs launched at 0556.

1005 Gunnery Department set to condition One Easy due to reported unidentified aircraft in vicinity.

1037 Sounded general quarters due to reported unidentified aircraft bearing 250°T, 4 miles.

1042 Aircraft identified as friendly. Secured from general quarters. Gunnery Department set to condition One Easy.

1111 Completed recovery of 7 TBMS and 8 F6Fs launched at 0740.

1234 Completed launching 8 TBMs (led by Lt-Comdr. John P. Barron) for a second strike against Okinawa Shima. The VT-46 Avengers were assigned targets working with USS INTREPID pilots by the Air Coordinator, bombing, rocketing and strafing a large factory and villages. Damage was not assessed.

1537-1539 Launched 3 F6Fs for CAP.

1543 Gunnery Department secured from condition One Easy.

1553 Changed course into the wind and launched 9 F6Fs, for a total of 12 launched as CAP.

1602-1616 Recovered 8 TBMs launched at 1234. One crashed into the barrier, without damage to ship or injury to personnel.

1720 S1c James Jefferson Mallard Clevenstine (he was called Mallard by his family) died as a result of wounds received in action aboard this ship on 18 March 1945.

1811-1825 Recovered 12 F6Fs launched 1539 and 1553.

1833 Secured from flight quarters, Air Department set to condition 14.

1838 Sounded torpedo defense.

1938 Secured from torpedo defense.

2350 Ceased zigzagging, changed course to 130°T.

GN Two loads of bombs and rockets left our deck again headed for Okinawa. Heard that our ship has sent over the most tonnage of all CVLs in this strike at Japan proper. Ten or twelve more days to go and I'm wondering if we can stand the strain. Many more days like today and we'll all be fit for the bughouse. Hope we don't have a 2 AM reveille like we did this AM. GN

GL Still bombing & rocketing Okinawa for invasion troops which will land on the first. 175,000 men and 1,400 ships – bigger than Normandy invasion. BB's still shelling. British task group is operating down south. GL

Saturday 31 March 1945   *Ryukyu Islands, Okinawa — Love Minus One*
James Jefferson Mallard Clevenstine buried at sea

0451 Steaming as before, off Okinawa Shima in TU 58.4.1. Sounded flight quarters.

0547-0556 Launched 12 F6Fs for CAP.

0635 Received report of unidentified aircraft bearing 330°T, 50 miles.

0641 Gunnery Department set to condition One Easy.

0645 Tokuna Shima was sighted over the horizon, bearing 335°T, 52 miles.

0742-0747 Launched 8 TBMs on a support strike against targets on Okinawa, assigned while orbiting "Point William". With a solid overcast at 2,000', heavy AA emplacements, a factory, barracks, caves, trenches and a radio tower were hit with bombs and rockets, in strikes led by Lt.-Comdr. Barron.

0815 Mustered crew on stations.

0921 Changed course to 110°T. Completed launching 8 F6Fs for a CAP.

0954 Completed recovering CAP of 12 F6Fs launched at 0556.

1040 F1c F.E. Krzyanski was admitted to sick bay for a sprained knee. He slipped descending a ladder.

1109 Completed recovering 8 TBMs launched at 0747.

1216 Completed launching 12 F6Fs for CAP, and 7 TBMs for a strike. Orbiting "Point King", they could not strike primary targets due to aircraft from other carriers, so they individually attacked targets of opportunity including highway bridges, small factories, barracks, small villages and fortified caves.

1233 Completed recovering 8 F6Fs launched at 0921.

1249 Changed course to 270°T, decreased speed to 15 knots.

1320 Held quarters for burial services.

1333 All vessels in this Task Group followed the INDEPENDENCE in half-masting colors.

1338 S1c James J. M. Clevenstine was solemnly buried at sea at 26° 43.9' North Latitude, 129° 33.3' East Longitude. He had held on for 12 days, and died last night, after developing peritonitis. He had received wounds to the abdomen by the tracer element from a 5" shell during the attack on the morning of 18 March 1945.

1339 Two-blocked the colors.   1340 Secured from quarters.

1358 Changed speed to 18 knots, then changed course to 110°T,

1511 Changed course to 090°T, changed speed to 23 knots. Unidentified aircraft reported bearing 015°T, 14 miles. Gunnery Department set to condition One.

1520 Aircraft identified as friendly. Gunnery Department set to condition One easy.

1535 Completed launching 8 F6Fs.

1611 Completed recovering 12 F6Fs, and 7 TBMs launched at 1216.

1615 Commenced zigzagging independently while some ships of the formation refueled destroyers.

1808-1818 Completed recovering the CAP of 8 F6Fs launched at 1535.

1828 Secured from flight quarters and set condition 14.

1936 Secured from torpedo defense.

2352 Changed course to 150°T.

Captain Kindell noted in the SOL as he left the bridge:

"Courses when not into the wind will be mostly North westerly, and then South westerly until morning. The weather forecast is for good weather. No friendly contacts are expected.

By dispatch today the OTC reminded all ships that they are expected to dodge torpedoes independently. The OTC will maneuver the group in avoiding submarines and torpedoes, but ships are not to wait for signals when endangered. Also ships are not to conform to emergency course signals immediately if to do so would prevent them from taking necessary individual action or would interfere with other ships doing the same."

During the night they remained in the same general area.

GN Two more loads of bombs and rockets over to Okinawa Shima. Clevenstine of first division buried. Hit about a week ago by a fragment of a 5" shell fired no doubt by one of our own guns. Japs were in pretty close that time. GN

AD At sea - Okinawa. GQ 0520. Secured 0620. Planes striking targets on island. No attacks on task group. Tomorrow they invade Okinawa. AD

Sunday 1 April 1945   *Ryukyu Islands, Okinawa Invasion*

Steaming as before, as part of Task Unit 58.4.1 accompanied by USS YORKTOWN (OTC, Rear Admiral A.W. Radford, Commander Carrier Division Six), USS INTREPID, and USS LANGLEY. Task Unit 58.4.1 is a part of Task Force 58 (Vice Admiral M.A. Mitscher - Bunker Hill, Flagship) in the Fifth Fleet (Admiral R.A. Spruance - USS INDIANAPOLIS, Flagship). Besides the carriers, this Task Group is operating with three battleships, two large cruisers, two AA cruisers, and four divisions of destroyers. Guide is USS NEW JERSEY, bearing 270°T, 2,000 yards, cruising disposition 5-VB, course 150°T, speed 18 knots.

Today, marines and soldiers of the Tenth Army are landing on the southwestern beaches of Okinawa Shima. Okinawa's defenses were well entrenched, prepared with care to extract a toll from the Marines and GI's that would have to slug it out in the islands mud. There are 485 square miles of rugged terrain with terraces, ridge lines with fortified well hidden caves & tunnel complexes, ravines and rolling hills, with pre-registered cross fire and very determined defenders.

0445 Sounded flight quarters.

0543-0556 Launched 16 F6Fs. Eight were for a CAP over the beaches and eight for CAP over our Group. Lt. Richard B. McNees, orbiting over a DD, spotted a Val 50' above the water. He and Ensign Everett R. Robinett commenced an attack, bracketing the maneuvering Val. Other hunters were lurking. Four FM-2s (Wildcats built by General Motors) closed at high speed on the Val's 6 o'clock to make the kill, just as the Val had turned in to meet Ens. Robinett's attack.

0632 Secured from flight quarters. Air Department set to condition 13.

0845 Sounded flight quarters.

0923-0935 Recovered 16 F6Fs launched at 0556.

0948 Gunnery Department set condition One Easy due to possibility of air attack.

1204-1211 Launched 12 F6Fs for CAPs. Four proceeded north of Okinawa. Eight covered this Group.

1352-1405 Launched 8 F6Fs and 8 TBMs. 4 F6Fs and 8 TBMs flew out as a strike to support the troops. Lt. Comdr Barron led the group to a prearranged point west of Okinawa, directly over the invasion fleet, to orbit. Two sections of Hellcats led by Lt. Schroeder provided cover for the TBMs. They were assigned heavy gun and AA positions one mile east of Naha airfield to bomb, rocket and strafe. The covering fighters joined the *"well-executed"* attack along with 11 planes from USS SAVO ISLAND. They had been advised to remain above 1,500' on bombing runs, due to heavy flack.

1535-1547 Recovered 12 F6Fs launched at 1211.

1725 Completed recovering 8 F6Fs launched at 1405.

1802-1814 Recovered 8 TBMs launched at 1405.

1820 Air Department secured from flight quarters.

1838 Sounded routine torpedo defense.

1850-1854 USS FRANKS was alongside starboard quarter to deliver mail.

1947 Secured from Torpedo defense. Gunnery Department set condition One Easy.

2300 Commenced zigzagging on base course 240°T, remaining in the same area during the night.

GL Invasion has started on Okinawa. We are sending in planes to support the troops. During the day a total of 6 Bettys were shot down. Our troops are 500 yards inland and we have partial control of the airfield. GL

AD At sea Okinawa. Marines and Army are landing on Okinawa. We are helping with air cover. Invasion going to schedule. AD

GN Easter Sunday today and we had it pretty easy. Only one load over the island. Had turkey for dinner and it hit the spot. 175,000 men make a landing on Okinawa today and from the latest reports they are going strong. Also got some good news from the other theater of war and that one may be over soon. I hope. For some reason I dreamt of Stoney and imagined him dead. Hope I get word of him soon. GN

Captain Kindell noted in the SOL as he left the bridge:
"Our flight deck is spotted forward as a standby for an emergency landing by night fighters. Be prepared to man landing stations quickly if such a landing must be made."

Monday 2 April 1945   *Ryukyu Islands, Okinawa Invasion*

Steaming as before, supporting the Tenth Army ashore on Okinawa. 0300 Sounded flight quarters.

0420 Sounded torpedo defense due to an enemy aircraft approaching the formation.

0444 Secured from torpedo defense.

0500 Completed launching 8 F6Fs as a CAP over Okinawa.

0603 Landed 1 night fighter from USS YORKTOWN.

0753 Completed launching 8 F6Fs and 6 TBMs for a sweep over Okinawa. Launched the YORTOWN fighter that had landed at 0603. Hindered by low ceilings, pinpoint bombing was not possible.

The pilots attacked targets of opportunity; 8 small fishing boats, a landing craft, villages, warehouses, barracks and fortified caves along the shore line.

0809 Gunnery Department secured from torpedo defense.

0821 Completed recovery of 8 F6Fs launched at 0500.

0855 Completed launching 4 F6Fs for a CAP over Okinawa. These Hellcats reported to a FDO on a destroyer near Ie Shima. Upon retirement, they strafed the towns of Awa and Takee.

1004 Sounded torpedo defense. At 1108 completed recovery of 1 F6F launched at 0753.

1124 Completed recovery of 7 F6Fs launched at 0753.

1135 Completed recovery of 6 TBMs launched at 0753.

1227-1237 Completed launching 8 F6Fs and 6 TBMs for an invasion support sweep. As with the previous sweep, no military targets of substantial value could be found, so targets of opportunity were selected, attacking fortified caves, trenches, trucks, a tank, behind enemy lines, and the towns of Kaniku, Yakata, and Jaba. Attacks were made in good weather, unhindered by other aircraft giving the hunters *"time to locate worthwhile objectives"*.

1241-1244 Completed recovery of 4 F6Fs launched at 0855.

1325 AMM3c Alexander R. Jarrett was admitted to sickbay with a fractured left foot. The ship rolled while he was pushing an aircraft causing the right tire to roll over his foot.

1356-1358 Launched 4 F6Fs for CAP over our radar picket line of destroyers.

1539-1543 Completed recovery of 8 F6Fs and 6 TBMs launched at 1237.

1659 Gunnery Department set to One Easy on orders from OTC.

1812 Completed recovery of 4 F6Fs launched at 1358.

1818 Secured from flight quarters. Air Department set to condition 14.

2109 Changed speed to 23 knots, course to 165°T.

2116 The night was noted as being "especially dark" before the moon came up. While resuming station after acting as plane guard, USS FRANKS collided with USS NEW JERSEY. Commenced steering various courses at various speeds maintaining position in the formation.

2120 USS YORKTOWN assumed guide, bearing 205°T, 2,800 yards. Early reports indicated that the damage to both ships apparently seems negligible. Later sources state the USS FRANKS (DD-554) suffered damage to her bridge and that her captain, Commander David R. Stephan was fatally injured. USS FRANKS would retire to Puget Sound via Ulithi and Pearl Harbor for an overhaul.

2147 USS NEW JERSEY assumed guide 250°T, 2,800 yards.

2336 Commenced zigzagging (Plan No.6) on base course 165°T.

Captain Kindell noted in the SOL as he left the bridge;
"We are proceeding to the Southeast to a fueling area.
We should pass Rasa Island 35 miles to port about 0030. It is 107 ft. high and should show on radar.
There is another Task Group coming back up from the same area. Should pass, presumably about midnight. It is TG 58.3. May show on radar.
Call me if anything unexpected shows up or happens."
(Note: Rasa Island today is called Oki Daito. It is 240 miles SE of Okinawa.)

GL During the night a Jap convoy was sighted trying to reinforce Okinawa (1 cruiser, 2DD's, 4 cargo ships, landing craft). 4 night fighters and 6 TBF's were launched from Yorktown and Langley. Cruiser was hit and other ships strafed. Invasion going to schedule. GL

GN Started working again at 2 AM for about the eighth day in a row. We had better be getting some good uninterrupted sleep soon or we will all wind up in sick bay. Looks like we have at least another week at least to go. Bogies have been around for the last few days but they get splashed before any damage is done. Thank God. Made two deck load strikes on Okinawa again today and were ready for a third but it never came off. Thought we would use fire bombs for the first time but then decided against it in favor of regular bombs of which the Nips have been receiving many here lately. GN

US Submarine Exclusion Zone.
Any subs in the marked area were assumed to be the enemy!
Note the "Shoot first, ask questions later" remark!

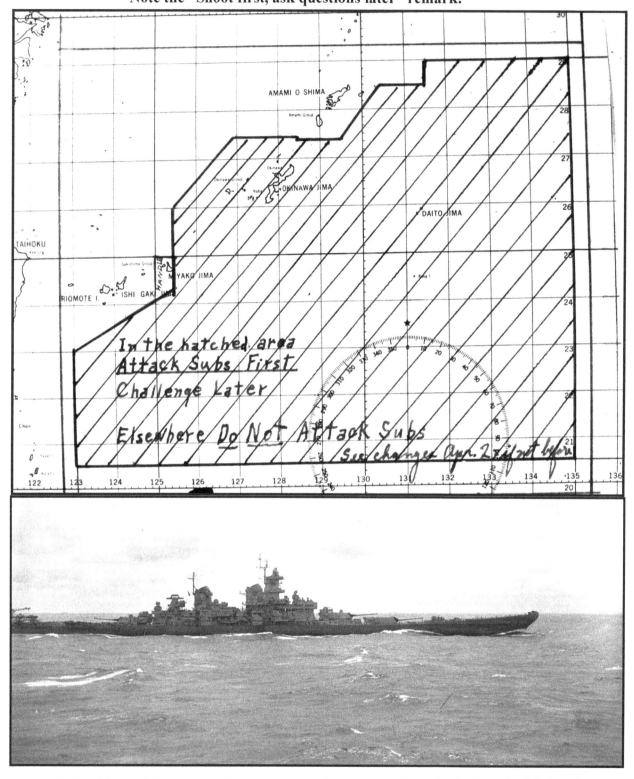

Battleship USS WISCONSIN (BB-63) as seen by the crew from the deck of the Mighty-I.
Other vessels in the Task Group are on the horizon. (Date possibly 5 April. Photo from Ed Schultz)

Tuesday 3 April 1945   *Ryukyu Islands, Okinawa Invasion*

0210 Steaming as before to join a fueling group. Sounded flight quarters.

0507-0607 Manned torpedo defense stations.

0611 Secured from flight quarters. Air Department set to condition 14.

0700 Changed to cruising disposition 5-R.

USS FRANKS left the formation to proceed to Ulithi. When the tankers were sighted, the groups did not attempt to join. Large swells and high wind made fueling prohibitive. They were suffering the effects of a nearby typhoon, and steamed west in search of better conditions.

1530 Closing on the tankers, they changed course downwind and dropped the speed to 10.5 knots, to commence fueling. Guide USS MONONGAHELA, bearing 260°T, 5,000 yards.

1826 USS INDEPENDENCE designated guide. Ships that went alongside tankers had cast off and the Task Group separated from the fueling group.

1959 Changed course to 020°T.

1907 USS NEW JERSEY designated as guide. INDEPENDENCE bears 080°T, 2,000 yards from guide.

2337 Changed course to 180°T. Both groups stayed in the same general area throughout the night.

Captain Kindell noted in the SOL as he left the bridge;
"We are slowly going East to where the weather was so bad this morning. It will possibly be worse. The tankers are going back there too.
Another Task Group is heading for the same spot from the North. Rendezvous at daylight probably.
We will no doubt attempt to fuel tomorrow.
No other friendly contacts are expected.
Call me if the weather really fouls up, or if anything unexpected occurs."

GL *Supposed to refuel today but riding out a storm. Last night the New Jersey rammed or side swiped a destroyer – Franks. Visibility poor and it took off for Ulithi. About 300 miles from Okinawa.* **GL**

Wednesday 4 April 1945   *Fueling and Rearming*

Steaming as before in the fueling area at the edge of a Typhoon.

0633 Commenced maneuvering to come along port side of USS CIMARRON.

0725 Came along port side of AO-22, USS CIMARRON to refuel.

0727-0841 USS MCGOWAN was along side the port quarter to transfer photos, gunnery gear and Lt (jg) M.E. Stewart for transfer to the USS YORKTOWN.

1019 USS CIMARRON cast off having pumped 218,262 gallons of fuel oil and 37,125 gallons of gasoline. Not completely refueled, cast off due to heavy seas, when it became imprudent to continue.

1020 Commenced maneuvering to gain position alongside USS LASSEN.

1140 Commenced receiving ammunition from USS LASSEN.

1452-1518 USS HAZLEWOOD was alongside port quarter to deliver mail and freight.

1618-1622 USS HAZLEWOOD returned alongside to deliver 1 bag of mail.

1735 USS LASSEN cast off having delivered bombs, rocket parts and fuses.

1737 Sounded flight quarters.

1738 Commenced maneuvering to regain position in the formation.

1801 Gained station in fueling formation, USS CIMARRON guide, bearing 068°T, 2,200 yards.

1810 Commenced maneuvering to recover replacement aircraft.

1817 Recovered 1 replacement F6F from CVE-99, USS ADMIRALTY ISLANDS.

1818 Commenced maneuvering to regain station in formation.

1837 Formation completed fueling and rearming operations. USS FLINT designated guide, course 030°T, speed 10 knots, bearing 210°T, 6,000 yards.

1844 Changed course to 210°T, then changed disposition to 5R, axis 030°T. USS NEW JERSEY designated guide, bearing 210°T, 2,000 yards.
1857 Changed speed to 18 knots.
2232 Began zigzagging on base course 255°T, heading west to calmer water off Sakishima Gunto.

GN Still blowing pretty bad but it did let up a bit. Refueled in the morning and rearmed in the afternoon. Worked from noon to midnight and was really pooped. Had a chance to write a few letters in the morning and took advantage of it. Didn't get quite the load we wanted due no doubt to the inclement weather. GN

Thursday 5 April 1945   *Ryukyu Islands, Okinawa Invasion - Saki Shima*

0522 Steaming in to strike the enemy on Sakishima Gunto. Sounded general quarters.
0628 Secured from routine general quarters. Gunnery Department set to One Easy, as 2,000' broken to overcast conditions with scattered showers made it ideal for a surprise enemy aircraft attack on the ship.
0629 Commenced forming cruising disposition 5VB.
0700 Sounded flight quarters.
0753-0813 Launched 11 F6Fs and 8 TBMs for a strike against Nobara Airfield on Miyako Shima. With no airfield facilities at Nobara, runways were bombed, and a town and factory southeast of Nobara was strafed. The target area had a ceiling of 1,500', with intense AA fire west of the target.
0816 Changed course to 020°T.
0851 USS WISCONSIN designated guide by OTC, bearing 184°T, 4,100 yards.
0859-0904 Launched 4 F6Fs for a SubCAP over the lifeguard rescue submarine.
0910 USS NEW JERSEY designated guide by OTC, bearing 210°T, 2,000 yards.
1020 Sheered out to port to avoid hitting a drifting mine.
1119-1141 Recovered 11 F6Fs and 8 TBMs launched at 0813.
1419 Launched 12 F6Fs. Eight were for a CAP, and four were tasked with SubCAP over the rescue submarine.
1431 Recovered 4 F6Fs launched at 0904.
1445 Secured from flight quarters. Air Department set to condition 13.
1732 Sounded flight quarters.
1832 Recovering aircraft, a F6F crashed into the barrier fouling the flight deck. INDEPENDENCE sent orbiting aircraft to other carriers so they would not have to land after sunset.
1844 USS LANGLEY recovered 2 VF-46 F6Fs due to the fouled deck from the barrier accident.
1845 USS INTREPID and USS YORKTOWN recovered 4 F6Fs each, launched from INDEPENDENCE at 1419.
1846 Recovered 1 F6F launched at 1419, completing recovery of all 12 F6Fs launched at 1419.
2100 AMM3c Anthony M. Simonie was admitted to sickbay with puncture wounds to his back. While working in a F6F, a detonator in the IFF gear went off sending two small fragments of the radio into Anthony's back.
2310 Changed course to 090°T.
Today, Admiral R.A. Spruance, Commander, Fifth Fleet, transferred his flag to the USS NEW MEXICO. The USS INDIANAPOLIS (hit by a kamikaze on March 31st) was in need of repairs.
The Task Group headed East at 23 knots.

GN Off to the wars again. We are relieving the British fleet who have been operating in and around Nakashima**. Hope we are a bit more successful for we heard that they had ships hit, two of them carriers. Also heard today from fairly good authority that we are to be awarded the Navy Unit Citation when we hit port. Heard rumors to the effect that we will be going back to night carrier operations and that will be OK by me. One bomb and rocket load today and that's about all we'll send over for the next few days in my opinion. GN (** Note: Nakashima was incorrect, should be Saki Shima)

GL Early in the morning night chickens splashed two Zekes trying to land on Okinawa. Langley planes splashed 2 Zekes 10 miles from target. We are in 1 Easy again. All is going to schedule on Okinawa. One of our planes cracked up and the others had to land on the Yorktown and Intrepid. GL

Friday 6 April 1945   *Ryukyu Islands, Okinawa Invasion - Fueling and Replenishing Ammo*
IJN "Operation Ten-Go"

0720 Steaming as before, retiring toward the southeast to fuel. There are 4 INDEPENDENCE F6Fs on the USS YORKTOWN, 4 F6Fs on the USS INTREPID, and 2 F6Fs on the USS LANGLEY.

0722 Changed course to 030°T. Speed is 10 knots. The Task Group commenced fueling operations.

0807-0812 USS MCNAIR was alongside port quarter to receive photographs for delivery to USS YORKTOWN.

0830 Mustered crew on stations. Sounded flight quarters.

0907 Changed course and speed for flight operations.

0927 Completed recovering 10 VF-46 F6Fs, launched from YORKTOWN, INTREPID and LANGLEY. They flew a CAP prior to returning to the INDEPENDENCE.

0928 Commenced maneuvering to gain position alongside the assigned tanker.

0938 Secured from flight quarters. Air Department set to condition 14.

1017 Came along port side of USS KASKASKIA.

1047-1104 USS MCNAIR was alongside port quarter to pick up a pilot for transfer to the USS BOUGAINVILLE to pick up a replacement aircraft.

1112 The after deckhouse of the USS KASKASKIA brushed against INDEPENDENCE, causing minor damage to the shield of the 40mm mount No. 11. The minor collision or brushing of the ships was said to have been due to "The seas causing excessive yawing".

1206-1235 USS MCGOWAN was alongside the port quarter to transfer on board 5 officers reporting for duty in Air Group 46. (Lt. C.O. Jones and Ensigns L.V. Adgate, J.V. Ballard, R.T. Dyer and Z. Plecha.)

1233 Sounded flight quarters.

1255 USS KASKASKIA cast off having delivered 182,032 gallons of fuel oil and 32,240 gallons of aviation gasoline.

1316 Regained position in the fueling disposition. Course 060°T. USS LACKAWANNA guide, bears 030°T, 3,000 yards.

1327-1332 USS MCNAIR was along starboard side amidships to deliver freight.

1410 Commenced maneuvering for air operations.

1415-1429 Launched 7 TBMs and 8 F6Fs on a strike to neutralize airfields on Minami Daito Shima. This was in response to Task Groups 58.1 and 58.3 coming under heavy air attacks during the morning.

1430 Commenced maneuvering to approach an ammunition ship.

1510 Came alongside USS SHASTA to our starboard.

1513 The crew of the USS INDEPENDENCE was securing from flight quarters. As this was taking place, the crew of IJN's YAMATO was preparing to weigh anchor in Tokuyama. The IJN had activated "Operation Ten-Go". Battleship YAMATO would sortie from the Inland Sea thru Bungo Strait as the *"Surface Special Attack Force"* with light cruiser YAHAGI and eight destroyers. The IJN plan was to thunder into the Allied Okinawa invasion force to decimate the invasion transports. YAMATO's captain Rear Admiral Kosaku Ariga would then beach her to use her heavy guns in support of the Japanese Army's defense of Okinawa. Its sailors would join to reinforce the Army. It was said Japanese Operation *"Ten-Ichi"* would decide the fate of the Japanese Empire.   (Japan's fate had long ago been sealed)

1704 USS INDEPENDENCE was detached from Task Group 58.4 by orders of Rear Admiral R.A. Radford. Pursuant to orders of Commander, Task Group 58.4, INDEPENDENCE is to proceed independently in company with USS UHLMAN and USS COLAHAN to join Task Unit 58.4.5.

1729 Cast off from USS SHASTA having received bombs, rockets and fuses. Sounded flight quarters.

1744 Commenced recovering aircraft.

1751 A TBM-3 piloted by Ens. John A. Tschirhart crashed into the barrier, causing minor damage to the flight deck. No personnel injuries. The Avenger (Bu.No.23392) was damaged beyond repair.

1822 Completed recovery of 7 TBMs and 8 F6Fs launched at 1429, and 1 F6F (as a replacement) from the USS BOUGAINVILLE. Two aircraft struck the barrier, causing minor damage to the flight deck and the aircraft, with no injuries to the pilots or aircrew. During one of these crashes S1c Clarence H. Miller and S2c Howard E. Figgins jumped from the flight deck to the catwalk, each receiving minor injuries.

1827 Secured from flight quarters. Air Department set to condition 14.

1829 Gunnery Departments went to torpedo defense.

1850 Reported for duty to CTU 58.4.5 in USS FLINT. USS FLINT is guide, bearing 090°T, 2,500 yards, course 130°T, speed 20 knots. OTC (and CTU) Captain C.R. Wells. INDEPENDENCE is now with USS FLINT, USS OAKLAND and several destroyers.

1929 Secured from torpedo defense.

1939 Secured shaft No.3 to make a test.

1944 With testing completed, cut in No.3 shaft.

2311 Changed course to 050°T.

This TU is staying in the fueling area tonight to join TG 58.2 tomorrow.

DL The real Japanese kamikaze onslaught against U.S. ships off Okinawa began on Friday, 6 April 1945.

The Official Chronology of the U.S. Navy in World War II reports that on this day alone, DD Bush was sunk. Four kamikazes irreparably damaged DD Colhoun, which was then scuttled by DD Cassin Young. LST 347 was sunk in air attack. DD Rooks and LDE Foreman were damaged. DMS Emmons was damaged by five suiciders, DD Mullany was damaged by two, as was DE Witter. Kamikazes damaged DD Morris and APD Daniel T. Griffin.

So it went. The record shows over eighteen U.S. vessels of all types and sizes were impacted during this one day. The number of men who died or suffered wounds was not listed. Only the men themselves, and the Navy, knew those details. The folks back home would learn them later. No wonder Nimitz complained. This was no place for the fast carriers to be hanging around. The Japanese didn't even have to search. We were right where they wanted us. DL

GN Good day so far. Got up at 6 AM and it was really a good night's sleep. Had hit the rack at nine so all's well. Refueled in the morning and then got busy with a load of bombs. Heard that two units of the task force were under attack in the morning so I guess we'll hunt up the field the Nips are using. If we find it, it won't look so good by the time we leave. The boys planted their eggs and we heard that they had no airborne opposition. AA fire was meager and inaccurate.

While they were off on that mission an ammo ship pulled alongside and we got another load of bombs and rockets. With incinerator on the blink we had a lot of fun breaking all the wood to splinter size before it went overboard. Heard today that we are going to join Adm. Bogan's outfit. Two of the unit have been under attack all day long and we are probably going north to help them out a bit. Hope he's as considerate to us as he was before. I think he knows we are a CVL and not a CV as some of the other big boys out here have an idea. GN

Saturday 7 April 1945　　　*Ryukyu Islands, Okinawa Invasion - Change Task Group*
Fueling and Replenishing Ammo, IJN Fleet Units sunk off Kyushu
IJN YAMATO sunk

Steaming as before in company of Task Unit 58.4.5 with USS FLINT (OTC), USS OAKLAND and four destroyers of DesDiv 105, in the fueling area, course 050°T, speed 10 knots. Guide, USS FLINT bears 090° T, 2,500 yards. Air Department is in condition 14.

0810 Commenced maneuvering to approach the port side of an assigned ammunition ship.

0836 Alongside USS LASSEN for rearming operations.

0854 Rearming operations canceled by order of CTU 58.4.5.

0857 Cast off from USS LASSEN, having received no ordnance.

0900 Received USS COLAHAN on the port quarter to transfer electrical parts.

0907 USS COLAHAN cast off. Commenced maneuvering to gain station in the Task Unit.

0946 Regained position in Task Unit 58.4.5.

1004 In accordance with a secret dispatch dated 5 March 1945, USS INDEPENDENCE was ordered by CTU 58.4.5 to proceed independently to join Task Unit 58.2.1. She began maneuvering to take up the new position.

1028 USS INDEPENDENCE joined Task Unit 58.2.1 with USS RANDOLPH (OTC, Rear Admiral G.F. Bogan, who is also CTU 58.2) and USS ENTERPRISE. Course 315°T, speed 20 knots. USS OAKLAND is guide, bearing 060°T, 2,000 yards.

1055 USS OWEN came along port quarter to transfer mail, then cast off due to pending formation, course and speed changes. Changed course to 065°T, speed 15 knots.

1114 Changed course to 310°T, speed 24 knots.

1136-1147 USS OWEN was alongside on the port quarter to deliver mail.

1540 USS LANGLEY was detached from CTU 58.4.1 and ordered to proceed as assigned.

1640-1653 USS UHLMANN was alongside on the port quarter to deliver mail.

The Task Group did not stop to refuel, but proceeded north and west at 24 knots.

GL 58.1 & 3 were under attack all day. We are leaving 58.4 and starting a new 58.2. Destroyer Calhoun[1] was hit by a Banazi, also USS Forbes and Morris, no word on causalities. 58.1 & 3 still under attack. USS Bennett hit by Banazi. USS Bush hit & reported sunk. We sure have been lucky, it seems every time we leave a TG to join another, the one we left was attacked. During the last two days 200 planes have been shot down by ships guns & planes. GL* (Note: In addition to destroyers BUSH and COLHOUN*[1], ammunition ships LOGAN VICTORY & HOBBS VICTORY were sunk.)

By days end, the last hope of the once powerful Imperial Japanese Navy was settled into its new berth atop eons of silt on the bottom of the East China Sea. The mighty and fearsome YAMATO and her Battle Group had cleared the Bongo Strait, steamed into the Pacific down the coast of Kyushu, thru the Osumi Strait into the East China Sea. YAMATO, commissioned shortly after the attack on Pearl Harbor, had taken 4 years to build at the Kure Naval Arsenal. With a deadly array of 3 triple 18"guns, YAMATO was once was flagship of the IJN Combined Fleet serving at the Battles of Midway, the Philippine Sea, and Leyte Gulf, where she steamed in over the horizon to surprise and terrorize the escort carriers of "Taffy 3" with their highly motivated bold heroic defenders in the Battle off Samar.

The final battle of YAMATO was closer to Kyushu Japan than its destination, nowhere near the US invasion fleet off the shores of Okinawa. Designed for ship-on-ship combat, YAMATO accompanied by light cruiser YAHAGI and four (of the eight) destroyers, ASASHIMO, HAMAKAZE, ISOKAZE and KASUMI fell victim to the determined fierce onslaught of US Naval carrier aviation. Hit by at least nine torpedoes and five 1,000 lb bombs, YAMATO would be lost with her captain (Ariga) as well as Commander-in-Chief Seiroku Ito, and an estimated 3,055 members of her 3,332 man crew.

The curtain had at last closed on the final performance and last gasp of the IJN surface fleet.

Sunday 8 April 1945   *Ryukyu Islands, Okinawa Invasion*

Steaming as before with carriers USS RANDOLPH and USS ENTERPRISE. Course 270°T, speed 18 knots, USS OAKLAND guide, bearing 240°T, 2,000 yards, in an operating area off Okinawa Shima. Since 6 April, the Japanese have been sending out heavy air assaults against our forces.

0420 Sounded flight quarters.

0522-0532 Launched 12 F6Fs for CAP.

0615 Secured from general quarters.

0616 Completed launching 3 TBMs for ASP, and at 0630 1 TBM for ASP.

0655 Commenced maneuvering to gain position in the formation. Axis rotated to 130°T, course 330°T.

0718 Unidentified aircraft reported bearing 148°T, 12 miles. At 0730 it was identified as friendly TBM.

0805 Completed launching 8 F6Fs for CAP and 4 TBMs for ASP to relieve an earlier launch.

0811-0830 Recovered 12 F6Fs and 4 TBMs launched from 0532 to 0630.

0900 USS BALTIMORE, USS PITTSBURGH, with DDs USS WEDDERBURN, USS TWINING and USS STOCKTON joined this Task Group, taking stations within the formation.

1109-1145 Launched 12 F6Fs to relieve the CAP. VT-46 ASP TBMs were relieved by 4 TBMs from the USS RANDOLPH.

1152-1212 Recovered 4 TBMs and 8 F6Fs launched at 0805.

1335 USS WASHINGTON, NORTH CAROLINA and their destroyer screen joined this Task Group.

1515 Completed launching 8 F6Fs as a relief CAP.

1602 Completed recovery of 12 F6Fs launched at 1145.   1726 Observed an explosion on the horizon believed to have been caused by a bomb jettisoned by a friendly aircraft.

1616 TBM Avenger (Bu.No. 23392) from the 1751 barricade crash on 6 April was jettisoned overboard.

1825-1835 Recovered 8 F6Fs launched at 1515.

1851 Secured from flight quarters.

1951 Gunnery Department set to normal conditions.

2357 Changed course to 350°T. The Task Group remained in the same general area overnight.

Captain Kindell noted in the SOL as he left the bridge:
"Oakland bears 310° — 2,000 yds.
As we operate in "Eagle" tomorrow we will probably run back NW part of the night.
No friendly contacts are expected.   Call me if anything unusual occurs or is sighted.
Okino Daito Shima was more or less in front of us at 2000, distance 92 miles.
We will probably turn back NW before we get close."

Monday 9 April 1945   *Ryukyu Islands, Okinawa Invasion*

0420 Steaming as before with Task Unit 58.2.1 off Okinawa. Sounded flight quarters.

0506 Sounded routine general quarters.

0535 Completed launching 12 F6Fs for CAP and 4 TBMs for ASP.

0606 Secured from general quarters, Gunnery Department set to condition One Easy.

0805 Completed launching 8 F6Fs and 4 TBMs as relief for our patrols launched at 0535.

0817 Completed recovering 4 TBMs launched at 0535.

0839 Completed recovering 12 F6Fs launched at 0535.

1150 Completed launching 12 F6Fs for CAP and 4 TBMs for ASP.

1216 Completed recovering 8 F6Fs and 4 TBMs launched at 0805.

1544 Completed launching 8 F6Fs for CAP.

1547-1616 Completed recovering 8 F6Fs and 4 TBMs launched at 1150.

1827 Completed recovering 8 F6Fs launched at 1544.

1847 Secured from flight quarters. Air Department set to condition 14.

The Gunnery Department was at condition One Easy all day until 1907 as Japanese air raids were expected. They had not found the Task Group, but hit the forces off the beaches of Okinawa.

2333 Commenced zigzagging on base course 345°T, remaining in the same general area overnight.

GL Still hitting Okinawa. Expecting attack today, that is why we have been staying in 1 Easy.
2 Val's shot down over targets. We have CAP & ASP today. GL

GN Flew CAP and ASP again today. Belted ammo again today and have about 85,000 rounds ready by this time. Got some good news today and that was that a remnant of the Jap Navy came out and they were smashed around but good. They lost one wagon, two cruisers and three cans. Three cans also were left but burning. Looks like the war may be over soon we hope. Still operating in vicinity of Okinawa. GN
    (Note: 1 BB - YAMATO, 1 CL and 4 DDs were lost. Refer back to 7 April 1945)

Tuesday 10 April 1945   *Ryukyu Islands, Okinawa Invasion*

Steaming as before with Task Unit 58.2.1 off Okinawa. Received a report from the USS BROWN, operating 30 miles to the south, that her crew had an enemy submarine under attack.

0730 Sounded flight quarters.

0834 Completed launching 12 F6Fs for a fighter sweep over airfields at Tokuna Shima and Kikai Shima. The raid encountered bad weather over the target area, with heavy rain and hail. The "rocks in the clouds" (Hail) removed paint from the leading edges of wings and engine cowls. Pilots had visibility reduced to 1/4 mile in rain approaching the target, with very low to broken ceilings over targets. At Kikai Shima airfield (200' ceiling) they attacked AA positions and camouflaged revetments. Tokuna was obscured due to weather (zero-zero visibility), so Uke Shima, was targeted instead.

Near Uke Shima they sunk a small troop transport boat (resembling an LST), and strafed a small town.

0842 Gunnery Department secured from condition One Easy.

0903 Made daily inspection of the magazines. Conditions normal

1055 USS COLAHAN came alongside to starboard quarter to receive a transformer and gun parts.

1216 Completed recovering 11 F6Fs launched at 0834. The remaining Hellcat from that strike (Ens. Thomas Delehaunty) was separated from his group due to weather.

1233 One F6F en route from the USS RANDOLPH with photographs crashed into the water roughly 300 yards off our port quarter. USS WEDDERBURN recovered both the pilot and the photographs.

1302-1310 USS WEDDERBURN was alongside the starboard quarter to deliver the photographs.

1327 Recovered the straggling F6F launched at 0834 (Ens. Thomas Delehaunty).

1328 Commenced maneuvering to regain position in the formation.

1347 Regained position in the formation on course 060°T. Changed speed to 17 knots.

1435 USS ENTERPRISE, USS OAKLAND and 2 screening destroyers left the Task Group to report to Task Group 58.3.

1445 Gained new position in the formation, USS PITTSBURGH designated guide.

1507 Completed launching 12 F6Fs for a sweep over this mornings targets. Pilots encountered a solid weather front. Minami Daito Shima was attacked instead. Weather was still adverse, so bombing and rocket attacks[1] were made on buildings south of the airport.

1518 USS FLINT was designated guide.

1546 Gained station off guide, USS FLINT, course 230°T, bearing 130°T, 2,000 yards.

1828 Recovered 12 F6Fs launched at 1507. 1835 Changed course to 130°T, speed 20 knots.

1842-1942 Gunnery Department manned routine torpedo defense stations.

[1] The US Navy developed (with a Caltech 3.5 inch dia. solid fuel rocket motor) a Forward Firing Aircraft Rocket (FFAR) which utilized a modified 5 inch shell on the nose as a warhead. The speed was roughly 450 mph. They began use in late 1943. In mid 1944 the new High Velocity Aircraft Rocket (**HVAR**) became operational. It featured a 5 in rocket motor with nearly twice the speed (roughly 950 mph.), triple the 1 mile range, and almost twice the near 80 Lb. weight at 140 lbs.

Captain Kindell noted in the SOL as he left the bridge: *"Somewhere around midnight if we continue SE, we may pass close to Rasa Island. Check its position with our D.R. We are heading for a fueling rendezvous."*

GN Strike day for us. Made a morning and afternoon strike on some airfields that the Nips are supposedly using to harass our boys on Okinawa. Belted ammo again all day. That latter is getting to look like an all time job. GN

The Air Group Commander (Commander C.W. Rooney) made the following recommendations on the Aircraft Action Report:

"AGC suggestions for added installations in the F6F-5:

(1) One or two fighters of each CVL group should be equipped to carry ASH radar (AN/APS-4). On fighter sweeps in extreme weather or reduced visibility leaders could then make landfalls on strange coasts, confident of safety of the flight.

(2) Radar altimeters should be installed as soon as practicable. When flights are launched in extremely adverse weather where pilots must fly for hours practically on the wave tops these instruments would greatly alleviate pilot fatigue as well as greatly increasing the safety of possible night operations.

(3) Heaters should continue to be installed in new VF. In these latitudes a CAP at 20,000 feet reduces

pilot efficiency seriously after an hour. Windshield fogging is also a serious problem when steep descents are made."

This begins to give the reader a feel for what the pilots were up against as they flew the war, from the flight deck, to the doorstep of the enemy during this period. They were often attacking the enemy with very low ceilings, rain, hail, targets obscured by smoke, haze or cloud with possible zero-zero visibility, and turbulence. The enemy took objection to the affront of being bombed, rocketed or strafed by shooting back. Add to this mix of hazards, other aircraft in close proximity within those very same elements. Also, if the ordinance the pilot dispensed from his delivery platform flying at a very low altitude (lower then good practice due to weather) had no delayed fusing, and something does go boom, they then faced gravity defying debris violently coming up at them.

In a compilation of Combat Action Reports for this period, the following statement was made with regard to the morning raids launched 0830 on this date:

"The accomplishment of this twelve plane flight in staying together and getting through to the assigned target in spite of frontal weather conditions is regarded as best possible proof of the value of combat instrument instruction which all pilots have received."

Wednesday 11 April 1945   *Fueling and Replenishing Ammo*

Steaming as before with Task Unit 58.2.1 off Okinawa, retiring toward the southeast to a fueling area.
0430 Sounded flight quarters.
0453 Sounded torpedo defense.
0520 Completed launching 8 F6Fs for CAP and 4 TBMs for ASP.
0601 Secured from flight quarters. Air Department set to condition 14.
0602 Secured from torpedo defense. Dawn today brings low scud down to 200'and showers.
0655 Commenced maneuvering while making an approach on the assigned tanker.
0750 Came along port side of USS CHICOPEE. Fueling course 300°T, speed 10 knots.
0755-0801 USS MARSHALL was alongside port quarter. Transferred Ensign R.E. Fitzgerald for transport to USS WINDHAM BAY to pick up a replacement TBM.
0818 Transferred US Mail to the USS CHICOPEE.
0941-0945 USS LEWIS HANCOCK came alongside port quarter with officer messenger mail.
1008 Concluded pumping from USS CHICOPEE, having received 175,438 gallons of fuel oil and 36,525 gallons of aviation gasoline.
1026 Commenced maneuvering for flight operations. Showers with 1,500' overcast.
1035 Completed launching 2 TBMs for ASP and 9 F6Fs for CAP.
1059 Completed recovery of 8 F6Fs and 4 TBMs launched at 0520.
1051 Commenced maneuvering making an approach on ammunition ship, USS LASSEN.
1103 Secured from flight quarters.
1144 Came along port side of USS LASSEN.
1211 USS COLAHAN came alongside our port quarter to deliver officer messenger and US Mail, then cast off.
1323 USS THE SULLIVANS came alongside our port quarter to receive radio parts, then cast off.
1404 Completed rearming from USS LASSEN, having received bombs, rocket parts, and ammunition.
1408 AOM3c Harry Severson was admitted to sick bay for treatment of a fractured wrist received as the result of a fall. He had been taping guns on a F6F when he slipped from the edge of the flight deck into a gun bucket.
1458 Sounded flight quarters.
1520 Completed recovery of 9 F6Fs and 2 TBMs launched at 1035, and 1 replacement TBM flown over from the USS WINDHAM BAY by Ensign Fitzgerald.
1535 Commenced maneuvering to gain position on guide USS MILLICOMA.

1627 USS FLINT was designated guide, bearing 270°T, 2,000 yards.
1629-1639 USS HICKOX was alongside port quarter to deliver an oxygen pump.
INDEPENDENCE departed from the replenishment group and headed back toward Okinawa.
1820 Commenced zigzagging on base course 355°T.

GL We are refueling and rearming. I guess we could stay out indefinitely as we are going to take provisions on soon from a supply ship. Got a report that the destroyer Kidd was hit by a Tojo (Banzai). We had a movie in the hangar deck also. *GL* (Note: USS KIDD, TRATHEN and SAMUEL S. MILES took casualities)

GN Refuel and rearming day for us. Possibly stores will come aboard too for we are getting light in that commodity. *GN*

25
President Franklin D. Roosevelt Dies

Thursday 12 April 1945   *Ryukyu Islands, Okinawa Invasion - A New Commander*

Steaming as before with Task Unit 58.2.1 off Okinawa Shima with USS RANDOLPH, in Task Unit 58. 2.1 in cruising disposition 5-R, course 355°T, speed 20 knots. USS FLINT is guide, bearing 270°T, 2,000 yards. Air Department is in condition 14.
0523-0530 Launched 8 F6Fs. Four were tasked with low CAP over the group. The other four were assigned CAP over the line of radar picket destroyers. It was anticipated the Japanese would do their best against the fleet again today.
0844 Three bogies reported approaching the formation from 070°T, 10 miles.
0853 Bogies identified as a friendly CAP.
0859 Launched 8 F6Fs to relieve the 0530 launch.
0920-0934 Recovered 8 F6Fs launched at 0530.
0952 Changed position in formation. New station off guide, USS FLINT on course 180°T, speed 20 knots, bearing 270°T, 1,500 yards. This formation change was made to tighten distance between ships.
1203 Completed launching 8 F6Fs to relieve the 0859 launch.
1227 Completed recovery of 8 F6Fs, launched at 0859.
1440 Flying RAPCAP, the FDO on the picket DD vectored the two sections (4 Hellcats, 2 per section) to bogies 15 miles from the DD.
1455 Ensign Thomas M. Delehaunty, flying at 5,000' with Lt.(Jg) Carleton T. Jones, sighted 3 Zeros with bombs strapped to the bottom of their fuselages, obviously Kamikazes. The Zekes were at the same altitude, on the same course, in a flat V formation. Delehaunty shot down the trailing Zeke on the left (cockpit 6 o'clock level) and Jones fired a long burst at the trailing Zeke on the right. Both Hellcat pilots pulled up left and right respectively and commenced a second run on the remaining two Zekes. Delehaunty shot down the lead Zeke (his second kill) from 4 o'clock level with a burst into the engine. Jones, seeing his Zeke split S, followed him down. He applied water injection and jettisoned his belly tank to catch his prey. Jones made the kill on his second pass from 500' astern. His victim crashed into the sea in flames.
1503 Completed launching 8 F6Fs to relieve the 1203 launch.
1509 Sounded torpedo defense. Several more bogies were reported approaching from the north. At the same time, our ships close in to Okinawa were taking a heavy attack.
1515 Increased speed to 25 knots.
1519 Sounded general quarters.
1538 Completed recovery of 8 F6Fs, launched at 1203.
1554 Set condition One Easy. All enemy aircraft in our vicinity were shot down or had turned back.

1804-1808 Recovered 8 F6Fs, launched at 1503.

1834 Secured from flight quarters. Air Department set to condition 14.

1958 Gunnery Department secured from condition One. Air Department stayed in condition 14.

2344 Changed course to 090°T.

This morning, Japanese command had a difficult time grasping the entire scope and location of the invading forces. It was not until near 1500 that Japanese leaders felt they had a sufficient understanding of the situation.

During the morning Japanese Army fighters were sent out from Kyushu. Fifteen at 0700, and three groups of twenty four each from between 1100 to 1200 for the 400 mile flight toward Okinawa.   Thirty four Shiden (George was the Allied designation) fighters fought over Kikaiga-shima (north of Okinawa).

Forty torpedo bombers with Okas hit the fleet from 1445 to 1600. They were supported by approximately sixty Army Kamikazes. Twenty fighter bombers (with 2 reconnaissance planes) also attacked the fleet at roughly the same time.

Fourteen land based bombers attacked at dusk, from 1915 to 1940. A night attack force of thirty heavy Bombers and Gingas struck from 1940 to 2145.

The cost to our ships and the causalities to the crews manning them was high. The Japanese would expend experienced aviators and needed aircraft. The task forces around Okinawa claimed nearly 300 Japanese planes shot down.

Our outer defense and early warning line of picket destroyers had been taking a pounding, with the USS CASSIN YOUNG, USS LINDSEY, USS PURDY, and USS STANLY taking hits. USS MANNERT L. ABELE was sunk. DDs BENNION, ZELLARS, CONKLIN, DEs RALL, RIDDLE, WHITEHURST, LCSs, a LSM, and the battleship USS TENNESSEE were also damaged.

Harry S. Truman

Early this evening, at 4:35 P.M (US Eastern time zone), in Warm Springs Georgia, President Franklin D. Roosevelt suddenly died of a cerebral Hemorrhage. Former Assistant Secretary of the Navy, former Governor of New York, in office for 12 years, Franklin Delano Roosevelt had been responsible for the creation of the INDEPENDENCE class of carriers. He left behind an unimaginable void to fill. Approximately three hours after FDR's death, Vice President Harry S. Truman was sworn in to become our 32nd* president. A new commander was now hastened to the helm, the burden of decision and weight of wartime command, suddenly tumbled upon his shoulders. (* 33rd if counting **non concurrent** double terms of Grover Cleveland. Harry Truman had no middle name, just the initial S, to honor both of his grandfathers.)

GL *Early in the night a bogie was splashed by a night chicken. We could see it from the ship. 9 planes were shot down by gunfire and planes. We are sending up only CAP today as Tokyo says they are sending out an all out attack again. TG 58.2 are in 1 Easy, 120 miles from Okinawa. Judy & Oscar were splashed by CAP near TG. Pilots report good hunting up till now 28 Vals, 12 Bettys, and Jills were splashed. USS Cassin Young took a banzai. Bogies are all around. LST & minesweeper just took banzai. Our pilots have shot down 5 planes, Zekes. Up till 5 o'clock 89 planes have been splashed. Our pickets are under constant attack, have splashed six Zekes. DD USS Stanly has been hit. Expecting lots of trouble tonight.* **GL**

Friday 13 April 1945   *Ryukyu Islands, Okinawa Invasion*

0430 Steaming as before. Sounded flight quarters.
0457 Sounded routine general quarters.
0531 Completed launching 8 F6Fs as CAP. Today, all day, we will fly the same type of Combat Air Patrols as yesterday. Four were tasked with low CAP over the group. The other four were assigned CAP over our line of radar picket destroyers.
0557 All Departments set to One Easy.

This Morning, they received news of the death of President, Franklin D. Roosevelt.

0859-0902 Launched 8 F6Fs. Clear skies with light wind will prevail thru the 16th.
0911-0922 Recovered 8 F6Fs launched at 0531.
1030 Passed floating debris that appeared to be part of a wrecked aircraft.
1042 USS MILLER reported sighting a life raft believed to contain two Japanese (one living and one dead), and is investigating. The MILLER rescued the one Japanese survivor.
1249 Completed launching 8 F6Fs for CAP.
1308 Completed recovery of 8 F6Fs launched at 0902.
1506 Completed launching 8 F6Fs for CAP.
1536 Completed recovery of 8 F6Fs launched at 1249.
1556 Secured from condition One Easy.
1815 Completed recovery of 8 F6Fs launched at 1506.
1829 Secured from flight quarters. Air Department was set to condition 14.
2322 Commenced zigzagging on base course 300°T.

GN *Same story. Standing by waiting for the Japs to come out after us. It seems that they do start but are always thwarted in one way or another. If the CAP fails the pickets generally get them. These cans have been taking a beating in the last few days and a goodly number of them are hurt in one way or another. I guess we have to pay some price though. Ran the total to over a hundred Nips shot down in two days.* **GN**

HC *C.A.P. over Okinawa. Received word that the president died. It's a shame he couldn't see the end of the war.* **HC**

Saturday 14 April 1945   *Ryukyu Islands, Okinawa Invasion*

0430 Steaming as before off Okinawa. Sounded flight quarters.
0531 Completed launching 4 F6Fs as CAP over our radar picket line of destroyers.
0800 Half masted the colors following motions of OTC, due to the death of President, Franklin D. Roosevelt.
0901 Launched 12 F6Fs and 8 TBMs. 4 F6Fs relieved the destroyer picket CAP. The other 16 aircraft proceeded out on a strike on Okinawa. Reported to have been *"poorly coordinated and poorly executed"* due to poor communications with the CASCU (radio frequency handoff problems and cluttered

radio channels), the Hellcats hit *"harmless deserted buildings"* near Machinato Airfield. Avengers did better striking a damaged radio station and barracks, as well as caves and trenches near Naha.

0943 Completed recovery of 4 F6Fs launched at 0531.

0954 Formation changed to 5-V, axis rotated to 080°T. Commenced maneuvering to gain station in new disposition.

1148 Completed launching 8 F6Fs. 4 F6Fs relieved the destroyer picket CAP and 4 formed a low CAP around our group. INDEPENDENCE maintained these patrols all afternoon, relieving the CAP at 1500.

1239 Changed course to 095°T, changed speed to 26 knots. Completed recovering 12 F6Fs and 7 TBMs launched at 0901.

1327 Sounded torpedo defense, on report of inbound enemy aircraft.

1336 Observed smoke on the horizon from an enemy aircraft shot down by fighters from the USS RANDOLPH.

1337 Changed course to 260°T.

1342 Observed firing on the horizon bearing 295°T, as Task Group 58.1 shot down an enemy airplane with AA fire.

1349 Observed firing on the horizon bearing 000°T.

1353 Observed a large plume of smoke on the horizon, bearing 005°T, believed to be from an enemy aircraft shot down by fighters from the USS YORKTOWN.

1406 Observed firing on the horizon bearing 010°T.

1500 Completed launching 8 F6Fs.

1532 Completed recovery of 8 F6Fs launched at 1148, and 1 TBM launched at 0901. This TBM piloted by Lt.(jg) B.B. LeTulle made an emergency landing and refueled at Kadena Airfield on Okinawa.

1544 Secured from torpedo defense. Gunnery Department set to condition One Easy.

1831-1839 Recovered 8 F6Fs launched at 1500.

1841 Gunnery Department set to condition One Easy, as had become standard near sunset.

1846 Darkened ship.

1913 Secured from flight quarters. Air Department set to condition 14.

1940 Enemy planes reported 20 miles out.

1944 Enemy plane, shot down 15 miles away, was visible burning to the north.

1945 Changed speed to 23 knots and course to 210°T. Several bogies reported approaching. Ships in this formation opened fire.

1948 Sounded general quarters. Observed firing by several ships of TG 58.2 growing persistent. For the next hour and 30 minutes, enemy planes were around the fringes of the formation. The OTC maneuvered the formation in a series of emergency turns during this time.

1953 Changed course to 050°T.

2018 Bogie reported to be closing from 358°T, 12 miles. Firing by pickets was observed on the horizon, bearing 020°T.

2024 Bogie reported to be closing from 250°T, 5 miles. Observed a cluster of 10 or more flares just outside the screen, bearing 340°T.

2025 Changed course to 190°T. This Task Group commenced firing on an enemy aircraft. The INDEPENDENCE, having no 5" guns, remained silent.

2029 Enemy plane previously fired upon, was crippled and seen to crash and burn fiercely, bearing 350°T, distance 6 miles.

2030 Changed course to 250°T.

2032 Observed a cluster of 12 flares, believed dropped from an enemy plane, bearing 020°T, distance 10 miles. Two minutes later INDEPENDENCE crew observed firing in the direction of a new group of 12 flares, bearing 030°T, 7 miles.

2041 All ships in the formation commenced firing on enemy aircraft which had entered the formation, flying overhead.

2045 Bogie reported closing the formation, bearing 130°T, distance 9 miles.

2047 Observed firing on the horizon, bearing 220°T.
2105 Bogie reported closing on the formation from 000°T, 8 miles. Changed course to 060°T.
2125 Secured from general quarters. Gunnery Department set condition One Easy.
2139 Gunnery Department secured from condition One Easy, set to condition 3.
2321 Commenced zigzagging on base course 250°T.

GN Got off a strike this morning. Gave us something to do anyhow. Was getting tired of playing poker which has been going on for two days. Belted ammo again all day and did a good job even though both machines are going to pieces slowly. One of our TBM's landed on Okinawa today because of radio trouble. Had bogies all around for two hours in the evening and we stayed at GQ all the time. One was shot down close by but other disappeared. Had us really going for a while with flares on both the port and starboard side and us going straight ahead. Forgot to mention the news of the President's death in yesterday's report. GN

AD Planes striking Island Today. At about 2000 tonight we went to GQ. Jap planes were all around us dropping windows and flares. There was plenty of shooting going on too. They dropped their fish but luckily none of our ships were hit. One plane was hit and after burning furiously it hit the drink. This sailor was scared as hell. They were shooting over my head. Secured from GQ 2200. AD

HC C.A.P. over Okinawa. They damaged 2 of our cans which were in our picket line, bogies came out this evening and dropped flares. We got 2 of them and the rest took a powder, lucky guys. First time I saw flares, and I didn't like it in the least. HC

GL Had bogie early in the morning, it was splashed. 70 miles from Okinawa. Today we are sending in strikes. CAP shot down 9 planes. Can see some of them burning on horizon. Intercepted Jap message calling for all out attack against 58. Tonight little after TD we had bogies around us. Night chicken splashed Betty starboard beam, we could see him burning. They started dropping flares all around us and all hell broke loose. Ships shot down two more. One passed overhead with light on and was splashed. Got word USS Sigsbee was hit, Miami took her in tow. Secured from 1 Easy around 22:00. GL (USS SIGSBEE took a kamikaze hit killing 23. She was towed to Guam, then on to Pearl Harbor where a complete 60 feet of her stern was replaced.)

Sunday 15 April 1945   *Ryukyu Islands, Okinawa Invasion, Kyushu Strike*

0430 Steaming as before off Okinawa. Sounded flight quarters.
0537 Completed launching 8 F6Fs, 4 for low CAP around the formation, and 4 for RAPCAP over the destroyer radar picket line.
0842-0844 Launched 4 F6Fs to relieve the RAPCAP over the destroyer radar picket line.
0939 Completed recovering 8 F6Fs launched at 0537.
1141-1201 Completed launching 8 F6Fs and 7 TBMs for a support strike against the enemy on southern Okinawa. 4 of the 8 F6Fs were utilized to relieve the RAPCAP over the destroyer radar picket line. No aerial opposition was encountered during the Okinawa strike, which targeted an ammo dump and buildings near Naha, and towns along the SE coast (Okota, Shinzato and Sashik). The TBMs struck an artillery position & ammo dump, a barracks and possible gun positions.
1205 Completed recovering 4 F6Fs launched at 0844.
1322 Completed launching 8 F6Fs for a special combined 90 plane fighter sweep over southern Kyushu. The primary target for INDEPENDENCE raiders was to have been Kushira Airfield, facing Shibushi Bay to the east. The 3 Japanese airfields were located roughly 3 miles apart on Osumi Peninsula between Kagoshima and Shibushi Bays.
Launched 300 miles out, Lt Commander Robert A. Weatherup, leading the INDEPENDENCE Hellcats, noticed a large number of Japanese aircraft (estimated 100) on the ground at Kanoya, with aircraft taxing

out for takeoff. Weatherup elected to divert to take advantage of the opportunity and led the VF-46 Hellcats for a run against Kanoya, shooting down 2 single engine fighters as they were taking off, splashing the first one on a stern pass at 400', followed by a high wingover killing the second one at 800' while climbing.

Ensign Peter Kooyenga shot down a single engine fighter, from above, roughly 75' off the runway. Lt.(jg) A.W.C. Thomas was in pursuit of an unidentified plane when he saw a twin engine plane on his port beam. Thomas turned into the Japanese twin and shot it down from level at 4 o'clock. Fourteen Japanese aircraft were listed as probably destroyed on the ground (with credit going to Lt. Comdr. Weatherup, Lt.(jg) Gentry, Lt.(jg) Sparks, Lt. Schroeder and Lt. Rivers). Ensign Kooyenga returned with a large hole shot in his wing by AA, landing safely back aboard with a shredded aileron.

1330 INDEPENDENCE held memorial services on the hangar deck in honor of late President Franklin D. Roosevelt. By order from OTC we had already half-masted the colors from 1100-1130.

1443 Completed launching 3 F6Fs relieving the RAPCAP over the destroyer radar picket line.
1540 Completed recovering 12 F6Fs and 7 TBMs launched at 1201.
1654 Completed recovering 8 F6Fs launched at 1322.
1727-1731 USS OWEN was alongside the starboard quarter to receive mail.
This evening, in the ready room, **VF-46 celebrated the one year anniversary of its commissioning** with a cake baked by INDEPENDENCE bakers and brandy medicinally dispensed by "Doc" Hudson.
2250 Two destroyers were detached to investigate a disappearing surface contact. It was thought to be a possible submarine. As stated, it disappeared. Not to be found.

Captain Kindell noted in the SOL: " *It looks like we might be heading to a fueling area.*
Follow signals as to courses and speeds as sent by the OTC in Randolph.
Courses should be southerly and southeasterly. Our position is 1.5 110, Randolph is guide at 15.250,
Axis is 180°T, guide bears 090°T 2800 yds.
New voice calls go into effect at midnight. No friendly contacts are expected during the night.
Call me if anything unusual shows up."

HC Hit Kanoya, Kyushu. Shot up planes on ground and shot four out of the air (our air group). One plane came back with a hole in its stbd wing big enough to drive a truck through. HC

GN Off on another mission today. Still looking for the airfields from which the Nips are operating. Sent one deckload strike of bombs and rockets over. Didn't hear the results. Prepared a load of rockets about 1300 for an emergency takeoff and they did something with them. Some of our fighters together with some from the Randolph caught some Japs leaving a field in the vicinity and really gave them the works. They shot three out of the air boosting their total to seventeen and shot up everything on the ground that was worth shooting. I don't know how many the Randolph got credit for but it was probably good. At this time it can fairly accurately be said that the Japs can't have too many planes left. Our pilots now claim that shooting the Nips is like shooting sitting ducks so they must be in a bad way for trained pilots also. So much the better in my estimation. Belted ammo again all day. Expect to refuel and rearm tomorrow. Had about fifteen depth charges go off about 8:30 at night and fairly close by. GN

Monday 16 April 1945   *Retiring to Refuel and Rearm*

Steaming as before off Okinawa with Task Unit 58.2.1 with USS RANDOLPH (OTC and guide), in cruising disposition 5-V, base course 145°T, speed 22 knots, bearing 090°T, 2,800 yards. Air Department is in condition 14. We are retiring toward the southeast to refuel and reprovision.
0650 Commenced maneuvering to gain position in the fueling formation.
0723 Commenced maneuvering to gain position on ammunition ship USS VESUVIUS.
0827 Came along port side of the USS VESUVIUS to begin rearming operations.

0913-0925 USS BENHAM was alongside the port quarter to transfer guard mail and US Mail.

1049 Cast off from the USS VESUVIUS having received bombs, rocket parts, fuses, ammunition and 20 spools of line for the throwing gun*.   (*Used to shoot a light line to another vessel to enable pulling over progressively heaver lines for underway replenishment, transfer of personnel, etc.)

1050 Commenced maneuvering to gain position on the assigned tanker, USS CACHE.

1133 Came along port side of USS CACHE to begin taking on fuel.

1156-1205 USS STEPHEN POTTER came alongside the port quarter to receive radio parts.

1349 Cast off from the USS CACHE having received 241,197 gallons of fuel oil, 34,825 gallons of aviation gasoline, 20 drums of lubricating oil, 3 fifty foot lengths of 2 1/2" fire hose, 1 bottle of helium.

1350 Commenced maneuvering to gain position in column astern Cruiser Division Ten, and other various ships, for AA gunnery exercises on towed sleeves, completing gunnery exercises at 1455.

1500 INDEPENDENCE commenced maneuvering for flight operations.

1508 Completed launching 8 F6Fs assigned to CAP, and 4 TBMs for ASP.

1510 Secured from flight quarters. Air Department set condition 13. Formation changed to disposition 5-V (modified).

1558-1604 USS CUSHING was along the starboard side amidships.

1650 USS RANDOLPH designated guide, course 020°T, bearing 315°T, 2,600 yards.

1700 Departed the replenishing group and steamed toward an operating area off Okinawa Shima.

1727 Sounded flight quarters.

1743 Recovered 1 F6F launched at 1508 due to oil leak.

1820-1832 Recovered 7 F6Fs and 4 TBMs launched at 1508. Changed course to 270°T, speed 16 knots.

1837 Secured from flight quarters. Air Department set to condition 14.

2330 Changed course to 310°T.

AD No attacks on our group. Saw movie on the hangar deck and also mail call. What more could a guy ask for? Home. 104 planes shot down by CAP. AD

GN Refueled and rearmed while underway. Brought aboard a goodly number of belted .50 cal but it looks like we'll have to keep on belting anyhow. Heard we are going back to 58.4 today and its quite possible we'll really have to go to work again. It seems that there will only be two outfits out here now, 58.2 and 58.4. The others may be retiring or just splitting up. Don't know at the moment. GN

Tuesday 17 April 1945   *Ryukyu Islands, Okinawa Invasion*
Task Group 58.2 dissolved

Steaming as before off Okinawa with Task Unit 58.2.1. Task Group 58.2 has been dissolved. INDEPENDENCE has been operating with only one other carrier (USS RANDOLPH) since 10 April. USS HANCOCK, assigned to this group, took a kamikaze hit on 7 April 1945 (killing 72 and wounding 82) requiring repairs, steamed to Ulithi Atoll.

0504 INDEPENDENCE took charge of USS FLINT and DesDiv 105 on orders of the Task Group Commander, Rear Admiral G.F. Bogan, and left the formation of TG 58.2 to proceed to join TG 58.4. Steered on various courses at various speeds to gain position in TG 58.4, formation disposition 5-R.

0600 Reported for Duty to CTG 58.4 in USS YORKTOWN, guide bearing 090°T, 4,000 yards. Besides INDEPENDENCE, the other carriers in the group are USS YORKTOWN and USS LANGLEY. Since CVL-22 last operated with this group, USS INTREPID had been hit and returned to Ulithi Atoll.

0620 Disposition changed to 5-VB.

0752 Commenced zigzagging on base course 170°T, Plan No. 24.

0822 Sounded torpedo defense on order of OTC and CTG 58.4. (Rear Admiral G.F. Bogan)

0824 Completed launching 20 F6Fs. Twelve were for TCAP over Okinawa. Eight Hellcats were for CAP over this group, the two divisions led by Lt. Frank D. Fogde and Lt. Angus T. Morrison under direction of the INDEPENDENCE FDO.

0830 Secured from flight quarters. Air Department set to condition 11.

0831 Sounded general quarters. Enemy planes were reported in the area.

Hellcats in the CAP were vectored out to meet the threat. They were advised that a dog fight was in progress 40 miles ahead and that an attack on the TG was approaching. At 30 miles out the F6F-5s were instructed to orbit at angels 20, then given vectors toward the northwest, then west for the intercept. Lt. Frank D. Fogde tallyhoed three Judys (with radial engines) flying SE at angels 12. Judy #1 & #2 were 500 yards ahead and left of Judy #3.

Lt. Fogde made a highside run putting bursts into Judy #3, passing over it with a sharp left turn to come around on the tails of #1 & #2. He fired 1800 rounds at the 3 Judys, most of them into the tails of #1 & #2 from astern. He shot down both #1 & #2 Judys, following them down from 8,000' to 2,000', getting close enough to get Japanese oil on his windshield.

Lt. Angus T. Morrison attacked Judy #3 from 5 o'clock astern. He continued to close, putting rounds into the engine, without apparent effect. *"Exasperated at this refusal of the Jap plane to burst into flames Lt. Morrison bore closer and closer until pulling out above, he clipped the vertical stabilizer off the Judy and took a 12 pound portion of it with him, 14" X 12", which embedded in the leading edge of his starboard wing 18" outboard of his guns. In colliding he also took a good sized nick out of the two propeller blades 4" long by 1 1/2" deep. The Judy finally succumbed to these unexpected offensive tactics, spiraled in from 1,000' and seen to explode as it hit the water."*

The Judys were thought to have been equipped with armor or self-sealing fuel tanks (they were not). They did not burn easily when hit, as had been the norm with many Japanese aircraft.

0859 Changed course to 000°T to recover aircraft.

0927 Observed TG 58.3, bearing 300°T, 14 miles, firing on an unidentified aircraft.

0928 Observed enemy aircraft taken under fire by TG 58.3 burst into flames and crash within the formation. An empty parachute was observed from the plane, floating down within the formation.

0930 Bogie reported closing on this formation bearing 300°T, 9 miles.

0937 Observed TG 58.3 firing on another unidentified aircraft.

1020 Recovered 2 F6Fs launched at 0824. One Hellcat was flown by Lt. Morrison, landing with the piece of enemy stabilizer embedded in his wing (Photo on right below).

Secured from general quarters.

Gunnery Department set to condition One Easy.

1048 Followed movements of OTC half-masting the colors.

1056 Gunnery Department set to condition One by orders of OTC.

1100 Two blocked the colors following movements of OTC.

1139 Changed course to 070°T to recover aircraft.

1204 Completed recovery of 18 F6Fs.

1324 Completed launching 12 F6Fs for a TCAP over Okinawa.

1446 Completed launching 8 F6Fs for a CAP over this group.

1542-1654 USS HAZELWOOD was alongside to receive 48,551 gallons of fuel oil.

1701 This TG changed the formation to disposition 5-VB.

1727 Completed recovering 12 F6Fs launched at 1324.

1813 USS BATAAN reported to this TG for duty.

1827 Followed movements of USS BENHAM half masting colors.

(The USS BENHAM had causalities from a near miss by a Kamikaze and friendly Naval gunfire.)

Lt. Angus T. Morrison with damaged wing.

1833 Completed recovering 8 F6Fs launched at 1446, and 2 F6F(N)s from USS YORKTOWN.

The 2 YORKTOWN night fighters were maintained in ready alert for immediate launching until USS LANGLEY took over night fighter duty at 2300.

1845 Gunnery Department set to routine condition One.

1857 Two blocked the colors following movements of USS BENHAM.

1944 Gunnery Department secured from condition One.

2200 Changed course to 250°T. TG 58.4 formed cruising disposition 5-R.

GL TF 58.4 had GQ and we went into Easy 1 all day. Our fighters shot down 3 Judys. One of our planes landed with a piece of Jap plane imbedded in his wing. There was firing everywhere on the horizon. Heard Intrepid & Enterprise was hit and headed for repairs. Score for yesterday 186 planes, 76 by ships, the rest by planes. Had bogie at 30,000 feet – turned out to be a Betty and was splashed. GL

AD Okinawa. 0845 GQ. Task Group on our port side were under attack and put up a terrific sky full of flack. No Japs reached our group. Could see this action clearly. The Task Group shot down 7 planes and the CAP 72. AD

This may be a good time to remind the reader that diary entries involving numbers of combat statics often disagree and may not be accurate. They are well intended in jotting down the war and facts surrounding them as they understood it. They were recorded without the benefit of time and historical analysis to verify validity. And who knows what their sources may have been. But the diary entries give us insight to the war as the crew lived it, felt it, and thought they understood it. It is thru the lens of the human perspective, often made hazy thru that wonderfully descriptive phrase, "The Fog of War".

Wednesday 18 April 1945   *Ryukyu Islands, Okinawa Invasion*

Steaming as before off Okinawa in Task Unit 58.4.1 with USS YORKTOWN (OTC & guide), USS LANGLEY and USS BATAAN. Rear Admiral A.W. Radford CTU in YORKTOWN.
0135 Commenced zigzagging, Plan No.6, on base course 250°T.
0143 Made an emergency turn to the left to 190°T due to reported sonar contact, bearing 020°T. This was later classified to be a non-submarine.
0249 Resumed zigzagging on base course 260T.
0454-0558 Manned (routine) general quarters stations.
0509 Completed launching 12 F6Fs for target CAP over Okinawa, and 2 F6F(N)s for return to USS YORKTOWN.
0628 Secured from flight quarters. Air Department set to condition 13.
0730 Sounded flight quarters. Winds are increasing with scattered clouds.
0816 Completed launching 8 F6Fs for CAP.
0903 Completed recovery of 12 F6Fs launched at 0509.
1014 Completed launching 8 TBMs and 4 F6Fs for a support strike directed by the CASCU. The targets were a hill honeycombed with caves and pillboxes with possible stores. The target area near the southeastern end of Okinawa, was hit with bombs and rockets, then strafed. The assigned area was said to contain an ammo dump, but no secondary explosions were observed.
1137 Completed launching 8 F6Fs for CAP.
1204 Completed recovery of 8 F6Fs launched at 0816.
1332 Completed recovery of 8 TBMs and 4 F6Fs launched at 1014.
1432 USS MISSOURI designated guide, bearing 213°T, 1,800 yards.
1442 Completed launching 8 F6Fs for CAP.
1501 Completed recovering 8 F6Fs launched at 1137.
1745 Sounded flight quarters.
1826 Completed recovery of 8 F6Fs launched at 1442.
Captain Kindell noted in the SOL as he left the bridge: *" We are not far from Daito Jima so get a radar bearing on it from time to time. No other landfall is expected. No friendly contacts are expected."*

GN Strike day for us. We are going in to support the army on Okinawa. Had a morning and noon strike. Not too much otherwise. Did hear some depth charges go off nearby and one can of our group was credited with sinking a sub. This is about the third day in a row that tin cans in our group have picked up some unfamiliar sounds and dropped ash cans. GN

AD Okinawa. Early morning we contacted subs. Cans were firing depth charges. Otherwise all was quiet during the day. AD

Note: On this date, IJN submarine I-56*[1.] (Shoda) was <u>reported</u> sunk by action involving our DDs COLLETT, HEERMANN, MCCORD, MERTZ and UHLMANN along with VT-47 from USS BATAAN. The action occurred roughly 106 miles northeast, 327° from Minami-Daito. Accurate operational records from sunk submarines are lost when a sub lays entombed in roughly 2,500 fathoms of salt water. Only oil and floating debris, so briefly on the surface, serve as a headstone to mark its grave. If position reports are correct, between the hours of 2000 (last night) on 17 April, and 0800 this morning USS INDEPENDENCE had moved southwest almost directly across (within 5 miles) from where the sub was reported sunk (based only on a straight line plot of the position reports, without plotting known course changes). It is possible that the sonar contact made at 0143 today, recorded in the Deck Log as a non-sub, MAY very well have been IJN submarine I-56 prior to her sinking. We will never know. She was lost with 116 crew members & six "Kaiten" pilots. (*[1.] Actual Sub ID is still unknown with certainty)

Thursday 19 April 1945   *Ryukyu Islands, Okinawa Invasion*

0430 Steaming as before off Okinawa in Task Unit 58.4.1. Sounded flight quarters.

0525 Launched 8 F6Fs for a CAP over the destroyer radar picket line.

0549 Launched 12 F6F-5s and 8 TBMs for a special strike as a concerted effort by all carriers. We would hit the Japanese positions in heavily concentrated strikes in support of our troops.

INDEPENDENCE aircraft joined with squadrons from the LANGLEY and BATAAN to bomb (500lb. GP), rocket and strafe the village of Shuri.

This support was later described in a dispatch to the fleet by our ground forces as "magnificent".

0843-0853 Recovered 8 F6Fs launched at 0525.

0906-0923 Completed recovering 8 TBMs and 12 F6Fs launched at 0549.

0948 Secured from flight quarters. Air Department set to condition 13.

1347 Air Department called to flight quarters, however a weather front passing Okinawa brought rain and zero-zero visibility necessitating the cancelation of an afternoon strike.

1452 Secured from flight quarters. Air Department set to condition 14.

From March 23rd thru today, Japan had sent out over 1400 sorties against the US fleet and our forces at Okinawa. This included mine laying and reconnaissance. Roughly 600 of those planes were acknowledged as lost by the Japanese (source - Fading Victory The Diary of Matome Ugaki 1941-1945).

A 1945 US Air Force photo of Ie Shima, 2.9 miles north, off Okinawa.

*AD 4/19/45 Kyushu All is quiet around Task group. Ernie Pyle reported killed on Ie Shima by Jap machine gun fire. He was on the Cabot for a while. **AD***

GN Made another early morning strike on Okinawa supporting the army. Had a real load ready to go in the afternoon but that was called off on account of bad weather. That latter was probably one of the biggest strikes this ship has ever prepared to send against the enemy but as luck would have it we had to put it all away. Got word that Ernie Pyle was killed on one of the nearby islands. Big guns in the wagons of our group could be seen and heard shelling the island. Made a $5 bet* with Joe Tinta that Yanks would come out better in American League race than Cleveland. Hope I'm well on my way before it comes time to collect. GN (* George won the bet with Joe .. No record if he collected)

Note: Ernie Pyle died yesterday April 18th on Ie Shima. The crew got word today. Riding in a jeep near a road junction, they were fired on by a Japanese machine gun. Taking cover in a ditch with Lt. Colonel Joseph B. Coolidge and three other men, Ernie caught a bullet in the left temple. He died instantly.

Friday 20 April 1945   *Ryukyu Islands*, Refueling and *Replenishing*

Steaming as before toward a replenishing area in Task Unit 58.4.1 with USS YORKTOWN, USS LANGLEY and USS BATAAN, in cruising disposition 5-R zigzagging on base course 095°T, speed 22 knots. YORKTOWN is guide bearing 140°T, 4,000 yards. 0442-0542 Gunnery Department manned all torpedo defense stations.

0515 Sounded flight quarters.
0623 Commenced maneuvering to enter the fueling formation and come alongside ammunition ship USS VESUVIUS.
0655 Secured from flight quarters. Air Department remained in condition 14.
0711 Came along port side of USS VESUVIUS, speed 10 knots. Guide is USS NESHANIC bearing 028°T, 5,500 yards.
0747 USS MELVIN came along port side to transfer mail, casting off at 0754.
0800 Mustered crew on stations. Rain, 200' ceilings and low visibility.
0918 Cast off from USS VESUVIUS having received bombs, rocket parts, fuses and 40mm rounds.
0925 Commenced maneuvering to take position 1,000 yards astern of our assigned tanker.
0940 Sounded flight quarters.
1004 Launched 4 F6Fs for CAP. Cruiser observation planes are flying ASP.
1007 Secured from flight quarters. Air Department stayed in condition 14.
1048 Commenced maneuvering to approach tanker USS CIMARRON, course 230°T, speed 10 knots.
1133 USS NORMAN SCOTT came alongside the port quarter.
1138 Came along side USS CIMMARON.
1207 Having completed transferring 3 officers and 4 enlisted personnel reporting for duty to this ship, USS NORMAN SCOTT cast off.
1249 USS REYNOLDS (DE-42) commenced delivering droppable fuel tanks on our port quarter.
1410 Sounded flight quarters.
1436 USS CIMARRON cast off having received from it 245,000 gallons of fuel oil, 35,100 gallons of aviation gasoline, 6 drums of lubricating oil, and stores. At 1437 the USS REYNOLDS cast off.
1454 Changed course to 030°T, speed 18 knots.
1503-1506 Recovered 4 F6Fs launched at 1004. Changed course to 220°T.
1525 Changed speed to 10 knots. Changed course to 280°T.
1532 USS MERCURY was designated guide, bearing 197°T, 3,700 yards.
1555 USS MCGOWAN came alongside the port quarter.
1647 USS MCGOWAN cast off having delivered 25 droppable fuel tanks and 1 aircraft propeller.
1700 USS YORKTOWN designated guide, bearing 140°T, 4,000 yards.
1720 Commenced maneuvering to gain station off our guide.
1736 Commenced zigzagging on base course 320°T, speed 20 knots.
1826 Secured from flight quarters. Air Department is in condition 14. Changed speed to 22 knots.
2356 Commenced zigzagging on base course 355°T, speed 22 knots (224 rpm).

AD Refueled, resupplied, rearmed. Movie on the hangar deck and mail call. AD

Steaming toward an operating area for support of the troops on Okinawa.

0044 Gunnery set to condition One, two unidentified aircraft reported on radar near the Task Group.

0142 Gunnery Department set to condition 3, the aircraft having been shot down by night fighters.

GL Splashed 1 Betty early this AM. Could see him go down in flames. GL

0350 Sounded flight quarters.

0452-0456 Launched 8 F6Fs for CAP.

0507 Changed speed to 22 knots, course to 070°T. Commenced maneuvering to form disposition 5-V. Guide is USS YORKTOWN, bearing 140°T, 4,000 yards.

0546 Changed the formation to cruising disposition 5-VB, axis 020°T.

0811-0816 Launched 8 F6Fs for CAP. Visibility 12 miles with scattered clouds at 4,000'.

0828 Recovered 1 F6F launched at 0456.

0835-0840 Recovered 7 F6Fs launched at 0456.

1110-1114 Launched 8 F6Fs for CAP over Okinawa.

1159-1212 Recovered 8 F6Fs launched at 0816.

1302 Completed launching 4 TBMs led by Lt. Norris E. Hanford for a strike against enemy positions on Okinawa. Under the direction of CASCU with planes from our 3 other carriers, the Avengers attacked a barracks (with bombs) near Yonabaru, and enemy machine gun positions (using rockets) south of the barracks.

1435 Secured from torpedo defense. Gunnery set to condition One Easy.

1440-1445 Launched 8 F6Fs for CAP.

1534 Completed recovering 1 TBM launched at 1302, and 8 F6Fs launched at 1114. The TBM had developed a hydraulic leak and returned.

1558 Gunnery Department set to condition One by order of OTC.

1635-1640 Recovered 3 TBMs launched at 1302.

1733 Gunnery Department set to condition 3.

1827 Completed recovery of 8 F6Fs launched at 1445.

1843 Darkened ship, secured from flight quarters. Air Department set to condition 14. Gunnery Department set to condition One.

1942 Secured from torpedo defense. Gunnery Department set to condition 3.

1947 Formed cruising disposition 5-R.

2001 Formed cruising disposition 5-V.

2046 Changed course to 000°T, sounded torpedo defense. Gunnery Department set to condition One. Destroyers in the Task Group were firing on an unidentified aircraft approaching the formation.

2117 Secured from torpedo defense. Gunnery Department set to condition 3. The enemy aircraft retired beyond range of our radar.

2200 Formed cruising disposition 5-R.

2341 Gunnery Department set to condition One by order of OTC (unidentified aircraft in the area).

2354 Changed speed to 23 knots. Changed course to 150°T.

GN Our CIC got info that the Japs have prepared an all out smash against us so we will probably be on the alert all day. Gunnery dept was called out at 0100 for enemy planes were overhead. Night planes from another carrier splashed them and they were identified as a Betty and an Irving so the day started out on the warm side. Off and on all day the gunnery dept was called to torpedo defense but they didn't get in close enough to get shot down. We had one smash at the enemy at Okinawa. GN

The 20th BOMBER COMMAND (of the **20th Air Force**) had been bombing the Japanese homeland with B-29 raids since mid 1944, operating out of India and China. It was joined in its raids by the **21st Bomber Command** operating out of the Marianas in early 1945.

On the 17th, 18th, 21st and 22nd of April, 1945, the 20th Air Force B-29s flew out for raids targeting Japanese air bases on Kyushu and Shikoku Islands. Over 600 sorties were flown on those missions, targeting those airfields. The B-29s would continue to target airfields in Japan flying close to 1100 additional sorties thru mid May. This in addition to a wide array of other missions, including aircraft factories. It is important to the story of the Mighty-I, and the entire fleet.

In addition to the toll in Japanese military assets, it was also impacting communication and intelligence. The raids created delays, confusion and more important, upset planning for strikes against our fleet. We kept the Japanese off balance and on the defensive with the mobility of our carrier raids as we struck, moved, then struck again. The B-29s had the same impact. The Japanese didn't know when or where we would strike next.

Raids tied up Japans pilots and aircraft for homeland defense and intercept missions against those frequent B-29 missions. Japanese fighters taking off in an attempt to intercept the incoming B-29s had difficulty returning to the airfields where they were based due to runway and facility damage, both old damage, and fresh destruction from the current raid. Japanese assets needed to be disbursed in smaller numbers at many scattered locations. This would cause further problems for organization, planning, logistics and implementation.

Admiral Ugaki noted in his diary; *"Scattered children are difficult to assemble."*

The simple fact is if an airplane (and pilot) is reserved for homeland defense, it is not therefore available to hit the fleet. The B-29s were functionally helping the Navy with perhaps as much value as our very own Combat Air Patrols. They were helping to keep potential Kamikazes off our backs.

Other impacts of the B-29 raids were on Japans fuel supply. Aviation gasoline was in critically short supply. In addition to fuel supplies destroyed in the raids, fuel consumed for intercept missions was not available for training new pilots.

Japanese pilot proficiency was declining making combat missions safer and easier for INDEPENDENCE pilots and aircrews. Low time Japanese pilots were sitting ducks for the comparatively heavily trained and combat proficient pilots catapulting off the Mighty-I.

Then there was the wear and tear on personnel. Japanese pilots, aircrew, mechanics and staff were becoming tired from loss of sleep, on top of working long hours under increasingly difficult conditions, which was impacting morale and performance. Life in shelters and trenches was less pleasant now that B-29s were raining down bombs with increased regularity. INDEPENDENCE pilots caused the same problems for the Japanese when they raided Kyushu, but right now INDEPENDENCE was tasked elsewhere, on a rather short leash, tethered to Okinawa.

The 20th Air Force was keeping the Japanese homeland busy to the fleets great benefit. (B-29 fire bombing raids would cause large scale destruction to Japanese cities and industry.)

Sunday 22 April 1945   *Ryukyu Islands, Okinawa Invasion*

Steaming as before off Okinawa in Task Unit 58.4.1 with USS YORKTOWN, USS LANGLEY and USS BATAAN. Ship is darkened, Air Department is in condition 14. There are several unidentified enemy aircraft in the vicinity.

0033 Gunnery Department set to condition One Easy.
0036 Gunnery Department set to condition 3.
0206 Formed cruising disposition 5-R.
0400 Sounded flight quarters. At 0449 the crew manned routine general quarters stations.
0503 Completed launching 8 F6Fs for CAP over our radar line picket destroyers.
0529 Task Group changed from disposition 5-R to 5-VB.
0550 Secured from general quarters. Air Department is in condition 13.
0745 Sounded flight quarters.
0839-0848 Completed recovery of 8 F6Fs launched at 0503.

0859-0950 USS MELVIN along starboard side amidships receiving 33,729 gallons of fuel oil, and transferring 21 TBM belly tanks to this ship.

1000-1003 Launched 4 TBMs led by Lt. E.A. Zurlinden for a strike against fortified caves on a hillside one mile east of the village of Shuri, behind Japanese lines.

1126-1131 Launched 8 F6Fs for CAP in scattered to broken clouds at 2,500', increasing high clouds.

1200 Engineering Department reported to the bridge that metallic chips and foreign matter were found in the hydraulic oil of the steering system. There was the possibility that valves may not function properly, with possible loss of steering control as a result. The OTC was notified of the condition.

1316 Launched 4 F6Fs for a TCAP (Target CAP) over airfields on Tokuno Shima and Kikai. They bombed the coral runway at Tokuno before beginning their patrol, encountering rain over the islands.

1335 Completed recovery of 4 TBMs launched at 1003.

As Lt(jg) John R. Fielding was preparing for launch, he actuated his flap switch to lower the flaps as customary for catapulting. The bomb on his left wing rack dropped to the flight deck. This was because of a "jury rig" manual release system, while waiting for a better manual release to be installed in the aircraft. Lt(jg) Richard M. Rogg had the same failure, preparing for launch, dropping his left bomb on the flight deck one hour later.

1353 Sounded torpedo defense. Gunnery Department set to condition One. Bogie closing on the formation from 269°T, 19 miles.

1359 Ships in this formation fired on an unidentified aircraft high overhead near USS YORKTOWN.

1402 Observed firing on the horizon to the east.

1418 Secured from torpedo defense and set condition One Easy.

1435 Gunnery Department set to condition One as ordered by OTC.

1442-1448 Launched 4 F6Fs to relieve the TCAP over airfields on Tokuno Shima and Kikai, and 4 TBMs (led by Lt. Foster C. Kay) for a support strike mission against a gun emplacement position on the east end of Senaga Shima, a small island off the west coast of Okinawa, 1 mile south of Naha Airfield. The F6Fs also escorted a photo plane for photographic coverage of Tokuno Airfield. With the photo mission complete, they dropped bombs on the southern end of the airstrip, then flew their TCAP. Ensign James William "Bill" Pruett tallyhoed a bogie over Kikai Shima, dropped his tank, applied water injection, catching a Tojo trying to land on Kikai Airfield. Pruett fired at the Tojo from 7 o'clock level, killing the pilot. The Tojo rolled over and exploded as it hit the ground. (maps - pages 575 & 612)

1455 Two bogies were fired on by ships of this formation, and were shot down by fighters from USS YORKTOWN.

1500 Gunnery Department set to condition One Easy as ordered by OTC.

1527 Completed recovery of 8 F6Fs launched at 1126.

1638 Sounded general quarters as ordered by OTC, in expectation of an air attack.

1654 Completed recovery of 4 F6Fs launched at 1316.

1709 All Departments set to condition One Easy.

1822-1838 Recovered 4 F6Fs and 4 TBMs launched at 1448, and 2 F6F(N)s from USS YORKTOWN.

1847 Gunnery Department set to condition One.

1856 Secured from flight quarters.

Air Department set to condition 14.

1923 Formed cruising disposition 5-R.

2100 Launched the 2 USS YORKTOWN F6F(N)s for a night patrol, then to return to YORKTOWN.

2355 Changed course to 300°T.

Captain Kindell on the bridge

GN *Gunnery dept called out again a few times at night. Got word that a fish narrowly missed the Yorktown and in turn was not too far off our stern. Cans dropped quite a few depth charges as seems to be the routine operation lately. Must be quite a few subs operating near us and trying to get in on us. One Jap plane splashed in the early afternoon from thirty thousand feet by one of our cans. Really coming in high lately. Got word today that the Navy is taking quite a beating in this operation and hope our luck holds out a while longer. Should be getting out of here fairly soon now. GQ called late in afternoon. One Jap plane at 35,000 ft. He went into a dive and hadn't traveled far when both wings broke off. Either a direct hit or some unknown factor. Fell among one of the other outfits. Our force is now composed of the Yorktown, Langley, Bataan and ourselves and those banzais are just as likely to head for one of us as for a CV. Would like to have about two more at least of those big jobs close at hand.* ***GN***

GL *Last night – early this AM had planes attack. Yorktown reported torpedo wake across the stern. We were just behind her but didn't see it. Shot down 1 Betty & then we secured. Had GQ in afternoon, our pickets shot down 4 planes. Yorktown fighters got another & CAP got 15. Two others were shot down 30,000 feet over TG.* ***GL***

Shooting down one snooper may not sound like much, but each one mattered. The loss of Japanese search planes to naval gunfire and carrier based Combat Air Patrols had been having an impact on Japanese planning, implementation and effectiveness.

Today, the Japanese sent out approximately 40 fighters, 5 Judys and 8 bombers against the fleet. Many more were to have been sent out but were delayed or canceled due to loss of intelligence. These delays, cancelations and confusion would continue to hamper Japanese military leaders.

Monday 23 April 1945   ***Ryukyu Islands, Okinawa Invasion***

Steaming as before on a 300°T course at 18 knots off Okinawa in Task Unit 58.4.1. Ship is darkened.
0415 Sounded flight quarters.
0515 Commenced launching 8 F6Fs. Four were tasked with a TCAP over Kikai and Amami Oshima. Four were sent to serve as a RAPCAP over a destroyer radar picket line. The TCAP Hellcats over Kikai and Amami Oshima first dropped bombs on the southern end of Tokuna Airfield.
0608 Task Group changed to disposition 5-VB.
0843 Completed launching 8 F6Fs for a TCAP and bombing attack on Kikai Airfield, taking out AA positions southeast of the field. Flack was at first heavy, thinning as gun crews took shelter during the bombing. The area around Akaoga in Amami Oshima was strafed during the CAP.
0903 Completed recovery of 8 F6Fs launched at 0515.
1140 Completed launching 8 F6Fs to relieve the TCAP over Kikai and Amami Oshima, and 9 TBMs for a support strike over Okinawa. Orbiting over "Point Jig", CASCU assigned artillery and pillboxes as targets, one mile east of Machinato Airfield. The target was identified by our troops on the ground, marked with phosphorous shells. The AAR noted:

"Communications were good and identification of the target was very satisfactory. However, with the low ceiling and hazy visibility prevailing, plus the large number of planes deployed in so small an area, the danger of collision was constantly a threat and detracted from bombing accuracy. Besides the attacking carrier groups, there was a continual milling around of L-5s, O6SUs and SOCs. Effectiveness of attacks would be enhanced by clearing air over target of all extraneous planes, especially when weather conditions are not favorable for heavy traffic."

The 8 Hellcats were assigned the TCAP over Kikai and Amami Oshima. They first dropped bombs on camouflaged AA revetments and trenches southeast of the field.
1433 Completed launching 12 F6Fs for a CAP.
1522 Completed recovery of 8 F6Fs and 9 TBMs launched at 1140.
1545 Air Department secured from flight quarters, and set to condition 13.

1739 Sounded flight quarters.

1819 Completed recovery of 12 F6Fs launched at 1433, and 2 F6F(N)s from USS YORKTOWN, to have ready for a night CAP.

1837 Secured from flight quarters. Air Department set to condition 14.

1848 Commenced zigzagging on base course 130°T. Sounded torpedo defense.

1922 Formed cruising disposition 5-R.

2300 Commenced zigzagging on base course 120°T, returning to the southeast for the night.

Captain Kindell noted: *"In the morning one of our submarines, which is damaged, will be in the vicinity. Probably will not be sighted however."*

GN *Fairly quiet today. Three sweeps over island. Two light ones and one real heavy. Met some air opposition and bagged another plane for themselves making twenty in all.* **GN**

AD *Okinawa. All quiet, no scares at all. Planes still bombing Isle. The Army on Okinawa has started their offensive push but still no gains. I guess we will stay here until they secure the isle.* **AD**

HC *Strike Okinawa and C.A.P. over Kikai and Amami-O-Shima. TD half the day until late at night.* **HC**

Tuesday 24 April 1945   *Ryukyu Islands, Okinawa Invasion*

0440 Steaming as before, returning to a replenishment area. Sounded routine torpedo defense. Gunnery Department set to condition One. Sounded flight quarters. At 0540 they secured from torpedo defense.

0605 Air Department set to condition 13.

0608 Commenced maneuvering to enter fueling formation and make an approach on USS MERCURY. USS AUCILLA designated guide. Fueling course 300°T, speed 10 knots.

0635 Air Department set to condition 14.

0643 Came along port side of cargo ship USS MERCURY to begin to reprovsion.

0710-0727 USS CUSHING came alongside to the port quarter to transfer from us five pilots from the INDEPENDENCE for the purpose of ferrying aircraft from a CVE, and photographs and press releases for delivery to the USS YORKTOWN. The USS SHANGRI LA and USS IOWA joined the fueling disposition, and will remain with Task Unit 58.4.1 after fueling.

0952 Cast off from USS MERCURY having received provisions.

0953 Commenced maneuvering to gain position on the assigned tanker.

1020 Came alongside to our starboard, the tanker USS TAPPAHANNOCK.

1113-1132 USS HEERMANN was alongside the port quarter transferring an officer and mail onboard.

1209 Cast off from USS TAPPAHANNOCK without completing fueling, having transferred to her 9 officers and enlisted men for transportation to Pearl Harbor and the United States. Separation from the tanker was due to requirements for a 170° formation course reversal.

1222 Changed course to 110°T.

1255 Came alongside to the USS TAPPAHANNOCK to complete fueling.

1338 USS CUSHING came alongside the port quarter to transfer ferry pilots.

1344 Sounded flight quarters.

1353 USS CUSHING cast off.

1402 Cast off from USS TAPPAHANNOCK having received 207,138 gallons of fuel oil and 30,100 gallons of aviation gasoline.

1425 Launched 2 F6F(N)s for return to USS YORKTOWN and 5 flyable F6F duds for transfer to the USS BOUGAINVILLE. Launched 4 F6Fs for CAP, and 3 TBMs for ASP.

1518 Recovered 5 F6Fs flown over from the USS BOGAINVILLE as replacement aircraft.

1541 Came alongside ammunition ship USS MAUNA LOA for rearming.

1615-1637 USS HAZELWOOD came alongside the port quarter to deliver freight.

1655 Cast off from USS MAUNA LOA.

1656-1700 USS LYMAN came alongside the port quarter to transfer US Mail.
1750 Gained station in formation, USS BATAAN designated guide (at 1704).
1820 Recovered 4 F6Fs and 3 TBMs launched at 1425 for the CAP and ASP. INDEPEDENCE also landed aboard 1 fighter for transfer to the USS SANGAMON.
1826 Secured from flight quarters. Air Department set to condition 14.
They stayed in the vicinity of the fueling group overnight.

AD Refueled and supplied. Movies on Hangar deck. AD

Admiral Matome Ugaki noted in his diary he had 620 aircraft in his command, with only 370 operational. He had noted 620 missing since March 25th, and 80 destroyed on the ground.

Wednesday 25 April 1945   *Ryukyu Islands, Replenishing*

Steaming as before, in the replenishment area. USS BATAAN is guide, course is 185°T, speed 17 knots. Guide bears 120°T, 2,000 yards. Air Department is in condition 14.
0438-0538 Manned torpedo defense stations.
0440 Sounded flight quarters.
0614 Changed speed to 10 knots.
0622 Commenced maneuvering to make approach on tanker USS SARANAC, guide now USS LACKAWANNA.
0701 USS JEFFERS came alongside the port quarter to transfer materials.
0742 Gained position alongside USS SARANAC.
0827 Cast off from USS SARANAC to launch aircraft.
0840 Completed launching 5 F6Fs, 4 F6Fs for CAP, and 3 TBMs for ASP. One of the F6Fs is to be ferried to USS SANGAMON.
0842 Secured from flight quarters.
0845 Commenced maneuvering to make approach on USS SARANAC.
0858 Came alongside USS SARANAC.
0940-0945 USS LYMAN was alongside the port quarter to deliver guard mail.
1034 Cast off from USS SARANAC having received lube oil, provisions, mail and 2 seamen for duty aboard this vessel.
1039 Commenced maneuvering to make approach on ammunition ship USS MAUNA LOA.
1103 Came alongside USS MAUNA LOA.
1136 Sounded flight quarters.
1152 Cast off from USS MAUNA LOA.
1207 Commenced maneuvering to gain flying station.
1210 USS BATAAN designated guide.
1225 Completed recovery of 4 F6Fs and 3 TBMs launched at 0840.
1227 Air Department set to condition 14.
1244 Gained position in the formation off guide, USS BATAAN, bearing 120°T, 2,000 yards in disposition 5-R, course 350°T, speed 18 knots.
2300 Commenced zigzagging on base course 160°T.

GN Rearmed and reprovisioned ship again. At long last we got some chow aboard. Had got dry stores yesterday and really supplemented that today with all kinds of provisions. Flew CAP and ASP again though the other ships with us had a mission to perform over some enemy held territory. Looks like the war in Europe is just about over what with the Russians having at least half of Berlin. More power to them. GN

AD Rearmed. Movies on hangar deck, also mail call. AD

GL Reprovisioned – fresh stores – food isn't to good but this ought to help out. Stew & rice – rice & stew. GL

Thursday 26 April 1945　　　　　*Ryukyu Islands, Okinawa Invasion*

Steaming as before off Okinawa in Task Unit 58.4.1 with USS YORKTOWN (OTC), USS LANGLEY, USS BATAAN and USS SHANGRI LA. Ship is darkened, Air Department is in condition 14.
0404 USS YORKTOWN designated as guide, course 000°T, speed 18 knots in cruising disposition 5-R, bearing 115°T, 2,800 yards.
0420 Sounded flight quarters.
0516-0520 Launched 8 F6Fs for CAP.
0531 USS BATAAN was detached from this Task Group to report to CTG 58.3.
0604 Disposition changed to 5-VB.
0618 Gained position in formation on guide USS IOWA, course 230°T, bearing 100°T, 2,000 yards.
0843 Completed launching 8 F6Fs for a TCAP over Tokuno. 500 lb. bombs were dropped on Tokuno Airfield runway, taxiway and revetments. Villages were strafed at Tokuno. A sulfur refinery and bunk houses were strafed on neighboring island Tori Shima.　　(Note: Tokunoshima is roughly 70 miles NE of Okinawa in the line of islands leading directly toward Kyushu, Japan - Map page 612)
0904 Completed recovering 8 F6Fs launched at 0520.
1149 Completed launching 12 F6Fs for a CAP.
1203 Completed recovery of 8 F6Fs launched at 0843.
1224 Secured from flight quarters. Air Department set to condition 13.
1445 Completed launching 8 F6Fs for TCAP over Okinawa.
1517 Changed course to 330°T. Sighted northern Okinawa Jima Island, bearing 291°T, distance 42 miles. Light rain for the next 3 hours. They would stay within sight of land until after 1700.
1519 Completed recovery of 12 F6Fs launched at 1149.
1806-1811 Recovered of 8 F6Fs launched at 1445.
1829 Secured from flight quarters. Air Department set to condition 14.
1918 Formed cruising disposition 5-R.
2044 Gunnery Department set AA batteries to condition One by order of OTC.
2050 Gunnery Department set to condition 3.
2355 Commenced zigzagging on base course 220°T.

GN Bad weather hampered operations to a certain extent today. We were slated for three deck load strikes but only one of them materialized. We're in sight of Okinawa for a good while. Heard that the closest we got was 35 miles out but the island was too visible for me to agree to that. GN

GL Back again, in close enough to see whole island. Could see big guns firing & lots of smoke. Still helping the troops. GL

Friday 27 April 1945　　　　　*Ryukyu Islands, Okinawa Invasion*

Steaming as before off Okinawa in Task Unit 58.4.1. Guide is USS IOWA, bearing 150°T, 2,000 yards.
0421 Sounded flight quarters.
0448-0545 Manned (routine) general quarters stations.
0524 Completed launching 12 F6Fs for a TCAP over Okinawa. Scattered to broken clouds at 1,000' with a 20 knot NE wind.
0550 Completed recovery of 2 F6Fs launched at 0524.
0641 Completed launching 2 F6Fs.
0839 Completed launching 9 F6Fs for a CAP over Tokuno airfields. Target visibility was clear, with 6 tenths cloud cover at 2,000'. Tokuno Airfield was bombed and taxiways and revetments were strafed. CAP was flown over Tokuno and Tori Shima.

0909 Completed recovery of 10 F6Fs launched at 0524, 2 F6Fs launched at 0641 and 1 F6F at 0839.
1157 Completed launching 12 F6Fs as a CAP, and 6 TBMs. The 6 Avengers (led by Lt.-Comdr. Barron) were assigned to hit an enemy gun emplacement in the hills southwest of Shuri Village by the CASCU. Level bombing runs were made at 1,000' with 500# bombs, then an additional run was made with rockets. Pilots encountered *"meager and inaccurate flack"*, thought to be 37mm. This was the squadrons first use of HVARs (High Velocity Aircraft Rockets) and 8 of the 24 rockets were duds.
1215 Completed recovery of 8 F6Fs launched at 0839.
1248 Secured from flight quarters. Air Department set to condition 13.
1403 Sounded flight quarters.
1456 Completed launching 8 F6Fs as a TCAP over Tokuno. The Hellcats dropped bombs and strafed Tokuno Airfield, then dropped 1 bomb on a sulfur refinery and strafed 6 villages, starting fires. Two 500# bombs were dropped on a deep water dock. Two 30' boats and one 70' boat were destroyed.
1539 Completed recovery of 12 F6Fs and 6 TBMs launched at 1157.
1837 Completed recovery of the 8 F6Fs launched at 1456.
1937 Formed cruising disposition 5-R.
During the night they retired toward the southeast for a fueling rendezvous.

GN Made our three strikes today. One was heavy and the other two mediums. Weather is still not too good and to my mind April is April no matter what part of the world you are in. Raining one minute and sun shining the next. GN

GL Still attacking Okinawa & surrounding islands. There are sure a lot of them. Only 50 miles from Okinawa. 104 Jap planes splashed. GL

Saturday 28 April 1945   *Ryukyu Islands, Replenishing at Sea*

Steaming as before off Okinawa in Task Unit 58.4.1 with USS YORKTOWN (OTC), USS LANGLEY and USS SHANGRI LA. Ship is darkened, cruising disposition 5-R, zigzagging on base course 170°T. Guide is USS IOWA, bearing 060°T, 2,000 yards. No.1 engine is secured for repairs to a condenser. The Task Group is retiring to refuel, reprovision and rearm.
0334 Condenser is repaired, and the No.1 engine is placed in use again.
0415 Sounded flight quarters.
0443 Sounded routine torpedo defense. Gunnery Department set to condition One.
0519 Completed launching 4 F6Fs for CAP and 3 TBMs for ASP.
0542 Secured from routine torpedo defense and flight quarters. Air Department set to condition 13. Gunnery Department set to condition 3.
0552 Commenced maneuvering to enter fueling formation and make approach on ammunition ship USS MAUNA LOA, guide USS LACKAWANNA, fueling course 070°T, speed 10 knots.
0631 Came along port side of USS MAUNA LOA.
0633 Air Department set to condition 14.
0726 Cast off from USS MAUNA LOA having received bombs and fuses.
0728 Commenced maneuvering to gain position in fueling formation, guide bearing 070°T, 7,000 yards.
0815 Sounded flight quarters.
0820 Commenced maneuvering to gain position on the assigned tanker.
0907 Completed recovering 4 F6Fs and 3 TBMs launched at 0519.
0934 Came alongside USS SARANAC.
0937 Secured from flight quarters. Air Department set to condition 14.
0945-1009 USS UHLMANN was alongside port quarter to transfer US Mail.
1020-1022 USS HAZELWOOD was alongside port quarter to transfer officer messenger mail.
1148-1218 USS HAGGARD was alongside port quarter to transfer officer messenger mail, US Mail and three Ensigns (Henry N. Lawrence, Charles A. Jacobs, Jr. & David W. Margulies) for duty aboard this vessel.

1230 Cast off all lines from tanker, USS SARANAC, having received 169,761 gallons of fuel oil. INDEPENDENCE had transferred one officer to USS SARANAC to proceed to San Diego and an enlisted man for transfer to the hospital ship USS BOUNTIFUL.

1235 Commenced maneuvering make approach on USS MILLICOMA.

1238 USS VESUVIUS designated guide. At 1325, the USS MERCURY was designated guide.

1343 Came alongside USS MILLICOMA to take on provisions.

1447 Cast off all lines from USS MILLICOMA having taken aboard fresh and frozen provisions, and one barrel of lube oil. Commenced maneuvering to regain station within Task Group 58.4.

1512 The Task Group parted from the replenishing group and began steaming toward the northwest. INDEPENDENCE gained station 2.180 in cruising disposition 5-R, 2,000 yards off USS IOWA (guide).

2115 Commenced zigzagging on base course 310°T.

GN Refueled, rearmed and reprovisioned the ship again today. Weather pretty choppy and we flew CAP and ASP. Quiet day all around. GN

AD Refueled, replenished. Movies on hangar deck, also mail call. AD

Sunday 29 April 1945   *Ryukyu Islands, Okinawa Invasion*

0400 Steaming off Okinawa in Task Unit 58.4.1. Sounded flight quarters.

0515 Commenced launching 8 F6Fs for a CAP over Tokuno and Tori Shima. Tokuno airfield was bombed and strafed. A bridge was destroyed near the airfield.

0529 Commenced maneuvering to change to disposition 5-VB.

0700-0708 Launched 4 F6Fs and 9 TBMs for a strike on the Koniya seaplane base at Amami Oshima. The Hellcats (Ens. Pruett & Lt.(jg) Purcell) were tasked with a photo mission of the seaplane base, while the Avengers bombed buildings, ramps, revetments and fuel storage. Two Avengers took heavy AA damage (flown by Lt.(jg) D.R. Williams & Lt.-Comdr. Barron). Barron's Avenger was turned over to the CASU for disposition (repair or cannibalize for spare parts). Half the town of Koniya was burnt out.

0805 Changed course to 000°T.

0821 Sounded torpedo defense by order of the OTC. Unidentified aircraft bearing 080°T (from the east), at 35 miles. It was later identified as friendly.

0837 Completed launching 8 F6Fs for CAP.

0846 Completed recovery of 8 F6Fs launched at 0515.

0906 Secured from torpedo defense.

1020 Launched 1 F6F.

1039 Completed recovering 4 F6Fs, and 6 TBMs launched at 0708. The other 3 TBMs launched at 0708 were reported to have landed on Okinawa Jima.

1146 Completed launching 8 F6Fs assigned for TCAP and bombing over Tokuno Airfield.

1211-1219 Recovered 7 F6Fs launched at 0837 and 1 F6F launched at 1020.

1325-1333 INDEPENDENCE ("Rumcoke") launched 4 F6Fs and 5 TBMs for a second strike against Koniya seaplane base at Amami Oshima. The attacks were coordinated with aircraft from USS LANGLEY ("Patriot"). Bombing, rocket and strafing runs were made damaging shops, barracks, an administration building, revetments, the seaplane ramp, as well as a radio station on Kakeroma Shima.

1340-1342 Recovered 1 TBM launched at 0708 and 1 TBM launched at 1333 with engine problems. The TBM (launched at 0708) had first made an emergency landing at Yontan Airbase on Okinawa with battle damage from Japanese anti-aircraft fire. ARM2c James W. Bosserman required treatment in sickbay from shrapnel wounds in his right leg.

1456-1500 Launched 8 F6Fs for a TCAP.

1505-1524 Recovered 8 F6Fs launched at 1146.

1535 Secured from flight quarters. Air Department set to condition 13.

1557 Sounded flight quarters.

1613 Landed 4 TBMs and 4 F6Fs launched at 1333.

1625 Sounded torpedo defense by order of the OTC, due to enemy planes reported in the area.

1637 A ship in the formation opened fire on planes forward of the formation with its 5" guns. This ship went to general quarters. The aircraft were friendly F6Fs, the INDEPENDENCE CAP.

1657 INDEPENDENCE crew observed firing on the horizon.

1659 *"A Japanese plane, painted black, bearing no circular red insignia, approached the formation from the port quarter, was taken under fire by all ships' of the formation on that side, including this vessel, and was splashed on the port quarter of this vessel at about 3,000 yards distant."*

1703 Ships of the formation again opened fire. The USS HAGGARD was hit by a kamikaze and was visibly burning at 1705.

1730 INDEPENDENCE crew observed more firing on the horizon at 340°T. The USS HAZELWOOD was reported hit. Both destroyers were dead in the water but still afloat. The USS FLINT and USS SAN DIEGO were detached to take the crippled destroyers in tow to the naval base at Kerama Retto.

(The USS HAZELWOOD suffered causalities of 112 killed, including the C.O., and 26 wounded. The USS HAGGARD 13 killed and 38 wounded)

1754 Secured from general quarters. Air Department remained at flight quarters. Gunnery Department set to condition One Easy.

1826 Commenced recovering aircraft.

1831 A F6F-5 (Bu. No. 74137) crashed into the barrier on landing. No injuries.

1838 Completed recovering 8 F6Fs launched at 1500.

1851 Secured from flight quarters. Air Department set to condition 14.

1900 Formed cruising disposition 5-R.

2356 Changed course to 310°T, speed is 20 knots.

GL Had bogy early in morning but it faded. Just heard hospital ship Comfort hit by bogie (29 killed, 33 wounded, plane still on board) 50 miles from us. Bogies all around again, lots of firing on horizon. Destroyer Haggard hit by 2 bogies. Hazelwood took one – heavy casualties. DD's looking for men in the water. Yorktown CAP shot down 15 Zekes, Jakes & Oscars. Shangri-La opened fire on our planes and almost got one. Some of our planes shot up on raids landed on Okinawa air strip. It sure saved a few of our air boys. Hitting Tokuno with 500, 1,000 pounders & rockets, also napalm fire bombs. GL

AD Okinawa. All quiet in morning and early afternoon. GQ at about 1700. The Shangri-La was firing before I could get to my station on the bridge. She ceased firing, it was her own planes she was firing on. Never less the Japs are flying all around the Task Group. Soon our ships were firing intensely with 5". Then I spotted Jap plane coming around our fantail from port to stb. 100 yards. Our 40 & 20 mm batteries opened up and the Jap was splashed. It is believed that we knocked that one down, It hasn't been confirmed though. A little later heavy fire was observed on the horizon. A couple of our picket DD's were under attack by Banzai Boys. The DD Haggard was hit by two suicides. The DD Hazelwood was hit by one. Both ships were taken under tow. I could see one DD burning on the horizon. AD

Monday 30 April 1945   *Ryukyu Islands, Okinawa Invasion*
Adolph Hitler commits suicide

Steaming as before off Okinawa in Task Unit 58.4.1. Air Department is in condition 14.

0050 Formed cruising disposition 5V.

0056 Observed the fires of two enemy planes burning on the horizon southwest of us at 230°T.

0130 Gunnery Department set to condition One Easy by order of OTC. One remaining enemy plane continued to shadow-box with the group roughly 20 miles from the formation.

0137 Gunnery Department set to condition One by order of OTC, as the enemy plane had closed to within 11 miles.

0141 Ships in the Task Group opened fire on a plane. The enemy was driven off.

0254 Gunnery Department set to condition One Easy by order of OTC.

0339 Gunnery Department secured from condition One Easy, set to condition 3.

0355 Commenced pumping bilges.   0415 Sounded flight quarters.

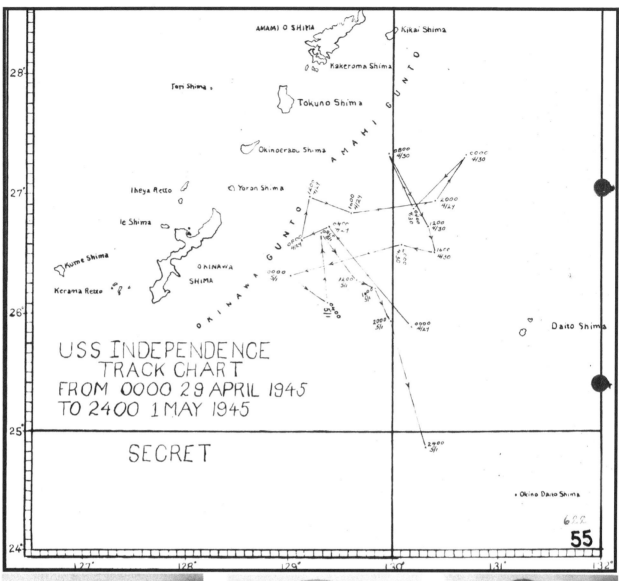

USS INDEPENDENCE
TRACK CHART
FROM 0000 29 APRIL 1945
TO 2400 1 MAY 1945

SECRET

Lt. Comdr. John P. Barron
VT-46

Lt. (Jg.) John A. Tschirhart
VT-46

Ens. Arthur Rosenburgh
VT-46

Chapter 25   612

0446 Sounded routine general quarters. At 0510 changed speed to 25 knots.

0521 Completed launching 8 F6Fs for a CAP to patrol between Tokuno and Tori Shima.

0528 Observed firing on the port beam, to the south, on the horizon at 190°T.

0533 Changed course to 000°T, speed 18 knots. At 0546 they secured from general quarters.

0749 Formed formation 5VC.

0751 Sounded torpedo defense by order of OTC. An enemy aircraft was in the vicinity.

0829 Completed launching 8 F6Fs for CAP.

0850 Completed recovering 8 F6Fs launched at 0521. At 0851 they secured from torpedo defense.

0857 Changed speed to 16 knots, formed cruising disposition 5VB.

0900 Secured from flight quarters.

1100 Sounded flight quarters.

1148 Completed launching 8 F6Fs.

1220 Completed recovering 8 F6Fs launched at 0829.

1455 Completed launching 8 F6Fs for a CAP to patrol between Tokuno and Tori Shima.

1513 Completed recovering 8 F6Fs launched at 1148.

1540 Jettisoned 1 F6F (Bu.No.71437) over the side, then secured from flight quarters. (29th. barricade accident)

1745 Sounded flight quarters.

1825 Completed recovering 8 F6Fs launched at 1455.

1840 Secured from flight quarters.   At 1850 thru 1943 manned torpedo defense stations.

1926 Formed cruising disposition 5R.

2350 Changed course to 160°T. Overnight they will remain in the same area. The USS INDEPENDENCE has been underway continually, without a break for the entire month.

GN *The day started early for the gunnery dept. Just at midnight they were called out again. Bogies in the neighborhood again. I was waiting for GQ but it never came. Two planes were shot down by night chickens and I guess they secured from TD shortly thereafter. Seems we expect plenty of Japs today and all the whole outfit is flying as CAP. About 8 o 'clock gunnery was called out again but it didn't last too long. One of the Shangri La's planes shot a Nip down from 26,000 feet. Confirmed about the Comfort being hit by a banzai, which is still on the ship. She is proceeding to port under her own power. Heard that Old Muss* was killed by his own people. Rumors are rife that we will be going back to the states before very long. Hope they have some foundation. Also heard that we have used close to 300 ton of bombs so far in this operation and that is quite some going.* *GN*

GL *One-Easy all night, shot down 1 Betty & Irving. Their flames sure looked beautiful. About 9AM had TD and two Zeros were splashed. The pilots parachuted on our port side.* *GL*

*On 27 April 1945, Benito Mussolini was captured. The following day on the 28th, he was executed.

On 30 April 1945, Adolph Hitler committed suicide in his bunker in Berlin. The war in Europe was rapidly drawing to a close.

Tuesday 1 May 1945   *Ryukyu Islands, Okinawa Invasion*

Steaming as before off Okinawa Shima in tactical and strategic support of the U.S. Tenth Army on Okinawa, in Task Unit 58.4.1 with USS YORKTOWN (OTC), USS LANGLEY and USS SHANGRI LA. INDEPENDENCE is in a Carrier Unit of TG 58.4, Rear Admiral A.W. Radford, part of Task Force 58 under Vice Admiral M.A. Mitscher, his flagship USS BUNKER HILL. This Task Group consist of 4 carriers, 3 battleships, 2 large cruisers with screening destroyers, in disposition 5R, course 160°T, speed 18 knots. USS IOWA is guide bearing 140°T, 2,000 yards. Air Department is in condition 14.

0056 USS FLINT rejoined the formation, having towed a damaged destroyer to Kerama Retto.

0415 Sounded flight quarters.

0516 Completed launching 8 F6Fs for a CAP from Amami Oshima to Kikai. Commander Rooney led the flight tasked with strafing attacks on shipping near Kominato and in Naze Ko after the CAP.

0543 Formed cruising disposition 5VB, a tighter formation allowing better mutual protection in case of air attack.

0608 Formation axis changed to 160°T to conform to a shift in the wind.

0644 Recovered 1 F6F launched at 0516.

0800 Mustered crew on stations. Completed launching 8 F6Fs for a CAP over the Task Group.

0834 Completed recovery of 7 F6Fs launched at 0516.

0854 Secured from flight quarters. Air Department set to condition 13.

1045 Sounded flight quarters.

1145 Completed launching 8 F6Fs for a CAP from Amami Oshima to Kikai, and 6 TBMs for an air support strike over Okinawa. The TBMs, led by Lt. Zurlinden, orbited "Point Bolo" where the CASCU directed them to attack a concentration of enemy troops, trucks and guns on a road (within 1 mile of our own troops). After the strike, they landed at Yontan Airfield to pick up squadron personnel beached since April 29th, when they made an emergency landing, before returning to the INDEPENDENCE.

1203 Completed recovery of 8 F6Fs launched at 0800.

1457-1501 Launched 8 F6Fs for a CAP over the Task Group.

1517-1521 Recovered 8 F6Fs launched at 1145.

1751-1759 Completed recovery of 5 TBMs launched at 1145, and completed recovery of 1 TBM launched at 1145, and 1 TBM (Donald William's plane repaired with parts from John Barron's plane) from Okinawa Jima having made an emergency landing there on 29 April.

1823 Completed recovery of 8 F6Fs launched at 1501.

1841 Secured from flight quarters.

1919 Formed cruising disposition 5R.

2340 Commenced zigzagging on base course 170°T, retiring toward the south during the night to join up with a replenishing group.

GN A new month starts and I hope it is the last one in this vicinity for quite some time. Had one deck load over Okinawa and flew CAP practically all day. All quiet on the western front as far as action goes. GN

DL A mood of dread settled over the ship. We decided we were living in a dice game. We had suffered a torpedo hit and we felt we knew something about that--the ship would take a beating and a number of men would die and you could hope you were not one of them. But with the fierce kamikazes all around, flown by animals who wanted to die, your chances of survival were mighty small. If your ship was large enough, it would probably survive even though many more men were likely to give up the ghost. Would you be one of them? It really was a toss of the dice.

Sometime in May the word went out that from now on the Exec would not station himself in or near the bridge while the ship was under attack. He would be accompanied wherever he went by a Marine guard --sometimes two of them. He would select a proper place on the flightdeck, staying clear of the aircraft of course if we were flying. When the deck was clear he made his rounds not talking with anyone or seeming to have communication with anyone else. He would watch us work on the planes, watch the mech and metalsmiths at their labors, even the plane pushers between flights. He'd observe the guys playing endless games of mumbelty-peg on the deck.

His proper place, it seemed, was to become available if a kamikaze would come through the screen of ships' fire and crash into the bridge--a favorite target of those pilots. This had happened to too many ships. Losing your skipper and navigator at one blow without immediate replacement would momentarily cripple any vessel.

(It had happened to Uncle Gib's ship, cruiser Columbia*. She was never a part of TF 58 or TF 38, but the rumor mill brought us word that The Gem had taken a bad hit in her superstructure from a kamikaze many miles from us. Not until the end of the war did I learn how narrowly he had missed being a victim of this assault.) (Note: *Cleveland class CL-56 was struck by a kamikaze on 1 January 1945 and again on 9 January)

Our personal role in this act of defense was to constantly wear our lifebelts just above the belts that held up our pants and supported the various tools we needed to do our job. Atop our heads we were forced to wear the unbelted steel helmet, which we hated most of all. No matter the weather, it was hot. And as close as you had to work on the airplanes, the helmets always seemed too big. We cursed them royally. It must be said that every sailor aboard had some sort of job. It was a job in an office or alongside a boiler below decks or the man was busy cleaning the heads or manning the guns and lookout stations. But flightdeck personnel were the busiest of all the bees. It was relatively easy for us to accept an early Flight Quarters call. While Turner Caldwell's planes were aboard we got used to working all night. But now that we were operating again as a day carrier, we found that "daytime" began about 0330 and ended about an hour after evening GQ. A long, strenuous day under a leaden sky that always contained a palpable menace in its clouds. **DL**

HC *Saw a hospital ship at night. Couldn't miss it if you were blind. It was all lit up. The bogies dropped a bomb on one*[1.]* on the 29th. The fleets madder than hell about that. C.A.P. over Amami O Shima and Kikai.* **HC** (*[1.]* Note: Herman is referring to the Kamikaze hit on the USS COMFORT)

Wednesday 2 May 1945   *Ryukyu Islands, Replenishing at Sea*

Steaming as before off Okinawa in Task Unit 58.4.1. The Task Group is retiring to refuel, reprovision and rearm. Since midnight a fully lighted hospital ship has been visible to the east.

0415 Sounded flight quarters.

0555-0559 Launched 4 F6Fs for CAP and 3 TBMs for ASP.

0608 Commenced maneuvering to gain position alongside the ammunition ship USS VESUVIUS.

0610 Secured from flight quarters. Air Department set to condition 13.

0710 USS HAILEY came alongside port quarter.

0721 Gained position on port side of USS VESUVIUS, course 100°T, speed 10 knots. Guide is USS MASCOMA.

0725 Air Department set to condition 14.

0732 USS HAILEY cast off.

0734-0737 USS HEERMANN was alongside port quarter.

0845 Cast off from USS VESUVIUS having received 99 - 500lb. bombs and 7 - 1,000lb. bombs.

0857 Sounded flight quarters.

0918 Completed recovering 3 TBMs and 4 F6Fs launched at 0559.

0931 Secured from flight quarters. Air Department set to condition 14.

1005 Came alongside USS MERCURY to receive provisions from her. Fueling course 060°T.

1011-1021 USS MELVIN was alongside port quarter to transfer 1 package.

1155 USS MERCURY cast off. Commenced maneuvering to approach USS MILLICOMA to refuel.

1246 Came alongside USS MILLICOMA.

1251-1257 USS BENHAM was alongside to transfer 1 bag of mail.

1301-1321 USS HAILEY was alongside to transfer mail and freight.

1326-1341 USS NORMAN SCOTT was alongside to receive spare parts.

1354 USS MERCURY designated as guide.

1448 Cast off from USS MILLICOMA having received 160,276 gallons of fuel oil and 31,600 gallons of aviation gasoline. INDEPENDENCE had also disembarked (to the tanker) 41 crew members for further transfer, most returning to the States.

1449 Commenced maneuvering to gain station on the guide, USS MERCURY.

1511 USS YORKTOWN was designated guide as they left the replenishment group and proceeded toward the northwest to return to the operating area off Okinawa Shima. The USS SAN DIEGO*[2.]* rejoined the formation, having towed a damaged destroyer to Kerama Retto. (*[2.]* See page 611 - 1730 entry)

1540 USS IOWA was designated guide, bearing 060°T, 2,000 yards, course 060°T, speed 15 knots.

1612 Completed recovery of 1 F6F and 1 TBM flown over from the USS WINDHAM BAY as replacement aircraft.

1819 Secured from flight quarters. Air Department set to condition 14.

1842-1942 Gunnery Department manned routine torpedo defense stations.
1943 Ceased zigzagging, returned to base course 300°T.

GN Refueled, rearmed and reprovisioned. Flew CAP and ASP. Got word that the Italian army in Italy had surrendered. No mail for the 58.4 at this time. Will probably pile up on us again. GN

AD Refueled, rearmed, replenished. Movies on hangar deck, no mail. AD

Today, the Soviet Union announced the fall of Berlin.

Thursday 3 May 1945   *Ryukyu Islands, Okinawa Invasion*
Germany Surrenders on night of 2-3 May to the American 9th Army

Steaming as before off Okinawa in Task Unit 58.4.1 with USS YORKTOWN (OTC), USS LANGLEY, USS BATAAN and USS SHANGRI LA. Ship is darkened, Air Department is in condition 14.
0415 Sounded flight quarters. First scheduled flights this morning were not launched due to weather.
0538 Formed cruising disposition 5VB.
0932 Changed course to 220°T, speed 18 knots, gaining station on guide USS IOWA, bearing 070°T, 2,000 yards.
1003 Completed launching 8 F6Fs for target CAP over Okinawa.
1030 Completed launching 2 F6Fs.
1146 Completed launching 4 F6Fs and 4 TBMs for a support strike against enemy lines on Okinawa. The strike targeted enemy troop concentrations 1/4 mile north of Shuri Town and a small village northeast of Yonaharu containing AA positions. One TBM-3 (Bu.No.69235), after being crippled by enemy AA gunfire over Yonabaru, was forced to make a water landing roughly 2 miles west of Naha. Lt.(jg) Burton B. Le Tulle with his two crewmen ARM3c Robert E. Collins and AMM3c Richard A. Hoberg were recovered in good condition by USS PAUL HAMILTON. They had received a 20mm shell hit causing a fire in the starboard wing. They spent only 15 minutes in a life raft before the destroyer picked them up.
1151 Completed recovering 2 F6Fs launched at 1003.
1202 Secured from flight quarters. Air Department set to condition 13.
1315 Sounded flight quarters.
1345 Completed recovering 6 F6Fs launched at 1003, & 2 F6Fs launched at 1030.
1501 Completed launching 8 F6Fs for TCAP over Okinawa Jima.
1519 Completed recovering 4 F6Fs launched at 1003, & 3 TBMs launched at 1146.
1545 Secured from flight quarters. Air Department set to condition 13.
1822-1829 Recovered 8 F6Fs launched at 1501.
1834 Sounded torpedo defense by order of OTC. No enemy aircraft were in the area, however it was felt that an attack was possible.
1845 Secured from flight quarters. Air Department set to condition 14.
1959 Gunnery Department secured from torpedo defense, set to condition 3.
2358 Changed course to 110T, speed is 25 knots.

GN First thing in the AM we got word of the unconditional surrender of the German army in Italy. Looks like the beginning of the end and I hope it is. Heard that we are to hit Honshu today. Weather is bad though and it may hamper us somewhat. The chaplain told us again that we had used 300 ton of bombs so far in this operation. That along with 1640 rockets and 185,000 rounds of .50 caliber makes for a bit of lead or steel that the Japs have received from this ship alone. Looks like someone is producing along the line. Instead of Honshu we made another hit on Okinawa. Lost a TBM on the mission and that makes three of them that we have lost on the last three missions. Gunners claim there is very little AA but it is very accurate. The crews of all three were saved. Called TD about 5 PM for a bogie in the neighborhood. He didn't show up in task group though the Yorktown chickens shot down four during the evening and night who did get too close. On the side porch for some air and did get to see a beaut of a fire on the Shangri La. One of her chickens* got fouled up in some way. Pilot was saved but didn't hear about the crew of the ship. GN (* F6F belly landing, belly tank causing fire - No injuries.)

Steaming as before off Okinawa in Task Unit 58.4.1

0155 Observed a burning enemy plane on the horizon, bearing 080°T. A four engine Emily flying boat was shot down by USS YORKTOWN night fighters.

0400 Three Betty bombers were shot down fifty miles out by night fighters.

0410 Sounded flight quarters.

0513 Completed launching 12 F6Fs for target CAP north of Okinawa Jima.

0538 Formed cruising disposition 5VB.

0632 Completed launching 4 F6Fs for a target CAP, 100 miles from the ship, over Kikai Shima. Lt. Morrison, Lt.(jg) Crampton and Ensigns Albertson and Agesen each released 1 bomb on Kikai Wan Airfield, and were in process of making a second bomb run when Angus Morrison shot down a Judy taking off from the airfield, 100' off the deck. The other 3 pilots stumbled into a dogfight in progress pulling out of their bombing run. YORKTOWN and RANDOLPH fighters were in a fight with 12 to 15 Japanese aircraft. It was a mix of Vals, Zekes, Judys, Tonys and Jills.

We'll let the Aircraft Action Report tell the events from here:

"The INDEPENDENCE planes became separated and it was every man for himself. After splashing the Judy Lt. Morrison pulled up and noticed a dog fight of 5 Jap planes and 2 F6F-5s at 4000 feet. At 8000 feet there was another dog fight. A Zeke dove away and made for Amami-O-Shima to take advantage of his protective coloring of the land. Lt. Morrison dropped his belly tank, put on water injection and got within range in a 10 mile chase. On a stern run Lt. Morrison burned the Zeke and he burst into flames and exploded at 500 feet into the hills. Ensign Bruce M. Agesen in a high speed climb from his dive ran into a dog fight and noticed two Tonys 300 feet above in a left climbing turn. Pulling up into a 60° climb he fired two healthy burst into the second one in column. He saw the Tony burst into flames and go into a dive and was then forced to recover his own plane from a spin. Several minutes later Ensign Agesen contributed several bursts into a Zeke, already smoking, which he saw crash into the water. He claims credit only for the destruction of a Tony.

Lt(jg) Joseph A. Crampton after witnessing the explosion of the Judy shot down by Lt. Morrison near the deck, pulled up from his dive bombing run and climbed to AG 9 where he joined a dog fight and soon thereafter got on the tail of a Zeke, firing within easy range which started a fire at the starboard wing root.

From the amount of smoke the Zeke gave off, his chances of returning to base were extremely remote. Lt (jg) Crampton was forced to pull away to the starboard when he noticed 20mm shells passing over the top of his plane from an enemy fighter in the rear. He flew for a few minutes alone until he noticed 2 F6F-5s trying without success to close on a Jill. When they turned away Lt(jg) Crampton closed in from the opposite side and rode the Jill's tail down over Kikai. When the Jill made a turn Lt(jg) Crampton opened fire and held it until the Jill burned and crashed. Ensign Albertson picked himself a Jill at 6000 feet, 5 miles from the NE tip of Amami-O-Shima and shot him down on a stern run from 800 foot range as the Jap pilot tried to make a turn to a northeast course around the tip of the island."

0640 Secured from flight quarters.

0751 A large group of unidentified planes were picked up by radar bearing 240°T, 125 miles away. The aircraft continued toward Okinawa. A report was later received that 39 planes had been shot down north of Okinawa.

The Diary of Matome Ugaki indicated 78 Japanese aircraft of the Sixth Army were sent out to "control the air", unequally split in three waves between 0730 and 0900. Additionally over 70 other Japanese aircraft were sortied. His Diary entry tomorrow, May 5th, will indicate that from Ugaki's perspective, the Japanese effort to have been a failure. On the 4th however, destroyers LUCE, MORRISON and LSMs 190 & 194 were sunk, with numerous other ships damaged. US Navy causalities were heavy!

0813 Gunnery Department set to condition One.

0815 Sounded flight quarters.

0825 Gunnery Department set to condition One Easy.

0844 Completed recovery of 12 F6Fs launched at 0513.

1000 Completed launching 12 F6Fs for a TCAP over north Okinawa.

1025 Completed recovery of 4 F6Fs launched at 0632.

1039 Gunnery Department secured from condition One Easy.

1137 Completed launching 4 F6Fs for a TCAP over Kikai. The 4 Hellcats each carried two 500# bombs. They released the 8 bombs to crater the Kikai Airfield. They returned after being relieved on station by USS LANGLEY aircraft. *"All Jap planes had been destroyed or fled by this time."*

1320-1330 Recovered 12 F6Fs launched at 1000.

1448-1453 Launched 12 F6Fs for a CAP over the Task Group.

1519-1521 Recovered 4 F6Fs launched at 1137.

1524 Secured from flight quarters. Air Department set to condition 13.

1745 Sounded flight quarters.

1833 Recovered 12 F6Fs launched at 1453.

1850 Secured from flight quarters. Air Department set to condition 14.

1936 Formed cruising disposition 5R.

2056 Commenced zigzagging on base course 170°T.

GN Two small strikes over Okinawa. Fighters from our ship splashed four Japs on the first run and one on the second making five in all. Heard that the Nips are now using Emily's for banzai jobs so they must be pretty hard up for aircraft. Set condition one for the gunnery dept about nine AM and it lasted for about an hour and a half. Must have been some Japs in the neighborhood for we heard that three of our cans got hit in one way or the other. The boys also got three probable's and the word is that the whole outfit has over a thousand planes from April 1st. Good going. GN

GL Early in morning 5 planes were splashed, 1 Emily, 3 Bettys, 1 unidentified. They sure burn pretty. Yorktown night fighters got them. In One Easy again as we expect an all out attack. Had several attacks and several bogies were splashed. 2:30PM so far today the score is 89 planes shot down in 50 mile area. Independence fighters shot down 7 planes. We are bombing Nansei Shoto. GL

AD Okinawa. Planes from our Task Force shot down about 90 Jap planes. Today our pilots got 5. No attacks on Task Group. AD

Saturday 5 May 1945   *Ryukyu Islands, Okinawa Invasion*

0410 Steaming as before off Okinawa in Task Unit 58.4.1. Sounded flight quarters.

0506-0518 Completed launching 12 F6Fs for a TCAP over north Okinawa.

0536 Changed the formation to 5VB, axis 050°T, course is 230°T, speed 22 knots.

0629-0632 Completed launching 4 F6Fs for CAP over Kikai Shima. These Hellcats bombed the airfield and revetments, and made strafing runs on buildings near Koniya seaplane base on Amami Oshima.

0810 Completed launching 1 TBM to proceed to Yontan Airfield on Okinawa to pick up the rescued pilot (Lt. Le Tulle) and aircrew (Robert Collins & Richard Hoberg) of the TBM that made the forced landing in the water off Naha on May 3rd.

0850 Completed recovering 12 F6Fs launched at 0518.

1004 Completed launching 12 F6Fs for a TCAP over north Okinawa.

1020 Completed recovering 4 F6Fs launched at 0632.

1130 Completed launching 4 F6Fs for CAP over Kikai Shima.

1332 Completed recovering 12 F6Fs launched at 1004.

1440-1454 Completed launching 16 F6Fs and 6 TBMs. 12 F6Fs were assigned CAP over the Task Group, and 4 F6Fs were to fly a CAP for a PBY seaplane on a rescue mission for downed pilots. The 6 TBMs, with ten 100lb. bombs each, were tasked with a strike over Kikai to neutralize the airfield.

They joined planes from YORKTOWN, LANGLEY and SHANGRI LA to crater the runway at Wan Airfield on Kikai Shima.

1457 USS MISSOURI accompanied by two destroyers were detached from this Task Group by orders of the OTC.

1504 USS YORKTOWN designated guide, course 035°T, bearing 065°T, 2,800 yards.

1512 Completed recovering 4 F6Fs launched at 1130.

1523 Recovered 1 TBM launched at 0810.

1715 Recovered 6 TBMs launched at 1454.

1726 Recovered 4 F6Fs launched at 1454. This was the CAP assigned to protect the PBY, which successfully picked up two pilots.

1829-1841 Completed recovering 12 F6Fs launched at 1454.

1859 Secured from flight quarters. Air Department set to condition 14.

1945 Changed to disposition 5R.

2241 Commenced zigzagging on base course 170°T.

GL Still bombing Okinawa. We are making fire bombs out of belly tanks. GL

AD Okinawa. Planes bombing Isle. Since we left Ulithi we have dropped 268 tons of bombs on the Japs, 8 torpedoes, 1641 rockets from our ship & squadrons only. AD

HC C.A.P. over Kikai. Japs tried to reinforce their troops with landing craft on west side of Okinawa but got the hell knocked out of them. HC

Sunday 6 May 1945   *Ryukyu Islands, Okinawa Invasion*

Steaming as before off Okinawa in Task Unit 58.4.1.

0440 Sounded flight quarters.

0508 Observed flares on the horizon in the direction of Okinawa Jima, bearing 295°T. These were assumed to be from the front lines on Okinawa, 60 miles away.

0511 Completed launching 8 F6Fs for a TCAP over Okinawa.

0541 Changed the formation to cruising disposition 5VB.

0700 Heavy ships of the formation, excluding INDEPENDENCE, commenced fueling destroyers.

0815 Completed launching 12 F6Fs. 8 Hellcats were assigned with a TCAP over Okinawa, and 4 were tasked with a photo reconnaissance mission over Minami Daito Jima Airfield.

0859 Completed recovering 8 F6Fs launched at 0511.

0915 Commenced zigzagging (Plan No.24) on base course 180°T.

Edward Schultz - PHOM2C

Tailhook release & tractor crew

0953 Sounded torpedo defense by direction of the OTC.

1008 Completed launching 8 F6Fs.

1010 Secured from torpedo defense. The approaching aircraft was identified as friendly.

1131 Completed launching 8 TBMs for a support mission over Okinawa. They were to strike at a strong point with artillery, revetments and fortified caves near Shuri Village. It was a joint strike with planes from YORKTOWN, LANGLEY and SHANGRI LA, carefully directed by the CASCU. Two runs were made, dropping bombs only when accuracy was assured. It was clear over target and there was no flack.

1140 Completed recovering 6 (of the 12) F6Fs launched at 0815.

1204 Completed recovering 6 F6Fs (the remainder of the Hellcats launched at 0815).

1344 Completed recovering 8 F6Fs launched at 1008.

1446 Launched 8 F6Fs for a TCAP over Okinawa.

1503 Recovered 8 TBMs launched at 1131.

1523 Secured from flight quarters. Air Department set to condition 13.

1549 Commenced zigzagging (Plan No.6) on base course 180°T.

1843 Completed recovering 8 F6Fs launched at 1446.

1937 Formed cruising disposition 5R.

1949 Commenced zigzagging (Plan No.6) on base course 165°T.

2056 USS SHANGRI LA in station 2.270 designated guide, bearing 355°T, 2,800 yards.

During the night they retired toward the south to a replenishing area.

Monday 7 May 1945   *Ryukyu Islands, Replenishing at Sea*

Steaming as before retiring to rendezvous with a replenishing group.

0410 Sounded flight quarters.

0510 Launched 4 F6Fs for CAP, and 3 TBMs for ASP.

0538 Changed disposition for refueling, course 070°T, speed 10 knots, guide USS PECOS. Commenced maneuvering to take position astern USS VESUVIUS.

0627 Came along port side of USS VESUVIUS.

0630 Secured from flight quarters, Air Department set to condition 14. Commenced receiving ammunition from USS VESUVIUS.

0735 Cast off from USS VESUVIUS having received eighty 500lb. bombs and 200 delay fuses. Changed course to 200°T.

0758 USS MERTZ came alongside port quarter.

0804 Sounded flight quarters.

0817 Completed launching 3 F6F "duds" to be transferred to USS BOUGAINVILLE. USS MERTZ cast off after having received ferry pilots for transfer to USS BOUGAINVILLE (to fly replacement aircraft back to the INDEPENDENCE) and exchanging guard mail.

0840 Completed recovering 4 F6Fs and 3 TBMs.

0842 Secured from flight quarters, Air Department set to condition 14.

0905 Came along port side of ammunition ship, USS WRANGELL.

1038 Cast off from USS WRANGELL having received bombs, fuses, napalm and 30 & 50 caliber ammunition.

1039 Commenced maneuvering to make an approach on USS MANATEE.

1104 Came alongside tanker USS MANATEE.

1315 USS HEERMANN came alongside the port quarter.

1338 Cast off from USS MANATEE, having received 212,191 gallons of fuel oil and 45,220 gallons of aviation gasoline, and 1 enlisted man for transfer to the States.

1342 USS HEERMANN cast off having delivered US Mail, US Registered Mail and an officer for duty aboard this vessel.

1343 Commenced maneuvering to gain position off supply ship USS MERCURY.

1515 Cast off from USS MERCURY having received provisions.

1520 Sounded flight quarters.

1557-1602 Recovered 4 F6Fs and 1 TBM as replacement aircraft from USS BOUGAINVILLE.

1610 Changed course to 000°T, speed 22 knots, formed up in disposition 5VB. Leaving the replenishing group. The USS LANGLEY temporally would stay with the replenishing group to allow her crew to perform repairs. Guide is USS YORKTOWN, bearing 205°T, 2,800 yards.

1620 Gunnery Department manned all torpedo defense stations in preparation for gunnery practice.

1633 Reformed to disposition 5VC to give ships clear arcs while firing on a towed sleeve.

1633 Commenced gunnery exercises, maneuvering as directed by OTC.

1650 Secured from flight quarters, Air Department set to condition 14.

1746 Task Group concluded gunnery exercises.

1750 Formed disposition 5R. Secured from torpedo defense.

2037 Commenced zigzagging, Plan No.6, on base course 290°T, returning to an operating area off Okinawa.

AD   Refueled, rearmed, movies on hangar deck. Also received mail.   AD

26
Germany Surrenders
The Pacific War grinds on!

Tuesday 8 May 1945   *Ryukyu Islands, Okinawa Invasion*

Steaming as before off Okinawa in Task Unit 58.4.1 with USS YORKTOWN (OTC and guide) and USS SHANGRI LA. Air Department is in condition 14.

0410 Sounded flight quarters. Rain today from 0400 lasting through 1800, wind E at 20 to 33 knots.

0955 Made daily inspection of the magazines.

1230 The flight schedule has been canceled and the ship has been notified to secure its aircraft for heavy weather by the OTC.

1412 Secured from flight quarters. Set condition 14.

INDEPENDENCE would end the day steaming south, zigzagging on base course 180°T, speed 15 knots.

GN   Had a big hop scheduled for today but bad weather caused a postponement. In fact we were told to stand by for hurricane weather and we did make everything secure. Did a bit of touching up on the paintwork.   GN

AD   Okinawa. 1 war over. At 2200 we received official word that Germany had surrendered unconditionally.   AD

On 4 May 1945 the German Command agreed to surrender. The actual signing on the Instrument of Surrender occurred three days later at Rheims on 7 May 1945, making it official.

Statement by **PRESIDENT TRUMAN** *on the surrender of Nazi Germany.* *
The White House. May 8, 1945.   (* source: ibiblio.org/hyperwar/ETO/Axis_Surrender)

Nazi Germany has been defeated.
The Japanese people have felt the weight of our land, air, and naval attacks. So long as their leaders and the armed forces continue the war the striking power and intensity of our blows will steadily increase and will bring utter destruction to Japan's industrial war production, to its shipping, and to everything that supports its military activity.
The longer the war lasts, the greater will be the suffering and hardships which the people of Japan will undergo-all in vain. Our blows will not cease until the Japanese military and naval forces lay down their arms in unconditional surrender.
Just what does the unconditional surrender of the armed forces mean for the Japanese people?

It means the end of the war.
It means the termination of the influence of the military leaders who have brought Japan to the present brink of disaster.
It means provision for the return of soldiers and sailors to their families, their farms, their jobs.
It means not prolonging the present agony and suffering of the Japanese in the vain hope of victory.
Unconditional surrender does not mean the extermination or enslavement of the Japanese people.
" We can repay the debt which we owe to our God, to our dead, and to our children only by work - by ceaseless devotion to the responsibilities which lie ahead of us."

At the emergence of the United States in World War II, the nation was ill prepared for an immediate response to the vast enormity of the material and manpower needs. We were caught " flatfooted " and needed time to capitalize on this nation's potential. It was decreed that a maximum effort would be made to take care of " Europe First ". We needed to help England and our European Allies defeat the larger threat of Nazi Germany, and make do as best we could in the Pacific. Now, there was no distraction. The full might of the US could be concentrated on Japan.

For troops in Europe, there was great cause for celebration. For the men in the Pacific, there was still a conflict in progress, and the crew of the Mighty-I steamed on. For the fleet, there would be more fuel oil to burn, Kamikazes to absorb, and an elusive peace to pursue, as the dogs of war continued to snarl.

Wednesday 9 May 1945   *Ryukyu Islands, Okinawa Invasion*

Steaming as before off Okinawa in Task Unit 58.4.1 with USS YORKTOWN (OTC and guide) and USS SHANGRI LA. Air Department is in condition 14.
0410 Sounded flight quarters. Weather had cleared enough to proceed with air operations.
0510 Completed launching 8 F6Fs for CAP.
0541 Formed disposition 5VB.
0659 USS MONSSEN came alongside to starboard for refueling.
0806 USS MONSSEN cast off, having received 32,334 gallons of fuel oil.
0818 Completed launching 8 F6Fs for CAP.
0857 Completed recovery of 8 F6Fs launched at 0510.
0910-0950 USS MERTZ was along the starboard side receiving 24,535 gallons of fuel oil.

1140 Completed launching 12 F6Fs and 8 TBMs. 8 F6Fs were for CAP, the remaining 4 to proceed with the TBMs for a support strike on Okinawa. Joining planes from the YORKTOWN and SHANGRI-LA, the flight was given a target area northeast of Shuri Town. It was described as a troop concentration, fortified caves and possible gun positions. Twenty four 500lb. bombs were dropped by the TBMs, an additional eight dropped by the Hellcats. A ground observer gave a "well done" adding that both Japanese mortar and artillery fire had been reduced.
1214 Completed recovery of 8 F6Fs launched at 0818. 1 TBM (just launched at 1140) was recovered due to a fuel leak.
1445 Completed launching 8 F6Fs as part of the Task Group CAP.
1513 Launched 1 replacement F6F for the CAP, for a plane returning with a hydraulic problem in the tail hook.
1530 Completed recovery of 8 F6Fs, and 7 TBMs launched at 1140.
1826-1832 Completed recovery of 7 F6Fs launched at 1445, and 1 F6F launched at 1513.
1845 Secured from flight quarters. Air Department set to condition 14.
2215 Commenced zigzagging on base course 180°T, speed 18 knots.

GN Bad weather never did materialize although it did blow a little bit. We got one deck load strike off.

*Heard we are headed for Ulithi again. Would be pleased just as much if we stayed out here unless there is a better possibility of getting transferred. We were supposed to go to Leyte but I imagine the admiral in 58.3 draws more water than our head man for we go back to the dump once more. Got definite word that the war in Europe was over as of yesterday. Had word of it but nothing definite. **GN***

Thursday 10 May 1945   *Ryukyu Islands, Okinawa Invasion*

0410 Steaming off Okinawa in Task Unit 58.4.1 with USS YORKTOWN (OTC and guide) and USS SHANGRI LA. Sounded flight quarters.
0515 Completed launching 8 F6Fs for a TCAP over Amami Oshima (also referred to as Amami Gunto). They flew up the west coast of Amami Oshima, over Tokuno Shima to Kikai Shima. There they cratered the airfield. Ensign Leland V. Adgate was hit by AA fire, having his wing tip blown off and a 2'x3' hole in the wing. Lt Morrison accompanied Adgate back to the ship. Six Hellcats led by Lt Fodge strafed 3 luggers at Kuji Wan and a light house the western point of Amami Oshima.
0533 Formed disposition 5VB.
0736 Sounded flight quarters.
0739 Changed course to 000°T.
0740 Suffered steering casualty with the rudder at left 12°, and lost steering control. INDEPENDENCE informed the OTC immediately who at 0742 ordered a further 40° turn to the left to 320°T. Shifted control of the steering aft and changed from starboard to port steering units.
0743 Regained steering control and shifted control back to the Pilot House.
0816 Completed launching 8 F6Fs for a TCAP over Okinawa Shima.
0855 Completed recovery of 8 F6Fs launched at 0515.
0958 Completed launching 8 F6Fs for a TCAP over Okinawa Shima.
1139 Completed launching 4 F6Fs and 8 TBMs for a support strike over Okinawa. The assigned targets were troop concentrations, camouflaged trucks and a supply dump.
1205-1212 Completed recovery of 8 F6Fs launched at 0816.
1329-1335 Completed launching 8 F6Fs for a TCAP over Amami Oshima. They cratered the runway at Tokuno Airfield. The F6F-5 (Bu.No.72288) flown by Ensign Robert D. Floodqust developed "engine trouble" after it was hit by 20mm shells, ditching at sea 4500 feet off Kikai Shima. A "Dumbo" flying boat picked him up in excellent condition. He was returned to the Mighty-I five days later in Ulithi.
1345-1350 Completed recovery of 8 F6Fs launched at 0958.
1418 Sounded torpedo defense. Unidentified aircraft approaching the formation from the north. Radar tracked it to within 10 miles, then lost it.
1446 Commenced launching aircraft.
1447 Secured from torpedo defense. Gunnery Department set to condition One Easy.
1450 Completed launching 8 F6Fs for a CAP over Okinawa. Camouflaged trucks were strafed.
1515-1527 Completed recovery of 4 F6Fs, and 8 TBMs launched at 1139.
1530 The problem that caused the steering casualty at 0740 was found to be a jammed gear in the Pilot House steering stand. Repairs have been effected.
1605 Gunnery Department secured from condition One Easy, set to condition 3.
1734-1740 Completed recovery of 7 F6Fs launched at 1335, minus the Hellcat that Ensign Floodqust had ditched.
1851 Completed recovery of 7 F6Fs launched at 1450. The F6F flown by Ensign Everett R. Robinett landed at Yontan Airfield with engine trouble due to a fuel pump problem. He was reported to have spent a sleepless night on a stretcher in an ambulance truck. The sleep was disrupted by air raids.
1858 Secured from flight quarters. Air Department set to condition 14.
1947 Formed disposition 5R.
2248 Commenced zigzagging on base course 270°T, speed 18 knots.

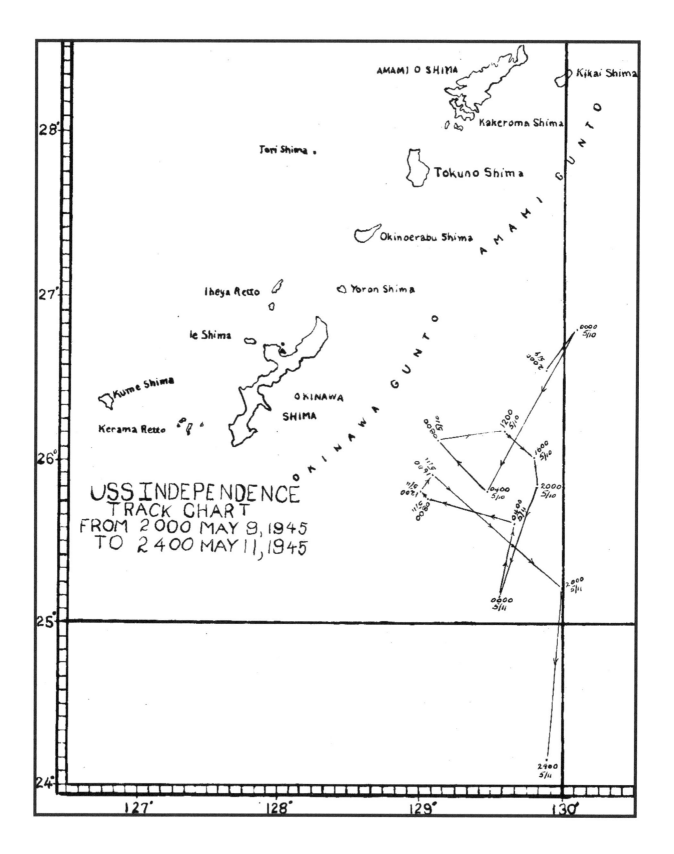

USS INDEPENDENCE
TRACK CHART
FROM 2000 MAY 9, 1945
TO 2400 MAY 11, 1945

Friday 11 May 1945   *Ryukyu Islands, Okinawa Invasion*

Steaming as before off Okinawa in Task Unit 58.4.1 with USS YORKTOWN (OTC and guide) and USS SHANGRI LA. Air Department is in condition 14.

0147 Sounded torpedo defense by order of OTC due to enemy aircraft approaching the task Group, 11 miles, bearing 005°T.

0257 Changed course to 130°T. Secured from torpedo defense. The enemy aircraft retired rapidly to the northeast with a night fighter in pursuit.

0410 Sounded flight quarters.

0518 Completed launching 12 F6Fs.

0533 Commenced maneuvering to form disposition 5VB.

0630 USS LANGLEY rejoined the formation.

0845 Completed recovery of 7 F6Fs launched at 0518.

0855 Resumed recovering aircraft. Formed cruising disposition 5 VC.

0856 Recovered 1 F6F launched at 0518.

0857 Sounded torpedo defense by order of OTC.

0903-0908 Recovered 4 F6Fs launched at 0518.

0944 Secured from torpedo defense. Gunnery Department set to condition One Easy.

1012 Gunnery Department set to condition One by order of OTC.

1013 Observed large plume of smoke arising from USS BUNKER HILL (on the horizon) believed to have been hit by a kamikaze. She continued to smoke and was visible to us for the next hour. (Photos next page)

1017 Observed enemy plane, shot down by fighters from USS LANGLEY, splash in the water, bearing 010°T, 10 miles.

1020 Sounded general quarters.

1023 Observed Task Group 58.3 firing on the horizon bearing 000°T, at an enemy plane.

1104 All departments set to condition One Easy.

1125-1134 Launched 12 F6Fs as CAP.

1144 Air Department set to condition 13. Gunnery Department set to condition One Easy.

INDEPENDENCE sighted life rafts, life jackets and other floating debris in the afternoon as they passed thru the area where the USS BUNKER HILL had been hit.

1245 Two motor-whale boats were sighted off the starboard quarter, distance approximately 7,000 yards. Their occupants were rescued by ships of this group.

1355 Formed cruising disposition 5VB.

1410 Sounded flight quarters.

1411 Sheered out to left to avoid hitting empty life rafts, life jackets and debris. A body was sighted in the water close aboard.

1444 Changed speed to 26 knots.

1446 Commenced launching aircraft.

1450 Sheered out to left to avoid hitting TBM-3 (Bu.No.68461) which crashed into the water almost dead ahead on takeoff, in light winds. The pilot, Lt.(jg) James M. Felker, and the two aircrew (ARM3c Edward S. Stepanian and AMM3c Authur A. Brinkmann) were observed to exit the plane before it sank.

1459 USS SHANGRI LA designated guide, bearing 345°T, 2,800 yards.

1500 Completed launching 4 F6Fs and 8 TBMS on a support strike, in addition to the TBM that splashed. The strike group was assigned to hit a ravine with enemy mortar positions. They attacked with bombs and rockets, putting their entire load into the ravine. They then strafed an assigned target believed to be camouflaged trucks.

1504 The pilot and the two crew members from the dunked TBM were picked up by the USS MELVIN in good condition.

1517-1535 Completed recovery of 12 F6Fs launched at 1134 and 1 F6F * that had landed at Yontan Field, Okinawa Jima due to engine trouble yesterday, 10 May 1945. (* Ensign Robinett)

Chapter 26   625

As the crews of all US vessels looked on in utter dismay .....
Deep within their gut they knew .... It could be them !
Daily they did their jobs, daily they lived with the threat.

1603 Gunnery Department secured from condition One Easy, set to condition 3.

By late afternoon, the USS BUNKER HILL was proceeding under her own power, being escorted to Ulithi. Vice Admiral Marc A. Mitscher, CTF 58, transferred his flag to the USS ENTERPRISE.

1623 USS YORKTOWN designated guide.

1755 Following the movements of the OTC, colors were half-masted.

1807 Changed course to 150°T, the Task Group had been previously ordered to proceed to Ulithi for replenishment, and overhaul.

1813 Two blocked the colors, following the movements of the OTC.

1820 USS SOUTH DAKOTA joined Task Group 58.4 to travel southeast with us.

1829-1839 Recovered 4 F6Fs and 8 TBMs launched at 1500.

1850 Secured from flight quarters. Air Department set to condition 14.

1927 USS SOUTH DAKOTA designated guide, course 145°T, bearing 300°T, 2,000 yards.

1933 Formed cruising disposition 5R. At 2346, changed course to 110°T.

Captain Kindell noted in the SOL: *"We seem to be on the way south to Ulithi, no land falls or contacts are expected."*

GL Early this AM had bogies – Betty splashed. Got word to expect big air attack. Set 1 Easy. 2 Jills & 1 Irving splashed, watched them burn all the way down. Bunker Hill was hit by 1,000 pounder & suicide plane. It is Mitscher's flag ship, she has only been out here 2 days. 5 planes shot down in that group, 20 by CAP. Bunker Hill dead in water, fires in engine room. 2 DD's and 1 cruiser standing by. We passed by her – big hole in flight deck, still burning. USS Hanley** attacked by 33 planes, shot down 19 by herself. Brother, that is shooting. After being hit she even got 4. DD Brown took a near miss by Banzai. About 2:30 in the afternoon we sighted life rafts & wreckage from Bunker Hill. 2 dead bodies floated under catwalk. DD's busy picking up out of sea, about 200 so far. GL

AD Okinawa. 1015 GQ was sounded and as I reached the flight deck I saw 2 Jap planes burning near the horizon. Our CAP shot them down. Our Task Group was not under attack however 58.2 was and the Bunker Hill was hit by two suicides. I could see her smoking on the Horizon. One DD shot down 19 planes today. AD

HC USS Bunker Hill was hit bad midships. Could see it burning. Don't know whether it was a bomb or a Banzai, went through to engine room. When explosions went off it threw a lot of men over the side, some jumped. Cruiser and 5 cans picked up most of them up and put them back aboard. Later in the day we saw 2 men afloat but both were dead. We were at GQ all morning, set condition 1 easy in the afternoon. HC

(Note: USS Bunker Hill suffered 346 men killed, 264 wounded, and 43 missing. She was hit by 2 kamikazes.)   (** The Destroyer was USS HUGH W. HADLEY. On picket duty, she was credited for roughly 20 Japanese aircraft. She was hit by; 1 bomb aft, 1 Oka / Baka piloted bomb released from a Betty, and 2 other kamikazes. She suffered 28 Killed and 67 wounded. She was towed to Ie Shima.)

Saturday 12 May 1945   *Retiring to Ulithi Atoll*

Steaming as before, with Task Unit 58.4.1 in company with USS YORKTOWN, USS SHANGRI LA and USS LANGLEY. Air Department is in condition 14.

0035 Commenced zigzagging on base course 145°T.

0133 Held steering casualty drill. Steering control was shifted to the central steering station.

0204 Shifted steering control aft. At 0233 shifted control back to the pilot house, completing the drill.

0508 Task group formed disposition 5-VB.

0835 USS YORKTOWN designated guide, course 020°T, speed 20 knots, bearing 255°T, 2,800 yards. Then the formation formed disposition 5-VC.

0845 Gunnery Department set to condition One for gunnery practice.
1100 Secured from torpedo defense having fired 1,950 rounds of 40mm, and 531 rounds of 20mm in practice on a towed sleeve.
1104 Formation shifted to disposition 5-VB.
1233-1243 USS MCGOWAN maneuvered alongside for the transfer of US Mail.
1236-1419 Gunnery Department went to torpedo defense stations for simulated dive bomber tracking exercises.
1351 Sounded flight quarters.
1447 Launched 4 F6Fs for CAP, and 3 TBMs for ASP.
1509 Formation shifted to disposition 5-VC.
1532 Gunnery Department manned torpedo defense stations for firing exercises.
1545 Secured from flight quarters.
1718 Secured from gunnery exercises and torpedo defense.
1728 Sounded flight quarters.
1729 Formed cruising disposition 5-R, changed speed to 16 knots, course is 165°T.
1755 USS SOUTH DAKOTA was designated guide, bearing 300°T, 2,000 yards.
1810 Recovered 4 F6Fs and 3 TBMs launched at 1447.

GN *Not much doing today. Did clean up the spaces a bit. Had ASP in the afternoon. On the way to Ulithi at about 14 knots.* *GN*

AD *Heading for Ulithi. Gunnery practice all day.* *AD*

Sunday 13 May 1945   *Retiring to Ulithi Atoll*

Steaming as before, with Task Unit 58.4.1 in company with USS YORKTOWN, USS SHANGRI LA and USS LANGLEY. Air Department is in condition 14. Task Group is in disposition 5R. Guide is USS SOUTH DAKOTA. Ship is darkened. Boilers 1 & 3 are in use.
0624-0640 USS MCGOWAN maneuvered along starboard side amidships to transfer the pilot and two aircrew (from Lt.(jg) Felker's TBM lost on 11 May, during the takeoff accident) back aboard.
0750 USS YORKTOWN designated guide.
0830-0948 Sounded torpedo defense for tracking drill and simulated attacks.
1047 Changed course to 120°T, speed 18 knots. Task Units 58.4.2 and 58.4.3, minus 8 destroyers, left the formation for gunnery exercises with their big guns.
1200 Secured from flight quarters. Air Department set to condition 14.
1445 Task Units 58.4.2 and 58.4.3 rejoined the formation, having completed exercises. USS SOUTH DAKOTA departed the formation for another destination.
1602 Commenced zigzagging on base course 145°T.
1805 Darkened ship.
2130 Commenced steering casualty drill. Transferred steering control to central station.
2231 Transferred steering control from central station to steering aft.
2301 Transferred steering control from steering aft to the pilot house, completing the steering casualty drill. They steamed through the night, zigzagging on base course 145°T, at 20 knots.

Monday 14 May 1945   *Ulithi Atoll*

Steaming as before, with Task Unit 58.4.1 in company with USS YORKTOWN (guide), USS SHANGRI LA and USS LANGLEY. Air Department is in condition 14. Task Group is in disposition 5R.
0506 Task group formed disposition 5VB on axis 105°T, speed 16 knots.
0630 Sounded flight quarters.
0724 Changed speed to 23 knots.

0726-0729 Launched 4 F6Fs for ASP before entering port. These aircraft landed at Falalop Airstrip.

0744 Task group formed cruising disposition 5VC to conduct AA practice against towed sleeves.

0745 Secured from flight quarters. Air Department set to condition 14.

0755 Changed speed to 18 knots.

0803 Sounded torpedo defense for gunnery practice.

1020 Changed course to 200°T.

1023 Sighted Ulithi Atoll, bearing 108°T, 18 miles.

1038 Secured from torpedo defense. Gunnery Department set to condition 3.

1100 Changed course to 190°T, speed 15 knots, while forming a column astern USS YORKTOWN.

1123 Changed course to 170°T, speed 18 knots. Gained station 3,000 yards astern guide.

1129 Changed course and axis to 245°T.

1144 Changed course and axis to 215°T, speed 16 knots.

1146 Commenced maneuvering while approaching Mugai Channel, Ulithi Atoll, Caroline Islands.

1208 Sounded general quarters for entering port.

1219 Passed buoys No.1 & 2 entering Mugai Channel.

1226 Secured from general quarters. Air Department set to condition 14. All other departments set to condition 3. Steering at various courses at various speeds while approaching anchorage.

1248 Anchored in berth 23, northern anchorage, in 23 fathoms of water, coral bottom, with 125 fathoms of chain to port anchor. In the anchorage were various supply ships and auxiliaries of the US Fleet, as well as a few combatant ships. CVL-22 had been underway for 61 days continuously since 14 March 1945, a new record for this ship. They immediately started an intensive schedule of replenishing, receiving a steady stream of small boats from supply and ammunition ships.

1300 Set all clocks ahead 1 hour to minus 10 time zone.

1412 Cut out boiler No.3 and secured it.

1630 Received 1 LCM from the boat pool.

1854 Set condition One for Gunnery Department.

1855-1955 LCT670 was along starboard side delivering mail.

1955 Gunnery Department secured from condition One. Set condition 3.

They would remain in condition 3 while at anchorage as a precaution against air attacks. The Air Group would participate in daily CAPs around the atoll, flying from Falalop Airstrip.

2115 Tanker USS NECHES moored along starboard side outboard of a camel with 6 manila lines.

GN Anchored in Ulithi at about 1300. Hope our stay here is very short. Hot as hell. GN

Tuesday 15 May 1945   *Ulithi Atoll*

0705 Anchored as before. USS NECHES and YOG 30 cast off, having delivered 388,914 gallons of fuel oil, and 33,100 gallons of aviation gasoline.

0825-1125 LCT 1102 was alongside forward delivering ammunition. (Deck Log error: Has LCM vs. LCT)

0910 After steering engines were placed out of commission for overhaul.

1035-1221 Barge was alongside delivering aviation supplies.

1250-1325 LCT 806 was alongside to receive 3 aircraft engines transferred to the engine pool for overhaul.

1426 Received message, flash Blue in the harbor. Sounded torpedo defense.

This unidentified aircraft turned out to be friendly.

1448 Received message, flash White. Secured from torpedo defense.

1450 Fox two-blocked. Commenced catapulting airplanes.

1453 Completed catapulting 1 F6F and 1 TBM to land at Falalop Island. Fox down.

1456–1520 Barge No. 312-2 was alongside port quarter delivering supplies.

1600-1620 Barge No. 34-626 was along starboard side delivering 1 F6F-5 from CASU 51.

1625-1930 LCT 797 was alongside port quarter delivering 3,000 gallons of aviation lube oil.

GN Painting all day. Hope we pull out soon. Reports are very conflicting on that score. Still hot as the devil and seems to be worse. GN

AD Anchored at Ulithi. The Enterprise was also hit by suicides. AD

(USS ENTERPRISE took a kamikaze hit on the 14th, blowing her massive forward elevator high into the air. She withdrew from combat on the 16th, not to return to the war. Mitscher, with the BUNKER HILL hit, had just transferred his flag to ENTERPRISE on the 11th. Once again uprooted, he transferred his flag, this time to the USS RANDOLPH.)

Wednesday 16 May 1945   *Ulithi Atoll*

Anchored as before. The ship is dimmed out. Boiler No. 1 in use for auxiliary purposes.
0320-0608 LCM 132 was alongside starboard quarter to deliver fresh provisions.
0800-1110 LCM 193 was alongside port quarter.
0805-1010 LCM 17-4 was alongside starboard quarter.
0830 Mustered crew on stations. LCT 760 alongside starboard bow to deliver bombs.
1014 LCM 129 alongside starboard quarter to deliver bomb fuses. LCM 80 alongside port quarter.
1110 LCM 35 alongside port quarter.
1204 LCT 760 cast off.
1345 Received two TBM3-Es from CASU 51.
1347 LCT 806 came alongside port quarter with salvage gear. (Deck Log error: Has LCM vs. LCT)
1614-1733 LCT 759 was along port side delivering lube oil.

Thursday 17 May 1945   *Ulithi Atoll*

Anchored as before. By 16 May, they completed most of the replenishing of the ship, before ComServRon TEN began moving his ships toward Leyte Gulf. During this period, daily recreation parties were sent to Mog Mog. Also during this period, they accomplished extensive repairs on the engineering plant, including steering engines.

This morning the USS LANGLEY, streaming a homeward bound pennant, and the USS BUNKER HILL got under way for the states.

GN Still around and still cleaning up the ship. Have an idea of what the peace time Navy must be like and it is not for me. GN

Friday 18 May 1945   *Ulithi Atoll*

Anchored as before. On this day they received aviation spares from LCT 882. This included aircraft engines, propellers and fuel drop tanks.

Saturday 19 May 1945   *Ulithi Atoll - Commander Daniel Fletcher Smith, Jr. becomes XO*

Anchored as before. Commander Daniel Fletcher Smith, Jr. replaced Commander Edwin James Stephen Young as Executive Officer of this vessel. Smith's last assignment was CAG 20 on the ENTERPRISE. This evening, before movies, a smoker was held on the hanger deck, featuring wrestling and boxing matches between crew members.

Sunday 20 May 1945   *Anchored in Ulithi Atoll*

0900 Mustered crew at quarters.

The Commanding Officer presented awards as follows:

The Distinguished Flying Cross
Commander Carl W. Rooney

Air Medal	**Purple Heart**
Commander Carl W. Rooney	Lt. Jack Rivers
Lt.(jg) Carlton T. Jones	ARM2c James W. Bosserman
Lt.(jg) William J. Schleis	AOM2c Elmer Vernon Rasor
Lt.(jg) Marlar E. Stewart	ARM3c Floyd Eugene Abbott
Lt.(jg) Richard M. Rogg	AM3c Raymond Bernard Franklin
	S1c George Robert Mc Coun

At 2130 the crew hoisted the No.2 motor whale boat into the skids.

Monday 21 May 1945 *Ulithi Atoll*

0800 Anchored as before. Mustered crew on stations. At 2015 today a LCM came along port side to deliver aviation stores, casting off at 2029.

GN Not much new. Just standing by now awaiting word of getting underway. All spaces are just about up to snuff or as good as we can do with them. GN

Tuesday 22 May 1945 *Ulithi Atoll*

0711 Anchored as before. Got underway to shift to a firing berth for gunnery practice, dropping anchor in berth A-4. They conducted AA firing practice on towed sleeves all morning, well into the afternoon. Gunners expended 2,083 rounds of 40mm ammunition, and 1,200 rounds of 20mm ammunition. During the course of their stay, personnel have been transferred, both on and off this ship. This evening, a draft of 79 men (largely Seamen Second Class) reported for duty.

Wednesday 23 May 1945 *Ulithi Atoll*

0830 Anchored as before. Mustered crew on stations.
0945-1132 Gunnery Department manned all torpedo defense stations for firing exercises.
1210 Tested port and starboard steering engines. Testing was satisfactory. Ready for getting underway.
1245 Made all preparations for getting underway.
1300 Underway from firing anchorage to shift berth within Ulithi Atoll. 1359 Anchored in berth 21, Ulithi Atoll in 22 fathoms of water, coral bottom, 125 fathoms of chain on port anchor. Our former berth is now occupied by the USS TICONDEROGA.

What was Ulithi like? This description is written in the Fighting Squadron Forty-Six (VF-46) History:
"Ulithi the Hairshirt
The chief difference between them is that you can remove a hairshirt. At 1255, 14 May the ship was dead in the water and the First Lieutenant marked the sounding, "By the deep twenty-six." We were at anchor for an alleged ten days of pleasure and rest. Ulithi had little to offer. There was no good swimming, no women (atoll) and the weather was extremely hot and enervating. After the novelty of Mog Mog's beer had worn off we were content to absorb Vitamin Dog by sun bathing on the Fo'cs'le in the afternoon, attend movies on the hangar deck in the evening and sleep until noon. Romance in the Pacific war was conspicuous by its absence. The ship, Chaplain FAILING officiating, provided a smoker consisting of wrestling and boxing contests between men and an excellent musical."

Thursday 24 May 1945   *Ulithi Atoll — Underway*

0330 Anchored as before. Lighted fires under No.4 Boiler.

0350 Cut No.4 Boiler into the main steam line.

0400 Set all clocks back one hour to zone minus 9.

0430 Made all preparations for getting underway.

0529 With Captain Kindell at the conn, Executive Officer and Navigator on the bridge, they got underway at 15 knots, maneuvering as necessary to conform to Mugai Channel.

0556 Sounded routine general quarters and tested general alarms.

0605 Took departure of Mugai Channel, Ulithi Atoll, passing between buoys No. 1 & 2 abeam and stood out with Task Group 58.4, including carriers USS YORKTOWN, USS SHANGRI LA and USS TICONDEROGA. The Group consisted of 3 large carriers, one light carrier, 2 battleships, 2 large cruisers, 2 anti-aircraft cruisers and our screening destroyers. OTC, Rear Admiral A.W. Radford in YORKTOWN, guide.

0658 Secured from general quarters.

0707 Formed disposition 5VC for gunnery exercises.

1004 Sounded torpedo defense for firing exercises.

1052 Sounded flight quarters.

1133 Reformed to disposition 5R.

1136 Secured from torpedo defense, having expended 1,422 rounds of 40mm and 1,580 rounds of 20mm ammunition.

1151 Completed recovery of 5 F6F replacement aircraft from Falalop Island.

1311 Launched 8 F6Fs and 6 TBMs to participate in a simulated strike.

1327 Secured from flight quarters.

1516 Recovered 1 TBM with an injured crewman. Charles W. Cooper was admitted to sick bay. He was injured when the tow line for the firing sleeve came loose, puncturing the fuselage in his radio compartment, severely lacerating his leg and his wrist. He would be sent to the USS BOUNTIFUL to recover.

1626 Completed recovery of the 8 F6Fs and the remaining 5 TBMs launched at 1311.

1659 Secured from flight quarters. Air Department set to condition 14.

1802-1902 Gunnery Department was at torpedo defense.

2217 Commenced zigzagging on base course 315°T, 22 knots.

Captain Kindell noted in the SOL: *"No friendly contacts are expected except the four DDs on the tracking exercise. Call me if anything unusual comes up."*

Friday 25 May 1945   *Ryukyu Islands, Okinawa Invasion*

0423 Steaming as before toward Okinawa in Task Unit 58.4.1 with USS YORKTOWN (OTC and guide), USS SHANGRI LA and USS TICONDEROGA.

0709 Formed cruising disposition 5VB.

0750 Commenced zigzagging on base course 320°T, 22 knots.

0758 Gunnery Dept. set to condition One for tracking exercises to defend against suicide bombers.

0800 Mustered crew on stations.

0936 Gunnery Department secured from condition One. Set condition 3.

1000 Sounded fire call. Fire reported in the after elevator pit, frame 115.

1006 Secured from fire quarters. Fire had been started in a bucket for drill purposes.

1030 Sounded flight quarters.

1139 Completed launching 3 TBMs for ASP and 8 F6Fs for CAP.

1200 Battleships and cruisers of Task Unit 58.4.2 (with their screening destroyers) departed the formation to conduct independent exercises.

1258-1305 Launched 8 F6Fs and 5 TBMs for a strike drill.

1318 Secured from flight quarters. Air Department set to condition 13.
1504 Sounded flight quarters.
1532-1544 Recovered 8 F6Fs and 3 TBMs launched at 1139.
1646 Completed recovery of 8 F6Fs and 5 TBMs launched at 1305.
1712 Secured from flight quarters. Air Department set to condition 14.
They finished the day zigzagging northwest on base course 320°T, at 20 knots.

GL Intense AA practice & battle problems. GL

Saturday 26 May 1945   *Ryukyu Islands, Okinawa Invasion*

Steaming as before toward Okinawa in Task Unit 58.4.1 with USS YORKTOWN (guide, bears 155°T, 2,800 yards - Rear Admiral A.W. Radford is OTC of 58.4 & 58.4.1), USS SHANGRI LA and USS TICONDEROGA.
TG is in disposition 5R. Boilers 1,2 and 4 are in use. Air Department is in condition 14.
0537 Formed cruising disposition 5VB.
0551 USS TRATHEN came along starboard side to take on fuel.
0630 Sounded flight quarters.
0645 USS TRATHEN cast off having received 18,273 gallons of fuel oil.
0727-0732 Launched 8 F6Fs and 2 TBMs. Four of the Hellcats were assigned CAP and the other four were utilized for radar calibration runs. The 2 Avengers were assigned ASP.
0746 Formed disposition 5VC for gunnery exercises.
0800 Mustered crew on stations. Secured from flight quarters. Air Department set to condition 13.
Sounded torpedo defense for firing exercises, practicing against a towed sleeve.
1028 Secured from torpedo defense. Expended 1,201 rounds of 40mm and 723 rounds of 20mm ammunition.
1030 Sounded flight quarters.
1031 Reformed cruising disposition 5VB.
1119 Completed recovery of 8 F6Fs and 2 TBMs launched at 0732.
1130 Secured from flight quarters.
1245 Commenced zigzagging on base course 315°T, speed 20 knots.
In the early afternoon they held gunnery AA coordination drills with no firing.
1415 Sounded flight quarters.
1429 Secured from condition One, having completed gunnery exercises. Set condition 3.
1515 Launched 4 F6Fs for CAP.
1522 Secured from flight quarters. Air Department set to condition 13.
1705 Formed cruising disposition 5R.
1744 Sounded flight quarters.
1836-1840 Recovered 4 F6Fs launched at 1515.
1905 Secured from flight quarters. Air Department set to condition 14.
2015 All ships commenced making smoke on order from OTC as an exercise.
2058 Ceased making smoke with the exercise having been completed. This had been an experiment to test the possible defensive value. Night fighters aloft on a bright moonlight night were to observe the coverage the smoke provided the fleet.
2232 Commenced zigzagging on base course 015°T, speed 18 knots.

Captain Kindell noted in the SOL: *"We expect to meet the fueling group and 58.1 and 58.3 in the morning. They should show on radar anytime in morning watch. No landfalls are expected."*

Sunday 27 May 1945   *Ryukyu Islands, Okinawa Invasion*

Steaming as before, proceeding toward a fueling rendezvous.

0140 Commenced zigzagging on base course 280°T.

0559 Task Group commenced fueling operations.

0600 Commenced maneuvering to gain position on our assigned tanker.

0622 Came along port side of USS ATASCOSA. At 0626, USS ATASCOSA was designated as guide in the fueling disposition, course 240°T, 10 knots.

0730 Sounded flight quarters.

0829 Completed launching 4 F6Fs for CAP and 3 TBMs for ASP.

0837 Secured from flight quarters. Air Department set to condition 13.

0900 Cast off from USS ATASCOSA having transferred to the tanker the Executive Officer, Commander Edwin J.S. Young for reassignment, and the mail. INDEPENDENCE received from the tanker fuel oil and aviation gasoline. Commenced maneuvering to regain position in formation disposition 5R.

0923 USS COLAHAN came alongside our port quarter. INDEPENDENCE transferred aircrewman ARM3c Charles W. Cooper to the USS COLAHAN for delivery to a hospital ship for long term recovery from injuries received on 24 May.

0928-0936 USS TRATHEN was alongside the starboard quarter to transfer officer messenger mail.

0944 USS COLAHAN cast off.

1118-1123 USS MELVIN was alongside the port quarter to transfer officer messenger mail.

1133 Sounded flight quarters.

1144 Sounded fire quarters for one alarm fire in the bake shop, second deck.

1149 Secured from fire quarters. Fire, caused by dripping grease onto an oven heating element, was extinguished without damage.

1209 Completed recovery of 4 F6Fs and 3 TBMs launched at 0829.

1241 Secured from flight quarters. Air Department set to condition 14.

1308-1320 USS WADLEIGH came alongside the starboard quarter for delivery of freight, and to transfer a ferry pilot to the USS TICONDEROGA (to pick up a replacement aircraft).

1322 USS YORKTOWN was designated guide. The Task Group completed fueling, and departed the tanker group at 1325. The Task Group continued on toward Okinawa.

1722 Sounded flight quarters.

1750 Changed speed to 17 knots.

1847 Recovered 1 F6F, flown from USS TICONDEROGA as a replacement aircraft.

1913 Secured from flight quarters. Air Department set to condition 14.

2133 Commenced zigzagging on base course 000°T.

GN Starting to get a wee bit cooler. We refueled today, brought aboard some mail. Young also left the ship and the new exec is officially underway. GN

RC Refueled, and " Bull Halsey " takes over, well here we go again. RC

Monday 28 May 1945   *Ryukyu Islands, Okinawa Invasion*

0000 At 2400 on the 27th (0000 this morning on 28 May) CVL-22 officially became part of Task Group 38.4 as Vice Admiral William F. Halsey, Commander Third Fleet, aboard the USS MISSOURI, replaced Vice Admiral Raymond A. Spruance. Tomorrow (on 29 May) Vice Admiral John Sydney McCain will replace Rear Admiral Mark A. Mitscher.

Task Force 38 now consisted of three carrier Task Groups.

TG 38.1 — Rear Admiral Joseph James ("Jocko") Clark

TG 38.3 — Rear Admiral Fredrick Carl Sherman

TG 38.4 — Rear Admiral Arthur William Radford

Steaming as before, headed north toward Okinawa in Task Unit 38.4.1 with USS YORKTOWN (guide, bears 105°T, 2,800 yards. Course 000°T, speed 19 knots. Rear Admiral A.W. Radford is OTC of 38.4 & 38.4.1), USS SHANGRI LA and USS TICONDEROGA. Task Group is in disposition 5R.

0356 Sounded torpedo defense due to reported unidentified aircraft on radar.

0409 Sounded flight quarters.

0416 Secured from torpedo defense after bogey retired from the area.

0437 Sounded routine general quarters.

0511 Completed launching 8 F6Fs for CAP over the Task Group.

0620 Changed course to 310°T. USS MISSOURI joined the formation.

0623 Reformed to cruising disposition 5VB.

0635 Changed speed to 18 knots. USS MISSOURI designated guide in station 0000, bearing 060°T, distance 2,000 yards.

VF-46 Squadron History would comment: *"together with 3 BBs, 2 CBs, 2 CLs, and 17 DDs comprised TG 38.4. We were surrounded by 27-16", 18-12", 217-5", and over 1000 each 40 mm and 20 mm guns, the greatest fire power ever assembled in one Task Group. Admiral HALSEY hoisted his flag in the U.S.S. MISSOURI whose position was directly ahead of us. It was comforting to see her guns "bristling" from port to starboard."*

0819 Completed launching 8 F6Fs for CAP over the Task Group.

0854 Completed recovery of 8 F6Fs launched at 0511.

0930 Sounded torpedo defense on order from OTC.

0935 Secured from torpedo defense. Aircraft was a friendly.

1215 Sounded torpedo defense.

1217 Secured from torpedo defense. Aircraft identified as friendly.

1311-1319 Recovered 8 F6Fs launched at 0819.

1433-1438 Completed launching 8 F6Fs for CAP over the Task Group.

1842 Completed recovery of 8 F6Fs launched at 1438.

1856 Reformed to cruising disposition 5R.

1903 Secured from flight quarters. Air Department set to condition 14.

2325 Commenced zigzagging on base course 245°T.

GN " Bull " Halsey officially took over as of midnight last night and we are now changed over again to 38.4. Started off good in the approved " Bull " style. Had TD about 4 AM with a bogie in the neighborhood and we at present time are about 90 miles off Okinawa. Gunnery called out a few times during the day but they never did get in too close. Had a B29 snooping around for a while during the day and that was surprising for usually the army tends strictly to their own knitting and leaves us be. Shangri La CAP bagged ten assorted Nip planes* before they could get out to us. Flew CAP. GN

(* SHANGRI LA's Air Group 85 bagged: 2 Oscars, 2 Nicks, 4 Franks, 1 Nate & 1 Val. "Willie Callan, now in VF-85, who flew with VF-6 off USS INDEPENDENCE in 1943 also was credited with a Zeke kill when the Japanese pilot splashed during a failed split-S trying to escape Callan's guns. His photo with "Butch" O'Hare & Alex Vraciu on page 171.)

Tuesday 29 May 1945   *Ryukyu Islands, Okinawa Invasion*

Steaming as before off Okinawa in Task Unit 38.4.1 with USS YORKTOWN (Rear Admiral A.W. Radford is OTC of 38.4 & 38.4.1), USS SHANGRI LA and USS TICONDEROGA. TG is in disposition 5R, axis 130°T, zigzagging on base course 245°T, speed 18 knots. Guide is USS MISSOURI, bearing 130°T, 2,000 yards. Air Department is in condition 14.

0407 Sounded flight quarters.

0456-0503 Launched 8 F6Fs for CAP over the Task Group.

0535 Air Department set to condition 13.

0731 Sounded flight quarters.

0800 Mustered crew on stations.

0815 Completed launching 8 F6Fs for RAPCAP over the radar picket line of destroyers.

0845 USS NORMAN SCOTT came alongside the starboard quarter to deliver officer messenger mail. She cast off, *"after dropping in the water, officer messenger mail"* to be delivered to this ship. Destroyer USS MCCORD was directed to recover the bag of mail.

0908 Completed recovery of 8 F6Fs launched at 0503.

0931-0933 USS MCCORD was alongside the starboard quarter to deliver the recovered bag of officer messenger mail.

1007 Vice Admiral J. S. McCain (Commander, Second Carrier Task Force, Pacific) assumed command of Task Force 38. His flagship, USS SHANGRI LA.

1142 Completed launching 8 F6Fs for CAP over the Task Group.

1217 Launched 1 F6F as a replacement.

1219-1225 Recovered 8 F6Fs launched at 0815, and 1 F6F launched at 1142.

1258 Secured from flight quarters. Air Department set to condition 13.

1402 Sounded flight quarters.

1443-1447 Completed launching 8 F6Fs for RAPCAP over the radar picket line of destroyers.

1518-1524 Recovered 7 F6Fs launched at 1142, and 1 F6F launched at 1217

1611 Launched 1 F6F.

1621 Recovered 1 F6F launched at 1447.

1847 Completed recovery of 7 F6Fs launched at 1447, and 1 F6F launched at 1611.

1912 Secured from flight quarters. Air Department set to condition 14.

1947 Formed cruising disposition 5R. At 2220 they commenced zigzagging on base course 355°T.

GL Attacking Okinawa, giving support. Shangri-la shot down 10 Japs over target, lost 3 of her own. Rest day was quiet, expecting bad weather. GL (Note: This occurred yesterday on 28 May - See write-up)

VF-46 Squadron History would note:
"Point Option is established once more at Okinawa.
The alleged vacation terminated 28 May when four CAPs were placed on the flight schedule. With Air Group 9 we were senior in the Task Group and hoped to receive strike for strike assignments with the CVs as we had in the good old days in Task group 58.3, but such was not our lot. The pre-dawn CAP became like the proverbial bed pan - - there every morning even on fueling days."

Wednesday 30 May 1945   *Ryukyu Islands, Okinawa Invasion*

Steaming as before off Okinawa in Task Unit 38.4.1.

0415 Sounded flight quarters.

0536-0544 Launched 16 F6Fs for a TCAP over Okinawa. Bad weather was present. Launch times had been delayed roughly 30 minutes, in hopes of clearing conditions.

0550 Formed cruising disposition 5VB.

0814 Sounded flight quarters.

0852 Completed recovery of 16 F6Fs launched at 0544.

A second planned TCAP for the day was canceled due to poor visibility over Okinawa. During this period, a frontal zone established between the Task Unit and Kyushu set up oscillations, pulsing out portions of it down to Okinawa. Low "scud" with ceilings down to 200' occurred on the 29th, 30th and 31st. Today, fog patches in the morning, mixed with the scud. But the weather was a dual edged blade as it deferred the planned strikes. It also grounded Japanese efforts to attack the fleet, both today and on the 31st. The southwest islands of Japan entered its rainy season.

1057 Sounded fire quarters. One alarm fire at frame 57, starboard side on the third deck.

1103 Secured from fire quarters. The fire was in the automatic control panel of the hangar deck sprinkling system, and was quickly extinguished. The control panel must be repaired before it can be used.

1445 Launched 8 F6Fs, then secured from flight quarters, setting the Air Department to condition 13.

1556 Electronic control panel for the sprinkler system was repaired, and is fully functional.

1752 Sounded flight quarters.

1850 Completed recovery of 8 F6Fs launched at 1445.

1918 Formed cruising disposition 5R.

1928 Secured from flight quarters. Air Department set to condition 14.

GN Pretty inactive again. Flew a big CAP in the morning and moderate size for the rest of the day. We're supposed to refuel and reprovision tomorrow but I think we strike instead. GN

Thursday 31 May 1945   *Ryukyu Islands, Okinawa Invasion*

Steaming as before off Okinawa in Task Unit 38.4.1.

This morning they were covered by a solid fog bank. Visibility varies from 200 to 800 yards laterally. However it appeared to be thin vertically, as they could see sun thru it, and above the thin layer the sky appeared to be clear. Flight operations, after the night patrols had landed, were of necessity curtailed. Roughly 3 hours after daybreak, the fog began to thin, giving them the ability to begin to see other vessels only 2,000 yards away. By 0800 the fog began to rapidly diminish.

0415 Sounded flight quarters.

0740 Launched 8 F6Fs for a CAP.

0750 Placed No.4 boiler out of commission for repair. During most of the period of time, since leaving Ulithi, the OTC had stated CVL-22 would not need speeds greater than 27 knots. Thus, they operated 3 boilers on the main steam line at any given time. This allowed them to shut down the forth to facilitate underway repairs and routine upkeep on the idled boiler.

0755 Formed cruising disposition 5VB.

0824 Completed launching 4 F6Fs, to augment the CAP launched at 0740.

1026 Completed launching 2 F6Fs and 6 TBMs for a support mission over Okinawa. The TBMs and F6Fs were tasked with an elevated crossroad near the village of Tomui, suspected to have camouflaged trucks parked along the roadside.

1202-1210 Recovered 12 F6Fs, 8 launched at 0740 and 4 launched at 0824.

1356-1406 Recovered 2 F6Fs and 6 TBMs launched at 1026.

1443-1448 Launched 8 F6Fs for a CAP.

1650 Recovered 1 F6F launched at 1448.

1855 Completed recovery of the 7 F6Fs remaining launched at 1448.

1911-2010 Manned (routine) torpedo defense stations.

1935 Secured from flight quarters. Air Department set to condition 14.

2014 Formed cruising disposition 5R, guide USS MISSOURI, distance 2,000 yards.

2241 Commenced zigzagging on base course 180°T, retiring toward the south to meet with our replenishment group in the morning.

GL Still hitting Okinawa, not much doing. We see lots of transports evacuating wounded. GL

Friday 1 June 1945   *Ryukyu Islands, Retiring to refuel*

0400 Steaming as before. Made radar contact with the tankers, bearing 238°T, 20 miles.

0503-0515 Launched 8 F6Fs for CAP and 3 TBMs for ASP.

0522 Sighted the tankers, bearing 260°T, 10 miles.

0531 Launched 1 replacement F6F.

0547 TG 38.4 commenced fueling exercises. USS MARIAS designated guide.

0618 Came along port side of the tanker USS MARIAS.

0801 USS MARIAS cast off having delivered 213,135 gallons of fuel oil, 28,400 gallons of aviation gasoline, and 11 drums of lubricating oil. CVL-22 transferred to the tanker, one enlisted man for transportation to the states. They next began maneuvering to approach the USS SHASTA to rearm.

0837-0838 USS MERTZ came alongside the port quarter to deliver guard mail.

0852-0858 USS MERTZ came alongside the port quarter to deliver aviation supplies, and receive one aircraft canopy for delivery to the USS TICONDEROGA.

0955 USS SHASTA cast off having delivered 175 cans of 40 mm ammunition and 18 500lb. bombs.

1042 Completed recovery of 8 F6Fs and 3 TBMs launched at 0515 and 1 F6F launched at 0531.

Commenced maneuvering to take position for gunnery exercises with USS IOWA (target control ship).
1106 Arrived on station with battleships for AA gunnery exercises against a controlled drone.
1109 Sounded torpedo defense gunnery exercises.
1118 Secured from flight quarters. Air Department set to condition 14.
1125-1137 USS HEERMANN came alongside the port quarter delivering aviation supplies.
1155 Completed gunnery exercises. Maneuvered to rejoin the fueling formation.
1203 Secured from torpedo defense.
1301 USS MISSOURI designated guide. With fueling operations completed they steamed away from the tanker group, forming cruising disposition 5R.
1330 Sounded flight quarters.
1413 Task Group formed disposition 5VB.
1427-1434 Launched 8 F6Fs for CAP, and 1 TBM for target towing duty.
1440 Secured from flight quarters. Air Department set to condition 13.
USS YORKTOWN designated formation guide.
1457 Formation reformed to disposition 5 VC to give clear firing arcs for gunnery exercises.
At approximately 1530 Gunnery Department manned all torpedo defense stations for gunnery exercises.
1647 Sounded flight quarters.
1652 Completed gunnery exercises.
1654 Task Group formed cruising disposition 5VB.
At approximately 1715 the USS MISSOURI was designated guide.
1738 Lighted fires under No.2 boiler.
1742 Recovered 1 TBM launched at 1434 for target towing.
1822 Cut No.2 boiler into the main steam line.
1850 Recovered 8 F6Fs launched at 1434.
1936 Secured from flight quarters. Air Department set to condition 14.
2235 Commenced zigzagging on base course 100°T.

GL *Refuel – rearmed – movies, but no mail.* **GL**

27

Target Japan

Saturday 2 June 1945   *Japan - Kyushu*

Steaming as before to an area east of Okinawa for a strike on Kyushu.
0410 Sounded flight quarters.
0503 Completed launching 8 F6Fs for RAPCAP over our radar picket line of destroyers.
0520 Formation reformed to disposition 5 VB to tighten the formation.
0604 Completed launching 12 F6Fs for a log range sweep over Kyushu.

The strike is well described as written in the Fighting Squadron Forty-Six (VF-46) History:

"The second day of June broke the monotony of CAPs, TCAPs, RAPCAPs, SUBCAPS and Barrier CAPS."
"The best way to shorten this war is to inflict damage on the enemy at every possible opportunity. Comdr. C.W. Rooney, U.S.N."
"On 2 June, Admiral McCain selected ten airfields in Southern Kyushu and divided them into four individual groups of targets for four carriers in 38.4. Twelve fighters from U.S.S. INDEPENDENCE joined by eight fighters from the U.S.S. YORKTOWN were assigned Miyazaki A/F, Iwakawa A/F and Miyakonojo A/F as primary, secondary and tertiary targets. Miyazaki, located on the east coast of Kyushu at 31°55'N by 131°25'E was the northern most objective of all targets assigned and hence the

farthest distant from the launching point. In order to cover all three airfields a minimum round trip of 750 miles had to be flown in such a manner as to allow for use of military power in the target area and return to the ship with at least 50 gallons (condition queen) of gas. In order to avoid loss of aircraft everything had to click with some luck thrown in.

Through a miscalculation of launching time of the two ships the U.S.S. INDEPENDENCE planes were forced to orbit over base for 1/2 hour using critical fuel before they were joined by 8 VF from the U.S.S. YORKTOWN. The twenty plane flight led by Comdr. Rooney then set course for the target and ninety miles north an active front was encountered and persisted until Tanega Shima, which necessitated instrument flying for 2/3 of the way into Miyazaki. In addition to carrying out the mission which was to destroy airborne and grounded aircraft at three assigned airfields, Comdr. Rooney led strafing attacks on Shibushi A/F, Inujo A/F on Tanega Shima, a locomotive, two sea trucks and a factory. The total bag for the day claimed by 9 VF of the INDEPENDENCE: 13 A/C destroyed and 7 A/C damaged on the ground, one locomotive destroyed, two sea trucks destroyed, one factory damaged and one radio tower damaged. Every opportunity was taken to inflict damage on the enemy! Q.E.D.

Seven out of the eight planes making the attack on Miyazaki were hit by enemy flack on the first pass. Two were severely damaged. Ensign Adgate with the starboard tip of his stabilizer blown off and his elevator destroyed flew back to base under the able wing of Lt.(jg) Shaw and made a perfect landing under a severe handicap.

Lt.(jg) Stewart, euphemistically and affectionately known as "Stew Babe" by the Skipper, was hit in the belly of his fuselage which destroyed his radio gear and electric compass. Losing contact with the flight he set a 185° "By guess and by god" heading for home which was a near miss.

With 60 gallons of gas left he determined at 1110, by the aid of his cloth survival chart, that he was over Kito Daito Shima, 200 miles east of Okinawa! A 280° course was then set and at 1230 with two gallons of gas left in his right main tank he sighted 4 DDs in the radar picket line. Making a water landing he was picked up at 1234 by the DD UHLMANN (689) and delivered f.o.b. to U.S.S. INDEPENDENCE at 0830 the following day for 10 gallons ice cream. He was worth the customary 25 gallons but the ship didn't have that much.

He was airborne 6 hours and 40 minutes, covered approximately 1050 miles and consumed 398 gallons of gas. (pilots time in the air verified from six hours to six hours and forty minutes).

All pilots who had the benefit of a wingman and instruments to fly with landed aboard with approximately 50 gallons of gas! Q.E.D.
The following inflicted serious damage on enemy aircraft and installations: Comdr. Rooney, Lt. C.O. Jones, Lts.(jg) Schleis, Rogg, Shaw and Pruett and Ensigns Dyer, Adgate and Ballard."

From this mission, two VF-46 Hellcats were lost, one with the water landing (Bu.No.77875), one with battle damage enough to be stricken. Six other Hellcats suffered AA damage; one with a rudder and elevator destroyed, one with damage to the hydraulic landing gear and wing flap, one with holes thru the prop and engine cowling, one with a hole in the starboard wing root, one a hole in the starboard wing, and one with radio gear destroyed, holes in the belly tank and fuselage.

0630 Secured from flight quarters. Air Department set to condition 13.
0844-0849 Completed recovery of 8 F6Fs launched at 0503.
1057-1102 Completed launching 8 F6Fs for CAP.
1147-1229 Completed recovery of 11 F6Fs launched at 0604.
1237 Sounded torpedo defense due to an unidentified aircraft.
1243 Secured from torpedo defense as the aircraft was friendly.
1448 On course 215°T. Changed course on an emergency turn signal to 135°T due to reported sub periscope sighting by a patrol aircraft 10 miles ahead of the formation. Several mines were sighted during the day.
1531 Completed recovery of 8 F6Fs launched at 1102.
1907-2007 Gunnery Department manned routine torpedo defense stations.

JAPAN

1945 Formed cruising disposition 5R.
2320 Commenced zigzagging on base course 100°T.

This evening the water was exceptionally luminescent, to the extent that at 25 knots the ships produced a bright green glow where the water was disturbed, lighting up bow waves and trailing water churned by the props that *"seemed to have wake lights burning."* with an iridescent splendor.
They steamed in the same general area through the night.

GN Got the word that we are about 130 miles east of Okinawa and around 300 miles from Kyushu. We made a fighter sweep over that latter place and had fair success. No air-borne opposition but heavy and accurate ack-ack was encountered. Two of our planes returned badly shot up while a third went into the drink. The pilot of that later plane was picked up though by the picket cans. Shot up quite a few sitting planes while over the target. GN

Sunday 3 June 1945   *Japan - Kyushu, and the Ryukyu Islands*

0400 Steaming as before in an area east of Okinawa for a strike on Kyushu. Sounded flight quarters.
0428 Sounded general quarters.
0501 Completed launching 8 F6Fs for a RAPCAP over our destroyer picket line.
0516 Formed cruising disposition 5VB.
0528 Secured from general quarters.
0600-0607 Launched 12 F6Fs to join 8 fighters from USS YORKTOWN in a fighter sweep over southern Kyushu. The weather was a repeat of yesterday, with a front to penetrate (too and from target). Two aircraft returned to land at 0853, one F6F (Ens. Bruce M. Agesen) having engine problems. The other 10 Hellcats made strikes at Miyazaki and Miyakonojo Airfields 350 miles from the ship, then Inujo and Tanega Shima on the return trip. Excellent photo coverage of the airfields on yesterdays raids showed 24 operational planes in the 54 bomber revetments at Miyazaki. They were now gone, probably in anticipation of another strike. Rockets were fired into revetments and the airfields were strafed. Villages were strafed on the return trip. Lt.(jg) James W. Pruett and Lt. Angus T. Morrison made photo runs over 6 airfields, receiving a dispatch "Excellent Kyushu photos. Well done." from CTG 38.4. Two enemy aircraft were destroyed and two damaged by VF-46 pilots in the raid. Pruett narrowly missed a flack hit from a Japanese AA position that was walking rounds in from astern, because of a timely call from Morrison; "Hey Pru, start jinking, they're going to shoot your tail off!" He did, they didn't! But it was close.

0626 Secured from flight quarters.
0636 Changed course to 210°T.
0755 USS UHLMANN came along side to transfer a passenger.
0801 USS UHLMANN cast off due to impending course change.
0802 Changed course to 000°T.
0820-0829 USS UHLMANN was alongside port quarter, returning Lt.(jg) Marlar E. Stewart, recovered from his water landing yesterday.
0853 Completed recovery of 10 F6Fs, 8 launched at 0501, 2 launched at 0607.
0939 Sounded torpedo defense due to an unidentified aircraft to the west, 64 miles out. Interception by the CAP was hindered by weather and the bogie eventually retired.
1104 Completed launching 8 F6Fs for CAP.
1114 Completed recovery of 10 F6Fs launched at 0607.
1130 Secured from torpedo defense.
1258-1305 Launched 9 F6Fs for a CAP ("Barrier Patrol") between Kikai Shima and Iheya Shima. They bombed and strafed Kikai Airfield, strafed revetments at Tokuno Airfield, as well as small beached boats and buildings on Tokuno.
1306-1307 Recovered 1 F6F launched at 1104
1455 Sounded flight quarters.

The CAP of 8 Hellcats launched at 1104 flew in foul conditions, penetrating a front with turbulence and heavy rain. The VF-46 Squadron history reported *"The weather became progressively worse in the afternoon and all agreed who flew on CAP that it was the most difficult instrument flying they had experienced"*. Two F6F-5 Hellcats became separated from the rest of the CAP and could not be raised by radio, and were not to be found on radar. They were feared to have been lost in a mid-air collision, roughly 60 miles east of Okinawa Shima (Bu.Nos. 77642 & 71969). They were last observed at 7,500' penetrating a front.

1528-1540 Recovered 5 F6Fs launched at 1104 and 1 F6F launched at 1305.

1706 Recovered 6 F6Fs launched at 1305.

1858 Secured from flight quarters. Air Department set to condition 14.

1906 Darkened ship. Two F6F-5s failed to return today. Dusk settled in on USS INDEPENDENCE and pilots Ensign Robert Theodore Dyer and Lt.(jg) Billy Robert Apgar were missing.

1916 Formation changed to cruising disposition 5R and returned to an operating area S.E. of Okinawa.

2224 CTG 38.4 (Rear Admiral Arthur William Radford) assumed tactical command of Task Force 38.

2230 Commenced zigzagging on base course 265°T.

Captain Kindell noted in the SOL:
"Get as good a look as possible at anything floating. We have two down pilots, in rubber boats we hope. Have smoke lights ready to drop. Call me if anything unusual or dangerous appears."

GN Had a few more fighter sweeps with rockets. On one of our early sweeps two of our planes failed to return. Shangri La also lost two[1.] *and whether they were due to enemy action or lost in the heavy overcast we don't know. GN*

([1.] SHANGRI LA Air Group 85, tasked with long range strikes on Kyushu airfields lost four pilots on this day: Lt. John H. Scroff flying a FG-1D was shot down by enemy fire near a beach - M.I.A.; Lt. Sigurd Lovdal crashed - structural failure tearing the tail off while diving chasing an enemy - M.I.A.; Lt.(Jg) Edward Dixon, Jr. missing in a flight near Kagoshima - M.I.A.; Robert J. Sundquist F4U-1D Zero-Zero weather - Spun into the sea - Missing .)

GL Kyushu again bombing & strafing. Dumbo (PBM rescue plane) made a daring rescue in Inland Sea, picked up a downed pilot right under the Jap's noses. Lost 2 planes. Lt. Apgar and Ens. Dyer. GL

George Leedecke was not the only one who was impressed enough with the daring "Dumbo" rescue to record it in his diary. Matome Ugaki also was impressed with the exploits of our brave flying boat crews, enough so to have also made the following entry in his diary[2.] on 2 June:
"Furthermore, at about 1500, when I was inspecting a dugout of the weather observation unit, an alert was sounded, and more than ten Grummans, followed by a Martin flying boat, came over Kagoshima Bay. After circling, the flying boat alighted on the bay and picked up crewmen of a plane shot down that morning, then flew away. I can't stand even to see an enemy submarine picking up survivors off shore, much less this arrogant behavior right in the middle of Kagoshima Bay"!

Our "arrogant behavior" would continue, and become much worse, over the sacred homeland of Matome Ugaki. At a time when many in Japan were aware of the futility of the continuation of the conflict, it is unfortunate that militants with views like Ugaki in power and control, would win out over those with better sense. Unable to stop the onrushing tide of the US and our allies, the destruction, suffering and the needless loss of life would continue.

The USS INDEPENDENCE steamed on into the night, returning to an operating area south east of Okinawa. Air Group CVLG46 was missing two aviators. There was a war to be won.

([2.] "Fading Victory - The Diary of Admiral Matome Ugaki 1941-1945" Naval Institute Press, provides excellent insight to the Japanese IJN perspective throughout the Pacific war.)

Monday 4 June 1945   *Ryukyu Islands, Okinawa Invasion, Iheya Shima*

Steaming as before in an area southeast of Okinawa. USS MISSOURI is guide, 2,000 yards from this vessel. Flight quarters was sounded prior to 0400 this morning.

0524 Completed launching 10 F6Fs and 8 TBMs. 8 F6Fs were for a RAPCAP, the remaining 2 were assigned to serve as target coordinators for the 8 TBMs, which were sent to support troops invading Iheya Shima. Iheya Shima is a small island roughly 20 miles north of Okinawa. Marines were landed (yesterday) on 3 June to secure the island. The strike reported to an Air Support Control Unit who had no targets for the TBMs. They checked in with CASCU on Okinawa, who also had no targets. Bombs were jettisoned in harmless water prior to the return to the carrier.

0634 Completed launching 8 F6Fs for a CAP over Okinawa.

0643 Secured from flight quarters. Air Department set to condition 13.

0815 Sounded flight quarters.

0841-0852 Recovered 10 F6Fs and 8 TBMs launched at 0524.

0932-0935 USS MELVIN was alongside starboard quarter to receive guard mail.

1021-1025 Recovered 8 F6Fs launched at 0634.

A typhoon was forecasted to be 300 miles to the southwest, moving northeast. The remainder of the days flight schedule was canceled. They began to prepare the ship for heavy weather, lashing aircraft down.

1035 USS YORKTOWN designated guide, bearing 205°T, 2,800 yards.

1608 Formed cruising disposition 5R. MISSOURI is guide, course 110°T, bearing 160°T, 2,000 yards. The Task Group steamed at 25 knots, course 110°T in the afternoon to clear the typhoons expected path.

1813 They changed course and speed to close on Task Group 38.3 and the tanker formation who were south of them, trying to outrun (and outguess) the storm.

2004 They joined up with the tanker group, dropping the speed to 12 knots, which was the limiting safe speed for the tankers and CVE escorts in the heavy weather.

Captain Kindell noted in the SOL:

"At twelve knots it should be a sleepy night. We are on course 110°T to escape the typhoon along with TG-38.1 and the tankers. Fuel in the morning if weather permits. However, if the 'phoon comes near my guess is that TG38 will not hold us in it just to keep the tankers company.
Formation 5R — Guide is Missouri at 0000. Axis; and bearing of Mo*., 160°T.   (* Missouri)
No land falls are expected and no land is near. No ships are on record as heading our way but many ships of TG38.1 and 30.1 are around and on the same course. Call me if the going gets rough."

An additional note on the same page was added the following day under Captain Kindell's signature:
"We ran right into the damn typhoon around daylight. Center showed on radar at distance 14 miles. No damage in our T.G. but the tankers and other T.G. went right thru the center. Considerable damage."

F6F "Hellcat" into the barricades

GN   Had an early bomb load over the target. Got word that the bombs were jettisoned as weather was very bad near target. Just heard that the ship expects to meet up with a typhoon shortly and to prepare for it. That typhoon weather starts in this neighborhood about June 15 and if only part of the scuttlebutt going around is true we should miss most of it.   GN

Tuesday 5 June 1945   *Typhoon Viper*

The ships War Diary tells the story of most of the day well:

C-O-N-F-I-D-E-N-T-I-A-L   c/o Fleet Post Office

Typhoon

5 June 1945   War Diary for USS INDEPENDENCE

Steaming as before outrunning a typhoon. The storm had recurved sharply to the east. As the wind went up in intensity and the barometer fell, we suspected we were not successfully outrunning the storm. We had to cease zigzagging at 0118; the seas made some courses too uncomfortable. With the storm still in the south-west heading east, we changed course to 300^0 T, at 0132. We later upped the speed to 16 knots, no longer penalizing ourselves to stay with the tankers. As the storm grew more intense, the Group changed course to 000^0 T, at 0251, thus placing the wind two points abaft the starboard beam and hoping for the best. At 0400 the storm center showed upon our radar scope bearing 220^0 T, 40 miles away. It chose a course of approximately 020^0 T, continuing to close. The barometer took a nose-dive, the true wind went up to sixty-five knots in gusts. The seas were so high and the spray so thick, that neighboring ships were not visible. The course was changed to keep the wind two points abaft the starboard beam until the storm center passed us. At 0700 the eye of the storm was indicated to be twelve miles south of us by radar. At that time, T.G. 38.1 which was also south of us was reported to have suffered damage to three ships. This ship rode the storm very well, suffering no damage and rolling no more than 20 degrees. After 0700, the storm passed quickly; the barometer recovered, the winds settled, and by noon the sky was largely clear. During the morning, the large carriers launched planes to search for the tankers and TG38.1. Finding them 100 miles to the Southeast, we changed course to close them.

At 1711, INDEPENDENCE joined the tankers, turning to course 270^0T (axis 180^0T) for fueling. At 1750, INDEPENDENCE was alongside the U.S.S. NECHES, refueling, the 1000th ship to be refueled by her. CVL-22 cast off at sunset, 1904, and took our station in disposition 5 R. They headed for an area which would put them in striking distance of Okinawa in the morning.

GN Hit into the typhoon area early in the morning. Had been batting along at good speed most of yesterday and all last night and thought we'd miss it but it wasn't long before we were right in the middle of it. Wind was up to 75 miles an hour but it wasn't like the others we've encountered and we were past the worst part by noon. Did a goodly bit of rolling for a time but we've seen it worse. Started to put on the steam again to get to the tankers before dark and we made it although we only got aboard part of the fuel we wanted. GN   HC Came close to typhoon. Worst water I have ever seen. HC

GL We are in middle of damn typhoon. I sure do dread these storms. Started clearing about noon, we refueled about 1700. A few ships were damaged by storm. GL

VF-46 Squadron History would note:
"TG38.4 outmaneuvered the elements escaping unscathed, but the allied ships were not so fortunate. CVs BENNINGTON and HORNET; CVEs SALAMA, WINDHAM BAY, BOUGAINVILLE and ATTU; CAs PITTSBURGH, DELUTH and DETROIT; DEs CONKLIN, DONALDSON and HILBERT; Oilers MILLICOMA, LACKAWANNA, SEBEC and CALIENTE all suffered damage of varying degree. At 0800 the worst of the storm had dissipated with pressure back to 999.0 mmlbs and wind 40 knots. By 1000 the wind had subsided to 28 knots."

Halsey misjudged the typhoon. Clark's Task Group and Beary's Fueling Group were caught in a nasty storm, tightly wound up and full of energy. Radford's Task Group (that USS INDEPENDENCE was in) just missed the worst of the typhoon's fury.

The typhoon had damaged 36 US naval vessels (as listed in the "United Sates Naval Chronology Of World War II").

Wednesday 6 June 1945   *Ryukyu Islands, Okinawa Invasion*

Steaming as before in an area off Okinawa, accompanied by USS YORKTOWN (OTC), USS TICONDERGA, and USS SHANGRI LA. USS MISSOURI is guide, bearing 180°T, 2,000 yards, on a course of 320°T in cruising disposition 5R.

0410 Sounded flight quarters.

0513 Launched 16 F6Fs for a CAP.

0548 INDEPENDENCE maneuvered to gain station on USS NECHES, designated guide.

0705 USS UHLMANN came along side the port quarter to transfer materials.

0710 Sounded flight quarters.

0711 USS UHLMANN cast off.

0733 Recovered 1 F6F with engine trouble, launched at 0513.

0824 Launched 7 TBMs for a ground support strike, and 2 F6Fs as strike coordinators. They dropped 500 lb. bombs on a ridge (Japanese positions) on Okinawa, holding up the advance of our troops. Ground observers gave their work a "Well done".

0901 Completed recovery of 15 F6Fs launched at 0513.

0915-0928 USS MCNAIR came alongside our starboard quarter to pick up 4 pilots*[1.] to ferry replacement aircraft back to this vessel.

   (*[1.] Lt.(Jg) M.B. Stuart, Lt.(Jg) N.J. Schleis, Ens. T.W. Delehaunty & Ens. J.R. Fielding)

0920 The fueling course and axis were changed to 270°T.

0932 USS MCCORD came alongside the port quarter to pick up an officer for TAD aboard that vessel.

0951 Commenced maneuvering to approach the USS CHICOPEE.

1030 Came alongside the fleet oiler USS CHICOPEE to receive additional fuel. Changed formation axis to 165°T, speed 10 knots.

1033-1037 USS COLAHAN was alongside the port quarter to deliver officer messenger mail.

1045-1100 USS LYMAN K. SWENSON was alongside the port quarter to transfer bomb fuses.

1102 -1103 Manned torpedo defense, due to a friendly aircraft which failed to identify itself.

1107-1120 USS HEERMANN was alongside the port quarter to transfer an officer aboard (Lt. Edward C. Slusher) for TAD to receive C.I.C. instruction..

1135 Launched 8 F6Fs for a CAP.

1140 Cast off form USS CHICOPEE, having completed receiving fuel oil.

1214-1222 Recovered 7 TBMs, and 2 F6Fs launched at 0824.

1228 Commenced maneuvering to approach the USS PLATTE.

1257 Came alongside USS PLATTE to transfer aviation gas.

1306-1316 USS BENHAM was alongside the port quarter to deliver mail, and to receive radio tubes and photographs.

1348 USS REMEY came alongside the port quarter to transfer a pilot Lt.(jg) J.K. Gentry to the USS YORKTOWN for treatment of pneumonia.

1349 USS PLATTE cast off.

1427 USS MISSOURI designated guide.

1450-1457 Launched a strike of 7 TBMs, and 2 F6Fs as strike coordinators. Their mission was like the 0824 launch, with the Avengers in direct support of the troops on the ground. The assigned targets were fortified caves in a ridgeline south of Naha Airfield.

1500 With fueling operations completed they separated from the tanker group.

1511 Gained station in disposition 5R, course 270°T, guide bearing 270°T, 2,000 yards.

1543 Completed recovering 8 F6Fs launched at 1135, and 4 replacement F6Fs ferried over from a CVE.

1602-1610 Sheered out from base course 090°T to jettison 1 F6F-5 (Bu# 77849).

1844-1855 Recovered 7 TBMs, and 2 F6Fs launched at 1457.

1908-2008 Gunnery Department manned all torpedo defense stations.

1911 Secured from flight quarters. Air Department set to condition 14.

2320 Commenced zigzagging on base course 030°T.

Captain Kindell noted in the SOL:
"Follow courses and speeds signaled by OTC in Yorktown.
Formation 5R axis 270°T.
Our position 2.180, Missouri guide bears 270°T — 2000 yds.
No landfalls and no ship contacts expected. The other T.G. is around, as is also the tanker group.
Lights of a hospital ship were seen earlier and will probably be seen again.
We stay around in this area - probably.
Call me if anything of concern shows up."

Thursday 7 June 1945   *Ryukyu Islands, Okinawa Invasion*

0410 Steaming as before in an area southeast Okinawa. Sounded flight quarters.

0505 Launched 8 F6Fs for a CAP.

0528 Formed cruising disposition 5VB.

0654 Launched a support strike of 7 TBMs, and 2 F6Fs as strike coordinators who worked with CASCU coordinators on the ground. Targets assigned were gun positions on Senaga Shima, a small island southwest of Okinawa. Bombing appeared to be accurate, taking out at least two gun emplacements.

0709 Secured from flight quarters. Air Department set to condition 13.

0812 Launched 1 F6F with Comdr. Carl W. Rooney to a conference on USS YORKTOWN.

0815 Sounded flight quarters.

0857-0904 Completed recovery of 8 F6Fs launched at 0505.

1025-1043 Completed recovery of 7 TBMs, and 2 F6Fs launched at 0654.

1140 Completed launching 12 F6Fs for a CAP.

1145 Maneuvered to avoid hitting an aircraft in the water (launched by the YORKTOWN).

1217 Completed recovery of 1 F6F launched at 0812 (YORKTOWN conference).

1325 Completed launching 6 TBMs, and 2 F6Fs for a support strike over Okinawa, and 6 F6Fs for a search mission for the two pilots (Ensign Robert Theodore Dyer and Lt.(jg) Billy Robert Apgar) missing, in bad weather, since 3 June 1945. The search had negative results. The strike on Okinawa was scheduled for 8 TBMs but only six were launched due to a bomb elevator failure making it impossible to bring enough ordnance to the flight deck on time for the strike. The assigned target was an enemy mortar position on a ridge near the village of Makabe. Bombs were scattered all over the hill as a result of difficulty with target identification.

1356 Secured from flight quarters. Air Department set to condition 13.

1445 Sounded flight quarters.

1526 Completed recovery of 12 F6Fs launched at 1140.

1614-1630 USS TRATHEN was alongside on port quarter to deliver catapult equipment.

1712 Completed recovery of 6 TBMs and 2 F6Fs launched at 1325.

1731 USS TRATHEN came back alongside on our port quarter to finish delivering catapult equipment.

1738 Secured from flight quarters. Air Department set to condition 14.

1744 USS TRATHEN cast off.

1905 Formed cruising disposition 5R.

2203 Commenced zigzagging on base course 080°T.

The Task force moved east during the night to a launching point 350 miles southeast of Kyushu.

GN   Two heavy strikes today on Okinawa before bomb elevator went on the blink. Heard later that that island is just about secured and it's about time methinks. Also heard that we head for Leyte on the tenth.
GN

Friday 8 June 1945   *Kyushu, Japan*

0345 Steaming as before. Sounded flight quarters.

0400 Shifted steering engines from starboard to port.

0446 Completed launching 8 F6Fs for a RAPCAP.

0457 Formed cruising disposition 5VB.

0735 Sounded flight quarters.

0817 Completed launching 8 F6Fs for a RAPCAP.

0851 Completed recovery of 8 F6Fs launched at 0446.

0900 Secured from flight quarters. Air Department set to condition 13.

1000 Large carriers sent out long range fighter bomber sweeps over southern Kyushu.

1100 Sounded flight quarters.

1146 Completed launching 8 F6Fs for a RAPCAP.

1223-1225 Completed launching 4 F6Fs to accompany 2 Kingfisher*[1] seaplanes from the USS WISCONSIN on an air-sea rescue mission. A pilot*[2] from the USS SHANGRI LA was reported to be in his life jacket and life raft. VF-46 Squadron History notes; *"This position was about 166 miles from Point Option. With no land marks to help, navigation had to be right on the nose with about five minutes to work out the problem on the plotting board. Lt. Badger led Ensign Ballard and Lts.(jg) Fielding and Delehaunty in escorting two Kingfishers from the WISCONSIN to a speck in the pacific 166 miles away which was the downed pilot! One Kingfisher landed in the rough sea and after making about eight passes got the pilot safely aboard. There followed a few tense minutes while the Kingfisher in attempting to take off was repeatedly slapped down by the relentless waves of the Pacific which kept trying to break off one of the wing tip floats. Finally after a two mile take off the pilot gradually lifted old faithful off the water and the flight, directed by Lt. Badger, returned safely back to base."* (*[1] Kingfisher photo on page 439) (*[2] Two SHANGRI LA F4U pilots had engine failure resulting in water landings. LT. (Jg) R.L. Meltebeke was picked up by the Kingfisher and Ens. N.L. Edwin was picked up by a destroyer.

1226-1234 Completed recovery of 8 F6Fs launched at 0817.

1239 Half-masted colors following the movements of the OTC.

1243 Secured from flight quarters. Air Department set to condition 13.

1317 Two-blocked the colors following the movements of the OTC.

1400 Sounded flight quarters.

1403 Gunnery Department manned all torpedo defense stations as the strike planes returned from Kyushu, in case Japanese planes tailed the strike back to the Task Group.

1444 Gunnery Department set to condition One Easy.

1450-1453 Completed launching 8 F6Fs for a RAPCAP.

1521-1526 Completed recovery of 8 F6Fs launched at 1146.

1547-1552 Completed recovery of 4 F6Fs launched at 1225.

1640 Gunnery Department secured from condition One Easy, set to condition 3.

1741 Completed recovery of 2 F6Fs launched at 1453, due to engine trouble.

1847-1854 Completed recovery of 6 F6Fs launched at 1453.

1930 Secured from flight quarters. Air Department set to condition 14.

1955 Formed cruising disposition 5R.

2207 Cruiser Division 16 (USS ALASKA, USS GUAM and USS FLINT) left the formation to carry out assigned orders.

2234 Commenced zigzagging on base course 170°T, steaming for a morning fueling rendezvous.

Saturday 9 June 1945   *Ryukyu Islands, Minami Daito Shima*
                                Refueling, Rearming & Reprovisioning

0127 Steaming as before. Commenced simulated steering casualty drills. Shifted steering control aft.

0225 Shifted steering control to central station. At 0322 shifted steering control back to the pilot house.

0646 The Task Group commenced fueling exercises. USS KANKAKEE designated guide, fueling course 065°T, 10 knots.

0647 Commenced maneuvering to approach USS COSSATOT.

0715-0842 Along port side of tanker USS COSSATOT to receive 130,641 gallons of fuel oil, 24,000 gallons of aviation gas and 12 drums of aircraft lubricating oil.

0842 Commenced maneuvering to approach ammunition ship USS LASSEN.

0906 Came along port side of USS LASSEN.

0914 Commenced rearming, while incrementally changing course to 100°T.

1103 Sounded flight quarters.

1148-1207 Launched 12 F6Fs for CAP, and 3 TBMs for ASP.

1246–1258 USS HEERMANN was alongside the port quarter to exchange mail and passengers.

1311 USS LASSEN cast off having delivered bombs, fuses, detonators and 40mm ammunition.

1445 Completed launching 9 F6Fs and 3 TBMs. 3 F6Fs were for a strike with the TBMs, targeting Minami and Kita Daito Shima. 6 F6Fs were for a TCAP to cover the strike aircraft. The primary purpose of the strike was to test and obtain data on Napalm fire bombs and GP bombs with VT fuses (airburst fused fragmentation bombs). A total of 112 aircraft participated in the raid, with Comdr. Carl Rooney acting air coordinator. 304 bombs were released and excellent photo coverage was obtained.

1446 Commenced maneuvering to approach USS ALDEBARAN.

1510 Came along port side of USS ALDEBARAN to take on provisions.

1512 Secured from flight quarters. Air Department set to condition 14.

1602 USS ALASKA and USS GUAM returned to the Task Group.

1637 USS LASSEN designated as guide.

1653 Sounded flight quarters.

1707 Cast off from USS ALDEBARAN having concluded receiving provisions.

1731 Recovered 12 F6Fs and 3 TBMs launched at 1207.

1735 USS MISSOURI designated guide.

1747 Gained station in disposition 5R, course 020°T, speed 18 knots guide bearing 140°T, 2,000 yards.

1831 Recovered 9 F6Fs and 3 TBMs launched at 1445, on a course of 150°T, speed 24 knots.

1842 Changed course to 270°T. At 2258 commenced zigzagging on base course 256°T.

GN Refuel, rearm and God alone knows what else today. The way the Bull operates we may yet make a strike at Tokyo before darkness falls. Not surprised in the least that we made a strike at Okinawa while taking on provisions. That was a pretty good day all in all. Heard we are heading for Leyte but are going to hit about every Jap held position on the way and are in no hurry. GN

Sunday 10 June 1945   *Ryukyu Islands, Minami Daito Shima*

Steaming near Daito Shima, in company with Task Unit 38.4.1.

0430 Sounded routine general quarters. Sounded flight quarters.

0507 USS YORKTOWN designated guide.

0516 USS MISSOURI designated guide. Formed cruising disposition 5VB.

0529 Secured from general quarters.

0640-0649 Completed launching a strike of 6 TBMs against Minami Daito Shima to test VT fused bombs. INDEPENDENCE also launched 6 F6Fs. Two were target coordinators and four were assigned to photograph the results. The bomb testing was considered successful. The targeted area consisted of buildings and AA positions located on the northeast quadrant of the island.

0715 Secured from flight quarters. Air Department set to condition 14.

0939 Sounded flight quarters.

1013 Completed recovery of 6 F6Fs and 6 TBMs launched at 0640.

1030 Secured from flight quarters. Air Department set to condition 14.

1215 Sounded flight quarters.

1300 Launched 2 TBMs to tow target sleeves for AA gunnery exercises.

1308 Secured from flight quarters. Air Department set to condition 14.

1317 USS FLINT designated guide.

1318 Commenced steering various courses at various speeds to gain station in disposition Easy Modified, a special formation for firing exercises.

1322 Sounded torpedo defense for firing exercises.

1333 Gained position in the disposition Easy Modified. Course is 030°T. Guide now bears 091°T, 11,000 yards.

1335 Commenced scheduled firing exercises.

1430 Sounded flight quarters.

1510 Concluded firing exercises and then secured from torpedo defense.

1513 Commenced maneuvering to gain station in disposition 5R.

1527 Gained station in disposition 5R.

1534 USS MISSOURI designated guide on course 050°T, bearing 100°T, 2,000 yards.

1541 Recovered 2 TBMs launched at 1300.

1605 Secured from flight quarters. Air Department set to condition 14.

1659 Changed course to 210°T, headed to Leyte Gulf for a period of rest and replenishment with Task Force 38.

1707 Task Unit 38.4.2 (less USS ALASKA, FLINT and SAN DIEGO) began topping off destroyers.

Captain Kindell noted in the SOL:

"We are now heading South on the way to Leyte. Same guide and formation. Axis is now 100°T. OTC in YORKTOWN is in tactical control.

No contacts are to be expected. No landfalls will be made on southerly courses.

Call me if anything unusual or dangerous appears. Watch the scope closely for mistakes of other ships, they seem to be getting more unreliable lately. (Fingers crossed !!)"

HC *We are on our way to Leyte and are starting to take pills for malaria, they taste like hell.* **HC**

GN *Made a strike at one of the numerous islands situated northeast of Okinawa. Flew CAP for a while after that and then launched some TBM's with sleeves so our Gunnery Department could get a crack at some kind of target.* **GN**

Monday 11 June 1945   *Retiring toward Leyte Gulf*

Kamikaze attacks had fallen off and we now had an operating air base on Okinawa. It had been decided that Task Force 38 could, at last, be released from Okinawa to strike at the Japanese homeland. But first, a deserved and needed rest.

Steaming toward Leyte Gulf in company with Task Unit 38.4.1, zigzagging on a southwesterly base course of 200°T, 18 knots, guide USS MISSOURI, bearing 100°T, 2,000 yards.

0410 Sounded flight quarters.

0512 Completed launching 3 TBMs for an ASP and 8 F6Fs for CAP.

0633 USS FLINT designated guide.

0656-0700 USS MERTZ was alongside the port quarter to pick up photographs.

0757 Changed course to 160°T. USS MISSOURI designated guide, bearing 150°T, 2,000 yards.

0813 Formed cruising disposition 5VB.

0815 Sounded flight quarters.

0840-0849 Recovered 3 TBMs and 8 F6Fs launched at 0512.

0902 Commenced a scheduled exercise (event 4) to track bogies.

0903 Sounded torpedo defense, manning our guns to track simulated attacking aircraft.

0910 Secured from flight quarters.

0912-0926 USS MCCORD was alongside port quarter to transfer to INDEPENDENCE Lt.(jg) R.A. Markham who completed temporary duty as a fighter director officer.

1020 Ceased gunnery exercises, then secured from torpedo defense.

1031 Commenced a scheduled exercise (event 5).

1155-1158 Launched 4 F6Fs for radar fade calibration, and 2 TBMS to tow target sleeves.

1215 Secured from flight quarters. Air Department set to condition 13.

1220 USS GUAM designated guide.

1223 Formed disposition 5VC for AA gunnery practice against towed sleeves.

1227 Gained position in disposition 5VC.

1230 Gunnery Department set condition One for firing exercises.

1254 Commenced firing against towed sleeve targets.

1445 Sounded flight quarters.

1500 The Task Group ceased scheduled exercises. Gunnery Department secured from condition One and set condition 3. Commenced maneuvering to regain station in disposition 5VB.

1526 Completed recovery of 4 F6Fs and 2 TBMs launched at 1158.

1545 Secured from flight quarters. Air Department set to condition 14.

1605 USS MISSOURI designated guide.

1910 Changed formation to disposition 5R.

1923 Commenced zigzagging on a base course of 205°T.

*GN Very easy day of it. Still on our way to Leyte and making slow time of it. *We flew ASP all day. Routine clean-up starts tomorrow and its going to be a headache. GN* (* Note: The INDEPENDENCE only flew ASP in the morning.)

GL Headed for the Philippines. Okinawa is almost secured. It has been a tough bloody battle especially for navy carriers and cans. GL

Tuesday 12 June 1945   *Retiring toward Leyte Gulf*

0430 Steaming toward Leyte Gulf. Sounded flight quarters.

0539 Completed launching 8 F6Fs for CAP.

0600 USS GUAM and USS ALASKA departed to conduct independent gunnery exercises.

0745 Sounded flight quarters.

0750-0755 Half-masted the colors following the movement of the USS TICONDEROGA.

0803 USS YORKTOWN designated guide.

0833 Launched 4 F6Fs and 2 TBMs. The TBMs were used as tow planes for target sleeves. The F6Fs made radar fade calibration test runs.

0844 Recovered 8 F6Fs launched at 0539.

0851 Formed disposition 5VC for gunnery exercises.

0905 Gunnery Department manned all torpedo defense stations for AA firing practice. USS GUAM and USS ALASKA rejoined the formation.

1102 Sounded flight quarters.

1115 Gunnery Department completed firing exercises and secured from torpedo defense.

1118 Formed disposition 5VB.

1152 Recovered 4 F6Fs and 2 TBMs launched at 0833.

1345 USS MISSOURI designated guide.

1545 Gunnery Department manned all torpedo defense stations for tracking exercises. Aircraft made simulated attacks on the formation.

1658 USS YORKTOWN designated guide. 1701 Formed cruising disposition 5R.

1716 Commenced zigzagging on base course 270°T.

1717 Secured from "Bogey Drill". Gunnery Department remained at torpedo defense due to an actual bogey reported bearing 240°T, 53 miles.

1725 Gunnery Department secured from torpedo defense. Bogey identified as a friendly transport.

1902 Commenced zigzagging on base course 235°T.

1917 USS MISSOURI designated guide, bearing 130°T, 2,000 yards.

They continued toward Leyte Gulf at 20 knots zigzagging on base course 235°T.

GL Gunnery practice & drills of all types. Randolph took on a P-38 which crashed. GL
(Note: The accident George noted occurred 5 days ago on 7 June 1945. A Lockheed F-5E "P-38 Lightning" (# 44-24559) crashed on the flight deck, during a mock strafing run, killing 4 and injuring 14 CV-15 crewmen.)

Fighting Squadron Forty-Six (VF-46) History notes:

"The ship's Hill-Billy orchestra, made up of a base fiddle, three guitars, two mandolins and a violin, entertained us in the Ready Room en route to Leyte. Favorite tunes repeatedly requested and rendered in their inimitable way included: Nelly (No.1 on the Hit Parade), Cindy, No Not a Word, No Letter Today, Rum and Coca Cola, Bill Bailey, Craw Dad Hole, Letter Edged in Black, Talkin' Blues, Back in the Saddle Again, Raggedy Ann, Red Wing, When the Work's All Done This Fall, New Moon Over My Shoulder, Golden Slippers.
At this writing, 12 June, there have been 179 written recommendations for pilot citations. This recalls Lt. Comdr. Ted Russell's (A.I.C.O. VT-46) remark that any pilot returning from combat in the Pacific theatre without an Air Medal will probably be a "conscientious objector.""

Wednesday 13 June 1945   ***Entered Leyte Gulf***
Air Group CVLG-46 relieved by Air Group CVLG-27

Steaming toward Leyte Gulf, accompanied by USS YORKTOWN (OTC), USS TICONDORGA, and USS SHANGRI LA. USS MISSOURI is guide, bearing 130°T, 2,000 yards, zigzagging on base course 235°T, in cruising disposition 5R at a speed of 20 knots.

0430 Sounded flight quarters.

0541 Launched 8 F6Fs for a CAP.

0607 Secured from flight quarters. Air Department set to condition 13.

0620 USS YORKTOWN designated guide.

0635 Task Group 38.4.2 and DesRon 54 left the formation to conduct independent exercises.

0652-0654 USS COLAHAN was alongside the port quarter to deliver officer messenger mail.

0858 Commenced maneuvering to gain position in column open order for gunnery exercises and for entering port.

0909 Task Unit 38.4.1 commenced gunnery exercises. Gunners fired automatic weapons at a towed sleeve.

0913 Gained position in column disposition, USS YORKTOWN is guide at head of the column, speed 18 knots, course & bearing 205°T, distance 3,000 yards.

0940 Sighted Suluan Island, bearing 230°T, 19 miles.

1014 Sounded torpedo defense for gunnery practice.

1044 Secured No.3 boiler.

1106 Completed recovery of 8 F6Fs launched at 0541.

1146 Secured from flight quarters. Air Department set to condition 14.

1155 USS SHANGRI LA designated guide, bearing & course 280°T, 2,000 yards.

1210 Sounded routine general quarters for entering port upon approaching entrance to jungle rimmed Leyte Gulf. At 1221 changed course to 310°T. At 1231, USS YORKTOWN was designated guide.

1235 Passed a line of Sono buoys abeam between Dinagat and Homonhon Islands, entering Leyte Gulf en route to San Pedro Bay, Philippine Islands.

1249 Secured from general quarters. Air Department set to condition 14.

1448 Passed channel buoy No.1 abeam to port. Commenced maneuvering, conforming to the channel entering San Pedro Bay.

1546 Anchored between berths 72 and 88, near Tacloban, San Pedro Bay, Leyte, in 10 fathoms of water, mud bottom, with 84 fathoms of chain to the starboard anchor. Ships present are various units of the U.S. Third and British Seventh Fleets, with auxiliaries and small craft. By days end, all of Task Force 38 was present.

1553 The Gunnery Department set in-port watch, a special harbor condition watch from sunrise to sunset while at anchor. At night, the ship dimmed out. At 1600 they let fires die out under No.2 boiler.

1615 LCM 177 came alongside to deliver on board 14 officers of VF27.

28
Air Group CVLG-27 Relieves Air Group CVLG-46

Air Group CVLG-27 is relieving Air Group CVLG-46.

GL Entered Philippines San Pedro Bay between Samar & Leyte. Spent 17 days here with liberty. Saw native girls on beach & traded with them. Plenty of work, mail & movies. GL

AD Leyte. Anchored at 1300. The whole Task Force is here. We are anchored between Leyte and Samar. Both Islands are visible. AD

Fighting Squadron Forty-Six (VF-46) History notes:
"The 13th turned out to be a lucky day for CVLG 46. Following YORKTOWN, SHANGRI LA, and TICONDEROGA in column the INDEPENDENCE making continuous soundings in San Pedro Bay, Leyte, "let go" the starboard anchor in 14 fathoms at 1400. Around 1700 the news that the Air Group Commander of CVLG 27 had come aboard as our relief was announced by an unrefined shout of joy which fairly shook the bulkheads in the Ready Room. Our tenuous hopes, some more fervent than others, had been answered! Strangely enough our replacement was the group we were scheduled to relieve on the U.S.S. PRINCETON last November. Picking up the pieces after the PRINCETON was sunk off Luzon 25 October they returned to the states for rehabilitation and reforming at Quonset and Sanford, Me. Equipped with twenty-one combat veterans in the Fighter Squadron our shoes were ably filled for the next operation which promises to be a tough one."

The following dispatch in the Fighting Squadron Forty-Six (VF-46) History also bears repeating, a message to Task Force 38:

Recognition of Services Rendered

From:	CTF 31	13 June 1945
To:	CTF 38	101530

Info: **Com 3rd Flt/CinCPac Adv. Hdqs.**

"On behalf of all those you leave behind here at OKINAWA I wish to extend hearty thanks and appreciation for the aggressive part you have played in bring this operation to a successful conclusion. Your protection and support have given us a very happy feeling of security and at the other end of the line you have caused a serious epidemic of nervous indigestion. Well done and come again soon."

Thursday 14 June 1945   *Anchored in San Pedro Bay, Leyte Gulf*
                                      Air Group 27 reports aboard
Anchored as before. Two gangways are in use, one port and one starboard.

During this period from 14 June 1945, replenishment of stores, ammunition and fuel would occur, and necessary repairs of a minor nature were undertaken. Recreation facilities at Osmena Beach were made available to the crew, one day in four, and Filipino crew members were given leave. Every morning quarters were held on the flight deck at 0800.

Officers reported aboard for duty with VF 27. Additional men would transfer on and off the ship during our stay.

Air Group 27 (CVLG-27) consisted of **Fighting Squadron Twenty Seven (VF-27)** and **Torpedo Squadron Twenty Seven (VT-27)**.

Air Group 27 reformed on 2 January 1945 at NAAF Sanford, Maine. The complement was joined by men from sister ship USS PRINCETON.

Lt.Cmdr. Frederic Abshire Bardshar was the Air Group Commander. His Executive officer was Lt. John Robinson Rodgers, Jr.
Commanding Officer for **VT-27** was Lt. John Gregory Dooling and his Executive Officer was Lt. Howard Lee Stalnaker.

VF-27 departed for NAAS Creeds Field on 1 March 1945. Pilots were carrier qualified in the Chesapeake Bay onboard the USS CHARGER.

VT-27 trained at NAAF Sanford, NAAF Creeds Field (surrounded by the "Great Dismal Swamp"), and at Boca Chica, Florida. Training included Air-to-Air gunnery, Air-to-Ground support, strafing, glide bombing, low level bombing, rockets, dummy & live torpedo runs, torpedo tactics, night flying and group exercises.

In late April the group disbursed for leave, and reassembly on the Pacific Coast in San Diego, CA. On 7 May they departed on the USS CAPE ESPERANCE CVE-88 bound for Pearl Harbor.

Air Group 27 received additional training at Hilo, and on Mighty-I's sister ship (The Mighty Moo) USS COWPENS off Pearl Harbor when they were alerted to their reassignment. On 10 June, they boarded R5D transports*[1] for the trip to the Philippines with orders to report aboard the INDEPENDENCE. The R5Ds flew via Johnston Island, Kwajelein, Guam, then Samar. (*[1] R5Ds were the Navy version of the Douglas C-54 "Skymaster", derived from the civilian 4 engine Douglas DC-4. It was produced 1942-1947. Photo next page.)

They came aboard USS INDEPENDENCE June 14th thru June 16th. Air Group 27 would fly in the departing Air Group's aircraft with Air Group 46 checker board tail markings for a short period of time until they were repainted and / or replaced.

1720-1727 Tug USS WANDANK was along starboard side with YOG-30, to be used as a camel, in preparation for fueling.
1800 USS CIMARRON came along starboard side to transfer fuel to this ship.

Original artwork for the **VF 27 squadron insignia** (Right)

Original artwork for the
VT 27 squadron insignia

Friday 15 June 1945   *Anchored in San Pedro Bay, Leyte Gulf - CVLG 46 Departs*

0629 Anchored as before. USS CIMARRON cast off having delivered 192,901 gallons of fuel oil, 24,500 gallons of aviation gasoline, and 15 barrels of lube oil.
1104 YTB 385 came alongside and removed YOG-30.
1310 LCT 1263 came along port side aft to pick up CVLG 46 for transportation to APL-13 for further transportation to Pearl Harbor, T.H.

Chapter 28   653

Fighting Squadron Forty-Six (VF-46) History describes their departure:

"On 15 June while still aboard the U.S.S. INDEPENDENCE, CTF 38 ordered us to disembark for housing aboard APL 13. A feverish perusal of available literature on ships of the Pacific Fleet was of no avail toward identifying our next haven. It wasn't until we had given three cheers for "Those we left behind and the good ship INDEPENDENCE" and were on our way in the LCI which transported us to its mooring off the coast of Samar that our curiosity was satisfied. APL 13 was an Auxiliary Personnel Lighter. To the laity, this is a powerless house boat with a deck below the main deck for refrigeration, engine room and quarters for passenger enlisted men, a main deck with recreation room, mess hall and crew's ship's company quarters, an upper deck which housed sick bay, the laundry and officers country and a super deck (pent house) for recreation. One of 35 of its kind built in the Charleston Navy Yard, Boston, APL 13 was towed by way of Panama Canal, [1] Pearl Harbor,* [2] Eniwetok and Ulithi * [2] to Leyte. She left Boston 22 December 1944 and arrived Leyte 1 June 1945 with a month taken out at Pearl for meditation and accumulation of poise for the trip across the Pacific at seven knots."*

(Author notes: Tug Boats * [1] ATA-102 to Pearl, * [2] MENOMINEE ATF-73 to Eniewetok, * [3] TERN ATO-142 to Leyte)

On 17 June they received orders to board the USS MAKASSAR STRAIT for Guam.
(Note: Air Group 46 would arrive in San Diego on 18 August, and be decommissioned on 14 September 1945)

Outgoing Air Group 46 had departed for the States, and the INDEPENDENCE welcomed Air Group 27 aboard, to settle in, as the ship worked with them in preparation to return to the Pacific war.

16-28 June 1945   *Anchored in San Pedro Bay, Leyte Gulf*

The crew continued taking on fresh goods, supplies and munitions.

Saturday 16 June 1945   *Anchored in San Pedro Bay, Leyte Gulf*

GN Heard today that both the Bennington and the Hornet will be going back soon. Both lost about 30 foot of their flight decks in that last typhoon so we didn't do too bad. Laid around practically all day with nothing to do. GN

RC Went ashore on Leyte the first time on land in 106 days. One day ashore here is plenty. RC

Sunday 17 June 1945   *Anchored in San Pedro Bay, Leyte Gulf*

GN Another lazy day. Not much doing although we are getting ready for the next brawl. Took aboard 42 -500 pound bombs - bringing that line of goods up to our capacity of 225. Got the dope that the Cowpens has already left Pearl bound out here. All kind of good rumors are making the rounds. GN

Tuesday 19 June 1945   *Anchored in San Pedro Bay, Leyte Gulf*

GN Brought aboard a load of fragmentation bombs that we expect to use on our first operation. Not much else doing. GN

Wednesday 20 June 1945   *Anchored in San Pedro Bay, Leyte Gulf*

TG 38.3 got underway, steaming out of the harbor for a short training cruise.

GN Attended school today aboard ship for that new VT fuse. Wrote a few letters. All else quiet. GN

Thursday 21 June 1945

Anchored in San Pedro Bay, Leyte Gulf

GN Started cleaning up all spaces. GN

Douglas R5D

Torpedo Twenty Seven - VT-27 Pilot and Air Crew

(Need names for each photo)

Fighting Twenty Seven - VF-27 Pilots

Air Group Twenty Seven - Non-flying officers and enlisted men

Friday 22 June 1945   *Anchored in San Pedro Bay, Leyte Gulf*

We got word that organized resistance on Okinawa Shima had ceased.

GN Heard today that we may get out for a gunnery run in a day or so. Would be okay by me. Inspection today and passed with flying colors. Brought a load of fuses aboard for the new bombs. GN

Saturday 23 June 1945   *Anchored in San Pedro Bay, Leyte Gulf*

0145 They received a report of a submarine from ComPhilSeaFron. They blacked out the ship, and the Executive Officer was notified of the warning, and the action taken. All watches were alerted.
0205 The bow sentry reported a dark unidentified object moving across the ship's bow. Sky Control was notified, and gun crews alerted. The forward 40mm guns and two 20mm guns were brought to bear with orders to open fire if the object approached dangerously close to the ship.
0220 The object was moving in direction of the USS TICONDEROGA. TICONDEROGA was notified by warning dispatch. Today TG 38.3 returned to the anchorage from its exercises.

Wednesday 27 June 1945   *Anchored in San Pedro Bay, Leyte Gulf*

0621 USS YORKTOWN, USS IOWA and USS ALASKA departed for a short training exercise. Rear Admiral Lewis E. Denfeld (USS WISCONSIN, Flagship) assumed tactical command of TG 38.4.
1750 USS IOWA and USS ALASKA returned from their exercise and Rear Admiral Oscar C. Badger (USS IOWA, Flagship) assumed tactical command of TG 38.4.

Thursday 28 June 1945   *Anchored in San Pedro Bay, Leyte Gulf*

0830 USS YORKTOWN returned and Rear Admiral A.W. Radford assumed tactical command of TG 38.4. At 2105 a probable air raid was reported by a shore based radar installation, followed by an all clear at 2010.

GN Getting places squared away for inspection. Underway tomorrow for some practice of one kind or another. GN

Friday 29 June 1945 *Leyte Gulf — Flight Operations*

0630 Anchored as before. Commenced turning over main engines by steam.
0645 Manned the special sea detail.
0646 Hoisted aboard the No.1 & No.2 motor whale boats.
0705 Commenced heaving short on the starboard anchor.
0710 All Departments ready for getting underway.
0720 Officer of the Deck shifted his watch to the bridge.
0726 USS INDEPENDENCE got underway, commencing to steer on various courses at various speeds conforming to the channel.
0730 INDEPENDENCE was joined by screening DDs USS UHLMANN and USS BENHAM as Task Unit 38.4.6, Captain Kindell OTC.
0748 Changed course to 149°T, speed 20 knots while departing San Pedro Bay for air operations and high speed engine runs in Leyte Gulf.
0822 Secured the special sea detail.
0850 Completed launching 8 F6Fs and 7 TBMs to conduct a search, then a simulated attack on the ship upon return.
1036-1045 Completed launching 16 F6Fs for CAP exercises.
1056 Recovered 1 F6F launched at 1045.

1159 Completed recovering 8 F6F and 7 TBMs launched at 0850.
1301 Completed launching 7 F6Fs and 6 TBMs for a search-attack training mission.
1315 Completed recovering the remaining 15 F6Fs launched at 1045.
1431 Completed recovering 7 F6F and 6 TBMs launched at 1301.
1458 Secured from flight quarters. Air Department set to condition 14.
A thunderstorm developed reducing visibility to 5,000 yards as they were returning to San Pedro Bay. Rains ceased before the ship anchored.
1533 Commenced maneuvering, passing channel buoy No.1 to port, conforming to channel entering San Pedro Bay.
1611 Anchored between berths 72 & 88, San Pedro Bay, Leyte Gulf, 13 fathoms of water, mud bottom.
1620 Secured steering gear.
1622 Set special sea detail. Secured boilers No.3 and 4.

GN Underway out in the bay for some practice landings and takeoffs. Inspection was not too good as I expected. What's good for some officers is not too good for others. Looks like we'll have a job squaring the joint away. GN

RC Got underway at 0730 for squadron to make some practice landings. Anchored at 1700. RC

GL Went out on a speed run & break in our squadron #27. GL

Saturday 30 June 1945 *Anchored in San Pedro Bay, Leyte Gulf*

1115 Anchored as before. Following the movements of the USS SAN JACINTO, half-masted the colors.
1130 Following the movements of the USS SAN JACINTO, two-blocked the colors.
1725-1732 LCM 55 was alongside port quarter delivering aviation supplies.

GN Had SP with the liberty party on the island of Samar and that's about all I want to see of the Philippines. Did get one can of beer which makes it about 15 in all for the year that we've been away from the States. GN

Sunday 1 July 1945 *Underway from San Pedro Bay, Leyte Gulf*

0405 Anchored as before. Lighted off fires under No. 3 boiler.
0430 Commenced jacking over all engines by hand.
0505 Tested steering engines.
0530 Lighted off fires under No. 2 boiler.
0545 Commenced heaving short on the starboard anchor to 30 fathoms.
0547 Cut in No. 3 boiler on main steam line.
0558 Tested all underway circuits and electrical equipment.
0620 Gunnery Department secured from special harbor condition 3.
0621 Commenced jacking over main engines by steam.
0630 Tested steering and annunciator systems.
0635 Made all preparations for getting underway.
0638 Officer of the Deck shifted his watch to the bridge.
0703 Cut in No. 2 boiler on main steam line.
0705 Underway from the anchorage, proceeding toward the channel. Commenced maneuvering to assume position in TG 38.4.1 (Rear Admiral A.W. Radford, commander Carrier Division Six in USS YORKTOWN) in column open order. They are part of Task Force 38 under Vice Admiral J.S. McCain in the Third Fleet, under Admiral W.F. Halsey.
0734 Changed course to 115°T, speed to 20 knots in station 2,000 yards astern of USS COWPENS.

Guide is USS YORKTOWN at head of column 8,000 yards ahead. CVL-22 is the fifth ship in column open order consisting of USS YORKTOWN, USS SHANGRI LA, USS BON HOMME RICHARD, USS COWPENS and USS INDEPENDENCE, with 2,000 yards interval between ships.

0800 Mustered crew on stations. They then secured the special sea detail.

0845 Secured No. 2 main engine for repairs.

0900 Formed column formation, interval 1,500 yards. Guide is USS YORKTOWN at head of column 6,000 yards.

0928 Lost steering control due to blown fuse on control panel, starboard steering unit.

0929 Shifted to port steering unit. Regained steering control.

1020 Passed by sonar buoys between Dinagat and Homonhon Islands at the entrance to Leyte Gulf.

1135 USS SHANGRI LA designated guide, formed disposition 5R.

1304 Secured from flight quarters, Air Department set to condition 14.

1305 USS FLINT designated guide. Commenced maneuvering to take station behind USS FLINT in column for AA gunnery exercises.

1338-1632 Gunnery Department manned all torpedo defense stations for firing exercises.

1638 Commenced maneuvering to form cruising disposition 5R.

1918 Commenced zigzagging on base course 060°T, 17 knots.

They were steaming north for strikes on Japan proper. In addition to the carriers, there are 3 battleships, one heavy cruiser, 2 anti-aircraft cruisers and screening destroyers. Throughout the night USS BON HOMME RICHARD and USS YORKTOWN exercised their night fighters in interceptions and join-ups. They also participated in intruder and heckler exercises.

RC Underway at 0705 for Tokyo. Several carriers are back from states after being repaired and have joined us. RC

Monday 2 July 1945   *Underway - Steaming toward Japan*

Steaming as before on a northeasterly course, in company with USS YORKTOWN (OTC and guide), USS SHANGRI LA, USS COWPENS, and USS BON HOMME RICHARD in TG 38.4.1 (Rear Admiral A.W. Radford, CTG)

0638-0748 USS CUSHING was along the starboard side receiving 27,905 gallons of fuel oil.

0803 USS COLAHAN came along starboard side to take on fuel.

0828 USS COLAHAN cast off having received only 12,412 gallons of fuel oil, so CVL-22 could change her course (into the wind) and speed for launching aircraft.

0842 Changed course to 220°T and commenced launching aircraft.

0857 Completed launching 24 F6Fs. 8 F6Fs were for CAP. 16 F6Fs held air training exercises.

0921 Changed speed to 15 knots. Changed course to 060°T. USS COLAHAN once again came along starboard side to continue to refuel.

0934 Secured from flight quarters. Air Department set to condition 13.

1020 USS COLAHAN cast off having received 18,002 gallons of fuel oil.

1100 Sounded flight quarters.

1150-1159 Launched 9 TBMs for air training exercises.

1248 Completed recovery of 24 F6Fs launched at 0857, and 1 fighter from the USS COWPENS.

1529 Completed launching 24 F6Fs for air training and tracking exercises, and additionally, launched the aircraft from the USS COWPENS to return to that vessel.

1542 Completed recovery of 9 TBMs launched at 1159.

1758-1821 Completed recovery of 24 F6Fs launched at 1529.

Throughout the night they zigzagged on base course 060°T and the USS BON HOMME RICHARD, operating independently with two DDs, again exercised her night fighters. She rejoined the formation in the morning.

HC Left Leyte and I am glad to get out of here, it is too damn hot and there is too much disease. HC

GL Just cruising & breaking in new pilots. GL

GN Broke out and made up rockets all day long. Cut my thumb wide open while working making writing a bit harder. GN

Tuesday 3 July 1945   *Steaming toward Japan*

0445 Steaming as before on a northeasterly course. 0530 Sounded flight quarters.
0642-0656 Launched 12 F6Fs and 7 TBMs for air training exercises.
0700 Secured from flight quarters. Air Department set to condition 13.
0714-0752 USS WEDDERBURN was alongside starboard receiving 16,620 gallons of fuel oil.
0757 USS FRANK KNOX came along starboard side to refuel.
0844 USS FRANK KNOX cast off having received 18,781 gallons of fuel oil.
0901 Recovered 1 returning TBM, launched at 0656, due to an oil leak.
0930 Sounded flight quarters.
1022 Completed recovery of 12 F6Fs and the remaining 6 TBMs launched at 0656.
1101-1145 USS SMALLEY was along the starboard side receiving 22,466 gallons of fuel oil.
1212 Completed launching 12 F6Fs and 9 TBMs for air training exercises. The Air Groups made simulated coordinated attacks on the Task Group.
1241 Secured from flight quarters. Air Department set to condition 13.
1501 Sounded flight quarters.
1545-1610 Recovered 12 F6Fs and 9 TBMs launched at 1212.
1808 The USS QUINCY, USS WISCONSIN, USS IOWA and USS MISSOURI (TG 38.4.2) joined TG 38.4 in cruising disposition 5R. USS MISSOURI designated guide, bearing 164°T, 2,500 yards.
2153 Commenced zigzagging on base course 060°T, 18 knots.
Tonight they continued on toward an operating area off Japan. The USS BON HOMME RICHARD exercised her night fighters.

GN Made up more rockets for our pilots to practice. Sure am getting so I don't like the look of rockets anymore. 7,000th landing today. GN

Wednesday 4 July 1945   *Independence Day - Steaming toward Japan*

Steaming as before in TG 38.4.1. Ship is darkened, zigzagging on a northeasterly base course 060°T, 18 knots, and boilers No.1, 2, & 3 are in use. Air Department is in condition 14.
0350 After gyro temporally out of commission due to accidental trip of circuit breaker on after distribution board, until the emergency diesel was cut in.
0358 Sounded flight quarters.
0415 After gyro restored on normal power.
0504 Completed launching 8 F6Fs for CAP and 3 TBMs for ASP.
0723 USS YORKTOWN assumed guide, course 230°T, bearing 218°T, 3,000 yards.
0735 Changed course to 070°T. Commenced maneuvering to form disposition 6VB.
0756 Completed launching 2 TBMs towing target sleeves for group AA practice.
0801 Commenced recovering aircraft.
0822 Formed disposition 6VC.
0833 Completed recovery of 8 F6Fs and 3 TBMs launched at 0504.
0850 Gunnery Department manned all torpedo defense stations for gunnery tracking exercises.
0900 Secured from flight quarters. Air Department set to condition 13.
1030 Sounded flight quarters.
1044 Gunnery Department secured from torpedo defense.

1047 Commenced maneuvering to form cruising disposition 5VB.

1115 USS MISSOURI designated guide, course 080°T, bearing 164°T, 2,500 yards.

1124-1125 Recovered 2 TBMs launched at 0756.

1148 Secured from flight quarters. Air Department set to condition 14.

1240-1342 Gunnery Department manned all torpedo defense stations for gunnery tracking exercises.

1426 Completed launching 2 TBMs towing target sleeves for group AA practice.

1437 USS YORKTOWN assumed guide.

1459 Formed disposition 5VB.

1505 Formed disposition 5VC.

1520 Gunnery Department manned all torpedo defense stations for gunnery exercises. Tactical command changed to USS IOWA.

1715 Sounded flight quarters. Task Group 38.4 completed gunnery exercises. USS INDEPENDENCE expended 4,253 rounds of 40mm and 2,225 rounds of 20mm ammunition firing on towed sleeves.

1717 OTC changed to USS YORKTOWN. At 1718 the Task Group changed to disposition 5R.

1720 Gunnery Department secured from torpedo defense.

1742 USS MISSOURI assumed guide.

1804 Recovered 2 TBMs launched at 1426.

1830 Air Department set to condition 14.

2210 Commenced zigzagging throughout the night on base course 050°T, speed 18 knots.

GN Sent a bit of 50 cal topside and made up more rockets. Hope that is the last of the small jobs. Big dinner today as usual on good old Independence Day. Had a stomach ache for a while but it passed off. GN

Thursday 5 July 1945 *Steaming toward Japan*

Zigzagging on base course 050°T, guide USS MISSOURI, bearing 014°T, 2,500 yards.

0603-0610 USS REMEY was alongside to port to deliver officer messenger mail.

0700 Sounded flight quarters.

0818 Completed launching 12 F6Fs and 9 TBMs for simulated coordinated attacks on the Task Group, and practice on approach procedures.

1140 Completed recovery of 12 F6Fs and 9 TBMs launched at 0818.

1200 Secured from flight quarters. Air Department set to condition 14.

1232 Formed cruising disposition 5VB.

1300 Gunnery Department manned all torpedo defense stations for tracking exercises.

1310-1315 USS WATTS was alongside starboard quarter to deliver officer messenger mail.

1330 Sounded flight quarters.

1419 Gunnery Department secured from torpedo defense.

1427-1434 Launched 12 F6Fs for CAP.

1440 Secured from flight quarters. Air Department set to condition 13.

1644 Sounded flight quarters.

1751 Completed recovery of 12 F6Fs launched at 1434.

1830 The USS BON HOMME RICHARD left the Task Group to operate independently (with 4 destroyers) during the night.

1843 Secured from flight quarters. Air Department set to condition 14.

1847 Formed disposition 5R.

1852 Commenced zigzagging on base course 050°T, at 18 knots.

GN Not too much doing. Fixed fan in morning making 411* more livable. Made up bunch of 3.25 rockets for early morning hop. GN (* 411 George refers to is likely a crew berthing compartment just forward the front wall of the hangar bay and 3 decks lower)

Friday 6 July 1945 *Steaming toward Japan - Air & Gunnery Exercises*

0320 Steaming as before en route to our fueling area. Sounded flight quarters.

0349-0448 Gunnery Department manned all torpedo defense stations.

0422 Completed launching 10 F6Fs. 8 were for CAP and 2 for SubCAP over our lifeguard submarines.

0540 USS BON HOMME RICHARD rejoined the Task Group.

0643 Having developed trouble, 2 F6Fs executed an emergency landing.

0749 Completed launching 12 F6Fs and 7 TBMs. 8 F6Fs for CAP. The TBMS were conducting strike exercises, and 4 F6Fs accompanied them (2 were tasked as photo planes). These aircraft made simulated attacks on the Task Group.

0758 Gunnery Department manned all torpedo defense stations for tracking exercises.

0809 Completed recovery of 8 F6Fs launched at 0422.

0815 Secured from flight quarters. Air Department set to condition 13.

0940 Sounded flight quarters.

1001 Completed launching 2 TBMs for a 100 mile weather search.

1010 Secured from flight quarters. Air Department set to condition 13.

1016 Secured from torpedo defense.

1110 Sounded flight quarters.

1225 Completed recovery of 12 F6Fs and 7 TBMs launched at 0749 and 2 TBMs launched at 1001.

1320 USS YORKTOWN designated guide.

1409-1410 Launched 2 TBMs as target tow planes for firing exercises.

1418 Secured from flight quarters. Air Department set to condition 13.

1419 Gained position in disposition 6VB.

1432 Formed cruising disposition 6VC in preparation for gunnery exercises.

1505 ComBatDiv 7 in USS IOWA designated OTC for conducting firing exercises.

1620-1659 Manned torpedo defense stations for gunnery firing practice on towed sleeves.

1700 Rear Admiral Radford (CTG 38.4 in USS YORKTOWN) resumed tactical command.

1708 Formed cruising disposition 6VB.

1758 Recovered 2 TBMs launched at 1409.

1815 USS MISSOURI designated guide, course 065°T, bearing 330°T, 3,000 yards.

1822 Secured from flight quarters. Air Department set to condition 14.

1834 Commenced maneuvering to gain station in cruising disposition 5R.

1850 Commenced zigzagging thru the night on base course 065°T, speed 18 knots.

Captain Kindell noted in the SOL:
"We are between Iwo and the Marianas. Ought to see B-29s tomorrow."

GN Inspection day again. Think that the Navy lives by field day and can't figure out whether we are at war or if this is a peace time Navy. Sent part of the rockets topside. Operating this time with 38.4 which comprises the Yorktown, Bon Homme Richard, Shangri La, Cowpens and ourselves as carriers. The Iowa, Wisconsin and Missouri as wagons. One heavy cruiser and two AA cruisers along with 22 cans. Quite an imposing force to my way of thinking. Two more of our forces like ours in the neighborhood and I heard one of the British so methinks it behooves the Japs to stay at home. We are Tokyo bound again and are supposed to get within 140 miles of that ruined city and 120 miles of the coast. The word is that the Nip has 96 airfields in the vicinity and 1600 planes on them. We have 1700 ourselves not to mention the Army* who'll be by with possible a few hundred more. GN

(* Note: Army aircraft were likely the Army Air force B-29s. Established as the part of the US Army on 1 August 1907, the Air force would become a separate branch on 18 September 1947 by passage of the National Security Act of 1947.)

Saturday 7 July 1945 *Steaming toward Japan - Gunnery Exercises*

Steaming as before en route to the fueling area.

0332-0432 Gunnery Department manned all torpedo defense stations.

0355-0404 Launched 10 F6Fs. 8 were for CAP, and 2 for CAP over lifeguard subs.

0433 Secured from flight quarters. Air Department set to condition 13.

0438 Formed cruising disposition 5VB.

0620 Sounded flight quarters.

0733 Completed launching 12 F6Fs and 9 TBMs. 8 F6Fs for CAP. The TBMs were conducting strike exercises, and 4 F6Fs went with them as photo planes.

0755 Completed recovery of 10 F6Fs launched at 0404.

0810 Sounded torpedo defense for tracking exercises.

0820 Secured from flight quarters. Air Department set to condition 13.

0944 Secured from torpedo defense.

1020 Sounded flight quarters.

1146 Recovered 12 F6Fs and 9 TBMs launched at 0733.

1214 Secured from flight quarters. Air Department set to condition 14.

1315 Sounded flight quarters.

1353 Completed launching 2 TBMs as target tow planes.

1404 Secured from flight quarters. Air Department set to condition 13.

1425 Commenced maneuvering to gain position in disposition 6VB.

1427 USS YORKTOWN designated guide.

1446 Formed disposition 6VC.

1447 ComBatDiv 7 in USS IOWA designated OTC for conducting firing exercises.

1606 Gunnery Department manned torpedo defense stations for firing exercises.

1639 With firing exercised completed, secured from torpedo defense.

1643 CTG 38.4 (Rear Admiral Radford) in USS YORKTOWN resumed tactical command.

1645 Sounded flight quarters.

1650 Commenced maneuvering to form disposition 5R.

1704 USS IOWA maneuvered to avoid a floating mine sighted off her port bow.

1734-1736 Recovered 2 TBMs launched at 1353.

2002 USS MISSOURI designated guide.

2235 Commenced zigzagging thru the night on base course 050°T, speed 17 knots.

Captain Kindell noted in the SOL:
"Reveille is scheduled for 0245. The night is practically non-existent so the need for night orders is the same. No changes from last night. We fuel in the morning."

GN Word is that we may get to go back after this operation if all goes well. The operation may last anywhere from 5 to 30 days and we're all hoping they'll be no accidents. Sent some more rockets topside for practice. The gunnery dep't is really being kept jumping around. They are being called all the time for gunnery and tracking drills. Put the rest of the rockets away and standing by for tomorrow. GN

Sunday 8 July 1945   *Refuel and Reprovision*

0315 Steaming as before to fuel and replenish. Gunnery Department manned torpedo defense stations. Sighted the tanker group at 0400 and commenced maneuvering to gain position to refuel and resupply.

0416 Secured from torpedo defense.

0503 Maneuvering to take position astern USS TAPPAHANNOCK, guide for the fueling operations.

0526 Came alongside tanker USS SEBEC, to the starboard.

0708-0716 USS MCNAIR was alongside the port quarter to transfer Lt. Commander Bardshar, Commander of Air Group 27, to the USS YORKTOWN for a conference.

0830 Cast off from USS SEBEC having received 469,622 gallons of fuel oil and 63,700 gallons of aviation gasoline. Commenced maneuvering to approach on the provision stores ship, USS ALDEBARAN.

0903 Came alongside of USS ALDEBARAN. Commenced receiving fresh provisions.

0938 Sounded flight quarters.

1018 Cast off all lines from USS ALDEBARAN having completed reprovisioning.

1031-1035 Completed launching 8 F6Fs for CAP.

1040 Secured from flight quarters. Air Department set to condition 13.

1055-1105 USS FRANK KNOX was alongside the port quarter to receive U.S. Mail and to transfer U.S. Mail and a passenger to this vessel.

1245-1251 USS MCNAIR was alongside the port quarter to deliver freight.

1330 Sounded flight quarters.

1425 USS MISSOURI designated guide.

1429 Completed recovery of 8 F6Fs launched at 1035.

1450-1455 USS WATTS was alongside the starboard quarter delivering a radar switch.

1500 Gained station in disposition 5R.

1539 Completed launching 2 TBMs for target towing.

1545 Secured from flight quarters. Air Department set to condition 14.

1555 USS YORKTOWN designated guide.

1607 Commenced maneuvering to form cruising disposition 6VC.

1620 Sounded torpedo defense for gunnery exercises, firing on towed sleeves.

1646 Sounded flight quarters.

1700 Half-masted colors by order of OTC following movements of USS QUINCY.

1703 Secured from torpedo defense.

1707 Commenced maneuvering to form cruising disposition 5R.

1710 Two-blocked the colors.

1735 Completed recovery of 2 TBMs launched at 1539.

1800 USS MISSOURI designated guide.

1815 Secured from flight quarters. Air Department set to condition 14.

1830-1840 USS STOCKHAM was alongside delivering U.S. mail and to transfer Lt. Commander Bardshar back aboard from the conference on USS YORKTOWN.

The USS CHICAGO joined Task Group 38.4 today.

They steamed zigzagging on base course 350°T at 19 knots thru the night.

Monday 9 July 1945 *Steaming toward Japan*

Steaming as before to an area east of Japan for strikes against Tokyo tomorrow.

0121 USS STODDARD (on picket duty in screen station 8) reported a possible submarine contact bearing 190°T, 1,000 yards.

0135 USS MCNAIR (in screen station 1) reported a possible sub contact bearing 305°T, 1,300 yards.

0250 USS STODDARD ordered by OTC to remain in the area of the possible sub contact.

0413 Formed cruising disposition 5VB.

0503 Task Group 38.4 commenced topping off destroyers.

0534-0632 USS WREN was along the starboard side to receive 21,483 gallons of fuel oil.

1100 Air Department set to condition 13.

1330 Sounded flight quarters.

1332 "Triton-5" from USS COWPENS tally-hoed and splashed a Dinah at 30,000'.

1340 A Frances was reported splashed over TG 38.1.

1431 Completed launching 8 F6Fs as CAP.

1440 Secured from flight quarters. Air Department set to condition 13.

1701 Sounded flight quarters.

1806 Completed recovery of 8 F6Fs launched at 1431.

Throughout the afternoon they zigzagged on a northwesterly course, and just after 1800 commenced a high speed run in on the target (course 320°T at 24 knots in cruising disposition 5R).

Captain Kindell noted in the SOL:

"Probably will make a long straight run at 25K* all night. Radio silence. Tomorrow a Tokyo area strike. Formation 5R Axis 0000. Guide MISSOURI, at 0000, bears 324°. OTC YORKTOWN.
No land anywhere out here. No ship sightings probable. Call me if anything unexpected appears."

(* 25 Knots)

AD *At sea. We were informed that we are going to strike Tokyo. This will be the first time for the 3rd fleet. The 5th fleet hit once in February.* ***AD*** (The "3rd Fleet" simply was a change of command back to Halsey.)

GN *Been running in all day to get as close to Japan as possible. From the dope we've been getting looks like we're in for trouble. Up topside again in evening but left soon as I was too cold. Another nice sunset and looks like a good day tomorrow.* ***GN***

Tuesday 10 July 1945   *Japan, Tokyo*

Steaming as before to an area east of Japan about 150 miles from Tokyo. Strike targets including airfields, military installations and industrial areas. INDEPENDENCE is in company with USS YORKTOWN (OTC), USS SHANGRI LA, USS COWPENS, and USS BON HOMME RICHARD in TU 38.4.1 (Rear Admiral A.W. Radford, CTG). Ship is darkened. USS MISSOURI is guide, course 320°T, bearing 324°T, 2,500 yards.

0244 Sounded flight quarters.

0258 Forward gyro failed due to a defective DC rectifier tube. Switched all repeaters to after gyro.

0325 Forward gyro back in service.

0350-0355 Launched 10 F6Fs. 8 Hellcats were for a CAP and 2 Hellcats were assigned as SubCAP over our lifeguard submarines. Weather today was excellent, CAVU with light to variable winds.

0415 Formed cruising disposition 5VB.

0722 Completed launching 8 F6Fs as a CAP over the Task Group, 9 TBMs for a strike, and 4 F6Fs for a photographic mission over the target area. The 9 TBM Avengers carried 54 260lb. fragmentation bombs for strikes on Kasumigaura, Kashima and Shimizu airfields. The destruction of enemy aircraft was the primary mission. Moderate AA was encountered, with no airborne opposition.

0726 Recovered 2 F6Fs launched at 0335.

0755 Completed recovery of the remaining 8 F6Fs launched at 0335.

1047 Launched 8 F6Fs for a CAP over the Task Group.

1123 Recovered 12 F6Fs and 9 TBMs launched at 0722.

1255-1300 Launched 9 TBMs for a strike on Konoike airfield, N.E. of Tokyo.

1320 Twin engine Japanese Dinah reported shot down over Task Group 38.1 by fighters from the USS COWPENS.

1322 Sounded torpedo defense due to enemy aircraft. Observed a large splash and black smoke, bearing 235°T, 10 miles, believed to have been the Dinah shot down over TG 38.1.

1324 Formed cruising disposition 5VC, placing a destroyer between each of the heavy vessels.

1335 Observed large explosion bearing 020°T, 6 miles.

1344 Secured from torpedo defense. Gunnery Department remained in condition One Easy.

1351 Formed cruising disposition 5VB.

1428-1444 Launched 16 F6Fs for a fighter sweep over costal airfields, with a strike on Yatabe Airfield. 12 Hellcats carried two 260 lb. fragmentation bombs each, and the other 4 Hellcats were assigned as photo planes. They bombed and strafed the few aircraft they encountered, reporting dummy aircraft at all airfields. 13 enemy planes were accessed as damaged. There was no airborne opposition. Flack was reported as light.

1451-1458 Recovered 8 F6Fs launched at 1047.

1706 Completed recovery of 9 TBMs launched at 1300.

1724 Completed recovery of 2 F6F photo planes launched at 1444, returning due to engine problems.

1830 Completed recovery of 14 F6Fs launched at 1444.

1920 Formed cruising disposition 5R.

1845-1931 Manned general quarters stations.

2034 Changed course to 100°T.
Throughout the night they retired from the target area on a northeasterly course at 25 knots.

Torpedo Squadron 27 noted: *"It began to look like the Japs would not come out to meet us; were waiting for invasion and husbanding available aircraft in widespread dispersal areas."*

From the Diary of Admiral Matome Ugaki: *"At noon the enemy broadcasted to the states from on board ship that they were attacking the Tokyo district with one thousand planes. They even mentioned the names of some ships. What insolence!"*

RC Hitting Tokyo, reveille was sounded at 0245 this morning, we were expecting them to come out with all they had but they didn't, just one plane shot down over task group all day long. They threatened to come out and "Bull Halsey" gave them our location but looks like they don't want to fight, for they didn't come. RC

(Authors note / observation: It is my opinion that it was NOT a matter of the Japanese not desiring to attack the US Fleet. They were short of necessary assets to do it. They had been ravaged by US Navy and Army Air Force bombing raids, low on aircraft, spare parts, trained pilots and fuel. The Imperial Japanese Navy was decimated. Transportation was interrupted, communication no doubt becoming difficult. Just gathering and coordinating the (logistics) scattered assets for rapid response would have been a major challenge. The decisions on use of valued precious remaining resources complicated by the above VT-27 observation was an all but impossible dilemma for Japans military leaders!

HC Big day today, striking Tokyo area. condition 1 Easy all day. Shot down one Dina on the horizon, another suicide job that didn't get in. The divine wind has lost its fury, or the fan broke. HC

GN Strike day on Japan. All told we sent over about 130 frag bombs and hope they went where they would do the most good. From all reports the air over Tokyo was bothered very much by American props and very little AA fire. No air borne opposition. GN

GL Tokyo – Reveille at 2:46, GQ 3:26 set 1 Easy. Our planes had 2 strikes with 265 pound bombs. No fighter opposition, light AA. 1 Frances splashed by guns of 58.1, 1 Dinah shot down by Cowpens. 1 destroyer sighted, no news yet. Quite a nice day. Destroyed 180 planes, sank 3 ships. Lots of mines in area. Our group is the only one striking Tokyo. Others are hitting Yokohama. GL

Wednesday 11 July 1945   *Japan, Retiring to Refuel*

0258 Steaming en route to an area for refueling. Commenced zigzagging on base course 025°T.
0312-0412 Manned general quarters stations.
0620 Sheered off course to avoid a floating mine, 4,000 yards off our bow.
0722-0727 Launched 8 F6Fs for CAP.
0839-0845 USS WATTS was along starboard side to receive photographs.
1105 Completed recovery of 8 F6Fs launched at 0727.
1158 Air Department set to condition 14.
1337-1345 Half-masted the colors following the movements of the USS YORKTOWN.
1822 Darkened the ship.
1823 USS BON HOMME RICHARD left the formation for night operations.
Throughout the night they zigzagged on base course 015°T, at 18 knots.

GN Heard last evening that we got an honorable mention from Admiral Nimitz in one of his talks stateside yesterday. He mentioned three other carriers and all of us are the old-timers out here. Today we retired and had pretty much a snap of it. Flew a very little CAP. We are headed north and it sure feels it. Getting mighty cold. Not enough opposition around Tokyo to keep " Bull " Halsey there so off we go a-hunting. There are supposed to be quite a few planes around Hokkaido so we'll go there and check on it. Supposed to refuel, rearm and reprovision ship tomorrow. Things are getting to look better all the time and looks as though " Bull " will take us a lot closer than the 110 miles away from Nipponland that he did this time. More power to him. GN

Missed the Nine Arresting Gear Cables
.....

Tail wheel in the air,
hook dragging on the deck,
notice the aircraft in front of the
fast moving VF-46 Hellcat.

Stopped by the Barricade Cables!

Thursday 12 July 1945 *Refueling*

Steaming as before en route to an area for refueling, zigzagging on base course 015°T, in cruising disposition 5R, guide USS MISSOURI. Air Department is in condition 14.

0153 Submarine sound contact and torpedo wakes reported by picket destroyers on our bow. Ceased zigzagging and came to course 090°T by order of the OTC.

0154 Changed speed to 25 knots. At 0201 changed course to 130°T.

0243-0341 Gunnery Department manned all torpedo defense stations.

0310 Air Department set to condition 12.

0330 Sighted the fueling group.

0345 Changed course to 0345°T. Began maneuvering into fueling position.

0342 Task Group commenced fueling exercises. Commenced maneuvering to gain position on USS MANATEE, designated guide on fueling course 330°T.

0500 Gunnery Department manned torpedo defense stations for firing exercises.

0503 Commenced maneuvering to gain position 800 yards astern the USS QUINCY for Anti-Aircraft exercises.

0519 Commenced gunnery exercises, firing at drones.

0543 Sounded flight quarters.

0555 Completed gunnery exercises and commenced maneuvering to gain the flying station.

0600 Gunnery Department secured from torpedo defense.

0622-0639 USS UHLMANN was alongside the port quarter to receive 4 pilots for transfer to the USS THETIS BAY to return with replacement aircraft.

0645-0657 Launched 8 F6Fs for CAP and 3 TBMs for ASP. Then commenced maneuvering to gain station 1,500 yards astern USS MANATEE, course 330°T, 8 knots. Formed disposition 5VB.

0751 Launched 2 TBMs to tow gunnery target sleeves.

0805 Commenced approach on the tanker USS MANATEE coming along side at 0817.

0841-1847 USS COLAHAN was alongside port quarter to transfer mail.

1023 Cast off from USS MANATEE having received 234,371 gallons of fuel oil and 22,700 gallons of aviation gasoline.

1139 Completed recovery of 8 F6Fs and 3 TBMs launched at 0657, and 2 TBMs launched at 0751.

1140-1206 UHLMANN was alongside port quarter to deliverer 4 pilots to ferry flyable duds to CVEs.

1209 Observed explosion in the water bearing 044°T, 12 miles distant.

1217 USS FLINT designated as guide.

1233 Completed launching 3 F6Fs and 1 TBM, flyable duds for delivery to the USS STEAMER BAY and the USS THETIS BAY respectively.

1254 Completed recovery of 3 F6Fs (Bu.No. 79637, 79817, 79839) and 1 TBM (Bu.No. 85887). These were replacement aircraft .

1314 USS REMEY came alongside the port quarter to deliver Lt. Commander Bardshar (CAG 27) back on board from his conference on the YORKTOWN.

1318 USS YORKTOWN designated guide.

1319 USS REMEY cast off.

1329 Gained station in disposition 5VB, guide USS YORKTOWN.

1412 Secured from flight quarters. Air Department set to condition 14.

1534 Formed cruising disposition 5R as the Task Group maneuvered to clear the fueling group.

1623-1630 USS STOCKHAM came alongside the port quarter to deliver mail.

1640 USS MISSOURI designated guide bearing 294°T, distance 2,500 yards.

1727 Changed course to 270°T, to steam thru the night toward an area southeast of Hokkaido.

Captain Kindell noted in the SOL:
"Tonight, run West to strike. Tomorrow night Northeast to strike again. Then Southeast to fuel."

GN Refueled toady but no provisions or arms came aboard. Didn't take too long and we were on our speedy way toward Hokkaido. Supposed to be virgin territory we are smacking and I hope we throw a surprise and the fear of God or of the US Navy in them. Cold as all get-out and looks like I'll have to break out more clothes soon. Have used a blanket the last few nights. GN

GL Refueled today. Pulled alongside tanker refueling Missouri. Saw Halsey on board as it is his flag ship. Have been lots of torpedo wakes, two passed by our fantail. Lots of trouble with subs but no hits yet. It is getting pretty cold. GL

Friday 13 July 1945   *Japan, Weather*

Steaming as before en route to an area southeast of Hokkaido. Today there are strikes planned against airfields and installations on most of Hokkaido.
0230 Sounded flight quarters.
0302-0402 Manned general quarters stations.
0405 Gunnery Department set to condition 3.
0756 Sounded torpedo defense by order of the OTC. Several unidentified planes sighted on radar.
0819 Secured from torpedo defense. The radar images indicating the presence of bogies turned out to be caused by weather returns.
Weather planes from USS BON HOMME RICHARD were sent out over the target area. They reported the ceiling 0 to 200' with visibility ranging from 0 to 1/2 mile. Widespread drizzle, rain, fog and reduced visibility over the target area, compounded early in the morning as high winds were experienced gusting to 50 knots. All air operations for the day were canceled. In heavy rain and choppy seas, they steamed in the general area throughout the day.
1308 Air Department secured from flight quarters.

Captain Kindell noted in the SOL:
"Coast is about 135nm west of us (2000)* so that's only about seven hours steaming. If we keep on this course until 0300 we can step ashore, fog or no fog. (*Note: 2000 refers to time of day)
No sightings are expected on friendly schedules. May see another sub or two by radar. Call me if anything of interest shows up."*

GL Hokkaido - Supposed to strike today but ceiling is zero, can't see 500 yards. No planes up all day. 75 miles from Japan. GL

AD At sea. We are supposed to strike some islands and the northern part of Honshu. Weather is bad so we are just cruising around. AD

Saturday 14 July 1945   *Japan, Honshu & Hokkaido*

Steaming as before in company with Task Unit 38.4.1, USS MISSOURI guide, in an area off Hokkaido.
0111 Pit log went out of commission for 5 minutes, put back in working order when trash was discovered in the end of the sword arm. (Note: This was used to register the speed of the ship, the sword arm is the pressure pickup).
0230 Sounded flight quarters.
0337 Completed launching 8 F6Fs for a CAP.
Weather was overcast at 5,000' with scattered large patches of fog and areas of drizzle. Attacks would be made thru holes in weather on alternate targets. The afternoon brought scattered clouds over the Task Group, with target conditions "average to undesirable".
0403 Formed cruising disposition 5VB. At 0406 the Gunnery Department set to condition One Easy. There was solid 1,500' overcast over the Task Group.
0447 Launched 1 F6F as a replacement for a F6F reporting high oil temperature.
0558 USS QUINCY, USS CHICAGO, and DesRon* 54 left the formation for assignment by CTG 38.
0612 USS YORKTOWN designated guide.   (* DesRon = Destroyer Squadron)

0620 USS COLAHAN picked up VF-27 pilot Ensign Julius Parker. He is reported to be in good condition. The F6F-5 developed an oil leak, high oil temperatures, and his engine froze. Unable to be taken aboard, and out of options, he made a water landing in his troubled Hellcat (Bu.No.77587).

0710 Launched 12 F6Fs and 9 TBMs. 8 Hellcats were assigned CAP, the other 4 were sent as photo planes, two returning due to engine trouble. The 9 TBMs made attacks against shipping in the harbor at Urakawa *[1.] and a 100 ton cargo vessel caught underway was forced to beach. A warehouse near town was left burning. The photo planes reported "considerable shipping" in Hakodate Harbor.

0711 Recovered 1 F6F launched at 0337. (*[1.] Error in VT-27 history - Urakawa, NOT Arakawa)

0721 Launched 2 F6Fs as replacements for 2 CAP planes.

0722 Recovered 2 F6Fs launched at 0710 due to 1 Hellcat having trouble with suction to his belly tank.

0730 Recovered 6 F6Fs launched at 0337 and 1 F6F launched at 0447.

0740 Recovered 2 F6Fs launched at 0710 (1 photo plane and his escort).

1042-1048 Launched 8 F6Fs for CAP.

1114-1130 Recovered 8 F6Fs and 9 TBMs launched at 0710, and 2 F6Fs launched at 0721.

1225 Sounded torpedo defense. Bogies were picked up on radar at 12,000' 80 miles out.

1232 Received word that 2 Bettys were tally-hoed by the TG 38.1 CAP. They splashed one, the second Betty getting away.

1244 Secured from torpedo defense. Gunnery Department set to condition One Easy.

1308 Completed launching 4 F6Fs and 9 TBMs. The F6Fs were Cap for the TBM strike launched against Japanese shipping at Muroran. They sank a lugger, made 2 bomb hits on a DE, one bomb hit on a 5,000 ton freighter transport. They strafed 2 other DEs, a freighter and another lugger. "There appeared to be serious damage inflicted on one of the destroyer escorts *[2.], the freighter and one of the small vessels". A radio & radar station on Ermio Saki was rocketed and strafed. Two planes returned to INDEPENDENCE "with wings ripped" by the anti-aircraft fire, described as intense.

(*[2.] The DEs were likely Costal Defense vessels 65 & 74. C.D. NO. 74 was struck by two bombs, one fore and one aft. It would sink with 22 killed and 20 injured.   C.D. NO.65 would also sink.)

1325 Secured from flight quarters. Air Department set to condition 13.

1522 Completed recovery of 8 F6Fs launched at 1048.

1717 Completed recovery of 4 F6Fs and 9 TBMs launched at 1308.

1950 Formed cruising disposition 5R.

Throughout the night they zigzagged on various courses to remain in the same general area.

Captain Kindell noted in the SOL:

"Do not expect to sight anything tonight. We will steam offshore all night"

GN We did manage to get off a few loads of bombs and as visibility was poor we got no reports as to the damage. Heard that our TBM ran into some large size Nip ferry boats and lit three of them. Should get more word in a few days. At one time we were within 66 miles of the target. TD was called about noon and a fighter from one of the other units splashed a Betty from angels 13 over the outfit. Will probably hang around for another day for another whack. GN

GL Weather cleared, we are striking. Cruisers left to shell beach & a few BB's from other groups. We done good. Our flyers got hits on 2 cargo ships, 1 destroyer, 3 ferries[3.]. We lost 1 F6F, 2 TBM's shot up. Air opposition light. AA fire heavy. GL* (*[3.] Nine train ferries were sunk or driven ashore and badly damaged by naval aircraft on the 14th, an additional two on the 15th)

Sunday 15 July 1945   *Japan, Honshu & Hokkaido*

Steaming in an area southeast of Hokkaido with carriers USS SHANGRI LA, USS COWPENS, and USS BON HOMME RICHARD in Task Unit 38.4.1 (USS YORKTOWN is OTC and guide).

0055 ComDiv 10 — USS QUINCY and USS CHICAGO with DesRon 54 rejoined the TG.

0100 Task Unit 38.4.2 (USS IOWA, USS MISSOURI and USS WISCONSIN, with screening Destroyers) left the formation for assignment.

0230 Sounded flight quarters.

0340 Completed launching 8 F6Fs for a CAP.

0412 Gunnery Department set to condition One Easy.

0452 Formed cruising disposition 5VB.

0655 Lost electrical load on aft distribution board, shifted load to diesel (generators).

0657-0735 Aft gyro out of commission due to diesel power failure.

0714 Completed launching 8 F6Fs for a CAP, 4 F6Fs and 9 TBMs. The 4 F6Fs were on the mission as both escort and photo planes for the TBMs. The TBMs led by Lt. John G. Dooling, on a shipping strike, sunk a DE off Hakodate in Southern Hokkaido. No aerial opposition was encountered. Adverse weather made finding targets extremely difficult. Railroad bridges and viaducts were attacked along the coast.

0736 Completed recovery of 8 F6Fs launched at 0340.

0831 Recovered 1 F6F (photo escort), with engine trouble, launched at 0714.

0945-0951 USS CUSHING was alongside the starboard quarter to deliver photos.

1051 Completed launching 8 F6Fs for DCAP over this Task Group.

1134 Completed recovery of 8 F6Fs launched at 0714.

1208-1223 Completed recovery of 9 TBMs and 3 F6Fs launched at 0714, and 1 F6F launched at 1051.

1338 Completed launching 12 F6Fs for a fighter sweep against installations, factories and warehouses in Urakawa (on Hokkaido). A radar & radio station on Ermio Saki was damaged by strafing and rockets.

1355 Secured from flight quarters. Air Department set to condition 13.

1434 Sounded flight quarters.

1538 Completed recovery of 7 F6Fs launched at 1051.

1717 Completed recovery of 12 F6Fs launched at 1338.

1748 Task Unit 38.4.2 rejoined TG 38.4

1830 Secured from flight quarters. Air Department set to condition 14.

1852 Sounded torpedo defense.

1913 Gunnery Department secured from torpedo defense, set to condition 3.

1916 USS MISSOURI designated guide, course 110°T, bearing 0294°T, 2,500 yards.

2019 Commenced zigzagging on base course 110°T, and would steam this base course throughout the night at 18.5 knots toward a fueling rendezvous.

GN Another hit at Hokkaido and it really started out to be a big one. Had an early morning strike over the island. One TBM spotted a DE on the way in and decided to try to finish it off. He did exactly that and reports have it that he made contact with all his four bombs. No DE after that. Started working on a large strike after that but it folded and we sent a small bomb and rocket job instead. Supposed to refuel, rearm and reprovision ship tomorrow after which we make another hit on Tokyo. GN

GL Striking again today same place. Bombed out a town, sank 1 DE. Bombed steel mills and warehouse. condition 1 Easy for two days now. GL

Monday 16 July 1945 *Japan, Refueling*

Steaming as before in an area east of Japan for a rendezvous with tankers.

0220 Sounded flight quarters.

0320-0325 Launched 8 F6Fs for CAP.

0400 Secured the after gyro due to low vacuum, shifting all navigation units to the forward gyro.

0520 Sighted the fueling group and commenced maneuvering to gain position in the fueling formation. USS MANATEE designated guide, fueling course 225°T, speed 10 knots (098 rpm).

0600 Resumed use of after gyro.

0620 Sounded flight quarters.

0627-0634 USS COLAHAN was alongside port quarter to deliver Ensign Julius Parker back aboard from his water landing July 14th.

0640-0647 USS MONSSEN was alongside the port quarter to receive a ferry pilot for transfer to the CVE USS THETIS BAY to pick up a replacement F6F.

0720 Completed recovery of 8 F6Fs launched at 0325.

0745 Secured from flight quarters. Air Department set to condition 14.

0804 Manned all fueling stations and fueling circuits.

0809-0810 USS MONSSEN was alongside the port quarter to pick up photographs.

0815 Maneuvered alongside tanker USS NECHES.

0841-0843 USS MCGOWAN was along side the port quarter to deliver guard mail.

1015 Cast off from USS NECHES having received 184,441 gallons fuel oil, and 25,000 gallons of aviation gasoline.

1206 Recovered 1 F6F replacement flown over from USS THETIS BAY.

1225-1235 USS STODDARD was alongside the port quarter delivering guard mail.

1254 Secured from flight quarters. Air Department set to condition 14.

1459 USS MISSOURI was designated guide.

1521-1534 USS MONSSEN was alongside the port quarter to deliver freight.

1659 Changed course to 250°T to clear the fueling group, zigzagging on this base course throughout the night at 18 knots.

GN We refueled but the rearming and reprovisioning will have to wait till later. Got a good look at some of the British jobs that are operating with us. They came along side and were in blues of all things. Hope they don't give our Exec any queer ideas for he has enough of those things now. GN

AD Receiving fuel. British Fleet fueled with us today. They are now going to operate with us. Their Fleet doesn't consist of much. Just one of our Task Groups is larger and at this time we have three Groups all operating together. The British have 3 carriers, 1 battleship, 2 cruisers and 14 DD's and DE's mixed. We have 6 CVL's & 9 CL's, about 7 battleships, about 12 cruisers and god knows how many DD's. AD

On this evening of no seemly particular importance Captain Kindell noted in the SOL:
" The Same old 5R but new axis - 045°T.
MISSOURI is guide at 0000 and bears 009°T 2500 yds.
OTC is El Toro at YORKTOWN. Tomorrow is another day.
Nothing to see tonight except our own group or by accident.
Call me if anything unusual appears."

Unrepping bombs from MAZAMA or VESUVIUS

29
The "Gadget" - A New Era Begins

Monday 16 July 1945 - *Continued*

Nothing unusual would appear, nothing noteworthy to disturb Captain Kindell, or that would find its way into the Deck Log. But tonight was not just another night. It would pass with significant consequence, and a new conspicuous marker placed in the pages of the history of mankind!

2029 Numerous crewmembers of the Mighty-I were standing watch, and many in their racks trying to sleep. Lookouts would not see it, the men on decks far below in the engine room would not feel it. The inconceivably enormous explosive blast, and its far reaching effects, would pass unnoticed as the INDEPENDENCE knifed on its zigzagging course thru the water off Japan.

At this instant, 0529 local time (15 July in the US), on a remote test range near Alamogordo New Mexico, a blazing blindly bright orb grew spectacularly in milliseconds from the previously insignificant "Trinity" site. The heat and shock wave thundered across the "Journey of the Dead Man" desert, with the equivalent energy of roughly 22,000 tons of TNT. The effect from the aftershock of the first detonation of an Atomic weapon, the "Gadget", from atop the (now vaporized)100' tower, would soon have significant consequence to the entire Pacific fleet, and well beyond.

But tonight, unknowing, crewmembers pulled up the blanket in their racks, manned the helm, stood watch on the bridge, serviced planes in the hangar bay, peered at the radar in CIC, and did what sailors needed to do on an aircraft carrier in time of war. Task Group 38 and the Mighty-I were fueled and steaming back to strike the enemy.

The "Gadget" .016 seconds after detonation. (For scale; those are a few large trees at the base of the cloud)

Tuesday 17 July 1945   *Japan, Tokyo & Nojima Cape*

Steaming east of Tokyo. Air Department is in condition 14. Engineering Department in condition 31, all other departments in condition 3.
0250 Sounded flight quarters.
0320 Sounded routine general quarters.
0352 Completed launching 8 F6Fs for a DCAP over this Task Group.
0416 Formed cruising disposition 5VB.

0420 Secured from general quarters. Gunnery Department set to condition One Easy.

0428 Large explosion observed in the water bearing 272°T, 10 miles. It was believed to be a jettisoned bomb from a fighter.

0659 Completed launching 10 F6F Hellcats. 8 were for CAP and 2 were assigned CAP over the lifeguard submarines (SubCAP).

0706 Completed launching 1 F6F to replace a F6F (on SubCAP) with an oil leak.

0759 Completed recovery of 9 F6Fs, 8 launched at 0352 and 1 launched at 0659.

1043-1046 Launched 8 F6Fs for CAP.

1129-1142 Recovered 9 F6Fs launched at 0659 and 1 launched at 1046.

They were to have launched sweeps and strikes against Tokyo today but bad weather prevented it. Cloud cover and poor visibility marred the day. The first sweep, made by planes from other carriers, dropped their bombs thru clouds with unobserved results. One of the SubCAP pilots reported sighting a possible sub wake as he returned to the ship.

1157-1209 After gyro was out of service due to defective rectifier tube.

1230 Secured from flight quarters. Air Department set to condition 13.

1430 Sounded flight quarters.

1502-1511 Completed recovery of 7 F6Fs launched at 1046.

1623 USS YORKTOWN designated guide, bearing 063°T, 3,000 yards. Sighted British battleship, bearing 323°T, 10,000 yards.

1641 Task Unit 38.4.2, USS IOWA, USS MISSOURI and USS WISCONSIN (with screening destroyers) left the formation to shell Japanese targets.

1826 Secured from flight quarters. Air Department set to condition 14. At 1836 they darkened ship.

1918 Formed cruising disposition 5R, USS YORKTOWN guide.

1947 Gunnery Department secured from condition One Easy. Set condition 3.

Throughout the night they steamed various courses while remaining in the same general area.

AD Tokyo. 100 miles off. We have been bombing and shelling Tokyo all morning. Just before noon weather closed in so we secured. We did get some pictures and there is a *battleship in drydock there. Tomorrow we are going in after it. No attacks on group. AD   (* The battleship NAGATO)

Wednesday 18 July 1945   *Japan, Tokyo Bay - Battleship NATAGO - We lose an aircrew*

Steaming in an area southeast of Tokyo. Air Department is in condition 14. Engineering Department in condition 31, all other departments in condition 3.

0307 Sounded flight quarters.

0350 8 Hellcats scheduled for CAP were ordered held in condition 11. Flight operations were delayed pending improvement of weather conditions. Weather delayed planned strikes on battleship NAGATO.

0828 Observed a mine exploded by destroyer gunfire 2,000 yards off the starboard bow.

0900 BatDiv 7 rejoined the formation with their destroyer screen.

0912 USS MISSOURI designated guide.

1125 Completed launching 8 F6Fs for CAP.

1131 Gunnery Department set to condition One Easy.

1341 Completed launching 6 F6Fs and 9 TBMs. 2 Hellcats were assigned for SubCAP. The remaining 4 Hellcats escorted the 9 TBM Avengers (armed with 1000# G.P. bombs) to join groups from other carriers to attack battleship NAGATO anchored at Yokosuka Naval Base. ** *"Our planes are believed to have scored six direct hits and 3 near misses."* (** from USS INDEPENDENCE War Diary)

An Avenger flown by Lt.(jg) Harry Roland Patterson was last seen diving on the target, Battleship NAGATO, and the entire crew is missing in action. He was believed to have crashed into the waters of Tokyo Bay.

Runs were made over 2 airfields however no planes were found.

1440 Completed launching 4 F6Fs for a SubCAP.

1517 Completed recovering 8 F6Fs launched at 1125.

1723-1726 USS MCNAIR was alongside the starboard quarter to receive a transmitter.

1750 Recovered 6 F6Fs and 8 TBMs launched at 1341. A TBM-3 (Bu.No.68707) flown by Lt.(jg) Harry Roland Patterson, with his crewmen ARM2c Lawrence Enoch Gardner and AOM3c Carmine Francis Marchese, failed to return from their combat mission over enemy territory.

1826 Recovered 4 F6Fs launched at 1440 for CAP.
1904 Secured from flight quarters. Air Department set to condition 14.
1917 Formed cruising disposition 5R.
1933 Gunnery Department secured from condition One Easy. Set condition 3.
2236 Commenced zigzagging on base course 120°T. They would steam on a long 500 mile run toward the next fueling rendezvous.

Torpedo Squadron 27 History describes the day: *"In line with hit-and-run tactics which characterized the operation from the beginning, the rampaging Task Force then swung to the south to sling its entire airborne strength at the battleship NAGATO, moored at Yokosuka Naval Base in Tokyo Bay. The preparatory briefings disclosed that in this case the degree of opposition would be of no question; the anti-aircraft defenses in the vicinity of Yokosuka presented the most intense concentration of flack to be encountered by carrier-based aircraft in the pacific war."*

Imperial Japanese Navy Battleship NAGATO

**Attacks by aircraft from numerous air groups on the 18th inflicted heavy damage
and killed the NAGATO's captain Rear Admiral Miki Otsuka.**

GN Gave it a good wallop today. So much smoke over the target and debris flying around that the pilots had a job picking out what they were to hit. One target was a battle wagon or 1/4 of the remaining Jap fleet and I think that was completely demolished. Lost a TBM in this operation and last seen it was diving on the target. Had two bogies on the screen during the day but nothing materialized. Joined up with the wagons again. They had left yesterday to shell the coast. GN

(Despite the attacks, NAGATO would remain afloat and see duty at Bikini Atoll as a target vessel in "Operation Crossroads" in 1946)

DL Our first job is striking Yokosuka naval base and airfields in the Tokyo area. Everything goes well, except — Suddenly the order comes down. We are to break up our living arrangements. The kamikazes have killed and wounded too many specialist sailors on every flattop they've hit. Mechanics, metals-smiths, radar repairmen, ordnancemen, catapult experts, plane pushers, tractor drivers, fuelers--no air-dale is to bunk within fifty feet anywhere on the ship with another man of the same classification. DL

GL Strike Tokyo area, our target BB Nagato. She is tied up to a pier in Yokohama Bay and camouflaged. Weather still cold and rainy. Limeys are also operating with us now. Our planes carried 1,000 pound bombs. 9VT – 4 VF. Also in bay is a cruiser and destroyer. Strikes called off because of weather. BB's went in to shell beach. GL

AD Tokyo. 120 miles off. Weather is bad this morning but this afternoon planes and battlewagons went in. It is believed that 144 1,000 lb bombs were dropped on battlewagon. Due to so much smoke they could not tell exactly how much damage was done. The going was tough for the planes due to intense AA fire. One of the TBM's from our ship failed to return. No attacks on task group. AD

Thursday 19 July 1945   *Japan, Retiring to Refuel*

Steaming as before retiring to refuel. Air Department is in condition 14. During the day they moved east trying to avoid a typhoon reportedly moving north, and are roughly two days from a fueling rendezvous.
0356-0401 Launched 8 F6Fs.
0535 Heavy ships of TG 38.4 (except INDEPENDENCE) began topping off destroyers.
0645 Sounded flight quarters.
0817 Recovered 8 F6Fs launched at 0401.
0854 Secured from flight quarters. Air Department set to condition 14.
1149 Commenced zigzagging on base course 130°T.
1205 Observed explosion of mine by gunfire from USS WALKER, bearing 198°T, 4,000 yards.
1310-1324 Half-masted colors following movements of USS SHANGRI LA. (Note: At 1351 SHANGRI LA aircrewman ARM3C A. Bonosconi, fatally wounded by shrapnel over Tokyo, was buried at sea.)
1405 Observed balloon, believed to be of Japanese origin, settle in the water on the port side, distance 4,000 yards. The balloon was shot down by aircraft from the USS SHANGRI LA.
1802 Changed course to 121°T, steaming throughout the night on this course at 22 knots.

GN Retiring to the fueling area today and everyone taking things easy. Few hops for us. Scuttlebutt still making the rounds about us going back but we should get a good idea tomorrow or the following day. Heard that fighters from one of the other ships held field-day on one of those state-side Jap balloons. Really smacked it too. GN

Friday 20 July 1945   *Refueling*

Steaming toward a fueling rendezvous. USS MISSOURI is guide. Air Department is in condition 14.
0100-0255 Discharged ballast. (Note: Sea water used as ballast in fuel voids, is discharged prior to refueling)
0439 Commenced maneuvering to approach tanker USS KENNEBAGO. USS LACKAWANNA designated guide.
0457 Alongside the USS KENNEBAGO to the starboard, fueling course 255°T at 8 knots.
0524-0542 USS WEDDERBURN was alongside the port quarter to receive pilots for transfer to a CVE to pick up replacement aircraft.
0525 USS BOSTON and USS SAINT PAUL joined Task Group 38.4, reporting for duty.
0647 Cast off from USS KENNEBAGO having received 157,644 gallons of fuel oil and 15,000 gallons of aviation gasoline.
0855-0927 USS WATTS was alongside the port quarter to deliver U.S. Mail.
0950-0955 USS MCNAIR was alongside the port quarter to deliver guard mail.
0723-0748 USS MELVIN was alongside the port quarter to deliver 4 personnel* reporting for duty.
 (* Lt. (Jg.) R.H. Wenzel, Ensigns A.W. Peterson & W.F. Philburn and Chief Gunner J.R. Strong reported aboard)
1034 Sounded flight quarters.
1115 Secured from flight quarters. Air Department set to condition 14.
1244-1246 USS REMEY was alongside the port quarter to exchange movies.
1300-1307 USS MCGOWAN was alongside the port quarter to deliver freight.
1314 USS UHLMANN was alongside the port quarter to receive 6 pilots of CLVG-27 for transfer to a CVE to pick up replacement aircraft.

1420 Completed launching 8 F6Fs for CAP over the Task Group.

1435 Secured from flight quarters. Air Department set to condition 13.

1502 Regained station in disposition 5R.

1600-1610 Half-masted colors following movements of the USS COWPENS.

1637 Sounded flight quarters.

1650-1712 USS WEDDERBURN was alongside our port quarter to transfer pilots to this vessel to fly flyable duds to a CVE. In addition, Ensign Daniel R. Berardinelli, AOM3c Michael H. Nagy and ARM3c Harold E. Gibson transferred aboard, reporting for duty with VT-27. Sadly, they would have not many days to live.

1738 Completed launching 7 F6Fs for transfer to a CVE as "surveyed" aircraft (flyable duds).

1755 USS SHANGRI LA was designated guide.

1757 Completed recovery of 8 F6Fs launched at 1420, and, 8 F6Fs and 1 TBM that are replacement aircraft flown over from a CVE.

1834 Gained station in formation disposition 5R. USS MISSOURI designated guide.

1853 Secured from flight quarters. Air Department set to condition 14.

2110 Sighted floating object close aboard to port. Notified OTC. Object turned out to be a 50 cal. ammunition box.

They steamed throughout the night with the replenishing group, course 255°T, speed 8 knots.

GN Refueled today. Had a few CAP hops. GN

Saturday 21 July 1945   *Rearming*

Steaming as before in a fueling area. Today the Task Group continues to refuel, rearm and reprovision.

0310-0404 Manned routine torpedo defense stations.

0336 USS INDEPENDENCE designated guide.

0704 USS LACKAWANNA designated guide.

0722 Commenced maneuvering to take position behind USS YORKTOWN for rearming.

0745 Gained station 1,200 yards astern USS YORKTOWN. Manned rearming stations.

0804 Commenced maneuvering to approach USS SHASTA.

0808 Came alongside port side of USS SHASTA to rearm.

1054 Cast off from USS SHASTA having received 115 500lb. G.P. bombs, 136 260lb. Fragmentation bombs, fuses and 96 cases of belted 50 caliber ammunition.

1122 Gained temporary station in formation off guide, USS LACKAWANNA.

1202 Observed explosion of a mine detonated by a destroyers gunfire.

1324-1340 USS MONSSEN was alongside the port quarter to deliver 4 personnel on board reporting for duty. (BKR1c J.C. Farley, SPA1c E.A. Scaff, QM3c S.H. Ackeret, SC3c L. Shaw)

1517-1521 USS WADLEIGH was alongside the port quarter to deliver officer messenger mail.

1737 USS ESCAMBIA was designated guide. Then at 1741 USS MISSOURI was designated guide.

They steamed throughout the night with the replenishing group, course 255°T, speed 8 knots.

GN Rearmed today but didn't get all we were looking for. Started to work on 413* and 413.5 as they are both quite empty. Quite a job too. GN (*Note: These were Ship's Stores compartments aft on the Platform Deck)

Sunday 22 July 1945   *Steaming with the Replenishment Group*

Steaming as before in a fueling area with the replenishment group. Today the Task Group will continue to refuel, rearm and reprovision.

0415 USS SHANGRI LA designated guide.

0514 Formed cruising disposition 5VB. USS LACKAWANNA designated guide.

0630 Sounded flight quarters.

0640-0648 USS TWINING was alongside the port quarter to deliver U.S. Mail.

0759 Completed launching 6 TBM avengers for ASP.

0815 Secured from flight quarters. Air Department set to condition 13.

1035 USS MISSOURI designated guide.

1200-1211 Recovered 6 TBMs launched at 0759.

1253-1308 Launched 12 F6Fs and 8 TBMs for training exercises.

1316 Recovered 1 TBM launched at 1308.

1327 Secured from flight quarters. Air Department set to condition 13.

1331-1335 USS WADLEIGH was alongside the starboard quarter to deliver guard mail.

1637 Commenced maneuvering to gain station 6 miles from the guide to conduct a limited visibility aircraft recovery drill. All other carriers did so in a similar manner but on different bearings.

During the afternoon the planes made bombing runs with bombs filled with water and strafing runs on target sleds towed by ships.

1748-1819 Recovered 12 F6Fs and 7 TBMs launched at 1308.

1800 Cleared the replenishing group.

1855 Formed disposition 5R. Throughout the night they zigzagged on course 255°T at 16 knots.

GL No provisions but took on some mail and had a movie. GL

Monday 23 July 1945   *Steaming toward Japan*

Steaming as before on a westerly course about 350 miles south of Honshu, headed toward a launching point for tomorrows planned strikes. The ship is darkened. Boilers No. 1, 2 and 3 are in use.

0638-1641 USS MCNAIR was alongside the starboard quarter delivering officer messenger mail.

0645 Sounded flight quarters.

0726-0728 Launched 2 TBMs to tow target sleeves.

0738 USS YORKTOWN designated guide, course 260°T, bearing 039°T, 3,000 yards.

0740 Commenced maneuvering to form disposition 6VC modified in preparation for gunnery exercises. This formation places all ships in a circle to give each ship a greater clear arc in which to fire.

0800 Task Group 38.4 commenced Anti-Aircraft gunnery exercises.

0837 Lighted fires under No.4 boiler.   At 0955 cut No. 4 boiler into the main steam line.

1011 Gunnery Department manned all torpedo defense stations for firing exercises.

1043 TG 38.4 secured from gunnery exercises. Secured from torpedo defense.

1101-1102 Recovered 2 TBMs launched at 0728.

1104 Commenced maneuvering to form disposition 6VB.

1213 USS MISSOURI designated guide. course 303°T.

1311 The Task Group changed speed to 20 knots and commenced the run in to strike Japan.

1553 Commenced zigzagging on base course 303°T.

Captain Kindell noted in the SOL:

"Guess where? July 23, 1945

Tomorrow a big day around Kure.

Tonight about NW by W to a strike point.

No land near and no ships, except our TF.

5R Axis 075T Position 25144

Missouri at 0000 bears 039T - 2500 yards, is guide.

OTC is in YORKTOWN.

Call Me if anything unexpected shows up."

Lt. Cdr. John Cyrille Vermeren

GN Finished on the mag[1] *spaces and restowed bodies*[2] *and motors. No sooner had them away than we got word of a 70 mile an hour wind headed our way. Lashed everything down and waited. Did kick us around a bit but not too bad.* **GN** (*[1] magazine) (*[2] Rocket bodies & motors)

The heavy weather that they lashed down for never appeared. Winds for this day increased to 40 knots with numerous showers. At 1400 the wind shifted to the west, decreasing to 30 knots and the barometer started to rise. By 1700 the wind shifted to the NW, decreasing to 15-20 knots and skies cleared. Cold air poured in from the north.

Tuesday 24 July 1945   *Japan, Honshu & Kure*

Steaming toward a position southeast of Shikoku. The target today is Kure.

0411 Sounded general quarters.

0450 Completed launching 13 F6Fs and 1 TBM. 8 F6Fs were for Cap over the Task Group. 4 F6Fs were for SubCAP over the lifeguard subs. 1 F6F and 1 TBM were tasked with a special weather search.

0511 Secured from general quarters. Gunnery Department set to condition One Easy.

0610 Formed disposition 5VB.

0640-0720 Task Group 38.4 heavies (except INDEPENDENCE) topped off destroyers.

0751 Completed launching 12 F6Fs and 8 TBMs. 8 F6Fs were for CAP over the TG. Four F6Fs were photo planes to proceed with the TBMs for a strike at Kure.

0810 Recovered 1 F6F launched at 0450 and 1 TBM, having "developed trouble", launched at 0751.

0903 Recovered 12 F6Fs launched at 0450.

0926 The CAP over one of the radar picket destroyers shot down an enemy aircraft.

0950 Completed launching 5 F6Fs. 4 were for SubCAP, one as a replacement for the CAP F6F that returned at 0810 after launch. After being relieved from their SubCAP they strafed shore targets in the vicinity of Tanabe.

1002 Recovered 1 F6F (described as a "dud") launched at 0950.

1145 Completed launching 8 F6Fs for CAP.

1219-1239 Recovered 11 F6Fs and 7 TBMS launched at 0751. One F6F-5P*[3] (Bu.No.77562) flown by Lt. Robert O. Zimmerman failed to return, having made a forced water landing off the coast of Shikoku, near the entrance to Bungo Suido after being hit by AA fire on a photo mission over Kure Naval Base. Lt. Zimmerman was initially believed to have been picked up by a lifeguard submarine, name unknown, with no reports as to his safety. His wingman was in radio contact with a nearby rescue submarine. (Lt. Robert O. Zimmerman was not recovered. ComSubPac reported a unidentified fighter pilot drowning under similar circumstances.) (*[3] the F6F-5P was a Hellcat converted for photo reconnaissance with aft mounted camera equipment)

1410 Completed launching 4 F6Fs and 8 TBMs carrying 500# bombs for our second strike of the day. The F6Fs were to serve as escorts and photo planes.

From the Torpedo Squadron 27 History:

"After six days of refueling and replenishing, Task Force Thirty-Eight struck again on 24 July with a concentration of the enemy's waning naval strength at Kure Naval Base as the objective. The squadron's first attack was led by Lieutenant Dooling and was directed against the new light cruiser OYODA moored midstream at the closed end of the deeply indented bay which is formed by the north-south arm of Eta Shima.

Five direct hits were scored on the decks of the ship with 500 pound bombs carried, and the vessel was left burning but afloat. Intense but inaccurate anti-aircraft fire was met and two enemy fighters were sighted, but they did not attack the striking force. In the afternoon Lieutenant Stalnaker's wing swept over the same area, attacking the heavy cruiser TONE and scoring three hits.. Ensign Cole, unable to get into position, for a run on TONE, dropped on OYODA, and reported two hits at add to the damage left by the morning strike. A lugger of approximately 700 gross tons was also attacked by strafing and was seen to explode and sink."

1432-1434 Recovered 3 F6Fs launched at 0950. One F6F-5 (Bu.No.78575) launched at 0950 flown by LT. Burdick V. Scoy Burtch, Jr. made a water landing and was reported rescued by a lifeguard submarine. He was one of the SubCAP pilots that had strafed the Tanabe area. He experienced intense AA fire with the aircraft taking enough damage to have required the water landing.

1517-1522 Launched 11 F6Fs. 7 F6Fs were for CAP and 4 were assigned SubCAP.

1602 Recovered 8 F6Fs launched at 1145.

1633 DesRon 53 left the formation for an assignment by the CTG 38.

1747 Sounded torpedo defense by order of the OTC, due to several unidentified enemy planes reported in the area.

1751 Formed cruising disposition 5VC. Guide is USS MISSOURI, course 300°T, bearing 039°T, 2,500 yards. 1758 Changed course to 125°T.

1801 Sighted large plume of smoke bearing 170°T, 20 miles, believed to be from a Dinah shot down by fighters from the USS RANDOLPH.

1911 Completed recovery of 8 TBMs and 4 F6Fs launched at 1410 and 11 F6Fs launched at 1522.

1936 Formed cruising disposition 5R.

2000 Secured from torpedo defense. condition 3 was set for the Gunnery Department.

2035 Secured from flight quarters. Air Department set to condition 14. Today had several radar reports of unidentified aircraft, which by now was considered unusual, as during the past few strikes, enemy planes had not ventured out in the vicinity. They steamed in the same general area throughout the night.

GN Strike day on Honshu. We are supposed to hit the Kure Naval Base and hope things work out well. All went fairly well. We are supposed to have got some good hits on a cruiser in the Inland Sea. Hit both that spot and the Kure Naval Base. Lost two planes. One over the base and another that was riddled by a cruiser camouflaged to look like a house. Both pilots are supposed to have been picked up by our submarine men. TD was called in the afternoon and a Tojo and another unidentified plane were shot down at 69 miles. GN

RC Hitting Honshu, Kure, Kobe and Maizuru. We lost two fighters, the pilots were picked up by our subs in Tokyo Bay. 3 Jap planes have been shot down in past two days over and around task group. In past operation 2 battlewagons, 2 heavy cruisers, 1 light cruiser, 1 large aircraft carrier, 1 escort carrier have been damaged and many small craft sunk. Nimitz reports 563 ships and small craft sunk or damaged and 635 planes destroyed by Halsey's Third Fleet in past 16 days. RC

AD Strike on Kure Naval Base, Honshu Japan. Planes went in to knock out all surface craft that was anchored there. 38.1 shot down one Jap over Task Group and our destroyer pickets got a couple. Two planes from our ship were shot down. Our pilots were picked up by our subs. AD

(Note: Though hopes were high for the safe return of both pilots, Lt. Robert O. Zimmerman was not recovered.)

Wednesday 25 July 1945 *Japan, Honshu - Kure, Kobe, and Maizuru*

Steaming toward a position southeast of Shikoku. The target today is Kure.

0330 Sounded flight quarters.

0438 Launched 12 F6Fs. 8 F6Fs were for CAP. 4 F6Fs were assigned lifeguard submarine CAP.

0503 Gunnery Department set to condition One Easy.

0505 Formed cruising disposition 5VB. Guide is USS MISSOURI.

0734-0739 USS NORMAN SCOTT was alongside the starboard quarter to pick up photographs for delivery to the OTC.

0738 Launched 10 F6Fs and 9 TBMs. 8 F6Fs were assigned CAP. 2 F6Fs were on a photo mission. The TBMS were on the squadrons first strike of the day. Originally tasked to strike Kure with aircraft from other carriers, weather forced attacks on alternate targets. Finding nothing else suitable, they bombed and strafed shipping and shore installations at Heki. A 100 gross ton Sugar Dog was sunk. The Avengers encountered heavy anti-aircraft fire, but returned safely.

0815 A Myrt (single engine Nakajima C6N reconnaissance plane) was splashed by CAP planes over the destroyer radar picket line.

0844-0850 Recovered 8 F6Fs launched at 0438.

0942-0944 Launched 4 F6Fs for lifeguard submarine CAP (SubCAP).

0952 Launched 1 F6F to replace a dud launched at 0944.

0957 Completed recovery of 5 F6Fs, 4 launched at 0438 and 1 launched at 0944 (returning to make an emergency landing).

1127-1130 Launched 8 F6Fs for CAP.

1141-1142 Recovered 2 F6F photo planes launched at 0738.

1225 Recovered the remaining 8 F6Fs and 9 TBMs launched at 0738.

1240 Maneuvered to avoid a mine 200 yards off the port bow.

1423 Recovered 3 F6Fs launched at 0944 and 1 F6F launched at 0952.

1455 Formed cruising disposition 5VC.

1512 Completed launching 8 F6Fs for CAP over the Task Group.

1549 Formed cruising disposition 5VB.

1600 Recovered 8 F6Fs launched at 1130.

1723 Changed course to 210°T to enable a PBM to land in the wake of the USS MISSOURI.

1725 The PBM landed in the middle of the formation, bearing 030°T, 3,000 yards from CVL-22. The seaplane was rescuing downed aircrew, and running low in fuel. It was not practical to refuel it from any ship present so the decision was made to scuttle it. The crew boarded the USS MISSOURI.

1748 Formed cruising disposition 5VC.

1750 The PBM (twin engine Martin "Mariner" patrol bomber flying boat) was scuttled 6 miles from this vessel.

1855 Sounded torpedo defense due to large groups of aircraft reported closing from the north.

1859-1903 Recovered 8 F6Fs launched at 1512.

1923 Two Graces were shot down by planes from the USS BON HOMME RICHARD 39 miles out. British carrier Task Group 37.1 aircraft shot down at least 1 Grace, possibly more. The Graces were carrying torpedoes. (20 years from this date in 1965 the author will be aboard the BHR steaming to the South China Sea)

1927 Sounded general quarters (the 1855 torpedo defense was upgraded to GQ).

1933 Formed cruising disposition 5V.

2010 Secured from general quarters. Gunnery Department set to condition One Easy. Air Department set to condition 14.

2038 Gunnery & C&R Departments set to condition 3.

2046 Formed cruising disposition 5R.

AD Retiring from area to meet tankers. At sundown we were called to GQ. Some Jap planes came out to attack us. All I could see was some gun firing on the horizon. None of our ships were hit but some Jap planes were shot down. AD

GN Couple of good strikes set for the Nips today. Got the first one off with no trouble but the second was cancelled on account of bad weather over the target. Just at sunset GQ was called first we've had in some time. Was on the flight deck at the time watching a picket or some other ship firing at God knows what. Heard at the time that the Limey's were catching hell but they splashed those planes. Night chickens from the Bon Homme Richard splashed two more at 29 miles. One was a Grace a new type torpedo plane and didn't know what the other was. Had us going for a while. GN

HC Hit home islands again. Picket line under attack, could see it on the horizon. P.B.M. landed in task group with survivors but damaged plane during landing. Tin can sank it, could see it all from the flight deck. HC

Thursday 26 July 1945   *Japan, Refueling and Rearming*

Steaming toward a fueling rendezvous with Task Unit 38.4.1, USS YORKTOWN is OTC (in company USS SHANGRI LA, USS COWPENS, and USS BON HOMME RICHARD) in cruising disposition 5R. Guide is USS MISSOURI. Air Department is in condition 14. Engineering department is in condition 31. All other departments are in condition 3.

0807 USS WASP reported for duty with Task Unit 38.4.1. (WASP had returned from bomb damage repairs in the Puget Sound Navy Yard at Bremerton Washington via Pearl Harbor, a strike at Wake, then on to Eniwetok.)

0808 Sighted tanker group 10 degrees off the starboard bow, bearing 120°T, 12 miles.

0842 Task Group 38.4 began fueling exercises. Commenced maneuvering to take position astern tanker USS CHICOPEE, acting as guide on fueling course 090°T.

0902 Commenced approach on USS CHICOPEE to begin fueling operations.

1055-1114 USS MERTZ was alongside to receive 2 pilots for delivery to a CVE to fly back onboard replacement aircraft.

1130 Cast off from USS CHICOPEE having received fuel oil, aviation gasoline, lube oil and breathing oxygen.

1132 Commenced approach on USS VESUVIUS in position 2,500 yards astern USS CHICOPEE .

1202 Commenced receiving ammunition from USS VESUVIUS.

1257-1304 USS MCNAIR was alongside port quarter to transfer CAG 27 (Lt. Cdr. Frederic Bardshar) and the Air Intelligence Officer to the USS YORKTOWN for a conference.

1523 Cast off from USS VESUVIUS having received 110 - 500lb. GP bombs (8 of which were damaged and jettisoned), 20 - 1,000lb. GP bombs, fuses, rocket motors, rocket bodies, and 105 cases of 50 cal ammunition.

1528 Sounded flight quarters.

1550 Regained normal station in formation with guide, USS CHICOPEE.

1600-1613 USS NORMAN SCOTT was alongside delivering freight and officer messenger mail.

1617 Completed recovery of 2 replacement F6Fs flown over from a CVE.

1652 Secured from flight quarters. Air Department set to condition 14.

1802 USS MISSOURI is designated guide. At 1837 Task Group 38.4 completed fueling exercises.

1925-1943 USS UHLMANN was alongside port quarter to transfer a passenger onboard this ship. They steamed with the replenishment group overnight on course 090°T, speed 10 knots.

GN Refueled and rearmed today. Brought a lot of stuff aboard but current rumor still has us on the way back early next month so most everyone is in good spirits. Heard last evening that they cancelled an order for flight deck lumber and that is all I've heard so far the best indication of an early return for us.
GN

Friday 27 July 1945 *Japan, Refueling and Rearming - Potsdam*

Steaming as before in company with the replenishment group. Task Unit 38.4.1 now consist of carriers INDEPENDENCE, YORKTOWN, COWPENS, SHANGRI LA, BON HOMME RICHARD and USS WASP. The Task Unit is beginning to take on the appearance of an entire Fleet. Guide is USS MISSOURI, 2,500 yards from this vessel. Ship is darkened and the Air Group is in condition 14.

0441 USS CHICOPEE was designated guide.

0640-0647 USS TWINING was alongside the port quarter to receive US Mail.

0723-0726 USS MERTZ was alongside the port quarter to deliver light freight.

0744 USS MISSOURI was designated guide.

0815 USS VESUVIUS was designated guide.

0828 Commenced maneuvering to gain station in a firing formation.

0900 Gunnery Department manned torpedo defense stations for firing exercises.

0914 TG 38.4 commenced firing exercises.

0947-1015 USS WATTS was alongside the port quarter to deliver the CAG-27 and the Air Intelligence

Officer back onboard from the conference aboard USS YORKTOWN.

1027 TG 38.4 ceased gunnery exercises. Secured from torpedo defense.

1037 USS SHANGRI LA designated guide. Formation changed disposition to 6R, placing the 6 carriers equally spaced on the 3 circle, and battleships & cruisers on the 5 circle. Course 090°T, 8 knots.

1105 USS MISSOURI designated guide.

1145 TU 38.4.1 cleared the fueling group.

1337-1334 USS WADLEIGH was alongside port quarter to deliver freight.

1402 Sounded flight quarters.

1505 Completed launching 8 F6Fs for CAP.

1513 Secured from flight quarters.

1640–1650 USS MERTZ was alongside the port quarter to transfer officer messenger mail.

1836 Completed recovery of the 8 F6Fs launched at 1505.

Throughout the night they steamed on course 315°T at 19 knots.

DL Friday 27 July 1945   Potsdam Declaration calling for unconditional surrender of Japan is issued. The Japanese ignore the ultimatum, prompting President Truman to approve dropping atomic weapons on Japan. DL

President Chiang Kai-shek, President Franklin D. Roosevelt, and Prime Minister Winston Churchill at the Cairo Conference in November 1943. They drafted the "Cairo Statement" or Declaration that would later be reaffirmed as the "Potsdam Declaration".

The Potsdam Declaration was issued by President Harry S. Truman, Prime Minister Winston Churchill and President Chiang Kai-shek on 26 July 1945. The following day, Churchill would leave office, being replaced by Clement Attlee.

Proclamation Defining Terms for Japanese Surrender   Issued, at Potsdam, July 26, 1945

(1) We - the President of the United States, the President of the National Government of the Republic of China, and the Prime Minister of Great Britain, representing the hundreds of millions of our countrymen, have conferred and agree that Japan shall be given an opportunity to end this war.

(2) The prodigious land, sea and air forces of the United States, the British Empire and of China, many times reinforced by their armies and air fleets from the west, are poised to strike the final blows upon Japan. This military power is sustained and inspired by the determination of all the Allied Nations to prosecute the war against Japan until she ceases to resist.

(3) The result of the futile and senseless German resistance to the might of the aroused free peoples of the world stands forth in awful clarity as an example to the people of Japan. The might that now converges on Japan is immeasurably greater than that which, when applied to the resisting Nazis, necessarily laid waste to the lands, the industry and the method of life of the whole German people. The full application of our military power, backed by our resolve, WILL mean the inevitable and complete destruction of the Japanese armed forces and just as inevitably the utter destruction of the Japanese homeland.

(4) The time has come for Japan to decide whether she will continue to be controlled by those self-willed militaristic advisers whose unintelligent calculations have brought the Empire of Japan to the threshold of annihilation, or whether she will follow the path of reason.

(5) Following are our terms. We will not deviate from them. There are no alternatives. We shall brook no delay.

(6) There must be eliminated for all time the authority and influence of those who have deceived and misled the people of Japan into embarking on world conquest, for we insist that a new order of peace, security and justice will be impossible until irresponsible militarism is driven from the world.

(7) Until such a new order is established AND until there is convincing proof that Japan's war-making power is destroyed, points in Japanese territory to be designated by the Allies shall be occupied to secure the achievement of the basic objectives we are here setting forth.

(8) The terms of the Cairo Declaration shall be carried out and Japanese sovereignty shall be limited to the islands of Honshu, Hokkaido, Kyushu, Shikoku, and such minor islands as we determine.

(9) The Japanese military forces, after being completely disarmed, shall be permitted to return to their homes with the opportunity to lead peaceful and productive lives.

(10) We do not intend that the Japanese shall be enslaved as a race or destroyed as a nation, but stern justice shall be meted out to all war criminals, including those who have visited cruelties upon our prisoners. The Japanese Government shall remove all obstacles to the revival and strengthening of democratic tendencies among the Japanese people. Freedom of speech, of religion and of thought, as well as respect for the fundamental human rights, shall be established.

(11) Japan shall be permitted to maintain such industries as will sustain her economy and permit the exaction of just reparations in kind, but not those which would enable her to rearm for war. To this end, access to, as distinguished from control of, raw materials shall be permitted. Eventual Japanese participation in world trade relations shall be permitted.

(12) The occupying forces of the Allies shall be withdrawn from Japan as soon as these objectives have been accomplished and there has been established, in accordance with the freely expressed will of the Japanese people, a peacefully inclined and responsible Government.

(13) We call upon the Government of Japan to proclaim now the unconditional surrender of all Japanese armed forces, and to provide proper and adequate assurances of their good faith in such action. The alternative for Japan is prompt and utter destruction.

30
Kure - OYODO Succumbs

Saturday 28 July 1945   *Japan,   Kure*

Steaming as before toward a position southeast of Shikoku. Today the schedule calls for the launching of strikes against shipping at Kure. Air Department is in condition 14.

0345 Sounded flight quarters.

0447-0452 Launched 8 F6Fs for DCAP and 4 F6Fs assigned to SubCAP.

0505 Commenced maneuvering to assume disposition 6VB.

0752 Completed launching 8 F6Fs for DCAP, 4 F6Fs for a photo mission over the target, and 9 TBM avengers for a strike on shipping at Kure. The TBMs attacked the light cruiser OYODO (see below).

0850 Completed recovery of 12 F6Fs launched at 0452.

0947 Completed launching 4 F6Fs for SubCAP.

1140 Completed launching 8 F6Fs for CAP.

1156 Recovered 1 TBM launched at 0752.

1149 Maneuvered to avoid an oil drum in the water, dead ahead 200 yards.

1222-1242 Recovered 12 F6Fs land 8 TBMs launched at 0752.

1358-1409 Completed launching 4 F6Fs and 9 TBMs for a second strike. The TBMs were loaded with 500# bombs and the F6Fs accompanied them on a photo mission.

From the Torpedo Squadron 27 History:

"On the morning of the 28 July, the weather broke and strikes against Kure were resumed. The morning strike on this date, led by Lieutenant Dooling, again hit luckless OYODA* - and this time it was for keeps. Four bombs from the squadron's Avengers crashed into the cruiser's decks, two amidships aft of the bridge, one aft of the stack in the hangar structure, and one astern on the fantail. As the strike retired, the ship was seen to be burning furiously along her entire superstructure aft of the bridge. When the afternoon strike came in to deliver the coup de grace, they found the ship, which had carried the flag of command in the battle of the Philippine Sea, capsized and lying on its side in the mud of Kure Harbor. Since no other strike groups are known to have attacked the ship following the morning's action, it is assumed that the damage inflicted was the finishing blow and the squadron feels justified in placing the destruction of the OYODA on top of the list of accomplishments for this cruise.

As mentioned above, the strike of the afternoon of 28 July was also directed against Kure. Originally assigned to attack the OYODA, and finding such effort unnecessary, the squadron dropped on the battleship HARUNA, scoring three hits and inflicting undetermined damage.

Finding himself in a propitious position for an attack on the TONE, Lieutenant Street made his drop on this ship and reported one hit with explosion on the water line aft of the bridge."

(* Note: OYODO is the correct spelling.)

1416-1421 Completed recovery of 4 F6Fs launched at 0947.

1516-1520 Completed launching 8 F6Fs for CAP.

1544-1620 Completed recovery of 8 F6Fs launched at 1140. Recovered 1 TBM launched at 1409.

1820 Completed recovery of 8 TBMs and 4 F6Fs launched at 1409.

1857 Completed recovery of 8 F6Fs launched at 1520. At 1905 they darkened ship.

1919 Secured from flight quarters. Air Department set to condition 14.

1927 Commenced maneuvering to assume disposition 6R, guide USS MISSOURI.

They retired, steaming on a southeasterly course throughout the night.

HC Hit Kure shipping. Today was the ship's 100th strike day. HC

DL *Today we struck the Inland Sea area between Nagoya and northern Kyushu and the Kure Naval Base. The weather was raw. We were wet going on watch and wetter coming off. I had a sloppy pair of bondockers that badly needed drying out, but nothing to replace them. Everybody was in the same soggy boat; they were a drag on our morale.*
But it was obvious that "things" were going on. The rumor wires were buzzing. Radiomen were (I think) sworn to secrecy. At chow the ideas we expressed concentrated on one major theme: War in Europe had been over more than two months. They could send enough men over here and get this blithering nonsense over with. No more sailors to die waiting for soldiers to come and finish the job; the soldiers knew what was needed and they'd brush the Japs away without trouble...or so we dreamed. We resumed work loading guns and hanging bombs and watching more flights go off, wondering again how many would be back and whether we'd have a habitable deck for them to come home to. *DL*

GN *Making another hit at Kure today. Want to finish up what the weatherman stopped us from doing a few days ago. Think we head north again after this strike. This is our 100th strike day against the enemy and in that time I think we have done our share of damage. Our squadron finally obliterated their target at Kure. They had a few ships to take out and one was a heavy cruiser*. Today they turned it over so it won't be much good to the Nips from here on out.* *GN* (* It was the IJN light cruiser OYODO noted below)

RC *Hitting Kure. Wasp joins our group of carriers making 4 heavy and 2 light carriers in group. Independence makes 100th strike today.* *RC*

Below: IJN light cruiser **OYODO** lying on her side in the mud at Kure. The four 500# bomb hits left her in a starboard list, taking on water and capsizing two hours later. Roughly 300 crewmen were killed.

Above - IJN's HURUNA under attack on 28 July 1945 at her mooring at Kure (photographed by an INTREPID aircraft).
Below - HURUNA's new mooring at rest on the silt bottom.   Photos (cropped) from the Naval History and Heritage Command

Sunday 29 July 1945   *Japan, Positioning to Strike*

They began traveling generally northeasterly to position themselves within a nights run of a launching point for strikes on Tokyo. The ship is darkened. Air Department is in condition 14.

0739-0743 USS NORMAN SCOTT was alongside port quarter to receive photographs to deliver to USS YORKTOWN.

0912 USS YORKTOWN designated guide.

0940 USS QUINCY, USS CHICAGO, USS SAINT PAUL and USS BOSTON with screening destroyers left the formation to proceed as assigned.

0950 USS MISSOURI was designated guide.

0953 CTG 38.4 resumed tactical command of TG 38.4.

1138-1143 Launched 8 F6Fs for CAP.

1327 Observed, heard and felt explosion of a mine caused by destroyer gunfire 2,000 yards to astern ten degrees to starboard.

1415 Sounded flight quarters.

1503 Completed launching 8 F6Fs for CAP over the Task Group.

1535 Completed recovery of 8 F6Fs launched at 1143.

1603 Secured from flight quarters. Air Department set to condition 13.

1745 Sounded flight quarters.

1838 Darkened ship.

1843 Completed recovery of 8 F6Fs launched at 1503.

1928 Secured from flight quarters. Air Department set to condition 14.

2357 Commenced zigzagging on base course 110°T.

The USS BON HOMME RICHARD sent in night hecklers over the target, requiring frequent turns into the wind.

Captain Kindell noted in the SOL:

"There is an island chain about eighty miles east of us - Aoga - Hachijo and that group. We are proceeding northward parallel to that chain. We will be very close to Japan in the morning"

Note: The islands of Aogashima and Hachijo are in a chain of volcanic islands (Izu Islands) extending in a north-south line pointing toward Sagami Bay (near Tokyo Bay).

GN Gave the Japs a rest today. We pulled out with the thought that they would come out after us as they knew where we were but it never did materialize. All quiet on the far western front. GN

0356 Steaming as before in an area south of Honshu. Sounded routine general quarters.

0435-0542 Launched 8 F6Fs. 4 were for CAP over the Task Force and 4 assigned SubCAP.

0500 Secured from general quarters. Gunnery Department set to condition One Easy. Air Department set to condition 11.

0510 Formed cruising disposition 6VB, USS MISSOURI guide.

0608 USS QUINCY, USS CHICAGO, USS SAINT PAUL and USS BOSTON with screening destroyers rejoined the formation.

0803 Completed launching 4 F6Fs for SubCAP.

0851 Completed launching 8 F6Fs and 8 TBMs to join other air groups for a strike on enemy shipping at Maizuru and airfields in the vicinity. 8 F6Fs attacked Mineyama airfield destroying 3 planes on the ground and heavily damaging buildings. They strafed 3 destroyer escorts and a small merchant ship outside Maizuru harbor. TBMs attacked shipping in the harbor seriously damaging a large transport and scoring hits on a patrol frigate and a medium freighter.

0930 Completed launching 4 F6Fs for SubCAP.

1015 Jettisoned 1 F6F5 (Bu.No. 78359) over the port quarter.

1140 USS YORKTOWN designated guide.

1200 Completed launching 4 F6Fs for CAP.

1257 Completed recovery of 12 F6Fs and 7 TBMs. 4 F6Fs launched at 0803, 8 F6Fs and 7 TBMs launched at 0851. One TBM-3E failed to return from a mission. The Avenger (Bu.No. 69326), flown by Ensign Daniel Ralph Berardinelli, with his aircrew, AOM3c Michael Harold Nagy and ARM3c Harold Eugene Gibson was seen to have been shot down by anti-aircraft fire and crashed into Maizuru Harbor during an attack on shipping. No survivors were seen. The three had just transferred onboard only ten days ago.

1406 Completed launching 12 F6Fs for a strike on Tokyo. 4 Hellcats were on a photo mission. The strike was directed against Utsunomiya Airfield, hitting aircraft in revetments, hangars, additionally nearby trains and a railroad terminal.

1437 USS MISSOURI designated guide 2,000 yards ahead of this vessel.

1534 Completed launching 4 F6Fs for CAP. One of the Hellcat pilots spotted a Nick at high altitude. The lucky Nick pilot escaped when his pursuers guns jammed.

1537 Completed recovering 4 F6Fs launched at 0930.

1619 Completed recovering 2 F6Fs (strike) launched at 1406 and 4 F6Fs (CAP) launched at 1200.

1825 Completed recovering the remaining 10 F6Fs launched at 1406 and 4 F6Fs launched at 1534.

1843 Darkened ship.

1847 Gunnery Department manned all torpedo defense stations.

1912 Secured from flight quarters. Air Department set to condition 14.

1935 Secured from torpedo defense.

1936 Commenced maneuvering to form disposition 6R.

2255 Lost power to forward gyro due to burnt out rectifier tube.

2257 Forward gyro operation restored.

USS BON HOMME RICHARD sent in night hecklers during the night, as the group steamed on southerly headings toward a fueling area.

GN Back in at them again. Honshu is our target once more and we had a couple of fair sized loads going over. Did quite a bit of damage and one of our TBM's failed to return. Observers said that it went up in a puff of smoke and there were no pieces. Very possible for he had not dropped his bombs up to the time of being hit. GN

HC Raided Honshu today and went in to 60 miles from the coast. Had hopes of seeing Fuji but it was cloudy. HC

Tuesday 31 July 1945   *Japan,   Refueling & Replenishing*

Steaming as before toward the south for a fueling rendezvous. USS YORKTOWN is guide.
0702 Sounded flight quarters.
0755 Completed launching 4 F6Fs for CAP.
0818 Jettisoned 1 TBM-3E (Bu.No. 69110) damaged operationally beyond repair.
0925-0930 USS WATTS was alongside starboard quarter to receive photographs.
1127 Completed launching 4 F6Fs for CAP.
1209 Completed recovery of 4 F6Fs launched at 0755.
1232 Secured from flight quarters. Air Department set to condition 13.
1321 Sounded flight quarters.
1331 Sighted replenishment group bearing 180°T, 18 miles.
1419 Completed recovery of 4 F6Fs launched at 1117.
1425 The Task Group commenced refueling. Commenced maneuvering to approach USS ALCYONE.
1445 Secured from flight quarters. Air Department set to condition 14.
1450-1454 Came along port side of AKA USS ALCYONE and commenced receiving provisions.
1555 USS NANTAHALA designated guide.
1710 Cast off from USS ALCYONE having received 6 tons of fresh and dry provisions.
1716 Commenced maneuvering to approach tanker USS ESCALANTE.
1825 Cast off and cleared USS ESCALANTE having received only part of our fuel oil and gasoline,
due to approaching darkness. Commenced maneuvering to gain station in disposition 6R.
1837 USS MISSOURI designated guide, course 295°T, bears 240°T, 3,000 yards, speed 10 knots.
They stayed with the replenishment group during the night to continue replenishment at dawn tomorrow.

GN Pulled out today to reprovision and rearm. Did take a lot of stores aboard but only got the gas and oil lines aboard when it got dark so it was put off till morning. GN

0925-0930 USS WATTS was alongside starboard quarter to receive photographs.

Wednesday 1 August 1945   *Japan,   Refueling & Replenishing - Man Overboard*

Steaming as before in company of the replenishment group so all units can refuel, rearm and reprovision, in Task Unit 38.4.1 (Rear Admiral A.W. Radford, Commander Carrier Division Six, USS YORKTOWN, Flagship). TU 38.4.1 is part of Task Group 38.4 (Rear Admiral A.W. Radford), a part of Task Force Thirty-Eight (Vice Admiral J.S. McCain, Commander Second Carrier Task Force, Pacific, USS SHANGRI LA, Flagship) in the Third Fleet (Admiral W.F. Halsey, Commander Third Fleet, USS MISSOURI, Flagship).

Ship is darkened. Air Department is in condition 14.

0413 Gunnery Department manned all torpedo defense stations for one hour until sunrise.

0443 USS NANTAHALA designated guide.

0457 Manned all fueling stations.

0458 Secured from torpedo defense. Commenced maneuvering to make approach on tanker USS CHIPOLA.

0521 Came alongside USS CHIPOLA to begin pumping fuel oil and aviation gasoline.

0602 Secured from flight quarters. Air Department set to condition 14.

0610-0640 USS SMALLEY was alongside the port quarter to receive four pilots who will return with replacement aircraft.

0700 USS CHIPOLA cast off, having completed the refueling. Commenced maneuvering to make approach on USS VESUVIUS.

0707 Manned all rearming stations.

0724 Came alongside USS VESUVIUS.

0845 Completed launching 2 F6Fs. 1 was a flyable dud for transport to the USS THETIS BAY. The other Hellcat was flown by CAG-27 (Comdr. Fredrick A. Bardshar) to land aboard the USS YORKTOWN for a conference.

0947 Cast off from USS VESUVIUS, having received bombs, rocket parts, detonators and fuses. Commenced maneuvering to regain station in the fueling disposition.

0950 Sounded flight quarters.

1020-1055 USS MC DERMUT was alongside the port quarter to transfer U.S. Mail and receive freight consisting of batteries.

1104 Completed recovery 2 F6F-5 and 2 TBM-3E replacements from USS THETIS BAY.

1105 Commenced maneuvering to gain position 800 yards astern USS CHICAGO in the USS WISCONSIN firing group for gunnery exercises.

1150 Gunnery Department manned all torpedo defense stations for AA firing exercises against a drone.

1201 USS VESUVIUS designated guide.

1218 Task Group completed gunnery exercises. Secured from torpedo defense. Commenced maneuvering to regain station in disposition 6R.

1250-1256 USS MC DERMUT was alongside the port quarter to deliver a bag of mail.

1530 USS SMALLEY was alongside the starboard quarter to transfer passengers to this vessel.

1549 First passenger in the boatswain's chair fell in water due to sudden slack in the whip.

1550 USS SMALLEY cast off to rescue man overboard.

1558 The passenger that had fallen overboard was recovered by USS SMALLEY "in good condition". Further transfer of passengers was suspended, no passengers having been received aboard the INDEPENDENCE. (Which begs the question:

   Is "in good condition" defined by the Navy as - slightly wet and less than drowned?)

1600 USS MISSOURI assumed guide.

1601 Secured from flight quarters. Air Department set to condition 14.

1616 Recovered 1 F6F launched at 0845 (for the YORKYOWN conference).

At 1633 they cleared the replenishment group and began steaming southeast, zigzagging at 16 knots.

Captain Kindell noted in the SOL:

At Sea 1Aug 1945

"We are going S.E. around the typhoon which is west of us. The strike schedule is out and its future is tied up with the typhoon.
The formation's the same as last night. The weather should not get worse as we go but should improve.
Follow signals of the OTC in Yorktown.
We expect to see nothing and nobody.
Call me if anything unusual happens or if the weather gets bad."

Thursday 2 August 1945

Steaming as before in cruising disposition 6R, USS MISSOURI guide.
0658-0738 USS STODDARD was alongside port quarter to transfer freight.
0858 USS IOWA designated guide.
0859 Commenced maneuvering to form disposition 6G.
0918 Gained station in special firing formation 6G, USS IOWA on course 300°T, bearing 327°T, distance 1,900 yards. CTU 38.4.2 in tactical command of TG 38.4 for gunnery exercises.
1029 Gunnery Department manned all torpedo defense stations for firing exercises against towed sleeves.
1114 Task Group 38.4 ceased gunnery exercises. CTG 38.4 assumed tactical command. Secured from torpedo defense.
1116 Commenced maneuvering to reform disposition 6R.
1213-1222 USS MC DERMUT was alongside port quarter to receive a passenger for transfer to the USS WISCONSIN.
1235 USS MISSOURI assumed guide.
1327-1350 USS SMALLEY was alongside the port quarter to transfer passengers to this vessel for duty with Torpedo Squadron VT-27, along with the pilot that flew the dud to USS THETIS BAY yesterday.
1650 ComBat Div 7 in the USS IOWA assumed tactical command of the Task Group for recovery of float planes.
1806 Rear Admiral Radford in USS YORKTOWN assumed tactical command of the Task Group.
2031 Commenced zigzagging on base course 270°T and continued on a westerly course thru the night.

GN Still rolling and pitching quite a bit and no strikes scheduled for today. Had target practice for the gunnery dept. GN

Friday 3 August 1945   *Refueling & Gunnery Exercises*

Steaming as before in cruising disposition 6R, USS MISSOURI guide. The ship is darkened. 0233 Changed course to 340°T.
0400 Tanker group reported bearing 056°T, 14 miles.
0421 Gunnery Department manned all torpedo defense stations.
0501 Task Group commenced fueling exercises.
0521 USS NECHES designated guide.
0643 Commenced maneuvering approach assigned tanker USS CACAPON.
0710 Came along port side of USS CACAPON.
0811 Cast off from USS CACAPON having received 58,390 gallons of fuel oil and 8,000 gallons of aviation gasoline.
0944 USS MISSOURI was designated guide.
0949 Task Group completed fueling exercises and has cleared the refueling group.
1101 USS IOWA designated guide.
1103 Task Group assumed disposition 6G. Rear Admiral O.C. Badger in USS IOWA assumed tactical command of TG 38.4 for gunnery exercises.

1118 Task Group commenced scheduled gunnery exercises.

1130 Sounded flight quarters.

1206 Task Group ceased gunnery exercises.

1208 CTG 38.4 reassumed tactical command.

1242 Completed launching 12 F6Fs and 9 TBMs.

1315 Recovered 1 TBM launched at 1241.

1327 Rear Admiral Badger in USS IOWA assumed tactical command of TG 38.4 for gunnery exercises.

1348 Recovered 1 TBM launched at 1241.

1353 Task Group 38.4 commenced scheduled gunnery exercises.

1418 Gunnery Department manned all torpedo defense stations for gunnery exercises.

1517 Task Group 38.4 ceased gunnery exercises. Secured from torpedo defense.

1520 CTG 38.4 reassumed tactical command. Commenced maneuvering to resume station in cruising disposition 6R.

1600 Sounded flight quarters.

1624 USS MISSOURI assumed guide.

1647 Completed recovery of 12 F6Fs and the 7 remaining TBMs launched at 1241.

1910 Commenced zigzagging on base course 330°T.

Captain Kindell in the SOL:

" Tomorrow on the way northward, more training. Next day - strike - weather permitting."

Today, as they refueled and held gunnery exercises, the Air Force flew one of its largest raids against the Japanese homeland with 820 B29 bombers. Major cities and industrial areas were decimated by the continuous destructive raids. Soon there would be difficulty finding large unscathed cities to target.

Saturday 4 August 1945   *Gunnery Exercises*

0409-0520 Steaming as before. Manned routine torpedo defense stations.

0610-0617 USS MELVIN was alongside port quarter to deliver VHF crystals and officer messenger mail.

0841 Launched 1 TBM for towing a target sleeve.

0901 Maneuvered to avoid the USS SHANGRI LA which had a steering casualty.

0906 USS SHANGRI LA regained steering control.

0912 USS WISCONSIN designated guide.

0915 Commenced maneuvering to gain station in disposition 6G. ComBat Div 7 (Rear Admiral O.C. Badger in USS IOWA) assumed tactical command of TG 38.4 for gunnery exercises.

0939-1059 Task Group 38.4 conducted scheduled gunnery exercises.

1102 Rear Admiral A.W. Radford resumed tactical command of TG 38.4.

1114 Commenced maneuvering to gain station in disposition 6R, USS WISCONSIN guide.

1133 Recovered 1 TBM launched at 0841.

1152 USS MISSOURI designated guide.

1309 Completed launching 12 F6Fs and 8 TBMs for simulated attacks on the Task Group.

1312 Recovered 1 TBM launched at 1309.

1318 Commenced maneuvering to gain station in disposition 6G. USS IOWA designated guide. Secured from flight quarters. Air Department set to condition 13.

1348 Recovered 2 F6Fs launched at 1309.

1407 Rear Admiral O.C. Badger in USS IOWA assumed tactical command of TG 38.4 for gunnery exercises. Task Group 38.4 commenced scheduled gunnery exercises.

1449 Gunnery Department manned all torpedo defense stations for gunnery exercises.

1512-1518 USS MC DERMUT was alongside the starboard quarter to deliver guard mail.

1530 Task Group 38.4 ceased gunnery exercises. Mighty-I had expended 1066 rounds of 40mm and 875 rounds of 20mm ammunition firing at towed sleeves.

Rear Admiral A.W. Radford in USS YORKTOWN resumed tactical command of TG 38.4.

1537 Commenced maneuvering to gain station in disposition 6R, guide USS IOWA.

1540 Secured from torpedo defense.

1629 Sounded flight quarters.

1632 USS MISSOURI designated guide.

1659-1716 Completed recovering 10 F6Fs and 7 TBMs launched at 1309.

1800 Secured from flight quarters. Air Department set to condition 14.

1832 Commenced zigzagging on base course 085°T. We would maintain this course thru the night.

1839 Lighted fires under No. 3 boiler.

2016 Cut in No.3 boiler into the main steam line.

2331 Secured No.1 boiler.

Captain Kindell in the SOL:
" We are cruising eastward and will probably will continue that tomorrow. No sightings are expected but after 0300 we will be near an area assigned to one of our submarines - the SEA HORSE."

Sunday 5 August 1945   *Gunnery Exercises and Tactics*

Steaming as before on a southeasterly course roughly 250 miles east of Tokyo.

0755– 0803 Launched 12 F6Fs for CAP and 1 TBM assigned tow plane for a target sleeve.

0814 Secured from flight quarters. Air Department set to condition 13.

0850 USS IOWA designated guide.

0907 Task Group 38.4 formed disposition 6G for gunnery exercises. ComBat Div 7 (Rear Admiral O.C. Badger in USS IOWA) assumed tactical command of TG 38.4 for gunnery exercises.

0912 Task Group 38.4 commenced scheduled gunnery exercises.

0918 Commenced zigzagging on base course 050°T.

0939 One F6F-5 Hellcat (Bu.No.78867) piloted by Lt.(jg) Edwin Free made an emergency water landing near our destroyer screen due to engine failure, bearing 260°T, off the port quarter astern 14,000 yards from this vessel.

1028 Gunnery Department manned all torpedo defense stations for gunnery exercises.

1030 Sounded flight quarters.

1040 USS WREN reported the rescue of Lt.(jg) Edwin Free.

1059 Task Group 38.4 completed scheduled gunnery exercises. INDEPENDENCE expended 961 rounds of 40mm and 395 rounds of 20mm ammunition firing at towed sleeves.

1101 Rear Admiral A.W. Radford in USS YORKTOWN resumed tactical command of TG 38.4.

1103 Commenced maneuvering to gain station in disposition 6R, guide USS IOWA.

1144 Completed launching 8 F6Fs and 8 TBMs for group tactics and simulated attacks.

1146 Recovered 1 TBM launched at 0803.

1215 Completed recovering 7 F6Fs launched at 0803 (minus 1 Hellcat lost in the water landing).

1352-1410 USS WREN was along the starboard side amidships, delivering injured pilot Lt.(jg) Edwin Free back aboard the INDEPENDENCE. Edwin Free was admitted to sickbay with abrasions to his arm, forehead and a possible fractured Thoracic Vertebrae.

1530 Completed recovering 8 F6Fs and 8 TBMs launched at 1144.

1601 Secured from flight quarters. Air Department set to condition 14.

1927 Boiler No.1 placed on main steam line.

1945 Boiler No.2 taken off main steam line.

They zigzagged on base course 050°T, at 17 knots throughout the night.

Captain Kindell wrote in the Standing Orders Log:
" No fueling tomorrow, next day yes.
We are going north tonight, well out in the Pacific, no ships, no islands, no sleep. See Plan of the Day.
Standard OTC and 6 Roger*.   (* Note: This refers to Disposition 6R)
Call me if anything unusual turns up, or if I doze off between now and 0305."

31
"Little Boy" and "Fat Man" Prevail

Monday 6 August 1945   *Gunnery Exercises, and beyond the horizon, "Little Boy"*

Steaming as before about 350 miles east of Tokyo. Task Unit 38.4.1 consist of carriers USS INDEPENDENCE, USS YORKTOWN, USS COWPENS, USS SHANGRI LA, USS BON HOMME RICHARD and USS WASP. The ship is darkened and the Air Department is in condition 14.
0335-0429 Manned routine torpedo defense stations.   0630 Sounded flight quarters.
0747 Completed launching 16 F6Fs for a training flight. The Hellcats bombed, rocketed, and strafed sleds towed by ships.

The time was 0816:08. The crew of the USS INDEPENDENCE had mustered on stations 15 minutes before. They secured from muster and were going about their normal morning work day duties.

Death was preceded by *"a blinding bluish light"* as the World's first use of an Atomic weapon in anger, **"Little Boy"** (a Uranium-235 fission devise with equivalent energy of roughly 15-16 kilotons of TNT) had just detonated approximately 1,900 feet above the city of Hiroshima, leaving roughly 70% of the city's buildings destroyed. The nuclear blast killed an estimated 80,000 people with more yet to die from injuries and the unknown effects of radiation exposure. It would take Tokyo most of the day to begin to grasp what had happened in Hiroshima, the best source perhaps the announcement by President Truman roughly 16 hours after the blast.

The city had been untouched until this date, to be able to study the aftereffects* of the new uranium weapon on a pristine target area.

(* Members of the US government later downplayed and covered up / censured the effects of radiation exposure on the Hiroshima victims. Sucked thru the dark veil into the vast vacuum of secrecy.)

(Suggested reading on the development and use of the nuclear bomb: "Nuclear Dawn" by Dr. James P. Delgado.)

Only 3 weeks had passed since "The Gadget" (a plutonium device) vaporized its tower in New Mexico.

1027-1030 USS WEDDERBURN was along the starboard quarter to receive a logistics report.
1125 Launched 1 TBM assigned tow plane for a target sleeve.
1154 Completed recovery of 16 F6Fs launched at 0747.
1205 Commenced maneuvering to gain station in disposition 6G, guide USS IOWA.
1225 Rear Admiral O.C. Badger in USS IOWA assumed tactical command of TG 38.4 for gunnery exercises.
1228 Task Group 38.4 commenced scheduled gunnery exercises.
1400 Gunnery Department manned all torpedo defense stations for gunnery exercises. During the exercises they expended 1040 rounds of 40mm and 777 rounds of 20mm ammunition firing at towed sleeves.
1427 Gunnery Department secured from torpedo defense, and set condition 3.
1457 Rear Admiral A.W. Radford in USS YORKTOWN resumed tactical command of TG 38.4. Commenced maneuvering to gain station in disposition 6R.
1512 Recovered 1 TBM launched at 1125.
1525 USS MISSOURI designated guide, course 160°T, bearing 240°T (starboard, abeam), distance 3,000 yards, at 16 knots.
1528 Changed course to 340°T. During the night they steamed on a northerly course at 18 knots.

HB Months before we dropped the first atomic bomb we heard scuttlebutt about some secret weapon that we had and were going to use, of course when they did drop the bomb it was something else. We could not believe it. HB

AD Heading for Japan. Today it was announced that we dropped an Atomic bomb on Japan. This may end this war a lot sooner. AD

DL Monday 6 August 1945

A USAAF B-29 bomber named "Enola Gay"[1] *drops atomic bomb on Hiroshima, Honshu. Twenty thousand tons worth of TNT, we hear. Stunning. How could any city absorb such power? Must have wrecked the whole town. Ordnancemen stared at each, impressed by the news and horrified.*

"War's over!" "We beat 'em!" The passageways are filled with exultant shouts. Men are actually dancing. They encroach upon the flightdeck, posing a danger to themselves until Marines are directed to hustle them off.

War went on. Weather went on. Everything we did seemed to be done under a period of waiting for the WORD. It did not come.[2] *DL*

(*[1] The "Enola Gay" today is on display at the Steven F. Udvar-Hazy National Air and Space Museum)

(*[2] Much of communication from Hiroshima was cutoff by the bomb. It would take time for Japanese leaders to fully learn of, and come to terms with, the true scale and nature of the unbelievable destruction. Then there would be the problem of sharp and disastrous military & political divisions.)

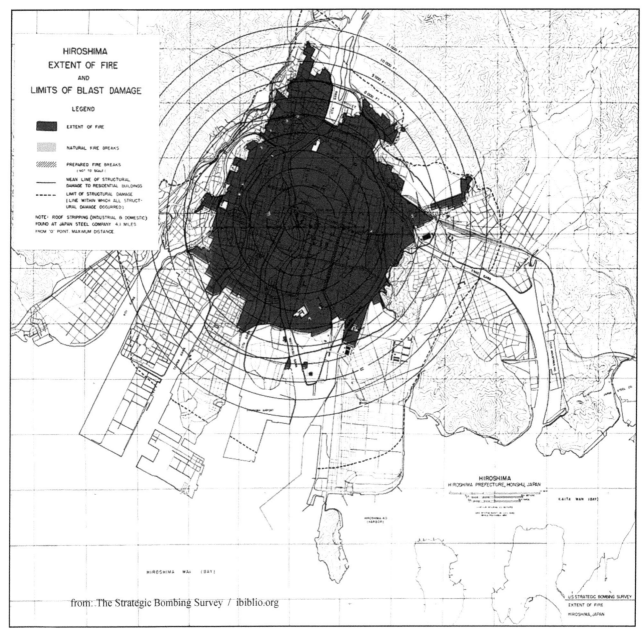

from: The Strategic Bombing Survey / ibiblio.org

The atomic genie was out of the bottle, and President Truman had unleashed General Leslie R. Groves to drop the weapons as fast as he could obtain them.

The mayhem train had left the station, was rushing down the tracks, and its deadly schedule made no allowance for Japanese indecision.

The US Fleet steamed on, committed to bring and end to the Pacific war.

Tuesday 7 August 1945   *Refueling*

0313 Steaming as before. Gunnery Department manned all torpedo defense stations, securing at 0413.
0444 USS NECHES designated guide.
0555-0606 USS BENHAM was alongside port quarter to receive a pilot to pick up a replacement F6F.
0723-0727 USS WADLEIGH was alongside port quarter to transfer guard mail.
0807 ComBat Div 7 assumed tactical command of TG 38.4 for gunnery exercises.
0821 Commenced maneuvering to approach assigned tanker USS TALUGA.
0852 Gained position along port side of USS TALUGA, course 270°T, 8 knots.
1013 Cast off from USS TALUGA having received 163,560 gallons of fuel oil, 24,000 gallons of aviation gasoline, 5 drums of lube oil. INDEPENDENCE transferred to the tanker 1 officer and 3 enlisted men, for transportation to other assignments.
1044 Recovered 1 replacement F6F.
1148-1155 USS BENHAM was alongside port quarter to transfer Lt. Burdick V. Burtch, the VF-27 Hellcat pilot rescued by the lifeguard submarine when he was shot down by AA fire on July 24th.
1201 USS YORKTOWN assumed tactical command of Task Group 38.4.
1329 USS MISSOURI designated guide.
1518 Task Group 38.4 cleared the fueling group.
2104 Lighted fires under No. 2 boiler.
2215 No. 2 boiler cut into the main steam line. Commenced zigzagging on base course 277°T.

3 to 7 August 1945 **GN** *Hung around a few hundred miles off the coast of Japan. Refueled twice in that time and can't understand why no strikes. Rumors have it that they have peace feelers out to us and also that there is a typhoon blowing in close. Typhoon or no I'm surprised at not striking. Made up loads of 3.25 rockets for the boys to practice with and hope they are having fun for it is certainly a pain to us.* **GN**

Wednesday 8 August 1945   *Japan, Honshu - Fog prevails*

0338 Steaming in an area roughly 120 miles east of Honshu. They were scheduled to launch strikes today but weather was so bad, the strikes were canceled. Fog was dense during the morning, clearing in the afternoon, but haze restricted visibility to 5 - 10 miles.
0711 Gunnery Department manned all torpedo defense stations due to reported unidentified aircraft.
0727 Secured from torpedo defense. Gunnery Department set to condition One Easy.
0740 Gunnery Department set to condition 3.
0943 Completed launching 4 F6Fs for CAP.
1102 Maneuvered to avoid a mine ahead.
1342-1350 Recovered 4 F6Fs launched at 0943.
1435 Secured from flight quarters. Air Department set to condition 14.

HC *Supposed to hit Hokkaido today but were fogged out. These damn people don't even have good weather.* **HC**

GN *Had two big strikes planned for today but nothing left the deck. The fog was very thick.* **GN**

This evening, at approximately 2300, the Soviet Union declared war against Japan, invading Manchuria after midnight. Adding to Japan's problems, B-29s destroyed over 70% of the city of Fukuyama.

Steaming as before. Today, they are in the Sendai area off Honshu. The ship is darkened and the Air Department is in condition 14. From 0329-0429 they manned (routine) general quarters stations.

0411 Completed launching 4 F6Fs for CAP over the Task Group.

0440 Commenced maneuvering to gain station in disposition 6VB, USS MISSOURI guide.

0539 Gunnery Department set to condition One Easy.

0541 Completed launching 4 F6Fs for SubCAP.

0756 Completed launching 13 F6Fs and 9 TBMs carrying 260 lb. fragmentation bombs for strikes against Koriyama Airfield, destroying parked aircraft and hangars. Additionally 4 trains were strafed.

0825 Completed recovery of 4 F6Fs launched at 0411 and 1 F6F launched at 0756.

1102 A B-29 bomber called "Bockscar" [1] dropped "Fat Man". The plutonium bomb devastated the secondary target, the city of Nagasaki. Photos page 700.   [1] Also referred to as "Bock's Car".

Weather was obscuring the primary target, which saved the city of Kokura. Over 40,000 initially died, and perhaps 60,000 injured. Many more would die from the aftereffects. Hills surrounding the industrial river valley would limit and concentrate the radius of total destruction to just over 1 mile radius, with fires following extending the damage consuming the area to the north. *"People close to the blast vaporized."*   The total area affected was roughly 43 square miles. with roughly 14,000 homes destroyed, targeting the industrial area saved the heavily populated residential area from the brunt of the damage. Reports[2] described damage to 2 Mitsubishi plants as "spectacular".([2] US DOE Manhattan Project)

1118-1125 Launched 8 F6Fs. 4 Hellcats were assigned CAP and 4 served as SubCAP.

1128-1155 Recovered 4 F6Fs launched at 0541, and 12 F6Fs & 9 TBMs launched at 0756.

1323 Completed launching 12 F6Fs and 9 TBMs for a return strike against Koriyama Airfield. 4 of the F6Fs were on a photo mission.

1440 Completed launching 4 F6Fs for CAP.

1446 Recovered 1 TBM, due to engine trouble, launched at 1323.

1458 Commenced maneuvering to form disposition 6VC due to reports of bogies in the area.

1459 Sounded torpedo defense by order of OTC due to bogies approaching the formation.

1515 Sounded general quarters.

1520 Completed recovery of 8 F6Fs launched at 1123.

1523 Completed recovery of 1 F6F launched at 1323.

1609 Course 050°T. USS CUSHING opened fire on a Grace over the Task Group. The Grace was observed to be fired on by other ships in this group. It burst into flames, and crashed close aboard to the USS WASP, bearing 240°T, 4,000 yards from this vessel. (photo next page)

1616 Observed firing on the horizon 10° off the stern.

1624 Changed course to 230°T. Observed firing on the horizon bearing 180°T.

1645 Secured from general quarters. Gunnery Department set to condition One Easy.

1704-1722 Recovered 12 F6Fs and 7 TBMs launched at 1323.

1823 Gunnery Department manned all torpedo defense stations.

1831 Darkened ship.

1833 Sounded general quarters due to unidentified aircraft observed by radar operators.

1845 Completed recovery of 4 F6Fs (CAP) launched at 1440.

1851 Secured from general quarters.

1902 Commenced maneuvering to form disposition 6R.

1909 Secured from flight quarters. Air Department set to condition 14.

2258 Commenced zigzagging on base course 243°T, 17.5 knots (175 rpm).

HC Struck at airfields about 100 miles north of Tokyo. We had a little excitement today, the Japs came out and tried to give us a bad time but didn't succeed. We shot one down, he sure did burn. We were at GQ all afternoon. HC

Photo # 80-G-455702   Japanese plane shot down off bow of USS Wasp, 9 August 1945

JAP GRACE SHOT DOWN OFF STARBOARD BOW OF U.S.S.WASP (CV-18)

U.S.S. BON HOMME RICHARD (CV-31)

DL *TF 38 pounded Japanese shipping and airfields ranging from northern Honshu and Hokkaido to the coast of Korea. Yes, we heard an announcement of the second atomic bomb, but we were so busy we could barely think about it. Until Tuesday.* *DL*

AD *Off Honshu 100 miles from Tokyo. Our planes are strafing. At 1500 GQ was sounded. Jap planes were all around our fleet. Our CAP were knocking them down as they came toward us. However some did get through. Two suicides hit one of our cans*[1] and to top that off one Jap was shot down a few thousand yards from us as she dived on the Wasp*[2] . He missed the Wasp by 25'. The Wasp got credit for shooting it down. We had another scare at 1800 but all was quiet. AD* (*[1] The DD USS BORIE was hit by a Kamikaze recciving minor damage) (*[2] The A/C diving on WASP was reported to be a Grace - CVL-22 Action Report)

GN *Made our two strikes today. Nips I guess didn't like it too well for they did send some planes out to get us. Sixteen were splashed in all within 50 miles and one was very close to the task force. In fact the Wasp hit her and she in turn tried to hit the Wasp but missed by about 25 foot. Had two GQ's when they got in close. One of the picket cans got hit by two banzais and hope he didn't fare too bad. Our CAP splashed a plane and that makes number one for them on our island structure. GN*

RC *Hitting northern Honshu. Russia declares war on Japan. Another atomic bomb was dropped on Japan. Task group under attack today. One destroyer was hit with two suicide dive bombers. One Zeke (dive bomber) dived on Wasp but was hit by ships guns and missed Wasp by 25 feet. RC*

**Before and after a USAAF B-29 called "Bockscar" **
dropped "Fat Man" over Nagasaki on
Thursday 9 August 1945, at 1102.**

Photo from: The Strategic Bombing Survey / Wikipedia.

(** The "Bockscar" today is on display at the
US Air Force Museum at the Wright-Patterson AFB.)

Friday 10 August 1945   *Japan, Honshu - Tokyo area*

Steaming as before roughly 150 miles off Honshu.

0300 Sounded flight quarters.

0336-0425 Manned general quarters stations.

0406-0408 Completed launching 4 F6Fs for CAP over the Task Group.

0507-0510 Completed launching 4 F6Fs for SubCAP.

0528 Commenced maneuvering to gain station in disposition 6VB, USS MISSOURI guide, course 000° T, bearing 240°T, distance 2,000 yards.

0615 USS BOSTON, USS CHICAGO, USS QUINCY and USS SAINT PAUL rejoined the task group.

0640 USS SCABBARDFISH (SS-397) made radio contact with the SubCAP F6Fs.

0720 Commenced launching aircraft.

0725 USS WREN came alongside port quarter to receive photographs.

0736 Completed launching 13 F6Fs and 8 TBMs. 4 Hellcats were for CAP and 1 was a replacement for a Hellcat just launched with hydraulic problems. The remaining 8 Hellcats and 8 Avengers joined aircraft from other carriers and attacked Iwaki Airfield, bombing and rocketing hangars, revetments and dispersal areas. 2 of our Hellcats rocketed a railway station near the airfield.

0738 Recovered 1 F6F launched at 0736, that could not retract his landing gear.

0840 Replacement air cover arrived on station to relieve the SCABBARDFISH CAP.

0852 Completed recovery of 4 F6Fs launched at 0408.

The 4 Hellcats catapulted at 0510, while on their SubCAP, ran into a small enemy surface vessel and proceeded to make strafing runs. One Hellcat (Bu# 78202) took hits from the vessel's anti-aircraft fire and developed an oil leak. Ensign George E. Van Hagen, short on options, was forced to make a water landing. George descended, disappearing into the concealing mist of a thick fog bank, unseen by his fellow fliers, and couldn't be located.

0956–1010 Recovered 3 (of the 4) F6Fs launched at 0510.

1040 DesRon 54 was detached from duty with TG 38.4 and departed for the states.

1047-1053 Recovered 1 F6F launched at 0736 due to engine trouble.

1115-1131 Launched 12 F6Fs. 4 F6Fs assigned to DCAP over the Task Group, 4 for SubCAP and 4 on a special search for Ensign Van Hagen.

1134-1155 Recovered 8 TBMs and the 11 remaining F6Fs launched at 0736, and 1 F6F just launched at 1131, returning due to engine trouble.

1331 Completed launching 4 F6Fs (photo) and 4 F6Fs and 9 TBMs for an afternoon attack on Koriyama Airfield, joining planes from other carriers on the mission. Target area visibility was poor and results were not observed.

1336 Recovered 2 F6Fs (photo plane & escort) launched at 1331, that returned - failure of landing gear to retract.

1446 Completed recovery of 2 F6Fs launched at 1331.

1452 USS SCABBARDFISH (** SS-397) changed course to pickup the downed F6F pilot.

1525 CVL-22 CIC reported Ensign Van Hagen was rescued by a friendly submarine.

(** SS-397 Deck Log times) Note: SCABBARDFISH Deck Log entries indicate that Van Hagen was visually sighted in the water at 1612 and that he was picked up at 1602 ? This should read 1622 (CVL-22 CIC was contacted at 1525) with a 1 hour time zone discrepancy between vessels.

1541 Completed launching 4 F6Fs for CAP over the Task Group.

1626-1629 Recovered 4 F6Fs launched at 1131.

1703-1714 Recovered 7 F6Fs launched at 1131.

1735-1755 Recovered 4 F6Fs and 7 TBMs launched at 1331.

1800 Recovered 1 TBM launched at 1331.

1822 Completed recovery of 4 F6Fs launched at 1541, and recovery of 1 TBM launched at 1331.

1923 Commenced maneuvering to gain position in disposition 6R, guide USS MISSOURI.
1939 Secured from flight quarters.

2050 Received a news report by radio that Japanese Government offered to accept Potsdam Ultimatum if they retain the Emperor.

2233 Commenced pumping bilges.

GN Made two very heavy strikes again today and all went well according to reports. One of our fighters was splashed but after a few hours in the water he was picked up by one of our subs. Got the report today that the Japs are willing to surrender and hope that the Pres. acts favorably on it. Looked like a bit of a mad house aboard last evening and I guess that there are any number like myself who want to go home and forget all about it. GN

RC Hitting Honshu. At 2100 Flash- Japan surrenders if they can keep their Emperor. RC

AD Receiving fuel. Our ship and 5 DD's left the Task Force for an errand trip to Iwo Jima. Tonight it was announced that Japan wanted to surrender. Believe me, there was a hell of a lot of excitement going on in the ship. I was in the ward room showing a movie when some officer came in yelling the war was over. No one paid much attention to the movie after that. AD

Japanese battleship NAGATO at anchor, probably at Yokosuka, in this photo taken by an INDEPENDENCE TBM.
(Note her stack is now missing)

Photo courtesy of Ed Schultz

Saturday 11 August 1945   *Refuel and depart for Iwo Jima*

0252 Steaming as before, toward a fueling area roughly 300 miles off Honshu. The ship is darkened and the Air Department is in condition 14. Sounded flight quarters.

0305 Aft gyro cut out for repairs.

0316 Sounded routine torpedo defense.

0347-0358 Launched 4 F6Fs for CAP and 4 TBMs for ASP.

0416 Secured from torpedo defense, and from flight quarters. Air Department set to condition 14.

0523 USS SABINE designated guide.

0525 Task Group 38.4 commenced fueling exercises.

0546 Commenced maneuvering to approach tanker USS KASKASKIA.

0713 Cast off from USS KASKASKIA having received fuel oil, aviation gasoline and transferring 1 person for return to the states.

0718 USS NECHES designated guide.

0741 Aft gyro back in operation.

0818-0822 USS UHLMANN was alongside the starboard quarter to transfer mail and photographs.

0835 USS INDEPENDENCE commenced maneuvering to clear the formation.

0836 Changed course to 225°T, speed increased to 20 knots in an effort to pass west of a typhoon moving up from the south. In accordance with dispatch orders of ComThird Fleet, dated 11 August 1945, they formed Task Unit 30.3.5 consisting of this vessel (OTC and guide) and DesDiv 100, consisting of USS COGSWELL, USS CAPERTON, USS INGERSOLL, USS KNAPP and USS HANK in screening disposition ASW 55. They are to proceed to a point within range to launch aircraft to fly to Iwo Jima with Lt. J. Sunderland carrying officer messenger mail.

0846 Completed launching 4 F6Fs for CAP and 3 TBMs for ASP.

0904 Completed recovery of 4 F6Fs and 4 TBMs launched at 0358.

0914 Secured from flight quarters.

0915-0925 USS HANK was alongside port quarter to transfer an Officer Messenger on board in accordance with orders of ComThird Fleet.

1147 Sounded flight quarters.

1221-1225 Launched 4 F6Fs for CAP and 3 TBMs for ASP.

1228-1233 Recovered 4 F6Fs and 3 TBMs launched at 0846.

1242 Secured from flight quarters. Air Department set to condition 13.

1444 Sounded flight quarters.

1520-1527 Completed launching 4 F6Fs for CAP and 3 TBMs for ASP.

1533-1545 Recovered 4 F6Fs and 3 TBMs launched at 1225.

1807 Completed recovery of 4 F6Fs and 3 TBMs launched at 1527.

2000 Changed course to 110°T to pass east of the typhoon which had moved northeasterly during the day.

RC Refueled in early morning and started for Iwo Jima with 5 destroyers on an important mission. RC

Sunday 12 August 1945   *Steaming to Iwo Jima*

Steaming as before (as Task Unit 30.3.5) toward a launch point near Iwo Jima. They are skirting to the eastward side of a typhoon. During the day they changed course by small intervals to 180°T, steaming through occasional squalls in 2-5 miles visibility, in haze. Wind at times was high with moderate swells and choppy seas. No flight operations were conducted today, cancelled because of weather.

RC Got radio flash that allies would accept Jap surrender only if Emperor took his orders from the Supreme Commander of Allied Forces (MacArthur). RC

GN Still headed in general direction of Iwo Jima and supposed to launch our planes today although storm is pretty bad. Were blown quite a ways off course and too far away to launch. GN

Monday 13 August 1945   *Iwo Jima - 8,000th Landing Aboard USS INDEPENDENCE*

0330 Steaming toward a point northeast of Iwo Jima. The ship is darkened and the Air Department is in condition 14. Sounded flight quarters.

0507 Secured from flight quarters. Air Department set to condition 14.

0600 USS HANK departed the Task Unit to proceed independently to Guam.

0700 Sounded flight quarters.

0755-0803 Launched 6 F6Fs and 6 TBMs. 2 F6Fs were for ASP. Officer Messenger Lt. J. Sunderland with the urgent mail proceeded to Iwo Jima on board a TBM.

0810 Secured from flight quarters. Air Department set to condition 13.

0901 Sounded flight quarters.

0930 Completed recovery of 1 TBM that had developed an oil leak, and 1 F6F escort launched at 0803.

0942 Secured from flight quarters. Air Department set to condition 13.

1050 USS KNAPP left the Task Unit to proceed independently to Iwo Jima.

1100 Sounded flight quarters.

1134 Completed launching 2 F6Fs for ASP.

1150 Task Unit 30.3.5 commenced scheduled fueling exercises, decreasing speed to 10 knots.

1157 Increased speed to 25 knots and commenced maneuvering to make slick for water landing.

1201 Ensign William Condon, in a F6F-5 (Bu.No.79817) launched at 0803, made an emergency water landing near USS CAPERTON, necessitated by a ramp strike where he lost the tail wheel & hook.

1202 Changed course to 270°T, reduced speed to 10 knots.

1212 USS CAPERTON rescued Ensign Condon, in good condition.

1224-1339 USS CAPERTON was along the starboard side amidships to deliver Ensign Condon back onboard, and received 56,880 gallons of fuel oil from this vessel.

1350-1503 USS INGERSOLL was along the starboard side amidships to receive 58,000 gallons of fuel oil from this vessel.

1508-1620 USS COGSWELL was along the starboard side amidships to receive 55,000 gallons of fuel oil from this vessel.

1622 Changed speed to 20 knots and completed launching 2 F6Fs for ASP.

1634 Completed recovery of 2 F6Fs launched at 1134. One of these aircraft made the 8,000th landing aboard USS INDEPENDENCE and the 1,000th landing without a barrier crash.

1657 Completed recovery of 5 TBMs and 3 F6Fs launched at 0803 for a messenger trip to Iwo Jima.

1726 Completed recovery of 2 F6Fs launched at 1622.

During the night they steamed northwest on course 315°T at 23 knots.

GN Storm has let up a bit and we did launch our TBM's and some fighters. One fighter in landing got waved off at the last moment and he left part of his tail hook on the deck. After four hours of CAP his gas was too low to make the nearest island so he made a water landing and did it very nicely. One of the cans picked him up. Got word that the Third Fleet was under attack and one unit was hit bad so I guess the war will go on for a while longer. GN

Tuesday 14 August 1945   *Steaming to rejoin 38.4 - Refuel & Reprovision*

Steaming as before as Task Unit 30.3.5, consisting of this vessel (OTC and guide) and DesDiv 100, consisting of USS COGSWELL, USS CAPERTON and USS INGERSOLL, proceeding in a northerly direction to rejoin TG 38.4. The screen is in disposition ASW 55. The Ship is darkened and the Air Department is in condition 14.

0330 Sounded flight quarters.

0411 SG radar contact bearing 342°T, 17 miles, identified as destroyer USS WADSWORTH.

0434 Completed launching 4 TBMs. 2 were assigned ASP and the other 2 delivered Officer Messenger mail to the USS WASP.

0740 Sighted TG 38.3, bearing 004°T, 18 miles.

0825 Sighted TG 38.4, bearing 005°T, 5 degrees starboard off the bow, distance 16 miles.

0907 DesDiv 100, consisting of USS COGSWELL, USS CAPERTON and USS INGERSOLL detached to report to CTU 38.4.5.

0912 Task Unit 30.3.5 was dissolved, USS INDEPENDENCE reporting for duty to CTG 38.4, and TG 38.4.1, Rear Admiral A.W. Radford. Commenced maneuvering to take up station in disposition 6R. The Task Group is in process of refueling. Tanker USS ESCAMBIA is guide.

0943-0953 USS STODDARD was alongside the port quarter to receive 3 pilots from CLVG-27 to pick up replacement aircraft.

1003 Commenced maneuvering to gain position along port side of the assigned tanker, USS SEBEC.

1042-1044 USS TWINING was alongside the port quarter to transfer a bag of guard mail to this vessel.

1126 Launched 1 F6F with CAG-27 to the USS YORKTOWN for a conference.

1310-1314 USS COLAHAN was alongside the port quarter to receive ACI* material and photographs.

1322 Cast off from USS SEBEC, having received 256,000 gallons of fuel oil, 14,000 gallons of aviation gasoline and 19 Hellcat belly tanks. Commenced maneuvering to recover aircraft. (*Air Combat Intelligence)

1342 Completed recovery of 2 F6Fs and 1 TBM, replacement aircraft.

1417 Recovered 2 TBMs launched 0434 for the mail flight to the USS WASP. Commenced maneuvering to regain station in disposition 6R.

1507 Joined with USS MISSOURI, leaving TG 38.4 to proceed to TG 38.1 to reprovision from the USS THUBAN.

1610 USS YORKTOWN designated guide of TG 38.4.

1646-1739 Alongside of USS THUBAN, to the starboard, taking on fresh and dried provisions.

1735 Sounded flight quarters.

1743 Commenced maneuvering, clearing TG 38.1, to regain station within TG 38.4.

1804 Recovered 1 F6F launched at 1126 (CAG from YORKTOWN conference).

1829 Regained station in TG 38.4.1.

1845 USS MISSOURI designated guide, course 300°T, bearing 240°T, 3,000 yards.

1856 Secured from flight quarters. Air Department set to condition 14.

GN Rejoined our old outfit today after a bit of a mix-up. We refueled and took some provisions aboard then struck off for ourselves. We had to pass through one of our units and the whole British fleet, but we got to our old gang at about dusk. Rumors are thick and fast about the war being over and done with. GN

The Japanese Imperial Conference made its final decision on the acceptance of the Potsdam Declaration. It contacted the Allied Powers through the Swiss Government, a neutral nation. General Douglas MacArthur is appointed Supreme Commander for the Allied Powers.

On this date, as the political pendulum was beginning to swing toward cessation of conflict, reality guided events for the fleet. In a communication sent out from the Admiral:

" NIP OFFICERS ARE STILL FIGHTING X THAT MEANS WE ARE STILL FACING AN ENEMY THAT HATES OUR CARRIERS LIKE THE DEVIL HATES HOLY WATER X UNTILL THEY SUR-RENDER AND ARE DISARMED REPEAT DISARMED THEY ARE DANGEROUS AND NEED KILL-ING X THE BEST PRESENT INSURANCE FOR OUR FORCES AND FUTURE INSURANCE FOR PEACE IS TO CARRY IT TO THEM WITH EVERY THING WE HAVE X CARRY ON X HALSEY "

Grassli
Charge d'Affaires ad interim of Switzerland

August 14, 1945.

Sir:
With reference to your communication of today's date,
transmitting the reply of the Japanese Government to the
communication which I sent through you to the Japanese
Government on August 11, on behalf of the Governments of the
United States, China, the United Kingdom, and the Union of
Soviet Socialist Republics, which I regard as full acceptance of
the Potsdam Declaration and of my statement of August 11, 1945,
I have the honor to inform you that the President of the United
States has directed that the following message be sent to you
for transmission to the Japanese Government:

"You are to proceed as follows:

"(1) Direct prompt cessation of hostilities by Japanese forces,
informing the Supreme Commander for the Allied Powers of the
effective date and hour of such cessation.

"(2) Send emissaries at once to the Supreme Commander for the
Allied Powers with information of the disposition of the
Japanese forces and commanders, and fully empowered to make any
arrangements directed by the Supreme Commander for the Allied
Powers to enable him and his accompanying forces to arrive at
the place designated by him to receive the formal surrender.

"(3) For the purpose of receiving such surrender and carrying it
into effect, General of the Army Douglas MacArthur has been
designated as the Supreme Commander for the Allied Powers, and
he will notify the Japanese Government of the time, place and
other details of the formal surrender."

Accept (etc.)

James F. Byrnes
Secretary of State.

Max Grassli, Esquire
Charge d'Affaires ad interim of Switzerland

32
Japan Surrenders !

Wednesday 15 August 1945   *Tokyo raid launched - Recalled*

Steaming in Task Unit 38.4.1 in an area 130 miles southeast of Tokyo, in company with USS YORKTOWN (OTC), USS COWPENS, USS SHANGRI LA, USS BON HOMME RICHARD (CTU 38.4.1 - Rear Admiral J.J. Ballentine) and USS WASP. The Task Group is in cruising disposition 6R, on base course 300°T, speed 18 knots, guide USS MISSOURI. The ship is darkened.
0315 Sounded flight quarters.
0416 Completed launching 4 F6Fs for a CAP.
0448 Gunnery Department set to condition One Easy.
0454 Commenced maneuvering to form disposition 6VB.
0519 Changed speed to 26 knots.
0526 Changed course to 190°T.
0542 Completed launching 4 F6Fs for SubCap, and 8 F6Fs with 7 TBMs loaded with 1,000 and 2,000 lb bombs respectively for a strike on Tokyo.
The raid is described in: The History of Torpedo Squadron Twenty Seven;
"During these days and nights the only thought in the minds of all was the question of whether or not the war was over. It was obvious that the end was merely a matter of days, but how many days remained to be answered. Orders were received on the night of the fourteenth to strike the following morning. The target designated was Tokyo-Shibaura Electric Plant # 2.
Next to the strike against Yokosuka, this target represented the most heavily defended of all those assigned for attack. The fact that the war might end momentarily, coupled with the realization of the hazards of the assigned target created a tension which had not existed on any previous mission. At 0530 item the strike was launched with Lieut. Dooling leading the nine TBM's; at 0640 the order came through from CinCPac to recall all strikes. Then it became a question of whether or not the strike had reached the target. Fortunately, the word got through to them before the coastline was crossed and, with no delay, they turned on reciprocal course to base. As the wheels of Lt. Dooling's plane touched the deck, President Truman's voice came over the speaker system announcing the end of hostilities."

The returning strike aircraft dropped their bombs into safe water prior to landing.
0633 INDEPENDENCE received the following message over TBS from Commander Third Fleet addressed to all ships and stations: **"We have received instructions from Commander in Chief Pacific Fleet to suspend air attack operations."**
0640 Received the following message from CTG 38.4 addressed to Task Unit 38.4.1:
"Have orders to recall all strike groups. Dearm all planes. Be prepared to maintain CAP."
0743 Completed launching 4 F6Fs.
0753 **Heard news broadcast that stated that President Truman had announced the Japanese have accepted unconditionally the surrender terms of the Potsdam conference.**
0800 Mustered crew on stations. **President Truman had announced on radio the Japanese Government had accepted the Potsdam surrender terms.**
0815 Completed recovering 8 F6Fs and 7 TBMs launched at 0542 and the 4 F6Fs launched at 0416.
0920 Cox J.M. Barfield was admitted into sickbay for treatment of a gunshot wound, stating that a shipmate was cleaning a 45 cal automatic and accidently pulled the trigger, wounding him in the left leg.
1132 Bogie reported visually by the Task Group, bearing 000°T, 8 miles. Changed course to 090°T, speed to 24 knots. Air Department set to condition 10.
1138 Gunnery Department manned all torpedo defense stations.
1148 Secured from torpedo defense. Gunnery Department set to condition One Easy. The bogey was

identified as friendly.

1200 The Imperial Prescript (edict) declaring the end of the war was broadcast by the Japanese Government. The Suzuki cabinet resigned.

1220 Completed recovering 4 F6Fs launched at 0743.

1535 Completed launching 8 F6Fs.

1540 Secured from flight quarters. Air Department set to condition 12.

1730 Sounded flight quarters.

1810 Completed recovering 8 F6Fs launched at 1535.

1820 All Divisions darkened ship.

1825 Commenced maneuvering to form disposition 6R.

1858 Secured from flight quarters. Air Department set to condition 14.

2213 Commenced zigzagging on course 000°T.

The war was over Wednesday 15 August 1945 (Western Pacific Date). INDEPENDENCE position at the time: 156 miles from Tokyo at 0800, 34 degrees 04.0 minutes North, 142 degrees 11.9 minutes East.

DL   Wednesday 15 August 1945
Planes from fast carrier Task Force 38 conduct raids in the vicinity of Tokyo. THEN came the announcement of the end of hostilities. Strike is cancelled while en route to objectives; pilots ordered to jettison ordnance and return to their carriers.

Word goes out that Bill Halsey sent a final combat command message, reading approximately: Shoot down any attacking aircraft in friendly fashion.

*We waited expectantly for our planes to return. The weather was okay but overcast and chill. All we ordnancemen were concerned about, however, was that somebody would return with a loose or hung-up bomb in the bay and kill us all. As each plane slammed down to the deck without incident the tension eased and we began to smile. I wanted to go over and slap Mister Porky on the back, but better sense killed my desire. I still wonder how he'd have reacted. Probably tossed me into the brig. **DL***

RC Hitting Tokyo. In the morning sent planes into Japan loaded with bombs and rockets. Just 4 minutes before the first planes reached their targets. They got word to drop bombs in the ocean and return to base for the war was over. We got the official word from President Truman at 0807 that the Japs had accepted our terms of surrender. Six Jap planes came out to look the fleet over about noon and were shot down[*1]. *They have been ordered to stay clear of fleet regardless of surrender. RC*
([*1] 3 Judys and 1 Zeke were confirmed shot down in the CVL-22 "Action Report")

During the operational period from 1 July 1945 (since leaving Leyte) through this date, the ship had on board air group CVLG-27. They were for the most part "Old Hands" in their craft, having served on sister CVL, the USS PRINCETON.

(the following is quoted from the CVL-22 Action Report)

" The INDEPENDENCE maintained 97% availability of aircraft which speaks for itself as to engineering efficiency. It is also of interest to note that on several occasions the INDEPENDENCE during the day, launched 200% of plane complement. A total of 3098 hours were flown by VF pilots who averaged 2 hours per day per pilot. VT pilots flew 1150 hours and averaged 1.6 hours per day per pilot. An average of 68% of total plane complement was flown each day."
During the previous thirteen and one half months the INDEPENDENCE had been away from the United States, the ship *"participated in practically every major operation which has been conducted. Throughout, the ship and the crew have aquitted (SIC*[2]) themselves in a manner that has reflected the highest credit upon the Navy."* (*[2] should be acquitted - used as related to performance and / or conduct)

Thursday 16 August 1945   *Off Tokyo - Snapshot*

Steaming as before in an area 300 miles southeast of Tokyo. The ship is darkened.

0430 The Task Group commenced fueling destroyers.

0653-0803 USS STODDARD was alongside the port quarter to deliver aircraft belly tanks.

1040 Commenced maneuvering to form special cruising disposition SNAPSHOT, guide USS MISSOURI, course 220°T, bearing 240°T, 1,500 yards. This formation placed all the elements of the Task Force close together to facilitate aerial photography of Task Force 38.

1202 Completed special exercises photographing the Task Force.

1205 Commenced maneuvering to form disposition 6R.

1239 Air Department set to condition 10.

1601 Air Department set to condition 14.

1610 HMS KING GEORGE V joined the formation in station 1,500 yards astern USS MISSOURI.

1924 Commenced zigzagging on base course 090°T. HMS KING GEORGE V cleared the formation to proceed as directed.

1959 Commenced zigzagging on base course 110°T.

The Emperor ordered immediate cessation of all hostilities.

HMS KING GEORGE V shot from the USS BON HOMME RICHARD. Behind her is USS NEW JERSEY.
(Freed from the war in the Atlantic, the Royal Navy contributed Task Force 57 for *"Operation Iceberg".*)

Friday 17 August 1945   *Off Tokyo - Snapshot*

Steaming as before. The ship is darkened and the Air Department is in condition 14.

0630 Sounded flight quarters.

0740 Completed launching 12 F6Fs for CAP.

0745 Secured from flight quarters. Air Department set to condition 13.

0746-0805 USS KNAPP was alongside port quarter to deliver 720 lbs. of laundry soap.

0920 Sounded flight quarters.

0940 Completed recovery of 1 F6F launched at 0740.

1100-1107 Completed recovery of 11 F6Fs launched at 0740. Commenced maneuvering to form special cruising disposition SNAPSHOT, guide USS MISSOURI, course 130°T, bearing 240°T, 1,500 yards.

1240 Completed special exercises photographing the Task Force.

1249 Commenced maneuvering to form disposition 6R.

1452 USS IOWA designated guide, course 135°T, bearing 025°T, 2,200 yards.

1455 Commenced maneuvering to form disposition 6G.

1517 Task Group 38.4 commenced scheduled gunnery exercises.

1620-1702 Gunnery Department manned all torpedo defense stations for firing exercises.

1702-1712 USS LANSDOWNE was alongside port quarter to transfer U.S. Mail and freight.

1713 Commenced maneuvering to form cruising disposition 6R.

1735 USS MISSOURI designated guide, course 210°T, bearing 240°T, distance 3,000 yards.

2235 Commenced zigzagging on base course 190°T.

RC Patrolling off Japan. Japs to send delegation to meet MacArthur in Manila. RC

17 August 1945 - Task Force 38 maneuvering off Japan

Saturday 18 August 1945   *Off Tokyo - Fueling*

0512 Steaming as before in an area 300 miles southeast of Tokyo. Commenced maneuvering to gain station in a fueling disposition for scheduled exercises, guide USS ATASCOSA.
0811 Maneuvered along port side of assigned tanker, USS SEBEC.
0955 Cast off from USS SEBEC, having transferred to her personnel for transportation to other assignments, and receiving fuel oil, lube oil and aviation gasoline.
1012 Gained station in disposition 6 R.
1625 USS MISSOURI designated guide.
1645 Maneuvered to avoid a possible mine and notified OTC of same.
1750 Darkened ship.
1815 Steamed clear of the fueling group.
2321 Commenced zigzagging on base course 290°T, speed 16 knots.

RC Patrolling off Japan. Jap delegates arrive in Manila. RC

Captain Kindell noted in the SOL:
"Tonite the three TG's retire to the N.E. and are to pass thru 'Point Drink' at <u>Dawn</u>.
Fleet axis will be E-W and Drink will be passed on southerly courses.
The oilers will clear to the S.E. and meet us again at dawn.
Tonight - Standard 6R and guide.
Maneuver according to OTC's transmissions.
No landfalls - No ships.
Call me if anything unusual comes up."

Sunday 19 August 1945   *Off Tokyo - Fueling, Provisioning, Transferring Personnel*

Steaming as before with Task Unit 38.4.1 with YORKTOWN (A.W. Radford CTG 38.4), WASP, SHANGRI LA, and BON HOMME RICHARD (J.J. Ballentine CTU 38.4.1) in an area southeast of Tokyo. The ship is darkened and the Air Department is in condition 14.
0444 USS ATASCOSA designated guide. Commenced maneuvering to go alongside USS THUBAN.
0505-0645 Along port side of USS THUBAN taking on provisions.
0700 Gained station in disposition 6R.
0829-0910 USS STODDARD was along starboard side to deliver mail and freight.
0956 Commenced maneuvering to go alongside USS OZARK (LSV-2).
1007-1136 Transferred personnel (the entire Marine Detachment) to the USS OZARK for duty ashore related to the occupation of Japan. They are to be landed on the beach near Tokyo, to take part in the initial occupation of Yokosuka Naval Base. INDEPENDENCE sent several specialists with the Marines.
1139 Commenced maneuvering to regain station in the formation.
1509-1545 USS WATTS was along starboard side amidships to deliver 11 passengers, mail and movies to this vessel.
1803 USS WASP designated guide, bearing 240°T, 6,000 yards.
1838 They cleared the fueling group and changed course to 000°T. USS YORKTOWN designated guide, bearing 180°T, 3,000 yards.
2036 Commenced zigzagging on base course 000°T, speed 16 knots.

Monday 20 August 1945   *Patrolling off Tokyo*

Steaming as before. The ship is darkened and the Air Department is in condition 14.
0437 They joined the fueling group again. USS PAMANSET designated guide. Commenced maneuvering to gain station in the formation.
0821-0826 USS TAYLOR was alongside the port quarter to transfer light mail.

1000 Sounded flight quarters.
1022 Commenced maneuvering to form disposition 6B.
1056-1106 Launched 12 F6Fs for a DCAP.
1114 Air Department set to condition 13.
1128-1136 USS CAPERTON was alongside the port quarter
to transfer U.S. Mail.
1412 USS MAZAMA designated formation guide.
1415 Sounded flight quarters.
1454-1501 Recovered 12 F6Fs launched at 1106.
1545 Secured from flight quarters.
Air Department set to condition 14.
1746 USS MISSOURI designated guide.
1828 They cleared the fueling group. Changed course to 000°T.

Captain Kindell noted in the SOL:
"Tomorrow is another fueling day in the same general area.
Tonight we are in a new one - 6B.
Our position 3.060
The MISSOURI is out at 1.090 and is guide.
She bears 227°T - 2,200 yards.
No ships or landfalls tonight.
Watch the H.M.S. ships. Maybe they're good, maybe not.
Call me if anything unusual comes up."
(Note: The HMS ships were of the British Fleet, Task Force 37, under Vice Admiral Rawlings.)

Ens. W. H. Kindell

Tuesday 21 August 1945 *Fueling, Provisioning and Rearming*

0400 Steaming as before in an area southeast of Tokyo. Made all preparations for fueling the ship.
0436 Commenced scheduled fueling exercises.
0447 USS MERRIMACK designated guide. Commenced maneuvering to approach tanker USS CHIPOLA on course 150°T, 8 knots.
0508 Alongside USS CHIPOLA taking on fuel oil and aviation gasoline.
0608 Cast off from USS CHIPOLA and commenced maneuvering to regain station in the formation, disposition 6R, guide USS MERRIMACK.
0827 HMS DUKE of YORK designated guide, bearing 247°T, 3,950 yards.
0830 Commenced emergency maneuvers to avoid a mine.
0904 USS STODDARD came alongside port quarter for ordnance disposal and personnel transfer.
0905 USS CHIPOLA designated guide.
0930 USS STODDARD cast off having received a passenger.
1009 Commenced maneuvering to approach ammunition ship USS MAZAMA.
1043 Came along the starboard side of USS MAZAMA for resupply of munitions.
1059-1115 USS INGERSOLL was alongside the port quarter to transfer a passenger.
1128-1135 USS WATTS was alongside the port quarter to deliver 5 bags of mail.
1231 Cast off from USS MAZAMA having received bombs, primer detonators, fuses and arming wires.
Commenced maneuvering to regain station in the formation, disposition 6R.
1312 Commenced zigzagging independently, base course 254°T, to keep the bridge clear of stack gas.
1517 Commenced maneuvering to take standby position astern USS THUBAN.
1553 Commenced maneuvering to approach USS THUBAN.
1602 Came along the port side of USS THUBAN to reprovision.
1732 Crane cable parted due to a heavy roll to port. Reprovisioning ceased.
1737 USS MISSOURI designated guide.

1740 F1c W.F. Neckerman was admitted to sickbay with a head laceration, injured while standing on a catwalk. The crane cable struck him when it parted.
1800 Gained station in disposition 6V, guide USS MISSOURI, bearing 227°T, 2,200 yards.
1830 The INDEPENDENCE cleared the fueling group.

Captain Kindell noted in the SOL:
"A Typhoon of some kind is S.E. of us. As the night orders from CTF 38 stand now we go S.W. until 1130 then 75° and later 30° to replenish some more tomorrow. The typhoon may change any or all of that.
If we get into a series of deep fast rolls a change of course 10° either way often breaks it up. Change back, of course, as soon as rolls diminish.
Call me if trouble shows up."

RC *Refueled, rearmed & re-provisioned ship. Typhoon due to hit us tonight.* **RC**

Wednesday 22 August 1945   *Fueling Continues, Mass Photo Flight*

Steaming in company with USS YORKTOWN (OTC and CTG Rear Admiral A.W. Radford), USS COWPENS, USS SHANGRI LA, USS BON HOMME RICHARD and USS ESSEX. Accompanying the group are members of the British Fleet: HMS DUKE OF YORK, HMS KING GEORGE V, HMS GAMBIA and HMS NEWFOUNDLAND.
0439 Commenced fueling exercises. USS PAMANSET designated guide.
0800 USS BENHAM came alongside the port quarter to receive a passenger for transfer to the USS SOUTH DAKOTA, then cast off.
0935-0943 USS WEEKS was alongside the port quarter to transfer back onboard Ensign George E. Van Hagen, shot down on 10 August and rescued by a friendly submarine.
0948-0950 USS COLAHAN was alongside the port quarter to deliver officer messenger mail.
1030 Sounded flight quarters.
1138 USS MISSOURI designated guide.
1145 Completed launching 9 TBMS and 8 F6Fs.
1228-1240 Launched 18 F6Fs for Air Group 27 to participate in a mass demonstration and photography of 961 Task Group aircraft, and surface units of Task Group 38.
1305 Secured from flight quarters. Air Department set to condition 13.
1430 Sounded flight quarters.
1516-1535 Recovered 8 F6Fs and 9 TBMs launched at 1145. They temporarily ceased landing operations to move aircraft to the hangar deck.
1626 Completed recovery of 18 F6Fs launched at 1240.
1648 Commenced maneuvering to regain station in disposition 6B.
1657 Secured from flight quarters. Air Department set to condition 14.
1804 Darkened ship.
1810-1820 USS NORMAN SCOTT was alongside the port quarter to transfer mail to this ship.

Captain Kindell noted in the SOL:
"The typhoon has moved off to N.E. Our present bad weather's a long wide front.
Probably rain all night, but visibility on and off fair to bad.
There is plenty of sea room around and no ships are expected.
Call me if anything unusual appears."

Thursday 23 August 1945   *Patrolling off Tokyo*

0325 Steaming 120 miles southeast of Tokyo. Sounded flight quarters.

0430 Completed launching 8 F6Fs.

0446 Secured from flight quarters. Air Department set to condition 13.

0700 Sounded flight quarters.

0800 Completed launching 8 F6Fs for CAP over the Task Group.

0901-0905 Recovered 8 F6Fs launched at 0430.

0952 Completed launching 1 TBM and 1 F6F for weather reconnaissance.

1125-1130 Completed launching 8 F6Fs for CAP.

1155 Gained flying station and commenced recovering aircraft.

1200 Completed recovery of 8 F6Fs. Commenced maneuvering to regain position in disposition 6B.

1210 Secured from flight quarters. Air Department set to condition 13.

1313-1317 USS SPERRY was alongside the starboard quarter to deliver officer messenger mail.

1400 USS MISSOURI, USS COWPENS, CruDivTen, DesDiv 100 and 105, and the British Units were detached from Task Group 38.4.

1408 USS YORKTOWN designated guide.

1413 Sounded flight quarters.

1439 Commenced maneuvering to gain position in disposition 5R.

1452 Commenced launching aircraft.

1500 Completed launching 8 F6Fs. USS WISCONSIN designated guide.

1526-1540 Recovered 1 TBM and 1 F6F launched at 0952 and 8 F6Fs launched at 1130. Commenced maneuvering to regain position in disposition 5R.

1550-1601 USS WALLACE L. LIND was alongside the port quarter to deliver 1 enlisted passenger to this vessel.

Captain Kindell noted in the SOL:

"Tonight we are en route to an area east of Japan, just around the bend from Tokyo. We stay there while Tokyo is occupied.

The T.F. which is with us now goes on north a hundred miles or so to the next area.

The other T.G. went the other way, to the Kyushu corner.

Tokyo Bay is in the S.W. corner of our area, so our airplanes can fly over and bring back the dope.

No land or ships expected.

Follow signals of O.T.C.

Call me if anything unexpected shows up."

Friday 24 August 1945   *Patrolling off Tokyo*

Steaming as before, southeast of Tokyo, in company with USS YORKTOWN (OTC), USS SHANGRI LA, USS BON HOMME RICHARD and USS ESSEX. USS WISCONSIN guide, distance 2,500 yards.

0335 Sounded flight quarters.

0424-0431 Launched 8 F6Fs for CAP over the Task Group.

0443 Secured from flight quarters. Air Department set to condition 12.

0551-0555 USS BULLARD was alongside the starboard quarter to deliver guard mail.

0730 Sounded flight quarters.

0804-0810 Recovered 8 F6Fs launched at 0431.

0836 Secured from flight quarters.

0907-0912 USS SPERRY was alongside the starboard quarter to deliver guard mail and U.S. Mail.

1213 USS VICKSBURG designated guide, course 270°T, bearing 211°T, distance 2,900 yards.

1216 Commenced maneuvering to gain station in firing disposition 5G.

1232 Task Group 38.4 commenced scheduled gunnery exercises.

1340 Gunnery Department manned all torpedo defense stations for gunnery exercises.

1430 Task Group 38.4 completed gunnery exercises. Secured from torpedo defense.

1435 Commenced maneuvering to gain station in reformed cruising disposition 5R.
2200-2204 USS SPERRY was alongside starboard quarter to deliver officer messenger mail.
2207 Changed speed to 14 knots, commenced zigzagging on base course 235°T.

Captain Kindell noted in the SOL:

> *" Here we are, T.G. 38.4, all alone in*
> *AREA STARS*
> *Which is East and Northeast of Tokyo"*

Vice Admiral Willis Augustus Lee, Jr.

Saturday 25 August 1945   *Patrolling off Tokyo*

0330 Steaming as before. Sounded flight quarters.
0427-0436 Launched 4 F6Fs for CAP over the Task group and 4 TBMs for a reconnaissance mission over Honshu.
0544-0551 Launched 4 F6Fs and 4 TBMs for a reconnaissance mission over Honshu.
0745 1 F6F launched at 0436 landed aboard the USS BON HOMME RICHARD with engine trouble.
0804 Completed launching 8 F6Fs, 4 for CAP over the Task Group and 4 for CAP over the USS FLINT, which was operating independently.
0837 Completed recovery of 3 F6Fs and 4 TBMs launched at 0436.
0937-0946 USS HANK was along the port side to deliver guard mail.
0938 USS VICKSBURG and USS NORMAN SCOTT left the formation to proceed as assigned.
0957-1004 Launched 4 F6Fs and 4 TBMs for a reconnaissance mission over Honshu.
1016 Completed recovering 4 F6Fs and 4 TBMs launched at 0551.
1053-1104 USS HANK was alongside the port quarter to transfer mail and movies.
1209 Completed launching 8 F6Fs and 5 TBMs. 4 F6Fs were for CAP over the Task Group. The other 4 F6Fs and the 5 TBMs flew a mission over prison camps to drop cigars, cigarettes and candy to the Prisoners of War.
1242 Completed recovering 8 F6Fs launched at 0804 and 1 F6F launched at 0436.
1346 Completed launching 4 F6Fs for CAP over the USS FLINT.
1427-1440 Recovered 4 F6Fs and 4 TBMs launched at 1004.
1541-1547 Launched 4 F6Fs CAP over the Task Group.
1619-1630 Recovered 8 F6Fs and 5 TBMs launched at 1209.
1730 Recovered 8 F6Fs, 4 launched at 1346 and 4 launched at 1547.

On this date, with the Pacific War now behind him, Vice Admiral Willis Augustus Lee, Jr. suffered a fatal heart attack.

Sunday 26 August 1945   *Patrolling off Tokyo*

0330 Steaming as before 120 miles southeast of Tokyo. Sounded flight quarters.
0439 Completed launching 8 F6Fs and 4 TBMs.
0530 USS INDEPENDENCE was ordered by OTC to cancel all carrier air operations for today and secure for heavy weather.
0721-0724 USS HANK was alongside the starboard quarter to receive photographs.
0731 Completed recovering 8 F6Fs and 4 TBMs launched at 0439.
1040-1107 USS HANK was along the starboard side to transfer freight.

Captain Kindell noted in the SOL:

"A typhoon is S.W. of us, quite a long way off. Its expected to pass into Japan well west of us. It may or may not. If not we should get a S.E. or S. hurricane swell and east to S.E. winds before morning."

RC *8/22–8/26 Patrolling. Dropped candy and cigarettes over prisoner of war camps in Japan. We're having typhoon weather, sea very rough. Signing of surrender terms delayed till September 2nd due to typhoon over and around Japan. Jap mine sweepers and U.S. mine sweepers clearing Tokyo Bay of mines.* **RC**

As Russell Carothers has noted in his diary, Tokyo bay was being prepared for the occupation by our Fleet and the surrender ceremonies. The ceremonies would be held on the deck of the USS MISSOURI. It was planned to anchor close to the spot where Commodore Perry anchored almost a century before.

Monday 27 August 1945   *Patrolling off Tokyo*

0442 Steaming as before. USS VICKSBURG and USS NORMAN SCOTT rejoined the formation.
0558 Completed launching 4 TBMs for a reconnaissance mission.
0650 USS INTREPID and USS ROWE joined the formation.
0819 Completed launching 8 F6Fs. 4 were for a Task Group CAP, and 4 for a reconnaissance mission.
1015 Completed launching 9 F6Fs and 5 TBMs. The Hellcats were assigned as a CAP over the USS MISSOURI, and the Avengers flew a reconnaissance mission.
1029 Completed recovery of 4 TBMs launched at 0558 and 1 F6F launched at 1015.
1123-1132 USS ROWE was along the starboard side to deliver mail.
1209 Completed launching 6 F6Fs and 3 TBMs. 4 F6F Hellcats flew CAP over the Task Group. 2 Avengers were on a reconnaissance mission. The remaining 2 F6Fs and 1 TBM flew a search mission.
1225-1227 USS MOALE was alongside the starboard quarter to transfer guard mail.
1243 Completed recovery of 8 F6Fs launched at 0819.
1314-1320 USS MOALE was alongside the starboard quarter to deliver guard mail.
1347 Completed launching 4 F6Fs for a reconnaissance mission over Honshu.
1454 Completed recovery of 8 F6Fs and 5 TBMs launched at 1015.
1513-1519 USS STODDARD was along the starboard side amidships to attempt transfer of passengers. It cast off without completing the transfer.
1545 Completed launching 4 F6Fs for CAP over the Task Group.
1607-1624 USS STODDARD was along the starboard side amidships to transfer 2 passengers.
1640 Completed recovery of 6 F6Fs and 3 TBMs launched at 1209.
1745 Completed recovery of 4 F6Fs launched at 1347 and 4 F6Fs launched at 1545.
1827-1841 USS AULT was alongside the port quarter to transfer 1 passenger and guard mail.
1844 Secured from flight quarters. Air Department set to condition 14.
2055 Changed course to 000°T. The typhoons that threatened had passed to the west over Honshu and on to China.

RC *Patrolling off Tokyo Bay with 12 battlewagons, 18 aircraft carriers, 6 escort carriers, 20 cruisers and 101 destroyers. There are also many transports, hospital ships and destroyer escorts out here waiting for word to move into the bay. Our planes fly over Japan and some have landed and taken off again. Japs have ceased firing on them.* **RC**

Tuesday 28 August 1945   *Patrolling off Tokyo*

Steaming as before, 120 miles southeast of Tokyo, in company with USS YORKTOWN (OTC), USS INTREPID, USS SHANGRI LA, USS BON HOMME RICHARD and USS ESSEX. USS WISCONSIN is guide, course 000°T, bearing 324°T, distance 2,500 yards. The ship is darkened.
0445 Completed launching 12 F6Fs and 4 TBMs. 8 Hellcats were for CAP over the Task Group.
4 Hellcats were assigned CAP over the USS FLINT (which was operating independently).
The 4 Avengers were assigned a reconnaissance mission.

0604 Completed launching 4 F6Fs and 4 TBMs.

0757 Completed launching 4 F6Fs for a CAP over USS FLINT.

0805-0817 USS WREN was alongside the port quarter to transfer photographs.

0825-0830 Completed recovery of 12 F6Fs and 4 TBMs launched at 0445 and 1 F6F launched at 0604.

1007 Completed launching 12 F6Fs, 8 for a CAP over USS MISSOURI, 4 for a CAP over USS FLINT.

1030 Completed recovery of 3 F6Fs and 4 TBMs launched at 0604.

1100-1125 USS WEEKS was along the starboard side amidships to deliver mail, freight and passengers.

1135 Completed launching 4 F6Fs for a CAP over USS FLINT.

1218 Completed recovery of 4 F6Fs launched at 0757.

1239-1243 USS SMALEY was along the starboard side to transfer registered and U.S. Mail.

1306-1323 USS WEEKS was along the starboard side to transfer passengers.

1335 Completed launching 4 F6Fs and 2 TBMs. The 4 F6Fs were for a CAP over USS FLINT, and the 2 Avengers were on a reconnaissance mission over Tokyo Bay.

1415 Completed recovery of 12 F6Fs launched at 1007.

1423 Secured from flight quarters. Air Department set to condition 13.

1426 USS WEEKS was along the starboard side to transfer freight.

1515 Sounded flight quarters.

1537 Completed recovery of 4 F6Fs launched at 1135.

1545-1551 USS WALDRON was alongside the port quarter to deliver U.S. Mail.

1749 Completed recovery of 4 F6Fs and 2 TBMs launched at 1335.

1815 Secured from flight quarters. Air Department set to condition 14.

2045 Secured No.4 main engine due to heavy oil drain.

2245 No.4 main engine repair completed.

RC Patrolling – The battlewagons Missouri and Iowa have moved into Tokyo Bay 30 miles off Tokyo. Jap delegates came aboard and met with Halsey's staff. Everything going very well so far. RC

US occupation forces began occupation of the Japanese mainland. General Headquarters of the US Army Forces Pacific moved from Manila to Yokohama.

Wednesday 29 August 1945   *Off Tokyo - Refueling and taking on provisions*

Steaming 250 miles southeast of Tokyo, in company with USS YORKTOWN (OTC), USS ESSEX, USS BON HOMME RICHARD and USS SHANGRI LA.

0330 Sounded flight quarters.

0433 Completed launching 8 F6Fs for CAP over the Task Group.

0442 Secured from flight quarters.

0446 They merged with the fueling group. USS SEBEC designated guide.

0604-0615 USS ROBERT K. HUNTINGTON was alongside delivering bales of rags.

0630 USS CHEVALIER cast off having delivered U.S. Mail.

0722 Recovered 1 F6F launched at 0433.

0822 Completed recovery of 7 F6Fs launched at 0433. Commenced maneuvering to approach assigned tanker USS KANKAKEE.

0855 Came along the port side of USS KANKAKEE.

0929-0936 USS MOALE was alongside the port quarter to deliver U.S. Mail.

1032-1050 USS ROWE was alongside the port quarter to deliver freight and U.S. Mail.

1053 Cast off from USS KANKAKEE, having taken on 213,720 gallons fuel oil, 61,500 gallons of gasoline, 5 drums of lube oil and miscellaneous supplies.

1145 USS STODDARD was along the starboard side to transfer passengers to USS ESSEX for transportation to the States.

1514 Commenced maneuvering to gain standby position astern USS ALDEBARAN.

1604-1652 Reprovisioned from USS ALDEBARAN.
1805-1810 USS KIMBERLY was alongside the port quarter to deliver freight.
1817 The Task Group cleared the fueling group.

Captain Kindell noted in the SOL:
"We have tankers, AKs, CVEs with us tonight.
More fueling and provisioning tomorrow."

RC Patrolling. The transports with landing forces have moved into the bay and many troops have gone ashore with no opposition. On the 31st MacArthur landed just outside Yokohama in his C-54. We're 430 days out of the states. RC

Thursday 30 August 1945   *Off Tokyo - Reprovisioning*

Steaming as before in a fueling area in company with USS YORKTOWN (OTC), USS ESSEX, USS BON HOMME RICHARD and USS SHANGRI LA. USS WISCONSIN is guide.
0425 They joined the fueling group. USS SEBEC was designated guide.
0448-0456 USS ROBERT K. HUNTINGTON was along the port quarter receiving outgoing U.S. Mail.
0545-0637 USS WALLACE L. LIND was alongside the port quarter receiving personnel for transfer to the USS ESSEX, then for further transfer to the States.
0556-0633 USS ENGLISH was along the starboard side amidships to receive personnel and gear for transfer to the USS ESSEX for further transfer to the States.
0803-0810 Launched 9 F6Fs for CAP.
0830 Secured from flight quarters.
0915 Made daily inspection of the magazines.
1055 Sounded flight quarters. Made all preparations for reprovisioning the ship.
1122 Left the formation to recover aircraft.
1137-1143 Recovered 9 F6Fs launched at 0810. Then commenced maneuvering for an approach on the USS THUBAN to reprovision.
1202 Came along the port side of USS THUBAN.
1207 Secured from flight quarters.
1409 Cast off from USS THUBAN having completed reprovisioning. Commenced maneuvering to gain station in the formation, in an AA firing disposition.
1441 On orders from OTC, commenced maneuvering for an approach on the USS ALDEBARAN.
1520 Stood clear of USS ALDEBARAN on orders from OTC, as formation changed course and speed.
1600 Changed course to 000°T, speed 14 knots.
1608 Commenced maneuvering for an approach on the USS ALDEBARAN.
1619-1652 INDEPENDENCE was along the port side of the USS ALDEBARAN taking on additional provisions. INDEPENDENCE then commenced maneuvering to gain station in the disposition, USS SEBEC guide, 6,000 yards.
1807 Darkened ship.
1827 Replenishment group was detached from the formation. USS WISCONSIN designated guide, course 000°T, bears 324°T, 2,500 yards.

AD Off Tokyo. Receiving supplies. AD

Friday 31 August 1945

Steaming as before in an area 100 miles off Tokyo.
0440 Completed launching 12 F6Fs and 4 TBMs. 8 F6Fs were for CAP over the Task Group, and 4 F6Fs were assigned CAP over USS FLINT. The TBMs flew reconnaissance patrols over Honshu.

0603 Completed launching 4 F6Fs, assigned CAP over USS FLINT, and 4 TBMs for reconnaissance patrols over Honshu.
0805 Completed launching 4 F6Fs.
0810-0840 Recovered 12 F6Fs and 4 TBMs launched at 0440.
0958-1007 Launched 13 F6Fs, 8 Hellcats for CAP over USS MISSOURI, 4 Hellcats for a CAP over USS FLINT. One extra F6F was launched to replace a Hellcat, just launched and returning to the ship.
1011-1019 Recovered 4 F6Fs and 4 TBMS launched at 0603 and 1 F6F launched at 1007.
1125-1126 Launched 4 F6Fs for a CAP over USS FLINT.
1210 Completed recovery of 4 F6Fs launched at 0805.
1400 Completed recovery of 12 F6Fs launched at 1007.
1554 Completed recovery of 4 F6Fs launched at 1126.
1543 Secured from flight quarters. Air Department set to condition 14.

AD Off Tokyo. Here it is the end of the month and the Peace Papers aren't signed*. Some soldiers Marines and sailors have landed at the naval Base at the mouth of Tokyo Bay already. **AD**

(Note: * Japan had just surrendered. Much needed to be done. Security was still a concern. Desirous to go home, many failed to consider the amount of time it would take to plan, arrange a secure site, procure agreement, legal documents and transport parties from all nations involved as signatories to the surrender, with the importance and weight of the occasion.)

Saturday 1 September 1945   Ensign Eugene Elwood Fellows Disappears

0457-0507 Steaming as before. Launched 10 F6Fs and 5 TBMs.
0512-0530 USS WEEKS was alongside starboard to receive passengers for transfer to USS ESSEX.
0548 Completed launching 8 F6Fs and 2 TBMs.

The LSO and his team brings them home

0612 USS MYLES C. FOX briefly came alongside the port quarter to deliver a V-belt for the ice cream machine.
0828 Completed recovery of 9 F6Fs and 5 TBMs launched at 0458, and 8 F6Fs and 2 TBMs launched at 0548.

1 F6F-5 (BU.No.79657) failed to return. While flying on a Combat Air Patrol, the division that Ensign Eugene Elwood Fellows was flying with passed through a solid overcast cloud bank. When the division emerged from the clouds, Ensign Fellows was missing. He was not seen again after that.
Rain began over the INDEPENDENCE as a front passed through. There would be intermittent rain all day, with winds to 20 knots.

0953 Secured from flight quarters. Air Department set to condition 12.
1145 USS YORKTOWN designated guide, distance 3,000 yards.
1519 Completed launching 2 F6Fs.
1740 USS ESSEX left the formation.
1752-1757 Recovered the 2 F6Fs launched at 1519.

RC Thousands of troops are landing today with no opposition. One Jap shot today for disobeying orders. RC

AD Off Tokyo. Tomorrow the official signing of the surrender of Japan will be held on the USS Missouri in Tokyo Bay AD

33
Official Surrender of Japan

Sunday 2 September 1945

Steaming as before in company with USS YORKTOWN (OTC), USS BON HOMME RICHARD, USS SHANGRI LA and USS WISCONSIN (guide), as Task Unit 38.4.1.
0330 Sounded flight quarters.
0520 Commenced maneuvering to gain station in disposition 4R.
0609 Sighted Nojima Saki, bearing 335°T, 35 miles.
0645 Completed launching 8 F6Fs.
0726 Completed launching 4 F6Fs and 8 TBMs.
0749 Completed launching 9 F6Fs.

At approximately 0900 the beginning of the formal surrender began in Tokyo Bay aboard USS MISSOURI. Over the next days, further ceremonies of surrender would occur across the Pacific. The Allies would need to locate and rapidly repatriate our prisoners held by Japan.

More than 4.5 million IJA soldiers & 1.8 million IJN sailors were allied prisoners, needing repatriation, and the infrastructure was in shambles. Japan would face severe food shortages. Another issue would be the Japanese holdouts not hearing of, or refusing to surrender. Back aboard INDEPENDENCE:

0910 Completed recovery of 8 F6Fs launched at 0645 and 2 F6Fs launched at 0749.
1034 Completed launching 9 F6Fs.
1134 Completed recovery of 6 TBMs launched at 0726, and 13 F6Fs. 7 F6Fs were launched at 0749, 4 F6Fs launched at 0726, and 2 launched at 1034, .
1151 Completed recovery of 2 TBMs launched at 0726.
1337 Completed launching 12 F6Fs (4 for a search and 8 for CAP) and 5 TBMs.
1508 Completed recovery of 7 F6Fs launched at 1034.
During the morning, the Mighty-I had been in sight of the Honshu mainland on both sides of Tokyo Bay and islands including; O Shima, To Shima, Udone Shima, Nii Shima, and Miyake Shima.

80-G-421130 Carrier planes over USS Missouri, 2 September 1945

1609 Completed recovery of 4 F6Fs launched at 1337.
1730 Completed recovery of 8 F6Fs and 5 TBMs launched at 1337.
1803 Darkened ship.   1810 Air Department secured from flight quarters.

DL   Three great things happened aboard ship in the ensuing days. While the highest brass signed papers aboard BB Missouri in Tokyo Bay on 2 September, our planes joined in a flight of about fifteen hundred aircraft in a grand ceremonial salute. This was to make sure the world, and history--as well as the old black-shoe battleship Navy men--would know which weapon had been the most effective in bringing the Japanese to this table. Even with the overcast, it was impressive. I watched tough men turn their heads away so that shipmates could not see their reaction. What the hell! Why not? We knew better than most what this aerial display had cost us. It was worth a few manly tears. I shed my share. DL

HB One of the biggest thrills of my life was when the Japanese surrendered, our planes from every carrier in all the task forces was put in the air and the flew over in mass, this was a sight to behold, planes as far as you could see. I knew we had many planes, but when you put them all in the air at one time it was simply the most exciting thing I have ever seen. HB

AD SEPTEMBER 2ND   VJ DAY   Today the Official Surrender Documents have been signed. Officials from all our Allied Nations were aboard the Missouri including the Jap officials. General Douglas MacArthur was The Boss. The Missouri was not visible to us because we were outside the bay. We could see land very clearly and it wouldn't take long for us to dock in Tokyo. We were that close. Fujiyama was clearly visible. AD

Top photo: Standing by the chair Lt. General Richard K. Sutherland on left watches Japan's Foreign Minister Mamoru Shigemitsu sign the Instrument of Surrender, assisted by Toshikazu Kase.
Bottom Photo: General Douglas MacArthur signs. Lt. General Jonathan M. Wainwright and Brittan's Lt. General Sir Arthur E. Percival are standing behind MacArthur.

RC   This morning the Unconditional Surrender Terms were signed in Tokyo Bay. MacArthur signed for all nations at war with Japan, Nimitz signed for U.S. while eight other representatives from their respective countries signed for China, Britain, Russia, Canada, Australia, France, New Zeeland and the Netherlands.   RC

Photo # 80-G-701293 FAdm. Nimitz signs Japanese surrender instrument

Behind Chester Nimitz stands MacArthur, Admiral William F. Halsey and Rear Admiral Forrest P. Sherman.

Photo # 80-G-353633 Adm. Halsey with VAdm. McCain, 2 Sept. 1945

On 6 September (just days after this photo was shot aboard USS MISSOURI) John S. McCain, will die, suffering a heart attack at his home on Coronado Island (San Diego). Halsey had insisted he attend the surrender ceremony, not realizing the extent of McCain's frail condition.

INSTRUMENT OF SURRENDER

We, acting by command of and in behalf of the Emperor of Japan, the Japanese Government and the Japanese Imperial General Headquarters, hereby accept the provisions set forth in the declaration issued by the heads of the Governments of the United States, China and Great Britain on 26 July 1945, at Potsdam, and subsequently adhered to by the Union of Soviet Socialist Republics, which four powers are hereafter referred to as the Allied Powers.

We hereby proclaim the unconditional surrender to the Allied Powers of the Japanese Imperial General Headquarters and of all Japanese armed forces and all armed forces under Japanese control wherever situated.

We hereby command all Japanese forces wherever situated and the Japanese people to cease hostilities forthwith, to preserve and save from damage all ships, aircraft, and military and civil property and to comply with all requirements which may be imposed by the Supreme Commander for the Allied Powers or by agencies of the Japanese Government at his direction.

We hereby command the Japanese Imperial General Headquarters to issue at once orders to the Commanders of all Japanese forces and all forces under Japanese control wherever situated to surrender unconditionally themselves and all forces under their control.

We hereby command all civil, military and naval officials to obey and enforce all proclamations, orders and directives deemed by the Supreme Commander for the Allied Powers to be proper to effectuate this surrender and issued by him or under his authority and we direct all such officials to remain at their posts and to continue to perform their non-combatant duties unless specifically relieved by him or under his authority.

We hereby undertake for the Emperor, the Japanese Government and their successors to carry out the provisions of the Potsdam Declaration in good faith, and to issue whatever orders and take whatever action may be required by the Supreme Commander for the Allied Powers or by any other designated representative of the Allied Powers for the purpose of giving effect to that Declaration.

We hereby command the Japanese Imperial Government and the Japanese Imperial General Headquarters at once to liberate all allied prisoners of war and civilian internees now under Japanese control and to provide for their protection, care, maintenance and immediate transportation to places as directed.

The authority of the Emperor and the Japanese Government to rule the state shall be subject to the Supreme Commander for the Allied Powers who will take such steps as he deems proper to effectuate these terms of surrender.

Signed at TOKYO BAY, JAPAN at ＿＿＿ on the ＿ SECOND ＿ day of ＿ SEPTEMBER ＿, 1945.

By Command and in behalf of the Emperor of Japan and the Japanese Government.

By Command and in behalf of the Japanese Imperial General Headquarters.

Accepted at TOKYO BAY, JAPAN at 0908 on the SECOND day of SEPTEMBER, 1945, for the United States, Republic of China, United Kingdom and the Union of Soviet Socialist Republics, and in the interests of the other United Nations at war with Japan.

Supreme Commander for the Allied Powers.

United States Representative

Republic of China Representative

United Kingdom Representative

Union of Soviet Socialist Republics Representative

Commonwealth of Australia Representative

Dominion of Canada Representative

Provisional Government of the French Republic Representative

Kingdom of the Netherlands Representative

Dominion of New Zealand Representative

Chapter 33

724

Monday 3 September 1945   *Off Tokyo, Reprovisioning*

Steaming as before in a fueling area in company with carriers USS YORKTOWN (OTC - Rear Admiral A.W. Radford), USS BON HOMME RICHARD and USS SHANGRI LA. Battleship USS WISCONSIN is guide.

0431 Completed launching 8 F6Fs. The Task group commenced fueling exercises. USS CIMARRON assumed guide.

0433 Commenced maneuvering to come alongside USS ALDEBARAN to reprovision.

0507 Came along the port side USS ALDEBARAN and commenced reprovisioning at 0541.

0743-0812 USS WEEKS was alongside the port quarter to transfer photographs, mail and a passenger.

0820 USS ALDEBARAN cast off. Sounded flight quarters.

0845 Completed recovery of the 8 F6Fs launched at 0431.

0847 Commenced maneuvering to come alongside USS KASKASKIA to take on fuel.

0923 Secured from flight quarters.

0925 Commenced pumping fuel oil from USS KASKASKIA.

1026 Cast off from USS KASKASKIA having taken on 131,520 gallons of fuel oil and 21,000 gallons of aviation gasoline. Commenced maneuvering to come alongside USS TALUGA.

1040-1147 Along the port side of fleet oiler USS TALUGA transferring 25 officers and enlisted men for transportation for further assignment or release to inactive duty.

1240 Commenced maneuvering to take station for gunnery exercises firing at drones.

1243 Sounded torpedo defense.

1255 Gained station in column 800 yards astern USS WISCONSIN, course 100°T, 8 knots.

1417 Secured from torpedo defense.

1437 Regained station on USS CIMARRON, bearing 110°T, 5,600 yards.

1526-1545 USS WALDRON was alongside our port quarter to deliver aviation supplies.

1540 CTG 38.4 in USS YORKTOWN assumed tactical command of the Task Group.

1620 USS WISCONSIN, USS VICKSBURG, USS MYLES C. FOX and USS HAWKINS departed the Task Group.

1627-1633 USS WALDRON was once again alongside the port quarter to deliver aviation supplies.

1652 USS ATLANTA assumed guide, bearing 000°T, 2,500 yards.

1921 Changed course to 295°T.

RC Refueled and re-provisioned RC

Tuesday 4 September 1945   *Off Tokyo, Patrolling*

0501 Steaming as before. The Task Group commenced fueling exercises. Speed changed to 8 knots, course 270°T, USS KASKASKIA designated guide.

0658 USS SMALLEY came along the port quarter to receive US Mail and to deliver towing sleeves.

0700 Sounded flight quarters.

0705 USS SMALLEY cast off.

0757 Completed launching 4 F6Fs.

0818 Secured from flight quarters. Air Department set to condition 13.

1100 Sounded flight quarters.

1144 Commenced maneuvering to our flying station.

1200 Completed recovering 4 F6Fs launched at 0757.

1210 Regained our station in the fueling disposition.

1224 Secured from flight quarters. Air Department set to condition 14.

1330 Sounded flight quarters.

1428 Launched 1 TBM.

1430 Secured from flight quarters. Air Department set to condition 14.

1538 USS YORKTOWN designated guide, course 320°T, bearing 044°T, 3,600 yards.
1540 Changed course to 000°T.
1655 Sounded flight quarters.
1730 Recovered 1 TBM launched at 1428.
1958 USS ATLANTA assumed guide, bearing 000°T, 2,500 yards.

RC Patrolling, censorship lifted on letters today. ***RC***   ***AD*** *Off Honshu on patrol.* ***AD***

Wednesday 5 September 1945   *Off Tokyo, Patrolling. We become Task Unit 38.1.1*

0330 Steaming as before. Sounded flight quarters.
0444-0448 Launched 4 F6Fs, and 4 TBMs for a reconnaissance flight over the Tokyo area.
0515 Secured from flight quarters.
0639 Task Unit 38.4.9 departed from the Task Group to report to CTG 38.2 for duty.
0715 Sounded flight quarters.
0800 Task Unit, 38.4.1 was ordered to become Task Unit 38.1.1, consisting of carriers
INDEPENDENCE, BON HOMME RICHARD, COWPENS (to report at a later date), SHANGRI LA,
and YORKTOWN, with Rear Admiral A.W. Radford in YORKTOWN in tactical command.
0821 Completed launching 12 F6Fs and 4 TBMs.
0845 USS DULUTH and USS TOPEKA reported for duty in Task Group 38.1.
0900 Completed recovery of 4 F6Fs and 4 TBMs launched at 0448.
0916 Secured from flight quarters.
1045 Sounded flight quarters.
1151 Completed launching 11 F6Fs and 4 TBMs.
1205-1217 Recovered 12 F6Fs and 4 TBMs launched at 0821, and 1 F6F launched at 1151.
1328-1332 Launched 4 F6Fs and 4 TBMs.
1337 Secured from flight quarters.
1352 USS YORKTOWN designated guide.
1401 Sounded flight quarters.
1415-1416 Recovered 2 F6Fs launched at 1332.
1420 Secured from flight quarters.
1517 Sounded flight quarters.
1528 USS TOPEKA designated guide,
         course 055°T, bearing 000°T, 2,500 yards.
1556-1555 Recovered 10 F6Fs and 4 TBMs launched at 1151.
1614 Secured from flight quarters.
1700 Sounded flight quarters.
1732-1735 Recovered 2 F6Fs and 4 TBMs launched at 1332.
1801 Secured from flight quarters.
         Air Department set to condition 14.
2118 Changed course to 230°T.

RC   Patrolling and getting damn sick of patrolling.
Received word from Admiral that USS Independence would
stay out here indefinitely doing patrol duty. ***RC***

AD   Off Honshu on patrol. ***AD***

Thursday 6 September 1945 *Off Tokyo, Patrolling*

0345 Steaming as before. Sounded flight quarters.
0453-0502 Launched 4 F6Fs and 4 TBMs.
0510 The Task Group (38.1) began topping off the destroyers.
0520 Secured from flight quarters.

ACMM Walter Charles Zarembra
V-1 Div. Arresting Gear Crew

726

0510 The Task Group (38.1) began topping off the destroyers.

0520 Secured from flight quarters.

0530-0622 Destroyer USS ROGERS was along the starboard side to be refueled.

0626-0628 USS COLLETT pulled along the port quarter to deliver Officer Messenger Mail.

0629 USS ROGERS cast off having received 26,620 gallons of fuel oil.

0630 USS ERBEN came along the starboard side to be refueled.

0725 Sounded flight quarters.

0737 USS ERBEN cast off having received 40,180 gallons of fuel oil.

0833 Completed launching 12 F6Fs and 4 TBMs.

0858 Recovered 4 F6Fs and 4 TBMs launched at 0502.

1201 Completed launching 12 F6Fs and 4 TBMs.

1226 Recovered 12 F6Fs and 4 TBMs launched at 0833.

1342 Completed launching 4 F6Fs and 4 TBMs. USS YORKTOWN designated guide.

1606 Completed recovering 12 F6Fs and 4 TBMs launched at 1201.

1628 USS TOPEKA designated guide.

1630 Secured from flight quarters.

1705 Sounded flight quarters.

1746 Completed recovering 4 F6Fs and 4 TBMs launched at 1342.

1803 Darkened ship. Changed course to 180°T.

1819 Secured from flight quarters. Air Department set to condition 14.

Friday 7 September 1945 *Off Tokyo, Patrolling*

0345 Steaming as before. Sounded flight quarters.

0507 Completed launching 4 F6Fs and 4 TBMs.

0527 USS HEERMANN came along starboard side amidships to be refueled.

0611 USS HEERMANN cast off having received 21,130 gallons of fuel oil.

0832 Completed launching 12 F6Fs and 4 TBMs.

0901 Completed recovering 4 F6Fs and 4 TBMs launched at 0507.

Howard Edsel Figgins

0919 Secured from flight quarters.

1100 Sounded flight quarters.

1157 Completed launching 12 F6Fs and 4 TBMs.

1229 Completed recovering 12 F6Fs and 4 TBMs launched at 0832.

1339 Completed launching 4 F6Fs and 4 TBMs.

1420 USS YORKTOWN designated guide.

1451 USS TOPEKA designated guide.

1605 Completed recovering 12 F6Fs and 4 TBMs launched at 1157.

1620 Secured from flight quarters.

1820 Darkened ship.

1827 Secured from flight quarters. Air Department set to condition 14.

2245 Changed course to 270°T.

Saturday 8 September 1945 *Refuel the Cans. The Marines return & navigation lights burn*

0400 Steaming as before in company with Task Unit 38.1.1.

0501 Completed launching 4 F6Fs and 3 TBMs.

0511 USS YORKTOWN designated guide.

0519 Secured from flight quarters.

0535 Commenced fueling destroyers. USS ROBERT K. HUNTINGTON came along the starboard side.

0556 USS ROBERT K. HUNTINGTON cast off having received 12,990 gallons of fuel oil.

0609-0630 USS LOWRY was along the starboard side receiving 14,340 gallons of fuel oil.

0645 USS SHANGRI LA assumed guide.

0646-0706 USS MOALE was along the starboard side receiving 13,870 gallons of fuel oil.

0716-0740 USS ERBEN was along the starboard side receiving 11,950 gallons of fuel oil.

0828 USS TOPEKA was designated guide.

0848 Completed launching 4 F6Fs and 3 TBMs.

0911 Completed recovering 4 F6Fs and 3 TBMs launched at 0501.

1012-1023 USS O'BRIEN was alongside to port transferring Officer Messenger Mail.

1034 USS YORKTOWN designated guide.

1045 Sounded flight quarters.

1112-1135 USS GARRARD was along the starboard side amidships to return the landing force of US Marine Corp personnel who took part in the initial occupation of Yokosuka Naval Base. They had departed the INDEPENDENCE on 19 August to participate in the rapid deployment. Transfer of the 46 Marines was carried out utilizing a cargo net and crane.

1116 Completed launching 4 F6Fs and 3 TBMs.

1250 Completed recovering 4 F6Fs and 3 TBMs launched at 0848.

1350 Completed launching 4 F6Fs and 3 TBMs.

1355 Secured from flight quarters.

1433 USS TOPEKA was designated guide.

1530 Sounded flight quarters.

1602 Completed recovering 4 F6Fs and 3 TBMs launched at 1116.

1735-1740 Recovered 4 F6Fs and 3 TBMs launched at 1350.

1750 Changed course to 190°T, speed 10 knots.

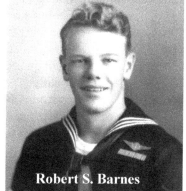

Robert S. Barnes

RC   *MacArthur enters Tokyo and raises American flag.*   *RC*

DL   *The second great thing to happen on Independence took place Saturday evening, 8 September. We turned all the lights on!*

> *Our OD had recorded it carefully:*
> *"Time zone –9*
> *"18-20*   (Author's note: 18-20 refers to the time period - 1800 thru 2000 - for the Deck Log entries)
> *"Steaming as before.*
> *"1806 Lighted all navigation lights on order of OTC, and did not darken ship. This is the first time since the U.S.S. Independence was commissioned that she has burned navigation lights and has not darkened ship under way."*

As if by magic, the flightdeck was suddenly populated by dozens, and a few minutes later by hundreds, of men not at all accustomed to life topside. They swarmed seemingly from the deepest innards of the hull. Some actually blinked at the dying daylight. I knew nobody in the crowd nor did any other AOM. We were astonished, until Bill I think, recognized that they spent their entire shipboard existence below decks--most often below the waterline. Not once had any white light been snapped on while the ship was at sea. The illumination had transformed the existence of everyone—none more so than these denizens of the deep. But I think everyone felt a little nervous until slowly, one by one, warships in the distance lit their own lights. It was a lovely panorama but it took awhile to begin enjoying it.   *DL*

Sunday 9 September 1945

0410 Steaming as before. Sounded flight quarters.

0505 The Task Group began fueling operations. USS TALUGA assumed guide.

0512 Completed launching 4 F6Fs.

0704-0716 USS LOWRY was alongside the starboard quarter. Pilots were transferred onboard for transport to the CVE USS MUNDA to ferry aircraft back. At 0800 they sounded flight quarters.

0905 Completed recovering 4 F6Fs launched at 0512, and landed onboard 1 torpedo plane from the USS YORKTOWN.

0920-0927 USS NORMAN SCOTT was alongside the port quarter to take onboard this ship two patients for emergency treatment.

0936 USS COLLETT came alongside the port quarter to transfer mail and materials and an officer for temporary duty. At 0937 the ship secured from flight quarters.

1000 USS COLLETT cast off.

1031-1041 USS NORMAN SCOTT was alongside the port quarter to receive back the two patients transferred aboard for medical treatment, and a medical officer from the NORMAN SCOTT who came aboard for consultation.

1053 Launched the torpedo plane that landed at 0905 for return to the YORKTOWN. They also launched 2 TBMs for transfer to the USS BON HOMME RICHARD.

1054 Secured from flight quarters. Air Department set to condition 14.

1116 Maneuvered along the port side of the tanker USS CIMARRON. Changed speed to 8 Knots.

1132 USS LOWRY came alongside the port quarter for the transfer of four officers aboard this vessel.

1315 Sounded flight quarters.

1320 Cast off from the USS CIMARRON having received 317,750 gallons of fuel oil, 67,300 gallons of aviation gasoline, and transferring to the CIMARRON mail and four officers to return to the US for release from active duty.

1328-1338 USS LOWRY was back alongside for the return of two ferry pilots to this ship.

1348 Changed speed to 17 knots.

1358 Recovered onboard 2 replacement TBMs.

1359 Commenced maneuvering to make an approach on the USS ALCYONE, taking a standby position 1,000 yards astern the SHANGRI LA and the ALCYONE.

1430 Secured from flight quarters. Air Department set to condition 14.

1446 Came along the port side of the USS ALCYONE.

1455-1518 USS SAMUEL N. MOORE was alongside to deliver freight and aviation gear.

1630 USS NORMAN SCOTT came alongside to deliver lube oil.

1640 Cast off from USS ALCYONE.

1641 USS NORMAN SCOTT cast off.

1714 Regained station in the formation, disposition 4R, USS TOPEKA guide.

2201 Changed course to 005°T, speed 13 knots.

RC Still patrolling, new point system comes out. We got word we're entering Tokyo Bay on the 16th. RC

Monday 10 September 1945   *Patrolling*

0457 Steaming with Task Unit 38.1.1. Completed launching 4 F6Fs and 3 TBMs.

0504 Secured from flight quarters. Air Department set to condition 13.

0517 Regained position in disposition 5R, guide USS TOPEKA, course 050°T, 10 knots.

0529-0611 USS NORMAN SCOTT was along the starboard side to receive 12 officers and enlisted men for further transfer on a temporary assignment, and take on 10,490 gallons of fuel oil.

0750 Sounded flight quarters.

0820 Completed launching 12 F6Fs and 3 TBMs.

0851 Completed recovering 4 F6Fs and 3 TBMs launched at 0457.

0907 Secured from flight quarters. Air Department set to condition 13.

1045 Sounded flight quarters.

1047-1053 USS CHEVALIER was alongside the port quarter to receive mail.

1059-1108 USS HEERMANN was alongside the port quarter to transfer a passenger to our ship.

1145 Completed launching 4 F6Fs and 3 TBMs.

1159-1216 USS MYLES C. FOX was alongside the port quarter to transfer mail.

1228 Completed recovering 12 F6Fs and 3 TBMs launched at 0820.

1331 Completed launching 4 F6Fs and 3 TBMs.

1350 Secured from flight quarters.

1518 Sounded flight quarters.

1550 Completed recovering 4 F6Fs and 3 TBMs launched at 1145.

1608 Secured from flight quarters.

1700 Sounded flight quarters.

1722-1727 Recovered 4 F6Fs and 3 TBMs launched at 1331.

1735 USS BON HOMME RICHARD with a screen of 3 destroyers departed the formation to proceed to its night flying station.

2132 Changed course to 280°T.

Tuesday 11 September 1945   *Off Tokyo, Patrolling*

Steaming as before. Today INDEPENDENCE patrolled in company with Task Group 38.1. The Air group and deck crews got a rest, with no flight operations.

Wednesday 12 September 1945   *Off Tokyo, Patrolling.*

Steaming with (TG 38.1) BON HOMME RICHARD, COWPENS, SHANGRI LA and YORKTOWN.

0503 Completed launching 4 F6Fs and 3 TBMs.

0509 Secured from flight quarters.

0536-0617 USS TAUSSIG was alongside the starboard side receiving 15,250 gallons of fuel oil.

0720 Sounded flight quarters.

0759 Completed recovering 4 F6Fs and 3 TBMs launched at 0503.

0826 Secured from flight quarters.

0910-0922 USS BARTON was alongside the port quarter to exchange US Mail and deliver OM Mail.

1231 Sounded flight quarters.

1303-1305 Launched 4 F6Fs.

1325-1332 Launched 8 F6Fs and 3 TBMs.

1338 Secured from flight quarters.

1605-1625 USS NORMAN SCOTT was along the port side to transfer officers and enlisted men back onboard from a temporary assignment on 10 September.

1649 Sounded flight quarters.

1726 Completed recovering 4 F6Fs launched at 1305, and 8 F6Fs and 3 TBMs launched at 1332.

1806 Secured from flight quarters. Air Department set to condition 14.

2230 Changed course to 270°T.

Thursday 13 September 1945   *Off Tokyo, Patrolling*

Steaming on patrol off Tokyo

0410 Sounded flight quarters.

0458-0502 Launched 4 F6Fs and 3 TBMs for a reconnaissance flight over Tokyo.

0515 Secured from flight quarters.

0530-0607 USS FRANKS was alongside starboard amidships to take on 12,018 gallons of fuel oil and receive personnel transferred for further duty.

0815 Sounded flight quarters.

0915-0925 Launched 12 F6Fs and 4 TBMs.

0931-0936 Recovered 4 F6Fs and 3 TBMs launched at 0502.

0949 Secured from flight quarters.

1214 Sounded flight quarters.

1344 Completed recovering 12 F6Fs and 4 TBMs launched at 0925.

1519-1524 USS DORTCH was alongside the starboard quarter to receive guard mail.

1602 USS YORKTOWN assumed guide.

1727 USS OAKLAND designated guide, course 270°T, bearing 324°T, 2,500 yards.

2059 Changed course to 205°T.

Friday 14 September 1945   *Off Tokyo, Patrolling*

Steaming as before.

0441 Commenced maneuvering to assigned station in a fueling disposition, gaining station at 0456. USS PLATTE designated as guide.

0610 Commenced maneuvering to come alongside fleet oiler USS PLATTE, arriving alongside to the starboard to take on fuel at 0643.

0822 Cast off from USS PLATTE having taken on 155,600 gallons of fuel oil and 22,500 gallons of aviation gasoline. In addition, we transferred 7 enlisted men to the tanker for transportation to a US Naval Hospital on the continent.

0825 Commenced maneuvering to regain position in disposition 5R.

0840-0849 USS LOWRY was alongside the port quarter to receive a pilot onboard for transport to ferry a F6F back.

0905-0914 USS NORMAN SCOTT was alongside the port quarter to receive clothing from this ship.

0920 Sounded flight quarters.

0926 USS COTTEN came alongside the port quarter to transfer OM Mail.

0931 Launched 1 flyable F6F dud to be flown to the USS BON HOMME RICHARD.

0942 USS COTTEN cast off.

0943 USS OAKLAND designated guide.

1100 Sounded flight quarters.

1128-1135 USS ALLEN M. SUMNER was alongside the port quarter to receive US Mail.

1159 Completed launching 8 F6Fs and 4 TBMs.

1211 Recovered 1 F6F replacement.

1213 Secured from flight quarters.

1218-1225 USS LOWRY was alongside the port quarter to return a pilot (who ferried over the dud F6F from the BON HOMME RICHARD).

1231 USS YORKTOWN designated guide.

1238 Maneuvered to gain station in special formation 5G, arriving on station at 1250.

1300-1500 Conducted scheduled gunnery exercises.

1508 Regained station in disposition 5R.

1530 Sounded flight quarters.

1540 USS OAKLAND designated guide.

1553 Completed recovering 8 F6Fs and 4 TBMs launched at 1159.

1626 Secured from flight quarters.

1924 Changed course to 000°T.

Saturday 15 September 1945   *Off Tokyo, Patrolling*

0410 Steaming as before. Sounded flight quarters.

0458 Completed launching 4 F6Fs and 3 TBMs.

0922 Completed launching 12 F6Fs and 4 TBMs.

0938 Completed recovering 4 F6Fs and 3 TBMs launched at 0458.

0943 Secured from flight quarters.

1131-1133 USS HEERMANN was alongside the port quarter to deliver guard mail.

1215 Sounded flight quarters.

1317 Completed launching 8 F6Fs.

1326 Forward gyro out of commission.

1331 Forward gyro returned to operational condition.

1335 Completed recovering 12 F6Fs and 4 TBMs launched at 0922.

1353 Secured from flight quarters.

1405 Held quarters for muster on the flight deck, for the presentation of awards.

1441 Forward gyro again out of commission.

1522 Forward gyro restored to operational condition.

1607-1648 USS FRANKS was alongside the port quarter to transfer mail and return officers that had completed temporary duty.

1721 Completed recovering 8 F6Fs launched at 1317.

2318 Changed course to 240°T.

Photo from: Lt. Cdr. John Cyrille Vermeren

34
Dropped Anchor in Tokyo Bay

Sunday 16 September 1945   *Entered Tokyo Bay*

Steaming as before in company with Task Unit 38.1.1.

0430 Changed course to 300°T, speed 15 knots.

0500 Sighted land bearing 020°T, 20 miles.

0509 Changed course to 0320°T.

0525 USS YORKTOWN assumed guide.

0536 Task Unit 38.1.1 departed Task Group 38.1 to proceed independently to enter Tokyo Bay.

0545 Commenced maneuvering to gain station No.4 in column 6,000 yards astern USS YORKTOWN, course 310°T, 15 knots.

0645 Sighted Suno Saki light bearing 060°T, 20,000 yards.

0655 Entered the Inland waters, and commenced maneuvering entering into port.

0720 Commenced maneuvering conforming to the Sugami Channel while proceeding to Tokyo Bay.

0837 Entered Tokyo Bay and maneuvered to anchorage.

0920 Anchored in area "F", berth No.74, Tokyo Bay, Japan in 15.5 fathoms of water with 105 fathoms of chain to the port anchor, on a mud bottom.

0921 All engines stopped.

0928 Secured main engines.

0930 Set port watch.

1125 Lieutenant M.H. Planck departed the ship proceeding to the USS PIEDMONT with $5,000 of ship's funds to exchange for Japanese currency. Lt. Planck returned onboard at 1340 with 75,000 yen.

RC   Entered Tokyo Bay this morning about 0800, weather cloudy and pretty cool. As the fleet enters single file all hands from all ships are on topside in whites. Few Jap ships can be seen on our way in, some have been bombed and are still afloat while others that have been sunk and nothing but the mast can be seen above the water. There are few Jap fishing boats out here paddling around. We dropped the anchor at 0900, the first time to be stopped in 78 days, this is the longest we have been underway at one time. Many battles have been fought, many ships have been hit and several sunk and many lives have been lost to get here and the Japs haven't got enough fighting ships left to even give one group of the fast moving, hard hitting third fleet a battle. It has been a great show and take it from me all hands are glad to know its over for our victories have been costly. **RC**

AD *Tokyo Bay. Anchored 0920. We are anchored directly off of Yokohama. The fleet plus all kinds of Aux. ships and landing ships are also here. Coming through the bay we passed several Jap fishing craft. Guess we gave them a show alright.* **AD**

DL *The third thing that happened—astonishing, stunning, unbelievable—was the sudden coming apart of our personnel. A new "Point System" was the trigger. This brainstorm act was first intended to bring older men with lots of combat experience home from the wars in Europe. But Europe was only one part of the war, so its effectiveness immediately rolled over to include men in the Pacific— many of whom had been fighting longer than those in Europe.*

The greatest mad scramble for "points" began throughout the ship. Men who had trouble adding half a dozen numbers became experts at summing up their points. Married men with children seemed to have the largest advantage; combat added a few more points. I had my own number, and I was sure they'd get me out soon. But many left the ship long before I did. It was painful to watch. There was no formality. One day they were here, the next day they were gone. Travel arrangements were hurriedly set up. Any bottom headed for the States—battleship, tin can, cruiser, stores vessel-- would do. With no time to be lost, deep friends were often ignored in the confusion. Many officers occupied the same boat. We ordnancemen were deprived of LCDR Harry (which we regretted) and lost the hovering menace of Porky Pig, lieutenant junior grade. They simply disappeared without a word. All men became strangers. They suddenly bore looks in their eyes of homes and girlfriends, of kids and wives and a life so different than the one they'd been committed to.

I lost Rebel—gone one day and never heard from again; I hope he remembered Yankee Labudde. Gone too was Windy, but not lost forever. We had time in '87 and '89 to compare notes. And there was Phil, of course. How would he have handled what our ship went through after he was removed from her? And Dan? There were others. Only a couple more have emerged from obscurity, handsome Bobbie not included.

Comparing two pictures shows the contrast. A January 1945 photo was taken eastbound en route to Pearl from Ulithi. We were about to give up our claim as the only night carrier in the fleet. This photo shows the ordnance group at almost full strength. Well over fifty men.

The final picture was taken in Yokohama Bay on 16 September 1945. It shows such a woeful diminution in ordnancemen that we have been instructed to share the stage with the aviation torpedomen. They had been our friendly competitors, a much smaller group.

But they too have lost men to "Points". Porky and LCDR Harry have vanished. The only ordnance CPO is a grinning B.C. Tom, Bill, Bob, and Nose are still there, as are Abie and M.U. who once considered beating hell out of me because I once objected to his unwillingness to make up his mind. (He could have, too.) I am perched to the right, a somewhat bitter smile on my face at having to wear a third class stripe on my undress whites. Stores was never able to come up with a suitable second class badge.

Incidentally, at the moment the photographer shot this exposure, handsome battleship Wisconsin slid slowly and majestically by three hundred yards to port. I took a lot of ribbing about that coincidence.

This was the last formal portrait of what was left of our group. I would not see many of these men again for forty years*. Most of them disappeared from my life. I see their faces, hear their voices. They speak from a well of memory. (* Don would encounter them at a newly formed CVL-22 Reunion Group)

A few of us rode the ship's whaleboat on a liberty tour into wrecked, abandoned Yokohama. I had no eager curiosity to do this, but I went. I walked with someone a few hundred yards, and then we separated. He felt I was taking too much time just looking around.

Chapter 34   733

Nothing in my life had stunned me as did the sight of this ravaged landscape—and I had helped make it so. I was awestruck. The waterfront purposely was not too badly damaged, but within another hundred yards everything was leveled. I saw what our bombs and the Air Force's bombs had done. It was flat. U.S. bulldozers had carved a passageway through the debris, but otherwise there was nothing to see except an endless swath of congealed junk. Debris, burned and still smoking, had been left rotting in a field waiting for someone to shovel it out of sight.

I wandered down a rude pathway, looking around, sniffing the air, looking skyward, trying, I suppose, to imagine what it must have been like to have this enormous area in flames all around you.

Well, some people had survived. I had just decided to give up and go back to the ship when I was accosted by what I took to be a family, led by a determined old woman. (Old? How could I tell?) Two or three little children were at her feet. One owned a brave smile that forced me to smile in return. The other two were bashful and reluctant to show their faces to this creature from another world. By the woman's side was an old man. But again, how old? He was crippled, hanging onto a cane, but his age could have been no more than ten years greater than mine. I discovered that I didn't trust him. He was kamikaze pilot age and didn't deserve trust.

The lady examined my face closely. She saw what was there and apparently approved. She reached out a hand and offered me a wrapped, folded scroll and before I could walk away she uncovered it. It was a rather striking Japanese woman in a kimono, pretty enough but no Betty Grable. She whispered a price and I bought the thing and folded it in my arm picking through the seventy yen the ships' disbursing officer had issued to us. I didn't (and don't) know how much I paid for it in American. What I could not bear was the gesture of welcome, the obsequious thanks, the folded hands, the effort to prompt her children to duplicate her gratitude. I felt victor's guilt. I had helped ruin her city and here she was, trying to thank me for it.

Back on the ship, I stuffed the object into my sea bag, and later procured another bag and placed it in there, rolled and barely covered. A gift for my mother if it survived the long trip home.
DL

Monday 17 September 1945   *Anchored in Tokyo Bay*

Anchored as before in berth Fox 74, Tokyo Bay, Japan. Various units of the United States, British Pacific Fleet, the Imperial Japanese Navy and various harbor craft are present.
0800-0820 Mustered the crew at quarters.
During the day a number of officers and enlisted men were rotated on and off from shore, assigned temporary duty as Shore Patrol. Liberty parties would also go ashore on Japanese soil.
1120 Forty one Enlisted men from the USS WEST VIRGINIA reported onboard for duty.

Tuesday 18 September 1945   *Anchored in Tokyo Bay*

0300 Anchored as before. The barometer is falling steadily and the wind is blowing at 30 knots. Preparations are being made to secure the vessel for typhoon weather.
0130 A LCM that was transporting stores was damaged by sea water.
0225-0330 Lighted fires under No.3 boiler and cut it into the main steam line.
0400 Commenced turning over all main engines 20 rpm ahead. Set the underway sea watch. Gunnery Department set condition 2 lookouts.
0526 LCM 15-15 had been secured to the fantail with one wire and two manila lines. No personnel were aboard and it drifted away northward.
0620 Veered port anchor chain to 125 fathoms.
0702 Let go the starboard anchor with 20 fathoms of chain to hold steady and prevent excessive yawing. The wind was picking up, gusting to 55 knots and heavy swells developed.
0800 Mustered crew on stations.
1240 Heaved in the starboard anchor.
1310 Heaved in the port anchor to 105 fathoms of chain at waters edge, and let go the starboard anchor with 20 fathoms of chain.

1330 All engines stopped. The wind decreased to 33 knots and the swells subsided slightly. At 1600 they secured the underway bridge watch and lookouts.

1615 With the wind velocity decreasing, main control was authorized to secure the rudder amidships.

1740 Heaved in and secured the starboard anchor, secured No.3 boiler, and unrigged the palisades on the flight deck.

Thirteen officers departed the ship for transportation to the United States on the USS TICONDEROGA.

Wednesday 19 September 1945   *Anchored in Tokyo Bay*

0800 Anchored as before. Held quarters for muster.

0925-1026 LCI 376 was alongside our starboard quarter to embark personnel. 137 enlisted men departed the USS INDEPENDENCE for transportation to the United States.

1610-1714 LCT 642 was tied up to our starboard side forward to unload supplies.

During the day a number of officers and enlisted men were rotated on and off from shore, assigned temporary duty as Shore Patrol. Liberty parties went ashore.

Thursday 20 September 1945   *Anchored in Tokyo Bay*

Anchored as before in berth Fox 74, Tokyo Bay, Japan. The regular in port watch is set. Officers and enlisted men were rotated on and off from shore, assigned temporary duty as Shore Patrol. Liberty parties went ashore.

At 1410 Lieutenant M.H. Planck departed the ship proceeding to the USS PIEDMONT with 10,560 yen to exchange for US currency.

1455-1705 LCT 525 was along our starboard side unloading fresh supplies and provisions.

1910-2250 LCT 705 unloaded stores along our starboard side.

RC   *Anchored in Tokyo Bay. Went ashore the 20th in Yokosuka, Japan. The Jap people well know we are the victors and step aside for you. Many buildings have been hit by bombs, some are in ashes while parts of some are still standing. Few stores were open such as they were, I saw no food stores and few fish markets. One day is enough to go ashore over there.   RC*

Friday 21 September 1945   *Anchored in Tokyo Bay, a helicopter lands*

Anchored as before. The regular in port watch is set. The port gangway is rigged in. Officers and enlisted men were rotated on and off from shore, assigned temporary duty as Shore Patrol. Liberty parties went ashore.

21 September 1945 - The first documented landing of a helicopter on the USS INDEPENDENCE flight deck.

0942 A helicopter (No. 345343 from Aircraft Repair Unit No.6) landed on the forward end of the flight deck, departing at 1005. This was the first documented landing of a helicopter on the INDEPENDENCE.
1252-1430 A trash lighter was alongside our port quarter.
1610 USS COWPENS and USS YORKTOWN shifted berths.

AD   Tokyo Bay. Went on liberty today. Went to Yokohama and then thumbed to Tokyo. Everything is pretty badly bombed. While in Tokyo I saw the Radio Tokyo building, Imperial Hotel where MacArthur is, and several other places of interest. The Japs were very friendly towards us. I took the train back to Yokohama, did some bartering, and then came back to the ship.   AD

RC   Supposed to get underway today for Saipan but orders were changed till tomorrow. Got word we would be in some west coast port for Navy Day.   RC

Saturday 22 September 1945   *Departed Tokyo Bay to proceed to Saipan*

Anchored as before in berth Fox 74, Tokyo Bay, Japan. The regular in port watch is set.
0222 Lighted fires under No.2 boiler, cutting it in to the main steam line at 0400.
0400 Made all preparations for getting underway.
0417-0440 LCT 1007 was alongside the starboard quarter delivering freight.
0446 Turned over main engines by steam.
0510 All Departments reported they were ready to get underway.
0532 Got underway as Task Unit 58.1.7, proceeding to Saipan, Mariana Islands. They steamed out of Tokyo Bay, in compliance with orders from CTG 58.1 dated 21 September 1945.
0600 USS ALLEN M. SUMNER joined the INDEPENDENCE as a screen.
0624 Abeam Kannon Saki Light, they proceeded south at 16 knots.
0800 Mustered crew on stations, changing course to 140°T at 0805.
1705 Changed course to 158°T.

Sunday 23 September 1945   *At sea, steaming to Saipan*

Steaming as before as Task Unit 58.1.7 with USS ALLEN M. SUMNER.
1231 Sounded flight quarters.
1321-1325 Launched 8 F6Fs "for routine flight".
1433-1438 Recovered the 8 F6Fs launched at 1325.
1442 Secured from flight quarters.

Monday 24 September 1945   *At sea, steaming to Saipan*

Steaming as before. USS ALLEN M. SUMNER is operating independently ahead.
0800 Held quarters for muster. Then, Captain Kindell held meritorious mast for the presentation of decorations to the officers of Air Group CVLG 27.
0942 USS ALLEN M. SUMNER picked up a "doubtful" sound contact off the port beam and proceeded to investigate. At 1002 it was classified as a non-submarine.
1031-1042 USS ALLEN M. SUMNER was alongside to exchange motion pictures, then took station 2,500 yards ahead of this vessel.
1200 Sounded flight quarters.
1258-1303 Launched 2 F6Fs for delivery to Saipan in preparation for the exchange of Air Groups.
1324 Secured from flight quarters.
1715 Sighted Farallon De Pajaros Islands, bearing 090°T, 45 miles.
2235 Sighted USS KALININ BAY bearing 135°T, 9 miles.
2250 Passed USS KALININ BAY astern.

Tuesday 25 September 1945   *Let go the port anchor at Saipan*
                    Air Group CVL-27 departs, Air Group CVLG-21 reports aboard

0800 Steaming as before. Mustered crew on stations, and sounded flight quarters.
0855-0907 Launched 1 F6F and 7 TBMs for delivery to Saipan. USS ALLEN M. SUMNER has assumed station 2.5000 as plane guard.
0955 Commenced recovering aircraft.
1000 On a course of 135°T, sighted Saipan Island, bearing 167°T, 53 miles.
1016 Recovered 16 replacement F6Fs flown onboard from Saipan, changed course to 167°T.
1120 Sighted Tinian Island, bearing 180°T, 23 miles.
1223 USS ALLEN M. SUMNER proceeded independently to anchorage.
1230 Sounded quarters for entering into port.
1259 Dropped port anchor between berths L-30 and L-31, Garapan Anchorage, Saipan, in 15 fathoms of water, sand and coral bottom, with 75 fathoms of chain.
1325 LCM 162 reported for duty.
1347 Barge No.B-30 was tied up to our starboard side to transfer un-flyable aircraft off the ship.
1410 A Shore Patrol party left the ship.
1415 Our new Air Group, CVLG 21, reported aboard for duty.
1420 Officers and enlisted men of Air Group CVLG 27 were detached. The Officers proceeded to the "Flight Personnel Rehabilitation Camp" on Guam.
1550 Barge No.B-30 cast off with 2 F6Fs.

AD   Saipan. Arrived at 1300. Saipan certainly looks different than it did one year ago. They have it pretty well built up now. We are sending our old squadron CVL-27 off and taking on CVL-21.   AD

Wednesday 26 September 1945   *Anchored at Saipan*

Anchored as before. Port gangway is rigged in. As in Tokyo Bay, they sent Shore Patrol and liberty parties to the beach.
0800-1400 YO-116 was along our port side pumping to us 129,780 gallons of fuel oil.
1421-1543 YO-109 was along our port side to deliver 1,500 gallons of aviation gasoline.
1750-1840 LCM-156 was along the starboard side to deliver stores aboard.

Thursday 27 September 1945   *Anchored at Saipan*

Anchored as before. The in port watch is set.
0930 Lieutenant M.H. Planck departed the ship proceeding to the Fleet Disbursing Center with 8,430 yen to be exchanged for US currency. He returned at 1220 with the same amount of yen and $300,000 in US currency. INDEPENDENCE sent Shore Patrol and liberty parties to the beach.

AD Saipan. We are supposed to be in a west coast port for Oct. 27. That is really good news.   AD

Friday 28 September 1945   *Anchored at Saipan*

Anchored as before. The in-port watch is set.
0840 Fifty two enlisted men from Air Group Twenty Seven reported back onboard for duty. The men had departed two days ago and though the reason is unknown, it would appear that a decision was made that the USS INDEPENDENCE would be the best available method to return them to the US mainland.
1050 Rigged the starboard gangway due to the sea rising above the gangway platform.
1105 Sounded fire quarters due to a fire in the bake shop. No damage to the ship occurred.

1124 Secured from fire quarters.

AD   Saipan. Went on liberty at Fleet Recreation on the island. Had 4 beers, 2 cokes and also went swimming.   AD

RC   At anchor. Went ashore today on Saipan, was ashore here just one year ago. It has changed plenty in the past year. There are still a few Japs left in the hills that haven't surrendered.   RC

Saturday 29 September 1945   *Anchored at Saipan*

Anchored as before.

Sunday 30 September 1945   *Saipan*

0620 Anchored as before. Turned over the main engines by steam.
0630 Made all preparations for getting underway.
0657 Got underway, departing the anchorage, maneuvering seaward.
0713 Sounded flight quarters.
0720 USS ALLEN M. SUMNER joined us as our screen.
0800 Mustered crew on stations.
0809 Completed launching 8 F6Fs.
1016 Completed launching 8 F6Fs.
1049 Completed recovery of 8 F6Fs launched at 0809.
1102 Secured from flight quarters. The 8 F6Fs launched at 1016 landed on Saipan at 1110, due to deteriorating weather conditions.
1302 Manned all special sea and anchor details.
1323 USS ALLEN M. SUMNER departed to return to anchorage independently.
1327 Maneuvered toward the anchorage, dropping anchor between berths L-30 and L-31 at Garapan Anchorage, Saipan.

RC   Underway at 0700 to give squadron some practice landings. Anchored at 1344.   RC

Monday 1 October 1945   *Saipan*

0655 Completed making preparations for getting underway as TU 58.1.12.
0707 Underway, departing the anchorage, maneuvering seaward for air group training.
0758-0805 Launched 12 F6Fs.
0840 Completed recovery of the 8 F6Fs that diverted to Saipan yesterday due to weather.
0918 Recovered 1 F6F launched at 0805.
1003 Completed launching 12 F6Fs.
1008 Commenced recovery of aircraft launched at 0805. Lt. L.B. Norris hit the No.1 barricade while landing, with minimal damage, no injuries, and the F6F still in operational condition.
1040 Recovered the remainder of the F6Fs launched at 0805.
1158-1207 Launched 12 F6Fs.
1400 Completed recovery of 12 F6Fs launched at 1207.
1430 Secured from flight quarters.
1435 USS ALLEN M. SUMNER departed to return to anchorage independently.
1438 Commenced maneuvering toward our anchorage.
1453 Anchored between berths L-30 and L-31 at Garapan Anchorage, Saipan, with 75 fathoms of chain in 15 fathoms of water.
1456 Secured main engines.
1615 Let out 20 fathoms more chain to the port anchor.
1930 The barometer was falling, the winds now between 30 to 35 knots with heavy rain. They set a watch on the open bridge.

Tuesday 2 October 1945   *Saipan*

0400 Anchored as before. They began lighting off boilers and cutting them into the main steam line.
0615 Turned over the main engines by steam.
0630 Made all preparations for getting underway.
0656 With anchor lifted, and screws in motion, INDEPENDENCE proceeded seaward.
0710 Sounded flight quarters.
0713 Secured the special sea details and set the underway watch.
0713 USS ALLEN M. SUMNER joined up as a screen.
0810 Completed launching 16 F6Fs.
0910 Completed launching 16 F6Fs.
1024 Commenced recovery of aircraft launched at 0810.
1029 Again today, Lt. L.B. Norris was to prove his skill at getting successfully into the air, but seemed to be encountering difficulty mastering the fine art of landing. His F6F careened off to port and went over the side, getting caught in antenna booms and wires. Two antenna booms were bent, along with damage to the catwalk and hand-railing. The Hellcat, already dangling over the side, was jettisoned. Lt. Norris was admitted to sickbay for treatment of a fractured left hand. Stopped all engines and maneuvered to port.
1136 Completed recovery of 22 F6Fs, with 1 jettisoned, and
9 remaining F6Fs sent to land on Saipan.
1156 Secured from flight quarters.
1345 Commenced maneuvering as they proceeded to anchorage.
1408 Anchored between berths L-30 and L-31 at Garapan Anchorage,
Saipan. Let fires die out under No.1 & 2 boilers,
with No.2 boiler taken out of service for minor repairs.

Wednesday 3 October 1945   *Saipan*

0630 Anchored as before. Made all preparations for getting underway.
0656 Got underway, departing the anchorage, maneuvering seaward.
0757-0808 Launched 13 F6Fs.
0829 Recovered 1 F6F launched at 0808.
0830 Launched 1 F6F.
0835 Recovered 1 F6F launched at 0830.
0838 Launched 1 F6F.

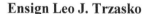

Ensign Leo J. Trzasko

0908 Ensign Leo J. Trzasko crashed through the barricade, tearing out two barrier cables, and over turned near the island. The Hellcat nosed up, a gas tank ruptured and the fuel ignited. A small fire occurred on the side of the forward elevator near the island, and some burning fuel streamed down the elevator well down into the elevator pit. Within 2 minutes of the accident the fire was reported under control, with slight fire damage to the flight deck, hangar deck and some paint burned. Ensign Trzasko was admitted to sickbay with second degree burns to his face, hands and legs.
0956 The damaged Hellcat (Bu.No.79487) was jettisoned over the starboard side.   (Photo on page 741)
1006-1047 Recovered 19 F6Fs, 11 that were launched at 0808, 1 F6F launched at 0838 and 7 that were sent to Saipan on the 2nd.
1105 Secured from flight quarters.
1200 Sounded flight quarters.
1228-1235 Launched 12 F6Fs.
1330-1340 Launched 11 F6Fs.
1345-1425 Recovered 2 F6Fs that were sent to Saipan on the 2nd, and 12 F6Fs launched at 1235.
1534-1547 Recovered 11 F6Fs launched at 1340.

Photos courtesy of John Doherty)

3 October 1945 - Ensign Leo Trzasko's F6F. Leo's told his sons (Tom & Peter) after the war that the tail hook broke on landing, causing the barricade incident.
Other photos clearly show the missing hook.

1612 Secured from flight quarters.
1628 Maneuvered to enter Saipan Harbor proceeding toward our anchorage.
1721 Anchored between berths L-31 and L-35, Garapan Anchorage, Saipan.
1730 Secured main engines.

Thursday 4 October 1945   *Saipan, taking departure*

Anchored as before.
0842-1225 Yard oiler YO-116 was secured to our port side delivering 141,380 gallons of fuel oil.
1155-1234 A barge along the starboard side picked up a F6F for transfer to CASU 47, Saipan.
Today INDEPENDENCE received aboard 87 passengers for transportation to the nearest Naval Hospital in the rear. Additionally, 258 men reported aboard INDEPENDENCE for transportation to a Receiving Station in the United States for further processing.
1440 LCM-109 delivered aboard the body of VF-94 pilot Lt. R.C. McAbu for "emergency treatment". The examination by a medical officer found Lt. McAbu to be cyanotic and without a pulse.
1600 Commenced making preparations for getting underway.
1607 A picket boat cast off taking the body of Lt. R.C. McAbu.
1618 Commenced heaving short on the port anchor.
1718 Got underway, departing Garapan Anchorage, Saipan seaward.
1730 Took departure of Garapan Harbor, Saipan. Steadied on course 225°T at 12 knots.

AD   Saipan. Picked up passengers for the States. Underway to Guam.   AD

Friday 5 October 1945   *At sea, underway to Guam, underway to the United States*

Steaming in company with USS ALLEN M. SUMNER as Task Unit 58.1.12 en route to Guam.
0200 Sighted Guam on the horizon, distance 25 miles, bearing 165°T.
0310 Changed course to 235°T, changing course again at 0601 to 055°T.
0631 Commenced maneuvering to conform to the movements of the USS BON HOMME RICHARD outside the Apra Harbor, Guam. The wind had picked up and the BON HOMME RICHARD had broken loose from her mooring overnight. Due to weather they would remain outside the harbor with the BON HOMME RICHARD and dispatched the ALLEN M. SUMNER into Apra Harbor to pick up passengers, mail and freight for transportation to the US.
0702 Reported for duty to USS BON HOMME RICHARD forming Task Unit 58.1.11.
1550 Commenced maneuvering to form up in column 1,500 yards astern of USS BON HOMME RICHARD (guide and OTC).

RC   Supposed to tie up at Guam this morning but sea was rough. Destroyer went in and picked up our mail and a few passengers, and we headed north this evening to meet the rest of our group. Carrier Bon Homme Richard joins up with us.   RC

Saturday 6 October 1945   *At sea, underway*

Steaming in company with USS BON HOMME RICHARD and destroyers USS ALLEN M. SUMNER, USS ROBERT K. HUNTINGTON and USS MOALE, on coarse 032°T, 18 knots.
0712 USS ALLEN M. SUMNER came alongside starboard amidships to deliver passengers, luggage and freight. Forty five officers from CVLG-27 (that had departed the ship on September 25th) reported back aboard, picked up at Guam, for transportation to the US mainland. *(Note: Fighting Squadron Twenty Seven would be decommissioned in Seattle, Washington on 26 October, 1945)*
0824-0833 USS ROBERT K. HUNTINGTON was alongside the port quarter delivering guard mail.
0941-1016 Pumped 22,900 gallons of fuel oil to USS ALLEN M. SUMNER. She then cast off.
1055 F2c E.B. Fitzgerald was admitted to sickbay for treatment to sickbay with first degree burns he received on his left side and abdomen from steam while removing a valve from a pipe in the aft fire room.
1704 Changed course to 352°T, speed 18 knots.
2058 Sighted 3 ships bearing 022°T (off our starboard bow), 16.5 miles. They would pass abeam within 9 miles at 2155 of the three AOs.

AD   Underway. We are to rendezvous with a couple of other carriers at Point Frisco which is 100 miles off Tokyo, then proceed to the States.   AD

Sunday 7 October 1945   *At sea, underway*

Steaming as before in Task Unit 58.1.11.

Monday 8 October 1945   *At sea, underway*

Steaming as before in Task Unit 58.1.11.
0730-0837 USS ALLEN M. SUMNER along the starboard side to take on 38,130 gallons of fuel oil.
0900 All engines were stopped as USS BON HOMME RICHARD received small boats from the destroyers.
0930 Sounded quarters for muster, personnel inspection and flight deck parade.
0957 All engines ahead standard.

1022 Secured from personnel inspection.
2220 Ensign John Brown was admitted to sickbay for treatment, with a diagnosis of acute appendicitis.

RC Steaming north, weather getting cooler. RC

Tuesday 9 October 1945   *At sea, underway*

Steaming as before.
0808 Task Unit 58.1.11 dissolved as they rendezvoused with a fueling group, and maneuvered to gain station in the disposition.
0845 Commenced maneuvering to approach tanker USS MERRIMACK, with first line over to the tanker at 0850.
1147 Cast off from the USS MERRIMACK having received 207,120 gallons of fuel oil from the tanker, and pumping 71,500 gallons of aviation gasoline to the tanker. During this period of time USS HEERMANN delivered guard mail.
1148 Commenced maneuvering to take position in disposition 6R, guide USS MERRIMACK.
1211-1249 USS WALKER was along the starboard side delivering freight.
1353 USS SHANGRI LA designated guide. At 1354 Task Group 58.1 completed fueling exercises.
1500 USS OAKLAND designated as guide 3,000 yards off the starboard quarter.

AD At sea - Point Frisco. AD

RC Refueled this morning. We joined up with the carriers Yorktown, Shangri-la, Hancock and the Cowpens, with 3 cruisers and 16 destroyers. At 1445 we headed for the United States, our basic course 080. RC

Wednesday 10 October 1945   *At sea, underway to Portland, Oregon*

Steaming with Task Group 58.1 in company with USS COWPENS, USS HANCOCK, SHANGRI LA, USS YORKTOWN, USS DULUTH, USS OAKLAND, USS TOPEKA and the screen of destroyers. CTF is Vice-Admiral John H. Towers in SHANGRI LA.
1056 Task Group 58.1 has been changed to Task Group 38.1, under the same command.
1245-1250 USS ROBERT K. HUNTINGTON was along side the port quarter to deliver guard mail.

Thursday 11 October 1945   *At sea, underway to Portland, Oregon*

0344 Steaming with Task Group 38.1. Captain Kindell reported hearing four shots in volleys of two outside his cabin, from the direction of the water.
0500 The OTC dispatched two destroyers to search for possible survivors due to the gunshot reports from this ship.
0803 The Task Group commenced topping off destroyers.
0810-0829 USS HUNTINGTON was along the starboard side to transfer 3 passengers to this vessel.
0842-0942 USS DULUTH was along the starboard side to receive 106 passengers for transportation to San Pedro, California.
0945-1009 USS HEERMANN was on the starboard side to transfer 2 patients for medical examination.
1542-1553 USS HEERMANN returned to receive onboard, the two personnel it had transferred at 1009.

Friday 12 October 1945   *At sea, underway to Portland, Oregon*

Steaming with Task Group 38.1.
0230 A small fire had broken out in the aviation tool room, caused by a loose aircraft battery that struck a trash can, igniting the contents. The fire was immediately extinguished.

Chapter 34   743

0323 The forward gyro went out of commission. All repeaters were transferred to the after gyro.
0339 The forward gyro operation was restored. The repeaters were transferred back to the forward gyro.
0822-0847 USS HEERMANN was along the starboard quarter to receive guard mail.

Saturday 13 October 1945 *At sea, underway to Portland, Oregon*

1330-1336 USS NICHOLAS was alongside the port quarter to receive guard mail.

Saturday 13 October 1945 *Crossing the I. D. L. - Repeat the 13th*

0000 Steaming as before. Set all clocks to zone plus 12, making this date the same date as yesterday.
0747 Crossed the 180th meridian from west to east.
1503-1509 USS LOWRY was alongside the port quarter to deliver freight.
1933 A one alarm fire broke out forward of the Chief's quarters on the second deck. They secured from fire quarters 6 minutes later with the fire put out, one mattress destroyed, 3 others mattresses damaged.
2203 USS COWPENS reported a man overboard.
2241 USS COWPENS in company with two destroyers was ordered to conduct a search for the man reported overboard, and rejoin no later than 1200, 14 October.

Sunday 14 October 1945 *At sea, underway to Portland, Oregon*

1015 USS COWPENS rejoined the formation, with negative results searching for the man overboard.
1200-1210 USS FRANKS was along the starboard side to transfer movies.

Monday 15 October 1945 *At sea, underway to Portland, Oregon*

Steaming as before. Today, the CVs topped off destroyers.

Tuesday 16 October 1945 *At sea, underway to Portland, Oregon*

0651-0701 USS HEERMANN was alongside to transfer guard mail.
1004 Changed course to 045°T, forming up in cruising disposition 3R, with USS DULUTH, USS TOPEKA (OTC) and a screen of destroyers as Task Unit 38.1.3. INDEPENDENCE is guide.
1019 Changed course to 083°T, 17.5 knots.

Wednesday 17 October 1945 *At sea, underway to Portland, Oregon*

Steaming as before with Task Unit 38.1.3.
1600 USS DULUTH and 5 destroyers departed the formation to proceed to Seattle. INDEPENDENCE was now in company USS TOPEKA and destroyers USS ALLEN M. SUMNER, USS FRANKS, USS HEERMANN, USS MOALE, USS TAYLOR AND USS WOODWORTH. Commenced forming in column with USS TOPEKA (OTC and guide) on course 091°T, 18 knots.

Thursday 18 October 1945 *At sea, underway to Portland, Oregon*

0100 Steaming in Task Group 38.1.3. Changed course to 096°T, speed is 17 knots. Guide bears 099°T, 1,000 yards.
0906 INDEPENDENCE designated guide due to steering casualty onboard the TOPEKA.
0921 USS TOPEKA assumed guide.

35
Moored in Portland, Oregon
& Operation Magic Carpet

Friday 19 October 1945   *At sea, underway to Portland, Oregon*

0010 Steaming as before. Picked up land on radar, distance 68.3 miles.

0355 Changed course to 085°T.

0405 Sighted Columbia River Lightship, bearing 112°T, 2,400 yards. They commenced maneuvering in column formation with 1,000 yard separation.

0510 Sounded flight quarters.

0557 Stopped all engines.

0616 Pilot boat came along the port side and a US Coast Guard Pilot proceeded to the bridge.

0628 Changed speed to 5 knots and commenced launching aircraft.

0646 Completed launching 12 F6Fs to proceed to NAS Astoria, Oregon.

0649 Secured from flight quarters.

0703 Passed outer bar buoy No.2 abeam to starboard, entering inland waters, maneuvering to conform to the channel.

0759 A pilot boat came along the starboard side dropping off a second USCG pilot. He proceeded to the bridge, replacing the first pilot, who departed the ship.

0808 Passed Astoria No.2 buoy 75 yards abeam to starboard, and continued steaming up the Columbia River toward Portland with the USCG pilot at the conn.

1343 Entered the Willamette River.

1513 Moored starboard side to Terminal 1, Berth No.2, Portland Oregon, assisted by tugs SIMONS and WILLAVIS.

1615 The USCG pilot departed the ship.

1700 Passengers commenced departing the ship, setting foot on US mainland soil, alive, and home from the war.

2030 250 gallons of fresh milk was brought aboard.

DL   We picked up a load of Marines and GI's from various places including Iwo and Saipan and headed east and north. Time was wasting. We made knots. It didn't snow but everyday got colder. Some of these troops had been in the warm Pacific a long time and they damn near froze. Every extra blanket went to them. The big running doors on the hangar were rolled down day and night. The men mostly wanted to sleep but their officers routed them out for exercise on the deck every day.

We sailed the Great Circle route and approached the coast with the bow filled to overflowing with men eager to see the land of home. I was among them. We crossed the bar carefully at Astoria. There were people waving and steam whistles sounding. All along the riverbanks as the Willamette got narrower there were more hordes looking us over, welcoming us home. Bands played, school kids waved flags. After awhile we stopped lamenting that this wasn't San Francisco.

It was raining when we docked. We were the biggest of the ships in the group. There was a cruiser and a couple of cans and a submarine--but everybody seemed to wish to come aboard Independence.

Captain Kindell had given us fair warning about the reception, but it was splendid. The first evening every free sailor escorted girls about the hangar, bringing them topside through the rigging, letting their buddies get views of female anatomy (some of it uncovered) as it made its way up the bulk-heads. Officers blanched, but nobody got hurt and later it paid off in tales told to grandchildren not yet fathered. Portland was great.   DL

RC   Started up the Columbia River this morning about 0600 for Portland. Hundreds of people were standing on the docks of every city or town along the river watching and waving to the warships as they went by. With us are two cruisers and four destroyers. We tied up to the dock at 1515 this afternoon in Portland Oregon. It has been cold, foggy and raining all day long but regardless of the weather, the shores of the USA certainly looks good to us. We have covered about 200,000 miles since leaving Philadelphia March 12, 1943.   RC

AD   Arrived Portland Oregon. We went up the Columbia River then down the Willamette and docked in downtown Portland. It is wonderful to be back in the States.   AD

20 October, 1945 - Portland, Oregon. CVL-22 is being moved to a berth along the harbor wall near the Morrison bridge, after backing thru the draw span of the Burnside bridge under tow.

Saturday 20 October 1945   *Moored in Portland, Oregon*
                                 CVLG-21 Departs

Moored as before, starboard side to Terminal 1, Berth No.2, Portland Oregon.
0830 Mustered crew at quarters.
1021 Commenced jacking over main engines in preparation for getting underway.
1025 Air Group CLVG 21 officers and enlisted men departed, detached from the ship with orders to report to Commander Fleet Air, Seattle, Washington.
1315 Made all preparation for getting underway.
1340 USCG pilot came on board.
1410-1446 Tug boats PORTLAND and JAMES W secured to the bow to assist in shifting berths. Tug MULKEY would also assist.
1508 Cast off all lines and got underway with the USCG pilot at the conn and the captain on the bridge. Steaming with the assistance of 3 tugs; They moored port side to Berth Baker, Terminal 2, at the sea wall at the foot of Pine Street, west side of the Willamette River, Portland Oregon. They were moored in 4.5 fathoms of water, mud bottom.
1638 Secured the main engines.
1706 All tugs cast off and minutes later the USCG pilot departed the ship.
1743 Secured the special sea details and set the regular in port watch.

AD   Portland Oregon. Liberty 1500 to 0730. Went dancing at Jantzen Beach to the music of Louie Armstrong.   AD

Sunday 21 October 1945   *Moored in Portland, Oregon*

Moored as before, port side to Terminal 2, Berth B, Portland Oregon. Receiving fresh water and telephone service from the dock.
1300 Rigged the ship for visitors.
1420 Rear Admiral C.F. Holden came aboard with his party, departing at 1535.
1428 Governor of Oregon Earl Snell came aboard with his party, departing at 1540.
1450 Memorial Services were held on the forward end of the hangar deck.
1700 All visitors left the ship.

RC   10/20-28   Tied up in Portland. The Governor of Oregon and the Mayor of Portland were aboard on the 21st. Thousands of people went through the ship this past week, it was open to visitors each afternoon from 1300 to 1630.   RC

Sunday 28 October 1945   *Moored in Portland, Oregon*

1146 Moored as before. The Russians invaded. Rear Admiral Ramishville, USSRN, Commodore Sedik, USSRN and their wives (accompanied with an interpreter) came onboard, "inspected" the INDEPENDENCE, and departed at 1159. They obviously were not invited to see much, or dine with the captain, with only 13 minutes onboard. The other event of note for the day was a traffic accident on the corner of Everett and N.W. 18th Ave. in Portland where a pair of crumpled front fenders were produced by an INDEPENDENCE "carryall" and a 1941 Pontiac sedan taxi of the Union Cab Co. No injuries.

Monday 29 October 1945   *Departing Portland, Oregon, seaward for San Francisco*
                               Final Flight Quarters

During the stay in Portland, crew changes occurred, with men detached to be discharged, or for reassignment. A number of new replacement crew members reported aboard, and a number of men boarded for transportation to San Francisco.

0040 Moored as before. Admitted to sickbay for treatment of minor shock, F2c E. B. Fitzgerald was outstretched trying to reach for the address of a girl on the dock, when he extended beyond his limit, gravity intervened, and Fitzgerald fell overboard.

0521 Commenced jacking over main engines.

0722 Disconnected from fresh water and telephone services on the dock.

0800 Mustered crew on stations. USS TOPEKA got underway.

0822 Two USCG channel pilots came onboard.

0913 Got underway with the assistance of tugs PORTLAND and HENDERSON.

Commenced maneuvering down the Willamette River to the confluence of the Willamette River and the Columbia River, conforming to the channels.

1000 Tugs PORTLAND and HENDERSON cast off.

1057 Sounded flight quarters.

1119 INDEPENDENCE entered the Columbia River.

1140-1154 Launched 18 F6Fs. Pilots were from VF-21, now detached and assigned to NAS Astoria, Oregon.

1200 Secured from flight quarters.

Flight quarters would never again be sounded aboard USS INDEPENDENCE.

1636 USCG pilot boat came alongside to remove the two river pilots, replaced by a different pilot.

1740 All engines were stopped. At 1744 the remaining river pilot departed and at 1747 with all engines ahead, they proceeded seaward.

1755 INDEPENDENCE entered the Pacific Ocean, taking departure of the Columbia River.

They steamed south on course 187°T, 15.5 knots.

1853 Sighted the Tillamook Light, bearing 097°T, 8.8 miles and at 1902 Cape Meares Light was sighted bearing 157°T, 29 miles.

2013 Observed Yaquina Head Light, passing it abeam to port at 2346, distance 14 miles.

Tuesday 30 October 1945 *At sea, underway to San Francisco, California*

Steaming independently as before, operating in accordance with a dispatch of ComThirdFleet, Admiral William F. Halsey. Boilers No. 2 & 4 in use.

0800 Mustered crew at quarters.

0855 Passed a tanker on the starboard bow, 1,500 yards.

Wednesday 31 October 1945 *At sea, underway to San Francisco, California*

0327 Steaming as before. Changed course to 115°T.

0451 Sighted Farallon Light, bearing 113°T, 26 miles, and Point Reyes Light, bearing 071°T, 23 miles.

0550 Passed Point Reyes Light abeam.

0623 Changed course to 070°T.

0717 Passed San Francisco Lightship abeam to port, 1,500 yards.

0724 Commenced maneuvering as we entered the channel steaming toward San Francisco Bay.

0805 Passed under San Francisco Oakland bay bridge.

0814 Yard tug YTB 396 transferred a bay pilot onboard.

0853 With aid from yard tugs 180 and 396, they moored with the starboard side to the north side of pier No.3, NAS Alameda, California.

0902 Yard tugs cast off from the port side.

0907 Secured main engines.

During the morning, roughly 300 officers and enlisted men in transit disembarked. They also offloaded aviation supplies.

1410 Received stores onboard and 400 gallons of milk from the Carnation Company.

Thursday 1 November 1945   *Steamed from NAS Alameda to Hunters Point*

Moored as before, starboard side to the north side of pier No.3, NAS Alameda, California.
0430 Lighted off No. 4 boiler.
0530 Commenced jacking over main engines. At 0635 they cut No.4 boiler into the main steam line.
0655 Disconnected fresh water supply from the pier.
0715 All departments reported ready for getting underway.
0842 With a harbor pilot on the bridge, and yard tug YT-396 secured to the bow, they proceeded to get underway, maneuvering to clear the berth at NAS Alameda, and steamed to Hunters Point.
1015 Moored with the port side to berth No.3, U.S. Naval Drydocks, Hunters Point, San Francisco with the assistance of yard tugs.
1058 Commenced connecting steam, fresh water, electricity and telephone services from the dock.

Friday 2 November 1945   *Moored at Hunters Point*

Moored as before port side to berth No.3, U.S. Naval Drydocks, Hunters Point, San Francisco. The in port watch is set. INDEPENDENCE would supply men for Shore Patrol, the crew had liberty, and departed for (and return from) leave throughout their stay at Hunters Point. Then, there was a seemingly never-ending supply of work details. Chipping paint, repainting, cleaning, a long list of maintenance.
0800 Sounded quarters for muster.
1030-1105 Lt. Planck went to the Federal Reserve Bank, San Francisco, returning with $20,000.
1335-1338 Fire quarters was held due to a mess cook placing a wet cloth on an electrical panel, the ensuing short circuit causing minor damage.
1520 A lighter (YSR-24) and a floating crane (YD-88) tied up along the starboard side amidships.

AD   San Francisco. We are getting 1,000 bunks on the hangar deck.   AD

Tuesday 13 November 1945   *Moored at Hunters Point - "Operation Magic Carpet"*

Moored as before port side to berth No.3, U.S. Naval Drydocks, Hunters Point, San Francisco.
During the stay at Hunters Point, work was done to perform necessary maintenance to the ship, and prepare the INDEPENDENCE for the next mission, "Operation Magic Carpet". Magic Carpet was the task of bringing the troops home from the Pacific. To fulfill their roll in this assignment, sleeping racks or bunks were welded on the hangar bay deck to receive passengers. The INDEPENDENCE would steam out of San Francisco without an Air Wing. She was now relegated for this mission, to become a troop transport. No glamour in the task on the surface. But what more important roll could she now play in a peacetime Navy to a soldier or sailor waiting for the longed-for return to U.S. soil, to home, family and friends. And daily while in port, before the first Magic Carpet run, new replacements reported for duty, as INDEPENDENCE sailors, now home from the war were departing.
0830 Commenced conducting dock trials to confirm the repairs were correct, systems functional, and the ship was ready for sea.
0850 Secured from dock trials until 1030.
0900 Commenced taking on fresh provisions from the U.S. Navy Provision Pier 56 (delivered by truck).
1030 Commenced dock trials.
1035 Yard oiler YO-105 came alongside the starboard quarter.
1130 Completed receiving stores.
1140 Dock trials were completed.
1300 With orders to report to the Navy Receiving Station San Francisco, 327 officers and men were detached from the ship for discharge or reassignment.
1420 YO-105 cast off having delivered 133,580 gallons of fuel oil.
2135 Power to the vessel supplied from the dock was transferred to the ships generator No.1.

Wednesday 14 November 1945   *Moored at Hunters Point - "Operation Magic Carpet"*

Moored as before port side to berth No.3, U.S. Naval Drydocks, Hunters Point, San Francisco. Our No.2 boiler is lighted off for baking purposes.

Thursday 15 November 1945   *Steamed from Hunters Point - "Operation Magic Carpet"*

0500 Moored as before. Lighted fires under No.3 boiler.
0620 Disconnected services from the dock.
0630 Commenced preparations for getting underway.
0730 Tested main engines by steam.
0800 Made all preparations for getting underway.
0802 Got underway for Guam, maneuvering at standard speed, 15 knots, to stand out of San Francisco Bay.
0907 Passed Point Bonita 1 mile abeam to starboard, taking departure of the channel.
1023 Passed Farallon Islands 2 miles abeam to starboard on a course of 270°T, 16 knots.
1545 Changed course to 264°T.

Friday 16 November 1945   *At sea with orders to proceed to Guam*

Steaming as before, independently, to Port Apra, Guam, Mariana Islands per dispatch No.122215.

Sunday 18 November 1945   *At sea steaming to Guam - "Magic Carpet"*

0435 Steaming on course 256°T, 17 knots. Sighted 3 unidentified ships to port on the horizon, opposite course.
1643 Changed speed to 22 knots to clear a heavy storm.
1931 Reduced speed to 16 knots.

Monday-Wednesday 19-21 November 1945 *At sea steaming to Guam*

On Monday the 19th, the crew was exercised at fire quarters. Tuesday the 20th, a man overboard drill was held.

Thursday 22 November 1945   *At sea steaming to Guam, crossed the I.D.L.*

0910 Course, 270°T. Sighted Midway Island bearing 291°T, 20 miles.
1020 Passed Sand Island, Midway Islands, six miles abeam to starboard.
1211 Passed over 100 fathom curve on Pogy Bank.
1214-1223 Passed over uncharted 39 fathom plateau, 2 to 3 miles wide adjacent to Pogy Bank. They experienced ground swells.
1850 Crossed the International Date Line at Latitude 27°06.1 N.
2400 Set all clocks ahead 24 hours.

AD 11/22/45 At sea. We had our Thanksgiving Dinner today. International Dateline.   AD

Tuesday 27 November 1945   *At sea, diverted to Saipan*

1030 Sounded torpedo defense for the purpose of gunnery exercises, and began maneuvering to gain position for the Gunnery Department to conduct balloon target firing practice.
1121 Secured from torpedo defense. Resumed course, 148°T at 16 knots.
1459-1520 Conducted abandon ship exercises.

2300 Changed course to 253°T. They had received a dispatch (No.270937) directing INDEPENDENCE to divert to Saipan, Mariana Islands.

AD   At sea. We are going to Saipan instead of Guam.   AD

Wednesday 28 November 1945   *At sea, steaming to Saipan - "Magic Carpet"*

Steaming as before, independently, to Saipan.
2220 Made radar land contact on the Island of Saipan, bearing 240°T, 59 miles.

Thursday 29 November 1945   *Anchored at Saipan - "Magic Carpet"*

0005 Steaming as before. Sighted lights on Saipan Island, distance 40 miles.
0330 Passed Saipan Harbor entrance buoy. At 0545 they set all special sea and anchor details.
0610 Commenced maneuvering toward an anchorage between berths L27 & L30, Garapan Anchorage.
0639 Anchored on 11 fathoms of water, 80 fathoms of chain to the port anchor, coarse sand bottom.
0920 A swell overturned the No.2 motor whale boat while it was coming alongside a gangway on the starboard side of the ship. There were no injuries to the 3 man crew. The boat was lifted into the No.1 whale boat skid.
1130 A camel was secured along the port side by a harbor tug.

AD   Saipan - Pulled in today. Went on the beach for movies.   AD

Friday 30 November 1945   *Anchored at Saipan*

Anchored as before, Garapan Anchorage between berths L27 and L30, Saipan.
0800-1040 Yard Oiler YO-116 was along the port side pumping 60,740 gallons of fuel oil.
1210-1706 Yard Oiler IX127 (USS RACCOON) delivered 390,970 gallons of fuel oil, then cast off.
1938 A yard tug came along side and removed the camel.

Saturday 1 December 1945   *At sea, steaming - Saipan to Iwo Jima*

0900 Anchored as before. Made all preparations for getting underway under dispatch No.300517.
0923 Got underway, maneuvering out of Garapan Harbor, Saipan steaming to Iwo Jima.
0936 They passed a buoy off Mutcho Point abeam 3,000 yards to starboard and departed the harbor.
0937 Secured the special sea and anchor details.
1012 On course 355°T, speed 15 knots, Anatahan Island was sighted 5 degrees off the starboard bow, 57 miles.
1406 They steamed past Anatahan Island abeam 3.5 miles to starboard. Changed course to 012°T.
1527 Passed Saragan Island abeam, 6 miles to starboard.
1800 Guguan abeam 3 miles to starboard.
1916 Passed Alamagan Island abeam, 4 miles to starboard.
2030 Changed course to 342°T.
2151 Passed Pagan Island 3.8 miles off the starboard beam.

Sunday 2 December 1945   *At sea, steaming - Saipan to Iwo Jima*

0000 Steaming as before. Passed Agrihan Island abeam 11.4 miles to starboard.
0534 Passed Maug Island abeam to starboard.
0720 Passed Japanese destroyer escort T-9 abeam 3,000 yards to port.
0805 Passed Farallon de Pajaros Island 7 miles abeam to port.
2030 Changed course to 329°T.

Monday 3 December 1945   *Arrived, dropped anchor, and departed Iwo Jima*

0152 Steaming as before. CIC reported Minami Iwo Jima 48 miles off the port bow, bearing 300°T.

0400 Changed course to 315°T.

0415 Sighted the Aero beacon on Iwo Jima dead ahead, distance 37 miles.

0435 Passed Minami Iwo Jima abeam to 15 miles port.

0545 Manned all special sea and anchor details.

0610 Commenced maneuvering as necessary to proceed into the anchorage.

0641 Anchored in berth No.181, Iwo Jima Anchorage, Volcano Islands, using 140 fathoms of chain to the port anchor on a volcanic sand bottom.

0647 Floyd E. Beeghly was on the anchor detail. He listened to the racket as the port anchor clunked and rattled as it went absent without leave. The brake had failed on the capstan followed by a shackle giving way. Escaping to the volcanic sand bottom of the anchorage, in 37 fathoms of water, the chain rapidly played out of the chain locker. 161.5 degrees off the summit of Mt. Suribachi, the 9 ton anchor (Serial No. 15937) and 170 fathoms of chain were claimed by Davey Jones for King Neptune's domain.

0840 USS INDEPENDENCE commenced loading passengers. They welcomed onboard 1624 Army enlisted men, 117 Army officers, 201 Navy enlisted men and 4 Navy officers. Between 0840 and 1145 they took aboard 1946 service men for transportation to Los Angeles, California.

1215 Commenced heaving short our starboard anchor.

1246 Got underway for Los Angeles Harbor, California, maneuvering to clear the Iwo Jima anchorage.

1257 USS INDEPENDENCE and the returning troops took departure of the anchorage, passing Kangoku Island 2,800 yards abeam to starboard. They set course 080°T at 17 knots, saying goodbye to Iwo Jima, and their port anchor.

AD We anchored here at 0700. I was up and over on the island by 0730. I had to pick up movies. There were no docks there. All they had were some Jap ships beached and by walking through them we reached the beach.

I never even saw a tree on that island. What a rat hole. By being on it you could understand why we suffered so many casualties. From the center or tops of the island the Japs could see everything. We picked up about 2,000 soldiers and at 1200 we were underway for the States.   AD

Tuesday 4 December 1945   *At sea, steaming to Los Angeles*

Steaming independently on base course 073°T, 17 knots, changing course at 1800 to 080°T.

Friday 7 December 1945   *At sea, steaming to Los Angeles - "Magic Carpet"*

Steaming independently on base course 086°T. At 0800 they mustered crew at quarters.

1030 Mustered passengers at quarters.

Saturday 8 December 1945   *At sea, steaming to Los Angeles - Cross the IDL*

Steaming independently on base course 090°T at 18 knots.

0643 Passed USS BARNSTABLE (APA-93) 8,500 yards abeam to port.

0800 Mustered crew at quarters. At 1030 they mustered passengers at quarters.

1115 Passed USS OZARK (LVS-2) 4 miles abeam to starboard.

1400 Crossed the International Date Line.

Saturday 8 December 1945 (Again - IDL)   *At sea, steaming to Los Angeles*

Once again, they repeated a day / date, due to crossing the International Date Line yesterday from west to east. At 0648 they passed USS SARITA (AKA-39) abeam, 8 miles to port.

0815 Passed the USS RENATE (AKA-36) abeam 1,500 yards to port.

1906 Passed the USS PRESIDENT MONROE (AP-104) 2.5 miles abeam to starboard.

2020 Increased speed to 18.5 knots to clear bad weather.

The days that followed thru and including 14 December were much the same, with crew musters, a Captains inspection, passing ships, and an eagerness to arrive back home.

Saturday 15 December 1945   *Los Angeles & San Pedro Harbors*

0512 Sighted the south light on Santa Barbara Island.
0610 Passed by Santa Barbara Island abeam to the starboard.
0830 Commenced maneuvering toward a berth in Los Angeles Harbor.
0853 Anchored in berth A6, Los Angeles Harbor, in 7 fathoms of water, mud bottom.
0928 A harbor pilot came onboard.
0955 Got underway to shift from an anchorage to a pier.
1055 Moored starboard side to pier 231, San Pedro Harbor, San Pedro, California.
1117 The 1946 passengers they took aboard at Iwo Jima began to depart the ship, to plant their feet again on U.S. soil. They would proceed for processing at separation centers.
1142 Additionally, 83 crewmembers were released for separation.
1345 Completed disembarking the passengers and crew scheduled to leave the ship in San Pedro.
1410 Made all preparations for getting underway.
1504 With a harbor pilot on the bridge they got underway with assistance from tugs. INDEPENDENCE maneuvered to shift to an anchorage from berth 231 and proceeded to berth C-5.
1520 The tugs cast off.
1610 Anchored in berth C-5, in the Los Angeles Outer Harbor, in 6.5 fathoms of water with 40 fathoms of chain. At 2110 YF 871 secured supply barges alongside the port quarter, then cast off.

AD   Docked at Long Beach, Calif. We let the troops off then anchored in the outer bay. Had liberty at 1800.   AD   (Note: The "Los Angeles Harbor" complex is bordered by the cities of Long Beach, San Pedro and Wilmington)   Note: **Today Lt. Cmdr. J. H. Arnold became Executive Officer.**

Tuesday 18 December 1945   *Anchored in Los Angeles Harbor*

Anchored as before. Today they took on fuel oil and 90 tons of fresh frozen provisions, delivered by a supply barge.

Wednesday 19 December 1945   *Anchored in Los Angeles Harbor*

Anchored as before. Today INDEPENDENCE took aboard additional fuel oil and diesel oil, and provisions. USS AMSTERDAM (CL-101) stood in. (CVL-22 hull was originally USS AMSTERDAM CL-59)

Friday 21 December 1945   *Departed Los Angeles Harbor - "Magic Carpet"*

0730 Anchored as before. Made all preparations for getting underway. 0800 Mustered crew at stations.
0904 Commenced maneuvering as we got underway to proceed seaward out of the Outer Channel of Los Angeles Harbor .
0920 Steamed past the breakwater with the Los Angeles Harbor light abeam to starboard, proceeding under orders to Port Apra, Guam. At 0931 they secured the special and anchor detail.
2036 Changed course to 279°T, speed 16 knots.

22-28 December 1945   *At sea steaming to Guam - "Magic Carpet"*

Steaming (as ordered in dispatch No.122249) to Port Apra, Guam to bring the troops home.
The days passed at sea with typical morning musters, sighting and passing various ships, many with the same assignment, transport our soldiers, sailors and airmen back to the US. Miles of ocean left behind in the wake and the ship's clocks reset at roughly one half hour per day as they progressed across invisible time zones. Not a vacation cruise for the crew as work was as usual with Firemen running and maintaining the boilers to keep a head of steam, running the evaporators to produce fresh water, C&R Department checking the bilges. Cooks, bakers and mess cooks feeding the crew, along with the seeming endless cleanup in the galleys and mess decks. Christmas passed on December 25th.

They would have a large flight deck to land on (compared to usual rooftops), four stacks to shimmy down, but alas ... no Santa.

Saturday 29 December 1945 (IDL)   *At sea, steaming to Guam*

0150 Steaming on base course 261°T, making 18 knots. Sighted USS SEA DEVIL, 18 miles to port.
0903 Passed USS FREMONT on a reciprocal course 7 miles abeam to port.
1305 Sighted Pearl Reef dead ahead, changing course to maneuver around.
2400 Set all ships clocks ahead 24 hours as they steamed across the International Date Line.

Monday 31 December 1945   *At sea steaming to Guam*

Steaming to Guam, they lost Sunday with one quick stroke of the clock as they as crossed the International Date Line, east to west. New Years eve was upon them, as they prepared to say good-by to 1945.

Tuesday 1 January 1946   *At sea steaming to Guam - New Years Day*

AD   At sea, 1 January 1946. Happy New Year!   AD

Wednesday 2 January 1946   *At sea, diverted to Saipan*

Once again they are diverted, by dispatch No.242234 dated 31 December 1945 from the Commander Marianas, modifying the original orders. Guam is a short distance from Saipan, both islands in the Marianas chain.

Saturday 5 January 1946   *At sea, steaming to Saipan - "Magic Carpet"*

0300 Saipan was picked up by the ships radar on their bow, bearing 255°T, 67 miles.
0520 Sighted the lights on Saipan.
0731 Commenced maneuvering to conform to the channel as they proceeded to the anchorage.
0800 Anchored between berths L-10 and L-13 in Garapan Harbor, Saipan in 14 fathoms of water.
1345 INDEPENDENCE lowered a Grumman J2F "Duck" floatplane from the flight deck, over the side into the water with the ships crane. After its flight, it returned to be hoisted aboard again at 1530.

Sunday 6 January 1946   *Anchored, Garapan Harbor, Saipan - "Magic Carpet"*

Anchored as before between berths L-10 and L-13 in Garapan Harbor, Saipan.
1340 They lowered a Grumman J2F "Duck" floatplane from the flight deck, over the side into the water with the ships crane. After its flight, it returned to be hoisted aboard again at 1510.
Shore patrol and liberty parties went ashore and crew members played basketball on the Hangar deck.

Wednesday 9 January 1946   *Anchored, Garapan Harbor, Saipan*

1500 Anchored as before. A mid-air collision between 2 F4Us from USS BOXER occurred, with one Corsair hitting the water roughly 1 mile off the Mighty-I's bow. The pilot was rescued by LCI 971. The other Corsair crashed into the water several miles off the port quarter, the pilot not found.
1550 Yard tug YTL452 shifted a camel to the starboard bow, then cast off.

10-14 January 1946   *Anchored, Garapan Harbor, Saipan - "Magic Carpet"*

Anchored as before. Thursday they took on 233,940 gallons of fuel oil from yard oiler YO-116. Friday, still thirsty, they pumped onboard another 226,537 gallons of fuel oil from YO-116. Not yet satisfied, they took on another 103,598 gallons from YO-147. She bumped the CVL-22 and broke some life net support rails. The USS RELIEF dropped anchor 100 yards from INDEPENDENCE, and they could look out across the anchorage to see the USS HORNET, sister carrier BELLEAU WOOD, MUNDA, ANTIETAM, KWAJALEIN, HOLLANDIA, ADMIRALTY ISLANDS, STEAMER BAY and numerous other vessels and small craft of the fleet. Shore Patrol and liberty parties went ashore.
At 0610 on Saturday, the No.2 motor whale boat was discovered to have gone AWOL, having broken

These photos were <u>possibly</u> taken at Hunters Point * or possibly <u>San Pedro</u> area while the ship was being readied for "Magic Carpet" or "<u>Crossroads</u>". She is moored port side to the dock, and many of the guns have been removed. Note the Grumman Duck on the bow. USS CABOT (CVL-28) is the carrier aft. * In my hi res photo, the 28 is <u>clearly</u> visible on the other carrier's flight deck, yet I find no Deck Log entries for Cabot being present, only the San Jacinto? Oil wells are present in large numbers in another photo shot the same time, indicating the Los Angeles / San Pedro harbor complex.

loose during the night. The stray was recovered undamaged and returned at 0955 by the USS FREDERICK FUNSTON (APA-89). The camel was removed from the starboard bow by YTB-452. Monday INDEPENDENCE took aboard Army Air Force troops for transportation to the U.S.

Tuesday 15 January 1946   *Garapan Harbor, Saipan - Underway*

Anchored as before between berths L-10 and L-13 in Garapan Harbor, Saipan.
A number of LCTs tied up to on the starboard side transferring personnel aboard for transportation to the U.S. INDEPENDENCE has taken on 211 officers and 1555 enlisted men.
1200 Made all preparations for getting underway, under orders - dispatch No. 110525.
1349 Got underway, maneuvering to clear the anchorage and the Garapan Harbor.
1443 Took departure of Saipan as they passed 2,200 yards abeam to port, Nafutan Point, at 16 knots.
1613 Steaming on base course 076°T.

Wednesday 16 January 1946   *At sea, steaming to San Pedro - "Magic Carpet"*

Steaming east as before independently from Saipan to San Pedro, California.
0800 Mustered the crew at quarters. At 1030 they mustered the passengers at quarters.

Friday 18 January 1946   *At sea, steaming to San Pedro*

Steaming east as before independently from Saipan to San Pedro, California, base course 080°T.
1219 Sighted USS SHIPLEY BAY bound for Pearl Harbor.
1512 Passed Wake Island 1.9 miles off our port beam.

AD   Passed by Wake Island today. It certainly was a small island. Not a green thing was on it.   AD

Sunday 20 January 1946   *At sea, steaming to San Pedro - Crossed the IDL*

Steaming as before. Today at 2400 we changed to zone plus 12 changing the date to Sunday 20 January 1946 (repeating Sunday the 20th. due to crossing the International Date Line from west to east).

AD   20 Jan 1946 At sea. International Date Line. The food on here since we left Saipan has really been something to squawk about. They are feeding us battle rations.   AD

INDEPENDENCE Medical Department in late 1945   Photo courtesy of John Underriner

Chapter 35   759

36
Operation Crossroads and Beyond

Tuesday 22 January 1946   *At sea, steaming to San Pedro*

0425 Steaming as before. They picked up Kaula Island on radar 30 miles ahead.
0615 Passed 6 miles abeam to port off Kaula Island.
0625 Sighted Niihau Island 20.5 miles off the port quarter.
0700 Sighted Kauai Island 20.5 miles off the port quarter.
0740 Passed Niihau Island abeam to port.
1017 Passed 6.3 miles abeam Makahuena Point Light on Kauai Island.
1136 Sighted Oahu 49 miles off our starboard bow. They continued on, passing between Kauai and Oahu, the Hawaiian Islands falling slowly astern as they steamed east.

On 22 January 1946 Dispatch No. 221810 was sent from the CNO: (Released by R.L. Conolloy)

UPON RELEASE FROM TRANSPORT DUTY ABOUT 29 JANUARY INDEPENDENCE (CVL22) IS ASSIGNED TO CINCPAC TO BE USED AS A TARGET IN OPPERATION CROSSROADS VICE RANGER (CV4).
CINCPAC **REDUCE PERSONNEL TO MINIMUM NECCESSARY FOR SLOW SPEED STEAMING.**
THIS MODIFIES CNO CONFIDENTIAL SERIAL 084P414 OF 14 NOVEMBER. NOT TO OR NEEDED BY ALL.
MY 162210 ALSO REFERS. **ASSIGNMENT OF INDEPENDENCE TO 19TH FLEET HEREBY CANCELLED.**

On 24 January 1946 Dispatch No. 240212 directed:

UPON RELEASE MAGIC CARPET COMSERVPAC DIRECT INDEPENDENCE (CVL 22) REPORT COMWESSEAFRON FOR DUTY.
COMWESSEAFRON **REDUCE PERSONNEL AND STRIP VESSEL** IN ACCORDANCE WITH CNO 221810 AND 222055.
UPON COMPLETION SAIL VESSEL TO PEARL TO ARRIVE 15 FEB OR AS SOON THEREAFTER AS PRACTABLE.
DIRECT VESSEL ON ARRIVAL PEARL REPORT COM 14 FOR BERTHING AND TRANSFER JOINT TASK FORCE 1 WHEN DIRECTED BY CINCPAC.

On 25 January 1946 Dispatch No. 250255 from COMSERVPAC directed:

UPON ARRIVAL SAN PEDRO AND COMPLETION DISCHARGE PASSENGERS ABOUT 29 JANUARY INDEPENDENCE CVL 22 DETACHED FROM TG 16.12 AND MAGIC CARPET DUTY.
REPORT TO COMWESSEAFRON FOR DUTY IN COMPLIANCE CINCPAC 240212. MODIFY CTG 16.12 ACCORDINGLY.

The above dispatches would forever change the life and destiny of the proud WWII veteran USS INDEPENDENCE.

Why us, the crew members might have asked? The Mighty-I had an honored history, did she not?

The answer perhaps might be:

The world, the United States, was shifting to a peacetime economy. We now had an overly abundant supply of new vessels. The very design of the USS INDEPENDENCE perhaps doomed it from the first day the work had begun to convert her from the light cruiser USS AMSTERDAM. Remember, her conversion was a stopgap measure. She was not properly designed as an aircraft carrier from her keel up.

USS INDEPENDENCE CVL-22 with her crew served her nation proudly in time of dire need, leaving in her historic wake, fulfillment of her purpose and mission in the best tradition of Naval Service!

The US Navy now had a good number of new ESSEX class carriers afloat. The Mighty-I, rather than a destiny of mothballs, was ordered to serve her nation once more, to help garner data so following vessels might better allow their crews to survive newly emerging weapons in future possible conflicts.

Monday 28 January 1946   *Moored at San Pedro, California - "Magic Carpet"*

Steaming as before.
0409 Sighted San Nicholas Island Light 8 miles off the port quarter.
0433 Passed San Nicholas Island Light 5.4 miles abeam to port.
0615 Passed Santa Barbara Island 8 miles abeam to port.
0630 Sighted Santa Catalina Island 14.3 miles off the starboard quarter.
0724 Passed Santa Catalina Island 4 miles abeam to starboard.
0858 Commenced maneuvering to conform to the entry into San Pedro Harbor.
0924 With a harbor pilot at the conn, aided by yard tug PORT VINCENT, INDEPENDENCE moored starboard side to pier 231, Terminal Island, San Pedro, California.
1100 Commenced disembarking the Army and Navy personnel they brought aboard at Saipan.
1230 Made all preparations for getting underway.
1302 Got underway, assisted by yard tugs YT 437 and YT 539, proceeding to berth B-6.
1417 Anchored at berth B-6, San Pedro Harbor, in 7 fathoms of water, with 40 fathoms of chain.

Tuesday 29 January 1946   *Anchored at San Pedro, California*

Today, yard tugs delivered 2 camels along the port side.

Wednesday 30 January 1946   *Anchored at San Pedro, California*

Today they offloaded munitions to an ammunition barge delivered alongside by a yard tug, and took on fuel oil from an oiler barge brought alongside by civilian tug LEBEC.
1055-1410 Received 7 tons of fresh provisions from an LCM.

Thursday 31 January 1946   *Anchored at San Pedro, California*

INDEPENDENCE received additional fuel oil from another barge, completed offloading ammunition and discharged the aviation gasoline to a gasoline barge.

Sunday 10 February 1946   *Moved to pier 3, berth 31, Terminal Island Navy Yard*

0800 Mustered crew at quarters. At 0900 they made all preparations for getting underway.
0916 With a harbor pilot at the conn, the ship got underway, maneuvering to conform to the channel.
1005 Aided by yard tugs YT 437 and YT 509, they entered the slip, securing port side to pier 3, berth

31 at the Terminal Island Navy Yard, San Pedro, California.
1145 Commenced receiving services from the dock.

Saturday 16 February 1946 *Moored - Terminal Island Navy Yard*

Today, 54 men were transferred from the USS INDEPENDENCE to separation centers for discharge.

AD Docked Terminal Island. Anthony D'Aiuto, E.M. "E Division" left the Independence to be discharged today. *AD* (Goodbye Anthony, thanks for your diary entries.)

Thursday 28 February 1946 *Moored - Terminal Island Navy Yard*

0800 Commander Raleigh C. Kirkpatrick relieved Commander Daniel F. Smith as Executive Officer.

Saturday 2 March 1946   *Shifted mooring to anchorage in Long Beach*
                              Begin preparations for "Operation Crossroads"

Began preparing ship for A Bomb tests at Bikini Atoll. "Operation Crossroads". Shipmates would begin to see the crew thin out as the mission for the ship had changed. The Mighty-I was designed to pursue targets. In a roll reversal, it now would become one.

0620 Disconnected services from the pier.
0715 Assisted by yard tugs, with a harbor pilot on the bridge, they got underway from berth 31, pier 3, Terminal Island, maneuvering as they proceed to berth E-9, Long Beach, San Pedro Harbor, California.
0758 Anchored in berth E-9, Long Beach, San Pedro Harbor, California.
0802 Ammunition barge YF 1116 was moved alongside by YTB 255 to deliver munitions.
1147 Ammunition barge YF 656 was moved alongside to deliver munitions.

Sunday 3 March 1946   *Anchored in San Pedro Harbor, California*

Anchored as before in berth E-9 with 40 fathoms of chain, in 40' of water, gray sand bottom.
Ships present include USS NEW JERSEY, ARKANSAS, NEVADA, PENSACOLA, SALT LAKE CITY, SAINT PAUL, SPRINGFIELD, VICKSBURG, ASTORIA, WILKES BARRE, DAYTON and USS CHENANGO.
During the day the crew continued to take aboard on a mix of bombs and bullets, working until 1940.

Monday 4 March 1946   *Anchored in San Pedro Harbor, California*

Anchored as before.

Tuesday 5 March 1946   *Underway from San Pedro Harbor to San Diego*

0800 Anchored as before. Mustered crew on stations. Got underway to proceed to San Diego, California in accordance with dispatch 012153, maneuvering to clear the harbor.
0814 Commenced steaming on base course 145°T at 20 knots.
1313 Commenced maneuvering to enter and conform to the San Diego channel. A civilian pilot came aboard and took the conn., with the Captain and Navigator on the bridge.
1333 Entered San Diego Harbor.
1428 Moored starboard side to berth "N", North Island, Calif. At 1507 the pilot departed the ship.

Wednesday 6 March 1946 *Underway from North Island, San Diego, California*

0835 The crew completed taking onboard a mix of 14 aircraft including four F6F-5Ns (Bu.No.s 77349, 77433, 77492, 77569), five TBM-3Es (Bu.No.s 69063, 69116, 69124, 69239, 692750), and two SB2C-4Es (Bu.No.s 31856, 31857) (the remaining two of the 14 unidentified). They then removed the J2F6 Grumman Duck (Bu.No. 32730).
0958 With a civilian harbor pilot on the bridge (F.D Pennoyer), and aided by tugs YTB- 148 & YTB-270, INDEPENDENCE commenced getting underway.

1000 Commenced maneuvering to conform to the harbor channel, taking departure of North Island en route to San Pedro Harbor. The Harbor pilot departed at 1049.
1100 They steamed north, 327°T at 20 knots.
1508 Commenced maneuvering to conform to the harbor channel, with a civilian pilot (A. Jorgansen) at the conn., the Captain, XO and Navigator on the bridge.
1603 Moored portside to pier 3, berth 31, U.S. Naval Drydocks, Terminal Island, San Pedro, Calif. The ship would receive fresh water and telephone service from the dock.

Wednesday 13 March 1946 *Moored in San Pedro, California*

Moored as before portside to pier 3, berth 31, Terminal Island, San Pedro, Calif.
Today the ship commenced taking on equipment and personnel for "Operation Crossroads".

Thursday 21 March 1946 *Moored in San Pedro, California*

Moored as before (since 6 March) portside to pier 3, berth 31, Terminal Island, San Pedro, Calif.
Today the captain's son, Ensign William H. Kindell reported aboard. (photo page 712)

Friday 22 March 1946 *Moored in San Pedro, California*

1300 A group of approximately 300 men disembarked for reassignment. There have been a number of reassignments on a daily basis with men both reporting aboard, and departing for other duty.

Monday 25 March 1946 *Moved from our mooring to an anchorage*

Moored as before portside to pier 3, berth 31, Terminal Island, San Pedro, Calif.
0842 Commenced getting underway with assistance from tugs YT-394 & YT509 and began maneuvering to depart thru the breakwater entrance to proceed to an anchorage.
0944 Anchored in berth E-6, San Pedro Harbor, California in 7 fathoms of water, 40 fathoms of chain.

Thursday 28 March 1946 *Underway for maneuvering exercises*

0830 Anchored in berth E-6 in San Pedro Harbor. Made all preparations for getting underway.
0920 Set the special sea and anchor details.
1132 Got underway, maneuvering to clear the harbor.
1143 Departed San Pedro Harbor for exercises at sea in the southern section of the western sea frontier.
1403-1417 Exercised the crew at fire quarters.
2230 Passed Santa Barbara Island 9.5 miles abeam to starboard.

Friday 29 March 1946 *At sea, conducting maneuvering exercises*

0113 Maneuvered to avoid an LST.
0930-1145 Conducted maneuvering exercises steering various courses at various speeds.
1418 Commenced maneuvering to proceed to the anchorage.
1451 Anchored in berth O-2, San Pedro Harbor, San Pedro, California in 7 fathoms of water.

Monday 1 April 1946 *Underway for maneuvering exercises*

Anchored in berth O-2, San Pedro Harbor, San Pedro, California. Anchorage bearings: Rivera Hotel 027°T, Hilton Hotel 013°T, Breakwater light 290°T, Breakwater light 157°T.
0840 Made all preparations for getting underway.
0918 Steamed out of San Pedro Harbor.
0920 Stopped all engines to take aboard Army personnel from an LCM.
0924 Resumed steaming at 12 knots.
1036-1430 Maneuvered on various courses at various speeds during a ship-handling exercises.
1530 Commenced maneuvering as necessary while proceeding back to the anchorage.
1550 Anchored in berth O-2, San Pedro Harbor, San Pedro, California.

Tuesday 2 April 1946   *Underway for maneuvering exercises*

0902 Anchored as before. Got underway maneuvering to clear the harbor steaming seaward.
1040-1046 Held Man Overboard drill.
1103-1400 Maneuvered on various courses at various speeds during a ship-handling exercises.
1510 Commenced maneuvering as necessary while proceeding back to the anchorage.
1521 Anchored in berth O-2, San Pedro Harbor, San Pedro, California. Here they would remain until the 23rd.

Tuesday 23 April 1946   *Underway to shift berths*

0830 Anchored as before. Made all preparations for getting underway.
0915 Tested steering engines and enunciators.
1258 Assisted by a harbor pilot and 2 yard tugs, got underway to shift berths from berth O-2, San Pedro Harbor, to berth 31, pier 3 Terminal Island, San Pedro, California.
1445 Moored port side to berth 31, pier 3 Terminal Island, San Pedro, California.

Wednesday 24 April 1946   *Moored - Terminal Island Navy Yard*

1235 During the stay, men both reported for duty and were transferred off the INDEPENDENCE. A group of 44 men reported onboard for duty today. Another 61 reported aboard on April 25th. The transfers, both reporting onboard and transferring from the ship, would continue.
2445 A tug came alongside with a barge to pump out our bilges.

Thursday 26 April 1946   *Shifted berths*

Moored as before, port side to berth 31, pier 3 Terminal Island, San Pedro, California.
0830 Commenced making preparations for getting underway.
1014 Proceeded with the assistance of a harbor pilot and 2 yard tugs to shift berths.
1100 Anchored in berth O-2, San Pedro Harbor, San Pedro, California.

INDEPENDENCE stripped down and ready for "Crossroads". Note many empty gun tubs.

1120 F2c William Phillips was admitted to sickbay for multiple lacerations to his face and chest, suffered during the "explosion" of a glass gauge in No.2 aft boiler room.

Thursday 2 May 1946   *Underway, en route San Pedro to Pearl Harbor*

Anchored as before in berth O-2, San Pedro Harbor, San Pedro, California.
0830 Commenced making preparations for getting underway.
0940 Set the special sea and anchor details.
0955 Got underway, maneuvering to depart the harbor.
1015 Departed San Pedro Harbor seaward bound for Pearl Harbor, Hawaii at 16 knots.

Friday 3 May 1946   *Underway, en route San Pedro to Pearl Harbor*

Steaming as before independently to Pearl Harbor in accordance with movement order # 314-46.
0403 Shifted steering control to steering aft. They had lost steering control in the pilot house.
0510 Restored steering control to the pilot house. Steamed toward Hawaii on base course 265°T.
They would sight numerous vessels on their journey west.

Tuesday 7 May 1946   *At sea, en route to Pearl Harbor*

2310 Picked up land on radar 64 miles off the starboard bow.

Wednesday 8 May 1946   *Moored - Pier F-1, Ford Island, Pearl Harbor, T.H.*

0123 Steaming independently. Picked up Maui Island on the radar, 58 miles off the starboard bow.
0253 Sighted Kauiki Head Light (south side of Hana Bay, Maui) 20 miles ahead.
0657 Commenced a series of course changes to conform to the N.E. coast lines of the islands of Maui and Molokai.
0945 Passed Molokai Light abeam to port as INDEPENDENCE steamed toward Oahu Island.
1237 Passed Diamond Head Light to port.
1453 Passed into the channel entrance to Pearl Harbor, having taken onboard a harbor pilot.
1536 Moored port side to the dock, Pier F-1, Ford Island, Pearl Harbor.
2000 Started receiving services from the dock.

Wednesday 22 May 1946   *Underway, en route from Pearl Harbor to Bikini Atoll*

Moored port side to the dock, Pier F-1, Ford Island, Pearl Harbor.
0800 Held quarters for muster.
0900 Commenced making preparations for getting underway.
1028 Got underway from Pier F-1, Ford Island, Pearl Harbor, maneuvering to clear the channel as the Mighty-I steamed seaward.
1113 Departed Pearl Harbor steaming south.
1200 INDEPENDENCE joined up with USS STACK and came to a more westerly course.

Sunday 26 May 1946   *Underway to Bikini Atoll - "Operation Crossroads"*

Steaming to Bikini Atoll, Marshall Islands in company with USS STACK.
1426 Crossed the International Date Line.

Tuesday 28 May 1946   *Underway to Bikini Atoll - "Operation Crossroads"*

0920-1140 Took on ballast. They sighted USS PENNSYLVANIA and 2 escorts. At 0930 they reversed course and disappeared in the haze.

Wednesday 29 May 1946   *Underway to Bikini Atoll - "Operation Crossroads"*

1004 Passed Bikar Island, Bikar Atoll 7.6 miles abeam to port (Bikar Atoll is in the Ratak chain of islands and Atolls in the Marshals, east of Bikini).

Thursday 30 May 1946 *Arrive at Bikini Atoll - "Operation Crossroads"*

This morning from 0035 thru 0240 the crew sighted and / or passed numerous vessels as they drew close to the destination, maneuvering as necessary to avoid conflicts.
0510 Picked up Bikini Atoll on radar 11 miles off the port bow. Our course, 262°T.
0515 Sighted Enyu Island, Bikini Atoll, 6 miles ahead, and Bikini Island 11 miles, bearing 280°T.
0524 Directed USS STACK to proceed independently.
0853 Set the special sea and anchor details. Commenced maneuvering to enter Bikini Lagoon.
1017 Moored in the assigned berth in the target area, assisted by tugs.
INDEPENDENCE was moored with 8 fathoms of chain to a forward buoy and 21 fathoms of 10 inch manila line to an aft buoy in 29 fathoms of water, sand bottom.

Friday 31 May 1946 *Moored - Target area, Bikini Atoll - "Operation Crossroads"*

Moored as before in assigned berth in the target area in Bikini Lagoon, Bikini Atoll, Marshall Islands. Boiler No.2 is in use for auxiliary purposes.
0800 Held quarters for muster. At 0805 the USS SARATOGA stood in the anchorage.

Saturday 1 June 1946 *Moored - Target area, Bikini Atoll - "Operation Crossroads"*

1850 & 2050 The stern lines on BB NAGATO and USS SALT LAKE CITY parted from their buoys.
2230 The stern line parted and CVL-22's stern swung 70° to port, no ships within the swing radius.

Sunday 2 June 1946 *Moored - Target area, Bikini Atoll - "Operation Crossroads"*

Moored as before. A 1 7/8 inch steel wire was secured from our stern to the aft buoy.
1845 A fire was reported in the No.2 boiler casing. Boiler fuel was cutoff to cut the boiler fires and a steam smothering system was opened.
1903 Lighted fires under No.2 boiler (to dry the boiler out).
1915 Fire reported out in No.2 boiler casing.
1917 Lighted fires under No.1 boiler.
2000 Let fires die out under No.2 boiler.
2001 Cut No.1 boiler into the main steam line. At 2005 cut out No.2 boiler from main steam line.

Sunday 9 June 1946 *Moored - Target area, Bikini Atoll - "Operation Crossroads"*

1445 The PRINZ EUGEN (former German cruiser) stood in.

Friday 14 June 1946 *Moored - Target area, Bikini Atoll - "Operation Crossroads"*

0800 Mustered crew at quarters.
1000 Target Vessel Group Commander Rear Admiral F.G. Fahrion came aboard, departing at 1035.
1340 U.S. Navy Task Force Commander Vice Admiral W.H.P. Blandy came aboard with his inspection party, departing at 1430.

USS Saratoga (CV-3) sinks after "Baker Test"

Overview - "Operation Crossroads" - Bikini Atoll

"Crossroads" was designed to further the understanding of the effects of weapons similar to those already used at the "Trinity" test site, Hiroshima and Nagasaki. Planning for the tests at Bikini called for the "precision" measurement of what occurs when a atomic bomb is used against naval vessels and other military hardware and material such as aircraft, tanks, electronic and electrical devices, etc.

Vice Admiral William H.P. Blandy directed "Crossroads" as the name selected as he felt that the Atomic Bomb was a turning point for "perhaps civilization itself".

Three tests were conducted: *(note: A third <u>atomic test</u> was initially authorized by President Truman, but not conducted, the three allocated weapons said then, to have been one third of our atomic arsenal.)*
"Queen"- A non-atomic *(dry-run)* test to assure readiness.
"Able" - An **air drop** / detonation of a weapon like the device used for Trinity and Nagasaki.
"Baker" - An **underwater** detonation of a weapon like the device used for Trinity and Nagasaki.
"Charlie" - A third atomic test (underwater) was planned but was not conducted due to problems with contamination from the Baker test.

Following the war, the armed forces had an excess of materials available. The US Navy had roughly 1,200 vessels, far in excess of the foreseeable needs. USS INDEPENDENCE was one of a lengthy list of roughly 94 target vessels *(numbers range from 84 to "over 90" depending on which source is viewed)* selected from a surplus fleet.

For the Able test, USS INDEPENDENCE would be anchored astern of former battered antagonist Japanese battleship NAGATO *(already in shambles),* and between battleship USS NEVADA and cruiser USS SALT LAKE CITY.

USS NEVADA would sport a fresh coat of garish red-orange paint, as she was selected to be the unfortunate target vessel. Thus, so that the aim point was clear to the eye peering thru the bombsight of the B-29 selected for the Able test drop. USS INDEPENDENCE was honored with front row seat.

The MIGHTY-I would float in uncomfortably close proximity as a reluctant, defiant victim-participant, slightly battle worn, dressed in traditional navy gray.

The condition of the Mighty-I just prior to the Crossroads tests is stated in the "Commanding Officers Report" as follows:

> *"The material condition of the ship was good, particularly the watertight integrity. Complete tests on watertight closures were made just before leaving San Pedro in May 1946. All machinery was in working order although some parts, particularly the boilers, showed the effects of long and hard use, with no Navy Yard overhaul since July 1944. Catapults, elevators, arresting gear, and other special equipment were in good condition.*
> *The special equipment on board for the test included the Signal Corps radar and radio sets, Air Corps tank trucks and trailers, deck exhibits of airplane structural materials, etc. This material had no effect one way or the other on the ability of the ship to resist damage. The ship was loaded with gasoline, bombs, ammunition, fuel and aircraft, but this was not special equipment as it is normal for a carrier to carry all these."*

For the entire operation, approximately 160 aircraft and 220 ships would be involved, with approximately 45,400 participants. Roughly 90 percent were navy personnel. They were **Joint Task Force 1 (JTF)**. More than 10,000 measuring devices, including 200 cameras, were said to have been utilized.

After the tests, some vessels had succumbed to the shock and brutality of the weapons, and aided by gravity, sought the bottom of the lagoon for a lasting refuge from the tormentors. Others would be sunk off Bikini, Kwajalein or Hawaii. Eight of the major target ships, along with two submarines were towed to the US or Hawaii for further testing.

Chapter 36   767

Saturday 15 June 1946   *Moored - Target area, Bikini Atoll - "Operation Crossroads"*

0915 Quarters for Captains inspection, flight deck parade.
1030 ARS 22 damaged INDEPENDENCE between frames 9 and 15, dishing and gashing the starboard side in during initial boarding team rehearsal. A ladder was damaged on frame 11.

Sunday 16 June 1946 *Moored - Target area, Bikini Atoll - "Operation Crossroads"*

Today efforts were made to improve the mooring, heaving in the port anchor chain, and a securing 8 ton spring buoy on the starboard anchor chain 20 feet from the regular buoy.

Friday 21 June 1946   *Moored - Target area, Bikini Atoll - "Operation Crossroads"*

0800 Mustered crew at quarters.
1100 Mooring lines were changed to an arrangement deemed to be more robust.
1257-1330 INDEPENDENCE conducted a "Q" day evacuation of group 1, consisting of 9 officers and 136 enlisted men for transportation to the USS ROCKWALL (APA-230).
1545 Commenced closing all watertight hatches, drains, and secured ventilators below the second deck in most of the ship except engineering spaces in B section.

Saturday 22 June 1946   *Moored - Target area, Bikini Atoll - "Operation Crossroads"*

0800 Mustered crew on stations.
0950-1007 The ship conducted evacuation of group 2, consisting of 8 officers and 107 enlisted men for transportation to the USS ROCKWALL.
1013 Started the forward emergency generator for ships lighting and power.
1045 Secured No.4 Generator.
1057 Let fires die out under No.4 boiler. C&R Department closed all watertight hatches and doors, all vent and drain valves and fire main cut-outs.
1230 Secured all electrical distribution switch boards.
1255 Secured the forward emergency generator and all ships lighting and power.
1306-1325 INDEPENDENCE conducted evacuation of group 3, consisting of 11 officers and 63 enlisted men for transportation to the USS ROCKWALL.
1335 Captain Noland Kindell and his party of 4 officers and 7 enlisted men departed the ship.
The USS INDEPENDENCE is "completely secured and evacuated", left in a condition of maximum watertight integrity.
 All personnel have been evacuated to the USS ROCKWALL.

Monday 24 June 1946   *"Queen" Day - Bikini Atoll - "Operation Crossroads"*

All personnel are aboard USS ROCKWALL cruising in area Marmon. Today is a practice rehearsal for the "Able" bomb run.
0830 A practice run was made over the target ship.
0915 A 2,000 pound high-explosive fragmentation air burst bomb and a flash bomb were released over the target, successfully exploding mid-air.
1600 USS ROCKWALL entered Bikini Lagoon to execute reentry and boarding plans.
1735 Captain Kindell and his boarding party of 10 officers and 22 enlisted men boarded the INDEPENDENCE to conduct an inspection of the ship, evaluating the bomb damage.
1737 Set the watch.
1738 Vice-Admiral Blandy and his party came alongside in an "L" boat to obtain a report of the damage, casting off at 1739.

1832 First group of Team Baker (6 officers and 25 enlisted men) reported aboard.

1845 Second group of Team Baker (4 officers and 16 enlisted men) reported aboard.

1910 Cut in the emergency diesel generator on the lighting circuit.

1915 Lighted fires under No.4 boiler

2130 No.4 generator was brought online.

2205 Secured the emergency diesel generator. The C&R Department opened all watertight doors, ports, hatches, ventilation system, drains and fire main cutouts. All power, light and ventilation was restored. Bomb Damage Assessment: Both elevators were slightly dished and the forward windshield blown out of the Captains' Gig due to concussion. Fragment damage consisted of scratches to the flight deck, holes thru 3 planes, a hole in the fire truck windshield, one hole in a P-47, and a hole in a Signal Corps radio.

Tuesday 25 June 1946   *Moored - Target area, Bikini Atoll - "Operation Crossroads"*

Throughout the day additional personnel reported back onboard from the USS ROCKWALL.

Friday 28 June 1946   *Moored - Target area, Bikini Atoll - "Operation Crossroads"*

0800 Moored as before. Mustered crew at quarters.

1150-1210 Admiral Cooke and Vice-Admiral Blandy were aboard for an informal visit.

Saturday 29 June 1946   *Moored - Target area, Bikini Atoll - "Operation Crossroads"*

0800 Mustered crew on stations.

0930 Made daily inspection of the magazines. Magazines were secured for test "Able".

1100-1135 A Joint Task Force One (JTF-1) inspection party was aboard the ship.

1253 Lighted fires under No.4 boiler.

1320 Second Division men in evacuation group No.1 departed to proceed to the USS ROCKWALL.

1340 Admiral MacNeal came aboard with his inspection party.

1347-1355 Divisions M,B, K,H, N and E in evacuation group No.1 departed to proceed to the USS ROCKWALL.

1355   Admiral Hall came aboard with his inspection party of Navy Officers, Army Officers, Military & foreign observers, and correspondents.

1400 Admiral MacNeal with his inspection party departed.

1413 Divisions S1, S2, S3 and V in evacuation group No.1 departed to proceed to the ROCKWALL.

A total of 5 officers and 133 enlisted men have left the ship per evacuation plans for test "Able".

1415 No.4 boiler cut into the main steam line.

1445 Admiral Hall departed with his party. Secured No.1 generator.

1555-1559 Let fires die out under No.1 boiler and secured it.

Sunday 30 June 1946   *Moored - Target area, Bikini Atoll - "Operation Crossroads"*

0800 Mustered crew on stations. Commenced closing all watertight hatches, drains, and secured ventilators and fire main cutouts.

1017 Group II (8 officers and 103 enlisted men) evacuated to the USS ROCKWALL.

1033-1056 Secured No.3 generator. Started forward emergency diesel generator. Secured No.4 Generator, and let fires die out under No.4 boiler.

1233 Secured forward emergency diesel generator along with all power and light on this vessel. Completed closing all watertight fittings for maximum watertight integrity.

1315 Evacuated 6 officers and 62 enlisted men of Group III to the USS ROCKWALL.

1335 General Joseph Stillwell and Admiral Hoover boarded the ship with their inspection party, departing at 1402.

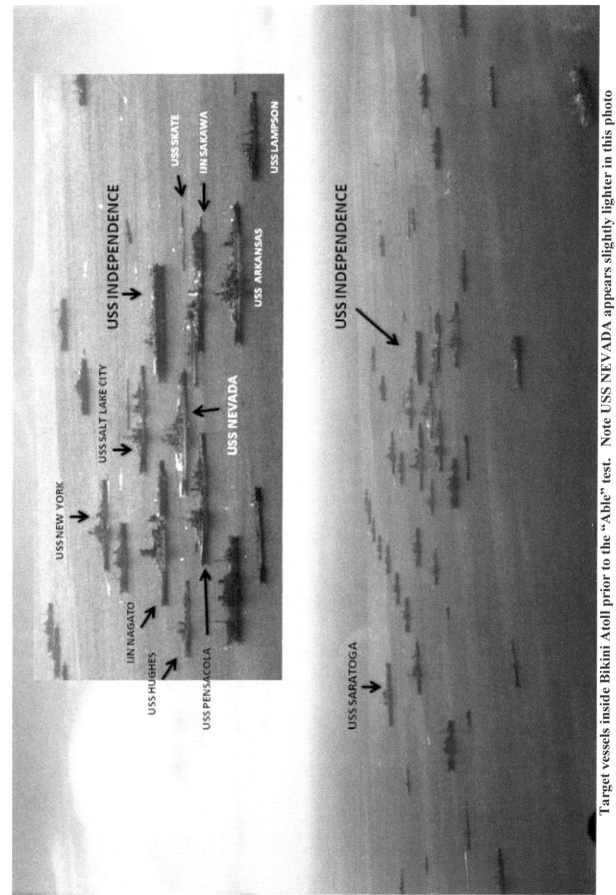

Target vessels inside Bikini Atoll prior to the "Able" test. Note USS NEVADA appears slightly lighter in this photo due to it being painted roughly pink / orange to stand out to the B-29 crew as the target for their bomb drop.

Prior to the "Able" test, "Dr. C.W. Lampson (right) explains device that determines exact spot of detonation to (left to right) Ron Richardson, Dr. A. B. Arons and CDR. R.C. Kirkpatrick, USN" aboard INDEPENDENCE.   CDR. Raleigh C. Kirkpatrick came aboard in January 1946 as the CVL-22 Navigator & Tactical Officer, becoming Executive Officer on 28 February 1946.

Newspaper photo of the stern of the INDEPENDENCE with damage sustained at Bikini Atoll 5 years after the "Able" & "Baker" bomb test. Photo shot in San Francisco Bay in 1951.
Note her name on the ship's stern plate. Her raised steel letters would be observed once again in 2016 by ROV "Hercules" in the deep dark depths of the Pacific.

1412 Captain Kindell with 7 officers and 12 enlisted men departed the USS INDEPENDENCE to the USS ROCKWALL. The USS INDEPENDENCE is now completely secured and no personnel remain onboard. The ship is ready for test "Able".

Monday 1 July 1946   *"Dave's Dream" - Bikini Atoll - Test "Able"*

0859 Roughly 80 JTF aircraft were aloft. The bomb bay doors of "Dave's Dream" were open. Major Harold Wood released the Mk3A "Fat Man" type bomb from the Boeing B-29. At approximately 520 feet above sea level, the detonation occurred. A blinding 21 kiloton flash followed instantly by the searing heat and shock wave expanding out in circular globe that rapidly took on the form of a vertical mass moving rapidly upward.
An angry boiling column of released energy zoomed upward toward the stratosphere and began to billow outward. A colossal mutant cauliflower like atomic mushroom had sprung from Bikini's lagoon.

Below the column, five target ships surrendered to the horrific burst of energy and would settle to the bottom of the Bikini Lagoon. Six vessels were seriously damaged. Seventeen ships were damaged to a lesser degree, and the damage to forty three vessels was classified as negligible. The orange-red paint coating USS NEVADA did not assure accuracy. The "Able" test bomb had drifted off target over roughly 2,000 feet. The detonation occurred off the port stern quarter of INDEPENDENCE. Close in, and above the GILLIAM, the battered attack transport would sink rapidly. DDs ANDERSON and LAMPSON & APA CARLISLE sank, as did IJN's Agano-class light cruiser SAKAWA.

Vessels within 500 yards of the blast were sunk or severely damaged. Beyond 1,500 yards, the damage was said to be minor. The "Able" test was said to have gone smoothly.

What of the INDEPENDENCE? They could not learn the full story today. The error in the drop, due to drifting from target vessel NEVADA lessened the close in exposure and damage to INDEPENDENCE. There was a fire aft. It would have to burn. It would take three days before teams could go aboard to survey the damage created by the indignity of "Able". But she had remained afloat.
The Japanese torpedo didn't put her on the bottom in 1943. Today she survived "Fat Man".

The USS ROCKWALL at 0900 was observing the "Able" test at approximately 23 miles from the detonation. ROCKWALL steamed back into the lagoon to drop anchor at 1722.

Thursday 4 July 1946   *Bikini Atoll target area - The aftermath of test "Able"*

The INDEPENDENCE had been towed and moored in a berth by a salvage party. Three days have passed since the test. The initial boarding team went onboard and declared re-boarding to be radiologically safe.
1341 Captain Kindell and his team re-boarded the INDEPENDENCE.
1353 Team "Able" made up of 13 officers and 28 enlisted men re-boarded and began inspection of the ship accompanied by 1 Radiological Monitor. The O.O.D. and Q.M. watches were set on the forecastle.
1400 Team "Baker" came aboard and at 1440 moved to the front end of the flight deck.
1547 A group from the USS BURLESON boarded to photograph, inspect and pick up animals.
1630-1715 Evacuated the ship, securing the watch.

Friday 5 July 1946   *Bikini Atoll target area - Surveying the damage*

0800 Held quarters for muster aboard the USS ROCKWALL.
0845 Captain Kindell and his team re-boarded the INDEPENDENCE.
0905 Team "Able" with selected personnel from "Baker" re-boarded the ship, setting the O.O.D. and Q.M. watches on the forecastle. (O.O.D. = Officer of the Deck,   Q.M. = Quartermaster)
1040-1230 Congressmen Engle and Gillespie with Colonel Fredrick were onboard to inspect the ship.
1405 Started the forward emergency diesels to provide lights forward of frame 69.
1530 Commenced evacuation of the ship.
1555 Secured the forward emergency diesels.
1620   Completed evacuation of the ship, securing the watch.

Saturday 6 July 1946   *Bikini Atoll target area - Surveying the damage*

0800 Held quarters for muster aboard the USS ROCKWALL.
0845 Captain Kindell and his team re-boarded the INDEPENDENCE.
0910 Team "Able" with selected personnel from "Baker" re-boarded the ship, setting the O.O.D. and Q.M. watches on the forecastle.
0955-1055 Vice-Admiral Blandy, General McAuliffe and 6 officers (inspection party) were aboard.
1013 Started the forward emergency diesels to provide lights forward of frame 69.
1540 Commenced evacuation of the ship.
1550 Secured the forward emergency diesels.
1645 Completed evacuation of the ship, securing the watch.

Sunday 7 July 1946   *Bikini Atoll target area - Surveying the damage*

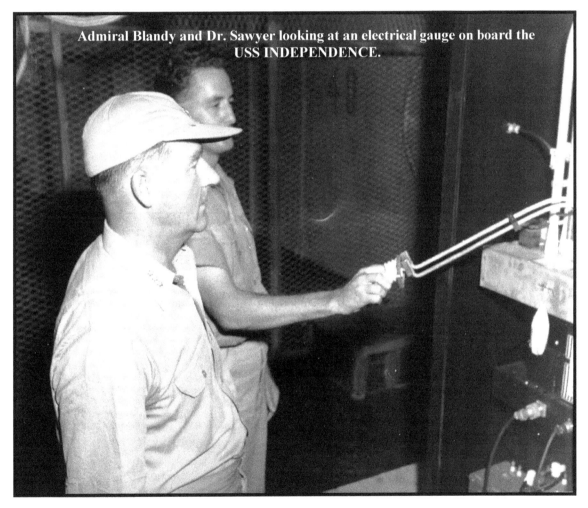

Admiral Blandy and Dr. Sawyer looking at an electrical gauge on board the USS INDEPENDENCE.

0800 Held quarters for muster aboard the USS ROCKWALL.
0850 Captain Kindell and his team re-boarded the INDEPENDENCE. General work parties with selected officers boarded the ship, setting the O.O.D. watch on the forecastle.
0904 Started the forward emergency diesels to provide lights forward of frame 69.
1530 Commenced evacuation of the ship.
1600 Secured the forward emergency diesels.
1705 Completed evacuation of the ship, securing the O.O.D. watch. Three signalmen were left aboard for an anchor watch.

INDEPENDENCE   SARATOGA

Slightly difficult to discern in shadow, the above photo shows the port side from the bow. She is still burning after the "Able" blast. The port side of the INDEPENDENCE bore the brunt of the blast, with the port stern quarter showing the worst of the exposure (*photo next page*).

* "Independence, "an impressive edifice of junk" that the bomb had blown into "a cocked hat""
(* James P. Delgado - Nuclear Dawn)

The following is a brief description of damage from Test "Able" :

Three full days after the test, crew members were finally allowed to re-board.
The draft was essentially the same as pretest conditions.
There was no noticeable damage to the hull below the waterline.
There was a four degree starboard list. The list attributed to loss of port side plating, gun buckets, catwalks, flight deck and the shift in weight toward the starboard of items displaced by the event.
The direction of pressure and shock from the initial blast was from aft, port side, 60 degrees off the centerline.
During the event, the ship developed a deep roll of roughly 40 degrees to starboard.
Surprisingly, despite the shock wave and the deep roll, pictures, clocks, battle lanterns, etc. remained in place in the forward part of the ship.
The aft port side overhanging corner of the flightdeck is gone.
Between the elevator wells, the flightdeck resembles a house roof, pitched upward toward the center.
Both elevator platforms were up prior to the test. Both aircraft elevator platforms are now gone. They simply vanished without leaving marks on the ship, blown up and off by the pressure wave.
The elevator rams, and two sets of elevator machinery appear to be intact.
The motor / pump / tank assembly for the port catapult was displaced starboard roughly 8 inches, making the port catapult inoperable. Up on the flight deck, the tracks for both catapults were undamaged.

Port stern quarter. Note the two crew members on the fantail

The unprotected wood on the flight deck did not at first show any heat effect. Gradually, it began blackening and after 13 days, looked distinctly charred.

At the time of re-boarding, the gray paint showed little noticeable discoloration, or effect. After several days the paint progressively turned dark, almost black and was all peeling. The red in the Japanese flags painted on the island structure have all turned white.

The aviation gasoline stowage, 40,000 gallons in 2 tanks was not damaged.

Ammunition in the ready lockers around the flight deck was not damaged. Below, protected in the magazines, bombs and rockets were not disturbed.

Had guns been in place in all provided locations, it was estimated that 50 percent of the 40mm guns and all centralized fire control would have been lost.

A slow fire, of unknown origin, had started with the blast on the stern of the ship somewhere within the blown in port quarter. It spread slowly thru compartments above the third deck. It reached the torpedo storage area off the hangar deck during the afternoon of July 1st.

Twelve torpedo warheads burned. A hole 2 feet by 12 feet was blown through the starboard side above the third deck, between frames 127 & 128, by an exploding torpedo. But the damage was comparatively small. The fire reached the aft elevator pit igniting tires on an Army F-1 trailer (displaced into the pit) at around 1700. The fire then consumed some flight deck planking aft of the rear elevator all the next day and into the night. The fire died out during the night of 2 July. The fire had progressed and burned for forty eight hours because there was no crew onboard to put it out.

Chapter 36   775

Twelve of the aircraft on board had no fuel or the fire would have been throughout the ship as the aircraft were torn to shreds both on the deck and in the hangar.

The shock wave had bounced the king post of the ships crane out of its bearing mount (generally undamaged but tilted off its proper angle), and snapped off the ships mast structure.

The pressure wave that followed blew out the elevators, expanded the hangar deck, pushed upward the flight deck, blew inward exposed doors, bent the radio masts over the flightdeck, tore away catwalks, boat booms, gangways and gun buckets, striped nude the island structure of searchlights, masts, the lookout platform and antennas. All radar antennas were gone.

After the pressure wave subsided, a strong wind developed in a direction toward the point of the explosion.

The ships control station on the bridge and the control station at the port forward corner of the flight deck were both operable. The ships steering gear and rudder were operable, the engine telegraph, gyro, compass and all compass repeaters but one, were operable. The bridge floor and side plates were warped, but the bridge was still usable.

Below in CIC, much of the equipment had relatively little damage but was effectively out of commission due to the loss of all the radar antennas.
In Radio 1 & 2, the transmitters and receivers were intact, but all antennas had been demolished.
The ships Loran set in the chart room took a thrashing, and was demolished.
Most of the machinery was in good condition. The main engines and generators, the two 150 KW diesel generators, the boilers and evaporators were all functional.
The four stacks (boiler uptakes) were bent over during the event and needed to be cleared, however it turned out to be a good thing as this sealed off access by the pressure wave into the boilers, saving them from possible catastrophic damage.

Two gassed airplanes had been on the stern. They were blown away without starting any fires.
The deep roll to the starboard cleaned house. A P-47 ended up in the front elevator pit, a trailer went into the aft elevator pit (the trailer with the tires that burned). The deep roll put another aircraft halfway up the starboard side of the hangar, and slid all the ships furniture starboard.
The hangar deck and flight deck were not usable, however the decks were deemed fit to walk on, though dangerous aft of the elevator opening.

The port side of the hangar was blown in, and every other supporting I-beam was broken at the hangar level, leaving fragile support at best for areas of the reshaped flight deck. The starboard side of the hangar was holed and partially blown out by plating from the port side and by aircraft being blown onto and through it. Shops and storerooms in the stern were demolished.
The port quarter was blown in by external pressure.
Many exposed doors were blown inward, not showing as much strength as supporting bulkheads and structures. On the port side many walkways and gun tubs are missing or bent upward at angles rendering them useless.

The fantail is only usable on the starboard side.
The underwater water hull was basically intact, and suffered only minor leakage through a shaft seal which was easily corrected retightening the packing.
There was some wrinkling of the hull below the main deck due to torque during clockwise rotation of the stern at the time of the "Able" bomb explosion. This was caused by uneven pressure applied to the high aft port side as the shock and pressure waves progressed along the hull.
The armor plate main deck was crushed down as much as a foot in some places in the elevator wells by high pressure within the hangar. The hangar deck protected the main deck in other areas.
The galley and mess areas are usable.
The crew's quarters sustained damage rendering them roughly half usable.

The chief's quarters were demolished, the officers quarters and messes are usable.
Every ventilation vent duct had splits or blowouts from the pressure. The ventilation system showed no signs of carrying heat, smoke or fire below decks to any extent.

Had this not been a test, and had a crew been onboard, everyone on any weather deck or in the hangar deck would have been killed or blown overboard. There would have been many causalities below deck due to pressure, shock, concussion, collisions. It was felt that 50 percent (75 percent of the Air Department) crew would have been killed or injured during daylight hours, less at night since much of the living quarters took less punishment.

The ship would need approximately 6 months in a yard for repair.

The fighting efficiency of the USS INDEPENDENCE has been reduced to zero.

Hank Schmalen *"I will try to state briefly my duties on the U.S.S. Independence during Operation Crossroads. I was a MM2/C in the "A" Division assigned to evaporators. We operated the evaporators with no extra preparations or precautions until leaving the Independence for berthing on a Liberty type troop transport ship. We were on the transport ship during the test until after the Baker detonation. During each test we were topside and covered our eyes with our arms. We were allowed to look immediately after each detonation.*

I was assigned to a boarding party but did not go on the first re-entry the morning after test Able. This was for scientists and personnel to check damage and radiation levels. I did go aboard the next morning. A memorable thing about going aboard the Independence was having to climb a rope ladder which was hanging from the flight deck near the bow.

The Independence had heavy damage in certain places but was quite normal in others (except for radiation of course). Something I've always remembered was a fire engine which was lashed down on the port side aft of the flight deck. It was partly blown apart and burned except as nice as could be, were the wheels with four Firestone tires, still like brand new.

I was on the boarding crew which went over each morning until late afternoon. We did this until the day before the Baker test. We were given a new change of greens each day but I don't remember being monitored for radiation each day, if at all. We were given "K-rations" to eat for lunch each day but being young and not knowing better we ate some canned fruit salad which had gone through the test. After test Baker, we were transferred to a repair ship (the Ajax AR-1) for transport back to Hawaii and subsequently back to the States for leave and re-assignment." ***Hank Schmalen***

(Posted on a Atomic Veterans History Project web site, used with the permission of Keith Whittle)

Monday 8 July 1946   *Bikini Atoll target area - Surveying the damage*

0800 Held quarters for muster aboard the USS ROCKWALL.
0850 Captain Kindell and his team reboarded the INDEPENDENCE. Team "Able" with selected personnel from "Baker" reboarded the ship, setting the O.O.D. and Q.M. watches on the forecastle.
0920 Started the forward emergency diesels to provide lights forward of frame 69.
1000 Made inspection of the magazines finding some of the stowage in disarray.
1530 Commenced evacuation of the ship.
1725 Secured all power and lights. Completed evacuation of the ship, securing the O.O.D. watch.

Tuesday 9 July 1946   *Bikini Atoll target area - Moved to a new berth*

0800 Held quarters for muster aboard the USS ROCKWALL. The USS INDEPENDENCE was towed by a salvage party to a new assigned berth, arriving at the new berth at 1030.
The day passed much like the previous days with work parties returning to the INDEPENDENCE and disembarking to return to the USS ROCKWALL at roughly the same time.

View of the port side (stern on the right)

View of the starboard side (bow on the right)

This photo was taken on 22, 23 or 24 July 1946

Wednesday 10 July 1946   *Bikini Atoll target area*

Today, pretty much a repeat of yesterday, except at 0750 Captain Kindell proceeded to the USS MOUNT MCKINLEY to attend a conference.

Thursday 11 July 1946   *Bikini Atoll target area*

0745 INDEPENDENCE crew commenced boarding using a cargo net on the side of the forecastle.
0801 Started the forward emergency diesels to provide power and lights.
1345-1600 Rear Admiral Solberg was aboard with his inspection party.
1505-1605 Major General Kepner was aboard with his party.
1540-1645 Evacuated the ship. One officer and 8 enlisted men remained aboard as watch standers.

Friday 12 July 1946   *Bikini Atoll target area*

0740 Crew members disembarked from the ROCKWALL to board INDEPENDENCE .
0845 Jacked over No.1 and 4 main engines.
This morning, USS SARATOGA stood into the target area. The crew of the gallant lady didn't know it (though they may have guessed it), but she had only few short days to remain afloat.
0945 Lighted fires under No.2 boiler.
1320 Started No.1 turbo generator, placing it online and securing the diesel generator at 1359.
1530-1615 Evacuated the ship, with the exception of 37 men.

Wednesday 17 July 1946   *Bikini Atoll target area - Moved to a new berth*

Moored in the Bikini Atoll target area, with the No.2 boiler in use for auxiliary purposes.
0710 A tug began making preparations for moving us to a new berth.
0755 The ships work party, in small boats, came aboard from the ROCKWALL.
0940 Moved from the forward buoy, aided by tugs, toward a new berth.
1037 Dropped the port anchor, with a tug standing by to assist mooring to a buoy with the starboard anchor chain. Today the INDEPENDENCE took on fuel oil and diesel fuel.

Monday 22 July 1946   *Bikini Atoll target area*

1115 Moored as before. LCT 1187 was alongside delivering a TBM.
1300 USS INDEPENDENCE received a SB2C, delivered from the CV-3, USS SARATOGA.

Wednesday 24 July 1946   *Bikini Atoll target area - Moved to a new berth*

Moored in the assigned berth in the Bikini Atoll target area.
0800 Captain Kindell boarded the USS INDEPENDENCE with his party.
1145 Commenced evacuating the ship. All watertight doors, hatches, fittings, ventilation, fire mains, flushing and drain systems were secured.
1230 Secured the forward emergency generator and all power and lights.
1316 Captain Kindell and his party departed the ship. The INDEPENDENCE was completely evacuated and in a condition of maximum watertight integrity in preparation for the "Baker" test.

Thursday 25 July 1946   *"Operation Crossroads" - Bikini Atoll target area - Test "Baker"*

It was the calm before the storm in the once peaceful lagoon. Inside the lagoon the average depth was roughly 120 feet. Lesser damaged vessels might have appeared to have floated serenely at their moorings in the target zone, had it not been for all the pre-Baker activity. There would be no B-29 drop for today's test. Instead, today the bomb was suspended 90 feet below the surface beneath LSM-60.
(See photo of LSM-60 on Index page 853)
Major vessels circling the weapon were USS INDEPENDENCE, USS PENSACOLA, USS ARKANSAS, USS NEW YORK and USS SARATOGA. Further out, the once feared Japanese battleship NAGATO, battered and pummeled by our forces until she looked to be a floating junkyard.

But despite our best efforts, NAGATO still floated. She was moored between USS NEVADA and USS SALT LAKE CITY. NEVADA was not the zero point for this test. The former German heavy cruiser PRINZ EUGEN (having battled the British alongside the dreaded BISMARCK) was moored still further distant.

INDEPENDENCE personnel were safely onboard the USS ROCKWALL approximately 16 miles upwind from the nuclear device. INDEPENDENCE herself had an isle seat close enough to center stage, only 1390 yards from "surface zero".
Sixty eight target vessels were at their moorings within the lagoon, and additionally, twenty four smaller craft were beached on the atoll.

At 0835 a blinding flash was rapidly followed by a globe of water, steam and debris blooming upward from the surface rapidly expanding out and shooting for the heavens. It rose thousands of feet high and *"at its base a tidal wave of spray and steam rose to smother the fleet"*, a radioactive spray mixed with coral and sand stirred from the lagoon bottom that would cause more problems than had been anticipated. The massive outgoing tidal wave swept across the fleet and untold tons of water forced skyward would relent to gravity as its massive weight fell back upon the target area vessels still afloat.

The following is from a *"Defense Threat Reduction Agency"* Fact Sheet About Operation Crossroads:

"BAKER inflicted heavy damage on the target fleet. Eight ships, including SARATOGA were sunk; eight more were seriously damaged. Even more important for the remainder of the operation, the detonation caused most of the target fleet to be bathed in radioactive water spray containing debris from the nuclear device, mixed with material dredged from the lagoon bottom.

The water in the lagoon near surface zero was intensely radioactive for several days. By July 30, many target ships remained too radioactive for boarding, and it was becoming apparent that the target fleet was much more heavily contaminated than had been expected. For all but 12 target vessels, the target fleet remained too radiologically contaminated to allow more than brief onboard activities.

Most of the thorough inspection and documentation of BAKER's effects, a primary objective of Operation CROSSROADS, was seriously delayed.
Within a week after the detonation, JTF commanders realized that they had to attempt to decontaminate the target vessels, even though they acknowledged that " since the nature and extent of contamination of the targets was completely unexpected, no plans had been prepared for organized decontamination measures." Beginning on August 1, work crews drawn from the target ships' companies sprayed and scrubbed the ships' exteriors-always under the supervision of radiation safety (rad-safe) monitors equipped with radiac instruments. Initially, decontamination proceeded slowly because safe time aboard some of the target ships was severely limited, sometimes to only a few minutes. Also, removing the radioactive particles imbedded in the paint, rust, and organic materials of the ships was a very slow and labor-intensive process. Crews experimented with a variety of techniques and decontaminating agents-including blasting with ground coconut shells, rice, ground coffee, and sand-but none worked well enough to significantly speed up the process.

In the meantime, radioactive contaminants in the water had spread to the lagoon anchorage of the support fleet. This became a serious problem as contamination accumulated in the ships' evaporators, saltwater piping, and marine growth on the outside of their hulls, potentially exposing shipboard personnel to low-level radiation.

By August 10, the increasing contamination of the support fleet, the futile decontamination effort of the target fleet, and finally the persistence of alpha radiation emitters (e.g., plutonium) on the ships forced the JTF to order an end to the decontamination work in Bikini and the towing of salvageable ships to Kwajalein Atoll, where they could be serviced in uncontaminated water. The move was completed by the end of September.

A major task at Kwajalein was to offload ammunition stored aboard some target ships before it became dangerously unstable, even though the ships were still contaminated. The work, which had to be carried out under strict radiation safety conditions, continued into fall 1946.

Eight of the major target ships and two submarines were eventually towed back to the United States and Hawaii for radiological inspection. Thirteen target ships that were only slightly contaminated were re-manned and sailed back to the United States. The remaining target ships were sunk off Bikini Atoll, off Kwajalein Atoll, or near the Hawaiian Islands between 1946 and 1948. The support ships were decontaminated as necessary at Navy shipyards in the United States and rejoined the fleet after receiving operational clearance. "

In addition to SARATOGA succumbing to "Baker", USS ARKANSAS, submarines USS APOGON and USS PILOTFISH were lost. And ravaged NAGATO finally settled to the bottom 5 days later.

USS ROCKWALL (in San Francisco Bay) - host to the INDEPENDENCE crew at Bikini Atoll

Monday 12 August 1946   *Bikini Atoll - Transfer to the USS AJAX*

The crew of the USS INDEPENDENCE have not been able to re-board due to radiation levels. Today all USS INDEPENDENCE personnel and gear were transferred from the USS ROCKWALL to the USS AJAX (AR-6).

Sunday 18 August 1946   *Bikini Atoll - Re-board the CVL-22*

0915 Captain Kindell with 2 officers, 3 chief petty officers and 24 enlisted men (and 2 additional officers who were radiation monitors) boarded the USS INDEPENDENCE . They proceeded to open up the ship and inspected it for lack of oxygen, toxic gasses, explosive gasses, and the levels of radioactivity.
The physical damage to the ship by the second atomic bomb was minimal. The principal problem appears to be high levels of radioactivity on all surfaces exposed to weather. Water levels in spaces monitored were considered to be normal, and the ship was within standards of normal list and trim.

1000 Approximately 160 officers and enlisted men began transferring to the USS ARTEMIS (AKA-21) for transportation to Pearl Harbor.
1330 The team aboard the INDEPENDENCE departed for return to the USS AJAX.

Monday 19 August 1946   *Bikini Atoll - Re-board the CVL-22*

0930 Captain Kindell with his inspection party (and 2 radiation monitors) boarded the USS INDEPENDENCE again today. Visual inspection of compartments revealed no noticeable additional damage other than "derangement" of loose items and furniture. The forward emergency diesel generator (to provide power and lights) was started, and both port and starboard anchor windlasses were tested.
1310 Secured the forward emergency diesel generator. Minutes later the team evacuated the ship, returning to the AJAX.

Tuesday 20 August 1946   *Bikini Atoll - Re-board the CVL-22*

Captain Kindell with his work detail of 3 officers, 3 C.P.O.s and 39 enlisted men (accompanied by 3 radiation safety monitors) boarded the USS INDEPENDENCE again today.
0810 Started the forward diesel generator.
0835 The inspection party of the Director of Ship Material boarded to inspect the engineering spaces, hull electrical systems and armament.
1200 The port anchor was secured for sea. The inspection party of the Director of Ship Material departed the ship.
1310 Secured the forward emergency diesel generator.
1320 The crew evacuated the ship, returning to the AJAX.

Wednesday 21 August 1946   *Bikini Atoll - Re-board the CVL-22*

Captain Kindell with his work party of 2 officers, 3 C.P.O.s and 37 enlisted men (and 1 radiation safety monitor) boarded the USS INDEPENDENCE again today.
0930 Started the forward diesel generator. The crew then began pumping water from the engineering spaces, and began closing up and securing the ship per a JTF memorandum to all target vessels.

1230 Shut down the forward emergency diesel generator, and closed up and secured the ship.
1300 The crew evacuated the ship, returning to the AJAX.

Sunday 25 August 1946   *Bikini Atoll - Begin the tow to Kwajalein Atoll*

USS INDEPENDENCE began its journey back to the US, as USS MUNSEE (ATF-107) took her in tow to Kwajalein Atoll. INDEPENDENCE arrived in Kwajalein Atoll on 27 August 1946 and was anchored.

Wednesday 28 August 1946   *Kwajalein Atoll - USS INDEPENDENCE is Decommissioned*

On 27 and 28 August, Captain Kindell and the remaining officers and crew were transferred officially off the USS INDEPENDENCE, (for the most part via USS AJAX) for transportation to Pearl Harbor. USS AJAX would anchor at Pearl Harbor on September 6th where most of the INDEPENDENCE crew would disembark.

The last entry in the INDEPENDENCE Deck Log, Wednesday 28 August 1946 states:

"In accordance with Commander Advance Echelon, JTF-1 ltr., CTG 1.2/A4-1/P16-2 (91:Nu) Serial 918 of 22 August 1946, the U.S.S. INDEPENDENCE (CVL-22) was decommissioned this date at Kwajalein Atoll, Marshall Islands."

Decommissioned USS INDEPENDENCE, now referred to by the navy as Ex-INDEPENDENCE, would remain at Kwajalein Atoll for seven months where she underwent radiological and decontamination studies.

15 May, 1947 Ocean tugs USS HITCHITI and USS PAKANA towed USS INDEPENDENCE to San Francisco, arriving at Hunters Point on 16 June 1947.

(USS NEW YORK & USS NEVADA would be taken to Pearl Harbor. USS PENSACOLA, HUGHES & SALT LAKE CITY were sent to Puget Sound Naval Shipyard. The CRITTENDEN & GASCONADE would join INDEPENDENCE at the San Francisco Naval Shipyard, with submarines SKATE & SKIPJACK sent on to Mare Island.)

1946

Adm. William H.P. Blandy and Mrs. Blandy with Adm. Frank Lowry.

They are cutting an "Operation Crossroads" cake.

INDEPENDENCE berthed at Hunters Point Shipyard for NRDL studies (note 22 on her flight deck).
Top photo: The "Gun Mole" is at the upper right where the large crane is.
Another vessel at is the end of the pier where the INDEPENDENCE will later be relocated.

Bottom photo: INDEPENDENCE - Hunters Point Shipyard relocated at the "Gun Mole".

The Final Years

INDEPENDENCE was one of six "Operation Crossroads" contaminated target ships towed to
San Francisco Bay. The nearest to the " zero-point ", and longest studied, she would be the last to leave.

In 1946 the CNO ordered the establishment of an organization *"tasked with applying radiological safety within the Navy"*. This was in recognition of problematic new issues as a direct result of the scientific development and utilization of nuclear weapons, and the opportunity "Operation Crossroads" provided to study exposed vessels (and other assets) including effects on personnel.
 "The military services recognized that changes would be required for both offensive and defensive measures in any future conflicts".

The initial organization was the "RSS", to become referred to as the "RADLAB".
" Original tasking for RSS included development of radiation detection instrumentation, equipment for protection of personnel onboard ships, and development of methods and equipment for decontamination of ships". " The original charter was intended to support OPERATION CROSSROADS". The return to HPS of "Crossroads" vessels would begin the expansion of the original mission.

Hunters Point Shipyard (HPS) was selected as the most logical location (over its other facilities) to effectuate the studies due to the close proximity to the University of California at Berkeley (across the bay near Oakland), and Stanford University (further south - deep within the bay near Palo Alto).
The HPS facilities would be named NRDL - Naval Radiological Defense Laboratory.
At NRDL, *"extensive research and experimentation on decontamination methods, personnel protection, and development of radiation detection instrumentation"*.
In "1948, the RADLAB was formalized as the NRDL with a greatly expanded mission" with a staff of 3 in 1946, to 200 by March 1949.
(This page- italic quotations from HPS HRA)

INDEPENDENCE - Flight Deck at Hunters Point

"Since its return from OPERATION CROSSROADS, the carrier ex-INDEPENDENCE was retained for use by the RADLAB and subsequently by NRDL for experimentation, testing of decontamination methods, storage of radioactive wastes, and as a dockside laboratory".

Decommissioned INDEPENDENCE was moored at the San Francisco Naval Yard at Hunters Point undergoing damage, decontamination, and radiological studies by the NRDL (Navy Radiological Defense Laboratory). She spent some time in Dry Dock 4 and later (1950) she was docked at the "Gun Mole" - Berths 16 & 17 also known as the "Regunning Pier" *"where NRDL had a field laboratory that managed work on the carrier".* At the "Gun Mole" she was berthed and contaminated equipment was removed *[1]. It was "*also a loading point for radioactive wastes*".

When Independence arrived, there was a problem of 274,000 gallons of radioactively contaminated fuel-oil to contend with. The fuel appears to have been burned (with Bu.Ships & Bu.Med " *safety Precautions* " monitoring the air in the bay) throughout mid 1947 in the ships boiler fireboxes.

Eventually, turbines, boiler condenser units, other machinery, electrical and electronic components, hatch covers, etc., were declared radiologically safe and would be removed for reuse. Some machinery; boilers, condensers and turbines were loaded aboard cargo transport USS ANDROMEDA and shipped to Navy's Guided Missile Test Center at Point Mugu to be installed as a steam power plant.

Thoroughly surveyed and documented, INDEPENDENCE was used for further radiological and decontamination studies until 1951.

The NRDL was done with her, and had no further use for the ex-INDEPENDENCE.

" Ex-INDEPENDENCE, loaded with radioactive waste from NRDL and other generators, was towed to sea and sunk in January 1951".

"Mr. Fong[2] recalled experimentation done on the ex-INDEPENDENCE to test the levels of exposure sailors would receive from detonation of an atomic weapon. To do this, a Co-60 source was placed in a plastic pipe that ran the length of the INDEPENDENCE. The source was moved through the pipe by water so they could get uniform exposure rates and check the attenuation effect of the decks and compartments. Dosimeters were hung throughout the ship to measure the exposure that the sailors would have received".*

"Among his memories of working at NRDL and HPS, Mr. Sartor[3] remembers evaluating various procedures for decontaminating the flight deck of the ex-INDEPENDENCE after OPERATION CROSSROADS. He said the ship was docked at the end of the Gun Mole.*
He remembered the residual sandblast material on the INDEPENDENCE was washed overboard to the Bay. At the time the ship was to be towed to sea and sunk, the Navy informed all Bay area facilities storing radioactive waste that they could load all their radioactive waste onto ex-INDEPENDENCE"

The *ex-INDEPENDENCE *[4] and two other* target ships contained fuel oil *"contaminated with low levels of plutonium and mixed fission products".* Air in the general bay area was monitored as the fuel oil was consumed in the ships boilers. Those air quality / contaminant levels from the HRA are not noted here.

(This page- italic quotations from HPS HRA)
([1] HRA Table 6-4)
([2] *Mr. Filbert Fong - "Mr. Fong was employed by NRDL from 1957 to 1969". "Mr. Fong worked in the Health Physics Division of NRDL. The Health Physics Division was responsible for overseeing safe use of radioactive materials and machines that produced ionizing radiation".*)
([3] *Mr. James Sator - "Mr. Sartor worked for Dr. Ed Thompson in the Technical Development Branch".*)
([4] INDEPENDENCE had 274,000 gallons.)

The Final Disposition

A letter to the Chief of Naval Operations stamped 23 December 1949 addressed the condition of the ship, still radioactive, (additionally, other contaminated materials had been moved on board) to help with the determination of the final disposition of the INDEPENDENCE.

INDEPENDENCE at Hunters Point

The consideration of disposing of her as scrap were overweighed by the cost of remediating the above mentioned hazards, and the possibility of *"subjecting the Navy to possible medico-legal litigation"*. The scrap value also questionable due to the large available supply of steel scrap from other sources. Then, there was the possible benefit to future ship design if she was used for proposed weapons testing and concluded *"it is considered that disposition of INDEPENDENCE by sinking incident to the underwater explosion tests proposed in reference (b) will serve the best interests of the Navy."*

She was loaded with radioactive waste *" from the NRDL, and other generators"* *[5.]

*[5.] Source: Hunters Point Shipyard - Final **H**istorical **R**adiological **A**ssessment - Historical Use of General Radioactive Materials 1939 - 2003.

On 16 January 1951 "Operation Order ComWestSeaFron No. 1-51" was issued. A new Task group would take form. INDEPENDENCE would proceed out to sea again, this time in company of Task Group 98.5. At sea she was now destined to remain, by order of the CNO.

The underwater explosion test was jointly sponsored by Bu. Ships and Bu. Ordnance, to be conducted by the Underwater Explosion Research Division of Naval Shipyard, Norfolk, VA.

Task Group 98.5 (Capt. W. H. Pickton, USN) consisted of the following elements:

    98.5.1 "Towing Unit"
                USS SARSI (ATF-111)
    98.5.2 "Surface Photographic Unit"
                USS SARSI (ATF-111)
                USS CAHOKIA (ATA-186)
                USS GEORGE A. JOHNSON (DE-583)
    98.5.3 "Air Photographic Unit" consisting of 1 R4D and 1 SNB
    98.5.4 "Test Unit"
    98.5.5 "Explosives Unit" consisting of one Explosive Ordnance Disposal Team

Orders were to *"tow the ex-CVL 22 to sea and sink it by underwater explosion, making photographic record of its movements under explosion stresses, to dispose of the hulk and to obtain technical information useful in the design of ships and weapons."*

- USS SARSI was tasked to supply boat service for the Explosives Unit.
- USS CAHOKIA was to assist the USS SARSI with towing as needed.
- The USS GEORGE A. JOHNSON in addition to its photographic duties would also provide boat service for the Explosives Unit if / as needed.

The additional directive was contained in the orders: *"Do not board the ex-CVL 22 except in line of duty and only after being properly cleared and instructed by the Naval Radiological Defense Laboratory, San Francisco."*

The ex-CVL 22 was to be towed to sea the first day the (actual and forecasted) weather and state of the sea permitted favorable conditions (during the period of 24 January - 7 February), with little wind or sea. Part of the concern was to provide good visibility and stable platforms for the Photographic Units.

The test was to: *"be conducted approximately forty miles southwest of San Francisco Lightship"* *[1.]*.
It had been anticipated the Task Group could not make the tow with enough daylight remaining on the first day.
(*[1.]* San Francisco Light Ship was stationed 8.6 miles off Point Bonita Lighthouse.)

On Monday 22 January 1951 a 0900 conference was scheduled to be held within the Administration Building, San Francisco Naval Shipyard, to assist in the coordination of the Task Group and support services for carrying out the orders.

From the Orders:

Tuesday 23 January 1951 at or before 0800 the SARSI was to be berthed at Naval Shipyard,
San Francisco, while CAHOKIA and GEORGE A. JOHNSON were to be berthed at Naval Station Treasure Island, and all necessary preparations would be made to conduct their tasked assignments.

At 1200 on each succeeding day (until test completion) the TG Commander was to obtain a special 48 hour weather forecast for the S.F. Bay, the Golden Gate, and an area extending 60 miles seaward from San Francisco.

By 1600 the ex-INDEPENDENCE was to have been made ready for the tow and the test.

During the period from 24 January - 7 February 1951, when conditions were favorable:

H hour was defined as the hour the ex-CVL 22 was unmoored.

H-1 hour: The Test Unit and the Explosives Unit were to embark on the USS CAHOKIA, stowage of charges to be checked, and proceed underway.

H hour :   At the Naval Yard, San Francisco the ex-CVL 22 was to be unmoored and turned over to the USS SARSI. The USS CAHOKIA was to rendezvous with the SARSI off Hunters Point and one shipyard YTB was to assist with the tow until released seaward of the main channel.

H+ 30 minutes: GEORGE A. JOHNSON would get underway, and at roughly H+1 hour would rendezvous with the SARSI and remain within visual signaling distance.

Bikini aftermath - Two tugs tow INDEPENDENCE out from Hunters Point for scuttling.
Note the range poles positioned along the length of the ship for study of the photography of the
effects of the scuttling charges.
Tugs are possibly the USS SARSI and the USS CAHOKIA .

Photo courtesy of: The National Park Service

- At an hour and one half prior to the "test', the aircraft were to be requested. They were to report on station when ready.
- The SARSI was to bring the tow into the wind at less than one knot, and then launch a boat.
- The Explosives Unit would rig the charge and report when ready.
- The vessels photographing the event were to take stations as follows:

SARSI	500 - 700 feet 15 degrees on the port bow.
JOHNSON	700 - 900 feet broad on the port beam.
CAHOKIA	500 - 700 feet 15 degrees on the port quarter.

- The photo planes were to circle at the best safe altitude and distance for their photo assignment.
- The "Test" charge was to be detonated.

The Tow   (See photos next page)

On 25 January 1951 conditions were favorable and H hour arrived. At 0440 Naval Shipyard Pilot Oakley (he had twice before piloted the CVL-22 in San Francisco Bay) boarded the USS SARSI. At 0730 USS CAHOKIA rendezvoused with SARSI and at 0735 SARSI (formation guide) took the INDEPENDENCE under tow from Hunters Point, passing under the Oakland Bay Bridge at 0839. USS George A. JOHNSON rendezvoused at 0905. At approximately 0941 on the morning of the 25th, INDEPENDENCE passed under the Golden Gate Bridge for the last time. At 1008, the tow took departure of San Francisco Bay proceeding to an area offshore, southwest of the Farallon Islands.

The Sinking

On 26 January 1951 at 0705 the Task Group arrived in the "Operational Area". The sea was reasonably flat, with light unsettled chop, under overcast skies. Sea birds circled as Task Group 98.5 elements assumed their positions and performed their assigned duties.

Per SARSI crew member George H. Cornell (verbal 2015 by phone), two charges were placed on the keel centerline. Deck logs (and George's notes) all slightly differ on the times observed.

At 0952 explosive charges attached to the Bikini battered hulk were fired, and the tow line was cut releasing the tow connection. The ship slowly developed a port list, and in roughly 15-20 minutes she had rolled over, settling on her port side, settling slightly down by the stern.

With her stern low in the water, and a large vertically billowing water froth from escaping air became evident at the stern. Minutes later only her bow and forward end of her flight deck were visible.

Water continued to fill her voids, and, with buoyancy depleted, the former USS AMSTERDAM CL-59 / USS INDEPENDENCE CV / CVL-22 began her stern first slide into the cold grasp of the sea, her crisp cruiser bow, now upright, vanished as she slipped beneath.

By 1024 the hulk of the INDEPENDENCE had sunk from sight leaving a large temporary "Boil" on the surface to mark the site of her unceremonious burial at sea.

Soon there remained only the light unblemished chop as Task Group 98.5 dissolved and the remains of the once "Mighty-I" settled into the new resting place deep on the sloping floor of the vast Pacific.

Note: On 29 January 1951, she was said to have been sunk in a test of "new aerial and undersea weapons" by the US Navy <u>*in coverage by the press.*</u>

The former USS INDEPENDENCE was stricken by the Navy.

San Francisco - Under tow, out to sea

The Deep Blue Sea - Davy Jones Locker

The flags on striped range poles are in place to help measure the hull displacement, captured on high speed film footage during the blast.

This photo (Flight Deck side) viewed from GEORGE A. JOHNSON
Top 3 photos on next page are view from hull bottom side

Roughly 0920 to 0930, 26 January, 1951

USS INDEPENDENCE took on water from her new Navy induced wounds, and rolled over on her port side. As air was displaced by water, her buoyancy lost the battle with gravity, and she went down stern first.

Next page: Not US Navy photos. They are 35mm (color) photos of the sinking.

Bottom left: The poor quality photo on the showing the final demise of a proud lady as CVL-22, her bow raised as if for one last breath, she is almost engulfed by the mighty Pacific.

Bottom right: Only the boil of escaping air and a circling seagull, both capturing in a brief fleeting moment, serve as her headstone, if seen today ... Perhaps a ghostly apparition!

Photo courtesy of George H. Cornell from aboard USS SARSI ATF-111
Blast plus 15 minutes

Note the photo aircraft
The DD is the GEORGE A. JOHNSON

Photo courtesy of George H. Cornell from aboard USS SARSI ATF-111
Blast plus 17 minutes

Photo courtesy of George H. Cornell from aboard USS SARSI ATF-111
Blast plus 19 minutes

Photo courtesy of George H. Cornell
from aboard USS SARSI ATF-111

Blast plus 20 minutes

"THE BOIL"

They had been shipmates !

DL   We had been shipmates. Our experiences had been intense and personal. At last I saw these men for what they, and I, had been during that harsh existence. A few had been drafted, most had enlisted. And what were we? Well, we were not the former admirals, not the ship skippers and navigators, not the anonymous deck officers or the vaunted airplane pilots whose exploits the history books recorded and the movies extolled. Only a handful had ever fired a gun "in anger," as the dreary saying goes. Few had seen the face of the enemy from the flightdeck of our carrier until the Fleet had steamed victorious into Tokyo Bay beneath leaden skies and an umbrella of the planes that had helped get us there.

What had to be done on any ship, we had done. We had swabbed the decks, chipped the rust, painted and repainted the endless compartments and magazines, loaded mountains of stores from canned beans to toilet paper. We had armed and rearmed the aircraft, serviced or changed their engines on rolling decks, patched bullet holes and reconstructed rudders and ailerons shattered by anti-aircraft fire, dodged knife sharp propellers, given thumbs-up to the pilots (many of whom called us Deck Apes) as they were launched into their hazardous missions, kept a sharp eye down the flightdeck while they were recovered hours later—and were glad when they came back at all. We former landlubbers had feared for our lives in raging typhoons while our betters were still trying to find out where the storms were coming from. We had cooked the food and baked the bread and manned the gedunk stand and the barbershop and, once a month when the Eagle shit, had pocketed our pitiful pay in cash or left it to accumulate on the Books.

And the Mighty-I ...

The last time I had seen Mighty I was pretty much like the first, except that I was older and alone. She was tied to a long, gray dock at Hunters Point, waiting to go to sea on her last voyage, this one to bring men home from afar before joining a horde of warships fated to be targets of experimental atomic explosions at an obscure Pacific island called Bikini. No longer was there a need for aviation ordnancemen.

I was wearing my regulation dress blues and my pea coat. Alongside one leg I had perched my seabags with most of my worldly goods including the Japanese portrait. In my small dittybag, neatly folded and officially signed, were my leave and discharge papers. No Phil was by my side. I kept thinking of him. Welcome aboard, sailor! he had told me on that May day so long ago.

At the quarterdeck I signed off for the last time, waiting in line. The JOOD was a bright-faced young ensign fresh out of Annapolis who had just come aboard. (I suppressed a desire to ask him if he had known a midshipman named Judd, my dear friend with whom I had enlisted). But I didn't know him. He didn't know any of us.
I put the dittybag down, turned aft, and snapped my ship, U.S.S. Independence CVL-22 , a final salute.

DON LABUDDE

USS INDEPENDENCE
CVL-22

In Honor of

"Would one day be eternity
I would spend it out at sea"

Annie Cordelia Adams

George Woodrow Obenour
"Obie"
VF(N)-41
12 October 1944

Jack Stanley Berkheimer
"Berky"
VF(N)-41
16 December 1944

Donald Richard Powers
VF(N)-41
16 Dec 1944

In Honor of

Bela Sobek
20 Nov 1943

Daniel Lee Rinick
23 Aug 1944

In GRATEFUL MEMORY OF

Bela Sobek

WHO DIED IN THE SERVICE OF HIS COUNTRY AT

Sea, Pacific Area, U.S.S. Independence, 20 November 1943

HE STANDS IN THE UNBROKEN LINE OF PATRIOTS WHO HAVE DARED TO DIE

THAT FREEDOM MIGHT LIVE, AND GROW, AND INCREASE ITS BLESSINGS.

FREEDOM LIVES, AND THROUGH IT, HE LIVES—

IN A WAY THAT HUMBLES THE UNDERTAKINGS OF MOST MEN

Franklin D Roosevelt

PRESIDENT OF THE UNITED STATES OF AMERICA

Fredrick Paul Lockwenz
23 Nov 1943

James Jefferson Mallard Clevenstine
30 Mar 1945

Bascom Eugene Gates
VF-6
30 Jul 1945

In Honor of

William Andrew Shipman
"Bill"
VF(N)-41
23 August 1944

Joseph Samuel Allen
"Joe Sam"
VF(N)-41
14 December 1944

Emmett Russell Edwards
"Eddy"
VF(N)-41
6 January 1945

"Life is like an onion. You peel it back one layer at a time, and sometimes you weep." - Carl Sandburg

Billy Robert Apgar
VF-46
3 June 1945

Edward Jilberto Rohner
VF-22
28 Mar 1943

Earl Willis Marsh
VF-22
11 Nov 1943

In Honor of

John B. L. Ashton and **Oliver Ashton** (Right)
Wounded in Action and **Missing in Action**
20 November 1943
(Brothers serving aboard, John survived)

George Edward Castro
F3c
22 November 1943

Warren Elias Callahan
VC-22
18 Jun 1943

Reuben Woodrow Baughman
"Woody"
VC-22
18 Jun 1943

Thomas J. Orzada
52nd AAF
18 Jun 1943

In Honor of

Carmine Francis Marchese
VT-27
18 July 1945

Lawrence Enoch Gardner
VT-27
18 July 1945

Harry Rowland Patterson
VT-27
18 July 1945

Daniel Ralph Berardinelli
VT-27
30 July 1945

Michael Harold Nagy, Jr.
VT-27
30 Jul 1945

Harold Eugene Gibson
VT-27
30 Jul 1945

Robert Oshme Zimmerman
VF-27
24 July 1945

Eugene Elwood Fellows
VF-27
1 September 1945

In Honor of

In Honor of

IN HONOR OF THESE MEN, KILLED OR MISSING
WHILE SERVING ON BOARD USS INDEPENDENCE CVL-22

Photos on page: 794- 798

EDWARD JILBERTO ROHNER	ENSIGN	28 March 1943	794
WARREN ELIAS CALLAHAN	LTJG	18 June 1943	795
REUBEN WOODROW BAUGHMAN	ARM3c	18 June 1943	795
ROBERT BRATCHER LOCKER	LTJG	14 September, 1943	172
JAMES SAMUEL BEHRENS	ENSIGN	27 October, 1943	
WILLIAM MARVIN MARTIN	ARM3c	27 October, 1943	
ROY ALFRED UTTER	AMM3c	27 October, 1943	
EARL WILLIS MARSH	LT	11 November 1943	794
JOHN CONEY KELLEY	LT	11 November 1943	
BASCOM EUGENE GATES, JR.	ENSIGN	11 November 1943	793
OLIVER ASHTON	F1c	20 November 1943	795
JOSEPH EDMOND BYRNE	S2c	20 November 1943	
GEORGE EDWARD CASTRO	F3c	20 November 1943	795
JOE ERWIN FRETWELL	S1c	20 November 1943	
JOHN LLOYD GRANT	F2c	20 November 1943	
WALTER ROBERT HUNT	S2c	20 November 1943	
EDWARD NEWMAN JONES	S1c	20 November 1943	
WALLACE GARDNER LEE	S1c	20 November 1943	
JAMES BOYDELL Mac KENZIE Jr.	GM3c	20 November 1943	
JOSEPH THERMON McGOWAN	S2c	20 November 1943	
EDWARD Mc LEAN	COXSWAIN	20 November 1943	
CLARENCE THORNTON ROBERTS	COXSWAIN	20 November 1943	
JOSEPH CHRISTY SEDGWICK	S2c	20 November 1943	
BELA SOBEK	S2c	20 November 1943	793
THOMAS EUGENE STREETER	COXSWAIN	20 November 1943	
LAWRENCE LEWIS SWARTZ	S1c	20 November 1943	
FREDRICK PAUL LOCKWENZ	S2c	23 November 1943	793
EDWARD JOHN GLASER	ARM3c	22 July 1944	
JAMES EDWARD HOGAN	S2c	4 August 1944	
DANIEL LEE RINICK	AOM2c	23 August 1944	793
WILLIAM ANDREW SHIPMAN	ENSIGN	23 August 1944	794
JOSEPH F. MOORE	ENSIGN	12 October 1944	
GEORGE WOODROW OBENOUR	ENSIGN	12 October 1944	792
JOSEPH SAMUEL ALLEN	ENSIGN	14 December 1944	794
FREDRICK H. HANKINS	LT	14 December 1944	
JACK STANLEY BERKHEIMER	ENSIGN	16 December 1944	792 & 476
DONALD RICHARD POWERS	ENSIGN	16 December 1944	
CALVIN MILTON BECKER	S1c	18 December 1944	
EMMETT RUSSELL EDWARDS	ENSIGN	6 January 1945	794
FREDERICK EUGENE LIEBER	LTJG	24 March 1945	
RALPH JUNIOR REEDER	LTJG	29 March 1945	
JAMES JEFFERSON MALLARD CLEVENSTINE	S1c	30 March 1945	793
ROBERT THEODORE DYER, JR.	ENSIGN	3 June 1945	
BILLY ROBERT APGAR	LTJG	3 June 1945	794
LAWRENCE ENOCH GARDNER	ARM2c	18 July 1945	796
CARMINE FRANCIS MARCHESE	AOM3c	18 July 1945	796
HARRY ROWLAND PATTERSON	LTJG	18 July 1945	796
ROBERT OSHME ZIMMERMAN	LT	24 July 1945	796
DANIEL RALPH BERARDINELLI	ENSIGN	30 July 1945	
HAROLD EUGENE GIBSON	ARM3c	30 July 1945	796
MICHAEL HAROLD NAGY, Jr.	AOM3c	30 July 1945	796
EUGENE ELWOOD FELLOWS	ENSIGN	1 September 1945	796

In Honor of

USS INDEPENDENCE CVL-22

Captains

Oh Captain!   My Captain!   Our fearful trip is done;
The ship has weather'd every rack, the prize we sought is won;
The port is near, the bells I hear, the people all exulting,
While follow eyes the steady keel, the vessel grim and daring

Walt Whitman

Captains

Captain George Remington Fairlamb, Jr.   14 January 1943 - 27 September 1943
Comdr. Rudolph Lincoln Johnson   27 September 1943 - 26 July 1944
Captain Edward Coyle Ewen   26 July 1944 - 11 February 1945
Captain Noland M. Kindell   11 February 1945 - 28 August 1946

Captain George Remington Fairlamb, Jr.

Captain Rudolph Lincoln Johnson

Captain Edward Coyle Ewen

Captain Noland M. Kindell

Captain George Remington Fairlamb, Jr.
USS INDEPENDENCE (CVL-22)
14 January 1943 - 27 September 1943

Captain Fairlamb was aboard the
USS LEXINGTON CV-2 in 1936 (then a Lieut.
Commander), and CO (Commander) of
IX-64 - USS WOLVERWINE, a coal fired pad-
dlewheel training carrier on Lake Michigan
(pleasure steamer conversion).

Comdr. Rudolph Lincoln Johnson
USS INDEPENDENCE (CVL-22)
27 September 1943 - 26 July 1944

Rudolph Lincoln Johnson was born in Battle
Lake, Minnesota February 12, 1900.

He graduated Annapolis and was commissioned
as an Ensign on 2 June 1922.
He retired 30 June 1952 with the rank of Rear
Admiral and died at the US Naval Hospital,
Chelsea, Mass. on 21 July 1959. He was buried
with full military honors in the Arlington National Cemetery.

Captain R.L. Johnson with Admiral Montgomery

Captain Edward Coyle Ewen
USS INDEPENDENCE (CVL-22)
 26 July 1944 - 11 February 1945

Captain Ewen was born 26 May 1897 at
Portsmouth, New Hampshire.

He received the Navy Cross:
*"for extraordinary heroism and distinguished service
in the line of his profession as Commanding Officer of
the Light Aircraft Carrier U.S.S. INDEPENDENCE
(CVL-22) in action against the enemy during September and October 1944, he (Capt. Ewen) brought to
bear the full offensive strength of a new weapon - the
Night Operating Carrier - with such a high degree of
fortitude and effectiveness as to break up enemy
planes and airborne trackers. The independent operation of this carrier during long periods of high jeop-
ardy was an admirable example of successful Navy
pioneering. "*

CAPT. N.M. KINDELL, U.S.N.　　COMDR. D.F. SMITH JR, U.S.N.　　LT. COMDR. J.H. ARNOLD,
COMMANDING OFFICER　　　　　EXECUTIVE OFFICER　　　　　　AIR OFFICER

Captain Noland M. Kindell
USS INDEPENDENCE (CVL-22)　11 February 1945 - 28 August 1946
Captain Noland M. Kindell was born 8 December 1896 in Bradford, Ohio.
He joined the US Navy reserves on 24 April 1917.
He reported for flight training at the Massachusetts School of Technology, Naval Aviation Detachment, on17 September 1917 as Seaman 2c.
On 13 February 1918 he attained the grade of Ensign, and appointed as a Naval Aviator at NAS Pensacola, FL 25 February 1918. He reported to the US Naval Aviation Forces in Paris France in 1918.
By 1924 he had soloed in 6 different aircraft.
He was placed on the retired list on 1 October 1948 with a rank of Rear Admiral with retired pay based on the rank of Captain.
He was recommended for promotion to the rank of Rear Admiral by Rear Admiral A.W. Radford in a letter report of fitness dated 29 June 1945.
The letter stated:
"2. The period covered by this report was one of long sustained offensive operations under the most varied and exacting conditions. The INDEPENDENCE and her attached air group made an outstanding contribution to the accomplishments of the Task Group. She was handled with skill and judgment (SIC) at all times, and her operations were notable for precision and dependability. Her performance reflected great credit on the commanding officer. Captain KINDELL is capable and thorough, and I am pleased to have him in command of a carrier of this group."

USS INDEPENDENCE CVL-22

The Admirals

"The burdens that make us groan and sweat,
The troubles that make us fume and fret,
Are the things that haven't happened yet."

George Bain

Fleet Admiral Ernest J. King, Secretary of the Navy James V. Forrestal, Fleet Admiral Chester W. Nimitz

Admirals Raymond A. Spruance, Marc A. Mitscher, Chester W. Nimitz, Willis A. Lee, Jr.

Fleet Admiral William F. Halsey

Admiral Arthur W. Radford

Admiral John H. Towers

Admiral Gerald F. Bogan   (1949)

Admirals   810

Admiral Marc A. Mitscher (1946)

Admiral John S. McCain, Sr.

Admiral Forrest P. Sherman
(Deputy Chief of Staff under Nimitz)

Vice Admiral Frederick C. Sherman

Admirals   811

USS INDEPENDENCE CVL-22

Crew Photos

"If you want to build a ship,
 don't drum up people together to collect wood
 and don't assign them tasks and work,
  but rather teach them to long for the endless immensity of the sea"

Antoine de Saint-Exupery

Crew Photos

CHIEF PETTY OFFICERS OF THE USS INDEPENDENCE CVL 22...25 AUGUST 1945

STANDING left to right

Moe. CPhM: Franceschini, CEM: Kiecher. ACMM; Shepard, ACMM; Freeman, CEM; Kellner, ACMM; Glager. CWT; Bass. CMM: Einhorn, CBM; Saxon, CMoMM; Lewis, ACOM; Smith, CRM; Seely, CTM; Winderweedle.ACOM; Powski. ACMM Gardner, CPR; Day. CGM

KNEELING left to right

Krantz, CBM: Galland, CWT; Weatherford, CSK; Carlson, CY. Mathes.CWT; Rhyne, CCM; Coleman.CAerM; Eddy, CCS: Smith,CMM:

Brown, CBM: VanHolten, ACMM; Zaremba, ACMM: Charpid. CSK: McKinny, CSM: Haug. ACRM: Clogston, CMM

SEATED left to right

Reese, ACMM: Forsythe, ACMM: Gregory, CSF; Colby, ACMM; Zeremba, CRM; Quillian. CEM; Ando, CSK; Buick, CMM: Abbott, ACMM: Latos, CY; Hillaker, CBM; Haulin. CFC; Pfarr, CEM: Anderson. ACMM: Shiro. CMM

CPOs (photo possibly shot 7 February 1945) Need names

A Division, Catapult Machine Shop - September 1945

Back Row (L to R)

Ens. Dewitte, MM1c Swift, MoMM1c Libby, MoMM3c Shurden, MM3c Boyle, F1c Goudy, F1c Atkenson, M1c Stoffel, MMR2c Paluska, F1c McLaughlin, MM2c Cooke, MMS2c McCune

Center Row

MM1c Black, MoMM2c Miller, S2c Soule, Y3c Balint, MM1c Webber, M2c Thomas, MM3c Koster, MM3c Robinson, MM2c Leader, F1c McKinney, MMS2c MacIntosh

Front Row

CMoMM Saxon, Y3c Krzyanski, MM3c Malaro, MMR3c Hearnsberger, MM2c Christy, F1c Meadows, Mach. Smith

Photo & crew names provided by George V. Balint

The "Airdales" - 16 September 1945 - Tokyo Bay

Back Row (Standing L to R)

ACMM Laremba, Ltjg Bevier, AM Plato, AMM Lathrop, AM Croft, AM Judd, ARM Ruhl, ACMM Robert G. Vander Zanden, ABM(GA) Thurston, PTRV Tutor, ABM(GA) Oniel, AMM Crabtree, AMM Seoert, ABM(GA) Charnley, Lt Chambers

Center Row

AMM Culver, AEM Prime, AMM Gearheart, AMM Surprise, AMM Krajewski, AEM Burke, AMM Nelson, PTRV Lowell, PR McLaughlin, ARM Slane, AMM Medlin, ABM(GA) Godin, AMM Cottone, MACH Sears

Front Row

ARM Ticktin, AMM Mesich, AMM Mulville, AMM Johns, AM Herndon, AM Croxford, AMM Seitz, AMM Pelton AMM Schrader, AMM Groner, ABM(GA) Cattiti, ABM(GA) Fleming

Air Ordinance Group

<u>**Fourth (Top) Row - L to R**</u>

James P. Davis, William Noel, Alexander C. May, Nelson R. Denton, William D. Mitchell, Hubert H. Warner, Harold J. Shaw, Donald E. Fry, James F. Hanelly, Howell W. Winderweedle, Harris, George E. Newbauer, Newell, Constatino G. Macrone

<u>**Third Row - L to R**</u>

Lynwood C. Coward, James E. Hudson, Donald E. LaBudde, Emil A. Steckelman, Melvin W. Senzig, Lee C. Bradenberger, Francis L. Fore, Gerald Maxwell, Harry Severson, Joseph E. Rook, Charles J. Horth, Ralph B. Hale, Thomas W. WoodallRaymond K. Foor, Albert J. Shactman, Hugh E. Bohn, Miltcn U. Norris

<u>**Second Row - L to R**</u>

Robert T. Maddox, Brown, Thomas R. Cosgrove, Lewis, Trey L. Haynes, Dennis J. Sullivan, Joseph S. Tinta, Nelson, Martin, Robert A. Parks, Eugene T. DeLage, Walter W. McQuatters, Harold Mundy, Vito A. Pino, William J. Elisee, Robert R. Goudy

<u>**First (bottom) Row - L to R**</u>

Edwin A. Malone, Charles E. McKie, Harry T. Steeves, Lee, Charles J. Arnold, Russell J. Seelye, Arthur J. Reese, Harry C. Green, Gustav A. Maigler, Thomas M. Harkness, Norris L. Pratt, Richard A. Roloff, Thomas F. Gannon, Edwin S. Morton, Briscoe

(some first names unknown)

The "Signal Gang" September 1945

Back Row

Ens. Bill Philburn, Dean Miller, Jim Haney, Don Lovold, Don Gorecki, Tom Kirchoff, George McCurdy, Bob Powell, Dick Mueller, Art Davis, Ted Vawter, Lt. Jackson

Front Row

Lt. Krause, Don Maiki, Jim Thornton, Al Montgomery, Tom Seger, Bob Spinharney, John Burkard, Art Moore, Ed Deering, Lew Mazzella, Roy Contraras, Jim Waldron, Lt. Wentz

Photo & crew names provided by Bob Spinharney

Crew Photos
818

E Division - Tokyo Bay - September 1945

(Power, Lighting, Distribution and Interior Communications)

<u>Top row (standing) - L - to - R</u>

Walter J. Putz, Allison A. Ploss, Edward W. Purdy, Rodney MacDugall, Gerald E. Adams, Russell G. Palmer, Edmond P. Conroy, Alfred Butniak, Vernon A. Shisler, James W. Jopp, Louis Ladouceur, Paul E. Lowman, Myron P. Miller.

<u>Middle row - L - to - R</u>

Ensign Albert W. Lawrence, Walter Legehbauer, Ralph F. Lawson, Jerome W. Jackson, Joseph J. Raulinaitis, Kenneth Isom, Joseph J. Krapf Jr, George H. Quackenbush, Carl F. Anderson, Wilfred J. Burns, John A. Korbe, Vincent W. Peterson, Joseph Agular, Richard Holton, Robert L. Rabus.

<u>Bottom row - L - to - R</u>

CEM Kermit A. Freeman, Robert O. Finley, John H. Rahm, Russel J. Carothers, John Pankovich, Edward A. Bosio, Richard H. Bullock. Gerald F. O'Callaghan, John T. McAlhany, CEM Fred L. Pfarr.

Missing: Anthony D'auito, Herbert B. Taylor

The Lighting Shop

Top row L - to - R: Cortland L. Olson, Unknown, Allison A. Ploss, James W. Jopp, Ralph F. Lawson, Anthony D'auito, Russell G. Palmer, Joseph J. Krapf Jr.

Bottom row L - to - R:

Unknown, Wilfred J. Burns, Richard Holton, Edward A. Bosio, Russell J. Carothers, Chief Blair

K-2 Division Radio Techs

Top Row L - to - R: Frank W. Polzek, Clair H. Jensen, Donald J. Brady, Rowland H. Choate
Bottom Row L - to R: Felix F. Biondi, Nicholas Forlano, Sandford Adler

Crew Photos

Electricians Mates

Standing L to R : Myron Miller, Paul Lowman, Harry Scheier, Gerald O'Callahan, Jim Jopp
Kneeling L to R : Lewis Lodouceur, Edward Bosio, Russ Carothers, Kermit Freeman

Storekeepers

Standing (Left - to - Right): Unknown, CSK Arthur J. Ando, CSK Herman M. Charpied,
S2c Jean R. Goemmer, SK3c Lewis A. Harwell Jr., S2c Vincent D. Manning
Kneeling: Unknown, S2c Joseph J. Del Torre, S2c Raymond A. Conklin, S2c Norman B. Slater

K Division - Communication Department

Top (back) Row Standing - L to R
Ensign F. W. Botts, Jr., Lt. E.V. Atkinson, Chief Eggling

Center Row Standing - L to R
William Patrick Moroney, Jr., Ingard Dahl, Donald Vernon Lovold, Donald Sylvester Gorecki, Theodore Eric Vawter, Dean Gilbert Miller, Robert Powell, Joe Robinson, Shellie Nichols Kennaday, Richard J. Muller, Wilson Grant McKinny

Bottom (front) Row Kneeling - L to R
Leonard John Schlosser, Duilio "Lew" Mazzella, Robert Edward Spinharney, Albert Washburn Montgomery, Richard Siepler, Arthur Daniel Moore, Thomas William Seger, Edwin Donald Deering, Arthur Lloyd Davis

Crew Photos

K-2 Division Tokyo Bay, 9/21/1945

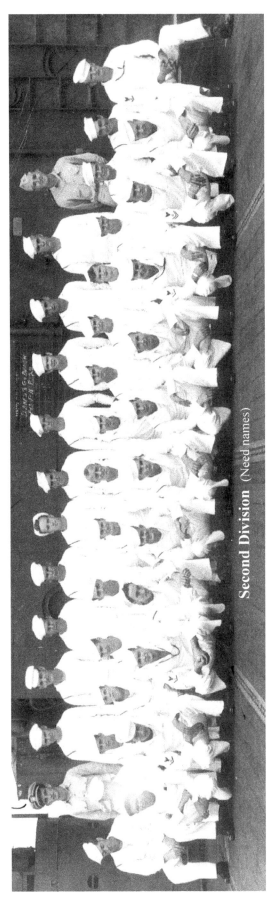

Second Division (Need names)

823

V-3 Division

Top Row (standing)- Left to Right

Lt. Kroll, H.B. Taylor, George Newburn, Elbert Boone, William Given, Unidentified, Windstrup, Robert D. Martin, Dickens, John G. Lee, Roy Bernard, Wayne M. Dontje, Elmo Bowers, C. A. Ross, Daniel Lutz, William R. Hodges, D.C. Schieck, H.H. Wilkins, Daniels, Julius Schien, Ens. Scott, Lt(jg) Vogel, Lt(jg) Springer

Center Row)- Left to Right

Lt. Fritz, Chief Smith, Emery C. Kamps, T.D. Tate, Al Hiegel, Harry A. Miller, William G. Graham, Charles W. Hibben, J. Roth, Joseph C. Meyer, Smith, J.R. Seyler, James N. Boren, Robert J. Geer, Mooney, Richard J. Detleson, Makai, Hersel S. Lashbrook, R.G. Taylor, Ens. Tittle, Ens. Hogan

Bottom Row)- Left to Right

Unidentified, Lt(jg) Lawler, Fredrick R. Fraser, Kenneth M. Lockwood, Gordon W. Hefford, Cornell, Charles J. McLean, Everett D. Bratt, Donald S. Peebles, McElhany, Gerald Jacobson, Wallace S. Powers, D. Summerlin, G.L. Thomas, Frank D. Maggilini, Lt. Wilson, Lt(jg) Evans

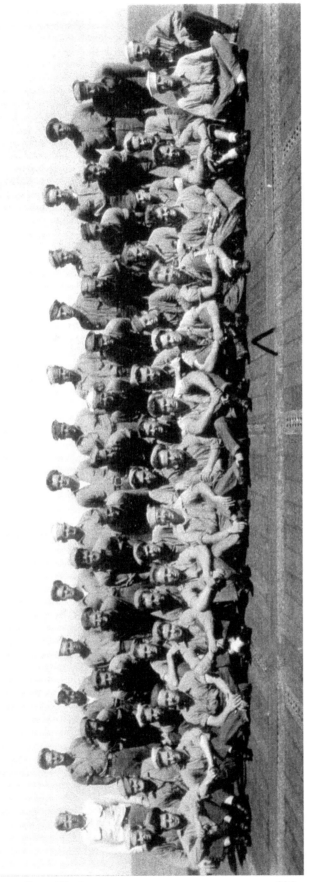

4th Division, 6 February 1945

4th Row (standing L - to - R): Ens. Oliver E. Niebruegge, William A. Giver Jr., Edgar F. Stobaugh, Edward J. Houle, William R. Howe, Alexander T. Massengale, James M. Richardson, Ralph H. Washabaugh, Charles E. Crane, Glen E. Wolfe ?, Harry E. Hart ?, Clyde L. Chappell, Micro Strmel

3rd Row: Alfred J. Mc Laughlin, Joseph P. Scarbulis, William R. Mc Whorter, Charles A. Moreno, Robert T. Musgreave, Joe Sandoval,George E. Sheperdson, Robert C. Bethke, Albert L. Cravens, Richard W. Schimscat, Max E. Loy, William J. Forbes

2nd Row: Andrew J. Mc Cann Jr., Keller, James E. Shanks, James B. Long, Frank S. Hintz, Joseph G. Herbert, Frederick M. Metzger.Robert B. Layton, William Hoffman Jr., Ruben Parish, Calvin G. Atnip, John J. Brady, unknown, Edward E. Hadefeli ?

1st Row (sitting L - to - R): George W. Mc Curdy, Joseph C. Manning, Oscar E. Mayo, William T. MacHamer, Stanley S. Malachowski, Joseph M. Clark, Joseph Hollock, Leonard R. Gregory, Joseph Brucato, George R. Hine, Andrew D. Aldi, Leo F. Cameron, Amedee Dezercie

V-6 Division

<u>**Top Row standing – Left to Right**</u>

Henry Theodore Haug, Robert Burns Abbott, Leo Edward Selewach, Earl William Fleschert, Horbart Nelson Anderson, William Francis Parnapy, Edward Jacob Heine, John Charles Tye, Edward Michael Stumpfel, Carroll Lee Tinsley, Eugene Elmer Buck, Smith, Lt.(jg) Victor Befus, Lt.(jg) Bevier, Ens. R.B.Bentley

<u>**Middle Row seated**</u>

Smith, Donnall D. Whitsett, Rex Lee Stansell, Adolph Adam Sikora, Evert Richard Thornley, Lara Elwin Jenkins, Lawrence Booker Wilson, Francis Joseph Catanzarita, Raymond Robert Blaige, Teddy Frank Swirniak, Richard Paul Hingle, John Martin Severt, James William Worstell, MACH E.L. Sears, Lt. Chambers, Lt. Hicox

<u>**Bottom Row**</u>

Orville Henry Wadel, Robert G. O'connor, Martin F. Sweeney, Gordon B. Rieger, Francis James Duke, Rudolph G. Mollner, John Joseph Zemba, Leo J. St Arnauld, Dominic John Albanese, Edward Jack Dudo, William George Fluellen, Moore, Henry Jacob Brand

bar

Crew Photos 826

Crew Photos

827

V6 - C&R (Construction & Repair) Division 1945

Top row (standing) - L - to - R

Lt.CDR. Joseph Daniel Jeffords, Stanley William Blohoweak, Columbus Andy McNeese, Bud Medich, William Joseph Miller, Basil William Lotocky, Alfred Rossetti, Francis Donald Spack, Ferris Eugene Young, Carlos Jules Wileman, Richards, Robert Gentry Richmond, Keith Wyant Gates, Charles William Lamb, LeRoy Charles Bouquet, George Wesley McIver, Jr., Lt. Verrel Othel McNabb

Middle row - L - to - R

Lt. Oliver Pearl Taylor, John Edward D'Atri, Anthony Schiappa, Calvin Glendon Athip, Jacob William Cansler, Henry Mady, unknown, James Robert Stratton, Columbus Pezzuti, Alvin Bart Cook, Robert Preston, John Joseph Brady, Leonard Ames, Norman Frederick Ohle, Clement Thomas Cajski, George Daniel Allen, Clarence James Ruder, Ens. Walter Wilson Gilbert

Bottom row - L - to - R

Lt. Henry Newman Lawrence, Junior Carl Fletcher, Ernest Eugene Preslar, Franklin Stanley Kistler, Frank Wilbur Robinson, Paul Donald Skinner, Edsel Earl Haney, Richards, Herman Lee Bell, Herman Bo Backlund, Floyd Edmund Beeghly, John Emil Balmer, Robert Laroy Lyon, David Torres Armijo, Earl Jerry Presto, Angelo Joseph Rich, Lt. Robert John McQuaid, Lt. Davidson

Richards*   one is Douglas Maldwyn Richards, and the other is Lotus Carl Richards. Unknown which is which.

Gunners Mates - 6th Division

Top Row (standing - L to R): Chief Morris Flemming, Lou Albano, Bill Bradley, Walter Radwonski, Carl Anderson, Alex Massengale (?), unknown, Al Henkler, Walter Saudey, Bill Rackawack, unknown, unknown, Chief Woodrow Day

Middle Row: Leonard Conradt, Tom Harmon, Henry Rushing, Jim Taylor, Tom Pearson, John Collins, Mike Dadonna, John Rhine, George Gray, Ted Hackett, Unknown

Front Row (sitting): Ray Bessemer, Earl Carpenter, unknown, unknown, unknown, unknown, unknown, George Laughlin, unknown, Joe Whalen

(Need Division & Names)

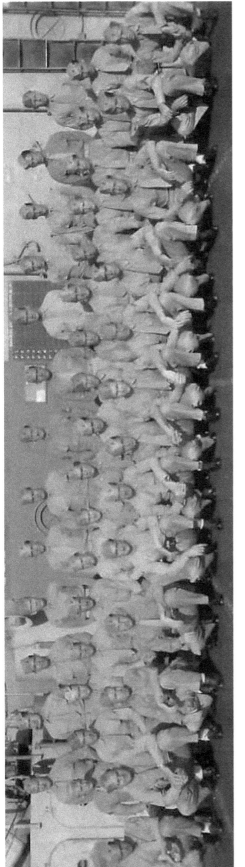

Marines - 1945

Top Row: Fitzgerald, Purcell, Swinney, D. Jones, Sanford, Vossin, Protheroc, Capt. James B. Carpenter, Lt. Ketler, Stylinski, O'Dcnnell, Butynski, Haenelt Felty, Barkyoumb, Putman, Rush, Kerpatrick, Horton, Short, Burk, Graham, Gladson, Hebert, Babola, Peterson, Kisling, Kennedy, Cieslaki, Mirck

Bottom Row: Hooker, Booterbaugh, U.B. Jones, Neidlein, Nutter, Bixby, Harmon, Turner, Dice, Baker, Russell, Nowak, Walter

(Need Division & Names)

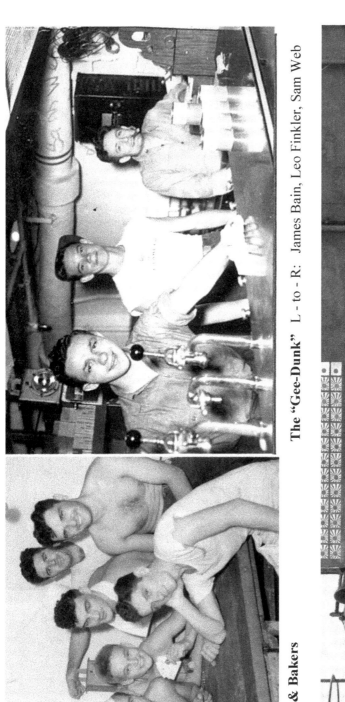

Crew Photos

Cooks & Bakers

The "Gee-Dunk" L - to - R: James Bain, Leo Finkler, Sam Web

USS INDEPENDENCE Stewards (Photo shot outside of Tokyo Bay, 1945 Need names)

830

Aboard the Aircraft Carrier U.S.S. Independence

Members of the crew of the aircraft carrier U.S.S. Independence photographed on the flight deck of the flat top. Planes on the deck with wings folded form a background. The carrier anchored at the foot of Stark Street, Portland, is here for the Navy Day celebration. The members of the crew were honored guests at the party of the Williams Ave. U.S.O. and scheduled for another entertainment when units of the fleet are anchored here.

Kneeling front row, left to right: Stm. 1c Willie J. Thomas, Cincinnati, Ohio; Stm. 1c Wilbert Ferguson, Trenton, N. J.; Stm. 2c Bill Clark, Philadelphia, Penn; Stm. 1c Burton Floyd Norfolk, Va.; Stm. 1c O. M. Austin Norfolk, Va.; Stm. 2c Gerald Clay, St. Louis, Missouri; Stm. 2c Robert Calhoun, Jr., Florence, Ala.; Stm. 1c L. A. Brown, Bloomington, Ill.

Back row standing, left to right: Stw. 2c Ed Watkins, Nashville, Tenn.; Stm. 1c J. W. Woodward, Pittsburgh, Pa.; Stm. 1c D. H. Holley, Dallas, Texas; Stm. J. M. Carson, Corpus Christie, Texas; Stm. 2c Wm. Brown, Muskogee, Okla.; Stm. 1c Earl Scott, Oakland, Calif.; Stw. 2c E. A. Pickett, Michigan; Stm. 1c J. G. Broome, LaGrande, Ga.; Stw. 1c John J. Scruggs, Baltimore, Maryland; Stm. 1c T. H. Williams, Atlanta, Ga.; Stm. 1c J. J. Thomas, Louisiana; Stm. 1c C. H. David, Tampa, Fla.; Stw. 2c Dennis Randall, St. Petersburgh, Florida; Stm. 1c J. Daniels, Cleveland, Ohio; Stm. 1c T. Barber, Columbia, South Carolina; Stm. 2c G. M. Clark; Stw. 1c A. A. Williams, Fredricksburg, Va.; Stm. 1c G. W. Williams, Jacksonville, Fla.

—Photo by Margaret C. Robinson

USS INDEPENDENCE Stewards   (Newspaper clipping - Portland Oregon)

Cooks and Bakers

Back Row Standing: ?, ?, Daniel W. Thompson, Chester C. Ireton Jr., Erwin C. Zeilinger, Charles W. Carrico, James C. Farley, Walter S. Pushea, William P. Lyman, ?, ?, Lt. Alegrmon H. Kerr

Middle Row: Patrick M. Ternes, ?, Francesco Bosco, Mike Buben, Wesley Swaka, Robert J. Ward, Leon Francia, George Bednar, ?, William Lederer, Lawrence S. Coulson, Gonsalo L. Aja, ?, John F. Beyer,

Front Row L-to-R: John E. Burkard?, ?, ?, Joseph DeVrins Jr. ?, Eugene E. Bull, Victor J. Thompson, James D. Kohl, Frederick E. Bass,

Jack M. Parker ?,

Need names and Division

INDEPENDENCE Cooks

Photographers Mates

USS INDEPENDENCE
CVL-22

Squadron Data

CVL-22 Dates Aboard
CVL-22 Aircraft Markings
Squadron Logos

"Up, up the long delirious burning blue
I've topped the wind-swept heights with easy grace"

John Gillespie Magee, Jr.

Air Groups or Squadrons - Dates Aboard the CVL-22

Carrier Air Group 22	16 March 1943	- 27 November 1943
VF-6	4 August 1943	- 26 November 1943
VF-33	(Rabaul only)	11 November 1943
CVLG(N)-41	6 July 1944	- 10 February 1945
CVLG-46	13 March 1945	- 14 June 1945
CVLG-27	14 June 1945	- 25 September 1945
CVLG-21	25 September 1945	- 20 October 1945

CVL-22 Aircraft Markings

VF-22, VT-22 & VC-22   1943
Had no large tail markings. Note the Air Group
Number / Squadron Type / A/C #
VF-6 Hellcats also had no large tail markings. Note
the older National Aircraft Insignia (Converted around
October 1943)

See other photos throughout the book for other views.

VT(N)-41 & VF(N)-41   1944
The "Shademaid's" tails were marked with a
number in a circle.

(Note: VF-33 not shown - aboard only during Rabaul.)

(Note: VF & VT 21 not shown. They were only aboard
for a few weeks after the war)

VF-46 & VT 46   1945
Air Group 46 appeared to be aboard CVL-22 both
with "Checkerboard" markings and without.
The Avenger in the photo was in Torpedo Forty Six,
aircraft No. 9 (which had nothing to do with the A/C
Bu. No.)

VF-27 & VT 27   1945
Air Group 27 was aboard CVL-22 initially with
"Checkerboard" markings, flying Air Group-46
aircraft after the Air Group change.
The "Checkerboard" scheme was later removed with
aircraft repainted* as in the photo below. The lower
photo was shot early September 1945. The Hellcats
in the photo have external fuel drop tanks. Also see
pages 413, 740, 741 for VF-27 Hellcat marking
photos. (*Or replaced)
The Avenger below has a Radar Pod (AN/APS-4)

CVL-22 Squadron Logos

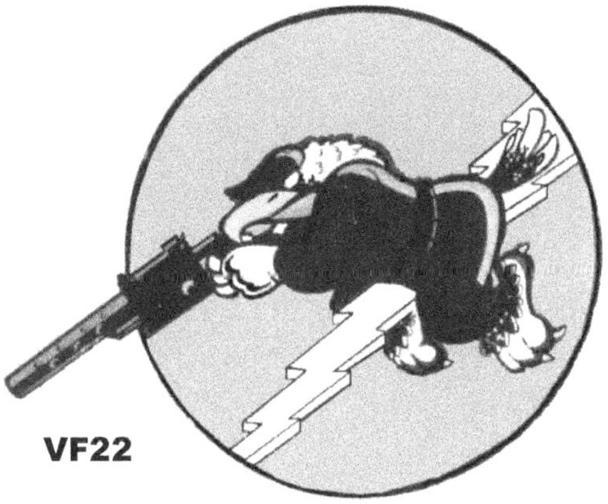

VF22

**VT-22
&
VC 22**

VF 6

"Shademaids"

**VT(N)-41
&
VF(N)-41**

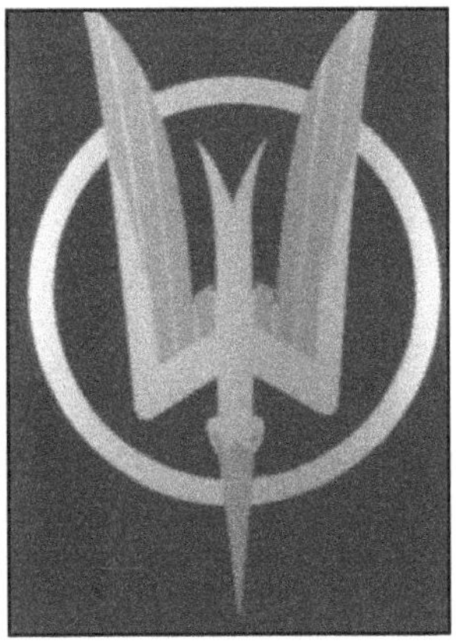

VF 46

VT 46

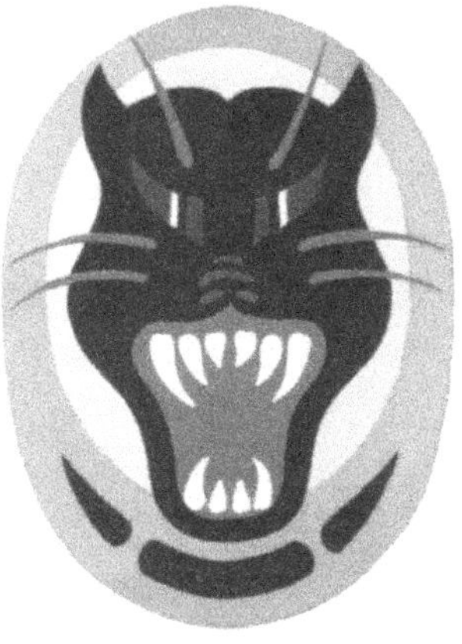

VF 27

VT 27

USS INDEPENDENCE CVL-22

Specifications

And what say you ...
About the sea?
Or perhaps the MIGHTY-I ?

USS Independence - Basic Specifications

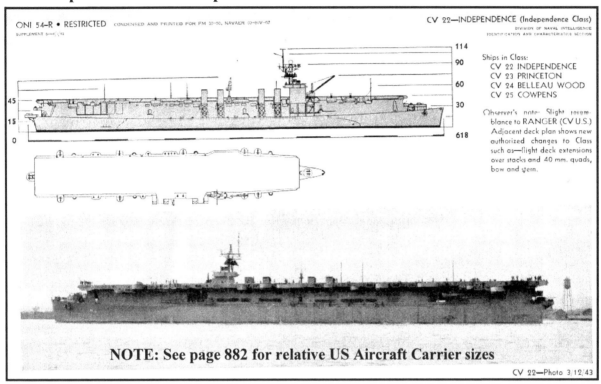

NOTE: See page 882 for relative US Aircraft Carrier sizes

Length of hull:	600' at the water line. 622.5' total length overall. (39" double bottom)
Beam:	At or below water line: 71', 6.5". (Extreme Beam 71', 9.25") Extreme Beam above main deck: 109'2"
Displacement:	Displacement to 22'6" water line 13,105 tons (7,565 tons when first launched) 11,000 tons / 14,800 Tons, mean displacement, ready for war. 15,100 max.
Draft:	26 Feet.
Length of Flight Deck:	552 Feet (as you can see in the photo, it did not extend to the bow).
Width of Flight Deck:	An average of 73 Feet, with an 8 foot wide x 60 foot long apron near the island / forward elevator on the port side. Wood flight deck with no armor.
Hangar Bay:	285 Feet long by 55 feet wide.
Catapults:	One H2-1 Pneumatic / Hydraulic installed on the port side. A second catapult (starboard) was retrofitted later in the war.
Boilers:	Four Babcock and Wilcox Three Drum "Express" double cased, divided furnace, single uptake boilers with B&W Carolina oil burners, 565 psi at 850° with pressure atomizers spraying fuel oil into the fire brick lined burners.
Propulsion:	Four 25,000 shaft horsepower (100,000 combined shaft horsepower total) General Electric geared (cross compound double reduced) steam turbine sets of one H.P., one Cruising and one L.P. with the Astern on the LP turbine per propeller shaft. 350 propeller shaft rpm with a 385 rpm safety over-speed safety trip (main steam supply, with a manual reset).

USS Independence - Basic Specifications Continued

Frame Data:	150 Frames, Spacing 4', Center Frame 75
Propellers:	Four, four-bladed solid manganese bronze, 11',10" diameter on 16.25" shafts, (2 left hand, two right hand). Manufactured by New York Shipbuilding Corp.
Speed:	31.5 knots (estimated contract data speed was 32.5 knots at 13,185 tons displacement) (A recorded speed of 34.4 knots was obtained on 16 June 1944)
Steering Gear	Electro-Hydraulic
Rudder Area	287 Sq. feet
Generators	Four GE steam impulse turbine, 6 stage geared. 600 KW / 750 KVA each, 450 volt, 60 cycle, 3 phase A.C., 961 Amps full load Two Diesel 250 KW / 312 KVA 450 volt, 60 cycle 3 phase auxiliary generators. Manufactured by The Cooper-Bessemer Corp.
Elevators:	Two, Lampson Design
Fuel Oil Capacity:	749,200 gallons (Approx. full load capacity, 95% full)
Aviation Gasoline Capacity:	Approx. 117,643 gallons (safe expendable capacity). 12 stations provided to service aircraft, 6 port side, 6 starboard side. 8 of the stations on catwalks for servicing planes on the flight deck, 4 located on the hangar deck.
Diesel Oil capacity:	26,450 (95 % full)
Potable water	Approx. 68,700 Gallons
Reserve Feed Water	Approx. 48,300 Gallons
Compliment:	Approx. 1570 men (additional added in the hangar bay during Magic Carpet). Originally designed for 114 officers, 65 C.P.O's and 1,236 enlisted men. Specs totaled 1456 berths plus 28 hospital spaces.
Armament: guns	Originally fitted with single 5 inch (5/38) guns on bow and on the stern, these were replaced with two Quad 40mm Bofors mounts (1 bow, 1 stern) after her shakedown cruise. Eight (ten later) 40mm Bofors twin mounts with 7 MK51gun directors. Two additional 40mm twin mounts were added in early 1944 during her repairs at Hunters Point. (Paperwork indicates 1 added gun but a photo shows 2)
	Sixteen 20mm Oerlikon Guns. Air cooled, 160 rounds per min. These were reduced to a total of four in early 1944 during her repairs at Hunters Point. (source for CVL-22 gun count - "General Information Book" for CVL22, CVL23, CVL24, Serial No. 61 from the Office of the Supervisor of Shipbuilding for the USN, NYSB, 1943)
	The 20mm & 40mm guns had Mark 14 gun sights (no magnification) prior to 1944. It was recommended to utilize Mark 15 sights in an Action report (see 12 October 1943). It is possible this was carried out during the repairs at Hunters Point in 1944, but I found no supporting documents.
Search Lights:	Two 24" and two 12"
Armor:	This vessel had no side belt armor. Steel for the armor was in short supply at time of construction. In 1944 side belt armor was not procured due to the amount of work involved, the expense, delay and "small gain in protection achieved".

Specifications

USS Independence - Basic Specifications Continued

Radar:
SK Air Search Radar with IFF
SG Surface Search Radar
SC-2 Radar (later removed and retrofitted with SM Radar in 1944 during her repairs at Hunters Point per note below).   (See page 279)
SM Radar replaced the SC-2 Radar in 1944 during her repairs at Hunters Point.
(See page 279)

Aircraft Homing: USS INDEPENDENCE was equipped with a YE aircraft homing beacon.
(Antennas in this section - See photos on pages 32-33, 52, 57-58, 397)

Radio Transmitting and Receiving Equipment (partial listing - note; dates not clarified) :

RADIO I

3 RBA-1 --- Receiver - 15-600 kc		1 TBV-1 --- Receiver
7 RBB-1 --- Receiver - 0.5-4.0 kc		1 TBM-7 --- Transmitter
7 RBC-1 --- Receiver - 4.0-27 mc		1 LR
1 RBU-1 --- Receiver		

RADIO II

1 LR
1 RAK-8 / RAL-8 --- Receivers - general purpose com. receivers 15-600 kc / 0 .3-23 mc
1 TAQ --- Main radio transmitter (medium frequency, hi power)
            (later replaced by TAJ-11 Transmitter)
1 TBK --- Radio transmitter (hi frequency)
2 TBM-7 --- Main radio communication between the Fighter Director Command and fighter
            aircraft. Later replaced (probably in February 1945 in Pearl Harbor) by TDQ (hi freq.
            transmitter) and RCK (hi freq. receiver). It was located outside the CIC doorway.
1 TBU --- Radio transmitter (medium frequency, medium power)

ELSEWHERE

1 DP - Island
1 DF - Portable (Direction Finding)
1 YE - Tower --- Transmits homing bearing signals and Morse Code letters for aircraft
            guidance.
1 YG - Portable (Aircraft Homing Beacon) [See page 397 for antenna / antenna mast photo]
1 RBH - Radar Plot --- Receiver - 300 kc-1200 kc and 1700 kc-17 mc
1 RBH - Air Plot --- Receiver - 300 kc-1200 kc and 1700 kc-17 mc
1 RBK-1 C.I.C. --- Receiver
1 RAS - Aerological --- Receiver - 190-30000 kc
3 BC Receivers
1 TBS - Bridge --- "Talk Between Ships" Transmitter / Receiver - For Line-of-sight
            Communication within a Task Force, Task Group, convoy, etc.
            (very hi frequency, low power)
1 TBX - Storage --- Portable Transmitter / Receiver (short range, medium to hi frequency)
1 TBY - Storage --- Portable self powered "Talk Between Ships" Transmitter / Receiver -
            20000-80000 kc   Line-of-sight distances
2 TBW - Storage --- Transmitter - 350-1000 kc and 3000-18100 kc (stored in a passageway
            outside of CIC)

Note: The Radio Transmitter Room was located Portside between frames 101 & 106
Note: An additional antenna mast was added to the ship at Hunters Point in early 1944. Not in photos
            taken prior to Hunters Point in 1944, located between the last two exhaust stacks, the new mast
            appears in later photos. There were additional radio antennas mounted on the stacks at that time.
(See photo of new antenna mast on page 397.)

USS Independence - Basic Specifications Continued

Anchors :   Two 18,000 lb. (Initially 13,000 lb until the 18,000 lb anchors were shipped.)
                     175 fathoms of chain port, 125 fathoms of chain starboard.

Windlass: Two vertical units (1 port, 1 starboard) hoisting 18,000 lb. anchors at 31 feet per minute.

Crane Capacity: 14,000 lbs

Boats: Two 26' motor whaleboats

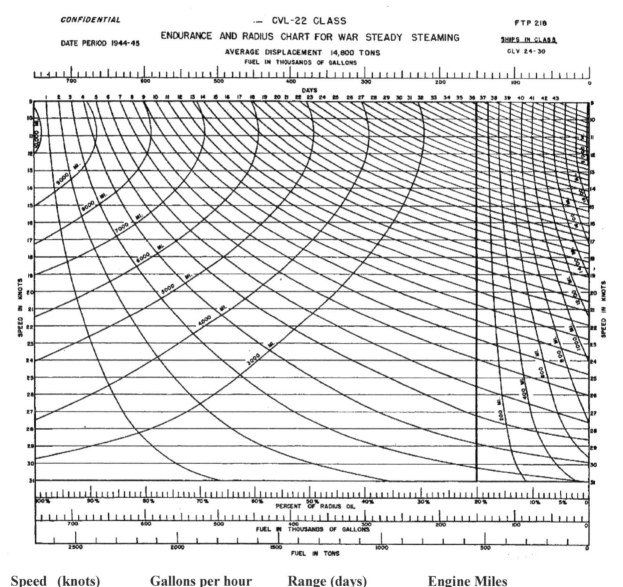

Speed (knots)	Gallons per hour	Range (days)	Engine Miles
9.8	639 - 814	43	10,070
20.7	2,116 - 2,698	13	6,650
25.9	3,655 - 4,659	7.5	4,710

USS INDEPENDENCE
CVL-22

Maps / Charts

&

Dispositions

"And I Tell
Where storms and stars come from"

Carl Sandburg

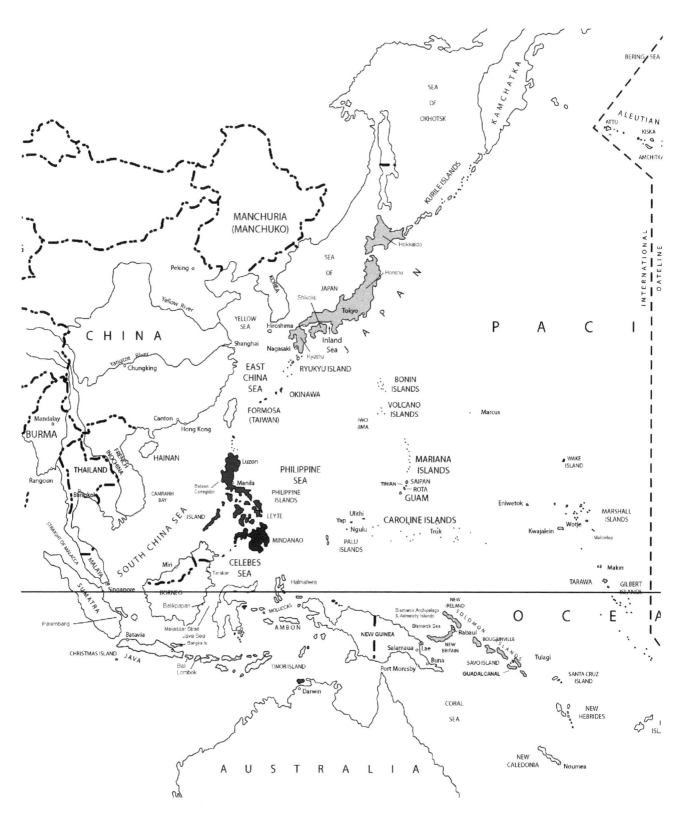

(Note: Palu Islands is misspelled - should be Palau Islands)

Map of the Pacific Ocean (Left Side)

Maps / Charts   846

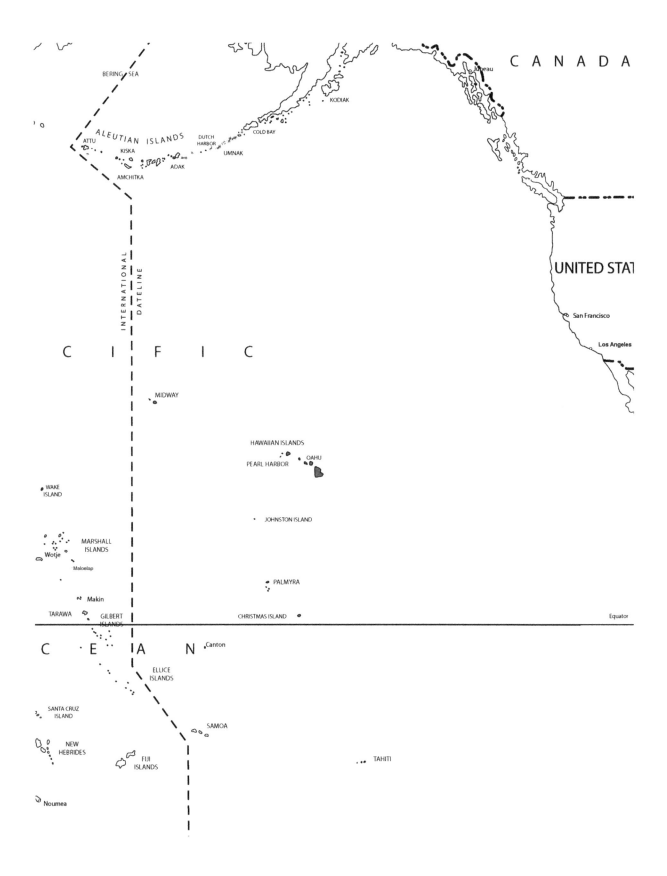

Map of the Pacific Ocean (Right Side)

Maps / Charts

847

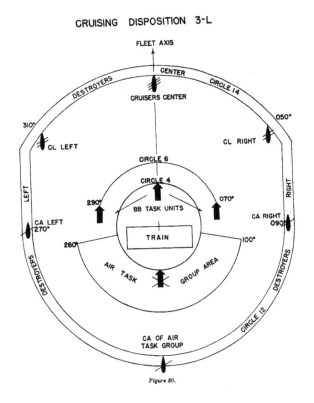

CRUISING DISPOSITION 3-L

Figure 20.

CRUISING DISPOSITION 3-R

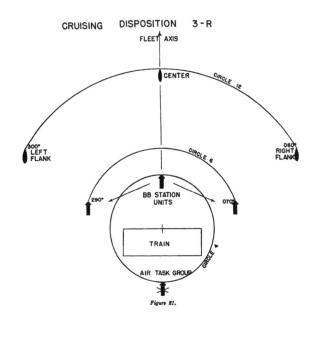

Figure 21.

CRUISING DISPOSITION 3-V

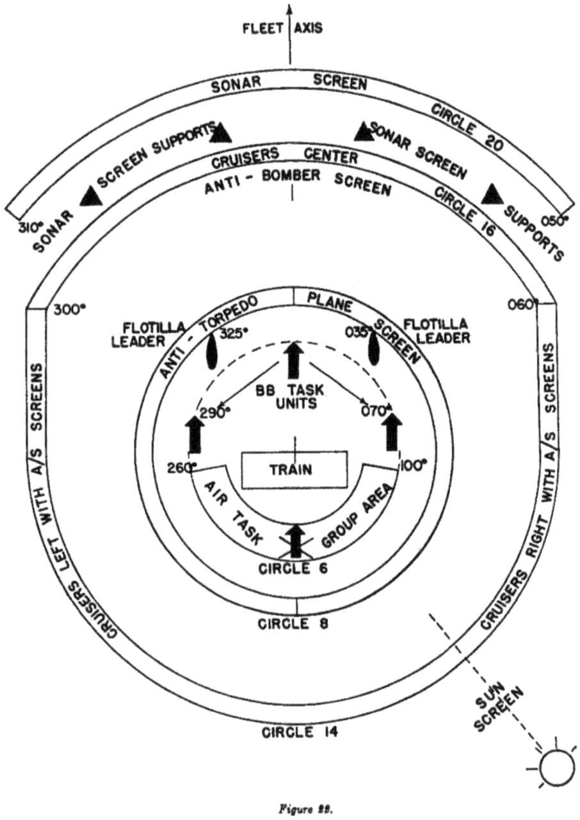

Figure 22.

CRUISING DISPOSITION 4-V

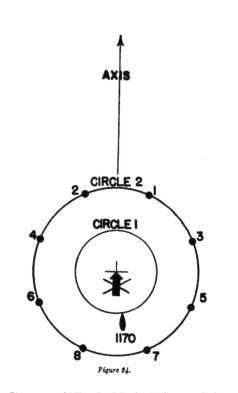

Figure 24.

Task Group / Task Unit Dispositions

SPECIAL CRUISING DISPOSITION 5F (FUELING)

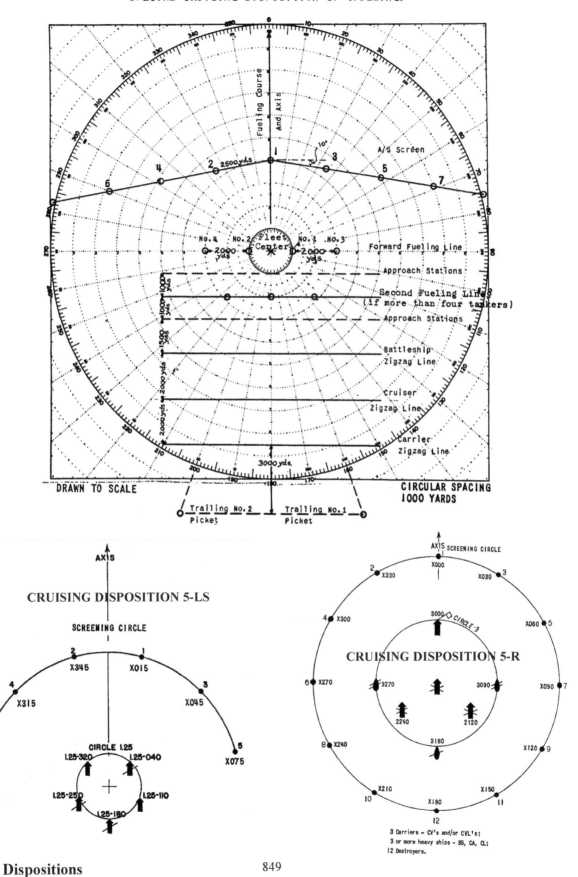

Dispositions

849

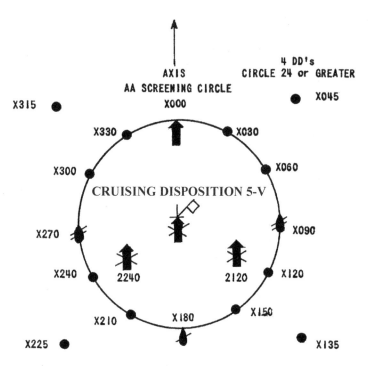

4 DD's
CIRCLE 24 or GREATER

AXIS
AA SCREENING CIRCLE

CRUISING DISPOSITION 5-V

3 Carriers - CV and/or CVL's;
3 or more heavy ships - BB, CA, CL;
12 Destroyers.

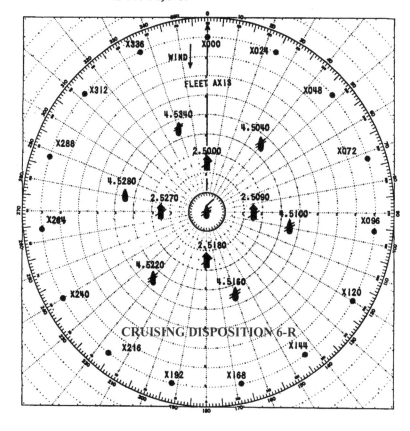

CRUISING DISPOSITION 6-R

4 CARRIERS
7 HEAVY SHIPS BB, CA, CL
15 DESTROYERS

Dispositions   850

USS INDEPENDENCE CVL-22

Index

"I must go down to the sea again,
to the lonely sea and the sky,
and all I ask is
A tall ship and a star to steer her by"

John Masefield

Index

Shell Sizes

30 Cal   50 Cal   20MM   40MM

Index

Index

Index

Index

Index

Index

Index
Ship   Name,   Hull Number,   Class,   Description,   page #

LSM-60 at Bikini Atoll. It was used to suspend the bomb in the "Baker" test (Operation Crossroads" page 781).

Index

Index   Ship   Name,   Hull Number,   Class,   Description,   page

USS INDEPENDENCE in San Francisco Bay May - June1944

Index
Ship Name, Hull Number, Class, Description, page #

Cartoons by Joe Rodgers with the Lucky Rabbit
(on this page and following pages)
**were on the cover of the ship's
"Breakfast Bulletin".
The "Breakfast Bulletin"**
(printed aboard the ship) **featured
"Radio Press News" of home,
of the war in Europe and the Pacific.**

Index

CVL-22 Ship's Reunion Group Patch / Logo

Index

Photographers Mates
L to R
Frederick "Fred" E. Owen - Phom3c**, Wilfred "Bill" I. Finucci -** Phom1c**, Edward "Ed" Schultz -** Phom2c,
unidentified, Ernest "Ernie" W. D'Ambrosi - Chief Phom

Thanks to Ed Schultz for some of the photos in this book

USS INDEPENDENCE CVL-22

EPILOGUE

"Twilight and evening bell
And after that the dark!"

Alfred, Lord Tennyson

Epilogue   2015 Joint Mission

Like a punch drunk prize fighter just staggering to his feet from a near knockout blow, the mustard yellow Boeing Echo Ranger's propeller spun up and accelerated the blunt nosed AUV upward, and partially out of the water, on a small swell. With a mind of its own, and seemingly unsure of its bearings, or with a grim determination that its correct track ought to be pointed in our direction, the heavy little sub began a rapidly arching path toward the NOAA Research Vessel *"FULMAR"* as it settled back in the water. It was an *"Aw-shucks"* moment (to be polite)!

The first thought that filled my cranium was … the USS INDEPENDENCE took a torpedo on 20 November 1943, and the question arose ... was this to be a case of history trying to present us with a rerun? I can just hear the call to the Coast Guard now … *"R/V FULMAR taking on water, hull penetrated by Boeing torpedo!"*

Captain Dave Minard rapidly began maneuvering the agile FULMAR out of harm's way as *"Echo Ranger"* closed, and that yellow **AUV** we were trying to herd took a modestly less threatening path on its own, to begin its mission, submerging out of sight below the surface of the glimmering waters of the Pacific, off Half Moon Bay California, probably with a cat-eating-the-mouse grin on its bow.

A test dive of the **A**ntonymous **U**nderwater **V**ehicle was now in progress, prior to the joint mission to locate and gather 3D side scan sonar images of the INDEPENDENCE, in order to ascertain the health of the hulk of that historic vessel … scuttled by the US Navy 64 years ago. See the book back cover.

The WWII aircraft carrier, now home to well over a half century of marine growth, is at rest on the bottom, undisturbed by the effort on the ocean's surface to check on her condition (nearly 2,700' above).

The EX-INDEPENDENCE (to the Navy … always the "Mighty-I" to her crew) came to rest on its keel, upright with a slight list and her bow lower than the stern due to a sloping bottom. She appears reasonably intact, considering her condition in 1951 when explosive charges began her stern first downward voyage, collimating with a slightly bow low collision with the ocean floor. Her hull is possibly fractured aft of the island, and sections of flight deck are understandably missing, but, unlike many maritime hulks that lay broken and scattered on the bottom, the INDEPENDENCE appears to be in reasonably fair condition, from what could be determined by the newly obtained sonar imaging.

She is now a member on the list of historically significant vessels within the domain of the National Marine Sanctuaries.

This was a joint mission by the **NOAA Maritime Heritage Program**, in a cooperative agreement with **Boeing Unmanned Undersea Systems** (providing the *"Echo Ranger"*) , utilizing **Coda Octopus** 3D (dual frequency) side scan sonar (*Echoscope©)* technology.

The "Echo Ranger", approx. 18.5 feet long, weighing 10,500 lb. designed for a 10K ' dive depth.

NOAA's *"R/V FULMAR"* in the background while crews in two support Zodiac type inflatable boats make ready the Boeing *"Echo Ranger"*. The FULMAR and her team will tow the Echo Ranger roughly 30 miles out to sea (and back) for the mission to image the INDEPENDENCE with the new Coda Octopus 3D side scan sonar.

Photo on Left
Half Moon Bay, CA. Boeing "Echo Ranger" is being raised from the water by crane from the Pillar Point Harbor Pier. "Echo Ranger" was being readied for tow to the operational area by NOAA's Research Vessel FULMAR. Unmanned - autonomous, the mission is per-programmed. It uses an Inertial Navigation System aided by additional onboard devices to compensate for typical INS navigation drift.

Epilogue - 2015 Mission

3D Sonar Image of the INDEPENDENCE
17 March 2015

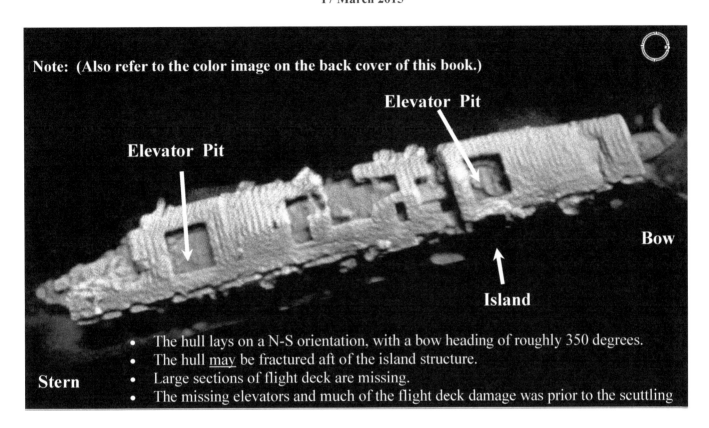

Note: (Also refer to the color image on the back cover of this book.)

Elevator Pit

Elevator Pit

Bow

Island

Stern

- The hull lays on a N-S orientation, with a bow heading of roughly 350 degrees.
- The hull <u>may</u> be fractured aft of the island structure.
- Large sections of flight deck are missing.
- The missing elevators and much of the flight deck damage was prior to the scuttling

Above photo (and color back cover photo) courtesy of: **Coda Octopus** and **NOAA Office of National Maritime Sanctuaries**

Boeing "Echo Ranger" being lowered by crane from the pier at Pillar Point Harbor.

EX USS INDEPENDENCE   2016 NAUTILUS Mission

The **2015 joint mission** to gain a 3D side scan image of the USS INDEPENDENCE hull on the floor of the Pacific helped gather valuable information to set the stage for Dr. Robert Ballard's mission the following year.

In **2016**, I was invited to again participate, this time as a "Scientist Ashore (Historian)" with the new mission to visit the INDEPENDENCE. This was a joint mission with NOAA's Maritime Heritage Division and Ocean Exploration Trust (OET). My eyes were curiously and intently glued upon two computer monitor screens at home via "Telepersence".

Aboard were two deep diving ROVs (Remote Operating Vehicles) that would be deployed to provide live streaming video feed that the world could watch on the *"Nautilus Live"* web site from their computers. The NAUTILUS crew would spend roughly four days (Monday, Tuesday, Thursday, Friday) operating the NAUTILUS and her two ROVs to provide the streaming video and a survey of the wreck with still photos. This was to be the first time the INDENPENDENCE would be seen by human eyes (abet via video) since her sinking in January 1951.

The two ROVs were the *"Argus"* and the *"Hercules"*. Both ROVs were piloted remotely by a crew in the NAUTILUS ROV control room. (See next page) Tethered on a long cable providing power, control commands and video, the *Argus* and *Hercules* were piloted independently in tandem to operate as a team to perform their assigned research work far below the surface. With the INDENPENDENCE lying in roughly 2,700 feet of water, it would take a lot of cable feeding out from the NAUTILUS to the *Argus* far below. The NAUTILUS would be station keeping (maintaining her position) against wind and surface currents, while differing currents at various depths would push & pull on all that cable, tugging on the *Argus*, making it a poor platform for detailed bottom photography and sample collection. To solve that problem, *Hercules* is tethered to *Argus* with a short cable. The *Argus* maneuvers taking the brunt of the long cable loads and NAUTILUS movements to accommodate the *Hercules*. This makes the *Hercules* a rather stable platform to maneuver and perform its assigned work, having only to correct for local currents and obstacles in its path. The *Argus* controllers also keeps a watchful eye (lighting & video feed camera) on the *Hercules* from above, and keeps *Hercules* in the big picture while *Hercules* controllers concentrate on the close up work at hand. It becomes a *Hercules centric* mission with the *Augus* and the *NAUTILUS* crews now there to support the all important research being done by *Hercules.*

The INDENPENDENCE sits upright on the bottom in reasonably good condition when you consider her repaired war wounds from Tarawa, the wear and tear from action in the Pacific, the horrendous abuse of the two Atomic bombs at Bikini, and the insults to her hull by the two torpedo charges used to scuttle her, as well hydraulic loads within the water column in the descending trip far below culminating in the impact with the ocean bottom. Initially rolling over on her port side and slowly sinking stern first, INDEPENDENCE disappeared from sight in a frothy boil of air bubbles released from her hull. Beneath the surface INDEPENDENCE shifted to a slightly bow-low upright attitude during her descent thru the water column. She impacted the bottom upright slightly bow-low as evidenced by some hull side plate crush damage near the bow beneath the location just aft of the quad 40mm Bofers gun mount.   (See painting by multi-talented artist / photographer / diver Danijel Frka on page 871)

Cloaked in deep darkness (as was her role as a night carrier decades before), her time under the sea has not as yet added a lot of noticeable physical damage to the hull. Much of the wood covering her flight deck is missing. She has a new life as a host to fish, sponges and other forms of marine growth. She appeared to human eyes much like a ghostly murky apparition with a very limited viewing made possible by lights on the ROVs. Only small segments of her large width / length / height would be revealed at any given time as lights and cameras passed up, down and along the wreck, much as looking thru the beam from your car headlights on a very dark rainy night.

At least two gun tubs with their marine growth encrusted weapons sit on the bottom alongside the ship, torn loose during her final impact. They had been weakened from the stress and strain of the Bikini nuclear blasts, hull vibration during the war, and her trip to the bottom. Some sections of flight deck have torn away, or lay resting folded back over . Visualize her appearance not as the carrier ORISKANY more recently sunk as a recreational diving reef, but with the torn and battered scars from the "Able" and "Baker" blasts at Bikini. A Hellcat fighter rests within her hangar bay, worn and encrusted by the sea, a reminder of the ship's intended life when our nation had a dire need to defend our shores, return the war to the then enemy, and restore peace to the massive Pacific.

The 2016 mission to the EX-INDEPENDENCE extended her historical connection to humanity that may otherwise have ended on 26 January 1951 when a few sailor's eyes aboard vessels of Task Group 98.5 last witnessed the upraised bow of the vessel when she slid stern first from sight. As *Argus & Hercules* ascended at the mission's end, she was once again in the dark, out of human sight to be left undisturbed in Neptune's Kingdom.

Epilogue - 2016 Mission   876

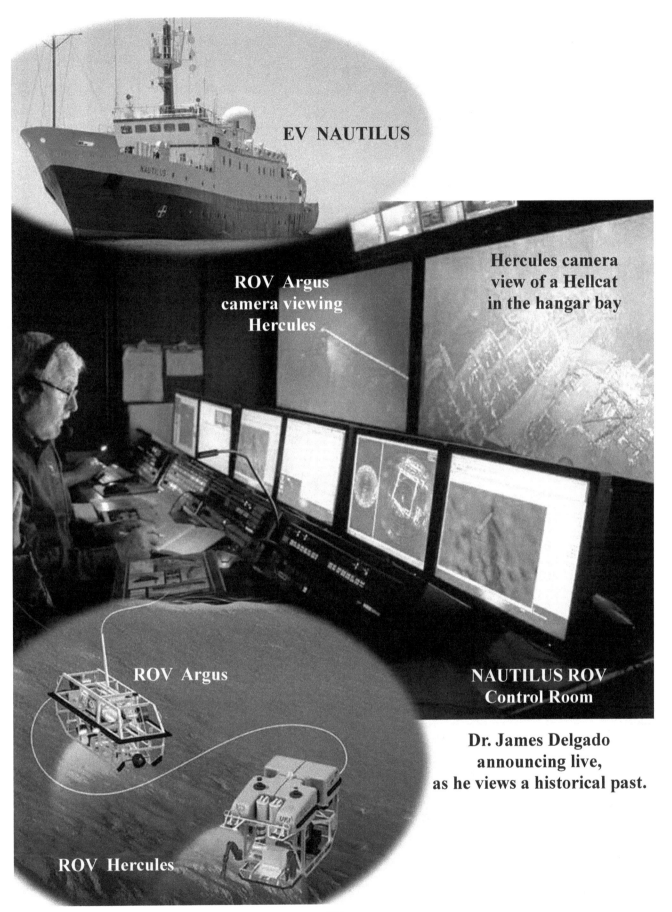

EV NAUTILUS

ROV Argus camera viewing Hercules

Hercules camera view of a Hellcat in the hangar bay

NAUTILUS ROV Control Room

ROV Argus

ROV Hercules

Dr. James Delgado announcing live, as he views a historical past.

Epilogue - 2016 Mission

Painting By Danijel Frka depicting ROV *Hercules* exploring in the hangar bay with ROV *Argus* cameras and lighting keeping watch for hazards to the *Hercules* and its cable from above.

Painting By Danijel Frka: The original is a splendid color painting commissioned by Russ Matthews, used with the kind permission of Danijel, Russ and James Delgado. Gifted by Russ Matthews to Dr. James Delgado, now in his collection.

This B & W rendition is the artist (Danijel Frka) depiction of INDEPENDENCE as she was viewed during the collimation of the 4 days of live streaming video from the mission led by Dr. Robert Ballard with Dr. James Delgado in 2016.

Dr. James Delgado explained the inception and organization of the 2015 & 2016 missions in the following email excerpts (edited for brevity):

" I was first "introduced" to USS Independence in 1989 when I was the head of the National Park Service's Maritime Heritage Program (then known as the National Maritime Initiative) and the NPS's Submerged Cultural Resources Center (now known as the Submerged Resources Center) was contacted by the Department of Energy to conduct a survey of the sunken ships of Operation Crossroads at Bikini; the team that ultimately went was Dan Lenihan, the Chief of SCRU, his Deputy, archaeologist Larry Murphy, archaeologist Larry Nordby, scientific illustrator Jerry Livingston, and me. We spent two field seasons at Bikini in 1989 and again in 1990, working with DOE's contractor, Holmes & Narver, and the U.S. Navy's Mobile Diving and Salvage (MDSU) Unit 1 and Explosive Ordinance Demolition Team 1, both from Pearl Harbor."

"The US Geological Survey announced they had a small sonar target thought to be Independence in 1990". "That, and the very visible role played by Independence at Bikini made it a follow up "target of opportunity" for a time when a mission could document it."

I joined NOAA as Director of Maritime Heritage in 2010. In discussions with NOAA OER archaeologist Frank Cantelas and Chris Beaverson of OER, Chris mentioned that a CRADA (Coooperative Reserarch and Development Agreement) with Boeing offered an opportunity to take a closer sonar look at the Independence target; OER arranged that, with Boeing funding for the full systems test of Echo Ranger, and because the wreck was within the boundaries of Monterey Bay National Marine Sanctuary (but managed by what was then the Gulf of the Farallones NMS), we provided the RV Fulmar as a test platform/tow boat. That is how that mission came to be; Bob Schwemmer, as our West Coast Maritime Heritage Coordinator, joined the team as co-director with Frank and me.

Echo Ranger's imagery *[1.] *gave us the outline of the hull, indications of damage, and the open elevator and what Chris thought might be an aircraft. That was the impetus for a return mission.* *[2.]

Because there was an extensive history of NOAA interest in the nuclear waste dumping, and Independence, and what I suspected was misinformation and fear based on a lack of empirical scientific knowledge (having spent considerable time with DOE and Los Alamos National Laboratory during the Bikini missions) I contacted Kai Vetter at UC Berkeley/Lawrence Livermore and invited his RadWatch team to join us. They funded their lab work; we provided the berth and full access.

At that time, we were planning a multiple year mission with Bob Ballard and the Ocean Exploration Trust, who receive NOAA funding from OER, and as part of that, a West Coast mission to the various sanctuaries was a key element. In the planning, I worked with the West Coast Regional Director, Bill Douros, GFNMS Superintendent Maria Brown, GNMS Research Coordinator Jan Roletto, and Bob Schwemmer to set maritime heritage priorities, and Independence was one of the top priorities for not only archaeology but additional radiation monitoring and a biological assessment of the marine life growing on the wreck, which was Jan's scientific priority in addition to the archaeology. Jan was overall principal investigator for the overall cruise of E/V Nautilus in the sanctuary; I was the archaeological principal investigator. Joining us on the mission was Russ Matthews, with Megan Lickliter-Mundon on call via telepresence, both focusing on the aircraft as the aviation archaeology principal investigators, and Kelly Elliott of NOAA, whose 2008 Master's Thesis had been on the archaeological potential of Independence. Dr. Michael Brennan, OET's archaeologist and on-board expedition leader, was also a key member of the team. We also had online participation from the archaeologists with the Navy History and Heritage Command (NHHC).

We also again had RadWatch on board, and collected sponges from the wreck for analysis by them.

There are no plans at this time to return to Independence"

*[1.] 2015 RV FULMAR mission (sonar imagery). One of the sonar images they kindly provided is on the back cover of this book.   *[2.] 2016 EV NAUTILUS (Dr. Robert Ballard) video / photo survey mission.

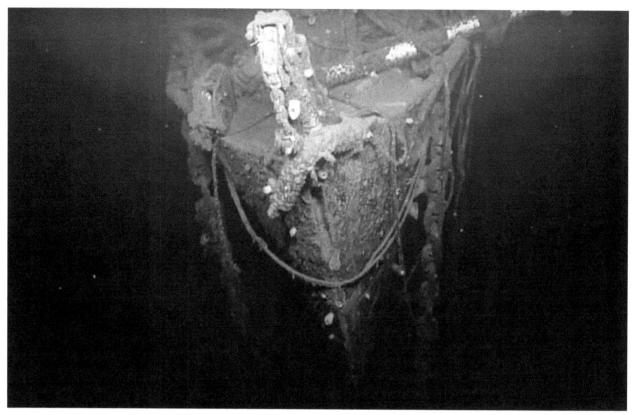

Bow of the INDEPENDENCE with mooring chains still attacked from Bikini Atoll.
One of the numerous striped poles used for high speed photo analysis during the scuttling test,
originally vertical, is laying over at the top of the above photo. (See photo page 786)

**Twin 40mm Bofors gun tub on the Gallery Level next to the flight deck,
with glass sponges & marine growth that now inhabit the ship.**

Above photos are monitor screen shots from the 2016 mission videos. Thanks to Exploration Trust / NOAA.

"Christmas Tree" mounted on the empty quad Bofors 40mm gun tub for measuring the pressure of the atomic bomb blast at Bikini Atoll in 1946. To the right is the gun director tub.

20mm Oerlikon gun tub torn lose from the Gallery Level, sitting on the bottom beside the hull.

Above photos are monitor screen shots from the 2016 mission videos. Thanks to Exploration Trust / NOAA.

F6F "Hellcat" captured on video taken by ROV "Hercules" in the hangar bay.

Above photos are monitor screen shots from the 2016 mission videos. Thanks to Exploration Trust / NOAA.

Epilogue - 2016 Mission   882

USS INDEPENDENCE
CVL-22

Contributors

&

Dedication

"Grey ship, grey ship,
do you hear them calling?
The voices of my people gone before me?"

J.R. Tolkien

Contributors To This Publication

It is with sincere appreciation that I thank and give heartfelt recognition to the following people and organizations for their assistance with information, data and the research material that made this historical document possible:

Harry E. Abbott - A good friend who provided constructive insight, critique and review.
David F. Anderson - McCain / Towers letters from NARA & additional background information.
Herman Bell - Diary / Memoirs, interviews & background information.
Allie Willis ("Willie") Callan - VF6 photos, interviews & background information: He authored "Sea Eagle".
Pat Caffee - Photos.
Nathan Canestaro - USS COWPENS AARS
Frank Capka - Memoirs.
Harvey Carlisle - Diary / memoirs.
Russell J. Carothers - Diary / memoirs.
Evelyn Cherpak - **Naval War College** - Assistance with research.
Conway Creative Writers Group (Dan & Shirley Barham) for encouragement and introspective guidance.
George H. Cornell - Photos (USS SARSI crewmember).
Blair Cunningham - **Coda Octopus** - Photos from data collected by the 3D sonar.
Anthony D'Aiuto - Diary / memoirs, interviews & background information.
James Delgado - **NOAA Office of National Marine Sanctuaries** (now with SEARCH) - Photos, data, NOAA Missions. Dr. Delgado was responsible for my participation in the 2015 & 2016 missions.
John J. Doherty - Photos.
Karl O. Drexel - Memoirs.
Exploration Trust / NOAA (Maritime Heritage) - 2016 mission photos
Danijel Frka - Painting of the EX-USS INDEPENDENCE on the ocean bottom
Craig Fuller - (Aviation Archaeology Investigation & Research) - Accident information.
Margaret Gardner - Photos / data of Air Group CVLG(N)-41 / (Shademaid), interview, background information on CVLG(N)-41 and her late husband Emmett Russell Edwards.
Leo B. Ghastin, Jr. - VF-27 Squadron History.
Jean Richard Goemmer - Diary / memoirs.
Charles R Goemmer - His brother's diary & background information.
Dale J. (Joe) Gordon - **Naval History and Heritage Command** - Photos and Squadron history.
Phil Hays - Drawings of the CL Engine Rooms.
Lisa L. Heinrich - Photos of her father (Cy Heinrich) & background information.
Mark Herber - Data / information related to the USS ESSEX.
Matt Herbison - Independence Seaport Museum, Penn's Landing - Research assistance.
Alphonse ("Al") Hiegel - Good friend - provided photos & records he collected as CVL-22 historian, background information, historical insight and assistance, interviews, as well as proof reading a later addition of this document.
Ben Houden - VF(N)-41 Pilot. Background information, documentation, interview.
Donald Irvin, Aerographers Mate 2c - Photo and INDEPENDENCE Track Chart Maps.
Donald E. Labudde - Memoirs - "The Sea Time, A Bluejacket's Memoir"
Dorothy Labudde - Don's unpublished book / memoir and background on Don, interview.
Raymond A. Luyet - Technical information.
Irvin Howard ("Hebe") Lee - (VFN-41 pilot) - "Shademaid".
Michael Lee - Background on his father, Irvin Howard Lee.
George J. Leedecke - Diary / memoirs.
Paul Leedecke - Photos.
Thomas L. Macchiarella - BRAC Program Management - HRAs
Craig A. Mackey - Air force Historical Research Agency - Aircraft Accident report
Russ Matthews (& James Delgado) - Permission to use the Danijel Frka painting he commissioned.
Charles Edward McKie - Diary / memoirs.
Sy E. Mendenhall - VF-6 Pilot - photos, interview.
NARA (National Archives at College Park) - Copies of CVL-22 Deck Logs, War diaries, After Action Reports (aviation & surface), Battle Damage Reports, Chronological Logs, Communication Logs, photographs, and hundreds of misc. documents too long to list.
Hugh Miller - Standing Orders Log
Wallace "Bud" Miller - Historical charts & material from his father, a pilot (and Ace) in VF(N)-41
Joseph R. Minville - Photos.

Contributors To This Publication

George Newbauer - Diary / memoirs.
Pam Orlando - NOAA Office of National Marine Sanctuaries - Deck Log pages for TG 98.5 from NARA
Herschel Pahl - VF6 photos, interview (Herschel wrote a book - "Point Option").
Ruben F. (Pete) Peterson - VF(N)-41 pilot - interview and background information.
Dr. Milton F. Popp - Diary / memoirs.
Allan Resman - VT-46 photos and information.
Joe Rogers - Ships cartoons, newsletters, "Breakfast Bulletins", interview and background information.
Rick Russell - USNI Press - Advice on publishing, approval to quote from "Fading Victory".
Harvey B. Sein, - Paper , 1958 -"U.S.S. INDEPENDENCE—PIONEER NIGHT CARRIER"
John G. Scruggs - Photos of his division, interview & background information.
Edwin R. Seace - Photos, newspaper articles and background information.
Doug Siegfried - Tailhook Association - Squadron Histories of VF-3, VF-6, VF-22 ,VF(N)-41 and photos of
　　　　squadron logos from the US Navy Historical Center.
Ed Schultz (Photographers Mate - Phom2c) - Photographs
Robert Schwemmer - NOAA Office of National Marine Sanctuaries - Photos, data, NOAA Mission.
John Underriner - Photos & letters from his grandfather: Lt. Cdr. John C. Vermeren (CVL-22 doctor)
USS INDEPENDENCE CVL-22 Reunion Group - photos, data, interviews and background information.
USS INDEPENDENCE CVL-22 veterans family members - Photos and information.
Curtis A. Utz - Naval History and Heritage Command - For redirecting me to the NARA for US Naval History.
Alex Vraciu - VF-6 pilot - Background information on Air Group Six.
Steve Wiper - Classic Warships Publishing - Photos and technical idea exchange.
To the numerous shipmates & their families who kindly provided photos and historical material.
And last but not least, my wife **Marcia L. Lambert** for her assistance with the project.
With my sincere apologies for any of the numerous people I may have neglected to acknowledge.

Books used for reference / background information include (but not limited to):

A Glorious Way To Die	Russell Spurr	New Market Press
Afternoon of the Rising Sun	Kenneth I. Friedman	Presidio Press
Battle of Surigao Strait	Anthony P. Tully	Indiana University Press
Blossoms in The Wind	M.G. Sheftall	NAL Caliber
Born To Die - The Cherry Blossom Squadrons	Hagoromo Society	Ohara Publications
Bull Halsey	E.B. Potter	Naval Institute Press
Downfall - The End of the Imperial Japanese Empire	Richard B. Frank	Penguin Books
Fading Victory - The Diary of Admiral Matome Ugaki 1941-1945		Naval Institute Press
Fire From The Sky - A Diary Over Japan	Ron Greer & Mike Hicks	Greer Publishing
Halsey's Typhoon	Bob Drury & Tom Calvin	Atlantic Monthly Press
Hellcat	Barrett Tillman	Naval Institute Press
How They Won The War in The Pacific	Edwin P. Hoyt	The Lyons Press
March of the Mighty I During World War II	Frank R. Capka	Self Published
Nimitz	E.B. Potter	Naval Institute Press
O'hare The Hero - Setting the Record Straight	Herman Backlund	Self Published
Point Option	Herschel Pahl	Dogwood Printing
Sea of Thunder	Evan Thomas	Simon & Schuster
Shademaid	**I.H. Lee**	Self Published
Squadron Histories of Air Group 27 & Air Group 46		
That Gallent Ship: USS Yorktown	Robert J. Cressman	Naval Institute Press ?
The Battle For Leyte Gulf	C.Vann Woodward	The Battery Press, Nashville
The Big E	Edward P. Stafford	Naval Institute Press
The Independence Light Aircraft Carriers	Andrew Faltum	The Nautical & Aviation Pub. Co.
The Invention That Changed The World	Robert Buderi	Touchstone Simon & Schuster
The Official Chronology of the US Navy in WWII	**Robert J. Cressman**	Naval Institute Press
	Bob's work was relied on heavily as reference for the opening background on the Pacific War.	
"The Sea Time, A Bluejacket's Memoir"	**Donald E. Labudde**	Unpublished
War Plan Orange	Edward S. Miller	Naval Institute Press

Any errors within this book should be considered to be mine. Please contact the author if you note any errors or omissions.

USS INDEPENDENCE CVL-22 became the first carrier of the INDEPENDENCE Class to have a second catapult installed.

Proper spotting / handling of the mix of aircraft was critical both on the catapults and on the forward elevator during operations.

These following 7 pages lay out the study.

guide line

1. NOSE IF CAN BE TAXIED TO CATAPULT POSITION WITH WINGS SPREAD.
2. BEST SEQUENCE IS TO TAXI PORT PLANE INTO POSITION, AND THE STARBOARD PLANE; ORDER MAY BE REVERSED AT SLIGHT COST IN TIME.
3. PORT PLANE CAN FOLD WINGS WHEN ON CATAPULT, IF NECESSARY.
4. PORT PLANE MUST BE LAUNCHED FIRST, UNLESS ITS WINGS ARE FOLDED.
5. GUIDE LINE PAINTED ON DECK IS TRACK FOR LEFT WHEEL OF STARBOARD PLANE, INSURING CLEARANCE BETWEEN RIGHT WING AND ISLAND STRUCTURE.
6. BRIDLE ON STARBOARD PLANE NOT HOOKED ON TILL PORT PLANE TAKES OFF.

Appendix 1 - Aircraft spotting with two catapults

886

Appendix 1 - Aircraft spotting with two catapults

1. BOTH TBM'S POSITIONED WITH WINGS FOLDED.
2. BOTH CAN SPREAD WINGS, WHEN POSITIONED, INDEPENDENT OF WINGS OF EACH OTHER.
3. LIFELINE FORWARD OF CRANE WAS MADE REMOVABLE TO PERMIT MOVEMENT OF RIGHT WING.
4. PORT PLANE MUST TAKE OFF FIRST IF BOTH HAVE WINGS SPREAD (SEE 2A).
5. STARBOARD PLANE CAN TAKEOFF FIRST IF PORT PLANE'S WINGS ARE FOLDED (SEE 2B).
6. CATAPULT POSITIONER ESSENTIAL TO MINIMIZE POSSIBILITY OF DAMAGING TAIL AGAINST CRANE (SEE 2C).

Appendix 1 - Aircraft spotting with two catapults

888

Appendix 1 - Aircraft spotting with two catapults

Appendix 1 - Aircraft spotting with two catapults

Appendix 1 - Aircraft spotting with two catapults

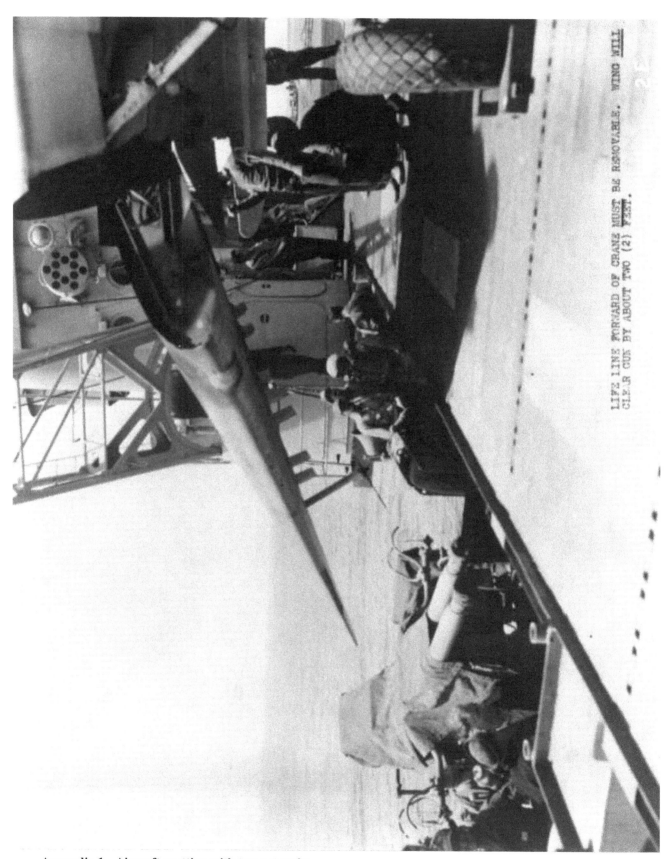

Appendix 1 - Aircraft spotting with two catapults

Appendix 2 - VF-46 F6F accident on 24 March 1945   (See page 568)

US CARRIER - Relative Size - 1943

CV

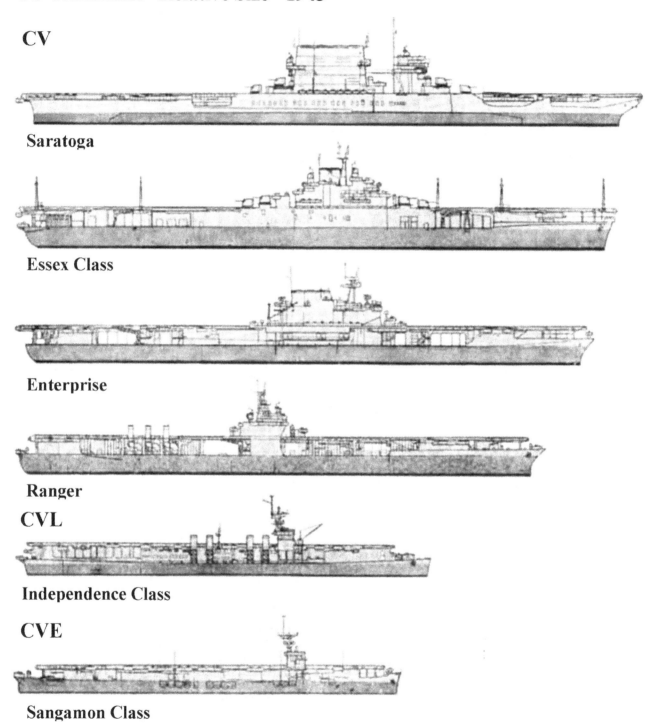

Saratoga

Essex Class

Enterprise

Ranger

CVL

Independence Class

CVE

Sangamon Class

Appendix 3 - US Aircraft Carrier Relative Size

USS INDEPENDENCE CVL-22 Awards

- **American Campaign Medal**
- **Asiatic-Pacific Campaign Medal (8 Stars)**

  1. **Pacific Raids**
  2. **Treasury-Bougainville Operation**
  3. **Gilbert Islands Operation**
  4. **Western Caroline Islands Operation**
  5. **Leyte**
  6. **Luzon**
  7. **Okinawa**
  8. **Third Fleet Operations Against Japan**

- **World War II Victory Medal**
- **Navy Occupation Service Medal ("Asia Clasp")**
- **Philippine Presidential Unit Citation**
- **Philippine Liberation Medal**

This book is dedicated to:

THE CAPTAINS

Upon who's shoulders fell the burden of command.

THE CREWS

Who's individual and collective skills, toils, sweat and dedication moved the mighty ship
as they faced seen and unseen threats on the Road to Tokyo.

 # THE AVIATORS

Both pilots and aircrews who had the hope, intestinal fortitude and audacity to believe
they could launch from the Mighty-I's flight deck, deliver the war to the enemy,
return to the ship, and live to fight another day.

THE SHIP

A massive complex machine of war, crafted of steel,
nourished on crude, driven by steam.
On her decks and through her portals passed her life's blood ....
The Captains, Crew and Aviators.

And especially to those that did not return,
who's families suffered a loss of their loved one.

Printed in the USA
CPSIA information can be obtained
at www.ICGtesting.com
LVHW081149190224
772231LV00005B/47